Accounting for Governmental & Nonprofit Entities

Seventeenth Edition

Jacqueline L. Reck, Ph.D., CPA

James E. and C. Ellis Rooks
Distinguished Professor in Accounting
University of South Florida

Suzanne L. Lowensohn, Ph.D., CPA, CGMA

Associate Professor of Accounting
Colorado State University

Mc Graw Hill Education

ACCOUNTING FOR GOVERNMENTAL & NONPROFIT ENTITIES, SEVENTEENTH EDITION

Published by McGraw-Hill Education, 2 Penn Plaza, New York, NY 10121.

This book is printed on acid-free paper.

1 2 3 4 5 6 7 8 9 0 DOW/DOW 1 0 9 8 7 6 5

ISBN 978-1-259-25311-9
MHID 1-259-25311-2

www.mhhe.com

DEDICATION TO EARL R. WILSON

Professors Jackie Reck and Suzanne Lowensohn dedicate the 17th edition of *Accounting for Governmental & Nonprofit Entities* to Professor Emeritus Earl R. Wilson. Professor Wilson served as an author of this textbook from the 9th edition (1992) through the 16th edition. As a result of Professor Wilson's innovation and dedication, the textbook is recognized nationally and has been adopted by hundreds of institutions. When the GASB issued the financial reporting model standard in 1999, Professor Wilson convinced his co-authors that the dual-track approach used in the textbook would be a better pedagogical approach to teaching the two bases of accounting than teaching the conversion method that is presented as part of Chapter 9 of the textbook. We believe he was correct in advocating the approach that has been taken in the textbook, and to our knowledge we are the only textbook offering this approach to teaching the two accounting and reporting bases for the government reporting model.

Professor Wilson is also responsible for the Smithville_Bingham software that is offered with the textbook. He originally contracted a programmer to work with him in developing the Smithville electronic practice set. Later his work was brought 'in-house' at McGraw-Hill and has been moved to a Web-based platform making it more accessible and easier for students and instructors to use. Since the initial development of Smithville, we have added Bingham, and with the 16th edition we introduced a shortened version of Smithville. We will continue to provide and add to this valuable teaching tool that was first developed by Professor Wilson.

Professor Wilson is also responsible for Chapter 17, "Accounting and Reporting for the Federal Government." He believed that a government and not-for-profit textbook was incomplete if it did not include information on the federal government. As a result, he researched and wrote the chapter on accounting and reporting for the federal government. We continue to believe this is an important chapter in our textbook.

Professor Wilson's contributions to the textbook were based on his wealth of experience as a researcher, teacher, and his participation in the government community. Among his many accomplishments are the following:

- Professor Emeritus of Accountancy at the University of Missouri—Columbia.
- Academic fellow with the Governmental Accounting Standards Board (GASB).
- Member of the Governmental Accounting Standards Advisory Council, the U.S. Comptroller General's Advisory Council on Governmental Auditing Standards, the American Institute of CPAs Government Accounting and Auditing Committee.
- President of the American Accounting Association Government and Nonprofit (AAA-GNP) Section.
- Author/co-author of numerous research articles in journals such as *The Accounting Review; Journal of Accounting Research; Contemporary Accounting Research; Journal of Accounting and Public Policy; Journal of Accounting, Auditing, and Finance; Research in Governmental and Nonprofit Accounting; and Public Budgeting and Finance.*
- Recipient of the enduring Lifetime Contribution Award from the AAA-GNP section.
- Recipient of the Cornelius Tierney/Ernst & Young Research Award from the Association of Government Accountants.
- Outstanding Teacher of the Year from the Kansas City MU Business Alumni Association; Outstanding Educator of the Year and Outstanding CPA in Government from the Missouri State CPA.

- Chair or committee member for more than 30 doctoral dissertations, many in the area of governmental accounting.

On a more personal note, Professors Reck and Lowensohn thank Professor Wilson for his guidance and patience as he taught us the "textbook process." Originally, Professor Wilson intended the 15th edition to be his last with the textbook, but we persuaded him to stay for the 16th edition. Since he has been an Emeritus professor for a number of years, persuasion did not work on the 17th edition. Professor Wilson has decided that he is ready to "fully" retire and spend more time with his golf game. We hope he enjoys his well-deserved retirement!

About the Authors

Jacqueline L. Reck

Serves as the associate dean of financial management and academic affairs for the College of Business and is the James E. and C. Ellis Rooks Distinguished Professor in Accounting at the University of South Florida. She received a BS degree from North Dakota State University, BS and MAcc degrees from the University of South Florida, and her PhD from the University of Missouri–Columbia. She is a certified public accountant (Florida).

Dr. Reck worked for state government for several years before joining academia. Currently, she is active in several professional associations. In addition to teaching governmental and not-for-profit accounting, Dr. Reck serves on the Governmental Accounting Standards Advisory Council and frequently presents continuing professional education workshops and sessions. She has provided workshops on governmental and not-for-profit accounting for local accounting firms and the state auditor general's staff. Dr. Reck has received several teaching and research awards and has chaired or served on several doctoral dissertation committees.

Dr. Reck has published articles in *Contemporary Accounting Research; Journal of Accounting and Public Policy; Research in Governmental and Nonprofit Accounting; Journal of Public Budgeting, Accounting and Financial Management;* and the *Journal of Information Systems*, among others. She joined as an author on the 14th edition.

Suzanne L. Lowensohn

Is an associate professor of Accounting at Colorado State University. She received a BS and a MAcc degree from the University of South Florida, and her PhD from the University of Miami. She is a certified public accountant (Florida) and a chartered global management accountant.

Dr. Lowensohn has served on the Governmental Accounting Standards Board Intangible Issues Task Force and Comprehensive Implementation Guide Advisory Committee, on the Government Finance Officers Association Special Review Executive Committee, on the Colorado Society of Certified Public Accountants Governmental Issues Committee, on the AICPA FARS Content Subcommittee, and as president of the Government and Nonprofit Section of the American Accounting Association. Prior to joining academia, she worked for KPMG and performed numerous governmental audits.

Professor Lowensohn has published articles in *Journal of Accounting and Public Policy; Research in Governmental and Nonprofit Accounting; Accounting and the Public Interest; Journal of Accounting Literature; Issues in Accounting Education;* and *Behavioral Research in Accounting,* among others. She joined as an author on the 16th edition.

Preface

For more than 60 years, *Accounting for Governmental & Nonprofit Entities* has been the leader in the market. It is a comprehensive governmental and not-for-profit accounting text written for students who will be auditing and working in public and not-for-profit sector entities. Originally published in 1951 and written by Professor R. M. Mikesell, this book—and the many subsequent editions revised by Professors Leon Hay, Earl Wilson, Susan Kattelus, Jacqueline Reck, and Suzanne Lowensohn—have given generations of instructors and students a comprehensive knowledge of the specialized accounting and financial reporting practices of governmental and not-for-profit organizations, as well as an understanding of how those organizations can better meet the information needs of a diverse set of financial statement users and decision makers. The vision of these original authors continues to be reflected in this 17th edition, and their strategy of providing a large and innovative set of instructional support materials prepared and tested in the classroom by the authors continues to be a guiding principle today. The current author team brings to this edition their extensive experience teaching government and not-for-profit courses as well as insights gained from their professional experience, scholarly writing, and professional activities. The result is a relevant and accurate text that includes the most effective instructional tools.

ORGANIZATION AND CONTENT

The 17th edition of *Accounting for Governmental & Nonprofit Entities* is separated into three parts: Part One covers state and local governments (Chapters 2 through 9), Part Two focuses on accountability for public funds (Chapters 10 through 12), and Part Three examines not-for-profit organizations (Chapters 13 through 16) and the federal government (Chapter 17). Chapter 1 continues to form a broad foundation for the more detailed material in Chapters 2 through 17. The order of the chapters is the same as the last edition. The chapters are ordered to facilitate a variety of courses and formats used by adopters of the text. For example, a course focused on state and local governments may cover Chapter 1 and Parts One and Two, while a course focused on not-for-profit organizations may cover Chapter 1 and Parts Two and Three. Part Two is a bridge between the public and not-for-profit sectors that includes accountability topics (e.g., financial analysis, auditing, and budgeting) applicable to all types of entities that receive public funds.

KEY CHANGES IN THIS EDITION

With the 17th edition, we are pleased to integrate McGraw-Hill's Connect and LearnSmart educational technology systems. Connect is a digital teaching and learning platform for homework completion and review that helps improve student performance over a variety of critical outcomes while aiding instructor grading and assessment efficiency. LearnSmart is an adaptive study tool that helps identify specific topics and learning objectives individual students need to study.

As always, readers can count on this edition to include authoritative changes from the Governmental Accounting Standards Board, Financial Accounting Standards Board, Federal Accounting Standards Advisory Board, American Institute of Certified

Public Accountants, Office of Management and Budget, Internal Revenue Service, and Government Accountability Office. Update bulletins will be provided periodically on the text Web site as new authoritative statements are issued.

Since publication of the 16th edition, **important** changes affecting accounting, financial reporting, and auditing for governmental and not-for-profit organizations have occurred, which include:

- Governmental Accounting Standards Board concepts statements and standards (particularly Statements 67 and 68) have been issued, and these describe new financial reporting elements and alter certain financial statements.
- The Office of Management and Budget has issued streamlined guidance relative to accounting and auditing federal grant funds in the *Uniform Administrative Requirements, Cost Principles, and Audit Requirements for Federal Awards.*
- The American Institute of Certified Public Accountants has issued clarified auditing standards.

Each of the changes in this abbreviated list has been incorporated into the text.

Several notable improvements have been made in this edition of the text. Chapter 3 includes new material on government budgets. Chapter 4 has been reorganized, so that interfund activities are covered after general governmental transactions have been introduced. Chapter 8 now illustrates external financial statements for an investment trust pool. Chapter 10 introduces Electronic Municipal Market Access (EMMA). Chapters 11 and 12 incorporate changes under the new OMB super circular. Chapters 15 and 16 have been reformatted to better identify differences between the accounting for governmental and nongovernmental not-for-profit organizations. Finally, all end-of-chapter material is now sequentially numbered to facilitate problem assignment, and the instructor's manual identifies learning objectives and assessment areas associated with each end of chapter item.

This edition continues to feature two comprehensive and effective computerized practice sets, the City of Bingham and the City of Smithville. As with the prior edition, a short version of the City of Smithville practice set is available for those instructors who wish a less comprehensive case. Both practice sets are downloadable from the publisher's Web site.

INNOVATIVE PEDAGOGY

For state and local government accounting, the authors have found that *dual-track* accounting is an effective approach in showing the juxtaposition of government-wide and fund financial statements in GASB's integrated model of basic financial statements. It allows students to see that each transaction has an effect on the fund financial statements (that are designed to show fiscal compliance with the annual budget), on the government-wide financial statements (that demonstrate accountability for operational performance of the government as a whole), or both. This approach better serves students who will design and use accounting information systems, such as enterprise systems, to allow information to be captured once and used for several purposes. Accounting for federal agencies as well as nongovernmental, not-for-profit entities closely parallels this approach as traditional fund accounting may be appropriate for keeping track of resources with restricted purposes, but citizens and donors also need to see the larger picture provided by the entity as a whole. The dual-track approach is further described inside the front cover of this text.

Governments will continue to prepare fund-based statements throughout the year and convert to accrual-based government-wide statements at the end of the year until they invest in information systems that can deliver real-time information for decision making. We want students to think beyond being transaction-bookkeepers and aspire to design and use the systems that will make government-wide financial information available when managers and citizens need it. The City of Bingham and City of Smithville Continuous Computerized Problems are teaching tools that develop these skills and perspective. The authors feel so strongly that this general ledger software tool helps students understand the material that we again provide it with the text. Students have enthusiastically told us that they like "learning by doing" and that these continuous computerized problems helped them to understand the concepts in the book.

TARGET AUDIENCE

The text continues to be best suited for senior and graduate accounting majors who plan to sit for the certified public accountant (CPA) exam and then audit governmental or not-for-profit entities. Public administration and other students who plan to provide financial management or consulting services to government and not-for-profit entities report that the text provides a more comprehensive set of competencies than traditional public budgeting texts. Students in not-for-profit management education programs find that the coverage of accounting, financial reporting, auditing, taxation, and information systems for both governmental and not-for-profit entities provides the exposure they need to work across disciplines and sectors. Finally, students preparing for the certified government financial manager (CGFM) exam will also find Chapters 1 through 11 useful for Examination 2. We encourage all students who use this book to consider the challenges and rewards of careers in public service—in federal, state, and local governments as well as not-for-profit organizations.

SUPPLEMENT PACKAGE

The following ancillary materials are prepared by the authors to ensure consistency and accuracy and are available on the textbook's Web site, *www.mhhe.com/reck17e*.

- Instructor's Guide and Solutions Manual.
- PowerPoint lecture presentations.
- Test Bank (including a computerized version using EZ Test software).
- McGraw-Hill's Connect online homework system and LearnSmart adaptive study tool.
- The City of Bingham and City of Smithville Continuous Computerized Problems—general ledger practice sets, downloadable from the publisher's Web site.
- The City of Bingham and City of Smithville Instructor's Version software, providing guidance for instructors, solution data files, and solution page image (.pdf) files for all required financial statements, schedules, and reports.

Students can also access the PowerPoint lecture presentations for each chapter at the Online Learning Center on the text's Web site, *www.mhhe.com/reck17e*.

Acknowledgments

We are thankful for the encouragement, suggestions, and counsel provided by many instructors, professionals, and students in writing this book. They include the following professionals and educators who read portions of this book and previous editions in various forms and provided valuable comments and suggestions:

Kimball Adams
City of Largo, Florida
Terry D. Balkaran
Queens College
Kelli A. Bennett
City and County of Denver
Irfan Bora
Rutgers University
Barbara Chaney
University of Montana
Michael Crawford
Crawford & Associates
Ruth W. Epps
Virginia Commonwealth University
Mary Foelster
American Institute of Certified Public Accountants
Michael Givens
City of Jacksonville, Florida
Debra Gula
University of South Florida
Kristen Hockman
University of Missouri—Columbia
Larita Killian
IUPUI—Columbus Center
Barbara Lippincott
Tampa, Florida
Allen McConnell
University of Northern Colorado
G. Michael Miller
City of Jacksonville, Florida
Dean Mead
Governmental Accounting Standards Board
Joel Provenza
City of Jacksonville, Florida
Walter A. Robbins
University of Alabama
Gail Sanderson
Lebanon Valley College
Ken Schermann
Governmental Accounting Standards Board
Mark Sutter
El Paso, Texas
Christopher Tenn
Colorado State University
Relmond P. Van Daniker
Association of Government Accountants
Shunda Ware
Atlanta Technical College
Tammy Waymire
Northern Illinois University

We acknowledge permission to quote pronouncements and reproduce illustrations from the publications of the Governmental Accounting Standards Board, American Institute of Certified Public Accountants, and International City/County Management Association. Dr. Reck thanks her family for their support and dedicates her work to the memory of Albert for the inspiration he continues to provide. Dr. Lowensohn would like to express appreciation to her loving family—Tom, Grant, and Tara—for their support and patience and to her friend and colleague, Dr. Laurence Johnson, for his professional guidance.

Although we are extremely careful in checking the text and end-of-chapter material, it is possible that errors and ambiguities remain in this edition. As readers encounter such, we urge them to let us know, so that corrections can be made. We also invite every user of this edition who has suggestions or comments about the material in the chapters to share them with one of the authors, either by regular mail or e-mail. The authors will continue the service of issuing Update Bulletins to adopters of this text that describe changes after the book is in print. These bulletins can be downloaded from the text Web site at *www.mhhe.com/reck17e.*

Dr. Jacqueline L. Reck
School of Accountancy
University of South Florida
4202 East Fowler Avenue, BSN 3403
Tampa, FL 33620
jreck@usf.edu

Dr. Suzanne Lowensohn
Colorado State University
College of Business
257 Rockwell Hall
Fort Collins, Colorado 80523-1271
Suzanne.Lowensohn@colostate.edu

Brief Contents

Table of Contents

Chapter 14

Not-for-Profit Organizations—Regulatory, Taxation, and Performance Issues 575

Chapter 15

Accounting for Colleges and Universities 605

Chapter 16

Accounting for Health Care Organizations 647

Chapter 17

Accounting and Reporting for the Federal Government 685

City of Bingham and City of Smithville Continuous Computerized Problems

Note: To download the City of Bingham or City of Smithville computerized problem, visit the Student Edition of the Web site for this textbook: *www.mhhe.com/reck17e.*

A great way to understand the GASB financial reporting model is to be actively engaged in learning through these "hands-on" continuous problems for small governmental entities. The City of Bingham and City of Smithville web supplement is general ledger software in which students record transactions in the appropriate general journals of each city. Transaction analysis is the first and most important step in the accounting cycle of any organization. After journal entries have been recorded, the software conveniently posts changes to all accounts in general and to subsidiary ledgers. From this point, students can preview trial balances, export them to a Microsoft Excel file, and then prepare financial statements from those data.

This instructional supplement substantially aids students' learning by requiring them to decide whether each transaction has an effect on the *fund financial statements,* the *government-wide financial statements,* or both. The City of Bingham and City of Smithville are built on the *dual-track approach* described on the adjacent page. Students can apply the conceptual framework that connects the government-wide financial statements (that report on the flow of total economic resources of the government using the accrual basis of accounting) and the fund financial statements (that report on the flow of current financial resources using the modified accrual or near-cash basis of accounting).

STUDENTS

Several examples are provided here to show how the software facilitates learning. When a government sends out property tax bills for the year, this transaction is recorded in the General Fund general journal because it impacts the governmental funds statement of revenues, expenditures, and changes in fund balance and in the governmental activities general journal because it has an impact on the government-wide statement of activities. Within each practice set, you can easily toggle among the journals for each fund and governmental activity. Drop-down menus make it easy to decide which revenue account should be increased or decreased, as the chart of accounts is embedded in the software. Journal entries must balance before one can proceed. When the government records its budget or encumbers items related to purchase orders, however, these journal entries affect only the governmental funds. Budgetary account titles are available for selection in the governmental funds general journals but not in the governmental activities general journal because funds, not governmental activities, capture information to show compliance with the short-term, legally approved budget. Conversely, depreciation expense of general capital assets is recorded only in the general journal of governmental activities because the accrual basis of accounting captures and matches the cost of using up the utility of capital assets with the time period in which the assets generate revenues.

INSTRUCTORS

This software can be used in several ways. You can project it each day as part of the classroom experience and discuss transactions that are keyed to the chapter under discussion. Depending on your objectives, you can require a small set of the transactions be recorded for each fund or governmental activity or you can assign either of the full problems as a semester-long case. Regardless of how you choose to use the cases, we recommend that students work on the City of Bingham or City of Smithville problem as they are studying the related chapter in the text and turn in each chapter as they go along. You may find that small student work groups provide an efficient way for students to learn from each other.

We continue to be encouraged by our students' positive reaction as they *learn by doing* the City of Bingham and City of Smithville Continuous Computerized Problems.

The Dual-Track Accounting Approach

The GASB reporting model requires government-wide, accrual-based financial statements to provide information that goes beyond the familiar fund accounting information. Analysts increasingly use government-wide "big picture" information in performance analysis, and some council members find that, relative to fund accounting information, accrual-based statements are better suited to demonstrate accountability for interperiod equity. For example, these statements provide the information necessary to explore critical questions such as, Has the government shifted the liability for current services to future generations? However, to date, governmental accounting software vendors have not provided governments with systems that can directly produce government-wide financial statements on the required accrual basis, particularly on an interim basis, such as monthly.

Beginning with the 12th edition of this text in 2001, the authors committed themselves to the importance of providing government-wide and fund accounting information by introducing a *dual-track* approach to recording governmental transactions. The dual-track approach captures both government-wide and fund accounting information at the same time an event is recognized, thereby allowing for the direct production of both government-wide and fund financial statements. As students will learn, some transactions affect the government-wide statements only (e.g., depreciation expense) and others affect the fund financial statements only (e.g., budgetary entries). However, the majority affect both types of statements, although in different ways (e.g., expensing versus capitalizing long-lived assets). The fund financial statements reflect a short-term measurement focus that is intended to assist statement users in assessing *fiscal accountability*—how financial resources were raised and spent. The government-wide financial statements reflect a medium- to long-term measurement focus intended to assist users in assessing *operational accountability*—whether governmental services were efficiently and effectively provided. Both perspectives are important.

The dual-track approach helps students understand how two different sets of accounting records are used to collect financial data as transactions occur. One set of records collects information using the short-term measurement focus and near-cash basis of accounting traditionally used in governmental fund accounting. This set of records includes a chart of accounts, general journal, general ledger, trial balances, and financial statements for each fund. The other set of records collects the same underlying information using a long-term measurement focus similar to that used by business; that is, the accrual basis of accounting. The second set of records assists in preparing statements for governmental activities and business-type activities. Each time we illustrate or explain what, if any, effect a transaction will have on the fund and governmental activities record.

The text does illustrate the reclassification approach in Chapter 9 because that approach is used in practice by most governments. Governments that continue to release only fund financial information throughout the year and must then convert (or reclassify) the data to government-wide information for the purposes of the financial statement preparation and year-end audit are not as accountable or transparent as governments that make GAAP-based information available throughout the year.

Governments, even small ones, are complex entities and there is no easy approach to learning the external governmental financial model. But the authors believe that the dual-track approach is conceptually superior to the reclassification approach in that it gives students the tools to understand "why" and "how" financial statements are prepared and used. A greater conceptual understanding of governmental financial statements also makes it easier for students to understand the reclassification approach when it is encountered. The dual-track pedagogy can help students see the short- and long-term effects of the decisions made by government managers and oversight bodies from the perspective of all stakeholders.

Chapter One

Introduction to Accounting and Financial Reporting for Governmental and Not-for-Profit Entities

Learning Objectives

After studying this chapter, you should be able to:

1-1 Identify and explain the characteristics that distinguish government and not-for-profit entities from for-profit entities.

1-2 Identify the authoritative bodies responsible for setting financial reporting standards for (1) state and local governments, (2) the federal government, and (3) not-for-profit organizations.

1-3 Contrast and compare the objectives of financial reporting for (1) state and local governments, (2) the federal government, and (3) not-for-profit organizations.

1-4 Explain the minimum requirements for general purpose external financial reporting for state and local governments and how they relate to comprehensive annual financial reports.

1-5 Identify and describe the required financial statements for the federal government and not-for-profit organizations.

WELCOME TO GOVERNMENTAL AND NOT-FOR-PROFIT ACCOUNTING

Welcome to the new world of accounting for governmental and not-for-profit organizations! Initially, you may find it challenging to understand the many new terms and concepts you will need to learn. Moreover, if you are like most readers, you will question at the outset why governmental and not-for-profit organizations use accounting and financial reporting practices that are different from those used by for-profit entities.

As you read this first chapter of the text, the reasons for the differences between governmental and not-for-profit accounting and for-profit accounting should become apparent. Specifically, government and not-for-profit organizations serve entirely different purposes in society than do business entities. Because such organizations are largely financed by taxpayers, donors, and others who do not expect benefits proportional to the resources they provide, management has a special duty to be accountable for how those resources are used in providing services. Thus, the need for managers to be accountable to citizens, creditors, oversight bodies, and others has played a central role in shaping the accounting and reporting practices of governmental and not-for-profit organizations.

This first chapter will give you a basic conceptual understanding of the unique characteristics of governmental and not-for-profit organizations and how their accounting and financial reporting concepts and practices differ from those of for-profit organizations. By the time you finish subsequent chapters assigned for your course, you should have an in-depth practical knowledge of government and not-for-profit accounting and financial reporting.

WHAT ARE GOVERNMENTAL AND NOT-FOR-PROFIT ORGANIZATIONS?

Governmental and not-for-profit organizations are vast in number and range of services provided. In the United States, governments exist at the federal, state, and local levels and serve a wide variety of functions. The most recent census of governments reports that there are 90,056 local governments, in addition to the federal government and 50 state governments. These 90,056 local governments consist of 3,031 counties, 19,519 municipalities, 16,360 towns and townships, 12,880 independent school districts, and 38,266 special district governments that derive their power from state governments.[1]

States, counties, municipalities (for example, cities, towns, and villages), and townships are **general purpose governments**—governments that provide a wide range of services to their residents (such as police and fire protection; sanitation; construction and maintenance of streets, roads, and bridges; and culture and recreation). Independent school districts, public colleges and universities, and special districts are **special purpose governments**—governments that provide only a single function or a limited number of functions (such as education, drainage and flood control, irrigation, soil and water conservation, fire protection, and water supply). Special purpose governments have the power to levy and collect taxes and to raise revenues from other sources as provided by state laws to finance the services they provide.

Not-for-profit organizations also exist in many forms and serve many different functions in society. These include private colleges and universities, various kinds of community service and health care organizations, certain libraries and museums, professional and trade associations, fraternal and social organizations, and religious organizations. Currently, there are nearly 2.3 million not-for-profit organizations in the U.S.[2]

[1] U.S. Department of Commerce, Bureau of the Census, *2012 Census of Governments,* Table 2, *http://www.census.gov/govs/cog2012/.*

[2] The National Center for Charitable Statistics reports that there were 1.6 million registered not-for-profit organizations in the U.S. as of 2010 (Amy S. Blackwood, Katie L. Roeger, and Sarah L. Pettijohn, *The Nonprofit Sector in Brief: Public Charities, Giving and Volunteering, 2012,* Washington, D.C: Urban Institute Press, p. 1). Also reported by the National Center for Charitable Statistics were 325,421 religious congregations as of November 2013. (Urban Institute, National Center for Charitable Statistics Web site, *http://nccs.urban.org/statistics/quickfacts.cfm*).

DISTINGUISHING CHARACTERISTICS OF GOVERNMENTAL AND NOT-FOR-PROFIT ORGANIZATIONS

Governmental and not-for-profit organizations differ in important ways from business organizations. An understanding of how these organizations differ from business organizations is essential to understanding the unique accounting and financial reporting principles that have evolved for governmental and not-for-profit organizations.

In its *Statement of Financial Accounting Concepts No. 4,* the **Financial Accounting Standards Board (FASB)** noted the following characteristics that it felt distinguished governmental and not-for-profit entities from business organizations:

a. Receipts of significant amounts of resources from resource providers who do not expect to receive either repayment or economic benefits proportionate to the resources provided.

b. Operating purposes that are other than to provide goods or services at a profit or profit equivalent.

c. Absence of defined ownership interests that can be sold, transferred, or redeemed or that convey entitlement to a share of a residual distribution of resources in the event of liquidation of the organization.[3]

The **Governmental Accounting Standards Board (GASB)** distinguishes government entities in the United States from both not-for-profit and business entities by stressing that governments exist in an environment in which the power ultimately rests in the hands of the people. Voters delegate that power to public officials through the election process. The power is divided among the executive, legislative, and judicial branches of the government, so that the actions, financial and otherwise, of government executives are constrained by legislative actions, and executive and legislative actions are subject to judicial review. Further constraints are imposed on state and local governments by the federal government. In the United States higher levels of government encourage or dictate activities of lower level governments. Higher levels of government finance the activities (partially, at least) by an extensive system of intergovernmental grants and subsidies that require the lower levels to be accountable to the entity providing the resources, as well as to the citizenry. Revenues raised by each level of government come, ultimately, from taxpayers. Taxpayers are required to provide resources to governments even though they often have little choice about which government services they receive and the extent to which they receive them.[4]

This relative lack of taxpayer choice is also identified in a GASB white paper that notes that "most governments do not operate in a competitive marketplace, face

[3] Financial Accounting Standards Board, *Statement of Financial Accounting Concepts No. 4,* "Objectives of Financial Reporting by Nonbusiness Organizations" (Norwalk, CT, 1980 as amended), par. 6. In 1985 the FASB replaced the term *nonbusiness* with the term *not-for-profit.* Other organizations use the term *nonprofit* as a synonym for *not-for-profit.* The term *not-for-profit* is predominantly used in this text.

[4] Based on discussion in GASB *Concepts Statement No. 1,* pars. 14–18. Governmental Accounting Standards Board, *Codification of Governmental Accounting and Financial Reporting Standards as of June 30, 2010* (Norwalk, CT, 2010), Appendix B.

virtually no threat of liquidation, and do not have equity owners."[5] The white paper further states:

> Governmental accounting and financial reporting standards aim to address [the] need for public accountability information by helping stakeholders assess how public resources were acquired and either used during the period or are expected to be used. Such reporting also helps users to assess whether current resources were sufficient to meet current service costs (or whether some costs were shifted to future taxpayers) and whether the government's ability to provide services improved or declined from the previous year.[6]

SOURCES OF FINANCIAL REPORTING STANDARDS

As shown in Illustration 1–1, Rule 203 of the American Institute of Certified Public Accountants (AICPA) Code of Professional Conduct formally designates the FASB, GASB, and FASAB as the authoritative bodies to establish **generally accepted accounting principles (GAAP)** for state and local governments, the federal government, and business organizations and nongovernmental not-for-profit organizations, respectively. In practice, the "authority to establish accounting principles" means the "authority to establish accounting and financial reporting standards." In addition, for publicly held business organizations, FASB standards are officially recognized as authoritative by the Securities and Exchange Commission (SEC) (Financial Reporting Release No. 1, Section 101, and reaffirmed in its April 2003 Policy Statement).

Authority to establish accounting and reporting standards for not-for-profit organizations is split between the FASB and the GASB because a sizable number of not-for-profit organizations are governmental in nature, particularly public colleges

ILLUSTRATION 1–1 **Primary Sources of Accounting and Financial Reporting Standards for Businesses, Governments, and Not-for-Profit Organizations**

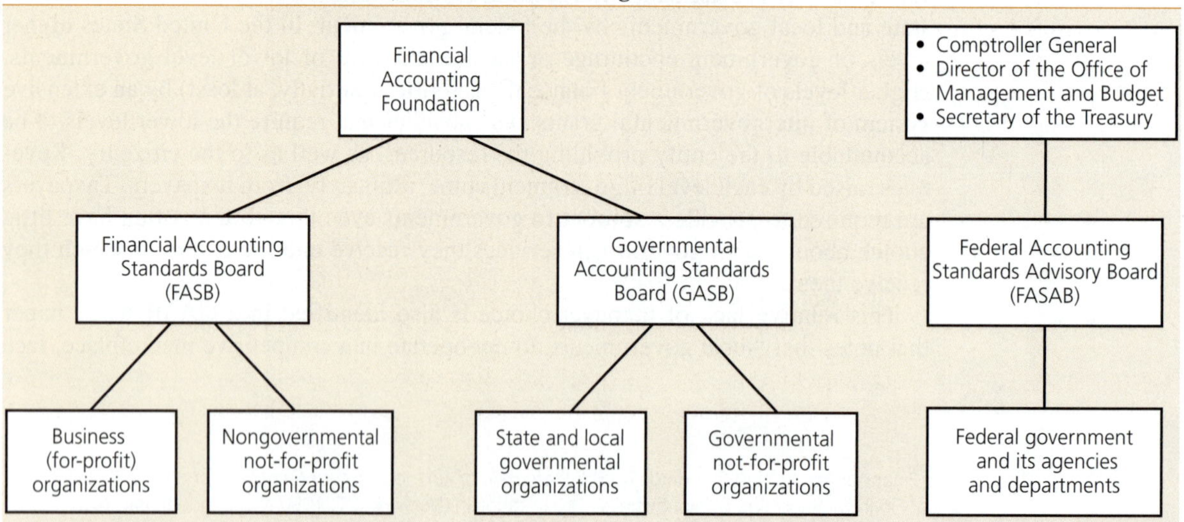

[5] Governmental Accounting Standards Board, *White Paper "Why Governmental Accounting and Financial Reporting Is—and Should Be—Different"* (Norwalk, CT, 2013, revised), Executive Summary, p. ii.

[6] Ibid.

and universities and government hospitals. The FASB is responsible for setting accounting and reporting standards for not-for-profit organizations that are independent of governments. Governmental not-for-profit organizations follow standards established by the GASB.

The GASB and the FASB are parallel bodies under the oversight of the Financial Accounting Foundation. The foundation appoints the members of the two boards and supports the boards' operations. The federal Sarbanes-Oxley Act greatly enhanced financial support for the FASB by mandating an assessed fee on corporate security offerings. The Dodd-Frank Wall Street Reform and Consumer Protection Act (2010) required the establishment of an accounting support fee to fund the GASB. In February 2012 the Financial Industry Regulatory Authority (FINRA) established such a fee.[7]

Because of the method of support and the lack of ties to any single organization or government, the GASB and the FASB are referred to as "independent standards-setting boards in the private sector." Before the creation of the GASB and the FASB, financial reporting standards were set by groups sponsored by professional organizations: The forerunners of the GASB (formed in 1984) were the National Council on Governmental Accounting (1973–84), the National Committee on Governmental Accounting (1948–73), and the National Committee on Municipal Accounting (1934–41). The forerunners of the FASB (formed in 1973) were the Accounting Principles Board (1959–73) and the Committee on Accounting Procedure (1938–59) of the American Institute of Certified Public Accountants.

Federal statutes assign responsibility for establishing and maintaining a sound financial structure for the federal government to three officials: the Comptroller General, the Director of the Office of Management and Budget, and the Secretary of the Treasury. In 1990, these three officials created the **Federal Accounting Standards Advisory Board (FASAB)** to recommend accounting principles and standards for the federal government and its agencies. It is understood that, to the maximum extent possible, federal accounting and financial reporting standards should be consistent with those established by the GASB and, where applicable, by the FASB.

OBJECTIVES OF FINANCIAL REPORTING

GASB *Concepts Statement No. 1,* "Objectives of Financial Reporting," states that "**Accountability** is the cornerstone of all financial reporting in government. . . . Accountability requires governments to answer to the citizenry—to justify the raising of public resources and the purposes for which they are used."[8] The board elaborated:

> Governmental accountability is based on the belief that the citizenry has a "right to know," a right to receive openly declared facts that may lead to public debate by the citizens and their elected representatives. Financial reporting plays a major role in fulfilling government's duty to be publicly accountable in a democratic society.[9]

Illustration 1–2 shows several ways that state and local government financial reporting is used in making economic, social, and political decisions and assessing accountability. Closely related to the concept of accountability as the cornerstone of

[7] Financial Industry Regulatory Authority, Regulatory Notice 13–17, "GASB Accounting Support Fee," April 2013.

[8] GASB, *Codification,* Appendix B, *Concepts Statement No. 1,* par. 56.

[9] Ibid.

ILLUSTRATION 1–2 Comparison of Financial Reporting Objectives—State and Local Governments, Federal Government, and Not-for-Profit Organizations

State and Local Governments[a]	Federal Government[b]	Not-for-Profit Organizations[c]
Financial reporting is used in making economic, social, and political decisions and in assessing accountability primarily by: • Comparing actual financial results with the legally adopted budget. • Assessing financial condition and results of operations. • Assisting in determining compliance with finance-related laws, rules, and regulations. • Assisting in evaluating efficiency and effectiveness.	Financial reporting should help to achieve accountability and is intended to assist report users in evaluating: • Budgetary integrity. • Operating performance. • Stewardship. • Adequacy of systems and controls.	Financial reporting should provide information useful in: • Making resource allocation decisions. • Assessing services and ability to provide services. • Assessing management stewardship and performance. • Assessing economic resources, obligations, net resources, and changes in them.

[a]Source: *GASB Concepts Statement No. 1,* par. 32.

[b]Source: *FASAB Statement of Federal Accounting Concepts No. 1,* par. 134.

[c]Source: *FASB Concepts Statement No. 4,* pp. 13–15.

governmental financial reporting is the concept the GASB refers to as **interperiod equity.** This concept and its importance are explained as follows:

> The Board believes that interperiod equity is a significant part of accountability and is fundamental to public administration. It therefore needs to be considered when establishing financial reporting objectives. In short, *financial reporting should help users assess whether current-year revenues are sufficient to pay for services provided that year and whether future taxpayers will be required to assume burdens for services previously provided.* (Emphasis added.)[10]

Accountability is also the foundation for the financial reporting objectives the FASAB has established for the federal government. The FASAB's *Statement of Accounting and Reporting Concepts Statement No. 1* identifies four objectives of federal financial reporting (see Illustration 1–2) focused on evaluating budgetary integrity, operating performance, stewardship, and adequacy of systems and controls.

Unlike the FASB and the GASB, which focus their standards on *external* financial reporting, the FASAB and its sponsors in the federal government are concerned with *both* internal and external financial reporting. Accordingly, the FASAB has identified four major groups of users of federal financial reports: citizens, Congress, executives, and program managers. Given the broad role the FASAB has been assigned, its standards focus on cost accounting and service efforts and accomplishment measures, as well as on financial accounting and reporting.

Financial reports of not-for-profit organizations—voluntary health and welfare organizations, private colleges and universities, private health care institutions, religious organizations, and others—have similar uses. However, as Illustration 1–2 shows, the reporting objectives for not-for-profit organizations emphasize decision usefulness over financial accountability needs. The FASB *Statement of Financial Accounting Concepts No. 4* indicates that not-for-profit and business enterprises are similar in many ways and thus the emphasis on decision usefulness in reporting objectives.

[10] Ibid., par. 61.

Note that the objectives of financial reporting for governments and not-for-profit entities stress the need for the public to understand and evaluate the financial activities and management of these organizations. Readers will recognize the impact on their lives, and on their bank accounts, of the activities of the layers of government they are obligated to support and of the not-for-profit organizations they voluntarily support. Since each of us is significantly affected, it is important that we be able to read intelligently the financial reports of governmental and not-for-profit organizations. In order to make informed decisions as citizens, taxpayers, creditors, and donors, readers should make the effort to learn the accounting and financial reporting standards developed by the authoritative bodies. The standards are further explained and illustrated throughout the remainder of the text.

OVERVIEW OF FINANCIAL REPORTING FOR STATE AND LOCAL GOVERNMENTS, THE FEDERAL GOVERNMENT, AND NOT-FOR-PROFIT ORGANIZATIONS

Financial Reporting of State and Local Governments

Like the FASB, the GASB continues to develop concepts statements that communicate the framework within which the Board strives to establish consistent financial reporting standards for entities within its jurisdiction. The GASB, as well as the FASB, is concerned with establishing standards for financial reporting to *external* users—those who lack the authority to prescribe the information they want and who must rely on the information management communicates to them. The Board does not intend to set standards for reporting to managers and administrators or others deemed to have the ability to enforce their demands for information.

General Purpose External Financial Reporting

Illustration 1–3 displays the minimum requirements for general purpose external financial reporting under the governmental financial reporting model specified by

ILLUSTRATION 1–3 Minimum Requirements for General Purpose External Financial Reporting

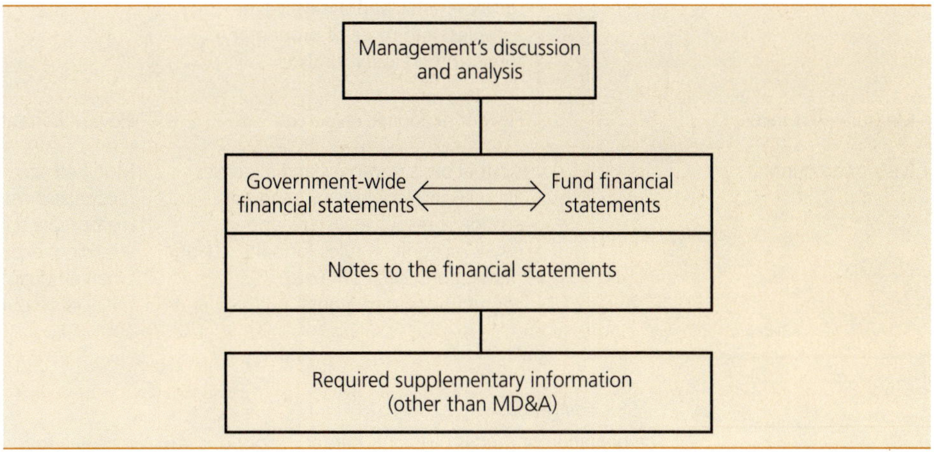

Source: GASB *Codification,* Sec. 2200.103.

the GASB.[11] Central to the model is the **management's discussion and analysis (MD&A).** The MD&A is **required supplementary information (RSI)** designed to communicate in narrative, easily readable form the purpose of the basic financial statements and the government's current financial position and results of financial activities compared with those of the prior year.

As shown in Illustration 1–3, the GASB prescribes two categories of **basic financial statements,** government-wide and fund. **Government-wide financial statements** are intended to provide an aggregated overview of a government's net position and changes in net position. You will notice that the GASB uses the term *net position* rather than the FASB term *net assets*; however, the terms are substantially the same. The government-wide financial statements report on the government as a whole and assist in assessing **operational accountability**—whether the government has used its resources efficiently and effectively in meeting operating objectives. The GASB concluded that reporting on operational accountability is best achieved by using essentially the same basis of accounting and measurement focus used by business organizations: the accrual basis and flow of economic resources measurement focus.

Fund financial statements, the other category of basic financial statements, provide more detailed financial information about the government. Certain funds, referred to as *governmental funds,* focus on the short-term flow of current financial resources rather than on the flow of economic resources.[12] The focus on current financial resources makes it easier for users assessing **fiscal accountability,** which relates to ensuring the government is complying with rules and regulations related to the use of financial resources. Because of the short-term focus, governmental funds use a modified accrual basis of accounting rather than the accrual basis. Under **modified accrual,** revenues are recognized in the period they are measurable and available for spending and expenditures (not expenses) are recognized when they create an obligation to be paid from current financial resources. The characteristics and roles of the government-wide and fund financial statements are summarized in Illustration 1–4.

ILLUSTRATION 1–4 Dual Roles of Governmental Financial Statements in Assessing Accountability

	Operational Accountability	Fiscal Accountability
Statements	Government-wide financial statements (governmental and business-type activities) and those of proprietary funds and fiduciary funds	Governmental fund financial statements
Measurement focus	Flow of economic resources	Flow of current financial resources
Basis of accounting	Accrual basis (revenues and *expenses* are recognized when exchange of economic resources occurs or per GASB recognition rules for nonexchange transactions, such as taxes, contributions, and grants)	Modified accrual basis (revenues are recognized when resources are measurable and available for current spending; *expenditures* are recognized when an obligation to spend current financial resources is incurred)

[11] GASB *Codification,* Sec. 2200.102.

[12] The definition of *fund* is given in Chapter 2. For now, you can view a fund as a separate set of accounts used to account for resources segregated for particular purposes.

Other funds, referred to as *proprietary* and *fiduciary funds,* account for the business-type and certain fiduciary (trust and agency) activities of the government. These funds follow accounting and reporting principles similar to those of business organizations.

As shown in Illustration 1–3, the notes to the financial statements are considered integral to the financial statements. In addition, governments are required to disclose certain RSI other than MD&A. These additional information disclosures are discussed in several of the following chapters.

Comprehensive Annual Financial Report

Serious users of government financial information need more detail than is found in the MD&A, basic financial statements, and RSI (other than MD&A). For state and local governments, much of that detail is found in the government's **comprehensive annual financial report (CAFR).** Although governments are not required to prepare a CAFR, most do so as a matter of public record and to provide additional financial details beyond the minimum requirements shown in Illustration 1–3. As such, the GASB provides standards for the content of a CAFR in its annually updated publication *Codification of Governmental Accounting and Financial Reporting Standards.* A CAFR prepared in conformity with these standards should contain the following sections.[13]

Introductory Section[14] The introductory section typically includes items such as a title page and contents page, a letter of transmittal, a description of the government, and other items deemed appropriate by management. The letter of transmittal may be literally that—a letter from the chief financial officer addressed to the chief executive and governing body of the government—or it may be a narrative over the signature of the chief executive. In either event, the letter or narrative material should cite legal and policy requirements for the report.

Financial Section The financial section of a comprehensive annual financial report should include (1) an auditor's report, (2) management's discussion and analysis (MD&A), (3) basic financial statements, (4) required supplementary information (other than MD&A), and (5) other supplementary information, such as combining statements and individual fund statements and schedules. Items (2), (3), and (4) represent the minimum requirements for general purpose external financial reporting, as depicted in Illustration 1–3. As you will recognize, a CAFR provides additional supplementary financial information beyond the minimum amount required by generally accepted accounting principles.

Laws regarding the audit of governments vary from state to state. Some states have laws requiring that all state agencies and all local governments be audited by an audit agency of the state government. In other states, local governments are audited by independent public accounting firms. In still other states, some local governments are audited by the state audit agency and some by independent public accounting firms.

[13] GASB, *Codification,* Sec. 2200.104–193.

[14] For a view of the introductory section, as well as the other sections of the CAFR, you may wish to look at the City and County of Denver, Colorado's CAFR at *http://www.denvergov.org/Default.aspx?alias=www.denvergov.org/finance.* Portions of Denver's CAFR for 2013 are included for illustrative purposes in various places in this text.

In any event, the auditor's opinion should accompany the financial statements reproduced in the report.

The financial section should contain sufficient information to disclose fully and present fairly the financial position and results of financial operations during the fiscal year. Laws of higher jurisdictions, actions of the legislative branch of the government itself, and agreements with creditors and others impose constraints over governments' financial activities and create unique financial accountability requirements.

Statistical Section In addition to the introductory and financial sections of the CAFR, which were just described, a CAFR should contain a statistical section. The statistical section typically presents tables and charts showing demographic and economic data, financial trends, fiscal capacity, and operating information of the government in the detail needed by readers who are more than casually interested in the activities of the government. The GASB *Codification* requires a specific set of statistical tables for inclusion in a CAFR. The statistical section is discussed at greater length in Chapter 9 of this text.

Financial Reporting of the Federal Government

U.S. Government-Wide Financial Reporting

For more than a decade, the Department of the Treasury has prepared a prototype consolidated financial report for the U.S. government as a whole.[15] The consolidated financial report includes a "plain language" *Citizen's Guide,* a management's discussion and analysis (MD&A), several financial statements,[16] and supplemental information that report both on the government's budget and proprietary financial activities, as well as reconciliation of the two. Of particular interest is a statement of social insurance (e.g., Social Security and Medicare, among other commitments) that reflects an excess of the present value of future actuarial expenditures over revenues at the end of FY 2013 of more than $53 trillion.

Readers may be shocked to learn that despite the enormous dollar amounts involved, the U.S. Comptroller General has never been able to issue an audit opinion on the federal government's consolidated financial statements. In general, serious financial management and data deficiencies are cited for the Comptroller General's continuing disclaimer of opinion. These deficiencies are explained in greater detail in Chapter 17.

Federal Department and Agency Financial Reporting

The federal Office of Management and Budget's (OMB) *Circular A-136* requires major federal departments and agencies to prepare a **performance and accountability report (PAR)** that includes an annual performance report (APR), annual financial

[15] The FY 2013 Consolidated Financial Report of the United States Government can be viewed and downloaded at *http://www.fms.treas.gov/fr/index.html.*

[16] Financial statements included in the U.S. Government's Consolidated Financial Report are comparative statements of net cost, statements of operations and changes in net position, reconciliation of net operating cost and unified budget deficit, statements of changes in cash balance from unified budget and other activities, balance sheets, and statements of social insurance. See Chapter 17 for more information about these statements.

statements, and a variety of management reports on internal control and other accountability issues. The PAR has four sections containing:

1. An MD&A, which serves as a brief overview of the entire PAR and clearly describes the department or agency's mission and organizational structure; its performance goals, objectives, and results; analysis of its financial statements; and analysis of information about internal controls and legal compliance.
2. Performance information. The annual performance report (APR) provides information about the agency's performance and progress in achieving its performance goals.
3. Basic financial statements. These include a balance sheet, statement of net cost (essentially an operating statement format that is presented with expenses reported before revenues; that is, program costs minus earned revenues results in net cost), statement of changes in net position (similar to changes in owners' equity in business accounting), statement of budgetary resources, statement of custodial activity, and statement of social insurance.
4. Other accompanying information, such as perspectives on the tax burden, size of the tax gap, challenges facing management, and revenue forgone.

Federal government financial reporting places a strong emphasis on management's performance, in addition to the reporting of financial information. Chapter 17 explains federal department and agency financial reporting requirements in much greater detail and provides examples of each financial statement.

Financial Reporting of Not-for-Profit Organizations (NFPs)

Most NFPs are nongovernmental in nature and, therefore, follow FASB accounting and financial reporting standards. The primary purpose of NFP financial statements is to provide decision-useful financial information to resource providers, principally donors, members, and creditors, among others. Resource providers have in common the need to assess (1) the services provided by an NFP and the ability of the NFP to continue to provide those services, and (2) management's performance and stewardship of resources.[17] To meet these reporting needs, FASB standards require NFPs to prepare a set of organization-wide financial statements that include a statement of financial position (balance sheet), a statement of activities (income statement), and a statement of cash flows.[18] In addition, NFPs classified as voluntary health and welfare organizations (health-related and community services organizations such as the YMCA, American Heart Association, and United Way) are required to provide a statement of functional expenses.[19] The latter statement classifies expenses into program and supporting services categories, in addition to *natural* classifications such as personnel, supplies, and travel. Chapter 13 provides examples of all these statements.

Many NFPs depend heavily on donor contributions to finance their operations. Donors often impose restrictions on the use of contributions, such as specifying that their contribution be used for a particular purpose or in a particular time period. **Donor-imposed restrictions** may be temporary or, in the case of certain

[17] FASB *ASC* 958-205-05-3.

[18] Ibid. 958-205-05-5.

[19] Ibid.

endowments, permanent. Permanent endowments require the NFP to maintain the principal amount of the contribution in perpetuity but permit the use of earnings on invested principal, either without restriction or for a particular restricted purpose.

FASB standards recognize the essential need for management to demonstrate accountability for donor-restricted resources. Specifically, the standards require that an NFP's statement of financial position report net assets (the excess of total assets over total liabilities) in three categories: permanently restricted, temporarily restricted, and unrestricted.[20] The statement of activities reports increases and decreases in each of the three categories of net assets.

In addition, it is important that an NFP's statement of activities report expenses incurred for direct support of programs separately from supporting expenses (more formally titled, management and general expenses) and fund-raising costs. Reporting expenses in this way is an important aspect of accountability since it allows donors, oversight bodies, and others to calculate what percentage of total expenses is being incurred for program purposes, rather than for overhead and fund-raising. Would you want to contribute to an NFP that spent more for administrative support and fund-raising than for its core mission?

As with state and local government and federal government financial reporting, a complete discussion of NFP financial reporting is deferred to later chapters of the text. Chapters 13 through 16 will provide you with a more comprehensive understanding of NFP accounting and financial reporting, both for nongovernmental and governmental NFPs.

EXPANDING THE SCOPE OF ACCOUNTABILITY REPORTING

Some governments publish highly condensed popular reports. These reports usually contain selected data from the audited financial statements, statistical data, graphic displays, and narrative explanations, but the reports themselves are not audited. In addition, many state and local governments have begun to identify and report nonfinancial performance measures. For nearly 20 years, the GASB has encouraged state and local governments to experiment with reporting **service efforts and accomplishments (SEA)** measures to provide more complete information about a government's performance than can be provided by basic financial statements, budgetary comparison statements, and schedules. Indicators of service efforts include inputs of nonmonetary resources as well as inputs of dollars. Indicators of service accomplishments include both outputs and outcomes; outputs are quantitative measures of work done, such as the number of juvenile cases handled, and outcomes are the impacts of outputs on program objectives, such as a reduction in the high school dropout rate or incidence of juvenile crime. Chapter 12 provides additional discussion of SEA measures.

OVERVIEW OF CHAPTERS 2 THROUGH 17

GASB Principles, Standards, and Financial Reporting

Part 1 of the text (Chapters 2–9) focuses on state and local governments. The principles that underlie GASB accounting and reporting standards are presented in Chapter 2.

[20] Ibid. 958-205-05-6.

Chapters 3 through 8 provide detailed illustrations of the effect of financial transactions on the funds and government-wide statements. Financial reporting for state and local governments is described in detail in Chapter 9.

Accountability for Public Funds

Part II of the text includes three chapters that describe ways that public financial managers provide accountability over funds entrusted to them. Chapter 10 provides information on how to analyze the financial performance of state and local governments based on financial and other information. Auditing techniques designed to assure the public that funds are properly recognized and spent efficiently and effectively are described in Chapter 11, with special attention devoted to areas of auditing that are unique to federal funds, such as single audits. Chapter 12 covers tools important to managers in demonstrating accountability for funds, such as budgeting, costing, and performance measurement.

Not-for-Profit Organizations and the Federal Government

Part III is a set of four chapters covering the unique accounting and financial reporting issues facing entities in the not-for-profit sector and a final chapter on accounting and financial reporting for the federal government. Chapter 13 provides detailed illustrations of the effect of financial transactions on the financial statements of not-for-profit organizations, much like Chapters 3 through 8 do for state and local governments. The governance and regulatory issues that a not-for-profit organization faces from the time of its incorporation through merger or dissolution, if any, are presented in Chapter 14. Chapters 15 and 16 present industry-specific accounting and financial reporting requirements for colleges and universities and health care organizations, respectively. Chapter 17 focuses on the federal government, the largest provider of public funds, and introduces federal offices that interact with state and local governments and not-for-profit organizations in a variety of ways; for example, the Government Accountability Office (GAO) and the Office of Management and Budget (OMB).

A CAVEAT

The first edition of this text was written by the late Professor R. M. Mikesell more than 60 years ago in 1951. Some words of his bear thoughtful rereading from time to time by teachers and students in all fields, not just those concerned with accounting and financial reporting for governmental and not-for-profit organizations:

> Even when developed to the ultimate stage of perfection, governmental accounting cannot become a guaranty of good government. At best, it can never be more than a valuable tool for promotion of sound financial management. It does not offer a panacea for all the ills that beset representative government; nor will it fully overcome the influence of disinterested, uninformed citizens. It cannot be substituted for honesty and moral integrity on the part of public officials; it can help in resisting but cannot eliminate the demands of selfish interests, whether in the form of individual citizens, corporations, or the pressure groups which always abound to influence government at all levels.[21]

[21] R. M. Mikesell, *Governmental Accounting,* rev. ed., Homewood, IL: Richard D. Irwin, 1956, p. 10.

Key Terms*

Accountability, *5*
Basic financial statements, *8*
Comprehensive annual financial report (CAFR), *9*
Donor-imposed restrictions, *11*
Federal Accounting Standards Advisory Board (FASAB), *5*
Financial Accounting Standards Board (FASB), *3*
Fiscal accountability, *8*
Fund financial statements, *8*
General purpose governments, *2*
Generally accepted accounting principles (GAAP), *4*
Governmental Accounting Standards Board (GASB), *3*
Government-wide financial statements, *8*
Interperiod equity, *6*
Management's discussion and analysis (MD&A), *8*
Modified accrual, *8*
Operational accountability, *8*
Performance and accountability report (PAR), *10*
Required supplementary information (RSI), *8*
Service efforts and accomplishments (SEA), *12*
Special purpose governments, *2*

* See the glossary at the back of the text for a definition of each term and concept.

Questions

1–1. Identify some differences between business organizations and government/not-for-profit organizations.

1–2. Using GP for general purpose government or SP for special purpose government, identify the following governments by type.
a. Stonington Village. _____
b. Lynnford Regional Library District. _____
c. Hillsborough County Consolidated School District. _____
d. Missoula, Montana. _____
e. Pulaski County Public Works District. _____
f. Hohenstein Township. _____

1–3. Which standard-setting bodies have responsibility for establishing accounting and reporting standards for (1) state and local governments, (2) business organizations, (3) not-for-profit organizations, and (4) the federal government and its agencies and departments?

1–4. The Beth House Museum is a nongovernmental not-for-profit organization. At the annual meeting, one of the new board members said, "I took a couple of accounting classes in college and we can choose to use either the FASB rules or the GASB rules." Do you agree with the board member? Why or why not?

1–5. Explain the meaning and significance of *interperiod equity*.

1–6. Explain the purpose of *operational accountability* and the purpose of *fiscal accountability*. Which category of financial statements is most useful in reporting on each of these accountability concepts?

1–7. What is the primary financial reporting objective for not-for-profit organizations? How does this differ from the primary financial reporting objective for a government?

1–8. What are the three sections of a comprehensive annual financial report (CAFR)? What information is contained in each section? How do the minimum requirements for general purpose external financial reporting relate in scope to the CAFR?

1–9. Identify and describe the four sections of a federal department or agency's *performance and accountability report.*

1–10. A not-for-profit organization is required to report expenses incurred for programs separately from management and general expenses and fund-raising costs. Explain who would use this information and why this separation matters.

Cases

1–11 Research Case—GASB. Examine the Governmental Accounting Standards Board's Web site (*www.GASB.org*) and prepare a brief report about its mission, standard setting process, board composition, and the role of the Governmental Accounting Standards Advisory Council. Can you determine how to obtain a copy of the most recent *Codification of Governmental Accounting and Financial Reporting Standards?* What would it cost to purchase or access this publication?

1–12 Research Case—FASB. On November 9, 2011, the chairman of the FASB announced that a standard-setting project intended to improve the financial reporting of not-for-profit organizations had been added to the FASB's agenda. Examine the Financial Accounting Standards Board's Web site (*www.FASB.org*) to find information about this project. Write a report outlining the objectives of the project and its current status. Include in your discussion what role the Not-for-Profit Advisory Committee (NAC) played in this project.

1–13 Research Case—FASAB. Examine the Federal Accounting Standards Advisory Board's Web site at *www.FASAB.gov* and prepare a brief report about its mission and structure and compile a list of organizations represented on its Accounting and Auditing Policy Committee. Can you obtain a copy of the full text of FASAB statements from this Web site? If not, how would you obtain a copy of a statement pertinent to federal agencies? What is the cost to purchase a statement?

1–14 Research Case—Comparing Financial Reporting Objectives. *GASB Concepts Statement No. 1*, "Objectives of Financial Reporting," states that "Accountability is the cornerstone of all financial reporting in government." *FASB Statements of Financial Accounting Concepts Statement No. 8,* "Conceptual Framework for Financial Reporting," states that "The objective of general purpose financial reporting is to provide financial information about the reporting entity that is useful to existing and potential investors, lenders, and other creditors in making decisions about providing resources to the entity." However, the FASB has acknowledged through *Statement of Financial Accounting Concepts No. 4,* "Objectives of Financial Reporting by Nonbusiness Organizations," that users of business and not-for-profit entities differ.

Required

Compare the financial reporting needs of the resource providers of government/not-for-profit organizations to the financial reporting needs of the resource providers of for-profit organizations.

1–15 Research Case—Federal Financial Reporting Objectives. *Statement of Financial Accounting Concepts 1*, "Objectives of Federal Financial Reporting" at (*http://www.fasab.gov/pdffiles/handbook_sffac_1.pdf*) identifies accountability and decision usefulness as the fundamental values of federal governmental financial accounting and reporting. The statement identifies four groups of users to whom the government owes accountability and the possible needs of each user group.

Required

Briefly describe the user groups, their needs for information, and how these tie into the four objectives of federal financial reporting identified in the statement.

Exercises and Problems

1–16 Examine the CAFR. Download a copy of the most recent comprehensive annual financial report (CAFR) for a city of your choice. Many cities with 25,000 or more population provide Internet access to their CAFRs.* Familiarize yourself with the city's CAFR and reread the section in this chapter titled "Financial Reporting of State and Local Governments." Be prepared to discuss in class the items suggested below.

a. Introductory Section.

What has the city included in the introductory section of its CAFR? Does it include the items identified in the section of the text titled "Comprehensive Annual Financial Report"?

b. Financial Section.

(1) *Audit Report.* Are the financial statements in the report audited by an independent CPA, state auditors, or auditors employed by the government being audited? Has the city received an unmodified audit report?

(2) *Basic Financial Statements.* Does the CAFR contain both government-wide financial statements and fund statements? How many financial statements have been included as part of the basic financial statements section of the CAFR?

(3) *Notes to the Financial Statements.* How many notes follow the required basic financial statements? Is there a phrase at the bottom of the basic financial statements indicating that the notes are an integral part of the financial statements?

(4) *Other Supplementary Information.* Following the notes to the financial statements, does the CAFR provide other supplementary information, such as combining and individual fund statements?

(5) *Management's Discussion and Analysis (MD&A).* Does the CAFR contain an MD&A? If so, where is it located and what type of information does it contain?

c. Statistical Tables.

What information has been included in this section of the CAFR?

1–17 Compare financial statements. For this exercise refer to the Denver government-wide statement of net position (p. 40), the Denver government-wide statement of activities (p. 42), the American Diabetes Association balance sheet (p. 528), and the American Diabetes Association statement of activities (p. 529).

* You can usually access a city's CAFR by doing a search on "City of (name)" and looking for a link to the city's departments. At that link, select Finance Department or a department with a similar function, such as Accounting and Budgeting, and look for "Financial Reports" or similar link.

Required

a. Compare Denver's statement of net position to the American Diabetes Association's balance sheet. What are some similarities and differences in the statement formats?

b. Compare Denver's statement of activities to the American Diabetes Association's statement of activities. What are some similarities and differences in the statement formats?

1–18 Multiple Choice. Choose the best answer.

1. Which of the following is a special purpose government?
   a. The State of Arkansas.
   b. Greene County.
   c. Rutgers University.
   d. Seattle, Washington.

2. Which of the following is *not* a distinguishing difference between governmental organizations and for-profit organizations?
   a. Lack of a profit motive.
   b. Revenue may be earned through exchange transactions.
   c. Absence of owners.
   d. Resources are provided by individuals and entities that may not directly benefit from the use of the resources.

3. Which of the following statements regarding primary sources of accounting and financial reporting standards is false?
   a. The GASB sets standards for all state and local governments.
   b. The FASB sets standards for all business and not-for-profit entities.
   c. The FASB and GASB are administered by the Financial Accounting Foundation.
   d. The FASAB sets standards for the federal government and its agencies and departments.

4. James Black is reviewing his city's financial reporting because he wants to run for the city council. He is concerned that the city is not using its resources effectively. James is primarily interested in:
   a. Fiscal accountability.
   b. Social accountability.
   c. Political accountability.
   d. Operational accountability.

5. The concept of *interperiod equity* refers to whether:
   a. Revenues equaled or exceeded expenditures for the year.
   b. Total assets (current and noncurrent) were sufficient to cover total liabilities (current and noncurrent).
   c. Current year revenues were sufficient to pay for current year services.
   d. Future taxpayers can expect to receive the same or higher level of services as current taxpayers.

6. What are the components that are included in the minimum requirements for general purpose external financial reporting?
   a. Introductory section, financial section, and statistical section.

b. MD&A, government financial statements, fund financial statements, notes to the financial statements, and RSI.
c. Letter from the chief financial officer, government financial statements, notes to the financial statements, and RSI.
d. MD&A, government-wide financial statements, notes to the financial statements, and RSI.

7. The basic financial statements of a state or local government include all of the following *except*:
a. An MD&A.
b. Government-wide financial statements.
c. Fund financial statements.
d. Notes to the financial statements.

8. Under GASB standards, financial information useful for assessing operational accountability is primarily reported in which financial statements?

	Government-wide Financial Statements	Fund Financial Statements
a.	No	Yes
b.	Yes	No
c.	Yes	Yes
d.	No	No

9. Which of the following is *not* a required section of a federal agency or department's performance and accountability report (PAR)?
a. A performance section, which includes an annual performance report (APR).
b. An MD&A.
c. A basic financial statements section.
d. A statement of nonparticipation in political matters.

10. The *primary* reason that not-for-profit (NFP) organizations should report expenses incurred for program purposes separately from those for supporting services such as management and general and fund-raising is that:
a. GASB standards require it.
b. Program managers need information about the cost of activities for which they are responsible.
c. Top managers need to know how much they are spending for nonprogrammatic management and general support.
d. Donors, potential donors, oversight bodies, and others need to know what percentage of total expenses are being incurred for carrying out the NFP's programs, rather than for overhead and fund-raising.

1–19 Matching. For each characteristic, concept, or financial reporting requirement listed on the next page, place a Y for yes in the type of organization column if the item applies to that type of organization or N for no if it does not apply. To answer some of the items, you may wish to take a look ahead to the illustrative operating statements in Chapters 2, 13, 15, 16, and 17 before answering.

Characteristic, Concept, or Financial Reporting Requirement	State and Local Governments	Federal Government	Nongovernmental Not-for-Profit Organizations
Organization-wide financial statements			
Management's discussion and analysis (MD&A)			
Annual performance report			
Modified accrual			
Reporting of program expenses separate from supporting expenses			
Absence of defined ownership interests			
Standards set by GASB			
Standards set by FASB			
Standards set by FASAB			
Standards focused on both internal and external users of financial information			

PART One

STATE AND LOCAL GOVERNMENTS

Chapter Two

Principles of Accounting and Financial Reporting for State and Local Governments

Learning Objectives

After studying this chapter, you should be able to:

2-1 Explain the nature of the three major activity categories of a state or local government: governmental activities, business-type activities, and fiduciary activities.

2-2 Explain the Governmental Accounting Standards Board's (GASB) integrated accounting and financial reporting model, including:

Elements and measurement approaches for the elements of the financial statements.

Government-wide financial statements.

Fund financial statements.

Definition of *fund* and principles of fund accounting.

Types of funds in each fund category and characteristics of each fund type.

2-3 Discuss the nature of major fund reporting and the criteria used to determine whether a fund should be reported as a major fund.

Chapter 1 presented a brief overview of the minimum requirements for general purpose external financial reporting under the GASB financial reporting model. This chapter expands on the previous discussion and focuses primarily on principles of accounting and financial reporting within GASB's integrated reporting model framework.

When the GASB was formed in 1984, it adopted 12 accounting and financial reporting principles that had been established by its predecessor standard-setting body, the National Council on Governmental Accounting (NCGA). Since that time, the GASB has modified several of the original 12 principles and added one principle for reporting long-term liabilities. A summary of these principles is presented in Appendix B at the end of this chapter. Certain of the principles are also discussed in this chapter.

ACTIVITIES OF GOVERNMENT

Chapter 1 explained that the characteristics of governmental organizations differ from those of for-profit business organizations. One key difference is that governments are not profit seeking but exist to meet citizens' demand for services, consistent with the availability of resources to provide those services. As shown in Illustration 2–1, most general purpose governments engage in three broad categories of service activities—governmental, business-type, and fiduciary. Although the types and levels of services vary from government to government, general purpose governments provide certain core services: those related to protection of life and property (e.g., police and fire protection), public works (e.g., streets and highways, bridges, and public buildings), culture and recreation facilities and programs, and educational, and social services. Governments must also incur costs for general administrative support such as data processing, finance, and personnel. Core governmental services, together with general administrative support, comprise the major part of what GASB *Concepts Statement No. 1* refers to as governmental-type activities.[1] In its more recent pronouncements, GASB refers to these activities as simply **governmental activities.** Chapters 3 through 6 of the text focus on various aspects of accounting for governmental activities.

Some readers may be surprised to learn that governments also engage in a variety of **business-type activities.** These activities include, among others, public utilities (e.g., electric, water, gas, and sewer utilities), transportation systems, toll roads, toll bridges, hospitals, parking garages and lots, golf courses, and swimming pools. Many of these activities are intended to be self-supporting by charging users for the services they receive. Operating subsidies from general tax revenues are not uncommon, however, particularly for transportation systems. Accounting for business-type activities is covered in Chapter 7 of the text.

ILLUSTRATION 2–1 Activities of Government

Governmental	Business-type	Fiduciary
• Administrative support (e.g., city manager's office, personnel, data processing, and finance) • Core government services (e.g., police and fire, public works, and culture and recreation)	• Business-like activities that are largely self-supported by user charges (e.g., public utilities, transportation systems, hospitals, and golf courses)	• Activities for which the government acts as an agent or trustee for parties outside the government (e.g., as an agent for billing and collecting taxes for other governments; as a trustee for employee pension plans and assets held in trust for the benefit of private parties)

[1] Governmental Accounting Standards Board, *Codification of Governmental Accounting and Financial Reporting Standards as of June 30, 2014* (Norwalk, CT, 2014), Appendix B, *Concepts Statement No. 1*, par. 10.

A final category of activity in which governments are involved is **fiduciary activities.** Governments often act in a fiduciary capacity, either as an agent or trustee, for parties outside the government. For example, a government may serve as an agent for other governments in administering and collecting taxes. Governments may also serve as a trustee for investments of other governments in the government's investment pool, for *escheat properties* that revert to the government when there are no legal claimants or heirs to a deceased individual's estate, and for assets being held for employee pension plans, among other trustee roles.

Under GASB standards, only *private-purpose* agency and trust relationships—those that benefit individuals, private organizations, and other governments—are reported as fiduciary activities. *Public-purpose* agency and trust activities, those that primarily benefit the general public and the government's own programs, are treated as governmental activities for accounting and financial reporting purposes. Accounting for fiduciary activities is covered in Chapter 8 of the text.

FINANCIAL REPORTING MODEL

As discussed in Chapter 1 (see Illustration 1–3), every state and local government should provide, at a minimum, basic financial statements, a management's discussion and analysis (MD&A) and certain other required supplementary information. To understand the basic principles of accounting and financial reporting for state and local governments, one must first understand GASB's integrated accounting and financial reporting model. This model is depicted in Illustration 2–2. Key to the integrated model is the requirement to provide two kinds of basic financial statements, government-wide and fund, each kind is intended to achieve different reporting objectives. Prior to a discussion of the financial statements, the elements appearing on the financial statements are introduced along with information on measurement of those elements.

Elements and Measurement

As will be shown, preparing two kinds of financial statements presents unique challenges to financial reporting for governments. One of those challenges is to define the elements of the financial statements. In *Concepts Statement No. 4*, "Elements of Financial Statements," the GASB defines the seven elements that will appear in the two kinds of financial statements. You will recognize some of the elements used in government financial statements as being similar to those used by business organizations; however, other elements will be unique to governments. The seven elements as defined by *Concepts Statement No. 4* are as follows:

1. Assets are resources with present service capacity that the government presently controls.
2. A deferred outflow of resources is the consumption of net assets by the government that applies to a future reporting period.
3. Liabilities are present obligations to sacrifice resources that the government has little or no discretion to avoid.
4. A deferred inflow of resources is the acquisition of net assets by the government that applies to a future reporting period.
5. Net position is the residual when assets + deferred outflows of resources − liabilities – deferred inflows of resources is calculated (net position appears in a statement of financial position).

ILLUSTRATION 2–2 The GASB Integrated Accounting and Financial Reporting Model

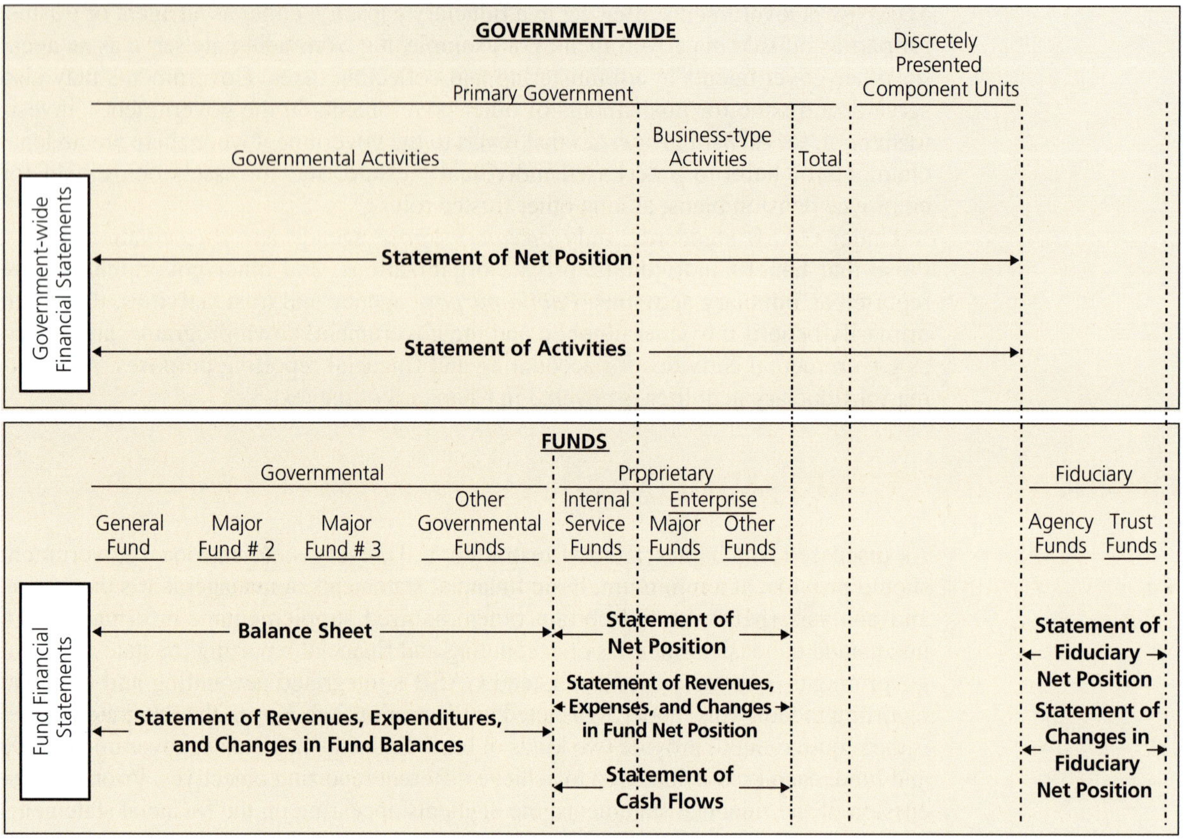

6. An inflow of resources is the acquisition of net assets by the government in the current reporting period (e.g., revenues and other resources).
7. An outflow of resources is the consumption of net assets by the government in the current reporting period (e.g., expenses, expenditures, and other uses of resources).[2]

The terms *inflow of resources* and *outflow of resources* are unique to governmental accounting and reporting standards as are the terms *deferred inflow of resources* and *deferred outflow of resources*. Due to the GASB standards requiring two bases of accounting, the elements inflow of resources and outflow of resources were defined to accommodate both bases.

Although a deferred outflow of resources has the effect of increasing a government's net position, it does not meet the definition of an asset; thus, GASB has created a separate element. Similarly, a deferred inflow of resources has the effect of decreasing a government's net position; however, it does not meet the definition of a liability. Deferred inflows and deferred outflows of resources are *only* used when required by a

[2] Governmental Accounting Standards Board, *Codification of Governmental Accounting and Financial Reporting Standards as of June 30, 2014* (Norwalk, CT 2014), Appendix B, *Concepts Statement No. 4,* pars. 8, 17, 24, 28, 32, 34 and 36. It should be noted that relatively few transactions will result in the recording of deferred outflows and deferred inflows of resources.

GASB standard. An example of a deferred inflow of resources would be resources received in a period prior to when the resources can be used (a timing issue). Since such an advance payment does not meet the definition of a liability, GASB standards require that it be recognized as a deferred inflow of resources. An advance debt refunding (covered in Chapter 6) could result in a deferred outflow (or inflow) of resources. If the resources used to refund the old bonds is greater than the net carrying value of the old bonds, a deferred outflow of resources results according to GASB standards. The difference does not properly meet the definition of an asset and it is not properly a "loss" since it relates to future periods over which the new debt has been substituted for the old debt.

You will notice in the financial reports that you examine that deferred inflows of resources and deferred outflows of resources are reported in separate sections of the balance sheet and/or statement of net position. As the different financial statements and the bases of accounting used by the financial statements are presented, the characteristics and relationships of the elements will become apparent.

In *Concepts Statement No. 6*[3], GASB indicates that those assets that are involved in the direct provision of services should be recorded and presented at the initial measurement amount. The initial amount is the transaction price or amount assigned when the asset is acquired (or a liability is reported). The GASB believes that the initial measurement amount is the amount most useful in providing information that can be used in determining the cost of services (e.g., capital assets). However, when assets are going to be converted to cash, *Concept Statement No. 6* indicates that a remeasurement amount should be used. A remeasured amount is the amount assigned when an asset (or liability) is remeasured at the financial statement date. Remeasurement amounts are useful when trying to determine the availability of resources to acquire services or meet obligations (e.g., investments). For liabilities, the GASB believes that a remeasured amount is more useful for those liabilities for which the timing and amount of payments may be uncertain (e.g., compensated absences). When determining initial amounts and remeasurement amounts, *Concepts Statement No. 6* identifies four possible measurement attributes: historical cost, fair value, replacement cost, and settlement amount. As the financial statements are presented and various classes of assets and liabilities are discussed, you will notice the different measurement approaches and attributes reflected in the financial statements.

Government-wide Financial Statements

The government-wide financial statements report on the governmental reporting entity as a whole but focus on the primary government. As illustrated by the City and County of Denver, Colorado's government-wide financial statements (see Illustrations A2–1 and A2–2 in Appendix A at the end of this chapter), as well as Illustration 2–2, the government-wide statements present the financial information for the governmental activities and business-type activities of the primary government in separate columns, although there is a total column for the primary government. The City and County of Denver also presents financial information about certain independent organizations for which the primary government is deemed to be financially accountable. This information is reported in the column captioned *Component Units.* Chapter 9 provides a detailed discussion of GASB reporting entity standards.

[3] Governmental Accounting Standards Board, *Concepts Statement No. 6*: Measurement of Elements of the Financial Statements (Norwalk, CT 2014).

The government-wide statements present all financial information using the **economic resources measurement focus** and the **accrual basis** of accounting—similar to the measurement focus and basis of accounting used in the financial statements of for-profit business organizations. Thus, as mentioned in Chapter 1, the government-wide financial statements report on the government's *operational accountability* and help to assess whether the government is covering the full cost of services over the long run.

The City and County of Denver's government-wide statement of net position (see Illustration A2–1) is essentially a balance sheet, which reports the government's fiscal year-end assets, deferred outflow of resources, liabilities, deferred inflow of resources, and net position.[4] Net position is the difference between total assets plus deferred outflows of resources and total liabilities plus deferred inflow of resources. It should be noted that Denver reports its net position in the three categories required by GASB standards—net investment in capital assets; restricted (for the purposes shown); and unrestricted. Although the net position section of the statement is different from a business entity's balance sheet, you will notice some similarities to the business entity balance sheet in that assets are listed in the order of liquidity and liabilities are separated into current and noncurrent.

Illustration A2–2 shows Denver's statement of activities. The statement of activities is the city's operating (resource flows) statement reporting expenses classified by program or function and revenues derived directly from the programs or functions. Revenues derived directly from programs or functions can be user charges or resources received directly from external sources, such as grants and contributions. The resulting net expense (i.e., program expense minus program revenue) of each program or function is reported in separate columns for governmental activities, business-type activities, and component units. General revenues, such as taxes of all kinds and transfers between governmental and business-type activities, often make up the bulk of a government's revenues and are reported in the bottom portion of the statement. You will notice that the change in net position for the year results in an increase (decrease) in the net position reported on the statement of net position. Programs/functions and revenue and expense classifications are described in the next chapter.

Because the government-wide financial statements display information in multiple columns, they are not fully consolidated in the manner of corporate financial statements. Receivables and payables between two or more programs or functions that are reported in the Governmental Activities column or between business-type segments reported in the Business-type Activities column are eliminated in preparing the financial statements. Receivables/payables between governmental and business-type activities, however, are not eliminated because they are reported in different columns. For example, Denver's statement of net position shows a receivable of $5,355,000 under the line item *internal balances* in the Governmental Activities column with an equal

[4] The City and County of Denver's financial statements provided in Appendix A and other excerpted information that is presented in later chapters are intended for illustrative educational purposes only. Omitted in this text are the auditor's report on the financial statements, the notes to the financial statements, and other required supplementary information. Moreover, depending on the time since this text was released, more current financial statements may be available. Those who have a need for financial information for credit analysis or other evaluative or decision purposes should refer to the City and County of Denver's audited financial statements in the comprehensive annual financial report (CAFR). The city's CAFR can be downloaded from *http://www.denvergov.org/Default.aspx?alias=www.denvergov.org/finance*.

contra-asset (payable) in the Business-type Activities column. These two amounts represent the *net* receivables and payables between these two activity categories.

Fund Financial Statements

Governments must also present *fund* financial statements or, more precisely, three sets of fund financial statements, one set for each of the three fund categories: governmental, proprietary, and fiduciary (see the lower half of Illustration 2–2). These categories correspond closely to the governmental, business-type, and fiduciary activities described earlier in this chapter. An observant reader will note, however, that although internal service funds are included in the proprietary funds category, their financial information usually is included as part of *governmental activities* in the government-wide financial statements. (Characteristics of these and other funds are described later in this chapter.) Thus, in most cases, only enterprise funds are reported as business-type activities in the government-wide statements. Internal service fund financial information is reported as part of governmental activities in the government-wide statements because these funds, though businesslike in operation, predominantly serve departments of the same government rather than the general public. If an internal service fund predominantly serves one or more enterprise funds, its financial information is reported in the Business-type Activities column of the government-wide statements. Financial reporting of internal service funds is discussed in depth in Chapter 7.

Governmental Fund Financial Statements

Governmental fund financial statements (see Appendix A, Illustrations A2–3 and A2–5) assist financial statement users in assessing *fiscal accountability* by reporting on whether financial resources were raised and expended in compliance with budgetary and other legal provisions. As such, these statements focus on current financial resources—cash and near-cash resources (principally receivables) that are available for expenditure. Since long-term obligations do not have to be paid in the current budgetary period, nor do noncurrent assets such as land, buildings, and equipment provide resources to pay current period obligations, neither is reported in the governmental funds. However, both are reported in the Governmental Activities column of the government-wide statement of net position as shown in Illustration A2–1.

Under the modified accrual basis of accounting used by governmental funds, revenues are recorded only if they are measurable and available for paying current period obligations. **Expenditures** are the amount of resources used to acquire an asset or service and are generally recognized when an obligation that will be paid from current financial resources has been incurred. As shown in Illustration A2–5, the governmental fund statement of revenues, expenditures, and changes in fund balances reports *expenditures* because outlays to acquire goods or services are more relevant than expenses in measuring the outflow of current financial resources. **Expenses,** on the other hand, are costs expired or used up in providing services and are more relevant at the government-wide level, as they provide a long-term measure of the cost of providing services.

Readers may be confused by the fact that the same underlying financial information for *governmental activities* is reported in two different ways: (1) using accrual basis accounting with an economic resources measurement focus on the government-wide financial statements and (2) using modified accrual basis accounting with a current financial resources focus on the fund statements. To ensure integration of these statements, total fund balances reported on the balance sheet—governmental funds (Illustration A2–3) must be reconciled to total governmental activities net position reported in the statement of net position (Illustration A2–1). The reconciliation can be displayed on the face of the balance sheet—governmental funds or, as Denver has done, separately as a stand-alone schedule (see Illustration A2–4). Similarly, GASB requires that operating statement results be reconciled for governmental activities. Accordingly, Denver presents a reconciliation (see Illustration A2–6) of the net changes in fund balances—total governmental funds reported on its statement of revenues, expenditures, and changes in fund balances—governmental funds (Illustration A2–5) to the change in net position of governmental activities reported on its statement of activities (Illustration A2–2). For now, it is sufficient to just be aware that such reconciliations are required; you will learn how to prepare reconciliations in Chapter 9 of this text.

Proprietary Fund Financial Statements

Proprietary fund financial statements present financial information for enterprise funds and internal service funds. Both types of funds operate essentially as self-supporting entities and, therefore, follow accounting and reporting practices similar to those of business organizations; that is, the accrual basis of accounting and a focus on the flow of economic resources. Enterprise funds and internal service funds are distinguished primarily by the kinds of customers they serve. Enterprise funds provide goods or services to the public, whereas internal service funds mainly serve departments of the same government. As required by GASB standards, the City and County of Denver reports proprietary funds financial information in three financial statements: a statement of net position—proprietary funds (Illustration A2–7), a statement of revenues, expenses, and changes in fund net position—proprietary funds (Illustration A2–8), and a statement of cash flows—proprietary funds (Illustration A2–9). An astute reader will note that these are very similar to the financial statements required for business organizations, although there are important differences, as will be discussed later in Chapter 7.

Fiduciary Fund Financial Statements

The final two required fund financial statements are those for the fiduciary funds. By definition, fiduciary funds account for resources that the government is holding or managing as an agent or trustee for an external party; that is, an individual, organization, or other government. Because these resources may not be used to support the government's own programs, GASB standards require that financial information about fiduciary activities be omitted from the government-wide financial statements; however, the information must be reported in two fund financial statements: a statement of fiduciary net position—fiduciary funds and a statement of changes in fiduciary net position—fiduciary funds. Both statements are prepared using accrual accounting with the economic resources measurement focus. These two statements for Denver are presented in Illustrations A2–10 and A2–11.

The discussion to this point has provided an overview of the integrated reporting model, which requires both government-wide and fund financial statements. As the following few chapters will make clear, *governmental activities* are reported quite differently in the two categories of financial statements. To fully comprehend these differences, one must first become familiar with the concept of a *fund* and the accounting characteristics associated with each fund and activity category.

FUND REPORTING

GASB's first accounting and financial reporting principle states:

> A governmental accounting system must make it possible both: (a) to present fairly and with full disclosure the funds and activities of the governmental unit in conformity with generally accepted accounting principles, and (b) to determine and demonstrate compliance with finance-related legal and contractual provisions.[5]

In the governmental environment, legal and contractual provisions often conflict with the requirements of generally accepted accounting principles (GAAP). As the first principle states, however, the accounting system must make it possible to present financial information that meets *both* requirements. Legal provisions related to budgeting revenues and expenditures, for example, often differ from GAAP accounting requirements regarding revenues and expenditures.

The necessity to report on fiscal accountability creates a need for governments to account for revenues and related expenditures that are legally or contractually constrained for specific purposes separately from revenues and expenditures without such constraints. The mechanism that has developed for providing such separate accounting is the fund. A **fund** is formally defined as:

> A fiscal and accounting entity with a self-balancing set of accounts recording cash and other financial resources, together with all related liabilities and residual equities or balances and changes therein, which are segregated for the purpose of carrying on specific activities or attaining certain objectives in accordance with special regulations, restrictions, or limitations.[6]

The concept of *fund* is fundamental to governmental accounting and reporting. As the definition states, a *fund* is a separate fiscal entity, which means it has its own resources, its own liabilities, and its own operating activity for the fiscal period. Furthermore, a fund conceptually has its own set of accounting records (e.g., journals and ledgers) allowing it to prepare separate financial statements. Thus, it is a separate accounting entity as well.

The latter part of the definition of fund is also worth noting: Specifically, a fund assists in *carrying on specific activities or attaining certain objectives in accordance with special regulations, restrictions, or limitations.* As this sentence implies, different funds are intended to achieve different objectives. Funds may be established by grant or contract provisions imposed by external resource providers, by constitutional provisions or enabling legislation of state or local governments, or by the discretionary action of reporting governments. The variety of purposes that may be served by different fund categories and types will become apparent in the discussion that follows.

Fund Categories

As mentioned earlier in the discussion of fund financial statements, there are three categories of funds: governmental, proprietary, and fiduciary (see Illustration 2–2). Accounting characteristics and principles unique to each fund category are discussed in the sections that follow.

[5] GASB *Codification,* Sec. 1100.101.

[6] Ibid., Sec. 1100.102.

Governmental Funds

The **governmental funds** category includes five types of funds: the General Fund, special revenue funds, debt service funds, capital projects funds, and permanent funds. Every state and local government has one and only one **General Fund,** although it may be called by a different name such as *General Revenue Fund, General Operating Fund,* or *Current Fund.* Other governmental funds will be created as needed.

The General Fund is the main operating fund of local governments. Most departmental operating activities, such as those of police and fire, public works, culture and recreation, education, and social services, as well as general government support services, such as the city manager's office, finance, personnel, and data processing, are typically recorded in the General Fund. Unless a financial resource is required to be recorded in a different fund type, it is usually recorded in the General Fund.

When tax or grant revenues or private gifts are restricted by external resource providers or committed by enabling legislation for particular operating purposes, such as the operation of a library or maintenance of roads and bridges, a **special revenue fund** is created. The number of special revenue funds used by state and local governments varies greatly, ranging from a few to many.[7] Nevertheless, GASB standards recommend that governments establish only the minimum number of funds needed to comply with legal requirements and to provide sound management. Using too many funds creates undue complexity and contributes to inefficient financial administration.

Governments that have bond obligations outstanding and certain other types of long-term general liabilities may be required by law or bond covenants to create a **debt service fund.** The purpose of a debt service fund is to account for financial resources segregated for making principal and interest payments on general long-term debt.[8] Some governments account for all debt service on general long-term debt in their General Fund, but governments ordinarily create one or more debt service funds if they have general long-term debt.

Governments often engage in capital projects to accommodate a growing population or to replace existing capital assets. These projects typically involve the purchase or construction of long-lived capital assets such as buildings, highways or bridges, or park land. To account for tax or grant revenues or bond proceeds earmarked for a capital project, as well as payments to architects, engineers, construction contractors, and suppliers, a **capital projects fund** is typically created. Multiple capital projects funds may be created if a government has multiple capital projects.

The fifth type of governmental fund is the *permanent fund.* A **permanent fund** is used to account for permanent endowments created when a donor stipulates that the principal amount of a contribution must be invested and preserved, but earnings on amounts so invested can be used for some public purpose. Public purposes include activities such as maintenance of a cemetery or aesthetic enhancements to public buildings. If the earnings from a permanent fund can be used to benefit only *private* individuals, organizations, or other governments, rather than supporting a program of

[7] Some governments establish special revenue funds for internal management purposes even though the fund's revenue inflows are not formally restricted or committed for particular purposes. Such discretionary funds should be reported as part of the General Fund for financial reporting purposes. GASB *Codification,* Sec. 1300.105.

[8] General long-term debt is distinguished from long-term debt issued and serviced by a proprietary or fiduciary fund. Payment of interest and principal on debt issued by proprietary or fiduciary funds and paid from the revenues of those funds is recorded in those funds rather than in a debt service fund.

the government and its citizenry, a private-purpose trust fund—a fiduciary fund—is used instead of a permanent fund.

Accounting and financial reporting standards for the governmental funds category, the five fund types just described, have evolved to meet the budgetary and financial compliance needs of government. Thus, it is hardly surprising that accounting for governmental funds focuses on the inflows and outflows of **current financial resources.** Current financial resources are cash or items such as receivables that will be converted into cash during the current fiscal period or that will be **available** soon enough after the end of the period to pay current-period liabilities. With the lone exception of property tax revenues, which GASB standards require to be collectible within 60 days of the end of the current fiscal year to be considered available, governments are free to establish their own definition of *available* and, therefore, which items to recognize in their financial statements as current financial resources and revenues.[9] Most governments have adopted a 60-day policy for all governmental fund revenues, although some governments have other policies that can range from 30 days to one year.

Because governmental funds account for the inflows and outflows of current financial resources, the balance sheet for governmental funds generally reports only current assets and current liabilities and **fund balances,** which is the difference between current assets and current liabilities.[10] One can readily see, for example, that no long-lived assets, such as land, buildings, and equipment, nor any long-term liabilities, such as bonds payable, are reported on the City and County of Denver's governmental funds balance sheet shown in Illustration A2–3.[11]

Proprietary Funds

Proprietary funds of a government follow accounting and financial reporting principles that are similar to those for commercial business entities. Use of these principles assist financial statement users to assess operational accountability for proprietary activities. As in business, if a government intends to charge users for the goods or services provided, its officials need to know the full cost of those goods and services, so they can determine appropriate prices or fees. Determining the full cost is also essential in deciding whether the government should continue to produce or provide particular goods or services or contract for them with an outside vendor. Accrual accounting, including depreciation of capital assets, is essential for governments to

[9] GASB standards require that governments disclose in the notes to their financial statements the length of time used to define *available* for purposes of revenue recognition in the governmental funds financial statements; see GASB *Codification,* Sec. 2300.106, par. a(5).

[10] As discussed earlier in this chapter GASB standards require that deferred outflows or inflows of resources be reported separately from assets and liabilities, respectively, if they are reported in governmental funds. The difference between (1) assets and deferred outflows and (2) liabilities and deferred inflows is still called fund balance.

[11] Some governmental accounting teachers use the example of a cookie jar or other container to illustrate the operation of a governmental fund. For example, you can visualize the General Fund, and each of the other governmental funds, as being a cookie jar. As revenues or other financing sources (cash and near-cash financial resources) flow into the cookie jar, it causes the balance of financial resources (the fund balance) in the cookie jar to rise. As financial resources (cash) are removed from the jar (or obligations are incurred to use cash later in the period or soon thereafter)—that is, as expenditures are made—the fund balance drops. It is necessary, of course, to keep an accounting record of (i.e., journalize) the inflows and outflows of financial resources as well as to maintain ledger accounts that indicate the nature of the financial resources (cash, short-term investments, receivables, and other near-cash assets), current liabilities owed by the fund, and the current fund balance. Although this is not a perfect analogy to the actual operation of a fund, it may help you to visualize its short-term, spending focus.

determine the full cost of providing business-type services and to report on the extent to which each service is covering its full cost of operation.

As Illustration 2–2 shows, there are two types of proprietary funds: *internal service funds* and *enterprise funds.* Legislative approval is ordinarily required to establish proprietary funds, although they may be required by law or contractual provisions such as debt covenants. The two funds differ primarily in terms of their objectives and the way the financial information of each type of fund is reported in the fund and government-wide financial statements. Accounting and financial reporting requirements for proprietary funds are covered in Chapter 7 of this text. Thus, only a brief overview is provided in this chapter.

Internal service funds are created to improve the management of resources and generally provide goods or services to departments or agencies of the same government and sometimes to other governments on a cost-reimbursement basis. Examples of services typically accounted for by internal service funds include central purchasing and warehousing of supplies, motor pools, centralized data processing, and self-insurance pools.

Enterprise funds *may* be used to account for activities in which goods or services are provided to the public for a fee that is the principal source of revenue for the fund. Unless the activities are insignificant in amount, GASB standards *require* the use of an enterprise fund if:

1. The activity is financed with debt that is secured solely by a pledge of the net revenues from fees and charges of the activity.
2. Laws or regulations require that the activity's costs of providing services, including capital costs (such as depreciation or debt service), be recovered with fees and charges rather than with taxes or similar revenues.
3. The pricing policies of the activity establish fees and charges designed to recover its costs, including capital costs.[12]

Fiduciary Funds

Fiduciary activities of a government report on operational accountability of those activities by using the same principles as proprietary fund and government-wide financial statements: the economic resources measurement focus and accrual basis of accounting. Again, it should be noted that fiduciary activities are reported *only* in the fiduciary fund statements (statement of fiduciary net position and statement of changes in fiduciary net position) and not in the government-wide statements (see Illustration 2–2). Examples of the two fiduciary fund statements for the City and County of Denver are provided in Illustrations A2–10 and A2–11. These statements present financial information for the pension trust funds, private-purpose trust fund, and agency funds.

The fiduciary fund category consists of agency funds and three types of trust funds: investment trust funds, pension (and other employee benefit) trust funds, and private-purpose trust funds. **Agency funds** generally are used when the government holds cash on a custodial basis for an external party (individual, organization, or government). An example is taxes collected by a government on behalf of other governments. There is no net position in agency funds since for every dollar of assets held there is a dollar of liability to the external party (total assets in the fund always equal total liabilities).

[12] GASB *Codification,* Sec. 1300.109.

Trust funds differ from agency funds primarily in the length of time and the manner in which resources are held and managed. In most cases, trust fund assets include investments whose earnings add to the net position of the fund and which can be used for a specified purpose. Examples of trust funds are **pension** (and other employee benefit) **trust funds** that hold assets in trust to provide retirement benefits for employees, **investment trust funds** used to report the equity of external participants (typically other governments) in a sponsoring government's investment pool, and **private-purpose trust funds** created to benefit private individuals, such as a fund to provide scholarships for the children of firefighters and police officers killed in the line of duty.

Accounting for trust funds is typically much more complex than just accounting for investments. For example, a large, legally separate state pension plan usually has significant capital assets such as land, buildings, and equipment to report in its financial statements. The expenses of the plan include personnel, supplies, utilities, depreciation, and other items, in addition to investment-related expenses.[13] Accounting for fiduciary funds is discussed in Chapter 8 of the text.

Classification of Fund Balances

The GASB requires that fund balances reported on the governmental fund balance sheet be classified according to the constraints on the use of the fund balances. In classifying fund balances, a government must first determine if any amount of the fund balance is *nonspendable*. Once it is determined how much of the fund balance is not spendable, the remaining *spendable* fund balance amount is identified according to any restrictions on how the funds may be used. Following are the fund balance classifications and classification descriptions identified in the financial reporting standards.

1. **Nonspendable fund balance.** These are amounts that are *(a)* not in spendable form or *(b)* legally or contractually required to be maintained intact. "Not in spendable form" includes items that are not expected to be converted to cash; for example, inventories, prepaid amounts, and long-term notes receivable. An example of an item that is legally or contractually required to remain intact is a permanent endowment.
2. **Restricted fund balance.** These are amounts that can be spent only for the specific purposes designated by external providers, constitutionally, or through enabling legislation. Restrictions are changed or lifted only with the consent of resource providers. Examples of external resource providers include creditors, grantors, and donors.
3. **Committed fund balance.** These are amounts that can only be used for the specific purposes determined by a formal action (e.g., legislation or ordinance) of a government's highest level of decision-making authority (e.g., county commission or city council). Commitments can only be changed or removed by taking the same formal action that imposed the constraint originally. It should be noted that enabling legislation differs from actions taken to commit funds. Enabling legislation provides authorization to raise revenue for a restricted

[13] Because fiduciary funds benefit only external parties, the account titles *revenues* and *expenses* are not used for these funds in the sponsoring government's fund financial statements. Instead, increases in fiduciary fund net position are called *additions* and decreases are called *deductions*.

purpose. The revenue component of enabling legislation prevents the use of the resources for anything other than the restricted purpose; whereas, committed funds can be used for another purpose by reversing the formal action that committed the resources.

4. **Assigned fund balance.** These are amounts intended to be used by the government for specific purposes that are neither restricted nor committed. *Intent* can be expressed in one of two ways: *(a)* the governing body can express its intent to use resources for a specific purpose or *(b)* the governing body can delegate authority to a body (e.g., a budget or finance committee) or an official (e.g., city manager) to express intent to use amounts for specific purposes. Additionally, it is implied that the amounts reported in special revenue, capital project, debt service, or permanent funds that have not been designated as restricted or committed are assigned.
5. **Unassigned fund balance.** This is the residual amount for the General Fund and includes all amounts that have not been classified as nonspendable, restricted, committed, or assigned. Unassigned amounts are technically available for any purpose.[14]

The General Fund is the only fund that will have a positive unassigned fund balance. If any other fund has expenditures that exceed the amounts restricted, committed, or assigned, it may be necessary for the fund to report a negative unassigned fund balance. The GASB does not allow negative restricted, committed, or assigned fund balances.

To assist in determining ending balances in each fund balance classification, the government should adopt a policy regarding whether it considers the restricted, committed, assigned, or unassigned amounts to be spent when an expenditure occurs for a purpose for which more than one classification amount is available. As an example, suppose the government has incurred a cost for which both a restricted and an assigned resource could be used. Generally, the government would want to spend those resources with the greatest limits on their use before spending resources with no limitations on their use. In the example given, the government might opt for a policy that would use the restricted resources first, before using the assigned resources.

Major Fund Reporting

GASB standards recognize that most financial statement users are unlikely to have a significant interest in all of the funds that a government may use. Instead, it is likely that their interest will be focused on larger dollar-amount funds. Consequently, GASB standards require that financial statements prepared for governmental funds and enterprise funds include a separate column for each *major fund*.[15] An additional column is provided in each statement for the total amounts for all *nonmajor funds* of that type—governmental or enterprise, as applicable. For example, Denver's governmental fund statements, shown in Illustrations A2–3 and A2–5 in Appendix A to Chapter 2, report the General Fund and one special revenue fund as major funds. Aggregate amounts for all nonmajor governmental funds are reported in the column headed *Other Governmental Funds*. Similarly, as shown in Illustrations A2–7, A2–8, and A2–9, Denver

[14] GASB, *Codification*, Sec. 1800, pars. 165–179.

[15] Ibid, Sec. 2200.158.

reports its Wastewater Management and Denver Airport System funds as major enterprise funds. Aggregate amounts for all other enterprise funds are reported in the *Other Enterprise Funds* column. Major fund reporting is not applicable to internal service funds or fiduciary funds.

Determination of Major Funds

By its nature the General Fund of a government is always considered a major fund. GASB standards require that any fund that meets the following size criteria also be designated as a **major fund**:

a. Total assets, liabilities, revenues, or expenditures/expenses of that governmental or enterprise fund are at least 10 percent of the corresponding element total (assets, liabilities, and so forth) for all funds of that category or type (that is, total governmental or total enterprise funds), *and* (emphasis added)

b. The same element that met the 10 percent criterion in (*a*) is at least 5 percent of the corresponding element total for all governmental and enterprise funds combined.[16]

In addition, any fund that a government considers of significant importance to financial statement users can be reported as major.

It is important to note that the same element of a fund must meet *both* the *a* and *b* criteria for mandatory reporting as a major fund. On occasion, a fund may meet both criteria in the preceding fiscal year but only one or perhaps neither of the criteria in the current year. In such a case, the government may elect to continue to report the fund as a major fund in the current year pending a future year determination.

To illustrate application of the major funds criteria, consider the information given in the accompanying table for the hypothetical Town of Truesdale, which is investigating whether certain governmental funds should be reported as major funds.

To determine whether a fund meets the 10 percent and 5 percent criteria, one must first calculate the threshold amounts for each element for total governmental funds and total governmental and enterprise funds, as displayed in the two rightmost columns of the table. It is then a simple matter to compare each fund's assets, liabilities, and so forth, to these threshold amounts.

Financial Statement Elements	Road Tax Fund	Debt Service Fund	Capital Projects Fund	10 Percent of Total Governmental Funds	5 Percent of Total Governmental and Enterprise Funds
Assets	$1,369,238	$3,892,020	$19,273,676	$4,492,627	$4,082,141
Liabilities	172,439	62,530	368,727	86,792	1,562,368
Revenues	4,289,876	6,836,472	6,286,240	6,073,695	3,942,318
Expenditures/ Expenses	3,986,746	5,622,890	9,846,935	5,952,221	3,834,623

[16] GASB, *Codification*, Sec. 2200.159

Fund by fund comparisons to the 10 percent and 5 percent amounts show that for assets, only the Capital Projects Fund meets both criteria for reporting as a major fund. The Road Tax Fund meets the 10 percent criterion for liabilities but not the 5 percent criterion and meets the 5 percent criterion for both revenues and expenditures but not the 10 percent criterion. Consequently, the Road Tax Fund need not be reported as a major fund. Although the Debt Service Fund does not meet either of the criteria for its assets or liabilities and only the 5 percent criterion for its expenditures, its revenues meet both the 10 percent and 5 percent criteria. Therefore, it should be reported as a major fund. To summarize, in addition to its General Fund, the Town of Truesdale must report its Debt Service Fund and Capital Projects Fund as major governmental funds. In addition, the Town of Truesdale would use the same process to investigate whether any enterprise funds are major funds, using totals for all enterprise funds rather than governmental funds for the 10 percent comparisons.

Nonmajor Fund Reporting

Although the GASB requires nonmajor funds to be aggregated and reported in a single column, internal managers and perhaps a small number of external financial statement users may have an interest in the financial information for individual nonmajor funds. To meet these needs, many governments provide supplementary combining financial statements for nonmajor governmental and enterprise funds in their comprehensive annual financial report (CAFR). These statements provide a separate column for the financial information of each nonmajor fund as well as total column amounts that are the same as the totals reported in the Nonmajor Governmental Funds or Nonmajor Enterprise Funds columns of the basic financial statements. Such a statement, the combining statement of revenues, expenditures, and changes in fund balances, governmental nonmajor funds for the nonmajor governmental funds of Sioux City, Iowa, is presented in Illustration 4–6 in Chapter 4. As shown in that statement, all of Sioux City's nonmajor governmental funds are special revenue funds except for the Cemetery Trust Fund, which is a permanent fund.

SUMMARY OF GOVERNMENT-WIDE AND FUND CHARACTERISTICS

Illustration 2–3 summarizes the characteristics and principles of accounting and reporting for government-wide and fund categories. One topic not discussed in this chapter is budgetary accounting, which is a main topic of Chapter 3. As shown in Illustration 2–3, budgetary accounts are integrated into the accounts of certain governmental funds, primarily the General Fund and special revenue funds, and often other governmental funds as well. Chapter 3 also covers other important subjects such as how governmental activity revenues and expenses are classified in the government-wide statements and how revenues and *expenditures* are classified in the governmental funds.

In the next few chapters, you will become familiar with the "dual-track" approach the authors have developed to record the different effects of certain transactions on the *governmental fund* financial statements and the *Governmental Activities* column of the government-wide financial statements. The differences in recording transactions reflect the different bases of accounting used by governmental funds and governmental activities.

ILLUSTRATION 2–3 Summary of Government-Wide and Fund Characteristics

Characteristics	Government-wide	Governmental Funds	Proprietary Funds	Fiduciary Funds[c]
Types of funds	NA[a]	General, special revenue, debt service, capital projects, permanent	Enterprise, internal service[b]	Agency, investment trust, pension trust, private-purpose trust
Primary accountability focus	Operational accountability	Fiscal accountability	Operational accountability	Operational accountability
Measurement focus	Economic resources	Current financial resources	Economic resources	Economic resources
Basis of accounting	Accrual	Modified accrual	Accrual	Accrual
Required financial statements	Statement of net position; statement of activities	Balance sheet; statement of revenues, expenditures, and changes in fund balances	Statement of net position; statement of revenues, expenses, and changes in fund net position; statement of cash flows	Statement of fiduciary net position; statement of changes in fiduciary net position
Balance sheet/statement of net position accounts	Current and noncurrent assets and deferred outflows of resources, current and noncurrent liabilities and deferred inflows of resources, net position	Current assets and deferred outflows of resources, current liabilities and deferred inflows of resources, fund balances	Current and noncurrent assets, and deferred outflows of resources, current and noncurrent liabilities and deferred inflows of resources, net position	Current and noncurrent assets and deferred outflows of resources, current and noncurrent liabilities and deferred inflows of resources, net position[d]
Operating or change statement accounts	Revenues, expenses	Revenues, expenditures, other financing sources/uses	Revenues, expenses, capital contributions and transfers in/out	Additions, deductions[e]
Budgetary accounting	Not formally integrated into the accounts	Formally integrated into accounts of certain funds	Not formally integrated into the accounts	Not formally integrated into the accounts

[a]Funds are not applicable to the government-wide statements.

[b]Financial information for internal service funds is usually reported in the Governmental Activities column of the government-wide statements unless the funds predominantly benefit enterprise funds. In that case, internal service fund information would be reported in the Business-type Activities column.

[c]Fiduciary activities are reported only in the fund statements, not in the government-wide statements.

[d]Agency funds have no net position since total assets equal total liabilities for these funds.

[e]Because fiduciary fund resources benefit external parties and cannot be used to provide governmental services, increases in fiduciary fund net position are not revenues of the government, nor are decreases expenses of the government. Instead, increases in fiduciary position, are reported as *additions* and decreases are reported as *deductions.* Since agency funds have no net position, they cannot have additions or deductions.

Appendix A

Illustrative Financial Statements from the City and County of Denver, Colorado

ILLUSTRATION A2–1

CITY AND COUNTY OF DENVER, COLORADO
Statement of Net Position
December 31, 2013 (dollars in thousands)

	Primary Government			
	Governmental Activities	**Business-type Activities**	**Total**	**Component Units**
Assets				
Cash on hand	$ 10,684	$ —	$ 10,684	$ —
Cash and cash equivalents	657,616	103,612	761,228	22,411
Investments	—	627,937	627,937	—
Receivables (net of allowances):				
Taxes	416,351	—	416,351	86,167
Notes	74,166	—	74,166	—
Accounts	21,538	58,244	79,782	539
Accrued interest	3,323	7,061	10,384	202
Other	—	—	—	11,726
Due from other governments	38,424	—	38,424	—
Internal balances	5,355	(5,355)	—	—
Inventories	3,018	9,663	12,681	—
Prepaid items and other assets	3,783	2,920	6,703	1,295
Restricted assets:				
Cash and cash equivalents	56,113	123,547	179,660	159,527
Investments	—	1,330,481	1,330,481	9,300
Accounts receivable	—	9,038	9,038	—
Accrued interest receivable	—	3,765	3,765	—
Other receivables	—	3,383	3,383	—
Prepaid items	—	4,388	4,388	—
Long-term receivables (net of allowances)	47,794	14,320	62,114	157,065
Denver Water CIS (net of amortization)	—	3,369	3,369	—
Prepaid expense	—	4,487	4,487	—
Prepaid bond insurance and other assets	934	—	934	6,756
Interest rate swaps	—	38,232	38,232	—
Assets held for disposition	13,256	—	13,256	—
Capital assets:				
Land and construction in progress	380,878	765,747	1,146,625	40,444
Buildings, improvements, infrastructure, collections, and equipment, net of accumulated depreciation	2,468,017	2,997,140	5,465,157	218,870
Total Assets	**4,201,250**	**6,101,979**	**10,303,229**	**714,302**

continued

ILLUSTRATION A2–1 (*Continued*)

CITY AND COUNTY OF DENVER, COLORADO
Statement of Net Position
December 31, 2013 (dollars in thousands)

	Primary Government			
	Governmental Activities	**Business-type Activities**	**Total**	**Component Units**
Deferred outflow of resources				
Accumulated decrease in fair value of hedging derivatives	20,692	13,967	34,659	—
Deferred loss on refunding	16,073	215,700	231,773	30,134
Liabilities				
Vouchers payable	66,120	40,341	106,461	8,427
Accrued liabilities	58,072	47,087	105,159	49,316
Unearned revenue	16,449	39,289	55,738	113
Interest rate swaps	26,221	201,820	228,041	—
Advances	9,480	—	9,480	2,402
Due to taxing unit	441	—	441	—
Due to other governments	—	5,324	5,324	4,759
Liabilities payable from restricted assets	—	114,133	114,133	—
Noncurrent liabilities:				
Due within one year	110,317	146,489	256,806	23,662
Due in more than one year	1,673,275	4,577,107	6,250,382	899,011
Total Liabilities	**1,960,375**	**5,171,590**	**7,131,965**	**987,690**
Deferred inflow of resources				
Gain on refundings	—	3,535	3,535	—
Property taxes	347,482	—	347,482	74,910
Net Position				
Net investment in capital assets	1,366,632	(192,372)	1,174,260	(112,232)
Restricted for:				
Capital projects and grants	336,815	18,095	354,910	71,756
Emergency use	39,087	—	39,087	252
Debt service	86,117	653,222	739,339	60,803
Donor and other restrictions:				
Expendable	11,004	—	11,004	4,005
Nonexpendable	3,000	—	3,000	—
Other purposes	5,914	—	5,914	—
Unrestricted (deficit)	81,589	677,576	759,165	(342,748)
Total Net Position (Deficit)	**$1,930,158**	**$1,156,521**	**$ 3,086,679**	**$(318,164)**

ILLUSTRATION A2–2

CITY AND COUNTY OF DENVER, COLORADO
Statement of Activities
For the Year Ended December 31, 2013 (dollars in thousands)

		Program Revenues			Net (Expense) Revenue and Changes in Net Assets			
					Primary Government			
Functions/Programs	**Expenses**	**Charges for Services**	**Operating Grants and Contributions**	**Capital Grants and Contributions**	**Governmental Activities**	**Business-type Activities**	**Total**	**Component Units**
Primary Government								
Governmental Activities:								
General government	$ 398,733	$ 87,988	$ 26,716	$ 64	$(283,965)	$ —	$(283,965)	
Public safety	563,651	87,996	29,023	—	(446,632)	—	(446,632)	
Public works	92,425	68,666	19,370	29,408	25,019	—	25,019	
Human services	114,624	376	68,244	—	(46,004)	—	(46,004)	
Health	54,453	2,322	9,056	—	(43,075)	—	(43,075)	
Parks and recreation	29,687	8,891	864	39,223	19,291	—	19,291	
Cultural activities	119,018	52,740	1,115	339	(64,824)	—	(64,824)	
Community development	35,142	25,615	15,800	478	6,751	—	6,751	
Economic opportunity	21,218	12,248	9,224	—	254	—	254	
Interest on long-term debt	70,030	—	—	—	(70,030)	—	(70,030)	
Total Governmental Activities	**1,498,981**	**346,842**	**179,412**	**69,512**	**(903,215)**	**—**	**(903,215)**	
Business-type Activities:								
Wastewater management	105,679	115,872	—	7,289	—	17,482	17,482	
Denver airport system	801,786	661,637	103,513	31,412	—	(5,224)	(5,224)	
Environmental services	9,354	8,586	—	—	—	(768)	(768)	
Golf course	10,474	9,522	—	—	—	(952)	(952)	
Total Business-type Activities	**927,293**	**795,617**	**103,513**	**38,701**	—	**10,538**	**10,538**	
Total Primary Government	**$2,426,274**	**$1,142,459**	**$282,925**	**$108,213**	**(903,215)**	**10,538**	**(892,677)**	
Component Units	**$ 283,398**	**$ 82,388**	**$ 5,536**	**$ —**				$(195,474)

continued

ILLUSTRATION A2–2 (*Continued*)

CITY AND COUNTY OF DENVER, COLORADO
Statement of Activities
For the Year Ended December 31, 2013 (dollars in thousands)

	Net (Expense) Revenue and Changes in Net Assets			
	Primary Government			
	Governmental Activities	Business-type Activities	Total	Component Units
General revenues:				
Taxes:				
Facilities development admissions	8,721	—	8,721	—
Lodgers	63,482	—	63,482	1,600
Motor vehicle ownership fee	21,000	—	21,000	—
Occupational privilege	44,515	—	44,515	—
Property	331,914	—	331,914	80,403
Sales and use	539,348	—	539,348	25,723
Specific ownership	193	—	193	194
Telephone	8,964	—	8,964	—
Investment and interest income	2,525	24,357	26,882	10,987
Other revenues	35,368	948	36,316	12,038
Transfers	275	(275)	—	—
Total General Revenues and Transfers	**1,056,305**	**25,030**	**1,081,335**	**130,945**
Change in net position	153,090	35,568	188,658	(64,529)
Net position (deficit)—January 1, as previously reported	1,782,262	1,151,011	2,933,273	(246,182)
Change in accounting principle—GASB 65	(5,194)	(30,058)	(35,252)	(7,453)
Net position—January 1, as restated	1,777,068	1,120,953	2,898,021	(253,635)
Net Position (Deficit)—December 31	**$1,930,158**	**$1,156,521**	**$3,086,679**	**$(318,164)**

ILLUSTRATION A2–3

CITY AND COUNTY OF DENVER, COLORADO
Balance Sheet—Governmental Funds
December 31, 2013 (dollars in thousands)

	General	Human Services	Other Governmental Funds	Total Governmental Funds
Assets				
Cash on hand	$ 143	$ 518	$ 10,023	$ 10,684
Cash and cash equivalents	195,214	42,844	368,034	606,092
Receivables (net of allowances of $123,807)				
Taxes	170,018	58,119	188,214	416,351
Notes	2,804	—	71,362	74,166
Accounts	20,109	7,533	40,217	67,859
Accrued interest	1,440	—	1,570	3,010
Interfund receivable	12,528	21	1,392	13,941
Due from other governments	—	1,659	36,765	38,424
Prepaid items and other assets	268	—	3,515	3,783
Restricted assets:				
Cash and cash equivalents	48,203	—	7,910	56,113
Assets held for disposition	11,436	—	1,820	13,256
Total Assets	**$462,163**	**$110,694**	**$730,822**	**$1,303,679**
Liabilities and Fund Balances				
Liabilities:				
Vouchers payable	$ 17,037	$ 5,422	$ 41,805	$ 64,264
Accrued liabilities	32,423	2,467	1,607	36,497
Due to taxing units	274	—	167	441
Interfund payable	2,122	2,241	6,049	10,412
Unearned revenue	939	1,322	14,188	16,449
Advances	—	505	6,975	7,480
Compensated absences	—	—	62	62
Total Liabilities	**52,795**	**11,957**	**70,853**	**135,605**
Deferred Inflows of Resources				
Property tax	109,343	58,346	180,011	347,700
Unavailable revenues—long-term receivables	12,690	—	33,979	46,669
Total Deferred Inflows of Resources	**122,033**	**58,346**	**213,990**	**394,369**
Fund Balances:				
Nonspendable	268	—	6,515	6,783
Restricted	62,443	40,391	372,617	475,451
Committed	23,594	—	37,804	61,398
Assigned	—	—	29,043	29,043
Unassigned	201,030	—	—	201,030
Total Fund Balances	**287,335**	**40,391**	**445,979**	**773,705**
Total Liabilities and Fund Balances	**$462,163**	**$110,694**	**$730,822**	**$1,303,679**

ILLUSTRATION A2–4

CITY AND COUNTY OF DENVER, COLORADO
Reconciliation of the Balance Sheet—Governmental Funds to the Statement of Net Position
December 31, 2013 (dollars in thousands)

Amounts reported for governmental activities in the statement of net position are different because:	
Total fund balance-governmental funds.	$ 773,705
Capital assets used in governmental activities, excluding internal service funds of $19,329, are not financial resources and, therefore, are not reported in the funds.	2,829,566
Accrued interest payable not included in the funds.	(21,092)
Deferred inflow of resources related to property taxes and long-term receivables are not available to pay for current-period expenditures and therefore, are not recorded in the funds.	48,011
Deferred outflow of resources are not financial resources and therefore are not reported in the funds and include:	
Accumulated decrease in fair value of hedging derivatives	20,692
Loss on refunding	16,073
Interest rate swap liability.	(26,221)
Prepaid bond insurance, net of accumulated amortization.	934
Internal service funds are used by management to charge the cost of these funds to their primary users-governmental funds. The assets and liabilities of the internal service funds are included in governmental activities in the statement of net position.	21,983
Long-term liabilities, including bonds payable, are not due and payable in the current period and therefore are not reported in the governmental funds (this excludes internal service liabilities of $50,099).	(1,733,493)
Net position of governmental activities	**$1,930,158**

ILLUSTRATION A2–5

CITY AND COUNTY OF DENVER, COLORADO
Statement of Revenues, Expenditures, and Changes in Fund Balances—Governmental Funds
For the Year Ended December 31, 2013 (dollars in thousands)

	General	Human Services	Other Governmental Funds	Total Governmental Funds
Revenues				
Taxes:				
Facilities development admission	$ —	$ —	$ 8,721	$ 8,721
Lodgers	17,602	—	45,880	63,482
Motor vehicle ownership fee	21,000	—	—	21,000
Occupational privilege	44,504	—	11	44,515
Property	108,522	55,990	167,402	331,914
Sales and use	493,002	—	46,346	539,348
Specific ownership	—	—	193	193
Telephone	2,710	—	6,254	8,964
Special assessments	—	—	1,702	1,702
Licenses and permits	42,916	—	1,499	44,415
Intergovernmental revenues	27,669	67,587	111,622	206,878
Charges for services	167,864	376	56,929	225,169
Investment and interest income	1,890	—	113	2,003
Fines and forfeitures	54,818	—	2,651	57,469
Contributions	49	657	6,380	7,086
Other revenue	10,265	442	44,957	55,664
Total Revenues	**992,811**	**125,052**	**500,660**	**1,618,523**

continued

ILLUSTRATION A2–5 (*Continued*)

CITY AND COUNTY OF DENVER, COLORADO
Statement of Revenues, Expenditures, and Changes in Fund Balances—Governmental Funds
For the Year Ended December 31, 2013 (dollars in thousands)

	General	Human Services	Other Governmental Funds	Total Governmental Funds
Expenditures				
Current:				
General government	181,635	—	76,773	258,408
Public safety	475,654	—	77,009	552,663
Public works	98,178	—	71,951	170,129
Health	44,636	—	9,569	54,205
Human services	—	114,079	—	114,079
Parks and recreation	55,279	—	11,713	66,992
Cultural activities	39,192	—	58,846	98,038
Community development	15,998	—	19,032	35,030
Economic opportunity	574	—	20,747	21,321
Debt service:				
Principal retirement	2,633	3,644	93,248	99,525
Interest	2,152	1,130	69,560	72,842
Capital outlay	—	—	45,877	45,877
Total Expenditures	**915,931**	**118,853**	**554,325**	**1,589,109**
Excess (deficiency) of revenues over (under) expenditures	76,880	6,199	(53,665)	29,414
Other Financing Sources (Uses)				
Sale of capital assets and assets held for disposition	—	743	(615)	128
Issuance of certificates of participation	—	—	34,030	34,030
Payments to escrow	—	—	(256,518)	(256,518)
Bond premium	—	—	19,659	19,659
Bond proceeds	—	—	48,660	48,660
Bond proceeds—refunding	—	—	209,700	209,700
Insurance recoveries	305	8	436	749
Transfers in	38,589	75	69,457	108,121
Transfers out	(55,287)	(75)	(53,121)	(108,483)
Total Other Financing Sources (Uses), Net	**(16,393)**	**751**	**71,688**	**56,046**
Net change in fund balances	60,487	6,950	18,023	85,460
Fund balances—January 1	226,848	33,441	427,956	688,245
Fund Balances—December 31	**$287,335**	**$ 40,391**	**$445,979**	**$ 773,705**

ILLUSTRATION A2–6

CITY AND COUNTY OF DENVER, COLORADO
Reconciliation of the Statement of Revenues, Expenditures and Changes in Fund Balances—Governmental Funds to the Statement of Activities
For the Year Ended December 31, 2013 (dollars in thousands)

Amounts reported for governmental activities in the statement of activities are different because:	
Net change in fund balances—total governmental funds	$ 85,460
Governmental funds report capital outlays as expenditures. However, in the statement of activities the cost of those assets is allocated over their estimated useful lives and reported as depreciation expense. This is the amount by which capital outlay exceeded depreciation expense in the current period:	
Capital outlay, including sale of assets	114,098
Depreciation expense (excluding internal service)	(146,546)
Revenues in the statement of activities that do not provide current financial resources are not reported as revenue in the funds.	31,834
The issuance of long-term debt and other obligations (e.g., bonds, certificates of participation, and capital leases) provides current financial resources to governmental funds, while the repayment of the principal of long-term debt consumes the current financial resources of governmental funds. Neither transaction, however, has any effect on change in net position. Also, governmental funds report the effect of premiums, discounts, and similar items when debt is first issued, whereas these amounts are amortized in the statement of activities. These differences in the treatment of long-term debt and related items consist of:	
General obligation bonds issued	(259,201)
Capital lease obligations	(34,030)
Principal retirement on bonds	269,765
Premium, discounts, and deferred gain (loss) on refunding	7,700
Capital lease principal payments	67,564
Principal payments on note payable	5,948
Principal payments on intergovernmental agreement	766
Some expenses reported in the statement of activities do not require the use of current financial resources and, therefore, are not reported as expenditures in governmental funds:	
Compensated absences (excluding internal service)	4,966
Accrued interest payable	2,812
Legal liability	2,762
Pollution remediation	47
Net OPEB obligation	(1,667)
Amortization of imputed debt-swap	522
Internal service funds are used by management to charge their cost to individual funds. The net expense of certain activities of internal service funds is reported within governmental activities.	290
Change in net position of governmental activities	**$153,090**

ILLUSTRATION A2–7

CITY AND COUNTY OF DENVER, COLORADO
Statement of Net Position—Proprietary Funds
December 31, 2013 (dollars in thousands)

	Business-type Activities—Enterprise Funds				Governmental Activities
	Wastewater Management	**Denver Airport System**	**Other Enterprise Funds**	**Total Enterprise Funds**	**Internal Service Funds**
Assets					
Current assets:					
Cash and cash equivalents	$ 7,423	$ 76,218	$ 19,971	$ 103,612	$ 51,524
Investments	7,830	447,196	—	455,026	—
Receivables (net of allowance for uncollectibles of $1,700):					
Accounts	12,829	43,275	2,140	58,244	1,473
Accrued interest	322	6,639	100	7,061	313
Inventories	—	9,496	167	9,663	3,018
Interfund receivable	491	1	4	496	1,894
Prepaid items and other assets	959	1,961	—	2,920	—
Restricted assets:					
Cash and cash equivalents	—	121,554	1,993	123,547	—
Investments	5,506	581,398	—	586,904	—
Accounts receivable	—	9,038	—	9,038	—
Accrued interest receivable	—	3,750	15	3,765	—
Other receivables	—	3,383	—	3,383	—
Prepaid items	—	4,388	—	4,388	—
Total Current Assets	**35,360**	**1,308,297**	**24,390**	**1,368,047**	**58,222**
Noncurrent assets:			—	743,577	—
Investments—restricted	23,025	720,552	—	172,911	—
Investments—unrestricted	32,744	140,167			
Capital assets:					
Land and construction in progress	25,709	734,514	5,524	765,747	5,653
Buildings and improvements	16,736	2,009,211	13,463	2,039,410	18,154
Improvements other than buildings	771,355	2,274,526	15,356	3,061,237	—
Machinery and equipment	15,783	768,354	5,399	789,536	6,790
Accumulated depreciation	(284,711)	(2,589,187)	(19,145)	(2,893,043)	(11,268)
Net capital assets	544,872	3,197,418	20,597	3,762,887	19,329
Long-term receivables (net of allowances)	—	10,320	4,000	14,320	—
CIS net	3,369	—	—	3,369	—
Prepaid expense and other	—	4,487	—	4,487	—
Interest rate swaps	—	38,232	—	38,232	—
Total Noncurrent Assets	**604,010**	**4,111,176**	**24,597**	**4,739,783**	**19,329**
Total Assets	**639,370**	**5,419,473**	**48,987**	**6,107,830**	**77,551**
Deferred Outflow					
Accumulated decrease in fair value of hedging derivatives	—	13,967	—	13,967	—
Deferred amount on refunding	737	214,963	—	215,700	—

continued

ILLUSTRATION A2–7 *(Continued)*

CITY AND COUNTY OF DENVER, COLORADO
Statement of Net Position—Proprietary Funds
December 31, 2013 (dollars in thousands)

	Business-type Activities—Enterprise Funds				Governmental Activities
	Wastewater Management	**Denver Airport System**	**Other Enterprise Funds**	**Total Enterprise Funds**	**Internal Service Funds**
Liabilities					
Current liabilities:					
Vouchers payable	$ 549	$ 37,911	$ 1,881	$ 40,341	$ 1,856
Revenue bonds payable	2,590	—	495	3,085	—
Accrued liabilities	1,151	42,341	481	43,973	421
Unearned revenue	16,986	22,026	277	39,289	—
Interfund payable	1,409	4,318	73	5,800	119
Advances	—	—	—	—	2,000
Capital lease obligations	548	—	290	838	760
Compensated absences	860	2,491	232	3,583	594
Construction payable	3,114	—	—	3,114	—
Due to other governments	5,324	—	—	5,324	—
Current liabilities (payable from restricted assets):					
Vouchers payable	—	51,934	—	51,934	—
Retainages payable	—	24,043	—	24,043	—
Notes payable	—	5,488	—	5,488	—
Accrued interest and other liabilities	—	26,534	—	26,534	—
Other accrued liabilities	—	11,622	—	11,622	—
Revenue bonds payable	—	133,495	—	133,495	—
Total Current Liabilities	**32,531**	**362,203**	**3,729**	**398,463**	**5,750**
Noncurrent liabilities:					
Interest rate swaps	—	201,820	—	201,820	—
Notes payable	—	20,316	—	20,316	—
Revenue bonds payable, net	48,586	4,480,582	3,498	4,532,666	—
Capital lease obligations	7,419	—	529	7,948	17,358
Compensated absences	1,944	6,423	801	9,168	590
Other accrued liabilities	7,009	—	—	7,009	—
Claims reserve	—	—	—	—	30,797
Total Noncurrent Liabilities	**64,958**	**4,709,141**	**4,828**	**4,778,927**	**48,745**
Total Liabilities	**97,489**	**5,071,344**	**8,557**	**5,177,390**	**54,495**
Deferred Inflows of Resources					
Gain on refundings	—	3,535	—	3,535	—
Other—long-term receivables	—	—	—	—	1,124
Net Position					
Net investment in capital assets	511,147	(719,304)	15,785	(192,372)	1,211
Restricted for:					
Capital projects	—	16,087	2,008	18,095	—
Debt service	—	653,222	—	653,222	—
Unrestricted	31,471	623,519	22,637	677,627	20,721
Total Net Position	**$542,618**	**$ 573,524**	**$40,430**	1,156,572	**$ 21,932**
Adjustment to reflect consolidation of internal service fund activities related to enterprise funds				(51)	
Net position of business-type activities				**$1,156,521**	

ILLUSTRATION A2–8

CITY AND COUNTY OF DENVER, COLORADO

Statement of Revenues, Expenses and Changes in Fund Net Position—Proprietary Funds
For the Year Ended December 31, 2013 (dollars in thousands)

	Business-type Activities—Enterprise Funds				Governmental Activities
	Wastewater Management	**Denver Airport System**	**Other Enterprise Funds**	**Total Enterprise Funds**	**Internal Service Funds**
Operating Revenues					
Charges for services	$ 115,872	$ 661,637	$ 17,794	$ 795,303	$ 40,712
Other revenue	—	—	314	314	1,044
Change in claims reserve	—	—	—	—	2,089
Total Operating Revenues	**115,872**	**661,637**	**18,108**	**795,617**	**43,845**
Operating Expenses					
Personnel services	21,430	125,608	8,202	155,240	9,633
Contractual services	19,687	194,666	5,905	220,258	668
Supplies and materials	1,589	111,661	1,687	114,937	21,430
Depreciation and amortization	16,499	184,721	1,011	202,231	1,854
District water treatment charges	44,860	—	—	44,860	—
Claims payments	—	—	—	—	7,903
Other operating expenses	—	—	2,753	2,753	2,469
Total Operating Expenses	**104,065**	**616,656**	**19,558**	**740,279**	**43,957**
Operating income (loss)	11,807	44,981	(1,450)	55,338	(112)
Nonoperating Revenues (Expenses)					
Investment and interest income	(555)	25,205	(293)	24,357	(307)
Passenger facility charges	—	103,032	—	103,032	—
Intergovernmental revenue	888	—	—	888	—
Disposition of assets	60	—	—	60	—
Grants	—	481	—	481	—
Interest expense	(1,479)	(183,359)	(224)	(185,062)	(615)
Other expense	—	(1,265)	—	(1,265)	—
Total Nonoperating Revenues (Expenses)	**(1,086)**	**(55,906)**	**(517)**	**(57,509)**	**(922)**
Income (loss) before capital grants, contributions, and transfers	10,721	(10,925)	(1,967)	(2,171)	(1,034)
Capital grants and contributions	7,289	31,412	—	38,701	—
Transfers in	—	—	—	—	637
Transfers out	(25)	—	(250)	(275)	—
Change in net position	17,985	20,487	(2,217)	36,255	(397)
Net position—January 1, as previously reported	525,297	582,336	42,742	1,150,375	22,329
Change in accounting position—GASB 65	(664)	(29,299)	(95)	(30,058)	—
Net position—January 1, as restated	524,633	553,037	42,647	1,120,317	22,329
Net Position—December 31	**$ 542,618**	**$ 573,524**	**$ 40,430**	**$ 1,156,572**	**$ 21,932**
Change in net position of enterprise funds				$ 36,255	
Adjustment to reflect consolidation of internal service fund activities related to enterprise funds				(687)	
Change in net position of business-type activities				**$ 35,568**	

ILLUSTRATION A2–9

CITY AND COUNTY OF DENVER, COLORADO
Statement of Cash Flows—Proprietary Funds
For the Year Ended December 31, 2013 (dollars in thousands)

	Business-type Activities—Enterprise Funds				Governmental Activities
	Wastewater Management	Denver Airport System	Other Enterprise Funds	Total Enterprise Funds	Internal Service Funds
Cash Flows From Operating Activities					
Receipts from customers	$ 115,741	$ 635,398	$17,723	$ 768,862	$40,740
Payments to suppliers	(57,393)	(283,886)	(11,228)	(352,507)	(23,431)
Payments to employees	(21,603)	(125,379)	(8,067)	(155,049)	(9,742)
Other receipts	—	—	(3,686)	(3,686)	1,994
Interfund activity	(9,003)	(19,274)	—	(28,277)	—
Claims paid	—	—	—	—	(7,903)
Net Cash Provided (Used) by Operating Activities	**27,742**	**206,859**	**(5,258)**	**229,343**	**1,658**
Cash Flows From Noncapital Financing Activities					
Operating grants received	—	425	—	425	—
Transfers in	—	—	—	—	637
Transfers out	(25)	—	(250)	(275)	—
Net Cash Provided (Used) By Noncapital Financing Activities	**(25)**	**425**	**(250)**	**150**	**637**
Cash Flows From Capital and Related Financing Activities					
Proceeds from capital debt	—	740,737	(641)	740,096	—
Bond issue costs	—	(3,347)	—	(3,347)	—
Principal payments	(5,677)	(182,702)	—	(188,379)	(728)
Interest payments	(2,122)	(166,797)	(231)	(169,150)	(616)
Passenger facility charges	—	105,630	—	105,630	—
Payments on capital assets acquired through construction payables	(2,502)	(82,719)	—	(85,221)	—
Acquisition and construction of capital assets	(11,681)	(182,723)	840	(193,564)	(162)
Reimbursement from City for capital asset costs and proceeds from sale of assets	60	834	—	894	—
Contributions and advances	1,565	38,050	—	39,615	—
Intergovernmental revenues	888	—	—	888	—
Net Cash Provided (Used) by Capital and Related Financing Activities	**(19,469)**	**266,963**	**(32)**	**247,462**	**(1,506)**
Cash Flows From Investing Activities					
Purchases of investments	(215,237)	(5,023,863)	—	(5,239,100)	—
Proceeds from sale of investments	205,527	4,504,798	—	4,710,325	—
Sale of assets held for disposition; payments to maintain assets held	—	2,241	—	2,241	—
Insurance proceeds from remediation of asset held for disposition	—	4,724	—	4,724	—
Interest received	396	27,397	(290)	27,503	(401)
Interest rate swap settlements	—	(38,139)	—	(38,139)	—
Net Cash Provided by Investing Activities	**(9,314)**	**(522,842)**	**(290)**	**(532,446)**	**(401)**

continued

ILLUSTRATION A2–9 (*Continued*)

CITY AND COUNTY OF DENVER, COLORADO
Statement of Cash Flows—Proprietary Funds
For the Year Ended December 31, 2013 (dollars in thousands)

	Business-type Activities—Enterprise Funds				Governmental Activities
	Wastewater Management	**Denver Airport System**	**Other Enterprise Funds**	**Total Enterprise Funds**	**Internal Service Funds**
Net increase (decrease) in cash and cash equivalents	(1,066)	(48,595)	(5,830)	(55,491)	388
Cash and cash equivalents – January1	8,489	246,367	27,794	282,650	51,136
Cash and Cash Equivalents—December 31	**$ 7,423**	**$ 197,772**	**$21,964**	**$ 227,159**	**$51,524**
Reconciliation of Operating Income (loss) to Net Cash Provided by Operating Activities					
Operating income (loss)	$ 11,807	$ 44,981	$ (1,450)	$ 55,338	$ (112)
Adjustments to reconcile operating income to net cash provided (used) by operating activities:					
Depreciation and amortization	16,499	184,721	1,011	202,231	1,854
Miscellaneous revenue	—	1,331	—	1,331	—
Accounts receivable, net of allowance	(529)	(7,227)	(58)	(7,814)	(394)
Interfund receivable	(387)	—	(4,000)	(4,387)	(168)
Inventories	—	1,028	(1,032)	(4)	(339)
Prepaid items and other assets	30	(2,018)	—	(1,988)	—
Vouchers payable	(67)	4,655	1,131	5,719	532
Unearned revenue	785	9,587	(13)	10,359	—
Accrued and other liabilities	(711)	(31,020)	(848)	(32,579)	(109)
Interfund payable	315	821	1	1,137	2,107
Deferred revenue	—	—	—	—	376
Claims reserved	—	—	—	—	(2,089)
Net Cash Provided (Used) by Operating Activities	**$ 27,742**	**$ 206,859**	**$ (5,258)**	**$ 229,343**	**$ 1,658**

Noncash Activities

The Airport System issued bonds in the amount of $719,915,000 in 2013 in order to refund debt and fund capital projects. Original issue premiums on bonds of $24,464,553 were realized on the issuance of bonds.

Assets acquired through capital contributions	$ 5,724	$ —	$ —	$ 5,724	$ —
Unrealized loss on investments	—	(46,782)	—	(46,782)	—
Unrealized gain on derivatives	—	45,113	—	45,113	—
Capital assets acquired through accounts payable	3,114	74,954	—	78,068	—
Amortization of bond premiums and deferred losses and gains on bond refunding	191	5,342	—	5,533	—

ILLUSTRATION A2–10

CITY AND COUNTY OF DENVER, COLORADO
Statement of Fiduciary Net Position—Fiduciary Funds
December 31, 2013 (dollars in thousands)

	Pension, Health, and Other Employee Benefit Trust Funds	Private-Purpose Trust Funds	Agency Funds
Assets			
Cash on hand	$ —	$268	$ 2,377
Cash and cash equivalents	41,501	577	29,464
Securities lending collateral	230,030	—	—
Receivables (net of allowance for uncollectibles of $5,627):			
Taxes	—	—	675,376
Accounts	327	—	135
Accrued interest	1,743	—	—
Investments, at fair value:			
U.S. Government obligations	61,939	—	—
Domestic stocks and bonds	841,381	—	—
International stocks	567,092	—	—
Mutual funds	80,565	—	—
Real estate	648,729	—	—
Other	441,066	—	—
Total Investments	**2,640,772**	**—**	**—**
Capital assets, net of accumulated depreciation	5,407	—	—
Total Assets	**2,919,780**	**845**	**$707,352**
Liabilities			
Vouchers payable	5,596	282	418
Securities lending obligation	230,030	—	—
Other accrued liabilities	—	—	16,141
Due to taxing units	—	267	690,793
Total Liabilities	**235,626**	**549**	**$707,352**
Net Position			
Net position held in trust for pension benefits	2,030,539	—	
Net position held in trust for OPEB benefits	79,877	—	
Net position held in trust for deferred compensation benefits	573,738	—	
Net position held in trust for other purposes	—	296	
Net Position Held in Trust for Pension Benefits and Other Purposes	**$2,684,154**	**$296**	

ILLUSTRATION A2–11

CITY AND COUNTY OF DENVER, COLORADO
Statement of Changes in Fiduciary Net Position—Fiduciary Funds
For the Year Ended December 31, 2013 (dollars in thousands)

	Pension, Health, and Other Employee Benefit Trust Funds	Private-Purpose Trust Funds
Additions		
Contributions:		
City and County of Denver	$ 53,424	$ —
Denver Health and Hospital Authority	7,138	—
Plan members	67,040	—
Total Contributions	**127,602**	—
Investment earnings:		
Net appreciation in fair value of investments	301,828	—
Interest and dividends	123,640	—
Total Investment Earnings	**425,468**	—
Less investment expense	(13,169)	—
Net Investment Earnings	**412,299**	—
Securities lending earnings	442	—
Securities lending expenses:		
Borrower rebates	902	—
Agent fees	(336)	—
Net Earnings from Securities Lending	**1,008**	—
Total Net Investment Earnings	**413,307**	—
Total Additions	**540,909**	—
Deductions		
Benefits	258,583	—
Refunds of contributions	1,093	—
Administrative expenses	3,850	—
Other deductions	—	(3)
Total Deductions	**263,526**	**(3)**
Change in net position	277,383	3
Net position—January 1	2,406,771	293
Net Position—December 31	**$2,684,154**	**$296**

Appendix B

Summary Statement of Governmental Accounting and Financial Reporting Principles

Following is a summary statement of accounting and financial reporting principles for state and local governments, as paraphrased from GASB Standards.[17] Principles summarized here that have not been discussed in Chapters 1 and 2 will be covered in depth in following chapters.

[17] GASB *Codification*, Sec. 1100 through 2100.

1. **Accounting and Reporting Capabilities**
   A governmental accounting system must make it possible both: (a) to present fairly and with full disclosure the funds and activities of the government in conformity with generally accepted accounting principles, and (b) to determine and demonstrate compliance with finance-related legal and contractual provisions.

2. **Fund Accounting Systems**
   Governmental accounting systems should be organized and operated on a fund basis. A fund is defined as a fiscal and accounting entity with a self-balancing set of accounts recording cash and other financial resources, together with all related liabilities and residual balances, and changes therein, which are segregated for the purpose of carrying on specific activities or attaining certain objectives in accordance with special regulations, restrictions, or limitations. Fund financial statements should be used to report detailed information about the primary government, including its blended component units. The focus of governmental and proprietary fund financial statements is on major funds.

3. **Types of Funds**
   The following types of funds should be used by state and local governments to the extent that they have activities that meet the criteria for using those funds.
   a. **Governmental Funds**
   (1) *The General Fund*—to account for all current financial resources except those required to be reported in another fund.
   (2) *Special Revenue Funds*—to account for and report the proceeds of specific revenue sources that are restricted or committed to expenditure for specified purposes other than debt service or capital projects.
   (3) *Capital Projects Funds*—to account for and report financial resources that are restricted, committed, or assigned to expenditure for capital outlays, including the acquisition or construction of capital facilities and other capital assets.
   (4) *Debt Service Funds*—to account for and report financial resources that are restricted, committed, or assigned to expenditure for principal and interest.
   (5) *Permanent Funds*—to account for and report resources that are restricted to the extent that only earnings, and not principal, may be used for purposes that support the primary government's programs (those that benefit the government or its citizenry). [Note: Similar permanent trusts that benefit private individuals, organizations, or other governments—that is, private-purpose trust funds—are classified as fiduciary funds, as shown below.]
   b. **Proprietary Funds**
   (6) *Enterprise Funds*—*may* be used to report any activity for which a fee is charged to external users for goods or services. An enterprise fund *must* be used if (a) the activity is being financed with debt that is secured solely from the fees and charges for the activity, (b) laws and regulations require that the costs of providing services, including capital costs such as depreciation or debt service, be recovered from fees and charges, or (c) pricing policies of the activity are intended to recover its costs, including capital costs.
   (7) *Internal Service Funds*—to account for the financing of goods or services provided by one department or agency to other funds, departments, or agencies of the governmental unit, or to other governmental units, on a cost-reimbursement basis.
   c. **Fiduciary Funds** (and similar component units). These are *trust* and *agency funds* that are used to account for assets held by a governmental unit in a trustee capacity

or as an agent for individuals, private organizations, and other governmental units. These include:

(8) *Agency funds.*
(9) *Pension (and other employee benefit) trust funds.*
(10) *Investment trust funds.*
(11) *Private-purpose trust funds.*

4. **Number of Funds**
Governmental units should establish and maintain those funds required by law and sound financial administration. Only the minimum number of funds consistent with legal and operating requirements should be established, however, because unnecessary funds result in inflexibility, undue complexity, and inefficient financial administration.

5. **Reporting Capital Assets**
A clear distinction should be made between general capital assets and capital assets of proprietary and fiduciary funds. Capital assets of proprietary funds should be reported in both the government-wide and fund statements. Capital assets of fiduciary funds should be reported in only the statement of fiduciary net position. All other capital assets of the governmental unit are general capital assets. They should not be reported as assets in governmental funds but should be reported in the Governmental Activities column in the government-wide statement of net position.

6. **Valuation of Capital Assets**
Capital assets should be reported at historical cost. The cost of a capital asset should include capitalized interest (not applicable to general capital assets) and ancillary charges necessary to place the asset into its intended location and condition for use. Donated capital assets should be reported at their estimated fair value at the time of the acquisition plus ancillary charges, if any.

7. **Depreciation of Capital Assets**
Capital assets should be depreciated over their estimated useful lives unless they are either inexhaustible or are infrastructure assets using the modified approach as set forth in GASB standards. Inexhaustible assets such as land and land improvements should not be depreciated. Depreciation expense should be reported in the government-wide statement of activities; the proprietary fund statement of revenues, expenses, and changes in fund net position; and the statement of changes in fiduciary net position.

8. **Reporting Long-Term Liabilities**
A clear distinction should be made between fund long-term liabilities and general long-term liabilities. Long-term liabilities directly related to and expected to be paid from proprietary funds should be reported in the proprietary fund statement of net position and in the government-wide statement of net position. Long-term liabilities directly related to and expected to be paid from fiduciary funds should be reported in the statement of fiduciary net position. All other unmatured general long-term liabilities of the government should not be reported in governmental funds but should be reported in the Governmental Activities column in the government-wide statement of net position.

9. **Measurement Focus and Basis of Accounting in the Basic Financial Statements**
a. **Government-wide Financial Statements**
The government-wide statement of net position and statement of activities should be prepared using the economic resources measurement focus and the accrual basis of accounting. Revenues, expenses, gains, losses, assets, and liabilities resulting from exchange and exchange-like transactions should be recognized when the exchange takes place. Revenues, expenses, assets, and liabilities resulting from nonexchange transactions should be recognized in accordance with [*Codification*] Section N50, "Nonexchange Transactions."

b. **Fund Financial Statements**

In fund financial statements, the modified accrual or accrual basis of accounting, as appropriate, should be used in measuring financial position and operating results.

(1) Financial statements for governmental funds should be presented using the current financial resources measurement focus and the modified accrual basis of accounting. Revenues should be recognized in the accounting period in which they become available and measurable. Expenditures should be recognized in the accounting period in which the fund liability is incurred, if measurable, except for unmatured interest on general long-term liabilities, which should be recognized when due.

(2) Proprietary fund statements of net position and revenues, expenses, and changes in fund net position should be presented using the economic resources measurement focus and the accrual basis of accounting.

(3) Financial statements of fiduciary funds should be reported using the economic resources measurement focus and the accrual basis of accounting.

(4) Transfers between funds should be reported in the accounting period in which the interfund receivable and payable arise.

10. **Budgeting and Budgetary Control**

a. An annual budget(s) should be adopted by every governmental unit.

b. The accounting system should provide the basis for appropriate budgetary control.

c. A common terminology and classification should be used consistently throughout the budget, accounts, and financial statements.

11. **Budgetary Reporting**

a. Budgetary comparison schedules should be presented for the General Fund and each major special revenue fund that has a legally adopted budget as part of the required supplementary information (RSI). Governments may elect to present the budgetary comparisons as part of the basic financial statements.

12. **Transfer, Revenue, Expenditure, and Expense Account Classification**

a. Transfers should be classified separately from revenues and expenditures or expenses in the basic financial statements.

b. Proceeds of general long-term debt issues should be classified separately from revenues and expenditures in the governmental fund financial statements.

c. Governmental fund revenues should be classified by fund and source. Expenditures should be classified by fund, function (or program), organization unit, activity, character, and principal classes of objects.

d. Proprietary fund revenues should be reported by major sources, and expenses should be classified in essentially the same manner as those of similar business organizations, functions, or activities.

e. The statement of activities should present *governmental* activities at least at the level of detail required in the governmental fund statement of revenues, expenditures, and changes in fund balances—at a minimum by *function.* Governments should present *business-type* activities at least by *segment.*

13. **Annual Financial Reports**

a. A comprehensive annual financial report (CAFR) should be prepared and published, covering all activities of the primary government (including its blended component units) and providing an overview of all discretely presented component units of the reporting entity—including introductory section, management's discussion and analysis (MD&A), basic financial statements, required supplementary information other than MD&A, combining and individual fund statements, schedules, narrative explanations, and statistical section. The reporting entity is the primary government (including its blended component units) and all discretely presented component units according to [*Codification*] Section 2100, "Defining the Financial Reporting Entity."

b. The minimum requirements for general purpose external financial reporting are:
   (1) Management's discussion and analysis.
   (2) Basic financial statements. The basic financial statements should include:
      (a) Government-wide financial statements.
      (b) Fund financial statements.
      (c) Notes to the financial statements.
   (3) Required supplementary information other than MD&A.

c. As discussed in [*Codification*] Section 2100, the financial reporting entity consists of (1) the primary government, (2) organizations for which the primary government is financially accountable, and (3) other organizations for which the nature and significance of their relationship with the primary government are such that exclusion would cause the reporting entity's basic financial statements to be misleading or incomplete. The reporting entity's government-wide financial statements should display information about the reporting government as a whole, distinguishing between the total primary government and its discretely presented component units as well as between the primary government's governmental and business-type activities. The reporting entity's fund financial statements should present the primary government's major funds individually and nonmajor funds in the aggregate. Included as part of the primary government are any blended component units. Funds and component units that are fiduciary in nature should be reported only in the statements of fiduciary net position and changes in fiduciary net position.

d. The nucleus of a financial reporting entity usually is a primary government. However, a governmental entity other than a primary government (such as a component unit, joint venture, jointly governed organization, or other stand-alone government) serves as the nucleus for its own reporting entity when it issues separate financial statements. For all of these entities, the provisions of [*Codification*] Section 2100 should be applied in layers "from the bottom up." At each layer, the definition and display provisions should be applied before the layer is included in the financial statements of the next level of the reporting government.

Key Terms

Selected References

Governmental Accounting Standards Board. *Codification of Governmental Accounting and Financial Reporting Standards as of June 30, 2014.* Norwalk, CT, 2014.

Questions

2–1. Identify and briefly describe the three broad categories of service activities that most general purpose governments perform.

2–2. Describe how the reporting objectives for government-wide and governmental fund financial statements are different.

2–3. Explain the *modified accrual basis* of accounting. Why is it used for governmental fund financial statements?

2–4. What are the three categories of funds prescribed by GASB standards and which fund types are included in each? Which basis of accounting is used by each category?

2–5. What is the primary reason that governmental entities need to use funds for financial reporting? How are funds established?

2–6. What is meant by the terms *deferred outflows of resources* and *deferred inflows of resources*? When are these accounts used?

2–7. How do *expenses* and *expenditures* differ?

2–8. Proprietary fund accounting is more like for-profit accounting than the accounting for any other category of fund. Explain why you think this is the case, using the two types of proprietary funds as examples.

2–9. Identify the fund balance classifications and give an example of what might be included in each classification identified.

2–10. Identify the criteria for determining if a governmental or enterprise fund must be reported as a *major fund*. What other funds should or may be reported as major funds?

Cases

2–11 Accounting and Reporting Principles. For more than 100 years, the financial statements of the Town of Fordville have consisted of a statement of cash receipts and a statement of cash disbursements prepared by the town treasurer for each of its three funds: the General Fund, the Road Tax Fund (special revenue fund), and the Sewer Fund (enterprise fund). As required by state law, the town submits its financial statements to the Office of the State Auditor; however, its financial statements have never been audited by an independent auditor.

Because of its growing population (nearing 15,000) and increasing financial complexity, the town has hired Emily Ramirez, who recently obtained her CPA certificate, to supervise all accounting and financial reporting operations. Having worked two years for a CPA firm in a nearby town, Ms. Ramirez gained limited experience auditing not-for-profit organizations, as well as compiling financial statements for small businesses. Although she has little knowledge of governmental accounting, she is confident that her foundation in business and not-for-profit accounting will enable her to handle the job.

Using her experience with not-for-profit organizations, for the year ended December 31, 2017, Ms. Ramirez prepared the following unaudited financial statements for the Town of Fordville. Study these financial statements and answer the questions that follow.

TOWN OF FORDVILLE
Balance Sheet
December 31, 2017
(unaudited)

Assets	
Cash	$ 1,740
Taxes receivable	18,555
Investments	7,468
Due from other governments	28,766
Land, buildings, and equipment (net of accumulated depreciation of $132,640)	287,580
Total assets	$344,109
Liabilities and Net Assets	
Accounts payable	$ 3,892
Due to other governments	11,943
Total liabilities	15,835
Net assets—unrestricted	299,893
Net assets—temporarily restricted	28,381
Total net assets	328,274
Total liabilities and net assets	$344,109

TOWN OF FORDVILLE
Statement of Activities
Year Ended December 31, 2017
(unaudited)

Revenues	
Property taxes	$121,290
Charges for services	3,580
Sewer fees	6,859
Investment income	239
Total revenues	131,968
Expenses	
Government services	115,958
Sewer services	7,227
Miscellaneous	8,462
Total expenses	131,647
Increase in net assets	321
Net assets, January 1, 2017	327,953
Net assets, December 31, 2017	$328,274

Required

a. Assume that you are the CPA Ms. Ramirez has contacted about the possibility of performing an audit of the Town of Fordville's financial statements. Based on your preliminary review, what concerns would you have about these financial statements? Do the statements appear to conform to generally accepted accounting principles (GAAP)? In what respects, if any, do the financial statements depart from GAAP?

b. Assume, instead, that you are a member of the town council or a citizen. What concerns would you have with these financial statements?

2–12 Evaluation of a city's basic financial statements. Following is a description of the basic financial statements extracted from an example city's management's discussion and analysis (MD&A). Review the description and respond to the requirements at the end of the case.

Government-wide Financial Statements

The basic financial statements include two government-wide financial statements: the statement of net position and the statement of activities. The government-wide financial statements report information about the city as a whole using accounting methods similar to those used by the private sector. The statement of net position and statement of activities divide the city into the following:

- **Governmental activities**—All of the city's basic services are considered to be governmental activities, including public safety, public works, health, parks, planning, cultural and economic development and general administration. These activities are supported primarily with general city revenue such as sales taxes, property taxes, fines and specific program revenue like permit fees and grants.
- **Business-type activities**—All the city's enterprise activities are included here. These operations derive revenues from charges for services that are intended to recoup the full cost of operations. Three of these operations require subsidies from tax revenue (airport, transit and recreation services). The city does not include any component units in its financial statements.

Fund Financial Statements

Another major section of the basic financial statements is the fund financial statements. The fund financial statements provide detailed information about each of the city's most significant funds, called "major funds." All "nonmajor" funds are summarized and presented in a single column. The city has three kinds of funds:

- **Governmental funds**—Most of the city's basic services are included in governmental funds. These fund statements are prepared on a modified accrual basis, which means they measure only current financial resources and uses. Capital assets and other long-lived assets, along with long-term liabilities, are not presented in the governmental fund statements. Because this information does not encompass the long-term focus of the government-wide financial statements, additional information is provided to explain the differences between them.
- **Proprietary funds**—These statements include both enterprise funds and internal service funds. Statements are prepared on the accrual basis and include all their assets and liabilities, current and long-term. This is the same basis used in the government-wide financial statements.
- **Fiduciary funds**—These statements include activity of funds that report trust responsibilities of the city. These funds are summarized by type: pension, other employee benefit, and private-purpose trust. These assets are restricted in purpose and do not represent discretionary assets of the city. Therefore, these assets are not presented as a part of the government-wide financial statements.

Required

a. Review the foregoing description of the example city's basic financial statements and prepare a detailed listing of the ways that this city's basic financial statements do or do not conform to GASB standards, as described in this chapter.

b. In the description of the city's governmental funds, explain the meaning of the sentence: *Because this information does not encompass the long-term focus of the government-wide financial statements, additional information is provided to explain the differences between them.*

2–13 Research Case—Fund Balances. The City and County of Denver allocates its governmental fund balances among the classifications specified by GASB standards (see Illustration A2-4). Go to Denver's Web site and locate its CAFR report for the 2013 fiscal year (Hint: Look for the Finance Department). Using the information provided in the notes to the financial statements, identify some of the reasons provided for classifying fund balance amounts as nonspendable, restricted, committed, and assigned.

Exercises and Problems

2–14 Examine the CAFR. Utilizing the CAFR obtained for Exercise/Problem 1–15, examine the financial statements included in the financial section and answer the following questions. If the CAFR you have obtained does not conform to GAAP, it is recommended that you obtain one that does.

a. Government-wide Statements. What are the titles of the two government-wide statements? Are total assets larger for governmental activities or business-type activities? Which function or program has the highest net cost? What kinds of general revenues are available to cover the net cost of governmental activities? Were business-type activities "profitable"? That is, is the excess of revenues over expenses positive?

b. Governmental Funds. Does the report state the basis of accounting used for the General Fund? What types of assets and liabilities are included on the governmental funds balance sheet? Is this reporting consistent with the basis of accounting being followed?

c. Identify which of the major funds, if applicable, are special revenue funds, debt service funds, capital projects funds, and permanent funds. Are you able to determine which funds are considered nonmajor? (Hint: look for supplementary information.) What fund balance categories are being used?

d. Proprietary Funds. List the names of the proprietary fund types included in the financial statements. Do the financial statements provide evidence that all proprietary funds use accrual accounting?

e. Fiduciary Funds. List the names of the fiduciary funds included in the fund financial statements. Identify whether each of these is an agency fund, investment trust fund, pension (and other employee benefit) trust fund, or private-purpose trust fund. Do the financial statements provide evidence as to what basis of accounting these funds use?

f. Notes to the Financial Statements. Read the notes to the financial statements, so that you can refer to them as needed in subsequent chapters. What significant accounting policies are discussed in the first note? With regard to revenue recognition, how do the notes define the term *available for paying current period obligations*?

2–15 Multiple Choice. Choose the best answer.

1. Which of the following statements is true regarding the definition of a fund?
   a. A fund is a fiscal entity that is designed to provide reporting that demonstrates conformance with finance-related legal and contractual provisions separately from GAAP reporting.
   b. A fund is an accounting entity that is designed to enable reporting in conformity with GAAP without being restricted by legal or contractual provisions.
   c. A fund is a mechanism developed to provide accounting for revenues and expenditures that are subject to certain restrictions separate from revenues and expenditures that are not subject to restrictions.
   d. A fund exists to assist in carrying on activities and attaining objectives where there are no specific rules or restrictions.

2. Which of the following statements is true regarding the basic financial statements of a state or local government?
   a. Separate columns should be provided in the government-wide financial statements for governmental activities and business-type activities.
   b. Governmental fund and proprietary fund financial statements should provide a separate column for each major fund.
   c. Aggregate information about all nonmajor governmental funds or nonmajor enterprise funds should be reported in a single column of the governmental fund or proprietary fund financial statements.
   d. All of the above.

3. Which of the following sets of elements are common to both governmental financial statements and for-profit financial statements?
   a. Assets and net position.
   b. Deferred outflows of resources and liabilities.
   c. Assets and liabilities.
   d. Net position and liabilities.

4. The measurement focus and basis of accounting that should be used for the governmental *fund* financial statements are:

	Measurement Focus	Basis of Accounting
a.	Current financial resources	Modified accrual
b.	Current financial resources	Accrual
c.	Economic resources	Modified accrual
d.	Economic resources	Accrual

5. Which of the following amounts that are identified at the end of the fiscal year would be classified as a restricted fund balance?
   a. Resources the city manager has set aside for a major street repair.
   b. A federal grant that is to be used for playground equipment.
   c. Significant amounts of inventory.
   d. Endowment resources that the city must maintain in perpetuity.

6. Separate reporting for major funds is needed because
   a. Users of governmental financial statements are usually interested in the details of every fund used by a government.
   b. It is illegal to aggregate funds where the elements of the fund represent at least 5 percent of the corresponding element for all funds of the same type.
   c. Users of governmental financial statements need to be able to examine the activities and resources of fiduciary funds.

d. Users of governmental financial statements need to be able to examine funds that represent large dollar amounts of a government's resources and activities.

7. Assets and liabilities of activities for which the government is acting in either an agency or trustee capacity for individuals, organizations, or other governments should be reported in:
   a. The fiduciary column of the government-wide financial statements.
   b. The fiduciary fund financial statements.
   c. Both government-wide and fiduciary fund statements.
   d. Neither government-wide nor fiduciary fund statements.
8. Under the modified accrual basis of accounting:
   a. Revenues are recognized at the time an exchange transaction occurs.
   b. Expenditures are recognized as the cost of an asset expires or is used up in providing governmental services.
   c. Revenues are recognized when current financial resources become measurable and available to pay current-period obligations.
   d. Expenses are recognized when an obligation occurs for costs incurred in providing services.
9. Financial information about an internal service fund should be reported in the proprietary fund financial statements and the:
   a. Governmental Activities column of the government-wide financial statements.
   b. Business-type Activities column of the government-wide financial statements.
   c. Either *a* or *b*, depending on whether the internal service fund predominantly serves governmental activities or business-type activities.
   d. None of the above.
10. A certain city reports the following year-end total assets:

General Fund	$18,400,000
Library Fund (a special revenue fund)	2,900,000
Debt Service Fund	2,600,000
Total governmental funds	26,300,000
Total governmental and enterprise funds combined	51,250,000

   Based on this information, which funds should be reported as *major funds*?
   a. General Fund only.
   b. General Fund and Library Fund.
   c. General Fund and Debt Service Fund.
   d. All three funds should be reported as major funds.

2–16 Matching Fund Types with Fund Categories. For each of the following fund types, indicate its fund category by placing either "GF" for governmental funds, "PF" for proprietary funds, or "FF" for fiduciary funds in the space provided before each item.

Fund Type

______ Agency fund
______ Permanent fund
______ Debt service fund
______ Internal service fund
______ Pension (and other employee benefit) trust fund
______ Special revenue fund

______ Enterprise fund
______ General Fund
______ Investment trust fund
______ Capital projects fund
______ Private-purpose trust fund

2–17 Matching Funds and Identifying Characteristics with Fund and Government-wide Financial Reporting Categories. For each fund or government-wide category listed in the left-hand column, choose the letter(s) of the applicable fund type or characteristic in the right-hand column. Multiple letters may apply to each category.

Fund or Government-wide Category	**Fund Type or Characteristic**
1. Governmental funds	*a.* Operational accountability
2. Proprietary funds	*b.* Modified accrual
3. Fiduciary funds	*c.* Agency funds
4. Governmental activities, government-wide	*d.* Statement of cash flows
5. Business-type activities, government-wide	*e.* Fiscal accountability
	f. Debt service funds
	g. Current and noncurrent assets and liabilities
	h. Internal service funds
	i. Integrated budgetary accounts
	j. Revenues and expenses
	k. Additions and deductions

2–18 Matching Funds with Transactions. Choose the letter of the sample transaction in the right-hand column that would most likely be reported in the fund listed in the left-hand column.

Fund	**Example**
1. Agency	*a.* Construction of public buildings.
2. Capital projects	*b.* Costs of a central purchasing and warehouse function.
3. Debt service	*c.* Gifts in which the principal must be invested and preserved but the investment earnings must be used to provide scholarships to children of police officers who died in the line of duty.
4. Enterprise	*d.* Administrative expenses of the city manager's office.
5. General	*e.* Assets held for external government participants in the government's investment pool for the purpose of earning investment income.
6. Internal service	*f.* Gifts in which the principal must be invested and preserved but the investment earnings can be used for public purposes.
7. Investment trust	*g.* Costs of operating a municipal swimming pool.
8. Pension (and other employee benefit) trust	*h.* Taxes collected on behalf of another governmental unit.
9. Permanent	*i.* Assets held in trust to provide retirement benefits for municipal workers.
10. Private-purpose trust	*j.* Principal and interest payments on general long-term debt.
11. Special revenue	*k.* Grant revenues restricted for particular operating purposes.

2–19 Fund Balance Classifications. Section A provides a list of the results of Georgetown's analysis of its fund balances at its fiscal year end. Section B provides a list of the possible classifications for reporting the items listed in Section A.

Section A

_____1. At year end a special revenue fund has a $50,000 fund balance on which there are no constraints.

_____2. Georgetown has a $1,000,000 emergency reserve fund it set aside. According to the town ordinance, funds can only be used from this fund with approval of two-thirds of the town council.

_____3. Georgetown determined that the General Fund has $22,000 in inventory it should report on its fund financial statements.

_____4. Georgetown issued bonds that sold at a premium. Using the authority allowed her by the governing body, the city manager made the decision to set aside the $100,000 premium to pay the principal on the debt when it comes due in a future period.

_____5. The federal government has provided a grant for emergency housing assistance that can only be used for low income families. Georgetown determined $250,000 of the grant funds remained at year-end.

Section B

a. Nonspendable
b. Restricted
c. Committed
d. Assigned
e. Unassigned

Required

Using the choices provided in Section B, identify under which fund balance classification Georgetown should report each of the dollar amounts listed in Section A.

2–20 Major Funds. Forest City has recently implemented GAAP reporting and is attempting to determine which of the following special revenue funds should be classified as "major funds" and, therefore, be reported in separate columns on the balance sheet and statement of revenues, expenditures, and changes in fund balances for the governmental funds. As the city's external auditor, you have been asked to provide a rationale for either including or excluding each of the following funds as a major fund. Prepare a memo to the city manager that gives your recommendation and explanation. Selected information is provided below.

FOREST CITY
As of (for the year ended) June 30, 2017

	Gas Tax Revenue Fund	Housing and Urban Development Grant Fund	Forest City Library Fund	All Governmental Funds	All Governmental and Enterprise Funds
Total assets	$160,748	$175,111	$101,549	$1,563,867	$3,497,398
Total liabilities	72,551	85,433	0	867,533	1,487,225
Total revenues	138,336	169,964	120,589	1,537,399	2,987,487
Total expenditures	124,225	130,583	119,812	1,496,223	2,684,531

Chapter Three

Governmental Operating Statement Accounts; Budgetary Accounting

Learning Objectives

After studying this chapter, you should be able to:

3-1 Describe how operating revenues and expenses related to governmental activities are classified and reported in the government-wide financial statements.

3-2 Distinguish, in governmental funds, between Revenues and Other Financing Sources and between Expenditures and Other Financing Uses.

3-3 Explain how revenues and expenditures are classified in the General Fund and other governmental funds.

3-4 Explain how budgetary accounting contributes to achieving budgetary control over revenues and expenditures, including such aspects as:

Recording the annual budget.

Accounting for revenues.

Accounting for encumbrances and expenditures.

Accounting for allotments.

Reconciling GAAP and budgetary amounts.

3-5 Describe governmental accounting systems.

3-6 Explain the classification of revenues and expenditures of a public school system.

As discussed in Chapters 1 and 2, the Governmental Accounting Standard Board's integrated financial reporting model is designed to meet the diverse needs of financial statement users and achieve the broad reporting objectives set forth in GASB *Concepts Statement No. 1.* Fund-based financial statements are intended to provide detailed financial information about the governmental, business-type, and fiduciary activities of the primary government. To meet users' broader information needs about the government as a whole, the GASB reporting model requires—in addition to fund-based financial statements—a management's discussion and analysis (MD&A) and two government-wide financial statements: a statement of net position or a balance sheet and a statement of activities. This chapter focuses on the latter statement as well as on the operating statement prepared for governmental funds.[1]

CLASSIFICATION AND REPORTING OF EXPENSES AND REVENUES AT THE GOVERNMENT-WIDE LEVEL

The format prescribed for the government-wide statement of activities (see Illustration 3–1) displays the net expense or revenue of each function or program reported for the governmental activities of the government. The GASB defines functions and programs in the following manner: **Functions** group related activities that are aimed at accomplishing a major service or regulatory responsibility, such as Public Safety or Highways and Streets. **Programs** group activities, operations, or organizational units that are directed to the attainment of specific purposes or objectives, such as Highway Beautification or Youth Sports.[2]

In some cases, an activity such as public safety could be identified as a function of one government and a program of another; however, the important thing to note is that functions and programs represent major activities or services of a government.

As shown in Illustration 3–1, the net expense (reported in parentheses if net expense) or net revenue for each function or program is reported in the right-hand column of the top portion of the statement. One will note that the format of the top portion of the statement is as follows:

Expenses − Program Revenues = Net (Expense) Revenue

According to the GASB, reporting in the net expense or revenue format "identifies the extent to which each function of the government draws from the general revenues of the government or is self-financing through fees and intergovernmental aid."[3] The sum of general revenues and any special or extraordinary items is then added to Net (Expense) Revenue to obtain the change in net position for the period (see Illustrations A2–2 and 3–1).

Reporting Direct and Indirect Expenses

Except for extraordinary or special item expenses, described later in this section, expenses generally are reported by function or program (see Illustration 3–1). **Direct expenses**—those that are specifically associated with a function or program—should

[1] GASB *Concepts Statement No. 4* refers to statements reporting inflows and outflows of resources as *resource flows statements*. The authors prefer the more commonly used term *operating statement* to refer to statements that report resource inflows and outflows and changes in fund balances or net position, as appropriate. An operating statement essentially summarizes the financial operations of a government for a specified accounting period. See GASB *Concepts Statement No. 4, Elements of Financial Statements*, par. 27, Governmental Accounting Standards Board, *Codification of Governmental Accounting and Financial Reporting Standards, as of June 30, 2014* (Norwalk, CT, 2014), Appendix B.

[2] GASB, *Codification,* Sec. 1800.116.

[3] GASB *Codification,* Sec. 2200.126.

ILLUSTRATION 3–1 **Format of Government-wide Statement of Activities, Governmental Activities**

			Program Revenues				
Functions/Programs	Expenses	—	Charges for Services	Operating Grants and Contributions	Capital Grants and Contributions	=	Net (Expense) Revenue
Primary Government:							
Function/Program 1	$ xxx,xxx		$ xxx,xxx	$ xxx,xxx	$ xxx,xxx		$ (xxx,xxx)
Function/Program 2	xxx,xxx		xxx,xxx		xxx,xxx		(xxx,xxx)
Function/Program 3	xxx,xxx		xxx,xxx	xxx,xxx			(xxx,xxx)
Function/Program 4	xxx,xxx			xxx,xxx	xxx,xxx		(xxx,xxx)
Function/Program 5	xxx,xxx		xxx,xxx	xxx,xxx	xxx,xxx		(xxx,xxx)
Interest on long-term debt	xx,xxx						(xx,xxx)
Total governmental activities	$x,xxx,xxx		$x,xxx,xxx	$x,xxx,xxx	$x,xxx,xxx		$(x,xxx,xxx)
General Revenues:							
Taxes:							
Property taxes							xxx,xxx
Sales taxes							xxx,xxx
Other taxes							xx,xxx
Grants and contributions not restricted to particular programs							xx,xxx
Investment earnings							xx,xxx
Special item—Gain on sale of government land							xx,xxx
Extraordinary item—Loss due to volcanic eruption							(xx,xxx)
Total general revenues, special items, and extraordinary items							x,xxx,xxx
Change in net position							xx,xxx
Net position—beginning							xxx,xxx
Net position—ending							$ xxx,xxx

be reported on the line for that function or program. **Indirect expenses**—those that are not directly linked to an identifiable function or program—can be reported in a variety of ways. A typical indirect expense is interest on general long-term liabilities. In most cases, interest on general long-term liabilities should be reported as a separate line item rather than being allocated to functions or programs (observe, for example, how it is reported as the last line before total governmental activities in Illustration 3–1).

Governments should report *at a minimum* major functions such as those described on page 79 of this chapter or those depicted in Illustration A2–2 for the City and County of Denver. The GASB encourages governments to provide additional information for more detailed programs if such information is useful and does not detract from readers' understanding of the statement.

Some readers might find it surprising that depreciation expense usually is reported as a direct expense. Depreciation expense for capital assets that are clearly identified with a function or program should be included in the expenses of that function or program. Similarly, depreciation expense for infrastructure assets (such as roads and bridges) should be reported as a direct expense of the function responsible for the infrastructure assets (for example, public works or transportation). Depreciation expense for shared assets should be allocated to functions on an appropriate basis (for example, square footage of building use). Depreciation expense for assets that essentially benefit all functions, such as the city hall, may be reported as a separate line item or on the same line as the General Government or similar function. If a government opts to report unallocated depreciation expense as a separate line item, it should indicate that the amount reported on that line does not include depreciation expense reported as part of direct expense of functions or programs.[4]

Program Revenues and General Revenues

Reporting in the net (expense) revenue format requires a government to distinguish carefully between **program revenues** and **general revenues.** As shown in Illustrations A2–2 for the City and County of Denver and 3–1, *program revenues* are reported in the functions/programs section of the statement of activities, where they reduce the net expense of each function or program or produce a net revenue. *General revenues* are not directly linked to any specific function or program and thus are reported in a separate section in the lower portion of the statement.

Three categories of *program revenues* are reported in the statement of activities: charges for services, operating grants and contributions, and capital grants and contributions. Charges for services include charges to customers or others for both governmental and business-type activities. Charges for services within the governmental activities category include items such as licenses and permits (for example, business licenses and building permits), fines and forfeits, and operating special assessments sometimes charged for services provided outside the normal service area or beyond the normal level of services. A typical example of the latter is snow removal for or maintenance of private lanes or roads that connect with public roads normally maintained by the government. Charges to other governments for services, such as incarceration of prisoners, also are reported in the Charges for Services column.

Grants and contributions restricted by other governments, organizations, or individuals for the *operating* purposes of a particular function or program are reported in a separate column from those restricted for *capital* purposes. GASB requires that

[4] Ibid., Sec. 2200.132.

multipurpose grants and contributions be reported as *program revenues* if "the amounts restricted to each program are specifically identified in either the grant award or grant application."[5] Otherwise, multipurpose grants and contributions should be reported as *general revenue.*

Earnings from endowments or permanent fund investments that are restricted for a specific public purpose in the endowment contract or agreement should be reported as program revenue in the appropriate grants and contributions category. Unrestricted earnings from such sources should be reported as general revenue. In addition, *all* taxes, even those specified by law for a particular use (e.g., motor vehicle fuel taxes that can be used only for road and bridge purposes), should be reported as general revenue.

As noted earlier, the distinction between program and general revenues allows financial statement users to evaluate whether specific functions or programs are self-sufficient or require general revenues to cover net costs. For example, in Illustration 2–2, program revenues for Denver's public safety function fall well below program expenses, so general revenues, such as taxes, help to pay for police services.

Reporting Special Items and Transfers

In the GASB reporting model, extraordinary items and special items must be reported as separate line items below General Revenues in the statement of activities to distinguish these nonrecurring items from normal recurring general revenues. Separate reporting of such items, as shown in Illustration 3–1, serves to inform citizens and other report users when governments engage in the unusual practice of balancing their budget by selling government assets or other similar practices. **Extraordinary items** are defined in the same manner as in business accounting: "transactions or other events that are both unusual in nature and infrequent in occurrence."[6] **Special items** are items *within management's control* that may be either unusual in nature or infrequent in occurrence. An example of a special item is one-time revenue from the sale of a significant governmental asset. Extraordinary items should be reported as the last item on the statement of activities; special items should be reported before extraordinary items. Significant items that are beyond management's control but are unusual or infrequent in nature (such as a loss due to civil riot) should be recorded as normal expenses, expenditures, or revenue, as appropriate, and be disclosed in the notes to the financial statements.

Other items that should be reported on separate lines below General Revenues (see Illustrations A2–2 and 3–1) are contributions to the principal amounts of endowments and permanent funds and transfers between funds reported as part of governmental activities and funds reported as part of business-type activities. Interfund transactions between governmental and business-type activities that involve the sale of goods or services (such as the sale of water from a water utility enterprise fund to the General Fund) are reported as program revenue and expenses, not as transfers. The reader should note that when transfers are reported, as shown in Illustration A2–2, they are reported as an inflow in one activities column and as an outflow in the other activities column but are eliminated from the Primary Government Total column.

The preceding discussion covers the major points relating to the government-wide operating statement—the statement of activities. Some of the unique aspects of *governmental fund* accounting are discussed next, focusing on governmental funds.

[5] Ibid., Sec. 2200.138.

[6] Ibid., Sec. 2200.143.

STRUCTURE AND CHARACTERISTICS OF THE GENERAL FUND AND OTHER GOVERNMENTAL FUNDS

The General Fund has long been the accounting entity of a state or local government that accounts for current financial resources raised and expended for the core governmental services provided to the citizenry. The General Fund is sometimes known as an *operating fund* or *current fund;* the purpose, not the name, is the true test of identity. A typical government now engages in many activities that for legal and historical reasons are financed by sources other than those available to the General Fund. Whenever a revenue source is restricted by an outside donor or grantor, or a tax or other revenue source is authorized by a legislative body for a specified purpose, a government should create a special revenue fund to demonstrate that all revenue from that source was used for the specified purpose only. A common example of a special revenue fund is one used to account for state gasoline tax receipts distributed to a local government; in many states, the use of this money is restricted to the construction and maintenance of streets, highways, and bridges.

As discussed in Chapter 2, there are three other fund types besides the General Fund and special revenue funds that are classified as governmental funds. Those other fund types are *debt service funds, capital projects funds,* and *permanent funds.* The essential characteristics of all governmental fund types were described in Chapter 2. This chapter illustrates in greater depth the manner in which generally accepted accounting principles (GAAP) are applied to the General Fund and special revenue funds. Illustrative accounting transactions for a permanent fund are provided in Chapter 4. Accounting and reporting for capital projects funds and debt service funds are discussed in Chapters 5 and 6, respectively.

Governmental Fund Balance Sheet and Operating Statement Accounts

It should be emphasized that the General Fund and all other funds classified as governmental funds account for only current financial resources (cash, receivables, marketable securities, and, if material, prepaid items and inventories). Economic resources, such as land, buildings, and equipment utilized in fund operations, are not recorded by these funds because they are not normally converted into cash. Similarly, governmental funds account for only those liabilities that will be paid with fund assets. As discussed in Chapter 2, general capital assets and general long-term liabilities are reported only in the Governmental Activities column of the statement of net position at the government-wide level.

The arithmetic difference between the amount of (1) current assets and deferred outflows and (2) current liabilities and deferred inflows recorded in governmental funds is the *fund balance*. Residents of a governmental jurisdiction have no legal claim on any excess of liquid assets over current liabilities; therefore, the fund balance is not analogous to the capital accounts of an investor-owned entity. Accounts in the fund balance section of governmental fund financial statements include accounts established to disclose that portions of the fund balance are not available for spending or that constraints have been placed on the purposes for which they can be expended.[7]

[7] As explained in Chapter 2, the spendable portion of fund balance is classified according to constraints imposed on the purposes for which particular revenues can be spent. The types of constraints include amounts restricted, committed, or assigned. All other spendable amounts of fund balance are reported as *unassigned.* Generally, however, only the General Fund will report unassigned fund balance. GASB *Codification,* Sec. 2200.157.

In addition to the balance sheet accounts just described, governmental funds record financial transactions in operating statement accounts classified as Revenues, Other Financing Sources, Expenditures, and Other Financing Uses. *Revenue* is defined as increases in fund financial resources other than from financing sources such as interfund transfers and debt issue proceeds. Transfers into a fund and the proceeds of debt issues and sales of government assets are examples of inflows classified as **other financing sources** of the fund.

Expenditure is a word that represents the cost to purchase a good or service, whereas *expense* represents the cost of a good or service consumed or expired during the period. Recall that governmental funds are concerned only with flows of current financial resources, not with determination of income or cost of services. Thus, governmental funds report expenditures, not expenses. In the case of employee payroll, utilities, professional travel, and other similar items, expenditures and expenses are essentially the same. In other cases, such as the purchase of equipment using governmental fund resources, an expenditure is recorded in the associated fund for the full cost of the equipment—which differs greatly from depreciation expense, the cost of the utility of the equipment deemed to have been consumed during the year. Depreciation expense is not recorded in the governmental fund because it does not represent the use of current financial resources. At the time of the purchase, the cost of the equipment is recorded as a capital asset of government activities at the government-wide level. The related depreciation expense is recorded as an adjusting entry at year-end.

Other financing uses, such as transfers of financial resources from one fund to another fund, have the same effect on fund balance as expenditures: Both decrease the fund balance at year-end when the temporary accounts are closed. An example of an operating transfer is a transfer of a portion of General Fund revenues to a special revenue fund, such as a library fund. The General Fund should debit Other Financing Uses—Interfund Transfers Out in the appropriate amount and credit Cash. The special revenue fund should debit Cash in the same amount and credit Other Financing Sources—Interfund Transfers In. Subsequently, the special revenue fund should recognize expenditures as transferred resources are expended for authorized operating purposes. Illustrative journal entries are provided in Chapter 4.

Total inflows and outflows for the operating statement accounts of the governmental funds are reported each period in a statement of revenues, expenditures, and changes in fund balances, such as the one presented in Illustration A2–5. Illustration 3–2 presents the format for such a statement in somewhat simpler form.[8] Other financing sources increase fund balances in the same manner as revenues. Similarly, other financing uses decrease fund balances in the same manner as expenditures. GASB standards emphasize, however, that other financing sources (uses) should be distinguished from revenues and expenditures. The format of the operating statements shown in Illustrations A2–5 and 3–2 accomplishes this objective by reporting other financing sources (uses) in a separate section below the revenues and expenditures sections.

The next section introduces the use of budgetary accounts in the General Fund and certain other governmental fund types that may be included in the government's formal budget. Illustration 3–3 displays the relationship between budgetary accounts and the balance sheet and operating statement accounts. When reviewing Illustration 3–3,

[8] If there are any extraordinary and special items, as defined earlier in this chapter, those items should be reported in a separate "extraordinary and special items" section below the other financing sources/uses section.

ILLUSTRATION 3–2 **Format of Governmental Funds Statement of Revenues, Expenditures, and Changes in Fund Balances**

	General	Major Fund #2	Major Fund #3	Other Governmental Funds	Total Governmental Funds
Revenues					
Property taxes	$ xxx,xxx			$ xx,xxx	$ xxx,xxx
Sales taxes	xxx,xxx	$ xx,xxx			xxx,xxx
Fines and forfeits	xx,xxx			xx,xxx	xx,xxx
Licenses and permits	xx,xxx				xx,xxx
Other revenue sources	xx,xxx	xx,xxx	$ xx,xxx	xx,xxx	xxx,xxx
Total revenues	x,xxx,xxx	xxx,xxx	xx,xxx	xxx,xxx	x,xxx,xxx
Expenditures					
General government	xx,xxx	xx,xxx		xx,xxx	xxx,xxx
Public safety	xxx,xxx				xxx,xxx
Health and welfare	xx,xxx			xx,xxx	xxx,xxx
Other functions	xxx,xxx	xxx,xxx	xxx,xxx	xx,xxx	xxx,xxx
Total expenditures	x,xxx,xxx	xxx,xxx	xxx,xxx	xxx,xxx	x,xxx,xxx
Excess (deficiency) of revenues over expenditures	(xx,xxx)	x,xxx	(xx,xxx)	x,xxx	xx,xxx
Other Financing Sources (Uses)					
Capital-related debt issued			xxx,xxx		xxx,xxx
Transfers in	xxx,xxx				xxx,xxx
Total other financing sources (uses)	xxx,xxx		xxx,xxx		xxx,xxx
Net changes in fund balances	x,xxx	x,xxx	x,xxx	x,xxx	xx,xxx
Fund balances—beginning	xx,xxx	xx,xxx	xx,xxx	x,xxx	xxx,xxx
Fund balances—ending	$ xx,xxx	$ xx,xxx	$ xx,xxx	$ x,xxx	$ xxx,xxx

note that both the operating statement accounts and the budgetary accounts are temporary accounts that are closed to their respective fund balance accounts at year-end. With the exception of encumbrances, the temporary budgetary accounts are closed at year-end to Budgetary Fund Balance by reversing the original budgetary entries. If encumbrances are still outstanding at year-end and the government's policy is to honor the encumbrances, there is no need to close the Encumbrances account at year-end. If the government will not honor the outstanding encumbrances at year-end, the Encumbrances account should be closed by debiting Encumbrances Outstanding and crediting Encumbrances.

Another noteworthy observation in Illustration 3–3 is that each operating statement account has a budgetary counterpart: Revenues and Estimated Revenues; Expenditures and both Appropriations and Encumbrances (defined in the next section); Other

ILLUSTRATION 3–3 Comparison of Balance Sheet, Operating Statement, and Budgetary Accounts

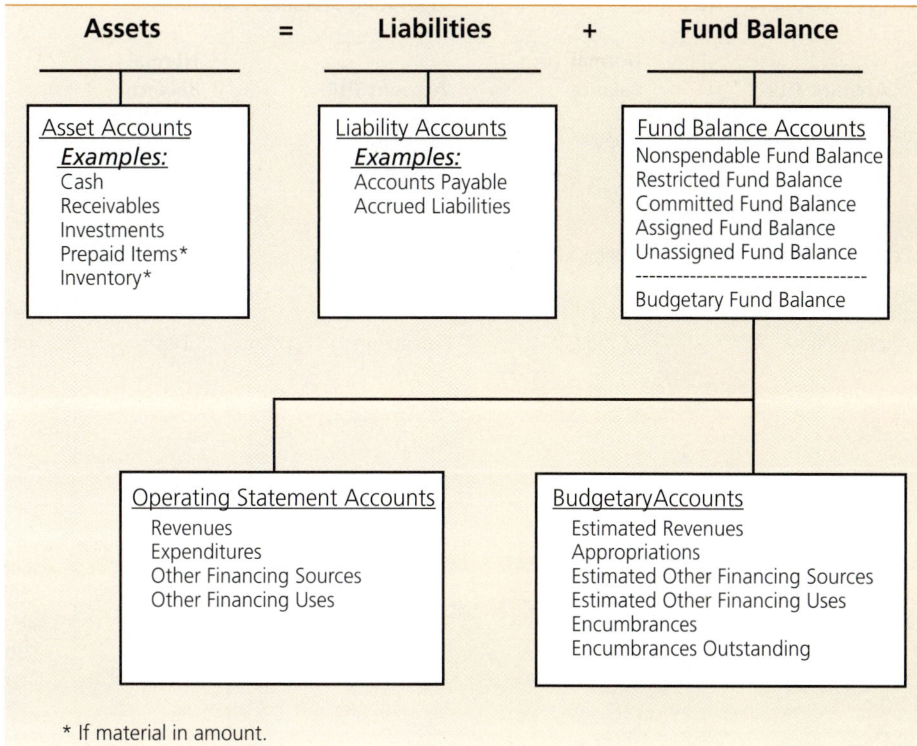

Financing Sources and Estimated Other Financing Sources; and Other Financing Uses and Estimated Other Financing Uses. A tip that may prove useful in understanding budgetary accounting is that, with the exception of Encumbrances, the **budgetary accounts** have normal balances that are the opposite of the corresponding operating statement accounts. For example, since the Revenues account has a normal credit balance, the Estimated Revenues account has a normal debit balance. The use of opposite account balances facilitates budgetary comparisons and makes it easy to determine whether actual amounts are under or over the budgeted amounts. The Encumbrances account has the same normal debit balance as the Expenditures account because an encumbrance represents a commitment prior to an expenditure, as discussed later in this chapter. Illustration 3–4 shows the normal balances of each budgetary account and its corresponding operating statement account.

REPORTING BUDGETED AND ACTUAL RESULTS

Since governments are responsible for public funds that often carry restrictions on their use, budgeting and financial management are among the most important aspects of a local government's operations. The budgeting process within a government is quite extensive and begins with budget projections at the program or departmental level, integration of budget projections by the budget office, public hearings, and final approval by the government's administrative body. The budget process is described

ILLUSTRATION 3–4 Relationship between Budgetary and Operating Statement Accounts

Budgetary Accounts		Operating Statement Accounts		
Account Title	**Normal Balance**	**Account Title**	**Normal Balance**	**Budgetary Status**
Estimated Revenues	Debit	Revenues	Credit	Net balance indicates deficit (excess) of operating (actual) vs. budgeted revenues.
Estimated Other Financing Sources	Debit	Other Financing Sources	Credit	Net balance indicates deficit (excess) of actual OFS vs. budgeted OFS.*
Appropriations	Credit	Expenditures	Debit	Appropriations minus the sum of Expenditures and Encumbrances indicates remaining or overspent expenditure authority.
Estimated Other Financing Uses	Credit	Other Financing Uses	Debit	Net balance indicates the amount of remaining or overspent interfund transfer authority.
Encumbrances	Debit	NA	NA	See Appropriations line above. An encumbrance has a normal debit balance because it is a commitment to make an expenditure and often is considered the same as an expenditure for budgetary purposes.

NA = Not applicable, since there is no corresponding operating statement account.

*OFS = Other Financing Sources.

within a government's notes to the financial statements. This topic is covered in more detail in Chapter 12.

The fact that budgets are legally binding upon administrators has led to the integration of budgetary accounts into the general ledgers of the General Fund and special revenue funds, and other funds that are required by state laws to adopt a budget. GASB standards require that a budget to actual comparison schedule be provided for the General Fund and for each *major* special revenue fund for which a budget is legally adopted.[9] GASB recommends that these schedules be provided as required supplementary information (RSI), which should be placed immediately following the notes to the financial statements. Alternatively, governments may report the budgetary comparison information in a budgetary comparison *statement,* a statement of revenues, expenditures, and changes in fund balances—budget and actual—which would then be part of the basic financial statements.[10]

Illustration 3–5 presents an example of a budgetary comparison schedule for the General Fund of the City and County of Denver. GASB standards require, at a minimum,

[9] GASB *Codification,* Sec. 2200.182. See Chapter 2 or the glossary for the definition of *major fund.*

[10] Ibid., footnote 35.

ILLUSTRATION 3–5

CITY AND COUNTY OF DENVER, COLORADO
Required Supplementary Information
General Fund and Human Services Special Revenue Fund
Budgetary Comparison Schedule (in thousands)
For the Year Ended December 31, 2013

	General Fund				Human Services Special Revenue Fund			
	Budget				Budget			
	Original	Final	Actual	Variance with Final Budget	Original	Final	Actual	Variance with Final Budget
Revenues								
Taxes	$ 625,584	$ 678,417	$ 687,340	$ 8,923	$ 52,662	$ 55,315	$ 55,990	$ 675
Licenses and permits	22,799	29,683	42,916	13,233	—	—	—	—
Intergovernmental revenues	26,901	27,614	27,669	55	85,044	85,864	79,195	(6,669)
Charges for services	165,203	172,865	167,864	(5,001)	584	584	376	(208)
Investment and interest income	3,382	4,055	1,890	(2,165)	—	—	—	—
Fines and forfeitures	61,778	58,856	54,818	(4,038)	—	—	—	—
Contributions	—	—	49	49	—	—	657	657
Other revenue	5,427	4,041	10,265	6,224	8,698	14,773	442	(14,331)
Total Revenues	**911,074**	**975,531**	**992,811**	**17,280**	**146,988**	**156,536**	**136,660**	**(19,876)**
Budget Basis Expenditures								
General government	218,044	220,924	184,252	36,672	—	—	—	—
Public safety	476,511	482,892	475,974	6,918	—	—	—	—
Public works	102,383	103,224	100,360	2,864	—	—	—	—
Human services	—	—	—	—	140,788	158,314	130,461	27,853
Health	44,163	44,687	44,636	51	—	—	—	—
Parks and recreation	53,115	56,046	55,519	527	—	—	—	—
Cultural activities	36,542	40,081	39,192	889	—	—	—	—
Community development	15,953	16,502	15,998	504	—	—	—	—
Total Budget Basis Expenditures	**946,711**	**964,356**	**915,931**	**48,425**	**140,788**	**158,314**	**130,461**	**27,853**
Excess (deficiency) of revenues over budget basis expenditures	(35,637)	11,175	76,880	65,705	6,200	(1,778)	6,199	7,977
Other Financing Sources (Uses)								
Sale of capital assets	—	—	—	—	—	—	743	743
Insurance recoveries	—	—	305	305	—	—	8	8
Capital leases	—	—	—	—	—	—	—	—
Transfers in	34,700	36,550	38,589	2,039	75	75	75	—
Transfers out	(50,915)	(63,103)	(55,287)	7,816	(75)	(75)	(75)	—
Total Other Financing Sources (Uses)	**(16,215)**	**(26,553)**	**(16,393)**	**10,160**	—	—	**751**	**751**
Excess (deficiency) of revenues and other financing sources over budget basis expenditures and other financing uses	**$ (51,852)**	**$ (15,378)**	$ 60,487	**$75,865**	**$ 6,200**	**$ (1,778)**	**6,950**	**$ 8,728**
Fund balances - January 1			226,848				33,441	
Fund Balance - December 31			**$287,335**				**$ 40,391**	

the presentation of both the originally adopted and final amended budgets and actual amounts of inflows, outflows, and balances. A variance column, such as that included in Denver's budgetary comparison schedule, is encouraged but not required since a financial statement user could calculate the variances himself or herself.

Individual fund budgetary comparisons are required to be presented at the legal level of budgetary control, which represents the administrative level (e.g., fund, program, organization unit) at which expenditures may not exceed appropriations without a formal budgetary amendment.[11] Meaningful budgetary comparisons also require that the actual amounts in the schedule be reported using the government's budgetary basis. Some governments, for example, budget their revenues on the cash basis. If the Actual column of the budgetary comparison schedule (or statement) uses a non-GAAP budgetary basis, such as the cash basis, either the schedule captions or column heading for actual amounts should so indicate.

Budgetary practices of a government may differ from GAAP accounting practices in ways other than basis. GASB standards identify timing, entity, and perspective differences. Discussion of these differences is beyond the scope of this text; it is sufficient to emphasize that GASB standards require that the amounts shown in the Actual column of the budgetary comparison schedule conform in all respects with practices used to develop the amounts shown in the budget columns of the schedule, so that there is a true comparison. Standards further require that either on the face of the budgetary comparison schedule or on a separate schedule, the amounts reported in the Actual column of the budgetary comparison schedule must be reconciled with the GAAP amounts shown in the statement of revenues, expenditures, and changes in fund balances. For the City and County of Denver, the General Fund revenues and expenditures in Illustration 3–5 are equal to the amounts reported in Illustration A2–5; the $11,608 difference between both revenue and expenditures for the Human Services Fund is identified in a separate schedule as grantor revenues and expenditures treated differently for budgetary purposes.

TERMINOLOGY AND CLASSIFICATION FOR BUDGETARY AND OPERATING STATEMENT ACCOUNTS

Government budgets may be described as legally approved plans of financial operations embodying the authorization of expenditures for specified purposes to be made during the budget period and the proposed means of financing them. The sequence of budget preparation in practice is often the same as the sequence in the preceding sentence: Departmental expenditure requests are developed first; then plans are made to finance or reduce the requested expenditures. For that reason, the discussion in this chapter follows the same sequence. Governmental budgeting is discussed in more detail in Chapter 12.

Classification of Appropriations and Expenditures

An appropriation is a legal authorization to expend cash or other financial resources for goods, services, and facilities to be used for specified purposes, in amounts not to exceed those authorized for each purpose. When liabilities authorized by an appropriation have been incurred, the appropriation is said to be *expended.* Thus, budgeted

[11]GASB *Codification,* Sec. 2400.121.

appropriations are sometimes called *estimated expenditures.* Expenditures, then, are expended appropriations. According to GASB standards, expenditures should be classified by (1) fund, (2) function or program, (3) organization unit, (4) activity, (5) character, and (6) object.[12] A common terminology and classification should be used consistently throughout the budget, the accounts, and the financial reports of each fund.

Classification by Fund

The primary classification of governmental expenditures is by fund since a fund is the basic fiscal and accounting entity of a government. Within each fund, the other five classifications itemized in the preceding paragraph are used to facilitate the aggregation and analysis of data to meet the objectives of financial reporting set forth in Chapter 1.

Classification by Function or Program

As explained earlier in the chapter, the GASB distinguishes between functions and programs. Examples of common functional classifications are the following:

General Government
Public Safety
Highways and Streets
Health and Welfare
Culture and Recreation

A good example of program classification is found in the budget of Cook County, Illinois, where county agencies are grouped into program areas which include:

Corrections
Courts
Health
Control of Environment
Economic Human Development
Assessment & Collection of Taxes
Election
Transportation

Classification by Organization Unit

Classification of expenditures by **organization unit** is considered essential to management control, assuming the organizational structure of a given government provides clear lines of responsibility and authority. Some examples of organization units that might be found in a city are:

Police Department
Fire Department
Building Safety Department
Public Works Department
City Attorney
City Clerk
Personnel Department
Culture and Recreation Department

The key distinction between classification of expenditures by organization unit and classification by program or function is that responsibility for a department is fixed, whereas a number of departments may be involved in the performance of a program or a function. Both management control within a department and rational allocation of resources within the government require much more specific identification of expenditures (and costs and expenses) than is provided by the major classifications illustrated thus far. The next step needed is classification by activity.

[12] GASB, *Codification,* Sec. 1800.116.

Classification by Activity

An **activity** is a specific and distinguishable line of work performed by an organization unit. For example, within the public works department, activities such as the following may be performed:

Solid waste collection—residential
Solid waste collection—commercial
Solid waste disposal—landfill
Solid waste disposal—incineration

Activity classification is more meaningful if responsibility for the performance of each activity is fixed, performance standards are established, and a good management accounting system is installed to measure input of resources consumed (dollars, personnel time, equipment, and facilities used) relative to units of service outputs. Such information is useful to those interested in assessing the efficiency of government operations.

Classification by Character

Classification by **character,** as defined by the GASB, is based on the fiscal period that benefits from a particular expenditure. A common classification of expenditures by character recognizes three groups:

Current expenditures
Capital outlays
Debt service

Current expenditures are expected to benefit the period in which the expenditure is made. Capital outlays are expected to benefit not only the period in which the capital assets are acquired but as many future periods as the assets provide service. Debt service includes payment of interest on debt and payment of debt principal; if the debt has been wisely incurred, residents have received benefits in prior periods from the assets acquired by use of debt financing, are receiving benefits currently, and will continue to receive benefits until the service lives of the assets expire.

Character classification of expenditures is potentially important to taxpayers and other citizens. Properly used, it could give them valuable information for assessing the cost of government during a given period. Generally speaking, expenditures for debt service relate to actions incurred by previous administrations. Capital outlays are expenditures expected to provide benefits in future periods; however, as discussed earlier in this chapter, GASB standards do not allow depreciation expense to be recorded in governmental funds, but require that depreciation expense on general capital assets be reported in the government-wide statement of activities (see the section titled "Depreciation of Capital Assets" in Appendix B of Chapter 2). It appears that expenditures in the *current* expenditures class are the most influential on the public mind, strongly influencing attitudes toward responsible officials.

A fourth character class, *intergovernmental,* is suggested by the GASB for use by governments that act as an intermediary in federally financed programs or that transfer "shared revenues" to other governments.

Classification by Object

The **object** of an expenditure is the article or service for which the expenditure was made. Object classes may be viewed as subdivisions of character classifications. One scheme of object classification includes the following major classes:

Personal services	Capital outlays
Supplies	Debt service
Other services and charges	

Many other object classifications are encountered in practice, generally more detailed than those listed above. Greater detail can, of course, be achieved by the utilization of subclasses under the major titles. Thus personal services may be subdivided on the basis of permanence and regularity of employment of the persons represented; and each subclass may be further subdivided to show whether the services performed were regular, overtime, or temporary. Employee benefits may be recorded in as much detail as desired as subclasses of the personal services class. "Other services and charges" must be subdivided if the class is to provide any useful budgeting and control information. Professional services, communication, transportation, advertising, printing and binding, insurance, public utility services, repairs and maintenance, rentals, aid to other governments, and miscellaneous are possible subdivisions.

Debt service, also listed as both an object of expenditure and a character class, should be subdivided to provide sufficient evidence that all interest payments and principal payments that should have been made in a certain fiscal period were actually made (or the appropriate liability recorded).

Classification of Estimated Revenues and Revenues

Revenue forecasts help administrators to determine that proposed expenditures presented in the operating budget can be financed by resources available under the laws of the budgeting jurisdiction and higher jurisdictions. *Revenue,* in the governmental budgeting sense, usually includes all financial resource inflows—all amounts that increase the fund balance of a fund. Examples include interfund transfers and debt issue proceeds, as well as taxes, licenses and permit fees, fines, forfeits, and other revenue sources described in the following sections of this chapter. In addition to those inflows, governments sometimes budget a portion of the beginning of year fund balance to finance proposed expenditures, particularly if the fund balance exceeds the government's established minimum fund balance policy. Well-managed governments typically maintain a minimum fund balance of 10 to 25 percent of a year's operating expenditures to provide a financial cushion should revenues fall short of forecasts or unexpected expenditures occur.

It should be emphasized that a government and the funds thereof may raise revenues only from sources available to them by law. Often, the law that authorizes a government to utilize a given revenue source to finance general governmental activities, or specific activities, also establishes the maximum rate that may be applied to a specified base in utilizing the source or establishes the maximum amount that may be raised from the source during the budget period.

The primary classification of governmental revenue is by *fund.* Within each fund, the major classification is by *source.* Within each major source class, it is desirable to have as many secondary classes as needed to facilitate revenue budgeting and accounting. Secondary classes relating to each major source are discussed below under each source caption. Major revenue source classes commonly used are these:

Taxes	Charges for Services
Special Assessments	Fines and Forfeits
Licenses and Permits	Miscellaneous Revenues
Intergovernmental Revenues	

The operating budget and the accounting system for each governmental fund should include all revenue sources available to finance activities of that fund. The General Fund of most governments will ordinarily need all seven major classes itemized above; in some governments, additional major classes may be needed. Each special revenue fund will need to budget and account for only those revenues legally mandated or restricted for use in achieving the purpose for which the special revenue fund was created. Similarly, debt service funds budget and account for those sources of revenue that are to be used for payment of interest and principal of tax-supported and special assessment long-term debt. Revenues and other financing sources earmarked for construction or acquisition of general capital assets are budgeted and accounted for by capital projects funds.

Taxes

Taxes are of particular importance because (1) they provide a large portion of the revenue for all levels of government and (2) they are compulsory contributions to finance the cost of government. Taxes, like all governmental fund revenues, are recognized on the modified accrual basis. Under this basis, revenues and other financing sources are recognized when they are measurable and available. *Available* means that the revenue or other financing source is expected to be collected during the current fiscal period or soon enough thereafter to pay current period obligations. In the case of property taxes, GASB requires collection within 60 days after the end of the current period.[13] For all other items, each government establishes its own definition of *available*. However, 60 days is commonly used for all revenues and other financing sources.

Ad valorem (based on value) **property taxes** are a mainstay of financing for many local governments but are not used as a source of revenue by many state governments or by the federal government. Ad valorem taxes may be levied against real property and personal property. Some property taxes are levied on a basis other than property values, one illustration being the tax on some kinds of financial institutions in relation to the deposits at a specified date. Other kinds of taxes are sales taxes, income taxes, gross receipts taxes, death and gift taxes, and interest and penalties on delinquent taxes.

The valuation of each parcel of taxable real property, and of the taxable personal property owned by each taxpayer, is assigned by a process known as **property assessment.** The assessment process differs state by state, and in some states by jurisdictions within the state. The tax rate is set by one of two widely different procedures: (1) The government simply multiplies the assessed valuation of property in its jurisdiction by a flat rate—either the maximum rate allowable under state law or a rate determined by the governing body—or (2) the property tax is treated as a residual source of revenue. In the latter event, revenues to be recognized from all sources other than property taxes must be budgeted; the total of those sources must be compared with the total proposed appropriations in order to determine the amount to be raised from property taxes, subject, of course, to limits imposed by law or legislative policy, economic conditions, and political feasibility. Illustration 3–6

[13] GASB *Codification*, Sec. P70.104.

ILLUSTRATION 3–6

TOWN OF MERRILL
General Fund
Estimate of Amount to Be Raised by Property Taxes
For Fiscal Year Ending December 31, 2017
As of Current Date—July 31, 2016

Estimated resource requirements:		
Estimated expenditures, remainder of FY 2016		$ 4,200,000
Appropriations proposed for FY 2017		8,460,000
Estimated fund balance needed at beginning of FY 2018		510,000
Total estimated resource requirements		13,170,000
Estimated resources available and to be raised, other than from property taxes:		
Actual current fund balance (July 31, 2016)	$ 654,000	
From second installment of FY 2016 taxes	2,430,000	
From miscellaneous resources, remainder of FY 2016	1,960,000	
From all nonproperty tax sources in FY 2017	4,544,000	
Total estimated resources other than FY 2017 property taxes		9,588,000
Amount required from FY 2017 property taxes		$ 3,582,000

shows an estimate of the total amount of revenues to be raised from property taxes under the assumption that property taxes are a residual source of revenues. The heading of Illustration 3–6 indicates that it is for the Town of Merrill's General Fund. A similar computation could be made for each fund for which property taxes are levied.

Illustration 3–6 shows that the amount of revenue to be raised from property taxes must, in this case, be estimated six months before the beginning of the next fiscal year. This is one step in determining the tax levy for the year. A second step is the determination from historical data and economic forecasts of the percentage of the tax levy expected to be collectible. (Even though property taxes are a lien against the property, personal property may be removed from the taxing jurisdiction and some parcels of real property may not be salable or valuable enough for the taxing jurisdiction to recover accumulated taxes against the property.) Therefore, the levy must be large enough to allow for estimated uncollectible taxes. For example, assume the Town of Merrill can reasonably expect to collect only 96 percent of the year 2017 property tax levy for its General Fund. Thus, if tax revenue is to be $3,582,000 (per Illustration 3–6), the gross levy must be $3,582,000 ÷ 0.96, or $3,731,250.

When the gross levy is known, the tax rate may be computed on the basis of the assessed valuation of taxable property lying within the taxing jurisdiction. The term **taxable property** is used in the preceding sentence in recognition of the fact that property owned by governments and property used by religious and charitable organizations are often not taxable by the local government. In addition, senior citizens, war veterans, and others may have statutory exemption from taxation for a portion of the assessed valuation of property. Continuing the example, assume the net assessed valuation of property taxable by the General Fund of the Town of Merrill is $214,348,000. In that case, the gross property tax levy ($3,731,250) is divided by the net assessed valuation ($214,348,000) to determine the property tax rate. Depending on the tax law in a particular state, the rate would be expressed as "$1.75 per $100 assessed valuation" or "$17.41 per $1,000 assessed valuation"—rounding up the actual decimal fraction (0.017407) to two places to the right of the decimal, as is customary. The latter rate is typically referred to as 17.41 mills.

Interest and Penalties on Delinquent Taxes

A **penalty** is a legally mandated addition to a tax on the day it becomes delinquent (generally, the day after the day the tax is due). Penalties should be recognized as revenue when they are assessed. *Interest* at a legally specified rate also may apply to delinquent taxes for the length of time between the day the tax becomes delinquent until the day it is ultimately paid or otherwise discharged; interest revenue should be accrued at the time financial statements are to be prepared.

Sales Taxes, Income Taxes, and Gross Receipts Taxes

GASB standards provide that revenue from sales taxes, income taxes, and gross receipts taxes be recognized, net of estimated refunds, in the accounting period in which underlying transactions (e.g., sales and earnings) occur.

Special Assessments

Special assessments differ from ad valorem real property taxes in that the latter are levied against all taxable property within the geographic boundaries of the government levying the taxes, whereas the former are levied against certain properties. The purpose of a special assessment is to defray part or all of the cost of a specific improvement or service that is presumed to be of particular benefit to the properties against which the special assessments are levied. Briefly, when routine services (street cleaning, snow plowing, and so on) are extended to property owners outside the normal service area of the government or are provided at a higher level or at more frequent intervals than for the general public, "service-type" special assessments are levied. Service-type special assessments are accounted for by the fund that accounts for similar services rendered to the general public—usually the General Fund or a special revenue fund. Special assessments for capital improvements should be accounted for by a capital projects fund during the construction phase and by a debt service or agency fund during the debt service phase if debt financing is used. (See Chapter 6 for additional details about capital improvement special assessments.)

Licenses and Permits

Licenses and permits include those revenues collected by a government from individuals or business concerns for various rights or privileges granted by the government. Some licenses and permits are primarily regulatory in nature, with minor consideration to revenue derived, whereas others are not only regulatory but also provide large amounts of revenue, and some are almost exclusively revenue producers. Licenses and permits may relate to the privilege of carrying on business for a stipulated period, the right to perform a particular activity that may affect the public welfare, or the right to use certain public property. They are found extensively at the state level and serve both regulatory and revenue functions. Commonly found among licenses and permits are building permits, vehicle licenses, amusement licenses, business and occupational licenses, animal licenses, and street and curb permits. Regardless of the governmental level or the purpose of a license or permit, the revenue it produces is ordinarily recorded when cash is received.

Intergovernmental Revenue

Intergovernmental revenues include grants and other financial assistance. These may be government-mandated nonexchange transactions (for example, certain state sales taxes required by law to be shared with local governments) or voluntary nonexchange transactions (for example, federal or state grants for which local governments compete). In either case, the recipient government does not provide significant value to the grantor government for value received. GASB defines *grants and other financial assistance* as

> transactions in which one governmental entity transfers cash or other items of value to [or incurs a liability for] another governmental entity, an individual, or an organization as a means of sharing program costs, subsidizing other governments or entities, or otherwise reallocating resources to the recipients.[14]

Governmental funds should recognize grants and other financial assistance as revenues in the period in which all time restrictions and eligibility requirements (such as a matching requirement) imposed by the grantor government have been met and the resources are available to pay current period obligations. Revenue recognition rules and the complexities of accounting for intergovernmental revenues are discussed in Chapter 4.

Charges for Services

As discussed earlier in this chapter, charges for services of the governmental funds (and governmental activities at the government-wide level) include all charges for goods and services provided by a governmental fund to enterprise funds, individuals and organizations, and other governments. A few of the many revenue items included in this category are court costs; special police service; street, sidewalk, and curb repairs; receipts from parking meters; library use fees (but not fines); and tuition.

Classification of expenditures by function is discussed earlier in this chapter. The grouping of Charges for Services revenue may be correlated with the functional classification of expenditures. For example, one functional group of expenditures is named General Government, another Public Safety, and so on. In providing general government service, a government may collect revenues such as court cost charges, fees for recording legal documents, and zoning and subdivision fees. Charges for services should be recognized as revenue when measurable and available if that is prior to the collection of cash.

Fines and Forfeits

Revenue from fines and forfeits includes fines and penalties for commission of statutory offenses and for neglect of official duty; forfeitures of amounts held as security against loss or damage, or collections from bonds or sureties placed with the government for the same purpose; and penalties of any sort, except those levied on delinquent taxes. Library fines are included in this category. If desired, Fines and Forfeits may be the titles of two accounts within this revenue class, or they may be subgroup headings for more detailed breakdowns.

Revenues of this classification should be accrued to the extent practicable. Unlike property taxes, however, fines and forfeits may not be estimated with any reasonable degree of accuracy. Because of these uncertainties, revenues from fines and forfeits may be recognized when received in cash if accrual is not practicable.

Miscellaneous Revenues

Although the word *miscellaneous* is not informative and should be used sparingly, its use as the title of a revenue category is necessary. It (1) substitutes for other possible source classes that might have rather slight and infrequent usage and (2) minimizes the need for forcing some kinds of revenue into source classifications in which they do not generically belong. While the miscellaneous revenues title represents a compromise, its existence aids in sharpening the meanings of other source classes. The heterogeneous nature of

[14] GASB *Codification,* Sec. N50.504.

items served by the title is indicated by the diversity of items found in this category: interest earnings (other than on delinquent taxes), rents and royalties, contributions from public enterprises (utilities, airports, etc.), **escheats** (taking of property in default of legally qualified claimants), and contributions and donations from private sources.

Some items of miscellaneous revenues, such as interest earnings on investments, might well be accrued, but mostly they are recorded when received in cash. Also, interest earnings that are significant in amount may be reported as a separate classification.

BUDGETARY ACCOUNTING

The use of budgetary accounts enhances budgetary control by permitting comparison of actual revenues and expenditures to budgeted amounts. Budgetary control is further enhanced by clear and logical classification of revenues and expenditures and by formally recording the budget in the accounts of the General Fund and other funds for which a budget is approved. The use of subsidiary ledgers, which permit recording revenues and expenditures—both actual and budgeted amounts—in the same level of detail as the budget, also helps to achieve sound budgetary control.

Three primary budgetary control accounts are needed to achieve budgetary control in the General Fund (and other funds for which a budget is adopted): **Estimated Revenues, Appropriations,** and **Encumbrances.** Subsidiary ledger accounts should be provided in whatever detail is required by law or for sound financial administration to support each of the three control accounts.[15] Budgeted interfund transfers and debt proceeds may be recorded in two additional budgetary control accounts: **Estimated Other Financing Sources** and **Estimated Other Financing Uses.** Again, these control accounts should be supported by subsidiary detail accounts as needed. The sum of detail account balances at any point in time should agree with the corresponding balance in the control account. For example, the sum of revenue detail account balances should always agree with the balance of the Revenues control account.

Recording the Budget

To illustrate the journal entries necessary to record a budget, assume the following amounts have been legally approved as the budget for the General Fund of a certain government for the fiscal year ending December 31, 2017. As of January 1, 2017, the first day of the fiscal year, the total Estimated Revenues should be recorded in the General Fund general ledger control account, and the amounts expected to be recognized during 2017 from each revenue source specified in the budget should be recorded in subsidiary ledger accounts. An appropriate entry would be:

		General Ledger		Subsidiary Ledger	
		Debits	*Credits*	*Debits*	*Credits*
1.	Estimated Revenues	1,277,500			
	Budgetary Fund Balance		1,277,500		
	Estimated Revenues Ledger:				
	Taxes			882,500	
	Intergovernmental Revenues			200,000	
	Licenses and Permits			195,000	

[15] As discussed in Appendix A at the end of this chapter, other structures are found in practice in contemporary accounting information systems, including separate ledger files for general ledger and budgetary accounts, and for encumbrance accounting.

The total Appropriations and Other Financing Uses legally budgeted for 2017 for the General Fund of the same government should also be recorded in the General Fund control accounts, and the amounts appropriated for each function itemized in the budget should be recorded in subsidiary ledger accounts. The journal entry using assumed budget amounts would be:

2.	Budgetary Fund Balance	1,636,500		
	Appropriations		1,362,000	
	Estimated Other Financing Uses		274,500	
	Appropriations Ledger:			
	General Government			1,150,000
	Public Safety			212,000
	Estimated Other Financing Uses Ledger:			
	Interfund Transfers Out to Other Funds			274,500

It is, of course, acceptable to combine the two entries illustrated above and make one General Fund entry to record Estimated Revenues, Appropriations, and Estimated Other Financing Uses; in this case there would be a debit to Budgetary Fund Balance for $359,000 (the amount by which Appropriations and Estimated Other Financing Uses exceed Estimated Revenues). Even if a single combined entry is made in the General Fund general ledger accounts, that entry must provide for entry of the budgeted amounts in each individual subsidiary ledger account as shown in the illustrations of the two separate entries.

Budgetary Control of Revenues

To establish accountability for revenues and permit budgetary control, actual revenues should be recognized in the general ledger accounts of governmental funds by credits to the Revenues account (offset by debits to receivable accounts for revenues that are accrued or by debits to Cash for revenues recognized when received in cash). The general ledger Revenues account is a control account supported by Revenues subsidiary ledger accounts kept in exactly the same detail as the Estimated Revenues subsidiary ledger accounts. For example, assume the General Fund of the government for which budgetary entries are illustrated in the preceding section collected revenues in cash during the month of January from Licenses and Permits, $13,200, and Intergovernmental Revenues, $61,900. In an actual case, entries should be made on a current basis and cash receipts should be deposited each working day; however, for the purpose of this chapter, the following entry illustrates the effect on the General Fund accounts of collections during the month of January 2017:

		General Ledger		Subsidiary Ledger	
		Debits	***Credits***	***Debits***	***Credits***
3.	Cash	75,100			
	Revenues		75,100		
	Revenues Ledger:				
	Licenses and Permits				13,200
	Intergovernmental Revenues				61,900

ILLUSTRATION 3–7

NAME OF GOVERNMENTAL UNIT
Revenues Ledger
General Fund

Class: Licenses and Permits — Number: 351.1

Date	Item	Reference	Estimated Revenues DR.	Revenues CR.	Balance DR. (CR.)
2017					
January 1	Budget estimate	J1	$195,000		$195,000
31	Collections	CR6		$13,200	181,800

Comparability between Estimated Revenues subsidiary accounts and Revenues subsidiary accounts is necessary, so that periodically throughout the fiscal year actual revenues from each source can be compared with estimated revenues for that source. Material differences between estimated and actual revenues should be investigated by administrators to determine whether (1) estimates were made on the basis of assumptions that may have appeared realistic when the budget was prepared but are no longer realistic (in that event, the budget needs to be revised, so that administrators and legislators have better knowledge of revenues to be realized during the remainder of the fiscal year) or (2) action needs to be taken, so that revenues estimated with reasonable accuracy are actually realized (i.e., one or more employees may have failed to understand that certain revenue items are to be collected). Illustration 3–7 shows a form of Revenues subsidiary ledger detail account for Licenses and Permits in which the Debit column is subsidiary to the Estimated Revenues general ledger control account and the Credit column is subsidiary to the Revenues general ledger control account.

A schedule of Actual and Estimated Revenues is illustrated in Chapter 4. Normally, during a fiscal year, the amount of revenue budgeted from each source will exceed the amount of revenue from that source realized to date; consequently, the Balance column will have a debit balance and may be headed Estimated Revenues Not Yet Realized, or simply Unrealized Revenues.

Budgetary Control of Encumbrances and Expenditures

When enacted into law, an appropriation is an authorization for administrators to expend financial resources on behalf of the government not to exceed the amounts specified in the appropriation ordinance or statute, for the purposes set forth in that ordinance or statute, during the period of time specified. An appropriation is considered *expended* when the authorized liabilities have been incurred. Penalties are imposed by law on an administrator who expends more than appropriated or who makes expenditures for any purpose not covered by an appropriation or after the authority to do so has expired. Prudence, therefore, dictates that each purchase order and each contract be reviewed before it is signed to determine that a valid and sufficient appropriation exists to which the expenditure can be charged when goods or services are received. If the review indicates that a valid appropriation exists and there is a sufficient balance to cover the amount of the purchase order or contract being reviewed, the purchase order or contract legally may be issued. If the appropriation balance is insufficient to cover the amount of the purchase order, local ordinances often permit either the department head or finance director to transfer limited appropriation amounts between line items within the same department.

When a purchase order or contract has been issued, it is important to record the fact that the appropriation has been *encumbered* in the amount of the purchase order or contract. The word *encumbered* is used, rather than the word *expended* because the amount is only an estimate of the liability that will be incurred when the purchase order is filled or the contract executed. It is reasonably common for quantities of goods received to differ from quantities ordered, and it is not uncommon for invoice prices to differ from unit prices shown on purchase orders. The use of appropriation authority may be somewhat tentative inasmuch as some suppliers are unable to fill orders or to perform as stipulated in a contract; in such cases, related purchase orders or contracts must be canceled.

Note that the issuance of purchase orders and/or contracts has two effects: (1) The encumbrance of the appropriation(s) that gave the government the authority to order goods or services and (2) the starting of a chain of events that will result in the government expending resources when the purchase orders are filled and the contracts executed. Both effects should be recorded in order to help administrators avoid over-expending appropriations and plan for payment of liabilities on a timely basis. The accounting procedure used to record the two effects is illustrated by Entry 4. The first effect is recorded by the debit to the budgetary account *Encumbrances.* Encumbrances is a control account that is related to the *Appropriations* control account discussed previously and to the *Expenditures* control account discussed in relation to Entries 5a and 5b. In order to accomplish the matching of Appropriations, Expenditures, and Encumbrances necessary for budgetary control, subsidiary account classifications of all three must correspond exactly (see Illustration 3–8).

The account credited in Entry 4, *Encumbrances Outstanding,* is a budgetary account that allows a double bookkeeping entry for originating encumbrances when purchase orders are placed and for reversing encumbrances when goods or services are received or purchase orders are canceled. It is not a control account in the sense that its detail appears in subsidiary ledger accounts.

Entries 4, 5a, and 5b illustrate accounting for encumbrances and expenditures for the General Fund of the government for which entries are illustrated in previous sections of this chapter. Entry 4 is made on the assumption that early in January purchase orders are issued pursuant to the authority contained in the General

ILLUSTRATION 3–8

NAME OF GOVERNMENTAL UNIT
Appropriations, Expenditures, and Encumbrances Ledger

Code No.: 0607-03
Fund: General
Year: 2017 Function: General Government

		Encumbrances			Expenditures		Appropriations	
Date	**Reference**	**Debits**	**Credits**	**Balance**	**Debits**	**Cumulative Balance**	**Credits**	**Available Balance**
Jan. 2	Budget (Entry 2)						$1,150,000	$1,150,000
3	Purchase orders issued (Entry 4)	$38,000		$38,000				1,112,000
17	Invoices approved for payment (Entries 5a, 5b)		$35,000	3,000	$35,100	$35,100		1,111,900

Fund appropriations; assumed amounts chargeable to each function for which purchase orders are issued on this date are shown in the debits to the Encumbrances subsidiary accounts.

		General Ledger		Subsidiary Ledger	
		Debits	***Credits***	***Debits***	***Credits***
4.	Encumbrances—2017	45,400			
	Encumbrances Outstanding—2017		45,400		
	Encumbrances Ledger:				
	General Government			38,000	
	Public Safety			7,400	

When goods or services for which encumbrances have been recorded are received and the suppliers' invoices are approved for payment, the accounts should record the fact that appropriations have been *expended,* not merely encumbered, and that an actual liability, not merely an expected liability, exists. Entry 5a reverses Entry 4 to the extent that purchase orders are filled (ordinarily some of the purchase orders recorded in one encumbrance entry will be filled in one time period, and some in other time periods). It is important to note that since estimated amounts were used when encumbrances were recorded, the reversing entry must also use the estimated amounts. Thus, the balance remaining in the Encumbrances control account and in the Encumbrances Outstanding account is the *total* estimated dollar amount of purchase orders and contracts outstanding. The estimated dollar amount of purchase orders outstanding against each appropriation is disclosed by the subsidiary accounts, as shown in Illustration 3–8.

		General Ledger		Subsidiary Ledger	
		Debits	***Credits***	***Debits***	***Credits***
5a.	Encumbrances Outstanding—2017.	42,000			
	Encumbrances—2017		42,000		
	Encumbrances Ledger:				
	General Government				35,000
	Public Safety				7,000
5b.	Expenditures—2017	42,400			
	Vouchers Payable		42,400		
	Expenditures Ledger:				
	General Government			35,100	
	Public Safety			7,300	

Expenditures and the liability account must both be recorded at the actual amount the government agrees to pay the vendors who have filled the purchase orders (see Entry 5b). The fact that estimated and actual amounts differ causes no accounting difficulties as long as goods or services are received in the same fiscal period as ordered. The accounting treatment required when encumbrances outstanding at year-end are filled, or canceled, in a following year is illustrated in Chapter 4.

The encumbrance procedure is not necessary for every type of expenditure transaction. For example, although expenditures for salaries and wages of governmental employees must be chargeable against valid and sufficient appropriations, many governments do not find it necessary to encumber the departmental personnel services appropriations for estimated payrolls of recurring, relatively constant amounts. Departments having payrolls that fluctuate greatly from one season to another may follow the encumbrance procedure to make sure the personnel service appropriation is not overexpended.

From the foregoing discussion and illustrative journal entries, it should be apparent that administrators of governments need accounting systems designed to provide at any given date during a fiscal year comparisons for each item in the legal appropriations budget of (1) the amount appropriated, (2) the amount of outstanding encumbrances, and (3) the cumulative amount of expenditures to this date. The net of the three items is accurately described as *Unencumbered Unexpended Appropriations* but can be labeled more simply as *Available Appropriations* or *Available Balance.*

Classification of appropriations, expenditures, and encumbrances was discussed in a preceding section of this chapter. In order to provide needed comparisons, classifications of expenditures and encumbrances must agree with the classifications of appropriations mandated by law. In many jurisdictions, good financial management may dictate all three elements be classified in greater detail than required by law. In most cases, budgetary control over expenditures follows the logical flow depicted below:

APPROPRIATION → ENCUMBRANCE → EXPENDITURE → DISBURSEMENT

At intervals during the fiscal year, a Schedule of Budgeted and Actual Expenditures and Encumbrances should be prepared to inform administrators and members of the legislative branch of the data contained in the subsidiary ledger records. An example of such a schedule is illustrated in Chapter 4 (see Illustration B4–2). Also in Chapter 4, the entries needed at year-end to close budgetary and operating statement accounts are illustrated (Entries 25a and 25b, Chapter 4).

Accounting for Allotments

In some jurisdictions, it is necessary to regulate the use of appropriations, so only specified amounts may be used from month to month or from quarter to quarter. The purpose of such control is to prevent expenditure of all or most of the authorized amount early in the year without providing for unexpected requirements arising later in the year. A common device for regulating expenditures is the use of allotments. An **allotment** may be described as an internal allocation of funds on a periodic basis usually agreed upon by the department heads and the chief executive.

Allotments may be formally recorded in ledger accounts. This procedure might begin with the budgetary entry, in which Unallotted Appropriations would replace Appropriations. If this is desired, a combined entry to record the budget would be (using the numbers given in Entries 1 and 2, omitting entries in subsidiary accounts—which would be as illustrated previously with one exception—the subsidiary ledger credit accounts in Entry 2 would be designated as Unallotted Appropriations instead of Appropriations):

	General Ledger		Subsidiary Ledger	
	Debits	*Credits*	*Debits*	*Credits*
Estimated Revenues	1,277,500			
Budgetary Fund Balance	359,000			
Unallotted Appropriations		1,362,000		
Estimated Other Financing Uses		274,500		

If it is assumed that $342,000 is the amount formally allotted for the first period, the following entry could be made (amounts allotted for each function are shown in the subsidiary ledger entries):

Unallotted Appropriations..............	342,000		
Allotments		342,000	
Allotments Ledger:			
General Government..................			289,000
Public Safety			53,000

Expenditures should be recorded periodically as invoices are received by using departments or divisions in the manner previously described.

CONCLUDING REMARKS

The illustrative journal entries shown in this chapter to record the budget have no impact on the government-wide statement of activities. Operating transactions shown, however, may be treated differently at the government-wide level than in the General Fund or other governmental funds. Because the illustrative transactions presented in this chapter were intended to illustrate budgetary control over revenues and expenditures, the possible effects of those transactions at the government-wide level were ignored. In Chapter 4, the dual effects of accounting transactions are analyzed and appropriate journal entries are made in both the general journal for the General Fund and the general journal used to record government activities at the government-wide level.

Appendix A

Accounting Information Systems

In a governmental accounting system, an account number structure provides for appropriate classification of revenues and expenditures, as well as for the desired classification of assets, liabilities, and fund balances. Many alternative governmental accounting software systems are available. The general ledger module of most systems can easily accommodate all of the revenue and expenditure detail accounts needed for effective budgetary control.

Instead of using general ledger control accounts and related subsidiary ledgers, governmental accounting systems often use separate files or ledgers for proprietary and budgetary reporting. For example, the general ledger module of one leading fund accounting software system includes both a general ledger and a budget ledger. Actual revenues and expenditures are posted to the general ledger, and budget amounts are posted to the budget ledger. Of course, the same account numbers and titles used in the budget ledger are used in the general ledger to permit budgetary comparison reporting. In addition, the system provides a separate encumbrance ledger to record encumbered amounts and monitor budgetary compliance. Selecting the type of transaction from a menu on the screen determines in which ledger (or ledgers) a particular transaction is posted. All such systems must provide transaction detail reports and other documentation of entries and postings in order to provide an adequate "audit trail."

In an accounting information system, the account number structure is an important design feature—one that affects the ease of financial operation and preparation of financial statements. Most account number structures provide for the multiple expenditure classifications prescribed by the GASB or similar classifications. Consider, for example, the following five-segment account number structure used by one Midwest city:

XXX	–	XXXX	–	XXX	–	XX	–	XX
(1)		(2)		(3)		(4)		(5)

The five segments of numbers represent the following classifications:

Segment	Represents
1	Fund (e.g., 110 = General Fund; 224 = Library Operating Fund; 550 = Water Fund; etc.)
2	First two positions of the segment represent department; other two positions represent divisions within a department (e.g., 2120 = Police Operations; 2125 = Police Major Crimes; 2127 = Narcotics; etc.)
3	First two positions of segment represent activity; third position represents subactivity (Note: This city uses segment 3 to indicate type of account rather than activity and subactivity. For example, 100–199 = Assets; 200–299 = Liabilities; 300–399 = Equity; 400–499 = Revenues; and 500–699 = Operating Expenses; etc.)
4	Element (broad object of expenditure category) (e.g., 01 = Personnel Services; 12 = Supplies and Materials; 75 = Debt Service, Interest; etc.)
5	Detailed object of expenditure (e.g., some detailed objects associated with Personnel Services are 01 = Salaries and Wages, Permanent Positions; 05 = Salaries and Wages, Temporary Positions; and 41 = Salaries and Wages, Overtime; etc.)

Even though the classification scheme just described does not agree precisely with the expenditure classifications required by the GASB, it conforms in all essential respects with the GASB classifications. Segment (1) accomplishes classification by fund. Segment (2) permits classification by department and division, where divisions, in most cases, represent particular activities, for example, operations, major crimes, narcotics, and other activities of the police department. Because the *Division* classification in segment (2) meets the GASB activity classification requirement, the city uses segment (3) to indicate what kind of account (asset, liability, and so forth) is being used for a particular transaction. Segments (4) and (5) permit adequate object of expenditure detail. Although the account structure provides no specific classification for functions or programs, it is relatively easy to aggregate appropriate departmental accounts to provide totals by function or program for financial reporting or management purposes. Similarly, the lack of a specific character classification is of little concern since object of expenditure accounts are provided for debt service, capital outlays, and intergovernmental activity.

To illustrate the use of this account number structure to code an actual transaction, consider how the purchase of diesel fuel by the Public Works Department, Street Cleaning activity would be coded for entry into the computer:

110	–	6023	–	534	–	12	–	40
General Fund		Public Works—Street Cleaning		Operating Expenses		Supplies and Materials		Other Supplies—Fuel, Oil, and Lubricants

If, as is likely, the diesel fuel is purchased from an internal service fund of the city, a liability account, Due to Other Funds, would also be credited. In this case, the transaction must also be recorded as a sale (Billings to Departments) and a receivable (Due from General Fund) in the internal service fund. If the fuel is purchased from an external source, either Accounts Payable or Vouchers Payable would be credited.

In actual practice, the interface programs used for most accounting systems make it relatively simple to move around within the account number structure. Though systems differ markedly, department or finance personnel or accounting clerks usually enter the appropriate numbers for funds, department, activity, type of account, expenditure object, and dollar amount or choose these items from drop-down help menus. Function keys are often programmed to produce help menus for account number segments, particularly for expenditure objects.

For transactions that can be entered by department personnel, such as purchase requisitions, internal control considerations usually restrict entry and data access to only certain funds and types of accounts. For these transactions, the fund and department/division information often defaults to that applicable to a particular department or division. In addition to the information embedded in the account number, purchasing and accounts payable programs also must provide lists of vendor numbers and names, usually in drop-down menu form. Some systems automatically complete the vendor identification information as soon as a few distinguishing keystrokes are entered. Vendor detail records usually permit instant display of vendor account status, including outstanding purchase orders, invoices received, due dates, invoices paid, and payments pending.

Generally, any account number segments not needed for a transaction have zeros inserted or, in some systems, may be masked. For example, for the city whose account number structure was illustrated earlier, recording revenues or paying vouchers payable requires no data to be entered for segments (4) and (5), so zeros are automatically inserted for those segments. Data classified according to an entity's account number structure can easily be aggregated within any segment, or group of segments, to provide a wide variety of custom financial reports, in addition to predefined reports and financial statements.

This discussion has focused on the systems that have evolved to meet the *fund* accounting needs of government. Many, if not most, governments use their fund accounting computer systems, supplemented by spreadsheet and report writer interfaces that permit the reclassifications of fund-based information needed to prepare government-wide financial statements. The disadvantage of this approach is that government-wide statements are often not available for the use of citizens and other users until the end of the reporting period when the reconciling worksheets are prepared.

Appendix B

Accounting for Public School Systems

There are about 13,000 independent public school systems in the United States. Although they are classified as special purpose governments, these school systems follow the same generally accepted accounting principles as state and local governments—the accounting and reporting standards issued by GASB.[16] The approximately 1,500 "dependent" school

[16] Dean Michael Mead, *What You Should Know about Your School District's Finances: A Guide to Financial Statements* (Norwalk, CT: GASB, 2012).

systems are accounted for as part of their parent general purpose government, either a state, county, municipality, or township. Public school systems, both independent and dependent, often follow specialized accounting and reporting procedures prescribed by a state oversight department or agency. Further, all state oversight departments or agencies collect revenues and expenditures data for all pre-kindergarten through grade 12 public schools in their state and provide these data to the National Center for Educational Statistics (NCES) so the NCES can prepare the annual "National Public Education Financial Survey."[17] For the sake of uniformity, most school systems follow the system of classification for revenues and expenditures recommended by the NCES. This system of classification is discussed next. In addition, independent public school systems must prepare the MD&A and basic financial statements required by GASB standards.

CLASSIFICATION OF EXPENDITURES OF PUBLIC SCHOOL SYSTEMS

The NCES system of expenditure classifications expands on the GASB classifications discussed in this chapter, reflecting the standardized national data collection and reporting requirements imposed by the NCES on all states. Specifically, the NCES account code structure provides for nine expenditure classification categories: fund, program, function, object, project, level of instruction, operational unit, subject matter, and job class.[18] Generally, school systems need to report data for the classifications required by the education oversight body in their state, which may vary from state to state.

The *program* classification is critically important for effective management of public education at the local, state, and federal levels. The NCES identifies nine broad classes of programs, including regular elementary/secondary education programs, special programs, vocational and technical programs, other instructional programs—elementary/secondary, nonpublic school programs, adult/continuing education programs, community/junior college education programs, community service programs, and co-curricular and extracurricular activities. Numerous detailed program classifications are possible within each broad category. For example, *special programs* may include service programs related to mental or physical impairment, emotional disturbance, and developmental delay, among many other services. Similarly, *vocational and technical programs* include programs intended to prepare students for careers in 16 broad-based career areas, such as agriculture and natural resources, architecture and construction, information technology, and law and public safety.

The NCES *function* classification relates to the activity for which goods or services are acquired. Functions are classified into the five broad areas of instruction, support services, operation of noninstructional services, facilities acquisition and construction, and debt service. In addition, the NCES provides account codes for 61 subfunctions, of which 14 are required for reporting to NCES. The required subfunctions are instruction; support services—students; support services—instruction; support services—general administration; support services—school administration; central services; operation and maintenance of plant; student transportation; other support services; food service operations; enterprise operations; community services operations; facilities acquisition and construction; and debt service.

[17] An extensive list of NCES reports and resources is available on the Internet at *http://www.NCES.ed.gov.*

[18] The following discussion of expenditure and revenue classifications is based on the account classification codes provided in National Center for Education Statistics, *Financial Accounting for Local and State School Systems: 2009 Edition* (Washington, DC: U.S. Department of Education, Core Finance Data Task Force, The National Forum on Education Statistics, 2009).

Consistent with GASB standards, the NCES *object* classification describes the service or goods acquired by a particular expenditure. The NCES provides for nine major object categories: personal services—salaries; personal services—employee benefits; purchased professional and technical services; purchased property services; other purchased services; supplies; property; debt service and miscellaneous; and other items. As with programs and functions, numerous detailed object accounts are provided for each major object category, although only certain of those are identified for mandatory use and reporting to the NCES.

The *project* classification provides coding for projects that are funded from local, state, or federal sources, plus an additional code for projects that do not require specialized reporting to a local, state, or federal funding source. To meet reporting requirements imposed by some states on public school systems, the NCES provides a *level of instruction* classification, consisting of such categories as elementary, middle, secondary, postsecondary, and programs for adult/continuing education. Finally, there are three optional-use expenditure classifications for *operational unit, subject matter,* and *job-class.* The operational unit classification provides the option of reporting by separate attendance centers, budgetary units, or cost centers. Subject matter could include such categories as agriculture, art, business, and science. Job-class relates to classifications used for personnel, such as administrative, professional, clerical, and technical.

CLASSIFICATION OF REVENUES OF PUBLIC SCHOOL SYSTEMS

Revenues of public school systems, both those dependent upon a general purpose government and independent school systems, should be classified in the manner prescribed by the NCES, as refined by the appropriate state oversight body. Generally, public school revenues should be classified by fund, source, and project/reporting code. The NCES publication cited in footnote 20 provides the following revenue classifications:

- 1000 Revenue from local sources
  - 1100 Taxes levied/assessed by the school system
  - 1200 Revenue from local governmental units other than school districts
  - 1300 Tuition
  - 1400 Transportation fees
  - 1500 Investment income
  - 1600 Food services
  - 1700 District activities
  - 1800 Community services activities
  - 1900 Other revenue from local sources
- 2000 Revenue from intermediate sources
  - 2100 Unrestricted grants-in-aid
  - 2200 Restricted grants-in-aid
  - 2800 Revenue in lieu of taxes
  - 2900 Revenue for/on behalf of the school district
- 3000 Revenue from state sources
  - 3100 Unrestricted grants-in-aid
  - 3200 Restricted grants-in-aid
  - 3800 Revenue in lieu of taxes
  - 3900 Revenue for/on behalf of the school district
- 4000 Revenue from federal sources
  - 4100 Unrestricted grants-in-aid direct from the federal government

- 4200 Unrestricted grants-in-aid from the federal government through the state
- 4300 Restricted grants-in-aid direct from the federal government
- 4500 Restricted grants-in-aid from the federal government through the state
- 4700 Grants-in-aid from the federal government through intermediate governments
- 4800 Revenue in lieu of taxes
- 4900 Revenue for/on behalf of the school district

5000 Other financing sources

- 5100 Issuance of bonds
- 5200 Fund transfers in
- 5300 Proceeds from the disposal of real or personal property
- 5400 Loan proceeds
- 5500 Capital lease proceeds
- 5600 Other long-term debt proceeds

6000 Other items

- 6100 Capital contributions
- 6200 Amortization of premium on issuance of bonds
- 6300 Special items
- 6400 Extraordinary items

Additional detail provided in the NCES revenue classification structure has been omitted from the foregoing list. For example, under classification 1100, taxes levied/assessed by the school system, are additional detail classifications for ad valorem taxes, sales and use taxes, and income taxes, among others.

"Intermediate" sources of revenue are administrative units or political subdivisions between the local school system and the state. "Grants-in-aid" from intermediate, state, or federal governments are contributions from general revenue sources of those governments, or, if related to specific revenue sources of those units, are distributed on a flat grant or equalization basis. "Revenue in lieu of taxes," analogous to payment from an enterprise fund to the General Fund discussed in Chapter 7, are payments made out of general revenues of intermediate, state, or federal governments to a local school system because the higher level governments own property located within the geographical boundaries of the local school system that is not subject to taxation. "Revenue for/on behalf of the school district" includes all payments made by intermediate, state, or federal governments for the benefit of the local system; payments to pension funds, or a contribution of fixed assets, are examples.

GASB financial reporting provides information to users of public school financial statements similar to that for state and local governments. As do other state and local governments, public school systems prepare basic financial statements, which include "district-wide" and fund financial statements, an MD&A, and other required supplementary information. Users are thus better able to assess how much the school owns and owes, its present financial status and future outlook, what it costs to educate students, and the tax burden placed on citizens and businesses to finance education.[19] District-wide statements report on traditional governmental activities of a public school district, essentially the activities related to educating students, as well as business-type activities, for example, food services or after-school latchkey programs. Accountants and auditors need to be aware of state laws and regulations affecting public schools' commercial activities, such as the sale of products, direct advertising, corporate-sponsored education materials, and exclusivity agreements with soft drink companies.[20]

[19] Ibid.

[20] General Accounting Office, *Public Educational Commercial Activities in Schools,* GAO/HEHS-00-156, September 2000.

Key Terms

Selected References

American Institute of Certified Public Accountants. *Audit and Accounting Guide. State and Local Governments.* New York, 2014.

Governmental Accounting Standards Board. *Codification of Governmental Accounting and Financial Reporting Standards as of June 30, 2014.* Norwalk, CT, 2014.

Mead, Dean Michael. *What You Should Know about Your School District's Finances: A Guide to Financial Statements-2nd Edition.* Norwalk, CT: Governmental Accounting Standards Board, 2012.

U.S. Department of Education, National Center for Education Statistics. *Financial Accounting for Local and State School Systems: 2009 Edition* (NCES 2009–325). Core Finance Data Task Force, The National Forum on Education Statistics. Washington, DC, 2009.

Questions

3–1. Explain the different purposes of the fund-based and government-wide financial statements of a state or local government and the primary differences between the fund-based and government-wide operating statements.

3–2. In relation to the government-wide statement of activities, define *direct expenses* and *indirect expenses* and why it is important to distinguish between them.

3–3. Describe the format prescribed by the GASB for the government-wide statement of activities and how that format benefits financial statement users.

3–4. Indicate whether the following revenues should be classified as *program revenues* or *general revenues* on the government-wide statement of activities.

a. Unrestricted operating grants that can be used at the discretion of the city council.
b. Capital grants restricted for highway construction.
c. Charges to other governments for police assistance at a special event.
d. A special assessment for snow removal.
e. Licenses and permits.
f. Motor vehicle fuel taxes restricted for road repair.
g. Investment earnings restricted for art preservation.

3–5. Explain the essential differences between *revenues* and *other financing sources* and between *expenditures* and *other financing uses.* How is each of these items reported on the governmental funds statement of revenues, expenditures, and changes in fund balances.

3–6. Indicate whether each of the following expenditure items should be classified as a function, program, organization unit, activity, character, or object.

a. Mayor's Office.
b. Public Safety.
c. Residential trash disposal.
d. Accident investigation.
e. Salaries and wages.
f. Debt service.
g. Environmental protection.
h. Health and Welfare.
i. Police Department.
j. Printing and postage.

3–7. Distinguish among appropriations, allotments, expenditures, encumbrances, and expenses.

3–8. State whether each of the following items should be classified as taxes, licenses and permits, intergovernmental revenues, charges for services, fines and forfeits, or miscellaneous revenue in a governmental fund.

a. Sales and use taxes levied by the government.
b. Payments by citizens for use of the city pool.
c. Building permits to construct a deck at a residence.
d. Traffic violation penalties.
e. Federal community development block grant.
f. Donation of bonds by a wealthy resident.
g. Charges to a local university for extra city police protection during sporting events.
h. Barbers and hairdressers' registration fees.

3–9. For which funds are budgetary comparison schedules or statements required? Should the *actual* revenues and expenditures on the budgetary comparison schedules be reported on the GAAP basis? Why or why not?

3–10. Explain how expenditure and revenue classifications for public school systems differ from those for state and local governments.

Cases

3–11 Research Case—Revenue and Expense/Expenditure Classification. Locate a comprehensive annual financial report (CAFR) using a city's Web site. Many cities, particularly those with a population greater than 25,000, publish their CAFRs on the city's official Web site. At the city's Web site, access a list of the city's departments and select "Department of Finance," or the one most similar to that name. With a little navigation, the CAFRs link can usually be located. Examine the city's government-wide statement of activities and statement of revenues, expenditures, and changes in fund balances—governmental funds and prepare a brief report responding to the following questions.

a. Referring to the government-wide statement of activities, explain how the program revenues and expenses are classified. Are expenses and program revenues reported using a function or program classification? Do any function or program categories show net revenues, or do they all show net expenses? Is the fact that most, if not all, functions or programs show a net expense a problem? Why or why not?

b. Explain how *revenues* are classified and reported on the statement of revenues, expenditures, and changes in fund balances. Compare the amount reported for property taxes in this statement to the amount reported as general revenue on the statement of activities. Do the two amounts agree? If not, can you think of a reasonable explanation for the difference?

c. Explain how *expenditures* are classified and reported on the statement of revenues, expenditures, and changes in fund balances. Compare these amounts to the amounts reported as expenses for the same functions or programs on the statement of activities. Do the amounts agree? If not, can you think of a reasonable explanation for the differences?

3–12 Research Case—Budgetary Comparison Statements; Budget Basis Compared with GAAP. Refer to Case 3–11 for instructions about how to obtain the CAFR for a city of your choice. Using that CAFR, go to the required supplementary information (RSI) section, immediately following the notes to the financial statements, and locate the *budgetary comparison schedule* (note: this schedule may be titled *schedule of revenues, expenditures, and changes in fund balances—budget and actual*) for the General Fund and major special revenue funds. If this schedule is not included in the RSI, then the city you have selected is one that elects to prepare an audited statement of revenues, expenditures, and changes in fund balances—budget and actual as part of the basic financial statements. Also, locate the GAAP operating statement for governmental funds called the statement of revenues, expenditures, and changes in fund balances—governmental funds in the basic statements (note: this statement does not contain any budgetary information). Examine the schedule and/or statements, as the case may be, and prepare a brief report that responds to the following questions.

a. Are revenues and/or expenditures presented in greater detail in the budgetary comparison schedule (or statement) than in the GAAP operating statement? If so, why, in your judgment, is this the case?

b. Do actual revenues on the budgetary comparison schedule agree in amount with those on the GAAP operating statement? If they differ, is there an explanation provided either in the notes to the financial statements or notes to the RSI to explain the difference? What explanations are provided, if any?

c. Do actual expenditures on the budgetary comparison schedule agree in amount with those on the GAAP operating statement? If they differ, is there an explanation provided either in the notes to the financial statements or notes to the RSI to explain the difference? What explanations are provided, if any?

d. If no differences were noted in either *b* or *c* above, go to item *e.* If differences were noted, was there a notation in the heading of the budgetary comparison schedule/statement indicating "Non-GAAP Budgetary Basis" or an indication of budget basis in the column heading for actual revenues and expenditures?

e. Does the budgetary comparison schedule/statement contain a variance column? If so, is the variance the difference between actual and original budget or the difference between actual and final budget?

f. Scan the notes to the financial statements and/or the notes to RSI to locate the note disclosure discussing budgetary information. Which funds are required to adopt budgets? Has a budgetary comparison statement or schedule been presented for each major special revenue fund with a legally required budget? What is the legal level of budgetary control? Did expenditures exceed appropriations in any funds?

3–13 Estimating and Setting the General Fund Property Tax Rate in a Challenging Economic and Political Environment.

Background: The city manager of University City is finalizing the budget proposal that must be submitted to the city council 60 days prior to the July 1 start of the next fiscal year, FY 20X2. An economic recession has significantly reduced the city's revenues over the past two years, particularly sales taxes and building permit fees. Despite strong political pressures on city council members to sustain current city services, the legal requirement to balance the budget has forced the council to cut certain services and staffing levels over the past two years. Federal financial assistance has prevented even deeper cuts, but will be sharply reduced at the end of FY 20X1. Even though the economy has gradually improved, reduced federal support will make achieving a balanced budget even more difficult in FY 20X2.

Constraints and planning factors: The city council has mandated that there be no increase in fees and taxes in FY 20X2. Although retail sales and housing starts are projected to increase modestly in FY 20X2, the assessed valuation of taxable property is projected to decrease an additional 5 percent in FY 20X2, reflecting the continuing decline in property values. Moreover, General Fund operating costs, particularly employee health insurance and energy, are expected to outpace revenue growth. Consequently, the city manager is recommending a third consecutive year of no salary and wage increases for city employees. The following financial information is provided as of May 1 of FY 20X1.

General Fund

Assessed valuation, taxable property (projected assessed valuation, beginning of FY 20X2)	$4,947,752,800
Estimated expenditures, remainder of FY 20X1	12,786,100
Recommended appropriations, FY 20X2	78,502,900
Required spendable fund balances, beginning of FY 20X3	15,223,000
Actual spendable fund balances, May 1 of FY 20X1	18,250,000
Estimated revenues from all sources, remainder of FY 20X1	11,705,000
Estimated revenues from sales taxes and other non-property tax sources, FY 20X2	66,414,000

Analysis and estimation of required property tax rate for FY 20X2: After analyzing the preceding information, constraints, and planning factors, respond to the following questions. (Keep in mind, however, that the city council may impose further changes to the budget as a result of the several budget hearings that will be held over the next two months.)

a. What amount of estimated revenues is required from property taxes for FY 20X2? (Hint: Make your calculation using the format shown in Illustration 3–6.)

b. What tax rate will be required in FY 20X2 to generate the amount of revenues from property taxes calculated in question *a*?

c. Assuming the property tax rate for FY 20X1 was $0.20 per $100 of assessed valuation of taxable property, will the tax rate calculated in question *b* violate the city council mandate of no increase in taxes? If so, how would you justify the rate calculated in question *b*, since the city council will likely be sensitive to adverse public reaction to an increased tax rate?

3–14 **Research Case—State-Mandated Financial Accounting and Reporting Requirements for Texas Schools.** As noted in Appendix B to this chapter, most, if not all, state governments require public school districts to report financial and other data to the appropriate state agency, so the state can report standardized school data to the National Center for Educational Statistics (NCES). Texas has one of the most rigorous school district reporting requirements in the nation. A state law called the Texas Education Code requires each school district to adopt a standard financial accounting system prescribed by the Texas Education Agency (TEA). District accounting systems must also conform to generally accepted accounting principles (GAAP). Each district must also have an annual independent audit.

Access the Texas Education Agency Web site at *www.tea.state.tx.us*. At the TEA home page, select "F" from the A-Z Index, then select the TEA's *Financial Accountability System Resource Guide* link and open "Module 1—Financial Accounting and Reporting (FAR)." When the FAR has opened, use the index to locate and move to Section 1.4 "Account Codes." Review Sections 1.4.2 through 1.4.9 and respond to the following questions.

a. Look at Exhibit 29, which depicts the prescribed Account Code Structure for Texas public school districts and discuss whether the code structure is adequate to meet both GASB and NCES revenue and expenditure/expense classification requirements.

b. Do the *function* and *program* categories prescribed in Sections 1.4.3 and 1.4.15 agree with the classifications discussed in Appendix B? If not, how do they differ?

3–15 **Accounting Information Systems.** In reading Appendix A of this chapter, you may have been struck by the fact that many governmental accounting information (GAI) software systems appear to be incapable of handling the full reporting requirements of a governmental entity. A 2006 Market Research Report published by the Government Finance Officers Association (GFOA) titled "Budgeting Technology Solutions" categorized available software into three types: Excel Add-on, Corporate Performance Management (CPM) Systems, and Relational Systems. Write a two- to three-page paper discussing the current status of governmental accounting information (GAI) software. Describe the three types of software identified in the GFOA report. What (if any) progress has been made since the GFOA's 2006 report? Have additional types of software been identified and/or developed? What does the future hold for GAI software?

Exercises and Problems

3–16 **Examine the CAFR.** Utilizing the CAFR obtained for Exercise 1–16, in Chapter 1, review the governmental fund financial statements and related data and government-wide financial statements. Note particularly these items:

a. **Statement of Activities at the Government-wide Level.** Has the government prepared statements in compliance with the GASB financial reporting model? Does the statement of activities appear on one page or two pages? What is the most costly governmental function or program operated by the government? How much of the cost of governmental activities was borne by taxpayers in the form of general revenues? Did the entity increase or decrease its governmental activities unrestricted net position this year? Did the entity increase or decrease its business-type activities unrestricted net position this year?

b. **Statement of Revenues, Expenditures, and Changes in Fund Balances for Governmental Funds.**

(1) *Revenues.* What system of classification of revenues is used in the governmental fund financial statements? List the three most important sources of General Fund revenues and the most important source of revenue for each major governmental fund. Does the reporting entity depend on any single source for as much as one-third of its General Fund revenues? What proportion of revenues is derived from property taxes? Do the notes clearly indicate recognition criteria for primary revenue sources?

Are charts, graphs, or tables included in the statistical section of the CAFR that show the changes over time in reliance on each revenue source?

(2) *Expenditures.* What level of classification of expenditures is used in the governmental fund financial statements (e.g., fund, function or program, organization unit, activity, character, object)? List the three largest categories of General Fund expenditures; list the largest category of expenditure of each major governmental fund.

Are charts, tables, or graphs presented in the statistical section of the CAFR to show the trend of General Fund expenditures, by category, for a period of 10 years? Is expenditure data related to nonfinancial measures such as population of the government or workload statistics (e.g., tons of solid waste removed or number of miles of street constructed)?

(3) *Other Financing Sources (Uses).* Are other financing sources and uses reported in a separate section of the statement of revenues, expenditures, and changes in fund balances, below the revenues and expenditures sections? Do the line items indicate the nature of each financing source or use?

c. **Budgetary Comparison Schedule or Statement.** Does the government present budgetary comparisons as a basic governmental fund financial statement, or as required supplementary information (RSI) immediately following the notes to the financial statements? Is the budgetary comparison title a *schedule* rather than a *statement?* Does the budgetary comparison present the original budget and the final amended budget? Does the budgetary schedule present actual data using the budgetary basis of accounting? Has the government presented one or more variance columns? Does the CAFR indicate that budgetary reporting practices differ from GAAP reporting practices? If so, does it explain how the practices differ?

3–17 Multiple Choice. Choose the best answer.

1. Which of the following best describes the recommended format for the government-wide statement of activities?
   a. Revenues minus expenses equals change in net position.
   b. Revenues minus expenditures equals change in net position.
   c. Expenses minus program revenues equals net (expense) revenue. Net (expense) revenue plus general revenues equals change in net position.
   d. Program revenues minus expenses minus general revenues equals changes in net position.

2. Which of the following is an acceptable method of reporting depreciation expense for depreciable assets used by governmental activities?
   a. Report as a general expense in the bottom section of the statement of activities.
   b. Report as a direct expense of the function or program with which the related depreciable assets are identified.
   c. Report as an indirect expense on a separate line, or as an expense of the general government (or similar) function, for depreciable assets that benefit all functions or programs.
   d. Either *b* or *c*.
3. GASB standards require that fund balances of governmental funds be classified according to whether the fund balance is spendable or nonspendable. *Spendable* fund balances are further classified as:
   a. Reserved, unreserved, and designated.
   b. Restricted, committed, assigned, and unassigned.
   c. Restricted, unrestricted, encumbered, and unencumbered.
   d. Restricted, reserved, and unreserved.
4. When determining *taxable property* for the purpose of property tax levy, which of the following would likely be excluded from the calculation?
   a. Property owned by governments.
   b. Property exempted from taxation by the government.
   c. Property used by religious or charitable organizations.
   d. All of the above.
5. One characteristic that generally distinguishes *other financing uses* from *expenditures* is that other financing uses:
   a. Arise from interfund transfers out.
   b. Decrease fund balances when they are closed at year-end.
   c. Are not included in budgetary entries.
   d. Have a normal credit balance.
6. An internal allocation of funds on a periodic basis, which is often used to regulate the use of appropriations over a budgetary period, is called:
   a. An encumbrance.
   b. A budgetary levy.
   c. An ad valorem assessment.
   d. An allotment.
7. According to GASB standards, *expenditures* may be classified by:
   a. Fund, function or program, organization unit, source, and character.
   b. Fund, function or program, organization unit, activity, character, and object.
   c. Fund, appropriation, organization unit, activity, character, and object.
   d. Fund, organization unit, encumbrance, activity, character, and object.
8. Under GASB requirements for external financial reporting, one would find the budgetary comparison schedule (or statement) in the:
   a. Required supplementary information (RSI).
   b. Basic financial statements.
   c. Either *a* or *b*, as elected by the government.
   d. Neither *a* nor *b*.
9. Before placing a purchase order, a department should check that available appropriations are sufficient to cover the cost of the item being ordered. This type of budgetary control is achieved by reviewing:
   a. Appropriations minus expenditures.
   b. Appropriations plus expenditures minus encumbrances.

c. Appropriations minus estimated revenues.
d. Appropriations minus the sum of expenditures and encumbrances.

10. Spruce City's finance department recorded the recently adopted General Fund budget at the beginning of the current fiscal year. The budget approved est\imated revenues of $1,100,000 and appropriations of $1,000,000. Which of the following is the correct journal entry to record the budget?

	Debits	Credits
a. Estimated Revenues	1,100,000	
Budgetary Fund Balance		100,000
Appropriations		1,000,000
b. Appropriations	1,100,000	
Budgetary Fund Balance		100,000
Estimated Revenues		1,000,000
c. Revenues Receivable	1,000,000	
Budgetary Deficit	100,000	
Appropriations		1,100,000
d. Memorandum entry only.		

3–18 Recording Budget and Ending Fund Balances. The following information is provided about the Town of York's General Fund operating statement and budgetary accounts for the fiscal year ended September 30, 2016. (Note: The town has no restricted, committed, or assigned fund balances.)

Estimated revenues	$32,150,000
Revenues	32,190,000
Appropriations	32,175,000
Expenditures	32,185,000
Fund Balance—Unassigned September 30, 2015	500,000

Required

a. Prepare the journal entry to record the budget.
b. Did the Town of York engage in imprudent budgeting practice by authorizing a greater amount of expenditures than revenues estimated for the year, or potentially violate town or state balanced-budget laws?
c. Calculate the end-of-year balance for the Fund Balance—Unassigned that would be reported on the town's balance sheet prepared as of September 30, 2016. Show all necessary work.

3–19 On February 15, 2016, the Town of Evergreen police chief's administrative assistant is preparing a purchase order to place an order for a new computer. The computer is estimated to cost $1,600. Prior to submitting the purchase order, he is required to verify that an appropriation is available in a sufficient amount to cover the cost of the new computer. His computer display shows the following current information for the Police Chief Equipment account and Office Supplies account.

Account No. 1010012058510 Year 2016		**Department/Activity Object**		**Police Department/Chief Equipment**	
		Encumbrances			
Date	**Reference**	**Originated**	**Closed**	**Expenditures**	**Available Appropriation**
Jan 2	Budget				4,500
Jan 21	PO 13-65	3,000			1,500
Jan 30	Voucher 13-794		3,000	2,990	1,510

Account No. 1010012058300 Year 2016		Department/Activity Object		Police Department/Chief Office Supplies	
		Encumbrances			Available
Date	Reference	Originated	Closed	Expenditures	Appropriation
Jan 2	Budget PO				5,000
Jan 15	16-98	500			4,500
Jan 30	Voucher 13-794		500	495	4,505

Required

Review the Police Chief accounts as of February 15, 2016, and answer the following questions, assuming you are the administrative assistant.

a. Is the available appropriation balance sufficient to authorize placing the purchase order for the new computer?

b. You notice an available appropriation balance in the office supply account. Under what circumstances might the Office Supplies appropriation balance be used for the equipment purchase?

3–20 Recording Adopted Budget. The Town of Willingdon adopted the following General Fund budget for fiscal year 2017:

Estimated revenues:	
Taxes	$15,000,000
Intergovernmental revenues	1,000,000
Licenses and permits	400,000
Fines and forfeits	150,000
Miscellaneous revenues	100,000
Total estimated revenues	$16,650,000
Appropriations:	
General government	$8,000,000
Public safety	6,000,000
Public works	1,550,000
Health and welfare	950,000
Miscellaneous	100,000
Total appropriations	$16,600,000

Required

Prepare the general journal entries to record the adopted budget at the beginning of FY 2017. Show entries in the subsidiary ledger accounts as well as the general ledger accounts.

3–21 Recording Encumbrances. During July 2016, the first month of the 2017 fiscal year, the Town of Willingdon issued the following purchase orders and contracts (see Problem 3–20):

General government	$ 800,000
Public safety	400,000
Public works	75,000
Health and welfare	65,000
Miscellaneous	25,000
Total purchase orders and contracts	$1,365,000

Required

a. Show the general journal entry to record the issuance of the purchase orders and contracts. Show entries in subsidiary ledger accounts as well as general ledger accounts.

b. Explain why state and local governments generally record the estimated amounts of purchase orders and contracts in the accounts of budgeted governmental funds, whereas business entities generally do not prepare formal entries for purchase orders.

3–22 Recording General Fund Operating Budget and Operating Transactions. The Town of Bedford Falls approved a General Fund operating budget for the fiscal year ending June 30, 2017. The budget provides for estimated revenues of $2,700,000 as follows: property taxes, $1,900,000; licenses and permits, $350,000; fines and forfeits, $250,000; and intergovernmental (state grants), $200,000. The budget approved appropriations of $2,650,000 as follows: General Government, $500,000; Public Safety, $1,600,000; Public Works, $350,000; Culture and Recreation, $150,000; and Miscellaneous, $50,000.

Required

a. Prepare the journal entry (or entries), including subsidiary ledger entries, to record the Town of Bedford Falls's General Fund operating budget on July 1, 2016, the beginning of the Town's 2017 fiscal year.

b. Prepare journal entries to record the following transactions that occurred during the month of July 2016.

1. Revenues were collected in cash amounting to $31,000 for licenses and permits and $12,000 for fines and forfeits.
2. Supplies were ordered by the following functions in early July 2016 at the estimated costs shown:

General Government	$ 7,400
Public Safety	11,300
Public Works	6,100
Culture and Recreation	4,200
Miscellaneous	900
Total	$29,900

3. During July 2016, supplies were received at the actual costs shown below and were paid in cash. General Government, Culture and Recreation, and Miscellaneous received all supplies ordered. Public Safety and Public Works received part of the supplies ordered earlier in the month at estimated costs of $10,700 and $5,900, respectively.

	Actual Cost	Estimated Cost
General Government	$ 7,300	$ 7,400
Public Safety	10,800	10,700
Public Works	6,100	5,900
Culture and Recreation	4,100	4,200
Miscellaneous	900	900
Total	$29,200	$29,100

c. Calculate and show in good form the amount of budgeted but unrealized revenues in total and from each source as of July 31, 2016.

d. Calculate and show in good form the amount of available appropriation in total and for each function as of July 31, 2016.

3–23 Subsidiary Ledgers. The printout of the Revenues and Appropriations subsidiary ledger accounts for the General Fund of the City of Augusta as of March 31, 2017, appeared as follows:

REVENUES LEDGER

Account	Ref.	Year	Account Title	Est. Revenues Dr(Cr)	Revenues Cr(Dr)	Balance Dr(Cr)
3/4020			**Taxes—Real Property**			
	101	2017	Budget Authorization	750,000		750,000
	102	2017	Received in Cash		200,000	550,000
3/4050			**Licenses and Permits**			
	101	2017	Budget Authorization	100,000		100,000
	102	2017	Received in Cash		10,000	90,000
3/4070			**Intergovernmental Revenue**			
	101	2017	Budget Authorization	50,000		50,000
	102	2017	Received in Cash		15,000	35,000
	103	2017		12,500		47,500

APPROPRIATIONS LEDGER

Account	Ref	Account/ Description	Encumbrances Increase Dr	Encumbrances Decrease (Cr)	Encumbrances Balance Dr(Cr)	Expenditures Dr(Cr)	Expenditures Balance Dr(Cr)	Appropriation Cr(Dr)	Balance Cr(Dr)
5/6/7020		**Genaral Government**							
	101	Budget Authorization						635,000	635,000
	102	Payroll				150,000	150,000		485,000
	102	Utilities and Other				15,000	165,000		470,000
5/6/7030		**Public Safety**							
	101	Budget Authorization						125,000	125,000
	102	Payroll				25,000	25,000		100,000
5/6/7050		**Health and Welfare**							
	101	Budget Authorization						85,000	85,000
	102	Goods Recived				15,000	15,000		70,000
5/6/7070		**Miscellaneous**							
	101	Budget Authorization						50,000	50,000

Required

Assuming that this printout is correct in all details and that there are no other General Fund revenue or expenditure transactions, answer the following questions. *Show all necessary computations in good form.*

a. What were the original approved budget amounts for Estimated Revenues and for Appropriations?

b. (1) Was the Estimated Revenues budget adjusted during the year?
(2) If so, by how much?
(3) If so, was the original budget increased or decreased?

c. (1) What are the current balances of the Estimated Revenues and Appropriations control accounts?
(2) What are the current balances of the Revenues and Expenditures control accounts?
(3) What do these balances indicate?

3–24 Governmental Accounting System—Departmental Budgetary Comparison Report. Review the computer generated budgetary comparison report presented below for the Lincoln City Culture and Recreation Department as of July 1 of its fiscal year ending December 31, 2016, and respond to the questions that follow.

LINCOLN CITY
FY 2016 Detail Report, Departmental Expenditures

Run date: July 1, 2016
08-00 Culture and Recreation Department

Account Number	Account Title	FY 2016 Budget	Expenditures 2016 to Date	Encumbrances Outstanding	Available Appropriations
01 08-00 6110	Personnel Services	$1,172,661	$533,472	$ 0	$639,189
01 08-00 7110	Materials and Supplies	376,457	207,683	27,424	141,350
01 08-00 7210	Conferences and Training	3,800	1,426	0	2,374
01 08-00 7310	Contractual Services	276,840	102,687	89,642	84,511
01 08-00 7410	Utilities	192,248	98,249	0	93,999
01 08-00 7810	Capital Outlay	57,924	21,387	3,600	32,937
01 08-00 7910	Other	248,673	172,538	6,742	69,393

Required

a. Explain the account code structure being employed by Lincoln City. Does that structure appear consistent with the expenditure classifications required by GASB standards? Does it allow for more detailed expenditure classifications, if desired? For example, could materials and supplies be further classified as recreational supplies, office supplies, building supplies, and so forth?

b. What is the likely reason there are no outstanding encumbrances for the Personnel Services, Conferences and Training, and Utilities accounts?

c. Does it appear that the Culture and Recreation Department may overexpend its appropriation for any accounts before the end of FY 2016? If so, which accounts may run short?

d. Does it appear that the Culture and Recreation Department may underexpend any of its appropriations for FY 2016? If so, which accounts may have excessive spending authority?

e. What factors may explain the expenditure patterns observed in parts *c* and *d*?

3–25 Government-wide Statement of Activities. The following alphabetic listing displays selected balances in the governmental activities accounts of Westover Village as of June 30, 2017. Prepare a (partial) statement of activities using the format shown in Illustrations 3–1 and A2–2 (see Appendix A in Chapter 2). Assume that beginning net position is $1,643 (in thousands) and that there were no changes in net position during the year other than those reflected in the selected account balances shown. For simplicity, assume that the village does not have business-type activities or component units.

WESTOVER VILLAGE
Governmental Activities
Selected Account Balances (in thousands)
For the Year Ended June 30, 2017

	Debits	***Credits***
Expenses—Culture and Recreation	12,352	
Expenses—General Government	9,571	
General Revenues—Property Taxes		56,300
General Revenues—Unrestricted Grants and Contributions		1,200
Expenses—Health and Sanitation	6,738	
Expenses—Interest on Long-term Debt	6,068	
General Revenues—Investment Earnings		1,958
Expenses—Public Safety	34,844	
Program Revenue—Culture and Recreation—Charges for Services		3,995
Program Revenue—Culture and Recreation—Operating Grants		2,450
Program Revenue—General Government—Charges for Services		3,146
Program Revenue—General Government—Operating Grants		843
Program Revenue—Health and Sanitation—Charges for Services		5,612
Program Revenue—Public Safety—Capital Grants		62
Program Revenue—Public Safety—Charges for Services		1,198
Program Revenue—Public Safety—Operating Grants		1,307
Special Item—Gain on Sale of Park Land		3,473

Chapter Four

Accounting for Governmental Operating Activities—Illustrative Transactions and Financial Statements

Learning Objectives

After studying this chapter, you should be able to:

4-1 Analyze typical operating transactions for governmental activities and prepare appropriate journal entries at both the government-wide and fund levels.

4-2 Prepare adjusting entries and a pre-closing trial balance.

4-3 Prepare closing journal entries and year-end General Fund financial statements.

4-4 Account for interfund and intra- and inter-activity transactions.

4-5 Account for transactions of a permanent fund.

4-6 Distinguish between exchange and nonexchange transactions, and define the classifications used for nonexchange transactions.

In Chapter 3, the use of general ledger budgetary control accounts (Estimated Revenues, Estimated Other Financing Sources, Appropriations, Estimated Other Financing Uses, and Encumbrances) and related operating statement accounts (Revenues, Other Financing Sources, Expenditures, and Other Financing Uses) was discussed and illustrated. The necessity for subsidiary ledgers, or equivalent files, supporting the budgetary control accounts and related operating statement accounts was also discussed. In this chapter, common transactions and events, as well as related recognition and measurement issues, arising from the operating activities of a hypothetical local government, the Town of Brighton, are discussed, and appropriate accounting entries and financial statements are illustrated.

ILLUSTRATIVE CASE

The Town of Brighton's partial government-wide statement of net position, showing only the governmental activities, and its General Fund balance sheet, both at the end of the 2016 fiscal year, are presented in Illustration 4–1. Because this chapter focuses on *governmental* operating activities, only the financial information for the Governmental Activities column is presented at this time. The Town of Brighton does have business-type activities, but those activities are discussed in Chapter 7 of the text. Although the town has no discretely presented component units, the column is shown in the statement of net position simply to illustrate the recommended financial statement format.

Measurement Focus and Basis of Accounting

As discussed at several points in the earlier chapters, the government-wide statement of net position reports financial position using the economic resources measurement focus and the accrual basis of accounting—in short, using accounting principles similar to those used by business entities. In contrast, the General Fund balance sheet reports financial position using the current financial resources measurement focus and the modified accrual basis of accounting. Although both of these statements represent financial position at the same point in time, even a casual comparison reveals significant differences.

Perhaps the most striking difference between the two statements shown in Illustration 4–1 is that the statement of net position reports both current and noncurrent assets and liabilities, whereas the General Fund balance sheet reports only current financial resources and current liabilities to be paid from current financial resources. *Current financial resources* include cash and items (such as marketable securities and receivables) expected to be converted into cash in the current period or soon enough thereafter to pay current period obligations. Prepaid items and inventories of supplies, if material, are also included in current financial resources.

Another major difference is that the information reported in the Governmental Activities column of the statement of net position includes financial information for *all* governmental activities, not just for the General Fund. For example, the Town of Brighton also has debt service funds whose cash and receivables are combined with those of the General Fund in the Assets section of the statement of net position. The investments reported in the statement of net position belong to the debt service funds. In fact, it will be noted that $77,884 of net position is restricted for purposes of paying debt service (principal and interest) on long-term debt. (*Note:* The debt service funds are discussed in Chapter 6.)

There are some other less important but still noteworthy differences. One such difference involves format. The Town's statement of net position is in the GASB-recommended net position format (that is, assets minus liabilities equals net position)[1] rather than the traditional balance sheet format (assets equals liabilities plus fund equity). However, GASB standards permit governments the option of preparing a government-wide *balance sheet* rather than a statement of net position.

An alert reader may have noted that the statement of net position reports financial information in a more condensed manner than does the General Fund balance sheet. The primary reason for reporting more aggregated financial information is that the government-wide financial statements, along with the required management's

[1] The Town of Brighton has no deferred outflows or inflows of resources. If there were deferred outflows or inflows, then net position would be defined as (a) the sum of assets and deferred outflows of resources minus (b) the sum of liabilities and deferred inflows of resources equals net position. See Chapter 2, for a discussion of deferred outflows and inflows of resources.

ILLUSTRATION 4–1

TOWN OF BRIGHTON
Statement of Net Position
December 31, 2016

	Primary Government			
	Governmental Activities	**Business-type Activities**	**Total**	**Component Units (None)**
Assets				
Cash	$ 257,500	(Omitted intentionally)		
Investments	40,384			
Receivables (net)	619,900			
Inventory of supplies	61,500			
Capital assets (net)	19,330,018			
Total Assets	20,309,302			
Liabilities				
Vouchers payable	320,000			
Accrued interest payable	37,500			
Due to federal government	90,000			
Bonds payable	1,500,000			
Total Liabilities	1,947,500			
Net Position				
Net investment in capital assets	17,830,018			
Restricted for:				
Debt service	77,884			
Unrestricted	453,900			
Total Net Position	$18,361,802			

TOWN OF BRIGHTON
General Fund Balance Sheet
December 31, 2016

Assets		
Cash		$190,000
Taxes receivable—delinquent	$660,000	
Less: Allowance for uncollectible delinquent taxes	50,000	610,000
Interest and penalties receivable on taxes	13,200	
Less: Allowance for uncollectible interest and penalties	3,300	9,900
Total Assets		$809,900
Liabilities and Fund Balance		
Liabilities:		
Vouchers payable		$320,000
Due to federal government		90,000
Total Liabilities		410,000
Fund balance—unassigned		399,900
Total Liabilities and Fund Balance		$809,900

discussion and analysis (MD&A), are intended to provide a broad overview of the government's financial position. Additional detail is provided in the notes to the financial statements (not provided in this chapter for sake of brevity), as well as in the fund financial statements.

A final point should be noted about the General Fund balance sheet before discussing illustrative budgetary and operating transactions. Fund balance, as shown in Illustration 4–1, is equal to the total assets minus total liabilities of the General Fund. In the case of the Town of Brighton, the unassigned fund balance of $399,900 reported in the General Fund is $54,000 less than the $453,900 reported for unrestricted net position in the government-wide statement of net position. In practice, these amounts are often markedly different, reflecting the two bases of accounting used as well as the fact that most governments will have financial information for other governmental fund types reported as part of the governmental activities unrestricted net position. At any rate, neither net position at the government-wide level nor fund balances at the fund level are analogous to the stockholders' equity of an investor-owned entity. Residents have no legal claim on any net position or fund balances of the government.

DUAL-TRACK ACCOUNTING APPROACH

Governmental fund operating activities and transactions have different effects on the Town of Brighton's government-wide financial statements and fund financial statements. Certain activities (e.g., those relating to the General Fund budget) have no effect on the government-wide financial statements. Most operating activities or transactions affect both the General Fund and governmental activities at the government-wide level, but in different ways. Still other activities, such as recording depreciation expense or accruing interest on general long-term debt, affect only the government-wide financial statements and are not recorded at all in the General Fund or in any other governmental fund. Examples of the latter journal entries are provided in Chapters 6 and 9.

Despite the GASB requirement to prepare government-wide financial statements, in addition to fund financial statements, nearly all governments continue to use traditional fund accounting software systems. These systems record transactions that occur during the year in the appropriate governmental funds, but are unable to directly provide the accrual accounting information needed to prepare the government-wide financial statements. To compensate for this deficiency, most governments manually convert their fund-based financial information to the accrual basis by preparing spreadsheets, as illustrated in Chapter 9. Most municipal accounting software vendors have helped simplify this approach by developing report generators that selectively aggregate data needed for the government-wide statements. Nevertheless, the authors believe that the reclassification approach is deficient in the sense that the general ledger accounts do not provide all the information needed to prepare government-wide financial statements. Among other problems, the reclassification approach may limit the preparation of government-wide financial statements to once a year and may present audit trail and accounting record retention problems.

To capture the dual effects of transactions at the government-wide and governmental fund levels, this text adopts a *dual-track* approach to analyzing and recording transactions based on manual accounting procedures. Although this approach is designed to facilitate ease of learning, it also provides all the accounting information needed to prepare both government-wide and fund financial statements.

ILLUSTRATIVE JOURNAL ENTRIES

For the illustrative journal entries that follow, if the account titles or amounts differ in any respect, *separate* journal entries are illustrated for the General Fund general journal and the governmental activities (government-wide) general journal. For activities or transactions in which the entries would be identical, only a single journal entry is illustrated. In these cases, the heading for the entry indicates that it applies to both journals.

Recording the Budget

As discussed in Chapter 3, the budget should be recorded in the accounts of each governmental fund for which a budget is legally adopted. For purposes of review, Entry 1, which follows, illustrates an entry to record the budget in the general journal for the General Fund of the Town of Brighton for fiscal year 2017. (The entry is shown in combined form to illustrate that format. The ledger detail shown is assumed to be that needed to comply with laws applicable to the Town of Brighton. Because the Estimated Revenues, and Appropriations, accounts apply only to the fiscal year 2017 budget and will be closed at the end of the year, it is not necessary to incorporate "2017" in the title of either.)

		General Ledger		Subsidiary Ledger	
		Debits	***Credits***	***Debits***	***Credits***
	General Fund:				
1.	Estimated Revenues	3,986,000			
	Budgetary Fund Balance	194,000			
	Appropriations		4,180,000		
	Estimated Revenues Ledger:				
	Property Taxes			2,600,000	
	Interest and Penalties on Delinquent Taxes			13,000	
	Sales Taxes			480,000	
	Licenses and Permits			220,000	
	Fines and Forfeits			308,000	
	Intergovernmental Revenue			280,000	
	Charges for Services			82,000	
	Miscellaneous Revenues			3,000	
	Appropriations Ledger:				
	General Government				660,000
	Public Safety				1,240,000
	Public Works				1,090,000
	Health and Welfare				860,000
	Culture and Recreation				315,000
	Miscellaneous				15,000

Encumbrances and Purchasing Transactions

Purchase orders for certain supplies and contracts for services were placed with outside vendors in the amount of $59,090. Entry 2 on the next page shows the journal entry required to record the estimated cost of supplies ordered and service contracts signed. Because some encumbrance documents issued in 2017 may not be filled until early 2018, sound budgetary control dictates that "2017" be added to the Encumbrances general ledger control account and the corresponding Encumbrances Outstanding. The amounts chargeable to specific appropriations of 2017 are debited to detail accounts in the Encumbrances Subsidiary Ledger. (Recall that budgetary entries affect only funds for which a budget is legally adopted; they have no effect at the government-wide level.)

		General Ledger		Subsidiary Ledger	
		Debits	**Credits**	**Debits**	**Credits**
	General Fund:				
2.	Encumbrances—2017	59,090			
	Encumbrances Outstanding—2017		59,090		
	Encumbrances Ledger:				
	General Government			18,500	
	Public Works			15,000	
	Culture and Recreation			20,590	
	Health and Welfare			5,000	

When supplies and services ordered during the current year have been received and found to be acceptable, the suppliers' or contractors' billings or invoices should be checked for agreement with the original interdepartmental requisitions, purchase orders, or contracts as to prices and terms, as well as for clerical accuracy. If all details are in order, the billing documents are approved for payment. If, as is usual practice, the estimated liability for each order was previously recorded in the Encumbrances control account in the general ledger, as well as in subsidiary Encumbrance Ledger accounts, entries must be made to reverse the encumbrances entries for the originally estimated amounts. In addition, entries are required to record the actual charges in the Expenditures control account and subsidiary Expenditures Ledger accounts. Expenses and/or assets must also be recorded in governmental activities accounts at the government-wide level, as appropriate.

Assume that only a portion of the supplies and contracts with outside vendors were filled or completed during the year at an actual cost of $19,700, for which the estimated cost had been $22,415. For purposes of illustration, the appropriations assumed to be affected are shown in Entries 3 and 3a for the General Fund.

	General Fund:				
3.	Encumbrances Outstanding—2017	22,415			
	Encumbrances—2017		22,415		
	Encumbrances Ledger:				
	General Government				2,300
	Public Works				5,600
	Culture and Recreation				14,415
	Health and Welfare				100
3a.	Expenditures—2017	19,700			
	Vouchers Payable		19,700		
	Expenditures Ledger:				
	General Government			2,300	
	Public Works			5,500	
	Culture and Recreation			11,800	
	Health and Welfare			100	

		General Ledger		Subsidiary Ledger	
		Debits	**Credits**	**Debits**	**Credits**
	Governmental Activities:				
3b.	Expenses—General Government	2,300			
	Expenses—Public Works	5,500			
	Expenses—Culture and Recreation	11,800			
	Expenses—Health and Welfare	100			
	Vouchers Payable		19,700		

In addition to supplies, the General Fund purchased a new copier during the year. It was ordered at a cost of $15,000.

	General Fund:				
4a.	Encumbrances—2017	15,000			
	Encumbrances Outstanding—2017		15,000		
	Encumbrances Ledger:				
	Public Safety			15,000	

The copier was received at an actual cost of $14,550. Entry 4c shows that long-lived assets are not accounted for in the General Fund because governmental funds are used only to account for the inflows and outflows (i.e., expenditures) of current financial resources used to purchase the equipment. Entry 4d records the asset in the Governmental Activities journal since the copier will provide service benefits in the future.

	General Fund:				
4b.	Encumbrances Outstanding—2017	15,000			
	Encumbrances—2017		15,000		
	Encumbrances Ledger:				
	Public Safety				15,000
4c.	Expenditures—2017	14,550			
	Vouchers Payable		14,550		
	Expenditures Ledger:				
	Public Safety			14,550	
	Governmental Activates:				
4d.	Equipment	14,550			
	Vouchers Payable		14,550		

Payment of Liabilities

Checks were drawn to pay the $339,700 balance of vouchers payable ($320,000 balance at the end of 2016 plus the $19,700 amount from Entry 3a) and the $90,000 amount due to the federal government at the end of 2016. The following entries would be made for the General Fund and governmental activities at the government-wide level:

		General Ledger		Subsidiary Ledger	
		Debits	**Credits**	**Debits**	**Credits**
	General Fund and Governmental Activities:				
5.	Vouchers Payable	339,700			
	Due to Federal Government	90,000			
	Cash		429,700		

Note that entries to subsidiary appropriation or expenditure accounts in the General Fund are unnecessary since those entries were made previously when the goods and services were received.

Some readers may question how more cash can be disbursed in Entry 5 than is available. This is no cause for concern, as the examples in this chapter are summarized transactions. Throughout the year revenues are also being collected, as illustrated in a later section. Should tax revenues be received later than needed to pay vendors on a timely basis, governments typically issue *tax anticipation notes* to meet those short-term cash needs, as discussed later in this chapter.

Payrolls and Payroll Taxes

The gross pay of employees of General Fund departments for the month of January 2017 amounted to $252,000. The town does not use the encumbrance procedure for payroll. Deductions from gross pay for the period amount to $19,278 for employees' share of FICA tax; $25,200, employees' federal withholding tax; and $5,040, employees' state withholding tax. The first two will have to be remitted by the town to the federal government, and the last item will have to be remitted to the state government. The gross pay is chargeable to the appropriations in the General Fund as indicated by the Expenditures Ledger debits. Assuming that the liability for net pay is vouchered, the entry in the General Fund is:

	General Fund:				
6a.	Expenditures—2017	252,000			
	Vouchers Payable		202,482		
	Due to Federal Government		44,478		
	Due to State Government		5,040		
	Expenditures Ledger:				
	General Government			35,040	
	Public Safety			156,120	
	Public Works			29,160	
	Health and Welfare			19,080	
	Culture and Recreation			12,600	

In addition, the following entry would be required to record the payroll transaction in the governmental activities general journal at the government-wide level, using the accrual basis (expenses rather than expenditures):

		General Ledger		Subsidiary Ledger	
		Debits	***Credits***	***Debits***	***Credits***
	Governmental Activities:				
6b.	Expenses—General Government	35,040			
	Expenses—Public Safety	156,120			
	Expenses—Public Works	29,160			
	Expenses—Health and Welfare	19,080			
	Expenses—Culture and Recreation	12,600			
	Vouchers Payable		202,482		
	Due to Federal Government		44,478		
	Due to State Government		5,040		

Recording the salaries and wages expenses in the manner shown in Entry 6b permits reporting direct expenses by function, as shown in Illustration A2–2 (see Appendix A in Chapter 2) and as described in Chapter 3 in the discussion on expense classification in the government-wide statement of activities. If a government prefers to also record the expenses by natural classification (that is, as salaries and wages expense), it will be necessary to add additional classification detail; for example, Expenses—General Government—Salaries and Wages.

Payment of the vouchers for the net pay results in the following entry in both the General Fund and governmental activities journals:

	General Fund and Governmental Activities:				
7.	Vouchers Payable	202,482			
	Cash		202,482		

In as much as the town is liable for the employer's share of FICA taxes ($19,278), it is necessary that the town's liability be recorded, as shown in Entry 8a.

	General Fund:				
8a.	Expenditures—2017	19,278			
	Due to Federal Government		19,278		
	Expenditures Ledger:				
	General Government			2,681	
	Public Safety			11,943	
	Public Works			2,230	
	Health and Welfare			1,460	
	Culture and Recreation			964	

Entry 8b is also required to record the payroll expense on the accrual basis at the government-wide level.

	Governmental Activities:				
8b.	Expenses—General Government	2,681			
	Expenses—Public Safety	11,943			
	Expenses—Public Works	2,230			
	Expenses—Health and Welfare	1,460			
	Expenses—Culture and Recreation	964			
	Due to Federal Government		19,278		

Accounting for Property Taxes

Entry 1 of this chapter shows that the estimated revenue for fiscal year 2017 from property taxes levied for the Town of Brighton General Fund is $2,600,000. If records of property tax collections in recent years, adjusted for any expected changes in tax collection policy and changes in local economic conditions, indicate that approximately 4 percent of the gross tax levy will never be collected, the *gross tax levy* must be large enough so that the collectible portion of the levy, 96 percent, equals the needed revenue from this source, $2,600,000. Therefore, the gross levy of property taxes for the General Fund of the Town of Brighton must be $2,708,333 ($2,600,000 ÷ 0.96). In an actual situation, property situated in the Town of Brighton also would be taxed for other funds of that town; for various funds of other general purpose governments, such as the county in which the property in the Town of Brighton is located; the various funds of special purpose governments that have the right to tax the same property, such as one or more independent school districts or a hospital district; and perhaps the state in which the town is located.

Recording the Property Tax Levy

The gross property tax levies for each fund of the Town of Brighton, and for each other general purpose and special purpose government, would be aggregated and divided by the assessed valuation of property within the geographical limits of that government, in order to determine the *tax rate* applicable to property within each jurisdiction. If the tax rate is at the maximum allowed by law or is fixed by law, then the levy is calculated as the allowable tax rate times the assessed valuation of taxable property. The assessed valuation is first divided by $100 or $1,000, depending on how the tax rate is expressed.

In many states, a county official prepares bills for all taxes levied on property within the county; another county official acts as collector of all property taxes levied for the county and all governments within the county. Although the billing and collecting functions may be centralized, the taxes levied for each fund must be recorded as an asset of that fund. If the accounts are to be kept in conformity with generally accepted accounting principles, the portion of the taxes expected to be collectible (0.96 of the total levy, in this example) must be recorded as revenues of that fund, and the portion expected to be uncollectible (0.04 of the total levy), must be recorded in a "contra-asset" account, as illustrated by Entries 9a and 9b.

		General Ledger		Subsidiary Ledger	
		Debits	**Credits**	**Debits**	**Credits**
	General Fund:				
9a.	Taxes Receivable—Current....................	2,708,333			
	Allowance for Uncollectible Current Taxes...............................		108,333		
	Revenues..		2,600,000		
	Revenues Ledger:				
	Property Taxes..................................				2,600,000
	Governmental Activities:				
9b.	Taxes Receivable—Current....................	2,708,333			
	Allowance for Uncollectible Current Taxes...............................		108,333		
	General Revenues—Property Taxes....		2,600,000		

As Entry 9a shows, in the General Fund when the general ledger control account, Revenues, is credited, an entry must also be made in the Revenues Subsidiary Ledger. Taxes Receivable—Current is also a control account, just as is the Accounts Receivable account of a business entity; each is supported by a subsidiary ledger that shows how much is owed by each taxpayer or customer. Ordinarily, the subsidiary ledger supporting the real property taxes receivable control is organized by parcels of property according to their legal descriptions; unpaid taxes are liens against the property regardless of changes in ownership. Because of its conceptual similarity to accounting for business receivables, taxes receivable subsidiary ledger accounting is not illustrated in this text.

Property tax revenue is an example of a **nonexchange revenue**—one in which the government receives value without directly giving equal value in exchange. More specifically, it is classified under GASB standards as an **imposed nonexchange revenue.** For imposed nonexchange revenues, a receivable should be debited when there is an enforceable claim, as in the case of a property tax levy, and a revenue should be credited in the year for which the tax was levied. In governmental funds, recall that revenue is recognized when measurable and available. For property taxes, GASB specifies that available means collected within the current period or within 60 days of year end.[2] The $2,600,000 credit to Revenues in Entry 8a indicates that the Town of Brighton expects to collect that amount during 2017 or within 60 days after the end of fiscal year 2017. If the town expected to collect a portion of the $2,600,000 later than 60 days after fiscal year-end, it should credit that portion to Deferred Inflow of Resources—Property Taxes and reclassify it to Revenues in the period in which the revenues are collected. Note, however, that even if a portion of revenues is deferred in the General Fund because of the availability criterion, the full $2,600,000 is recognized as General Revenues—Property Taxes in the governmental activities journal at the government-wide level. This is so because availability to finance current expenditures is not a revenue recognition criterion under the accrual basis used at the government-wide level.

Collection of Current Taxes

Collections of property taxes levied in 2017 for the General Fund of the Town of Brighton amount to $2,042,033. Since the revenue was recognized at the time of the levy (see Entry 9a), the following entry is made in both the General Fund and governmental activities journals.

		General Ledger		Subsidiary Ledger	
		Debits	***Credits***	***Debits***	***Credits***
	General Fund and Governmental Activities:				
10.	Cash	2,042,033			
	Taxes Receivable—Current		2,042,033		

Reclassification of Current Property Taxes. Assuming that all property taxes levied by the Town of Brighton in 2017 were legally due before the end of the year, any balance of current taxes receivable at year-end is properly classified as **delinquent taxes** rather than current. The related allowance for estimated uncollectible taxes should also

[2] GASB *Codification,* Sec. P70.104.

be reclassified as contra to the Taxes Receivable—Delinquent account. The entry to accomplish the reclassification, using amounts assumed to exist in the accounts at year-end, is:[3]

		General Ledger		Subsidiary Ledger	
		Debits	**Credits**	**Debits**	**Credits**
	General Fund and Governmental Activities:				
11.	Taxes Receivable—Delinquent	666,300			
	Allowance for Uncollectible Current Taxes	108,333			
	Taxes Receivable—Current		666,300		
	Allowance for Uncollectible Delinquent Taxes		108,333		

Accrual of Interest and Penalties on Delinquent Taxes. Delinquent taxes are subject to interest and penalties as discussed previously. If the amount of interest and penalties earned/imposed in 2017 by the General Fund of the Town of Brighton is $13,320, and it is expected that only $10,800 of that amount can be collected, the following entries are necessary:

	General Fund:				
12a.	Interest and Penalties Receivable on Taxes	13,320			
	Allowance for Uncollectible Interest and Penalties		2,520		
	Revenues		10,800		
	Revenues Ledger:				
	Interest and Penalties on Delinquent Taxes				10,800
	Governmental Activities:				
12b.	Interest and Penalties Receivable on Taxes	13,320			
	Allowance for Uncollectible Interest and Penalties		2,520		
	General Revenues—Interest and Penalties on Delinquent Taxes		10,800		

Collection of Delinquent Taxes[4]

Delinquent taxes are subject to interest and penalties that must be paid at the time the tax bill is paid. It is possible for a government to record the amount of penalties at the

[3] If an entry was not made at the time of the tax levy to defer recognition of revenue for property taxes that are estimated to be collected after the first 60 days of the following year, a year-end adjusting entry will be needed to record the deferral. Deferral of revenue recognition is unnecessary at the government-wide level because availability for spending is not a criterion for recognizing revenues under the accrual basis of accounting.

[4] Some governments choose to sell the collection rights to unpaid property taxes in tax lien public auctions. Buyers pay the delinquent tax, interest to the date of the purchase, and an administrative fee in return for the right to collect the delinquent tax payment and interest. With such sales, the government would no longer maintain receivable balances for the delinquent taxes or interest.

time the taxes become delinquent. Interest may be computed and recorded periodically, particularly at the end of a fiscal period. It must also be computed and recorded for the period from the date of last recording to the date when a taxpayer pays delinquent taxes. Assume that taxpayers of the Town of Brighton have paid delinquent taxes totaling \$440,000, on which interest and penalties of \$6,800 had been recorded as receivable at the end of 2016. Also, assume that additional interest of \$400 was paid for the period from the first day of 2017 to the dates on which the delinquent taxes were paid. Since it is common for the cashier receiving the collections to be permitted to originate source documents that result in credits only to Taxes Receivable—Current, Taxes Receivable—Delinquent, or Interest and Penalties Receivable on Taxes, the \$400 interest earned in 2017 should be recorded in a separate entry, as shown in Entries 13a and b.

		General Ledger		Subsidiary Ledger	
		Debits	**Credits**	**Debits**	**Credits**
	General Fund:				
13a.	Interest and Penalties Receivable on Taxes	400			
	Revenues		400		
	Revenues Ledger:				
	Interest and Penalties on Delinquent Taxes				400

The corresponding entry at the government-wide level is:

		Debits	Credits
	Governmental Activities:		
13b.	Interest and Penalties Receivable on Taxes	400	
	General Revenues—Interest and Penalties on Delinquent Taxes		400

Collection of the delinquent taxes as well as interest and penalties thereon is summarized in Entry 14, which is the entry that should be made in both the General Fund and governmental activities journals. Note that these collections during 2017 are from the delinquent taxes receivable reported on the 2016 General Fund balance sheet and the Governmental Activities column of the government-wide statement of net position (see Illustration 4–1).

		Debits	Credits
	General Fund and Governmental Activities:		
14.	Cash	447,200	
	Taxes Receivable—Delinquent		440,000
	Interest and Penalties Receivable on Taxes		7,200

Write-off of Uncollectible Delinquent Taxes. Just as officers of profit-seeking entities should review aged schedules of receivables periodically to determine the adequacy of allowance accounts and authorize the write-off of items judged uncollectible, so should officers of a government review aged trial balances of taxes receivable and other receivables. Although the levy of property taxes creates a lien against the underlying property in the amount of the tax, accumulated taxes may exceed the market value of the property, or, in the case of personal property, the property may have been removed from the jurisdiction of the government. When delinquent taxes are deemed uncollectible, the related interest and penalties must also be written off. If the treasurer of the Town of Brighton receives approval to write off delinquent taxes totaling $26,300 and related interest and penalties of $1,315, the entry for both the General Fund and governmental activities would be:

		General Ledger		Subsidiary Ledger	
		Debits	*Credits*	*Debits*	*Credits*
	General Fund and Governmental Activities:				
15.	Allowance for Uncollectible Delinquent Taxes	26,300			
	Allowance for Uncollectible Interest and Penalties	1,315			
	Taxes Receivable—Delinquent		26,300		
	Interest and Penalties Receivable on Taxes		1,315		

When delinquent taxes are written off, the tax bills are retained in the files in case it becomes possible to collect the amounts in the future. If collections of written-off taxes are made, it is highly desirable to return the tax bills to general ledger control by making an entry that is the reverse of the write-off entry, so that the procedures described in connection with Entries 13 and 14 can be followed.

Other Revenues

Revenues from sources such as sales taxes, licenses and permits, fines and forfeits, charges for services, and certain other sources are often not measurable until received in cash. However, under the modified accrual basis of accounting, if such revenues are measurable in advance of collection and are available for current period expenditure, they should be accrued by recording a debit to a receivable and a credit to Revenues. During fiscal year 2017, the Town of Brighton has collected revenues in cash from the sources shown in Entry 16a.

	General Fund:				
16a.	Cash	365,000			
	Revenues		365,000		
	Revenues Ledger:				
	Sales Taxes				105,800
	Licenses and Permits				100,000
	Fines and Forfeits				151,000
	Charges for Services				7,000
	Miscellaneous Revenues				1,200

Of the preceding revenues, sales taxes are reported as *general revenues* at the government-wide level; licenses and permits, fines and forfeits, and charges for services are appropriately recorded as *program revenues*. Licenses and permits are attributed to the general government function. Fines and forfeits were assessed by the Public Safety function in the amount of $91,000 and by the Public Works function in the amount of $60,000. Charges for services were received from customers of the Culture and Recreation function. Miscellaneous revenues cannot be identified with a specific function and thus are recorded as *general revenues* at the government-wide level. Based on this information the entry that should be made in the journal for governmental activities is shown in Entry 16b.

		General Ledger		Subsidiary Ledger	
		Debits	**Credits**	**Debits**	**Credits**
	Governmental Activities:				
16b.	Cash	365,000			
	Program Revenues—General Government—Charges for Services		100,000		
	Program Revenues—Public Safety—Charges for Services		91,000		
	Program Revenues—Public Works—Charges for Services		60,000		
	Program Revenues—Culture and Recreation—Charges for Services		7,000		
	General Revenues—Sales Taxes		105,800		
	General Revenues—Miscellaneous		1,200		

Readers may be confused by classifying Fines and Forfeits as Charges for Services since generally we associate Charges for Services with **exchange** or **exchange-like transactions** in which value is given for value received (see the appendix to this chapter). GASB considered this issue and decided that Charges for Services does not preclude a transaction such as Fines and Forfeits. Furthermore, Fines and Forfeits is not appropriately classified as either Operating Grants and Contributions or Capital Grants and Contributions (see program revenue classifications in Illustration A2–2 and Illustration 3–1). Thus, in substance, the GASB decided to classify Fines and Forfeits as Charges for Services to avoid the need to add a fourth category of program revenues in the government-wide statement of activities.[5]

Tax Anticipation Notes

In the December 31, 2017, Statement of Net Position and General Fund Balance Sheet of the Town of Brighton, two items, Vouchers Payable and Due to Federal Government, are current liabilities. Assuming there was a need to pay these in full within 30 days after the date of the balance sheet, the town treasurer would need to do some cash forecasting because the balance of Cash in the General Fund is not large enough to pay the $410,000 debt. In addition to this immediate problem, the treasurer may face the problem that cash disbursements during a fiscal year tend to be approximately level month by month, whereas cash receipts from major revenue sources are concentrated in just a few months. For example, property tax collections may be concentrated in two separate months, such as May and November, when the installments are due. Receipts from the state or federal government of revenues collected by superior

[5] GASB, *Codification*, Sec. 2200. 137.

ILLUSTRATION 4–2 Determination of Required Tax Anticipation Note Financing, January 1 through March 31, 2017

Estimated Expenditure Requirements:		
Budgeted expenditures (25% of $4,180,000)	$1,045,000	
Current liabilities payable	410,000	$1,455,000
Estimated Resources Available:		
Cash available at January 1, 2017	190,000	
Collections of delinquent taxes, interest, and penalties	425,000	
Collection of budgeted FY 2017 revenues	140,000	755,000
Estimated Amount of Required Tax Anticipation Note Financing		$ 700,000

jurisdictions for distribution to a local government are also often concentrated in one or two months of the year.

Forecasting Amount of Tax Anticipation Borrowing

Knowing cash receipt and disbursement patterns, the treasurer of the Town of Brighton may, for example, forecast the need to disburse approximately one-fourth of the budgeted appropriations, or $1,045,000 (one-fourth of $4,180,000), during the first three months of fiscal year 2017, before major items of revenue are received. This amount plus current liabilities at the beginning of the year, $410,000, equals $1,455,000 expected cash disbursements in the period for which the forecast is made. The town's experience suggests that a conservative forecast of collections of delinquent taxes and interest and penalties thereon during the forecast period will amount to $425,000. Furthermore, assume the treasurer's review of the items in the Estimated Revenues budget indicates that at least $140,000 will be collected in the forecast period. Therefore, total cash available to meet the estimated $1,455,000 of disbursements is $755,000 ($190,000 cash as of the beginning of the period, plus the $425,000 and $140,000 items just described), leaving a deficiency of $700,000 to be met by borrowing. Determination of the $700,000 required tax anticipation note financing is summarized in Illustration 4–2.

The taxing power of the government is ample security for short-term debt; banks customarily meet the working capital needs of a government by accepting a **tax anticipation note** from the government. Additional discussion of cash budgeting is provided in Chapter 12. If the amount of $700,000 is borrowed at this time, the necessary entries in both the General Fund and governmental activities are:

		General Ledger		Subsidiary Ledger	
		Debits	***Credits***	***Debits***	***Credits***
	General Fund and Governmental Activities:				
17.	Cash	700,000			
	Tax Anticipation Notes Payable		700,000		

Repayment of Tax Anticipation Notes

As tax collections begin to exceed disbursements, it becomes possible for the Town of Brighton to repay the local bank for the money borrowed on tax anticipation notes. Just as borrowing the money did not involve the recognition of an other financing source, the repayment of the principal extinguishes the liability of the General Fund and is not an expenditure. Payment of interest, however, must be recognized as the expenditure of an appropriation because it reduces the fund balance of the fund. Assuming the interest is $13,500, and the amount is properly chargeable to Miscellaneous appropriations, the entry is:

		General Ledger		Subsidiary Ledger	
		Debits	*Credits*	*Debits*	*Credits*
	General Fund:				
18a.	Tax Anticipation Notes Payable	700,000			
	Expenditures—2017	13,500			
	Cash		713,500		
	Expenditures Ledger:				
	Miscellaneous			13,500	

Procedures of some governments would require the interest expenditures to have been recorded as an encumbrance against Miscellaneous appropriations at the time the notes were issued, and the liability for the principal and interest to have been vouchered before payment. Even if these procedures were followed by the Town of Brighton, the net result of all entries is achieved by Entry 18a.

A similar entry, shown as Entry 18b, is made at the government-wide level except that an expense rather than expenditure is recorded for the interest charged on the note. This expense is deemed to be a direct expense of the General Government function.

	Governmental Activities:				
18b.	Tax Anticipation Notes Payable	700,000			
	Expenses—General Government	13,500			
	Cash		713,500		

SPECIAL TOPICS

This section of the chapter presents several special topics that result in additional journal entries, either in the General Fund or governmental activities journals, or both. Many additional transactions are assumed to have occurred during 2017, the recording of which would have been redundant of the transactions already illustrated.

Correction of Errors

No problems arise in the collection of current taxes if they are collected as billed; the collections are debited to Cash and credited to Taxes Receivable—Current. Sometimes, even in a well-designed and well-operated system, errors occur and must be corrected. If, for example, the assessed valuation of a parcel of property were legally reduced, but the tax bill erroneously issued at the higher valuation, the following correcting entry would be made when the error was discovered, assuming the corrected bill to be $364 smaller than the original bill. (The error also caused a slight overstatement of the credit to Allowance for Uncollectible Current Taxes in Entry 9, but the error in that account is not considered material and, for that reason, does not require correction.)

		General Ledger		Subsidiary Ledger	
		Debits	Credits	Debits	Credits
	General Fund:				
19.	Revenues	364			
	Taxes Receivable—Current		364		
	Revenues Ledger:				
	Property Taxes			364	

An entry similar to Entry 19 would also be made at the government-wide level to correct the overstatement of General Revenues—Property Taxes and Taxes Receivable—Current.

An audit may disclose errors in the recording of expenditures during the current year or during a prior year. If the error occurred during the current year, the Expenditures account and the proper Expenditures subsidiary account should be debited or credited as needed to correct the error. If it occurred in a prior year, however, the Expenditures account in error would have been closed to a fund balance account at the end of the prior year, so the correcting entry should be made to the appropriate fund balance account. Technically, overpayment errors of prior periods should also result in corrections to fund balance accounts. However, as a practical matter, collections from suppliers of prior years' overpayments may be budgeted as Miscellaneous Revenues and recorded as credits to the Revenues account, especially if the amount involved is minor.

Receipt of Goods Ordered in Prior Year

Although not yet discussed in this chapter, purchase orders and other commitment documents issued in 2016 and not filled or canceled by the end of that year totaled \$127,000. Since the Town of Brighton has a policy to honor all outstanding encumbrances, including those still outstanding at year-end, the Encumbrances account was not closed at the end of 2016. When the goods on order at the end of fiscal year 2016 are received in 2017, their actual cost is considered an expenditure of the 2016 appropriations to the extent of the amount encumbered in 2016; any additional amount must be charged to the 2017 appropriations.[6] When goods or services ordered in 2016 are received in 2017, it is convenient to debit the Expenditures—2016 account when the liability account is credited and eliminate the encumbrance in the normal manner. At the end of 2017, the Expenditures—2016 account is closed to fund balance accounts, along with Expenditures—2017 and all other operating statement accounts.

Assuming that all goods and services for which encumbrances were outstanding at the end of 2016 were received in 2017 at a total invoice cost of \$127,250, Entries 20a

[6] State laws vary considerably regarding the treatment of appropriations and encumbrances at year-end. In some states, appropriations do not lapse at year-end. In many others, appropriations lapse and goods encumbered at year-end require a new appropriation in the next year's budget or must be charged to the next year's normal appropriation. The authors recommend that the Encumbrances and Encumbrances Outstanding accounts remain open if the government is required or intends to honor the encumbered purchase orders or contracts in the next period. If the government must approve a new appropriation in the following year for encumbered amounts, then Encumbrances and Encumbrances Outstanding should be closed at year-end and reestablished at the beginning of the next year when the new appropriation has been approved.

and 20b are necessary in the General Fund, and Entry 20c is made in the governmental activities journal. Notice that only the estimated amount, $127,000, is charged to Expenditures—2016 since this was the amount of the encumbrance against the 2016 appropriation; the difference between the amount encumbered in 2016 and the total cost of the goods must be charged against the 2017 appropriation for Culture and Recreation.

		General Ledger		Subsidiary Ledger	
		Debits	**Credits**	**Debits**	**Credits**
	General Fund:				
20a.	Encumbrances Outstanding—2016	127,000			
	Encumbrances—2016		127,000		
	Encumbrances Ledger:				
	Culture and Recreation—2016				127,000
20b.	Expenditures—2016	127,000			
	Expenditures—2017	250			
	Vouchers Payable		127,250		
	Expenditures Ledger:				
	Culture and Recreation—2016			127,000	
	Culture and Recreation—2017			250	
	Governmental Activities:				
20c.	Expenses—Culture and Recreation	127,250			
	Vouchers Payable		127,250		

Revision of the General Fund Budget

Comparisons of budgeted and actual revenues, by sources, comparisons of departmental or program appropriations with expenditures and encumbrances, and interpretation of information that was not available at the time the budgets were originally adopted could indicate the need to legally amend the budget during the fiscal year. For example, the schedule of budgeted and actual revenues for the three months ended March 31, 2017 (Appendix B, Illustration B4–1), shows that more than 70 percent of the revenues budgeted for the General Fund of the Town of Brighton have already been realized because revenue from property taxes was accrued when billed, whereas revenues from all other sources were recognized when collected during the three-month period for which entries are illustrated. Consequently, administrators of the town must review the information shown in Illustration B4–1 and determine whether the budget appears realistic or whether changes should be made in light of current information about local economic conditions; possible changes in state or federal laws relating to grants, entitlements, or shared revenues; or other changes relating to license and permit fees, fines, forfeits, and charges for services. Similarly, revenue collection procedures and revenue recognition policies should be reviewed to determine whether changes should be made in the remaining months of the year. Assume that the Town of Brighton's General Fund revenues budget for 2017 has been reviewed as described and that the budget is legally amended to reflect that revenues from Charges for Services are expected to be $15,000 more than originally budgeted. Entry 21 records the amendment of the Revenues budget, as well as the amendment of the appropriations budget, as will be discussed following Entry 21.

		General Ledger		Subsidiary Ledger	
		Debits	**Credits**	**Debits**	**Credits**
	General Fund:				
21.	Estimated Revenues	15,000			
	Budgetary Fund Balance	15,000			
	Appropriations		30,000		
	Estimated Revenues Ledger:				
	Charges for Services			15,000	
	Appropriations Ledger:				
	Public Works			50,000	
	Public Safety				80,000

Information shown in Appendix B, Illustration B4–2 should be reviewed by administrators of the Town of Brighton to determine whether the appropriations legally approved for FY 2017 appear realistic in light of expenditures incurred in the first three months of 2017 and encumbrances outstanding on March 31 of that year. Illustration B4–2 shows that total cumulative expenditures and outstanding encumbrances approximate 30 percent of the total appropriations for 2017, which seems reasonable for one quarter of the fiscal year. By function, however, cumulative expenditures and outstanding encumbrances range from 3 percent of the Miscellaneous appropriation to almost 48 percent of the Public Safety appropriation. Assume that the Town of Brighton's General Fund appropriations have been reviewed and are legally amended to reflect a $50,000 decrease in the appropriation for Public Works and an $80,000 increase in the appropriation for Public Safety. Entry 21 reflects the legal amendment of appropriations, as well as the amendment of the revenues budget. Note the net increase in Appropriations of $30,000 is more than the net increase in Estimated Revenues of $15,000, requiring a decrease in Budgetary Fund Balance.

Comparisons of budget and actual should be made periodically during each fiscal year. In the Town of Brighton case, it is assumed that comparisons subsequent to the ones illustrated disclosed no further need to amend either the revenues budget or the appropriations budget.

Exchange Transactions with Proprietary Funds

Governments often enter into internal exchange transactions, which are reciprocal exchange transactions that occur internally between funds and activities rather than between the government and an external entity or person. The funds that participate in internal exchange transactions should recognize revenues and expenditures or expenses, as appropriate, within each respective fund as if the transaction involved the fund and an external entity. At the government-wide level, however, if the interfund transaction occurs between two governmental funds (or between a governmental fund and an internal service fund) or between two enterprise funds, then neither the Governmental Activities column nor the Business-type Activities column is affected at the government-wide level. This concept will be illustrated and further discussed later in the chapter.

Supplies Purchased from an Internal Service Fund

The Town of Brighton maintains an internal service fund to facilitate the purchase and distribution of commonly used supply items throughout town departments. (The internal service fund will be more closely examined in Chapter 7.) Interdepartmental requisitions for supplies with an estimated cost of $247,360 were submitted to the Town of Brighton's Supplies Fund. Assuming that the supplies were encumbered when ordered, Entry 22 below illustrates the journal entry required to record the receipt of the supplies from the internal service fund (Supplies Fund) at an actual cost of $249,750.

		General Ledger		Subsidiary Ledger	
		Debits	**Credits**	**Debits**	**Credits**
	General Fund:				
22.	Encumbrances Outstanding—2017	247,360			
	Encumbrances—2017		247,360		
	Encumbrances Ledger:				
	General Government				9,950
	Public Safety				72,000
	Public Works				145,300
	Culture and Recreation				15,585
	Health and Welfare				4,075
	Miscellaneous				450
22a.	Expenditures—2017	249,750			
	Due to Other Funds		249,750		
	Expenditures Ledger:				
	General Government			10,000	
	Public Safety			72,000	
	Public Works			145,100	
	Culture and Recreation			18,200	
	Health and Welfare			4,000	
	Miscellaneous			450	

Although the Town of Brighton records the purchase of supplies from the Supplies Fund at the amount billed, the expenses recorded in the governmental activities accounts at the government-wide level should be the cost of the goods to the Supplies Fund. In other words, the cost to the government as a whole is what the internal service fund paid for the goods to external parties and does not include the markup charged to departments by the Supplies Fund. As shown in Chapter 7, Entries 4a and b, the cost of the $249,750 of supplies issued to the General Fund was $185,000, so the markup is 35 percent on cost. Accordingly, the total direct expenses recorded at the government-wide level (see Entry 22b) is the $185,000 cost of supplies purchased from the Supplies Fund, distributed to functions based on assumed purchase patterns. Note that the account credited at the government-wide level for the supplies purchased from the Supplies Fund is Inventory of Supplies since $185,000 represents supplies issued that are no longer in the Supplies Fund's inventory and thus are no longer in inventory from a government-wide perspective, assuming that substantially all supplies purchased by General Fund departments will be consumed during the year. (Amounts of year-end inventory in the General Fund are considered immaterial and should be ignored.) Likewise, the government-wide cash balance is not affected by transactions between the governmental and internal service funds.

		General Ledger		Subsidiary Ledger	
		Debits	**Credits**	**Debits**	**Credits**
	Governmental Activities:				
22b.	Expenses—General Government	9,885			
	Expenses—Public Safety	54,889			
	Expenses—Public Works	105,522			
	Expenses—Culture and Recreation	17,741			
	Expenses—Health and Welfare	3,037			
	Inventory of Supplies		185,000		

When the liability is later paid, the entry in the General Fund will be as follows:

	General Fund:				
23.	Due to Other Funds.	249,750			
	Cash		249,750		

Services Provided by an Enterprise Fund

The Town of Brighton operates a water utility fund, which provides fire hydrants and water service for fire protection at a flat annual charge. (The Water Utility Fund will be more closely examined in Chapter 7.) Fire protection is logically budgeted as an activity of the Fire Department, a General Fund department. Assuming the amount charged by the water utility to the General Fund for hydrants and water service is $30,000, and the fire department budget is a part of the Public Safety category in the Town of Brighton example, the General Fund should record its liability as shown in entry 24a below. (The encumbrance entries have been omitted for brevity.)

	General Fund:				
24a.	Expenditures—2017	30,000			
	Due to Other Funds		30,000		
	Expenditures Ledger:				
	Public Safety			30,000	

The corresponding entry to record the inter-activities transaction (between the governmental activities and business-type activities) at the government-wide level is given as Entry 24b. Recall that since receivables/payables between governmental and business-type activities are reported in different columns on the government-wide statement of net position, year-end interfund receivable/payable balances will appear in the line item **internal balances** within their respective columns. (The year-end reclassification will be illustrated in Chapter 9.) The balances will appear as receivables and payables within the fund financial statements.

	Governmental Activities:				
24b.	Expenses—Public Works	30,000			
	Internal Balances		30,000		

Governmental utility property is not assessed for property tax purposes, but it is common for governmental utilities to make an annual "payment in lieu of taxes (PILOT)" contribution to the General Fund in recognition of the fact the utility does receive police and fire protection and other services. In fact, an amount in lieu of taxes is often billed to the utility's customers; the aggregate amount collected is simply passed on to the General Fund.

If the water utility of the Town of Brighton pays $25,000 to the General Fund in lieu of taxes for an amount that fairly represents the value of services received from the general government,[7] the required journal entries for the General Fund and governmental activities are:

		General Ledger		Subsidiary Ledger	
		Debits	***Credits***	***Debits***	***Credits***
	General Fund:				
25a.	Due from Other Funds	25,000			
	Revenues		25,000		
	Revenues Ledger:				
	Charges for Services				25,000
	Governmental Activities:				
25b.	Internal Balances	25,000			
	Program Revenues—General Government—Charges for Services		25,000		

Internal exchange transactions of the nature illustrated in Entries 23 through 25 affect both the fund and government-wide financial statements. The GASB refers to these transactions as *interfund services provided and used.* The funds that participate in internal exchange transactions should recognize revenues and expenditures or expenses, as appropriate, as if the transaction involved each fund and an external entity. Other types of internal transactions between funds and between governmental and business-type activities are discussed in a later section of this chapter.

Adjusting Entries

Inventories of Supplies

Governments may account for their supplies within the General Fund or other governmental funds using either the *purchases method* or the *consumption method.* Using the **purchases method,** expenditures for supplies equals the total cost of supplies purchased during the year, even if the amount of supplies consumed is less than or greater than the amount purchased. Thus, the purchases method is consistent with the modified accrual basis of accounting used by the General Fund and other governmental funds. The purchases method is generally associated with a periodic inventory system, so the balance of the Inventory of Supplies account is increased or decreased as necessary at year-end to agree with the valuation based on a physical count. In addition, the balance of an account titled Fund Balance—Nonspendable—Inventory of Supplies is increased or decreased by the same amount as the inventory account to indicate that the inventory reported on the balance sheet is not available for spending.

[7] If the amount billed to the government-owned utility is based on a calculation of the property taxes an equivalent investor-owed utility would pay, or some portion thereof, rather than the value of services provided and received, then the transaction is not treated as an exchange transaction. In that case, the transaction is reported as an interfund transfer and neither expenses nor revenues are reported. GASB *Codification*, Sec. 1800.102.a(2).

The **consumption method** is consistent with the accrual basis of accounting, as resources (i.e., supplies) consumed in providing services is the essence of an expense. Thus, GASB standards require the use of the consumption method for government-wide and proprietary fund reporting. Using this method, the General Fund recognizes expenditures equal to the amount of supplies *consumed* during the year rather than the amount purchased. Accordingly, budgetary appropriations for supplies are based on estimated consumption rather than estimated purchases.

To illustrate and contrast the purchases and consumption methods, assume the following information for supplies purchases and usage of a certain city for its 2017 fiscal year.

Balance of inventory, January 1, 2017	$ 55,000
Purchases during 2017	260,000
Supplies available for use	315,000
Less: Balance of inventory, December 31, 2017	65,000
Supplies consumed during 2017	$250,000

Purchases Method

Under the purchases method, the summary entry in the General Fund to record supplies purchased during the year, assuming all supplies are purchased from external vendors and all invoices have been paid, is (encumbrance entries and subsidiary detail are omitted for simplicity):

	General Ledger		Subsidiary Ledger	
	Debits	**Credits**	**Debits**	**Credits**
General Fund:				
Expenditures	260,000			
Cash		260,000		

At year-end, a physical inventory revealed that $65,000 of inventory remained on hand. The entry to record the $10,000 increase in inventory from the beginning balance and the corresponding classification of fund balance is given as:

General Fund:				
Inventory of Supplies	10,000			
Fund Balance—Nonspendable—Inventory of Supplies		10,000		

Consumption Method

If the city uses a *perpetual inventory system* and reports inventories under the consumption method in both the General Fund and governmental activities, the following entries are required. To record purchases of supplies for the year, assuming the same data as before, the journal entry is (encumbrance entries and subsidiary detail are omitted for simplicity):

General Fund and Governmental Activities:				
Inventory of Supplies	260,000			
Cash		260,000		

During the 2017 fiscal year, the General Fund will debit Expenditures and credit Inventory of Supplies each time supplies are issued for consumption. In total, supplies costing $250,000 were consumed during the year. The journal entry to summarize consumption of supplies for the year (omitting encumbrance and subsidiary detail entries) is given as:

	General Ledger		Subsidiary Ledger	
	Debits	***Credits***	***Debits***	***Credits***
General Fund:				
Expenditures	250,000			
Inventory of Supplies		250,000		

At year-end, it is not necessary to adjust the balances of the Expenditures and Inventory of Supplies accounts. However, an adjusting entry is required to reclassify fund balance for the $10,000 increase in inventory of supplies during the year. The adjusting entry is:

General Fund:				
Fund Balance—Unassigned	10,000			
Fund Balance—Nonspendable—Inventory of Supplies		10,000		

At the government-wide level, *Expenses* will be debited rather than Expenditures and Inventory of Supplies will be credited each time supplies are issued for consumption. The required summary entry to record supplies consumed during the year is:

Governmental Activities:				
Expenses (Function or program detail omitted)	250,000			
Inventory of Supplies		250,000		

No year-end adjusting entry is necessary at the government-wide level because reclassification of fund balance to show the increase in nonspendable inventory applies only at the governmental fund level where the focus is on current financial resources.

In these examples, the entries in the General Fund are somewhat more complex because of the need to increase or decrease the balance of the Fund Balance—Nonspendable—Inventory of Supplies account at the fund level. One can expect that the requirement to report inventories using the consumption method at the government-wide level may lead to increased use of this method for the General Fund as well.

Pre-Closing Trial Balance

Assume that all illustrated journal entries for the transactions and events pertaining to the Town of Brighton's 2017 fiscal year have been posted to the general and subsidiary ledgers. In addition, numerous other transactions and events were journalized and posted during the year but were not shown in this chapter because they were similar to those that were illustrated. As a result of all transactions and events recorded for the year (both those that were illustrated and those that were not), the balances of all balance sheet, operating statement, and budgetary accounts before closing entries are presented in the following trial balance:

TOWN OF BRIGHTON
General Fund
Pre-Closing Trial Balance
As of December 31, 2017

	Debits	*Credits*
Cash	$ 145,800	
Taxes Receivable—Delinquent	701,813	
Allowance for Uncollectible Delinquent Taxes		$ 123,513
Interest and Penalties Receivable on Taxes	13,191	
Allowance for Uncollectible Interest and Taxes		3,091
Due from Other Funds	25,000	
Vouchers Payable		405,800
Due to Federal Government		126,520
Due to State Government		39,740
Due to Other Funds		30,000
Estimated Revenues	4,001,000	
Revenues		4,015,000
Appropriations		4,210,000
Expenditures—2016	127,000	
Expenditures—2017	4,130,760	
Encumbrances—2017	70,240	
Encumbrances Outstanding—2017		70,240
Budgetary Fund Balance	209,000	
Fund Balance—Unassigned		399,900
	$9,423,804	$9,423,804

Closing Entries

At fiscal year-end, all temporary accounts, both budgetary and operating, must be closed to the appropriate fund balance account. Budgetary accounts are closed by simply reversing the original budgetary entry (or entries) made at the beginning of the fiscal year, as well as any amended budget entries made during the year. As discussed earlier in the chapter, the Encumbrances account need not be closed to Encumbrances Outstanding at year-end if the government is required or intends to honor the encumbrances outstanding at year-end. Encumbrance details are not reported in the financial statements but rather are disclosed in the notes to the financial statements. An exception occurs if outstanding encumbrances apply to restricted, committed, or assigned resources. In that case, the encumbered amount may be reported in the balance sheet as part of that classification of fund balance (restricted, committed, or assigned, as applicable). Even then, the word *encumbrance* never appears on the balance sheet.

Closing the operating accounts increases the balance of the general ledger Fund Balance—Unassigned account by the excess of revenues and other financial resources over expenditures and other financing uses. If there is an operating deficit (revenues and other financing sources are less than expenditures and other financing uses), then fund balance is decreased. Entries 25a and b illustrate the entries needed to close the budgetary and operating accounts, using account balances shown in the Pre-Closing Trial Balance.

		General Ledger		Subsidiary Ledger	
		Debits	*Credits*	*Debits*	*Credits*
	General Fund:				
25a.	Appropriations	4,210,000			
	Estimated Revenues		4,001,000		
	Budgetary Fund Balance		209,000		
25b.	Revenues	4,015,000			
	Fund Balance—Unassigned	242,760			
	Expenditures—2017		4,130,760		
	Expenditures—2016		127,000		

Entries 25a and b illustrate closing entries for the operating and budgetary *control* accounts of the General Fund but not for the detailed subsidiary ledger accounts.

In a manual accounting system, such as that illustrated in this chapter, closing the subsidiary ledger accounts is generally unnecessary because new subsidiary ledger accounts are prepared for each fiscal year. In a computerized accounting system, closing entries may be required for detail operating and budgetary accounts, depending on the account structure employed.

Reclassification of Fund Balances

The Town of Brighton has only a few revenue sources that have constraints placed on the purposes for which they can be expended. As allowed by GASB standards, the town has established a policy of spending its constrained resources before spending unconstrained resources for those purposes. Thus, restricted, then committed, and finally assigned resources are spent in that order.[8] Under this policy, constrained resources are generally consumed before the end of the year, leaving only a few amounts that require reclassification of fund balances at year-end. The town determines those amounts at year-end by inspecting its accounting and administrative records and making the appropriate entries to reclassify fund balances.[9] The town has determined that only two constrained revenues remain unspent at the end of fiscal 2017, $17,500 of sales taxes *committed* for constructing a hiking trail in one of the town parks and $23,700 of General Fund resources that the town manager has *assigned* for acquisition and installation of downtown security cameras. Journal entry 26 shows the required reclassification of fund balances in the General Fund. (*Note*: The required entry in the governmental activities journal at the government-wide level for the restricted net position is shown in Chapter 9.)

	General Fund:				
26.	Fund Balance—Unassigned	41,200			
	Fund Balance—Committed—Culture and Recreation		17,500		
	Fund Balance—Assigned—Public Safety		23,700		

[8] GASB *Codification*, Sec.1800.178.

[9] Governments that receive constrained revenues from multiple sources may find it necessary to incorporate detail accounts in their general and subsidiary ledgers to track these revenues and specific expenditures from these sources during the year. The Town of Brighton has not found it necessary to employ such real-time tracking.

General Fund Financial Statements

As discussed in earlier chapters, the General Fund of every government is considered a *major fund*. Accordingly, all governmental fund financial statements will include a separate column for the General Fund financial information, as well as for all other major governmental funds, as shown in Illustrations A2–3 and A2–5 for the City and County of Denver and Illustrations 9–5 and 9–6 for the hypothetical Town of Brighton. For internal management purposes, a government may find it useful to prepare additional financial statements for the General Fund that are more detailed than the governmental fund statements. Such financial statements prepared for the Town of Brighton's General Fund are shown in Illustrations 4–3 and 4–4.

The Town of Brighton's General Fund balance sheet includes two major sections, *Assets* and *Liabilities and Fund Balances*. The Town of Brighton has opted to net the $25,000 receivable from the Water Utility Fund (see Entry 24a) against the $30,000 payable to that fund (see Entry 23a), so that only the $5,000 net amount payable to the Water Utility Fund is reported as *Due to other funds* in the Liabilities section of the balance sheet in Illustration 4–3. It is not acceptable, however, to offset receivables or payables from one fund against those of a different fund.

A second financial statement should be presented for the General Fund, a statement of revenues, expenditures, and changes in fund balance (see Illustration 4–4). Illustration 4–4 presents the actual revenues and actual expenditures that resulted from transactions illustrated in this chapter and other transactions not illustrated because they were similar in nature. Note that the Town of Brighton reported no other financing sources or uses during 2017. The fact that there were no interfund transfers in or out of

ILLUSTRATION 4–3

TOWN OF BRIGHTON
General Fund Balance Sheet
As of December 31, 2017

Assets		
Cash		$145,800
Taxes receivable—delinquent	$701,813	
Less: Allowance for uncollectible delinquent taxes	123,513	578,300
Interest and penalties receivable on taxes	13,191	
Less: Allowance for uncollectible interest and penalties	3,091	10,100
Total Assets		$734,200
Liabilities and Fund Balances		
Liabilities:		
Vouchers payable	$405,800	
Due to federal government	126,520	
Due to state government	39,740	
Due to other funds	5,000	
Total Liabilities		$577,060
Fund Balances:		
Committed—culture and recreation	17,500	
Assigned—public safety	23,700	
Unassigned	115,940	
Total Fund Balances		157,140
Total Liabilities and Fund Balances		$734,200

ILLUSTRATION 4–4

TOWN OF BRIGHTON
General Fund
Statement of Revenues, Expenditures, and Changes in Fund Balances
For the Year Ended December 31, 2017

Revenues:		
Property taxes	$2,599,636	
Interest and penalties on delinquent taxes	11,400	
Sales taxes	485,000	
Licenses and permits	213,200	
Fines and forfeits	310,800	
Intergovernmental revenue	284,100	
Charges for services	107,464	
Miscellaneous revenues	3,400	
Total Revenues		$4,015,000
Expenditures:		
2017:		
General government	649,400	
Public safety	1,305,435	
Public works	1,018,900	
Health and welfare	850,325	
Culture and recreation	292,500	
Miscellaneous	14,200	
Expenditures—2017	4,130,760	
2016:		
Culture and recreation	127,000	
Total Expenditures		4,257,760
Excess of Expenditures over Revenues		(242,760)
Other Financing Sources (Uses):		
Interfund transfers in	–0–	
Interfund transfers out	–0–	
Total Other Financing Sources		–0–
Change (Decrease) in Fund Balances		(242,760)
Fund Balances, January 1, 2017		399,900
Fund Balances, December 31, 2017		$ 157,140

the General Fund is important information that should be reported. Information shown as Illustration 4–4 would be presented in the General Fund column of the Statement of Revenues, Expenditures, and Changes in Fund Balances—Governmental Funds (see Illustration 9–6).

GASB standards require a budgetary comparison schedule, as shown previously in Illustration 3–5, or, alternatively, a statement of revenues, expenditures, and changes in fund balance—budget and actual for the General Fund, as well as for each *major* special revenue fund for which a budget is legally adopted. Illustration 4–5 presents a budgetary comparison schedule for the Town of Brighton General Fund. Note that columns must be provided for both the legally adopted budget amounts and the final amended amounts.

ILLUSTRATION 4–5

TOWN OF BRIGHTON
General Fund
Schedule of Revenues, Expenditures, and Changes in Fund Balance—Budget and Actual
(Non-GAAP Presentation)
For the Year Ended December 31, 2017

	Budgeted Amounts			
	Original	Final	Actual Amounts Budgetary Basis	Variance with Final Budget Over (Under)
Revenues:				
Taxes:				
Property taxes	$2,600,000	$2,600,000	$2,599,636	$ (364)
Interest and penalties on taxes	13,000	13,000	11,400	(1,600)
Sales taxes	480,000	480,000	485,000	5,000
Total Taxes	3,093,000	3,093,000	3,096,036	3,036
Licenses and permits	220,000	220,000	213,200	(6,800)
Fines and forfeits	308,000	308,000	310,800	2,800
Intergovernmental revenue	280,000	280,000	284,100	4,100
Charges for services	82,000	97,000	107,464	10,464
Miscellaneous revenues	3,000	3,000	3,400	400
Total Revenues	3,986,000	4,001,000	4,015,000	14,000
Expenditures and Encumbrances:				
General government	660,000	660,000	658,850	(1,150)
Public safety	1,240,000	1,320,000	1,318,500	(1,500)
Public works	1,090,000	1,040,000	1,038,300	(1,700)
Health and welfare	860,000	860,000	858,650	(1,350)
Culture and recreation	315,000	315,000	312,500	(2,500)
Miscellaneous	15,000	15,000	14,200	(800)
Total Expenditures	4,180,000	4,210,000	4,201,000	(9,000)
Excess of Expenditures over Revenues	(194,000)	(209,000)	(186,000)	23,000
Decrease in Encumbrances Outstanding	—	—	(56,760)	(56,760)
Decrease in Fund Balance for Year	(194,000)	(209,000)	(242,760)	(33,760)
Fund Balances, January 1, 2017	399,900	399,900	399,900	-0-
Fund Balances, December 31, 2017	$ 205,900	$ 190,900	$ 157,140	$(33,760)

The amounts in the Revenues section of the Actual column in Illustration 4–5 present the same information as shown in the Revenues section of Illustration 4–4 because in the Town of Brighton example, the General Fund revenues budget is on a GAAP basis, the same as actual revenues. However, the amounts in the Expenditures section of the Actual column of the budgetary comparison schedule (Illustration 4–5) differ from the expenditures shown in Illustration 4–4 because, under GAAP, expenditures chargeable to 2016 appropriations of $127,000 and expenditures of the 2017 appropriations of $4,130,760 are reported in Illustration 4–4. Also, in the GAAP operating statement, Illustration 4–4, encumbrances are not reported in the Expenditures section of the statement. In contrast, GASB standards require the amounts in the Actual column of Illustration 4–5 to conform with budgetary practices; therefore, in that statement, encumbrances outstanding at the end of 2017 are added to 2017 expenditures because both are uses of the 2017 appropriation authority.

Note that expenditures for 2016 are excluded from the budget and actual schedule because that schedule relates only to the 2017 budget. GASB standards require differences between the amounts reported in the two statements (Illustrations 4–4 and 4–5) to be reconciled in a separate schedule or in the notes to the required supplementary information. For example, the notes to the budgetary comparison schedule for the Town of Brighton might include the following reconciliation of General Fund Expenditures reported in the two operating statements illustrated:

Expenditures for 2017, budgetary basis	$4,201,000
Less: Encumbrances Outstanding as of December 31, 2017	(70,240)
Expenditures—2016	127,000
Expenditures for 2017, GAAP basis	$4,257,760

SPECIAL REVENUE FUNDS

As noted in Chapters 2 and 3, special revenue funds are needed when a significant revenue source is restricted or committed for a specific operating purpose, other than those served by proprietary or fiduciary funds. An example of a special revenue fund created to demonstrate legal compliance is a Street Fund, which is largely financed by a local government's share of the motor fuel tax levied by the state to be used only for maintenance and construction of streets, roads, and bridges. Another example of a special revenue fund is a Library Operating Fund created to account for a special tax levy to support the operations of a library. A final example is a trust fund in which both the investment principal and the investment earnings are available to support a government program or the citizenry. A common example of the latter is an expendable gift that can be used only to purchase works of art for public buildings.

Accounting for Operating Grants

Grants received by a local government from the state or federal government—or received by a state from the federal government—are often restricted for specified operating purposes. If the grant revenue finances a substantive part of the specified operating purpose, then the use of a special revenue fund is required. Many grants provide that the grantor will pay the grantee on a reimbursement basis. In such instances, GASB standards require that the grant revenue not be recognized until qualifying expenditures have been incurred. Other grants may impose a **time requirement,** which specifies that the amount is intended for a future accounting period. Resources received before time requirements are met, but after all other eligibility requirements have been met, should be reported as an asset and a deferred inflow of resources by the recipient.[10]

As an example of appropriate accounting procedures, assume that a local government has been awarded a state grant to finance a fine arts program, but the state will provide reimbursement only after the grantee has made expenditures related to the fine arts program. This is an example of a **voluntary nonexchange transaction** in which

[10] GASB *Codification,* Sec. N50.112. See Appendix A to this chapter for a more detailed discussion of revenue and expense/expenditure recognition for both exchange and nonexchange transactions.

an **eligibility requirement** (incurrence of allowable costs) must be met before the local government can recognize an asset and revenue. Assuming that the grantee government has incurred qualifying expenditures, or expense at the government-wide level, the required entries (detail omitted) in both the special revenue fund and the governmental activities journals would be:

	Debits	Credits
Special Revenue Fund and Governmental Activities:		
Expenditures (or Expense)	50,000	
Vouchers Payable (or Cash)		50,000
Cash	50,000	
Revenues		50,000

The latter entry, of course, records the reimbursement, which presumably would be shortly after the expenditures were incurred. As with prior entries in this chapter, the revenue account title in the governmental activities journal would designate that the grant was a program-specific operating or capital grant.

Financial Reporting

Special revenue fund accounting and financial reporting are essentially the same as for the General Fund, as described earlier in this chapter. In addition to amounts for the General Fund, amounts for *major* special revenue funds would be included in the balance sheet and statement of revenues, expenditures, and changes in fund balances prepared for the governmental funds. A budgetary comparison schedule is also provided as required supplementary information (RSI) for each major special revenue fund for which a budget is legally adopted. Elsewhere in the financial section of the government's comprehensive annual financial report (CAFR), a combining balance sheet and combining operating statement should be provided for all *nonmajor* governmental funds, including nonmajor special revenue funds. An example of a combining statement of revenues, expenditures, and changes in fund balances for nonmajor governmental funds is presented in Illustration 4–6 for the City of Sioux City, Iowa.

INTERFUND ACTIVITY

Transactions involving the sales and purchases of goods and services in a reciprocal exchange transaction between two funds were discussed earlier in this chapter. Other interfund transactions are discussed in this section.

Interfund Loans

Interfund loans are sometimes made from one fund to another with the intent that the amount be repaid. If the loan must be repaid during the current year or soon thereafter, the lending fund should record a current receivable, and the borrowing fund should record a current liability. If an interfund loan did not require repayment for more than one year, the word "Noncurrent" would be used rather than "Current" to signify the noncurrent nature of the loan.[11] This is illustrated by the following journal entries,

[11] Governments also use the accounts "Due to (from) Other Funds" and "Advances from (to) Other Funds" to record current and noncurrent interfund loans, respectively. The authors prefer to reserve the use of "Due to (from) Other Funds" for operating transactions only; that is, internal exchange transactions. Although used for decades, the term "Advances" is somewhat vague.

ILLUSTRATION 4–6

CITY OF SIOUX CITY, IOWA
Combining Statement of Revenues, Expenditures, and Changes in Fund Balances
Governmental Nonmajor Funds
For the Year Ended June 30, 2013

	Special Revenue Funds							Permanent Fund	
	Storm Water Drainage	Road Use	Community Development	Housing	Main Street	Events Facilities	Transit Operations	Cemetery Trust	Total Governmental Nonmajor Funds
Revenues									
Taxes	$ —	$ —	$ —		$ 119,776	$ —	$ —	$ —	$ 119,776
Intergovernmental Revenue	—	8,538,778	2,860,068	4,537,562	—	42,478	1,868,666	—	17,847,552
Revenue from Use of Property	—	9,115	—	900	—	4,629,070	64,446	34,270	4,737,801
Charges for Services	1,322,270	—	311	—	—	799,355	1,344,511	—	3,466,447
Interest	8,812	—	320,074	1,748	—	—	—	—	330,634
Miscellaneous	—	63,017	5,710	74,724	—	585,318	127,300	—	856,069
Total Revenue	1,331,082	8,610,910	3,186,163	4 ,614,934	119,776	6,056,221	3,404,923	34,270	27,358,279
Expenditures									
Current:									
Public Works	135,962	8,203,133	—	—	—	—	4,188,780	—	12,527,875
Culture and Recreation	—	—	—	—	—	7,602,578	—	—	7,602,578
Community and Economic Development	—	—	2,356,006	4,890,430	307,000	—	—	—	7,553,436
Capital Projects	—	—	614,420	—	—	—	—	—	614,420
Total Expenditures	135,962	8,203,133	2,970,426	4,890,430	307,000	7,602,578	4,188,780	—	28,298,309
Excess (Deficiency) of Revenues Over Expenditures	1,195,120	407,777	215,737	(275,496)	(187,224)	(1,546,357)	(783,857)	34,270	(940,030)
Other Financing Sources (Uses)									
Transfers In	212,202	899,596	—	—	187,227	1,463,141	796,177	—	3,558,343
Transfers Out	(1,258,144)	(616,199)	(8,584)	—	—	—	(118,219)	—	(2,001,146)
Total Other Financing Sources (Uses)	(1,045,942)	283,397	(8,584)	—	187,227	1,463,141	677,958	—	1,557,197
Net Change in Fund Balance	149,178	691,174	207,153	(275,496)	3	(83,216)	(105,899)	34,270	617,167
Fund Balance (Deficit) - Beginning of Year	428,319	391,564	8,833,397	1,346,689	41,688	(946,145)	62,523	1,058,731	11,216,766
Fund Balance (Deficit) - End of Year	$ 577,497	$1,082,738	$9,040,550	$1,071,193	$ 41,691	$(1,029,361)	$ (43,376)	$1,093,001	$11,833,933

assuming that the General Fund makes a long-term loan in the amount of $100,000 to the Central Stores Fund, an internal service fund.

	General Ledger		Subsidiary Ledger	
	Debits	***Credits***	***Debits***	***Credits***
General Fund:				
Interfund Loans Receivable—Noncurrent	100,000			
Cash		100,000		
Internal Service Fund:				
Cash	100,000			
Interfund Loans Payable—Noncurrent........		100,000		

Because the noncurrent interfund loan receivable represents assets that are not spendable for the current year's appropriation in the General Fund, an amount of the Fund Balance—Unassigned account equal to the noncurrent loan balance should be reclassified as nonspendable, as shown in the following entry.

General Fund:		
Fund Balance—Unassigned	100,000	
Fund Balance—Nonspendable—		
Noncurrent Loans Receivable		100,000

An interesting question is whether the illustrated interfund loans require journal entries at the government-wide level. The answer is no since GASB standards require that most internal service fund amounts be reported in the Governmental Activities column of the government-wide financial statements. Interfund receivables and payables between two funds that are both included in governmental activities have no effect on the amounts reported in the government-wide statement of net position. In contrast, an interfund loan between a governmental fund and a proprietary fund would require an entry in the governmental activities journal.

Interfund Transfers

Interfund transfers are nonreciprocal in the sense that the receiving fund is not expected to repay the amount transferred. Some interfund transfers are periodic, routine transfers. For example, resources may be transferred from the General Fund to subsidize the operations of an activity, such as a library, or a public transportation system. An additional example is an interfund transfer made to establish or liquidate a fund. The creation of a fund by transfer of assets and/or resources from an existing fund to a new fund, or transfers of residual balances of discontinued funds to another fund, results in the recognition of an other financing source rather than a revenue by the new fund (or a transfer in if the recipient fund is a proprietary fund) and an other financing use rather than an expenditure by the transferor fund (or as a transfer out rather than an expense if the transferor is a proprietary fund).

Intra- versus Inter-Activity Transactions (Government-wide Level)

In all the preceding examples, if the interfund transaction occurs between two governmental funds (or between a governmental fund and an internal service fund) or between two enterprise funds, that is, an **intra-activity transaction,** then neither the

Governmental Activities column nor the Business-type Activities column is affected at the government-wide level. Interfund loans or transfers between a governmental fund (or internal service fund) and an enterprise fund results in an **inter-activity transaction.** These transactions are reported as *Internal Balances* on the government-wide statement of net position (see Illustration A2–1) and "Transfers" in the statement of activities (see Illustration A2–2). Except for internal exchange transactions between governmental funds and internal service funds, for which any element of profit or loss is eliminated prior to preparing the government-wide financial statements, other internal exchange transactions should be reported as revenues and expenses in the statement of activity.

PERMANENT FUNDS

Governments often receive contributions under trust agreements in which the principal amount is not expendable, but earnings are expendable. Most of these trusts are established to benefit a government program or function, or the citizenry, rather than an external individual, organization, or government. Trusts of the first type are called **public-purpose trusts;** trusts of the second type are called **private-purpose trusts.**

GASB standards require that public-purpose trusts for which the earnings are expendable for a specified purpose, but the principal amount is not expendable (also referred to as *endowments*) be accounted for in a governmental fund called a **permanent fund.** Public-purpose trusts for which both principal and earnings thereon can be expended for a specified purpose are accounted for in a special revenue fund, again a governmental fund type. Accounting issues involving private-purpose trusts, a type of fiduciary fund, are discussed in Chapter 8.

Budgetary Accounts

Budgetary accounts generally should not be needed for permanent funds because transactions of the fund result in changes in the fund principal only incidentally; by definition, the principal cannot be appropriated or expended. However, public-purpose expendable trust funds may be required by law to use the appropriation procedure to ensure adequate budgetary control over the expenditure of fund assets since they are accounted for in special revenue funds. If the appropriation procedure is required, the use of the budgetary accounts discussed earlier in this chapter is also recommended. The following paragraphs illustrate a public-purpose nonexpendable trust that is accounted for as a permanent fund.

Illustrative Case

As an illustration of the nature of accounting for permanent fund trust principal and expendable trust revenue, assume on November 1, 2017, Wilma Wexner died, having made a valid will that provided for the gift of marketable securities to the City of Concordia to be held as a nonexpendable trust. For purposes of income distribution, the net income from the securities is to be computed on the accrual basis but does not include increases or decreases in the fair value of investments. Income, so measured, is to be transferred to the city's Library Operating Fund, a special revenue fund. Accounting for the Library Operating Fund is not illustrated here because it would be very similar to General Fund accounting already covered in depth in this chapter. For the sake of brevity, corresponding entries in the general journal for governmental activities at the government-wide level are also omitted.

The gift was accepted by the City of Concordia, which established the Library Endowment Fund (a permanent fund) to account for operation of the trust. The following securities were received by the Library Endowment Fund:

	Interest Rate per Year	Maturity Date	Face Value	Fair Value as of 11/1/18
Bonds of AB Company	6%	1/1/18	$640,000	$652,000

Journal Entries—Permanent Fund

The Library Endowment Fund's receipt of the securities is properly recorded at the fair value of the securities as of the date of the gift because this is the amount for which the trustees are responsible. Although the face value of the bonds will be received at maturity (if the bonds are held until maturity), GASB standards require that investments in bonds maturing more than one year from receipt be reported at fair value.[12] Thus, the entry in the Library Endowment Fund to record the receipt of the securities at initiation of the trust on November 1, 2016, is:

		Debits	Credits
	Permanent Fund:		
1.	Investment in Bonds	652,000	
	Accrued Interest Receivable	12,800	
	Revenues—Contributions for Endowment		664,800
	[Interest accrued on the bonds of Company AB ($640,000 × 6% × 4/12 = $12,800), assuming semiannual interest was last received on July 1, 2016]		

As of January 1, 2017, semiannual interest of $19,200 is received on the AB Company bonds, of which only the two months of interest earned since the endowment was created can be transferred to the Library Operating Fund. The entry for the receipt of bond interest and the revenue earned for transfer to the Library Operating Fund is:

		Debits	Credits
	Permanent Fund:		
2.	Cash	19,200	
	Accrued Interest Receivable		12,800
	Revenues—Bond Interest		6,400

As the bond interest was received in cash, the Library Endowment Fund has sufficient cash to pay the amount to be transferred to the Library Operating Fund for interest earned since the endowment was created. Assuming that cash is transferred as of January 3, 2017, Entry 3 is:

		Debits	Credits
	Permanent Fund:		
3.	Other Financing Uses—Interfund Transfers Out	6,400	
	Cash		6,400

[12] GASB *Codification,* Sec. I50.105.

Interest accrued on June 30, 2017, amounted to $19,200, the same amount received early in January 2017. The fair value of the Library Endowment Fund investments as of June 30, 2017, the last day of the City of Concordia's fiscal year, is given below.

	Fair Value as of 11/1/16	Fair Value as of 6/30/17	Change in Fair Value
Bonds of AB Company	$652,000	$674,000	$22,000

Entry 4a records the accrual of interest earned for transfer to the Library Operating Fund. Entry 4b records the adjusting entry to record the change in fair value of investments at the end of the fiscal year, compared with the prior fair value recorded for the investments. Entry 4c records the liability to the Library Operating Fund. As reflected by Entry 4c, the $22,000 revenue from change in fair value of investments is not expendable, but rather adds to the nonexpendable principal of the endowment.

		Debits	Credits
	Permanent Fund:		
4a.	Accrued Interest Receivable	19,200	
	Revenues—Bond Interest		19,200
4b.	Investment in Bonds	22,000	
	Revenues—Change in Fair Value of Investments		22,000
4c.	Other Financing Uses—Interfund Transfers Out	19,200	
	Due to Library Operating Fund		19,200

The closing entry at the end of the fiscal year, June 30, 2017, is shown in Entry 5.

		Debits	Credits
	Permanent Fund:		
5.	Revenues—Contributions for Endowment	664,800	
	Revenues—Bond Interest	25,600	
	Revenues—Change in Fair Value of Investments	22,000	
	Other Financing Uses—Interfund Transfers Out		25,600
	Fund Balance—Nonspendable—Principal of Permanent Fund		686,800

In Entry 5, one can see that $25,600, the total interest earned on bonds was transferred during the year to the Library Operating Fund; the net change (increase) in fair value of investments, $22,000, and the original contribution are added to the Fund Balance. If the net increase in the value of investments were permitted under the trust agreement to be used for library operating purposes, the entire $47,600 (sum of earnings and increase in fair value) would have been transferred out, and the addition to the fund balance account would have been just the $664,800 original contribution.

At year-end, financial statements for the Library Endowment Fund would be presented in essentially the same formats as the General Fund balance sheet and General Fund statement of revenues, expenditures, and changes in fund balance shown in Illustrations 4–3 and 4–4. If the Library Endowment Fund meets the criteria for a major fund, its balance sheet and operating statement information will be included as a column in the balance sheet—governmental funds and statement of revenues, expenditures, and changes in fund balances—governmental funds, examples of which are presented in Illustrations A2–3 and A2–5 in Chapter 2. If the fund is determined to be a nonmajor fund, it would be reported in the combining balance sheet and operating statement presented in the CAFR for the nonmajor governmental funds (see Illustration 4–6 for an example of the latter type of financial statement).

As indicated previously, entries in the Library Operating Fund are omitted for the sake of brevity since accounting for special revenue funds is similar to that for the General Fund. Thus, at the beginning of the 2017 fiscal year (July 1, 2016) a budgetary entry would have been recorded; that entry would have been amended on November 1, 2016, the date the Library Endowment Fund was created, to reflect the Estimated Other Financing Sources (interfund transfers in) expected from the endowment and to authorize expenditures of all or a portion of those resources in the Library Operating Fund. Each time Other Financing Uses—Interfund Transfers Out are recorded in the Library Endowment Fund, Other Financing Sources—Interfund Transfers In would be recorded in the same amount in the Library Operating Fund.

Chapters 3 and 4 have focused on operating activities that are recorded in the General Fund, special revenue funds, permanent funds, and in governmental activities at the government-wide level. Chapter 5 discusses accounting for general capital assets and capital projects funds, while general long-term debt and debt service funds are discussed in Chapter 6.

Appendix A

Concepts and Rules for Recognition of Revenues and Expenses (or Expenditures)

EXCHANGE TRANSACTIONS

Current GASB standards provide guidance for the accounting recognition of revenues and expenses on the accrual basis in the government-wide financial statements and revenues and expenditures on the modified accrual basis in the governmental fund financial statements.[13] Recognition rules for *exchange transactions* and *exchange-like transactions,* those in which each party receives value essentially equal to the value given, are generally straightforward; for operating transactions, the party selling goods or services recognizes an asset (for example, a receivable or cash) and a revenue when the transaction occurs and the revenue has been earned. The party purchasing goods or services recognizes an expense or expenditure and liability (or reduction in cash). As discussed in Chapter 2, under the *modified accrual* basis of accounting, if a governmental fund provides goods or services to another party or fund, it should recognize an asset (receivable or cash) and a revenue if the assets (financial resources) are deemed *measurable* and *available.* If a governmental fund *receives* goods or services from another party or fund, it should recognize expenditures (not expense) when the fund liability has been incurred. In most cases, exchange

[13] GASB *Codification* Secs. 1600 and N50.

transactions of governmental funds result in measurable and available assets being received or a fund liability being incurred when the transaction occurs and thus result in immediate recognition of revenues and expenditures. For example, the General Fund should recognize a revenue immediately when a citizen is charged a fee for a building permit and an expenditure when a purchase order for supplies has been filled.

NONEXCHANGE TRANSACTIONS

Nonexchange transactions are defined as external events in which a government gives or receives value without directly receiving or giving equal value in exchange.[14] Accounting for nonexchange transactions raises a number of conceptual issues. Two key concepts that affect a resource recipient's recognition of revenues (or a resource provider's recognition of expenses/expenditures) are *time requirements* and *purpose restrictions.*[15]

Time requirements relate either to the period when resources are required to be used or when use *may* begin. Thus, time requirements determine the *timing* of revenue or expense (expenditure) recognition—that is, whether these elements should be recognized (recorded in the accounts) in the current period or deferred to a future period. **Purpose restrictions** refer to specifications by resource providers of the purpose or purposes for which resources are required to be used. For example, a grant may specify that resources can be used only to provide transportation for senior citizens. The *timing* of revenue recognition is unaffected by purpose restrictions. Rather, the purpose restrictions should be clearly reported as restrictions of net position in the government-wide statement of net position or as restricted fund balance in the governmental funds balance sheet.

For certain classes of nonexchange transactions, discussed later in this section, revenue and expense recognition may be delayed until program *eligibility requirements* are met. Eligibility requirements may include, in addition to time requirements, specified characteristics that program recipients must possess or reimbursement provisions and contingencies tied to required actions by the recipient. GASB standards provide the example of state-provided reimbursements to school districts for special education. To meet the specified eligibility requirements, (1) the recipient must be a school district, (2) the applicable school year must have started, and (3) the district must have incurred allowable costs. Only when all three conditions are met can a school district record a revenue and the state record an expense.[16]

Nonexchange transactions are subdivided into four classes: (1) *derived tax revenues* (e.g., income and sales taxes), (2) *imposed nonexchange revenues* (e.g., property taxes and fines and penalties), (3) **government-mandated nonexchange transactions** (e.g., certain education, social welfare, and transportation services mandated and funded by a higher level of government), and (4) *voluntary nonexchange transactions* (e.g., grants and entitlements from higher levels of government and certain private donations).[17]

RECOGNITION OF NONEXCHANGE TRANSACTIONS

Illustration A4–1 provides a summary of the recognition criteria applicable to each class of nonexchange transactions, both for the accrual basis of accounting and for modified accrual. Assets and revenues in the **derived tax revenues** category are generally

[14] GASB *Codification,* Sec. N50.104.

[15] Ibid., par. 109.

[16] Ibid., par. 902. Example 8.

[17] Ibid., par. 104.

ILLUSTRATION A4–1 Summary Chart—Classes and Timing of Recognition of Nonexchange Transactions

Class	*Recognition*
Derived tax revenues Examples: sales taxes, personal and corporate income taxes, motor fuel taxes, and similar taxes on earnings or consumption	**Assets*** Period when *underlying exchange has occurred* or when resources are received, whichever is first. **Deferred inflows of resources** When modified accrual accounting is used, resources that are not "available." **Revenues** Period when *underlying exchange has occurred*. (Report advance receipts as a liability.) When modified accrual accounting is used, resources also should be "available."
Imposed nonexchange revenues Examples: property taxes, most fines and forfeitures	**Assets*** Period when an *enforceable legal claim has arisen* or when resources are received, whichever is first. **Deferred inflows of resources** When resources are received or recognized as receivable before (a) the period for which property taxes are levied or (b) the period when resources are required to be used or when use is first permitted for all other imposed nonexchange revenues in which enabling legislation includes time requirements. When modified accrual accounting is used, resources that are not "available." **Revenues** Period when *resources are required to be used* or first period that use is permitted (for example, for property taxes, the *period for which levied*). When modified accrual accounting is used, resources *also* should be "available." (For property taxes, apply Section P70.)
Government-mandated nonexchange transactions Examples: federal government mandates on state and local governments **Voluntary nonexchange transactions** Examples: certain grants and entitlements, most donations	**Assets* and Liabilities** Period when *all eligibility requirements have been met* or (for asset recognition) when resources are received, whichever is first. **Deferred inflows of resources** Receipt of resources before time requirements are met, but after all other eligibility requirements have been met. When modified accrual accounting is used for revenue recognition, resources that are not "available". **Deferred outflows of resources** Payment of resources before time requirements are met, but after all other eligibility requirements have been met. **Revenues and expenses or expenditures** Period when *all eligibility requirements have been met*. (However, when a provider precludes the sale, disbursement, or consumption of resources for a specified number of years, until a specified event has occurred, or permanently [for example, permanent and term endowments], report revenues and expenses or expenditures when the resources are, respectively, received or paid and report resulting net position, equity, or fund balance as restricted.) When modified accrual accounting is used for revenue recognition, resources *also* should be "available."

*If there are purpose restrictions, report restricted net position (or restricted fund balance for governmental funds).

Source: GASB *Codification*, Sec. N50.901. Adapted for subsequent standard changes.

recognized in the period in which the underlying exchange occurs; the period in which income is earned for income taxes and when sales have occurred for sales taxes.

For *imposed nonexchange revenues,* an asset (receivable or cash) is recognized when there is an enforceable legal claim or when cash is received, whichever is first. Revenues should be recognized in the period in which the resources are required to be used or the first period when their use is permitted. For property taxes, revenues usually are recognized in the period for which the taxes are levied. In governmental funds, the additional criterion of availability for use must be met. Current standards, as interpreted, define *available* in the context of property taxes as meaning "collected within the current period or expected to be collected soon enough thereafter to be used to pay liabilities of the current period."[18] *Soon enough thereafter* means not later than 60 days after the end of the current period.[19]

A common set of recognition rules applies to the remaining two classes of nonexchange transactions: *government-mandated* and *voluntary nonexchange.* An asset (a receivable or cash) is recognized when all eligibility requirements have been met or when cash is received, whichever occurs first. For example, although cash has not been received from a grantor, when a program recipient meets matching requirements imposed by the grantor agency in order to become eligible for a social services grant, a receivable (Due from [Grantor]) would be recorded. Revenues should be recognized only when all eligibility criteria have been met. If cash is received before eligibility requirements are met, the recipient records an asset and a liability; however, if cash is received in the period prior to intended use (that is, there is a time requirement), deferred inflow of resources should be reported rather than a liability or a revenue. In the period when the time requirement expires, the account Deferred Inflow of Resources will be debited and Revenues will be credited.

Appendix B

Interim Financial Reporting

Unlike publicly traded corporations, state and local governments usually are not required to provide quarterly or other interim financial statements to external parties. Although there is no requirement for *external* interim reporting, all state and local governments should prepare interim financial schedules for the *internal* use of administrators and legislators. The frequency and nature of interim reports are at the discretion of each government. At a minimum, quarterly budgetary comparison schedules should be prepared showing actual revenues to date compared with budgeted revenues and actual expenditures and outstanding encumbrances to date compared with appropriations. Schedules such as these for the Town of Brighton, prepared as of the end of the first quarter of the 2017 fiscal year, are presented as Illustrations B4–1 and B4–2. (*Note:* The amounts of revenues, expenditures, and encumbrances shown in these schedules are the amounts assumed to exist through March 31, 2017.) Such schedules are essential to sound budgetary control and often include an additional column showing prior year revenues and expenditures/encumbrances for the same period. So that appropriate officials can take timely action to correct unexpected revenue or expenditure/encumbrance variances, it may be necessary to prepare interim budgetary comparison schedules on a monthly, or even weekly, basis, rather than quarterly. This is particularly true for larger governments.

[18] GASB, *Codification*, Sec. P70.104.

[19] Ibid.

ILLUSTRATION B4–1

TOWN OF BRIGHTON
General Fund
Schedule of Budgeted and Actual Revenues
For the Three Months Ended March 31, 2017

Sources of Revenues	Estimated	Actual	Estimated Revenues Not Yet Realized
Taxes:			
Property taxes	$2,600,000	$2,599,636	$ 364
Interest and penalties on taxes	13,000	400	12,600
Sales taxes	480,000	105,800	374,200
Total taxes	3,093,000	2,705,836	387,164
Licenses and permits	220,000	100,000	120,000
Fines and forfeits	308,000	151,000	157,000
Intergovernmental revenue	280,000	—	280,000
Charges for services	70,000	7,000	63,000
Miscellaneous revenues	15,000	1,200	13,800
Total General Fund Revenue	$3,986,000	$2,965,036	$1,020,964

ILLUSTRATION B4–2

TOWN OF BRIGHTON
General Fund
Schedule of Budgeted and Actual Expenditures and Encumbrances
For the Three Months Ended March 31, 2017

Function	Appropriations	Expenditures of 2017 Appropriations	Outstanding Encumbrances	Available Appropriations
General government	$ 660,000	$ 129,100	$15,750	$ 515,150
Public safety	1,240,000	592,400	—	647,600
Public works	1,090,000	330,060	9,100	750,840
Health and welfare	860,000	67,700	5,825	786,475
Culture and recreation	315,000	72,000	6,000	237,000
Miscellaneous	15,000	450	—	14,550
Total General Fund	$4,180,000	$1,191,710	$36,675	$2,951,615

Key Terms

Consumption method, *134*
Delinquent taxes, *121*
Derived tax revenues, *149*
Eligibility requirements, *142*
Exchange transaction, *125*
Exchange-like transaction, *125*
Government-mandated nonexchange transactions, *149*
Imposed nonexchange revenue, *121*
Inter-activity transactions, *145*
Interfund loans, *142*
Interfund transfers, *144*
Internal balances, *132*
Intra-activity transactions, *144*
Nonexchange revenue, *121*
Nonexchange transactions, *149*
Permanent fund, *145*
Private-purpose trusts, *145*
Public-purpose trusts, *145*
Purchases method, *133*
Purpose restrictions, *149*
Tax anticipation note, *126*
Time requirements, *141*
Voluntary nonexchange transactions, *141*

Selected References

American Institute of Certified Public Accountants. Audit and Accounting Guide. *State and Local Governments.* Revised. New York, 2015.

Governmental Accounting Standards Board. *Codification of Governmental Accounting and Financial Reporting Standards, as of June 30, 2014.* Norwalk, CT, 2014.

Questions

4–1. Explain why some transactions for governmental activities at the government-wide level are reported differently than transactions for the General Fund. Give some examples of transactions that would be recorded in the general journals of (*a*) only the General Fund, (*b*) only governmental activities at the government-wide level, and (*c*) both.

4–2. When preparing the statement or schedule of revenues, expenditures, and changes in fund balance on the budgetary basis, how are encumbrances outstanding at year end treated if they will be honored in the upcoming year?

4–3. In many cases, property taxes comprise a significant source of revenue and cash receipts for a government. If property tax cash collections typically occur during one or two collection periods, how do governments manage working capital needs?

4–4. During a recession citizens and governments see a substantial decline in the value of homes. How might this decline in value impact the a government's gross property tax levy?

4–5. If the General Fund of a certain city needs $6,720,000 of revenue from property taxes to finance estimated expenditures of the next fiscal year and historical experience indicates that 4 percent of the gross levy will not be collected, what should be the amount of the gross levy for property taxes? Show all computations in good form.

4–6. How does accounting in a governmental fund for the purchase of supplies from an outside vendor differ from the purchase of supplies from an internal service fund?

4–7. Explain why some governments may account for inventories of supplies using the *purchases* method in the General Fund and the *consumption* method at the government-wide level? How would the amount reported for expenditures in the General Fund compare with the amount of expenses reported at the government-wide level if the two methods of inventory accounting are used?

4–8. The computer department of a certain city, a General Fund department, charges other funds for data processing services. At the end of the fiscal year, the General Fund is owed $5,000 by the City Library Fund (a special revenue fund) and $8,000 by the City Electric Fund (an enterprise fund) for service billed but still unpaid. How would these interfund receivables and payables be reported in the Governmental Activities column of the government-wide statement of net position?

4–9. How does a *permanent fund* differ from public-purpose trusts that are reported in special revenue funds? How does it differ from private-purpose trust funds?

4–10. Name the four classes of nonexchange transactions defined by GASB standards and explain the revenue and expenditure/expense recognition rules applicable to each class.

Cases

4–11 Analyzing Reports of Operations. Using the finance or similarly named department link of a county's Web site, download either the county's entire comprehensive annual financial report (CAFR) or, if possible, just the portion of the CAFR that contains the basic financial statements. Print a copy of the government-wide statement of activities and a copy of the statement of revenues, expenditures, and changes in fund balances—governmental funds, along with the reconciliation between these two statements, and respond to the requirements below.

The county administrator presented these statements at the last county commission meeting. Unfortunately, she opted not to take a governmental accounting course in college, and when the commission members began to question why these two statements were so different, she was unable to answer their questions. She has asked you, as finance director, to prepare her for the next meeting by explaining (in clear, easy-to-understand terms) the purposes for which each operating statement is intended and how and why the operating results differ.

Required

a. Examine the two operating statements in detail, paying particular attention to the lines on which changes in net position and changes in fund balances are reported and develop a list of reasons why the two numbers are not the same.

b. Prepare a succinct and understandable explanation of the results of operations of this government, comparing and contrasting both operating statements. Be sure that you use language that a non-accountant commission member would be able to understand.

4–12 Policy Issues Relating to Volatility of Taxable Property Values. Park City experienced unusual volatility of taxable property values over a particular five-year period. For the first three years of this period, the "pre-recession period," average property values in the city increased by more than 35 percent. Then, almost without warning, the nation plunged into a sudden and deep recession, and like communities in many states, Park City experienced a steep drop in property values. During the year the recession occurred and the year following, the market value of residential property in Park City decreased by an average 50 percent.

Park City has found that changes in the assessed valuation of taxable property often lags behind changes in the market value of the property. State law requires that the Park County Equalization Board reassess residential and other taxable properties located in the county only when actual sales of properties occur. Properties that have not sold must be reassessed at least every three years. To spread its workload the equalization board reassesses approximately one-third of taxable property in the county each year. This means that during the pre-recession market value growth period, many properties had assessed valuations well below market value. Even worse, during the recession period, despite the fact that the market value of some residential properties had dropped below the amount of mortgage debt owed on them (so-called "under-water properties"), many of these same properties continued to be assessed at values well above actual market values.

Property owners who believe their assessed valuations are in error or above market value can file formal appeals with the state Equalization Review Commission (hardly anyone seems to file an appeal for under-assessments).

In judging property assessment appeals, the commission relies heavily on actual sales data but also has broad authority under state law to exercise professional judgment in deciding whether and how much to adjust appellants' property assessment. Over the years, many property owners, particularly those with unsuccessful appeals, have complained that the appeal process is too political.

Required

a. Read and evaluate the foregoing information about Park City's taxable property assessments. Then, put yourself in the position of a homeowner and explain what concerns you may have and what plausible actions you might take in each of the following situations. (1) During the first two years of the pre-recession period, your property had not yet been reassessed, so your assessed property value may have been undervalued since average assessed valuation had increased in the city. (2) During the third year of the pre-recession period, you received notice that the assessed valuation of your property was increased by 35 percent. (3) During the year of and year following the recession, your property now has a market value less than what you owe on your mortgage, yet the assessed valuation of your property has increased each of those years. Moreover, property tax rates have increased somewhat because average assessed valuation in the city has decreased.

b. Now put yourself in the role of city manager of Park City and explain what issues you will likely face as you develop a budget and recommend a property tax rate to the city council during (1) the pre-recession period and (2) the recession period.

4–13 Research Case—Delinquent Taxes. When property taxes become delinquent, governmental entities often accrue interest and penalties on the delinquent taxes or choose to sell the rights to collect such taxes, interest, and penalties to external parties. Select a local municipality of your choice. Using information from the government's Web site, respond to the questions below. (Hint: Search for delinquent tax collection process, delinquent property taxes—FAQs, tax lien, etc.)

Required

a. What happens if a taxpayer fails to pay property taxes on time? When do taxes become delinquent? What happens if a taxpayer fails to pay delinquent taxes? At what point does a tax lien attach to the property? What interest charges and other penalties or fees are assessed to the delinquent taxpayer?

b. If delinquent property taxes or tax liens are sold at public auction, what rights are purchased by the buyer? Is there a possibility, at some point in time, that the tax lien buyers can attain legal title to the property for which they hold the tax lien? (This may be called a treasurer's deed.) If so, describe this process.

4–14 Reporting Multipurpose Grant Transactions in the Funds and Government-wide Financial Statements of Local Government Recipients. In this case, local governments receive reimbursements from the state government's Department of Social Services for expenditures incurred in conducting an array of locally administered programs that benefit troubled teens. The state program provides reimbursement up to a maximum amount based on grant applications submitted annually by each local government and provides notification of the amounts approved prior to the grant year. Each local government determines which kinds of teen programs and what mix of services are most appropriate for its community. Reimbursements are made only after services have been provided and documented claims for reimbursements have been submitted to the state. Due to backlogs near year end, such reimbursements may take several months to process and, hence, approval and payment may not take place in the same fiscal year that claims are submitted to the state. GASB standards relevant to this grant state:

> Multipurpose grants (those that provide financing from more than one program) should be reported as program revenue if the amounts restricted to each program are specifically identified in either the grant award or the grant application. Multipurpose grants that do not provide for specific identification of the programs and amounts should be reported as general revenues.

Required

a. Explain how the local governments should record the grant award. When should asset and revenue recognition occur? Please explain your answer.

b. Considering the GASB guidance on multipurpose grants provided above, *how* should the grant be reported on the fund and government-wide financial statements? Please explain your answer.

Exercises and Problems

4–15 Examine the CAFR. Utilizing the comprehensive annual financial report obtained for Exercise 1–16, follow these instructions.

a. **Governmental Activities, Government-wide Level.** Answer the following questions. (1) Are governmental activities reported in a separate column from business-type activities in the two government-wide financial statements? (2) Are assets and liabilities reported either in the relative order of their liquidity or on a classified basis on the statement of net position? (3) Is information on expenses for governmental activities presented at least at the functional level of detail? (4) Are program revenues segregated into (*a*) charges for services, (*b*) operating grants and contributions, and (*c*) capital grants and contributions on the statement of activities?

b. **General Fund.** Answer the following questions. (1) What statements and schedules pertaining to the General Fund are presented? (2) What purpose is each statement and schedule intended to serve? (3) Are any noncurrent or nonliquid assets included in the General Fund balance sheet? If so, are they offset by equal amounts classified as "nonspendable" fund balances? (4) Are any noncurrent liabilities included in the General Fund balance sheet? If so, describe them. (5) Are revenue classifications sufficiently detailed to be meaningful? (6) Has the government refrained from reporting expenses rather than expenditures?

c. **Special Revenue Funds.** Answer the following questions. (1) What statements and schedules pertaining to the special revenue funds are presented? (2) Are these only combining statements, or are there also statements for individual special revenue funds? (3) Are expenditures classified by character (i.e., current, intergovernmental, capital outlay, and debt service)? (4) Are current expenditures further categorized at least by function?

4–16 Multiple Choice. Choose the best answer.

1. When equipment was purchased with General Fund resources, which of the following accounts would have been debited in the General Fund?
   a. Expenditures.
   b. Equipment.

c. Encumbrances.
d. No entry should be made in the General Fund.

2. Goods for which a purchase order had been placed at an estimated cost of $1,600 were received at an actual cost of $1,550. The journal entry in the General Fund to record the receipt of the goods will include a:
a. Debit to Encumbrances Outstanding for $1,600.
b. Credit to Vouchers Payable for $1,550.
c. Debit to Expenditures for $1,550.
d. All of the above are correct.

3. Which of the following items would be reported as *General* Revenue on the government-wide statement of activities?
a. Parking fines.
b. Federal grants earmarked for specific programs.
c. Animal licensing fees.
d. Sales taxes earmarked for maintenance of roads and bridges.

4. Garden City has calculated that General Fund property tax revenues of $4,608,000 are required for the current fiscal year. Over the past several years, the city has collected 96 percent of all property taxes levied. The city levied property taxes in the amount that will generate the required $4,608,000. Which of the following general journal entries would correctly record the property tax levy?

a. Taxes Receivable—Current	4,608,000	
Allowance for Uncollectible Current Taxes		184,320
Revenues		4,423,680
b. Taxes Receivable—Current	4,800,000	
Allowance for Uncollectible Current Taxes		192,000
Revenues		4,608,000
c. Taxes Receivable—Current	4,608,000	
Deferred Inflow of Resources—Property Taxes		184,320
Revenues		4,423,680
d. Taxes Receivable—Current	4,800,000	
Deferred Inflow of Resources—Property Taxes		192,000
Revenues		4,608,000

5. Carroll City levies $200,000 of property taxes for its current fiscal year. One percent of the tax levy is expected to be uncollectible. The city collects $170,000 of its taxes during the year and another $25,000 during the first two months of the following year. In addition, the city collected $3,000 of prior year taxes during the first two months of the current fiscal year and another $2,000 during the remainder of the current fiscal year. What amount of property tax revenues should the city report in the *governmental fund* financial statements for the current fiscal year?
a. $200,000.
b. $198,000.
c. $197,000.
d. $195,000.

6. Carroll City levies $200,000 of property taxes for its current fiscal year. One percent of the tax levy is expected to be uncollectible. The city collects

$170,000 of its taxes during the year and another $25,000 during the first two months of the following year. In addition, the city collected $3,000 of prior year taxes during the first two months of the current fiscal year and another $2,000 during the remainder of the current fiscal year. What amount of property tax revenues should the city report in the *government-wide* financial statements for the current fiscal year?

a. $200,000.
b. $198,000.
c. $197,000.
d. $195,000.

7. The Village of Frederick borrowed $1,000,000 from a local bank by issuing 4 percent tax anticipation notes. If the village repaid the tax anticipation notes six months later after collecting its next installment of property taxes, the General Fund journal entry to record the repayment will include:
   a. A debit to Tax Anticipation Notes Payable for $1,000,000.
   b. A debit to Expenditures for $20,000.
   c. A debit to Expenditures for $1,020,000.
   d. Both *a* and *b*.

8. Which of the following transactions is reported on the government-wide financial statements?
   a. An interfund loan from the General Fund to a special revenue fund.
   b. Equipment used by the General Fund is transferred to an internal service fund that predominantly serves departments that are engaged in governmental activities.
   c. The City Airport Fund, an enterprise fund, transfers a portion of boarding fees charged to passengers to the General Fund.
   d. An interfund transfer is made between the General Fund and the Debt Service Fund.

9. Clarion Township was approved for a grant from the federal government. The grant provides for reimbursement up to $200,000 for expenditures incurred to weatherize homes for low-income persons. Upon notification that the grant had been approved, but before weatherization activities have begun, Clarion Township should:
   a. Make no journal entry.
   b. Debit Due from Federal Government for $200,000.
   c. Credit Deferred Inflow of Resources for $200,000.
   d. Both *b* and *c*.

10. The City of Marshfield uses the *purchases method* for recording its inventory of supplies in the General Fund. Rather than using a perpetual inventory system, inventories are updated at year-end based on a physical count. Physical inventories were $112,000 and $128,000 at December 31, 2016 and 2017, respectively. The adjusting journal entry on December 31, 2017, will include a:
    a. Debit to Inventory of Supplies for $16,000.
    b. Debit to Expenditures for $16,000.
    c. Credit to Inventory of Supplies for $16,000.
    d. Credit to Expenditures for $16,000.

4–17 Recording Encumbrances and Expenditures. During fiscal year 2017, the City of Hickory Hills issued purchase orders to various vendors in the amounts shown for the following functions of the city:

General Government	$ 164,200
Public Safety	302,000
Public Works	224,400
Culture and Recreation	181,700
Health and Welfare	168,100
Miscellaneous	24,600
Total	$1.065,000

All goods ordered during the year were received at the following actual costs:

General Government	$ 159,800
Public Safety	301,700
Public Works	226,800
Culture and Recreation	181,700
Health and Welfare	171,300
Miscellaneous	25,600
Total	$1.066,900

Required

a. Prepare a summary journal entry in the General Fund general journal to record the issuance of purchase orders during fiscal year 2017. In addition, show subsidiary detail for the Encumbrances ledger.

b. Prepare summary journal entries in the General Fund general journal to record the receipt of and payment for goods during fiscal year 2017. In addition, show subsidiary detail for the Encumbrances and Expenditures ledgers.

c. Does the fact that the actual cost of goods received during the year exceeded the estimated cost when ordered suggest a budgetary or management problem?

4–18 On July 1, 2017, the beginning of its fiscal year, Ridgedale County recorded gross property tax levies of $4,200,000. The county estimated that 5 percent of the taxes levied would be uncollectible. As of April 30, 2018, the due date for all property taxes, the county had collected $3,900,000 in taxes. The county imposed penalties and interest in the amount of $14,500 but only expects to collect $12,800 of that amount. At the end of the fiscal year (June 30, 2018), the county had collected $53,000 in delinquent taxes and $4,800 in interest and penalties on the delinquent taxes.

Required

a. Prepare journal entries to record the tax levy on July 1, 2017, in the General Fund. (Ignore all entries in the governmental activities journal.)

b. Prepare a summary journal entry to record the collection of taxes as of April 30.

c. Prepare the journal entry necessary to reclassify the uncollected tax amounts as delinquent.

d. Prepare the journal entry necessary to record interest and penalties.

e. Prepare a summary journal entry to record the collection of delinquent taxes, interest, and penalties.

f. How does the reporting of revenues from taxes differ from a for-profit company's recording of revenues and uncollectible accounts?

g. Suppose that a portion of the delinquent taxes considered collectible will not be collected until November of 2018 (i.e., more than 60 days after year-end). Would this information affect the accounting treatment of the taxes?

4–19 Calculating Required Tax Anticipation Financing and Recording Issuance of Tax Anticipation Notes. The City of Troy collects its annual property taxes late in its fiscal year. Consequently, each year it must finance part of its operating budget using tax anticipation notes. The notes are repaid upon collection of property taxes. On April 1, 2017, the city estimated that it will require $2,500,000 to finance governmental activities for the remainder of the 2017 fiscal year. On that date, it had $770,000 of cash on hand and $830,000 of current liabilities. Collections for the remainder of FY 2017 from revenues other than current property taxes and from delinquent property taxes, including interest and penalties, were estimated at $1,100,000.

Required

a. Calculate the estimated amount of tax anticipation financing that will be required for the remainder of FY 2017. Show work in good form.

b. Assume that on April 2, 2017, the City of Troy borrowed the amount calculated in part *a* by signing tax anticipation notes bearing 6 percent per annum to a local bank. Record the issuance of the tax anticipation notes in the general journals of the General Fund and governmental activities at the government-wide level.

c. By October 1, 2017, the city had collected a sufficient amount of current property taxes to repay the tax anticipation notes with interest. Record the repayment of the tax anticipation notes and interest in the general journals of the General Fund and governmental activities at the government-wide level.

4–20 Adjusting and Closing Entries. At the end of fiscal year 2017, the City of Columbus General Fund pre-adjusting trial balance showed the following balances for operating and budgetary accounts and fund balance accounts.

	Debits	***Credits***
Appropriations		$6,224,000
Estimated Other Financing Uses		2,776,000
Estimated Revenues	$7,997,000	
Encumbrances	0	
Expenditures	6,192,000	
Other Financing Uses	2,770,000	
Revenues		7,980,000
Budgetary Fund Balance	1,003,000	
Fund Balance—Nonspendable—Inventory of Supplies		140,000
Fund Balance—Unassigned		1,990,000

The City of Columbus uses the *purchases* method of accounting for its inventory of supplies in the General Fund. The city uses a periodic inventory system in which the amount of inventory used during the year and the amount on hand at the end of the year are determined by a physical inventory. During the year, $220,000 of supplies were purchased and recorded as expenditures. These purchases are included in the final expenditures balance of $6,192,000 shown above. The physical inventory revealed a supplies balance of $152,000 at the end of fiscal year 2017, an increase of $12,000 from the prior year.

Required

a. Provide the required adjusting journal entry (or entries) in the General Fund general journal at the end of 2017.

b. Provide the required journal entries in the General Fund general journal to close the operating statement and budgetary accounts at the end of 2017.

4–21 Special Revenue Fund, Voluntary Nonexchange Transactions. The City of Waterville applied for a grant from the state government to build a pedestrian bridge over the river inside the city's park. On May 1, 2017, the city was notified that it had been awarded a grant of up to $200,000 for the project. The state will provide reimbursement for allowable expenditures. On May 5 the special revenue fund entered into a short-term loan with the General Fund for $200,000, so it could start bridge construction. During FY2017 the special revenue fund expended $165,000 for allowable bridge construction costs, for which it submitted documentation to the state. Reimbursement was received from the state on December 13, 2017.

Required

For the special revenue fund, provide the appropriate journal entries, if any, that would be made for the following. (Assume the city has a fiscal year-end of December 31.)

1. May 1, 2017, notification of grant approval.
2. May 5, 2017, loan from General Fund.
3. During FY 2017, bridge expenditures and submission of reimbursement documentation.
4. December 13, 2017, receipt of the grant reimbursement funds.
5. December 31, 2017, adjusting and closing entries.

4–22 Transactions and Budgetary Comparison Schedule. The following transactions occurred during the 2017 fiscal year for the City of Evergreen. For budgetary purposes, the city reports encumbrances in the Expenditures section of its budgetary comparison schedule for the General Fund but excludes expenditures chargeable to a prior year's appropriation.

1. The budget prepared for the fiscal year 2017 was as follows:

Estimated Revenues:	
Taxes	$1,943,000
Licenses and permits	372,000
Intergovernmental revenue	397,000
Miscellaneous revenues	62,000
Total estimated revenues	2,774,000
Appropriations:	
General government	471,000
Public safety	886,000
Public works	650,000
Health and welfare	600,000
Miscellaneous	86,000
Total appropriations	2,693,000
Budgeted increase in fund balance	$ 81,000

2. Encumbrances issued against the appropriations during the year were as follows:

General government	$ 58,000
Public safety	250,000
Public works	392,000
Health and welfare	160,000
Miscellaneous	71,000
Total	$931,000

3. The current year's tax levy of $2,005,000 was recorded; uncollectibles were estimated as $65,000.
4. Tax collections from prior years' levies totaled $132,000; collections of the current year's levy totaled $1,459,000.
5. Personnel costs during the year were charged to the following appropriations in the amounts indicated. Encumbrances were not recorded for personnel costs. Since no liabilities currently exist for withholdings, you may ignore any FICA or federal or state income tax withholdings. (*Note:* Expenditures charged to Miscellaneous should be treated as General Government expenses in the governmental activities general journal at the government-wide level.)

General government	$ 411,000
Public safety	635,000
Public works	254,000
Health and welfare	439,000
Miscellaneous	11,100
Credit to Vouchers Payable	$1,750,100

6. Invoices for all items ordered during the prior year were received and approved for payment in the amount of $14,470. Encumbrances had been recorded in the prior year for these items in the amount of $14,000. The amount chargeable to each year's appropriations should be charged to the Public Safety appropriation.
7. Invoices were received and approved for payment for items ordered in documents recorded as encumbrances in Transaction (2) of this problem. The following appropriations were affected.

	Actual Liability	Estimated Liability
General government	$ 52,700	$ 52,200
Public safety	236,200	240,900
Public works	360,000	357,000
Health and safety	130,600	130,100
Miscellaneous	71,000	71,000
	$850,500	$851,200

8. Revenue other than taxes collected during the year consisted of licenses and permits, $373,000; intergovernmental revenue, $400,000; and $66,000 of miscellaneous revenues. For purposes of accounting for these revenues at the government-wide level, the intergovernmental revenues were operating grants and contributions for the Public Safety function. Miscellaneous revenues are not identifiable with any function and, therefore, are recorded as General Revenues at the government-wide level.
9. Payments on Vouchers Payable totaled $2,505,000.

Additional information follows: The General Fund Fund Balance—Unassigned account had a credit balance of $96,900 as of December 31, 2016; no entries have been made in the Fund Balance—Unassigned account during 2017.

Required

a. Record the preceding transactions in general journal form for fiscal year 2017 in both the General Fund and governmental activities general journals.

b. Prepare a budgetary comparison schedule for the General Fund of the City of Evergreen for the fiscal year ending December 31, 2017, as shown in Illustration 4–5. Do not prepare a government-wide statement of activities since other governmental funds would affect that statement.

4–23 Interfund and Interactivity Transactions. The following transactions affected various funds and activities of the Town of Big Springs.

1. The Fire Department, a governmental activity accounted for within the General Fund, purchased $100,000 of water from the Water Utility Fund, an enterprise fund.
2. The General Fund made a long-term loan in the amount of $50,000 to the Central Stores Fund, an internal service fund that services town departments.
3. The General Fund paid its annual contribution of $100,000 to the debt service fund for interest and principal on general obligation bonds due during the year.
4. The $5,000 balance in the capital projects fund at the completion of construction of a new Town Hall was transferred to the General Fund.
5. A special revenue fund was awarded a $250,000 reimbursement grant. The General Fund advances $50,000 to the special revenue fund to cover initial costs associated with the grant's purpose.

Required

a. Make the required journal entries in the general journal of the General Fund and any other fund(s) affected by the interfund transactions described. Also make entries in the governmental activities journal for any transaction(s) affecting a governmental fund. Do not make entries in the subsidiary ledgers.

b. Why is it unnecessary to make entries in a business-type activities journal for any transaction(s) affecting enterprise funds?

4–24 Operating Transactions, Special Topics, and Financial Statements. The City of Hinton's General Fund had the following post-closing trial balance at April 30, 2016, the end of its fiscal year:

	Debits	*Credits*
Cash	$ 97,000	
Taxes Receivable—Delinquent	583,000	
Allowance for Uncollectible Delinquent Taxes		$189,000
Interest and Penalties Receivable	26,280	
Allowance for Uncollectible Interest and Penalties		11,160
Inventory of Supplies	16,100	
Vouchers Payable		148,500
Due to Federal Government		59,490
Fund Balance—Nonspendable—Inventory of Supplies		16,100
Fund Balance—Unassigned		298,130
	$722,380	$722,380

During the year ended April 30, 2017, the following transactions, in summary form, with subsidiary ledger detail omitted, occurred:

1. The budget for FY 2017 provided for General Fund estimated revenues totaling $3,140,000 and appropriations totaling $3,100,000.
2. The city council authorized temporary borrowing of $500,000 in the form of a 120-day tax anticipation note. The loan was obtained from a local bank at a discount of 6 percent per annum (debit Expenditures for the discount in the General Fund journal and Expenses—General Government in the governmental activities journal).
3. The property tax levy for FY 2017 was recorded. Net assessed valuation of taxable property for the year was $43,000,000, and the tax rate was $5 per $100. It was estimated that 3 percent of the levy would be uncollectible.
4. Purchase orders and contracts were issued to vendors and others in the amount of $2,060,000.
5. The County Board of Review discovered unassessed properties with a total taxable value of $500,000. The owners of these properties were charged with taxes at the city's General Fund rate of $5 per $100 assessed value. (You need not adjust the Allowance for Uncollectible Current Taxes account.)
6. $1,961,000 of current taxes, $383,270 of delinquent taxes, and $20,570 of interest and penalties were collected.
7. Additional interest and penalties on delinquent taxes were accrued in the amount of $38,430, of which 30 percent was estimated to be uncollectible.
8. Because of a change in state law, the city was notified that it will receive $80,000 less in intergovernmental revenues than was budgeted.
9. Total payroll during the year was $819,490. Of that amount, $62,690 was withheld for employees' FICA tax liability, $103,710 for employees' federal income tax liability, and $34,400 for state taxes; the balance was paid to employees in cash.
10. The employer's FICA tax liability was recorded for $62,690.

11. Revenues from sources other than taxes were collected in the amount of $947,000.
12. Amounts due the federal government as of April 30, 2017, and amounts due for FICA taxes, and state and federal withholding taxes during the year were vouchered.
13. Purchase orders and contracts encumbered in the amount of $1,988,040 were filled at a net cost of $1,987,570, which was vouchered.
14. Vouchers payable totaling $2,301,660 were paid after deducting a credit for purchases discount of $8,030 (credit Expenditures).
15. The tax anticipation note of $500,000 was repaid.
16. All unpaid current year's property taxes became delinquent. The balances of the current tax receivables and related uncollectibles were transferred to delinquent accounts.
17. A physical inventory of materials and supplies at April 30, 2017, showed a total of $19,100. Inventory is recorded using the purchases method in the General Fund; the consumption method is used at the government-wide level. (*Note:* A periodic inventory system is used both in the General Fund and at the government-wide level. When inventory was purchased during the year, Expenditures were debited in the General Fund journal and Expenses were debited in the governmental activities journal.)

Required

a. Record in general journal form the effect of the above transactions on the General Fund and governmental activities for the year ended April 30, 2017. Do not record subsidiary ledger debits and credits.

b. Record in general journal form entries to close the budgetary and operating statement accounts in the General Fund only. Do not close the governmental activities accounts.

c. Prepare a General Fund balance sheet as of April 30, 2017.

d. Prepare a statement of revenues, expenditures, and changes in fund balance for the year ended April 30, 2017. Do not prepare the government-wide financial statements.

4–25 Permanent Fund and Related Special Revenue Fund Transactions. Jacqueline Ponce de Leon, a descendent of Juan Ponce de Leon, made a cash contribution of $1,500,000 to the City of Fountains to create and maintain a large dramatic fountain in front of City Hall in honor of her ancestor. For accounting purposes, the city created the Ponce de Leon Endowment Fund. The endowment requires the city to invest and conserve the principal amount of the contribution in perpetuity. Earnings must be used to maintain and operate the fountain in a "pristine manner." Any changes in fair value are treated as adjustments of fund balance of the permanent fund and do not affect earnings. Earnings are transferred each year to the Ponce de Leon Fountain Maintenance Fund, a special revenue fund. Information pertaining to transactions of the endowment and special revenue funds for the fiscal year ended June 30, 2017, follows.

1. The contribution of $1,500,000 was received and recorded on December 31, 2016.
2. On December 31, 2016, the city purchased a certificate of deposit in the amount of $1,000,000 that yields 5% per year payable on June 30 and December 31. On that date, the city also purchased bonds having a face value of $400,000 for $406,300. The bonds mature on July 1, 2025 (102 months

from the date of purchase) and pay interest of 6 percent per year semiannually on June 30 and December 31. Assume the interest payment for December 31, 2016, was paid to the previous owner prior to the city's purchase of the bonds.

3. On June 30, 2017, interest on the certificate of deposit and the bonds was received by the endowment fund.
4. Interest from both the certificate of deposit and the bonds was transferred to the Ponce de Leon Fountain Maintenance Fund.
5. On June 30, 2017, the market value of the bonds was $409,600. The value of the certificate had not changed.

Required

a. Prepare in general journal format the entries required in the Ponce de Leon Endowment Fund to record the transactions occurring during the fiscal year ending June 30, 2017, including all appropriate adjusting and closing entries. (*Note:* Ignore related entries in the governmental activities journal at the government-wide level and the Fountain Maintenance Fund.)

b. Prepare the following financial statements:

(1) A balance sheet for the Ponce de Leon Fountain Endowment Fund as of June 30, 2017.

(2) A statement of revenues, expenditures, and changes in fund balance for the Ponce de Leon Fountain Endowment Fund for the year ended June 30, 2017.

c. What type of trust is the Ponce de Leon Fountain endowment? Does the fund require budgetary entries? Why or why not?

Chapter **Five**

Accounting for General Capital Assets and Capital Projects

Learning Objectives

After studying this chapter, you should be able to:

5-1 Describe the nature and characteristics of general capital assets.

5-2 Account for general capital assets, including: acquisition, maintenance, depreciation, impairment, and disposition.

5-3 Explain the purpose, characteristics, and typical financing sources of a capital projects fund.

5-4 Prepare journal entries for a typical capital project, both at the fund level and within the governmental activities category at the government-wide level.

5-5 Prepare financial statements for capital projects funds.

Chapters 3 and 4 illustrate that long-lived assets such as office equipment, police cruisers, and other items may be acquired by expenditure of appropriations of the General Fund or one or more special revenue funds. Long-lived assets used by activities financed by the General Fund or other governmental funds are called **general capital assets.** General capital assets should be distinguished from capital assets that are specifically associated with activities financed by proprietary and fiduciary funds. Capital assets acquired by proprietary and fiduciary funds are accounted for by those funds.

Capital assets include land, buildings, land and building improvements, construction work in progress, vehicles, machinery, equipment, works of art and historical treasures, infrastructure assets, and intangible assets. They are generally acquired by outright purchase, by construction (either utilizing the government's own workforce or the services of private contractors), or by capital lease agreement. Acquisitions of general capital assets that require substantial amounts of money ordinarily cannot be financed from General Fund or special revenue fund appropriations within a single budgetary period. Thus, they are commonly financed by issuance of long-term debt to be repaid from tax revenues, special assessments against property deemed to be particularly benefited by the long-lived asset, grants from other governments, transfers from

ILLUSTRATION 5–1 **General Capital Asset Acquisition: Governmental Funds and Government-wide Governmental Activities**

General Fund and/or Special Revenue Funds	Capital Projects Funds	Government-wide Governmental Activities
Used to account for capital outlay expenditures from annual budget appropriations. General capital assets acquired are recorded in the governmental activities general ledger at the government-wide level.	Used to account for construction or other major capital expenditures from debt proceeds, capital grants, special assessments, and other sources restricted, committed, or assigned for capital asset acquisition. General capital assets acquired and related long-term debt to be serviced from tax revenues or from special assessments are recorded in the governmental activities general ledger at the government-wide level.	Used to account for the cost and depreciation of general capital assets acquired by expenditures of the General Fund, special revenue funds, and capital projects funds. Also used to account for general capital assets acquired under capital leases and for those acquired by gift. Used to account for all general capital asset-related long-term debt.

other funds, gifts from individuals or organizations, capital leases, or a combination of several of these sources. If money received from these sources is restricted, committed, or assigned to the purchase or construction of specified general capital assets, it is recommended that a **capital projects fund** be created to account for and report resources restricted, committed or assigned for such projects. When deemed useful, capital projects funds may also be used to account for the acquisition of major general capital assets, such as buildings, under a capital lease agreement. Leases involving equipment are more commonly accounted for by the General Fund.

As discussed and illustrated in Chapter 4, governmental funds account only for current financial resources; therefore, these funds do not record capital assets acquired by the funds. Rather, general capital assets purchased or constructed with governmental fund resources are recorded in the governmental activities general ledger at the government-wide level. Illustration 5–1 summarizes the fund types and activities at the government-wide level as they relate to general capital asset acquisition. It shows that general capital assets may be acquired from expenditures of the General Fund, special revenue funds, or capital projects funds. The cost or other carrying value of general capital assets and any related long-term debt is recorded in the general ledger for the governmental activities category at the government-wide level. This chapter focuses on capital projects fund accounting and financial reporting. Chapters 3 and 4 discuss accounting and financial reporting for the General Fund, special revenue funds, and permanent funds.

ACCOUNTING FOR GENERAL CAPITAL ASSETS

Management should maintain an inventory record for each asset, or group of related assets that exceeds the minimum dollar capitalization threshold established by the government, as well as other important assets, such as computers or computer software that might fall below the threshold level but warrant tracking. Inventory records help achieve accountability and should provide all information needed for planning an effective maintenance program, preparing budget requests for replacements and additions, providing for adequate insurance coverage, and assigning the responsibility for custody of the assets.

Governmental Accounting Standards Board (GASB) standards require that general capital assets be recorded at historical cost. **Historical cost** includes acquisition cost plus ancillary costs necessary to put the asset into use.[1] Ancillary costs may include items such as freight and transportation charges, site preparation costs, and set-up costs. If the cost of a capital asset was not recorded when the asset was acquired and is unknown when accounting control over the asset occurred, it is acceptable to record an estimated cost. If general capital assets are donated, they are recorded at their fair value at the time of receipt, plus ancillary charges. Revenue related to the donation is recognized in the government-wide statement of activities and classified as program revenue or general revenue consistent with the criteria discussed in Chapter 3.

As demonstrated in Chapter 4, Entries 4c and 4d, acquisition of a general capital asset represents an expenditure in a governmental fund but requires capitalization of an asset in the appropriate governmental activities account. Following the GASB reporting model, general capital assets are reported in the Governmental Activities column of the statement of net position, net of accumulated depreciation, when appropriate. Any rational and systematic depreciation method is allowed. Depreciation is not reported for inexhaustible assets such as land and land improvements, capitalized collections of works of art or historical treasures whose useful lives are not diminished by display or other applications, and infrastructure assets that are accounted for using the *modified approach*.[2] (The modified approach is explained later in this chapter.) The term amortization rather than depreciation is used when referring to intangible assets.

Even though general capital assets are acquired for the production of general governmental services rather than for the production of services that are sold, reporting depreciation on general capital assets may provide significant benefits to users and managers alike. Reporting depreciation expense as part of the direct expenses of functions and programs in the Governmental Activities column of the government-wide statement of activities (see Illustration A2–2) helps to determine the full cost of providing each function or program. Depreciation expense on capital assets used in the operations of a government grant–financed program is often an allowable cost under the terms of a grant. In addition, depreciation expense may provide useful information to administrators and legislators concerned with the allocation of resources to programs, departments, and activities. To a limited extent, a comparison of the accumulated depreciation on an asset with the cost of the asset may assist in budgeting outlays for replacement of capital assets.

Required Disclosures about Capital Assets

GASB standards require certain disclosures about capital assets in the notes to the basic financial statements, both the general capital assets reported in the Governmental Activities column and those reported in the Business-type Activities column of the government-wide financial statements.[3] These disclosures should be divided into the major classes of capital assets of the primary government (as discussed in the following section) and should distinguish between general capital assets and those reported in business-type activities. Capital assets that are not being depreciated are disclosed separately from those assets that are being depreciated. In addition to disclosure of

[1] Governmental Accounting Standards Board, *Codification of Governmental Accounting and Financial Reporting Standards, as of June 30, 2014* (Norwalk, CT, 2014), Sec. 1400.102.

[2] Ibid., par. 104.

[3] GASB, *Codification,* Sec. 2300.117–119.

their general policy for capitalizing assets and for estimating the useful lives of depreciable assets, required disclosures about each major class of capital assets include:

1. Beginning-of-year and end-of-year balances showing accumulated depreciation separate from historical cost.
2. Capital acquisitions during the year.
3. Sales or other dispositions during the year.
4. Depreciation expense for the current period with disclosure of the amounts charged to each function in the statement of activities.
5. Disclosures describing works of art or historical treasures that are not capitalized and explaining why they are not capitalized. While the GASB encourages capitalization of all collections or individual works of art or historical treasures, governments can opt *not* to capitalize if the collection is (1) held for public exhibition, education, or research in furtherance of public service rather than for financial gain; (2) protected, kept unencumbered, cared for, and preserved; and (3) subject to an organizational policy that requires the proceeds from sales of collection items to be used to acquire other items for collections.[4] If collections are capitalized, they should be included in the disclosures described in items 1 through 4.

Illustration 5–2 presents capital asset note disclosures for the City and County of Denver. These disclosures conform in all respects to required items 1–4 above, and an additional note states that the city capitalizes all assets with a cost over its $5,000 capitalization threshold, with the exception of internally generated software which has a threshold of $50,000. Relative to item 5, artwork collections are not capitalized because these assets are held for public exhibition rather than financial gain. Items are protected and preserved and proceeds from any sales, where allowed, must be used to acquire other items for collection.

Denver's capital asset disclosures are presented in two sections, representing Governmental Activities and Business-type Activities. Within each section, capital assets not being depreciated (land, land rights, and construction in progress) are reported separately from those that are being depreciated, as required by GASB standards. Such information should be useful for both internal and external decision makers as it reports on beginning balances for each major class of capital assets, additions to and dispositions or reclassifications from each class, and the ending balance of each class. The same information is provided for accumulated depreciation. Lastly, the disclosure presents the amount of depreciation expense that was charged to each function of governmental activities and each business-type activity at the government-wide level.

Classification of General Capital Assets

The capital asset classifications shown in Illustration 5–2 are typical of those used by state and local governments. Additional or similarly named accounts may be needed to better describe the asset classes of any given governmental entity. As discussed previously in this chapter, general capital assets typically are those acquired using the financial resources of a governmental fund. Many of these assets, however, are not used exclusively in the operations of any one fund, nor do they belong to a fund.

[4] These GASB *Codification* Section 1400.109 criteria, all of which must be met in order not to capitalize, are identical to those in FASB *ASC* 958-360-20 for nongovernmental not-for-profit organizations (see Chapter 13 for discussion).

ILLUSTRATION 5–2 Illustrative Capital Assets Disclosure

CITY AND COUNTY OF DENVER, COLORADO
Capital Assets Disclosure
For the Year Ended December 31, 2013

Capital asset activity for the year ended December 31, 2013, was as follows (in thousands):

Primary Government

	January 1	Additions	Deletions	Transfers	December 31
Governmental Activities:					
Capital assets not being depreciated:					
Land and land rights	$ 291,843	$ 4,514	$ —	$ —	$ 296,357
Construction in progress	88,056	45,776	—	(49,311)	84,521
Total capital assets not being depreciated	**379,899**	**50,290**	**—**	**(49,311)**	**380,878**
Capital assets being depreciated:					
Buildings and improvements	2,256,276	29,546	(1,342)	14,549	2,299,029
Equipment and other	302,418	25,286	(7,369)	267	320,602
Collections	62,324	4,657	(13,917)	677	53,741
Intangibles	10,797	145	—	1,929	12,871
Infrastructure	1,334,365	38,814	(210)	31,889	1,404,858
Total capital assets being depreciated	**3,966,180**	**98,448**	**(22,838)**	**49,311**	**4,091,101**
Less accumulated depreciation for:					
Buildings and improvements	(591,743)	(70,902)	1,896	—	(660,749)
Equipment and other	(244,444)	(26,381)	7,333	—	(263,492)
Collections	(44,844)	(3,870)	13,881	—	(34,833)
Intangibles	(507)	(2,753)	—	—	(3,260)
Infrastructure	(616,466)	(44,494)	210	—	(660,750)
Total accumulated depreciation	**(1,498,004)**	**(148,400)**	**23,320**	**—**	**(1,623,084)**
Total capital assets being depreciated, net	**2,468,176**	**(49,952)**	**482**	**49,311**	**2,468,017**
Governmental Activities Capital Assets, net	**$ 2,848,075**	**$ 338**	**$ 482**	**$ —**	**$ 2,848,895**
Business-type Activities:					
Capital assets not being depreciated:					
Land and land rights	$ 322,202	$ 143	$ —	$ 13	$ 322,358
Construction in progress	186,350	292,361	(45)	(35,277)	443,389
Total capital assets not being depreciated	**508,552**	**292,504**	**(45)**	**(35,264)**	**765,747**
Capital assets being depreciated:					
Buildings and improvements	2,038,012	41	(4,594)	5,951	2,039,410
Improvements other than buildings	3,048,009	5,725	(2,993)	10,496	3,061,237
Machinery and equipment	791,280	10,480	(31,041)	18,817	789,536
Total capital assets being depreciated	**5,877,301**	**16,246**	**(38,628)**	**35,264**	**5,890,183**
Less accumulated depreciation for:					
Buildings and improvements	(951,900)	(60,967)	2,107	—	(1,010,760)
Improvements other than buildings	(1,162,758)	(81,593)	1,103	—	(1,243,248)
Machinery and equipment	(608,394)	(59,166)	28,525	—	(639,035)
Total accumulated depreciation	**(2,723,052)**	**(201,726)**	**31,735**	**—**	**(2,893,043)**
Total capital assets being depreciated, net	**3,154,249**	**(185,480)**	**(6,893)**	**35,264**	**2,997,140**
Business-type Activities Capital Assets, net	**$ 3,662,801**	**$ 107,024**	**$ (6,938)**	**$ —**	**$ 3,762,887**

Note: Interest costs of $27,721 were capitalized during 2013.

continued

ILLUSTRATION 5–2 (*Continued*)

Depreciation expense was charged to the functions of the primary government as follows (in thousands):

Governmental activities:	
General government	$ 23,535
Public safety	17,775
Public works, including depreciation of infrastructure	52,181
Human services	882
Health	548
Parks and recreation	22,738
Cultural activities	28,865
Community development	22
Capital assets held by internal service funds	1,854
Total	**$148,400**

Source: City and County of Denver, Notes to the Financial Statements, 2013, Note D.

Consider, for example, that general capital assets include courthouses and city halls, public buildings in general, the land on which they are situated, highways, streets, sidewalks, storm drainage systems, equipment, and other tangible assets with a life longer than one fiscal year. The following paragraphs present a brief review of generally accepted principles of accounting for typical categories of capital assets based on applicable GASB standards.

Land

The cost of land acquired by a government through purchase should include not only the contract price but also such related costs as taxes and other liens assumed, title search costs, legal fees, surveying, filling, grading, draining, and additional costs of preparing the land for its intended use. Governments are frequently subject to damage suits in connection with land acquisition, and the amounts of judgments levied are considered capital costs of the property acquired. Land acquired through forfeiture should be capitalized at the total amount of all taxes, liens, and other claims surrendered plus all other costs incidental to acquiring ownership and perfecting title. Land acquired through donation should be recorded on the basis of appraised value at the date of acquisition; the cost of the appraisal itself should not be capitalized, however.

Buildings and Improvements Other than Buildings

Buildings are structures erected above ground for the purpose of sheltering persons or property, while building improvements include alterations, renovations, or betterments that materially extend the useful life of a building or increase its value, or both. Hence, routine or minor repairs to buildings are not considered building improvements. Land improvements include land attachments of a permanent nature, walks, retaining walls, parking lots, fencing and landscaping. Land improvements that are inexhaustible and produce permanent benefits are not depreciable; however, land improvements that are part of a structure or that deteriorate over time, such as fences, should be depreciated.[5]

The historical cost of buildings and improvements acquired by purchase includes the cost of purchased items, as well as legal and other costs necessary to put the capital

[5] GASB, *Comprehensive Implementation Guide* 7.13.4.

asset into acceptable condition for its intended use. Likewise, capital assets constructed by outside contractors are capitalized at the contract price, plus incidental costs incurred to prepare the asset for use. However, determination of the cost of buildings and improvements obtained through construction by some agency of the government (sometimes called force account construction) is slightly more difficult. In these cases, costs should include not only all direct and indirect expenditures of the fund providing the construction but also materials and services furnished by other funds.

The value of buildings and improvements acquired by donation should be established by appraisal. As in the case of land, one reason for setting a value on donated buildings and improvements is to aid in determining the total value of capital assets used by the government and for reports and comparisons. However, more compelling reasons exist for setting a value on buildings and certain improvements: the need for obtaining proper insurance coverage and the need to substantiate the insurance claim if loss should occur. Finally, the cost of donated general capital assets is also required to be reported in the Governmental Activities column of the government-wide financial statements.

Machinery and Equipment

Machinery and equipment are usually acquired by purchase. Occasionally, however, machinery and equipment may be constructed by the government. In such cases, the same rules will apply as for buildings and improvements constructed by governmental employees. The cost of machinery and equipment purchased should include items conventional under business accounting practice: purchase price, transportation costs if not included in purchase price, installation cost, and other direct costs of readying the asset for use. Cash discounts on machinery and equipment purchased should be treated as a reduction of costs. Donated equipment should be recorded in the same manner and for the same reasons as donated buildings and improvements.

Construction Work in Progress

General capital assets acquired with capital projects fund resources would be recorded in essentially the same manner as if they had been acquired by the General Fund. As described later in this chapter, construction expenditures by capital projects funds are ordinarily closed to fund balance accounts at the end of each year, but the amounts are not capitalized in the funds financing the construction. In the governmental activities general journal, Construction Work in Progress is the account used to capitalize the accumulated cost of partially completed general capital assets. Construction Work in Progress is reported on the statement of net position with other assets not being depreciated. Once construction is complete, the capital asset is reclassified from Construction Work in Progress into the proper capital asset category and depreciation begins, as appropriate.

Infrastructure Assets

Infrastructure assets are capital assets, such as highways, streets, sidewalks, storm drainage systems, and lighting systems that are stationary in nature and normally can be preserved for a longer life than most other capital assets. The GASB reporting model requires all state and local governments to report the cost of their infrastructure assets in the government-wide statement of net position. Unless a government adopts the *modified approach* discussed below, it must also report depreciation expense for infrastructure assets in its government-wide statement of activities.

Under the **modified approach,** a government can elect not to depreciate certain *eligible* infrastructure assets, provided that two requirements are met.[6] The two requirements are:

(1) The government manages the eligible infrastructure assets using an asset management system that includes (*a*) an up-to-date inventory of eligible assets, (*b*) condition assessments of the assets and summary of results using a measurement scale, and (*c*) estimates each year of the annual amount needed to maintain and preserve the eligible assets at the condition level established and disclosed by the government, and

(2) The government documents that the eligible infrastructure assets are being preserved approximately at (or above) the condition level established and disclosed (see item 1, (*c*) above).

What constitutes adequate documentation requires professional judgment. At a minimum, the government must provide documentation that (1) complete condition assessments are made at least every three years and (2) the three most recent condition assessments provide reasonable assurance that the eligible infrastructure assets are being preserved at or above the established condition level.

If requirements are met and adequate documentation is maintained, all expenditures incurred to preserve the eligible infrastructure assets should be expensed in the period incurred. Additions and improvements to the eligible assets should be capitalized. As long as the conditions are met, there is evidence that the eligible assets have an indefinite useful life and thus do not need to be depreciated. If the government subsequently fails to maintain the assets at or above the established and disclosed condition level, it must revert to reporting depreciation for its infrastructure assets and discontinue its use of the modified approach.

Intangible Assets

Intangible assets are defined by the GASB as capital assets that lack physical substance, have a useful life of more than one reporting period, and are nonfinancial in nature. Examples of government intangible assets include patents, copyrights, easements, water rights, and computer software. The GASB standards allow for recognition of intangible assets if the asset is separable or if the asset arises from contractual or other legal rights.[7] An asset would be considered separable from the government if, for example, it could be sold, transferred, or exchanged, either individually or in combination with a related asset, liability, or contract. The GASB standards also specifically address capitalization rules for intangible assets, including computer software that are internally generated by government personnel or third parties on behalf of the government. Because intangible assets are considered general capital assets, all guidance related to general capital assets is applicable.

General Capital Assets Acquired under Capital Lease Agreements

As will be explained in some detail in Chapter 6, state and local governments generally have limits on the amount of long-term debt they may issue. Consequently, governments that are reaching their legal debt limit often use leases to acquire capital assets.

[6] GASB, *Codification,* Section 1400.105, specifies eligible assets as those that are part of a network of infrastructure assets or a subsystem of a network. For example, all roadways in a state might be considered a network, and interstate highways and state highways could be considered subsystems of that network.

[7] GASB, *Codification,* Sec. 1400.141.

GASB *Codification* Section L20 addresses accounting and financial reporting standards for a number of forms of leases, two of which are important to governmental lessees: operating leases and capital leases.[8] If a particular lease meets any one of the following classification criteria, it is a **capital lease.**[9]

1. The lease transfers ownership of the property to the lessee by the end of the lease term.
2. The lease contains an option to purchase the leased property at a bargain price.
3. The lease term is equal to or greater than 75 percent of the estimated economic life of the leased property.
4. The present value of rental or other minimum lease payments equals or exceeds 90 percent of the fair value of the leased property less any investment tax credit retained by the lessor.

If no criterion is met, the lease is classified as an **operating lease** by the lessee. Rental payments under an operating lease for assets used by governmental funds are recorded as expenditures of the period. In many states, statutes prohibit governments from entering into obligations extending beyond the current budget year. Because of this legal technicality, governmental lease agreements typically contain a "fiscal funding clause," or cancellation clause, which permits governmental lessees to terminate the agreement on an annual basis if funds are not appropriated to make required payments. GASB standards specify that lease agreements containing fiscal funding or cancellation clauses should be evaluated. If the possibility of cancellation is judged remote, the lease should be disclosed in financial statements and accounts in the manner specified for capital leases.[10]

As an example of accounting for the acquisition of general capital assets under a capital lease agreement, assume that a government signs a capital lease agreement to pay $10,000 on January 1, 2016, the scheduled date of delivery of certain equipment to be used by an activity accounted for by a special revenue fund. The lease calls for annual payments of $10,000 at the beginning of each year thereafter; that is, January 1, 2017, January 1, 2018, and so on, through January 1, 2025. There will be 10 payments of $10,000 each, for a total of $100,000, but GASB standards require entry in the accounts of the present value of the stream of annual payments, not their total. Since the initial payment of $10,000 is paid at the inception of the lease, its present value is $10,000. The present value of the remaining nine payments must be calculated using the borrowing rate the lessee would have incurred to obtain a similar loan over a similar term to purchase the leased asset. Assuming the rate to be 10 percent, the present value of payments 2 through 10 is $57,590. The present value of the 10 payments is, therefore, $67,590. GASB standards require a governmental fund (including, if appropriate, a capital projects fund) to record the following entry at the inception of the capital lease:

	Debits	*Credits*
Special Revenue Fund:		
Expenditures	67,590	
Other Financing Sources—Capital Lease Agreements		67,590

[8] As this textbook goes to press, the GASB's technical agenda includes a major project regarding leases, with guidance slated to be issued in the fourth quarter of 2016.

[9] GASB, *Codification,* Sec. L20.105.

[10] GASB, *Codification*, Sec. L20.108–110.

The corresponding entry in the governmental activities general journal at the government-wide level to record the equipment and long-term liability under the capital lease is as follows:

	Debits	Credits
Governmental Activities:		
Equipment	67,590	
Capital Lease Obligations Payable		67,590

Costs Incurred after Acquisition

Governmental accounting procedures should include clear-cut provisions for classifying costs incurred in connection with capital assets after the acquisition cost has been established. Outlays closely associated with capital assets will regularly occur in amounts of varying size, and responsible persons will be charged with deciding whether these should be recorded as additions to assets. In general, any outlay that clearly adds to the utility or function of a capital asset or enhances the value of an integral part of it may be capitalized as part of the asset. Thus, drainage of land, addition of a room to a building, and changes in equipment that increase its output or reduce its cost of operation are clearly recognizable as additions to assets.

Special difficulty arises in the case of large-scale outlays that are partly replacements and partly additions or betterments. An example would be replacement of a composition-type roof with a roof of more durable material. If the old roof is replaced, the outlays should not be capitalized unless the cost of the old roof is removed from the accounts; however, to the extent that the project provides a better roof, outlays should be capitalized. The distribution of the total cost in such a case is largely a matter for managerial determination. The distribution of the outlay having been decided, the estimated amount of addition or betterment might be added to the asset if capitalization thresholds or other critera are met. Better results are sometimes obtained by crediting the appropriate asset account for the cost of the replaced part, thus removing the amount, and then debiting the asset account for the total cost of the replacing item.

Reduction of Cost or Asset Disposal

Reductions in the recorded cost of capital assets may be brought about by a number of events, including sale, retirement from use, destruction, replacement of a major part, and theft or loss. Reductions may relate to the total amount expended for a given item or items, or they may pertain only to the cost applicable to a specific part. Thus, if an entire building is demolished, the total cost of the structure should be removed from the appropriate accounts; but if the demolition applies only to a wing or some other definitely identifiable portion, the cost eliminated should be the amount estimated as applying to the identifiable portion. The cost of capital assets recorded in the governmental activities ledger may sometimes be reduced by the transfer of an asset to an enterprise fund, or vice versa.

Accounting for cost reductions consisting of entire assets is a relatively simple matter if adequate asset records have been kept. If the reduction is only partial, the cost shown in the capital assets record must be modified to reflect the change with a complete description of what brought about the change. Additionally, if the cost reduction is related to a transfer of capital assets between funds within the same financial reporting entity both historical cost and associated accumulated depreciation should also be transferred in the capital asset records.

Because depreciation is recorded on general capital assets, the removal of a capital asset from the governmental activities general ledger may be accomplished by crediting the ledger account recording the asset's cost and debiting Accumulated Depreciation and Cash if the item was sold. Gains or losses should be recognized if the value received differs from the book value of the assets removed. The gains and losses are reported on the government-wide statement of activities.

Assuming a building that cost $100,000 and with $80,000 of accumulated depreciation is retired, the following entry in the governmental activities general journal would be required:

	Debits	Credits
Governmental Activities:		
Loss on Disposal of Building	20,000	
Accumulated Depreciation—Buildings	80,000	
Buildings		100,000

No entry is required within the General Fund because the cost of the building was recognized as an expenditure and closed to fund balance in the year of acquisition. Property records for the building should receive appropriate notations about the transaction and then be transferred to an inactive file.

In the event that cash is disbursed or received in connection with the disposal of general capital assets, the Cash account would be debited or credited as part of the required entries, and a gain or loss would be recorded, as appropriate. Assuming that in the preceding example the General Fund incurred $3,000 for the demolition of the building, an entry in the following form should be made on the General Fund books:

General Fund:		
Expenditures	3,000	
Cash		3,000

The corresponding entry that should be made at the government-wide level is:

Governmental Activities:		
Loss on Disposal of Building	23,000	
Accumulated Depreciation—Buildings	80,000	
Buildings		100,000
Cash		3,000

If cash is received from the sale of a general capital asset, some question may arise as to its disposition. Theoretically, the cash should be directed to the fund that provided the asset, but this may not always be practicable. If the asset was provided by a capital projects fund, the contributing fund may have been liquidated before the sale occurs. Unless otherwise prescribed by law, disposition of the results of a sale will be handled as decided by the legislative body having jurisdiction over the asset and will be recorded in the manner required by the accounting system of the recipient fund. When the general capital asset sale occurs, the General Fund (or appropriate governmental fund) debits Cash (or a receivable) for the selling price and credits Other Financing Sources—Proceeds of Sales of Assets.

Asset Impairments and Insurance Recoveries

GASB standards provide accounting and reporting guidance for impairment of assets, as well as for insurance recoveries. The GASB defines an **asset impairment** as a *significant, unexpected decline in the service utility of a capital asset.*[11] Impairments occur as a result of unexpected circumstances or events, such as physical damage, obsolescence, enactment of laws or regulations or other environmental factors, or change in the manner or duration of the asset's use.[12] Unless an impairment is judged to be temporary, the amount of impairment should be measured using one of three approaches: *restoration cost approach,* the estimated cost to restore the utility of the asset (appropriate for impairments from physical damage); *service units approach,* the portion of estimated service utility life of the asset that has been estimated lost due to impairment (appropriate for impairments due to environmental factors or obsolescence); and *deflated depreciated replacement cost approach,* the estimated current cost of a replacement asset with similar depreciation and deflated for the effects of inflation (appropriate for impairment due to change in the manner or duration of use).[13] Barring evidence to the contrary, asset impairments should be considered permanent.

When an asset impairment has occurred, the estimated amount of impairment is reported as a write-down in the carrying value of the asset. The loss due to impairment is recorded as a program expense in the government-wide statement of activities for the function using the asset, and as an operating expense in the statement of revenues, expenses, and changes in fund net position of proprietary funds, if applicable. If the impairment is significant in amount and results from an event that is unusual in nature or infrequently occurring, or both, then the loss should be reported as either a special item or extraordinary item, as appropriate.

Impairment losses are reported net of any insurance recoveries that occur during the same fiscal year. Insurance recoveries occurring in a subsequent year should be reported as other financing sources in governmental fund operating statements, as program revenues in the government-wide statement of activities, and as nonoperating revenues in proprietary fund operating statements. Finally, restorations and replacements of impaired capital assets should be reported separately from both the impairment loss and any insurance recovery.

Service Concession Arrangements

In recent years, a number of governments have entered into **service concession arrangements (SCAs)** to generate revenue and cash flows from their capital assets or to improve the efficiency of public services. Under an SCA, a government transfers the rights and obligations of an asset to another legally separate governmental or private sector entity. This external entity, the operator, provides public services

[11] GASB, *Codification,* Sec. 1400.180.

[12] Ibid, par. 184.

[13] Ibid, pars. 187–190.

through the use of the asset, collecting related fees in return for an up-front payment to the transferring government. For example, a private company might pay a large fee to a county in exchange for the right to operate the county's parking garage and collect fees from those who park in the garage for the following 20 years. The county maintains control over the types of services provided and has ability to modify or approve the rates that can be charged for the services. Risks associated with the building, financing, and operation of the public assets often are shared between the government and the external entity.

GASB *Codification* Section S30 includes accounting and financial reporting standards for both transferors and governmental operators. In general, standards require that the transferring government continue reporting the transferred asset as a capital asset and any related contractual obligations as liabilities. The government will record the operator's payment or receivable, a liability for the present value of significant contractual obligations (i.e., commitments to maintain the asset in a specified condition, insurance costs, etc.), and a corresponding deferred inflow of resources for the difference between the two. The *deferred inflow* is recognized as revenue over the term of the arrangement. If the operator is a governmental entity, the operating government will report an intangible asset at cost for its right to access the facility and collect third-party fees. The intangible asset is then amortized over the term of the arrangement.

CAPITAL PROJECTS FUNDS

The reason for creating a fund to account for capital projects is the same as the reason for creating special revenue funds—to provide a formal mechanism to enable administrators to ensure revenues and other financing sources dedicated to a certain purpose are used for that purpose and no other. For example, grants or other resources provided by state and federal agencies to help finance capital acquisitions made by local governments necessitate establishment of accounting and reporting procedures that can provide information showing compliance with terms of the grants. Furthermore, the use of a fund helps ensure that all required information is provided when it is needed. Also, capital projects financed through general obligation debt should be accounted for in a capital projects fund.

Capital projects funds differ from the General Fund and special revenue funds in that the latter categories have a year-to-year life, whereas capital projects funds have a project-life focus. In some jurisdictions, governments are allowed to account for all capital projects within a single capital projects fund. In other jurisdictions, laws are construed as requiring each project to be accounted for by a separate capital projects fund. Even in jurisdictions that permit the use of a single fund, managers may prefer to use separate funds to enhance control over each project.

Accounting for a capital project, either in a new capital projects fund or within an existing single fund, begins when a capital project or a series of related projects is legally authorized; the fund is closed when the project or series is completed. Appropriation accounts need not be used because the legal authorization to engage in the project is in itself an appropriation of the total amount that may be obligated for the construction or acquisition of the capital asset specified in the project authorization. Estimated revenues need not be recorded because few contractors will start work on a project until financing is ensured through the sale of bonds or the receipt of grants or gifts. To provide control over the issuance of contracts and purchase orders, which may be numerous and which may be outstanding for several years in construction projects, it is recommended that the encumbrance procedure described in Chapter 3 be used. Since the purpose of the capital projects fund is to account for the receipt and expenditure of financial resources earmarked for capital projects, its balance sheet reports only financial resources and the liabilities to be liquidated by those resources. Neither the capital assets acquired nor any long-term debt incurred for the acquisition is recorded in a capital projects fund; these items are recorded in the governmental activities general ledger at the government-wide level, as discussed earlier in this chapter and in Chapter 6.

Illustrative Transactions—Capital Projects Funds

GASB standards require the use of the same basis of accounting for capital projects funds as for the other governmental fund types. Proceeds of debt issues should be recognized by a capital projects fund at the time the issue is sold rather than the time it is authorized because authorization of an issue does not guarantee its sale. Proceeds of debt issues should be recorded as Proceeds of Bonds or Proceeds of Long-Term Notes rather than as Revenues, and they should be reported in the Other Financing Sources section of the statement of revenues, expenditures, and changes in fund balance. Similarly, tax revenues raised by the General Fund or a special revenue fund and transferred to a capital projects fund are recorded as Interfund Transfers In and reported in the Other Financing Sources section of the operating statement.

Taxes raised specifically for a capital projects fund would be recorded as revenues of that fund, as would special assessments to be used for the construction of assets that will be of particular benefit to certain property owners. Grants, entitlements, or shared revenues received by a capital projects fund from another government are considered revenues of the capital projects fund. Interest earned on investments of the capital projects fund is also considered revenue if the interest is available for expenditure by the capital projects fund. If, by law, the interest must be used for service of general long-term capital debt, the interest should be transferred to the appropriate debt service fund.

In the following illustration of accounting for representative transactions of a capital projects fund, it is assumed that the town council of the Town of Brighton authorized an issue of $1,200,000 of 6 percent bonds as partial financing of a fire station expected to cost approximately $1,500,000; the $300,000 additional financing was to be contributed by other governments. The project, utilizing land already owned by the town, was completed partly by a private contractor and partly by the town's own workforce. Completion of the project occurred within the current year. Transactions and entries related to the project are shown here, all of which are assumed to occur in fiscal year 2017. For economy of time and space, vouchering of liabilities is omitted.

The $1,200,000 bond issue, which had been approved by voter referendum, was officially approved by the town council. No formal entry is required to record voter and town council approval. A memorandum entry may be made to identify the approved project and the means of financing it.

To defray engineering and other preliminary expenses incurred prior to the debt issuance, the sum of $50,000 was borrowed on a short-term basis from National Bank. Because this transaction affects both the Fire Station Capital Projects Fund and governmental activities at the government-wide level, the following entry is made in both journals:

		Debits	Credits
	Fire Station Capital Projects Fund and Governmental Activities:		
1.	Cash	50,000	
	Short-Term Notes Payable		50,000

Total purchase orders and other commitment documents issued for supplies, materials, minor equipment, and labor required for the part of the project to be performed by the town's employees amounted to $443,000. (Since the authorization is for the project, not for a budget year, it is unnecessary to include 2017, or any other year, in the account titles.) The following budgetary control entry is made in the capital projects fund but is not recorded at the government-wide level.

	Fire Station Capital Projects Fund:		
2.	Encumbrances	443,000	
	Encumbrances Outstanding		443,000

A contract, in the amount of $1,005,000, was signed for certain work to be done by a private contractor. As with Entry 2, only the capital projects fund is affected.

	Fire Station Capital Projects Fund:		
3.	Encumbrances	1,005,000	
	Encumbrances Outstanding		1,005,000

Special engineering and miscellaneous costs that had not been encumbered were paid in the amount of $48,000. These costs are deemed to be properly capitalized as part of the fire station.

	Fire Station Capital Projects Fund:		
4a.	Construction Expenditures	48,000	
	Cash		48,000
	Governmental Activities:		
4b.	Construction Work in Progress	48,000	
	Cash		48,000

Entries 4a and 4b highlight a major difference between accounting for a governmental fund and governmental activities at the government-wide level. Accounting for a governmental fund focuses on the inflows and outflows of current financial resources on the modified accrual basis; accounting for governmental activities focuses on the inflows and outflows of economic resources, including capital assets, on the accrual basis used in accounting for business organizations. This accounting difference will later be included in the reconciliation between the fund and government-wide financial statements prepared in Chapter 9.

The contractor submitted a bill for work completed in the amount of $495,000.

		Debits	Credits
	Fire Station Capital Projects Fund:		
5a.	Encumbrances Outstanding	495,000	
	Encumbrances		495,000
5b.	Construction Expenditures	495,000	
	Contracts Payable		495,000
	Governmental Activities:		
5c.	Construction Work in Progress	495,000	
	Contracts Payable		495,000

Entries 5a and 5b record conversion of an estimated liability to a firm liability eligible for payment upon proper authentication. Contracts Payable records the status of a claim under a contract between the time of presentation and verification for vouchering or payment.

Payment in full was received from the other governments that had agreed to pay part of the cost of the new fire station.

		Debits	Credits
	Fire Station Capital Projects Fund:		
6a.	Cash	300,000	
	Revenues		300,000
	Governmental Activities:		
6b.	Cash	300,000	
	Program Revenues—Public Safety—Capital Grants and Contributions		300,000

The National Bank loan was repaid with interest amounting to $1,000.

		Debits	Credits
	Fire Station Capital Projects Fund:		
7a.	Interest Expenditures	1,000	
	Short-Term Notes Payable	50,000	
	Cash		51,000
	Governmental Activities:		
7b.	Expenses—Interest on Notes Payable	1,000	
	Short-Term Notes Payable	50,000	
	Cash		51,000

The reader will note that the $1,000 of interest expenditure (expense) recorded in Entries 7a and 7b is not capitalized as part of the total cost of the new fire station. GASB standards prohibit capitalization of interest incurred during the construction of *general capital assets*. However, as is illustrated and discussed in Chapter 7, interest is capitalized as part of self-constructed capital assets recorded for business-type activities and enterprise funds.

On June 15, 2017, the Town of Brighton issued at par bonds with a par value of $1,200,000 and dated June 15, 2017. Thus, there was no accrued interest as of the date of issue. Entries 8a and 8b show the contrast between how the bond issue is recorded in the general journals for the capital projects fund and governmental activities at the government-wide level. Since the bond issue increases current financial resources in the capital projects fund, the credit in Entry 8a is to Other Financing Sources—Proceeds of Bonds rather than to a liability account. As shown in Entry 8b, the long-term liability is recorded in the governmental activities general journal as a credit to Bonds Payable, reflecting the economic resources measurement focus used at the government-wide level. This difference represents another item that will appear in the reconciliation between the fund and the government-wide financial statements prepared in Chapter 9.

		Debits	Credits
	Fire Station Capital Projects Fund:		
8a.	Cash	1,200,000	
	Other Financing Sources—Proceeds of Bonds		1,200,000
	Governmental Activities:		
8b.	Cash	1,200,000	
	Bonds Payable		1,200,000

The contractor's initial claim was fully verified and paid (see Entries 5b and 5c).

	Fire Station Capital Projects Fund and Governmental Activities:		
9.	Contracts Payable	495,000	
	Cash		495,000

Actual invoices for the items encumbered in Entry 2 amounted to $440,000. Although the encumbrances entry only affects the capital projects fund, payment of the invoices affects both the capital projects fund and governmental activities at the government-wide level.

	Fire Station Capital Projects Fund:		
10a.	Encumbrances Outstanding	443,000	
	Encumbrances		443,000
10b.	Construction Expenditures	440,000	
	Cash		440,000
	Governmental Activities:		
10c.	Construction Work in Progress	440,000	
	Cash		440,000

Billing for the balance owed on the construction contract was received from the contractor.

		Debits	Credits
	Fire Station Capital Projects Fund:		
11a.	Encumbrances Outstanding	510,000	
	Encumbrances		510,000
11b.	Construction Expenditures	510,000	
	Contracts Payable		510,000
	Governmental Activities:		
11c.	Construction Work in Progress	510,000	
	Contracts Payable		510,000

Inspection revealed only minor imperfections in the contractor's performance, and on correction of these, the liability to the contractor was paid.

	Fire Station Capital Projects Fund and Governmental Activities:		
12.	Contracts Payable	510,000	
	Cash		510,000

All requirements and obligations related to the project having been fulfilled, the operating statement accounts were closed in the capital projects fund to Fund Balance—Restricted. Project resources consisted of voter-approved debt proceeds and funding from other governments specifically intended for the fire station; hence the use of these funds is restricted. Governmental activities general ledger accounts will be closed in Chapter 9.

	Fire Station Capital Projects Fund:		
13.	Revenues	300,000	
	Other Financing Sources—Proceeds of Bonds	1,200,000	
	Construction Expenditures		1,493,000
	Interest Expenditures		1,000
	Fund Balance—Restricted		6,000

Since the project has been completed, it is appropriate to terminate the capital projects fund. The only remaining asset of the fund after the 13 transactions illustrated is Cash in the amount of $6,000 restricted for fire station construction. State laws often require that assets no longer needed in a capital projects fund be transferred to the fund that will service the debt incurred for the project, a debt service fund. Transfers of this nature are called **interfund transfers** and are reported as other financing uses by the transferor fund and other financing sources by the transferee fund in the statement of revenues, expenditures, and changes in fund balance (see Illustration 5–3). The entries to record the transfer and termination of the Town of Brighton Fire Station Capital Projects Fund are:

	Fire Station Capital Projects Fund:		
14a.	Other Financing Uses—Interfund Transfers Out	6,000	
	Cash		6,000
14b.	Fund Balance—Restricted	6,000	
	Other Financing Uses—Interfund Transfers Out		6,000

Similar entries would be required to record the interfund transfers in by the debt service fund. No entry is required at the government-wide level since the transfer occurs *within* the governmental activities category.

The cost of the fire station constructed by the Town of Brighton is recorded in the governmental activities general journal at the government-wide level. Because all capitalizable costs have previously been recorded as construction work in progress during the period of construction, the only entry required is to reclassify the amount in that account to the Buildings account, as shown in the following entry.

		Debits	Credits
	Governmental Activities:		
15.	Buildings	1,493,000	
	Construction Work in Progress		1,493,000

Illustrative Financial Statements for a Capital Projects Fund

Inasmuch as all balance sheet accounts of the Town of Brighton Fire Station Capital Projects Fund are closed in the case just illustrated, there are no assets, liabilities, or fund equity to report in a balance sheet. The operations of the year, however, should be reported in a statement of revenues, expenditures, and changes in fund balances, as shown in Illustration 5–3. Because it is assumed that the Town of Brighton is not required to adopt a legal budget for its capital projects funds, it does not need to prepare a budgetary comparison schedule or statement for the capital projects fund type.

At the government-wide level, the completed fire station is reported as a capital asset, net of accumulated depreciation (if any depreciation expense is recorded in the first year in which the asset is placed into service), in the Governmental Activities column of the statement of net position (see Illustration A2–1). The $1,200,000 of tax-supported bonds issued for the project is reported as a long-term liability in the Governmental Activities column of the statement of net position. If any depreciation

ILLUSTRATION 5–3

TOWN OF BRIGHTON
Fire Station Capital Projects Fund
Statement of Revenues, Expenditures, and Changes in Fund Balances
For the Year Ended December 31, 2017

Revenues:		
From other governments		$ 300,000
Expenditures:		
Construction	$1,493,000	
Interest	1,000	1,494,000
Excess of revenues over (under) expenditures		(1,194,000)
Other financing sources (uses):		
Proceeds of bonds	1,200,000	
Interfund transfer out	(6,000)	1,194,000
Excess of revenues and other financing sources/uses over expenditures		–0–
Fund balances, January 1, 2017		–0–
Fund balances, December 31, 2017		$ –0–

expense is recorded for the portion of a year that the fire station has been in service, it would be reported as a direct expense of the Public Safety function in the statement of activities (see Illustration A2–2).

Alternative Treatment of Residual Equity or Deficits

In the example just presented, a modest amount of cash remained in the Fire Station Capital Projects Fund after the project had been completed and all liabilities of the fund were liquidated. If expenditures and other financing uses are planned and controlled carefully so that actual costs do not exceed planned costs, revenues and other financing sources of the capital projects fund should equal, or slightly exceed, the expenditures and other financing uses, leaving a residual fund equity. If, as in the example presented, long-term debt has been incurred for the purposes of the capital projects fund, the residual equity is ordinarily transferred to the fund that is to service the debt. If the residual equity has come from grants or shared revenues restricted for capital acquisitions or construction, legal advice may indicate that any residual equity must be returned to the source(s) of the restricted grants or restricted shared revenues.

Even with careful planning and cost control, expenditures and other financing uses of a capital projects fund may exceed its revenues and other financing sources, resulting in a negative fund balance, or a deficit. If the deficit is a relatively small amount, the legislative body of the government may be able to authorize transfers from one or more other funds to cover the deficit in the capital projects fund. If the deficit is relatively large, and/or if intended transfers are not feasible, the government may seek additional grants or shared revenues from other governments to cover the deficit. If no other alternative is available, the government would need to finance the deficit by issuing debt in whatever form is legally possible and feasible under market conditions then existing.

Bond Premium, Discount, and Accrued Interest on Bonds Sold

Governments that issue bonds or long-term notes to finance the acquisition of capital assets commonly sell the entire issue to an underwriter or a syndicate of underwriters on the basis of bids or negotiated terms. The underwriters then sell the bonds or notes to institutions or individuals who often have agreed in advance to purchase a specified amount of bonds from the underwriters.[14] Statutes in some states prohibit the initial sale of an issue of local government bonds at a discount. Accordingly, it is usual to set the interest rate high enough to enable the underwriters to pay the issuer at least the par, or face, value of the bonds; it is not unusual for underwriters to pay issuers an amount in excess of par, known as a *premium.* State statutes, local ordinances, or bond indentures often require that initial issue premiums be used for debt service. In such cases only the par value of the bonds is considered as an other financing source of the capital projects fund; the premium is considered as an other financing source of the debt service fund. Therefore, the sale of bonds at a premium would require an entry in the capital projects fund for the face of the bonds (as shown in Entry 8a of this chapter) and an entry in the debt service fund for the premium. At the government-wide level, a premium would be recorded as an additional component of the general long-term liability for the bonds. As in accounting for business organizations, the premium should be amortized, using the effective-interest method, over the life of the bonds.

[14] Issue costs associated with general long-term debt, such as underwriter fees, attorney and rating agency fees or bond insurance, should be reported as expenditures, rather than a reduction of bond proceeds. GASB, *Codification,* Sec. 1800.126.

The amount of amortization is the difference between the actual cash paid for interest and the calculated amount of effective interest expense for the period.

It may happen that the issuing government receives one check from the underwriters for the total amount of the par and premium. If procedures of that government indicate that it is desirable to record the entire amount in the capital projects fund, the following entries are appropriate (using assumed amounts). (*Note:* This entry and the one that follows are not part of the Town of Brighton Fire Station Capital Projects Fund example.)

	Debits	Credits
Capital Projects Fund:		
Cash	1,509,000	
Other Financing Sources—Proceeds of Bonds		1,500,000
Due to Other Funds		9,000

This entry accounts for the bond premium as a liability of the capital projects fund because it must be remitted to the debt service fund. In the debt service fund, an entry would be made to debit Due from Other Funds and credit Other Financing Sources—Premium on Bonds. Some accountants prefer to credit Other Financing Sources—Premium on Bonds rather than Due to Other Funds in the capital projects fund, particularly if the disposition of the premium is still to be determined on the sale date. Some accountants also include the amount of the premium as part of the credit to Other Financing Sources—Proceeds of Bonds in the capital projects fund. If either of these alternative procedures is used, it is necessary to make a second entry in the capital projects fund debiting Other Financing Uses—Interfund Transfers Out and crediting Due to Other Funds.

In those jurisdictions in which it is legal for bonds to be sold initially at a discount, using the same face amount as the bonds in the entry above, except the debt proceeds are less than the face amount of the bonds, the entry might be:

Capital Projects Fund:		
Cash	1,491,000	
Other Financing Uses—Discount on Bonds	9,000	
Other Financing Sources—Proceeds of Bonds		1,500,000

Crediting Other Financing Sources—Proceeds of Bonds for $1,500,000 carries the implication that, if necessary, the discount is expected to be counterbalanced at a future date by receipt of money from another source, perhaps the General Fund. When the money from another source is received, the capital projects fund should debit Cash and credit either Revenues or Other Financing Sources, depending on the source of the money. When it is known in advance that the discount will not be made up by transfers from other sources, the initial entry would include a debit to Cash and a credit to Other Financing Sources—Proceeds of Bonds, each for par value less discount.

When bonds are sold between interest payment dates, the party buying the bonds must pay up front the amount of interest accrued from the date the bonds are issued (the starting date for purposes of calculating interest) to the date the bonds are actually sold as part of the total price of the bonds. Thus, assuming two months of interest have already accrued by the sale date, and interest is paid semi-annually, the two months of interest that bondholders pay at the sale date yields the equitable result that they earn a *net* four months of interest, although they will receive a full six months of interest only four months after the sale date. In a governmental fund, accrued interest sold should conceptually be credited to Interest Expenditure and be offset against the six-month interest expenditure recorded on the first interest payment date following the sale of the bonds. In practice, however, accrued interest sold is generally recorded as a revenue of the debt service fund. This practice simplifies budgetary control by permitting the government to budget appropriations for and record an expenditure for the full six months of interest that must be paid on the first interest payment date. At the government-wide level, however, cash received on the sale date for accrued interest would be credited either as Accrued Interest Payable or Interest Expense, as in accounting for businesses.

Retained Percentages

It is common to require contractors on large-scale contracts to give performance bonds, providing for indemnity to the government for any failure on the contractor's part to comply with terms and specifications of the agreement. Before final inspection of a project can be completed, the contractor may have moved its work force and equipment to another location, thus making it difficult to remedy possible objections to the contractor's performance. Also, the shortcoming alleged by the government may be of a controversial nature with the contractor unwilling to accede to the demands of the government. Results of legal action in such disagreements are not predictable.

To provide more prompt adjustment on shortcomings not large or convincing enough to justify legal action and not recoverable under the contractor's bond, as well as those the contractor may admit but not be in a position to rectify, it is common practice to withhold a portion of the contractor's payment until final inspection and acceptance have occurred. The withheld portion is normally a contractual percentage of the amount due on each segment of the contract.

In the Town of Brighton illustration, the contractor submitted a bill for $495,000, which, on preliminary approval, was recorded previously in Entry 5b in the Fire Station Capital Projects Fund as follows:

	Debits	Credits
Capital Projects Fund:		
Construction Expenditures	495,000	
Contracts Payable		495,000

Assuming that the contract provided for retention of 5 percent, current settlement on the billing would be recorded as follows:

Capital Projects Fund:		
Contracts Payable	495,000	
Cash		470,250
Contracts Payable—Retained Percentage		24,750

This same entry would also be made in the governmental activities general journal at the government-wide level. Alternatively, the intention of the government to retain the percentage stipulated in the contract could be recorded at the time the progress billing receives preliminary approval. In that event, the credit to Contracts Payable in the first entry in this section would be $470,250, and the credit to Contracts Payable—Retained Percentage in the amount of $24,750 would be made at that time. The second entry, therefore, would be a debit to Contracts Payable and a credit to Cash for $470,250.

On final acceptance of the project, the retained percentage is liquidated by a payment of cash. In the event that the government recording the retention finds it necessary to spend money on correction of deficiencies in the contractor's performance, the payment is charged to Contracts Payable—Retained Percentage. If the cost of correcting deficiencies exceeds the balance in the Contracts Payable—Retained Percentage account, the excess amount is debited to Construction Expenditures in the Fire Station Capital Projects Fund and to Buildings (or other appropriate capital asset account) in the governmental activities general journal.

Claims and Judgments Payable

Claims and judgments often, although not always, relate to construction activities of a government. If a claim has been litigated and a judicial decision adverse to the government has been rendered, there is no question as to the amount of the liability that should be recorded. If claims have not been litigated or judgments have not been made as of the balance sheet date, liabilities may be estimated through a case-by-case review of all claims, the application of historical experience to the outstanding claims, or a combination of these methods.[15]

GASB standards specify that the amount of claims and judgments recognized as expenditures and liabilities of governmental funds is limited to the amount that would normally be liquidated with expendable resources then in the fund; however, the full known or estimated liability should be reported in the Governmental Activities column of the government-wide statement of net position.

Bond Anticipation Notes Payable and the Problem of Interest Expenditures

A government may experience delays in perfecting all details connected with bond issuance or may postpone a bond sale until a large portion of the proceeds is needed. In such cases, governments often obtain temporary financing by use of **bond anticipation notes.** The "bond anticipation" description of the debt signifies an obligation to retire the notes from proceeds of a proposed bond issue. If the following two conditions are met, then the liability for bond anticipation notes should be treated as a long-term liability:[16]

1. All legal steps have been taken to refinance the bond anticipation notes.
2. The intent is supported by an ability to consummate refinancing the short-term notes on a long-term basis.

[15] GASB standards (GASB *Codification,* Sec. C50.110–114) require that if information is available prior to issuance of the financial statements that indicates it is probable that an asset has been impaired or a liability has been incurred at the date of the financial statements and the amount of the loss can be estimated with a reasonable degree of accuracy, the liability should be recognized.

[16] GASB *Codification,* Sec.1500.111–114 and B50.101.

In cases in which the bond anticipation notes are secured by approved but unissued bonds and the intent is to repay the notes from the proceeds of the bond issue, it would appear that the two criteria have been met and thus bond anticipation note issues in such cases would be reported as a long-term liability in the Governmental Activities column of the government-wide statement of net position and as an other financing source (Proceeds of Bond Anticipation Notes) in the capital projects fund.

As an example of a bond anticipation note that meets the two criteria provided, assume that a particular city issued $500,000 of 6 percent bond anticipation notes under a written agreement that the notes will be retired within six months using the proceeds of a previously approved $5,000,000 bond issue. When the bond anticipation notes are issued, the journal entries for the capital projects fund and governmental activities would be as follows:

	Debits	Credits
Capital Projects Fund:		
Cash	500,000	
Other Financing Sources—Proceeds of Bond Anticipation Notes		500,000
Governmental Activities		
Cash	500,000	
Bond Anticipation Notes Payable		500,000

Six months later, the bonds are issued at par and the bond anticipation notes are retired using a portion of the bond proceeds. Cash from other sources is assumed to be used to pay interest on the bond anticipation notes. The required journal entries are as follows:

	Debits	Credits
Capital Projects Fund:		
Cash	5,000,000	
Other Financing Sources—Proceeds of Bonds		5,000,000
Other Financing Uses—Retirement of Bond Anticipation Notes	500,000	
Interest Expenditures	15,000	
Cash		515,000
Governmental Activities:		
Cash	5,000,000	
Bonds Payable		5,000,000
Bond Anticipation Notes Payable	500,000	
Expenses—Interest on Long-Term Debt	15,000	
Cash		515,000
(*Note:* Interest expense is $500,000 × .06 × 6/12 = $15,000)		

As indicated in the preceding example, interest almost always must be paid on bond anticipation notes. Both practical and theoretical problems are involved in the payment of interest on liabilities. Practically, payment of interest by the capital projects fund reduces the amount available for construction or acquisition of the assets, so the administrators of the capital projects fund would wish to pass the burden of interest payment to another fund. Logically, the debt service fund set up for the bond issue should bear the burden of interest on bond anticipation notes and possibly on judgments, but at the time this interest must be paid, the debt service fund may have no assets. It would also appeal to the capital projects fund's administrators that interest on the bond anticipation notes and judgments should be paid by the General Fund (or any other fund with available cash). If such interest payments have been included in the appropriations budget by the General Fund (or other fund), the payment is considered legal; if not, the legislative body might authorize the other fund to pay the interest.

If the capital projects fund bears the interest on bond anticipation notes or other short-term debt, either initially or ultimately, an expenditure account must be debited. In Entry 7a illustrated earlier in this chapter, interest paid on short-term notes payable was debited to Interest Expenditures rather than to Construction Expenditures because GASB requirements prohibit the capitalization of construction-period interest on general capital assets. Entry 7b showed that the $1,000 paid for interest also was not capitalized as part of the cost of the assets for the fire station project.

Investments

Interest rates payable on general long-term debt have typically been lower than interest rates that the government can earn on temporary investments of high quality, such as U.S. Treasury bills and notes, bank certificates of deposit, and government bonds with short maturities. Consequently, there is considerable attraction to the practice of selling bonds as soon as possible after a capital project is legally authorized and investing the proceeds to earn a net interest income. This practice also avoids the problems and costs involved in financing by bond anticipation notes, described in the preceding section. However, arbitrage rules under the Internal Revenue Code constrain the investment of bond proceeds to securities whose yield does not exceed that of the new debt. Application of these rules to state and local governments is subject to continuing litigation and legislative action, so competent legal guidance must be sought by governments wishing to invest bond proceeds in a manner that will avoid incurring an *arbitrage rebate* and possible difficulties with the Internal Revenue Service.

Interest earned on temporary investments is available for use by the capital projects fund in some jurisdictions; in others, laws or local practices require the interest income to be transferred to the debt service fund or to the General Fund. If interest income is available to the capital projects fund, it should be recognized on the modified accrual basis as a credit to Revenues. If it will be collected by the capital projects fund but must be transferred to another fund, an additional entry is required to record an interfund transfer out. If the interest will be collected by the debt service fund, or other fund that will recognize it as revenue, no entry by the capital projects fund is necessary.

Multiple-Period and Multiple-Project Funds

Thus far, discussion of capital projects fund accounting has proceeded on the assumption that initiation and completion of projects occur in the same fiscal year. However, many projects large enough to require a capital projects fund are started in one year and ended in another. Furthermore, a single comprehensive authorization may legalize two or more purchase or construction projects as segments of a master plan of improvements. Both multiple-period and multiple-project activities require some deviations from the accounting activities that suffice for one-period, one-project accounting.

The first difference appears in the budgeting procedure. Whereas for a one-period operation a single authorization might adequately cover the project from beginning to end, annual budgets, in one form or another, may be desirable or even required for those extending into two or more periods. This practice is used as a means of keeping the project under the legislative body's control and preventing the unacceptable deviations that might result from a one-time, lump-sum approval of a long-term project. Likewise, a large bond issue, to be supplemented by grants from outside sources, may be authorized to cover a number of projects extending over a period of time but not planned in detail before initiation of the first project. Such an arrangement requires the fund administration to maintain control by giving final approval to the budget for each project only as it comes up for action.

For a multiple-project fund, it is necessary to identify encumbrances and expenditures in a way that will indicate the project to which each encumbrance and expenditure applies in order to check for compliance with the project budget. This can be accomplished by adding the project name or other designation (e.g., City Hall or Project No. 75) to the encumbrance and expenditure account titles. This practice facilitates preparation of cash and expenditure statements for multi-project operations.

In accounting for encumbrances for multi-period projects, there is some difference of opinion as to the desirable procedure to follow in relation to encumbrances outstanding at the end of a period. In the management of the General Fund, for example, operations in terms of amounts of revenues and expenditures during a specified standard period of time (quarter, half year, etc.) provide measures of budgetary accomplishment. Because capital projects are rarely of the same size and may be started and ended at any time of year, periodic comparisons are of little significance. Furthermore, although the personnel of a legislative body may change at the beginning of a year during which a capital project is in progress, the change is unlikely to affect materially the project's progress. Although the operations of a capital projects fund are project-completion oriented, with slight reference to time, GASB standards require Expenditures, Proceeds of Bonds, and Revenues accounts to be closed to the appropriate fund balance accounts at year-end to facilitate preparation of capital projects fund financial statements for inclusion in the government's annual report on a basis consistent with year-end statements of other funds. The authorization (appropriation) for a capital project, however, does not expire at the end of a fiscal year but continues for the life of the project.

The required closing procedure does produce year-end capital projects fund balance sheets that appear similar to those of the General Fund and special revenue funds illustrated in preceding chapters. The similarity of appearance and terminology may be misleading, however. The spendable fund balance accounts of the General Fund or a special revenue fund represent net financial resources available for appropriation, whereas the spendable fund balances of a multiple-period capital projects fund, classified as restricted, committed, or assigned, represent net financial resources already set aside for the acquisition of specified capital facilities. The fund balance accounts of a multiple-period capital projects fund are comparable to an unexpended unencumbered appropriation item of the General Fund at an interim period; they are not comparable to the year-end fund balance accounts of such funds.

Capital Projects Financed by Special Assessments

Earlier in this chapter it was noted that one common source of financing construction of general capital assets is by issuance of long-term debt to be repaid by special assessments. A **special assessment** is a compulsory levy made against certain property to defray part or all of the cost of a specific improvement or service that is of particular benefit to the assessed property and may also be of benefit to the general citizenry. Generally, a group of property owners agrees to the formation of a special assessment district, sometimes called a *local improvement district,* to facilitate a capital improvement project (e.g., street improvements within a housing development). Subject to state laws, the local government acts on behalf of those property owners by arranging for financing, overseeing the progress and completion of the project, and collecting the assessments to pay any debt incurred to finance the project.

A special assessment district may be an independent special purpose government created under the laws of the state in which it is located, or a component unit of a county, city, or other general government. In some cases, special assessment transactions are administered directly by a general purpose government. If a special assessment district is an independent special purpose government, it will need to account for the construction phase of a capital project, the debt service phase of the project, and the resulting general capital assets and related long-term debt as described in this chapter and Chapter 6. The same observations apply to a special assessment district that is a component unit of a primary government, which should be reported in a discrete presentation in the basic financial statements of the governmental financial reporting entity, as discussed briefly in Chapters 2 and 4, and in greater detail in Chapter 9.

If the financial activities of a special assessment district are so intertwined with those of the primary government that the balances and transactions meet the criteria for blending (see discussion related to Illustration 9–1), it is logical that special assessment transactions be administered directly by the primary government. In that event the accounting and reporting standards set forth in this chapter apply to capital projects financed in whole or in part by special assessments with a few minor modifications and additions.[17]

General capital assets financed wholly or partially through collections of special assessments are recorded in the same manner as any other general capital assets in the governmental activities category at the government-wide level.

Financial Reporting for Capital Projects Funds

Each capital projects fund that meets the definition of a *major fund* (see the Glossary for a definition) must be reported in a separate column of the balance sheet—governmental funds (see Illustration A2–3) and the statement of revenues, expenditures, and changes in fund balances—governmental funds (see Illustration A2–5). Nonmajor capital projects funds would be reported in a column with other nonmajor governmental funds in these two basic financial statements.

Governments are also encouraged but not required to provide as supplementary information combining financial statements for all nonmajor funds. Combining financial statements present each nonmajor fund as a separate column. These statements usually would not be included within the scope of the auditor's examination other than indirectly as part of the audit of the basic financial statements.

The required basic financial statements and notes thereto, along with the recommended combining financial statements, should meet most external report users' needs for information about capital projects funds. Internal management and those with oversight responsibility for capital projects may need additional information, however, of a more detailed nature. Additional information that may be useful for internal management or oversight purposes includes information about whether the amount and quality of work accomplished to date is commensurate with resources expended to date and project plans, and whether the remaining work can be accomplished within the established deadlines with remaining resources.

[17] GASB, *Codification*, Sec. S40.

Key Terms

Asset impairment, *178*
Bond anticipation notes, *189*
Capital leases, *175*
Capital projects fund, *168*
General capital assets, *167*
Historical cost, *168*
Infrastructure assets, *173*
Intangible assets, *174*
Interfund transfers, *184*
Modified approach, *174*
Operating leases, *175*
Service concession arrangements (SCAs), *178*
Special assessment, *192*

Selected References

Governmental Accounting Standards Board. *Codification of Governmental Accounting and Financial Reporting Standards, as of June 30, 2014.* Norwalk, CT, 2014.

Governmental Accounting Standards Board. *Comprehensive Implementation Guide as of June 30, 2014.* Norwalk, CT, 2014.

Questions

5–1. What are general capital assets? How are they reported in the fund and government-wide financial statements?

5–2. Explain what disclosures the GASB requires for capital assets in the notes to the financial statements.

5–3. Compare and contrast the valuation of general capital assets of a government to the valuation of assets of a for-profit entity. What special issues may arise in valuing a government's assets that generally do not occur in a for-profit company?

5–4. How does one determine whether a particular lease is a capital lease or an operating lease? What entries are required in the general journals of a governmental fund and governmental activities at the government-wide level to record a capital lease at its inception?

5–5. What are examples of intangible assets held by governments? How are they recorded?

5–6. What is the accounting difference between using the modified approach for infrastructure assets and depreciating infrastructure assets? Under the modified approach, what happens if infrastructure assets are not maintained at or above the established condition level?

5–7. If a capital project is incomplete at the end of a fiscal year, what happens to Encumbrances and all operating statement accounts at year-end?

5–8. Both a capital projects fund general ledger and the governmental activities general ledger at the government-wide level are affected by transactions related to construction of a new capital asset for a government. Describe the major differences in how activities are recorded in the capital projects fund and the governmental activities general ledger. Why do these differences occur?

5–9. What two measures help protect a government from failure on a contractor's part to comply with the terms and specifications of a construction agreement? Describe each measure and its primary purpose.

5–10. What is a service concession arrangement, and why might a government choose to enter into such an arrangement? Provide examples of general capital assets that might be subject to service concession arrangements.

Cases

5–11 Using the Modified Approach or Depreciation. You are an auditor in a regional public accounting firm that does a large volume of governmental audits and consulting engagements. The finance director of a large metropolitan city has asked you for assistance in determining whether it should use the modified approach or depreciate its infrastructure assets. The city is particularly interested in which accounting approach other large metropolitan cities have chosen.

Required

a. Examine several comprehensive annual financial reports (CAFRs) of large cities. Create a table that lists the cities and the methods they have chosen to report their general infrastructure assets.

b. Prepare a memo to your client summarizing the results of your research. Be sure to address the finance director's specific concern about what other large cities are doing with respect to reporting of infrastructure assets.

5–12 Criteria for Intangible Asset Recognition. In preparation for the annual meeting of Barker County, the finance committee was meeting to discuss the financial reports that would be presented to the Board of Commissioners. The committee included a newly elected commissioner, Michelle Backin, who graduated about 15 years ago with a business degree from the local college. After a long discussion about why the presentation of the financial information was so different from what she had learned in her accounting principles course, the county treasurer, Jack Black, was wrapping up the meeting.

"Are there any final questions from anyone on the committee?" Jack asked. Michelle raised her hand.

"I just have one more question. Since the county has the power to tax, shouldn't there be an intangible asset in the government-wide financial statements that reflects the value of that power? Isn't it similar to owning a patent or trademark that allows you to produce future revenue? And I know that patents and trademarks are intangible assets."

Jack looks at you, and says "Why don't you answer this question for Michelle?"

Required

a. First, present to Michelle the requirements that need to be met for an intangible asset to be recorded in the county's financial statements. Your discussion should be in language that a person without significant accounting knowledge would understand.

b. Using those requirements, explain in detail whether the power to tax meets the definition of an intangible asset.

c. Is there a point in time when the power to tax creates an asset? Explain.

5–13 Recording and Reporting of Damaged Capital Assets. A tornado damaged a part of the City of Westbrook's Police Station. Some of the costs related to the damage included the following:

1. The building wiring had to be replaced. Since the wiring was over 20 years old, replacing the wiring allowed the city to bring the wiring up to current code and accommodate the increasing technology needs of the police station.
2. A large section of the interior walls (dry-wall) had to be replaced and painted. The same type of material was used in replacing the interior walls.
3. All hardwood floors were replaced with the same materials.

4. Office furniture that had been gathered for transfer to the city's surplus storage facility was damaged beyond repair. Replacement furniture was on order but had not been received by the date of the tornado.
5. The police station's radio dispatch equipment suffered water damage.

Required

a. Discuss how to determine if the police station should be considered impaired, and if it is impaired, how accounting and reporting should be handled.

b. Discuss whether you would classify the costs incurred to repair the building as enhancements or replacements.

c. Discuss the accounting treatment of the damaged furniture and radio dispatch equipment.

5–14 Considerations Involving a Service Concession Arrangement. You are a town council member in the seaside town of Pleasantville. Poor economic conditions and unusually severe weather conditions have affected tourism in the town, leading to significantly reduced sales, income, and hotel resort tax collections. Town revenue is 50 percent below budget, while expenditures remain constant at budgeted levels; hence, a sizable budget deficit is imminent. A group of investors has approached the town council with a proposal to take over operations of metered parking areas and the municipal beach parking garage for 20 years. In return for the anticipated parking revenues, the town will receive a $1 million up-front payment and retain full ownership of the parking operations at the end of the agreement. The town will also have some control over rates charged and will collect parking fines assessed. The town will continue to make debt payments related to the garage construction.

You perform some research and find that two larger cities in a neighboring state entered into a similar arrangement to mixed reviews. While city officials were praised for balancing their budgets and spending additional funds on local government programs, drivers complained about higher rates and frequent meter and parking garage malfunctions.

Required

a. What questions do you have about the proposal?

b. Evaluate the proposal on a long-term and short-term basis.

c. How do you think the agreement would affect the city's bond rating?

Exercises and Problems

5–15 Examine the CAFR. Utilizing the CAFR obtained for Exercise 1–16, answer these questions.

a. **General and Other Capital Assets:**

(1) **Reporting of Capital Assets.** Are capital assets reported as a line-item in the government-wide statement of net position? Are nondepreciable capital assets reported on a separate line from depreciable capital assets, or are they separately reported in the notes to the financial statements? Do the notes include capital asset disclosures, such as those for the City and County of Denver shown in Illustration 5–2? Does the disclosure show beginning balances, increases and decreases, and ending balances for each major class of capital assets, as well as the same information for accumulated depreciation for each major class? Are these disclosures presented

separately for the capital assets of governmental activities, business-type activities, and discretely presented component units? Do the notes specify capitalization thresholds for all capital assets, including infrastructure? Do the notes show the amounts of depreciation expense assigned to each major function or program for governmental activities at the government-wide level? Are the depreciation policies and estimated lives of major classes of depreciable assets disclosed? Do the notes include the entity's policies regarding capitalization of collections of works of art and historical treasures? If collections are capitalized, are they depreciated? Are accounting policies disclosed for assets acquired under capital leases?

(2) **Other.** Is the accumulated cost of construction work in progress recorded as an asset anywhere within the financial statements or notes? Which fund, or funds, account for cash received, or receivables created, from sales of general capital assets? Are the proceeds of sales of general capital assets reported as an other financing source or as revenue?

b. **Capital Projects Funds:**

(1) **Title and Content.** What title is given to the funds that function as capital projects funds, as described in this chapter? (Street Improvement Funds and Capital Improvement Funds are common titles, although these titles also are often used for special revenue funds that account for ongoing annual maintenance of roadways.) Where does the report state the basis of accounting used for capital projects funds? Is the basis used consistent with GASB standards discussed in this chapter? Are there separate capital projects funds for each project, several funds that account for related projects, or is only one fund used for all projects?

(2) **Statements and Schedules.** What statements and schedules pertaining to capital projects funds are presented? In what respects (headings, arrangement, items included, etc.) do they differ when compared to statements illustrated or described in the text? Are any differences merely a matter of terminology or arrangement, or do they represent significant deviations from GASB accounting and reporting standards for capital projects funds?

(3) **Financial Resource Inflows.** What is the nature of the financial resource inflows utilized by the capital projects funds? If tax-supported bonds or special assessment bonds are the source, have any been sold at a premium? At a discount? If so, what was the accounting treatment of the bond premium or discount?

(4) **Fund Expenditures.** How much detail is given concerning capital projects fund expenditures? Is the detail sufficient to meet the information needs of administrators? Legislators? Creditors? Grantors? Interested residents? For projects that are incomplete at the date of the financial statement, does the report compare the percentage of total authorization for each project expended to date with the percentage of completion? For those projects completed during the fiscal year, does the report compare the total expenditures for each project with the authorization for each project? For each cost overrun, how was the overrun financed?

(5) **Assets Acquired under Capital Leases.** Were any general capital assets acquired by the primary government or one or more component units under a capital lease agreement during the year for which you have statements? If so, was the present value of minimum lease rentals recorded as an Expenditure and as an Other Financing Source in a capital projects fund (or in any other governmental fund)? If the primary government or one or more component units leased assets from another component unit, how are the assets, related liabilities, expenditures, and other financing sources reported in the basic financial statements or in another section of the CAFR of the reporting entity?

5–16 Multiple Choice. Choose the best answer.

1. Under GASB standards, which of the following would be considered an example of an intangible asset?
   a. A lake located on city property.
   b. Water rights associated with the springs that supply the water to the lake.
   c. The city's irrigation system, which uses water from the lake.
   d. None of the above would be considered an intangible asset.

2. Two new copiers were purchased for use by the city clerk's office using General Fund resources. The copiers cost $15,000 each; the city's capitalization threshold is $5,000. Which of the following entries would be required to completely record this transaction?

	Debits	Credits
a. General Fund		
Expenditures	30,000	
Vouchers Payable		30,000
b. Governmental Activities		
Expenses	30,000	
Vouchers Payable		30,000
c. General Fund		
Expenditures	30,000	
Vouchers Payable		30,000
Governmental Activities		
Equipment	30,000	
Vouchers Payable		30,000
d. General Fund		
Expenditures	30,000	
Vouchers Payable		30,000
Governmental Activities		
Expenses	30,000	
Vouchers Payable		30,000

3. Maxim County just completed construction of a new town hall to be used for its governmental offices. The employees have moved in and the new building is officially in use. The county used a capital projects fund to account for the construction of the building, and the building came in under budget. There is a fund balance of $12,000. The county should:
   a. Transfer the remaining funds to the General Fund to pay operating expenses.

b. Transfer the remaining funds to the debt service fund which will be handling the long-term debt incurred for the construction of the building.
c. Return the excess to the source of the restricted funding.
d. All of the above may be appropriate ways to treat the fund balance.

4. A capital projects fund would probably *not* be used for which of the following assets?
a. Construction and installation of new shelving in the mayor's office.
b. Financing and construction of three new fire substations.
c. Purchase and installation of an entity-wide integrated computer system (such as SAP).
d. Replacing a bridge.

5. Machinery and equipment depreciation expense for general capital assets totaled $163,000 for the reporting period. Which of the following correctly defines the recording of depreciation for general capital assets?

	Debits	Credits
a. Depreciation Expenditure	163,000	
Accumulated Depreciation		163,000
b. Depreciation Expense	163,000	
Machinery and Equipment		163,000

c. Depreciation expense is allocated and recorded at the government-wide level with a debit to the functions or programs of government and a credit to accumulated depreciation.
d. Since depreciation does not involve the use of financial resources it is not necessary for the government to record it at the fund level or government-wide level.

6. Which of the following is a correct statement regarding the use of the *modified approach* for accounting for eligible infrastructure assets?
a. Depreciation on eligible infrastructure assets need not be recorded if the assets are being maintained at or above the established condition level.
b. Depreciation on eligible infrastructure assets must still be recorded for informational purposes only.
c. The government must document that it is maintaining eligible infrastructure assets at the condition level prescribed by the GASB.
d. All of the above are correct statements.

7. The City of Deauville entered into a service concession arrangement (SCA) with Water Wonders, Inc. to operate the city pool for the next 20 years. Water Wonders has agreed to pay the city $3,000,000 up front as a part of this agreement. According to the agreement, Water Wonders will be responsible for operating the pool, and the city will continue to be responsible for costs related to maintaining it. In addition, Water Wonders has the right to collect fees from the public for their use of the pool, although the rates are subject to approval by the city. The city should:
a. Remove the cost of the pool and the related accumulated depreciation from its records because it has effectively transferred the asset to Water Wonders.
b. Record the receipt of the cash payment, a liability for the cost of required future maintenance, and a deferred inflow of resources for the difference between the cash payment and the liability.

c. Record the payment as a cash receipt and as an other financing source for the General Fund.
d. Set up a proprietary fund to record all transactions related to the SCA.

8. Callaway County issued $10,000,000 in bonds at 101 for the purpose of constructing a new County Recreation Center. State law requires that any premium on bond issues be deposited directly in a debt service fund for eventual repayment of bond principal. The journal entry to record issuance of the bonds will require a (an):
   a. Credit to Bonds Payable in the capital projects fund.
   b. Credit to Other Financing Sources—Proceeds of Bonds in the capital projects fund.
   c. Credit to Other Financing Sources—Premium on Bonds in the debt service fund.
   d. Both *b* and *c* are correct.

9. Centerville enters into a capital lease for new copiers in all its city hall offices. In the General Fund, it should report:
   a. Equipment balances equal to the lease payments made during the year.
   b. Capital expenditures equal to the lease payments made during the year.
   c. Equipment balances equal to the capitalizable cost of the fixed assets regardless of the amount of lease payments made during the year.
   d. Capital expenditures equal to the capitalizable cost of the fixed asset regardless of the amount of lease payments made during the year.

10. The following balances are included in the subsidiary records of Sinclair:

Town hall building	$5,000,000
Town pool (supported by user fees)	1,000,000
Town pool maintenance equipment	25,000
Police cars	200,000
Equipment	75,000
Office supplies	10,000

What is the total amount of general capital assets held by the town?
   a. $5,275,000.
   b. $5,285,000.
   c. $6,275,000.
   d. $6,285,000.

5–17 General Capital Assets. Make all necessary entries in the appropriate governmental fund general journal and the government-wide governmental activities general journal for each of the following transactions entered into by the City of Loveland.

1. The city received a donation of land that is to be used by Parks and Recreation to develop a public park. At the time of the donation, the land had a fair value of $5,200,000 and was recorded on the donor's books at a historical cost of $4,500,000.
2. The Public Works Department sold machinery with a historical cost of $35,100 and accumulated depreciation of $28,700 for $6,000. The machinery had originally been purchased with special revenue funds.
3. A car was leased for the mayor's use. Since the term of the lease exceeded 75 percent of the useful life of the car, the lease was capitalized. The first payment was $1,000 and the present value of the remaining lease payments was $30,000.

4. During the current year, a capital projects fund completed a new public safety building that was started in the prior year. The total cost of the project was $9,720,000. Financing for the project came from a $9,000,000 bond issue that was sold in the prior year, and from a $720,000 federal capital grant received in the current year. Current year expenditures for the project totaled $1,176,000. The full cost is attributed to the building since it was constructed on city-owned property.
5. Due to technological developments, the city determined that the service capacity of some of the technology equipment used by general government had been impaired. The calculated impairment loss due to technology obsolescence was $1,156,000.

5–18 Capital Asset Disclosures. Carmel County has prepared the following schedule related to its capital asset activity for the fiscal year 2017. Carmel County has governmental activities only, with no business-type activities.

CARMEL COUNTY
Capital Asset Disclosures
For the Year Ended December 31, 2017

	January 1	Change	December 31
Total capital assets not being depreciated (land, infrastructure, machinery under capital lease, and construction work in progress)	$61,721,000	$ 9,158,000	$70,879,000
Total capital assets being depreciated (buildings, equipment, and collections)	13,421,000	1,647,000	15,068,000
Less total accumulated depreciation	(3,464,000)	(558,000)	(4,022,000)
Capital assets, net	$71,678,000	$10,247,000	$81,925,000

Required

a. Does the above capital asset footnote disclosure comply with the GASB requirements? Explain.

b. Does the county use the modified approach to account for infrastructure assets? Explain.

5–19 Capital Assets Acquired under Lease Agreements. The City of Rochester signed a 30-year agreement with East Coast Real Estate, Inc. to lease a newly constructed building for city services. The city agrees to make an initial payment of $1,000,000 and annual payments of $809,375 for the next 29 years. Using an assumed borrowing rate of 6 percent, the present value of the lease payments is approximately $12,000,000. At the time the lease agreement is signed, the building had an appraised market value of $13 million and an estimated life of 40 years.

Required

a. Using the criteria presented in this chapter, determine whether the city should consider this lease agreement a capital lease. Explain your decision.

b. Provide the journal entries the city should make for both the capital projects fund and governmental activities at the government-wide level to record the lease at the date of inception.

c. Which financial statement(s) prepared at the end of the first year would show both the asset and the liability related to this capital lease?

5–20 Asset Impairment. On July 20, 2017, the building occupied by Sunshine City's Culture and Recreation Department suffered severe structural damage as a result of a hurricane. It had been 48 years since a hurricane had hit the Sunshine City area, although hurricanes in Sunshine City's geographic area are not uncommon. The building had been purchased in 2007 at a cost of $2,000,000 and had accumulated depreciation of $500,000 as of July 2017. Based on a restoration cost analysis, city engineers estimate the impairment loss at $230,000; however, the city expects during the next fiscal year to receive insurance recoveries of $120,000 for the damage.

Required

a. Should the estimated impairment loss be reported as an extraordinary item? As a special item? Explain.

b. Record the estimated impairment loss in the journal for governmental activities at the government-wide level.

c. How should the insurance recovery be reported in the following fiscal year? (You need not provide the journal entry or entries here.)

5–21 Recording Capital Projects Fund Transactions. In Fulbright County, the Culture and Recreation Department constructed a library in one of the county's high growth areas. The construction was funded by a number of sources. Below is selected information related to the Library Capital Project Fund. All activity related to the library construction occurred within the 2017 fiscal year.

1. The county issued $6,000,000, 4 percent bonds, with interest payable semi-annually on June 30 and December 31. The bonds sold for 101 on July 30, 2016. Proceeds from the bonds were to be used for construction of the library, with all interest and premiums received to be used to service the debt issue.
2. A $650,000 federal grant was received to help finance construction of the library.
3. The Library Special Revenue Fund transferred $250,000 for use in construction of the library.
4. A construction contract was awarded in the amount of $6,800,000.
5. The library was completed on June 1, 2017, four months ahead of schedule. Total construction expenditures for the library amounted to $6,890,000. When the project was completed, the cost of the library was allocated as follows: $200,000 to land, $6,295,000 to building, and the remainder to equipment.
6. The capital projects fund temporary accounts were closed to Fund Balance—Restricted. The resources are restricted because they were obtained from bonded debt issued exclusively for library construction. The capital projects fund was closed by transferring remaining funds to the debt service fund for use in library construction debt repayment.

Required

Make all necessary entries in the capital projects fund general journal and the governmental activities general journal at the government-wide level.

5–22 Statement of Revenues, Expenditures, and Changes in Fund Balances. The pre-closing trial balance for the Chance County Woodland Park Capital Projects Fund is provided on the next page.

	Debits	Credits
Cash	$ 987,000	
Grant Receivables	600,000	
Investments	1,000,000	
Contract Payable		$1,263,500
Contract Payable—Retained Percentage		66,500
Encumbrances Outstanding		1,625,000
Revenues		707,000
Encumbrances	1,625,000	
Construction Expenditures	4,150,000	
Other Financing Sources—Proceeds of Bonds		4,700,000
	$8,362,000	$8,362,000

Required

a. Prepare the June 30, 2017, statement of revenues, expenditures, and changes in fund balances for the capital projects fund.

b. Has the capital project been completed? Explain your answer.

5–23 Multiple-Project Fund Transactions. During FY 2017, the voters of Surprise County approved construction of a $21 million police facility and an $11 million fire station to accommodate the county's population growth. The construction will be financed by tax-supported bonds in the amount of $30 million, a $1 million economic stimulus grant, and a portion of future use tax revenues. During 2017, the following events and transactions occurred.

1. Issued $100,000 of 6 percent bond anticipation notes to cover preliminary planning and engineering expenses.
2. Incurred architecture and engineering costs in the amount of $60,000. They were split evenly between the two projects.
3. Entered into a construction contract for $32 million—$21 million was for the police facility and $11 million was related to the fire station.
4. Issued the $30 million, 20-year 5% bonds at 101. (The premium should be recorded in a debt service fund. You do not need to record this entry.)
5. Paid off the bond anticipation notes that had been outstanding 180 days. (Interest is an expenditure of the capital projects fund.)
6. An invoice for $16 million was received from the contractor for a portion of police facility construction ($10 million) and fire station construction ($6 million).
7. Half of the grant funds were received in cash. The remainder is anticipated in 2018; however, the grantor notified the county that there is no guarantee that the federal government will appropriate the 2018 portion.
8. The initial construction invoice, less 5% retainage, was paid.
9. The fire station was completed, and a final invoice for the remaining $5 million was received. All fire station construction charges incurred can be capitalized as buildings.
10. Following inspection, the fire station invoices were paid in full.
11. At year-end, the contractor billed the county an additional $7.5 million for the police facility; however, the police facility was incomplete.
12. Temporary accounts were closed at year-end. Assume that the fund balances are all restricted.

Required

a. Prepare journal entries to record the preceding information in a single Surprise County Construction Fund and the governmental activities general journal at the government-wide level.

b. Prepare a Surprise County Construction Fund balance sheet for the year ended December 31, 2017.

c. Prepare a Construction Fund statement of revenues, expenditures, and changes in fund balances for the year ended December 31, 2017.

d. How would these capital expenditures for the police facility and fire station appear on the Surprise County's government-wide statements of net position and activities?

5–24 Capital Projects Transactions. In 2017, Riverside began work on an outdoor amphitheater and concession stand at the city's park. It is to be financed by a $3,500,000 bond issue and supplemented by a $500,000 General Fund transfer. The following transactions occurred in 2017:

1. The General Fund transferred $500,000 to the Park Building Capital Projects Fund.
2. A contract was signed with Restin Construction Company for the major part of the project on a bid of $2,700,000.
3. Preliminary planning and engineering costs of $69,000 were vouchered for the Great Pacific Engineering Company. (This cost had not been encumbered.)
4. A payable was recorded for an $18,500 billing from the Water and Sewer enterprise fund for the cost of extending water pipes to the new concession stand.
5. An invoice in the amount of $1,000,000 was received from Restin for progress to date on the project.
6. The $3,500,000 bonds were issued at par.
7. The amount billed by the contractor (see Transaction 5) less 5 percent retainage was paid.
8. Temporary investments were purchased at a cost of $1,800,000.
9. Closing entries were prepared as of December 31, 2017. Assume that $2,500,000 of the encumbrances outstanding will be paid from the bond proceeds and are therefore considered restricted resources.

Required

a. Prepare journal entries to record the preceding information in the general ledger accounts for the Park Building Capital Projects Fund. (You may ignore the entries that would also be required in the governmental activities general journal at the government-wide level.)

b. Prepare a balance sheet for the Park Building Capital Projects Fund as of December 31, 2017.

c. Prepare a statement of revenues, expenditures, and changes in fund balances for the period.

Chapter Six

Accounting for General Long-term Liabilities and Debt Service

Learning Objectives

After studying this chapter, you should be able to:

6-1 Explain what types of liabilities are classified as general long-term liabilities.

6-2 Make journal entries in the governmental activities general journal to record the issuance and repayment of general long-term debt.

6-3 Prepare note disclosures for general long-term debt.

6-4 Describe the reasons for statutory debt limits and explain the terms *debt margin* and *overlapping debt*.

6-5 Explain the purpose and types of debt service funds.

6-6 Make appropriate journal entries to account for activities of debt service funds.

The use of long-term debt is a traditional part of the fiscal policy of state and local governments, particularly for financing the acquisition of general capital assets. Although some governments have issued taxable debt, the interest earned on most debt issued by state and local governments is exempt from federal taxation and, in some states, from state taxation. The tax-exempt feature enables governments to raise large amounts of capital at relatively low cost. For example, total long-term debt outstanding for state and local governments amounted to $2.94 trillion at the end of 2013.[1] Because of the relative ease with which governments can issue debt, most states have acted in the public interest to impose statutory limits on the debt that can be incurred by state and local governments. Consequently, effective management of state and local governmental debt requires good legal advice and a sound understanding of public finance.

This chapter describes the types of debt and other long-term liabilities that are termed "general long-term liabilities." **General long-term liabilities** are those that arise from activities of governmental funds and that are not reported as fund liabilities of a proprietary or fiduciary fund. General long-term liabilities are reported as

[1] U.S. Federal Reserve, *Federal Reserve Statistical Release,* "Flow of Funds Accounts of the United States," Washington, D.C., Federal Reserve, March 6, 2014, Table D.3, p. 5.

liabilities in the Governmental Activities column of the government-wide statement of net position but are not reported as liabilities of governmental funds. This chapter also discusses the concepts of direct and overlapping debt, statutory debt limit, and debt margin. Finally, the chapter explains the nature and types of debt service funds, and debt service accounting at the fund and government-wide levels for various types of general long-term liabilities, as well as accounting for refunding of debt.

GENERAL LONG-TERM LIABILITIES

The primary focus of this chapter is general long-term liabilities arising from financing activities, such as the issuance of bonds and notes, and capital leases. In addition, long-term liabilities can arise from the operating activities of governments. Examples of long-term liabilities related to operating activities include claims and judgments, compensated absences, pensions and other postemployment benefits, and obligations related to landfills and pollution remediation. Compensated absences, pollution remediation obligations, and claims and judgments are briefly discussed later in this chapter. Other types of long-term liabilities are discussed in Chapter 7 (landfill obligations) and Chapter 8 (pensions and other postemployment benefits).

Accounting for Long-term Liabilities

When studying this chapter, the reader is reminded that governmental fund types (General, special revenue, capital projects, debt service, and permanent funds) account for only short-term liabilities to be paid from fund assets.[2] While, the proceeds of long-term debt may be placed in one of these fund types (usually a capital projects fund), the long-term liability itself must be recorded in the governmental activities accounting records at the government-wide level. As shown in illustrative Entries 8a and 8b in Chapter 5, most increases in general long-term liabilities arising from debt issuances are recorded as an other financing source in a governmental fund and as a general long-term liability at the government-wide level.

As a general rule, entries are made in the governmental activities general journal at the government-wide level to reflect increases or decreases in general long-term liabilities. Increases in long-term liabilities that arise from operating activities, for example, estimated losses from long-term claims and judgments, are recorded only at the government-wide level by debiting an expense and crediting a liability. Also, any portion of special assessment debt that will be repaid directly by the government (e.g., to finance the portion of a special assessment project deemed to have public benefit) should be reported like any other general long-term liability of the government.

Proprietary funds and perhaps certain private-purpose trust funds account for both long-term debt serviced by the fund and short-term debt to be repaid from fund assets.

[2] Conceivably a permanent fund could have a long-term liability, for example, if a permanent fund consisted of a gift of income-producing real property that the government accepted subject to a long-term mortgage note. In establishing the permanent fund as a governmental fund type, the GASB cited its belief that most such funds hold only financial resources (e.g., investments in financial securities and cash). Thus, it is not clear whether any permanent funds in practice hold assets other than financial assets, and the probability is low that any permanent funds have long-term liabilities. Moreover, GASB standards provide no guidance on how income-producing real property and long-term liabilities could be accounted for as a governmental fund.

As discussed in subsequent chapters, the liabilities of enterprise funds should be displayed on the face of the statement of the issuing fund if that fund may realistically be expected to finance the debt service; however, if the liability also is secondarily backed by the full faith and credit of the government, the contingent general obligation liability of the government should be disclosed in a note to the financial statements. Likewise, if contingency clauses associated with enterprise fund tax-supported debt become effective because resources of the enterprise fund are insufficient for debt service, the unpaid portion of the debt is recorded as a liability of governmental activities at the government-wide level.

Long-term Liability Disclosures

In any given year, it is common for new debt issues to be authorized, for previously authorized debt to be issued, and for older issues to be retired. When a combination of liability events takes place, a schedule detailing changes in long-term debt is needed to inform report users of the details of how long-term liabilities have changed. The general long-term liability disclosures required by GASB reporting standards effectively meet these needs by providing detail of beginning of period long-term liabilities, additions to and reductions of those liabilities, ending liabilities, and the portion of the liabilities payable within one year. Illustration 6–1 presents this disclosure schedule for the City and County of Denver.

In addition to the disclosures about long-term liabilities presented in Illustration 6–1, information about the amount of debt principal and interest that will be due in future years is useful information to financial managers, bond analysts, and others having an interest in assessing a government's requirements for future debt service expenditures. One form of such a schedule, representing a disclosure from the notes to the financial statements for Denver, prepared in conformity with GASB standards, is shown in Illustration 6–2. The reader should note that the interest portion of the scheduled future debt service payments is *not* a present liability and should not be presented as such. To do so would not be in conformity with generally accepted accounting principles.

Debt Limit and Debt Margin

The information provided in the debt schedules already illustrated in this chapter is primarily useful to administrators, legislative bodies, credit analysts, and others concerned with the impact of long-term debt on the financial condition and activities of the government, particularly with reference to the resulting tax rates and taxes. Another matter of importance is the legal limit on the amount of long-term indebtedness that may be outstanding at a given time, in proportion to the assessed value of property within the government's jurisdiction.[3] Because a government's power to issue bonds constitutes an ever-present hazard to the welfare of its property owners in particular and its taxpayers in general, this authority is ordinarily limited by legislation. The purpose of legislative limitation is to obtain a prudent balance between public welfare and the rights of individual citizens. In some jurisdictions, most bond

[3] Even though tax-rate limitation laws may be in effect for a government, the limitation on bonded indebtedness is usually needed because the prevailing practice is to exempt the claims of bondholders from any tax-rate restrictions. This is to say that, even though a law establishing maximums for tax rates is in the statutes, it will probably exclude debt service requirements from the restrictions of the law.

ILLUSTRATION 6–1 **Illustrative Long-term Liabilities Disclosure**

CITY AND COUNTY OF DENVER, COLORADO
Changes in Long-term Liabilities
For the Year Ended December 31, 2013

Long-term liability activity for the year ended December 31, 2013, is as follows (in thousands):

Governmental Activities	January 1	Additions	Deletions	December 31	Due within one year
Legal liability	$ 6,603	$ 941	$ 3,703	$ 3,841	$ —
Pollution remediation	456	—	47	409	47
Compensated absences:					
Classified service employees - 3,072	97,841	15,582	20,586	92,837	4,676
Career Service employees - 5,507	46,396	25,453	25,540	46,309	3,695
Net other postemployment benefit obligation	9,045	1,667	—	10,712	—
Claims payable	32,886	3,908	5,997	30,797	9,398
General obligation bonds[1]	901,188	259,201	250,070	910,319	48,254
GID general obligation bonds	5,290	—	370	4,920	385
Excise tax revenue bonds	230,650	—	19,325	211,325	20,175
Capitalized lease obligations	447,679	34,030	68,292	413,417	23,127
Unamortized premium	40,927	19,659	13,478	47,108	—
Intergovernmental agreement	4,508	—	766	3,742	560
Other governmental funds - note payable	13,804	—	5,948	7,856	—
Total Governmental Activities	**$ 1,837,273**	**$ 360,441**	**$ 414,122**	**$ 1,783,592**	**$ 110,317**

continued

ILLUSTRATION 6–1 (*Continued*)

	January 1[4]	Additions	Deletions	December 31	Due within one year
Business-type Activities					
Wastewater Management					
Revenue bonds	$ 48,555	$ —	$ 2,540	$ 46,015	$ 2,590
Unamortized premium	5,435	—	274	5,161	—
Capitalized lease obligations	8,500	—	534	7,966	548
Notes payable	2,603	—	2,603	—	—
Compensated absences	2,836	43	74	2,805	860
Other long-term liabilities	5,046	2,684	721	7,009	—
Total Wastewater Management	**72,975**	**2,727**	**6,746**	**68,956**	**3,998**
Denver Airport System:					
Revenue bonds	3,897,420	719,915	175,940	4,441,395	133,495
Unamortized premium	167,603	24,464	19,385	172,682	—
Notes payable	32,566	—	6,762	25,804	5,488
Compensated absences	8,999	3,373	3,458	8,914	2,491
Total Denver Airport System	**4,106,588**	**747,752**	**205,545**	**4,648,795**	**141,474**
Nonmajor enterprise funds:					
Revenue bonds	4,450	—	470	3,980	495
Unamortized net premium	19	—	6	13	—
Capitalized lease obligations	1,269	—	450	819	290
Compensated absences	911	1,105	983	1,033	232
Total nonmajor enterprise funds	**6,649**	**1,105**	**1,909**	**5,845**	**1,017**
Total Business-type Activities	**$4,186,212**	**$751,584**	**$214,200**	**$4,723,596**	**$146,489**
Major Component Units:					
Revenue bonds[2]	$ 350,811	$ —	$ 4,772	$ 346,039	$ 4,900
Increment bonds and notes payable[3]	469,133	286,566	196,161	559,538	18,393
Compensated absences	130	102	102	130	—
Total Major Component Units	**$ 820,074**	**$286,668**	**$201,035**	**$ 905,707**	**$ 23,293**

[1]Additions to general obligation bonds represent mini-bond accretion of $842. Ending balance includes compound interest from the 1999A and 2007 mini-bonds of $6,371.
[2]Includes unamortized premium of $6,179.
[3]Includes unamortized premium of $26,750.
[4]As restated.
Source: City and County of Denver, Notes to the Financial Statements, Year Ended 2013, Note G, Tables 31 and 32.

ILLUSTRATION 6–2 Future Debt Service Requirements

CITY AND COUNTY OF DENVER, COLORADO
Future Debt Service Requirements
For the Year Ended December 31, 2013

The debt service requirements to maturity for general obligation bonds at December 31, 2013, are as follows (in thousands):

	Governmental Activities			
	General Government		General Improvement District	
Year	Principal[1]	Interest[2]	Principal	Interest
2014	$ 48,294	$ 42,745	$ 385	$ 308
2015	51,970	39,045	405	291
2016	54,270	36,759	595	273
2017	56,825	34,143	105	248
2018	59,930	31,675	110	240
2019–2023	243,900	134,874	685	1,072
2024–2028	273,135	74,327	960	797
2029–2033	115,615	9,721	1,345	410
2034	—	—	330	23
Total	**$903,939**	**$403,289**	**$4,920**	**$3,662**

[1]Does not include $3,112 and $3,269 of compound interest on the Series 1999A and 2007 mini-bonds respectively, unamortized premium of $33,527, or deferred amount on refunding of ($14,484).

[2]Excludes Build America Bonds interest subsidy. The City is eligible to receive $84 million over the remaining life of its Direct Pay Build America Bonds to subsidize interest payments.

Source: City and County of Denver, Colorado, Notes to the Financial Statements, December 31, 2013, Note G, Table 22.

issues must be approved by referendum; in others, by petition of a specified percentage of taxpayers.

Before continuing a discussion of debt limitation, it seems appropriate to clarify the meaning of the terms *debt limit* and *debt margin.* **Debt limit** means the total amount of indebtedness of specified kinds that is allowed by law to be outstanding at any one time. The limitation is likely to be in terms of a specified percentage of the assessed or actual valuation of property within the government's jurisdiction. It may relate to either a gross or a net valuation. The latter is logical but probably not prevalent because debt limitation exists as a device for protecting property owners from confiscatory taxation. For that reason, tax-paying property *only* should be used in regulating maximum indebtedness. In many governmental jurisdictions, certain property is legally excluded even from *assessment.* This includes property owned by governments, churches, charitable organizations, and some others, depending on state laws. Exemptions, which apply to property subject to assessment, are based on homestead or mortgage exemption laws, military service, and economic status, among others. Both exclusions and exemptions reduce the amount of tax-paying property.

Debt margin, sometimes referred to as *borrowing power,* is the difference between the amount of debt limit calculated as prescribed by law and the net amount of outstanding indebtedness subject to limitation. The net amount of outstanding indebtedness subject to limitation differs from total general long-term indebtedness because certain debt issues may be exempted from the limitation by law, and the amount available in debt service funds for debt repayment is deducted from the outstanding debt in order to determine the amount subject to the legal debt limit. Total general long-term indebtedness must, in some jurisdictions, include special assessment debt and debt serviced by enterprise funds if such debt was issued with covenants that give the debt tax-supported status in the event that collections of special assessments or enterprise fund revenues are insufficient to meet required interest or principal payments. Debt authorized but not issued as of the end of a fiscal year should be disclosed and considered in evaluating debt margin, as it may be sold at any time. Although it would be in keeping with the purpose of establishing a legal debt limit to include the present value of capital lease obligations along with bonded debt in the computation of legal debt margin, state statutes at present generally do not specify that the liability for capital lease obligations is subject to the legal debt limit.

Debt information disclosed within governmental financial statements is monitored closely by bond rating analysts and others. Illustration 6–3 provides ratios relating the City and County of Denver's general obligation debt relative to the taxable value of property over a 10-year period. Legal debt margin calculations for Denver are shown in Illustration 6–4 over the same 10 years. Denver's general indebtedness is limited by charter to 3 percent of actual property valuation. Contrast that with the specific limitations imposed by the City of Portland, Maine, shown in Illustration 6–5. Portland must adhere to debt limitations in total as well as by purpose.

Overlapping Debt

Debt limitation laws ordinarily establish limits that may not be exceeded by each separate governmental entity affected by the laws. This means the county government may incur indebtedness to the legal limit, a township within that county may do likewise, and a city within the township may become indebted to the legal limit, with no restriction because of debt already owed by larger territorial units in which it is located. As a result, a given parcel of real estate or object of personal property may be the basis of debt beyond the legal limit and also may be subject at a given time to assessments for the payment of taxes to retire bonds issued by two or more governments. When this situation exists, it is described as **overlapping debt.**

The extent to which debt may overlap depends on the number of governments represented within an area that are authorized to incur long-term indebtedness. These may include the state, county, township, city, and various special purpose governments, such as a school district. To show the total amount of indebtedness being supported by taxable property located within the boundaries of the reporting government, a statement of direct and overlapping debt should be prepared. Direct debt is the debt that is being serviced by the reporting government. To this direct debt should be added amounts owed by other governments that levy taxes against the same properties on which the direct debt is based. A statement of direct and overlapping debt for the City and County of Denver is presented in Illustration 6–6. Note that the overlapping debt applies to debt issued by a transportation authority, a reclamation district, and a school district which share property boundaries with the City and County of Denver.

ILLUSTRATION 6–3 Legal Debt Margin

CITY AND COUNTY OF DENVER, COLORADO
Legal Debt Margin Information
Last Ten Fiscal Years (in thousands)

Calculation of Legal Debt Margin for Fiscal Year 2013	
Total Estimated Actual Valuation	**$79,581,379**
Maximum general obligation debt, limited to 3% of total valuation	$ 2,387,441
Outstanding bonds chargeable to limit	903,939
Less amount reserved for long-term debt	26,513
Net chargeable to bond limit	**877,426**
Legal Debt Margin – December 31	**$ 1,510,015**

	2004	2005	2006	2007	2008	2009	2010	2011	2012	2013
Debt limit	$1,886,034	$1,975,265	$2,009,975	$2,304,393	$2,356,914	$2,485,329	$2,494,539	$2,314,276	$2,300,923	$2,387,441
Total net debt application to limit	355,492	380,984	453,021	402,994	567,928	649,694	976,103	902,541	862,872	877,426
Legal debt margin	**$1,530,542**	**$1,594,281**	**$1,556,954**	**$1,901,399**	**$1,788,986**	**$1,835,635**	**$1,518,436**	**$1,411,735**	**$1,438,051**	**$ 1,510,015**
Total net debt applicable to the limit as a percentage of debt limit	**18.85%**	**19.29%**	**22.54%**	**17.49%**	**24.10%**	**26.14%**	**39.13%**	**39.00%**	**37.50%**	**36.75%**

Notes: Section 7.2.5, Charter of the City and County of Denver: The City and County of Denver shall not become indebted for general obligation bonds, to any amount, which, including indebtedness, shall exceed three percent of the actual value as determined by the last final assessment of the taxable property within the City and County of Denver.

Source: City and County of Denver, Colorado, Comprehensive Annual Financial Report, Statistical Section, 2013, page 165.

ILLUSTRATION 6–4

CITY AND COUNTY OF DENVER, COLORADO
Ratios of General Bonded Debt Outstanding
Last Ten Fiscal Years (in thousands, except per capita amount)

	2004	2005	2006	2007	2008	2009	2010	2011	2012	2013
General obligation bonds	$378,977	$404,667	$472,309	$422,924	$551,679	$616,209	$969,229	$941,484	$895,649	$903,939
Less amounts available in debt service fund	(23,485)	(23,683)	(19,288)	(19,930)	(21,751)	(26,436)	(34,280)	(38,943)	(32,777)	(26,513)
Total	**$355,492**	**$380,984**	**$453,021**	**$402,994**	**$529,928**	**$589,773**	**$934,949**	**$902,541**	**$862,872**	**$877,426**
Percentage of estimated actual taxable value of property	0.57%	0.58%	0.68%	0.53%	0.67%	0.71%	1.12%	1.17%	1.13%	1.10%
Per capita	$ 621	$ 657	$ 778	$ 681	$ 885	$ 966	$ 1,558	$ 1,519	$ 1,412	$ 1,392

Note: Details regarding the City's outstanding debt can be found in the notes to the financial statements.

Source: City and County of Denver, Colorado, Comprehensive Annual Financial Report, Statistical Section, 2013, Page 163.

ILLUSTRATION 6–5 Detailed Example of Legal Debt Margin

CITY OF PORTLAND, MAINE
Legal Debt Margin Information
Last Ten Fiscal Years
(dollars in thousands)

	2013	2012	2011	2010	2009	2008	2007	2006	2005	2004
Assessed value per State Property Tax Division	$7,552,150	$7,659,250	$7,909,900	$8,196,900	$8,283,450	$8,289,850	$7,653,400	$7,039,000	$6,289,900	$5,501,100
Debt limit - 15% of assessed value	1,132,823	1,148,888	1,186,485	1,229,535	1,242,518	1,243,478	1,148,010	1,055,850	943,485	825,165
Less outstanding debt applicable to debt limit	288,016	274,612	272,137	258,291	247,655	235,893	250,519	248,613	246,515	248,505
Legal debt margin	$ 844,807	$ 874,276	$ 914,348	$ 971,244	$ 994,863	$1,007,585	$ 897,491	$ 807,237	$ 696,970	$ 576,660
Total outstanding debt applicable to the limit as a percentage of debt limit	25.42%	23.90%	22.94%	21.01%	19.93%	18.97%	21.82%	23.55%	26.13%	30.12%

The debt limit is restricted by State statute based on the assessed value per the State above and the percentages below.

	2013	2012	2011	2010	2009	2008	2007	2006	2005	2004
Municipal purposes - 7.5%										
Debt limit	$ 566,411	$ 574,444	$ 593,243	$ 614,768	$ 621,259	$ 621,739	$ 574,005	$ 527,925	$ 471,743	$ 412,583
Less outstanding debt applicable to debt limit	177,292	174,002	174,351	178,469	177,096	173,708	182,078	174,895	179,932	183,619
Debt margin for municipal purposes	$ 389,119	$ 400,442	$ 418,892	$ 436,299	$ 444,163	$ 448,031	$ 391,927	$ 353,030	$ 291,811	$ 228,964
Outstanding debt applicable to the limit as a percentage of debt limit for municipal purposes	31.30%	30.29%	29.39%	29.03%	28.51%	27.94%	31.72%	33.13%	38.14%	44.50%
School purposes - 10%										
Debt limit	$ 755,215	$ 765,925	$ 790,990	$ 819,690	$ 828,345	$ 828,985	$ 765,340	$ 703,900	$ 628,990	$ 550,110
Less outstanding debt applicable to debt limit	37,105	38,087	38,242	34,985	22,171	24,554	27,837	29,605	29,187	24,717
Debt margin for school purposes	$ 718,110	$ 727,838	$ 752,748	$ 784,705	$ 806,174	$ 804,431	$ 737,503	$ 674,295	$ 599,803	$ 525,393
Outstanding debt applicable to the limit as a percentage of debt limit for school purposes	4.91%	4.97%	4.83%	4.27%	2.68%	2.96%	3.64%	4.21%	4.64%	4.49%

continued

ILLUSTRATION 6–5 *(Continued)*

	2013	2012	2011	2010	2009	2008	2007	2006	2005	2004
Storm and sanitary sewer purposes - 7.5%										
Debt limit	$ 566,411	$ 574,444	$ 593,243	$ 614,768	$ 621,259	$ 621,739	$ 574,005	$ 527,925	$ 471,743	$ 412,583
Less outstanding debt applicable to debt limit	73,619	62,523	59,544	44,837	48,388	37,631	40,604	44,113	37,396	40,169
Debt margin for sewer purposes	$ 492,792	$ 511,921	$ 533,698	$ 569,931	$ 572,871	$ 584,108	$ 533,401	$ 483,812	$ 434,347	$ 372,414
Outstanding debt applicable to the limit as a percentage of debt limit for sewer purposes	13.00%	10.88%	10.04%	7.29%	7.79%	6.05%	7.07%	8.36%	7.93%	9.74%
Airport, water and other special district purposes - 3%										
Debt limit	$ 226,565	$ 229,778	$ 237,297	$ 245,907	$ 248,504	$ 248,696	$ 229,602	$ 211,170	$ 188,697	$ 165,033
Less outstanding debt applicable to debt limit	—	—	—	78	235	392	550	707	864	1,024
Debt margin for special district purposes	$ 226,565	$ 229,778	$ 237,297	$ 245,829	$ 248,269	$ 248,304	$ 229,052	$ 210,463	$ 187,833	$ 164,009
Outstanding debt applicable to the limit as a percentage of debt limit for special districts	0.00%	0.00%	0.00%	0.03%	0.09%	0.16%	0.24%	0.33%	0.46%	0.62%
Maximum total debt limit - 15%	$1,132,823	$1,148,888	$1,186,485	$1,229,535	$1,242,518	$1,243,478	$1,148,010	$1,055,850	$ 943,485	$ 825,165

ILLUSTRATION 6–6

CITY AND COUNTY OF DENVER, COLORADO
Direct and Overlapping Governmental Activities Debt
As of December 31, 2013

	Debt Outstanding	Percentage Applicable	City and County of Denver Share of Debt
Direct Debt			
General Obligation bonds	$ 903,939		
General Improvement District bonds	4,920		
Capital leases	413,417		
Housing and Urban Development notes	7,856		
Intergovernmental agreement	3,742		
Less amount reserved for long-term debt	26,513		
Total Net Direct Debt	**1,303,619**		
Overlapping Debt			
Regional Transportation District	3,293,780	30.1%[2]	$ 991,428
Metro Wastewater Reclamation District	669,971	40.8%[3]	273,348
School District[1]	2,420,302	100.0%	2,420,302
Total Overlapping Debt	**6,384,053**		**3,685,078**
Total Net Direct and Overlapping Debt	**$7,687,672**		**$4,988,697**

[1]Does not include $33,527 unamortized premium or ($14,484) deferred amount on refunding applicable to general obligation bonds.

[2]Percentage calculated on estimated Scientific and Cultural Facilities District sales and use tax for Denver City and County compared to State total, per the Colorado Department of Revenue, Office of Research and Analysis.

[3]Percentage calculated on Denver's wastewater charges compared to the entire metro district per Metro Wastewater Reclamation District.

Source: City and County of Denver, Colorado, Comprehensive Annual Financial Report, Statistical Section, 2013, Page 164.

DEBT SERVICE FUNDS

When long-term debt has been incurred for capital or other purposes, revenues must be raised in future years to make debt service payments. Debt service payments, including both periodic interest payments and the repayment of debt principal when due, are typically specified in a *bond indenture,* the legal document which describes key terms of the bond offering. Revenues from taxes that are restricted for debt service purposes are usually recorded in a *debt service fund,* as are subsequent expenditures for payments of interest and principal. A debt service fund is used only for debt service activities related to *general* long-term liabilities—those reported in the Governmental Activities column of the government-wide statement of net position. Debt service related to long-term liabilities reported in proprietary and fiduciary funds is reported in those funds, not in a debt service fund.

Number of Debt Service Funds

In addition to debt service for bond liabilities, debt service funds may be required to service debt arising from the use of notes or warrants having a maturity more than one year after date of issue. Debt service funds can also be used to make periodic payments required by capital lease agreements. Although each issue of long-term or intermediate-term debt is a separate obligation and may have legal restrictions and servicing requirements that differ from other issues, GASB standards provide that, if legally permissible, a single debt service fund can be used to account for the service of all issues of tax-supported and special assessment debt. Subsidiary records of that fund can provide needed assurance that budgeting and accounting meet the restrictions and requirements relating to each issue. If legal restrictions do not allow for the debt service of all issues of tax-supported and special assessment debt to be accounted for by a single debt service fund, as few additional debt service funds as is consistent with applicable laws should be created. In this chapter, a separate debt service fund for each bond issue is illustrated simply as a means of helping the reader focus on the different accounting procedures considered appropriate for each type of bond issue encountered in practice.

Use of General Fund to Account for Debt Service

In some jurisdictions, laws do not require accounting for the debt service function by a debt service fund. Unless the debt service function is very simple, it may be argued that good financial management would dictate the establishment of a debt service fund even though not required by law. If neither law nor sound financial administration requires the use of debt service funds, the function may be performed within the accounting and budgeting framework of the General Fund. In such cases, the accounting and financial reporting standards discussed in this chapter should be followed for the debt service activities of the General Fund.

Budgeting for Debt Service

In addition to possible bond indenture requirements, good politics and good financial management suggest that the debt service burden on the taxpayers be spread evenly rather than lumped in the years that debt issues or installments happen to mature. To assist with sound financial management, the debt service fund is considered both a budgeting and an accounting entity. As such, a budget is prepared for the debt service fund. If taxes for payment of interest and principal on long-term debt are recorded directly in the debt service fund, they are budgeted as estimated revenues of the debt service fund. Interest on the investments recorded in the debt service fund is also budgeted as estimated revenue by the debt service fund. When recognized, taxes and interest earnings are recorded as revenues. Transfers made from other funds to the debt service fund are budgeted as an estimated other financing source and when the transfers are recognized, they are recorded as *interfund transfers in*. If resources, such as taxes, are to be raised by another fund and transferred to the debt service fund, they must be included in the revenues budget of the fund that will raise the revenue (often the General Fund). The amount to be transferred to the debt service fund will be budgeted as an estimated other financing use and recorded as an *interfund transfer out* when the transfer of funds to the debt service fund is recognized.

Although the items may be difficult to budget accurately, debt service funds often receive premiums and accrued interest on debt issues sold. Accrued interest on debt sold is commonly considered revenue of the recipient debt service fund; premium on debt sold is another financing source. Similarly, as illustrated in Chapter 5, if capital projects are completed with expenditures less than revenues and other financing sources, the residual equity may be transferred to the appropriate debt service fund. Persons budgeting and accounting for debt service funds should seek competent legal advice on the permissible use of both premiums on debt sold and interfund transfers of the residual equity of capital projects funds. In some cases, one or both of these items must be held for eventual debt repayment and may not be used for interest payments; in other cases, both premiums and interfund transfers in of equity may be used for interest payments.

ILLUSTRATION 6–7 Modified Accrual Basis of Recognition of Expenditures for Long-term Debt Interest and Principal

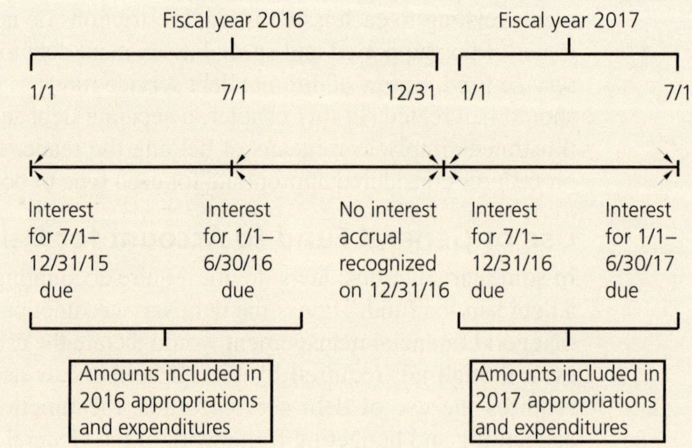

The appropriations budget of a debt service fund must provide for the payment of all interest on general long-term debt that will become legally due during the budget year and for the payment of any principal amounts that will become legally due during the budget year. GASB standards require debt service fund accounting to be on the same basis as is required for general and special revenue funds. One peculiarity of the modified accrual basis used by governmental fund types (which is not discussed in Chapter 3 because it relates primarily to debt service funds) is that interest on long-term debt is generally not accrued in the debt service fund but is accrued at the government-wide level. For example, if the fiscal year of a government ends on December 31, 2016, and the interest on its bonds is payable on January 1 and July 1 of each year, the amount payable on January 1, 2017, would generally not be considered a liability in the balance sheet of the debt service fund prepared as of December 31, 2016. The rationale for this recommendation is that the interest is not legally due until January 1, 2017. (See Illustration 6–7.) The same reasoning applies to principal amounts that mature on the first day of a fiscal year; they are not liabilities to be recognized in statements prepared as of the day before. In the event 2016 appropriations include January 1, 2017, interest and/or principal payment, the appropriations and expenditures (and resulting liabilities) should be recognized in 2016.[4]

Types of Serial Bonds

Several decades ago, governmental issues of long-term debt commonly matured in total on a given date, resulting in a large "balloon" payment. In that era, bond indentures often required the establishment of a "sinking fund," sometimes operated on an

[4] While governmental fund liabilities and expenditures for debt service on general long-term debt are generally recognized in the reporting period that debt payments are due to correspond with appropriations, GASB *Codification,* Section 1500, pars. 122 and 123, provide for an exception. If a government has deposited or transferred financial resources dedicated for payment of debt service to the debt service fund *and* payment of principal and interest is due early in the following year (defined as less than one month), then the expenditure and related liability may be recognized in the debt service fund prior to year-end.

actuarial basis. The purpose of a **sinking fund** is to set aside resources for the substantial debt payment due at maturity. Today a large majority of tax-supported bond issues are serial bond issues in which the principal matures in installments allowing the issuer to make payments of principal that match revenue expectations over that time period. Four types of serial bond issues are found in practice: regular, deferred, annuity, and irregular. If the total principal of an issue is repayable in a specified number of equal annual installments over the life of the issue, it is a **regular serial bond** issue. If the first installment is delayed for a period of more than one year after the date of the issue but subsequent installments fall due on a regular basis, the bonds are known as **deferred serial bonds.** If the amount of annual principal repayments is scheduled to increase each year by approximately the same amount that interest payments decrease (interest decreases because the amount of outstanding bonds decreases), so that the total debt service remains reasonably level over the term of the issue, the bonds are called **annuity serial bonds. Irregular serial bonds** may have any pattern of repayment that does not fit the other three categories.

Accounting for Regular Serial Bonds—First Year

Accounts recommended for use by debt service funds are similar to but not exactly the same as those recommended for use by the General Fund and special revenue funds. Because the number of sources of revenues and other financing sources is relatively small in a typical debt service fund, as is the number of purposes for which expenditures are made, it is generally not necessary to use control and subsidiary accounts such as those used by the General Fund. Moreover, because debt service funds do not issue purchase orders or contracts for goods and services, the use of encumbrance accounting is unnecessary. Thus, the budgetary accounts typically used for a debt service fund are Estimated Revenues, Estimated Other Financing Sources, Appropriations, Estimated Other Financing Uses, and Budgetary Fund Balance. The actual operating accounts usually include only a few revenue accounts, Other Financing Sources (for interfund transfers in and bond issue premiums), Expenditures—Bond Interest, Expenditures—Bond Principal, and, in the case of certain bond refunding transactions, Other Financing Uses. Similarly, relatively few balance sheet accounts are found in a debt service fund. Accounts typically include current asset accounts such as Cash, Investments, Taxes Receivable (and related estimated uncollectible accounts), and Due from Other Funds. Liability accounts might include Bond Interest Payable and Bond Principal Payable. Fund equity typically consists of fund balance accounts that are restricted, committed, or assigned to expenditure for principal and interest.

For the convenience of bondholders, the payment of interest and the redemption of matured bonds is ordinarily handled through the banking system. Usually the government designates a bank as paying agent or fiscal agent to handle interest and principal payments for each issue. Therefore, the assets of a debt service fund often include "Cash with Paying (or Fiscal) Agent" and the appropriations, expenditures, and liabilities may include amounts for the service charges of paying agents. Investment management may be performed by governmental employees or by banks, brokers, or others who charge for the service; investment management fees are a legitimate charge against investment revenues. While most governmental bond issuances are handled by bond underwriters,[5] for the sake of simplicity, the debt service examples in this

[5]For a discussion of the underwriting process, see the Municipal Securities Rulemaking Board Web site at http://www.msrb.org/Municipal-Bond-Market/How-the-Market-Works.aspx.

chapter assume that the issuing government issues checks directly to bondholders for interest and redemption of principal.

Accounting for debt service of regular serial bonds furnishes the simplest illustration of recommended debt service fund accounting. Assume the bonds issued by the Town of Brighton as partial financing for the fire station construction project (discussed in Chapter 5, under the heading "Illustrative Transactions—Capital Projects Funds") are regular serial bonds maturing in equal annual amounts over 20 years. The total face value of the issue was $1,200,000; all bonds in the issue bear interest of 6 percent per year, payable semiannually on June 15 and December 15. The bonds were dated June 15, 2017, and sold on that date at par. During 2017 the only expenditure the debt service fund will be required to make will be the interest payment due December 15, 2017, in the amount of $36,000 ($1,200,000 × 0.06 × 1/2 year). Assuming that revenues to pay the first installment of bonds due on June 15, 2018, and both interest payments due in 2018 will be raised in 2018 from a special sales tax recorded directly in the debt service fund, the budget for 2017 need only provide resources in the amount of the 2017 interest expenditure. The entry to record the budget for the year ended December 31, 2017, including $6,000 residual equity to be transferred from the Fire Station Capital Projects Fund, is:

		Debits	Credits
	Serial Bond Debt Service Fund:		
1.	Estimated Revenues	30,000	
	Estimated Other Financing Sources	6,000	
	Appropriations		36,000

(*Note:* Entry 1 has no effect at the government-wide level since budget entries are made only in governmental funds.) If sales tax revenues in the amount of $31,200 are collected in cash for debt service, the entry is:

	Serial Bond Debt Service Fund:		
2a.	Cash	31,200	
	Revenues		31,200

The corresponding entry in the governmental activities general ledger at the government-wide level is:

	Governmental Activities:		
2b.	Cash	31,200	
	General Revenues—Sales Taxes—Restricted for Debt Service		31,200

As illustrated in Chapter 5, the $6,000 residual equity of the Fire Station Capital Projects Fund was transferred to the debt service fund. The entry required in the latter fund is:

		Debits	Credits
	Serial Bond Debt Service Fund:		
3.	Cash	6,000	
	Other Financing Sources—Interfund Transfers In		6,000

Governmental activities at the government-wide level are unaffected since the transfer is between two funds within the governmental activities category.

On December 15, 2017, when the first interest payment is legally due, checks totaling $36,000 are written to the registered owners of these bonds. The debt service fund records the expenditure and the corresponding entry is made to record interest expense at the government-wide level:

	Serial Bond Debt Service Fund:		
4a.	Expenditures—Bond Interest	36,000	
	Cash		36,000
	Governmental Activities:		
4b.	Expenses—Interest on Long-term Debt	36,000	
	Cash		36,000

As of December 31, 2017, an adjusting entry would be made to accrue one-half of a month's interest expense ($1,200,000 × 0.06 × 1/12 × 1/2) on the accrual basis at the government-wide level, as would be the case in accounting for business organizations. As was discussed earlier, the debt service fund recognizes an expenditure in the period the interest is legally due; it does not record an accrual at the end of the reporting period. This accounting difference will later be included in the reconciliation between the fund and government-wide financial statements prepared in Chapter 9.

	Governmental Activities:		
5.	Expenses—Interest on Long-term Debt	3,000	
	Interest Payable		3,000

All budgetary and operating statement accounts are closed by the following entries:

	Serial Bond Debt Service Fund:		
6a.	Appropriations	36,000	
	Estimated Revenues		30,000
	Estimated Other Financing Sources		6,000
6b.	Revenues	31,200	
	Other Financing Sources—Interfund Transfers In	6,000	
	Expenditures—Bond Interest		36,000
	Fund Balance—Restricted—Debt Service		1,200

In addition, all temporary accounts of the governmental activities general ledger would be closed at year-end. Because that ledger has many temporary accounts besides those related to debt service, closing entries for governmental activities are presented in Chapter 9 for fiscal year 2017.

Second Year Transactions

In the second year of the Serial Bond Debt Service Fund, the fiscal year ending December 31, 2018, the following journal entries would be required.

The special sales tax for debt service is estimated to produce revenues of $135,000 for the year. From these revenues, two interest payments (the interest due on June 15, 2018, and December 15, 2018) of $36,000 and $34,200, respectively, and a principal redemption payment of $60,000 due on June 15, 2018, must be paid. Entry 7 shows the entry required at January 1, 2018, to record the budget for FY 2018.

		Debits	Credits
	Serial Bond Debt Service Fund:		
7.	Estimated Revenues	135,000	
	Appropriations		130,200
	Budgetary Fund Balance		4,800

During the year, actual revenues from the special sales tax were $134,100. Entries 8a and 8b summarize these collections.

	Serial Bond Debt Service Fund:		
8a.	Cash	134,100	
	Revenues		134,100
	Governmental Activities:		
8b.	Cash	134,100	
	General Revenues—Sales Taxes—Restricted for Debt Service		134,100

On June 15, 2018, interest of $36,000 and the first redemption of principal in the amount of $60,000 ($1,200,000 ÷ 20 years) were paid to bondholders of record, as shown in Entries 9a and 9b.

	Serial Bond Debt Service Fund:		
9a.	Expenditures—Bond Principal	60,000	
	Expenditures—Bond Interest	36,000	
	Cash		96,000
	Governmental Activities:		
9b.	Bonds Payable	60,000	
	Expenses—Interest on Long-term Debt	33,000	
	Interest Payable	3,000	
	Cash		96,000

The semiannual interest payment due on December 15, 2018, was paid on schedule, as reflected in Entries 10a and 10b, based on a remaining principal of $1,140,000 at 6 percent interest per annum.

		Debits	Credits
	Serial Bond Debt Service Fund:		
10a.	Expenditures—Bond Interest	34,200	
	Cash		34,200
	Governmental Activities:		
10b.	Expenses—Interest on Long-term Debt	34,200	
	Cash		34,200

On December 31, 2018, interest expense and interest payable were accrued in the amount of $2,850 ($1,140,000 × .06 × 1/12 × 1/2):

	Governmental Activities:		
11.	Expenses—Interest on Long-term Debt	2,850	
	Interest Payable		2,850

All temporary accounts of the debt service fund were closed on December 31, 2018, as shown in Entries 12a and 12b.

	Serial Bond Debt Service Fund:		
12a.	Appropriations	130,200	
	Budgetary Fund Balance	4,800	
	Estimated Revenues		135,000
12b.	Revenues	134,100	
	Fund Balance—Restricted—Debt Service		3,900
	Expenditures—Bond Interest		70,200
	Expenditures—Bond Principal		60,000

In subsequent years, the pattern of journal entries will be the same as that of the preceding entries, except that actual sales taxes realized will vary from year to year and the amount of interest will decline each year as the principal is reduced. If revenues are insufficient in any year to meet debt service requirements, available fund balance amounts that have been set aside for debt service can be used to augment current year revenues. If fund balances are insufficient to cover the shortfall, then an interfund transfer from the General Fund would likely be used. Making all interest and principal redemption payments by their due date is critically important, as a missed or late payment could adversely impact the entity's bond rating and significantly increase future borrowing costs.

Debt Service Accounting for Term Bonds

Term bond issues mature in their entirety on a given date, in contrast to serial bonds, which mature in installments. Required revenues of term bond debt service funds may be determined on an "actuarial" basis or on less sophisticated bases designed to produce approximately level contributions during the life of the issue.

In order to illustrate the use of an actuarial basis, the following example assumes that the Town of Brighton has a term bond issue amounting to $1,500,000 with a 20-year life. The term bonds bear semiannual interest at a nominal (or stated) annual rate of 5 percent, payable on January 1 and July 1. Revenues and other financing sources of this particular debt service fund are assumed to be property taxes levied directly for this debt service fund and earnings on investments of the debt service fund. The amount of the tax levy is computed in accord with annuity tables on the assumption that revenues for principal repayment will be invested and will earn 6 percent per year, compounded semiannually. For every year of the life of the issue, the budget for the Term Bonds Debt Service Fund of the Town of Brighton, reflecting the conditions just described, will include two required additions of $19,893.57 each for investment for eventual principal repayment, and two amounts of $37,500 each for interest payment, for a total of $114,787.14.[6]

Assuming the bonds were issued in the preceding fiscal year on January 1, 2016, and actual additions and actual earnings were both exactly as budgeted, the Term Bonds Debt Service Fund of the Town of Brighton would have the following trial balance as of December 31, 2016.

	Debits	Credits
Cash	$37,500.00	—
Investments	40,383.95	—
Fund Balance—Restricted—Debt Service	—	$77,883.95
Totals	$77,883.95	$77,883.95

[6] Using either the annuity tables found in most accounting texts or a calculator, one will find that the future amount of $1 invested at the end of each period will amount to $75.4012597 at the end of 40 periods, if the periodic compound interest is 3 percent (as specified in this example). Since the amount needed for bond repayment at the end of 40 six-month periods is $1,500,000, the tax levy for bond principal repayment must yield $1,500,000 divided by 75.4012597, or $19,893.57, at the end of each six-month period throughout the life of the bonds. Tax revenue must be sufficient to cover each bond interest payment of $37,500 ($1,500,000, the face value of the bonds, × 5 percent, the annual nominal interest rate, × 1/2 year) plus the two required additions of $19,893.57 for sinking fund investment, for a total revenue of $114,787.14 per year. The computation is (all amounts rounded to nearest cent):

Year	Period	Addition at End of Period	3 Percent per Period	Balance at End of Period
2016	1	$19,893.57	$ -0-	$19,893.57
	2	19,893.57	596.81	40,383.95
2017	3	19,893.57	1,211.52	61,489.04
	4	19,893.57	1,844.67	83,227.28

The balance at the end of Period 2 is the total of investments and the total of fund balance in this case since actuarial assumptions were met exactly in 2016. The sum of the interest for Period 3 and Period 4 is $3,056.19, the required earnings for the second year.

The budget will include earnings on debt service fund investments computed in accord with actuarial requirements. For 2017, the second year of the Term Bonds Debt Service Fund's operation, the actuarial assumption is that the fund will earn 6 percent per year, compounded semiannually; the required earnings for the year amount to $3,056.19 (see footnote 6 for calculation). Therefore, Estimated Revenues is debited for $117,843.33 ($114,787.14 + $3,056.19) to reflect estimated property taxes and interest amounts. The appropriations budget would include only the amounts becoming due during the budget year, $75,000 (two interest payments, each amounting to $37,500). The entry to record the budget for fiscal year 2017 follows.

		Debits	Credits
	Term Bond Debt Service Fund:		
1.	Estimated Revenues	117,843.33	
	Budgetary Fund Balance		42,843.33
	Appropriations		75,000.00

If the debt service fund is to accumulate the amount needed to retire the term bond issue at maturity, both additions and earnings must be received, and invested, in accord with the actuarial assumptions. Therefore, the tax levy for this fund must yield collections in the first six months totaling at least $57,393.57, so that $19,893.57 can be invested and $37,500 can be paid in interest to bondholders, both as of the end of the first six-month period. Collections during the second six months must also total $57,393.57, for the same reason. Realistically, it is unlikely that collections would ever total exactly $57,393.57 in either six-month period. If collections were less than that amount in either period, this fund would have to borrow enough to make the required investments; there is no question that the interest would have to be paid when due, as discussed earlier in this chapter. Assuming that collection experience of the Town of Brighton indicates that a tax levy in the amount of $120,000 is needed in order to be reasonably certain that collections during each six-month period will equal the needed amount, the entries to record the levy and the expected uncollectibles amounting to $3,000 are as follows:

		Debits	Credits
	Term Bond Debt Service Fund:		
2a.	Taxes Receivable—Current	120,000.00	
	Estimated Uncollectible Current Taxes		3,000.00
	Revenues		117,000.00
	Governmental Activities:		
2b.	Taxes Receivable—Current	120,000.00	
	Estimated Uncollectible Current Taxes		3,000.00
	General Revenues—Property Taxes—Restricted for Debt Service		117,000.00

The required interest payment was made on January 1, 2017, as reflected in Entries 3a and 3b.

		Debits	Credits
	Term Bond Debt Service Fund:		
3a.	Expenditures—Bond Interest	37,500.00	
	Cash		37,500.00
	Governmental Activities:		
3b.	Interest Payable	37,500.00	
	Cash		37,500.00

(*Note:* Interest expense and interest payable were accrued at the government-wide level for the second six months of FY 2016, but not in the debt service fund as the interest was not yet due on December 31, 2016.) Since cash was available in the debt service fund and the interest payment is made early in 2017, an accrual could have been made in 2016 (see footnote 5); however, since the interest payment is budgeted in 2017, this option was not exercised here.

Actual tax collections during the first six months of FY 2017 were $57,400. Entries 4 and 5 would be required in the journals of both the debt service fund and governmental activities to record the collections and subsequent addition to sinking fund investments at June 30, 2017.

		Debits	Credits
	Term Bond Debt Service Fund and Governmental Activities:		
4.	Cash	57,400.00	
	Taxes Receivable—Current		57,400.00
5.	Investments	19,893.57	
	Cash		19,893.57

Entries 6a and 6b record the addition of $1,261.99 of interest on June 30, 2017, which is added to the Investments account. Note that the actual interest earned during this six-month period is $50.47 more than the estimated earnings of $1,211.52 for the period because the actual earnings rate for the period was slightly higher than the 6 percent per annum rate used in actuarial computations.

		Debits	Credits
	Term Bond Debt Service Fund:		
6a.	Investments	1,261.99	
	Revenues		1,261.99
	Governmental Activities:		
6b.	Investments	1,261.99	
	General Revenues—Investment Earnings—Restricted for Debt Service		1,261.99

The interest payment of $37,500 due on July 1, 2017, was made as scheduled, as shown in Entries 7a and 7b.

		Debits	Credits
	Term Bond Debt Service Fund:		
7a.	Expenditures—Bond Interest	37,500.00	
	Cash		37,500.00
	Governmental Activities:		
7b.	Expenses—Interest on Long-term Debt	37,500.00	
	Cash		37,500.00

During the second six months of the year, property tax collections for debt service on the term bonds totaled $58,000 and the required addition to the sinking fund investments account was made on December 31, 2017, as shown in Entries 8 and 9.

	Term Bond Debt Service Fund and Governmental Activities:		
8.	Cash	58,000.00	
	Taxes Receivable—Current		58,000.00
9.	Investments	19,893.57	
	Cash		19,893.57

At December 31, 2017, interest of $37,500 on the term bonds was accrued at the government-wide level for the second six months of the year.

	Governmental Activities:		
10.	Expenses—Interest on Long-term Debt	37,500.00	
	Interest Payable		37,500.00

Interest earnings on sinking fund investments for the second six months of the year were recorded in the amount of $1,883.10, as shown in Entries 11a and 11b.

	Term Bond Debt Service Fund:		
11a.	Investments	1,883.10	
	Revenues		1,883.10
	Governmental Activities:		
11b.	Investments	1,883.10	
	General Revenues—Investment Earnings—Restricted for Debt Service		1,883.10

Taxes levied for 2017 but not collected during the year become delinquent as of December 31; however, the portion considered collectible is expected to be received within 60 days of year-end and can be included in tax revenue for 2017 under the modified accrual basis of accounting. The balance of the Estimated Uncollectible Current Taxes account is reviewed and determined to be reasonable. Entry 12 is made in the journals of both the Term Bond Debt Service Fund and governmental activities at the government-wide level to record the reclassification of the property tax accounts as delinquent.

		Debits	Credits
	Term Bond Debt Service Fund and Governmental Activities:		
12.	Taxes Receivable—Delinquent	4,600.00	
	Estimated Uncollectible Current Taxes	3,000.00	
	Taxes Receivable—Current		4,600.00
	Estimated Uncollectible Delinquent Taxes		3,000.00

All budgetary and operating statement accounts of the Term Bond Debt Service Fund were closed at December 31, 2017, as shown in Entries 13a and 13b. Related closing entries for governmental activities are made in Chapter 9.

	Term Bond Debt Service Fund		
13a.	Appropriations	75,000.00	
	Budgetary Fund Balance	42,843.33	
	Estimated Revenues		117,843.33
13b.	Revenues	117,000.00	
	Revenues	3,145.09	
	Expenditures—Bond Interest		75,000.00
	Fund Balance—Restricted—Debt Service		45,145.09

Although not illustrated in this chapter, accounting for deferred serial bonds has elements of both serial and term bond debt service fund accounting, reflecting the hybrid nature of deferred serial bonds. Illustrative debt service fund journal entries are not provided for these bonds, as they are similar to those provided for serial and term bonds.

Financial Reporting

Debt service activities are reported as part of governmental activities at the government-wide level. In addition, if a debt service fund qualifies as a major fund (see Glossary for definition), the financial information for that fund is reported in a separate column of the balance sheet—governmental funds and the statement of revenues, expenditures, and changes in fund balances—governmental funds. Financial information for debt service funds that do not qualify as major funds is aggregated and reported along with that for all other nonmajor governmental funds (i.e., special revenue, capital projects, and permanent funds) in an "Other Governmental Funds" column of the two financial statements just mentioned. Financial information for each nonmajor debt service fund is also reported in a separate column of the supplemental combining financial statements for nonmajor governmental funds in the financial section of the comprehensive annual financial report. For internal management purposes, it may also be desirable to prepare combining financial statements for the debt service funds only. A combining statement of revenues, expenditures, and changes in fund balances and a combining balance sheet for the debt service funds of the Town of

ILLUSTRATION 6–8

TOWN OF BRIGHTON
Debt Service Funds
Combining Statement of Revenues, Expenditures, and Changes in Fund Balances
For the Year Ended December 31, 2017
(amounts reported in whole dollars)

	Serial Bonds	Term Bonds	Total Debt Service Funds
Revenues:			
Taxes	$31,200	$117,000	$148,200
Investment earnings	–0–	3,145	3,145
Total revenues	31,200	120,145	151,345
Expenditures:			
Interest on bonds	36,000	75,000	111,000
Excess of revenues over (under) expenditures	(4,800)	45,145	40,345
Other financing sources (uses):			
Interfund transfers in	6,000	–0–	6,000
Increase in fund balances	1,200	45,145	46,345
Fund balances, January 1, 2017	–0–	77,884	77,884
Fund balances, December 31, 2017	$ 1,200	$123,029	$124,229

Brighton are presented in Illustrations 6–8 and 6–9. Illustration 6–10 presents a schedule of revenues, expenditures, and changes in fund balances—budget and actual for the debt service funds.

ILLUSTRATION 6–9

TOWN OF BRIGHTON
Debt Service Funds
Combining Balance Sheet December 31, 2017
(amounts reported in dollars)

	Serial Bonds	Term Bonds	Total Debt Service Funds
Assets:			
Cash	$1,200	$ 38,113	$ 39,313
Investments	–0–	83,316	83,316
Taxes receivable (net)	–0–	1,600	1,600
Total assets	$1,200	$123,029	$124,229
Fund Balances:			
Fund balance—restricted—debt service	$1,200	$123,029	$124,229

Accounting for Bond Premiums and Accrued Interest

This chapter's examples illustrate the accounting for serial and term bonds sold at par on or near the interest payment date. More often than not, governments sell bonds at a premium, and the bonds are sold between interest payment dates. As noted in Chapter 5,

ILLUSTRATION 6–10

TOWN OF BRIGHTON
Debt Service Funds
Combining Schedule of Revenues, Expenditures, and Changes in Fund Balances—Budget and Actual
For the Year Ended December 31, 2017
(amounts reported in dollars)

	Serial Bonds			Term Bonds			Total Debt Service Funds		
	Budget	Actual	Actual over (under) Budget	Budget	Actual	Actual over (under) Budget	Budget	Actual	Actual over (under) Budget
Revenues:									
Taxes	$30,000	$31,200	$1,200	$114,787	$117,000	$2,213	$144,787	$148,200	$3,413
Investment earnings	–0–	–0–	–0–	3,056	3,145	89	3,056	3,145	89
Total revenues	30,000	31,200	1,200	117,843	120,145	2,302	147,843	151,345	3,502
Expenditures:									
Interest on bonds	36,000	36,000	–0–	75,000	75,000	–0–	111,000	111,000	–0–
Excess of revenues over (under) expenditures	(6,000)	(4,800)	1,200	42,843	45,145	2,302	36,843	40,345	3,502
Other Financing Sources (Uses):									
Interfund transfers in	6,000	6,000	–0–	–0–	–0–	–0–	6,000	6,000	–0–
Increase in fund balances	–0–	1,200	1,200	42,843	45,145	2,302	42,843	46,345	3,502
Fund balances, January 1, 2017	–0–	–0–	–0–	77,884	77,884	–0–	77,884	77,884	–0–
Fund balances, December 31, 2017	$ –0–	$ 1,200	$1,200	$120,727	$123,029	$2,302	$120,727	$124,229	$3,502

state statutes, local ordinances, or bond indentures often require that initial issue premiums be used for debt service. Thus, the premium will either be directly recorded in the debt service fund as another financing source, as shown below, or promptly transferred to the debt service fund from the fund issuing the bonds.

	Debits	Credits
Debt Service Fund:		
Cash	59,000	
Other Financing Sources—Premium on Bonds		59,000

Recall that the premium on bonds payable is not amortized in the debt service fund. At the government-wide level, a premium would be recorded as an additional component of the general long-term liability for the bonds, and the premium should be amortized, using the effective-interest method, over the life of the bonds.

When bonds are sold between interest payment dates, the party purchasing the bonds pays interest accrued from the date the bonds are issued to the date the bonds are actually sold. In a debt service fund, accrued interest sold is generally recorded as a revenue, as follows:

Debt Service Fund:		
Cash	8,000	
Revenues		8,000

When the full interest payment is later recorded as an expenditure of the debt service fund, this revenue serves as a partial offset when calculating the change in fund balance. At the government-wide level, cash received on the sale date for accrued interest would be credited either as Accrued Interest Payable or Interest Expense, as in accounting for businesses.

Valuation of Debt Service Fund Investments

As shown in the term bond debt service fund example in this chapter, financial resources typically are accumulated in these types of debt service funds for eventual repayment of principal. Such resources should be invested prudently until they are needed for principal repayment. Interest earnings on investments in bonds and other securities purchased at a premium or discount generally would not be adjusted for amortization of any premiums or discounts. Current GASB standards require fair value accounting and reporting for most investments except for certain money market investments with maturities of less than one year.[7] All long-term investments in debt and equity securities held for repayment of general long-term debt principal are reported at fair value in the debt service fund balance sheet. All *changes* in the fair value of investments during the period, both realized and unrealized, are reported as revenue in the statement of revenues, expenditures, and changes in fund balances. At the government-wide level, all investment income, including realized and unrealized investment gains and losses, is reported on the statement of activities.

[7] GASB standards define fair value as "the amount at which an investment could be exchanged in a current transaction between willing parties, other than in a forced or liquidation sale." GASB, *Codification,* Sec. I50.105.

Deposit and Investment Disclosures

Bond issuances and subsequent debt service activities typically result in significant deposits and long-term investments being held for principal redemption. In addition, excess cash of the General Fund and other funds, pension plan assets, self-insurance pool reserves, and investment pools are also common sources of deposits and investments. Among other concerns, deposits and investments held in the custody of financial institutions impose risks such as exposure to loss due to interest rate increases, custodial credit risk related to the underlying creditworthiness of the financial institution, credit risk related to the creditworthiness of debt security issuers, and concentration risk from holding substantial portions of investment securities of a single issuer.

Interest rate risk may be reduced by holding fixed income securities with lower term to maturity (duration) and avoiding highly interest-rate-sensitive derivative investments. Derivative securities are financial instruments or contracts whose value is dependent upon some other underlying security or market measure such as an index or interest rates.[8] Custodial credit risk for deposits may be reduced by holding other securities as collateral. Such risk may be eliminated entirely if covered by depository insurance (e.g., Federal Deposit Insurance Corporation). Credit risk can be reduced by investing in bonds with high-quality ratings or that are backed by insurance. Concentration risk can be minimized through diversification of investments to avoid investing in securities of a single issuer that exceed 5 percent of total investments.

GASB standards require certain disclosures about *external investment pools,* as discussed in Chapter 8. For other investments, the government should describe in its notes to the financial statements (1) legal and contractual provisions for deposits and investments, including types of investments authorized to be held and any significant violations of legal or contractual provisions and (2) investment policies related to the kinds of risks described in the preceding paragraph.[9] Investment disclosures should be organized by type of investment. Additionally, the government should provide disclosures about specific risks. These disclosures include information about:[10]

1. Credit quality ratings of investments in debt securities, such as the ratings provided by the major national bond rating services (e.g., Moody's Investors Service, Standard & Poor's, and Fitch Ratings). A recommended format is to present aggregated amounts of investments by quality rating category.
2. Custodial credit risk; specifically investment securities or deposits that are not insured, deposits that are not collateralized, investments that are not registered in the name of the government, and both deposits and investments that are held by either (*a*) the counterparty (e.g., financial institution) or (*b*) the counterparty's trust department or agent but not in the government's name.
3. Concentration of credit risk, including disclosure of amount and issuer for investments in the securities of any one issuer that exceed 5 percent or more of total investments.
4. Interest rate risk of investments in debt securities, using one of five approved methods described in the standards.

[8] For a formal definition of *derivative,* see GASB, *Comprehensive Implementation Guide*, Appendix 6-1 glossary.

[9] GASB, *Codification,* Sec. I50.130–136.

[10] Ibid. pars. 137–143.

In addition, the government should disclose any deposits or investments that are exposed to foreign currency risk.

Debt Service Accounting for Special Assessment Debt

Special assessment projects, as introduced in Chapter 5, typically follow the same pattern as transactions of other capital projects. Specifically, construction activities are usually completed, using either interim financing from the government or proceeds of special assessment debt issuances (bonds or notes) to pay construction costs to contractors. Either at the beginning of the project or, more commonly, when construction is completed, assessments for debt service are levied against property owners in the defined special benefit district. The portion of the total assessment and applicable interest to be borne by each parcel of property within the district must be determined as specified by laws of the relevant jurisdiction. Often the amount to be paid by each owner is so large that laws allow the total special assessment against each parcel to be paid in equal installments over a specified period of years. Total annual assessment installments receivable and interest on the balance of unpaid installments usually approximate the amount of debt principal and interest payable during the same year.

If the government is obligated in some manner to make the debt service payments in the event that amounts collected from benefited property owners are insufficient, the debt should be recorded in the governmental activities journal at the government-wide level and a debt service fund should be used to account for debt service activities.[11] The portion of the special assessment debt that will be repaid from property owner assessments should be reported as "special assessment debt with governmental commitment" to recognize governmental backing of the debt, while the portion of special assessment debt that will be repaid from general resources of the government (the public benefit portion or the amount assessed against government-owned property) should be reported like other general long-term liabilities. If the government is not obligated in any manner for special assessment debt, the debt should *not* be recorded in any accounting records of the government.[12] In addition, the notes should disclose the amount of the debt and the fact that the government is in no way liable for repayment but is only acting as an agent for the property owners in collecting the assessments, forwarding the collections to bondholders, and initiating foreclosure proceedings, if appropriate. In the latter case, which is relatively rare, debt service transactions should be recorded in an *agency fund,* as explained in Chapter 8.

Assume that special assessment bonds, secondarily backed by the general taxing authority of a certain city, were previously issued to complete a street-widening project in a housing development within the city. Upon completion of the project the city levied assessments amounting to $480,000, payable in 10 equal installments with 5 percent interest on unpaid installments, on owners of properties within the housing development. As shown in Entry 1, all receivables are recorded at the time of the levy, but Revenues is credited only for the amount expected to be collected within one year from the date of the levy; Deferred Inflow of Resources is credited for the amount of deferred installments. Required budgetary entries, as shown earlier in this chapter for serial bond and term bond debt service funds, are omitted.

[11] GASB, *Codification,* Sec. 1500.120.

[12] Ibid.

	Debits	Credits
Debt Service Fund:		
1a. Assessments Receivable—Current	48,000	
Assessments Receivable—Unavailable	432,000	
Revenues		48,000
Deferred Inflow of Resources		432,000
Governmental Activities:		
1b. Assessments Receivable—Current	48,000	
Assessments Receivable—Unavailable	432,000	
Program Revenue—General Government—Capital Grants and Contributions		48,000
Deferred Inflow of Resources		432,000

All current assessments receivable due at year-end were collected along with interest of $24,000 (see Entry 2). Any amounts not collected by the due date should be reclassified by a debit to Assessments Receivable—Delinquent and a credit to Assessments Receivable—Current.

Debt Service Fund		
2a. Cash	72,000	
Assessments Receivable—Current		48,000
Revenues		24,000
Governmental Activities:		
2b. Cash	72,000	
Assessments Receivable—Current		48,000
Program Revenue—General Government—Capital Grants and Contributions		24,000

Special assessment bond principal in the amount of $48,000 and bond interest payable of $24,000 were paid on schedule.

Debt Service Fund:		
3a. Expenditures—Bond Principal	48,000	
Expenditures—Bond Interest	24,000	
Cash		72,000
Governmental Activities:		
3b. Special Assessment Debt with Governmental Commitment	48,000	
Expenses—Interest on Special Assessment Debt	24,000	
Cash		72,000

The second installment of assessments receivable was reclassified from the unavailable category to the current category. A corresponding amount of Deferred Inflow of Resources was reclassified as Revenues.

		Debits	Credits
	Debt Service Fund:		
4a.	Assessments Receivable—Current	48,000	
	Assessments Receivable—Unavailable		48,000
4b.	Deferred Inflow of Resources	48,000	
	Revenues		48,000
	Governmental Activities:		
4c.	Assessments Receivable—Current	48,000	
	Assessments Receivable—Unavailable		48,000
4d.	Deferred Inflow of Resources	48,000	
	Program Revenue—General Government—Capital Grants and Contributions		48,000

This pattern of journal entries will be repeated during each of the remaining nine years until all special assessment bonds have been retired.

Use of Debt Service Funds to Record Capital Lease Payments

In Chapter 5, under the heading "General Capital Assets Acquired under Capital Lease Agreements," an example is given of the computation of the present value of rentals under a capital lease agreement. The entry necessary in a governmental fund at the inception of the lease is illustrated in Chapter 5. The corresponding entry in the governmental activities general journal at the government-wide level is also given in Chapter 5 to show the capitalization of the asset acquired under the lease. That entry is reproduced here to illustrate how the liability is recorded.

Governmental Activities:		
Equipment	67,590	
Capital Lease Obligations Payable		67,590

As shown in this entry, at the inception of the lease an obligation is recognized at the government-wide level in an amount equal to the present value of the stream of annual payments. Although the lease agreement calls for a $10,000 initial lease payment on January 1, 2016, the full present value should be recorded as the liability until the initial payment has been recorded. Since governmental funds do not record long-term liabilities, no journal entry is made at the fund level for the liability.

Governments may use a General Fund, a special revenue fund, or a debt service fund to record capital lease payments since the annual lease payments are merely installment payments of general long-term debt. For illustrative purposes, it is assumed that the capital lease recorded in Chapter 5 is serviced by a debt service fund. The first $10,000 lease payment since it occurs on the first day of the lease, is entirely a payment on the principal of the lease obligation. Accordingly, the payment would be recorded as follows:

Debt Service Fund:		
Expenditures—Principal of Capital Lease Obligation	10,000	
Cash		10,000

	Debits	Credits
Governmental Activities:		
Capital Lease Obligations Payable	10,000	
Cash		10,000

On January 1, 2017, the second lease rental payment of $10,000 is made. As the accompanying table shows, only $4,241 of that payment applies to reduction of the principal of the lease obligation (the remaining $10,000–$4,241, or $5,759, represents interest on the lease). Thus, the following entries are required at the debt service fund and government-wide level.

	Debits	Credits
Debt Service Fund:		
Expenditures—Principal of Capital Lease Obligation	4,241	
Expenditures—Interest on Capital Lease Obligation	5,759	
Cash		10,000

	Debits	Credits
Governmental Activities:		
Capital Lease Obligations Payable	4,241	
Expenses—Interest on Capital Leases	5,759	
Cash		10,000

The payment due on January 1, 2017, and the payment due each year thereafter, will reflect a partial payment on the lease obligation and a payment of interest on the unpaid balance of the lease obligation. GASB standards specify that a constant periodic rate of interest must be used. In the example started in Chapter 5, the present value of the obligation is computed using the rate of 10 percent per year. It is reasonable to use the same interest rate to determine what part of the annual $10,000 payment is payment of interest and what part is payment of principal. The following table shows the distribution of the annual lease rental payments:

Payment Date	Amount of Payment	Interest on Unpaid Balance at 10 Percent	Payment on Principal	Unpaid Lease Obligation
				$67,590
1/1/16	$10,000	$ -0-	$10,000	57,590
1/1/17	10,000	5,759	4,241	53,349
1/1/18	10,000	5,335	4,665	48,684
1/1/19	10,000	4,868	5,132	43,552
1/1/20	10,000	4,355	5,645	37,907
1/1/21	10,000	3,791	6,209	31,698
1/1/22	10,000	3,170	6,830	24,868
1/1/23	10,000	2,487	7,513	17,355
1/1/24	10,000	1,736	8,264	9,091
1/1/25	10,000	909	9,091	-0-

The unpaid balance of the capital lease obligation is carried in the governmental activities general ledger at the government-wide level.

Accounting for Debt Refunding

Governments may elect to issue **refunding bonds** if debt service fund assets accumulated for debt repayment are not sufficient to repay creditors when the debt matures, if the interest rate on the debt is appreciably higher than the government would have to pay on a new bond issue, or if the covenants of the existing bonds are excessively burdensome. Under a bond refunding, new bonds are issued to retire previously issued bonds. The proceeds of the new bonds are either deposited in escrow to pay the debt service on the outstanding bonds when due or used to promptly retire the outstanding bonds. The proceeds of refunding bonds are accounted for as other financing sources of the debt service fund that is to repay the existing debt.

If a government has accumulated no assets at all for debt repayment, it is possible that no debt service fund exists. In such a case, a debt service fund should be created to account for the proceeds of the refunding bond issue and the repayment of the old debt. When the debt has been completely repaid, the debt service fund relating to the liquidated issue should be closed, and a debt service fund for the refunding issue should be created and accounted for as described in this chapter. If the refunding bond issue is not sold but is merely given to the holders of the matured issue in an even exchange, the transaction does not require entries in a debt service fund or at the government-wide level but should be disclosed adequately in the notes to the financial statements.

Advance Refunding of Debt

Advance refundings of tax-exempt debt are common during periods when interest rates are falling sharply. Complex accounting and reporting issues have surfaced relating to legal issues such as whether both issues are still the debt of the issuer. If the proceeds of the new issue are to be held for the eventual retirement of the old issue, how can the proceeds be invested to avoid conflict with the Internal Revenue Service over the taxability of interest on the debt issue? (Compliance with the arbitrage rules under the Internal Revenue Code Sec. 148 and related regulations is necessary for the interest to be exempt from federal income tax and, possibly, from state and local taxes.) Full consideration of the complexities of accounting for advance refundings resulting in defeasance of debt is presented in the GASB *Codification* Section D20. Defeasance of debt can be either "legal" or "in substance." **Legal defeasance** occurs when debt is legally satisfied based on certain provisions in the debt instrument, even though the debt is not actually paid. **In-substance defeasance** occurs when debt is considered settled for accounting and financial reporting purposes, even though legal defeasance has not occurred. GASB *Codification* Section D20.106 sets forth in detail the circumstances for in-substance defeasance. Briefly, the debtor must irrevocably place cash or other assets in trust with an escrow agent to be used solely for satisfying scheduled payments of both interest and principal of the defeased debt. The amount placed in escrow must be sufficiently large, so that there is only a remote possibility that the debtor will be required to make future payments on the defeased debt. The trust is restricted to owning only monetary assets that are essentially risk-free as to the amount, timing, and collection of interest and principal.

To illustrate accounting for advance refundings resulting in defeasance of debt reported in the governmental activities ledger at the government-wide level, assume that the proceeds from the sale of the refunding issue amount to $2,000,000 and that debt defeased amounted to $2,500,000. The proceeds are recorded in the fund receiving the proceeds (normally, a *debt service fund*) by an entry such as follows:

	Debits	Credits
Cash	2,000,000	
Other Financing Sources—Proceeds of Refunding Bonds		2,000,000

Payments to the escrow agent from resources provided by the new debt should be recorded in the debt service fund as an other financing use; payments to the escrow agent from other resources are recorded as debt service expenditures. Therefore, assuming $500,000 has previously been accumulated in the debt service fund for payment of the $2,500,000 bond issue, the entry to record the payment to the escrow agent is as follows:

Other Financing Uses—Payment to Refunded Bond Escrow Agent	2,000,000	
Expenditures—Payment to Refunded Bond Escrow Agent	500,000	
Cash		2,500,000

Disclosures about Advance Refundings

The *disclosure* guidance on debt refunding in GASB *Codification* Section D20 is applicable to state and local governments, public benefit corporations and authorities, public employee retirement systems, and governmental utilities, hospitals, colleges and universities, and to all funds of those entities.

Briefly, the disclosure requirements state that all entities subject to GASB jurisdiction are to provide a general description of any advance refundings resulting in defeasance of debt in the notes to the financial statements in the year of the refunding. At a minimum, the disclosures must include (1) the difference between the cash flows required to service the old debt and the cash flows required to service the new debt and complete the refundings and (2) the economic gain or loss resulting from the transaction. Economic gain or loss is the difference between the *present value* of the old debt service requirements and the *present value* of the new debt service requirements, discounted at the effective interest rate and adjusted for additional cash paid. Section D20.901–.917 provides examples of effective interest rate and economic gain calculations and of note disclosures.

OTHER LONG-TERM LIABILITIES

The primary focus of the chapter thus far has been general long-term liabilities arising from financing activities. Other long-term liabilities can arise from operating activities and would include liabilities such as compensated absences, pollution remediation obligations, and claims and judgments. In each of these types of long-term liabilities, described briefly on the next page, estimated expenses or losses are recorded at the government-wide level by debiting an expense and crediting a liability. Liabilities with average maturities greater than one year should be reported in the government-wide statement of net position in two components—the amount due within one year and the amount due in more than one year. In general, governmental fund claims are recognized as expenditures to the extent that the amounts are payable with expendable available financial resources.

Compensated Absences

Compensated absences are leaves of absence for which employees earn the right to be paid, such as vacation or sick leave. In the government-wide financial statements, vacation leave should be accrued as a liability as the benefits are earned by the employees if the leave is attributable to past service and it is probable that the employer will compensate the employees for the benefits through paid time off or cash payments at termination or retirement. On the other hand, paid time off for earned sick leave may be contingent on an illness-specific event that is outside the control of the employer and employee. Furthermore, some employers pay employees for all or a portion of accumulated sick leave upon termination of employment. Thus, sick leave should be accrued as a liability as the benefits are earned by the employees but only to the extent it is probable that the employer will compensate the employees for the benefits through cash payments conditioned on the employees' termination or retirement.

Entities that report compensated absences in governmental funds should recognize compensated absences expenditures each period using the modified accrual basis of accounting. That is, the amount of the compensated absences recognized as expenditures in these funds should be the net amount accrued during the year that normally would be liquidated with expendable available financial resources. Compensated absences liabilities that are general long-term liabilities should be reported in the Governmental Activities column in the statement of net position.

Pollution Remediation Obligations

Pollution remediation obligations arise from responsibilities related to the cleanup of hazardous wastes or hazardous substances resulting from existing pollution. A liability related to pollution remediation should be recognized if it is reasonably estimable and an obligating event has occurred. GASB identifies five types of obligating events: (1) the government is compelled to take remediation action due to imminent endangerment to the public health, (2) a violation of a pollution prevention permit has occurred, (3) the government is named or will be named as the responsible or potentially responsible party to a remediation, (4) the government has been or will be named in a lawsuit requiring its participation in remediation, and (5) the government commences or legally obligates itself to commence remediation.[13] Once it is deemed that an obligating event has occurred and the liability, or any component of the liability, is reasonably estimable, the liability is measured using the expected cash flow technique. Periodically, the amount of the estimated liability must be reevaluated. GASB identifies several stages or benchmarks in the remediation process where a reevaluation of the estimated liability should occur. In addition to recognizing the estimated liability, several note disclosures should be prepared to provide the reader with information concerning the liability and how the estimated liability was derived.

[13] GASB, *Codification*, Sec. P40, par. 109.

Claims and Judgments

Governmental entities are often party to **claims and judgments**, including lawsuits or demands for payment of damages related to the occurrence of an event, such as the destruction or damage of property and related injuries. The government will assess whether a loss contingency exists using probable/reasonably possible/remote criteria similar that that set forth for commercial entities. Governments should report an estimated loss from a claim as an expense and as a liability in the government-wide financial statements if a claim is probable and reasonably estimable. Claim amounts that are probable but not reasonably estimable should be disclosed in notes to the financial statements when there is at least a reasonable possibility that a loss or an additional loss may have been incurred. Governmental fund claims should be recognized as expenditures and liabilities to the extent that the amounts are payable with expendable available financial resources; that is, to the extent that the liabilities mature (come due for payment) each period.

Key Terms

Annuity serial bonds, *219*
Claims and judgment, *240*
Compensated absences, *239*
Debt limit, *210*
Debt margin, *210*
Deferred serial bonds, *219*
General long-term liabilities, *205*
In-substance defeasance, *237*
Irregular serial bonds, *219*
Legal defeasance, *237*
Overlapping debt, *211*
Pollution remediation obligations, *239*
Refunding bonds, *237*
Regular serial bonds, *219*
Sinking fund, *219*
Term bonds, *224*

Selected References

Governmental Accounting Standards Board. *Codification of Governmental Accounting and Financial Reporting Standards, as of June 30, 2014*. Norwalk, CT, 2014.
Governmental Accounting Standards Board. *Comprehensive Implementation Guide as of June 30, 2014*. Norwalk, CT, 2014.

Questions

6–1. How are *general long-term liabilities* distinguished from other long-term liabilities of the government? How does the financial reporting of general long-term liabilities differ from the financial reporting of other long-term liabilities?

6–2. What disclosures about long-term liabilities are required in the notes to the financial statements?

6–3. What is the purpose of a debt service fund? Does a debt service fund require budgeting? Why or why not?

6–4. Explain the financial reporting for special assessment bonds when (*a*) a government assumes responsibility for debt service should special assessment collections be insufficient, and when (*b*) the government assumes no responsibility whatsoever.

6–5. Although the most common type of general long-term liabilities are those arising from financing activities (e.g., bonds, notes, and capital leases), general long-term liabilities can also be created through operating activities. Provide examples of long-term liabilities other than those related to financing.

6–6. What is overlapping debt? Why would a citizen care about the amount of overlapping debt reported? Why would a government care about the amount of overlapping debt reported?

6–7. Governments are prevented from borrowing unlimited funds through the enforcement of debt limits. Explain the concept of a debt limit. How are debt limits computed? How is the concept of borrowing power or debt margin connected to debt limits?

6–8. How do term bonds differ from serial bonds? What, if any, impact does this difference have on the entries made to the debt service fund over the life of the bonds?

6–9. What are the GASB requirements for reporting investments held for the purpose of servicing government debt?

6–10. Under what circumstances might a government consider an advance refunding of general obligation bonds outstanding?

Cases

6–11 Evaluating Financing Options. Surf City is a rapidly growing city on the Mid-Atlantic coast, with a current population of 200,000. To cope with the growing vehicular traffic and the need for infrastructure expansion (e.g., streets, sidewalks, lighting, storm water drains, and sewage systems), members of the city council have recently engaged in debate about the merits of alternative mechanisms for financing expansion. The alternatives the council is exploring are: (1) a sales tax referendum to increase an existing one-half cent capital improvement tax by one-quarter cent on every dollar of sales; (2) a development fee of $0.50 per square foot imposed on real estate developers for new residential and commercial buildings; and (3) a term bond issue maturing in 20 years.

Public debate at recent city council meetings has been contentious, with developers arguing that the burden for infrastructure improvements would be disproportionately placed on homeowners and businesses, whereas reliance on a sales tax increase would permit part of the infrastructure burden to be borne by nonresidents who shop in and otherwise enjoy the benefits of Surf City. Some voters fear that a term bond will adversely impact their children when the large principal payment is due in 20 years. Developers have also argued that more of the existing one-half-cent capital improvement tax should be spent for street and sidewalk improvements and less should be spent for improvement of public buildings, parks, and biking trails.

Proponents of the proposed real estate development fee argue that new residential and commercial building is the main factor driving the growing demand for infrastructure development. Thus, they argue, it is most appropriate that new residents and new businesses shoulder much of the burden for expanding infrastructure. They further argue that the development fee will result in only a modest, largely invisible increase in the cost of each new building. Moreover, the incremental cost of the development fee should be recaptured as property values increase as a result of enhanced infrastructure. Finally, they argue that Surf City citizens enjoy better health and a generally higher quality of life as a result of park and biking trail improvements and that the existing one-half cent sales tax should continue to support recreational facilities.

Supporters of the bond option argue that borrowing the funds for expansion will allow for continued urban growth without placing undue burden on developers, business owners, or current residents. They point to the balloon payment and stress that over the upcoming 20 years the increased population base will be better able to fund the city's expansion. They worry that any tax increases will stifle growth and discourage tourists or other visitors from spending money in the city.

Required

Evaluate the advantages and disadvantages of each potential financing option from the viewpoint of (1) a city council member, (2) the city manager, (3) current homeowners and business owners, and (4) potential new homeowners or new business owners. Provide a written analysis of the options from the perspective of each party.

6–12 Policy Issues Relating to General Long-term Debt. In the midst of a lingering recession, a citizens group in your state has placed an amendment on an upcoming election ballot. The measure would prohibit new debt issuances by state or local governments, which would presumably reduce taxes as a result of less tax-supported debt. Supporters of the amendment claim the proposed measure will force government to operate more efficiently and cut bloated spending, while opponents fear that public services and the quality of life in the state will be severely affected if the amendment passes.

Required

a. Why do governments typically issue general long-term debt? What types of services might be limited if debt was no longer a financing option?

b. Consider each of the following statements regarding the amendment. Select at least one of the statements (numbered 1–4) to indicate your position on the proposed amendment. Incorporating the statement(s) selected, draft a memo supporting your position on the proposed amendment.

(1) The state has enough money to spend. Government officials can spend more wisely or even cut their spending.

(2) Voters' frustration with government spending is understandable; however, borrowing restrictions will require that the state and local governments raise fees, reduce construction, or reduce programs and services.

(3) Highly paid government lawyers have created loopholes, so taxpayers are spending millions on long-term debt interest that they never got the opportunity to approve.

(4) This measure is a direct reaction to poor treatment of taxpayers by government; however, this reaction is so far overreaching that it will ultimately kill state jobs and strip local governments' ability to provide police and fire protection and to educate our children.

6–13 The Case of the Vanishing Debt.

Facts: A county government and a legally separate organization—the Sports Stadium Authority—entered into an agreement under which the authority issued revenue bonds to construct a new stadium. Although the intent is for the authority to make debt service payments on the bonds from a surcharge on ticket sales, the county agreed to annually advance the Sports Stadium Authority the required amounts to make up any debt service shortfalls and has done so for several years. Accordingly, the county has recorded a receivable from the authority and the authority has recorded a liability to the county for all advances made under the agreement.

Ticket surcharge revenues that exceed $1,500,000 are to be paid to the county and to be applied first toward interest and then toward principal repayment of advances. Both parties acknowledge, however, that annual ticket surcharge revenues may never exceed $1,500,000, since to reach that level would require an annual paid attendance of 3,000,000. Considering that season ticket holders and luxury suite renters are not included in the attendance count, it is quite uncertain if the required trigger level will ever be reached.

The authority has twice proposed to raise the ticket surcharge amount, but the county in both cases vetoed the proposal. Thus, the lender in this transaction (the county) has imposed limits that appear to make it infeasible for the borrower (the authority) to repay the advances. Consequently, the authority's legal counsel has taken the position that the authority is essentially a pass-through agency with respect to the advances in that the authority merely receives the advances and passes them on to a fiscal agent for debt service payments. Moreover, they note that the bonds could never have been issued in the first place without the county's irrevocable guarantee of repayment since all parties knew from the beginning that the authority likely would not have the resources to make full debt service payments.

Based on the foregoing considerations, the authority's legal counsel has rendered an opinion that the liability for the advances can be removed from the authority's accounts. The county tacitly agrees that the loans (advances) are worthless since it records an allowance for doubtful loans equal to the total amount of the advances. Still, the county board of commissioners refuses to remove the receivable from its accounts because of its ongoing rights under the original agreement for repayment.

Required

a. Assume you are the independent auditor for the authority, and provide a written analysis of the facts of this case, indicating whether or not you concur with the authority's decision to no longer report the liability to the county for debt service advances.

b. Alternatively, assume you are the independent auditor for the county and, based on the same analysis you conducted for requirement *a,* indicate whether or not you concur with the county continuing to report a receivable for debt service advances on its General Fund balance sheet and government-wide statement of net position.

6–14 Assessing General Obligation Debt Burden. This case focuses on the analysis of a city's general obligation debt burden. After examining the accompanying table that shows a city's general obligation (tax-supported) debt for the last ten fiscal years, answer the following questions.

Required

a. What is your initial assessment of the trend of the city's general obligation debt burden?

b. Complete the table by calculating the ratio of Net General Bonded Debt to Assessed Value of taxable property and the Net General Bonded Debt per Capita. In addition, you learn that the average ratio of Net General Bonded Debt to Assessed Value for comparable-size cities in 2017 was 4.56 percent, and the average net general bonded debt per capita was $1,376. Based on time series analysis of your calculations and the benchmark information provided in this paragraph, is your assessment of the city's general obligation still the same as it was in part *a,* or has it changed? Explain.

Ratio of Net General Bonded Debt to Assessed Value and Net Bonded Debt per Capita (Last Ten Fiscal Years—$000s omitted)

Fiscal Year	Estimated Population	Assessed Valuation	Gross Bonded Debt	Less: Amount in Debt Service Fund	Net Bonded Debt	Net General Bonded Debt to Assessed Value	Net General Bonded Debt per Capita
2008	90,599	1,792,747	192,151	99,545	92,606	—	—
2009	92,061	1,939,316	206,856	100,690	106,166	—	—
2010	93,524	2,057,130	212,323	106,655	105,668	—	—
2011	94,986	2,197,710	221,287	102,518	118,769	—	—
2012	96,647	2,386,169	261,519	117,212	144,307	—	—
2013	97,610	2,585,416	291,736	120,326	171,410	—	—
2014	99,208	2,843,133	280,654	106,551	174,103	—	—
2015	100,477	3,080,629	278,042	105,945	172,097	—	—
2016	102,404	3,201,498	271,425	86,976	184,449	—	—
2017	103,428	3,325,203	309,788	95,158	214,630	—	—

Exercises and Problems

6–15 Examine the CAFR. Utilizing the comprehensive annual financial report (CAFR) obtained for Exercise 1–16, follow the instructions below.

a. **General Long-term Liabilities.**

(1) *Disclosure of Long-term Debt.* Does the report contain evidence that the government has general long-term liabilities? If so, does the report include a list of outstanding tax-supported debt issues; capital lease obligations; claims, judgments, and compensated absence payments to be made in future years; and unfunded pension obligations?

Has the government issued any special assessment debt? If the government is obligated in some manner, is the debt reported as a liability in the government-wide statement of net position? If the government has issued special assessment debt for which it is not obligated in any manner, do the notes discuss this debt?

Refer to the enterprise funds statement of net position as well as note disclosures for long-term liabilities. Are any enterprise debt issues backed by the full faith and credit of the general government? If so, how are the primary liability and the contingent liability disclosed?

(2) *Changes in Long-term Liabilities.* How are changes in long-term liabilities during the year disclosed? Is there a disclosure schedule for long-term liabilities similar to Illustration 6–1? If any new debt was issued by a governmental fund, are the proceeds of the debt issuance reported in the governmental fund financial statements as an "other financing source"?

Are interest payments and principal payments due in future years disclosed? If so, does the report relate these future payments with resources to be made available under existing debt service laws and covenants?

(3) *Debt Limitations.* Does the report contain information as to legal debt limit and legal debt margin? If so, is the information contained in the report explained in enough detail, so that an intelligent reader (you) can understand how the limit is set, what debt is subject to it, and how much debt the government might legally issue in the year following the date of the report?

(4) *Overlapping Debt.* Does the report disclose direct debt and overlapping debt of the reporting entity? What disclosures of debt of the primary government are made in distinction to debt of component units? Is debt of component units reported as "direct" debt of the reporting entity or as "overlapping debt"?

b. **Debt Service Funds.**

(1) *Debt Service Function.* How is the debt service function for tax-supported debt handled—by the General Fund, by a special revenue fund, or by one or more debt service funds? If there is more than one debt service fund, what kinds of bond issues or other debt instruments are serviced by each fund? Is debt service for bonds to be retired from enterprise revenues reported by enterprise funds?

(2) *Investment Activity.* Does the CAFR contain a schedule or list of investments of debt service funds? Does the report disclose increases or decreases in the fair value of investments realized during the year? Does the report disclose net earnings on investments during the year? What percentage of revenue of each debt service fund is derived from earnings on investments? What percentage of the revenue of each debt service fund is derived from taxes levied directly for the debt service fund? What percentage is derived from transfers from other funds? List any other sources of debt service revenue and other financing sources, and indicate the relative importance of each source.

(3) *Capital Lease Payments.* If general capital assets are being acquired under capital lease agreements, are periodic lease payments accounted for as expenditures of a debt service fund (or by another governmental fund)? If so, does the report disclose the portion of capital lease payments considered as interest and the portion considered as payment on the principal?

6–16 Multiple Choice. Choose the best answer.

1. Which of the following would *not* be considered a general long-term liability?
   a. The estimated liability to clean up the hazardous waste storage sites of the city's Public Works Department.
   b. Capitalized equipment leases of the water utility fund.
   c. Compensated absences for the city's Police Department.
   d. Five-year notes payable used to acquire computer equipment for the city's administrative offices.
2. Proceeds from bonds issued to construct a new city hall would most likely be recorded in the journal of the:
   a. Capital projects fund.
   b. Debt service fund.
   c. General Fund.
   d. Enterprise fund.
3. The liability for long-term debt issued to finance a capital project will appear in which financial statement?
   a. Government-wide statement of net position.
   b. Capital projects fund balance sheet.
   c. Debt service fund balance sheet.
   d. General fund balance sheet.

4. Which one of the following statements regarding debt margin is correct?
   a. Debt margin is the total amount of indebtedness of specified types of debt that is allowed by law to be outstanding at any one time.
   b. Debt margin is calculated without regard to debt that is authorized but not yet issued.
   c. Debt margin is the difference between the legal debt limit and the amount of net indebtedness subject to limitation.
   d. All of the above statements regarding debt margin are correct.
5. Budgeting entries for a debt service fund would:
   a. Not include an entry for estimated revenues since taxes are always recorded directly into the General Fund.
   b. Include an estimated adjustment to bonds payable equal to the amount of principal payments that will become legally due during the fiscal year.
   c. Include estimated other financing uses equal to the amount of interest payments that will become legally due during the fiscal year.
   d. Include appropriations for principal payments that will become legally due during the fiscal year.
6. On March 2, 2017, 20-year, 6 percent, general obligation serial bonds were issued by Mossy County at the face amount of $3,000,000. Interest of 6 percent per year is due semiannually on March 1 and September 1. The first principal payment of $150,000 is due on March 1, 2018. The county's fiscal year-end is December 31. What amounts are reported as interest expense in the government-wide financial statements and interest expenditure in the debt service fund for 2017?

	Interest Expense	Interest Expenditure
a.	$150,000	$ 90,000
b.	$ 90,000	$150,000
c.	$150,000	$150,000
d.	$150,000	$180,000

7. Debt service funds may be used to account for all of the following *except:*
   a. Repayment of debt principal.
   b. Lease payments under capital leases.
   c. Amortization of premiums on bonds payable.
   d. The proceeds of refunding bond issues.
8. Which of the following items would be reported in the Governmental Activities column of the government-wide financial statements?

	Premium on Bonds Payable	Noncurrent Portion of General Long-term Liabilities Payable
a.	Yes	No
b.	No	No
c.	No	Yes
d.	Yes	Yes

9. The liability for special assessment bonds for which the city is not obligated in any manner should be recorded in a (an):
   a. Debt service fund general journal.
   b. Agency fund general journal.

c. Governmental activities general journal.
d. None of the fund or governmental activities general journals but should be disclosed in the notes to the financial statements.

10. As a result of planning and setting aside funds to repay debt, substantial sums may be accumulated in accounts at financial institutions and in long-term investments. This subjects the government to which of the following types of risk?
    a. Interest rate risk, custodial credit risk, concentration risk, and reinvestment risk.
    b. Credit risk, concentration risk, interest rate risk, and market risk.
    c. Concentration risk, custodial credit risk, interest rate risk, and liquidity risk.
    d. Custodial credit risk, concentration risk, interest rate risk, and credit risk.

6–17 Long-term Liability Transactions. Following are a number of unrelated transactions for the Village of Centerville, some of which affect governmental activities at the government-wide level. None of the transactions has been recorded yet.

1. The General Fund collected and transferred $750,000 in tax collections to the debt service fund; $600,000 of this amount was used to retire outstanding serial bonds and the remainder was used to make the interest payment on the outstanding serial bonds.
2. A $5,000,000 issue of serial bonds to finance a capital project was sold at 102 plus accrued interest in the amount of $50,000. The accrued interest and the premium were recorded in the debt service fund. Accrued interest on bonds sold must be used for interest payments; the premium is designated by state law for eventual payment of bond principal.
3. The debt service fund made a $110,000 capital lease payment, of which $15,809 was interest. Funds used to make the lease payment came from a capital grant received by the special revenue fund.
4. Tax-supported serial bonds with a $2,800,000 par value were issued in cash to permit partial refunding of a $3,500,000 par value issue of term bonds. The difference was settled with $700,000 that had been accumulated in prior years in a debt service fund. Assume that the term bonds had been issued several years earlier at par.
5. Four months prior to year-end, 6 percent special assessment bonds totaling $500,000 were issued to fund a streetlight improvement project in a local subdivision. The bonds are secondarily backed by the village. The first $25,000 installment will be due from property owners six months after the initial bond issuance, but no debt payments are due in the first year.
6. Marketable equity securities held by the debt service fund increased in value by $10,000 during the year.

Required

Prepare in general journal form the necessary entries in the governmental activities and appropriate fund journals for each transaction. Explanations may be omitted. For each entry you prepare, name the fund in which the entry should be made.

6–18 Budgeted and Actual Debt Service Transactions. The City of Amarillo is authorized to issue $8,000,000, 3 percent regular serial bonds in 2017 for the construction of a new exit off the interstate highway within city limits. The bonds mature in equal annual amounts beginning on January 1, 2018, for 10 years and pay interest on January 1 and July 1. The city is required to use all accrued interest and premiums to service the debt. The funds to pay the interest will be transferred from the General Fund. The county's fiscal year-end is December 31.

Required

a. Prepare the budgetary entries for 2017 assuming that the bonds were scheduled to be issued on January 2. Assume that the January 1, 2018, principal and interest payments will be included in the 2018 budget.
b. The bonds were sold on February 1, 2017, at 101. Prepare the journal entries needed to record the issuance of the bonds, including the entries required in the debt service fund and any entries required in the governmental activities general ledger at the government-wide level.
c. Prepare the entry required to reflect the transfer of funds from the General Fund in the debt service fund. (You may ignore the entry in the General Fund.)
d. Prepare the journal entries needed to record first interest payment made on July 1, including the entries required in the debt service fund and any entries required in the governmental activities general ledger at the government-wide level. Assume that the straight-line method is used for premium amortization.
e. What, if any, adjustments would need to be made to the debt service fund or the governmental activities general ledger at the government-wide level during the fiscal year?

6–19 Capital Lease. In early 2017, McCormick County agreed to acquire a new recreation equipment storage facility under a capital lease agreement. At the inception of the lease, a payment of $750,000 will be made; four additional annual lease payments, each in the amount of $750,000, are to be made at the end of each year, beginning in late 2017. The total amount to be paid under this lease is $3,750,000. The county could borrow this amount for four years at an annual interest rate of 6 percent. Therefore, the present value of the lease at inception, including the initial payment, is $3,348,829. Assume that the fair value of the building at the inception of the lease is $3,600,000.

Required

a. Was this lease properly classified as a capital lease? Explain.
b. Show the entries required to record the inception of the lease in the capital projects fund, the debt service fund, and the governmental activities journal.
c. Show the entries required to record the payment at the end of the first year of the lease in both the debt service fund and governmental activities journal.
d. Which financial statement(s) prepared at the end of the first year would show both the asset and the liability related to this capital lease? At what amount would the liability be reported?

6–20 Legal Debt Margin and Direct and Overlapping Debt. In preparation for a proposed bond sale, the city manager of the City of Appleton requested that you prepare a statement of legal debt margin and a schedule of direct and overlapping debt for the city as of December 31, 2016. You ascertain that the following bond issues are outstanding on that date:

Convention center bonds	$3,600,000
Electric utility bonds	2,700,000
General obligation serial bonds	3,100,000
Tax increment bonds	2,500,000
Water utility bonds	1,900,000
Transit authority bonds	2,000,000

You obtain other information that includes the following items:

1. Assessed valuation of real and taxable personal property in the city totaled $240,000,000.
2. The rate of debt limitation applicable to the City of Appleton was 6 percent of total real and taxable personal property valuation.
3. Electric utility, water utility, and transit authority bonds were all serviced by enterprise revenues. By law, such self-supporting debt is not subject to debt limitation.
4. The convention center bonds and tax increment bonds are subject to debt limitation.
5. The amount of assets segregated for debt retirement at December 31, 2016, is $1,800,000.
6. The city's residents are also taxed by Clyde County for 25 percent of school district and health services debt. The school district has $15,000,000 in outstanding bonds, while health services has $8,000,000 in debt. Finally, one-third of the $2,400,000 of regional library outstanding debt is paid by taxes assessed on Appleton residents.

6–21 Debt Service Fund Trial Balance. Following is Grant County's debt service fund pre-closing trial balance for the fiscal year ended June 30, 2017.

GRANT COUNTY
Debt Service Fund
Pre-closing Trial Balance
June 30, 2017

	Debits	*Credits*
Cash	$ 214,000	
Investments	56,000	
Fund Balance—Restricted		$ 56,500
Budgetary Fund Balance		?
Estimated Other Financing Sources	7,125,000	
Estimated Revenue	1,607,500	
Revenue—Sales Taxes		1,582,000
Revenue—Investment Earnings		11,500
Other Financing Sources—Interfund Transfers In		145,000
Other Financing Sources—Proceeds of Refunding Bonds		7,000,000
Estimated Other Financing Uses		7,000,000
Appropriations		1,525,000
Expenditures—Bond Interest	525,000	
Expenditures—Bond Principal	1,000,000	
Other Financing Uses—Payment to Escrow Agent	7,000,000	

Required

Using information provided by the trial balance, answer the following.

a. Assuming the budget was not amended, what was the budgetary journal entry recorded at the beginning of the fiscal year?

b. What is the budgetary fund balance?

c. Did the debt service fund pay debt obligations related to capital leases? Explain.

d. Did the debt service fund perform a debt refunding? Explain.

e. Prepare a statement of revenues, expenditures, and changes in fund balances for the debt service fund for the year ended June 30, 2017.

6–22 Serial Bond Debt Service Fund Journal Entries and Financial Statements. As of December 31, 2016, Sandy Beach had $9,500,000 in 4.5 percent serial bonds outstanding. Cash of $509,000 is the debt service fund's only asset as of December 31, 2016, and there are no liabilities. The serial bonds pay interest semiannually on January 1 and July 1, with $500,000 in bonds being retired on each interest payment date. Resources for payment of interest are transferred from the General Fund, and the debt service fund levies property taxes in an amount sufficient to cover principal payments.

Required

a. Prepare debt service fund and government-wide entries in general journal form to reflect, as necessary, the following information and transactions for FY 2017.

(1) The operating budget for FY 2017 consists of estimated revenues of $1,020,000 and estimated other financing sources equal to the amount of interest to be paid in FY 2017. Appropriations must be provided for interest payments and bond redemptions on January 1 and July 1.

(2) Cash was received from the General Fund and checks were written and mailed for the January 1 principal and interest payments.

(3) Property taxes in the amount of $1,020,000 were levied (no estimate for uncollectible accounts has been made).

(4) Property taxes in the amount of $1,019,000 were collected.

(5) Cash was received from the General Fund and checks were written and mailed for the July 1 principal and interest payments.

(6) Adjusting entries were made and uncollected taxes receivable were reclassified as delinquent. At the fund level, entries were also made to close budgetary and operating statement accounts. (Ignore closing entries in the government activities journal.)

b. Prepare a statement of revenues, expenditures, and changes in fund balances for the debt service fund for the year ended December 31, 2017.

c. Prepare a balance sheet for the debt service fund as of December 31, 2017.

6–23 Term Bond Debt Service Fund Transactions. On July 1, 2016, the first day of its 2017 fiscal year, the City of Nevin issued at par $2,000,000 of 6 percent term bonds to construct a new city office building. The bonds mature in five years on July 1, 2021. Interest is payable semiannually on January 1 and July 1. A sinking fund is to be established with equal semiannual additions made on June 30 and December 31, with the first addition to be made on December 31, 2016. Cash for the sinking fund additions and the semiannual interest payments will be transferred from the General Fund shortly before the due dates. City officials assume a yield on sinking fund investments of 6 percent per annum, compounded semiannually. Investment earnings are added to the investment principal.

Required

a. Prepare a schedule in good form showing the required additions to the sinking fund, the expected semiannual earnings, and the end-of-period balance in the sinking fund for each of the 10 semiannual periods. (*Note:* The future amount of an ordinary annuity of $1 for 10 periods at 3 percent per period is $11.4638793.)

b. Create a term bond debt service fund and prepare journal entries in the debt service fund for the following:

(1) Record a budget for the fiscal year ended June 30, 2017. Include an accrual for all interfund transfers to be received from the General Fund during the year. An appropriation should be provided only for the interest payment due on January 1, 2017.

(2) On December 28, 2016, the General Fund transferred $234,461 to the debt service fund. The addition to the sinking fund was immediately invested in 6 percent certificates of deposit.

(3) On December 28, 2016, the city issued checks to bondholders for the interest payment due on January 1, 2017.

(4) On June 27, 2017, the General Fund transferred $234,461 to the debt service fund. The addition for the sinking fund was invested immediately in 6 percent certificates of deposit.

(5) Actual interest earned on sinking fund investments at year-end (June 30, 2017) was the same as the amount budgeted (see *a*). This interest adds to the sinking fund balance.

(6) All appropriate closing entries were made at June 30, 2017, for the debt service fund.

6–24 Comprehensive Capital Assets/Serial Bond Problem. Residents from the Town of Mountain View authorized a $5,000,000 renovation to their historic town hall on November 15, 2016. Financing for the project consists of $2,500,000 from a 5 percent serial bond issue, $1,500,000 from a state grant, and $1,000,000 from the General Fund. Debt service for the serial bonds will be provided by a one-quarter-cent city sales tax imposed on every dollar of sales in the city. Prepare all necessary journal entries to record the related transactions in the town's capital projects fund, debt service fund, and governmental activities at the government-wide level. You may ignore entries in the General Fund. The town has a calendar year-end.

a. Record the 2017 budget for the Serial Debt Service Fund. $350,000 of sales taxes are expected to be collected in 2017; the only appropriation is expected to be six months of interest on the serial bond.

b. The town transfers $1,000,000 from the General Fund to a newly established capital projects fund.

c. Planning and architect's fees for the town hall renovation are paid in the amount of $200,000.

d. The town hall renovation construction contract is awarded to a local contractor, Central Paving and Construction, for $4,500,000.

e. On April 1, 2017, the town issues serial bonds with a face value totaling $2,500,000 and having maturities ranging from one to 20 years at 102. The bonds bear interest of 5 percent per annum, payable semiannually on April 1 and October 1. Premiums on bonds issued must be deposited directly in the debt service fund and are restricted for debt service. (Remember to amend the debt service fund budget since this premium was not anticipated.) Premiums are amortized using the straight-line method over 40 interest periods.

f. The capital projects fund paid the city's Utility Fund $50,000 for wiring associated with the renovation. No encumbrance had been recorded for this service.

g. On October 1, 2017, the city mailed checks to bondholders for semiannual interest on the bonds.

h. Sales taxes earmarked for debt service of $350,000 were collected.

i. Central Paving and Construction submitted a progress billing to the town for $2,500,000. The city's public works inspector agrees that all milestones have been met for this portion of the work.

j. The town paid Central Paving and Construction the amount it had billed, except for 5 percent that was withheld as a retained percentage per terms of the contract.

k. Grant funds totaling $1,500,000 are received from the state historical society, since eligible expenditures have been made.

l. At year-end, closing entries are made; $1,000,000 of fund balance is assigned, and the remainder is restricted. (Ignore closing entries for governmental activities.)

m. Record the 2018 budget for the Serial Debt Service Fund; $300,000 of earmarked sales taxes are expected to be collected in 2018; appropriations include a $250,000 principal payment on April 1 and two serial bond interest payments.

n. Sales tax collections for debt service amounted to $250,000.

o. Central Paving and Construction submitted a final billing to the town for $2,000,000. Upon final inspection by the Public Works Department, a leak was discovered in the roof.

p. Public works employees installed a new sidewalk and landscaping at a total cost of $130,000.

q. The roof leak was repaired satisfactorily, and the city paid the final billing and all retainages.

r. The April 1 debt service payments are made.

s. The renovation is considered complete and appropriate amounts are reclassified as buildings and improvements other than buildings (i.e., landscaping). All capital projects fund nominal accounts are closed, and remaining cash in the capital projects fund is transferred to the debt service fund. (Remember to amend the debt service fund budget since this transfer was not anticipated.)

Chapter **Seven**

Accounting for the Business-type Activities of State and Local Governments

Learning Objectives

After studying this chapter, you should be able to:

7-1 Describe the characteristics of proprietary funds, including those unique to internal service and enterprise funds.

7-2 Distinguish between the purposes of internal service funds and enterprise funds.

7-3 Explain proprietary fund financial reporting requirements, including the differences between the reporting of internal service and enterprise funds in the government-wide and fund financial statements.

7-4 Describe accounting procedures and prepare journal entries and financial statements for an internal service fund.

7-5 Describe accounting procedures and prepare journal entries and financial statements for an enterprise fund.

7-6 Explain special topics in accounting for the business-type activities of state and local governments.

Chapters 3–6 addressed accounting and reporting for governmental funds. This chapter addresses accounting and reporting for proprietary funds. Governmental funds owe their existence to legal constraints placed on the raising of revenues and the use of resources. In contrast to the governmental funds, proprietary funds rely primarily on exchange transactions, specifically charges for services, to generate revenues. As a result, proprietary funds follow accounting principles that are similar to those of investor-owned businesses.

The focus on exchange transactions with parties outside of the government is the reason that the enterprise funds are reported in a separate Business-type Activities column at the government-wide level. In contrast, the exchange transactions recorded in internal service funds are primarily undertaken with other funds and departments within the government; hence internal service funds are typically reported as governmental activities at the government-wide level.

PROPRIETARY FUNDS

As shown in Illustration 2–2, there are two types of proprietary funds, internal service funds and enterprise funds. Traditionally, the reason for the creation of proprietary funds was to improve the management of resources. As governments become more complex, efficiencies can be gained by combining or centralizing services that are commonly found in several departments or funds. Examples of common services or functions that are frequently centralized by governments include purchasing, information systems, insurance, and central motor pools. More recently, with increased citizen resistance to tax increases, many governmental entities also rely on user charges as a means of financing operations formerly financed by tax revenues and intergovernmental revenues. Thus, proprietary funds are now frequently used to account for activities formerly found in governmental funds.

Because proprietary funds operate on user charges, it is important to determine whether user charges are sufficient to cover operating costs. Additionally, administrators and governing bodies need information that will allow them to determine that the costs of operating the fund are reasonable in relation to the benefits provided by the fund. For these reasons, accounting and operating activities of proprietary funds are conducted in a business-like manner, focusing on the economic flow of resources through the use of accrual accounting.

Internal service funds are used to account for the acquisition or production and the distribution of centralized goods and services that are provided to departments or agencies of the government, or to other governments, on a cost-reimbursement basis. Although internal service funds are accounted for *internally* as business-type activities, their transactions predominantly involve sales of goods and services, or other transactions with the General Fund and other governmental funds. For this reason, the Governmental Accounting Standards Board (GASB) requires the financial balances of most internal service funds to be reported in the Governmental Activities column at the government-wide level rather than the Business-type Activities column. At the fund level, internal service funds are reported in a separate column of the proprietary fund financial statements. (See Illustrations A2–7, A2–8, and A2–9 for examples of proprietary fund statements for the City and County of Denver.)

Enterprise funds account for activities that produce goods or services to be sold to the general public. Activities of enterprise funds are referred to as *business-type activities* for purposes of accounting and financial reporting at the government-wide level (see the City and County of Denver's statement of activities presented in Illustration A2–2). Similar to governmental funds, *major* enterprise funds must be identified and reported in separate columns of the fund financial statements, while nonmajor enterprise fund information is aggregated and reported in an Other Enterprise Funds column (see Illustrations A2–7, A2–8, and A2–9).

Assets Acquired under Lease Agreements

The acquisition of general capital assets under lease agreements is discussed in Chapter 5. Assets for use by proprietary funds may also be acquired under lease agreements. The criteria set forth in GASB *Codification* Section L20.105 (itemized in Chapter 5) are used to determine whether the lease is an operating lease or a capital lease.

Assets acquired under an operating lease belong to the lessor, not to the proprietary fund; accordingly, the annual lease payment is recorded as a rental expense of the fund,[1] and there is no depreciation expense on the assets acquired under an operating lease agreement. Assets acquired under a capital lease agreement by an internal service fund, or an enterprise fund, should be capitalized by that fund. The amount to be recorded by a proprietary fund as the *cost* of the asset acquired under a capital lease is the lesser of (1) the present value of the rental and other minimum lease payments or (2) the fair value of the leased property. The amount recorded as the cost of the asset is amortized in a manner consistent with the government's normal depreciation policy for owned assets of proprietary funds. The amortization period is restricted to the lease term, unless the lease (1) provides for transfer of title or (2) includes a bargain purchase option, in which case the economic life of the asset becomes the amortization period.

During the lease term, each minimum lease payment by the fund is to be allocated between a reduction of the obligation under the lease and interest expense in a manner that produces a constant periodic rate of interest on the remaining balance of the obligation. This allocation and other complexities that arise in certain events are described and illustrated in GASB *Codification* Section L20.

Financial Reporting Requirements

Accounting for proprietary funds is similar to that of investor-owned business enterprises of the same type. An enterprise fund established to account for a government-owned electric utility, for example, should follow accounting principles similar to those of investor-owned electric utilities. Accordingly, proprietary funds focus on the flow of economic resources recognized on the accrual basis, both within the fund and at the government-wide level. Thus, these funds account for all capital assets used in their operations and for all long-term liabilities to be paid from the revenues generated from their operations, as well as for all current assets, current liabilities, and deferred inflows and outflows, if applicable. Because proprietary funds follow business-type accounting principles, these funds prepare essentially the same financial statements that businesses do: a balance sheet (called either a statement of net position or a balance sheet); a statement of revenues, expenses, and changes in fund net position (equivalent to an income statement); and a statement of cash flows. These statements are prepared according to GASB standards, which differ in some respects from the statements identified by FASB for business organizations.

Statement of Net Position

For proprietary funds, governments generally present a statement of net position in a format that displays assets, plus deferred outflows of resources, less liabilities, less deferred inflows of resources, equals net position. Similar to profit-seeking businesses, the statement of net position (or a traditional balance sheet) for proprietary funds is classified; that is, current assets are shown separately from capital assets and other assets, and current liabilities are shown separately from long-term debt. Additionally, current assets are listed in the order of liquidity. If applicable, deferred outflows of resources should be reported in a separate section following assets and deferred inflows of resources should be reported in a separate section following liabilities. Unlike businesses, there is no owners' or stockholders' equity section on the statement of net position. Instead, GASB standards require the reporting of net

[1] GASB, *Codification,* Sec. L20. 104–108 establishes measurement criteria and recognition criteria for revenues and expenditures/expenses relating to operating leases with scheduled rent increases.

position, which is divided into three components: net investment in capital assets; restricted (distinguishing among major categories of restrictions); and unrestricted.[2] Net investment in capital assets is calculated as the total of gross capital assets, net of accumulated depreciation, less any outstanding debt related to the acquisition or construction of capital assets. If debt has been incurred for construction or acquisition of a capital asset, but the proceeds of the debt have not been spent by year-end, that debt is excluded in calculating net investment in capital assets. Restricted net position represents net resources with restrictions on use imposed by law or external parties. For example, if a bond is issued for construction of a capital asset, but is unspent at year-end, the proceeds from the bond would be considered restricted net position. Unrestricted net position represents the residual amount of net position after separately identifying net investment in capital assets and restricted net position.

Statement of Revenues, Expenses, and Changes in Fund Net Position

The period results of operations for a proprietary fund should be reported in a statement of revenues, expenses, and changes in fund net position, which is similar to the income statement of a profit-seeking business. GASB standards state that revenues are to be reported by major revenue source, with revenues used as security for revenue bonds identified. Unlike Financial Accounting Standards Board (FASB) standards, GASB standards also indicate that revenues should be shown net of any discounts or allowances. For example, rather than reporting bad debt expense, proprietary funds would record and report a contra-revenue account, such as Provision for Bad Debts, which would be netted against the Revenues account in the financial report. In the statement of revenues, expenses, and changes in fund net position, revenues and expenses are to be identified as operating or nonoperating, with subtotals for operating revenues, operating expenses, and operating income. Operating revenues and expenses are those related to the primary functions of the proprietary fund. Management judgment is necessary when defining which revenues and expenses are primary to the operations of the fund. The distinction between operating and nonoperating revenues and expenses is important for achieving effective management control, as well as for complying with GASB requirements. If interfund transfers, special items, extraordinary items, or capital contributions are also reported in the statement of revenues, expenses, and changes in fund net position they appear after the Nonoperating Revenues/Expenses section.

Statement of Cash Flows

GASB financial reporting standards require the preparation of a statement of cash flows as a part of the full set of financial statements for all proprietary funds. Unlike FASB, GASB requires the statement to be prepared using the direct method of presentation. The difference between the direct and indirect methods of preparing a statement of cash flows is the format for the operating activities section of the statement. While the indirect method reconciles an entity's net income to net cash provided by operating activities, the direct method reports all cash receipts and cash payments from operating activities. Both methods produce the same figure for cash from operating activities and do not affect investing or financing activities.

[2] If a government reports deferred inflows or deferred outflows of resources, these items will also affect net position classifications. Details on classification definitions including deferred inflows and outflows of resources are provided in GASB, *Codification*, Sec. 2200.118–125.

Categories of cash flows provided by FASB *ASC* 230 were deemed insufficient to meet the needs of users of governmental financial reports. Consequently, GASB standards provide four categories of cash flows: operating, noncapital financing, capital and related financing, and investing. In each category, the term *cash* also includes **cash equivalents** (defined as short-term, highly liquid investments).

Cash flows from *operating* activities include receipts from customers, receipts from sales to other funds, payments to suppliers of goods or services, payments to employees for services, payments for purchases from other funds (including payments in lieu of taxes that approximate the value of services received), and other operating cash receipts and payments.

Cash flows from *noncapital financing* activities include proceeds from debt not clearly attributable to acquisition, construction, or improvement of capital assets; receipts from grants, subsidies, or taxes other than those specifically restricted for capital purposes or those for specific operating activities; payment of interest on and repayment of principal of noncapital financing debt; and grants or subsidies paid to other governments, funds, or organizations except payments for specific operating activities of the grantor government.

Cash flows from *capital and related financing* activities include proceeds of debt and receipts from special assessments and taxes specifically attributable to acquisition, construction, or improvement of capital assets; receipts from capital grants; receipts from the sale of capital assets; proceeds of insurance on capital assets that are stolen or destroyed; payments to acquire, construct, or improve capital assets; and payment of interest on and repayment or refunding of capital and related financing debt.

Cash flows from *investing* activities include receipts from collection of loans; interest and dividends received on loans, debt instruments of other entities, equity securities, and cash management and investment pools; receipts from the sales of debt or equity instruments; withdrawals from investment pools not used as demand accounts; disbursements for loans; payments to acquire debt or equity instruments; and deposits into investment pools not used as demand accounts.

Budgetary Comparison Schedule

Unlike the General Fund and other major governmental funds for which a budget is legally adopted, proprietary funds are not required by GASB standards to record budgets in their accounting systems, nor are they required to present a budgetary comparison schedule. Some governments do, however, require all funds to operate under legally adopted budgets. In such cases GASB standards permit but do not require the integration of budgetary accounts in the manner described in Chapters 3 and 4 for the General Fund and special revenue funds.

INTERNAL SERVICE FUNDS

Internal service funds are established to improve financial management of governmental resources; yet, it is important to remember that establishment of a fund is ordinarily subject to legislative approval. The ordinance or other legislative action that authorizes the establishment of an internal service fund should also specify the source or sources of financial resources to be used for fund operations. For example, to start up an internal service fund, the General Fund or an enterprise fund may *contribute* assets to the fund, or the internal service fund may receive the assets in the form of a long-term *interfund loan* to be repaid over a number of years. Alternatively, the resources initially allocated to an internal service fund may be acquired from the proceeds of a tax-supported bond issue or by transfer from other governments that anticipate utilizing the services to be rendered by the internal service fund. Since internal service funds are established to improve the management of resources, it is generally considered that their accounting and operations should be maintained on a business basis.

Illustrative Case—Supplies Fund

Accounting for an internal service fund concerned with the functions of purchasing, warehousing, and issuing supplies is illustrated in this section. The illustrations assume that the financial objective of an internal service fund is to recover from operating revenues the full cost of operations with enough net income to allow for replacement of inventories in periods of rising prices and a sufficient increase in inventory quantities to meet the needs of using funds and departments whose scale of operations is increasing. The illustrations also assume that net income should be sufficient to allow for replacement of capital assets used by the internal service fund but that expansion of the facilities must be financed through contributions from other funds authorized in their appropriations budgets. Managers of internal service funds must prepare operating plans—budgets—as a management tool. The illustrations assume that the budgets of internal service funds are submitted to the legislative body and to the public for information but not for legal action. Therefore, the budget is not formally recorded in internal service fund accounts. Similarly, managers of businesses must be kept informed of the status of outstanding purchase orders and contracts, but encumbrances need not be recorded in the accounts to accomplish this.

In prior chapters a "dual-track" approach captured transactions using both the modified accrual (governmental funds) and the accrual (government-wide) basis of accounting. Because the internal service fund uses accrual accounting, the "dual-track" approach is not needed to capture the different bases of accounting since the basis is the same at the fund level and the government-wide level. However, the internal service fund is generally reported as a part of the Governmental Activities column of the government-wide financial statements. To ensure that double counting of revenues, expenses, and other transactions does not occur, GASB standards require the elimination of the effect of transactions between governmental funds and internal service funds.[3] For this reason, the "dual-track" approach is used in recording the following internal service fund transactions, thus ensuring that double counting does not occur at the government-wide level.

Assume that late in fiscal year 2016 the administrators of the Town of Brighton, upon approval of the town council, created an internal service fund to centralize the purchasing, storing, and issuing functions. The new Supply Fund was created on December 31, 2016, by transferring cash of $30,000 and supplies having a cost of $61,500 from the General Fund. These transfers were intended as permanent contributions to the Supply Fund and are not to be repaid. The transfers had no effect on governmental activities at the government-wide level since both the General Fund and the Supply Fund are reported as governmental activities. The post-closing trial balance for the newly created Supplies Fund is shown here.

[3] GASB *Codification of Governmental Accounting and Financial Reporting Standards, as of June 30, 2014* (Norwalk, CT: GASB, 2014), Sec. 1800.103.

TOWN OF BRIGHTON SUPPLIES FUND
Post-Closing Trial Balance
As of December 31, 2016

	Debits	Credits
Cash	$30,000	
Inventory of Supplies	61,500	
Net Position—Unrestricted		$91,500
	$91,500	$91,500

In order to provide cash to be used for acquisition of a building and the equipment needed to handle the supply function efficiently, the town's Water Utility Fund provides a long-term interest-free interfund loan of $130,000 to the Supplies Fund. The loan is to be repaid by the Supplies Fund in 20 equal annual installments. Entry 1a illustrates the entry to be made by the Supplies Fund for the receipt of the interfund loan; Water Utility Fund entries for this transaction are illustrated later in this chapter. As shown in Entry 1b, GASB standards require that interfund receivables and payables between governmental and business-type activities be presented as *internal balances.* While internal balances do not meet the definition of elements of financial statements, they are reported in the government-wide statement of net position for purposes of fairly presenting each reporting entity.[4]

		Debits	Credits
	Supplies Fund:		
1a.	Cash	130,000	
	Interfund Loan from Water Utility Fund—Current		6,500
	Interfund Loan from Water Utility Fund—Noncurrent		123,500
	Governmental Activities:		
1b.	Cash	130,000	
	Internal Balances		130,000

Assume that a satisfactory warehouse building is purchased for $95,000; $25,000 of the purchase price is considered the cost of the land. Necessary warehouse machinery and equipment are purchased for $25,000. Delivery equipment is purchased for $10,000. If the purchases are made for cash, the acquisition of the assets would be recorded as follows:

	Supplies Fund:		
2a.	Land	25,000	
	Buildings	70,000	
	Machinery and Equipment—Warehouse	25,000	
	Equipment—Delivery	10,000	
	Cash		130,000
	Governmental Activities:		
2b.	Land	25,000	
	Buildings	70,000	
	Equipment	35,000	
	Cash		130,000

[4] GASB, *Concepts Statement 4,* par. 40.

Additional supplies would be ordered to ensure inventories can meet expected demand for supplies. During 2017, it is assumed supplies are received and related invoices are approved for payment in the amount of $192,600; the entry needed to record the asset and the liability follows:

		Debits	Credits
	Supplies Fund and Governmental Activities:		
3.	Inventory of Supplies	192,600	
	Vouchers Payable		192,600

The Supplies Fund should account for its inventories on the perpetual inventory basis since the information is needed for proper performance of its primary function. Accordingly, when supplies are issued, the inventory account must be credited for the cost of the supplies issued. Since the fund acquiring the supplies from the internal service fund will be charged an amount in excess of the inventory carrying value, the receivable and revenue accounts must reflect the selling price. The markup above cost should be determined on the basis of budgeted expenses and other items to be financed from net income, in relation to expected requisitions by using funds. If the budget for the Town of Brighton's Supplies Fund indicates a markup of 35 percent on cost is needed, issues to General Fund departments (see Chapter 4, illustrative Entry 22a) of supplies costing $185,000 would be recorded by the following entries:

	Supplies Fund:		
4a.	Cost of Supplies Issued	185,000	
	Inventory of Supplies		185,000
4b.	Due from General Fund	249,750	
	Billings to Departments		249,750

For the effect of this transaction at the government-wide level see Chapter 4, Entry 22b.

If collections from the General Fund (see Chapter 4, illustrative Entry 23) during 2017 totaled $249,750, the entry is as follows:

	Supplies Fund:		
5.	Cash	249,750	
	Due from General Fund		249,750

No entry is required at the government-wide level since this transaction is between two funds that are both part of governmental activities.

Assuming that payroll and fringe benefits totaling $55,000 during the year were all paid in cash and distributed to the functional expense accounts in the amounts shown, Entry 6 is appropriate.

		Debits	Credits
	Supplies Fund:		
6a.	Administrative Expenses	11,000	
	Purchasing Expenses	19,000	
	Warehousing Expenses	12,000	
	Delivery Expenses	13,000	
	Cash		55,000
	Governmental Activities:		
6b.	Expenses—General Government	55,000	
	Cash		55,000

The town received a $1,000 cash grant from a state program promoting the use of compact fluorescent light bulbs in the supplies warehouse. Unlike the billing in Entry 4b, this revenue is from a source external to the town government; therefore, the transaction should be recorded in both the supplies fund and the governmental activities general journal. Shortly after receipt of the grant funds, the warehouse light bulbs were replaced at a cost of $1,000.

	Supplies Fund:		
7a.	Cash	1,000	
	Grant Revenue		1,000
7b.	Warehousing Expense	1,000	
	Cash		1,000
	Governmental Activities:		
7c.	Cash	1,000	
	Program Revenue—General Government—Operating Grants and Contributions		1,000
7d.	Expenses—General Government	1,000	
	Cash		1,000

If payments on vouchers during the year totaled $164,000, the entry is as follows:

	Supplies Fund and Governmental Activities:		
8.	Vouchers Payable	164,000	
	Cash		164,000

The interfund loan from the Water Utility Fund is to be repaid in 20 equal annual installments; repayment of one installment at the end of 2017 and reclassification of the next installment are recorded:

	Supplies Fund:		
9a.	Interfund Loan from Water Utility Fund—Current	6,500	
	Cash		6,500
9b.	Interfund Loan from Water Utility Fund—Noncurrent	6,500	
	Interfund Loan from Water Utility Fund—Current		6,500
	Governmental Activities:		
9c.	Internal Balances	6,500	
	Cash		6,500

The building used as a warehouse was estimated at the time of purchase to have a remaining useful life of 20 years; the warehouse machinery and equipment were estimated to have useful lives of 10 years, and the delivery equipment to have a useful life of 5 years. If the administrative and clerical office space occupies 10 percent of the area of the warehouse, 10 percent of the depreciation of the warehouse, $350, may be considered administrative expense. Similarly, if the purchasing office occupies 10 percent of the space in the warehouse building, 10 percent of the building depreciation, $350, may be considered purchasing expense. The remainder of the building is devoted to warehousing; therefore, 80 percent of the total building depreciation, $2,800, is to be charged to Warehousing Expenses. This account is also charged $2,500 for machinery and equipment depreciation expense. Delivery Expense is charged $2,000 for depreciation of equipment during the year. Entry 10a illustrates the allocation of depreciation to the Supplies Fund's functions. To simplify the illustration at the government-wide level, Entry 10b assumes that only the General Government function incurred supply expenses. In fact, most functions of government would incur supply expenses.

		Debits	Credits
	Supplies Fund:		
10a.	Administrative Expenses	350	
	Purchasing Expenses	350	
	Warehousing Expenses	5,300	
	Delivery Expenses	2,000	
	Allowance for Depreciation—Building		3,500
	Allowance for Depreciation—Machinery and Equipment—Warehouse		2,500
	Allowance for Depreciation—Equipment—Delivery		2,000
	Governmental Activities:		
10b.	Expenses—General Government	8,000	
	Accumulated Depreciation—Building		3,500
	Accumulated Depreciation—Equipment		4,500

Organizations that keep perpetual inventory records must adjust the records periodically to reflect shortages, overages, or out-of-condition stock disclosed by physical inventories. Adjustments to the inventory account are also considered adjustments to the warehousing expenses of the period. This illustrative case assumes that no adjustments were found necessary at year-end.

Assuming that all revenues and expenses applicable to 2017 have been properly recorded by the preceding entries, the operating statement accounts should be closed as of December 31, 2017:

	Supplies Fund:		
11.	Billings to Departments	249,750	
	Grant Revenue	1,000	
	Cost of Supplies Issued		185,000
	Administrative Expenses		11,350
	Purchasing Expenses		19,350
	Warehousing Expenses		18,300
	Delivery Expenses		15,000
	Excess of Net Billings to Departments over Costs		1,750

The government-wide revenue and expense accounts related to the Supplies Fund will be closed, along with all other governmental activities revenue and expense accounts, in Chapter 9.

Excess of Net Billings to Departments over Costs (or Excess of Costs over Net Billings to Departments, if operations resulted in a loss) is the account title generally considered more descriptive of the fund's results than Income Summary or Current Earnings, the titles commonly found in profit-seeking businesses. Regardless of the title used for the account summarizing the results of operations for the period, the account should be closed at year-end. The title of the account that records earnings retained in an internal service fund, as well as contribution to equity, is Net Position—Unrestricted.

		Debits	Credits
	Supplies Fund:		
12.	Excess of Net Billings to Departments over Costs	1,750	
	Net Position—Unrestricted		1,750

Illustrative Statements Using Supplies Fund

To ensure sound financial management, each government should prepare a statement of net position (or balance sheet), a statement of revenues, expenses, and changes in fund net position, and a statement of cash flows for each internal service fund.

Statement of Net Position

The statement of net position for the Supplies Fund of the Town of Brighton as of December 31, 2017, is shown as Illustration 7–1. As of December 31, 2017, the Supplies Fund investment in capital assets of $122,000 ($130,000 less $8,000 accumulated depreciation) is less than the balance of the interfund loan of $123,500 ($117,000 long-term liability plus $6,500 current portion due within one year). Thus, there is a negative net investment in capital assets to report.[5]

There are no assets restricted as to use by external resource providers or legislative action. As a result, the remaining net position for the Supplies Fund as of December 31, 2017 is unrestricted.

Statement of Revenues, Expenses, and Changes in Fund Net Position

Illustration 7–2 presents a statement of revenues, expenses, and changes in fund net position for the year ended December 31, 2017, for the Town of Brighton Supplies Fund. Because grant revenue is not a part of the primary activity of the Supplies Fund, it is shown below operating income.

Statement of Cash Flows

For the statement of cash flows (Illustration 7–3), the transactions of the Supplies Fund recorded in Entries 5, 6a, 7b, and 8 are classified as operating activities and are reported in the first section of the statement of cash flows. The grant revenue (see Entry 7a) is reported in the cash flows from noncapital financing activities section of the statement of cash flows. The transactions recorded in Entries 1a, 2a, and 9a are classified as capital and related financing activities and are reported in that section of the statement of cash flows. During 2017 there were no transactions that would be classified as investing activities. As required by GASB standards, the statement of cash flows is accompanied by a reconciliation of operating income with the net cash flow from operating activities.

[5] GASB, *Comprehensive Implementation Guide* 7.23.9.

ILLUSTRATION 7–1

TOWN OF BRIGHTON SUPPLIES FUND
Statement of Fund Net Position
As of December 31, 2014

Assets			
Current assets:			
Cash			$ 54,250
Inventory of supplies, at average cost			69,100
Total current assets			123,350
Capital assets:			
Land		$25,000	
Building	$70,000		
Less: Allowance for depreciation	3,500	66,500	
Machinery and equipment—warehouse	25,000		
Less: Allowance for depreciation	2,500	22,500	
Equipment—delivery	10,000		
Less: Allowance for depreciation	2,000	8,000	
Total capital assets			122,000
Total assets			245,350
Liabilities			
Current liabilities:			
Vouchers payable			28,600
Current portion of long-term liabilities			6,500
Total current liabilities			35,100
Long-term liabilities:			
Interfund loan from water utility			117,000
Total liabilities			152,100
Net Position			
Net investment in capital assets			(1,500)
Unrestricted			94,750
Total net position			$ 93,250

ILLUSTRATION 7–2

TOWN OF BRIGHTON SUPPLIES FUND
Statement of Revenues, Expenses, and Changes in Fund Net Position
For the Year Ended December 31, 2017

Operating revenues:		
Billings to departments		$249,750
Less: Cost of supplies issued		185,000
Gross margin		64,750
Operating expenses:		
Purchasing expenses	$19,350	
Administrative expenses	11,350	
Warehousing expenses	18,300	
Delivery expenses	15,000	
Total operating expenses		64,000
Operating income		750
Nonoperating revenues:		
Operating grant		1,000
Change in net position		1,750
Net position—January 1, 2017		91,500
Net position—December 31, 2017		$ 93,250

ILLUSTRATION 7–3

TOWN OF BRIGHTON SUPPLIES FUND
Statement of Cash Flows
For the Year Ended December 31, 2017

Cash Flows from Operating Activities:		
Cash received from customers	$249,750	
Cash paid to employees for services	(55,000)	
Cash paid to suppliers	(165,000)	
Net cash provided by operating activities		$29,750
Cash Flows from Noncapital Financing Activities:		
Operating grant received	1,000	
Net cash provided by noncapital financing activities		1,000
Cash Flows from Capital and Related Financing Activities:		
Advance from Water Utility Fund	130,000	
Partial repayment of advance from Water Utility Fund	(6,500)	
Acquisition of capital assets	(130,000)	
Net cash used for capital and related activities		(6,500)
Net increase in cash and cash equivalents		24,250
Cash and cash equivalents, 1/1/2017		30,000
Cash and cash equivalents, 12/31/2017		$54,250
Reconciliation of Operating Income to Net Cash Provided by Operating Activities		
Operating income		$ 750
Adjustments:		
Depreciation expense		8,000
Increase in inventory		(7,600)
Increase in vouchers payable		28,600
Net cash provided by operating activities		$29,750

External Financial Reporting of Internal Service Funds

The financial statements presented in Illustrations 7–1, 7–2, and 7–3 are prepared for internal management purposes. As indicated earlier, for external reporting purposes the Supplies Fund financial information would be aggregated with other internal service fund data and reported as a separate column of the statement of net position—proprietary funds; statement of revenues, expenses, and changes in net position—proprietary funds; and statement of cash flows—proprietary funds, each of which is prepared for all proprietary funds (see Illustrations A2–7, A2–8, and A2–9 for examples). In the government-wide statement of net position and statement of activities, internal service fund financial information is, in most cases, "collapsed" into and reported in the Governmental Activities column of both government-wide financial statements.

As shown by the journal entries for the Supplies Fund, collapsing information requires eliminating any interfund activity between a governmental fund and an internal service fund. Thus, under the dual-track approach those activities involving a transaction between a governmental fund (General Fund in the Town of Brighton illustration) and an internal service fund (Supplies Fund in the Town of Brighton illustration) are not recorded for governmental activities at the government-wide level.

If a portion of an internal service fund's operating income results from billings to enterprise funds, the GASB requirement to report internal service fund financial information in the governmental activities category tends to overstate unrestricted net position in that category and understate unrestricted net position in the business-type category. Usually this effect should not be material. If enterprise funds are the predominant participants in an internal service fund, the government should report the internal service fund's residual assets, deferred inflows and outflows of resources, and liabilities within the business-type activities column in the statement of net position.[6]

Dissolution of an Internal Service Fund

When an internal service fund has completed the mission for which it was established or its activity is terminated for any other reason (such as outsourcing the activity to an outside vendor), the fund should be dissolved. Liquidation may be accomplished in any one of three ways or in combinations thereof: (1) transfer the fund's assets to another fund that will continue the operation as a subsidiary activity, for example, a supply fund becoming a *department* of the General Fund; (2) distribute the fund's assets to another fund or to another government; or (3) convert all its noncash assets to cash and distribute the cash to another fund or other funds. Dissolution of an internal service fund, as for a private enterprise, would proceed by first paying outside creditors, followed by repayment of any long-term interfund loans outstanding and, finally, liquidation of remaining net resources. The entire process of dissolution should be conducted according to pertinent law and the discretion of the appropriate legislative body. Net resources contributed by another fund or government logically would revert to the contributor fund or government, but law or other regulations may dictate otherwise. If net position has been built up from charges in excess of costs, liquidation will follow whatever regulations may govern the case; if none exist, the appropriate governing body must decide on the recipient or recipients.

Special Topics Associated with Internal Service Funds

Administrative Issues

The accounting and operating of a fund on a business basis can lead to conflict between managers, who want the freedom to operate the fund like a business, and legislators, who wish to exercise considerable control over funds. For example, assume that administrators request the establishment of a fund for the purchasing, warehousing, and issuing of supplies used by a number of funds and departments. Because no internal fund exists at the time of the request, each fund or department will include in its budget an appropriation for supplies, an appropriation for salaries and wages of personnel engaged in purchasing and handling the supplies, and an appropriation for any operating expense or facility costs associated with the supply function. Accordingly, legislators are likely to believe that by maintaining control over these budgets, they will be able to control the investment in supplies and the use of supplies by each fund and department. On the other hand, if they approve the establishment of the requested supply fund, with the authority to generate operating revenues sufficient to maintain the fund, legislators may believe the supply function will no longer be subjected to annual legislative budget review and the legislature will "lose control" of the fund. Administrators are more likely to believe that if an internal service fund does not have the authority to generate operating revenues sufficient to maintain the fund and to spend those revenues at the discretion of fund management (rather than at the discretion of persons possibly more concerned with reelection than financial management), little will be gained by establishing the internal service fund.

[6] GASB, *Codification*, Sec. 2200.156.

The two opposing views should be somewhat balanced by the fact that, as shown in Illustration 7–4, the customers of an internal service fund are, by definition, other funds and departments of the government or of other governments. Therefore, each using fund and department must include in its appropriations budget request the justification for the amount to be spent (i.e., paid to the internal service fund) for supplies, so the legislative branch continues to exercise budgetary review over the amount each fund and department budgets for supplies. As shown in Illustration 7–4, departments and programs that require legislative appropriations to expend resources for goods and services should account for purchases of goods or services from internal suppliers (i.e., internal service funds or enterprise funds) in essentially the same manner as goods and services purchased from external suppliers. By setting pricing policies for the internal service fund and policies governing the use and retention of current earnings, the legislature can maintain considerable control over the function performed by the internal service fund but leave the fund managers freedom to operate at their discretion within the policies set by the legislative branch.

One of the more difficult problems to resolve to the satisfaction of persons with opposing views is the establishment of a pricing policy. "Cost" is obviously an incomplete answer: Historical cost of the supplies, whether defined as first-in, first-out; last-in, first-out; average; or specific identification, will not provide sufficient revenue to replace supplies issued if replacement prices have risen since the last purchase. Nor will it allow for an increase in the inventory quantities if the scale of governmental operations is growing. Payroll and other cash operating expenses of the internal service fund must be met; if the internal service fund has received a loan from another fund or another government, prices must be set at a level that will generate cash needed for debt retirement. If the internal service fund is to be operated on a true business basis, it must also be able to finance from its operations the replacement, modernization, and expansion of plant and equipment used in fund operations. Prices charged by the internal service fund, however, should be less than the using funds and departments would have to pay outside vendors for equivalent products

ILLUSTRATION 7–4 Relationship between Appropriations and Internal Service Funds

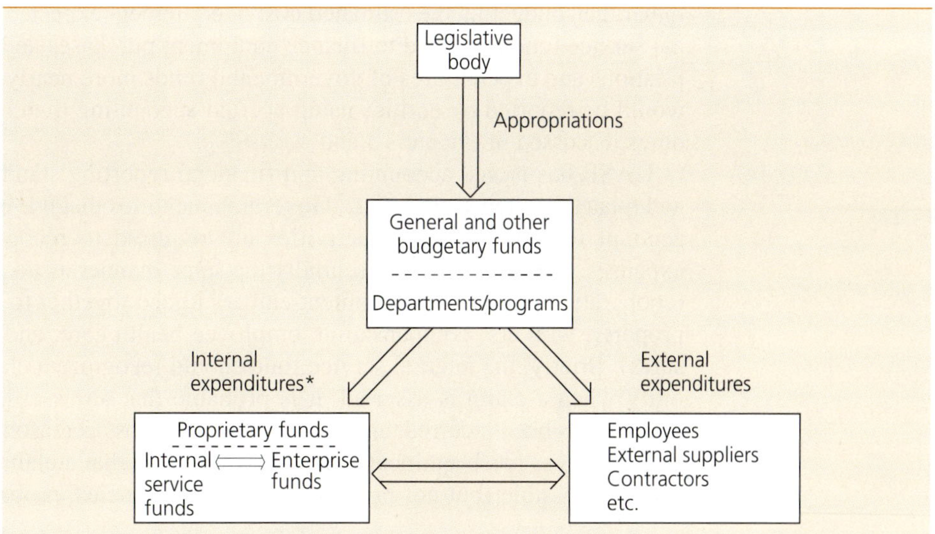

*Internal expenditures are more formally referred to as *interfund services provided and used* or *internal exchange transactions.*

and services if the existence and continued operation of the internal service fund is to be justified. Because of the considerations mentioned in this section, many different approaches to internal service fund operations are found in practice.

Internal Service Funds with Manufacturing Activities

The Supplies Fund of the Town of Brighton, for which journal entries and statements are illustrated earlier in this chapter, is responsible for purchasing, storing, and issuing supplies used by other funds and departments of the town. Many states and local governments have supplies funds similar to that of the Town of Brighton. It is also common to find that funds and departments use printing shops, asphalt plants, and other service units that produce a physical product or that facilitate the operations of the other funds and departments by performing maintenance or repair jobs or even performing a temporary financing function.

If an internal service fund performs a continuous process manufacturing operation, its accounting system should provide process cost accounts. If a service fund performs a manufacturing, maintenance, or repair operation on a job-order basis, the fund's accounting system should provide appropriate job-order cost accounts. To the extent that operations, processes, or activities are capable of being standardized, cost standards for materials, direct labor, and overhead should be established; in such cases, the accounting system should provide for the routine measurement and reporting of significant variances from the standards. Cost determination for government services is discussed in Chapter 12 of this text.

Internal Service Funds as Financing Devices

Governments may utilize internal service funds as devices to finance risk management, equipment purchases and operations (including centralized computer operations), and other functions that are facilitated by generating revenues from user charges to cover costs and expenses computed on an accrual basis. In the case of funds to finance equipment purchases and operations, including the operations of computers owned by the government, an internal service fund can include depreciation and, perhaps, expected increases in the cost of replacing assets, in the charge to the using funds, thus incorporating these costs in current appropriations of governmental funds, rather than budgeting the estimated cost of equipment expected to be replaced. If internal service funds are used to finance equipment purchases and operations, the appropriations and expenditures of governmental funds more nearly approximate costs that would be reported by entities using accrual accounting than is true under the procedures discussed in Chapters 3 and 4.

GASB has issued accounting and financial reporting standards for risk financing and related insurance activities.[7] Government entities that use internal service funds to account for risk financing activities are required to recognize revenues, claims expenses, and liabilities in essentially the same manner as do public entity risk pools (cooperative groups of government entities joined together to finance risks of loss to property, workers' compensation, employee health care, and similar risks or exposures). Briefly, the internal service fund should recognize a claims expense and a liability when a claim is asserted, it is probable that an asset has been impaired or a liability has been incurred, and the amount of the loss is reasonably estimable; or if an estimable loss has been incurred and it is probable that a claim will be asserted. Reasonably possible (but not probable) loss contingencies, probable losses that are not

[7] GASB, *Codification,* Sec. Po20.

reasonably measurable, and loss exposure in excess of the accrued liability should be disclosed in the notes to the financial statements. The disclosure should explain the nature of the contingency and an estimate of the possible loss, the range of the loss, or why the amount is not estimable.

Internal service fund charges to other funds for risk financing activities should be sufficient to recover the total amount of claim expenses recognized for the period or, alternatively, may be based on an actuarial method so that internal service fund revenues and expenses over time are approximately equal. Charges to other funds may also include a reasonable provision for expected future catastrophe losses. Internal service fund charges to other funds are recognized as revenues by the internal service fund and as expenditures by governmental funds or expenses by proprietary funds. Internal service fund charges in excess of the full cost amount should be reported as a nonoperating transfer by the internal service fund and an other financing use by the other funds. If the internal service fund fails to recover the full cost of claims over a reasonable period of time, the accumulated fund deficit should be charged to the other funds and reported by the other funds as an expenditure or expense, as appropriate.

ENTERPRISE FUNDS

Enterprise funds and internal service funds are both classified by the GASB as proprietary funds, although enterprise funds are used by governments to account for services provided to the general public on a user charge basis. Under GASB standards, a government must report certain activities in an enterprise fund if any of the following criteria are met.[8]

1. The activity is financed with debt that is secured *solely* by a pledge of the revenues from fees and charges of an activity. [Emphasis added by authors.]
2. Laws or regulations require that the activity's costs of providing services, including capital costs (such as depreciation or debt service), be recovered with fees and charges, rather than with taxes or similar revenues.
3. Pricing policies are designed to recover the costs of the activity, including capital costs.

These criteria are quite specific regarding when an enterprise fund *must* be used. For example, if debt issued is also backed by the full faith and credit of the government, even though it is intended to be repaid from revenues of a particular activity, that activity need not be reported in an enterprise fund. Similarly, if an activity is subsidized by a government's General Fund rather than fully covering its costs of providing services with fees or charges, that activity need not be reported in an enterprise fund. In either of these examples, the government could opt to report the activities in an enterprise fund. However, if governments support the activities *primarily* with general or special revenue sources rather than user charges, accounting for the activities is more appropriate in the General Fund or a special revenue fund.

Because the word *enterprise* is often used as a synonym for "business-type activity," it is logical that enterprise funds should use accrual accounting and account for all assets used in the production of goods or services offered by the fund. Similarly, if long-term debt is to be serviced by the fund, the fund does the accounting for the

[8] GASB *Codification,* Sec. 1300.109.

debt. It follows that enterprise funds are generally reported as part of the Business-type Activities column of the government-wide financial statements. Since internal service funds are generally reported as part of the Governmental Activities column, if only enterprise funds are included in the Business-type Activities column, the financial records of the enterprise funds can simply be added together for financial reporting purposes at the government-wide level. Any interfund transactions among enterprise funds should be eliminated because they would have no net effect on overall business-type activities.

The most common examples of governmental enterprises are public utilities, notably water and sewer utilities. Electric and gas utilities, transportation systems, airports, ports, hospitals, toll bridges, produce markets, parking lots, parking garages, and public housing projects are other examples frequently found. Because services of the types mentioned are intended to be largely self-supporting, they are generally accounted for by enterprise funds.

Almost every type of enterprise operated by a government has its counterpart in the private sector. In order to take advantage of the work done by regulatory agencies and trade associations to develop useful accounting information systems for the investor-owned enterprises, it is recommended that governmentally owned enterprises use the accounting structures developed for investor-owned enterprises of the same nature.[9] Budgetary accounts should be used only if required by law. The accounting for debt service and construction activities of a governmental enterprise occurs within the enterprise fund rather than by separate debt service and capital projects funds. Thus, the financial statements of enterprise funds are self-contained, and creditors, legislators, or the general public can evaluate the performance of a governmental enterprise on the same bases as they can the performance of investor-owned enterprises in the same industry.

By far the most numerous and important enterprise services rendered by local governments are public utilities. In this chapter, therefore, the example used is that of a water utility fund.

WATER UTILITY FUNDS

The statement of net position as of December 31, 2016, for the Town of Brighton Water Utility Fund is shown in Illustration 7–5. The statement appears fairly conventional, but terminology peculiar to utilities warrants discussion prior to proceeding to the illustrative transactions for the year ending December 31, 2017. Part of the difference in terminology relates to the fact that the Water Utility Fund is part of a regulated industry. As such, the primary regulatory bodies, the National Association of Regulatory Utility Commissioners (NARUC) and Federal Energy Regulatory Commission (FERC), influence the accounting for utilities.

[9] Most applicable private-sector guidance from FASB and AICPA pronouncements has been officially incorporated into the GASB codification. Additional accounting guidance, such as FASB statements issued after 2010 or industry-specific guidance, is considered "other accounting literature," as defined in *GASB Codification,* Sec. 1000, pars. 103 and 104, and may be followed by governments as long as they do not conflict with or contradict GASB pronouncements. It should also be noted that as this textbook goes to press the GASB has issued an exposure draft related to the hierarchy of GAAP, which further addresses "other accounting literature."

ILLUSTRATION 7–5

TOWN OF BRIGHTON
Water Utility Fund
Statement of Net Position
As of December 31, 2016

Assets			
Current and accrued assets:			
Cash		$ 126,000	
Customer accounts receivable	$69,000		
Less: Accumulated provision for uncollectible accounts	2,900	66,100	
Accrued utilities revenues		14,800	
Materials and supplies		28,700	
Total current and accrued assets			$ 235,600
Restricted assets:			
Cash		6,600	
Investments		556,000	562,600
Utility plant:			
Utility plant in service		3,291,825	
Less: Accumulated depreciation		440,325	
Utility plant—net		2,851,500	
Construction work in progress		125,000	
Net utility plant			2,976,500
Total assets			3,774,700
Liabilities			
Current liabilities:			
Accounts payable		33,200	
Customer advances for construction		21,000	
Total current liabilities			54,200
Liabilities payable from restricted assets:			
Customer deposits			23,700
Long-term liabilities:			
Revenue bonds payable (net of unamortized discount of $5,300)			1,744,700
Total liabilities			1,822,600
Net Position			
Net investment in capital assets			1,231,800
Restricted for debt service			538,900
Unrestricted			181,400
Total net position			$1,952,100

Current and Accrued Assets

The Cash and Materials and Supplies accounts shown in Illustration 7–5 in the Current and Accrued Assets section are not peculiar to utilities and need not be discussed here. The other two asset accounts in this section—Customer Accounts Receivable and Accrued Utilities Revenues—are related. The former represents billings to customers that are outstanding at year-end (and are reduced by an accumulated provision for uncollectible accounts). The latter results from the fact that utilities generally prepare billings to customers on the basis of meter readings, and it is not practical for utilities to read all meters simultaneously at year-end and bill all customers as of that time. Utilities that meter their service make extensive use of cycle billing, which, in substance, consists of billing part of their customers each day instead of billing by calendar months. Under this plan, meter reading, whether manual or electronic, is a continuous day-by-day operation, with billings following shortly after data collection. Individual meters are read on approximately the same day each month, or every other month, so that each bill covers approximately the same number of days of usage. Cycle billing eliminates the heavy peak load of accounting and clerical work that results from uniform billing on a calendar month basis. It does, however, result in a sizeable amount of unbilled receivables on any given date. Thus, in order to state assets and sales properly, accrual of unbilled receivables (Accrued Utilities Revenues, in regulatory terminology) is required as of the financial statement date.

Restricted Assets

The section following Current and Accrued Assets in Illustration 7–5 is captioned Restricted Assets, the caption most commonly used when the use of assets is restricted by contractual agreements or legal requirements. Some governments that use regulatory terminology report restricted assets of utilities under the broader caption, Other Property and Investments. Other Property and Investments may include, in addition to restricted assets, the carrying value of property not being used for utility purposes or being held for future utility use.

Cash and Investments are the only two items reported under the Restricted Assets caption of the balance sheet shown in Illustration 7–5. Those items are restricted for return of customer deposits and for retirement of revenue bonds pursuant to the bond covenants. The amount of assets segregated, $562,600, is offset by liabilities currently payable from restricted assets (in the case of the Town of Brighton, customer deposits of $23,700) and restrictions of net position (in this case, restricted for payment of debt service, $538,900). This *fund within a fund* approach permits segregation of assets, related liabilities, and restricted net position within a single enterprise fund. Net position should be restricted in the amount that has been restricted by each "fund" within the enterprise fund, as shown in Illustration 7–5. Other items commonly reported in the Restricted Assets section include assets set aside to fund depreciation for capital improvements or grants and contributions restricted for capital acquisition or improvement.

Utility Plant

Utility Plant in Service

Utility Plant in Service is a control account, supported in whatever detail is required by regulatory agencies and by management needs. For example, water utilities commonly have six subcategories of plant assets: intangible plant, source of supply plant, pumping plant, water treatment plant, transmission and distribution plant, and general plant. Each of the six subcategories is supported by appropriate subsidiary accounts. For example, intangible plant consists of the costs of organization, franchises, and consents, and any other intangible costs necessary and valuable to the conduct of utility operations. Source of supply plant consists of land and land rights; structures and improvements; collecting and impounding reservoirs; lake, river, and other intakes; wells and springs; infiltration galleries and tunnels; supply mains; and other water source plant. Each of the accounts within a subcategory is supported by necessary subsidiary records for individual assets detailing description, location, cost, date of acquisition, estimated useful life, salvage value, depreciation charges, and any other information needed for management planning and control, regulatory agency reports, financial statements, or special reports to creditors.

Construction Work in Progress

The other utility plant item shown on the statement of net position, Illustration 7–5, is Construction Work in Progress. This account represents the accumulated costs of work orders for projects that will result in items reportable as utility plant when completed and is supported by the work orders for projects in progress. Each work order, in turn, is supported by documents supporting payments to contractors and to suppliers or supporting charges for materials, labor, and overhead allocable to the project. Unlike self-constructed general capital assets, GASB requires interest capitalization for self-constructed assets of proprietary funds.[10]

Current Liabilities

Items commonly found in the Current Liabilities section of a utility statement of net position are shown under that caption in Illustration 7–5. Accounts Payable needs no comment here. The other item, Customer advances for construction, results from utilities' practice of requiring customers to advance to the utility a sizeable portion of the estimated cost of construction projects to be undertaken by the utility at the request of the customer. If the advances are to be refunded, either wholly or in part, or applied against billings for service rendered after completion of the project, they are classified as shown in Illustration 7–5. When a customer is refunded the entire amount to which he or she is entitled according to the agreement or rule under which the advance was made, the balance retained by the utility, if any, is reported as Contributions from Customers in the statement of revenues, expenses, and changes in fund net position. Other items commonly reported under Current Liabilities include accrued expenses, amounts due to other funds, and current portions of long-term liabilities. Some governments also report customer deposits under the Current Liabilities caption; however, this item is generally reported as a liability payable from restricted assets, as discussed below.

Liabilities Payable from Restricted Assets

Liabilities payable from restricted assets should be displayed separately from current liabilities, as shown in Illustration 7–5. In addition to customer deposits, the current portion of revenue bonds payable, if any, would be reported here since restricted assets have been set aside for that purpose. The Town of Brighton follows the common practice of most utilities and requires all new customers to deposit a sum of money with the utility as security for the payment of bills. In many jurisdictions, utilities are required to pay interest on customer deposits at a nominal rate. Regulatory authorities or local policy may require utilities to refund the deposits, and interest, after a specified period of time if the customer has paid all bills on time. The utility may be required, as was the Town of Brighton Water Utility Fund, to segregate cash or investments in an amount equal to the liability for Customer Deposits. Customer Advances for Construction are contractually different from Customer Deposits and are less likely to be reported separately as restricted assets and liabilities unless agreements with developers make it necessary to restrict assets for this purpose.

Long-term Liabilities

Bonds are the customary form of long-term liabilities. Bonds issued by a utility are usually secured by the pledge of certain portions of the utility's revenue; bonds of this nature are called **revenue bonds.** Some utility bonds are secured not only by a pledge

[10] Capitalization of interest cost is covered in GASB, *Codification*, Sec. 1400.120–137.

of a certain portion of the utility's revenues but also by an agreement on the part of the town's or city's general government to subsidize the utility in any year in which its normal revenue is inadequate for compliance with the terms of the bond indenture. Other utility bonds carry the pledge of the government entity's full faith and credit, although the intent is to service them from utility revenues rather than general taxes. The latter are, therefore, technically **general obligation bonds.** GASB standards require that general obligation bonds intended to be serviced from utility revenues be reported as a liability of the enterprise fund; however, the bonds should be included with other general obligation debt when computing the schedule of general bonded debt or any related ratios.[11] Similarly, special assessment debt may be assumed by an enterprise fund if the assets constructed by special assessment financing are used in enterprise fund operations.[12]

Governmentally owned utilities may have received long-term interfund loans from the government's General Fund or other funds. Also, enterprises may acquire assets under a capital lease arrangement. The portion of interfund loans, required lease payments, or bond or other debt issues to be paid within one year from the statement of net position date should be reported as a current liability; the remainder is properly reported in the Long-term Liabilities section of the utility statement of net position. Long-term bonds payable should be reported net of unamortized discount or premium, as shown in Illustration 7–5, or the unamortized discount or premium can be reported as an offset against bonds payable at par on the statement of net position.

Net Position

As discussed earlier in the chapter, proprietary funds report using three net position categories: net investment in capital assets; restricted; and unrestricted. The three categories of net position for the Water Utility Fund are shown in Illustration 7–5. Restrictions may be placed by law, regulation, or contractual agreement with creditors or other outside parties. Illustration 7–5 shows a typical restriction: A sinking fund created pursuant to a bond indenture for repayment of revenue bond principal. Unrestricted net position represents the residual amount of net position after segregating net investment in capital assets and restricted net position.

Illustrative Case—Water Utility Fund

The preceding discussion concerning the statement of net position accounts of a water utility addresses the essential characteristics of accounting necessary for both governmentally owned utilities and investor-owned utilities. In this section, accounting for typical transactions of a utility fund is illustrated in general journal entry format for fiscal year 2017, the year following the statement of net position presented in Illustration 7–5.

It is assumed that the Town of Brighton is located in a state that permits enterprise funds to operate without formal legal approval of their budgets. Utility or other enterprise management must prepare operating budgets and capital expenditure budgets as

[11] GASB, *Comprehensive Implementation Guide,* 9.25.4; and GASB, *Implementation Guide Statement 44,* Q&A, Question 77.

[12] In the case of special assessment debt, the portion that is a direct obligation of the enterprise fund or the portion expected to be repaid from enterprise fund revenues should be reported as a liability on the enterprise fund's balance sheet. As described in GASB *Codification* Sec. S40, par. 123, a governmental entity may choose to report all of the transactions and balances of a special assessment project within an enterprise fund to properly reflect the actual administration of a project.

management tools. For the illustrative case, it is assumed that the budgets are submitted to the town administrators, the town legislative body, and the public for information, not for legal action. Accordingly, the budget is not formally recorded in enterprise fund accounts. While utility management must be informed periodically of the status of outstanding construction contracts and purchase orders, encumbrances need not be recorded in the accounts in order to accomplish this.

The nature of the Accrued Utilities Revenues account was explained previously in the section "Current and Accrued Assets." For FY 2017, it is not feasible when customers' bills are prepared to determine whether a portion of the bill has been accrued and, if so, in what amount. The simplest procedure, therefore, is to reverse the accrual entry as of the start of the new fiscal year. Assuming that the entire December 31, 2016, Town of Brighton Water Utility Fund revenues accrual has been credited to Sales of Water, the following entry is appropriate as of January 1, 2017:

		Debits	Credits
1.	Sales of Water	14,800	
	Accrued Utility Revenues		14,800

Earlier in this chapter, recall that the Water Utility Fund advanced $130,000 to the Supplies Fund as a long-term loan. The entry by the Supplies Fund is illustrated in Entry 1a in the "Illustrative Case—Supplies Fund" section earlier in this chapter; the corresponding entry in the Water Utility Fund would be:

2.	Interfund Loan to Supplies Fund—Noncurrent	130,000	
	Cash		130,000

When utility customers are billed during the year, appropriate revenue accounts are credited. Assuming that during 2017 the total bills to nongovernmental customers amounted to $696,000, bills to the Town of Brighton General Fund amounted to $30,000, and all revenue was from the sale of water, the following entry summarizes the events:

3.	Customer Accounts Receivable	696,000	
	Due from General Fund	30,000	
	Sales of Water		726,000

If collections on receivables from nongovernmental water customers totaled $680,000, Entry 4 is needed:

4.	Cash	680,000	
	Customer Accounts Receivable		680,000

Materials and supplies in the amount of $138,000 were purchased during the year by the Water Utility Fund. The liability is recorded as:

		Debits	Credits
5.	Materials and Supplies	138,000	
	Accounts Payable		138,000

Materials and supplies chargeable to the accounts itemized in the following entry were issued during the year.

6.	Source of Supply Expenses	18,000	
	Pumping Expenses	21,000	
	Water Treatment Expenses	24,000	
	Transmission and Distribution Expenses	13,000	
	Construction Work in Progress	66,000	
	Materials and Supplies		142,000

Payrolls for the year were chargeable to the accounts shown in the following entry. Tax Collections Payable is the account provided in the NARUC and FERC systems to report the amount of taxes collected by the utility through payroll deductions or otherwise pending transmittal of such taxes to the proper taxing authority. Taxes Accrued is the account provided in the NARUC and FERC systems to report the liability for taxes that are the expense of the utility, such as the employer's share of social security taxes. The following entry assumes that the employer's share of social security taxes is charged to the same accounts that the employees' gross earnings are; it also assumes that checks have been issued for employees' net earnings.

7.	Source of Supply Expenses	8,200	
	Pumping Expenses	15,700	
	Water Treatment Expenses	17,500	
	Transmission and Distribution Expenses	76,250	
	Customer Accounts Expenses	96,550	
	Sales Expenses	17,250	
	Administrative and General Expenses	83,150	
	Construction Work in Progress	30,400	
	Taxes Accrued		13,800
	Tax Collections Payable		51,750
	Cash		279,450

Bond interest in the amount of $105,000 was paid; the bonds were issued to finance the acquisition of utility plant assets. Amortization of debt discount amounted to $530.

8.	Interest on Long-term Debt	105,530	
	Unamortized Discount		530
	Cash		105,000

Bond interest in the amount of $12,900 was properly capitalized as part of construction work in progress during the year. (The Town of Brighton does not impute interest on its own resources during construction.)

		Debits	Credits
9.	Construction Work in Progress	12,900	
	Interest on Long-term Debt		12,900

Construction projects on which costs totaled $220,000 were completed and the assets placed in service were recorded:

10.	Utility Plant in Service	220,000	
	Construction Work in Progress		220,000

Collection efforts on bills totaling $3,410 were discontinued. The customers owing the bills had paid deposits totaling $2,140 to the water utility; the deposits were applied to the bills, and the unpaid remainder was charged to Accumulated Provision for Uncollectible Accounts (Entry 11a). Restricted assets (cash) is reduced by $2,140, the amount of the decrease in Customer Deposits (Entry 11b). Cash may be restricted for a number of reasons, such as customer deposits or debt, so a government will maintain internal information regarding the nature of restrictions placed on cash.

11a.	Customer Deposits	2,140	
	Accumulated Provision for Uncollectible Accounts	1,270	
	Customer Accounts Receivable		3,410
11b.	Cash	2,140	
	Cash—Restricted		2,140

Customers' deposits amounting to $1,320 were refunded by check to customers discontinuing service (see Entry 12a). Deposits totaling $2,525 were received from new customers (see Entry 12b).

12a.	Customer Deposits	1,320	
	Cash—Restricted		1,320
12b.	Cash—Restricted	2,525	
	Customer Deposits		2,525

Customers' advances for construction in the amount of $14,000 were applied to their water bills; in accord with the agreement with the customers and NARUC recommendations, the remainder of the advances was transferred to Capital Contributions from Customers.

13.	Customer Advances for Construction	21,000	
	Customer Accounts Receivable		14,000
	Capital Contributions from Customers		7,000

Payments of accounts payable for materials and supplies used in operations totaled $67,200, and payment of accounts payable for materials used in construction totaled $66,000. Payments of taxes accrued amounted to $13,500, and payments of tax collections payable amounted to $50,000.

		Debits	Credits
14.	Accounts Payable	133,200	
	Taxes Accrued	13,500	
	Tax Collections Payable	50,000	
	Cash		196,700

The Water Utility Fund agreed to pay $25,000 to the town General Fund as a payment in lieu of property taxes. The entry in the General Fund is illustrated in Chapter 4 (see Chapter 4, illustrative Entry 25a). The following entry records the event in the accounts of the Water Utility Fund:

		Debits	Credits
15.	Payment in Lieu of Taxes	25,000	
	Due to General Fund		25,000

During the year, interest amounting to $44,500 in cash was received on restricted investments. The amount $1,375 is allocable to investments of customer deposit assets and is unrestricted as to use; the remaining $43,125 adds to the amount restricted for revenue bond repayment.

		Debits	Credits
16a.	Cash	1,375	
	Cash—Restricted	43,125	
	Interest and Dividend Income		44,500
16b.	Net Position—Unrestricted	43,125	
	Net Position—Restricted for Debt Service		43,125

At year-end, entries to record depreciation expense, the provision for uncollectible accounts, and unbilled customer accounts receivable should be made as illustrated by Entry 17. In accord with regulatory terminology, Uncollectible Accounts instead of Bad Debts Expense (FASB) or Provision for Bad Debts (GASB) is debited for the amount added to Accumulated Provision for Uncollectible Accounts. Amounts are assumed.

		Debits	Credits
17.	Depreciation Expense	102,750	
	Uncollectible Accounts	3,980	
	Accrued Utility Revenues	15,920	
	Accumulated Provision for Depreciation of Utility Plant		102,750
	Accumulated Provision for Uncollectible Accounts		3,980
	Sales of Water		15,920

In accord with the revenue bond indenture, $100,000 of unrestricted cash was invested in U.S. government securities for eventual retirement of revenue bonds. Net position is restricted in an amount equal to the increase in restricted assets. In addition, investments totaling $40,000 were made from restricted cash for eventual bond repayment.

		Debits	Credits
18a.	Investments—Restricted	140,000	
	Cash		100,000
	Cash—Restricted		40,000
18b.	Net Position—Unrestricted	100,000	
	Net Position—Restricted for Debt Service		100,000

Toward the end of 2017, the Supplies Fund paid its first installment of $6,500 to the Water Utility Fund as a partial repayment of the long-term advance. Entry 9a of the illustrative entries for the supply fund shown earlier in this chapter (see the section titled "Illustrative Case—Supplies Fund") illustrates the effect of the Supplies Fund on the accounts. The effect on the accounts of the Water Utility Fund is recorded by the following entry:

19.	Cash	6,500	
	Interfund Loan to Supplies Fund—Noncurrent		6,500

Nominal accounts for the year were closed:

20.	Sales of Water	727,120	
	Capital Contributions from Customers	7,000	
	Interest and Dividend Income	44,500	
	Source of Supply Expenses		26,200
	Pumping Expenses		36,700
	Water Treatment Expenses		41,500
	Transmission and Distribution Expenses		89,250
	Customer Account Expenses		96,550
	Sales Expenses		17,250
	Administrative and General Expenses		83,150
	Interest on Long-term Debt		92,630
	Payment in Lieu of Taxes		25,000
	Depreciation Expense		102,750
	Uncollectible Accounts		3,980
	Net Position—Unrestricted		163,660

In addition, Net Position—Net Investment in Capital Assets, would be decreased for depreciation and amortization of the debt discount and increased for the change in utility plant during the year.

Entry 21a reflects the adjustment for depreciation (Entry 17) and amortization of the bond discount (Entry 8). The increase to capital assets (Entries 6, 7, and 9), resulting in adjustment to net position, is shown in Entry 21b.

21a.	Net Position—Net Investment in Capital Assets	103,280	
	Net Position—Unrestricted		103,280
21b.	Net Position—Unrestricted	109,300	
	Net Position—Net Investment in Capital Assets		109,300

After these entries the balance of Net Position—Net Investment in Capital Assets is equal to total fund capital assets, less accumulated depreciation, net of capital asset-related debt.

Illustrative Statements Using Water Utility Fund

Statement of Net Position

The statement of net position for a water utility, and definitions of certain statement of net position categories and items peculiar to regulated utilities, have been explained in the sections of this chapter preceding the illustrative entries. The statement of net position of the Town of Brighton Water Utility Fund as of December 31, 2017, is shown as Illustration 7–6. Similar to what was done in Chapter 4 (Illustration 4–3), and in conformance with GASB standards, internal receivables and payables are netted. That is, the amount due to the General Fund is offset against the amount due from that fund, and only the net amount of the receivable, $5,000, is shown as an asset.

Statement of Revenues, Expenses, and Changes in Fund Net Position

The activity of the Town of Brighton's Water Utility Fund for the year ended December 31, 2017, is shown in Illustration 7–7, the statement of revenues, expenses, and changes in fund net position. In accordance with GASB standards, operating revenues are shown net of Uncollectible Accounts and revenues and expenses are identified as operating and nonoperating. The classifications and account titles used in the statement are consistent with NARUC and FERC recommendations. If NARUC and FERC had not been used, a contra-revenue account title such as Provision for Bad Debts would have been used rather than the title Uncollectible Accounts.

Statement of Cash Flows

GASB standards require that a statement of cash flows be prepared for all proprietary funds as part of a full set of annual financial statements. As discussed earlier in this chapter, GASB standards for preparation of a cash flow statement differ from FASB standards, the main difference being that GASB standards specify four major categories of cash flows rather than three. The statement of cash flows for the Town of Brighton for the year ended December 31, 2017 (Illustration 7–8), utilizes only three of the four categories of cash flows since the town had no cash flows from noncapital financing activities. The section *Cash Flows from Operating Activities* (Illustration 7–8) was provided by receipts from customers (Entry 4) and the net increase in refundable customer deposits (Entries 12a and 12b). Note that the application of customer deposits to pay overdue bills (Entries 11a and 11b) has no effect on total cash and cash equivalents. Cash from operating activities was used to pay employees (Entries 7 and 14). As suggested in the GASB *Comprehensive Implementation Guide* on reporting cash flows,[13] all employee-related items (in this case Taxes Accrued and Tax Collections Payable) have been added to the amount actually paid to employees. Payroll taxes and fringe benefits may be included in a separate line, called cash payments for taxes, duties, fines, and other fees or penalties, if significant in amount. Cash paid to employees for services in the amount of $312,550 is calculated as the net cash paid

[13] Governmental Accounting Standards Board, *Comprehensive Implementation Guide—2014* (Norwalk, CT, 2014), 2.29.2.

ILLUSTRATION 7–6

TOWN OF BRIGHTON
Water Utility Fund
Statement of Net Position
As of December 31, 2017

Assets			
Current and accrued assets:			
Cash		$ 4,865	
Customer accounts receivable	$67,590		
Less: Accumulated provision for uncollectible accounts	5,610	61,980	
Accrued utilities revenues		15,920	
Due from General Fund		5,000	
Materials and supplies		24,700	
Total current and accrued assets			$ 112,465
Restricted assets:			
Cash		8,790	
Investments		696,000	704,790
Utility plant:			
Utility plant in service		3,511,825	
Less: Accumulated depreciation		543,075	
Utility plant—net		2,968,750	
Construction work in progress		14,300	
Net utility plant			2,983,050
Other noncurrent assets:			
Interfund loan to Supplies Fund			123,500
Total assets			3,923,805
Liabilities			
Current liabilities:			
Accounts payable		38,000	
Taxes accrued		300	
Tax collection payable		1,750	
Total current liabilities			40,050
Liabilities payable from restricted assets:			
Customer deposits			22,765
Long-term liabilities:			
Revenue bonds payable (net of unamortized discount of $4,770)			1,745,230
Total liabilities			1,808,045
Net Position			
Net investment in capital assets			1,237,820
Restricted for debt service			682,025
Unrestricted			195,915
Total net position			$2,115,760

directly to employees, $279,450, less $30,400 capitalized as Construction Work in Progress (Entry 7) plus $63,500 paid for Taxes Accrued and Tax Collections Payable (Entry 14). Finally, cash from operating activities was used to pay suppliers (Entry 14). Although suppliers were paid $133,200 in total, only $67,200 of this amount applied to operating activities.

The section *Cash Flows from Capital and Related Activities* in Illustration 7–8 shows two uses of cash. The first item, acquisition and construction of capital assets, is calculated as the sum of $30,400 (Entry 7) and $66,000 (Entry 14 where amounts

ILLUSTRATION 7–7

TOWN OF BRIGHTON
Water Utility Fund
Statement of Revenues, Expenses, and Changes in Fund Net Position
For the Year Ended December 31, 2017

Utility operating revenue:		
Sales of water (net of $3,980 for uncollectible accounts)		$ 723,140
Operating expenses:		
Source of supply expenses	$ 26,200	
Pumping expenses	36,700	
Water treatment expenses	41,500	
Transmission and distribution expenses	89,250	
Customer account expenses	96,550	
Sales expenses	17,250	
Administrative and general expenses	83,150	
Depreciation expense	102,750	
Payment in lieu of taxes	25,000	
Total operating expenses		518,350
Utility operating income		204,790
Nonoperating income and deductions:		
Interest and dividend revenue	44,500	
Interest on long-term debt	(92,630)	
Total nonoperating income and deductions		(48,130)
Income before contributions		156,660
Capital contributions from customers		7,000
Change in net position		163,660
Total net position, January 1, 2017		1,952,100
Total net position, December 31, 2017		$2,115,760

recorded in Entry 6 were paid). The other item, interest paid on long-term bonds, reflects bond interest in the amount of $105,000 paid in cash (Entry 8).

The *Cash Flows from Investing Activities* section shows cash provided by interest and dividend income (Entry 16a), cash used to purchase investments (Entry 18a), and cash used to acquire an interfund loan (Entries 2 and 19).

As shown in Illustration 7–8, two reconciliations are required. The first reconciliation is necessary because the Town of Brighton's Statement of Cash Flows reports changes in *total* cash and cash equivalents, whereas the statement of net position shows two components of cash and cash equivalents: that included in Current and Accrued Assets and that included in Restricted Assets.[14] GASB standards also require a reconciliation of operating income to net cash provided by operating activities.

External Financial Reporting of Enterprise Funds

As shown in Illustrations A2–1 and A2–2, the totals for all enterprise funds, with interfund transactions between enterprise funds eliminated, are reported in the Business-type Activities columns of the government-wide financial statements. Governments must also prepare three fund financial statements for their major enterprise funds (see the Glossary for a definition of major funds) and the total of their internal service funds. These statements are the statement of net position (or balance

[14] Ibid., 2.31.2.

ILLUSTRATION 7–8

TOWN OF BRIGHTON WATER UTILITY FUND
Statement of Cash Flows
For the Year Ended December 31, 2017

Cash Flows from Operating Activities:	
Cash received from customers	$680,000
Cash provided from customer deposits	1,205
Cash paid to employees for services	(312,550)
Cash paid to suppliers	(67,200)
Net cash provided by operating activities	301,455
Cash Flows from Capital and Related Financing Activities:	
Acquisition and construction of capital assets	(96,400)
Interest paid on long-term bonds	(105,000)
Net cash used for capital and related financing activities	(201,400)
Cash Flows from Investing Activities:	
Interest and dividend income	44,500
Purchases of restricted investments	(140,000)
Interfund loan	(123,500)
Net cash used for investing activities	(219,000)
Net decrease in cash and cash equivalents	(118,945)
Cash and cash equivalents—January 1, 2017	132,600
Cash and cash equivalents—December 31, 2017	$ 13,655

Reconciliation of Cash and Cash Equivalents to the Statement of Net Position

	End of Year	Beginning of Year
Cash and cash equivalents in current and accrued assets	$ 4,865	$126,000
Restricted cash and cash equivalents	8,790	6,600
Total cash and cash equivalents	$ 13,655	$132,600

Reconciliation of Utility Operating Income to Net Cash Provided by Operating Activities

Utility operating income		$204,790
Adjustments:		
Depreciation expense	$102,750	
Increase in accounts payable	4,800	
Increase in accrued liabilities	2,050	
Decrease in customer deposits	(935)	
Decrease in inventories	4,000	
Increase in interfund receivables	(5,000)	
Increase in accrued receivables	(1,120)	
Decrease in customer accounts receivable	4,120	
Customer advances applied to customer receivables	(14,000)	
Total adjustments		96,665
Net cash provided by operating activities		$301,455

sheet), statement of revenues, expenses, and changes in fund net position, and statement of cash flows. Illustrative proprietary fund statements are presented in Illustrations A2–7, A2–8, and A2–9. As those statements show, a separate column is provided for internal service funds. The amounts shown in this column are the totals for all internal service funds since major fund reporting does not apply to the internal service funds.

Appendix

Special Topics in Accounting for the Business-type Activities of State and Local Governments

REGULATORY ACCOUNTING PRINCIPLES (RAP)

Investor-owned utilities, as well as governmentally owned utilities in some states, are required to report in a prescribed manner to state regulatory commissions. Electric and certain other utilities subject to the Federal Power Act must also file reports with the FERC. As mentioned within the chapter, both NARUC and FERC prescribe charts of accounts and uniform financial statement formats for reporting to regulatory agencies. Even though the Town of Brighton follows GAAP rather than **regulatory accounting principles (RAP)** in preparing its financial statements, the town uses some of the chart of accounts and some of the financial statement captions provided in regulatory publications. The illustrative financial statements shown earlier in this chapter are typical of those for water funds included in comprehensive annual financial reports.

For utilities that are required to report to a state rate regulatory commission or the FERC, accounting and reporting procedures under RAP are quite different from GAAP. Because plant assets and long-term debt are customarily a dominant share of the total assets and total debt of utilities and current assets and current liabilities are relatively insignificant in amount, the regulatory balance sheet format displays plant assets before current assets and long-term debt before current liabilities. In Illustration 7–5, for example, Utility Plant—Net amounts to almost 79 percent of total assets, and long-term debt is almost 96 percent of total debt.

Under regulatory reporting, Utility Plant in Service is stated at original cost. Original cost is a regulatory concept that differs from historical cost, a concept commonly used in accounting for assets of nonregulated businesses. In essence, **historical cost** is the amount paid for an asset by its present owner. In contrast, **original cost** is *the cost to the owner who first devoted the property to public service*. When a regulated utility purchases plant assets from another utility, it must record in its accounts the amounts shown in the accounts of the seller for the utility plant purchased and for the related accumulated depreciation. Any premium paid by the present owner over and above such cost less depreciation is in the general nature of payments for goodwill by nonutility enterprises. But utilities enjoy monopoly privileges and are subject to corresponding restrictions. One of the restrictions is that earnings shall not exceed a fair rate of return. Since goodwill is the capitalized value of excess earnings, utilities can have no goodwill (in the accounting sense). Premium on plant purchased is therefore accounted for as **Utility Plant Acquisition Adjustments.** The amount of acquisition adjustment capitalized is amortized over a period of time determined by the appropriate regulatory body; accumulated amortization is disclosed in the Accumulated Provision for Amortization of Utility Plant Acquisition Adjustments account.

For construction work in progress the Uniform System of Accounts for water, sewer, gas, and electric utilities published by NARUC contains a section on Utility Plant Instructions that, among other items, specifies the components of construction cost. Generally, the components are in agreement with those listed in any intermediate accounting text. One item long recognized in utility accounting and accepted by the FASB in *ASC* 980-835-25-1 is the **Allowance for Funds Used during Construction** (AFUDC).

AFUDC includes the net cost for the period of construction of borrowed funds used for construction purposes *and a reasonable rate on other funds so used*. Thus, interest paid, accrued, or imputed during the period of construction of a utility plant asset is included as a cost of the asset. Interest paid or accrued, known as the *debt component* of AFUDC, is deducted from Interest on Long-term Debt in the Other Income and Deductions section of the utility's operating statement. This practice accomplishes two things: (1) It discloses to financial statement readers the amount of interest that was capitalized during the year and (2) it reduces the reported interest expense, thus increasing reported net income for the period (presumably slowing down utilities' requests for rate increases). If construction is financed, in part, by use of resources generated by operations of the utility, regulatory authorities allow interest to be imputed on these "equity" funds and capitalized. Because imputed interest is not viewed by accountants as an expense, it is offset by reporting the *equity component* of AFUDC as nonoperating income.

Other asset sections of balance sheets prepared in the regulatory format are Other Property and Investments and Deferred Debits. One item usually reported in the former section is Special Funds, which is similar to the Restricted Assets section of the GAAP–format statement of net position shown in Illustrations 7–5 and 7–6. Thus, Other Property and Investments is broader in scope than Restricted Assets and may contain items other than restricted assets. One item typically reported under the Deferred Debits caption is Unamortized Debt Discount and Expense, which under GAAP is reported as an offset to the related long-term debt.

ACCOUNTING FOR NONUTILITY ENTERPRISES

Early in this chapter it was stressed that each governmentally owned enterprise should follow the accounting and financial reporting standards developed for investor-owned enterprises in the same industry. Generally, the standards developed by the Financial Accounting Standards Board and its predecessors have been accepted by the GASB as applying to internal service funds and enterprise funds.[15] Consequently, sections earlier in this chapter that discuss generally accepted accounting principles applicable to internal service funds apply equally to enterprise funds accounting for activities other than utilities.

ACCOUNTING FOR MUNICIPAL SOLID WASTE LANDFILLS

According to Environmental Protection Agency (EPA) estimates, there are approximately 1,908 municipal solid waste landfills (MSWLFs) in the United States.[16] An EPA Rule, "Solid Waste Disposal Facility Criteria" (40 *Code of Federal Regulations*, parts 257 and 258), establishes certain closure requirements for MSWLFs and imposes stringent criteria for location, design, and operation of landfills, groundwater monitoring and corrective action, postclosure care, and financial assurance. State governments are assigned primary responsibility for implementing and enforcing the EPA rule and may increase or reduce its provisions based on site conditions existing within their states.

MSWLF owners and operators may incur a variety of costs both during the period of operation and after closure. These costs include the equipment and facilities (including final covering of the MSWLF upon closure) and services for such items as

[15] See footnote 9.

[16] U.S. Environmental Protection Agency, "Municipal Solid Waste Generation, Recycling, and Disposal in the United States: Tables and Figures for 2012," (Washington, DC, 2014), Table 28.

postclosure maintenance and monitoring for a period of 30 years after closure. The EPA requires owners and operators to estimate in detail the current dollar cost of hiring a third party to close the largest area of an MSWLF expected to require a final cover and to care for the MSWLF over the 30-year postclosure period. Each year the closure and postclosure cost estimates must be adjusted for inflation and revised as necessary to reflect changes in plans or conditions. Owners and operators of MSWLFs must provide assurances that adequate financial resources will be available to cover the estimated costs of closure, postclosure care, and remediation or containment of environmental hazards when the landfill has been filled to capacity. Several forms of financial assurance are acceptable, including third-party trusts, surety bonds, letters of credit, insurance, or state-sponsored plans.

The GASB standards provide guidance both for measuring and reporting estimated total closure and postclosure costs. Reporting requirements for MSWLFs that use proprietary fund accounting are described briefly; more detail is provided in the GASB *Codification,* Section L10. An expense and a liability should be recognized each period for a portion of the estimated total current cost of MSWLF closure and postclosure care. The portion of total cost to be recognized is based on the units-of-production method, so that estimated total current cost is assigned to periods on the basis of landfill usage rather than the passage of time. Recognition begins in the period in which the MSWLF first accepts solid waste and continues each period until closure. For example, a town opens a landfill and estimates that the capacity of the landfill is 4,000,000 cubic yards. Once capacity is reached, the town currently estimates that it will cost $9,500,000 to close and care for the landfill after closure. Based on the GASB guidance, the estimated closure and postclosure cost for the first year would be $190,000, if 80,000 cubic yards of capacity is used in the first year. The journal entry to record the estimated cost would be:

	Debits	Credits
Provision for Landfill Closure and Postclosure	190,000	
Accrued Landfill Closure and Postclosure Liability........................		190,000

In subsequent years the annual cost will be calculated by multiplying the cumulative proportionate landfill used by the estimated total closure costs and subtracting any accrued landfill closure and postclosure liability figure. Estimated total closure and postclosure costs should be reevaluated each year during operation of the landfill, and the cumulative effect of changes in the estimated costs, if any, should be reported in the period of the change. Costs of equipment, facilities, services, or final cover acquired during the period are reported as a reduction of the accrued liability, not as capital assets. Equipment and facilities installed prior to commencement of operation of the landfill should be fully depreciated by the closure date.

Assets held by third-party trustees or in surety standby trusts to meet financial assurance requirements should be reported as "amounts held by trustee" in the Restricted Assets section of the statement of net position and as net position restricted for closure and postclosure costs. Earnings on such investments should be reported as revenue.

The GASB standards also provide guidance for reporting of MSWLFs in governmental fund types or by other entities such as colleges and universities. Accounting for MSWLFs in the General Fund, for example, requires that an expenditure and a fund liability be reported for the current closure and postclosure costs to the extent that an accrued liability would be settled with available fund resources; any remaining liability would be reported in the Governmental Activities column at the government-wide level, as discussed in

Chapter 6. Regardless of the fund type or entity reporting the MSWLF activities, the GASB standards require the following note disclosures.[17]

1. The nature and source of landfill closure and postclosure care requirements (federal, state, or local laws or regulations).
2. The recognition of a liability for closure and postclosure care costs based on landfill capacity used to date.
3. The reported liability for closure and postclosure care at the balance sheet date (if not apparent from the financial statements) and the estimated total current cost of closure and postclosure care remaining to be recognized.
4. The percentage of landfill capacity used to date and approximate remaining landfill life in years.
5. How closure and postclosure care financial assurance requirements, if any, are being met. Also, any assets restricted for payment of closure and postclosure care costs (if not apparent from the financial statements).
6. The nature of the estimates and the potential for changes due to inflation or deflation, technology, or applicable laws or regulations.

The costs of improving landfills to meet increased EPA standards, providing financial assurance, and complying with accounting and reporting requirements can be significant for many governments.

REQUIRED SEGMENT INFORMATION

As with investor-owned enterprises, governments are required to disclose segment information related to certain enterprise funds.[18] The GASB defines a segment as an identifiable activity or group of activities within the enterprise fund. Within an enterprise fund, only those segments with one or more bonds or other debt instruments outstanding, and with a revenue stream pledged to support the debt, are subject to segment disclosure requirements. Additionally, segment disclosure is not required if the enterprise fund is both a segment (only one identifiable activity or group of activities) and is reported as a major fund.

In reporting segment information, emphasis is placed on identifiable streams of revenues pledged for the support of revenue bonds along with related expenses, gains, losses, assets, and liabilities of the same activity. Disclosure requirements for segments are met by presenting condensed financial information in the notes. The condensed statement of net position should provide information on total assets, total liabilities, and total net position (by net position type). As noted earlier in the chapter regarding the statement of net position, if applicable, deferred outflows of resources should be reported in a separate section following assets and deferred inflows of resources should be reported in a separate section following liabilities. The condensed statement of revenues, expenses, and changes in fund net position should identify major sources of operating revenues, operating expenses, operating net income, nonoperating revenues and expenses, along with any capital contributions, special or extraordinary items, and transfers. At the bottom of the condensed statement of revenues, expenses, and changes in fund net position, the change in net position should be shown, along with beginning and ending net position balances. The GASB's format for the statement of cash flows should be followed when presenting the required condensed statement of cash flows for the segment.

[17] GASB, *Codification,* Sec. L10.115.

[18] Segment reporting is also required for a stand-alone entity that has one or more bonds or other debt instruments outstanding, with a revenue stream pledged to support the debt. (GASB, *Codification*, Sec 2500.101.)

Key Terms

Allowance for Funds Used during Construction, *284*
Cash equivalents, *257*
General obligation bonds, *274*
Historical cost, *284*
Original cost, *284*
Regulatory accounting principles (RAP), *284*
Revenue bonds, *273*
Utility Plant Acquisition Adjustment, *284*

Selected References

Governmental Accounting Standards Board. *Codification of Governmental Accounting and Financial Reporting Standards, as of June 30, 2014.* Norwalk, CT, 2014.
Governmental Accounting Standards Board. *Comprehensive Implementation Guide as of June 30, 2014.* Norwalk, CT, 2014.

Questions

7–1. What are the characteristics of a proprietary fund? How do internal service funds and enterprise funds differ?

7–2. Explain the reporting requirements for internal service funds and enterprise funds. Internal service funds and enterprise funds are both proprietary funds, so why do their reporting requirements differ?

7–3. A member of the city commission insists that the city's internal service fund prepare and submit a budget for commission approval. The commissioner argues that it is only through the budget that the commissioners will be able to ensure control over the internal service fund. Do you agree or disagree with the commissioner's argument? Explain your answer.

7–4. Although proprietary funds are often compared to for-profit businesses, there are several differences between accounting for proprietary funds and accounting for a for-profit organization. Identify and discuss at least one difference for each of the fund financial statements.

7–5. What is the purpose of the Restricted Assets section of an enterprise fund statement of fund net position? Provide examples of items that might be reported in the Restricted Assets section.

7–6. What are the three components of net position provided by GASB? Describe how a government assigns amounts to the classifications.

7–7. What is the accounting treatment if an internal service fund recovers more or less than the costs incurred by the fund?

7–8. When do GASB standards require interfund receivables and payables to be reported as *Internal Balances*?

7–9. What are regulatory accounting principles and how do they relate to enterprise fund accounting?

7–10. What is meant by "segment information for enterprise funds"? When is the disclosure of segment information required?

Cases

7–11 Internal Service Fund Reporting. Financial statements for the Building Maintenance Fund, an internal service fund of Coastal City, are reproduced here. No further information about the nature or purposes of this fund is given in the annual report.

COASTAL CITY BUILDING MAINTENANCE FUND
Balance Sheet
As of December 31, 2017

Assets	
Assets:	
Cash and investments	$452,879
Accounts receivable	2,116
Inventory	479,000
Prepaid expenditures	19,854
Total assets	$953,849
Liabilities and Fund Equity	
Liabilities:	
Accounts payable	$ 35,675
Other accrued liabilities	109,099
Accrued annual leave	227,369
Total liabilities	372,143
Fund equity:	
Fund balance—unspendable	479,000
Fund balance—unrestricted	102,706
Total liabilities and fund equity	$953,849

COASTAL CITY BUILDING MAINTENANCE FUND
Statement of Revenues, Expenditures, and Changes in Fund Balance
Year Ended December 31, 2017

Revenues:	
Billings to departments	$10,649,781
Miscellaneous	161,396
Other financing sources—Interfund Transfers In	125,000
Total revenues	10,936,177
Expenditures:	
Salaries and employee benefits	3,353,413
Supplies	3,409,096
Capital leases	59,302
Operating services and charges	495,143
Maintenance and repairs	3,536,443
Bad debts	1,750
Total expenditures	10,855,147
Excess of revenues over expenditures	81,030
Fund balance—January 1, 2017	500,676
Fund balance—December 31, 2017	$ 581,706

Required

a. Assuming that the Building Maintenance Fund is an internal service fund, discuss whether the financial information is presented in accordance with GASB standards.

b. If you were the manager of a city department that uses the services of the Building Maintenance Fund, what would you want to know in addition to the information disclosed in the financial statements?

7–12 Proprietary Fund Operating Statement. Casper County has prepared the following operating statement for its proprietary funds. The county has three enterprise funds and two internal service funds.

CASPER COUNTY
Income Statement
Proprietary Funds
For the Year Ended December 31, 2017
(amounts expressed in thousands)

	Total Enterprise Funds	Total Internal Service Funds	Total
Revenues			
Charges for services	$ 61,309	$10,621	$ 71,930
Investment income	1,086	59	1,145
Total Revenues	62,395	10,680	73,075
Expenses			
Personnel services	24,196	5,681	29,877
Supplies and materials	11,540	3,293	14,833
Interest expense	6,904	172	7,076
Depreciation	11,213	2,076	13,289
Loss on disposal of capital assets	200		200
Total Expenses	54,053	11,222	65,275
Net income (loss)	8,342	(542)	7,800
Special item—Loss on Sale	(3,794)		(3,794)
Net assets—January 1, 2017	288,611	3,337	291,948
Net assets—December 31, 2017	$293,159	$ 2,795	$295,954

Required

The statement as presented is not in accordance with GASB standards. Identify the errors and explain how the errors should be corrected in order to conform with GASB standards. Along with the information in Chapter 7, Illustration A2–8 will be helpful in identifying and correcting the errors.

7–13 Research Case: City and County of Denver Proprietary Funds. Use the 2012 CAFR for the City and County of Denver to respond to the following questions.

Required

a. Does the City and County of Denver report any internal service funds? If so, identify the internal service funds found in its financial statements and the primary purpose of each one.

b. Does the City and County of Denver use any enterprise funds? If so, identify the major funds found in its financial statements and the primary purpose of each one. If there are any nonmajor funds that are named, identify them.

c. The statement of net position for the Denver Airport System shows a negative net investment in capital assets. How is this possible and what are the implications? Does the net investment in capital assets figure change significantly in the 2013 CAFR?

d. The Denver Airport System has both restricted assets and liabilities payable from restricted assets. Are the restricted assets sufficient to pay the liabilities?

e. What is the largest expense (operating or nonoperating) for the Denver Airport System? Is there a connection between this item and your answer to part *c*? If so, explain.

f. For both the Wastewater and Denver Airport System, operating income was significantly lower than cash flows from operations. What is the largest adjustment in the reconciliation of operating income to operating cash flows for each fund?

g. Do any of the enterprise or internal service funds use capital or operating leases? How do you know?

h. Was the Central Services internal service fund created or disposed of during the fiscal year? Explain.

i. What type of fund is the Workers' Compensation fund? What is the most significant reconciling item between operating income and cash flows from operations? Does it appear that the fund's charges are appropriate compared to the expenses?

7–14 Enterprise Fund Golf Course Management.* Kaui County has operated a popular oceanside municipal golf course for more than 30 years. Local patrons as well as tourists enjoy reasonable rates in a picturesque setting. Ten years ago, the course was quite profitable, so the county created an enterprise fund and moved accounting for the golf operations from the General Fund to the new enterprise fund. Over the years, however, course usage has declined and costs have increased. During the current year the course suffered a $650,798 shortfall that had to be covered by the county's General Fund. In the upcoming fiscal year, the county projects the shortfall to be more than $1 million. Many have criticized the county for injecting money into a business that should be primarily funded through user charges. Supporters of the golf course note that the municipal course is part of the county's Parks and Recreation department, which benefits the entire community, hence county support of the course is warranted.

Required

a. Is the Kaui County golf course required to be accounted for as an enterprise fund? What are the accounting implications of operating the golf course as part of a General Fund department rather than an enterprise fund activity?

b. Assume you are a member of a task force that the county has appointed to address the current golf course situation. Consider each of the following options and draft a list of questions that come to mind as you evaluate the potential for each option.

(1) **Status Quo.** The county could continue to operate its golf course with all revenues, expenses, and employees belonging to the municipality.

(2) **Concession Agreements or Management Contracts.** The county could hire a management company to operate all aspects of the golf

*Portions of this problem were adapted from "The Dreaded 'P' Word—Outsource Options for Municipal Golf Courses," June 5, 2009, by Richard Singer, available at http://golfoperationsguru.wordpress.com/.

facility, or grant a license to an outside vendor to operate a portion of the facility. This option offers several combinations, whereby the county maintains control of the golf operations but outsources the golf pro shop, food and beverage operations, and course maintenance to one or more concessionaires.

(3) **Operating Lease.** The county could lease the golf facility to a private operator in exchange for an annual (or monthly/quarterly) lease payment to the municipality. The lease could be established to include certain lessee requirements, including capital investment in facility improvements, minimum standards of maintenance, and greens fee restrictions.

(4) **Selling the Golf Course.** The county could place the golf course up for sale. This removes the facility from the books of the municipality.

Exercises and Problems

7–15 Examine the CAFR. Utilizing the comprehensive annual financial report (CAFR) obtained for Exercise 1–16, follow these instructions:

a. **Internal Service Funds.**

(1) *Use of Funds.* What activities of the government are reported as being administered by internal service funds? (*Note:* Working capital funds, revolving funds, industrial funds, and intragovernmental service funds are other names used for funds of the type discussed in Chapter 7.) If internal service funds are not used by the reporting entity, does the report disclose how financing and accounting for activities such as purchasing, motor pools, printing, data processing, and other activities commonly used by more than one fund are handled? Does the report state the basis of accounting used for the internal service funds?

(2) *Fund Disclosure.* In the balance sheet(s) or statement(s) of net position displaying information for the internal service fund(s), are assets classified in accord with practices of profit-seeking businesses, or are current, capital, and other assets not separately displayed? If there are receivables other than from other funds or other governments, are allowances for estimated uncollectibles provided? Are allowances for depreciation deducted from related capital asset accounts?

Are current liabilities and long-term debt properly distinguished in the balance sheet? Are long-term loans from other funds properly distinguished from capital contributions received from other funds?

Are budgetary accounts (Estimated Revenues, Appropriations, Encumbrances) used by the internal service funds? From what sources were revenues actually obtained by each internal service fund? How are costs and expenses of each fund classified? Are noncash expenses, such as depreciation, separately disclosed? Do the revenues of each fund exceed the costs and expenses of the period? Compute the net income (or net loss) of each fund in this category as a percentage of its operating revenue for the period. Does the net income (or net loss) for any fund exceed 5 percent of operating revenues? If so, do the statements or the accompanying notes explain how the excess is being used or how the deficiency is being financed?

(3) *Statement of Cash Flows.* Is a statement of cash flows presented for internal service funds? If so, how does the cash provided by operations

shown in this statement relate to the revenues and expenses shown in the statement of revenues, expenses, and changes in net position, or other similarly titled operating statement? Are cash flows from financing activities presented separately for noncapital- and capital-related activities? Is there a section for cash flows from investing activities?

(4) *Government-wide Financial Statements.* Is there a column for business-type activities on the statement of net position and statement of activities? Is there any evidence that the internal service fund account balances were collapsed into the Governmental Activities column? If enterprise funds are the predominant participants in the internal service fund, do you see evidence that the internal service fund balances are reported in the Business-type Activities column of the government-wide statements?

b. **Enterprise Funds.**

(1) *Use of Funds.* What activities of the government are reported as being administered by enterprise funds? Does the government own and operate its water utility? Electric utility? Gas utility? Transportation system? Are combining statements presented in the financial section of the CAFR for all enterprise funds, or are separate statements presented for each enterprise fund? Do all enterprise funds use accrual accounting? Are all funds in this category earning revenues at least equal to costs and expenses? If not, how is the operating deficit being financed? Do the notes include segment information on individual enterprise funds where applicable (see "Required Segment Information" section of this chapter)?

Are sales to other funds or other governments separately disclosed? Are there receivables from other funds or other governments? How are receivables from component units, if any, disclosed? Is there any evidence that enterprise funds contribute amounts to the General Fund in lieu of taxes to help support services received by the enterprise? Is there any evidence that enterprise funds make excessively large contributions to the General Fund or any other funds?

(2) *Utility Funds.* Is it possible to tell from the report whether utilities of this government are subject to the same regulations as investor-owned utilities in the same state? (If the utility statements use account titles prescribed by the NARUC and the FERC, as described in this chapter, there is a good chance that the governmentally owned utilities are subject to at least some supervision by a state regulatory agency.) What rate of return on sales (or operating revenues) is being earned by each utility fund? What rate of return on total assets is being earned by each utility fund?

Is depreciation taken on the utility plant? Are accounting policies and accounting changes properly disclosed? If so, what method of depreciation is being used? Does each utility account for its own debt service and construction activities in the manner described in this chapter? What special funds or restricted assets are utilized by each utility?

(3) *Government-wide Financial Statements.* What proportion of the net position of the business-type activities are reported as net investment in capital assets, restricted, and unrestricted? Were the business-type activities profitable; that is, did revenues exceed expenses?

7–16 Multiple Choice. Choose the best answer.

1. Within the government-wide financial statements, the column for Business-type Activities will generally include:
   a. Internal service funds only.
   b. Enterprise funds only.
   c. All internal service fund and enterprise fund transactions added together and accounted for on the accrual basis of accounting.
   d. All enterprise fund transactions and only the internal service fund transactions undertaken with governmental funds on the accrual basis of accounting.
2. Which of the following would most likely be accounted for in an internal service fund?
   a. The city pool.
   b. The city's investments, which are pooled with the county's and the school district's investments.
   c. An asphalt plant used to supply the asphalt needed to resurface the city's streets.
   d. Proceeds from an endowment that are used to maintain the city's library.
3. Under GASB standards, the City of Parkview is required to use an enterprise fund to account for its nature center if:
   a. It charges fees to assist in paying for the maintenance of the nature center.
   b. The Nature Center was originally financed through the issuance of general obligation bonds.
   c. The ordinance that was passed to establish the nature center requires that all costs of the Nature Center be paid for by user fees.
   d. All of the above are true.
4. During 2017, the Gateway City government recorded a $15,000 transfer from the General Fund to an internal service fund; a $25,000 transfer from the General Fund to an enterprise fund; a $10,000 transfer from an enterprise fund to an internal service fund, and a $5,000 transfer from an enterprise fund to the General Fund. In the Business-type Activities column of the government-wide financial statements, Gateway City should report:
   a. Net transfers out of $5,000.
   b. Net transfers in of $10,000.
   c. Net Transfers in of $25,000.
   d. Net Transfers in of $35,000.
5. Which of the following events would generally be classified as nonoperating on an enterprise fund's statement of revenues, expenses, and changes in net position?
   a. Billing other funds of the same government for services.
   b. Loss on the sale of a piece of equipment.
   c. Depreciation expense.
   d. Administrative expense.
6. In reviewing the accounting records of the Transportation Services Fund, an internal service fund of Douglas City, you notice that the fund uses budgetary accounts. This is most likely because
   a. The administrators of the fund prefer to prepare a budget to use in managing the fund.
   b. GASB requires the use of budgetary accounts in internal service funds.

c. The city council must legally approve the fund's budget.
d. The accountants for the fund are unfamiliar with proper accounting procedures for a proprietary fund.

7. Under GASB standards, which of the following events would be classified as an investing activity on a proprietary fund's statement of cash flows?
a. Interest earned on certificates of deposit held by the proprietary fund.
b. Purchase of equipment for use by the proprietary fund.
c. Grant received to construct a building that will be used by the proprietary fund.
d. All of the above would be considered investing activities for reporting purposes.

8. An internal service fund used for insurance activities should recognize an expense and a liability when:
a. A claim has been made, it is reasonably possible that a liability has been incurred, and the amount will be reasonably estimable at some time in the near future.
b. A claim has not been made, but it is reasonably possible that a liability has been incurred or an asset has been impaired, and an amount can be reasonably estimated.
c. A claim has been made, it is probable that an asset has been impaired, and the amount will be reasonably estimable at some time in the near future.
d. A claim has been made, it is probable that a liability has been incurred, and the amount can be reasonably estimated.

9. During the year an enterprise fund purchased $230,000 worth of equipment. The equipment was acquired with a cash down payment of $30,000 and a $200,000 loan. A partial year of depreciation on the equipment was taken in the amount of $23,000. What is the net effect of this transaction on the net position accounts of the enterprise fund?
a. Net investment in capital assets is increased by $7,000.
b. Net investment in capital assets is increased by $30,000.
c. Net investment in capital assets is increased by $207,000.
d. Net investment in capital assets is increased by $230,000.

10. Tinsel Town had the following long-term liabilities at year end:

Revenue bonds to be repaid from tolls collected by the superhighway enterprise fund	$250,000
General obligation bonds issued for the Tinsel Town water utility, which will service the debt	200,000

What amount should be recorded as long-term liabilities in the proprietary fund financial statements?
a. $0.
b. $200,000.
c. $250,000.
d. $450,000.

7–17 Information Technology Internal Service Fund. Washington City created an Information Technology department in 2013 to centralize information technology (IT) functions for the city. The goal of the department was to reduce costs, avoid duplication of efforts, and provide up-to-date technology to all of the city's operations. The fund was designed to be self-supporting; that is, all costs are to be recovered through user fees, but any excess of fees over expenses should be less than 5 percent. The preclosing trial balance for the IT department as of December 31, 2016, is shown below.

	Debits	Credits
	(in thousands)	
Cash	$14,500	
Due from Other Funds	4,250	
Materials and Supplies Inventory	350	
Machinery and Equipment	53,600	
Accumulated Depreciation		$30,100
Accounts Payable		2,550
Payroll Taxes Payable		2,650
Due to Other Funds		1,200
Net Position—Net Investment in Capital Assets		23,500
Net Position—Unrestricted		12,700
	$72,700	$72,700

During the fiscal year ended December 31, 2017, the following transactions (summarized) occurred:

1. Gross employee wages were $57,600, including the employer's share of Social Security taxes amounting to $4,100. Federal income and Social Security taxes withheld from that amount totaled $18,725.
2. Office expenses in the amount of $3,700 were paid in cash.
3. Materials and supplies purchased on account during the year were $8,400.
4. Received a bill totaling $14,525 for utilities provided by Washington City's utility fund.
5. Cash paid to the federal government for payroll taxes was $23,000.
6. Cash paid to the Utility Fund was $14,500.
7. Accounts payable at year-end totaled $2,950.
8. Materials and supplies used during the year were $8,250.
9. Charges to departments during the fiscal year were as follows:

General Fund	$57,500
Special Revenue Fund	20,600

10. Unpaid balances at year-end were:

General Fund	$3,500
Special Revenue Fund	1,800

11. The depreciation for the year was $6,100.
12. Revenue and expense accounts for the year were closed.

Required

a. Prepare a statement of revenues, expenses, and changes in net position for the Information Technology Fund for 2017.

b. Prepare a statement of net position for the Information Technology Fund as of December 31, 2017.

c. Prepare a statement of cash flows for the Information Technology Fund as of December 31, 2017.

d. Given the goals of the fund as described above, evaluate the manager of the IT department.

7–18 Central Garage Internal Service Fund. The City of Ashville operates an internal service fund to provide garage space and repairs for all city-owned-and-operated vehicles. The Central Garage Fund was established by a contribution of $300,000 from the General Fund on July 1, 2017, at which time the land and building were acquired. The pre-closing trial balance at June 30, 2017, was as follows:

	Debits	Credits
Cash	$110,000	
Due from Other Funds	9,000	
Inventory of Supplies	90,000	
Land	50,000	
Building	250,000	
Allowance for Depreciation—Building		$ 20,000
Machinery and Equipment	65,000	
Allowance for Depreciation—Machinery and Equipment		12,000
Vouchers Payable		31,000
Net Position—Net Investment in Capital Assets		333,000
Net Position—Unrestricted		178,000
	$574,000	$574,000

The following information applies to the fiscal year ended June 30, 2017:

1. Supplies were purchased on account for $92,000; the perpetual inventory method is used.
2. The cost of supplies used during the year ended June 30, 2017, was $110,000. A physical count taken as of that date showed materials and supplies on hand totaled $72,000 at cost.
3. Salaries and wages paid to employees totaled $235,000, including related costs.
4. Billings totaling $30,000 were received from the enterprise fund for utility charges. The Central Garage Fund paid $27,000 of the amount owed. (At the government-wide level, record the payable amount as Internal Balances.)
5. Depreciation of the building was recorded in the amount of $10,000; depreciation of the machinery and equipment amounted to $9,000.
6. Billings to other departments for services provided to them were as follows:

General Fund	$270,000
Special Revenue Fund	127,000

7. Unpaid interfund receivable balances were as follows:

	6/30/16	6/30/17
General Fund	$2,500	$3,000
Special Revenue Fund	6,500	9,000

8. Vouchers payable at June 30, 2017, were $16,000.
9. For June 30, 2017, closing entries were prepared for the Central Garage Fund (ignore government-wide closing entry).

Required

a. Assume all expenses at the government-wide level are charged to the General Government function. Prepare journal entries to record all of the transactions for this period in the Central Garage Fund accounts and in the governmental activities accounts.

b. Prepare a statement of revenues, expenses, and changes in net position for the Central Garage Fund for the period ended June 30, 2017.

c. Prepare a statement of net position for the Central Garage Fund as of June 30, 2017.

d. Explain what the Central Garage Fund would need to report at the governmental activities level, and where the information would be reported.

7–19 Tribute Aquatic Center Enterprise Fund. The City of Saltwater Beach established an enterprise fund in 2015 to construct and operate Tribute Aquatic Center, a public swimming pool. The pool was completed and began operations in 2016. All costs, including repayment of debt, are to be paid by user fees. The fund's preclosing trial balance as of December 31, 2017, is shown below.

	Debits	**Credits**
Cash and Cash Equivalents	$ 182,240	
Accounts Receivable	5,225	
Supplies	8,225	
Restricted Cash and Cash Equivalents	942,000	
Land	1,400,000	
Buildings and Equipment	925,000	
Accumulated Depreciation—Buildings and Equipment		$ 41,625
Improvements Other Than Buildings	4,715,000	
Accumulated Depreciation—Improvements Other Than Buildings		212,175
Accounts and Accrued Payables		22,150
Current Portion of Long-Term Debt—Bonds		281,600
Bonds Payable		6,195,200
Net Position—Net Investment in Capital Assets		174,010
Net Position—Restricted		867,000
Net Position—Unrestricted		84,030
Charges for Services		2,040,000
Interest and Dividend Income		92,500
Personnel Expenses	1,034,000	
Utilities Expense	188,500	
Repairs and Maintenance	82,100	
Supplies Expense	67,200	
Depreciation Expense	136,960	
Interest Expense	323,840	
	$10,010,290	$10,010,290

Additional information concerning the Tribute Aquatic Center Fund follows.

1. All bonds payable were used to acquire property, plant, and equipment.
2. Each year a payment is required on January 1 to retire an equal portion of the bonds payable. The payment for the current year was paid on January 1, 2017.
3. Equipment was sold for cash at its carrying value of $9,250.
4. Total cash received from customers was $2,038,355 and cash received for interest and dividends was $92,500; of this amount $75,000 was restricted cash. There were no other changes to restricted cash during the year.

5. Cash payments included $1,038,800 for personnel expenses, $185,800 for utilities, $86,225 for repairs and maintenance, $323,840 for interest on bonds, and $65,900 for supplies.
6. The beginning balance in Cash was $99,300, Accounts Receivable was $3,580, Supplies was $9,525, and Accounts and Accrued Payables was $28,375. Accrued Payables include personnel expenses, utilities, and repairs and maintenance.
7. The net position categories shown on the preclosing trial balance have not been updated to reflect correct balances as of the December 31, 2017, year-end.

Required

a. Prepare the statement of revenues, expenses, and changes in fund net position for the Tribute Aquatic Center as of December 31, 2017.
b. Prepare the statement of net position for the Tribute Aquatic Center as of December 31, 2017.
c. Prepare the statement of cash flows for the Tribute Aquatic Center as of December 31, 2017.

7–20 Net Position Classifications. During 2017, the Town of Falmouth had a number of transactions that affected net position of its town skating rink, which is operated as an enterprise fund. You are provided with the following information for 2017:

1. The beginning net position balances are: net investment in capital assets, $679,800; restricted, $0; and unrestricted, $1,354,692.
2. Net income for the year was $162,759.
3. Depreciation expense totaled $54,000.
4. A piece of equipment with a carrying value of $26,100 was sold for $25,000.
5. Bonds for $500,000 were issued to construct a concession stand at the rink. At the end of the year, the concession stand was 50 percent complete, and construction work in progress totaled $248,000.
6. A $15,000 principal payment was made on a capital lease.
7. A new Zamboni ice resurfacing machine was purchased for $250,000. At the end of the year, a $30,000 note associated with the machine remains outstanding.

Required

Prepare the net position section of Falmouth's 2017 statement of net position.

7–21 Central Station Enterprise Fund. The Town of Elizabeth operates the old train station as an enterprise fund. The train station is on the national register of historic buildings. Since the town has held the building for such a long time, the Central Station Fund has no long-term debt. The only capital assets recorded by the Central Station Fund are machinery and equipment. Businesses rent space in the building and the town provides all services related to the operation and maintenance of the building. Following is information related to the fund's 2017 operating activities.

1. Rental income of $94,444 was accrued. Subsequently, cash in the amount of $90,210 was received on accounts.
2. Cash expenses for the period included: administrative services, $25,205; maintenance and repairs, $72,882; supplies and materials, $7,792; and utilities, $30,124.
3. The Central Station Fund received a $60,000 transfer of funds from the General Fund.

4. Adjustments were made for depreciation ($3,519) and for uncollectible accounts ($667).
5. At the end of the period, nominal accounts were closed.

Required

a. Prepare general journal entries to record the Central Station Fund's operating activities for the year.
b. Prepare a statement of revenues, expenses, and changes in fund net position. The net position balance at the beginning of the period was $60,129.
c. Based on the information provided, does it appear that the Central Station Fund is required to be recognized as an enterprise fund under GASB standards? Explain your answer.
d. Assuming you are the town's manager, discuss your concerns about the Central Station Fund.

7–22 Enterprise Fund Journal Entries and Financial Statements. Following is the June 30, 2017, statement of net position for the City of Bay Lake Water Utility Fund.

CITY OF BAY LAKE
Water Utility Fund
Statement of Fund Net Position
June 30, 2017

Assets		
Current assets:		
Cash and investments		$ 1,775,019
Accounts receivable (net of $13,367 provision for uncollectible accounts)		306,869
Accrued utility revenue		500,000
Due from General Fund		29,311
Interest receivable		82,000
Total current assets		2,693,199
Restricted assets:		
Cash		9,193
Capital assets:		
Land	$1,780,945	
Buildings (net of $3,420,000 in accumulated depreciation)	5,214,407	
Machinery and equipment (net of $5,129,928 in accumulated depreciation)	8,488,395	
Total capital assets (net)		15,483,747
Total Assets		18,186,139
Liabilities		
Current liabilities:		
Accounts payable	532,047	
Interest payable	131,772	
Current portion of long-term debt	400,000	
Total current liabilities		1,063,819
Liabilities payable from restricted assets:		
Customer deposits		9,193
Long-term liabilities:		
Revenue bond payable		11,600,000
Total Liabilities		12,673,012
Net Position		
Net investment in capital assets		3,483,747
Unrestricted		2,029,380
		$ 5,513,127

Required

a. For fiscal year 2017, prepare general journal entries for the Water Utility Fund using the following information.

(1) The amount in the Accrued Utility Revenue account was reversed.

(2) Billings to customers for water usage during fiscal year 2017 totaled \$2,982,557; \$193,866 of the total was billed to the General Fund.

(3) Cash in the amount of \$260,000 was received. The cash was for interest earned on investments and \$82,000 in accrued interest.

(4) Expenses accrued for the period were: management and administration, \$360,408; maintenance and distribution, \$689,103; and treatment plant, \$695,237.

(5) Cash receipts for customer deposits totaled \$2,427.

(6) Cash collections on customer accounts totaled \$2,943,401, of which \$209,531 was from the General Fund.

(7) Cash payments for the period were as follows: Accounts Payable, \$1,462,596; interest (which includes the interest payable), \$395,917; bond principal, \$400,000; machinery and equipment, \$583,425; and return of customer deposits, \$912.

(8) A state grant amounting to \$475,000 was received to help pay for new water treatment equipment.

(9) Accounts written off as uncollectible totaled \$10,013.

(10) The utility fund transferred \$800,000 in excess operating income to the General Fund.

(11) Adjusting entries for the period were recorded as follows: depreciation on buildings was \$240,053 and on machinery and equipment was \$360,079; the allowance for uncollectible accounts was increased by \$14,913; an accrual for unbilled customer receivables was made for \$700,000; accrued interest income was \$15,849; and accrued interest expense was \$61,406.

(12) The Revenue Bond Payable account was adjusted by \$400,000 to record the current portion of the bond.

(13) Closing entries and necessary adjustments were made to the net position accounts.

b. Prepare a statement of revenues, expenses, and changes in fund net position for the Water Utility Fund for the year ended June 30, 2017.

c. Prepare a statement of net position for the Water Utility Fund as of June 30, 2017.

d. Prepare a statement of cash flows for the Water Utility Fund as of June 30, 2017.

7–23 Enterprise Fund Statement of Cash Flows. Inglis City had a beginning cash balance in its enterprise fund of \$895,635. During 2017, the following transactions occurred:

1. Interest received on investments totaled \$42,400.
2. The city acquired additional equity investments totaling \$75,000.
3. A grant was received from the state in the amount of \$50,000 for summer interns.
4. Receipts from sales of goods or services totaled \$2,915,500.
5. Payments for supplies were made in the amount of \$1,642,100.
6. Payments to employees for salaries amounted to \$479,300.

7. Equipment was sold for $57,500. It had a book value of $56,625.
8. $25,000 was transferred to the General Fund.
9. Other cash expenses for operations were $89,200.
10. Long-term debt payments totaled $525,000.

Required

Prepare a statement of cash flows for the Inglis City enterprise fund. (Ignore the reconciliation of operating income to net cash provided by operating activities since insufficient information is provided to complete the reconciliation.)

7–24 Appendix—Solid Waste Enterprise Fund. Brown County operates a solid waste landfill for the citizens of the county. The following events occurred during the county's fiscal year ended September 30, 2017.

1. The county paid interest costs of $6,869,000; of this amount, $214,000 was required to be capitalized to construction work in progress. Amortization of bond premiums was $167,000.
2. The county is self-insured through an internal service fund for workers' compensation, automotive and general liability insurance. The Solid Waste Enterprise Fund participates in the county run program, and the amount paid for the year was $1,069,000.
3. The county's recorded value of investments as of September 30, 2017, was $129,638,000. Fair market value was determined to be $133,590,000.
4. The fund bills franchise haulers, and at September 30, 2017, the balance in Accounts Receivable was $4,687,000. The Allowance for Uncollectible Accounts showed a balance of $134,000, but an aging of accounts determined that the balance should be $179,000.
5. The county's landfill has a total space of 54,000 cubic yards (cy). The county has projected that future closure and postclosure care costs will be $60,600,000. The county's estimate of cubic yards consumed as of September 30, 2017, is 13,500 cy. The balance in the liability account for closure and postclosure costs as of September 30, 2016, was $13,350,000. (Hint: The current liability account balance should be subtracted from the total proportion of landfill cubic yards used to arrive at the current year's expense.)

Required

a. Prepare general journal entries to record the Solid Waste Disposal Fund's activities shown above.

b. Based on the information provided above, does it appear that the fund managers are complying with GASB standards for recognition of closure and postclosure care costs? Explain.

c. The county has set aside funds to meet its financial obligations related to closure and postclosure care costs in the amount of $12,670,000. Where would these funds be reported? Regulations require that solid waste disposal funds have current resources available to satisfy at least 90 percent of the estimated current liability. Does it appear that the Solid Waste Disposal Fund has met this requirement? Why or why not?

Chapter Eight

Accounting for Fiduciary Activities—Agency and Trust Funds

Learning Objectives

After studying this chapter, you should be able to:

8-1 Explain how trust and agency funds are used to report on the fiduciary activities of a government.

8-2 Distinguish among agency funds and trust funds (private-purpose, investment, and pension).

8-3 Describe the uses for and characteristics of agency funds.

8-4 Explain the activities of and accounting and financial reporting for commonly used agency funds.

8-5 Explain the purpose, accounting, and financial reporting for a cash and investment pool (including an investment trust fund); a private-purpose trust fund; and a pension trust fund.

8-6 Describe accounting for other postemployment benefits plans.

Governments are often involved in fiduciary activities whereby they hold assets that benefit individuals, organizations, or governments other than the reporting government. Because the resources related to such activities are not owned by the reporting government and cannot be used to support its programs, Governmental Accounting Standards Board (GASB) standards exclude the reporting of fiduciary activities in the government-wide financial statements. However, fiduciary activities are reported in fiduciary fund financial statements, the focus of this chapter.

Four types of fiduciary funds are used to account for private-purpose activities in which a government holds assets as an agent or trustee—agency funds, investment trust funds, private-purpose trust funds, and pension and other employee benefit trust funds (hereafter shortened to pension trust funds or just pension funds). Resources that are held in trust for the benefit of the government's own programs or its citizenry should be accounted for using a governmental fund rather than a fiduciary fund. Such public-purpose trusts should be accounted for as special revenue funds (see Chapter 4) if the resources are expendable for the trust purpose or as permanent funds (see Chapter 4) if the trust principal is permanently restricted.

In law, there is a clear distinction between an agency relationship and a trust relationship. In accounting practice, the legalistic distinctions between trust funds and agency funds are not of major significance. The important and perhaps the sole consideration from an accounting standpoint is what can and what cannot be done with the fund's assets in accordance with laws and other pertinent regulations.

Trust funds differ from agency funds principally in degree: When compared to agency funds, trust funds often exist over a longer period of time, represent and develop vested interests of a beneficiary to a greater extent, and involve more complex administration and financial accounting and reporting. Agency funds are used only if a government holds resources in a purely custodial capacity for others. The specific transactions and accounting procedures undertaken by fiduciary funds depend on the enactment that brought about creation of a particular trust or agency fund, plus all other regulations under which it operates. Regulations include pertinent statutes, ordinances, wills, trust indentures, and other instruments of endowment, resolutions of the governing body, statements of purposes of the fund, kinds and amounts of assets held, and others.

AGENCY FUNDS

The GASB standards identify **agency funds** as fiduciary funds used to account for assets held by a government acting as an agent for one or more other governments, for individuals, or for private organizations. Assets that are held in an agency fund belong to the party or parties for which the government acts as agent. Therefore, *agency fund assets are offset by liabilities equal in amount; no fund net position exists.* GASB requires agency fund assets and liabilities to be recognized on the accrual basis. Revenues and expenses are not recognized in the accounts of agency funds, however.

Unless use of an agency fund is mandated by law, by GASB standards, or by decision of the governing board, an agency relationship may be accounted for within governmental and/or proprietary funds. For example, local governments act as agents of the federal and state governments in the collection and remittance of employees' withholding taxes, retirement contributions, and social security taxes. In the absence of contrary legal requirements or administrative decisions, it is perfectly acceptable to account for the withholdings, and the remittance to federal and state governments, within the funds that account for the gross pay of the employees, as is shown by the illustrative entries in Chapter 4. In general, if an agency relationship is incidental to the primary purposes for which a given fund exists, the relationship is ordinarily discharged on a current basis, and the amounts of assets held as agent are small in relation to fund assets, there is no need to create an agency fund unless required.

Agency Fund for Special Assessment Debt Service

Readers of Chapters 5 and 6 of this text should recall that GASB standards specify that a government that has *no* obligation to assume debt service on special assessment debt in the event of property owners' default but does perform the functions of billing property owners for the assessments, collecting installments of assessments and interest on the assessments, and *from the collections,* paying interest and principal on the special assessment debt, should account for those activities by use of an agency fund.

To illustrate *agency fund* accounting for special assessment debt service activities, assume the same information as used in Chapter 6 except that the government is not obligated in any manner for the special assessment debt. When the assessments in the amount of $480,000, payable in 10 equal installments, were levied on benefited property owners, the following journal entry was made in the agency fund. Note that no entries are made in the government-wide journal because fiduciary funds are not reported in the government-wide financial statements.

		Debits	Credits
1.	Assessments Receivable—Current	48,000	
	Assessments Receivable—Noncurrent	432,000	
	Due to Special Assessment Bondholders—Principal		480,000

All current assessments receivable were collected (see Entry 2) along with $24,000 of interest (5 percent on the previous unpaid receivable balance). As indicated in Chapter 6, any amounts not collected by the due date should be reclassified as Assessments Receivable—Delinquent.

2.	Cash	72,000	
	Assessments Receivable—Current		48,000
	Due to Special Assessment Bondholders—Interest		24,000

Special assessment bond principal in the amount of $48,000 and interest in the amount of $24,000 were paid during the current year.

3.	Due to Special Assessment Bondholders—Principal	48,000	
	Due to Special Assessment Bondholders—Interest	24,000	
	Cash		72,000

The second installment of assessments receivable was reclassified at year-end from the noncurrent category to the current category.

4.	Assessments Receivable—Current	48,000	
	Assessments Receivable—Noncurrent		48,000

This pattern of journal entries will be repeated during each of the remaining nine years until all special assessment bonds are retired.

Tax Agency Funds

An agency relationship that often results in the creation of an agency fund is the collection of taxes or other revenues by one government for several of the funds it operates and for other governments. State governments commonly collect sales taxes, gasoline taxes, and many other taxes that are apportioned to state agencies and to local governments within the state. At the local government level, it is common for an elected county official to serve as collector for all property taxes owed by persons or corporations owning property within the county. Taxes levied by all funds and governments within the county are certified to the county collector for collection. The county collector is required by law to make periodic distributions of tax collections for each year to each fund or government in the proportion that the levy for that fund or government bears to the total levy for the year.

Tax agency fund accounting would be quite simple if all taxes levied for a given year were collected in that year. It is almost always true, however, that collections during any year relate to taxes levied in several prior years as well as taxes levied for the current year, and sometimes include advance collections of taxes for the following year. In many jurisdictions, not only does the total tax rate vary from year to year but the proportion that the rate of each government (and each fund) bears to the total rate also varies from year to year. Additionally, interest and penalties on delinquent taxes must be collected at statutory rates or amounts at the time delinquent taxes are collected; interest and penalties collected must be distributed to participating funds and governments in the same manner that tax collections are distributed. The following sections relate to administration of a tax agency fund.

Illustration of Composition of Total Tax Rates

Assume that the county collector of Campbell County is responsible for collecting the taxes due in 2017 for the funds and governments located within the county. Ordinarily, the taxes levied for each fund and government within the county are shown in columnar form in a newspaper advertisement as legal notice to taxpayers. In order to keep the illustrations in this text legible and comprehensible, Illustration 8–1 shows two columns of a legal advertisement. Real property tax statements are prepared for each parcel of property located within the jurisdiction for which the tax agency fund is operated. Whether each statement discloses the amount of tax that will be distributed to all of the tax agency fund's participants that levy taxes on that parcel, or shows only the total tax payable to the county collector, the collector's office must be able to compute and appropriately distribute all taxes collected to the appropriate funds and governments.

For example, Illustration 8–1 shows that a parcel of property located in Washington Township outside the City of Washington would be taxed at the rate of $7.10 per $100 of assessed valuation; if the parcel were inside the city limits, however, the tax rate would be $10.06. Therefore, if a parcel of property located in Washington Township outside the city had an assessed valuation of $10,000, the total real property tax payable in 2017 would be $710, but a parcel with the same assessed valuation located within the city would be taxed at $1,006. The subtotals in each column represent the taxes levied for each tax agency fund participant, and the taxes levied for each government are broken down into the taxes levied for funds of that government. The relationship between direct and overlapping debt is discussed in Chapter 6. Note that Illustration 8–1 shows that a person or organization owning property within the City of Washington is required to pay 66 cents of the total rate for debt service (20 cents to Campbell County, 38 cents to the school district, and 8 cents to the City of Washington). Illustration 8–2 summarizes the composition of taxes levied on properties within and outside the City of Washington.

In those states in which taxes are levied on personal property, the funds and governments that levy the personal property taxes are generally assumed to be the ones that levy taxes on the residence of the owner unless there is convincing evidence that the legal location of the personal property is elsewhere. Inasmuch as the tax rate levied for

ILLUSTRATION 8–1

Composition of Taxes to Be Collected by County Collector of Campbell County for the County Funds and Other Taxing Authorities For the Year 2017

	Washington Township	City of Washington
Total state rate	$0.01	$ 0.01
County funds:		
General	1.08	1.08
Capital projects	0.09	0.09
Debt service	0.20	0.20
Welfare	0.11	0.11
Total county rate	1.48	1.48
Library Fund	0.25	0.25
Township funds:		
General	0.07	0.07
Fire protection	0.23	—
Total township rate	0.30	0.07
School funds:		
General	4.50	4.50
Capital projects	0.18	0.18
Debt service	0.38	0.38
Total school rate	5.06	5.06
City funds:		
General		2.53
Street		0.33
Pension		0.25
Debt service		0.08
Total city rate		3.19
Total tax rates per $100 assessed valuation	$7.10	$10.06

ILLUSTRATION 8–2

2017 Taxes Payable to Campbell County Collector for Parcel with Assessed Valuation of $10,000

	Parcel Located	
Amount Levied by	**Outside City**	**In City**
State	$ 1.00	$ 1.00
County	148.00	148.00
Library	25.00	25.00
Township	30.00	7.00
School	506.00	506.00
City	—	319.00
Total	$710.00	$1,006.00

each tax agency fund participant often varies from year to year, it is necessary that all tax collections be identified with the year for which the taxes were levied as well as with the particular parcels for which taxes were collected.

Operation of the collector's office often requires the use of substantial administrative resources. Accordingly, it is common for the collector to be authorized to withhold a certain percentage from the collections for each government, and to remit to the county General Fund (or other fund bearing the expenditures for operating the tax agency fund) the total amount withheld from the collections of other governments.

Accounting for Tax Agency Funds

Taxes levied each year should be recorded in the accounts of the appropriate funds of each government in the manner illustrated in preceding chapters. Although an allowance for estimated uncollectible current taxes would be established in each fund, the *gross* amount of the tax levy for all funds should be recorded in the Tax Agency Fund as a receivable. Note the receivable is designated as belonging to other funds and governments, and the receivable is offset in total by a liability. Assuming total real property taxes certified for collection during 2017 amounted to $9,468,000, the entry would be as follows:

		Debits	Credits
	Tax Agency Fund:		
1.	Taxes Receivable for Other Funds and Governments—Current..........	9,468,000	
	Due to Other Funds and Governments..		9,468,000

It would be necessary for the county collector to keep records of the total amount of 2017 taxes to be collected for each of the funds and governments in the Tax Agency Fund in order to distribute tax collections properly. Assume that the 2017 taxes were levied for the following governments (to reduce the detail in this example, a number of the governments are combined):

State	$ 10,000
Campbell County	1,480,000
Washington School District	5,060,000
City of Washington	2,552,000
Other governments (should be itemized)	366,000
	$9,468,000

If collections of 2017 taxes during a certain portion of the year amounted to $4,734,000, the Tax Agency Fund entry would be:

		Debits	Credits
	Tax Agency Fund:		
2.	Cash	4,734,000	
	Taxes Receivable for Other Funds and Governments—Current........		4,734,000

The tax collections in an actual case must be identified with the parcels of property against which the taxes were levied because the location of each parcel determines the funds and governments that should receive the tax collections. Assuming for the sake of simplicity that the collections for the period represent collections of 50 percent of the taxes levied against each parcel in Campbell County and that the County General Fund is given 1 percent of all collections for governments other than the county as reimbursement for the cost of operating the Tax Agency Fund, the distribution of the $4,734,000 collections would be:

	Taxes Collected (50% of Levy)	Collection Fee (Charged) Received	Cash to Be Distributed
State	$ 5,000	$ (50)	$ 4,950
Campbell County	740,000	39,940	779,940
Washington School District	2,530,000	(25,300)	2,504,700
City of Washington	1,276,000	(12,760)	1,263,240
Other governments (should be itemized)	183,000	(1,830)	181,170
	$4,734,000	$ -0-	$4,734,000

If cash is not distributed as soon as this computation is made, the entry by the Tax Agency Fund to record the liability would be:

		Debits	Credits
	Tax Agency Fund:		
3.	Due to Other Funds and Governments	4,734,000	
	Due to State		4,950
	Due to Campbell County		779,940
	Due to Washington School District		2,504,700
	Due to City of Washington		1,263,240
	Due to Other Governments		181,170

If, as is likely, collections during 2017 include collections of taxes that were levied for 2016, 2015, and preceding years, computations must be made to determine the appropriate distribution of collections for each tax year to each fund and government that levied taxes against the property for which collections have been received.

When cash is distributed by the Tax Agency Fund, the liability accounts shown in Entry 3 should be debited and Cash credited. If cash is advanced to one or more funds or governments prior to a regular periodic distribution, the debits to the liability accounts may precede the credits. By year-end, all advances should be settled, all distributions computed and recorded, and all cash distributed to the funds and governments for which the Tax Agency Fund is being operated. Therefore, if all those events have taken place, the year-end balance sheet for the Tax Agency Fund would consist of one asset, Taxes Receivable for Other Funds and Governments—Delinquent, and one liability, Due to Other Funds and Governments.

Entries Made by Funds and Governments Participating in Tax Agency Funds

Each fund or government that receives a distribution must record the appropriate portion of the amount received and the collection fee paid in each of the funds it maintains. The fee paid is recorded as an expenditure. For example, the computation for the entries to be made by the various funds of Washington School District would be (using the rates shown in Illustration 8–1) as follows:

	2017 Rate	Collections of 2017 Taxes	Collection Fee Paid	Cash Received
School Funds:				
General	$4.50	$2,250,000	$22,500	$2,227,500
Capital projects	0.18	90,000	900	89,100
Debt service	0.38	190,000	1,900	188,100
Total	$5.06	$2,530,000	$25,300	$2,504,700

From the computations it can be seen that the entry made in the Washington School District General Fund for the 2017 collections distributed should be:

	Debits	Credits
Washington School District General Fund:		
Cash	2,227,500	
Expenditures	22,500	
Taxes Receivable—Current		2,250,000

Similar entries would be made in the other two funds of the Washington School District and in all the funds of governments that paid a tax collection fee to the county General Fund. The computation by the county of taxes and fees collected for the General Fund are as follows.

	2017 Rate	Collections of 2017 Taxes	Collection Fee	Cash Received
County Funds:				
General	$1.08	$540,000	$39,940	$579,940
Capital Projects	0.09	45,000	-0-	45,000
Debt Service	0.20	100,000	-0-	100,000
Welfare	0.11	55,000	-0-	55,000
Total	$1.48	$740,000	$39,940	$779,940

The entry to be made in the General Fund of Campbell County for the 2017 collections distributed should be:

Campbell County General Fund:		
Cash	579,940	
Taxes Receivable—Current		540,000
Revenues		39,940

"Pass-through" Agency Funds

Grants, entitlements, or shared revenues from the federal or a state government often pass through one level of government (primary recipient) before distribution to a secondary recipient. Accounting for such "pass-through" grants depends on whether the primary recipient government is deemed to have *administrative involvement* or *direct financial involvement* in the grants. According to GASB standards:

> A recipient government has administrative involvement if, for example, it (a) monitors secondary recipients for compliance with program-specific requirements, (b) determines eligibility of secondary recipients or projects, even if using grantor-established criteria, or (c) has the ability to exercise discretion in how the funds are allocated. A recipient government has direct financial involvement if, for example, it finances some direct program costs because of a grantor-imposed matching requirement or is liable for disallowed costs.[1]

Most often, the criteria for administrative or direct financial involvement are met, in which case the primary recipient government must recognize a revenue for the receipt and an expenditure or expense for the transfer in a governmental fund, private-purpose trust fund, or proprietary fund. If, however, neither administrative nor financial involvement is deemed to exist, then a pass-through agency fund must be used and no revenue or expenditure/expense is recognized.

To illustrate accounting for a pass-through agency fund, assume that $5 million of federal financial assistance is received by a state government from the federal government, the full amount of which must be passed to local governments according to predetermined eligibility requirements and in amounts according to a predetermined formula. Since the state government is serving merely as a "cash conduit" in this case, the use of a pass-through agency fund is deemed appropriate. The entry to record receipt of the $5 million in the pass-through agency fund would be:

	Debits	Credits
Cash	5,000,000	
Due to Other Governments		5,000,000

Assuming that all monies were disbursed to the secondary recipients during the current fiscal year, the pass-through agency fund entry would be:

Due to Other Governments	5,000,000	
Cash		5,000,000

Accounting for the receipt of cash or other assets from a pass-through agency fund by the recipient should be in conformity with GASB standards discussed previously: Governmental funds are to recognize all grants as revenue when the grant proceeds are available for use for the purposes of the fund and eligibility requirements have been met. Recall from Chapter 4 that if cash is received before eligibility requirements are

[1] GASB *Codification of Governmental Accounting and Financial Reporting Standards, as of June 30, 2014,* (Norwalk, CT: GASB, 2014), Sec. N50.128.

met, the recipient records an asset and a liability; however, if cash is received in the period prior to intended use (that is, there is a time requirement), Deferred Inflow of Resources should be reported rather than a liability or a revenue. Amounts should be transferred from Deferred Inflow of Resources to Revenues as time requirements are met. Proprietary funds recognize as nonoperating revenues the proceeds of grants for operating purposes or grants that may be expended at the discretion of the recipient government; if the terms of the grant restrict the use of the proceeds to the acquisition or construction of capital assets, the proceeds must be recorded as capital contributions (see Chapter 7).

Financial Reporting of Agency Funds

As mentioned earlier in this chapter, fiduciary activities are reported only in the fiduciary fund financial statements; they have no effect on the governmental or business-type activities of the primary government reported in the government-wide financial statements. As shown in Illustration A2–10, agency fund financial information is reported in a separate column of the statement of fiduciary net position. Only those assets held for external parties are reported by agency funds in the statement of fiduciary net position. Agency funds are not included in the statement of changes in fiduciary net position (see Illustration A2–11) because they have no net position (assets equal liabilities) and therefore cannot have *changes* in net position. The GASB standards do not require disclosure of the assets and liabilities of individual agency funds, but a government may optionally include in its comprehensive annual financial report a combining statement of net position displaying the assets and liabilities of each agency fund in separate columns.

TRUST FUNDS

In addition to agency funds, the fiduciary fund classification includes three types of trust funds—investment trust funds, private-purpose trust funds, and pension trust funds.

Historically, trust funds have been created to account for assets received by the government in a trust agreement in which the assets are to be invested to produce income to be used for specified purposes (such as cultural or educational). The majority of such trusts benefit the government's own programs or its citizenry. As discussed and illustrated in Chapter 4, trusts that benefit the government's own programs or citizens at large are accounted for as either special revenue funds or *permanent funds*. The type of fund used depends on whether the principal of the gift can be spent for the specified purposes (i.e., a special revenue fund) or is permanently restricted for investment, with only the earnings therefrom available to spend for the specified purposes (i.e., a permanent fund). As discussed in Chapter 4, both special revenue funds and permanent funds are governmental fund types. The GASB standards indicate that fiduciary funds are used when trusts benefit others, such as individuals, organizations, or other governments. Examples of trust funds are shown in the following sections.

INVESTMENT POOLS

It is common for governments to possess both long- and short-term investments, as well as idle cash within their funds. Effective management of investments can be enhanced by placing the investments of the funds in a pool under the control of the treasurer or a professional investment manager, either within the treasurer's office or in a financial institution such as a bank or investment firm. For additional information on management of investments, see the appendix to this chapter.

If the investment pool is an *internal* investment pool (participating funds are all within the same government) an agency fund may be used to account for the investments in the pool. However, under GASB standards, each participating fund is required to report its proportionate share of pooled cash and investments as fund assets. The assets and liabilities of the agency fund are not reported in the government's external financial statements.[2] For internal management purposes, it may be useful for participating funds to use the account title *Equity in Pooled Cash and Investments,* the account title used in the illustrative journal entries shown later in this section.

If the investment pool has external participants (other governments or organizations outside the government administering the pool), an **external investment pool** is used. GASB standards require that an **investment trust fund** be used to account for the assets, liabilities, net position, and changes in net position corresponding to the equity of the *external* participants.[3] The accounting for investment trust funds uses an economic resources measurement focus and the accrual basis of accounting.

Typically, the administering government of an external investment pool also participates in the pool; however, its equity is considered *internal* and is not reported in the financial statements of the investment trust fund. Instead, the net position and changes in net position relating to the internal portion of the pool are presented in the financial statements of each participating fund and in the governmental activities and business-type activities of the sponsoring government's government-wide financial statements. Recall that the financial information for investment trust funds is reported only in the fiduciary fund financial statements (see Illustrations A2–10 and A2–11) and is not reported in the government-wide financial statements.

Accounting for an external investment pool is presented in the remainder of this section.

Creation of an Investment Pool

Earnings on pooled investments and changes in fair value of investments are allocated to the participants having an equity interest in the pool in proportion to their relative contributions to the pool. To ensure an equitable division of earnings and changes in fair value it is necessary to revalue fund assets whenever contributions to the pool or distributions from the pool occur. The revaluation involves adjusting to fair value all investments in the pool, as well as all investments being brought into the pool or removed from the pool.[4] Each fund of the sponsoring government and each external participant that contributes investments to the pool should debit Equity in Pooled Investments, or some similar account, for the fair value of the investments, credit the Investments account for the carrying value (cost or fair value at the time the investments were previously marked to fair value), and credit or debit Revenues—Change in Fair Value of Investments, depending on whether the current fair value is higher or lower than carrying value, respectively. Changes in the fair value of investments are recognized as a component of investment income in both the fund and government-wide operating statements.

[2] GASB, *Codification,* Sec. I50.113.

[3] Ibid., Sec. I50.117.

[4] GASB standards define *fair value* as the price that would be received to sell an asset in an orderly transaction between market participants at the measurement date. *GASB Concepts Statement 6*, par. 38.

Illustration of the Creation of an Investment Fund

On January 10, 2017, Drew County decided to create a new investment pool to be accounted for as an *investment trust fund.* Operating expenses of the pool, primarily for personnel time, office supplies, and postage, are considered nominal and will not be charged to the pool. The initial participants in the pool are the county's own debt service fund and two external participants, the Town of Calvin's Debt Service Fund and the Calvin Independent School District's Capital Projects Fund. The equity pertaining to the Drew County Debt Service Fund represents an *internal* investment pool, so its proportionate equity share of the investment pool's assets is reported in the debt service fund for financial reporting purposes, not as part of the investment trust fund net position. The proportionate share of assets allocated to *external* participants, however, is properly reported in the financial statements of the investment trust fund.

Illustration 8–3 shows the specific cash and investments that were transferred on January 10, 2017, to create the Drew County Investment Pool.

At the time the Drew County Investment Pool is created, journal entries are required in the accounts of the Drew County Debt Service Fund, the Town of Calvin Debt Service Fund, the Calvin Independent School District Capital Projects Fund, and the investment trust fund to record creation of the fund. The journal entries in the Drew County Debt Service Fund and Drew County Investment Pool (the investment trust fund) to create the investment pool are shown in Entries 1a and 1b. Entries in the funds of the external participants would be similar to those for the Drew County Debt Service Fund and therefore are omitted for the sake of brevity.

		Debits	Credits
	Drew County Debt Service Fund:		
1a.	Equity in Pooled Investments	14,850,000	
	Cash		1,000,000
	Investments—U.S. Agency Obligations		13,373,000
	Revenues—Change in Fair Value of Investments		52,000
	Revenues—Investment Earnings		425,000

ILLUSTRATION 8–3 Assets Transferred to Create Drew County Investment Pool

Assets Transferred	Fair Value at 12-31-16	Fair Value at 1-10-17	Change in Fair Value	Accrued Interest
Drew County Debt Service Fund:				
Cash	$ 1,000,000	$ 1,000,000	$ –0–	$ –0–
U.S. agency obligations	13,373,000	13,425,000	52,000	425,000
Town of Calvin Debt Service Fund:				
U.S. Treasury notes	9,568,000	9,545,000	(23,000)	192,000
U.S. agency obligations	158,700	160,000	1,300	3,000
Calvin Independent School District Capital Projects Fund:				
U.S. agency obligations	2,789,000	2,800,000	11,000	76,900
Repurchase agreements	2,060,000	2,060,000	–0–	13,100
Totals	$28,948,700	$28,990,000	$41,300	$710,000

		Debits	Credits
	Drew County Investment Pool:		
1b.	Cash	1,000,000	
	Investments—U.S. Treasury Notes	9,545,000	
	Investments—U.S. Agency Obligations	16,385,000	
	Investments—Repurchase Agreements	2,060,000	
	Interest Receivable	710,000	
	Due to Debt Service Fund		14,850,000
	Additions—Deposits in Pooled Investments—Town of Calvin		9,900,000
	Additions—Deposits in Pooled Investments—Calvin Independent School District		4,950,000

A trial balance, prepared for the Drew County Investment Pool immediately after Entry 1b has been posted to the pool's general ledger, is presented in Illustration 8–4.

On February 1, 2017, Drew County sold tax-supported bonds in the amount of $15,000,000 to finance the construction of roads and bridges. The proceeds of the bonds are added to the pool for investment until such time as they are needed for capital projects fund disbursements. As of February 1, 2017, the U.S. Treasury notes in the pool have a current fair value of $9,535,000 ($10,000 less than the carrying value reported in the trial balance shown in Illustration 8–4), and the U.S. agency obligations in the pool have a fair value of $16,695,000 ($310,000 more than the carrying value reported in the trial balance); the fair value of the repurchase agreement is the same as reported in the trial balance. The balance of the Cash account was still $1,000,000 as of February 1, 2017. Therefore, total assets of the pool, revalued to fair value as of February 1, 2017, amount to $30,000,000 (a net increase of $300,000 over the carrying values previously reported).

In the investment pool accounts, the $300,000 increase in carrying value of assets should be credited to a liability account for the share of the internal participant

ILLUSTRATION 8–4

DREW COUNTY
Investment Pool
Trial Balance
As of January 10, 2017

Account Title	Debits	Credits
Cash	$ 1,000,000	
Investments—U.S. Treasury Notes	9,545,000	
Investments—U.S. Agency Obligations	16,385,000	
Investments—Repurchase Agreements	2,060,000	
Interest Receivable	710,000	
Due to Debt Service Fund		$14,850,000
Additions—Deposits in Pooled Investments—Town of Calvin		9,900,000
Additions—Deposits in Pooled Investments—Calvin Independent School District		4,950,000
Totals	$29,700,000	$29,700,000

(Drew County's Debt Service Fund) and to "additions" accounts (addition to net assets, similar to revenue) for the shares of the external participants, based on their equitable proportions in the pool just prior to the asset revaluation. The liability to the debt service fund, therefore, is increased by $150,000 (300,000 × 14,850/29,700); Additions—Change in Fair Value of Investments—Town of Calvin is credited for $100,000 (300,000 × 9,900/29,700); and Additions—Change in Fair Value of Investments—Calvin Independent School District is credited for $50,000 (300,000 × 4,950/29,700). Note that the equity of each participant in the pool remains proportionately the same (i.e., the amount due to the Town of Calvin is $10,000,000 after revaluing the investments to current fair value; total liabilities and net position [if the Additions accounts were closed] of the pool are $30,000,000; 10,000/30,000 = 9,900/29,700, etc.). The journal entry in the investment pool summarizing the revaluation of investments and the capital projects entry into the investment pool is given as follows:

		Debits	Credits
	Drew County Investment Pool:		
2.	Cash	15,000,000	
	Investments—U.S. Agency Obligations	310,000	
	Investments—U.S. Treasury Notes		10,000
	Due to Debt Service Fund		150,000
	Due to Capital Projects Fund		15,000,000
	Additions—Change in Fair Value of Investments—Town of Calvin		100,000
	Additions—Change in Fair Value of Investments—Calvin Independent School District		50,000

After revaluation of investments in the pool and receipt of $15,000,000 cash from proceeds of bonds sold to finance road and bridge construction, the Drew County Trial Balance of the Investment Pool is as shown in Illustration 8–5.

Operation of a Cash and Investment Pool

Although the capital projects fund invested $15,000,000 cash, upon admission to the pool, that fund no longer has a specific claim on the cash of the pool; rather, it (and the other funds and governments that are members of the pool) has a proportionate interest in the total assets of the pool and will share in earnings, gains, and losses of the pool in that proportion. Ordinarily, it is inconvenient and unnecessary to make allocations to liability accounts and additions accounts each time dividends or interest are received and for each revaluation of the portfolio to fair value (some pools revalue to fair value daily). It is simpler to accumulate the earnings in the *Undistributed Earnings on Pooled Investments* account and the unrealized and realized gains and losses in the *Undistributed Change in Fair Value of Pooled Investments* account (both of these accounts are clearing accounts) and to make periodic distributions from these accounts to the specific liability and additions accounts for pool participants.

The frequency of distributions depends on whether all cash of all participants is pooled along with investments or whether each participant retains an operating cash account. In the former case, the pool would have frequent receipts attributable to collections of revenues and receivables of the participants and would have daily

ILLUSTRATION 8–5

DREW COUNTY
Investment Pool
Trial Balance
As of February 1, 2017

Account Title	Debits	Credits
Cash	$16,000,000	
Investments—U.S. Treasury Notes	9,535,000	
Investments—U.S. Agency Obligations	16,695,000	
Investments—Repurchase Agreements	2,060,000	
Interest Receivable	710,000	
Due to Debt Service Fund		$15,000,000
Due to Capital Projects Fund		15,000,000
Additions—Deposits in Pooled Investments—Town of Calvin		9,900,000
Additions—Deposits in Pooled Investments—Calvin Independent School District		4,950,000
Additions—Change in Fair Value of Investments—Town of Calvin		100,000
Additions—Change in Fair Value of Investments—Calvin Independent School District		50,000
Totals	$45,000,000	$45,000,000

disbursements on behalf of the participants; in this case, the interest of each participant in the pool would have to be recomputed each day. If, however, a working cash balance is retained by each participant, the receipts and disbursements of pool cash would be much less frequent, and the distribution of gains and losses and earnings, as well as the recomputation of the equity of each participant in the pool, would be correspondingly less frequent.

As an example of accounting for earnings on investments of a pool, assume the pool shown in Illustration 8–5 collects interest of $1,610,000, including the $710,000 interest receivable. An appropriate entry would be:

		Debits	Credits
	Drew County Investment Pool:		
3.	Cash	1,610,000	
	Interest Receivable		710,000
	Undistributed Earnings on Pooled Investments		900,000

By the time the earnings are to be distributed, the fair value of all investments may have changed. Even if this is true, the proportionate interest of each participant will not have changed because each participant continues to bear gains and losses in the same proportion until a participant changes all participants' proportionate interest in the pool by contributing additional assets to the pool or taking assets out of the pool. Therefore, in this example, when earnings are distributed, the shares apportioned to the participants are Drew County Debt Service Fund, 15/45 or 3/9; Drew County

Capital Projects Fund, 15/45 or 3/9; Town of Calvin, 10/45 or 2/9; and Calvin Independent School District, 5/45 or 1/9. The entry in the Drew County Investment Pool to distribute $900,000 of earnings follows:

		Debits	Credits
	Drew County Investment Pool:		
4a.	Undistributed Earnings on Pooled Investments	900,000	
	Due to Debt Service Fund		300,000
	Due to Capital Projects Fund		300,000
	Additions—Investment Earnings—Town of Calvin		200,000
	Additions—Investment Earnings—Calvin Independent School District		100,000

After the distribution, each participant has the same proportionate interest in the assets of the pool as it had before the distribution.

As noted previously, internal management of the pool is enhanced if each participant that is a member of the pool maintains an asset account with a title such as Equity in Pooled Investments. The balance of this account in each member's fund should be the reciprocal of the pool's account that reports the pool's liability or net position balance to that participant (depending on whether the participant is an internal member or external member). Thus, in the Drew County example, the Drew County Debt Service Fund's Equity in Pooled Investments account had a debit balance of $15,000,000 as of March 31, 2017, before the earnings distribution. Upon notification of the earnings distribution on the pooled investments, the Drew County Debt Service Fund would make the following entry:

		Debits	Credits
	Drew County Debt Service Fund:		
4b.	Equity in Pooled Investments	300,000	
	Revenues—Investment Earnings		300,000

Interest and dividends earned on pooled investments would increase the participants' equity in the pool, as would realized gains on the sales of investments (excess of fair value on date of sale over carrying value) and any unrealized gains resulting from periodic revaluation of the pooled investment portfolio to fair value. Both realized losses on securities sold (deficit of fair value at prior revaluation date compared with fair value at the sale date) and any unrealized losses resulting from periodic revaluation of the portfolio decrease the equity of members of the pool. In the Drew County Investment Pool example, each member maintains an operating cash account. Consequently, the pool does not need to distribute gains and losses daily, so it accumulates realized and unrealized gains and losses in the *Undistributed Change in Fair Value of Pooled Investments* account. This procedure allows a netting of gains and losses in each account, so that only the net realized and unrealized gain (or loss) need be distributed to pool participants.

GASB standards require that realized and unrealized gains and losses—including adjustments to the initial carrying value of pooled investments noted earlier—be reported as a revenue on the operating statement. When identified separately as a component of investment income the change in the fair value of investments should be captioned "Net

Increase (Decrease) in the Fair Value of Investments" rather than being reported as separate amounts in the financial statement.[5] However, realized and unrealized gains and losses can be disclosed in the notes to the financial statements, if desired.[6] If a government intends to disclose realized and unrealized gains or losses or needs such information for internal management purposes, it may be useful to maintain a separate *Allowance for Changes in Fair Value of Pooled Investments* account (a contra-asset account) to record all changes in fair value rather than increasing and decreasing the balance of the investment accounts. This technique permits the investment accounts to be carried at cost.

Assume that during fiscal 2017, the realized gains on sales of pooled investments of the Drew County Investment Pool, all credited to the Undistributed Change in Fair Value of Pooled Investments, amounted to $235,000 (measured as excess of fair value at the sale dates over prior fair value). During the year, realized losses, all debited to the undistributed change account, totaled $50,000 (measured as the deficit of fair value at the sale dates under prior fair value). Thus, there was a net credit of $185,000 for realized gains and losses for the period. Similarly, assume the net effect of marking the portfolio to fair value is an unrealized gain of $265,000, which is credited to the undistributed change account. The net effect of recognizing these gains and losses ($185,000 + $265,000) in the accounts of the Drew County Investment Pool, pending distribution, is summarized in Entry 5.

		Debits	***Credits***
	Drew County Investment Pool:		
5.	Investments (specific investments should be debited or credited here)	450,000	
	Undistributed Change in Fair Value of Investments		450,000

Assuming that no participants have joined the pool or withdrawn from the pool and that the four participants that have continued to be members of the pool have not transferred assets to or withdrawn additional assets from the pool, the realized and unrealized net gains of $450,000 should be distributed to the participants in the proportions used for the distribution of earnings in Entry 4a (3/9, 3/9, 2/9, and 1/9). The distribution is shown in the following entry:

	Drew County Investment Pool:		
6.	Undistributed Change in Fair Value of Investments	450,000	
	Due to Debt Service Fund		150,000
	Due to Capital Projects Fund		150,000
	Additions—Change in Fair Value of Investments—Town of Calvin		100,000
	Additions—Change in Fair Value of Investments—Calvin Independent School District		50,000

[5] GASB, *Codification*, Sec. I50.112.

[6] GASB, *Codification,* Sec. I50.129. If the entity opts, however, to disclose realized gains and losses, they must be computed as the difference between the proceeds of the sale and the original cost of the investments sold. The entity should also disclose that: (1) the calculation of realized gains and losses is independent of a calculation of the net change in the fair value of investments, and (2) realized gains and losses on investments that had been held in more than one fiscal year and sold in the current year were included as a change in the fair value of investments reported in the prior year(s) and the current year.

At December 31, 2017, interest earnings of $720,000 had accrued and were recorded, as shown in Entry 7:

		Debits	Credits
	Drew County Investment Pool:		
7.	Interest Receivable	720,000	
	Undistributed Earnings on Pooled Investments		720,000

Assuming that the accrued interest was immediately distributed to pool participants in the same proportions listed for Entry 6, the following entry would be made to record the distribution:

		Debits	Credits
	Drew County Investment Pool:		
8.	Undistributed Earnings on Pooled Investments	720,000	
	Due to Debt Service Fund		240,000
	Due to Capital Projects Fund		240,000
	Additions—Investment Earnings—Town of Calvin		160,000
	Additions—Investment Earnings—Calvin Independent School District		80,000

Both Entries 6 and 8 would lead to entries to recognize an increase in each participant's Equity in Pooled Investments and revenue accounts. Those entries would be similar to Entry 4b and thus are not shown here.

After all earnings and changes in fair value have been recorded as in the entries illustrated, the equities and proportionate interests of the participants follow:

Debt service fund	$15,690,000, or 3/9 of total
Capital projects fund	15,690,000, or 3/9 of total
Town of Calvin	10,460,000, or 2/9 of total
Calvin Independent School District	5,230,000, or 1/9 of total
Total	$47,070,000

Withdrawal of Assets from the Pool

If a participant in a pool withdraws part of its equity from a pool, that participant's proportionate interest is decreased and all other participants' proportionate interest is increased. Before a withdrawal occurs, an allocation of proportionate shares of earnings, gains, and losses to date should be made. The same is true in the event of complete withdrawal of one or more participants from the pool.

Continuing with the Drew County Investment Pool example, assume that the debt service fund needs to withdraw $5,230,000 from the pool to retire matured bonds. Ignoring the fact that in most practical cases it would be necessary to first sell some investments, the entry in the investment trust fund for the withdrawal is given as follows:

		Debits	Credits
	Drew County Investment Pool:		
9a.	Due to Debt Service Fund	5,230,000	
	Cash		5,230,000

If the withdrawal had been from an external participant, the debit in entry 9a would have been to an account such as *Deductions—Withdrawal from Pooled Investments.* The corresponding entry in the debt service fund follows:

	Drew County Debt Service Fund:		
9b.	Cash	5,230,000	
	Equity in Pooled Investments		5,230,000

After withdrawal of $5,230,000 by the debt service fund, the proportionate interests in the pool become:

Debt service fund	$10,460,000,	or	25% of total
Capital projects fund	15,690,000,	or	37.5% of total
Town of Calvin	10,460,000,	or	25% of total
Calvin Independent School District	5,230,000,	or	12.5% of total
Total	$41,840,000		

Closing Entry

To assist in preparing financial statements, the additions accounts (see Entries 1b, 2, 4a, 6, and 8), which reflect changes in the external participants' proportionate interest due to net new deposits/withdrawals, investment earnings, and changes in fair value, must be closed to the appropriate net position accounts, as shown in Entry 10 below:

	Drew County Investment Pool:		
10.	Additions—Deposits in Pooled Investments—Town of Calvin	9,900,000	
	Additions—Deposits in Pooled Investments—Calvin Independent School District	4,950,000	
	Additions—Investment Earnings—Town of Calvin	360,000	
	Additions—Investment Earnings—Calvin Independent School District	180,000	
	Additions—Change in Fair Value of Investments—Town of Calvin	200,000	
	Additions—Change in Fair Value of Investments—Calvin Independent School District	100,000	
	Net Position Held in Trust for Participants—Town of Calvin		10,460,000
	Net Position Held in Trust for Participants—Calvin Independent School District		5,230,000

ILLUSTRATION 8–6

DREW COUNTY
Investment Pool
Statement of Net Position
As of December 31, 2017

Assets		
Cash		$ 4,642,500
Investments		10,777,500
Interest receivable		270,000
Total assets		15,690,000
Net Position		
Assets held in trust for pool participants—		
Town of Calvin	$10,460,000	
Calvin Independent School District	5,230,000	
Total net position		$15,690,000

ILLUSTRATION 8–7

DREW COUNTY
Investment Pool
Statement of Changes in Net Position
For the Year Ended December 31, 2017

Additions	
Deposits of participants	$14,850,000
Investment earnings	540,000
Increase in fair value of investments	300,000
Total additions	15,690,000
Deductions	
Total deductions	–0–
Change in net position	15,690,000
Net position, January 1, 2017	–0–
Net position, December 31, 2017	$15,690,000

Illustrative Financial Statements

Illustrative fiduciary fund statements are presented in Illustrations 8–6 and 8–7. These statements are prepared as of, or for the year ended, December 31, 2017, Drew County's fiscal year-end. These statements also provide the information to be reported in a column of the statement of fiduciary fund net position (see Illustration A2–10) and statement of changes in fiduciary fund net position (see Illustration A2–11). Only assets of the external pool participants, representing 37.5% of the total pool holdings, are reported in the statement of net position. The other $26,150,000 is reported within the two participating funds of the Drew County government as Equity in Pooled Investments rather than specific assets.

PRIVATE-PURPOSE TRUST FUNDS

Individuals or organizations may establish trust agreements to confer assets (or management of the assets) to another party at the present time or at a future date. The fair value of assets placed in trust is referred to as the *principal* or *corpus* of the trust. If the principal of the trust must be held intact (nonexpendable) to produce income, the trust is often called an *endowment*. The income from the assets of an endowment may be used only for the purposes specified by the trustor. Not all trusts require that the principal be held intact. Some trusts allow the principal to be spent (expended) for the purpose specified by the trust. Additionally, not all trusts make distinctions between the use of principal and income. For example, loan funds operated as trust funds usually require that both the principal and income be held intact, whereas public retirement systems are trusts whose principal and income are both expended for specified purposes.

Governments may act as administrators of trust agreements that provide public or private benefit. *Public trust funds* are those whose principal or income, or both, must be used for some public purpose. The beneficiaries of *private trust funds* are private individuals, organizations, or other governments. A common example of a private trust fund is a state-sponsored 529 savings plan, structured such that parents make after-tax contributions to an investment fund managed by the state government. Contributions are maintained by the government until withdrawn by parents or students to pay educational costs of the student.

Because most trusts administered by governments are created for public purposes (for example, to maintain parks and cemeteries or to acquire art for public buildings), they are considered governmental rather than fiduciary activities under GASB standards. Thus, nonexpendable public-purpose trusts are accounted for as permanent funds, and expendable public-purpose trusts are accounted for as special revenue funds. These governmental fund types were discussed and illustrated in Chapter 4.

There are relatively few private-purpose trust funds compared with public-purpose trust funds. Further, private-purpose trust funds follow accounting and financial reporting practices that are quite similar to those illustrated in the previous section on investment trust funds. The accounting for a private-purpose trust fund whose principal is permanently restricted for investment, with earnings available for a specified private purpose, is similar to that for the City of Concordia Library Endowment Fund illustrated in Chapter 4 as a permanent fund. The principal difference is that financial information for a private-purpose trust is reported in the statement of fiduciary net position and statement of changes in fiduciary net position, whereas that for a permanent fund is reported in the balance sheet—governmental funds and statement of revenues, expenditures, and changes in fund balances—governmental funds. Even though a private-purpose trust reports additions and deductions from net position (see Illustration 8–7 for an example), those items are measured in essentially the same manner as revenues and expenditures of a permanent fund. Because there is little difference in accounting and reporting for private-purpose trusts, permanent funds, and investment trust funds (already illustrated), no journal entries or financial statements are provided in this chapter for private-purpose trust funds.

PENSION TRUST FUNDS

The funding shortfall of public pension plans has made headline news in recent years, primarily due to improved reporting, and the extent of public resources involved. The GASB has devoted substantial effort over time to improve the transparency and usefulness of financial reporting of pension plans. In many instances enhanced disclosures demonstrated underfunded pension plans with pension assets valued well below pension liabilities. The situation was exacerbated by the national financial crisis, which further reduced the value of existing plan assets and negatively affected many state and local government revenue sources used to fund pension plans. While the extent of pension funding shortfall varies significantly by government, recent stock market gains have helped to improve the funding status of many plans. Futhermore, research indicates that on a nationwide basis pension costs currently account for only 3.7 percent of state and local spending[6]; however, the fact that the largest 100 plans held assets of roughly $3.2 trillion in 2013 raises public interest in the topic.[7]

GASB standards provide comprehensive guidance on pension accounting and financial reporting for defined benefit pension plans and for the plan sponsor and employer. The authoritative portions of these standards can be found in the GASB *Codification,* Sections Pe5 and P20, respectively. Two newly implemented statements, Statement No. 67, *Financial Reporting for Pension Plans—an Amendment of GASB Statement No. 25,* and Statement No. 68, *Accounting and Financial Reporting for Pensions—an Amendment of GASB Statement No. 27,* establish new requirements for how most governments calculate and report the costs and obligations associated with pensions.[8] The new guidance shifts to an accounting-based approach of reporting pension liabilities and expense under the economic resources measurement focus. This provides a broader perspective of the employers' net pension position than the prior funding-based approach, whose focus was primarily on employer contributions and progress toward funding benchmarks. This section provides an overview of the accounting and reporting requirements for pension plans, as well as the governmental employers that provide retirement benefits to their employees under such plans.

General Characteristics of Governmental Pension Plans

Pension plans are of two general types, *defined contribution plans* and *defined benefit plans.* A **defined contribution plan** specifies the amount or rate of contribution, often a percentage of covered salary, that the employer and employees must contribute to the members' accounts in the pension plan. The level of benefits payable upon retirement is determined by the total amount of contributions to a member's account and earnings on investments. Because future benefits are neither formula based nor guaranteed, the risk associated with defined contribution plans rests primarily with employees; the employer's responsibility essentially ends once the required contribution is made. Such plans ordinarily are *not* administered on an actuarial basis; therefore, accounting and financial reporting requirements for both the plan and the employer are straightforward and present few complications. Essentially, the plan reports the fair value of pension assets and any liability for accrued plan benefits; the employer reports expenditures/expenses for the amount contributed to the plan. Both the plan and the employer are required to provide in the notes to the financial statements a brief description of the plan, including identification of the pension plan as a

[6] National Association of State Retirement Administrators (NASRA) Issue Brief: State and Local Government Spending on Public Employee Retirement Systems, May 2014, available at http://www.nasra.org/files/Issue%20Briefs/NASRACostsBrief.pdf, (accessed June 18, 2014).

[7] U.S. Bureau of the Census, *Summary of the Quarterly Survey of Public Pensions for 2013:Q4,* Figure 1, available at www.census.gov/govs/qpr/ (accessed June 18, 2014).

[8] *GASBS 67* and *GASBS 68* apply to pension plans that are administered through trusts or equivalent arrangements, as discussed in this chapter. Other pension plans not administered through trusts and defined contribution plans that provide postemployment benefits other than pensions continue to follow the requirements of *GASBS 25* and *GASBS 50.*

defined contribution pension plan, classes of plan members covered, the number of plan members, participating employers, nonemployer contributing entities, and the authority under which the pension plan is established or may be amended.[9]

A **defined benefit plan** provides a specified amount of benefits to a retiree based on a formula that may include factors such as age, salary, and years of employment. Determining the present value of projected pension benefits involves numerous factors, such as employee mortality, employee turnover, salary progression, and investment earnings. To ensure that plan assets will be adequate to cover future benefits, professional actuaries are engaged to calculate the present value of benefits and the required contributions that must be made by employers and, in some cases, employees. The basic assumptions underlying actuaries' projections may change over time, giving rise to periodic revisions in the required contributions. Because of the need to rely extensively on actuaries' estimates, it is not surprising that accounting for defined benefit plans is much more complex than for defined contribution plans. The remainder of this section provides a summary overview of the accounting and financial reporting requirements for defined benefit pension plans.[10]

Defined benefit pension plans are classified as either **single-employer pension plans** (pensions are provided only to employees of the employer) or **multiple-employer pension plans** (pension benefits are provided to the employees of more than one employer). Multiple employer plans can be further designated as agent or cost-sharing. Under an **agent multiple-employer pension plan**, plan assets of numerous employers are pooled for investment purposes but accounts are maintained for the individual employer participants. A **cost-sharing multiple-employer pension plan** is one in which the pension obligations of many employers are pooled and plan assets can be used to pay the benefits of the employees of any employer that provides pensions through the pension plan.

The illustrative transactions and statements for defined benefit pension plan accounting discussed in this section are based on a single-employer plan. Readers should be aware, however, that many governments sponsor several employer pension plans for different classes of employees (for example, a plan for general employees and one or more separate plans for public safety employees). Furthermore, in some states, some or all local government employees participate in a statewide defined benefit pension plan rather than one sponsored by the local government. Such plans or groups of plans are often referred to as **Public Employee Retirement Systems (PERS).**

Pension plans are required to be reported in the basic fiduciary fund statements for the sponsoring government (see Illustrations A2–10 and A2–11). For those plans administered as legally separate entities that publish "stand-alone" financial statements, standards also require the reporting of the separate entities' pension fund financial information in the fiduciary funds statements of the sponsoring governments.

[9] GASB, *Codification,* Sec. Pe6.107, as amended by *GASBS 67.*

[10] While the financial crisis caused many governments to consider moving from a defined benefit plan to a defined contribution plan for new employees, defined benefit plans are still predominant. See Alicia H. Munnell, Jean-Pierre Aubry, and Mark Cafarelli, "Defined Contribution Plans in the Public Sector: An Update," State and Local Pension Plans Issue Brief 37, Center for Retirement Research at Boston College, April 2014; available at http://crr.bc.edu/wp-content/uploads/2014/04/SLP_37.pdf (viewed June 18, 2014).'

Required Financial Reporting for Defined Benefit Pension Plans

The GASB standards establish a financial reporting framework for defined benefit pension plans that includes required financial statements, note disclosures, and required schedules of historical trend information. Two financial statements are required:

a. A statement of fiduciary net position showing plan assets, deferred inflows of resources, liabilities, deferred outflows of resources, and net position. Plan assets should be reported at fair value. (See Illustrations 8–8 and 8–9.)

b. A statement of changes in fiduciary net position showing additions to plan net position, deductions from plan net position, and net increase (decrease) in plan net position. (See Illustration 8–10.)

ILLUSTRATION 8–8

JOHNSON COUNTY EMPLOYEE RETIREMENT SYSTEM
Statement of Fiduciary Net Position
June 30, 2017

Assets	
Cash	$ 51,213
Interest receivable	2,507,612
Investments (at fair value):	
Bonds	71,603,976
Common stocks	31,957,205
Commercial paper and repurchase agreements	12,570,401
Total assets	118,690,407
Liabilities	
Accounts payable and accrued expenses	401,581
Net position restricted for pensions	$118,288,826

ILLUSTRATION 8–9

JOHNSON COUNTY EMPLOYEE RETIREMENT SYSTEM
Statement of Fiduciary Net Position
June 30, 2017

Assets	
Cash	$ 62,434
Interest receivable	4,822,076
Investments (at fair value):	
Bonds	99,965,064
Common stocks	30,627,302
Commercial paper and repurchase agreements	11,215,833
Total assets	146,692,709
Liabilities	
Accounts payable and accrued expenses	251,650
Net position restricted for pensions	$146,441,059

ILLUSTRATION 8–10

JOHNSON COUNTY EMPLOYEE RETIREMENT SYSTEM
Statement of Changes in Fiduciary Net Position
For the Fiscal Year Ended
June 30, 2017

Additions:	
Contributions:	
Employer	$ 14,126,292
Plan members	8,009,400
Total contributions	22,135,692
Investment income:	
Net decrease in fair value of investments	(2,198,782)
Interest and dividends	14,262,845
Total investment income	12,064,063
Total additions	34,199,755
Deductions:	
Annuity benefits	3,134,448
Disability benefits	287,590
Refunds to terminated employees	2,057,265
Administrative expenses	568,219
Total deductions	6,047,522
Net increase in net position	28,152,233
Net position restricted for pensions:	
Beginning of year	118,288,826
End of year	$146,441,059

The following pension-related information should be disclosed in the notes to the financial statements, as applicable:[11]

a. Plan description:

1. The name of the pension plan; identification of the public employee retirement system or other entity that administers the pension plan; and identification of the pension plan as a single-employer, agent, or cost-sharing pension plan.
2. The number of participating employers (if the pension plan is a multiple-employer pension plan) and the number of nonemployer contributing entities, if any.
3. Information regarding the pension plan's board and its composition.
4. Classes of plan members.
5. The authority under which benefit terms are established or may be amended and the types of benefits provided through the pension plan.
6. A brief description of contribution requirements.

b. Pension plan investments:

1. Investment policies.
2. A brief description of how the fair value of investments is determined.

[11] *GASBS 67*, par. 30.

3. Identification of investments in any one organization that represent 5 percent or more of the pension plan's fiduciary net position.
4. The annual money-weighted rate of return on pension plan investments.

c. Receivables.
d. Allocated insurance contracts excluded from pension plan assets.
e. Reserves.
f. Deferred retirement option program (DROP) balances.

In addition the notes should disclose components of net pension liability, significant assumptions, and other inputs used to measure the total pension liability and the date of the actuarial valuation on which the total pension liability is based.[12]

Single-employer defined benefit (as illustrated in this chapter) and multiple-employer cost-sharing pension plans must also present the following schedules as required supplementary information:[13]

a. A 10-year schedule of changes in the net pension liability and selected ratios, including
1. The total pension liability.
2. The pension plan's fiduciary net position.
3. The net pension liability.
4. The pension plan's fiduciary net position as a percentage of the total pension liability.
5. The covered-employee payroll.
6. The net pension liability as a percentage of covered-employee payroll.

b. A 10-year schedule of contributions.
c. A 10-year schedule presenting for each fiscal year the annual money-weighted rate of return on pension plan investments.

The notes to the required schedules should provide:[14]

a. Identification of actuarial methods and significant actuarial assumptions used in calculating the actuarially determined contributions for the most recent year covered by the required supplementary schedules.
b. Factors such as changes in benefit terms, size or composition of employees covered by the plan, or actuarial methods or assumptions used that significantly affect the trends reported in the schedules.

Statement of Fiduciary Net Position

Illustrations 8–8 and 8–9 present the statement of fiduciary net position for the hypothetical Johnson County Employee Retirement System for fiscal years 2016 and 2017, respectively. Johnson County administers one pension plan. As shown, plan investments should be reported at fair value (last reported sales price) for all investments in securities that trade on active exchanges. Investments in mortgages should be based on

[12] Prior to *GASBS 67* and *GASBS 68* implementation, employers were required to disclose pension funding status. They reported the actuarially determined amount that should be contributed in the current year to maintain adequate funding status (i.e., annual required contribution) and the portion of that amount that was actually contributed. While this disclosure is no longer required by the GASB, some governmental entities may still be required by law to comply with minimum funding levels and will therefore continue to disclose an "annual required contribution".

[13] *GASBS 67*, par. 32.

[14] Ibid, par. 34.

the discounted present value of future interest and principal payments to be received. Investments in real estate should be reported at fair value based on independent appraisals. All other investments should be reported at estimated fair value, including institutional price quotes for debt securities for which trade prices are unavailable.

Depreciable assets of a pension fund, that is, capital assets held for use by the fund, should be reported at cost less accumulated depreciation. Cash, short-term investments (reported at cost), and receivables typically represent a minor part of the total assets of a pension fund. The assets of a pension fund are not classified as current and noncurrent; this distinction is not important since short-term liabilities typically are immaterial in relation to available plan assets. Fund liabilities, usually short-term (e.g., benefits due but unpaid, refunds for terminated employees, vouchers payable, accrued expenses, and payroll taxes payable), are reported as a deduction from assets; the difference is typically captioned *net position restricted for pensions.*

Statement of Changes in Fiduciary Net Position

The Johnson County Employee Retirement System Statement of Changes in Fiduciary Net Position for fiscal year 2017 is presented in Illustration 8–10. This statement reports employer and employee contributions and investment income as additions to net position rather than as revenues. Similarly, benefits paid, refunds of contributions, and administrative expenses are reported as deductions from net position rather than as expenses. The net increase (decrease) in net position is added to beginning-of-period net position to calculate end-of-period net position. Additions and deductions are recognized on the accrual basis.

Schedule of Changes in Net Pension Liability and Related Ratios

An example of a *schedule of net pension liability and related ratios* for Johnson County is presented in Illustration 8–11. This schedule displays elements of total pension liability, net pension liability, and changes in fiduciary net position for each of the last 10 fiscal years. **Total pension liability** is the portion of the present value of projected benefit payments to be provided through the pension plan that is attributed to past periods of employee service. It is actuarially determined using the pension plan's most recent valuation and arises primarily from past underfunding and changes in pension plan provisions. As shown in Illustration 8–11, the total pension liability section displays current year changes, including **service cost**, which is the portion of the actuarial present value of projected benefit payments that is attributed to the current year, interest on the total pension liability, benefit payments, and other changes to the total pension liability, such as differences in investment returns and recognition of a portion of deferred inflows of resources or deferred outflows of resources.

The next section of the schedule displays changes to plan fiduciary net position, which are similar to the items found on the statement of changes in fiduciary net position in Illustration 8–10. The plan fiduciary net position is basically equal to the market value of plan assets. The difference between the total pension liability and plan fiduciary net position is referred to as the **net pension liability.**

Following the net pension liability is a ratio indicating the percentage of the total pension liability that is held in trust for future pension payments. This ratio indicates the current funding position of the pension plan. Note that Johnson County's total pension liability has increased at varying amounts over the past 10-year period, however, its net position held in trust for pensions has not increased at the same rate. In fact plan fiduciary net position as a percentage of total pension liability currently stands at 42.37 percent and has been as low as 33.25 percent.

ILLUSTRATION 8–11

JOHNSON COUNTY EMPLOYEE RETIREMENT SYSTEM
Schedule of Changes in the County's Net Pension Liability & Related Ratios
Last 10 Fiscal Years
(in thousands)

	2017	2016	2015	2014	2013	2012	2011	2010	2009	2008
Total pension liability										
Service cost	$ 12,896	$ 12,627	$ 12,097	$ 11,788	$ 11,369	$ 10,676	$ 10,109	$ 8,859	$ 8,374	$ 6,898
Interest	36,808	34,856	32,104	29,698	27,627	25,156	23,198	21,633	18,073	16,618
Differences between expected and actual experience	3,378	(2,585)	(605)	(7,688)	(4,981)	3,669	5,150	2,288	3,408	2,505
Benefit payments (including refunds of employee contributions)	(20,304)	(19,143)	(17,749)	(16,213)	(15,094)	(14,644)	(13,121)	(12,054)	(11,354)	(10,311)
Net change in total pension liability	32,778	25,755	25,847	17,585	18,921	24,856	25,336	20,726	18,501	15,710
Total pension liability, beginning	312,825	287,069	261,222	243,637	224,716	199,860	174,525	153,799	135,298	119,588
Total pension liability, ending	345,603	312,825	287,069	261,222	243,637	224,716	199,860	174,525	153,799	135,298
Plan fiduciary net position										
Contributions—employee	$ 8,009	$ 1,838	$ 1,266	$ 652	$ 426	$ 704	$ 637	$ 588	$ 545	$ 487
Contributions—employer	14,126	7,352	5,063	2,609	1,702	2,814	2,549	2,351	2,178	1,948
Net investment income	12,064	33,346	(2,743)	(5,967)	28,360	23,822	32,828	6,654	11,897	(978)
Benefit payments (including refunds of employee contributions)	(5,479)	(19,143)	(17,749)	(16,213)	(15,094)	(14,644)	(13,121)	(12,054)	(11,354)	(10,311)
Administrative expenses	(568)	(559)	(472)	(439)	(351)	(383)	325	(319)	(273)	(270)
Net change in plan fiduciary net position	28,152	22,835	(14,635)	(19,358)	15,042	12,313	23,218	(2,781)	2,993	(9,124)
Plan fiduciary net position, beginning	118,289	95,454	110,089	129,447	114,405	102,092	78,874	81,655	78,662	87,786
Plan fiduciary net position, ending	146,441	118,289	95,454	110,089	129,447	114,405	102,092	78,874	81,655	78,662
Net pension liability, ending	$199,162	$194,535	$191,579	$151,133	$114,190	$110,312	$ 97,769	$ 95,651	$ 72,144	$ 56,638
Plan fiduciary net position as a percentage of total pension liability	42.37%	37.81%	33.25%	42.14%	53.39%	50.91%	51.08%	45.19%	53.09%	58.14%
Covered-employee payroll	$ 79,226	$ 74,192	$ 70,761	$ 69,328	$67,376	$ 64,864	$ 62,115	$ 55,062	$ 51,321	$ 46,634
Net pension liability as a percentage of covered-employee payroll	251.38%	262.22%	270.74%	217.98%	169.48%	170.07%	157.40%	173.72%	140.57%	121.45%

Covered payroll is the amount of payroll costs on which the contributions to the pension plan are based. Examples of covered payroll include an employee's base pay and could also include employee overtime if overtime is included as part of the pension plan's coverage. The schedule presents covered payroll and a ratio of net pension liability as a percentage of covered payroll. This ratio provides a measure of the size of the net pension liability relative to annual payroll for employees covered by the pension plan. For Johnson County, this ratio has risen and fallen; net pension liability currently stands at over two and a half times the annual covered payroll cost.

Schedule of Employer Contributions

The key information the reader should note in the *schedule of employer contributions* shown in Illustration 8–12 is the *actuarially determined contribution* and the portion of that amount that the employer has contributed in each of the last 10 fiscal years. The actuarially determined contribution is a target or recommended contribution to a defined benefit pension plan for the reporting period, based upon external actuarial calculations relative to the most recent asset measurement and benefit projections available. In this schedule, contributions are presented as a percentage of covered payroll. In Illustration 8–12, Johnson County has made annual contributions equal to the actuarially determined contribution.

Schedule of Investment Returns

The final required schedule presented as required supplementary information for defined benefit plans presents the annual *money-weighted rate of return* on pension plan investments for each of the last 10 fiscal years. This internal rate of return on pension plan investments is calculated net of pension plan investment expense and is adjusted for the changing amounts actually invested. Illustration 8–13 presents this schedule for Johnson County and shows that the County suffered investment losses in 2013 and 2014. Note how the investment returns fluctuated over the years and was a partial contributing factor to the growing net pension liability.

Illustrative Transactions for a Defined Benefit Pension Plan

Assume that the Johnson County Employee Retirement Plan started the fiscal year beginning July 1, 2016, with the statement of fiduciary net position presented in Illustration 8–8. During fiscal year 2017, the following transactions occurred that require journal entries as shown.

Interest receivable as of June 30, 2016, was collected:

		Debits	Credits
1.	Cash	2,507,612	
	Interest Receivable		2,507,612

Member contributions in the amount of $8,009,400 and employer contributions in the amount of $14,126,292 were received in cash:

2.	Cash	22,135,692	
	Additions—Member Contributions		8,009,400
	Additions—Employer Contributions		14,126,292

ILLUSTRATION 8–12

JOHNSON COUNTY EMPLOYEE RETIREMENT SYSTEM
Schedule of Contributions
Last 10 Fiscal Years
(in thousands)

	2017	2016	2015	2014	2013	2012	2011	2010	2009	2008
Actuarially determined contribution	$14,126	$ 7,352	$ 5,063	$ 2,609	$ 1,702	$ 2,814	$ 2,549	$ 2,351	$ 2,178	$ 1,948
Contributions in relation to the actuarially determined contribution	14,126	7,352	5,063	2,609	1,702	2,814	2,549	2,351	2,178	1,948
Contribution deficiency (excess)	$ —	$ —	$ —	$ —	$ —	$ —	$ —	$ —	$ —	$ —
Covered-employee payroll	$79,226	$74,192	$70,761	$69,328	$67,376	$64,864	$62,115	$55,062	$51,321	$46,634
Contributions as a percentage of covered-employee payroll	17.83%	9.91%	7.16%	3.76%	2.53%	4.34%	4.10%	4.27%	4.24%	4.18%

ILLUSTRATION 8–13

JOHNSON COUNTY EMPLOYEE RETIREMENT SYSTEM
Schedule of Investment Returns
Last 10 Fiscal Years

	2017	2016	2015	2014	2013	2012	2011	2010	2009	2008
Annual money-weighted rate of return net of investment expense	4.58%	3.77%	2.10%	−0.04%	−0.28%	9.81%	10.46%	9.31%	7.50%	7.14%

Annuity benefits in the amount of $3,134,448 and disability benefits in the amount of $287,590 were recorded as liabilities:

		Debits	Credits
3.	Deductions—Annuity Benefits	3,134,448	
	Deductions—Disability Benefits	287,590	
	Accounts Payable and Accrued Expenses		3,422,038

Accounts payable and accrued expenses paid in cash amounted to $3,571,969:

4.	Accounts Payable and Accrued Expenses	3,571,969	
	Cash		3,571,969

Terminated employees whose benefits were not vested were refunded $2,057,265 in cash:

5.	Deductions—Refunds to Terminated Employees	2,057,265	
	Cash		2,057,265

Investment income received in cash amounted to $9,440,769; $4,882,076 of interest income was accrued at year-end. In addition, the fair value of investments in bonds decreased during the year by $5,626,382 and the fair value of investments in common stocks increased by $3,427,600.

6a.	Cash	9,440,769	
	Interest Receivable	4,822,076	
	Additions—Investment Income		14,262,845
6b.	Investment in Common Stock	3,427,600	
	Deductions—Change in Fair Value of Investments	2,198,782	
	Investment in Bonds		5,626,382

Commercial paper and repurchase agreements carried at a cost of $1,354,568 matured, and cash in that amount was received:

7.	Cash	1,354,568	
	Commercial Paper and Repurchase Agreements		1,354,568

Common stocks carried at fair value of $6,293,867 were sold for that amount; $1,536,364 was reinvested in common stocks and the remainder in bonds. An additional amount of $29,229,967 was also invested in bonds:

		Debits	Credits
8a.	Cash	6,293,867	
	Investment in Common Stocks		6,293,867
8b.	Investment in Bonds	33,987,470	
	Investment in Common Stocks	1,536,364	
	Cash		35,523,834

Administrative expenses for the year totaled $568,219, all paid in cash:

9.	Deductions—Administrative Expenses	568,219	
	Cash		568,219

Nominal accounts for the year were closed:

10.	Additions—Member Contributions	8,009,400	
	Additions—Employer Contributions	14,126,292	
	Additions—Investment Income	14,262,845	
	Deductions—Annuity Benefits		3,134,448
	Deductions—Disability Benefits		287,590
	Deductions—Refunds to Terminated Employees		2,057,265
	Deductions—Administrative Expenses		568,219
	Deductions—Change in Fair Value of Investments		2,198,782
	Net Position Restricted for Pensions		28,152,233

Entries 1 through 10 result in the financial statements shown as Illustrations 8–9 and 8–10, when applied to the accounts existing at the beginning of the period as shown in Illustration 8–8.

Employer's Pension Accounting

The prior section addressed accounting for a pension trust fund by a pension fund sponsor. This section discusses accounting for the employer who provides pensions to its employees. Under a single-employer defined benefit plan, such as our chapter example, the sponsor and employer are one and the same. Pension activity will be recorded in a pension trust fund, while employer pension-related expenses, expenditures, deferred outflows of resources, applicable liabilities, and deferred inflows of resources will be recorded within fund and government-wide financial statements.

The GASB standards for the employer's accounting for defined benefit pension plans provide guidance for measurement, recognition, and display of the employer's pension information. Many of the note and statistical disclosures applicable to defined benefit pension plans, discussed in the preceding paragraphs, apply to the employer. If the plan (or PERS) is deemed to be part of the government's reporting entity, the employer need not make disclosures that would duplicate those made by the plan. If the plan issues a stand-alone financial report, however, the employer will have to make many of the same disclosures in the comprehensive annual financial report (CAFR) that the plan makes in its stand-alone report. Because of the similarity of the disclosures and supplementary information required of the employer to those enumerated previously for the plan, the reader is referred to the *GASBS 68*, pars. 37–47, for specific disclosure requirements applicable to the employer.

Whether a government employer accounts for payroll in a governmental fund or proprietary fund, or both, the primary measures to be calculated and reported are the *net pension liability* and the pension expense or expenditure.

Net Pension Liability

As noted earlier, the employer's *net pension liability* is measured as the *total pension liability* less the amount of fiduciary net position held for future pension payments. The total pension liability represents the portion of the present value of projected benefit payments to be provided through the pension plan to current active and inactive employees that is attributed to those employees' past periods of service based on actuarial valuations generally required to be performed at least every two years. The measurement process involves three essential steps: (1) projection of future benefit payments for current and former employees and their beneficiaries; (2) discounting those payments to their present value; and (3) allocating the present value over past, present, and future periods of employee service using the "entry age" actuarial cost method. The discount rate used in discounting should generally be the long-term expected rate of return on the pension plan investments if an appropriate strategy exists to achieve that return; however, under some circumstances a blend of the expected rate of return and a municipal borrowing rate is required.[15]

As shown in Illustration 8–11, the total pension liability includes current year changes, interest on the total pension liability, benefit payments, cumulative differences in investment returns, and recognition of a portion of deferred inflows of resources or deferred outflows of resources. The net pension liability representing an employer's unfunded pension liability is reported on the employer's government-wide statement of net position. The change in the net pension liability does not all get recognized as pension expense immediately. Certain changes can be deferred (shown as deferred inflows of resources or deferred outflows of resources) and amortized systematically over the average remaining years of employee service.

Pension Expenditure and Expense

Under *GASBS 68*, pension expenditures should be recognized equal to the total of (1) amounts paid by the employer to the pension plan and (2) the change between the beginning and ending balances of amounts normally expected to be liquidated with expendable available financial resources. The pension expense recorded is the change in the net pension liability, adjusted for amortized amounts related to differences arising due to changes in assumptions and differences between projected and actual earnings. It can be depicted as follows:

Service cost (actuarially determined benefits related to the current year)
+ Interest on total pension liability
+ Plan changes (recognized immediately)
+ Changes in fiduciary net position from other than investments
(e.g., admin expenses, member contributions)
− Projected earnings on plan investments
+/−Recognition of portion of deferred inflows/outflows
Pension expense for the period

Those amounts not expensed (i.e., the unamortized amounts) should be recognized as deferred outflows of resources or deferred inflows of resources.

[15] *GASBS 67*, par. 44.

Employer Recording and Reporting of Pension Expenditure/Expense

A governmental employer that reports pension expenditures in a governmental fund should recognize the expenditures on the modified accrual basis. Thus, the amount recognized will be the actual amount contributed to the plan during the year and the net annual change in amounts normally expected to be liquidated with expendable available financial resources. An appropriate entry to recognize pension expenditures (amounts assumed) in the General Fund of a city follows.

	Debits	Credits
General Fund:		
Expenditures—(various governmental functions)	157,982	
Cash		157,982

The governmental activities journal at the government-wide level would recognize pension cost on the accrual basis. On the accrual basis of accounting, pension expense includes current year benefits, interest on prior pension liabilities, plan changes, amortization of deferred amounts, and other changes to the net pension liability. The appropriate journal entry for governmental activities at the government-wide level would allocate the pension cost to the various functions of government by debiting expenses.

	Debits	Credits
Governmental Activities:		
Expenses—(various government functions)	166,863	
Cash		157,982
Net Pension Liability		8,881

If plan fiduciary net position exceeds the total pension liability, an asset can be recorded in the employer's government-wide statement of net position.

OTHER POSTEMPLOYMENT BENEFITS (OPEB)

In addition to accounting and reporting of pension plans, GASB also requires accounting and reporting for **other postemployment benefits (OPEB).** OPEB includes benefits other than pensions, such as health care, life insurance, and long-term care, among others. The accounting and reporting for OPEB has historically been quite similar to that of defined benefit pension plans; however, the GASB issues separate standards for OPEB. As this textbook goes to press, the GASB has issued two exposure drafts related to accounting and reporting for OPEB that would institute changes similar to those noted in *GASBS 67* and *GASBS 68* described earlier in the chapter. GASB standards do not currently require that governments fund the liability associated with OPEB; however, a decision not to fund OPEB could be considered negatively by bond rating agencies and therefore affect the cost of debt.

TERMINATION BENEFITS

In addition to the standards on pensions and OPEB, GASB has a standard relating to accounting for **termination benefits.**[16] This standard provides guidance on expense and liability recognition for voluntary and involuntary termination benefits. Voluntary termination benefits occur when employers provide an incentive to hasten an employee's voluntary termination of employment, such as a one-time cash payout. An involuntary termination benefit could relate to layoffs or reductions in force and include such items as career counseling and severance pay.

Appendix

Managing Investments

Prudent investment is important to the success of investment trust funds and defined benefit plan funds. The managers of these funds are charged with earning the maximum return possible on the portfolio of investments within the constraints of safety and liquidity. To aid managers, formal investment policies should be adopted by governments. A sound investment policy will:

1. Identify investment objectives.
2. Define risk tolerance.
3. Assign responsibility for the investment function.
4. Establish control over the investment process.[17]

For management of public investment pools, industry best practices include investment guidelines that suit the needs of pool participants, clear and transparent investment guidelines and portfolio reporting, regular review of compliance procedures and investment guidelines, and understanding impacts of ongoing regulatory change.[18]

An investment strategy that assesses liquidity needs, provides for a total return benchmark, and evaluates the success of meeting investment objectives will help maximize the return on the investment portfolio. Accurately assessing liquidity needs helps ensure that short-term investments will be able to provide cash when needed. However, any cash not needed in the short term should be invested in longer term, higher yielding investments.

The benchmark selected for the targeted rates of total return or yield should be consistent with the risk tolerance defined in the investment policy. There are several types of risk that affect deposits and investments; however, two major risks the investment manager should consider are credit risk and market risk. *Credit risk* relates to the probability of loss due to the issuer or counterparty not meeting its obligations. Thus, credit risk relates to the financial viability and dependability of the issuers of the securities, any insurers of the securities, and/or the custodians of the securities or collateral. *Market risk* is the risk that the fair value of

[16] GASB, *Codification,* Sec. T25.

[17] The preceding list is adapted from M. Corrine Larson, "Managing Your Investment Program in Today's Market," *Government Finance Review*, June 2002, p. 40.

[18] FitchRatings Fund and Asset Manager Rating Group Special Report, "Local Government Investment Pools: Best Practices Vary," June 13, 2014, available at http://www.fitchratings.com/creditdesk/reports/report_frame.cfm?rpt_id=742119 (accessed June 23, 2014).

the security will decline. Periodic evaluation of the investment portfolio will help ensure that the targeted return is met while not exceeding the risk tolerance defined in the investment policy. Because risk exposure is a critical element in the management of investments, GASB requires disclosures of investment policies related to risk.[19]

To meet the investment objectives, managers can choose from a wide array of investments. Some commonly used investment securities are obligations of the federal government (e.g., U.S. Treasury bills, bonds, and notes), repurchase agreements, bankers' acceptances, commercial paper, money market funds, and state and local bonds. Additionally, some investment policies allow for investment in corporate debt and equity securities and derivatives.

Some governments invest in derivative instruments. The GASB *Codification,* Section D40 requires that **derivatives** be reported at fair value on the fiduciary statement of net position. Changes in the fair value of derivative instruments used for investment purposes (or those derivatives that are deemed ineffective as hedging derivatives) are to be reported as part of investment earnings in the additions section of the statement of changes in fiduciary net position. If the derivative is used to hedge risk (e.g., interest or foreign currency), the change in fair value will be reported as a *deferred inflow* or a *deferred outflow* on the fiduciary statement of net position, provided the derivative meets the hedge effectiveness criteria identified in the GASB *Codification,* Section D40. Investment managers may want to keep the derivative standard in mind when making decisions about the best use of derivatives and the effectiveness of the derivatives.

When setting targets for rates of total return, managers need to be aware of Internal Revenue Code Sec. 148 rules on arbitrage. These rules significantly limit the ability of a government to realize arbitrage earnings by investing tax-exempt bond proceeds (e.g., general obligation bond proceeds received for future construction of a capital asset) in taxable investments with higher yields. Interest earnings in excess of those permitted by Internal Revenue Code rules must be paid to the federal government. There are severe penalties for violating the Internal Revenue Code rules on arbitrage.

Key Terms

Agency funds, *304*
Agent multiple employer pension plan, *325*
Cost-sharing multiple-employer pension plan, *325*
Covered payroll, *331*
Defined benefit plan, *325*
Defined contribution plan, *324*
Derivatives, *338*
External investment pool, *313*
Investment trust fund, *313*
Multiple-employer pension plan, *325*
Net pension liability, *329*
Other postemployment benefits (OPEB), *336*
Public Employee Retirement System (PERS), *325*
Service cost, *329*
Single-employer pension plan, *325*
Termination benefits, *337*
Total pension liability, *329*

Selected References

De Foor, Joya C. and Kay Chandler, "Innovations in Managing Public Funds: Benchmarking and Total Return," *Government Finance Review,* August 2007, p. 16.

Governmental Accounting Standards Board. *Codification of Governmental Accounting and Financial Reporting Standards, as of June 30, 2014.* Norwalk, CT, 2014.

———. *Comprehensive Implementation Guide, as of June 30, 2014.* Norwalk, CT, 2014.

[19] GASB, *Codification*, Sec. I50, pars. 137–143.

Questions

8–1. Explain the distinction(s) between *agency funds* and *trust funds.* What financial statements are prepared for each?

8–2. Identify the different types of trust funds and explain the purpose of each type.

8–3. Describe the basic activities conducted by a tax agency fund. What are some of the issues that make tax agency fund accounting complex?

8–4. Explain how the financial reporting of fiduciary funds differs from that of governmental funds.

8–5. What is a "pass-through" agency fund and under what conditions is it appropriate to use such a fund?

8–6. How does the accounting for an internal investment pool differ from the accounting for an external investment pool?

8–7. Compare a defined benefit pension plan with a defined contribution pension plan. If you were an employee, which type of plan would you prefer? Why?

8–8. Explain the difference between a private-purpose trust and a public-purpose trust. How does the reporting for the two types of trusts differ?

8–9. How does total pension liability differ from net pension liability?

8–10. Compare the accounting for pension expenditures in a governmental fund with the accounting for pension expenses at the government-wide level.

Cases

8–11 Research Case—CalPERS. While the examples in this chapter have focused on a single-employer plan, many states operate statewide plans, referred to as Public Employee Retirement Systems (PERS), to which multiple employers contribute. One of the largest PERS plans in the nation is operated in the State of California.

Required

To answer the following questions use the Web site found at *www.calpers.ca.gov.* The answers to the questions can be found in CalPERS's annual report or in the general information section provided on the site.

a. When was CalPERS established?
b. What types of employers contribute to CalPERS?
c. How many individuals are served by CalPERS?
d. How many and what types of funds are administered by CalPERS?
e. For the most recent reporting period, what is the value of total net position?
f. For the most recent reporting period, what was the change in pension fund net position?
g. What is the reporting relationship between CalPERS and the State of California?

8–12 Other Postemployment Benefit (OPEB) Plans. GASB standards require that governments report other postemployment benefits offered to employees, which in some cases will be huge. To investigate the extent of the problem, examine the required supplementary information (RSI) of the most recent CAFRs for the City of Boston (http://www.cityofboston.gov/auditing/reports/cafr.asp) and the City of New York (*www.comptroller.nyc.gov*).

a. Examine the Schedules of Funding Progress in the RSI. For the most recent year, how large is the unfunded actuarial accrued liability (UAAL) for Boston's OPEB-City and OPEB-Plan? What is the funded ratio and the UAAL as a percentage of covered payroll? *Hint:* the funded ratio is calculated as assets held for OPEB liabilities divided by the UAAL.

b. Examine the Schedule of Funding Progress for OPEB within the RSI of New York City's CAFR. For the most recent year, how large is the UAAL? What is the funded ratio and the UAAL as a percentage of covered payroll?

c. Compare the funded status of Boston and New York City's OPEB obligations.

8–13 Policy Issues Relating to Employee Pension Plans. Policymakers in your state have been talking about shifting from a defined benefit pension plan to a defined contribution pension plan or a hybrid alternative for new state employees. You work for a state legislator who asks you to research the pros and cons of making the change.

Required

Access the Center for State and Local Government Excellence's *Issue Brief* entitled, "A Role for Defined Contribution Plans in the Public Sector," at http://crr.bc.edu/briefs/a-role-for-defined-contribution-plans-in-the-public-sector/. The brief describes the differences between defined benefit and defined contribution plans. It also discusses hybrid plan alternatives. Prepare a memo for the legislator that addresses the following:

a. Briefly define a defined benefit plan and a defined contribution plan. What is a hybrid plan?

b. When considering a change of pension plan, what are the primary considerations mentioned in the *Issue Brief*?

c. What type of plan do most states offer? What states have recently changed their state plans?

d. Based upon your review of the *Issue Brief,* what would be your recommendation to the legislator? Briefly explain the reason for your recommendation.

8–14 Research Case—Evaluating New Pension Standards. In July, 2012, GASB issued two new statements, *GASBS Nos. 67* and *68*, related to governmental pension reporting. These new standards replace the pension accounting practices found in *GASBS Nos. 25* and *27*, and more closely align pension reporting for governments with that of for-profit organizations. *GASBS No. 67* was effective for plan fiscal years beginning after June 15, 2013, while *GASBS No. 68* was effective for plan fiscal years beginning after June 15, 2014.

Required

Search for one or more articles on *GASBS No. 67* and *GASBS No. 68* in professional journals or using an online search engine. Using the material you found, write a paper that succinctly compares and contrasts the old and new standards. Your final paragraph should state whether you believe the new standards improve governmental reporting of pensions or not, with at least one specific example to support your opinion.

Exercises and Problems

8–15 Examine a CAFR. Utilizing the annual report obtained for Exercise 1–16, follow these instructions:

a. Agency Funds. Does the government operate a tax agency fund or participate in a tax agency fund operated by another government? Does the government act as an agent for owners of property within a special assessment district and for the creditors of those property owners? Does the government operate one or more pass-through agency funds? If so, describe.

b. Investment Trust Funds. Does the government operate, or participate in, a cash and investment pool? If so, is the pool operated as an investment trust fund? If there is a cash and investment pool and it is not reported as an investment trust fund, how is it reported? Explain.

c. Private-purpose Trust Funds. Does the government operate one or more private-purpose trust funds? If yes, explain the purpose(s).

d. Pension Trust Funds. Are the government employees covered by a retirement fund operated by the government, by the state, by the federal Social Security Administration, or by two or more of these? If the government operates one or more pension plans, or retirement systems, is a reference made to the actuary's report in the notes to the financial statements? Is a net pension liability reported in the government-wide statement of net position and/or in a proprietary fund? Is all the pension information specified by GASB standards and discussed in Chapter 8 presented in the notes to the financial statements? Are all required supplementary schedules and related notes reported in the comprehensive annual financial report?

e. Fiduciary Fund Financial Statements. Are all fiduciary funds shown in a statement of fiduciary net position and a statement of changes in fiduciary net position? Does the financial report state the basis of accounting used for trust and agency funds? Are agency funds properly disclosed in the financial statements? Does the report contain a schedule or list of investments of trust funds? Are investments reported at fair value? Is the net increase (decrease) shown separately from interest and dividend income? If trust funds own depreciable assets, is depreciation taken?

8–16 Multiple Choice. Choose the best answer.

1. Which of the following is *not* a fiduciary fund?
   a. Permanent fund.
   b. Private-purpose trust fund.
   c. Investment trust fund.
   d. Agency fund.
2. Which of the following is an example of a trust fund?
   a. A fund used to account for the collection and distribution of taxes to several local governments.
   b. A fund used to distribute scholarships to the children of the city's police officers.
   c. A fund used to account for gasoline taxes collected for road maintenance.
   d. A fund used to account for risk management services provided to other funds of the government.
3. Fiduciary fund activities are *not* included in the government-wide financial statements:
   a. Because the resources in the funds are not owned by the government.
   b. Unless the government has an interest in the fund activities.
   c. If there is no fiduciary net position in the fund.
   d. When there are offsetting liabilities.
4. Tax agency funds:
   a. Are required to account for a government's collection and remittance of federal and state payroll taxes.
   b. Are used by a county's assessor to compute the amount of taxes due on the properties contained within the county.
   c. Are used to account for the collection and distribution of taxes when one government collects taxes for multiple purposes and governments.
   d. Are not allowed to charge for the services rendered to the various governmental funds and other governments.

5. An investment trust fund should be used when:
   a. A government manages investments for multiple internal participants.
   b. A government manages investments for itself and other external entities.
   c. A government receives an endowment from a citizen where only the income from the fund may be used to support a public library.
   d. A government hires an outside investment manager.
6. The city has installed sidewalks using special assessment debt. Special assessments paid over the next 10 years will be used to retire the debt. If property owners fail to pay the assessments the city is under no obligation to pay the assessments. Debt service related to the special assessment debt used to install the sidewalks should be recorded in what fund type?
   a. Private-purpose trust fund.
   b. Debt service fund.
   c. Agency fund.
   d Capital projects fund.
7. How are agency funds reported in a CAFR?
   a. Agency funds are reported in the statement of changes in fiduciary net position.
   b. Agency funds are reported in the Governmental Activities column of the government-wide statements.
   c. Agency funds are reported in the Business-type Activities column of the government-wide statements.
   d. Governments may opt to prepare a combining statement of net position to display the assets and liabilities of individual agency funds.
8. Fiduciary funds:
   a. Are accounted for using the accrual basis of accounting.
   b. Include trust, agency, and permanent funds.
   c. Are not included in a government's CAFR since they account for assets not owned by the government.
   d. Cannot recognize investment gains until the associated investment is sold.
9. Colby City has a single pension plan for its employees, all of whose salaries and wages are paid from the General Fund. Ordinarily, the city's General Fund should report an expenditure for its annual pension cost related to a defined benefit pension plan in an amount equal to the:
   a. Actual amount contributed to the plan.
   b. Value of current year benefits.
   c. Net annual change in amounts normally expected to be liquidated with expendable available financial resources.
   d. Both *a* and *c*.
10. When the defined benefit pension obligations of several employers are combined and the accounts of the employees of each employer are separately maintained, the plan is classified as:
    a. A single-employer pension plan.
    b. A multiple-employer benefit-sharing pension plan.
    c. An agent multiple-employer pension plan.
    d. A cost-sharing multiple-employer pension plan.

8–17 Multiple Choice. Choose the best answer.

1. Which of the following financial statements is prepared by fiduciary funds?
   a. Statement of activities.
   b. Statement of net position.

c. Statement of cash flows.
d. All of the above.

2. At the government-wide level, where are fiduciary funds reported?
   a. In the Governmental Activities column.
   b. In the Business-type Activities column.
   c. As an internal balance in the total column.
   d. Fiduciary funds are not reported at the government-wide level.

Items 3 through 5 relate to the following information.

The county collects taxes on behalf of the county, city, and a special purpose district. For 2017, the taxes to be levied by the government are:

County	$ 632,000
City	917,000
Special purpose district	26,000
Total	$1,575,000

3. What type of fund will the county use to account for tax collection and distribution?
   a. The county must use a trust fund.
   b. The county must use an agency fund.
   c. The county should use a special revenue fund.
   d. Unless mandated by law, the county may use a governmental or proprietary fund; however, an agency fund is typically used.
4. On the date the taxes are levied, the county would credit which of the following accounts in the fund used to account for tax collection and distribution?
   a. Due to Other Funds and Governments.
   b. Revenues—Taxes.
   c. Additions—Other Funds and Governments.
   d. Accrued Taxes.
5. If the county assessed a 1 percent administrative fee, it would be recorded by the county as a credit to:
   a. Revenue.
   b. Transfer In.
   c. Additions—Fund Equity.
   d. Due to County.

Items 6 through 8 relate to the following information:

The city council of the City of Great Falls decided to pool the investments of its General Fund with that of Great Falls School District and Great Falls Township, each of which carried its investments at fair value as of the prior balance sheet date. All investments are revalued to current fair value at the date of the creation of the pool. At that date, the prior and current fair value of the investments of each of the participants were as follows:

	Investments	
	Prior Fair Value	**Current Fair Value**
General Fund	$ 600,000	$ 590,000
Great Falls School District	3,600,000	3,640,000
Great Falls Township	1,800,000	1,770,000
Total	$6,000,000	$6,000,000

6. At the date of the creation of the investment pool, each of the participants should:
   a. Debit its Fund Balance account and credit its Investments account for the prior fair value of the assets transferred to the pool.
   b. Debit or credit its Investments account as needed to adjust its carrying value to current fair value. The offsetting entry in each fund should be to Fund Balance.
   c. Debit Equity in Pooled Investments for the current fair value of investments pooled, credit Investments for the prior fair value of investments pooled, and credit or debit Revenues—Change in Fair Value of Investments for the difference.
   d. Make a memorandum entry only.
7. One day after creation of the pool, the investments that had belonged to Great Falls Township were sold by the pool for $1,760,000.
   a. The loss of $40,000 is borne by each participant in proportion to its equity in the pool.
   b. The loss of $10,000 is borne by each participant in proportion to its equity in the pool.
   c. The loss of $40,000 is considered to be a loss borne by Great Falls Township.
   d. The loss of $10,000 is considered to be a loss borne by Great Falls Township.
8. One month after creation of the pool, earnings on pooled investments totaled $59,900. It was decided to distribute the earnings to the participants, rounding the distribution to the nearest dollar. The Great Falls School District should receive:
   a. $36,000.
   b. $35,940.
   c. $36,339.
   d. $37,000.

Items 9 and 10 are based on the following information.

Fairview County contributes to and administers a single-employer defined benefit pension plan on behalf of its covered employees. The following information is available for the current year:

Current year benefits	$150,000
Actual amount contributed to the plan	145,000
Amortization of deferred amounts	2,500
Net annual change in amounts normally expected to be liquidated with expendable available financial resources	600
Interest on prior pension liabilities	1,250

9. If the above information was for the General Fund, the current year pension expenditure would be equal to:
   a. $145,000.
   b. $145,600.
   c. $150,000.
   d. $153,750.
10. If the above information was for a proprietary fund, the current year pension expense would be equal to:
    a. $145,000.
    b. $145,600.
    c. $150,000.
    d. $153,750.

8–18 Tax Agency Fund. The county collector of Suncoast County is responsible for collecting all property taxes levied by funds and governments within the boundaries of the county. To reimburse the county for estimated administrative expenses of operating the tax agency fund, the agency fund deducts 1.5 percent from the collections for the town, the school district, and the other town. The total amount deducted is added to the collections for the county and remitted to the Suncoast County General Fund.

The following events occurred in 2017:

1. Current-year tax levies to be collected by the agency were:

County General Fund	$10,333,000
Town of Bayshore General Fund	4,840,000
Suncoast County Consolidated School District	6,550,000
Other towns	3,120,000
Total	$24,843,000

2. $13,700,000 of current taxes was collected during the first half of 2017.
3. Liabilities to all funds and governments as a result of the first half-year collections were recorded. (A schedule of amounts collected for each participant, showing the amount withheld for the county General Fund and net amounts due the participants, is recommended for determining amounts to be recorded for this transaction.)
4. All cash in the tax agency fund was distributed.

Required

a. Make journal entries for each of the foregoing transactions that affected the tax agency fund.

b. Make journal entries for each of the foregoing transactions that affected the Suncoast County General Fund. Begin with the tax levy entry, assuming 4 percent of the gross levy will be uncollectible.

c. Make journal entries for each of the foregoing entries that affected the Town of Bayshore General Fund. Begin with the tax levy entry, assuming 2 percent of the gross levy will be uncollectible.

d. Which financial statements would be prepared by the tax agency fund?

8–19 Special Assessment Debt. Residents of Green Acres, a gated community located in the City of Foothills, voted to form a local improvement district to fund the construction of a neighborhood park. The city agreed to administer the bonded debt; however, residents of Green Acres are solely responsible for repaying the bond issue. The following events are related to the special assessment park debt:

1. On January 1, 2017, the city assessed levies totaling $5,000,000 on properties within Green Acres. The levies are payable in 10 equal annual installments, beginning in the current year, with 5 percent interest due on unpaid installments.
2. All assessments associated with the current year's installment were collected by December 31, 2017, as was the interest due on the unpaid installments. A portion of assessments receivable equal to the 2018 installment was reclassified as current.
3. On January 1, 2018, the first principal payment of $500,000 was made to bondholders as was interest on the debt.

Required

a. What type of fund should the City of Foothills use to account for the special assessment debt?

b. Make journal entries for each of the foregoing events for the city.

c. How would this fund be reported in the City of Foothills' financial statements?

d. How would the special assessment debt be recorded in the City of Foothills' financial statements?

8–20 Identification of Fiduciary Funds. Following is a list of fund names and descriptions from comprehensive annual financial reports (CAFRs).

Required

Indicate which of the following are fiduciary funds. If not a fiduciary fund, identify which type of fund should be used to account for the activities and explain why that fund is most appropriate.

a. Tri-Centennial Fund. Accounts for money raised or contributed by several local area governments and other organizations. The purpose is to ensure availability of resources to celebrate the United States Tri-Centennial in 2076.

b. Perpetual Care Fund. Accounts for endowed gifts and investment earnings dedicated to perpetual care of the city's cemeteries.

c. Poudre River Public Library District Fund. Accounts for cash and investments held by the city on behalf of Poudre River Public Library District.

d. School Impact Fee Fund. The city collects school impact fees as part of the cost of building permits issued. Money must be remitted periodically to the local school district, a legally separate government that is not a component unit of the city.

e. Cultural Services and Facilities Fund. Accounts for revenues received from the Lincoln Center performing arts facility, the city museum, and General Fund subsidies used to promote cultural activities for city residents.

f. Payroll Fund. The city has established a fund in which all payroll deductions are reported.

g. Telephone Commissions Fund. The city collects commissions on pay telephones used by jail inmates. The funds are used to provide inmates such benefits as library resources and fitness equipment.

h. Block Grant Fund. The state receives federal funds for the homeless which it passes through to local not-for-profit organizations. The only responsibility the state has is to contribute an additional amount of funds (match) to the federal grant.

i. Health Benefits Fund. The county has agreed to pay a portion of the health insurance premiums for employees when they retire. Contributions for the benefit are paid into this fund.

j. Unclaimed Property Fund. The state has established a fund to account for abandoned and unclaimed property. The property is held in the fund for 10 years. If a legal claimant to the property is not found within the 10-year time period, the property reverts to the state.

8–21 Investment Trust Fund. The Albertville City Council decided to pool the investments of its General Fund with Albertville Schools and Richwood Township in an investment pool to be managed by the city. Each of the pool participants had reported its investments at fair value as of the end of 2016. At the date of the creation of the pool, February 15, 2017, the fair value of the investments of each pool participant was as follows:

	Investments	
	12/31/16	2/15/17
City of Albertville General Fund	$ 890,000	$ 900,000
Albertville Schools	4,200,000	4,230,000
Richwood Township	3,890,000	3,870,000
Total	$8,980,000	$9,000,000

Required

a. Prepare the journal entries that should be made by the City of Albertville, Albertville Schools, and Richwood Township on February 15 to record their participation in the investment pool. (Entries for the investment pool trust fund will be made later.)

b. Prepare the journal entries to be made in the accounts of the investment pool trust fund to record the following transactions for the first year of operations:

(1) Record the investments transferred to the pool; assume that the investments of the city's General Fund were in U.S. Treasury notes and the investments of both the schools and the township were in certificates of deposit (CDs).

(2) On June 15, the Richwood Township decided to withdraw $3,010,000 for a capital projects payment. At the date of the withdrawal, the fair value of the Treasury notes has increased by $30,000. Assume that the trust fund is able to redeem the CDs necessary to complete the withdrawal without a penalty but does not receive interest on the funds.

(3) On September 15, interest on Treasury notes in the amount of $50,000 was collected.

(4) Interest on CDs accrued at year-end amounted to $28,000.

(5) At the end of the year, undistributed earnings were allocated to the investment pool participants. Assume that there were no additional changes in the fair value of investments after the Richwood Township withdrawal. Round the amount of the distribution to each fund or participant to the nearest dollar.

c. Record the June 15 increase in each of the participant's funds.

d. Record the change in each participant's Equity in Pooled Investment account due to the September 15 treasury interest and December 31 CD interest accrual.

e. Explain how the investment trust fund would report the General Fund's interest in the investment pool and the Albertville School's interest in the investment pool.

8–22 Pass-through Agency Funds. Evergreen County acts as the disbursing agent for a state grant for the performing arts. The state is responsible for determining which local governments are eligible for the grant money and for following up to ensure that the recipients comply with the requirements of the grant. The county receives the grant funds and disburses them according to the schedule provided by the state. When the county was asked to participate, the county's attorney was concerned that the county might be held responsible for any disallowed costs. The state agreed to accept responsibility for any disallowed costs, so the county decided to act as the agent for the state for this grant.

The schedule for the grant funds for 2017 is shown below.

City of Boulder	$2,100,000
Aspen Township	1,400,000
Snowton	900,000
Firtree Village	600,000
Total	$5,000,000

Required

a. Prepare the general journal entries necessary to record Evergreen County's receipt of the money on December 31, 2017 (the end of its fiscal year) and disbursement of the grant funds on January 2, 2018.

b. Prepare the general journal entries required to record Aspen Township's receipt of the funds; assume that funds are to be used to construct a new performing arts center and all time and eligibility requirements have been met.

c. Since the county received the funds prior to its fiscal year-end, but didn't disburse them until after its fiscal year-end, how would the activities related to the grant be reported in the county's financial statements?

8–23 Fiduciary Financial Statements. Ray County administers a tax agency fund, an investment trust fund, and a private-purpose trust fund. The tax agency fund acts as an agent for the county, a city within the county, and the school district within the county. Participants in the investment trust fund are the Ray County General Fund, the city, and the school district. The private-purpose trust is maintained for the benefit of a private organization located within the county. Ray County has prepared the following statement of fiduciary net position.

RAY COUNTY
Statement of Fiduciary Net Position
Fiduciary Funds
June 30, 2017
(in thousands)

	Trust Funds	Agency Funds	Total
Assets			
Cash and cash equivalents	$ 104,747	$ 788	$ 105,535
Receivables	12,166	81,858	100,024
Investments:			
Short-term investments	241,645		241,645
Bonds, notes, and stock	972,226		992,226
Capital assets, at cost	20,000	6,000	
Total assets	1,350,784	88,646	1,439,430
Liabilities			
Accounts payable	61,447		61,447
Capital lease obligation		6,000	6,000
Net Assets			
Held in trust for:			
Organizations	193,400		193,400
County	219,187	10,638	229,825
City of Leetown	383,578	22,048	406,626
Leetown School District	493,172	50,960	548,132
Total net position	$1,289,337	$88,646	$1,377,983

Required

The statement as presented is not in accordance with GASB standards. Using Illustration A2–10 as an example, identify the errors (problems) in the statement and explain how the errors should be corrected.

8–24 Pension calculations. Bluff County's schedule of changes in net pension liability and related ratios is shown below.

Required

Compute the missing amounts.

BLUFF COUNTY EMPLOYEE RETIREMENT SYSTEM
Schedule of Changes in the County's Net Pension Liability and Related Ratios
Last Three Fiscal Years

	2017	2016	2015
Total pension liability			
Service cost	$ 123,225	$ 125,440	$ 127,950
Interest	(a)	182,580	169,960
Differences between expected and actual experience	1,250	(850)	625
Benefit payments (including refunds of employee contributions)	(248,000)	(g)	(217,960)
Net change in total pension liability	66,205	75,590	(o)
Total pension liability, beginning	2,083,715	(h)	1,927,550
Total pension liability, ending	(b)	(i)	(p)
Plan fiduciary net position			
Contributions—employee	$ 32,450	$ 36,240	(q)
Contributions—employer	98,620	102,530	91,550
Net investment income	18,990	(j)	(21,510)
Benefit payments (including refunds of employee contributions)	(64,500)	(42,780)	(51,330)
Administrative expenses	(3,290)	(3,110)	(2,840)
Net change in plan fiduciary net position	(c)	80,500	(r)
Plan fiduciary net position, beginning	(d)	(k)	1,011,680
Plan fiduciary net position, ending	1,220,490	(l)	1,057,720
Net pension liability, ending	$ 929,430	(m)	(s)
Plan fiduciary net position as a percentage of total pension liability	(e)	45.38%	47.33%
Covered-employee payroll	(f)	(n)	$ 489,810
Net pension liability as a percentage of covered-employee payroll	185.09%	194.86%	(t)

Chapter Nine

Financial Reporting of State and Local Governments

Learning Objectives

After studying this chapter, you should be able to:

9-1 Describe the concepts related to the financial reporting requirements of the GASB reporting model.

9-2 Explain the key concepts and terms used in describing the governmental reporting entity.

9-3 Apply the GASB criteria used to determine whether a potential component unit should be included in the reporting entity and, when included, the manner of reporting component units.

9-4 Identify and describe the contents of a comprehensive annual financial report (CAFR).

9-5 Prepare governmental fund financial statements and government-wide financial statements and understand how to reconcile the two.

9-6 Identify and explain financial reporting issues and topics.

Chapters 2 through 8 present extended discussions of the principles of accounting for governmental, proprietary, and fiduciary funds and governmental and business-type activities at the government-wide level. Chapters 1 and 2 provide overviews of Governmental Accounting Standards Board (GASB) financial reporting requirements, and financial reporting requirements for specific fund types are discussed in several chapters. This chapter presents the reporting requirements in more depth and discusses other governmental financial accounting issues and topics of interest to the reader. Prior to examining reporting requirements, a brief conceptual discussion of financial reporting is provided.

PROVIDING USEFUL FINANCIAL REPORTS

GASB *Concepts Statement 1*[1] identifies two objectives of government financial reports: to provide information that can be used to assess a government's accountability and to assist users in making economic, social, and political decisions. The primary

[1] Governmental Accounting Standards Board, *Codification of Governmental Accounting and Financial Reporting Standards as of June 30, 2014* (Norwalk, CT, 2014), Appendix B.

users of government financial reports are those external to government; principally, citizens, legislative and oversight bodies, and creditors. For the financial reports to be useful in meeting identified objectives, the GASB indicates that the information provided in the reports should be understandable, reliable, relevant, timely, consistent, and comparable.

An important part of providing useful information is communicating the information in a manner that is helpful to the user. GASB *Concepts Statement 3* provides guidance regarding where and how items of information should appear in financial reports to be the most useful.[2] The areas identified for communicating items of information are recognition in the financial statements, disclosures in the notes to the financial statements, presentation as required supplementary information, or presentation as supplementary information. The GASB indicates that an item of information that meets the definition of an element and is measurable with sufficient reliability should be recognized in the financial statements. A note should be used if it can help support an item recognized in a financial statement or provide information that is essential to the user's understanding of the item. An example of the relationship between recognized items and notes can be conveyed with the Investments account. Without a note disclosure relating information on fair values and risk exposure, the user is left without information that is relevant in assessing the quality and management of the government's investments.

Required supplementary information (RSI) and supplementary information are used to communicate information that is essential and useful, respectively. Without RSI the financial statements and related notes cannot be placed in the correct context. Examples of RSI include the budget to actual schedules (Chapter 3) and several pension disclosures (Chapter 8). Other supplementary information is useful but not essential in understanding the financial statements and related notes. Much of the supplementary information is found in the statistical section of the comprehensive annual financial report (CAFR).

As indicated, before an item can be recognized in the financial statements it must meet the definition of an element. GASB *Concept Statement 4* identifies the seven financial statement elements.[3] The elements (defined in Chapter 2) are assets, liabilities, deferred outflows of resources, deferred inflows of resources, net position, outflows of resources, and inflows of resources. Since governments use two bases of accounting, the GASB defines the elements in terms that will allow for recognition under both modified accrual and accrual accounting. For example, an outflow of resources can mean an expenditure or an expense.

GASB concept statements primarily serve the needs of standard-setters, providing them with guidance in writing standards that form the basis for the type and display of information found in the financial reports discussed in the remainder of the chapter.

THE GOVERNMENTAL REPORTING ENTITY

The average citizen—including accountants whose only experience has been with business organizations—has only a vague knowledge and little understanding of the overlapping layers of general purpose and special purpose governments that have some jurisdiction over us wherever we may live and work. Illustration 8–1,

[2] GASB, *Codification,* Appendix B.

[3] Ibid.

for example, shows that different levels of general purpose governments can levy taxes on property. The school funds in that illustration show that taxes are also levied by special purpose governments (an independent school district in that illustration). Omitted from the illustration, for the sake of brevity, are taxes levied by any *special districts.* Special districts are defined by the Bureau of the Census as "all organized local entities (other than counties, municipalities, townships, or school districts) authorized by state law to provide only one or a limited number of designated functions, and with sufficient administrative and fiscal autonomy to qualify as separate governments."[4] About 42.5 percent of the local governments in the United States are classified as special districts.[5]

Although the Census definition stresses the independence of special districts, in many instances they were created as a means to finance the services demanded by residents of a general purpose government. The services demanded could not be financed by the general purpose government because of constitutional or statutory limits on the rates or amounts the general purpose government could raise from taxes, other revenue sources, and debt. Building authorities are examples of special districts created to finance general purpose government projects.

In addition to independent special districts, certain governmental activities are commonly carried out by commissions, boards, and other agencies that are not considered as independent of a general purpose government by the Bureau of the Census but that may have some degree of fiscal and administrative independence from the governing board of the general purpose government. In past years, some governments included in their annual reports the financial statements of such semi-independent boards and commissions and even certain of the special districts, whereas other governments excluded them.

To improve uniformity in reporting and to promote the preparation of financial reports consistent with GASB *Concepts Statement 1,* the GASB *Codification,* Section 2100 provides authoritative guidance on defining the reporting entity, and Section 2600 presents guidance on reporting entity and component unit presentations and disclosure. The GASB *Codification,* Section 2100 also provides guidance for reporting certain affiliated organizations, such as fund-raising foundations. These sections provide the basis for the following discussion.

Defining the Financial Reporting Entity

Elected officials of state and local governments (*primary governments*) are accountable to their constituents. That accountability extends not only to the financial performance of the primary government, but also to any organizations that are financially dependent on the primary government or over which the primary government can impose its will. Thus, GASB takes the position that governmental financial reporting should report on all governments and organizations for which elected officials are accountable. Collectively, these governments and organizations are referred to as the *financial reporting entity*. Before proceeding further with the explanation of a financial reporting entity, it is important to more formally define the terms *primary government* and *financial reporting entity.*

As defined by the GASB, a **primary government** is a state government or general purpose local government. It can also be a special purpose government that has a separately elected governing body, is *legally separate*, and is *fiscally independent* of other state or local governments. A legally separate organization has an identity of its own as an "artificial person" with a personality and existence distinct from that of its

[4] http://www.census.gov/govs/local/definitions.html#s

[5] http://www.census.gov/govs/cog2012/

creator and others. A fiscally independent organization has the authority to determine its budget, levy its own taxes, set rates or charges, and issue bonded debt without approval of another government.

The GASB defines a **financial reporting entity** as the primary government and organizations for which the primary government is *financially accountable*. A primary government may also need to include an organization that does not meet the financial accountability criteria in order to prevent the financial statements from being misleading. Such an organization should be included as a *component unit.*

As seen in the preceding definition, a primary government is generally the basis for the financial reporting entity. However, other types of governments can also be the basis for a financial reporting entity if they issue separate financial statements. Examples of other types of governments that may serve as their own reporting entity are component units, government joint ventures, jointly governed organizations, or other stand-alone governments.

A primary government is **financially accountable** for another organization if the primary government appoints a voting majority of the organization's governing board and it is (*a*) able to impose its will on the organization *or* (*b*) there is a potential for the organization to provide specific financial benefits to, or impose specific financial burdens on, the primary government. The ability of the primary government to impose its will on an organization exists if the primary government can significantly influence the programs, projects, or activities of, or the level of services performed or provided by, the organization. Examples of activities that indicate significant influence is being exerted could include removing an organization's board members at will, modifying or approving an organization's budget or fee structures, overruling or modifying decisions made by an organization's governing body, and the hiring/dismissing of an organization's management. A financial benefit or burden relationship exists if the primary government *(a)* is entitled to the organization's resources; *(b)* is legally obligated or otherwise assumes the obligation to finance the deficits of, or provide financial support to, the organization; or *(c)* is obligated in some manner for the debt of the organization.

The primary government is also financially accountable for another organization if the organization is *fiscally dependent* on the primary government. A **fiscally dependent** organization is one that provides specific financial benefits to, or imposes specific financial burdens on, the primary government. Under these circumstances the primary government is considered financially accountable regardless of whether the organization has a separately elected governing board, a governing board appointed by another level of government, or a jointly appointed board.[6]

Component Units

Component units are included as part of the reporting entity. A **component unit** is defined as a legally separate organization for which the elected officials of the primary government are financially accountable. A component unit can also be another organization for which the nature and significance of its relationship with the primary government is so important that excluding it from the reporting entity's financial statements would make the statements misleading. Examples of component units include not-for-profit organizations, for-profit firms, or a nonprimary government. Because the reporting entity must include the component unit's financial information in its financial statements, the GASB has provided that the information can be included by blending the information or discretely presenting the information.

[6] GASB, *Codification*, Sec. 2100.133.

ILLUSTRATION 9–1 Decision Process for Inclusion or Exclusion of Potential Component Unit (PCU)

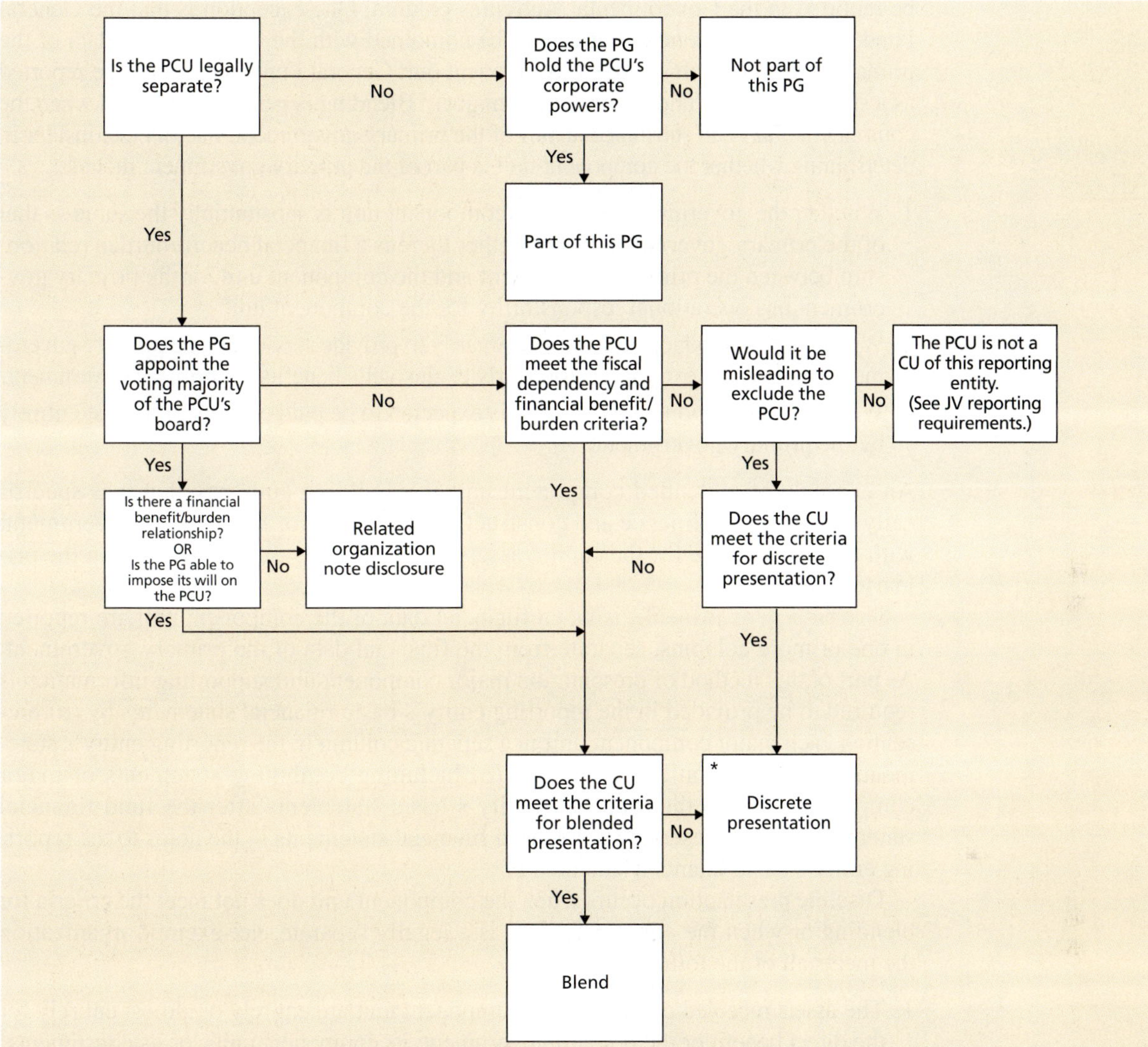

Legend: PCU = potential component unit; PG = primary government; CU = component unit; JV = joint venture
Source: Adapted from GASB, *Codification*, Sec. 2100.901.

Professional judgment is required to determine whether an organization should be included as a component unit. To assist management with this determination the GASB has developed the flowchart in Illustration 9–1. In addition to assisting in determining whether a component unit should be included in the financial statements, the flowchart also assists in determining whether the component unit information should be blended or discretely presented.

Blended presentation is when the component unit's financial data for its funds and activities are reported with the same fund types and activities of the primary government. For example, if a component unit has special revenue funds the funds should be reported in the same manner as special revenue funds for the primary government. A separate column should be used in the governmental funds financial statements if the fund is considered major; if the fund is not major it should be aggregated with other nonmajor funds. At the government-wide level the component unit special revenue fund data should be reported in the Governmental Activities column. One exception is that the General Fund data of a component unit cannot be combined with the General Fund data of the primary government. Instead, the component unit General Fund data should be reported as a special revenue fund (major or nonmajor).[7] Blending is generally required when the component unit is, in substance, a part of the primary government. Factors to consider in determining whether the component unit is part of the primary government include:

1. Whether the governing body of the component unit is substantially the same as that of the primary government, and whether there is a financial benefit/burden relationship between the primary government and the component unit, or the primary government has operational responsibility for the component unit.
2. Whether the component unit exists primarily to provide services to the primary government or otherwise exclusively, or nearly exclusively, benefits the primary government.
3. Whether the component unit's debt is expected to be paid entirely or almost entirely by the primary government.[8]

An example of a blended component unit is a building authority that was specifically established to finance and construct capital assets for the primary government, with the debt service for the capital assets provided by lease payments from the primary government.

Discrete presentation is when financial data of the component unit are reported in one or more columns, separate from the financial data of the primary government. As part of this method of presentation major component unit supporting information is required to be provided in the reporting entity's basic financial statements by *(a)* presenting each major component unit in a separate column in the reporting entity's statements of net position and activities, *(b)* including combining statements of major component units in the reporting entity's basic statements after the fund financial statements, or *(c)* presenting condensed financial statements in the notes to the reporting entity's basic financial statements.

Discrete presentation occurs when the component unit does not meet the criteria for blending or when the component unit is a legally separate, tax-exempt organization the meets all of the following criteria:

1. The assets received or held by the component unit are entirely or almost entirely for the direct benefit of the primary government, its component units, or its constituents.
2. The primary government, or its component units, is entitled to, or has the ability to otherwise access, a majority of the assets received or held by the component unit and these assets are significant to the primary government.
3. The assets received or held by an *individual organization* that the specific primary government, or its component units, is entitled to or has the ability to otherwise access are significant to the primary government.[9]

The term *major component unit* is not the same as *major fund.* A major component unit is determined by the nature and significance of its relationship to the primary government.[10] Factors to be considered in determining whether a component unit is

[7] GASB, *Codification,* Sec. 2600.114.

[8] GASB, *Codification*, Sec. 2600.113.

[9] GASB, *Codification*, Sec. 2100.140.

[10] GASB, *Codification*, Sec. 2600.108.

major include its financial relationship to the primary government and the importance of the component unit's services to the citizens.

The notes to the financial statements should contain a brief description of the component units of the financial reporting entity and the component units' relationships to the primary government. This disclosure should also explain the rationale for including the component units and whether the units are blended, discretely presented, or included in the fiduciary fund statements. Information about major component units may be presented in the condensed financial statements within the notes or in the combining statements that provide a separate column for each component unit, along with a total column for all component units. The notes should also include information about how separate financial statements for individual component units may be obtained. Those readers interested in more detailed information about component units are referred to GASB *Codification*, Section 2600.

Reporting by Other Government Organizations

The financial reporting information in the remainder of the chapter is provided from the perspective that the financial reporting entity is composed of a primary government and its component units. However, the information would also apply to other government organizations that issue separate financial reports. Examples of such organizations would include governmental joint ventures, jointly governed organizations, and other stand-alone governments. Additionally, if a component unit chooses to provide financial statements separately from the financial reporting entity of which it is a part, it would also rely on the information provided in this chapter. To aid in understanding the other types of government organizations that could issue separate financial reports, definitions of the organizations are provided in the next three paragraphs.

A **joint venture** is a legal entity or other organization that results from a contractual arrangement and that is owned, operated, or governed by two or more participants as a separate and specific activity subject to joint control, in which the participants retain *(a)* an ongoing financial interest or *(b)* an ongoing financial responsibility.[11] A government might enter into a joint venture to pool resources and share the risks and rewards of a project.

Like a joint venture a **jointly governed organization** is governed by representatives from each of the governments that create the organization. However, unlike a joint venture the participants do not have an ongoing financial interest or responsibility in the organization.

An **other stand-alone government** is a legally separate governmental organization that *(a)* does not have a separately elected governing body and *(b)* does not meet the definition of a component unit. By definition, joint ventures and jointly governed organizations would be considered other stand-alone governments. However, some special purpose governments could also meet the definition.

GOVERNMENTAL FINANCIAL REPORTS

Once the reporting entity has been determined in accordance with the criteria discussed in the preceding section, persons responsible for preparing financial reports for the reporting entity should follow the guidance given in currently effective authoritative literature to determine the content of financial reports to be issued for external users. Chapter 2 contains a summary of the standards set forth for the content of the comprehensive

[11] GASB, *Codification*, Sec. J50.102.

annual financial report (CAFR) of a state or local governmental reporting entity. Chapters 3 through 8 elaborate on the application of those standards to accounting and financial reporting for each of the funds and government-wide activities. Although much of the discussion in preceding chapters concerns general purpose external financial reporting, the needs of administrators, legislators, and other users not properly classifiable as "external" have been given some attention. In the following paragraphs, the discussion in preceding chapters is briefly summarized and placed in perspective.

Need for Periodic Reports

Individuals concerned with the day-to-day operations and activities of governmental funds should be familiar with much of the data processed by the accounting information system because it results from the events and transactions with which they are involved. However, it is easy for these individuals to become overconfident of their understanding of the data with which they are daily involved. Past events are not always as remembered, and the relative significance of events changes over time. Similarly, administrators at succeedingly higher levels in the organization may feel that participation in decision making and observation of the apparent results of past decisions make it unnecessary to conduct periodic analysis of accounting and statistical reports prepared objectively and with neutrality. The memory and perceptions of administrators at higher levels are also subject to failure. Therefore, it is generally agreed that it is useful for financial reports to be prepared and distributed at intervals throughout a fiscal period as well as at period-end.

Interim Financial Reports

Government administrators have the greatest need for interim financial reports, although members of the legislative branch of the government (particularly those on its finance committee) may also find interim reports useful. Although the particular statements and schedules that should be prepared on an interim basis are a matter of local management preference, the authors believe the following interim schedules provide the minimum useful information for budgetary and cash management purposes.

1. Schedule of actual and budgeted revenue (for the General Fund and special revenue funds and other funds for which budgets have been legally adopted).
2. Schedule of actual and budgeted expenditures (for the General Fund and special revenue funds and other funds for which budgets have been legally adopted).
3. Comparative schedule of revenue and expense (for each enterprise and internal service fund).
4. Combined schedule of cash receipts, disbursements, and balances—all funds.
5. Forecast of cash positions—all funds.

Other statements and schedules, in addition to those just listed, may be needed, depending on the complexity and scope of a government's activities. A statement of investments held and their cost and fair values is an example of an additional statement that may be useful. Schedules of past-due receivables from taxes, special assessments, and utility customers may also be needed at intervals. Interim reports of government-wide activities can be done only if the information system can capture the information.

Complete interim reports should be prepared and distributed at regular intervals throughout a fiscal period, generally monthly, although small governments that have little financial activity may find a bimonthly or quarterly period satisfactory. Partial interim reports dealing with those items of considerable current importance should be prepared and distributed as frequently as their information would be of value. For example, reports of the fair values of investments and of purchases and sales may be needed by a relatively small number of users on a daily basis during certain critical periods.

Annual Financial Reports

Governmental annual financial reports are needed by the same individuals and groups receiving interim reports. They are also often required to be distributed to agencies of higher governmental jurisdictions and to major creditors. Other users include citizens and citizen groups; news media; financial underwriters; debt insurers; debt rating agencies; debt analysts; libraries; other governments; associations of governmental administrators, accountants, and finance officers; and college professors and students.

Most larger governments prepare a comprehensive annual financial report (CAFR). The CAFR is the government's official annual report prepared and published as a matter of public record. A CAFR provides information beyond the minimum requirements of general purpose external financial reporting, which includes management's discussion and analysis (MD&A), basic government-wide and fund financial statements and related notes, and required supplementary information (RSI). In addition, the CAFR includes individual fund and combining financial statements, schedules, narrative explanations, a statistical section, and other material management deems relevant. For CAFRs containing audited financial statements, the auditor's report should also be included.

Introductory Section

As discussed in Chapter 1, the introductory section of a CAFR generally includes the table of contents, a letter of transmittal, and other material deemed appropriate by management.

The letter of transmittal should cite legal and policy requirements for the report. The introductory section may also include a summary discussion of factors relating to the government's service programs and financial matters. Matters discussed in the introductory section should not duplicate those discussed in the MD&A. Because the MD&A is part of the information reviewed (but not audited) by the auditor, it presents information based only on facts known to exist as of the reporting date. Since the introductory section is generally not covered by the auditor's report, it may present information of a more subjective nature, including prospective information such as forecasts or expectations.

Financial Section

The financial section should contain sufficient information to disclose fully and present fairly the financial position and results of financial operations during the fiscal year. The GASB *Codification,* Section 2200 identifies the minimum content for the financial section of a CAFR as consisting of the:

1. Auditor's report (discussed in Chapter 11)
2. MD&A
3. Basic financial statements
   a. Government-wide financial statements
      (1) Statement of net position (see Illustration A2–1)
      (2) Statement of activities (see Illustration A2–2)
   b. Fund financial statements
      (1) Governmental funds
         (a) Balance sheet (see Illustration A2–3)
         (b) Statement of revenues, expenditures, and changes in fund balances (see Illustration A2–5)

(2) Proprietary funds
   (a) Statement of net position (see Illustration A2–7)
   (b) Statement of revenues, expenses, and changes in fund net position (see Illustration A2–8)
   (c) Statement of cash flows (see Illustration A2–9)
(3) Fiduciary funds (including component units that are fiduciary in nature)
   (a) Statement of fiduciary net position (see Illustration A2–10)
   (b) Statement of changes in fiduciary net position (see Illustration A2–11)

c. Notes to the financial statements

4. Required supplementary information other than MD&A, including, but not limited to, the budgetary comparison schedule (see Illustration 3–5) and defined benefit pension plan schedules (see illustrations in Chapter 8)
5. Combining statements and individual fund statements and schedules[12]

State and local governments may provide in the financial section of the CAFR combining financial statements for nonmajor funds of each fund type and individual fund statements for the General Fund or for a nonmajor fund that is the only fund of a given type (for example, a debt service fund that is the only fund of that type). The GASB requires that all "lower" level statements, such as combining statements, be prepared and displayed in the same manner as "higher" level statements, such as the governmental funds financial statements.

Examples of all required basic financial statements were provided in Chapter 2; however, no example is provided in Chapter 2 for an MD&A. An example of an MD&A from the City and County of Denver is presented as Appendix B of this chapter. As shown in Appendix B, the MD&A should provide an overview of the government's financial activities and financial highlights for the year. The MD&A should provide a narrative explanation of the contents of the CAFR, including the nature of the government-wide and fund financial statements, and the distinctions between those statements. The remainder of the MD&A should describe the government's financial condition, financial trends of the government as a whole and of its major funds, budgetary highlights, and activities affecting capital assets and related debt. Finally, the MD&A should discuss economic factors, budget, and tax rates for the next year.

Statistical Section

In addition to the output of the accounting information system presented in the financial section of the governmental annual report, statistical information reflecting social and economic data, financial trends, and the fiscal capacity of the government are needed by users interested in obtaining a better understanding of the activity and condition of the government. The GASB indicates that generally the statistical section should present information in five categories to assist the user in understanding and assessing a government's economic condition.[13] To be most useful, the 10 most recent years of data should generally be included (unless otherwise indicated) in the schedules used to meet the requirements of the five categories defined by the GASB. Following are descriptions of the five categories.

1. **Financial trends information** provides the user with information that is helpful in understanding and assessing how a government's financial position has changed

[12] A combining statement has columns for all funds included on the statement; for example a combining statement for nonmajor enterprise funds would list each nonmajor enterprise fund in a separate column. See the City and County of Denver's CAFR for examples (*http://www.denvergov.org/Default.aspx?alias=www.denvergov.org/finance*).

[13] GASB, *Codification,* Sec. 2800.

over time. Schedules in this category are prepared at both the fund level and government-wide level. The focus is on showing the trend in fund balances and net position categories, including changes in net position and fund balances.

2. **Revenue capacity information** assists the user with understanding and assessing the government's ability to generate its own revenues (own-source revenues), such as property taxes and user charges. The schedules presented should focus on the government's most significant own-source revenues. Suggested schedules provide information on the revenue base (sources of revenue), revenue rates (including overlapping tax rate information), the principal revenue payors, and property tax levy and collection information.
3. **Debt capacity information** is useful in understanding and assessing the government's existing debt burden and its ability to issue additional debt. Four types of debt schedules are recommended—ratios of outstanding debt to total personal income of residents, information about direct and overlapping debt, legal debt limitations and margins, and information about pledged revenues.
4. **Demographic and economic information** assists the user in understanding the socioeconomic environment in which the government operates and provides information that can be compared over time and across governments. Governments should present demographic and economic information that will be most relevant to users, such as information on personal income, unemployment rates, and employers.
5. **Operating information** is intended to provide a context in which the government's operations and resources can be better understood. This information is also intended to assist users of financial statements in understanding and assessing the government's financial condition. At a minimum, three schedules of operating information should be presented—number of government employees, indicators of demand or level of service (*operating indicators*), and capital asset information.

Some of the information in the statistical section has been discussed previously. For example, the computation of legal debt limit, legal debt margin, and direct and overlapping debt and future debt service requirements, are all illustrated and discussed in Chapter 6. Other information listed by the GASB as recommended for presentation in the statistical section of the CAFR is generally self-explanatory.

PREPARATION OF BASIC FINANCIAL STATEMENTS

The basic financial statements that must be presented to meet minimum general purpose external financial reporting requirements were listed earlier in this chapter. Although examples of the basic statements of the City and County of Denver are provided in the appendix of Chapter 2, it is instructive to illustrate preparation of those statements for the Town of Brighton, the hypothetical town used for illustrative purposes in several of the preceding chapters. The prior chapters provided illustrative journal entries for fund and government-wide activities for the fiscal year ending December 31, 2017, as follows:

Chapter	Illustrative Entries for
4	General Fund/governmental activities
5	Capital projects fund/governmental activities
6	Serial bond debt service fund/governmental activities
	Term bond debt service fund/governmental activities
7	Supplies fund (an internal service fund)
	Water utility fund (an enterprise fund)

Recall from Chapter 7 that the Business-type Activities column of the government-wide statements simply reports information for the enterprise funds (internal service fund information is reported in the Governmental Activities column). Further, enterprise funds report using the same measurement focus (flow of economic resources) and basis of accounting (accrual) as the government-wide financial statements. Thus, unlike governmental activities, which use a different measurement focus and basis of accounting than governmental funds, there is no need for a separate set of accounting records to record government-wide business-type transactions. The accounting information reported in enterprise funds can easily be aggregated for reporting at the government-wide level. Since, in the case of the Town of Brighton, the water utility fund is the only enterprise fund, its financial information will simply be reported in the Business-type Activities column of the government-wide financial statements. Internal service funds also use the same measurement focus and basis of accounting as the government-wide financial statements. However, internal service funds are generally reported in the Governmental Activities column. Recall that in Chapter 7 entries were made at both the fund level and the government-wide level to simplify reporting and to avoid double counting transactions (recording in the governmental fund and internal service fund) when reporting at the government-wide level.

The Governmental Activities column of the government-wide financial statements for the Town of Brighton, presented later in this section, includes all pertinent financial information, other than budget related, arising from transactions of the General Fund, the capital projects fund, the two debt service funds, and the internal service fund. In addition, the direct expenses of the functions reported in the statement of activities include depreciation on general capital assets assigned to those functions. If general capital assets are shared by functions of government, depreciation is allocated to the functions on a rational basis, such as square footage of usage for functions that share public buildings.

All changes in government-wide net position that occurred due to transactions during fiscal year 2017 in the General Fund, capital projects fund, serial bond debt service fund, term bond debt service fund, and internal service fund are reflected in the pre-closing general ledger trial balance for governmental activities presented in Illustration 9–2. The amounts shown for certain accounts are assumed amounts that reflect many transactions that were not illustrated in Chapter 4.

Before preparing the government-wide financial statements, an adjusting entry should be made to record fiscal year 2017 depreciation expense for the general capital assets, as well as other appropriate adjusting entries. Using assumed amounts for depreciation and assuming that depreciation is assigned to functions in the amounts shown, the journal entry to record the adjusting entry for depreciation in the governmental activities general journal is as follows:

	Debits	Credits
Governmental Activities:		
Expenses—General Government	114,746	
Expenses—Public Safety	229,493	
Expenses—Public Works	672,288	
Expenses—Health and Welfare	95,622	
Expenses—Culture and Recreation	133,871	
Accumulated Depreciation—Buildings		527,240
Accumulated Depreciation—Equipment		428,980
Accumulated Depreciation—Improvements Other than Buildings		289,800

ILLUSTRATION 9–2

TOWN OF BRIGHTON
Pre-closing Trial Balance
Governmental Activities General Ledger December 31, 2017

	Debits	*Credits*
Cash	$ 239,363	
Taxes Receivable—Delinquent	706,413	
Allowance for Uncollectible Delinquent Taxes		$ 126,513
Interest and Penalties Receivable	13,191	
Allowance for Uncollectible Interest and Penalties		3,091
Inventory of Supplies	69,100	
Investments	83,316	
Land	1,239,600	
Buildings	15,545,248	
Accumulated Depreciation—Buildings		10,971,847
Equipment	6,404,477	
Accumulated Depreciation—Equipment		4,063,944
Improvements Other than Buildings	16,693,626	
Accumulated Depreciation—Improvements Other than Buildings		5,148,162
Vouchers Payable		434,400
Interest Payable		40,500
Due to Federal Government		126,520
Due to State Government		39,740
Internal Balances		128,500
Current Portion of Long-term Debt		60,000
Bonds Payable		2,640,000
Net Position—Net Investment in Capital Assets		17,830,018
Net Position—Restricted for Debt Service		77,884
Net Position—Unrestricted		453,900
Program Revenues—General Government—Charges for Services		238,200
Program Revenues—General Government—Operating Grants and Contributions		1,000
Program Revenues—Public Safety—Charges for Services		186,480
Program Revenues—Public Works—Charges for Services		124,320
Program Revenues—Culture and Recreation—Charges for Services		82,464
Program Revenues—Public Safety—Operating Grants and Contributions		100,000
Program Revenues—Health and Welfare—Operating Grants and Contributions		184,100
Program Revenues—Public Safety—Capital Grants and Contributions		300,000
General Revenues—Property Taxes		2,599,636
General Revenues—Sales Taxes		485,000
General Revenues—Interest and Penalties on Delinquent Taxes		11,400
General Revenues—Miscellaneous		3,400
General Revenues—Property Taxes—Restricted for Debt Service		117,000
General Revenues—Sales Taxes—Restricted for Debt Service		31,200
General Revenues—Investment Earnings—Restricted for Debt Service		3,145
Expenses—General Government	839,481	
Expenses—Public Safety	1,517,817	
Expenses—Public Works	1,654,736	
Expenses—Health and Welfare	944,884	
Expenses—Culture and Recreation	546,112	
Expenses—Interest on Notes Payable	1,000	
Expenses—Interest on Long-term Debt	114,000	
Totals	$46,612,364	$46,612,364

The pre-closing trial balance presented in Illustration 9–2 provides all of the information needed for the Governmental Activities column of the government-wide financial statements, including the effects of the preceding adjusting entry for depreciation.

Illustrative closing entries for the temporary accounts of the governmental activities were deferred in earlier chapters. The complete closing entry to close all temporary accounts of the governmental activities general ledger is given as follows:

	Debits	Credits
Governmental Activities:		
Program Revenues—General Government—Charges for Services	238,200	
Program Revenues—General Government—Operating Grants and Contributions	1,000	
Program Revenues—Public Safety—Charges for Services	186,480	
Program Revenues—Public Works—Charges for Services	124,320	
Program Revenues—Culture and Recreation—Charges for Services	82,464	
Program Revenues—Public Safety—Operating Grants and Contributions	100,000	
Program Revenues—Health and Welfare—Operating Grants and Contributions	184,100	
Program Revenues—Public Safety—Capital Grants and Contributions	300,000	
General Revenues—Property Taxes	2,599,636	
General Revenues—Sales Taxes	485,000	
General Revenues—Interest and Penalties on Delinquent Taxes	11,400	
General Revenues—Miscellaneous	3,400	
General Revenues—Property Taxes—Restricted for Debt Service	117,000	
General Revenues—Sales Taxes—Restricted for Debt Service	31,200	
General Revenues—Investment Earnings—Restricted for Debt Service	3,145	
Net Position—Unrestricted	1,150,685	
Expenses—General Government		839,481
Expenses—Public Safety		1,517,817
Expenses—Public Works		1,654,736
Expenses—Health and Welfare		944,884
Expenses—Culture and Recreation		546,112
Expenses—Interest on Notes Payable		1,000
Expenses—Interest on Long-term Debt		114,000

In addition to the closing entry just shown, entries are required to reclassify the three net position accounts to their correct amounts as of December 31, 2017. A comparison of the pre-closing trial balance (see Illustration 9–2) to the Governmental

Activities column of the statement of net position as of December 31, 2016 (see Illustration 4–1), shows that the balances of the two accounts Net Position—Net Investment in Capital Assets and Net Position—Restricted for Debt Service in the pre-closing trial balance are the same as those reported at the end of the prior year. The fact that the balances are the same tells the reader that these accounts have not yet been updated to reflect changes in either general capital asset transactions and related debt or changes in net position restricted for debt service.

From the information in the trial balance, the total amount of capital assets, net of accumulated depreciation, as of December 31, 2017, is calculated as $19,698,998. Therefore, the correct balance of Net Position—Net Investment in Capital Assets is $16,998,998 ($19,698,998, less related debt of $2,700,000), a decrease of $831,020 during the year. During the year capital debt increased by $1,200,000 (from $1,500,000 to $2,700,000) and accumulated depreciation increased $1,254,020 (including $8,000 on internal service fund depreciable assets). The increase in debt and the increase in accumulated depreciation would decrease the account Net Position—Net Investment in Capital Assets a total of $2,454,020. Yet it has already been shown that the value of the account only decreased $831,020; therefore, there must have been asset acquisitions of $1,623,000 ($2,454,020 in decreases adjusted for $1,623,000 in increases equals $831,020). The amount $1,623,000 can be verified by analyzing the transactions showing that the Town of Brighton Fire Station (see Entry 15 in Chapter 5) was completed during the year at a cost of $1,493,000, and $130,000 of capital assets were acquired by the internal service fund (see Entry 2b in Chapter 7).

Based on the assets reported in the combined debt service funds balance sheet presented in Illustration 6–9, assets reported in the governmental activities trial balance must include amounts totaling $124,229 for cash, investments, and taxes receivable that are restricted for debt service. However, accrued interest payable of $40,500 will be paid from these assets. Thus, the correct balance for Net Position—Restricted for Debt Service as of December 31, 2017, must be $83,729 ($124,229 less $40,500), an increase of $5,845 from its current balance of $77,884.

Based on the foregoing analysis, the journal entries to reclassify the governmental activities net position accounts to the appropriate amounts are given as:

	Debits	Credits
Governmental Activities:		
Net Position—Net Investment in Capital Assets	831,020	
Net Position—Unrestricted		831,020
Net Position—Unrestricted	5,845	
Net Position—Restricted for Debt Service		5,845

The Town of Brighton's government-wide statement of net position and statement of activities are presented in Illustrations 9–3 and 9–4. Compared with the trial balance shown in Illustration 9–2, it is apparent that the financial statements are highly condensed. For example, taxes receivable, interest and penalties receivable, and interest receivable are reported as a single receivables amount, net of related estimated uncollectible amounts. Detail of the receivables and uncollectibles should be disclosed in the notes to the financial statements. Similarly, because the detail of capital assets, including depreciation expense and accumulated depreciation, should be disclosed in the notes to the financial statements, it is acceptable to report the aggregate net amount

ILLUSTRATION 9–3

TOWN OF BRIGHTON
Statement of Net Position
December 31, 2017

	Primary Government			
	Governmental Activities	**Business-type Activities**	**Total**	**Component Units (None)**
Assets				
Cash	$ 239,363	$ 13,655	$ 253,018	
Receivables (net)	590,000	77,900	667,900	
Investments	83,316	696,000	779,316	
Inventory of supplies	69,100	24,700	93,800	
Capital assets (net)	19,698,998	2,983,050	22,682,048	
Total assets	20,680,777	3,795,305	24,476,082	
Liabilities				
Vouchers payable and accrued liabilities	641,160	62,815	703,975	
Internal balances	128,500	(128,500)	-0-	
Current portion of long-term debt	60,000		60,000	
Bonds payable	2,640,000	1,745,230	4,385,230	
Total liabilities	3,469,660	1,679,545	5,149,205	
Net Position				
Net investment in capital assets	16,998,998	1,237,820	18,236,818	
Restricted for debt service	83,729	682,025	765,754	
Unrestricted	128,390	195,915	324,305	
Total net position	$17,211,117	$2,115,760	$19,326,877	

for capital assets on a single line. The town has also decided to report all current liabilities, except for the current portion of long-term debt, as a single amount for vouchers payable and accrued liabilities. Such highly condensed reporting is consistent with the GASB's objective to "enhance the understandability and usefulness of the general purpose external financial reports of state and local governments" by providing an overview of the financial condition and results of activities of the government as a whole, in addition to more detailed fund financial statements and detailed disclosures in the notes to the financial statements.[14]

As shown in Illustrations 9–3 and 9–4, the two government-wide financial statements should also report amounts for discretely presented component units. Because the Town of Brighton has no component units, only primary government information is presented. To minimize line-item detail in the financial statements and thus make the financial statements easier to understand, immaterial amounts for specific items may be reported with the amounts for broadly similar items. For example, in the Town of Brighton's Statement of Activities, it would have been acceptable to report the

[14] *GASBS 34,* par. 1.

ILLUSTRATION 9–4

TOWN OF BRIGHTON
Statement of Activities
For the Year Ended December 31, 2017

		Program Revenues			Net (Expenses) Revenues and Changes in Net Position			
					Primary Government			
Functions/Programs	**Expenses**	**Charges for Services**	**Operating Grants and Contributions**	**Capital Grants and Contributions**	**Governmental Activities**	**Business-type Activities**	**Total**	**Component Units (None)**
Primary government:								
Governmental activities:								
General government	$ 839,481	$ 238,200	$ 1,000		$ (600,281)		$ (600,281)	
Public safety	1,517,817	186,480	100,000	$300,000	(931,337)		(931,337)	
Public works	1,654,736	124,320			(1,530,416)		(1,530,416)	
Health and welfare	944,884		184,100		(760,784)		(760,784)	
Culture and recreation	546,112	82,464			(463,648)		(463,648)	
Interest on long-term debt	114,000				(114,000)		(114,000)	
Interest on notes	1,000				(1,000)		(1,000)	
Total governmental activities	5,618,030	631,464	285,100	300,000	(4,401,466)		(4,401,466)	
Business-type activities:								
Water	610,980	723,140		7,000		$ 119,160	119,160	
Total primary government	$6,229,010	$1,354,604	$285,100	$307,000	(4,401,466)	119,160	(4,282,306)	
General revenues:								
Taxes:								
Property taxes levied for general purposes					2,599,636		2,599,636	
Property taxes levied for debt service					117,000		117,000	
Sales taxes					485,000		485,000	
Sales taxes for debt service					31,200		31,200	
Investment earnings for debt service					3,145	44,500	47,645	
Interest and penalties on delinquent taxes					11,400		11,400	
Miscellaneous					3,400		3,400	
Total general revenues					3,250,781	44,500	3,295,281	
Increase (decrease) in unrestricted net position					(1,150,685)	163,660	(987,025)	
Net position, January 1, 2017					18,361,802	1,952,100	20,313,902	
Net position, December 31, 2017					$17,211,117	$2,115,760	$19,326,877	

relatively small amount of revenue from interest and penalties on delinquent taxes as part of revenues from property taxes.

Fund Financial Statements

In addition to the MD&A and government-wide financial statements, the Town of Brighton would prepare several required fund financial statements. The latter include a balance sheet—governmental funds and a statement of revenues, expenditures, and changes in fund balances—governmental funds. The town would also prepare proprietary fund financial statements for the Supply Fund and the Town of Brighton Water Utility Fund. The statement of net position; statement of revenues, expenses, and changes in fund net position; and statement of cash flows for the funds were provided in Chapter 7 as Illustrations 7–6, 7–7, and 7–8, and thus are not shown again in this chapter.

Classification of Fund Balances

The Town of Brighton Balance Sheet—Governmental Funds in Illustration 9–5 reflects the fund balance classifications utilized by the Town of Brighton for its governmental funds. Financial reporting standards require that the fund balances reported

ILLUSTRATION 9–5

TOWN OF BRIGHTON
Balance Sheet
Governmental Funds
December 31, 2017

	General Fund	Other Governmental Funds	Total Governmental Funds
Assets			
Cash	$145,800	$ 39,313	$185,113
Receivables (net)	588,400	1,600	590,000
Investments		83,316	83,316
Total assets	734,200	124,229	858,429
Liabilities and Fund Balances			
Liabilities:			
Vouchers payable	405,800		405,800
Due to other governments	166,260		166,260
Due to other funds	5,000		5,000
Total liabilities	577,060		577,060
Fund Balances:			
Spendable:			
Restricted—Debt service		124,229	124,229
Committed—Culture and recreation	17,500		17,500
Assigned—Public safety	23,700		23,700
Unassigned	115,940		115,940
Total fund balances	157,140	124,229	281,369
Total liabilities and fund balances	$734,200	$124,229	$858,429

on the balance sheet be classified according to the constraints on the use of the fund balances. Recall from Chapter 2 that the fund balance classifications and classification descriptions provided by GASB include nonspendable, spendable—restricted, spendable—committed, spendable—assigned, and spendable—unassigned.

Chapter 4 identified that the town established a policy of spending restricted, committed, or assigned resources for particular purposes, in that order, before spending unconstrained resources. Governments with such spending priority policies generally end the fiscal year with few resource amounts requiring reclassification from unassigned fund balances to the constrained fund balance classifications. Prior to preparing financial statements, governments evaluate all fund balance classification amounts to determine whether fund balances need to be reallocated to properly reflect constraints as of year-end.

The Town of Brighton completed its evaluation and determined it does not have a material amount of inventory on hand. Therefore, no unassigned fund balances are allocated to the non-spendable fund balance classification. From Chapter 4, two constrained resources were unspent at the end of fiscal 2017; $17,500 of sales taxes *committed* for constructing a hiking trail in one of the town parks and $23,700 of General Fund resources that the town manager has *assigned* for acquisition and installation of downtown security cameras. In Chapter 6, the town determined that resources of the debt service fund were *restricted* for debt and principal repayment. Therefore, $124,229 of fund balances are identified as restricted. The remaining fund balances are considered *unassigned.* As a reminder, only the General Fund can have unassigned fund balances. Fund balances related to any other governmental fund must be classified as restricted, committed, or assigned.

Major Funds

Illustration 9–5 also presents information concerning major and nonmajor funds. The Fire Station Capital Projects Fund meets the criteria of a *major fund* (see the glossary for the definition of this term and the criteria for determining whether a fund is a major fund). Since the Fire Station Capital Projects Fund has no assets or liabilities at December 31, 2017, it does not appear in the Town of Brighton Balance Sheet—Governmental Funds. Therefore, no major funds are shown on the balance sheet, other than the General Fund. The nonmajor funds are combined in a single column headed Other Governmental Funds.

The Town of Brighton's Statement of Revenues, Expenditures, and Changes in Fund Balances is shown in Illustration 9–6. Because all governmental funds had activity during the year, they are all included in the operating statement. The two nonmajor funds (the Serial Bond Debt Service Fund and the Term Bond Debt Service Fund) are combined under the column headed Other Governmental Funds.

Required Reconciliations

GASB requires that the financial information reported in the governmental funds balance sheet be reconciled to that reported in the Governmental Activities column of the government-wide statement of net position. Similarly, the information reported in the governmental funds statement of revenues, expenditures, and changes in fund balances must be reconciled to that reported as governmental activities in the government-wide statement of activities. The need for reconciliation arises from the use of different measurement focuses and bases of accounting, as discussed at several points in prior chapters. Because enterprise funds are reported on the accrual basis, using the economic resources measurement focus, usually there will be no need for a reconciliation

ILLUSTRATION 9–6

TOWN OF BRIGHTON
Statement of Revenues, Expenditures, and Changes in Fund Balances
Governmental Funds
For Year Ended December 31, 2017

	General Fund	Fire Station Capital Projects Fund	Other Governmental Funds	Total Governmental Funds
Revenues				
Property taxes	$2,599,636		$117,000	$2,716,636
Interest and penalties	11,400			11,400
Sales taxes	485,000		31,200	516,200
Licenses and permits	213,200			213,200
Fines and forfeits	310,800			310,800
Intergovernmental	284,100	$ 300,000		584,100
Charges for services	107,464			107,464
Investment earnings			3,145	3,145
Miscellaneous	3,400			3,400
Total revenues	4,015,000	300,000	151,345	4,466,345
Expenditures				
Current:				
General government	649,400			649,400
Public safety	1,305,435			1,305,435
Public works	1,018,900			1,018,900
Health and welfare	850,325			850,325
Culture and recreation	419,500			419,500
Miscellaneous	14,200			14,200
Debt service:				
Interest		1,000	111,000	112,000
Capital outlay		1,493,000		1,493,000
Total expenditures	4,257,760	1,494,000	111,000	5,862,760
Excess (deficiency) of revenues over expenditures	(242,760)	(1,194,000)	40,345	(1,396,415)
Other Financing Sources (Uses)				
Proceeds of long-term capital debt		1,200,000		1,200,000
Interfund transfers in (out)		(6,000)	6,000	
Total other financing sources (uses)		1,194,000	6,000	1,200,000
Net change in fund balances	(242,760)	0	46,345	(196,415)
Fund balances, January 1, 2017	399,900	0	77,884	477,784
Fund balances, December 31, 2017	$ 157,140	$ 0	$124,229	$ 281,369

between the enterprise fund financial information and that of business-type activities at the government-wide level.

Items that typically differ between governmental fund statements and governmental activities at the government-wide level, and thus should be reconciled, include:

1. Capital outlays that are reported as expenditures in governmental funds but as capital assets at the government-wide level.

2. Disposition of capital assets that are reported as other financing sources in governmental funds but as reductions of capital assets and gains/losses at the government-wide level.
3. Depreciation on capital assets that is not reported in governmental funds but is reported as expenses and contra-assets at the government-wide level.
4. Issuance of long-term debt that is reported as other financing sources in governmental funds but as an increase in general long-term liabilities at the government-wide level.
5. Retirement of long-term debt that is reported as an expenditure in governmental funds but as a reduction of general long-term liabilities at the government-wide level.
6. Some revenues that do not provide current financial resources are not recognized in governmental funds but are recognized at the government-wide level.
7. Reporting expenses on an accrual basis at the government-wide level.
8. Interfund transfers between governmental funds, which are not reported at the government-wide level.
9. Adjusting for internal service funds' assets, liabilities, operating income (loss), and transfers.

Illustration A2–4 reconciles the City and County of Denver's total fund balance for governmental funds to the net position of governmental activities, while Illustration A2–6 reconciles changes in governmental fund balances to changes in governmental activities net position. GASB standards permit reconciliations to be provided on the face of the governmental fund basic financial statements or in accompanying schedules.

The reconciliation for the Town of Brighton's balance sheet of governmental funds (Illustration 9–5) to the statement of net position (Illustration 9–3) is presented in Illustration 9–7. Illustration 9–8 presents the reconciliation of the statement of revenues, expenditures, and changes in fund balances for the governmental funds (Illustration 9–6) to the statement of activities (Illustration 9–4).

ILLUSTRATION 9–7

TOWN OF BRIGHTON
Reconciliation of the Balance Sheet—Governmental Funds to the Statement of Net Position
December 31, 2017

Total fund balances—governmental funds	$ 281,369
Amounts reported for governmental activities in the statement of net position are different because:	
Capital assets used in governmental activities are not financial resources and therefore are not reported in the funds.	19,698,998
Long-term liabilities, including bonds payable, are not due and payable in the current period and therefore are not reported in the funds.	(2,700,000)
The assets and liabilities of the internal service fund are included in governmental activities in the statement of net position.	(28,750)
Accrued interest payable is not due in the current period and therefore is not included in the funds.	(40,500)
Net position of governmental activities	$17,211,117

ILLUSTRATION 9–8

TOWN OF BRIGHTON
Reconciliation of the Statement of Revenues, Expenditures, and Changes in Fund Balances—Governmental Funds to the Statement of Activities
For the Year Ended December 31, 2017

Net change in fund balances—governmental funds	$ (196,415)
Amounts reported for governmental activities in the statement of activities are different because:	
Governmental funds report capital outlays as expenditures. However, in the statement of activities, the cost of those assets is allocated over their estimated useful lives as depreciation expense. This is the amount by which capital outlays exceeded depreciation.	246,980
Bond proceeds provide current financial resources to governmental funds, but issuing debt increases long-term liabilities in the statement of net position. This is the amount of proceeds.	(1,200,000)
Some expenses reported in the statement of activities do not require the use of current financial resources and therefore are not reported as expenditures in governmental funds.	(3,000)
Internal service funds are used by management to charge the costs of certain activities to individual funds. The net revenue of the internal service fund is reported with governmental activities.	1,750
Change in net position of governmental activities	$(1,150,685)

Intra-entity Transactions

The Town of Brighton does not have any component units. As a result, the town does not record any intra-entity transactions. **Intra-entity transactions** are exchange or nonexchange transactions between the primary government and its blended or discretely presented component units. If the Town of Brighton did have a component unit, the method of recording transactions would be affected by whether the component unit was blended or discretely presented. Transactions between the primary government and *blended* component units follow the same standards as for reciprocal and nonreciprocal interfund activity discussed and demonstrated in the preceding chapters. Thus, if the blended component unit was treated as a governmental fund, the transactions between the component unit and governmental funds would not be reported at the government-wide level because the transactions occurred between two governmental funds. Transactions between the primary government and *discretely presented* component units are treated as if the component units are external entities and thus should be reported as revenues and expenses in the statement of activities. Amounts receivable and payable resulting from these transactions should be reported on a separate line in the statement of net position.

OTHER FINANCIAL REPORTING ISSUES AND TOPICS

The area of government financial reporting is dynamic, with new issues constantly arising. For those interested in the financial issues facing state and local governments, the GASB Web site (*www.gasb.org*) provides a great deal of information, including information about ongoing projects and its due process documents.

As this textbook goes to press, the time period for comment on a GASB exposure draft has just ended. The exposure draft relates to the modification of the GAAP hierarchy for state and local governments. Under the proposal the hierarchy would have just two levels. Level one of the hierarchy would be the statements issued by the GASB and level two would include GASB Technical Bulletins, GASB Implementation Guides, and literature of the American Institute of Certified Public Accountants that has been specifically cleared by the GASB. Of particular interest is the addition of the Implementation Guide to the GAAP hierarchy. As a result of this change, the Implementation Guide will become subject to the due process policies of the GASB. The comment period for the first exposure draft related to the Implementation Guide also ended at the time the textbook went to press.

For quite some time, the GASB worked on the Recognition and Measurement Attributes project. Recently the project was divided into two projects—recognition and measurement. The measurement portion of the project has resulted in a new concept statement, *Concepts Statement No. 6*: "Measurement of Elements of the Financial Statements." The recognition project remains under consideration. Several other projects on which the GASB is working include fiduciary responsibilities, lease accounting, and post-employment benefit reporting. Additional information on the status of these projects is available at the GASB Web site.

Three topics not currently addressed by the GASB standards, but which are of interest to government entities, are popular reporting, other comprehensive basis of accounting, and international government standards. These three topics are touched on in the remainder of the chapter.

Popular Reporting

Although the CAFR has evolved to meet the diverse information needs of financial report users (i.e., citizens, legislative and oversight bodies, and investors and creditors), it is widely recognized that most citizens are unable to read and comprehend the CAFR. To better communicate financial results to citizens, a growing number of governments prepare and distribute **popular reports** (also referred to as citizen-centric reports) that provide highly condensed financial information, budget summaries, and narrative descriptions. In fact, a recent survey of the 100 largest U.S. cities and counties found that of those responding, 75 percent provide citizens with some type of popular report.[15] All of these reports were available on the governments' Web sites. Popular reports are intended to supplement the CAFR, not replace it. Since they do not present minimum data required for complete and fair presentation, popular reports are considered "summary data" and are unaudited.[16]

For popular reports to be effective researchers have found that they need to make the information relevant to the citizen.[17] The reports need to focus on how the

[15] Juita-Elena, Yusuf, Meagan M. Jordan, Katharine A. Neill, and Merl Hackbart, "For the People: Popular Financial Reporting Practices of Local Governments," *Public Budgeting & Finance*, Spring 2013, pp. 95–113.

[16] Audit standards issued by the American Institute of Certified Public Accountants permit auditors to express their opinion that a popular report (and other forms of summary data) is fairly stated *in relation to* the complete audited financial statements from which it is derived. Current AICPA guidance does not permit auditors to express an opinion on whether popular reports are fairly presented in conformity with GAAP.

[17] Juita-Elena, Yusuf, and Meagan M. Jordan, "Effective Popular Financial Reports: The Citizen Perspective," *The Journal of Government Financial Management*, Winter 2012, pp. 44–49.

information being provided relates to the citizen and should link financial information to the government's performance. Interestingly, the research indicated that users were more interested in revenue information than expenditure information. In delivering the information to citizens the reports need to be short, readable for the average citizen, and visually appealing.

The GASB, the Association of Government Accountants (AGA) and the Government Finance Officers Association (GFOA) recognize the value of popular reports. In 2010 the GASB called for research on popular reporting that would provide information on the effectiveness of financial reporting. An examination of effectiveness is relevant given that both the AGA and the GFOA have award programs for popular reporting. The AGA award is the "Certificate of Excellence in Citizen-Centric Reporting," while the GFOA has an award entitled "Popular Annual Financial Reporting Award."

Other Comprehensive Basis of Accounting (OCBOA)

Chapters 1–9 of the textbook have focused on GAAP for state and local governments. However, a large number of state and local governments do not maintain internal accounting records on a GAAP basis and many do not report using GAAP. In place of GAAP, many of these governments use an **other comprehensive basis of accounting (OCBOA)**, which is also known as a *special-purpose framework*. *Statement of Auditing Standards* defines four bases of accounting other than GAAP that would be considered OCBOA.[18] The OCBOA most commonly used by state and local governments are cash or modified cash basis and regulatory basis of accounting.

Some of the reasons given for using OCBOA instead of GAAP include: OCBOA accounting records are easier to understand and maintain, the financial statements are easier to prepare and may be easier for users to understand, and the accounting and reporting is less costly than GAAP. However, use of OCBOA does not preclude the need to present information similar to that reported under GAAP. For example, if a government is using a cash or modified cash basis of accounting, it is expected to comply with presentation of financial statement requirements set forth in GAAP, including presentation of government-wide and fund financial statements, notes to the financial statements, and required supplementary information, such as management's discussion and analysis.[19] Readers interested in a more comprehensive discussion of OCBOA are referred to the following resources: AICPA's *Professional Standards; Applying OCBOA in State and Local Governmental Financial Statements;* and the Auditing and Accounting Guide, *State and Local Governments.*

International Accounting Standards

As in the corporate sector, the public sector also has an international accounting standards-setting body. The International Public Sector Accounting Standards Board (IPSASB) issues International Public Sector Accounting Standards (IPSAS) that have been adopted by many national governments. The purpose of the IPSASB is to provide high quality public sector accounting standards that can be used by governments and other public sector organizations around the world. Similar to its counterpart, the International Accounting Standards Board (IASB), the IPSASB uses due process in

[18] American Institute of Certified Public Accountants, *Codification of Statements on Auditing Standards,* AU section 623.04 (New York: AICPA, 2014).

[19] American Institute of Certified Public Accountants, Audit and Accounting Guide, *State and Local Governments* (New York: AICPA, 2014).

the issuance of standards. Prior to being issued, the proposed standard is made available for public comment in exposure draft form. Comments are considered by the Board prior to the issuance of the final standard. The IPSASB has issued more than 32 standards.[20]

The IPSASB supports efforts to achieve international convergence of all accounting standards. It is the IPSASB's belief that a uniform set of standards used globally by businesses and public sector entities will increase the quality and transparency of financial reporting.[21] However, given the differences that exist in public sector entities, it may be difficult to achieve international convergence among the public sector entities, much less between the public sector and business entities.[22] As with the IASB, IPSASB faces the problem that countries may be selectively adopting and implementing IPSASs. Not adopting standards in their entirety runs counter to the IPSASB objective of providing quality and transparent reporting.

The difficulty of achieving the IPSASB objective was recently demonstrated when the European Union (EU) considered adoption of IPSAS. A consultation report issued by the EU Member States determined that IPSAS were not suitable for a majority of the EU Member States. Therefore, instead of adopting IPSAS, the report recommended the establishment of European Public Sector Standards using the IPSAS as a reference.[23]

Appendix A

Converting Accounting Information from the Modified Accrual to the Accrual Basis of Accounting

As mentioned in Chapter 4, there are two basic approaches to obtaining the information necessary to prepare the government-wide financial statements. The first method is the dual-track approach used in this textbook, which requires an accounting information system capable of capturing two bases of accounting, the modified accrual basis and the accrual basis. The second approach, not as conceptually desirable, is to maintain one set of records on the modified accrual basis and, at the end of the reporting period, analyze all transactions occurring over the period and prepare a worksheet that converts the modified accrual basis transactions to the full accrual basis. It is this second approach that is used by a number of governments since most existing accounting information systems only provide for reporting governmental funds on a modified accrual basis. To familiarize readers with the worksheet process, a brief introduction is provided.

[20] *www.ipsasb.org*

[21] International Federation of Accountants, "International Public Sector Accounting Standards Board," Fact Sheet issued by IFAC. Retrieved from *www.ipsasb.org.*

[22] Alan Rob and Susan Newberry, "Globalization: Governmental Accounting and International Financial Reporting Standards," *Socio-Economic Review* 5 (2007), pp. 725–754.

[23] Caroline Aggestam-Pontoppidan, "The European Union Is Moving Toward Implementing European Public Sector Accounting Standards," *The Journal of Government Financial Management*, Fall 2013, pp 50–53.

The point of the worksheet is to convert account balances derived under the modified accrual basis of accounting to account balances on an accrual basis. Converting and extending the account balances provides management with the balances needed to prepare the government-wide statement of activities and statement of net position. The conversion is accomplished through a series of adjustments to a total governmental funds pre-closing trial balance. The types of adjustments made to the modified accrual balances are similar to the adjustments found in the reconciliation process shown in Illustrations 9–7 and 9–8. Some of the transactions requiring adjustments include:

1. Converting capital acquisitions from expenditures to capital assets.
2. Recording sales of capital assets.
3. Accounting for the depreciation of capital assets.
4. Converting issuance of debt from an operating statement account to a liability.
5. Converting payment of debt from an operating statement account to a liability adjustment.
6. Recording any accruals for expenses that are deferred under modified accrual since the payment is not legally due (e.g., interest due on long-term debt).
7. Adjusting assets and liabilities, and including the change in net position for internal service funds.
8. Eliminating interfund receivables and payables among governmental funds (such as a special revenue fund and the General Fund) and between governmental funds and internal service funds. Any remaining balance represents activity between the governmental funds and enterprise funds (business-type activities) and is transferred to an account titled Internal Balances. Internal Balances may have a debit or credit balance. When reported in the actual *financial statement,* Internal Balances between governmental and business-type activities are offsetting.
9. Interfund transfers in and interfund transfers out occurring among governmental funds, and between governmental funds and internal service funds, must be eliminated. Any remaining balance represents the transfers between governmental and business-type activities. When reported in the actual *financial statement,* transfers between governmental and business-type activities are offsetting.

A worksheet conversion example, using the Town of Brighton, is presented in Illustration A9–1. Since Brighton uses the dual-track approach to record keeping, it would not need to prepare a worksheet. However, the reader's familiarity with the Town of Brighton makes it easier to see how a worksheet conversion would work for a government that does not keep records on both the modified and accrual basis of accounting. The top portion of the worksheet presents the pre-closing trial balances for all governmental funds as of December 31, 2017. At the bottom of the worksheet are those accounts that would not appear in the governmental funds using the modified accrual basis but would appear under the accrual basis used by governmental activities. Examples of such accounts include capital asset and long-term debt accounts. Under the worksheet approach, the governmental activities accounts are only adjusted once a year, at the time the annual financial statements are prepared; thus, the balances in the worksheet represent the beginning balances, unadjusted for any activity during the 2017 fiscal year. For ease of explanation the following liberties have been taken with the worksheet—revenue information has been consolidated since no adjustments need to be made to revenues, and capital asset accounts have been consolidated into a single capital assets (net) account. The reader should keep in mind that the worksheet process has been simplified for illustrative purposes. Additional

ILLUSTRATION A9–1

TOWN OF BRIGHTON
Conversion Worksheet
For the Year Ended December 31, 2017

Fund Accounts	Fund Balances		Adjustments				Statement of Activities		Statement of Net Position	
	Debit	*Credit*	*ID*	*Debit*	*ID*	*Credit*	*Debit*	*Credit*	*Debit*	*Credit*
Cash	185,113		e	54,250					239,363	
Taxes Receivable—Delinquent	706,413								706,413	
Estimated Uncollectible Delinquent Taxes		126,513								126,513
Interest and Penalties Receivable	13,191								13,191	
Estimated Uncollectible Interest and Penalties		3,091								3,091
Due from Other Funds	25,000				f	25,000				
Inventory of Supplies			e	69,100					69,100	
Investments	83,316								83,316	
Vouchers Payable		405,800			e	28,600				434,400
Due to Federal Government		126,520								126,520
Due to State Government		39,740								39,740
Due to Other Funds		30,000	f	30,000						
Fund Balance		477,784								477,784
Revenues		4,463,200			e	1,000		4,464,200		
Revenues—Interest		3,145						3,145		
Other Financing Sources—Bond Proceeds		1,200,000	c	1,200,000						
Other Financing Sources—Interfund Transfers In		6,000	g	6,000						
Expenditures—General Government	649,400		b,h,e	190,081			839,481			
Expenditures—Public Safety	1,305,435		b	229,493	e	17,111	1,517,817			
Expenditures—Public Works	1,018,900		b	672,288	e	36,452	1,654,736			
Expenditures—Health and Welfare	850,325		b	95,622	e	1,063	944,884			
Expenditures—Culture and Recreation	419,500		b	133,871	e	7,259	546,112			
Expenditures—Miscellaneous	14,200				h	14,200				
Expenditures—Construction	1,493,000				a	1,493,000				
Expenditures—Interest	112,000		d	3,000			115,000			
Other Financing Uses—Interfund Transfers Out	6,000				g	6,000				
Total	6,881,793	6,881,793								

continued

ILLUSTRATION A9–1 *(Continued)*

Government-wide Accounts	Government-wide Beginning Balances									
Capital Assets (net)	19,330,018		a,b,e	368,980					19,698,998	
Accrued Interest Payable		37,500			d	3,000				40,500
Bonds Payable		1,500,000			c	1,200,000				2,700,000
Net Position		17,792,518			e	91,500				17,884,018
Total	19,330,018	19,330,018								
Interfund Loan Payable					e	123,500				123,500
Internal Balances					f	5,000				5,000
Total				3,052,685		3,052,685	5,618,030	4,467,345	20,810,381	21,961,066
Change in Net Position								1,150,685	1,150,685	
Total							5,618,030	5,618,030	21,961,066	21,961,066

work that would be necessary to prepare the actual government-wide financial statements would include:

1. Renaming expenditures as expenses because, through the conversion process, expenditures are adjusted to expenses.
2. Adding the fund balance (top portion) and the net position balance (bottom portion) yields the total net position balance needed for the statement of net position.
3. Separating the total net position balance into the three components for reporting in the statement of net position.
4. Identifying revenues as general or program for reporting in the statement of activities.
5. Recording the entries made in the worksheet to update account balances for governmental activities. However, no worksheet entries should be made in the fund journals.

The following key provides information concerning the figures presented in the adjustment column. An identification (ID) letter is used for tracing purposes.

a. Adjusts the capital projects expenditure into a capital asset (Chapter 5).
b. Records the annual depreciation on capital assets (Chapter 9).
c. Adjusts the Other Financing Sources—Proceeds of Bonds to a long-term liability (Chapter 5).
d. Records the accrual of interest on serial bond debt (Chapter 6).
e. Incorporates the internal service fund activity (Chapter 7 post-closing trial balance for 2016, Illustrations 7–1 and 7–2). *Note:* That for the internal service fund the expenses charged to general government increased the total expenses of the general government. The markup on supplies charged to government functions ($64,750) was allocated based on usage among the functions, effectively decreasing the total expenses of the functions of government.
f. Transfers net Due from Other Funds and Due to Other Funds balances to Internal Balances (Chapter 4).
g. Eliminates interfund transfers between governmental funds (Chapters 5 and 6) and between governmental funds and internal service funds (Chapters 4 and 7).
h. Reclassifies miscellaneous expenditures to general government expense. *Note:* At the government-wide level, Expenditure—Interest represents $114,000 interest on bonded debt and $1,000 interest on notes (see Chapter 6, and Chapter 5, respectively).

Appendix B

Management's Discussion and Analysis (MD&A)—City and County of Denver

Management of the City and County of Denver (City) offers readers of the basic financial statements this narrative overview and analysis of the financial activities of the City for the fiscal year ended December 31, 2013. Readers are encouraged to consider the information presented here in conjunction with additional information that is furnished in the letter of transmittal. The focus of the information herein is on the primary government.

FINANCIAL HIGHLIGHTS

- The City's assets and deferred inflows of resources exceeded its liabilities at the close of the fiscal year by $3,086,679,000 (net position). Of this amount, $759,165,000 (unrestricted net position) may be used to meet the City's ongoing obligations.
- The City's total net position increased by $188,658,000, or 6.5% from the restated beginning net position as a result of the change in accounting principle – GASB 65, *Items Previously Reported as Assets and Liabilities*.
- As of close of the current fiscal year, the City's governmental funds reported combined ending fund balances of $773,705,000, an increase of $85,460,000 from the prior year. Approximately 25.98% or $201,030,000 of the fund balance (unassigned fund balance) is available for spending at the government's discretion.
- At the end of the current fiscal year, unassigned fund balance of the General Fund was $201,030,000 which represents 20.7% of total General Fund expenditures, including transfers out.
- The City's total bonded debt increased by $529,930,000 during the year. Increases occurred in the general obligation bonds and revenue bonds.

OVERVIEW OF THE FINANCIAL STATEMENTS

This discussion and analysis is intended as an introduction to the City's basic financial statements. The basic financial statements comprise three components: 1) government-wide financial statements, 2) fund financial statements, and 3) notes to the basic financial statements. In addition to the basic financial statements, also provided are required and other supplementary information.

Government-wide Financial Statements

The government-wide financial statements are designed to provide readers with a broad overview of the City's finances, in a manner similar to a private-sector business.

The Statement of Net Position presents information on all of the City's assets, liabilities, and deferred inflows/outflows of resources, with the difference reported as net position. Over time, increases or decreases in net position may serve as a useful indicator of whether the financial position of the City is improving or deteriorating.

The Statement of Activities reports how the City's net position changed during the most recent year. All changes in net position are reported as soon as the underlying event giving rise to the change occurs, regardless of the timing of related cash flows. Thus, revenues and expenses are reported in this statement for some items that will only result in cash flows in future fiscal periods (e.g., uncollected taxes and earned but unused vacation and sick leave).

The governmental activities reflect the City's basic services, including police, fire, public works, sanitation, economic development, culture, and recreation. Sales and property taxes finance the majority of these services.

The business-type activities reflect private sector-type operations, such as Wastewater Management; the Denver Airport System, including Denver International Airport (DIA); and Golf Courses, where fees for services typically cover all or most of the cost of operations, including depreciation.

The government-wide financial statements include not only the City itself (referred to as the primary government), but also other legally separate entities for which the City is financially accountable. Financial information for most of these component units is reported separately from the financial information presented for the primary government itself. A few component units, although legally separate, function essentially as an agency of the City and, therefore, are included as an integral part of the City.

Fund Financial Statements

A fund is a grouping of related accounts used to maintain control over resources that have been segregated for specific activities or objectives. The City uses fund accounting to ensure and demonstrate compliance with finance-related legal requirements. All of the funds of the City can be divided into three categories: governmental funds, proprietary funds, and fiduciary funds.

Governmental funds are used to account for essentially the same functions reported as governmental activities in the government-wide financial statements. Governmental fund financial statements focus on near term inflows and outflows of spendable resources, as well as on the balances left at year-end that are available for spending. Consequently, the governmental fund financial statements provide a detailed short-term view that helps the reader determine whether there are more or fewer financial resources that can be spent in the near future to finance the City's programs. Because this information does not encompass the long-term focus of the government-wide statements, additional information is provided that reconciles the governmental fund financial statements to the government-wide statements explaining the relationship (or differences) between them.

The City maintains 22 individual governmental funds. Information is presented separately in the governmental funds balance sheet and in the governmental funds statement of revenues, expenditures, and changes in fund balances for the General Fund and Human Services special revenue fund, each of which is considered to be a major fund. Data from the other 20 governmental funds are combined into a single aggregated presentation. Individual fund data for these nonmajor governmental funds is provided in the form of combining statements elsewhere in this report.

The City adopts an annual appropriated budget for the General Fund and Human Services special revenue fund. A budgetary comparison schedule has been provided to demonstrate compliance with these budgets for the General Fund and Human Services fund in accordance with U.S. GAAP.

The City maintains two different types of ***proprietary funds***: enterprise funds and internal service funds. Enterprise funds are used to report the same functions presented as business-type activities in the government-wide financial statements. The City uses enterprise funds to account for its Wastewater Management, Denver Airport System, Environmental Services, and Golf Course funds. Internal service funds are an accounting device used to accumulate and allocate costs internally among the City's various functions. The City uses internal service funds to account for its fleet of vehicles, workers' compensation self-insurance, and asphalt plant operations. The internal service funds provide services which predominantly benefit governmental rather than business-type functions. They have been included within governmental activities with an adjustment to reflect the consolidation for internal service fund activities related to the enterprise funds in the government-wide financial statements.

Proprietary funds provide the same type of information as the government-wide financial statements, only in more detail. The proprietary fund financial statements provide separate information for Wastewater Management and the Denver Airport System, both of which are considered to be major funds of the City. Data for the other two enterprise funds and all of the internal service funds are combined into their respective single aggregated presentations. Individual fund data for the nonmajor enterprise funds and all of the internal service funds is provided in the form of combining statements elsewhere in this report.

The City uses ***fiduciary funds*** to account for assets held on behalf of outside parties, including other governments. When these assets are held under the terms of a formal trust agreement, a private-purpose trust fund is used.

Agency funds generally are used to account for assets that the City holds on behalf of others as their agent. Pension trust funds account for the assets of the City's employee retirement plans.

Fiduciary funds are not reflected in the government-wide financial statements because the resources of those funds are not available to support the City's own programs. The accounting used for fiduciary funds is much like that used for proprietary funds.

The ***notes to the basic financial statements*** provide additional information that is essential to a full understanding of the data provided in the government-wide and fund financial statements.

Other information in addition to the basic financial statements and accompanying notes is presented in the form of certain required supplementary information concerning the City's budgetary comparison schedules and the implicit rate subsidy on other postemployment benefits.

The combining statements supplementary information referred to earlier in connection with nonmajor funds, internal service funds, and nonmajor component units are presented immediately following the budgetary comparison required supplementary information.

Government-wide Financial Analysis

As noted earlier, net position may serve over time as a useful indicator of a government's financial position. In the case of the City, assets and deferred outflows exceeded liabilities and deferred inflows by approximately $3,086,679,000 at the close of the most recent fiscal year.

A portion of the City's net position, $759,165,000 (24.6%), is unrestricted and may be used to meet the City's ongoing financial obligations. This portion represents resources that are not restricted by external requirements nor invested in capital assets.

Net position of $1,174,260,000 (38%) reflects investment in capital assets (e.g., land, buildings, infrastructure, machinery, and equipment) less any related debt used to acquire those assets that is still outstanding. The City uses these capital assets to provide services to citizens; consequently, these assets are not available for future spending. Although the City's investment in its capital assets is reported net of related debt, it should be noted that the resources needed to repay this debt must be provided from other sources since the capital assets themselves cannot be used to liquidate these liabilities.

Net positions of the City also include $1,153,254,000 (37.4%) of restricted net position. These are resources subject to external restrictions as to how they may be used by the City. Table B9-1 reflects the City's net position (dollars in thousands) as of December 31, 2013 and 2012. Table B9-2 reflects the City's changes in net position (dollars in thousands) for the years ended December 31, 2013 and 2012.

Governmental activities increased the City's net position by $153,090,000 for the year ended December 31, 2013. Key elements of the increase are as follows:

- Property tax and sales and use taxes totaled 85.6% of all tax revenues and 52.7% of all governmental activities' revenues. Property tax recorded in the governmental funds totaled $331,914,000 for an increase of $44,852,000 (15.6%) while sales and use tax revenues of $539,348,000 were up $44,853,000 (9.1%) compared to 2012, reflecting a moderate growth in the 2013 economy.
- Investment income decreased by $8,734,000 (77.6%) due to the decrease in interest rates nationally, and a decrease in the unrealized gains for the investment portfolio.
- Total expenses decreased by $6,788,000 (.5%) primarily due to the cost savings measures developed by the City.

TABLE B9–1 Net position (dollars in thousands) as of December 31, 2013 and 2012

	Governmental Activities		Business-type Activities		Total Primary Government	
	2013	2012	2013	2012	2013	2012
Current and other assets	$1,352,355	$1,253,715	$2,339,092	$1,978,213	$ 3,691,447	$3,231,928
Capital assets	2,848,895	2,848,075	3,762,887	3,650,401	6,611,782	6,498,476
Total assets	**4,201,250**	**4,101,790**	**6,101,979**	**5,628,614**	**10,303,229**	**9,730,404**
Deferred outflows	36,765	43,816	229,667	42,900	266,432	86,716
Noncurrent liabilities	1,783,592	1,835,276	4,723,596	3,944,974	6,507,188	5,780,250
Other liabilities	176,783	528,068	447,994	575,529	624,777	1,103,597
Total liabilities	**1,960,375**	**2,363,344**	**5,171,590**	**4,520,503**	**7,131,965**	**6,883,847**
Deferred inflows	347,482	—	3,535	—	351,017	—
Net position						
Net investment in capital assets	1,366,632	1,315,237	(192,372)	(13,036)	1,174,260	1,302,201
Restricted	481,937	457,614	671,317	656,174	1,153,254	1,113,788
Unrestricted	81,589	9,411	677,576	507,873	759,165	517,284
Total net position	**$1,930,158**	**$1,782,262**	**$1,156,521**	**$1,151,011**	**$ 3,086,679**	**$2,933,273**

TABLE B9–2 **Changes in net position (dollars in thousands) for the years ended December 31, 2013 and 2012**

	Governmental Activities		Business-type Activities		Total Primary Government	
	2013	**2012[1]**	**2013**	**2012[1]**	**2013**	**2012**
Revenues						
Program revenues:						
Charges for services	$ 346,842	$ 324,826	$795,617	$ 854,783	$1,142,459	$1,179,609
Operating grants and contributions	179,412	253,319	103,513	675	282,925	253,994
Capital grants and contributions	69,512	33,557	38,701	29,886	108,213	63,443
General revenues:						
Facilities development admissions tax	8,721	8,986	—	—	8,721	8,986
Lodgers tax	63,482	57,956	—	—	63,482	57,956
Motor vehicle ownership fee	21,000	19,784	—	—	21,000	19,784
Occupational privilege tax	44,515	43,227	—	—	44,515	43,227
Property tax	331,914	287,062	—	—	331,914	287,062
Sales and use tax	539,348	494,495	—	—	539,348	494,495
Specific ownership tax	193	191	—	—	193	191
Telephone tax	8,964	9,979	—	—	8,964	9,979
Investment income	2,525	11,259	24,357	48,275	26,882	59,534
Other revenues	35,368	31,921	948	17	36,316	31,938
Total revenues	**1,651,796**	**1,576,562**	**963,136**	**933,636**	**2,614,932**	**2,510,198**
Expenses						
General government	398,733	247,659	—	—	398,733	247,659
Public safety	563,651	570,111	—	—	563,651	570,111
Public works	92,425	195,168	—	—	92,425	195,168
Human services	114,624	111,067	—	—	114,624	111,067
Health	54,453	53,755	—	—	54,453	53,755
Parks and recreation	29,687	80,480	—	—	29,687	80,480
Cultural activities	119,018	110,885	—	—	119,018	110,885
Community development	35,142	40,262	—	—	35,142	40,262
Economic opportunity	21,218	21,481	—	—	21,218	21,481
Interest on long-term debt	70,030	74,901	—	—	70,030	74,901
Wastewater management	—	—	105,679	99,179	105,679	99,179
Denver airport system	—	—	801,786	763,249	801,786	763,249
Other enterprise funds	—	—	19,828	15,944	19,828	15,944
Total expenses	**1,498,981**	**1,505,769**	**927,293**	**878,372**	**2,426,274**	**2,384,141**
Change in net position before transfers	152,815	70,793	35,843	55,264	188,658	126,057
Transfers	275	275	(275)	(275)	—	—
Change in net position	**153,090**	**71,068**	**35,568**	**54,989**	**188,658**	**126,057**
Net position - January 1, as previously reported	1,782,262	1,711,194	1,151,011	1,096,022	2,933,273	2,807,216
Change in accounting principle - GASB 65	(5,194)	—	(30,058)	—	(35,252)	—
Net position - January 1, as restated	1,777,068	1,711,194	1,120,953	1,096,022	2,898,021	2,807,216
Net position - December 31	**$1,930,158**	**$1,782,262**	**$1,156,521**	**$1,151,011**	**$3,086,679**	**$2,933,273**

[1] Amounts do not reflect the change in accounting principle - GASB 65 because it was not practical to do so.

General government expenses in 2013 were $398,733,000 (26.6%) of total expenses. Public safety expenses were $563,651,000 (37.6%) of total expenses. Public works' expenses were $92,425,000 (6.2%) of total expenses. Cultural activities were $119,018,000 (7.9%) of total expenses. Human services' expenses were $114,624,000 (7.7%) of total expenses. The remainder of the governmental activities expenses is comprised of health with $54,453,000 (3.6%), parks and recreation with $29,687,000 (2%), community development with $35,142,000 (2.3%), economic opportunity with $21,218,000 (1.4%), and interest on long-term debt of $70,030,000 (4.7%).

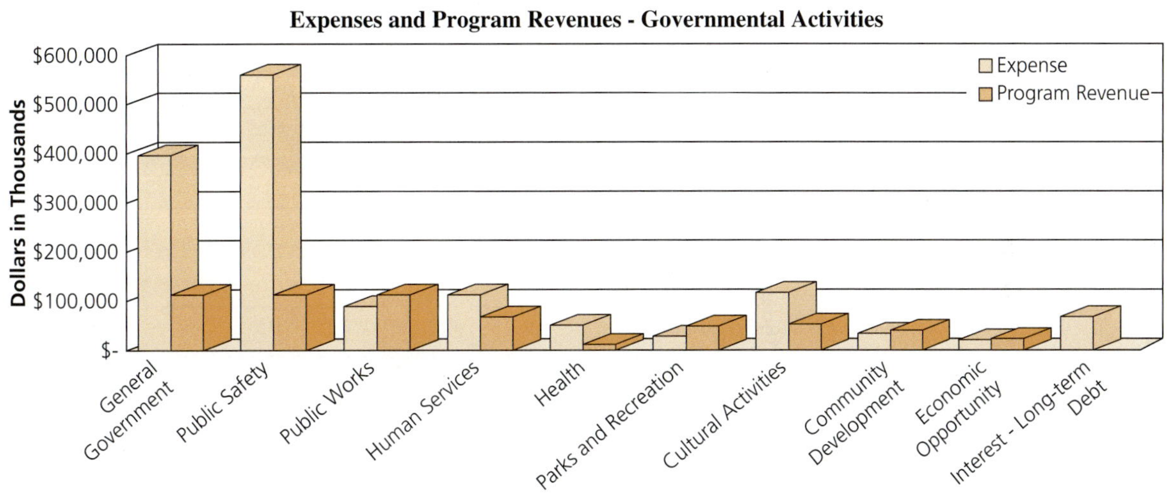

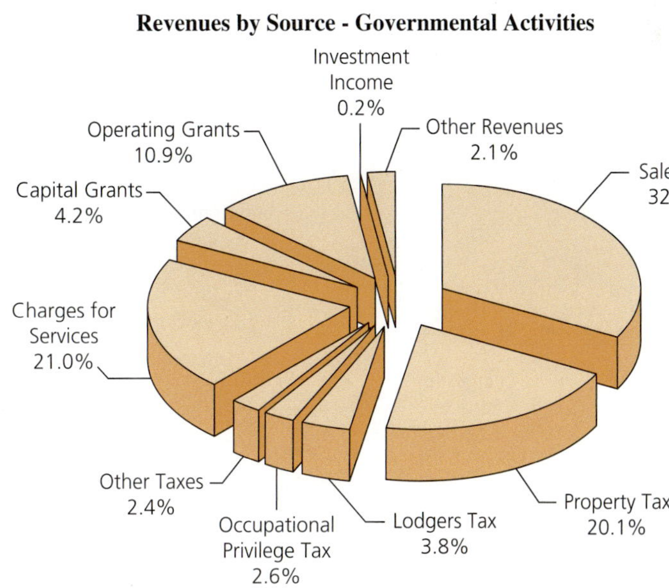

Business-type activities increased the City's net position by $35,568,000. Key elements of this modest increase are as follows:

- Total revenues of $963,136,000 were $29,500,000 (3.2%) higher compared to prior year amounts.
- Total expenses of $927,293,000 increased by $48,921,000 (5.6%) when compared to the prior year. Wastewater Management expenses in 2013 totaled $105,679,000 (11.4%) of total business-type activities. Denver Airport System expenses totaled $801,786,000 (86.5%) of business-type activities. The remaining $19,828,000 (2.1%) of expenses in business-type activities were related to Environmental Services and Golf activities.

Expenses and Program Revenues - Business-type Activities

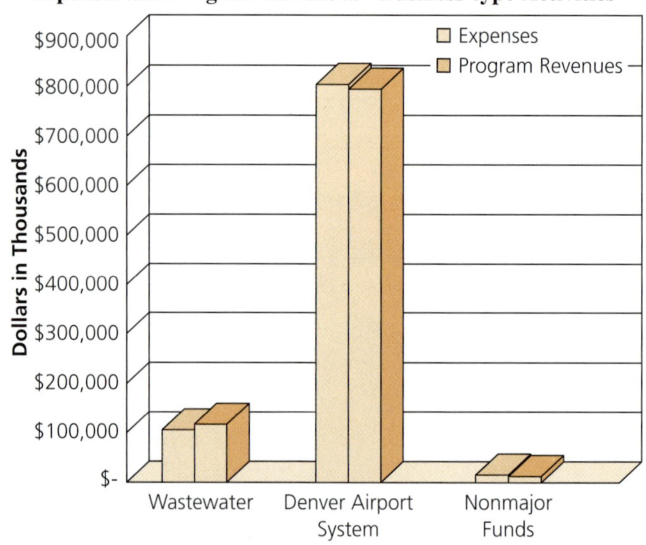

Revenues by Source - Business-type Activities

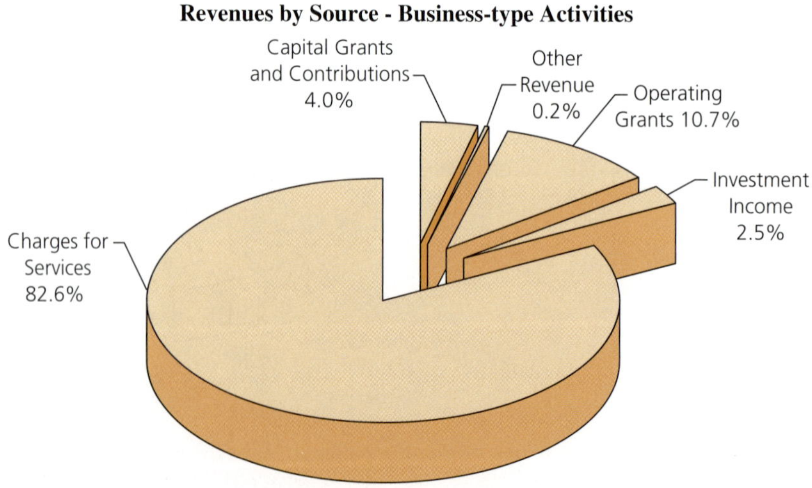

FINANCIAL ANALYSIS OF THE GOVERNMENT'S FUNDS

As noted earlier, the City uses fund accounting to ensure and demonstrate compliance with finance-related legal requirements.

Governmental Funds

The focus of the City's governmental funds is to provide information on current year revenues, expenditures, and balances of spendable resources. Such information is useful in assessing the City's near-term financing requirements. In particular, unassigned fund balance may serve as a useful measure of a government's net resources available for spending at the end of the fiscal year.

As of December 31, 2013, the City's governmental funds reported combined ending fund balances of $774,000, an increase of $85,460 in comparison with the prior year. Approximately 26% or $201,030,000 of the total fund balance amount constitutes unassigned fund balance, which is available for spending at the City's discretion.

The General Fund is the chief operating fund of the City. As of December 31, 2013, unassigned fund balance of the General Fund was $201,030,000, while total fund balance was $287,335,000. As a measure of the General Fund's liquidity, it may be useful to compare both unassigned fund balance and total fund balance to total fund expenditures. Unassigned fund balance represents 20.7% of total General Fund expenditures, including transfers out, of $971,218,000, while total fund balance represents 29.6% of the same amount.

The total fund balance of the City's General Fund increased by $60,487,000 (26.7%) during the year ended December 31, 2013. This is a result of recovering revenues following the economic downturn and cost savings measures implemented to reduce overall expenditures.

Almost every revenue source increased slightly in 2013 due to a recovery of the economy. Total General Fund revenues, including transfers in, of $1,031,400,000 increased by $96,045,000 or 10.3%. Certain revenues in the General Fund that increased from 2012 to 2013 include:

- Sales and use taxes earned were higher by $41,650,000. This increase is primarily attributable to improvements in the economy.
- Motor Vehicle ownership revenue increased by $1,216,000 as a result of an increase in vehicle registrations.
- Property taxes were higher by $29,323,000 primarily due to higher collections allowed by TABOR.
- Licenses and permits revenues increased by $9,010,000 largely due to an increase in construction activity as well as an increase in the value of the activity.
- Charges for services increased by $5,778,000. Factors contributing to this increase include additional revenue reimbursement from enterprise funds, growth in plan review revenue associated with improvements in local construction activity, and various other fee increases.
- Fines and forfeitures increased by $1,591,000. Factors contributing to this increase are higher collections in Photo Radar and traffic court fines.

Some revenues in the General Fund decreased from 2012 to 2013, including:

- Investment income decreased by $2,716,000 due to the investment portfolio securities' unrealized gains being less at year end than the prior year.

The national and local economies continued to recover in 2013 following the recession of 2009. The City continued to monitor 2013 expenditures. Total General Fund expenditures, including transfers out, increased by $47,022,000, or 5.1%. The primary drivers of this increase are personnel cost increases and transfers out.

The Human Services special revenue fund had a total fund balance of $40,391,000. This amounts to a net increase in fund balance of $6,950,000 during the current year. The underlying reasons for the change include increased cash and decreased liabilities at year-end when compared to 2012 due to increased property tax revenue resulting from an improving economy.

Proprietary Funds

The City's proprietary funds provide the same type of information found in the government-wide financial statements, but in more detail.

Total net position of Wastewater Management was $542,618,000 and for the Denver Airport System net position was $573,524,000. Net position for all enterprise funds increased $36,255,000. Other significant factors concerning the finances of the enterprise funds can be found in the discussion of the City's business-type activities.

GENERAL FUND BUDGETARY HIGHLIGHTS

Differences between the General Fund original budget and the final amended budget include a revision to both the projected revenues and expenditures.

Original revenue estimates for 2013, prepared in the summer of 2012, were based on a gradual growth in the economy. The original projection was for sales and use tax growth of 4.0% above 2012 amounts and an overall growth rate in the General Fund of 3.5% over 2012 revised figures. The revenue forecast, including transfers in, was revised upward by $66,307,000 or 7%, over original projections, during 2013 primarily due to the passage of ballot measure 2A in November 2012. The major revisions by individual revenue type are listed below:

- Property tax collections were revised up by $32,901,000, or 44.5%, due to restoring credited mills that had been used to stay under TABOR revenue growth limits.
- The sales and use tax estimate was revised upward by $12,181,000, or 2.6%, due to collections exceeding original growth expectations.
- The occupational privilege tax estimate was revised upward by $825,000, or 2.0%, to better align with year-to-date collections and projected job growth for the State.
- Licenses and permitting revenue projections were revised upward by $6,884,000, or 30.2%, due to an increase in construction activity.
- Transfers in was revised upward by $1,851,000, or 5.3%, to account for additional Convention Center excise tax revenue being transferred to the General Fund.

Differences between the final amended budget and actual revenues and expenditures are briefly summarized in the following paragraph. While the national economy continues to slowly improve, Denver's economy has performed stronger than anticipated and outperforms the nation.

In 2013, actual General Fund revenues, including transfers in, were approximately $23,757,000 higher than the revised budget for 2013, or 2.3%, primarily due to various revenues performing better than expected. General Fund budget basis expenditures were approximately $17,343,000 less than the final budget. This is due to achieving expected unspent appropriations, due in large part of savings measures put in place to respond to the recession, including compensation savings and equipment replacement deferrals.

CAPITAL ASSETS AND BONDED DEBT ADMINISTRATION

Capital Assets

The City's capital assets for its governmental and business-type activities as of December 31, 2013, were $6,611,782,000 (net of accumulated depreciation). This investment in capital assets includes land and land rights, collections, buildings and improvements, equipment and other, park facilities, and, for governmental activities, infrastructure (including streets, alleys, traffic signals, bridges, fiber optic cable, and trails). Infrastructure-type assets of business-type activities are reported as buildings and improvements. The City's capital assets by type at December 31, 2013 and 2012 are shown in **Table B9–3** (dollars in thousands):

TABLE B9–3

	Governmental Activities		Business-type Activities		Total Primary Government	
	2013	2012	2013	2012	2013	2012
Land and construction in progress	$ 380,878	$ 379,899	$ 765,747	$ 508,552	$1,146,625	$ 888,451
Buildings and Improvements	2,299,029	2,256,276	5,100,647	5,086,021	7,399,676	7,342,297
Equipment and other	320,602	302,418	789,536	791,280	1,110,138	1,093,698
Collections	53,741	62,324	—	—	53,741	62,324
Infrastructure	1,417,729	1,345,162	—	—	1,417,729	1,345,162
Less accumulated depreciation	(1,623,084)	(1,498,004)	(2,893,043)	(2,723,052)	(4,516,127)	(4,221,056)
Total	**$2,848,895**	**$2,848,075**	**$3,762,887**	**$3,662,801**	**$6,611,782**	**$6,510,876**

Major capital asset activity for the year ended December 31, 2013 included the following:

- Governmental Activities – The Police Command Vehicle Garage and Justice Center Staff Services Area projects were all placed in service in 2013 as part of the Better Denver Bond projects.
- Business-type Activities – Additions to the Wastewater Collection system of $14,734,000 occurred in 2013 and Denver Airport System continued construction on the South Terminal Redevelopment Program.

Additional information on the City's capital asset activity for the year can be found in **Note III-D** in the notes to basic financial statements.

Bonded Debt

At December 31, 2013, the City had total bonded indebtedness of $5,606,654,000 (excluding GID Bond of $4,920,000). Of this amount, $903,939,000 comprises debt backed by the full faith and credit of the City. The remainder of the City's debt, $4,702,715,000, represents bonds and commercial paper notes secured by specified revenue sources (i.e., revenue bonds of the Denver Airport System, Wastewater Management, and excise tax revenue bonds). The City has no outstanding commercial paper notes as of December 31, 2013.

As of December 31, 2013, the City's general obligation debt is rated AAA by Standard & Poor's rating agency, Fitch Ratings, and Moody's Investors Service.

On July 15, 2013, the Airport System issued $326,260,000 and $393,655,000 of Airport System Subordinate Revenue bonds Series 2013A and Series 2013B, respectively, in a fixed rate mode to finance a portion of the costs of the Airports 2013–2018 Capital Program.

Outstanding bonded debt at December 31, 2013, and 2012, is reflected in **Table B9–4** (dollars in thousands):

TABLE B9–4

	Governmental Activities		Business-type Activities		Total Primary Government	
	2013	**2012**	**2013**	**2012**	**2013**	**2012**
General obligation bonds	$ 903,939	$ 895,649	$ —	$ —	$ 903,939	$ 895,649
Revenue bonds	211,325	230,650	4,491,390	3,950,425	4,702,715	4,181,075
Total	**$1,115,264**	**$1,126,299**	**$4,491,390**	**$3,950,425**	**$5,606,654**	**$5,076,724**

Additional information on the City's bonded debt for the year can be found in **Note III-G** in the notes to the basic financial statements.

ECONOMIC FACTORS AND NEXT YEAR'S BUDGET

The original 2014 budget assumes moderate growth in the local economy. The 2014 General Fund original revenues, including transfers in, are projected to be $1,043,457,000, which is an increase of 1.2% from actual 2013 revenues. It is anticipated that 2014 revenues will be revised upward to reflect better than expected performance in 2013 and the early part of 2014. Measures have been taken to have expenditures be in line with anticipated revenues.

It is anticipated that fund balance will increase during 2014 and the City remains committed to growing General Fund reserves.

REQUESTS FOR INFORMATION

This financial report is designed to provide a general overview of the City's finances for all those with an interest in the government's finances. Questions concerning the information provided in this report or requests for additional financial information should be addressed to the Controller's Office, 201 West Colfax Avenue, Department 1109, Denver, CO 80202. The report is available online at www.denvergov.org/finance.

Key Terms

Blended presentation, *355*
Component unit, *354*
Discrete presentation, *356*
Financially accountable, *354*
Financial reporting entity, *354*
Fiscally dependent, *354*
Intra-entity transactions, *372*
Joint venture, *357*
Jointly governed organizations, *357*
Other comprehensive basis of accounting, (OCBOA), *374*
Other stand-alone government, *357*
Popular reports, *373*
Primary government, *353*

Selected References

American Institute of Certified Public Accountants, *Codification of Statements on Auditing Standards.* New York, 2014.

American Institute of Certified Public Accountants, Audit and Accounting Guide. *State and Local Governments.* New York, 2014.

Crawford, Michael A. AICPA Practice Aid Series, *Applying OCBOA in State and Local Governmental Financial Statements,* edited by Leslye Givarz. New York: AICPA, 2003.

Governmental Accounting Standards Board. *Codification of Governmental Accounting and Financial Reporting Standards, as of June 30, 2014.* Norwalk, CT, 2014.

Questions

9–1. Under GASB guidance when should an item be recognized on the face of the financial statements? Under what conditions, would the GASB indicate that a note disclosure should accompany an item that has been recognized on the financial statements?

9–2. State and general purpose local governments are considered primary governments. Under what circumstances would a special purpose government be considered a primary government?

9–3. A city manager was overheard saying, "Since we don't release them to the public, I don't see any value in taking the time to prepare interim reports." Explain why you agree or disagree with this statement.

9–4. What is a financial reporting entity and what organizations generally make up a financial reporting entity?

9–5. Explain the difference between a blended and discretely presented component unit, and explain how each is reported.

9–6. Explain the difference between a CAFR and general purpose external financial reports.

9–7. Assuming that a government has governmental, proprietary, and fiduciary funds, identify the nine financial statements that must be prepared for the CAFR.

9–8. Give examples of items (transactions) that would require reconciliation of total governmental fund balances to net position of governmental activities.

9–9. What is popular reporting? How does it compare to GAAP based reporting?

9–10. Define OCBOA and explain what, if any, relationship exists between GAAP and OCBOA reporting by a government.

Cases

9–11 Identification of Component Units. Following are descriptions of several relationships between primary governments and other organizations.*

Required

Using just the information provided, indicate whether you believe the primary government should include the organization as a component unit. Please explain your answer.

* Information used in this case is adapted from information provided in the GASB *Comprehensive Implementation Guide* (Norwalk, CT, 2010).

a. Tesser Municipal Hospital is a not-for-profit corporation, whose governing board is appointed by the Tesser city mayor. The hospital manages its day-to-day operations and sets its own fee schedule. The governing board provides preliminary approval of the hospital budget, with final approval required by the Tesser city council. Bonded debt for the hospital is repaid with the hospital's revenues.

b. The Atkins Convention and Visitor's Bureau is a not-for-profit organization funded by a hotel tax levied by the City of Atkins. By city statute, the hotel tax is set by the city and can be used only by the Convention and Visitor's Bureau.

c. The Sports Authority of Dawson County is a legally separate organization with its own elected board. It annually presents its budget to the Dawson County Commission for commissioners' input and recommendations. The Sports Authority incorporates those recommendations it deems beneficial.

d. The County Aviation Authority has issued bonds that are guaranteed by the City of Middle Falls. The Aviation Authority will use its revenues to service the debt. Middle Falls believes that the probability it will have to cover any debt service requirements related to the Aviation Authority bonds is remote.

e. Help for Kids is a not-for-profit organization that receives funding from Alice County. Each year Help for Kids is required to submit its audited financial statements and approved budget to Alice County. County commissioners review the financial statements and budgets to ensure that the resources provided by the county are being used in an approved manner.

9–12 MD&A and Statistical Tables. The MD&A for the 2013 City and County of Denver CAFR is included as Appendix B in this chapter. Following are two tables that have been adapted from the statistical section of the CAFR. Use the MD&A and the provided statistical tables to complete this case.

Required

a. What are the three largest sources of governmental funds revenue? What percentage of the governmental funds revenue is from each of these sources?

b. Sales tax is a large part of Denver's tax revenue. Using information from the MD&A and trend information from both statistical tables provided, discuss trends in Denver's sales tax revenues and your projection for sales tax revenues over the next two to three years.

c. What are the three largest sources of governmental funds expenditures? What percentage of the governmental funds expenditures does each of the three sources represent?

d. Compare the growth in the three largest revenue sources to the growth in the three largest expenditure sources over the past 10years. Using the information from the MD&A and the trend information discuss any changes in the overall expenditure growth patterns you have seen and would expect to see over the next two to three years.

CITY AND COUNTY OF DENVER, COLORADO

Changes in Fund Balance of Governmental Funds (Partial Statement)
Last Ten Fiscal Years
(Dollars in Thousands - Modified Accrual Basis of Accounting)

	2004	2005	2006	2007	2008	2009	2010	2011	2012	2013
Revenues										
Property taxes	$ 179,497	$ 212,778	$ 217,119	$ 227,188	$ 274,809	$ 259,963	$ 295,381	$ 288,106	$ 287,062	$ 331,914
Sales and use taxes	381,891	417,079	420,693	455,436	468,137	421,838	447,071	481,023	494,495	539,348
Other taxes	116,507	123,326	121,539	150,017	136,211	118,165	124,855	132,259	140,123	146,875
Special assessments	655	1,467	1,359	1,370	1,394	1,342	1,397	1,429	1,422	1,702
Licenses and permits	23,667	26,173	27,438	29,383	29,364	24,555	29,907	31,094	35,393	44,415
Intergovernmental revenue	192,256	170,760	188,010	211,351	247,386	208,031	213,568	227,776	236,892	206,878
Charges for services	130,888	121,920	160,030	156,564	189,494	190,940	196,642	200,728	219,691	225,169
Investment and interest Income	14,449	16,612	26,287	39,990	34,340	11,826	21,225	23,680	10,738	2,003
Fines and forfeitures	33,512	32,844	36,856	37,013	41,473	44,863	47,628	58,075	55,964	57,469
Contributions	18,951	13,698	15,871	8,668	9,022	5,741	5,961	8,661	6,515	7,086
Other revenue	37,520	26,729	38,246	40,376	40,167	50,664	53,840	64,905	51,030	55,664
Total revenues	**1,129,793**	**1,163,386**	**1,253,448**	**1,357,356**	**1,471,797**	**1,337,928**	**1,437,475**	**1,517,736**	**1,539,325**	**1,618,523**
Expenditures										
General government	166,375	170,543	203,266	236,694	255,008	249,526	243,697	239,138	242,091	258,408
Public safety	364,355	427,634	437,632	470,978	534,984	488,380	499,293	514,421	545,395	552,663
Public works	67,957	69,247	74,339	96,313	125,668	168,048	149,812	155,204	207,205	170,129
Health	45,767	46,533	47,739	48,694	52,191	52,734	53,035	52,415	52,848	54,205
Human services	98,234	98,041	112,112	129,451	139,013	128,592	11 9,083	114,004	110,784	114,079
Parks and recreation	48,840	50,224	52,297	59,791	100,928	100,182	58,212	63,895	61,761	66,992
Cultural activities	54,226	66,901	81,307	72,974	40,826	71,143	77,547	80,599	87,984	98,038
Community development	44,273	41,062	34,069	53,877	37,808	41,251	50,240	49,882	40,505	35,030
Economic opportunity	19,130	17,702	20,512	26,122	31,486	31,885	25,860	22,939	21,482	21,321
Principal retirement	66,784	88,669	79,837	81,685	70,807	65,590	70,387	81,269	87,393	99,525
Interest	56,037	52,227	56,525	53,387	82,598	61,351	60,773	79,425	75,351	72,842
Bond issue cost	297	205	1	421	833	3,272	3,041	289	—	—
Capital outlay	211,182	102,394	88,695	95,821	210,430	192,232	142,706	155,267	93,934	45,877
Total Expenditures	**1,243,457**	**1,231,382**	**1,288,331**	**1,426,208**	**1,682,580**	**1,654,186**	**1,553,686**	**1,608,747**	**1,626,733**	**1,589,109**
Deficiency of revenues under expenditures	(113,664)	(67,996)	(34,883)	(68,852)	(210,783)	(316,258)	(116,211)	(91,011)	(87,408)	29,414

CITY AND COUNTY OF DENVER, COLORADO
Sales and Use Tax by Category
Last Ten Calendar Years
(Dollars in Thousands - Modified Accrual Basis of Accounting)

	2004	2005	2006	2007	2008	2009	2010	2011	2012	2013
Apparel stores	$ 14,380	$ 15,207	$ 15,179	$ 16,474	$ 17,691	$ 16,241	$ 18,356	$ 20,237	$ 21,796	$ 22,778
General merchandise	16,583	16,356	16,892	16,209	16,953	14,699	16,921	16,825	17,161	17,704
Food stores	15,420	15,845	16,729	16,210	17,961	17,795	18,790	19,467	20,269	21,399
Eating and drinking establishments	53,763	56,824	60,252	60,097	67,878	64,798	68,520	75,531	77,886	85,211
Home furnishings, electronics and appliances	17,727	20,255	21,268	21,543	22,461	19,105	20,413	21,827	22,584	24,410
Building materials and farm tools	35,058	39,322	39,353	35,826	37,741	31,258	30,962	33,700	36,837	44,188
Auto dealers and supplies	40,394	38,860	38,093	38,350	39,584	33,927	35,853	41,544	44,371	50,021
Service stations	14,597	13,390	13,702	11,942	10,719	14,792	20,345	16,798	15,100	14,396
Public utilities	21,928	24,598	25,068	24,503	30,145	26,118	28,783	30,333	28,164	30,944
Manufacturing	31,124	33,720	35,808	34,033	34,947	29,666	31,526	35,073	36,415	40,651
Information producers and distributors	34,329	37,376	39,768	36,164	41,431	36,154	37,531	40,445	38,576	37,877
Other retail stores	28,409	27,543	25,506	44,383	40,913	29,743	34,631	47,463	51,512	52,656
All other outlets	58,179	77,783	73,075	99,702	89,713	87,542	84,440	81,780	83,824	97,113
Total	**$381,891**	**$417,079**	**$420,693**	**$455,436**	**$468,137**	**$421,838**	**$447,071**	**$481,023**	**$494,495**	**$539,348**
City direct sales tax rate	3.50%	3.50%	3.50%	3.62%	3.62%	3.62%	3.62%	3.62%	3.62%	3.62%

9–13 Classification of Fund Balances. In its notes to the financial statements the City of St. Petersburg, Florida provided the following information about the amounts and classifications for the St. Petersburg fund balances. Use the information provided by St. Petersburg to complete this case.

Required

a. St. Petersburg lists a number of nonspendable fund balances. Explain what characteristic(s) the advances would need to possess to be classified as non-spendable. Explain possible characteristics the Library fund balance possesses that would cause it to be classified as nonspendable.

b. Identify where St. Petersburg has reported unassigned fund balances and discuss whether you agree with St. Petersburg's decision and why.

CITY OF ST. PETERSBURG
Notes to the Basic Financial Statements
For the Fiscal Year Ended September 30, 2013

	General	Community Redevelopment Districts	Downtown Redevelopment District	Local Option Sales Surtax Improvement	Grants	Non major Governmental	Total Governmental Funds
Non Spendable							
Advances From Other Funds	$ 4,315,069	$ —	$ —	$ —	$ —	$ —	$ 4,315,069
Library	—	—	—	—	—	238,396	238,396
Kopsick Palm Arboretum	—	—	—	—	—	130,803	130,803
Prepaid Deposit and Inventory	452,771	40	—	—	—	16,459	469,270
Total Non Spendable	4,467,840	40	—	—	—	385,658	5,153,538
Restricted							
Redevelopment Districts	—	1,860,448	$5,004,028	—	—	—	6,864,476
Public Safety Capital Improvement	—	—	—	12,144,696	—	—	12,144,695
City & Neighborhood Infrastructure	—	—	—	23,528,151	—	—	23,528,151
Recreation and Culture Capital Improvement	—	—	—	10,192,465	—	—	10,192,465
City Facilities Capital Improvement	—	—	—	2,179,872	—	—	2,179,872
Fire Rescue and EMS Awards	—	—	—	—	—	29,271	29,271
Debt Service Payments	—	—	—	—	—	9,491,193	9,491,193
Public Safety	—	—	—	—	—	3,242,792	3,242,792
Housing Assistance	—	—	—	—	—	1,114,968	1,114,968
Recreation and Culture	—	—	—	—	367,011	9,335,574	9,702,585
Building Code Enforcement	—	—	—	—	—	3,139,748	3,139,748
Total Restricted	—	1,860,448	5,004,028	48,045,183	367,011	26,353,546	81,630,216
Committed							
General Capital Improvements	—	—	—	—	—	2,853,733	2,853,733
Transportation Improvements	—	—	—	—	—	588,020	588,020
Housing Capital Improvements	—	—	—	—	—	44,560	44,560
Land sale proceeds	7,500	—	—	—	—	—	7,500

continued

	General	Community Redevelopment Districts	Downtown Redevelopment District	Local Option Sales Surtax Improvement	Grants	Non major Governmental	Total Governmental Funds
Committed (continued)							
Economic Stability and Budget Shortfalls	22,819,412	—	—	—	—	—	22,819,412
Preservation Projects	924,482	—	—	—	—	—	924,482
Operating reappropriations	1,036,848	—	—	—	—	—	1,036,848
Qualified Target Industry (QTI) Tax	18,000	—	—	—	—	—	18,000
Recreation and Culture	258,782	—	—	—	—	11,276,550	11,535,332
Total Committed	25,065,024	—	—	—	—	14,762,863	39,827,887
Assigned							
General Capital Improvement	—	—	—	—	—	2,307,357	2,307,357
Housing Capital Improvement	—	—	—	—	—	339,496	339,496
Transportation Improvement	—	—	—	—	—	16,587,842	16,587,842
Downtown Parking Garage Improvement	—	—	—	—	—	668,729	668,729
Recreation and Culture	—	—	—	—	—	1,007,889	1,007,889
Total Assigned	—	—	—	—	—	20,911,313	20,911,313
Unassigned	10,197,562	—	—	—	—	(21,667)	10,175,895
Total Fund Balances	$40,030,426	$1,860,488	$5,004,028	$48,045,183	$367,011	$62,391,713	$157,698,849

9–14 Research Case—Popular Reports. Throughout Chapters 2-9 reference has been made to the City and County of Denver's Comprehensive Annual Financial Report (CAFR). In addition to issuing the CAFR the City and County of Denver issues a Popular Annual Financial Report (PAFR). To complete this case access the City and County of Denver's PAFR at its Web site (Hint: Look for the Finance department reports) and information on the GFOA PAFR Award program on the Government Finance Officers Association's (GFOA) Web site.

Required

a. The GFOA PAFR Award program lists four eligibility criteria in addition to the requirement that a government's CAFR report receive the Certificate of Achievement for Excellence in Financial Reporting. Evaluate Denver's PAFR relative to these four criteria and explain how you believe the Denver PAFR clearly meets the four criteria.

b. Due to the size and complexity of the CAFR, popular reports are encouraged as a method of increasing communication with various users of government financial information. Evaluate Denver's PAFR and explain whether you believe the PAFR meets each of the following three criteria—visually appealing for the reader, understandable, and provides relevant information. The criteria should be evaluated relative to the following user groups:

1. Citizens
2. Creditors

Exercises and Problems

9–15 Examine the CAFR. Utilizing the CAFR obtained for Exercise 1–16 and your answers to the questions asked in Exercise 1–16 and the corresponding exercises in Chapters 2 through 8, comment on the following:

a. Analysis of Introductory Section. Does the report contain all of the introductory material recommended by the GASB? Is the introductory material presented in such a manner that it communicates significant information effectively—do you understand what the government is telling you? On the basis of your study of the entire report, do you think the introductory material presents the information fairly? Comment on any information in the introductory section you feel is unnecessary, and explain why.

b. Analysis of Financial Statements.

1. Do the statements, notes, and schedules in the financial section present the information required by the GASB? Are Total columns provided in the basic financial statements and schedules for the primary government and the reporting entity? If so, are the Total columns for the current year compared with Total columns for the prior year?
2. Review your answers to the questions asked in Exercises 3–15 and 4–15 in light of your study of subsequent chapters of the text and your analysis of all portions of the annual report. Based on your current knowledge and understanding of government accounting, would you change or modify any of your earlier answers? If so, explain how you would change them and why you would change them.

c. Analysis of Statistical Section. Does the statistical section present information in the five categories defined by the GASB? What tables and schedules are presented for each category? Does the information provided in each category appear to meet the purpose of the category? Explain your response.

d. Service Potential of the CAFR. In your opinion, what are the most important information needs that a governmental annual report should fulfill for each of the following:

1. Administrators.
2. Members of the legislative branch.
3. Interested residents.
4. Creditors or potential creditors.

In what ways does the CAFR you have analyzed meet the information needs you have specified for each of the four groups, assuming that members of each group make an effort to understand reports equivalent to the effort you have made? In what way does the report fail to meet the information needs of each of the four groups?

9–16 Multiple Choice. Choose the best answer.

1. The members of the Museum Board of the City of Springfield are appointed by the City of Springfield City Council, which has agreed to finance any operating deficits of the museum. Under these conditions:
   a. The museum is a primary government.
   b. The city and the museum together are a financial reporting entity.
   c. The museum is a special district.
   d. The museum is a component unit of the city.
2. Interim government financial reports:
   a. Are not necessary because administrators and managers of the government are already familiar with the events and activities of the government on a day to day basis.

b. Should be prepared and distributed publicly at regular intervals.
c. Are important for budgetary and cash management purposes.
d. Are not necessary as long as the government prepares a comprehensive annual financial report (CAFR).

3. The comprehensive annual financial report (CAFR) of a governmental reporting entity should contain a statement of cash flows for:

	Governmental Funds	Proprietary Funds
a.	Yes	No
b.	Yes	Yes
c.	No	Yes
d.	No	No

4. Which of the following terms would be used when describing a primary government?
a. Fiscally independent.
b. Legally separate organization.
c. Separately elected governing body.
d. All of the above.

5. The city council of Lake Jefferson passed a resolution to establish a small botanical garden in the city park. The council decided to put aside funds in the amount of $22,000 to build and establish the botanical garden. At the end of the fiscal year, $3,000 of the funds had been spent. How should the remainder of the funds be reported?
a. Committed fund balance.
b. Assigned fund balance.
c. Restricted fund balance.
d. Nonspendable fund balance.

6. Which of the following require a statement of changes in net position?
a. Fiduciary funds.
b. Government-wide financial statements.
c. All governmental funds.
d. Both proprietary funds and fiduciary funds.

7. What are intra-entity transactions?
a. Nonexchange transactions between a primary government and its component units.
b. Exchange or nonexchange transactions between a primary government and its component units.
c. Exchange or nonexchange transactions between a primary government and any discretely presented component units.
d. Exchange transactions between a primary government and any blended component units.

8. Which of the following would *not* be included as a reconciling item in reconciling the governmental fund statement of revenues, expenditures, and changes in fund balance to the government-wide statement of activities?
a. Bond issuances reported as an other financing source in a governmental fund.
b. Interest accrued on long-term notes payable.
c. Acquisition of capital assets reported as an expenditure in the governmental fund financial statements.
d. Interest accrued on Property Taxes Receivable—Delinquent.

9. A positive unassigned fund balance can be found in which of the following funds?
   a. Special revenue fund.
   b. Debt service fund.
   c. General fund.
   d. All of the above.
10. Which of the following is generally considered an other comprehensive basis of accounting (OCBOA) acceptable for governments?
    a. Cash.
    b. Budgetary.
    c. Accrual.
    d. Reserve cash.

9–17 Primary Governments. The GASB defines a financial reporting entity as the primary government and the entities for which the primary government is financially accountable. Following is a list of entities being considered for classification as primary governments.

_____1. Waseca County government.
_____2. University of South Florida, a part of the State University System of Florida.
_____3. The Tri-County Independent School District, a legal entity, with an elected board and financial independence.
_____4. The State of Colorado.
_____5. Greenfield Sports Authority, a joint venture between Greenfield County and the Mighty Ducks Sports franchise.

Required

For each of the entities listed indicate with a Y (yes) if the entity would be considered a primary government and with an N (no) if it would not be considered a primary government. In addition, explain why you believe the entity should or should not be considered a primary government.

9–18 Comprehensive Set of Transactions. The City of Lynnwood was recently incorporated and had the following transactions for the fiscal year ended December 31, 2017.

1. The city council adopted a General Fund budget for the fiscal year. Revenues were estimated at $2,000,000 and appropriations were $1,990,000.
2. Property taxes in the amount of $1,940,000 were levied. It is estimated that $9,000 of the taxes levied will be uncollectible.
3. A General Fund transfer of $25,000 in cash and $300,000 in equipment (with accumulated depreciation of $65,000) was made to establish a central duplicating internal service fund.
4. A citizen of Lynnwood donated marketable securities with a fair value of $800,000. The donated resources are to be maintained in perpetuity with the city using the revenue generated by the donation to finance an after school program for children, which is sponsored by the culture and recreation function. Revenue earned and received as of December 31, 2017, was $40,000.
5. The city's utility fund billed the city's General Fund $125,000 for water and sewage services. As of December 31, the General Fund had paid $124,000 of the amount billed.
6. The central duplicating fund purchased $4,500 in supplies.

7. Cash collections recorded by the general government function during the year were as follows:

Property taxes	$1,925,000
Licenses and permits	35,000
User charges	28,000

8. During the year the internal service fund billed the city's general government function $15,700 for duplicating services and it billed the city's utility fund $8,100 for services.
9. The city council decided to build a city hall at an estimated cost of $5,000,000. To finance the construction, 6 percent bonds were sold at the face value of $5,000,000. A contract for $4,500,000 has been signed for the project; however, no expenditures have been incurred as of December 31, 2017.
10. The general government function issued a purchase order for $32,000 for computer equipment. When the equipment was received, a voucher for $31,900 was approved for payment and payment was made.

Required

Prepare all journal entries to properly record each transaction for the fiscal year ended December 31, 2017. Use the following funds and government-wide activities, as necessary:

General Fund	GF
Capital projects fund	CPF
Internal service fund	ISF
Permanent fund	PF
After School Fund (a special revenue fund)	SRF
Enterprise fund	EF
Governmental activities	GA

Each journal entry should be numbered to correspond with each transaction. Do *not* prepare closing entries.

Your answer sheet should be organized as follows:

			Amounts	
Transaction Number	Fund or Activity	Account Title	Debits	Credits

9–19 Reconciliation of the Governmental Funds Balance Sheet to the Statement of Net Position. The following information has been provided for the City of Elizabeth for its fiscal year ended June 30, 2017. The information provided relates to financial information reported on the city's statement of net position and its total governmental funds balance.

Revenues accrued but unavailable to pay the current period expenditures	$361,200
Capital assets	639,900
Accumulated depreciation on capital assets	353,400
Accrued interest on bonds and long-term notes payable	1,200
Bonds and long-term notes payable	174,200
Unamortized premium on bonds payable	700
Compensated absences	13,300
Total governmental fund balances	157,700
Total net position of governmental activities	616,000

Required

Using the information provided, prepare in good form a reconciliation of the governmental fund balances to the net position of governmental activities (Hint: See Illustration 9–7 and A2–4).

9–20 Net Position Classification. Section A provides a list of transactions or events that occurred during the year, followed by Section B, a list of the possible effects each transaction or event has on adjusting net position accounts at year-end, assuming that all temporary accounts have already been closed to the account Net Position—Unrestricted.

Section A

_____ 1. Depreciation was recorded for the year.
_____ 2. A fully depreciated computer was sold for $50.
_____ 3. Bonds issued to construct the new library were retired.
_____ 4. Construction expenditures were incurred for the new fire substation.
_____ 5. Grant funds that can only be used for a summer kids' camp remain unexpended at year-end.
_____ 6. An operating lease was entered into during the year.
_____ 7. A $3 million endowment was received during the year.
_____ 8. Several new fire trucks were purchased and 70 percent financed with long-term notes.
_____ 9. The capital projects fund transferred its residual fund balance to the debt service fund during the year.
_____10. A grant received in the prior year for afterschool recreational activities was expended.

Section B

a. Restricted Net Position is **increased** and Unrestricted Net Position is **decreased.**
b. Restricted Net Position is **decreased** and Unrestricted Net Position is **increased.**
c. Net Investment in Capital Assets is **increased** and Unrestricted Net Position is **decreased.**
d. Net Investment in Capital Assets is **decreased** and Unrestricted Net Position is **increased.**
e. None of the above.

Required

Identify how the net position categories would need to be adjusted for each of the transactions. For the statement in Section A, select the appropriate answer from Section B.

9–21 Change in Net Position of Governmental Activities. You have been provided with the following information concerning operating activity for Annette County. For the year ended June 30, 2017, the net change in total governmental fund balances was $(289,200), and the change in net position of governmental activities was $194,300. During the year, Annette issued $2,000,000 in general obligation bonds at a premium of 101. The bonds are to be used for a construction project. The county acquired $2,750,00 in capital assets and sold capital assets with a book value of $563,000 for $570,900. At the beginning of the period accrued liabilities were $470,000 and at the end of the period they totaled $494,000. Depreciation on capital assets totaled $595,000. Revenue accrued for the period but not available for use totaled $364,600.

Required

Using the information provided, prepare a reconciliation of the change in governmental fund balance to the change in net position of governmental activities.

9–22 Governmental Funds Statement of Revenues, Expenditures, and Changes in Fund Balances. You have recently started working as the controller for a small county. The county is preparing its financial statements for the comprehensive annual financial report and you have been given the following statement for review. You know that in addition to the General Fund the county has three other funds.

Statement of Revenues, Expenses, and Changes in Fund Balances
Governmental Funds
For the Year Ended December 31, 2017
(000s omitted)

	General Fund	Other Governmental Funds
Revenue and other financing sources:		
Taxes	$10,156	
Licenses and permits	612	
Charges for services	985	
Intergovernmental revenue	2,657	$1,437
Fines and forfeits	422	
Debt proceeds		5,919
Miscellaneous revenues	325	23
Total Revenues and Other Financing Sources	15,157	7,379
Expenses and other financing uses:		
General government and debt service	3,187	961
Public safety and capital outlay	6,257	689
Public works and capital outlay	3,269	2,310
Culture and recreation and capital outlay	2,088	1,748
Transfers out	604	
Total Expenses and Other Financing Uses	15,405	5,708
Net Change in Fund Balances	$ (248)	$1,671

Required

After reviewing the statement, you realize it is not in the GASB format. To help your staff correct the statement, please make a list of the modifications or corrections that should be made to the statement, so it can be presented in the proper format.

9–23 Government-wide Financial Statements. Following is the governmental activities pre-closing trial balance for the Town of Freaz. Freaz is a relatively small town and, as a result, it has only governmental funds (i.e., it uses no proprietary funds). There are no component units. To complete the financial statements for its annual report, the town must prepare a government-wide statement of net position and a statement of activities.

TOWN OF FREAZ
Pre-closing Trial Balance
As of June 30, 2017
(000s omitted)

	Debits	*Credits*
Cash	$ 3,639	
Investments	7,299	
Taxes Receivable—Delinquent	5,788	
Allowance for Uncollectible Delinquent Taxes		$ 49
Due from Other Funds	645	
Due from Other Governments	6,343	
Land	8,720	
Buildings	25,680	
Accumulated Depreciation—Buildings		8,021
Infrastructure	85,768	
Accumulated Depreciation—Infrastructure		45,603
Machinery & Equipment	28,720	
Accumulated Depreciation—Machinery & Equipment		13,785
Accounts Payable		7,764
Accrued Liabilities		4,765
Due to Other Funds		748
Current Portion of Long-term Debt		8,600
Bonds Payable		28,700
Net Position—Net Investment in Capital Assets		45,259
Net Position—Restricted for Debt Service		2,123
Net Position—Unrestricted		6,598
Program Revenues—General Government—Charges for Services		4,411
Program Revenues—Public Safety—Charges for Services		996
Program Revenues—Culture & Recreation—Charges for Services		359
Program Revenues—General Government—Operating Grants & Contributions		307
Program Revenues—Public Works—Capital Grants & Contributions		1,680
General Revenues—Property Taxes		13,665
General Revenues—Interest & Penalties		746
General Revenues—Interest Income		345
Expenses—General Government	2,468	
Expenses—Public Safety	11,577	
Expenses—Public Works	5,311	
Expenses—Culture & Recreation	1,817	
Expenses—Interest on Long-term Debt	749	
	$194,524	$194,524

Required

Using the trial balance provided by the town, prepare a government-wide statement of activities and a statement of net position. The restricted net position for debt service increased $87 for FY 2017. The net position accounts do not reflect FY 2017 depreciation of $1,080 that was allocated to the functions of government, or the town's decision to designate $900 for street repair. (All 000s omitted.)

9–24 Converting from Modified Accrual to Accrual Accounting. The Village of Rodale keeps its governmental fund accounting records on a modified accrual basis. At the end of the fiscal year, the village accountant must convert the modified accrual information to accrual information to allow for preparation of the government-wide financial statements. Following are several transactions identified by the accountant that will require conversion.

1. At the end of the year, depreciation expense of $674,300 was recorded on buildings and equipment.
2. Year-end salaries amounting to $39,123 were accrued.
3. During the year the village acquired a vehicle at a cost of $21,369 and depreciable office equipment at a cost of $7,680. (*Note:* the village uses a Buildings and Equipment account.)
4. The village made the final $50,000 payment on a long-term loan. Interest related to the loan was $2,250, half of which had been accrued at the end of the prior fiscal year.
5. The records indicate that the Due from Other Funds balance is $720. Of this amount, $480 is due from the Water Utility Fund for service provided by the general government; the remainder is due from a special revenue fund for services provided by the Police Department. The amount Due to Other Funds balance is $950, which the General Fund owes to the Water Utility Fund for water received.

Required

Prepare modified accrual to accrual adjustments for all of the transactions identified in Items 1–5. Your answer sheet should be organized as follows. In the first column, identify the account titles that will be affected by the adjustment. Use the second column to identify whether the account title provided is a modified accrual account or an accrual account. The adjustment columns should record the amount of the debit or credit that would need to be made to adjust information from modified accrual to accrual. Keep in mind that some transactions may not be recorded under modified accrual; in such cases, the debit and credit adjustments affect only accrual accounts since the adjustments are reflected at the government-wide level only.

		Adjustment	
Account Affected	**Modified Accrual/ Accrual Account**	**Debit**	**Credit**

PART **Two**

ACCOUNTABILITY FOR PUBLIC FUNDS

Chapter Ten

Analysis of Governmental Financial Performance

Learning Objectives

After studying this chapter, you should be able to:

10-1 Explain the importance of evaluating governmental financial performance.

10-2 Distinguish among and describe key financial performance concepts, such as: financial position, financial condition, and economic condition.

10-3 Explain the relationships among environmental factors, organizational factors, and financial factors in determining governmental financial condition.

10-4 Identify, calculate, interpret, and analyze key ratios that measure financial performance.

10-5 Describe how benchmarks can aid financial analysis and identify possible sources of government information that can be helpful when benchmarking.

At the end of the 20th century, considerable time and effort were used to increase the quality and transparency of government reporting. Combined efforts on the part of standard-setters, users, preparers, attestors, and bond raters led to higher quality governmental accounting principles, government auditing standards, and programs designed to recognize excellence in financial reporting.

THE NEED TO EVALUATE FINANCIAL PERFORMANCE

Despite improvements in financial reporting and increased public scrutiny, state and local governments have faced criticism from various groups, including the Securities and Exchange Commission, concerning what is perceived as inadequate financial transparency.

Financial transparency[1] is important for those outside government who need to assess government performance as they decide whether to locate in a city, work for public entities, or invest in municipal bonds. Bond investors and creditors have an interest in assessing the government's ability to make future interest and principal

[1] We define financial transparency as all relevant financial information that is fully and freely available to users.

payments, even in the face of adverse economic trends or other events (for example, natural disasters). Knowing that managers are employing a system to track financial trends provides investors and creditors with added confidence in the quality of the government's financial management, particularly if such trend data are shared with credit analysts. Credit analysts also have an interest in the government's ability to provide services in the long run, since experience has shown that, in times of fiscal crisis, expenditures for vital services often take priority over debt service payments.

Oversight bodies have responsibility for monitoring and, in some cases, establishing the fiscal policies of governments for which they have oversight responsibility. Some states, for example, impose uniform financial accounting and reporting systems that all municipalities within the state must follow. Oversight bodies typically have responsibilities to monitor administrators' compliance with laws and regulations.

Citizens should have an interest in their government's overall financial performance given the impact of taxes on individuals and their need for public services. Generally, citizens' interests are represented through intermediaries such as the media, taxpayer *watchdog* groups, special interest groups, and groups that serve the public interest.

While external financial reports are not primarily prepared for managers, ensuring that the government has the financial capacity to sustain desired services is the primary reason management monitors financial performance through its financial reports. Government managers need business skills in order to assess financial performance and thwart disaster from environmental factors. Managers need analytical tools and data offered by the financial statements as they adjust the size and structure of public service delivery systems.

GOVERNMENT FINANCIAL PERFORMANCE CONCEPTS

In an effort to meet the needs of financial statement users, such as citizens and taxpayers, the Governmental Accounting Standards Board (GASB) produced two guides to financial statements.[2] In the first guide, titled *What You Should Know about Your Local Government's Finances,* the GASB points out that government managers need to demonstrate to citizens that they are financially accountable for raising enough resources for the government to remain financially viable. Managers also need to demonstrate they spend resources responsibly. The unique relationship between involuntary tax financing and the provision of public goods and government services requires special care to assess whether government has met its duty to be accountable to citizens. In a related outreach effort to the analyst user community (broadly defined), the GASB produced a user guide titled *An Analyst's Guide to Government Financial Statements* in which it points out that the process of drawing meaning from financial statement data is an art form, not a science.[3] As indicated by these user guides, different people are interested in different aspects of financial health, and those doing the analyzing must focus on the concepts that are most relevant for their purposes.

Prior to examining systems for evaluating financial performance, it is important to distinguish among key terms related to accountability: financial position, financial condition, and economic condition.

[2] Dean M. Mead, *What You Should Know about Your Local Government's Finances: A Guide to Financial Statements* (Norwalk, CT: GASB, 2011). A related guide, also by Dean M. Mead, is *What You Should Know about Your School District's Finances: A Guide to Financial Statements* (2012).

[3] Dean M. Mead, *An Analyst's Guide to Government Financial Statements* (Norwalk, CT: GASB, 2012), p. 277.

Financial Position and Financial Condition

A review of the literature finds that in both the government and business sector the terms *financial condition* and *financial position* tend to be used interchangeably. Although not clearly differentiated by many users, an early GASB research study[4] did attempt to clarify the difference between the two terms. The research study indicates that **financial position** tends to be a short-term concept that focuses on the assets that are cash or are normally converted to cash in the near future and liabilities that require cash in the near future.[5] As can be seen, this definition of financial position is closely related to the concept of liquidity. By contrast, the GASB study defines **financial condition** as follows:

> The probability that a government will meet both its financial obligations to creditors, consumers, employees, taxpayers, suppliers, constituents, and others as they become due and its service obligations to constituents, both currently and in the future.[6]

The International City/County Management Association (ICMA) provides a different definition of financial condition in its publication titled "Evaluating Financial Condition: A Handbook for Local Government."[7] It defines financial condition as composed of four types of solvency: **cash solvency**—a government's ability to generate enough cash over a 30- or 60-day period to pay its bills; **budgetary solvency**—a government's ability to generate enough revenue over its normal budgetary period to meet its expenditures and not incur deficits; **long-run solvency**—a government's ability in the long-run to pay all the costs of doing business such as expenditures in the annual budget and those that appear only in the years in which they must be paid; and **service-level solvency**—a government's ability to provide services at the level and quality that are required for the health, safety, and welfare of the community and that its citizens desire. The ICMA's term *cash solvency* closely aligns with the GASB's definition of financial position; that is, both terms focus on the shorter-term, balance sheet concept addressing whether the government is able to meet its current obligations.

With regard to financial condition, both the GASB study and the ICMA handbook clearly indicate that *financial condition* is broader in scope than financial position. Financial condition includes both the willingness and capacity to meet financial and service obligations. As defined, financial condition is related to the accountability concept of *interperiod equity,* a term the GASB defines as determining "whether current-year revenues are sufficient to pay for the services provided that year and whether future taxpayers will be required to assume burdens for services previously provided."[8] Excessive shifting of the burden to pay for current services to future taxpayers may threaten the government's ability to sustain the current level of services or to expand services to meet future population growth.

[4] Robert Berne, Research Report, "The Relationship between Financial Reporting and the Measurement of Financial Condition" (Norwalk, CT: GASB, 1992).

[5] Ibid., pp. 16–17.

[6] Ibid.

[7] Karl Nollenberger, *Evaluating Financial Condition: A Handbook for Local Government,* 4th ed. (Washington, DC: International City/County Management Association, 2003); a revision of the original 1980 text by Sanford M. Groves and Maureen G. Valente.

[8] Governmental Accounting Standards Board, *Concepts Statement No. 1,* "Objectives of Financial Reporting" (Norwalk, CT: GASB, 1987), par. 61.

Economic Condition

In an effort to avoid confusion associated with the terms financial position and financial condition the GASB has opted to use the term *economic condition*.[9] The choice of the term economic condition also better reflects that in assessing the condition of a government, attention should focus on both the ability and willingness to meet financial and service obligations.[10] The GASB has tentatively defined **economic condition** as

> A composite of a government's financial position and its ability and willingness to meet its financial obligations and service commitments on an ongoing basis.[11]

As seen from the definition, GASB views economic condition as a composite measure for which it has identified three components: financial position, fiscal capacity, and service capacity. The GASB has tentatively defined each of the three components as follows

- *Financial position* is the status of a government's assets, deferred outflows, liabilities, deferred inflows, and net position, as displayed on the financial statements.
- **Fiscal capacity** is the government's ability and willingness to meet its financial obligations as they come due on an ongoing basis.
- **Service capacity** is the government's willingness and ability to meet its commitments and provide services on an ongoing basis.[12]

An important objective of the economic condition project is to determine whether providing additional information to users would be beneficial in determining economic condition. Based on the definition of economic condition, it would appear the information on economic condition would be beneficial to users attempting to assess a government's fiscal sustainability.

INTERNAL FINANCIAL TREND MONITORING

As mentioned earlier in this chapter, the ICMA has a handbook that can be used to track the financial performance of governments. It calls the tool described in the handbook the *financial trend monitoring system.* Credit market analysts, particularly analysts with the major rating agencies, have developed proprietary (in-house) approaches for evaluating the general obligation creditworthiness of governments that issue bonds. Although evaluation objectives differ slightly between internal and external evaluation systems and among the approaches used by external users, both types of systems focus on many of the same kinds of factors. Presumably, these systems can be useful as well for legislative and oversight bodies and citizen groups.

Illustration 10–1 shows the framework the ICMA developed for internal managers to use in evaluating financial condition. The financial trend monitoring system (FTMS) is comprised of environmental, organizational, and financial factors that influence a

[9] GASB *Statement No. 44*, "Economic Condition Reporting: The Statistical Section" (Norwalk, CT: GASB, 2004), par.49.

[10] Lisa Parker, Dean Mead, Dan Brown, and Jay Fountain memo to Economic Condition Reporting: Fiscal Sustainability Task Force Members. Definitions of "Economic Condition and Its Components, Including Fiscal Sustainability," GASB, May 17, 2010.

[11] Governmental Accounting Standards Board. See Project Pages: Economic Condition Reporting: Financial Projections at *www.gasb.org*.

[12] Ibid.

ILLUSTRATION 10–1 Factors Affecting Financial Condition

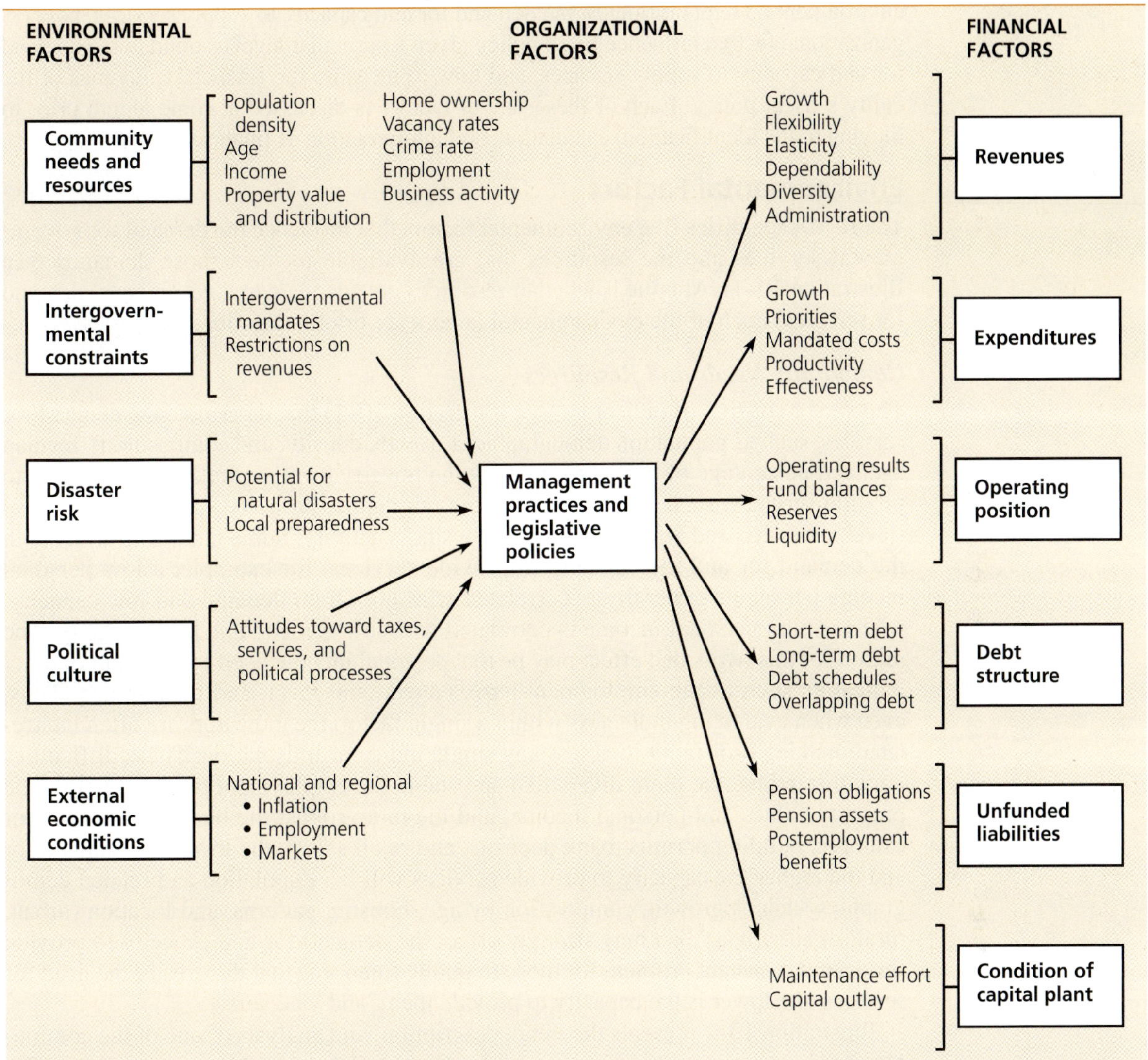

Source: Karl Nollenberger, *Evaluating Financial Condition: A Handbook for Local Government,* 4th ed. (Washington, DC: International City/County Management Association, 2003), p. 5.

government's financial condition, and that are measured by various indicators. The ICMA provides a large number of potentially useful indicators grouped into the factors corresponding to the environmental, organizational, and financial dimensions shown in Illustration 10–1. Some local governments use the FTMS to monitor their financial condition. The FTMS, together with various publications of the municipal credit market, has long been the main source of guidance for monitoring and evaluating governmental financial condition, including how to use financial and other information for these purposes. Examining changes in indicators over time and relationships among indicators can yield useful information on financial issues, such as whether revenue trends are adequate to meet expenditure trends and the adequacy of financial reserves to withstand revenue shortfalls or unforeseen expenditure requirements. However, making a reasonable judgment about the financial condition of a particular entity requires a sound understanding of how environmental factors influence the demand for and capacity to supply services, how organizational factors influence fiscal policy given a particular level or trend in the demand for and capacity to supply services, and how to measure the financial outcomes of the entity's fiscal policy. Each of these sets of factors is discussed at some length prior to moving to the identification, calculation, and interpretation of financial ratios.

Environmental Factors

The ICMA identifies five environmental factors that influence the demand for governmental services and the resources that are available to meet those demands (see Illustration 10–1). At issue is whether resources are adequate to meet citizens' demand for services. Each of the environmental factors are briefly described next.

Community Needs and Resources

This factor consists of indicators (see Illustration 10–1) that determine the demand for services, such as population demographics (growth, density, and composition), median age, and percentage of households below the poverty level, as well as the capacity to provide services, such as personal income per capita, property values, employment (level, diversity, and types), and level of business activity. Some indicators affect both the demand for and the capacity to provide services; for example, a low personal income per capita generally is correlated with both high demand and low capacity, whereas high personal income is correlated with low demand and high capacity. The reason for this two-sided effect may be that personal income itself is the result of other indicators such as the employment base, educational level, and median age. Thus, even when evaluating indicators within a single factor, the indicators are often interrelated, making it difficult to assess any single indicator in isolation. These difficulties notwithstanding, the more diversified and stable the employment base, the higher the property values and personal income, and the more robust the business activity (for example, building permits, bank deposits, and retail sales), the lower the demand for and the higher the capacity to provide services will be. Population and related demographics such as growth, composition by age, housing patterns, and location (urban, rural, or suburban) also may strongly affect the demand for and capacity to provide services. A constant problem for those in public finance is that the greater the need for services, the lower is the capacity to provide them, and vice versa.

Illustration 10–2 presents the trend, description, and analysis of one of the community needs and resources indicators of the City of Columbia, Missouri: Indicator 35, Rate of Employment. This information is taken from its Trend Manual for the years 2004 through 2013. It appears that unemployment rates jumped considerably in FY 2009. Although a 6.4 percent rate is considerably higher than the 2008 rate of 4.5 percent, it remained well below the national rate of 9.3 percent. As the economy has improved, Columbia's unemployment rate declined faster than the national rate in both 2011 and 2012. Based on the city's analysis, most of the fluctuation was associated with national manufacturing firms located in Columbia, although manufacturing jobs comprise less than 10 percent of the city's workforce.

Intergovernmental Constraints

Most local governments operate under various legal constraints imposed by the state government. Moreover, the federal government imposes constraints as a condition for receiving federal financial assistance. Among the state-imposed constraints may be legal limitations on the ability of local governments to raise revenues and issue debt.

ILLUSTRATION 10–2 **Indicator 35—Rate of Employment**

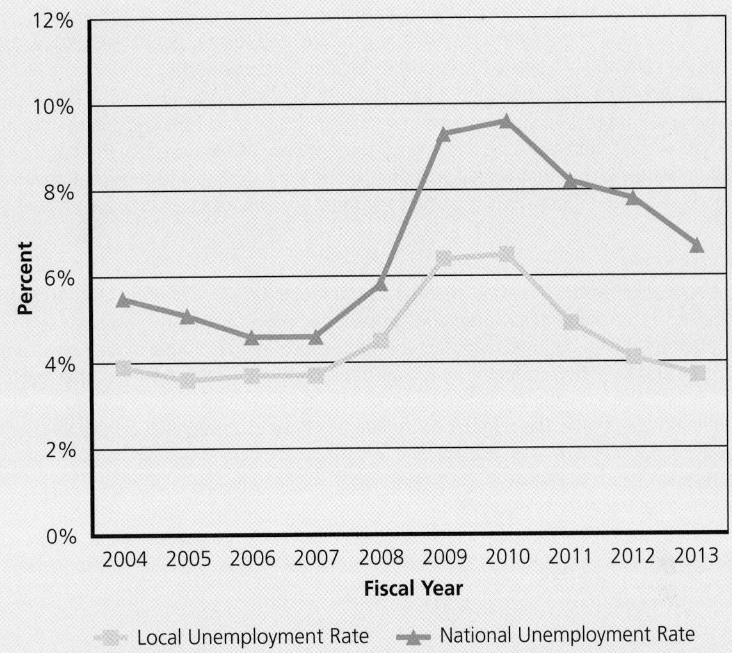

Warning Trend:

Increasing rate of unemployment or a decline in number of jobs provided within a community.

Formulation:

Unemployment rate and number of jobs in the community.

Fiscal Year	Local Unemployment Rate	National Unemployment Rate	Jobs in Community—Civilian Labor Force
2004	3.9%	5.5%	88,214
2005	3.6%	5.1%	91,210
2006	3.7%	4.6%	92,316
2007	3.7%	4.6%	93,159
2008	4.5%	5.8%	92,777
2009	6.4%	9.3%	93,236
2010	6.5%	9.6%	94,216
2011	4.9%	8.2%	95,300
2012	4.1%	7.8%	93,000
2013	**3.7%**	**6.7%**	95,900
10 Yr % Chg	*(5.13%)*	*21.82%*	*8.71%*

Description:

Unemployment and jobs in the community are considered together because they are closely related; for purposes of this discussion, they are referred to as "employment base." In addition, for comparative purposes, the national unemployment rate is included. Employment base is important because it is directly related to the levels of the business activity and personal income.

continued

ILLUSTRATION 10–2 (*Continued*)

Changes in the number of jobs provided by the community are a measure of and an influence on business activity. Changes in the rate of employment of the community's citizens are related to changes in personal income and thus are a measure of and an influence on the community's ability to support its local business sector.

If the employment base is growing, if it is sufficiently diverse to provide against short-run economic fluctuation, or downturn in one sector, and if it provides sufficient income to support the local business community, then it will have a positive influence on the city's financial condition. A decline in employment base as measured by the number of jobs, or the lack of employment, can be an early warning sign that overall economic activity will decline and thus that governmental revenues may decline (or at least not increase at the expected rate), particularly sales tax revenues.

Analysis:

The current economic factors have had an impact on the economy in Columbia. Although the unemployment base has been sufficiently diverse to cushion against temporary economic downfalls in any particular sector, most employment fluctuations have been associated with national manufacturing firms located in Columbia. Such jobs comprise less than 10% of the City's total workforce and have been effected by the current economic factors on a national level. The City of Columbia's largest workforce sector is the education, health and social services area which has enabled the City to continue to stay well below the national unemployment rate. The number of civilian jobs have increased 9% during this period.

* All figures have been restated to reflect annual amounts for each year reported by the Bureau of Labor
FY 2011 figures reflective of June 2012 reporting period.

Source: City of Columbia, Missouri, *Ten Year Financial Trend Model FY 2004–2013,* p. 309. The full report is available at *www.gocolumbiamo.com/finance/services/financial_reports/index.php.*

If such limitations exist, the current levels of revenues and debt subject to such limits should be compared to the authorized limits. Of particular importance is consideration of the extent to which legal limits may impede needed acquisition of capital assets and future growth in services. In addition to revenue raising constraints and debt limits, local governments are often burdened with unfunded mandates by higher level governments to provide specified services.

Disaster Risk

The need to consider and plan for natural disasters is incumbent on all top governmental officials. As the past few years have shown, no place is immune from such events, although some locations are more vulnerable than others. The question that should be asked is: What would happen if a major earthquake or hurricane were to strike or a terrorist attack were to occur? Related questions that need to be asked are these: (1) Does the city have sufficient insurance and reserves to cover possible losses? (2) Does the government have sufficient resources (and a plan) for evacuation, protection against looting, and cleanup? In addition to natural disasters, it can be equally difficult to prepare and budget for man-made disasters, for example, oil or chemical spills from industry.

Political Culture

This perhaps is the most difficult of all factors to measure but is certainly critically important to determining how the administration will react to the other environmental factors in shaping the government's fiscal policy. Political culture includes such factors as form of government (e.g., mayor-council—weak or strong, council-manager, commission) and the entity's economic, political, and social history. The entity's history may reveal underlying community philosophies regarding willingness to support higher taxes, issuances of long-term debt, and increased social services.

External Economic Conditions

No local or state government operates independently of the regional and national economy. Regional economic activity affects local business activity, employment, and income by influencing the demand for manufactured, agricultural, and service products as well as the levels of wholesale and retail sales. Similarly, inflation at the national level influences regional and local prices, including wages and the cost of debt financing. A good example of the impact of national events is the national subprime mortgage crisis, which negatively affected the prices and number of home sales. Recently, the local housing markets in most areas have seen significant improvements in both the price and number of home sales as the national economy overcomes the effect of the mortgage crisis. Although consideration of external economic conditions is essential to assessing the local economy, the linkages can be difficult to pinpoint and quantify.

Organizational Factors

As indicated by their pivotal location in Illustration 10–1, *management practices and legislative policies* play a crucial role in determining fiscal policy in response to the environmental factors just discussed. Sound financial management and the political will to resist easy solutions can minimize financial problems that might otherwise result from factors such as economic downturns, plant closings, or natural disasters. Financial crises often build over a number of years during economic recessions. Politicians may be either unwilling or unable to curtail expenditures for services in response to revenue shortfalls. Results of past policies, such as heavy reliance on debt or an excessive labor force, may make it difficult or infeasible to reduce expenditures sufficiently in the short run. Short-run solutions, such as deferring needed maintenance, curtailing capital expenditures, or underfunding pensions, may lead to even more serious problems in the future. Thus, sound financial management means planning for adverse environmental conditions or events and devising long-run solutions when problems do occur. Although management practices and legislative policies are critical determinants of financial condition, they are among the most difficult factors to measure. Evidence of mismanagement or management practices that sustain an operating deficit include using existing fund balances, short-term borrowing, internal borrowing, sale of assets, or one-time accounting changes to balance the budget. Other signs of deficient fiscal policies include deferring pension liabilities, deferring maintenance expenditures, failing to fund employee benefits, and ignoring full-life costs of capital assets.[13]

Financial Factors

Examples of governmental fund financial ratios typically used in assessing financial condition are shown in Illustration 10–3. Although the ratios contained in Illustration 10–3 represent what the authors consider key ratios, they are not intended to represent *all* ratios that might be useful in evaluating financial condition. In fact, the ICMA handbook provides for a total of 27 financial indicators across the six financial factors shown on the right-hand side of Illustration 10–1. For those interested, the handbook provides worksheets and an electronic spreadsheet that guides the user in defining the terms used in the ratios.

The data to calculate the financial ratios shown in Illustration 10–3 are readily obtainable from most CAFRs. Except for population, which is usually disclosed in the statistical section, data for most of the ratios can be obtained from the

[13] Nollenberger, *Evaluating Financial Condition,* pp. 147–52.

ILLUSTRATION 10–3 Selected Financial Ratios Based On CAFR Governmental Funds Information

Indicator	Computation[1]	Suggestions for Analysis
Revenues Measures:		
Revenues per capita	Total operating revenues[2] / Population	If per capita operating revenues are decreasing, the government may not be able to maintain existing service levels unless it finds new sources of revenue.
Intergovernmental revenues	General Fund intergovernmental revenues / Total General Fund revenues[2]	A large percent is a warning sign since it indicates the government is dependent on revenues is does not control.
Expenditures Measures:		
Expenditures per capita	Total operating expenditures[3] / Population	Determine which functions are increasing and if the increase represents increased services or new services. Are there sufficient revenues to pay for these?
Employees per capita	Number of municipal employees / Population (or households)	If personnel costs (as measured by the number of employees) are increasing at a greater rate than the population base, determine why this is happening.
Operating Position Measures:		
Revenues over expenditures	Total operating revenues[2] / Total operating expenditures[3]	This ratio should be evaluated for a trend. As a benchmark, an average of 1.05 or greater is considered very strong, with 1.0 considered average and 0.95 or less weak.
Operating surplus/deficit	General Fund operating surplus/deficit[4] / General Fund operating revenues[2]	Abnormally large deficits or consecutive deficits are warning signs. See Illustration 10–5 for additional information on interpreting the measure.
Fund balances	General Fund balances[5] / Operating revenues[2]	Declining fund balances as a percentage of net operating revenues can affect a government's ability to withstand financial emergencies.
Liquidity	Cash and short-term investments / Current liabilities	If this measure of a government's cash position is less than 1 then determine if this is a temporary situation or whether causes, such as receivables, may persist, leading to long-term solvency concerns.
Debt Indicators:		
Long-term debt	General obligation long-term debt[6] / Assessed valuation (or population or personal income)	An increase in this ratio may be an indication that the government's ability to repay the debt is diminishing. Warning signs would include debt that exceeds 10 percent of assessed value, an increase of 20 percent over the previous year, or an increase of 50 percent over the prior four years.
Current liabilities	Current liabilities / Operating revenues[2]	A value of 5 percent or greater, or an increasing trend are considered warning signs.
Debt service	Principal and interest payment of debt / General Fund operating revenue[2]	An increasing percent reduces expenditure flexibility. A warning sign would include a value greater than 20 percent. Values below 10 percent are considerd acceptable.

continued

ILLUSTRATION 10–3 (*Continued*)

Unfunded Liability Measures: (This category is only useful if the government manages its own pension plan.)		
Pension obligations	Pension obligations / Salaries and wages	An increasing amount of net pension obligation is a negative signal that should be investigated to determine if the trend of not funding annual pension cost is expected to continue.
Funded ratio	Actuarial value of pension plan assets / Actuarial accrued pension plan liability	Level of funding is an indicator of future financial condition.
Capital Plant Indicators:		
Capital outlay	Capital outlay from operating funds / Operating expenditures[3]	If a decline in the relationship between expenditures for general capital assets to operating expenditures persists over three years, the government may be deferring the replacement of capital assets, which adversely affects delivery of government services.

[1] Express amounts in constant dollars; that is, adjust for inflation using the consumer price index (CPI). See the U.S. Bureau of Labor Statistics Web site at *www.bls.gov/cpi* for how to access and use the CPI.

[2] Operating revenues are those that are available for general government operations, such as tax revenues, revenues from fees and user charges, and other local revenues, but excluding revenues restricted to capital acquisitions or improvements. The ratio being calculated indicates whether total governmental fund or total General Fund operating revenues should be used.

[3] Operating expenditures are those incurred for governmental operations. Excluded from consideration are capital outlays.

[4] General Fund operating deficit is calculated as operating revenues minus operating expenditures.

[5] General Fund fund balances include restricted, committed, assigned, and unassigned amounts.

[6] The long-term debt indicator provided is a simplification of the ICMA measure.

Source: Adapted from Karl Nollenberger, *Evaluating Financial Condition: A Handbook for Local Government* (Washington, DC: ICMA, 2003), and Craig S. Maher and Karl Nollenberger, "Revisiting Kenneth Brown's '10-Point Test'," *Government Finance Review*, October 2009, pp. 61–66.

statement of revenues, expenditures, and changes in fund balances—governmental funds (see Illustration A2–5) and the balance sheet—governmental funds (see Illustration A2–3). Data for the remaining ratios usually can be found in the notes to the financial statements.

The ratios displayed on Illustration 10–3 indicate whether all governmental funds or only the General Fund should be used in the calculation. However, analysts differ on preferences with some preferring to utilize General Fund data only, whereas others utilize combined data for all governmental fund types. This decision depends, in part, on how large the General Fund is relative to all governmental fund types. In calculating operating revenues, capital project fund revenues should be excluded since the capital project fund is not an operating fund. For purposes of calculating revenues and expenditures in these ratios, other financing sources are often added to revenues and other financing uses are often added to expenditures; although by definition other financing sources and uses are not considered revenues and expenditures. The government-wide financial statements offer additional opportunities for analysis of financial factors relating to the governmental entity as a whole and are discussed next.

ANALYZING GOVERNMENT-WIDE FINANCIAL STATEMENTS

The CAFR provides information about the government as a whole that should assist citizens, bond analysts, governing boards, and other financial statement users to answer questions that are not easily answered with disaggregated fund financial statements. The management's discussion and analysis and two accrual-based government-wide financial statements that focus on the flow of total economic resources in and out of the government offer a level of analysis about the real cost of government services, the means of financing them, and the financial condition of the government as a whole.

One firm that has developed a method to describe and report ratios designed to take advantage of aggregated information is Crawford & Associates, P.C., a public accounting firm that developed a financial analysis and rating tool to use in measuring a government's financial health and success. The firm suggests a number of performance indicators that measure financial position, financial performance, and financial capability from basic financial statements. A brief description of the questions best answered by some of these ratios is presented here, along with Crawford & Associates' "plain English" statement of the questions to be addressed by the performance measure.[14]

Financial Position Ratios:

1. *Unrestricted Net Position (Assets).* How do our rainy day funds look?
2. *Capital Asset Condition.* How much useful life do we have left in our capital assets?
3. *Debt to Assets.* Who really owns the government entity?
4. *Current Ratio.* Will our employees and vendors be pleased with our ability to pay them on time?
5. *Quick Ratio.* How is our short-term cash position?

Financial Performance Ratios:

6. *Change in Net Position (Assets).* Did our overall financial condition improve, decline, or remain steady over the past year?
7. *Interperiod Equity.* Who paid for the cost of operating the city—current, past, or future tax and rate payers?
8. *Sales Tax Growth.* What is the state of our local economy?
9. *BTA Self-Sufficiency.* Did current year business-type activities (BTA), such as utilities, pay for themselves?

Financial Capability Ratios:

10. *Revenue Dispersion.* How much of our revenue is beyond our direct control?
11. *Bonded Debt per Capita.* What is our long-term general obligation debt burden on our taxpayers?
12. *Available Legal Debt Limit.* Will we be able to issue more long-term general bonded debt, if needed?
13. *Property Taxes per Capita.* What is our property tax burden on our taxpayers?
14. *Sales Tax Rate.* Will our citizens be likely to approve an increase in sales tax rates, if needed?

Illustration 10–4 provides additional descriptions of the above ratios, along with formulas for calculating them. Other ratios that capture these dimensions are change in

[14] Crawford & Associates, P.C., *The Performeter®* (Oklahoma City, OK, 2008). See its Web site at *crawfordcpas.com.*

ILLUSTRATION 10–4 Financial Indicators Using the CAFR

Performance Measures	Description	Ratio
Financial Position:		
1. Unrestricted net position	A measure of the adequacy of the amount of the government's total unrestricted net position or level of deficit at the measurement date.*	Unrestricted net position / Total revenue
2. Capital asset condition	A measure of the extent to which the government's total depreciable capital assets, on average, are reaching the end of their useful lives, and, therefore, may need replacement.*	Accumulated depreciation / Average cost of depreciable capital assets
3. Debt to assets	A measure of the degree to which the government's total assets have been funded with debt as of the measurement date.*	Total liabilities / Total assets
4. Current ratio	A measure of the government's ability to pay its short-term obligations as they become due.*	Current assets / Current liabilities
5. Quick ratio	A more conservative measure of the government's liquidity that focuses on unrestricted cash and cash equivalents.	Unrestricted cash and cash equivalents / Current liabilities
Financial Performance:		
6. Change in net position	A measure of the change in the overall financial condition of the government that includes governmental and business-type activities (BTA) but not fiduciary activities or discretely presented component units.	Total ending net position (governmental and BTA) − Total beginning net position
7. Interperiod equity	A measure of whether the government has lived within its means for the year.*	Net revenues (gross revenues plus/minus the effect of internal transfers, special items and/or extraordinary items) / Total expenses
8. Sales tax growth	A measure of the state of the local economy by comparing current revenue collected to the prior year.	Change in sales and use tax revenue (current − prior year) / Prior-year sales and use tax revenue
9. BTA self-sufficiency	A measure of the extent to which the government's business-type activities (BTA) are funded with current-year service charge revenues, rather than prior year resources or subsidies from other funds.	BTA service charge revenues / BTA total expenses
Financial Capability:		
10. Revenue dispersion	A measure of the exposure to potential financial difficulties resulting from reliance on revenue sources beyond the direct control of the government.	Non-tax revenue sources / Total revenue (excluding special or extraordinary items)
11. Bonded debt per capita	A measure of the government's bonded debt burden on its taxpayers.	General bonded debt / Population
12. Available legal debt limit	A measure of the government's capacity to issue general bonded debt.	General bonded debt / Legal debt limit
13. Property taxes per capita	A measure of the government's property tax burden on its taxpayers.	Property tax levy / Population
14. Sales tax rate	A measure of the government's capacity to raise additional sales tax if needed.	Percentage sales tax rate

*Calculate for governmental activities and business-type activities separately and then for the total.

Source: Crawford & Associates, P. C., *The Performeter* ® 2008. See *www.crawfordcpas.com.*

overall financial position, reported as a percentage of total net position, and levels of reserves or deficits, employing expenses as a denominator instead of revenues. Chaney, Mead, and Schermann suggest these ratios, as well as general revenues minus transfers as a percentage of expenses, to measure financial performance. They also recommend change in net position plus interest expense as a percentage of interest expense as an additional solvency measure.[15]

Despite the complexity of evaluating government-wide financial condition, there are recognizable signals of fiscal stress. These include (1) a decline or inadequate growth in revenues relative to expenses, (2) a decline in property values, (3) a decline in economic activity (such as increasing unemployment, declining retail sales, and declining building activity), (4) erosion of capital plant, particularly infrastructure, (5) increased levels of unfunded pension and other postemployment obligations, and (6) inadequate capital expenditures. Warning signals such as these, particularly if several exist simultaneously, may indicate a potential fiscal crisis unless the government takes action to increase revenues or decrease spending.

USE OF BENCHMARKS TO AID INTERPRETATION

Regardless of how the ratios are calculated, the more difficult task is how to interpret the ratios to make an informed judgment about a government's financial condition. Checking each ratio in Illustration 10–3 and 10–4 against a target or acceptable range is a critical step in the process of analyzing financial performance. **Benchmarking** is a very useful tool in the continual process of monitoring performance of "the plan," allowing for identification of needed improvements in the delivery of government services.

A benchmark, broadly defined, is any target, range, or "red flag" that provides an analyst with a basis for comparison in order to draw conclusions about whether performance indicators suggest good or bad news. Appropriate benchmarks for comparisons can be found inside or outside of the government. Internal monitoring of trends over time within an organization is the most common method of assessing whether the government has performed better or worse than prior years. According to the Government Finance Officers' Association (GFOA), a government's past performance is usually the most relevant context for analyzing current-year financial data[16] and, at a minimum, five years of data should be compared. The ICMA's Financial Management Trend System is a good example of a tool that has been used by many governments as a way to compare current-period ratios to those of prior years for a variety of performance indicators. Illustration 10–5 shows the use of time-series trend monitoring by the City of Columbia, Missouri, for one indicator of financial condition—Excess of Revenues over Expenditures for the General Fund over a 10-year period. A narrative description of the ratio is provided as well as the mathematical formulation of the ratio. Graphical display of the trend in addition to data tables assists the analyst in drawing conclusions about the government's performance. Providing a "warning trend" helps the reader understand whether increasing or decreasing trends are positive

[15] Barbara A. Chaney, Dean M. Mead, and Kenneth R. Schermann, "The New Governmental Financial Reporting Model," *Journal of Government Financial Management,* Spring 2002, pp. 27–31. In this article, the authors calculate and compare these ratios for two cities with similar population size.

[16] Government Finance Officers' Association, *Recommended Practice: The Use of Trend Data and Comparative Data for Financial Analysis* (2003). Available at *www.gfoa.org*.

ILLUSTRATION 10–5 Indicator 16—Excess of Revenues over Expenditures: General Fund

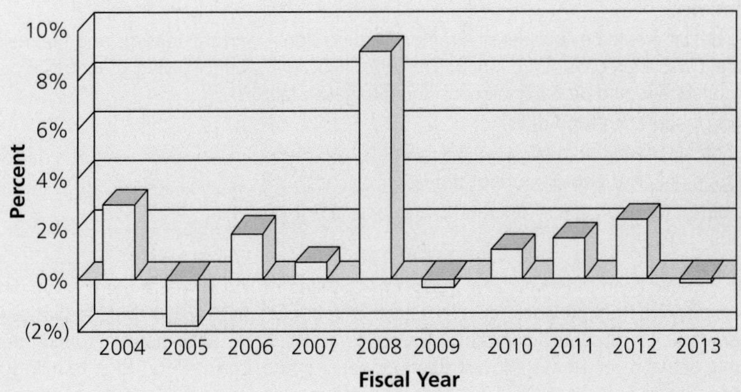

Warning Trend:
Increasing amount of General Fund operating deficits as a percent of operating revenues and transfers.

Formulation:

$$\frac{\text{General Fund operating (deficits)/surpluses}}{\text{Operating revenues and transfers}}$$

Fiscal Year	General Fund Operating Surplus/(Deficit)*	Operating Revenues**	General Fund Operating Surplus/(Deficit) as a Percentage of Operating Revenues and Transfers
2004	$1,745,541	$58,238,591	3.00%
2005	($1,147,015)	$60,917,104	(1.88%)
2006	$1,213,384	$66,716,295	1.82%
2007	$487,116	$70,693,991	0.69%
2008	$7,214,312	$78,898,068	9.14%
2009	($247,378)	$77,275,976	(0.32%)
2010	$945,091	$79,023,392	1.20%
2011	$1,313,361	$79,689,322	1.65%
2012	$1,903,482	$79,233,087	2.40%
2013	**($143,533)**	**$79,129,363**	**(0.18%)**
10 Yr % Chg	(108.22%)	35.87%	(106.05%)

Notes:
* *Not including encumbrances or appropriated fund balance*
** *Operating Revenues = General Fund Revenues + Operating Transfers from Other Funds + Appropriated Fund Balance*

Description:
An operating deficit will occur as operating expenditures exceed operating revenues. However, this does not necessarily mean the budget will be out of balance. Reserves (fund balances) and transfers are sometimes used to cover the difference. However, it does mean that the government is spending more than it is receiving. Continuing use of reserves and the unjustifiable transfer of funds to balance the deficit may indicate a revenue/expenditure problem. The existence of an operating deficit in one year is not cause for concern, but frequent and increasing deficits can indicate that current revenues are not supporting current expenditures, and that serious problems may lie ahead.

continued

ILLUSTRATION 10–5 (*Continued*)

Credit Industry Benchmarks:

A current year operating deficit would be considered a minor warning signal, and the reasons and manner of funding would be carefully examined before it was even considered a negative factor. However, the following situations would be looked at with considerably more attention and would probably be considered negative factors:

1. Two consecutive years of operating fund deficits.
2. A current year deficit greater than the previous year's deficit.
3. A current operating fund deficit in two or more of the last five years.
4. An abnormally large deficit (5% to 10% of operating revenues) in any one year.

Analysis:

For the period shown, there have been three years (FY 2005, FY 2009 and FY 2013) where there was a deficit. For each of these years the City used excess reserves from previous years to balance the budget. In FY 2008 the City was awarded a large non-motorized federal grant which caused a significant inflow of revenues. In FY 2013, actual expenditures were below budgeted expenditures but actual revenues were lower than budgeted in the area of PILOT (due to mild summer weather) and investment revenue due to governmental accounting standards reporting requirement to record investments at market on the last day of the fiscal year.

Source: City of Columbia, Missouri, *Ten Year Financial Trend Model FY 2004–2013*, p. 258. Full report available at *http://www.gocolumbiamo.com/finance/services/financial_reports/index.php*.

or negative signals. Illustration 10–5 also presents benchmark information from outside the government. A section called "Credit Industry Benchmarks" provides metrics and ranges that reflect credit analysts' assessment of what is appropriate for a government of this type.

Illustration 10–6 presents a comprehensive look at all the financial and economic indicators the City of Columbia, Missouri, tracks over time with a rating of whether the indicator has improved, declined, or remained the same from the prior year. Additionally, an indication is provided as to whether the trend is stable/improving, in need of close attention, or poorly performing (warning). A caveat to keep in mind in using external benchmarks is that comparison groups may not always be appropriate. A good example is that in a few states, local school districts are legally part of the government of the city in which they are located, whereas in most states school districts are independent governments. In some governments population may be the best denominator for a per capita ratio and in others households are more appropriate.

In addition to analyzing ratios, one should evaluate the stability, flexibility, and diversity of revenue sources; budgetary control over revenues and expenditures; adequacy of insurance protection; level of overlapping debt; and growth of unfunded employee-related benefits. Socioeconomic and demographic trends should also be analyzed, including trends in employment, real estate values, retail sales, building permits, population, personal income, and welfare. Much of this information is contained in the statistical section of the CAFR; the remainder can be obtained from the U.S. Bureau of the Census publications available from its Web site, *www.census.gov*.

Sources of Governmental Financial Data

Currently, there are no comprehensive benchmark values based on up-to-date financial data available for easy-to-use comparisons. Raw data, such as that compiled by the GFOA in its *Financial Indicators Database* from CAFRs submitted to the Certificate of Achievement for Excellence in Financial Reporting program, must be converted to useful geographic and population strata benchmarks.

ILLUSTRATION 10–6 FY 2013 Columbia Financial Trend Monitoring System—At a Glance

Indicator	Trend	Change
Revenue Indicators		
Revenues per Capita: General Fund	Gray	—
Restricted Revenues: General Fund	White	—
Elastic Tax Revenues: General Fund	White	—
Temporary Revenues: General Fund	White	—
Tax Revenues: General Fund	White	↑
Uncollected Property Taxes: General Fund	White	—
Service Charges Coverage: General Fund Building and Site Development Charges	White	↑
Revenue Surpluses/(Shortfalls): Estimated vs Actual—General Fund	Gray	—
Expenditure Indicators		
Expenditure per Capita: General Fund	White	—
Expenses per Capita: Utilities	White	—
Expenditures by Function: General Fund	White	—
Employees per Thousand Population: General Fund	White	—
Employees per Thousand Population: Utilities	White	—
Fixed Costs: General Fund	Black	—
Fixed Costs: Utilities	Gray	—
Fringe Benefits: General Fund	Black	—
Fringe Benefits: Utilities	Black	—
Expenditures (Over)/Under Budget: General Fund	White	—
Operating Position Indicators		
Excess of Revenues over Expenditures: General Fund	White	—
Enterprise Operating Position: Recreation Services	Gray	—
Operating Position Indicators cont.		
Enterprise Operating Position: Transit	Black	—
Enterprise Operating Position: Airport	Black	—
Enterprise Operating Position: Parking	Black	—
Enterprise Operating Position: Railroad	Gray	—
Enterprise Operating Position: Water and Electric	White	—
Enterprise Operating Position: Sewer	White	—
Enterprise Operating Position: Solid Waste	White	—
Enterprise Operating Position: Storm Water	Black	—
Fund Balance: General Fund	White	—
Liquidity: General Fund	White	—
Liquidity: Water and Electric	White	—
Liquidity: Sewer	White	—
Liquidity: Solid Waste	White	—
Liquidity: Storm Water	White	—
Liquidity: Parking	Gray	—
Debt Structure Indicators		
Current Liabilities: General Fund	White	—
Current Liabilities: Water and Electric	White	—
Current Liabilities: Sewer	White	—
Current Liabilities: Storm Water	Gray	—
Current Liabilities: Solid Waste	White	—
Current Liabilities: Parking	Gray	—
Debt Service: Water and Electric	White	—
Debt Service: Sewer	Gray	—
Debt Service: Parking	Gray	—

Changes from the previous year are indicated in the right column as: ↑ improved from previous year, ↓ declined from previous year, — no change from previous year.

Trend information is indicated by the buttons in the center column: black indicates a warning, gray indicates issues that need attention, white indicates stable or improving trend.

Source: City of Columbia, Missouri, *Ten Year Financial Trends Model FY 204-2013,* p. 233. Full report available at *http://www.gocolumbiamo.com/finance/services/financial_reports/index.php*.

Electronic Municipal Market Access

In 2009 a new source of municipal financial information was provided to the public. Through the Municipal Securities Rulemaking Board (MSRB), the Electronic Municipal Market Access, or EMMA, was established. EMMA is an online service that investors and others interested in the municipal securities market can access to obtain information about state and local governments who have issued debt. The MSRB indicates that EMMA serves as a resource to users who want to learn more about the municipal securities market; evaluate the features and risks of a specific municipal bond; and/or monitor municipal securities investment. EMMA provides a wealth of information about individual securities. In addition to the official statement, which is issued when a new bond or other debt offering is made to the public, other types of information provided include: the type of debt, initial offer price, the interest rate, the size of the debt issue, and the credit rating for the debt. After a government issues debt, it is required to provide continuing disclosures to the market. Among the required continuing disclosures is the CAFR. The best way to understand EMMA is to access it through its Web site at http://emma.msrb.org.

Credit Analyst Models

As discussed earlier in this chapter, credit analysts are concerned with assessing a government's ability to pay interest and principal when due. Credit analysts typically examine the same kinds of information that internal managers use in evaluating financial condition. Of course, internal managers have access to *all* information generated by the government for as far back as data have been retained, whereas credit analysts have access only to what management provides or what they require from management. Thus, internal managers have an informational advantage with respect to their own government. Credit analysts with the major bond rating agencies (FitchRatings, Moody's Investors Service, and Standard & Poor's) or with companies that insure bonds against default may have an informational advantage with respect to *benchmark* information, in that they have data from thousands of entities whose bonds are rated or insured. Moreover, these analysts develop extensive multiple-year libraries, including budgets and CAFRs, for the entities whose bonds are rated or insured, and they often visit the entity for discussions with management. Analysts with investment firms (underwriters and brokers) tend to collect and process much less information than do bond rating and insurer organizations. Rather, these analysts rely in part on agency ratings to help them properly determine the credit risk of municipal bonds.

The rating agencies are recognized as one of the primary groups of users of governmental financial reports, particularly, comprehensive annual financial reports (CAFR). They use financial measures discussed earlier in the chapter built on audited numbers in the government-wide and fund financial statements, management's discussion and analysis, notes to the financial statements, and statistical information in the last section of the CAFR. Rating agencies have recently revised their rating criteria for general obligation municipal debt issues. In part the rating criteria adjustments have been made in response to concerns that rating agencies tended to underrate governments' overall credit quality when considered relative to nongovernment entities.[17] The three major ratings agencies (FitchRatings, Moody's Investor Service, and Standard & Poor's) focus on similar criteria in conducting their rating analyses; however, the weight given to qualitative and quantitative data varies among the agencies. In making adjustments to their processes, rating agencies have focused on the development of more quantitative tools, such as scorecards, for assessing credit risk. The development of quantitative tools has the benefit of making the rating process more transparent to investors and issuers. However, the ability to assess credit risk still relies heavily on the ability to use forward-looking and qualitative factors in the ratings assignment process.

FitchRatings uses four factors when conducting its ratings assessment—economy, debt and other long-term liabilities, finances, and management. Since FitchRatings considers the factors interactive, it uses a dynamic weighting process in its assessment.[18] In January 2014, Moody's Investor Service issued revised rating criteria for assessing credit risk related to local government general obligation debt. The scorecard developed by Moody's includes four rating factors that are assigned a factor

[17] Christopher O'Leary, "Rating Agencies to Re-evaluate Ratings Criteria," *Investment Dealer's Digest*, August 23, 1999, pp. 7–9.

[18] Richard J. Raphael, FitchRatings Presentation at the GFOA Conference: Rating Methodology, May 19, 2014.

weighting. The broad factors and their weights are economy/tax base (30 percent), finances (30 percent), management (20 percent), and debt/pensions (20 percent). Each of the broadly identified rating factors has several subfactors that are considered in the rating process.[19] Standard & Poor's identifies seven factors it considers in assessing credit risk. These factors and their associated weights are: economy (30 points), management (20 points), budgetary flexibility (10 points), budgetary performance (10 points), liquidity (10 points), debt and contingent liabilities (10 points), and institutional framework (10 points).[20] Similar to Moody's, Standard & Poor's has subfactors that are considered in its rating process. You will notice that Moody's and FitchRatings have a different number of factors than Standard & Poor's, but the factors generally cover the same performance areas.

It should be noted that bond ratings are often viewed, particularly by investors, as crude indicators of long-term financial condition. For example, a Standard & Poor's AAA rating indicates a city is likely in better financial condition than a city with a BBB- rating (the lowest *investment grade* rating) but a user is unable to tell how much better from the ratings. Furthermore, ratings assigned to general obligation (GO) bonds often apply to all GO bonds of the same issuer, although GO bonds issued with state credit backing or other credit enhancement may carry a higher rating than the ordinary GO bonds of the same issuer.

This chapter describes the evaluation of financial condition. Continued sound financial condition indicates quality financial management and good financial performance. Achieving strong financial performance, however, does not ensure efficient and effective operating performance. Although it is difficult to provide an adequate level of services without sufficient financial resources, achieving efficient and effective use of *productive* resources requires innovative budgeting and management techniques. We defer discussion of these techniques until Chapter 12. In reading Chapter 12, keep in mind the importance of maintaining sound financial condition if service levels are to be sustained.

[19] Moody's Investor Service, *Rating Methodology: US Local General Obligation Debt*, January 15, 2014.

[20] Standard & Poor's Ratings Services, https://www.spratings.com/us-local-government-scenario-builder, accessed May 27, 2014.

Key Terms

Benchmarking, *420*
Budgetary solvency, *409*
Cash solvency, *409*
Economic condition, *410*
Financial condition, *409*
Financial position, *409*
Fiscal capacity, *410*
Long-run solvency, *409*
Service capacity, *410*
Service-level solvency, *409*

Selected References

Berne, Robert. *Research Report,* "The Relationship between Financial Reporting and the Measurement of Financial Condition." Norwalk, CT: GASB, 1992.

Chaney, Barbara A., Dean M. Mead, and Kenneth R. Schermann. "The New Governmental Financial Reporting Model," *Journal of Government Financial Management,* Spring 2002, pp. 27–31.

Governmental Accounting Standards Board. *Concepts Statement No. 1,* "Objectives of Financial Reporting." Norwalk, CT: GASB, 1987.

Mead, Dean M. *What You Should Know about Your Local Government's Finances: A Guide to Financial Statements.* Norwalk, CT: GASB, 2011.

———. *An Analyst's Guide to Government Financial Statements.* Norwalk, CT: GASB, 2000.

———. *What You Should Know about Your School District's Finances: A Guide to Financial Statements.* Norwalk, CT: GASB, 2012.

Maher, Craig, S., and Karl Nollenberger. "Revisiting Kenneth Brown's '10-Point Test'." *Government Finance Review*, October 2009, pp. 61–66.

Nollenberger, Karl. *Evaluating Financial Condition: A Handbook for Local Government,* 4th ed. Washington, DC: ICMA, 2003.

Questions

10–1. Describe some typical causes of municipal financial crises. How could an effective monitoring system reduce the risk of a financial crisis?

10–2. The GASB indicates that economic condition is composed of three components. Identify and define the three components of economic condition.

10–3. The International City/County Management Association (ICMA) describes four types of solvency within the concept of *financial condition.* Identify each type and explain why each is important to the long-term financial health of a government.

10–4. Identify some of the characteristics of a government's citizens that can affect the government's financial condition. Explain how the characteristics affect financial condition.

10–5. When conducting a financial analysis, ratios based solely on governmental fund financial statements would not be considered sufficient for assessing economic condition. Explain why this statement would be true.

10–6. Explain how organizational factors, such as management practices and legislative policies, affect a government's financial condition.

10–7. Should citizens be concerned if the *funded ratio* for pension plans decreases over time? Why?

10–8. Illustration 10–4, adapted from Crawford and Associates, lists several ratios under the heading Financial Position. Which of the ratios listed most closely aligns with the GASB research study definition of financial position provided on page 409? Explain why the ratios you selected align with the definition of financial position.

10–9. What is EMMA and when would someone want to use EMMA?

10–10. Identify factors that the rating agencies use in determining bond ratings. Which of the factors identified is beyond management control and how could this factor affect the government's finances?

Cases

10–11 Research Case—EMMA. Electronic Municipal Market Access (EMMA) provides investors and others interested in state and local government debt and financial information an excellent resource. By accessing EMMA an individual is able to learn about what type of debt is outstanding for a government of interest, and he/she is also able to learn about the debt's characteristics along with the financial performance of the entity. Access EMMA (http://emma.msrb.org) and using the Education and Browse Issuers sections complete this case.

Required

a. Use the Education Center to help answer the following questions:
1. What is a credit rating and when is a credit rating issued?
2. What is an official statement and what financial information is required in an official statement?

b. To answer the following questions, use the Browse Issuers, click on a state (your home state might be of interest to you), and then click on a city of interest. Finally, look for a debt issuance, while a general obligation issuance is preferred, any long-term debt issue should provide the information needed to answer the following questions. Be aware that not all governments will have outstanding debt issuances.
1. Is a credit rating provided for the debt issue you selected? If so, who issued the rating and what is the rating?
2. Was the debt initially issued at a premium or a discount?
3. Click on a CUSIP for your debt issue and indicate what financial information was included with the official statement. Check for continuing disclosures (there is a continuing disclosures button)—are CAFRs provided under continuing disclosures?

10–12 Municipal Credit Analysis.* In the 2010 CAFR, Detroit indicated that its general obligation debt rating had been downgraded by Moody's Investors Services from a Ba2 to a Ba3. Based on its fourth quarter Performance Dashboard[1], Detroit was subsequently downgraded to junk bond status as of the fourth quarter of 2012 by all three rating services (Caa2, Moody's; CCC-, Standard & Poor's; CCC-, Fitch). The audit of the 2011–2012 financial reports resulted in the following statement from its auditor, KPMG:

> "The City has an accumulated unassigned deficit in the General Fund of $326.6 million as of June 30, 2012, which has resulted from operating deficits over the last several years. The deficits raise significant liquidity risks regarding the City's ability to meet its financial obligations as they come due without raising revenues, cutting costs of services provided, and effectuating financial restructuring."[2]

As Detroit indicates in its 2012 CAFR report, the city faces socioeconomic factors that make it difficult for the city to regain its financial footing:

> The City of Detroit is the largest City in Michigan and the 18th largest City in the United States. However, as documented in the 2010 Census, the City's population continues to decline, which contributes to the declining property and income tax base. In addition, the City faces continued high unemployment (18.9% in October 2012), which hinders personal income tax collections. Resident home foreclosures and delinquent property tax levels are another financial concern. The weak economy has had an adverse impact on the State's budget resulting in cuts of revenue sharing to local governments. The City's revenue sharing for the year ended June 30, 2012 was $173.3 million or $66.0 million less than the year ended June 30, 2011.

* This case represents an update to the Detroit case that can be found in the 16th edition of the textbook.

[1] http://www.detroitmi.gov/DepartmentsandAgencies/Finance/PerformanceIndicators.aspx

[2] Comprehensive Annual Financial Report, Independent Auditors Report, Detroit, Michigan, 2012, p 2.

Although the City's current economic condition is poor, the future outlook for recovery and improvement is positive. Businesses are transferring employees from suburban cities to the City of Detroit. New residents are moving into the City's mid-town area.

Following are selected financial indicators from Detroit's CAFRs, which provide financial data that can be used to help identify financial trends the city has experienced with regard to its economic condition.

Selected 10-Year Trend Data from Detroit's CAFRs*

Measure	2012	2011	2010	2009	2008	2007	2006	2005	2004	2003
Cash and cash equivalents	$82	$123	$81	$116	$268	$59	$75	$50	$49	$47
Current liabilities	$1,038	$818	$871	$823	$858	$726	$698	$671	$481	$558
General fund balance	($269)	($91)	($91)	($267)	($142)	($91)	($107)	($34)	$69	($69)
Governmental fund total revenues	$1,524	$1,712	$1,630	$1,748	$1,773	$1,910	$1,839	$1,840	$1,867	$1,829
Governmental fund total expenditures	$1,586	$1,711	$1,665	$1,843	$1,908	$1,870	$2,061	$3,220	$2,170	$1,981
Debt per capita	$1,350	$1,456	$1,062	$880	$990	$936	$1,011	$1,028	$882	$702
Legal debt limit used	92.65%	84.82%	75.46%	59.10%	54.50%	49.67%	56.48%	52.36%	55.94%	44.02%
Debt service/operating expenditures	15.10%	13.70%	13.39%	14.41%	13.97%	13.00%	14.06%	5.76%	6.98%	6.91%

*Dollars are in millions.

In July of 2013 Detroit filed for bankruptcy.[3] Since its bankruptcy filing, numerous events have occurred that impact the city's economic condition.

[3] Michael Corkery and Matthew Dolan, "Detroit Bankruptcy Likely to Spark a Pension Brawl; Filing Will be a Test Case of How Far a City Can Go in Shedding Retiree Costs," *The Wall Street Journal* (online), July 20, 2013.

Required

a. Using the information provided in the case, the information provided in the Illustrations 10–3 and 10–4, and the information provided in the Credit Analyst Models section of the text provide an analysis of factors that would lead to the downgrading of the debt rating.

b. The City of Detroit's Finance Department provides quarterly performance indicators on financial sustainability and some economic indicators along with service performance. Additionally, the Emergency Manager for the bankruptcy provides quarterly filings on the Detroit Web site. These quarterly reports provide a status update on Detroit's financial situation. Using the information provided by the Finance Department and the Emergency Manager, assess the city's economic condition. As part of the assessment indicate whether you believe the city's condition has improved, worsened, or remained the same since 2012.

10–13 Financial Analysis.* In 2010 the city had failed to honor its guarantees on The Harrisburg Authority (THA) debt. (THA is a component unit of the city.) In 2011 Harrisburg filed for bankruptcy; however, the bankruptcy petition was denied by the court. The State of Pennsylvania appointed a receiver for the City of Harrisburg in 2011 to help with the city's economic recovery. The

* This case represents an update to the Harrisburg case presented in the 16th edition of the textbook.

following three paragraphs are taken from the mayor's transmittal letter in the 2012 CAFR report. Subsequent to the three paragraphs are two bar charts providing 10 years of information on General Fund balance and net position and a table providing 5 years of debt performance information.

> For perspective, 2009 was the year the City went from a 2008 statement of net position, where assets exceeded liabilities by $46,178,883, to a deficit in 2009 of $227,092,975. It was the year in which the contingent liability for The Harrisburg Authority Resource Recovery Facility debt guarantees of approximately $264 million would be recorded on the City's financial statements due to payment defaults on that debt.
>
> As of December 31, 2012, the City's liabilities exceeded its assets by $277,261,834, representing a further decrease of net position of $28,092,042. As of December 31, 2012, the City's governmental funds (General Fund, Grant Programs, Debt Service and other Non-Business Type Funds) reported combined ending fund balances of ($76,414,768), a decrease of $23,421,231 from 2011.
>
> The General Fund is the City's primary operating fund and the largest source of day-to-day service delivery. The Fund Balance of the General Fund decreased by $23,569,137 for the year ending December 31, 2012, from the prior year, primarily due to a significant drop-off in departmental earnings resulting from a $7 million decrease in administrative service charge revenue from the Water and Sewer Funds, higher expenditures incurred from a write-off of approximately $5 million of Incinerator amounts receivable from under guarantee agreements for principal and interest previously paid by the bond insurer, and an $11.2 million accrued liability associated with the settlement of reimbursable sewer related amounts owed to several suburban municipalities.

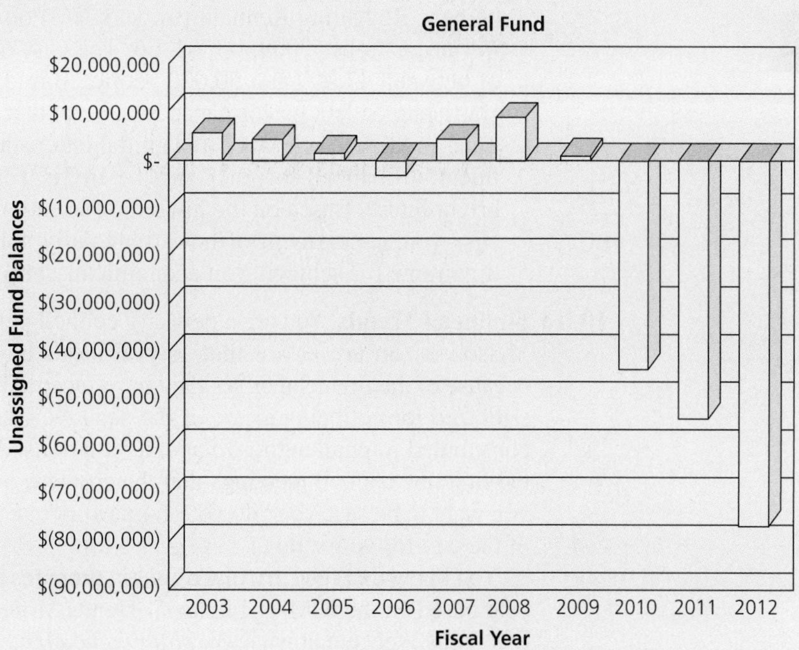

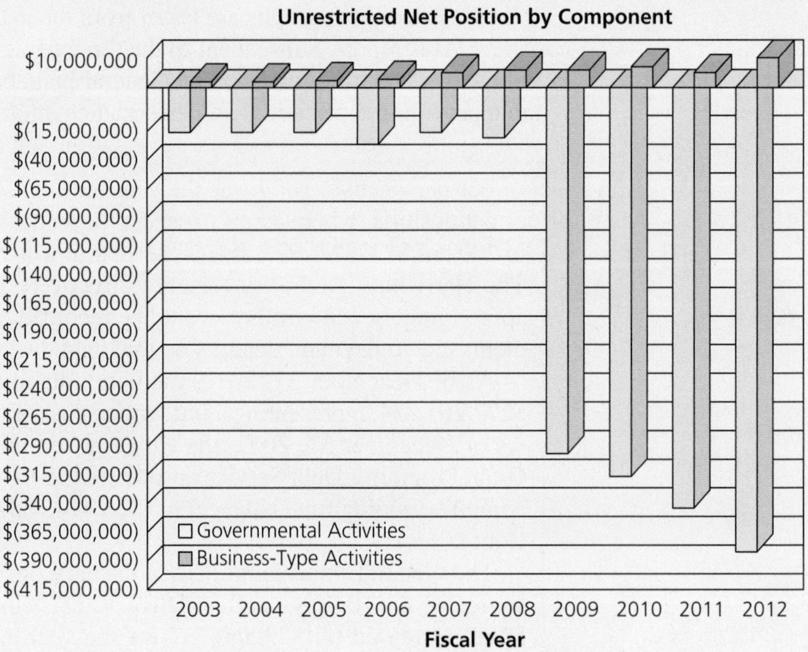

	Calculated Value for Each Year				
Performance Measure	**2008**	**2009**	**2010**	**2011**	**2012**
Debt Service for THA	182.5%	236.2%	354.7%	145.3%	142.9%
Bonded Debt per Capita	$1,998	$7,405	$6,343	$6,211	$6,043
Debt to Assessed Value	5.98%	21.85%	19.60%	19.17%	18.75%

Required

a. Using your library's resources, locate Craig S. Maher, and Karl Nollenberger. "Revisiting Kenneth Brown's '10-Point Test'." *Government Finance Review*, October 2009, pp. 61–66. The City of Harrisburg has a population of between 47,000 and 50,000 people. Based on its size, assess the City of Harrisburg's debt performance relative to that of comparably sized cities.

b. Later in the mayor's 2012 transmittal letter she indicates that the city is confident of financial solvency and the city is working toward an economically bright future. Based on the limited information you have been provided, discuss your assessment of how financially solvent the city appears and its timeframe for achieving an economically bright future.

10–14 Financial Trends. You are a new city council person for the City of Columbia, Missouri. You are aware that several cities have been in the news recently because of the financial crises they have faced. The governing bodies have been criticized for not being aware of the negative signals and trends that obviously contributed to challenging financial situations. Although you were assured at the first few council meetings that the city was overall in good financial shape, you want to be sure you "do your homework" and assess the financial condition of the city for yourself.

You know that the City of Columbia prepares a *Financial Trends* report each year based on the ICMA's Financial Trends Monitoring System and that it posts this on its Web site at *www.gocolumbiamo.com.*

Required

a. Go to the city's Web site and view a copy of the *Financial Trends* report. (*Hint:* Once at the Web site, click on City Government and you will find financial reports.) The trend report can be accessed by clicking on Financial Reports. Examine the trend information and make a list of any indicators that are negative.

b. Prepare a list of questions for the next city council meeting. Your questions should help you focus on whether you and the other council members should be concerned about any trends.

Exercises and Problems

10–15 Examine the CAFR. Utilizing the CAFR obtained for Exercise 1–16 and your answers to the questions asked in Chapters 1 through 9, assess the economic condition of the government. For purposes of this project, the term *economic condition* is as defined earlier in this chapter. Examine the following issues and questions.

a. Analysis of revenues and revenue sources.

(1) How stable and flexible are the city's revenue sources in the event of adverse economic conditions?

(2) Is the revenue base well diversified, or does the city rely heavily on one or two major sources?

(3) Has the city been relying on intergovernmental revenues for an excessive portion of its operating expenditures?

(4) What percentage of total expenses of governmental activities is covered by program revenues? By general revenues?

(5) Do any extraordinary or special items reported in the statement of activities deserve attention?

b. Analysis of reserves.

(1) Are the levels of financial reserves (i.e., spendable fund balances, contingency funds, and unrestricted net position) adequate to meet unforeseen operational requirements or catastrophic events?

(2) Do total governmental fund revenues exceed total governmental fund expenditures? Do General Fund revenues exceed General Fund expenditures? What has been the trend in the ratio of revenues to expenditures?

(3) Is an adequate amount of cash and securities on hand, or could the city borrow quickly to cover short-term obligations?

c. Analysis of expenditures and expenses.

(1) Do any components of expenditures and, at the government-wide level, expenses exhibit sharp growth?

(2) How flexible are expenditures? That is, are there large percentages of relatively nondiscretionary expenditures, such as for interest and public safety?

(3) How does the growth pattern of operating expenditures and expenses over the past 10 years compare with that of revenues?

d. Analysis of debt burden.

(1) What has been the 10-year trend in general obligation long-term debt relative to trends in population and revenue capacity?

(2) Are significant debts of other governments (e.g., a school district, a county) supported by the same taxable properties? What has been the trend for this "overlapping" debt?

(3) Are there significant levels of short-term operating debt? If so, has the amount of this debt grown over time?
(4) Are there any significant debts (e.g., lease obligations, unfunded pension liabilities, accrued employee benefits) or contingent liabilities?
(5) Are any risky investments such as derivatives disclosed in the notes to the financial statements?

e. Socioeconomic factors.

What have been the trends in demographic and economic indicators, such as real estate values, building permits, retail sales, population, income per capita, percent of population below the poverty level, average age, average educational level, employment and unemployment, and business licenses? (*Note:* Many of these items and other potentially useful information can be obtained from the Census Bureau's Web site *www.census.gov.*)

f. Potential "red flags" or warning signs.

(1) Decline in revenues.
(2) Decline in property tax collection rate.
   (a) Less than 92 percent of current levy collected?
   (b) Property taxes more than 90 percent of the legal tax limit?
   (c) Decreasing tax collections in two of the last three years?
(3) Expenditures increasing more rapidly than revenues.
(4) Declining balances of liquid resources and fund balances.
   (a) General Fund spendable fund balance deficit in two or more of the last five years?
   (b) General Fund assigned and unassigned fund balance less than 5 percent of General Fund revenues and other financial sources?
(5) Reliance on nonrecurring (i.e., special item) revenues to support current-period operations.
(6) Growing debt burden.
   (a) Short-term debt more than 5 percent of operating revenues?
   (b) Two-year trend of increasing short-term debt?
   (c) Short-term interest and current-year debt service on general obligation debt more than 20 percent of operating revenues?
   (d) Debt per capita ratio 50 percent higher than four years ago?
(7) Growth of unfunded pension and other employee-related benefits such as compensated absences and postemployment health care benefits.
(8) Deferral of needed maintenance on capital plant.
(9) Decrease in the value of taxable properties, retail sales levels, or disposable personal income.
(10) Decreasing revenue support from federal or state government.
(11) Increasing unemployment.
(12) Unusual climatic conditions or the occurrence of natural disasters.
(13) Ineffective management and/or dysfunctional political circumstances.

Required

a. Calculate, insofar as possible, the financial ratios in Illustrations 10–3 and 10–4 of the text. Evaluate the ratios in terms of the red flags, information provided in Illustration 10–3, benchmarks provided in Illustrations 10–5 and 10–6, and long-term trend data for each ratio, if available. List any assumptions you made.

b. Locate any additional data that you think may be useful in assessing the financial condition of this city; for example, see the U.S. Census Bureau's Web site at *www.census.gov* and the Web sites of cities you consider comparable in size or other attributes to this city.

c. Prepare a report on the results of your analysis. The report should have an appendix providing a few graphs and/or tables to support your analysis. In particular, graphs showing revenues, expenditures, and key debt ratios for the past 10 years and selected demographic and socioeconomic trends are helpful. You may want to include some of the ratios calculated in part *b* in an appendix. Be succinct and include only data relevant to your analysis. Organize your report along the lines of the ratios evaluated in part *a*.

10–16 Multiple Choice. Choose the best answer.

1. Evaluation of government financial performance is important for which of the following reasons?
   a. Credit analysts use it to determine whether bonds should be issued.
   b. Investors use it to make decisions about bond investments.
   c. Oversight bodies use it to develop new laws.
   d. Managers use it to evaluate day to day operations.
2. Which of the following terms or concepts focuses primarily on a government's ability to generate enough cash over a 30- or 60-day period to pay its bills?
   a. Interperiod equity.
   b. Financial position.
   c. Budgetary solvency.
   d. Cash solvency.
3. Why does GASB prefer to use the term economic condition rather than financial condition?
   a. Economic condition considers the probability that the government will meet both financial and service obligations currently and in the future but financial condition does not.
   b. Financial condition does not consider the ability to maintain service levels.
   c. Economic condition focuses on both the ability and willingness to meet financial and service obligations.
   d. Financial condition focuses primarily on liquidity.
4. Factors that influence a government's financial condition include which of the following?
   a. Financial factors, such as governmental fund financial ratios.
   b. Environmental factors, such as community needs and resources.
   c. Organizational factors, such as management practices and legislative policies.
   d. All of the above.
5. Which of the following environmental factors reveals the entity's underlying philosophies regarding willingness to support higher taxes, issuances of long-term debt, and increased social services?
   a. Political culture.
   b. Community needs and resources.
   c. External economic conditions.
   d. Management practices and legislative policies.

6. Which of the following would be an effective means of benchmarking?
   a. Comparing the city's key ratios to those of special purpose governments in the area.
   b. Comparing current-period ratios to published medians of the same ratios for cities of similar size or in the same geographic region.
   c. Comparing key ratios to published medians of the same ratios for larger cities in other parts of the country.
   d. Comparing current-period ratios to estimates for future periods.
7. Which of the following conditions *could* signal *decreasing* fiscal stress?
   a. Increasing unemployment.
   b. Decreasing property values.
   c. Increasing revenues relative to expenditures.
   d. Increasing levels of unfunded pension obligations and other postemployment retirement benefits.
8. Rating agencies, such as FitchRatings, Moody's Investor Service and Standard & Poor's, produce bond ratings that
   a. Are created using the exact same measures and weights.
   b. Allow users to know how much better one issuing entity's financial condition is than another's.
   c. Focus both on quantitative and qualitative factors using proprietary models.
   d. Are intended to be precise indicators of the government's long-term financial condition.
9. Which of the following suggests a government that is relying primarily on revenues it directly controls?
   a. Property taxes, 20%; charges for services, 70%; grants and contributions, 5%; investment income, 5%.
   b. Property taxes, 20%; charges for services, 60%; grants and contributions, 10%; investment income, 10%.
   c. Property taxes, 40%; charges for services, 40%; grants and contributions, 10%; investment income, 10%.
   d. Property taxes, 60%; charges for services, 5%; grants and contributions, 30%; investment income, 5%.
10. What is Electronic Municipal Market Access, or EMMA?
   a. A library-based service that provides information about state and local governments that have issued debt.
   b. A fee-based service that provides information to investors and credit analysts about government bond issues.
   c. An online service that allows users to learn more about the municipal securities market.
   d. A source of municipal finance information developed by the Securities and Exchange Commission.

10–17 Financial Condition. Write the letters *a* through *o* on a sheet of paper. Beside each letter, put a plus (+) if a high or increasing value of the item is generally associated with *stronger* financial condition, a minus (−) if a high or increasing value of the item is generally associated with a *weaker* financial condition, and NE if the item generally has *no effect* on the financial condition or the direction of the effect cannot be predicted.
a. Unfunded pension liability.
b. Operating deficit.

c. Revenues over expenditures.
d. Intergovernmental revenues.
e. Level of business activity.
f. Education level of citizens.
g. Unemployment rate.
h. Restrictions on revenues.
i. Personal income per capita.
j. Debt service.
k. Percentage of households below the poverty level.
l. Short-term borrowing.
m. Property values.
n. Population growth.
o. Political party of the mayor.

10–18 Benchmarks. Examine the following tables from the Financial Trend Monitoring Report for the Town of Oakdale that reports on fiscal year 2017. The performance indicators selected are *total revenue* and *revenue per capita.* The town provides three reference groups with which to compare Oakdale: Aaa-rated municipalities, comparison municipalities, and the state median. Since local government budgeting in this state is driven by the property tax levy cap, this is a key variable in comparing municipalities.

Aaa-Rated Municipality	FY17 Total Revenue	FY17 Rev per Cap	State Rank	Comparison Municipality	FY17 Total Revenue	FY17 Rev per Cap	State Rank
Delta	$ 49,794,904	$4,342	12	Dover	$356,895,723	$3,521	27
Monroe	111,784,312	3,683	21	**Oakdale**	**175,058,152**	**3,065**	**45**
Schoolcraft	47,219,656	3,605	24	Cook	71,477,390	2,954	51
Dover	356,895,723	3,521	27	Lakeview	245,812,303	2,932	53
Bentley	103,338,507	3,307	33	Frankenmuth	76,196,553	2,863	63
Oakdale	**175,058,152**	**3,065**	**45**	Walden	59,310,311	2,850	65
Harris	59,373,338	2,986	48	Superior	161,444,163	2,726	80
Cook	71,477,390	2,954	51	Cedar	89,441,958	2,644	97
Lakeview	245,812,303	2,932	53	Pittsfield	169,322,957	2,531	116
Caro	49,726,361	2,926	55	Lodi	99,100,870	2,338	168
Frankenmuth	76,196,553	2,863	63	Huron	120,977,460	2,169	210
Walden	59,310,311	2,850	65	Pineview	116,134,368	2,151	217

Aaa-Rated	FY17 Total Revenue	FY Rev per Cap		Oakdale
Median	$ 73,836,972	$3,026	Aaa-Rated LQ	1.01
Comparison RG Median	118,555,914	2,788	Comparison RG LQ	1.10
State Median	23,487,291	2,314	State LQ	1.32

where RG = reference group
LQ = location quotient showing how much above or below the median this government is.

Required

a. Prepare a histogram or bar graph that shows Oakdale in relation to the three reference groups, Aaa-rated median, comparison reference group, and state median for FY 2017 total revenue and a separate graph for FY 2017 revenue per capita.

b. Evaluate the financial performance of Oakdale for FY 2017. Use information from the tables and the graph you prepared for Part *a* to support your analysis.

c. What other performance measures would you like to see before you conclude the town is in good or bad shape for the fiscal year shown?

10–19 Financial Trend Monitoring System. The City of St. Cloud, Minnesota, annually prepares a trend report using the ICMA's Financial Trend Monitoring System. The table presented here captures trend information provided by St. Cloud in its 2013 Annual Financial Trend Report. For a description of the indicators included, see Illustration 10–3 in this chapter.

	Calculated Values for Each Year				
Indicator	**2008**	**2009**	**2010**	**2011**	**2012**
Operating revenues per capita	$778	$755	$738	$731	$692
Intergovernmental revenues	32.2%	33.5%	29.7%	29.8%	29.5%
Operating expenditures per capita	$741	$765	$742	$748	705
General Fund operating surplus/deficit	−2.4%	−0.6%	0.6%	−2.3%	−4.2%
General Fund balance	49.5%	50.2%	54.7%	57.3%	57.3%
Liquidity (quick ratio)	778%	951%	755%	576%	660%
Current liabilities	8.0%	6.5%	9.4%	12.6%	11.1%
Debt service	31.1%	40.8%	29.3%	37.6%	36.2%
Capital outlay	2.0%	2.3%	1.0%	4.7%	3.0%

Required

a. Based on the trend, which indicators indicate improving financial performance?

b. Based on the trend, which indicators indicate declining financial performance? Using Illustration 10–3, discuss what the decline indicates.

c. Discuss your overall assessment of St. Cloud's financial performance.

d. What additional information would be helpful in assessing St. Cloud's financial performance?

10–20 Comparative Ratios. The government-wide financial statements for the City of Arborland for a three-year period are presented on the following pages.

Additional information follows:

Population: Year 2017: 30,420, Year 2016: 28,291, Year 2015: 26,374. Debt limit remained at $20,000,000 for each of the three years. Net cash from operations is generally 80 percent of total revenues each year.

Required

a. Which of the financial performance measures in Illustration 10–4 can be calculated for the City of Arborland based on the information that is provided?

b. Calculate those ratios identified in part *a* for FY 2017. Show your computations.

c. Provide an overall assessment of the City of Arborland's financial condition using all the information provided, both financial and nonfinancial. Use information from the prior years to form your assessment.

CITY OF ARBORLAND
Statements of Net Position
As of December 31
(In Thousands)

	2017			2016			2015		
	Governmental Activities	Business-type Activities	Total	Governmental Activities	Business-type Activities	Total	Governmental Activities	Business-type Activities	Total
Assets									
Current assets:									
Cash	$ 5,540	$ 1,800	$ 7,340	$ 4,531	$ 1,663	$ 6,194	$ 3,452	$ 1,487	$ 4,939
Investments	733	291	1,024	638	181	819	769	179	948
Receivables (net)	2,747	1,809	4,556	2,947	1,608	4,555	1,865	1,472	3,337
Prepaid expenses	253	8	261	251	6	257	171	5	176
Inventories	26	58	84	101	48	149	167	49	216
Total current assets	9,299	3,966	13,265	8,468	3,506	11,974	6,424	3,192	9,616
Capital assets:									
Land	2,180	2,101	4,281	2,070	1,804	3,874	1,971	1,604	3,575
Depreciable assets	37,600	14,455	52,055	37,183	17,775	54,958	39,347	14,801	54,148
Accumulated depreciation	(15,039)	(5,782)	(20,821)	(16,732)	(9,776)	(26,508)	(19,680)	(7,402)	(27,082)
Total capital assets (net)	24,741	10,774	35,515	22,521	9,803	32,324	21,638	9,003	30,641
Total assets	34,040	14,740	48,780	30,989	13,309	44,298	28,062	12,195	40,257
Liabilities									
Accounts payable	1,580	467	2,047	412	376	788	1,633	295	1,928
Deferred revenue	32		32	30		30	42		42
Other, current	1,754	200	1,954	1,443	190	1,633	1,489	170	1,659
Total current liabilities	3,366	667	4,033	1,885	566	2,451	3,164	465	3,629
Bonds payable	15,900	6,500	22,400	16,900	7,500	24,400	15,900	6,500	22,400
Total liabilities	19,266	7,167	26,433	18,785	8,066	26,851	19,064	6,965	26,029
Net Position									
Net investment in capital assets	9,104	4,027	13,131	7,945	3,065	11,010	5,366	2,067	7,433
Restricted for:									
Capital projects	140	—	140	151	—	151	130	—	130
Debt service	933	—	933	1,033	—	1,033	818	—	818
Unrestricted (deficit)	4,597	3,546	8,143	3,075	2,178	5,253	2,683	3,163	5,846
Total net position	$14,774	$ 7,573	$22,347	$12,204	$ 5,243	$17,447	$ 8,997	$ 5,230	$14,227

CITY OF ARBORLAND
Statement of Activities
For the Year Ended December 31, 2017
(in thousands)

		Program Revenues			Net (Expense) Revenue and Changes in Net Position		
Functions/Programs	**Expenses**	**Charges for Services**	**Operating Grants and Contributions**	**Capital Grants and Contributions**	**Governmental Activities**	**Business-type Activities**	**Total**
Governmental Activities:							
General government	$ 5,716	$ 531	$ —	—	$ (5,185)	—	$ (5,185)
Judicial	1,926	716	99	—	(1,111)	—	(1,111)
Public safety	7,958	1,530	168	—	(6,260)	—	(6,260)
Health and sanitation	2,804	524	—	—	(2,280)	—	(2,280)
Culture and recreation	2,166	554	—	$495	(1,117)	—	(1,117)
Road maintenance	2,455	5	1,619	—	(831)	—	(831)
Interest on long-term debt	948	—	—	—	(948)	—	(948)
Total governmental activities	23,973	3,860	1,886	495	(17,732)	—	(17,732)
Business-type activities	2,895	5,218	—	7	—	$2,330	2,330
Total government	$26,868	$9,078	$1,886	$502	(17,732)	2,330	(15,402)
General Revenues:							
Property taxes					17,296		17,296
Grants and contributions not restricted to specific programs					2,190		2,190
Investment earnings					716		716
Special item—gain on sale of land					100	—	100
Total general revenues and special items					20,302		20,302
Change in net position					2,570	2,330	4,900
Net position—January 1					12,204	5,243	17,447
Net position—December 31					$14,774	$7,573	$22,347

CITY OF ARBORLAND
Statement of Activities
For the Year Ended December 31, 2016 (in thousands)

		Program Revenues			Net (Expense) Revenue and Changes in Net Position		
Functions/Programs	**Expenses**	**Charges for Services**	**Operating Grants and Contributions**	**Capital Grants and Contributions**	**Governmental Activities**	**Business-type Activities**	**Total**
Governmental Activities:							
General government	$ 4,133	$ 148	—	—	$ (3,985)	—	$ (3,985)
Judicial	1,737	209	$ 17	—	(1,511)	—	(1,511)
Public safety	5,239	1,943	30	—	(3,266)	—	(3,266)
Health and sanitation	2,129	147	—	—	(1,982)	—	(1,982)
Culture and recreation	3,762	322	—	$350	(3,090)	—	(3,090)
Road maintenance	1,055	—	501	—	(554)	—	(554)
Interest on long-term debt	804	—	—	—	(804)	—	(804)
Total governmental activities	18,859	2,769	548	350	(15,192)	—	(15,192)
Business-type activities	4,287	4,290	—	10	—	$ 13	13
Total government	$23,146	$7,059	$548	$360	(15,192)	13	(15,179)
	General Revenues:						
	Property taxes				13,619		13,619
	Grants and contributions not restricted to specific programs				3,664		3,664
	Investment earnings				916		916
	Special item—gain on sale of land				200	—	200
	Total general revenues and special items				18,399	—	18,399
	Change in net position				3,207	13	3,220
	Net position—January 1				8,997	5,230	14,227
	Net position—December 31				$12,204	$5,243	$17,447

CITY OF ARBORLAND
Statement of Activities
For the Year Ended December 31, 2015
(in thousands)

		Program Revenues			Net (Expense) Revenue and Changes in Net Position		
Functions/Programs	**Expenses**	**Charges for Services**	**Operating Grants and Contributions**	**Capital Grants and Contributions**	**Governmental Activities**	**Business-type Activities**	**Total**
Governmental Activities:							
General government	$ 3,922	$ 109	$ —	—	$ (3,813)	—	$ (3,813)
Judicial	1,601	198	57	—	(1,346)	—	(1,346)
Public safety	4,113	1,723	10	—	(2,380)	—	(2,380)
Health and sanitation	2,096	216	—	—	(1,880)	—	(1,880)
Culture and recreation	3,484	364	—	$ 320	(2,800)	—	(2,800)
Road maintenance	1,438	—	460	—	(978)	—	(978)
Interest on long-term debt	948	—	—	—	(948)	—	(948)
Total governmental activities	17,602	2,610	527	320	(14,145)	—	(14,145)
Business-type activities	2,637	3,708	—	20		$1,091	1,091
Total government	$20,239	$6,318	$527	$ 340	$(14,145)	1,091	(13,054)
General Revenues:							
Property taxes					13,100		13,100
Grants and contributions not restricted to specific programs					2,990		2,990
Investment earnings					681		681
Special item—gain on sale of land					150	—	150
Total general revenues and special items					16,921	—	16,921
Change in net position					2,776	1,091	3,867
Net position—January 1					6,221	4,139	10,360
Net position—December 31					$ 8,997	$5,230	$14,227

Chapter Eleven

Auditing of Governmental and Not-for-Profit Organizations

Learning Objectives

After studying this chapter, you should be able to:

11-1 Explain the essential elements of financial audits by independent CPAs, including:

The objective(s) of financial audits.

The source and content of generally accepted auditing standards (GAAS).

Audit report formats and opinions.

The audit process.

11-2 Explain what is meant by generally accepted government auditing standards (GAGAS), the source of GAGAS, and why and how GAGAS are broader than GAAS.

11-3 Explain the types of audits performed under GAGAS, including financial audits, attestation engagements, and performance audits.

11-4 Explain the essentials of a single audit, including:

The purpose and scope of a single audit.

Major program identification.

Audit work required.

Reports that must be submitted.

11-5 Discuss special topics related to audits of governments and not-for-profit organizations.

This chapter introduces auditing topics associated with governmental and not-for-profit entities. Similar to the accounting principles followed by such organizations, some of the auditing issues and standards used by auditors of governmental and not-for-profit entities are unique to the public sector. After reviewing fundamentals of financial audits, this chapter describes generally accepted government auditing standards, the single audit concept, and other audit-related subjects.

FINANCIAL AUDITS BY INDEPENDENT CPAs

Financial statements of governmental entities, colleges and universities, health care organizations, voluntary health and welfare organizations, and other not-for-profit organizations are prepared for external users by accountants and officials responsible for the financial management of the entity. In order for users of the financial statements to have the assurance that the statements have been prepared in conformity with accounting and financial reporting standards established by authoritative bodies, and that all material facts have been disclosed, the statements should be accompanied by a report of an independent auditor. Audits for this purpose are called financial audits. Audits or engagements conducted for other purposes are discussed later in this section.

The auditor's objective in performing a financial audit is to render a report expressing his or her opinion that the financial statements are presented fairly. "Present fairly" means in conformity with generally accepted accounting principles. Auditors provide opinions on financial statements that are based on *reasonable assurance* that the financial statements are free from material misstatements, which is not the same as ensuring or guaranteeing that the statements are free of errors and all fraud was detected.

Three levels of audit to which governments and not-for-profit entities may be subject are discussed in this chapter. The American Institute of Certified Public Accountants' (AICPA) generally accepted auditing standards (GAAS) for financial audits are discussed first. Most readers will be familiar with GAAS, so attention will be focused on the unique aspects of auditing government and not-for-profit entities under GAAS. A broader level of financial audit is provided by generally accepted government auditing standards (GAGAS), standards issued by the Government Accountability Office (GAO), which largely incorporate and add to the GAAS standards. Finally, the Single Audit Act is discussed. The single audit incorporates GAGAS and adds program compliance audit and internal control requirements to the financial audit standards provided by GAGAS. As can be seen, audit complexity increases as the level of the audit goes from GAAS to GAGAS to a single audit.

Generally Accepted Auditing Standards

In the case of state and local governments, audits may be performed by independent certified public accountants (CPAs) or by state or federal audit agencies. Generally, not-for-profit organizations electing or required to have an audit are audited by CPAs. In performing audits, CPAs are professionally and ethically obligated by Rule 202 of the AICPA's *Code of Professional Conduct* to follow **generally accepted auditing standards (GAAS)**—standards set by the Auditing Standards Board (ASB) of the AICPA and issued in the form of *Statements on Auditing Standards.*[1] State or federal auditors, whether or not they are CPAs, are also required to follow GAAS if GAAS are prescribed by law or policy for the audits they conduct.

Failure to follow GAAS can result in severe sanctions, including the loss of the auditor's license to practice as a CPA. It is the auditor's duty to adhere to auditing standards, and it is his or her technical qualifications and independence from the entity being audited that add credibility to reported financial information and increase financial statement users' confidence in the information.

[1] The *Public Company Accounting Reform and Investor Protection Act* (the Sarbanes-Oxley Act of 2002, H.R. 3763, July 25, 2002) created a federal oversight board with the authority to set and enforce generally accepted auditing standards for auditors of public companies. Auditors performing audits of governments and not-for-profit organizations continue to follow AICPA and GAO auditing standards.

GAAS provide general guidelines for audits and address the minimum responsibilities of the auditor, as well as objectives, requirements, and material designed to support the auditor in obtaining reasonable assurance regarding the financial statements under audit. They include specific reference to ethical requirements relating to an audit of financial statements, independence, professional skepticism, professional judgment, the sufficiency and appropriateness of audit evidence, and audit risk. The ASB develops and issues standards in the form of statements on auditing standards (SASs) that are then codified into AU-C sections of the AICPA *Professional Standards* and represent generally accepted auditing standards.

In 2011, the AICPA completed its Clarity Project, which involved complete recodification of GAAS. Former AU sections of the *Professional Standards* now have a revised format and the AU-C identifier to identify them as clarified auditing standards. Each AU-C section contains one or more objectives that assist the auditor in understanding what needs to be accomplished and deciding whether more needs to be done to achieve the objectives in the particular circumstances of the audit.[2] The auditor should comply with all AU-C sections relevant to the audit noting that, when appropriate, additional considerations specific to audits of governments are included within the application and other explanatory material of AU-C sections.

Format of the Audit Report

The culmination of a financial audit is the issuance of an audit report, which contains a formal opinion stating auditor conclusions regarding fair presentation of the audited financial statements. While a not-for-profit entity's unmodified audit report would appear similar to that of a corporate entity, a government audit report must be altered to reflect the fact that a government may have numerous units on which an opinion must be rendered. The basic elements of the standard GAAS report are a title that includes the word *independent*; the addressee; an introductory paragraph; a section with the heading "Management's Responsibility for the Financial Statements"; a section with the heading "Auditor's Responsibility"; a section with the heading "Opinion"; when applicable, a section subtitled "Report on Other Legal and Regulatory Requirements"; signature of the auditor; and date of the auditor's report.[3] Illustration 11–1 shows an alteration to the standard audit report provided for an unmodified audit opinion on an entity's financial statements.

The introductory paragraph of the auditor's report should identify the financial statements being audited and, in particular, refer to the audit of the financial statements of each *opinion unit* (discussed further in the following section). The section headed "Management's Responsibility for the Financial Statements" is not unique in audit reports of governments; however, the section headed "Auditor's Responsibility" will specify whether the audit is conducted under GAAS or GAGAS. The "Auditor's Opinion" section should include the heading "Opinion" or "Opinions", if there are multiple opinion units. If the government presents the required budgetary comparison information as a basic financial statement rather than as RSI, the opinion paragraph should also refer to the budgetary comparisons for those funds.

The auditor's report of a government should also include an "Other Matters" section because GASB requires basic financial statements to be accompanied by RSI, which is considered an other matter. Illustration 11–1 provides an example in which RSI is

[2] AU-C Section 200.A72.

[3] AU-C Section 700, pars. .23–.41.

ILLUSTRATION 11–1 **Unmodified Opinions on Basic Financial Statements Accompanied by Required Supplementary Information and Other Information**

Independent Auditor's Report

Report on the Financial Statements

We have audited the accompanying financial statements of the governmental activities, the business-type activities, the aggregate discretely presented component units, each major fund, and the aggregate remaining fund information of the City of Example, Any State, as of and for the year ended June 30, 20X1, and the related notes to the financial statements, which collectively comprise the City's basic financial statements as listed in the table of contents.

Management's Responsibility for the Financial Statements

Management is responsible for the preparation and fair presentation of these financial statements in accordance with accounting principles generally accepted in the United States of America; this includes the design, implementation, and maintenance of internal control relevant to the preparation and fair presentation of financial statements that are free from material misstatement, whether due to fraud or error.

Auditor's Responsibility

Our responsibility is to express opinions on these financial statements based on our audit. We conducted our audit in accordance with auditing standards generally accepted in the United States of America [and the standards applicable to financial audits contained in Government Auditing Standards, issued by the Comptroller General of the United States]†. Those standards require that we plan and perform the audit to obtain reasonable assurance about whether the financial statements are free from material misstatement.

An audit involves performing procedures to obtain audit evidence about the amounts and disclosures in the financial statements. The procedures selected depend on the auditor's judgment, including the assessment of the risks of material misstatement of the financial statements, whether due to fraud or error. In making those risk assessments, the auditor considers internal control relevant to the entity's preparation and fair presentation of the financial statements in order to design audit procedures that are appropriate in the circumstances, but not for the purpose of expressing an opinion on the effectiveness of the entity's internal control. Accordingly, we express no such opinion. An audit also includes evaluating the appropriateness of accounting policies used and the reasonableness of significant accounting estimates made by management, as well as evaluating the overall presentation of the financial statements.

We believe that the audit evidence we have obtained is sufficient and appropriate to provide a basis for our audit opinions.

Opinions

In our opinion, the financial statements referred to above present fairly, in all material respects, the respective financial position of the governmental activities, the business-type activities, the aggregate discretely presented component units, each major fund, and the aggregate remaining fund information of the City of Example, Any State, as of June 30, 20X1, and the respective changes in financial position, and, where applicable, cash flows thereof for the year then ended in accordance with accounting principles generally accepted in the United States of America.*

Other Matters

Required Supplementary Information

Accounting principles generally accepted in the United States of America require that the [identify required supplementary information, such as management's discussion and analysis and budgetary comparison information] on pages XX–XX and XX–XX be presented to supplement the basic financial statements. Such information, although not a part of the basic financial statements, is required by the Governmental Accounting Standards Board who considers it to be an essential part of financial reporting for placing the basic financial statements in an appropriate operational, economic, or historical context. We have applied certain limited procedures to the required supplementary information in accordance with auditing standards generally accepted in the United States of America, which consisted of inquiries of management about the methods of preparing the information and comparing the information for consistency with management's responses to our inquiries, the basic financial statements, and other knowledge we obtained during our audit of the basic financial statements. We do not express an opinion or provide any assurance on the information because the limited procedures do not provide us with sufficient evidence to express an opinion or provide any assurance.

Other Information

Our audit was conducted for the purpose of forming opinions on the financial statements that collectively comprise the City of Example's basic financial statements. The [identify accompanying supplementary information, such as the combining and

continued

ILLUSTRATION 11–1 (*Continued*)

individual nonmajor fund financial statements, and the other information, such as the introductory and statistical sections] are presented for purposes of additional analysis and are not a required part of the basic financial statements.

The [identify accompanying supplementary information] is the responsibility of management and was derived from and relates directly to the underlying accounting and other records used to prepare the basic financial statements. Such information has been subjected to the auditing procedures applied in the audit of the basic financial statements and certain additional procedures, including comparing and reconciling such information directly to the underlying accounting and other records used to prepare the basic financial statements or to the basic financial statements themselves, and other additional procedures in accordance with auditing standards generally accepted in the United States of America. In our opinion, the [identify accompanying supplementary information] is fairly stated, in all material respects, in relation to the basic financial statements as a whole.

The [identify the other information] has not been subjected to the auditing procedures applied in the audit of the basic financial statements, and accordingly, we do not express an opinion or provide any assurance on it.

Other Reporting Required by Government Auditing Standards

[In accordance with Government Auditing Standards, we have also issued our report dated [date of report] on our consideration of the City of Example's internal control over financial reporting and on our tests of its compliance with certain provisions of laws, regulations, contracts, and grant agreements and other matters. The purpose of that report is to describe the scope of our testing of internal control over financial reporting and compliance and the results of that testing, and not to provide an opinion on internal control over financial reporting or on compliance. That report is an integral part of an audit performed in accordance with Government Auditing Standards in considering City of Example's internal control over financial reporting and compliance.][†]

[Auditor's signature]
[Auditor's city and state]
[Date of the auditor's report]

[*]If a government presents required budgetary comparison information as basic financial statements instead of as required supplementary information, the opinion paragraph would be replaced with the following: "In our opinion, the financial statements referred to above present fairly, in all material respects, the respective financial position of the governmental activities, the business-type activities, the aggregate discretely presented component units, each major fund, and the aggregate remaining fund information of the City of Example, Any State, as of June 30, 20X1, and the respective changes in financial position and, where applicable, cash flows thereof and the respective budgetary comparison for the [indicate the major governmental funds involved] for the year then ended in conformity with accounting principles generally accepted in the United States of America."

[†]This bracketed wording would be added to an audit performed under *Government Auditing Standards.* See American Institute of Certified Public Accountants, Audit Guide, *Government Auditing Standards and Circular A–133 Audits* (New York: AICPA, 2014).

Source: American Institute of Certified Public Accountants, Audit and Accounting Guide, *State and Local Governments* (New York: AICPA, 2014), Appendix A, Example A-1.

included within the financial statements, the auditor has applied the limited procedures, and no opinion has been expressed on the contents. This is followed by an "Other Information" section, when applicable, to inform financial statement users that certain information, such as combining statements, budgetary comparison *schedules,* or data housed in the introductory and statistical sections of the financial report may not have been subject to the comprehensive audit procedures. The audit report in Illustration 11–1 assumes that the auditor has been engaged to provide an "in-relation-to" opinion on other information, and the auditor has concluded that the other information is fairly stated, in all material respects, in relation to the financial statements as a whole.

The final section of the audit report in Illustration 11–1 is required when an auditor addresses reporting responsibilities that are in addition to the auditor's responsibility under GAAS to report on the financial statements. A common example in the governmental arena, discussed in detail in a later section of this chapter, applies to audits conducted under GAGAS, which require the auditor to report on internal control over financial reporting and compliance with laws, regulations, and provisions of contracts or grant agreements.

Types of Opinions

If the auditor determines that the financial statements contain a departure from GAAP, the effect of which is material, or there has been a material change between periods in accounting principles, or in the method of their application, the auditor may not express an *unmodified opinion.* It is also possible that the auditor cannot express an unmodified opinion because the scope of the examination was affected by conditions that precluded the application of one or more auditing procedures the auditor considered necessary to complete the audit. If it is not appropriate for the auditor to express an unmodified opinion, the auditor should consult relevant authoritative pronouncements to determine whether a *qualified* or *adverse opinion* should be issued, or whether an opinion should be *disclaimed* for one or more of the opinion units.[4] See Illustration 11–2 for an example of a report modification. The table presented in the illustration is not a required element of the auditor's report; however, it is an acceptable method for the auditor to communicate that more than one type of opinion is being issued.

The Audit Process

To determine what is GAAP for various entities, the auditor must first identify the sources of accounting principles for the type of entity being audited and then assess the weight of authority given to different pronouncements and writings (i.e., the GAAP hierarchy). Authoritative guidance for each of three types of entities: state or local government, federal government, and nongovernmental (i.e., businesses or not-for-profit organizations) is shown in Illustration 11–3.[5] If the accounting treatment for a transaction or event is not specified by a pronouncement, an accountant or auditor may refer to nonauthoritative accounting literature identified by the GASB, FASB, or FASAB.

Before any audit work is done, there should be a clear understanding of the scope of each engagement by all interested parties. A written memorandum of the engagement, or **engagement letter,** specifying the scope of the work to be done, as well as the auditing standards to be applied to the engagement, should be prepared in advance and copies retained by both the auditor and auditee. A written record of the agreement is essential for the protection of both parties. The need for specific, written memorandums of the scope of engagements was forcefully pointed out to independent public accountants by a number of well-known liability cases.

Entities can engage more than one audit firm to conduct annual audits. For example, some government component units, such as airports, hospitals, and utilities, may have their own governing boards and select their own auditor, yet meet the criteria discussed in Chapters 2 and 9 for inclusion in the governmental reporting entity. The principal auditor for the primary government must in this case decide whether to make reference to the other auditor in his or her audit report or to assume responsibility for the work performed by the other auditor without reference in the audit report. If reference is made to the other auditor, the principal auditor's report should disclose the magnitude of the portion of the financial statements audited by the other auditor. An audit report making reference to another auditor is not a qualified report unless some other reason exists for qualification.

Auditing procedures deemed particularly applicable to audits of state and local governments and not-for-profit entities by independent CPAs are published in the AICPA Audit and Accounting Guides: *State and Local Governments, Health Care Entities,* and *Not-for-Profit Entities.* The audit guides and other authoritative auditing

[4] Expanded discussion of the nature of each of these types of opinions and the conditions that would warrant the use of each is contained in the AICPA pronouncements, available at *http://www.aicpa.org/Research/Standards/AuditAttest/Pages/ClarifiedSAS.aspx*

[5] As this textbook goes to press, the GASB has issued an exposure draft entitled "The Hierarchy of Generally Accepted Accounting Principles for State and Local Governments." Students are encouraged to check the status of governmental GAAP hierarchy at the GASB's Web site (*www.gasb.org*).

ILLUSTRATION 11–2 Report on Basic Financial Statements That Includes a Qualified Opinion on Major Governmental Funds Because of a GAAP Departure*

Independent Auditor's Report

[Same content until the Opinions section of Illustration 11–1.]

Summary of Opinions

Opinion Unit	Type of Opinion
Governmental Activities	Unmodified
Business-Type Activities	Unmodified
Aggregate Discretely Presented Component Units	Unmodified
Governmental Fund X	Qualified
Governmental Fund Y	Qualified
Governmental Fund Z	Unmodified
Enterprise Fund A	Unmodified
Enterprise Fund B	Unmodified
Aggregate Remaining Fund Information	Unmodified

Basis for Qualified Opinions on Major Governmental Funds

Management has not adopted a methodology for reviewing the collectibility of taxes receivable in the [*indicate the affected major governmental funds*] and, accordingly, has not considered the need to provide an allowance for uncollectible amounts. Accounting principles generally accepted in the United States of America require that an adequate allowance be provided for uncollectible receivables, which would decrease the assets and fund balances, and change the revenues in the [*indicate the affected major governmental funds*]. The amount by which this departure would affect the assets, fund balances, and revenues of the [*indicate the affected funds*] is not reasonably determinable.**†

Qualified Opinions

In our opinion, except for the effects of the matter described in the "Basis for Qualified Opinions on Major Governmental Funds" paragraph, the financial statements referred to above present fairly, in all material respects, the respective financial position of the [*indicate the affected major governmental funds*] of the City of Example, Any State, as of June 30, 20X1, and the respective changes in financial position thereof for the year then ended in conformity with accounting principles generally accepted in the United States of America.

Unmodified Opinions

In our opinion, the financial statements referred to above present fairly, in all material respects, the respective financial position of the governmental activities, the business-type activities, the aggregate discretely presented component units, [*indicate the major funds not affected by the qualification*], and the aggregate remaining fund information of the City of Example, Any State, as of June 30, 20X1, and the respective changes in financial position and, where applicable, cash flows thereof for the year then ended in conformity with accounting principles generally accepted in the United States of America.

[*Signature*]
[*Date*]

* Paragraph A-l (of Appendix A, Chapter 14 of the Audit and Accounting Guide *State and Local Governments*) describes conditions that may make modifications to this report necessary, such as when the financial statements include information from a prior period.

** Depending on the nature and magnitude of the GAAP departure, it is possible that the auditor's opinion on the governmental activities also would be qualified, as illustrated in Example A-10 (of Appendix A, Chapter 14 of the Audit and Accounting Guide *State and Local Governments*). Further, the same GAAP departure in the nonmajor governmental funds could affect the auditor's opinion on the aggregate remaining fund information. This example assumes that the auditor has concluded that the GAAP departure is not material to the governmental activities opinion unit or to the aggregate remaining fund information opinion unit. Another auditor could make a different professional judgment. (See paragraphs 14.07 and 14.08 of the Audit and Accounting Guide *State and Local Governments*). If a GAAP departure is material to more than one opinion unit, the explanatory paragraph should explain the nature and effect of the departure on each affected opinion unit.

† If a government presents budgetary comparison information as basic financial statements instead of as required supplementary information, the basis for modification paragraph also should explain the effect of the GAAP departure on the budgetary comparison information. This example assumes that the government budgets on a cash basis, and thus the GAAP departure would not affect the budgetary comparison information if it were presented as a basic financial statement.

Source: American Institute of Certified Public Accountants, Audit and Accounting Guide, *State and Local Governments* (New York: AICPA, 2014), Appendix A, Example A-5.

ILLUSTRATION 11–3 **GAAP Hierarchy Summary**

	Authoritative Accounting Principles		
	State and Local Governments	**Federal Governmental Entities**	**Nongovernmental Entities**
Category (*a*)	Officially established accounting principles—GASB Statements and Interpretations	Officially established accounting principles—FASAB Statements of Federal Financial Accounting Standards (Standards) and Interpretations	The FASB *Accounting Standards Codification* is the source of authoritative GAAP to be applied by nongovernmental entities. Rules and interpretive releases of the SEC under authority of federal securities laws are also sources of authoritative GAAP for SEC registrants.†
Category (*b*)	GASB Technical Bulletins, and the following pronouncements if specifically made applicable to state and local governments by the AICPA (and cleared by the GASB): AICPA Industry Audit and Accounting Guides and AICPA Statements of Position	FASAB Technical Bulletins and if made applicable to federal governmental entities by the AICPA and cleared by the FASAB: AICPA Industry Audit and Accounting Guides	
Category (*c*)	AICPA Practice Bulletins if specifically made applicable to state and local governments (and cleared by the GASB) and Consensus positions of the GASB Emerging Issues Task Force*	Technical Releases of the Accounting and Auditing Policy Committee of the FASAB	
Category (*d*)	Implementation guides ("Qs and As") published by the GASB staff, as well as industry practices widely recognized and prevalent	Implementation guides published by the FASAB staff, as well as practices that are widely recognized and prevalent in the federal government	

*As of the date of this textbook publication, the GASB had not organized such a group.

†An entity that has followed, and continues to follow, an accounting treatment that was labeled in category (*c*) or category (*d*) of the prior FASB GAAP hierarchy as of March 15, 1992, need not change to an accounting treatment within the FASB *Codification* if its effective date was before March 15, 1992. Also a number of accounting standards allow for the continued application of superseded accounting standards for transactions that have an ongoing effect in an entity's financial statements. In instances where the superseded guidance has not been included in the *Codification,* it is grandfathered in as authoritative. More details are available in FASB *ASC* 105.

Sources: GASB, *Codification,* Sec. 1000; Statement of Federal Financial Accounting Standards No. 34; and FASB *Accounting Standards Codification (ASC)* 105.

literature provide guidance to all auditors, not just independent CPAs, whose function it is to examine financial statements, and the underlying records, for the purpose of determining whether the statements present fairly the financial position as of a certain date, changes in financial position, and cash flows for a fiscal period, in conformity with generally accepted accounting principles.

The *State and Local Governments* guide emphasizes the importance of testing for compliance with laws and regulations that may have a material effect on the determination of financial statement amounts. The guide notes that the auditor is required to design the audit to provide reasonable assurance that the financial statements are free of material misstatement resulting from violations of laws and regulations, error, or fraud.[6]

Materiality for Government Audits

At the beginning of the auditing process, auditors must determine the potential for misstatements on the financial statements that could adversely impact a user's evaluation of the entity's financial condition. Auditors refer to **materiality** to indicate, in their judgment, the level at which the quantitative or qualitative effects of misstatements will have a significant impact on a user's evaluation. The AICPA's Audit and Accounting Guide, *State and Local Governments,* requires auditors to make separate materiality determinations for each opinion unit. **Opinion units** are (1) governmental activities, (2) business-type activities, (3) aggregate discretely presented component units, (4) each major governmental and enterprise fund, and (5) the aggregate remaining fund information (nonmajor governmental and enterprise funds, the internal service fund type, and the fiduciary fund types). The auditor's report, then, will contain an opinion regarding each opinion unit or assertions to the effect that an opinion on one or more opinion units cannot be expressed. Specific guidance for evaluating materiality is in Chapter 14 of the Audit and Accounting Guide (pars. 14.67–14.87).

Required Supplementary and Other Information

Auditors generally render an opinion on the fairness of the basic financial statements of governments and, if engaged to do so, on the combining and individual fund presentations. AU-C Sections 720, 725, and 730 cover auditor responsibilities regarding additional information that is included in a document containing audited financial statements.[7] Required supplementary information (RSI), such as the MD&A and budgetary comparison schedules, are outside the scope of the financial statement audit. Auditors apply certain limited procedures in connection with RSI to provide assurance that it is fairly presented *in relation to* the basic financial statements. These procedures, addressed in AU-C Section 730, include inquiries about the methods used to prepare RSI and comparison of RSI to information in the audited financial statements. If no significant exceptions are noted in regard to RSI, an explanatory paragraph that provides no assurance on the RSI is included after the opinion paragraph; however, report wording is modified for omission of RSI, a material departure from prescribed guidelines, an inability to complete required audit procedures, or unresolved doubts about whether the RSI adheres to prescribed guidelines. No modification is made to the opinion paragraph, since the supplementary information is not considered part of the audited information.

The auditor may also perform a limited review of the introductory and statistical sections of a comprehensive annual financial report (CAFR) and other supplementary information, although the level of responsibility for this material is much less than for RSI. GAAS terms the content not specifically required by GAAP to be included within the CAFR as *other information.* Auditors need only report on the other information when it is considered materially inconsistent with the financial statements or materially misstated; however, AU-C Section 720 allows auditors the option of providing a paragraph including no assurance on that other information. AU-C Section 725 provides guidance for auditors engaged to opine on supplementary information in relation to the

[6] American Institute of Certified Public Accountants, Audit and Accounting Guide, *State and Local Governments* (New York: AICPA, 2014), pars. 4.09–4.10.

[7] See American Institute of Certified Public Accountants, Audit and Accounting Guide, *State and Local Governments,* 2014, Chapter 4, for a discussion of the auditor's responsibilities for required supplementary information, supplementary information, and other information.

financial statements as a whole. Illustration 11–1 demonstrated an "in-relation to" statement for RSI and no assurance on other information.

GOVERNMENT AUDITING STANDARDS

Audit standards that are to be followed by auditors of federal organizations, programs, activities, and functions are much broader in scope than GAAS. The Government Accountability Office under the direction of the Comptroller General of the United States has developed government auditing standards. **Generally accepted government auditing standards (GAGAS)**[8] are set forth and explained in the publication *Government Auditing Standards;* because of the color of its cover, the document has historically been referred to as the *yellow book.* It is important for readers to understand that GAGAS may apply to audits of governments, not-for-profits, or for-profit entities that receive federal funds. Additionally, some governments are required by statute or ordinance to use GAGAS in audits of public funds. Therefore, GAGAS should apply whenever required by law or contract.

Generally accepted auditing standards (GAAS), described earlier in the chapter, are used as a basis for government auditing standards. Reasons that the standards established by the AICPA were deemed to be too narrow in scope for audits of recipients of public funds are expressed in the introduction of GAGAS:

> The concept of accountability for use of public resources and government authority is key to our nation's governing processes. Management and officials entrusted with public resources are responsible for carrying out public functions and providing service to the public effectively, efficiently, economically, ethically, and equitably within the context of the statutory boundaries of the specific government program. As reflected in applicable laws, regulations, agreements, and standards, management and officials of government programs are responsible for providing reliable, useful, and timely information for transparency and accountability of these programs and their operations. Legislators, oversight bodies, those charged with governance, and the public need to know whether (1) management and officials manage government resources and use their authority properly and in compliance with laws and regulations; (2) government programs are achieving their objectives and desired outcomes; and (3) government services are provided effectively, efficiently, economically, ethically, and equitably. Government auditing is essential in providing government accountability to legislators, oversight bodies, those charged with governance, and the public.[9]

The first edition (1972) of GAGAS presented a single set of auditing standards that were similar to GAAS. Subsequent revisions developed a progressively broader set of standards, reflecting the need to provide standards for performance audits and attestation engagements in addition to financial audits. The broader standards also reflect the unique auditing and operating environments of government and not-for-profit organizations.

Types of Audits and Engagements

GAGAS describes audits and engagements that cover a broad range of financial or nonfinancial objectives. The GAGAS framework includes three types of audits and

[8] Another acronym often used to denote government auditing standards is GAS, which is the abbreviation for the publication *Government Auditing Standards.* These terms are used interchangeably; however, the term GAGAS is used in this text.

[9] Comptroller General of the United States, *Government Auditing Standards, 2011 Revision* (Washington, DC: U.S. Government Accountability Office, 2011, pars. 1.01–1.03).

services: financial audits, attestation engagements, and performance audits. Illustration 11–4 lists the purposes and characteristics of these auditor services. Performance audits are often performed by internal auditors or state audit agencies. An engagement letter between the auditor and the organization should clearly specify what type of audit is to be performed and which auditing standards will be followed.

Financial audits are all audits covered under GAAS, such as financial statement audits, special reports (e.g., a report on a single account or instance of compliance), reviews of interim financial information, letters to underwriters, compliance audits, and service organization audits. In financial audits, the auditors express an opinion on the fairness of an entity's financial statements as well as whether the statements conform to GAAP. **Attestation engagements** include services related to providing various levels of assurance on other financial or nonfinancial matters, such as internal control, compliance, MD&A presentation, allowability and reasonableness of proposed contract amounts, final contract costs, and reliability of performance measures. **Performance audits** or operational audits are independent assessments of the performance and the management of the entity, program, service, or activity against objective criteria. Objectives include assessing effectiveness and results, economy and efficiency, and internal controls and compliance with laws and regulations.

The GAGAS field work and reporting standards for performance audits are unique in that the objective of performance audits is to provide evidence to assess performance of a governmental organization, program, activity, or function rather than to render a professional opinion. Thus, testing for compliance with laws and regulations, although of critical importance in a financial audit, may be relatively less so if the audit objective in a performance audit is to assess the efficiency and effectiveness of a program and there are no laws and regulations that would have a material effect on the program.

ILLUSTRATION 11–4 Types of Governmental Audits and Other Engagements

Financial Audits

The primary purpose of a financial statement audit is to provide an opinion about whether an entity's financial statements are presented fairly in all material respects in conformity with an applicable financial reporting framework.

Attestation Engagements

The primary purpose of an attestation engagement is to provide an examination, a review, or an agreed-upon procedure report on a subject matter or on an assertion about a subject matter.

- Examination—the purpose is to express an opinion on whether the subject matter examined is based on (or in conformity with) the recognized criteria or the assertion being made is presented (or fairly stated) based on the recognized criteria.
- Review—the purpose is to express a conclusion about whether any information came to the attention of the auditor on the basis of work performed indicating that the subject matter reviewed is not based on (or not in conformity with) the recognized criteria, or the assertion is not presented (or not fairly stated) based on the recognized criteria.
- Agreed-Upon Procedures—the purpose is specific to the procedures the auditor performs on an agreed-to subject matter.

Performance Audits

The purposes of performance audits vary widely and include assessments of program effectiveness, economy, and efficiency; internal control compliance; and prospective analyses. Performance audits are defined as engagements that provide findings or conclusions based on an evaluation of sufficient, appropriate evidence against criteria.

Source: *Government Auditing Standards* (Washington, DC: GAO, 2011), pars. 2.07–2.11.

GAGAS Financial Audits

As noted earlier, GAGAS standards incorporate all AICPA SASs and identify additional requirements for financial audits. With the release of the AICPA's clarified auditing standards and the elimination of redundancies in the 2011 GAGAS revision, however, there are fewer major differences now than ever before between financial audits conducted using GAAS and those using GAGAS. Illustration 11–5 shows the four general standards and the performance and reporting standards that GAGAS requires in addition to GAAS for financial audits. The standards also suggest that materiality and early communication of deficiencies be given special consideration in the governmental audit environment.

ILLUSTRATION 11–5 Generally Accepted Government Auditing Standards (GAGAS) for Financial Audits—GAO

General Standards

1. Independence standard: In all matters relating to audit work, the audit organization and the individual auditor must be independent in mind and in appearance.
2. Professional judgment: Auditors must use professional judgment in planning and performing audits and in reporting the results.
3. Competence: The staff assigned to perform the audit must collectively possess adequate professional competence needed to address the audit objectives and perform the work in accordance with GAGAS.
4. Quality control and assurance: The audit organization must establish and maintain a system of quality control and have an external peer review at least once every 3 years.

Additional GAGAS Requirements for Performing Financial Audits

1. Pertinent information should be communicated to individuals contracting for or requesting the audit. When performing the audit pursuant to a law or regulation or for a legislative committee, the auditor should communicate with the legislative committee that has oversight of the audited entity.
2. During audit planning, the auditors should evaluate whether the audited entity has taken appropriate corrective action to address findings and recommendations from previous engagements that could have a material effect on the financial statements.
3. Auditors should extend the AICPA requirements pertaining to the auditors' responsibilities for laws and regulations to also apply to consideration of compliance with provisions of contracts or grant agreements.
4. When audit findings involve deficiencies in internal control; noncompliance with provisions of laws, regulations, contracts, or grant agreements; fraud; or abuse, auditors should plan and perform procedures to develop the elements (criteria, condition, cause and effect) of the findings that are relevant and necessary to achieve the audit objectives.
5. Documentation should be provided concerning evidence of supervisory review of work performed. For any departures from the GAGAS requirements, auditors should document the impact on the audit and on the auditors' conclusions.

Additional GAGAS Requirements for Reporting on Financial Audits

1. When audits are conducted in accordance with GAGAS, a reference to GAGAS should be made in the audit report.
2. When the financial statement audit report contains an opinion or a disclaimer of opinion, a report on internal control over financial reporting and on compliance with laws, regulations, and provisions of contracts and grants must be provided as part of the report or as a separate report.
3. Based on the audit work performed, a report should be made on significant deficiencies and material weaknesses in internal control, and instances of fraud; noncompliance with provisions of laws and regulations; and violations of grant or contract provisions and abuse that are material.
4. When the report discloses deficiencies in internal control, the views of responsible officials concerning the audit report and any plans for corrective action should be included in the report.
5. When applicable, the report should indicate that confidential or sensitive information has been omitted from the report and the reason that such an omission is necessary.
6. Submission of reports should be made to appropriate officials, and audits should be made available to the public. Auditors should document any limitation on report distribution.

Source: *Government Auditing Standards* (Washington, DC: GAO, 2011), Chapters 3 and 4.

General Standards

As shown in Illustration 11–5, GAGAS includes four general standards. While the content of these general standards is consistent with concepts found in AU-C Section 200, the GAGAS standards are explicitly stated and, in some cases, include specific requirements. For example, relative to competency, language from the GAGAS standard places responsibility on audit organizations to ensure that assignments are performed by staff that collectively have the knowledge, skills, and experience for the assignment (par. 3.70). A specific GAGAS requirement to ensure that auditors conducting audits under GAGAS maintain their professional competence is that, every two years, each auditor should complete at least 80 hours of continuing professional education (CPE) that directly contributes to the auditor's professional proficiency to perform such work (par. 3.76). Of the 80 CPE hours, 24 hours should relate to government auditing, the government environment, or the specific or unique environment in which the entity operates (e.g., the not-for-profit environment). At least 20 of the CPE hours should be completed in each year of the two-year period.[10]

To further ensure the quality of government audits, the fourth general standard in GAGAS requires each audit organization to have an "appropriate internal quality control system" and undergo an external peer review at least once every three years by an audit organization independent of the audit organization being reviewed.[11] The purpose of the standard is to ensure that the audit organization has quality control policies and procedures in place that will provide reasonable assurance that the organization and its employees are complying with applicable standards, laws, and regulations (par. 3.83). Once policies and procedures are in place, they must be monitored and analyzed at least annually to ensure that systematic improvement is being made (pars. 3.93–3.95).

Additional GAGAS Requirements for Performing Financial Audits

The additional standards for performing financial audits contained in GAGAS emphasize the importance of communication; follow-up on prior findings and recommendations; detection of material misstatements; development of the elements of a deficiency finding; and documentation. The first additional standard relates to written communication. Due to the fact that more parties tend to be involved in a GAGAS audit, communication during the planning process is important.

The second additional standard relates to prior audit findings and recommendations, information that auditors should use in assessing risk and determining the nature, timing, and extent of current audit testing. The third additional standard on detection of material misstatements contains an item that is unique to GAGAS audits—abuse. According to par 4.07 of the standards, "abuse involves behavior that is deficient or improper when compared with behavior that a prudent person would consider reasonable and necessary business practice given the facts and circumstances. Abuse also includes misuse of authority or position for personal financial interests or those of an immediate or close family member or business associate." If abuse is detected, auditors may need to apply additional audit procedures.

The fourth additional standard relates to findings in internal control, fraud, noncompliance with provisions of laws, regulations, contracts, grant agreements, or abuse. The four elements of a deficiency finding that GAGAS indicate should be developed to ensure

[10] The GAO provides complete guidance concerning continuing education requirements in its publication *Government Auditing Standards: Guidance on GAGAS Requirements for Continuing Professional Education (GAO-05-568G),* which is available through the GAO Web site *(www.gao.gov).*

[11] Ibid., pars. 3.96–3.100.

audit objectives are met are: criteria (the basis for determining a deficiency, such as a law), condition (the deficiency as it currently exists), cause, and effect or potential effect.

The fifth additional standard relates to documentation. This is one area that is frequently deemed deficient in reviews of GAGAS audits submitted to the Federal Audit Clearinghouse. Audit documentation needs to be sufficient to enable another auditor with no previous connection to the audit to review and understand the documentation.

Additional GAGAS Requirements for Reporting on Financial Audits

The additional GAGAS reporting standards cover reporting on compliance, internal controls, report requirements, and distribution. Some of the additional standards relate to reporting information that is unique to government-awarded grants and contracts. For example, the standards permit auditors to exclude reporting certain privileged and confidential information. Other standards add to disclosure requirements. An example of additional disclosure is "when auditors detect instances of noncompliance with provisions of contracts or grant agreements or abuse that have an effect on the financial statements or other financial data significant to the audit objectives that are less than material but warrant the attention of those charged with governance, they should communicate those findings in writing to audited entity officials" (par. 4.26).

Ethics and Independence

GAGAS outlines basic ethical principles that should guide auditors who are applying governmental auditing standards. When auditors are considering the facts and circumstances of the subject matter they are auditing, they should do so within the framework provided by the ethical principles. The five fundamental ethical principles identified by GAGAS are: public interest; integrity; objectivity; proper use of government information, resources, and position; and professional behavior. Public interest refers to consideration of the collective well-being of those being served by the auditor (par. 1.15). The other ethical principles outlined by GAGAS are fairly self-explanatory. Ethical principles should be considered throughout the audit.

Ethical principles are especially salient when the audit organization is considering whether it meets the GAGAS independence standard. The independence standard requires that the highest degree of integrity and objectivity be maintained by any auditor (CPA, non-CPA, government financial auditor, or performance auditor) performing audits of federal, state, and local governments and not-for-profit entities that receive federal financial assistance, so that the public is best served. GAGAS's practical consideration of independence is covered in four sections that address: (1) a conceptual framework for making independence determinations (pars. 3.07–3.26); (2) requirements and guidance for audit organizations structurally located within the governments they audit (pars. 3.27–3.32); (3) requirements and guidance when performing nonaudit services, including indication of specific nonaudit services that would normally impair independence (pars. 3.33–3.58); and (4) requirements and guidance on documentation to support consideration of auditor independence (par. 3.59). Contents of sections 1, 3, and 4, which pertain to the independence of auditors external to the governmental entity, are discussed below.

Conceptual Framework for Independence

Because it is impossible to define every situation that creates threats to independence, GAGAS establish a conceptual framework that requires auditors to identify, evaluate, and apply safeguards to appropriately address threats to independence. The conceptual framework, shown in Illustration 11–6, achieves further harmonization with AICPA

ILLUSTRATION 11–6 GAGAS Conceptual Framework for Independence

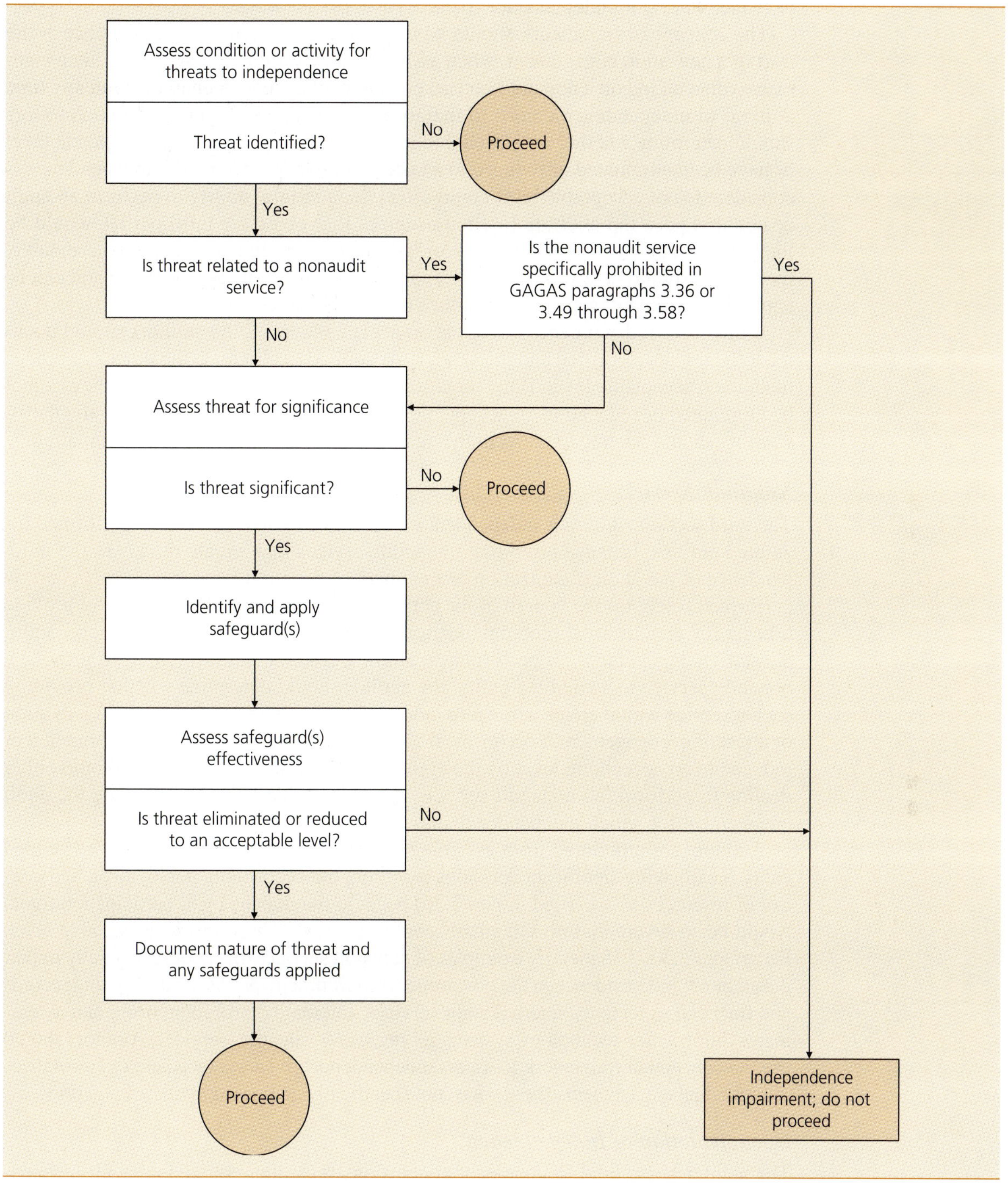

Source: *Government Auditing Standards, Internet Version* (Washington, DC: GAO, 2011), Appendix II.

and international standards and includes additional considerations for government audits. Threats to independence are circumstances that could impair independence and, therefore, should be evaluated. They include self-interest threat, self-review threat, bias threat, familiarity threat, undue influence threat, management participation threat, and structural threat (par. 3.14). Safeguards are controls designed to eliminate or reduce threats to independence (pars. 3.16–3.19).

The conceptual framework should be used to assess threats to independence at the start of a new audit engagement, when assigning new staff to an ongoing audit engagement, when taking on a nonaudit service engagement at an audited entity, and any time a threat to independence comes to the attention of the audit organization. Auditors should determine whether identified threats to independence are at an acceptable level or have been eliminated or reduced to an acceptable level. A threat to independence is considered "not acceptable" if it could affect the auditors' ability to perform an audit or could expose the auditors to circumstances that objective third parties would be likely to conclude compromised auditor judgment. Any time a threat is unacceptable, the auditor should determine whether appropriate safeguards are available and can be applied to eliminate the threats or reduce them to an acceptable level.

If threats to independence are not at an acceptable level, the auditors should document the threats identified and the safeguards applied to eliminate the threats or reduce them to an acceptable level. If the threats are considered so significant that they cannot be eliminated or reduced to an acceptable level through the application of safeguards, auditors should decline to perform the audit since independence has been impaired.

Nonaudit Services

The third section addresses independence issues when nonaudit work is performed for audited entities, because providing nonaudit services may create threats to the independence of the audit organization or members of the audit team. **Nonaudit work** is performed solely for the benefit of the entity requesting the work and does not provide a basis for conclusions, recommendations, or opinions as would a financial audit, attestation engagement, or performance audit. Before an auditor agrees to provide a nonaudit service to an audited entity, the auditor should determine whether providing such a service would create a threat to independence with respect to any GAGAS audit or attestation engagement it performs. If a threat is created that cannot be eliminated or reduced to an acceptable level by the application of safeguards, auditors should either decline to perform the nonaudit service or decline to perform or terminate the audit engagement for which independence may be impaired.

Auditors are prohibited from assuming a management responsibility for an audited entity (i.e., making significant decisions regarding the acquisition, deployment, and control of resources as specified in par. 3.36) because the management participation threat would be so severe that no safeguards could reduce the threats to an acceptable level. Paragraphs 3.50–3.58 identify examples of nonaudit services that could potentially impair the auditors' independence in the government environment: preparing accounting records and financial statements, internal audit services, internal control monitoring and assessments, information technology systems services, and valuation services. Auditors should use the conceptual framework to assess independence given the facts and circumstances of individual engagements for services not specifically addressed by these categories.

Documentation of Independence

The auditor is required to document conclusions regarding compliance with independence requirements and support for those conclusions. Such documentation should include discussion of threats identified and safeguards in place or applied that eliminated the threat or reduced it to an acceptable level; safeguards required if an audit organization is structurally located within a government entity and is considered independent based on those safeguards; consideration of the audited entity management's ability to effectively oversee a nonaudit service to be provided by the auditor; and the auditor's understanding with an audited entity for which the auditor will perform a nonaudit service.

SINGLE AUDITS

Federal grants-in-aid to state and local governments total over $500 billion annually. Although grants-in-aid originate from more than 1,000 different programs administered by more than 30 federal departments and agencies, about 89.2 percent of the grants-in-aid in 2013 were made by five departments: the Department of Health and Human Services (64.7 percent), Department of Transportation (10.7 percent), Department of Agriculture (6.1 percent), Department of Housing and Urban Development (4.0 percent), and the Department of Education (3.8 percent).[12]

History of the Single Audit

Until the mid-1980s each federal agency established accounting, reporting, and auditing requirements for each program it administered, and these requirements differed from agency to agency. Accordingly, each agency had the right to make on-site audits of grant funds and often did so. Since even relatively small local governments might have several active federal grants (each with different accounting, reporting, and auditing requirements), the amount of time spent keeping track of conflicting requirements and providing facilities for a succession of different groups of auditors became extremely burdensome. Efforts were made in the 1960s to standardize grant accounting, reporting, and auditing requirements but with only modest success. In 1979, the Office of Management and Budget (OMB) required that federal fund audits be made on an organizationwide basis, rather than on a grant-by-grant basis. This concept is called the **single audit.** The OMB's experience led to the enactment of the Single Audit Act of 1984. The purposes of the act are to:

1. Improve the financial management of state and local governments with respect to federal financial assistance programs,
2. Establish uniform requirements for audits of federal financial assistance provided to state and local governments,
3. Promote the efficient and effective use of audit resources,
4. Ensure that federal departments and agencies rely upon and use audit work done pursuant to the Single Audit Act.

Studies by the GAO found that the Single Audit Act of 1984 and the related requirements imposed by OMB's guidance had improved accountability over federal assistance, strengthened the financial management of state and local governments and not-for-profit organizations, and reduced the overall audit burden. However, thousands of single audits were being imposed on small entities that in aggregate represented only a small percentage of total federal assistance.

Amendments to Single Audit Requirements

Recognizing the need to further improve the Single Audit Act, Congress passed the Single Audit Act Amendments of 1996 (P.L. 104–156). These amendments include one additional purpose: to reduce audit burdens on state and local governments, Indian tribes, and not-for-profit organizations.

[12] Based upon 2013 data available at *USAspending.gov.*

The 1996 amendments also extended the statutory requirement for single audit coverage to not-for-profit organizations, established a risk-based approach for selecting programs for audit testing, and increased administrative flexibility by giving OMB the authority to revise certain audit requirements periodically without seeking further amendments to the Single Audit Act.

The 1996 amendments essentially replaced the 1984 Act. Revisions to OMB guidance took place in 1997, 2003, and 2013. The current guidance for single audits is contained within an extensive OMB document, *Uniform Administrative Requirements, Cost Principles, and Audit Requirements for Federal Awards,* issued in December 2013.[13] This single document provides streamlined guidelines for grant accounting and reporting and incorporates material previously issued in OMB "circulars." Since the guidance replaces eight OMB circulars, it is often referred to as the "super circular," "omni circular," or *Uniform Guidance* (the abbreviation used in this chapter).[14] It is anticipated that this guidance will be complemented by additional efforts to strengthen program outcomes through effective use of grant-making models, performance metrics, and evaluation.

Determining Who Must Have a Single Audit

Illustration 11–7 provides a flowchart to determine whether an entity must have a single audit or other type of audit. As Illustration 11–7 shows, nonfederal entities that expend $750,000 or more in a year in federal awards must have a single audit or a **program-specific audit** for that year. The election of a program-specific audit applies when an auditee expends federal awards under only one program or a cluster of related programs, and the program's (cluster's) laws, regulations, or grant agreements do not require an entitywide financial statement audit. A program-specific audit is usually performed on the financial statements of the particular program and examines matters related to the program such as internal controls and compliance with pertinent laws, regulations, and agreements. In many cases a program-specific audit guide will be available to provide detailed audit guidance for conducting the program-specific audit.

Nonfederal entities that expend less than $750,000 of federal awards during the fiscal year generally are exempt from federal audit requirements for that year. Nonetheless, any federal awarding agency may conduct or arrange for additional audits it deems necessary. Such additional audits should be rare, should build upon work performed for other audits, and should be paid for by the federal agency conducting or requesting the audit. Some states have voluntarily adopted federal GAGAS and single audit requirements that may apply under state audit mandates, even if federal awards expended are less than $750,000 and no other federal audit requirement exists. In other states that do not mandate their own requirements for GAGAS audits or single audits, annual audits of local governments and not-for-profit organizations, when required, are performed in conformity with AICPA GAAS, discussed earlier in this chapter.

[13] See United States Office of Management and Budget, *Uniform Administrative Requirements, Cost Principles, and Audit Requirements for Federal Awards,* 78 FR 78589, published in the Federal Register on December 26, 2013, available at *https://federalregister.gov/a/2013-30465*. Upon implementation, this guidance will also be available on the OMB Web site.

[14] OMB Circular A-133, *Audits of States, Local Governments, and Non-Profit Organizations,* was the primary document covering single audit guidance; while Circular A-50 addressed single audit follow-up. The remaining superseded circulars set forth cost principles and administrative requirements under grant programs, contracts, and other agreements, to state and local governments (OMB Circulars A-87 and A-102), educational institutions (OMB Circulars A-21 and A-110), other not-for-profit organizations (OMB Circulars A-122 and A-110), and in general (OMB Circular A-89).

ILLUSTRATION 11–7 Determining Applicability of the Single Audit

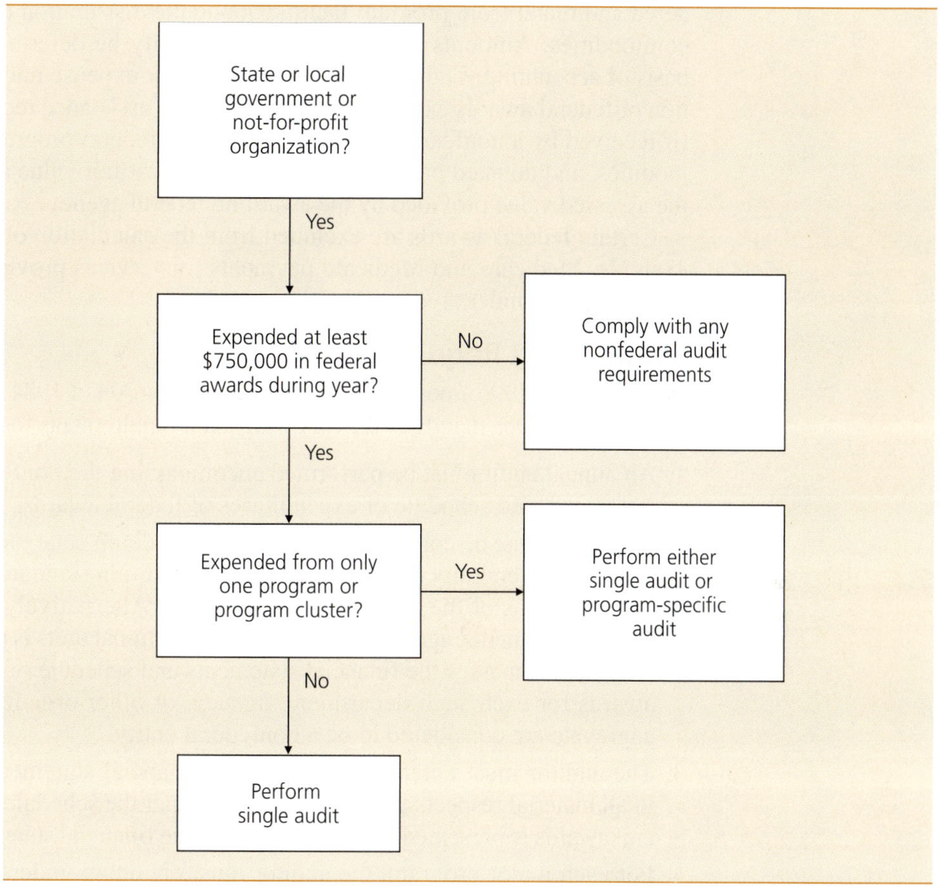

The *Uniform Guidance* defines a *nonfederal entity* as a state or local government, Indian tribe, institution of higher education, or non-profit organization. *Federal awards* are defined as:

> Federal financial assistance [defined by OMB as grants, loans, loan guarantees, property, cooperative agreements, interest subsidies, insurance, food commodities, direct appropriations, and other assistance] and federal cost-reimbursement contracts that nonfederal entities receive directly from federal awarding agencies or indirectly from pass-through entities.[15]

It is important to note that the required audit threshold is based on federal awards *expended* rather than *received.* Unfortunately, calculating federal awards expended is not as straightforward as it might seem. The basic rule is that a federal award has been expended at the point in time when activity occurs that requires the nonfederal entity to begin complying with laws, regulations, or contractual provisions relating to the award. Typical examples are expenditure/expense transactions (such as incurring labor costs, purchasing or using supplies, and paying utility bills) associated with grants, cost-reimbursement contracts, cooperative agreements, and direct appropriations; disbursement of funds by a pass-through entity to a subrecipient; the receipt of property; the receipt

[15] Office of Management and Budget, *Uniform Administrative Requirements, Cost Principles, and Audit Requirements for Federal Awards,* 78 FR 78589, §200.38.

or use of program income (such as charges to program beneficiaries for services rendered and rental from program facilities); and the distribution or consumption of food commodities. Amounts expended would normally be determined using the entity's basis of accounting. Thus, either an expenditure or expense may enter into the calculation of federal awards expended. Federal noncash assistance received, such as free rent (if received by a nonfederal entity to carry out a federal program), food stamps, commodities, and donated property, should be valued at fair value at the time of receipt or the assessed value provided by the awarding federal agency.

Certain federal awards are excluded from the calculation of awards expended. For example, Medicare and Medicaid payments for services provided are not included in the calculation unless required by the state.[16]

Single Audit Requirements

Pursuant to the 1996 amendments to the Single Audit Act of 1984 Subpart F of the OMB's *Uniform Guidance* mandates the following audit requirements for the single audit:

1. An annual audit must be performed encompassing the nonfederal entity's financial statements and schedule of expenditures of federal awards.
2. The audit must be conducted by an external federal, state, or local auditor in accordance with generally accepted government auditing standards (GAGAS) and cover the operations of the entire nonfederal entity. Alternatively, a series of audits that cover departments, agencies, and other organizational units is permitted if the series of audits encompasses the financial statements and schedule of expenditures of federal awards for each such department, agency, or other organizational unit, which in aggregate are considered to be a nonfederal entity.
3. The auditor must determine whether the financial statements are presented fairly in all material respects with GAAP and whether the schedule of expenditures of federal awards is presented fairly in relation to the financial statements taken as a whole.
4. For each major program, the auditor must obtain an understanding of the internal controls pertaining to the compliance requirements for the program, assess control risk, and perform tests of controls, unless the controls are deemed to be ineffective. (*Note:* OMB's *Uniform Guidance* requires the auditor to obtain an understanding of and conduct testing of internal controls to support a low assessed level of control risk; that is, as if high reliance will be placed on the internal controls.) In addition, for each major program the auditor shall determine whether the nonfederal entity has complied with laws, regulations, and contract or grant provisions pertaining to federal awards of the program. Auditors test compliance by determining if requirements listed for each program in the *Compliance Supplement* published by the OMB have been met. Auditors are required to use the *Compliance Supplement,* which details compliance auditing requirements for many federal programs, listed by *Catalog of Federal Domestic Assistance* (CFDA) title and number.
5. OMB's *Uniform Guidance* assigns certain responsibilities to federal awarding agencies and nonfederal entities that act as "pass-through" agents in passing federal awards to subrecipient nonfederal entities.

Compliance Audits

As noted in item (4) above, the *Uniform Guidance* requires the auditor to express an opinion that the auditee complied with laws, regulations, and grant or contract

[16] Ibid., §200.502

ILLUSTRATION 11–8 Sample Matrix of Compliance Requirements

	Types of Compliance Requirements													
	A	B	C	D	E	F	G	H	I	J	K	L	M	N
CFDA	Activities Allowed or Unallowed	Allowable Costs/ Cost Principles	Cash Management	Davis-Bacon Act	Eligibility	Equipment and Real Property Management	Matching, Level of Effort, Earmarking	Period of Availability of Federal Funds	Procurement and Suspension and Debarment	Program Income	Real Property Acquisition and Relocation Assistance	Reporting	Subrecipient Monitoring	Special Tests and Provisions
94 – Corporation for National and Community Service (CNCS)														
94.006	Y	Y	Y		Y		Y	Y				Y	Y	
94.011 94.016	Y	Y	Y		Y		Y	Y				Y		
96 – Social Security Administration (SSA)														
96.001 96.006	Y	Y	Y			Y		Y	Y			Y		Y
97 – Department of Homeland Security (DHS)														
97.024	Y	Y	Y		Y		Y	Y				Y	Y	
97.036	Y	Y	Y		Y		Y	Y				Y	Y	Y
97.039	Y	Y	Y		Y		Y	Y				Y	Y	
97.067	Y	Y	Y			Y	Y	Y				Y	Y	Y
98 – United States Agency for International Development (USAID)														
98.007 98.008	Y	Y	Y					Y		Y		Y		Y

Y - Yes, this type of compliance requirement may apply to the Federal program.
Shaded box Indicates the program normally does not have activity requiring the auditor to test this type of compliance requirement.

Source: Excerpt from *OMB Circular A-133 Compliance Supplement 2014,* page 2–10.

provisions that could have a direct and material effect on each major program. To gather sufficient evidence to support his or her opinion in such **compliance audits,** the auditor tests whether each major program was administered in conformity with administrative requirements contained in the *Uniform Guidance*. The auditor also tests for compliance with the detailed *compliance* requirements for major programs provided in the *Compliance Supplement* or other guidance provided by federal awarding agencies. The *Compliance Supplement*, updated by the OMB annually, identifies generic compliance requirements and suggested audit procedures for testing compliance with each requirement.[17] A matrix in part 2 of the *Supplement* identifies which of the generic compliance requirements apply to specific federal funding sources. See Illustration 11–8 for an excerpt from part 2 that specifies general compliance requirements for funding programs under four federal agencies. Note that the first column identifies individual programs by CFDA.

Part 4 of the *Supplement* provides grant-specific program information, compliance requirements, and audit procedures for each federal funding source organized by 19 federal agencies and programs that distribute funding. Generally, compliance requirements relate to matters such as allowed and unallowed activities; allowed and unallowed costs; eligibility of program beneficiaries; responsibilities of the nonfederal entity regarding matching, level of effort, and earmarking; management of equipment and real property acquired from federal awards; and required reporting.

Auditee Responsibilities

The *Uniform Guidance* also details the responsibilities of auditees (nonfederal entities). Auditees are responsible for identifying all federal awards received and expended, and the federal programs under which they were received. Identification of the federal program includes the Catalog of Federal Domestic Assistance (CFDA) title and number, award number and year, and name of the federal agency. In addition, auditees are responsible for maintaining appropriate internal controls and systems to ensure compliance with all laws, regulations, and contract or grant provisions applicable to federal awards. Finally, auditees must prepare appropriate financial statements and the schedule of expenditures of federal awards, ensure that audits are properly performed and submitted when due, and follow up and take appropriate corrective action on audit findings. The latter requirement includes preparation of a summary schedule of prior audit findings and a corrective action plan for current year audit findings.

Selecting Programs for Audit

Illustration 11–9 shows the procedures and criteria for selecting major programs for audit as described in the *Uniform Guidance.* A **major program** is a federal award program selected for audit using the procedures described below and shown in Illustration 11–9 or by request of a federal awarding agency. Use of a **risk-based approach** for selecting major programs for audit ensures that audit effort is concentrated on the highest risk programs. The risk-based approach is applied as follows:[18]

1. Identify the "larger" federal programs and analyze them according to the Type A criteria. Programs not meeting Type A criteria are identified as Type B programs. Type A programs are determined using the following sliding scale:

[17] The 2014 *Compliance Supplement* contains 14 general compliance requirements; however, in drafting the *Uniform Guidance*, the OMB disclosed plans to reduce the number of general compliance requirements over time.

[18] OMB *Uniform Guidance*, §200.518.

Total Federal Awards Expended	Threshold for Type A Program
$750,000 to $100 million	Larger of $750,000 or 3% (.03) of total federal awards expended
More than $100 million to $10 billion	Larger of $3 million or .3% (.003) of total federal awards expended
More than $10 billion	Larger of $30 million or .15% (.0015) of total federal awards expended

2. Identify low-risk Type A programs: programs previously audited in at least one of the two most recent audit periods as a major program, with no internal control deficiencies identified as material weaknesses, opinion modifications, or significant questioned costs in the most recent audit period; programs with no significant changes in personnel or systems that would have significantly increased risk; and programs that, in the auditor's professional judgment, are low risk, after considering such factors as the inherent risk of the program, the level of oversight exercised by federal awarding agencies and pass-through agencies, and the phase of a program in its life cycle. New programs, for example, tend to be more risky than more mature programs.

ILLUSTRATION 11–9 Risk-Based Approach for Selecting Major Programs for Audit

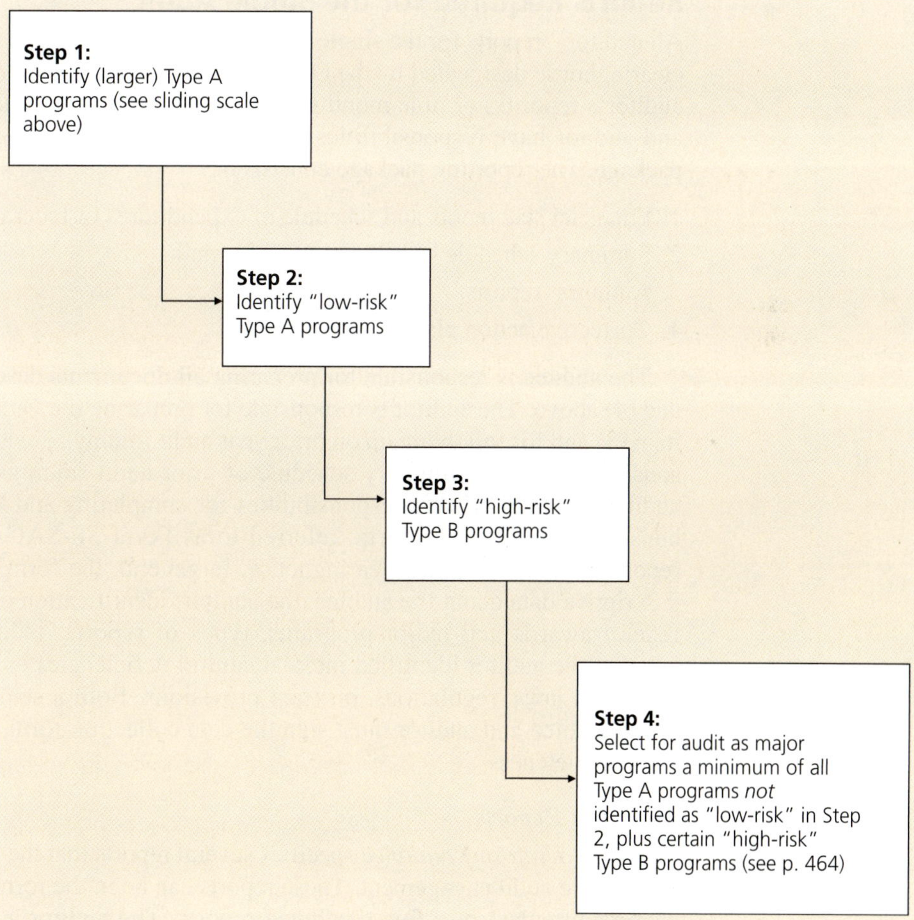

3. Identify Type B programs that, based on the auditor's professional judgment and criteria discussed above, are high risk. The auditor is not expected to perform risk assessments on relatively small federal programs. Risk assessments are performed only for those Type B programs that exceed 25 percent (0.25) of the Type A threshold determined in Step 1. Note, however, that the auditor is not required to identify more high-risk Type B programs than at least one fourth the number of low-risk Type A programs identified as low-risk under Step 2.
4. At a minimum, audit as major programs all Type A programs *not* identified as low risk and high-risk Type B programs identified in Step 3.

The *percentage of coverage rule* requires the auditing of as many major programs as necessary to ensure that at least 40 percent of total federal awards expended are audited. In addition to the possibility of reduced audit coverage resulting from individual Type A programs being classified as low risk, the *Uniform Guidance* also provides that the auditee itself can be classified as low risk and thereby receive even greater reduction in audit coverage. An auditee that meets the rather stringent criteria prescribed in Section 200.520 of the *Uniform Guidance* to be a low-risk auditee needs to have audited a sufficient number of major programs to encompass only 20 percent of total federal awards expended. In either percentage of coverage case, at a minimum, the major programs slated for audit in Step 4 must be audited.

Reports Required for the Single Audit

All auditors' reports for the single audit must be submitted electronically to the federal clearinghouse designated by the OMB within the earlier of 30 days after receipt of the auditor's report(s) or nine months after the end of the audit period. Both the auditee and auditor have responsibilities for particular reports that comprise the reporting package. The reporting package consists of:

1. Financial statements and schedule of expenditures of federal awards.
2. Summary schedule of prior audit findings.
3. Auditors' reports.
4. Corrective action plan.

The auditee is responsible for preparing all documents described in items (1), (2), and (4) above. The auditor is responsible for preparing the various auditors' reports in item (3) and for following up on prior year audit findings, including assessing the reasonableness of the summary schedule of prior audit findings. In addition, both the auditee and auditor have responsibilities for completing and submitting the comprehensive data collection form, referred to as Form SF-SAC, that accompanies the reporting package to the clearinghouse. In general, the form provides for extensive descriptive data about the auditee, the auditor, identification of types and amounts of federal awards and major programs, types of reports issued by the auditor, and whether the auditor identified internal control deficiencies or significant noncompliance with laws, regulations, or grant provisions. Both a senior-level representative of the auditee and auditor must sign the data collection form, certifying its accuracy and completeness.

Auditor's Reports

The OMB *Uniform Guidance* specifies several reports that the auditor must submit for each single audit engagement. These reports can be in the form of separate reports for each requirement or a few combined reports. The auditor's report on the financial statements should indicate that the audit was conducted in accordance with GAAS and GAGAS. The required single audit reports, whether made as separate reports or combined, must include:[19]

1. An opinion (or disclaimer of opinion) as to whether the financial statements are presented fairly in all material respects with GAAP and whether the schedule of expenditures of federal awards is fairly stated in all material respects in relation to the financial statements as a whole.
2. A report on internal control over financial reporting and compliance with federal statutes, regulations, and the terms and conditions of the federal award, noncompliance with which could have a material effect on the financial statements. This report must describe the scope of testing of internal control and compliance and the results of the tests, and where applicable, it will refer to the separate schedule of findings and questioned costs described in item (4) below.
3. A report on compliance for each major program and on internal control over compliance. This report must describe the scope of testing of internal control over compliance; include an opinion or modified opinion as to whether the auditee complied with federal statutes and regulations and the terms and conditions of federal awards that could have a direct and material effect on each major program; and refer to the separate schedule of findings and questioned costs described in item (4) below.
4. A schedule of findings and questioned costs, containing the following:
   (*a*) A summary of the auditor's results, including such information as type of opinion rendered on the financial statements, significant deficiencies or material weaknesses relating to internal control, material noncompliance affecting the financial statements, major programs audited, type of opinion on compliance for major programs and significant deficiencies or material weaknesses in internal control affecting major programs, other audit findings, identification of major programs, the dollar threshold used to distinguish between Type A and Type B programs, and a statement as to whether the auditee qualified as low risk.
   (*b*) Findings related to the audit of the financial statements required to be reported under GAGAS.
   (*c*) Audit findings and questioned costs. Audit findings are discussed next.

Reporting Audit Findings

As listed in item (4) above, auditors must prepare a schedule of findings and questioned costs. **Audit findings** reported in the schedule provide detail on matters such as internal control significant deficiencies or material weaknesses, instances of noncompliance, questioned costs, fraud and illegal acts, material violations of contract and grant agreements, and material abuse.

Regarding reporting on internal controls, item (4a) above refers to significant deficiencies or material weaknesses. A deficiency exists when "the design or operation of a control does not allow management or employees, in the normal course of performing their assigned functions, to prevent, or detect and correct misstatements on a timely basis," and it includes material weaknesses and significant deficiencies.[20] A **material weakness** is a deficiency in internal control "such that there is a reasonable

[19] Ibid, §200.515.

[20] American Institute of Certified Public Accountants, *Codification of Statements on Auditing Standards*, AU-C Section 265.07, available at *http://www.aicpa.org/Research/Standards/AuditAttest/Pages/Clarified SAS.aspx*.

possibility that a material misstatement of the entity's financial statements will not be prevented, or detected and corrected on a timely basis"; a **significant deficiency** is a deficiency in internal control "that is less severe than a material weakness, yet important enough to merit attention by those charged with governance."[21] Under GAGAS, auditors should include in the audit report any deficiencies in internal control that are significant within the context of the audit objectives based upon the audit work performed; deficiencies that are not significant to the objectives of the audit may be included in the report or communicated in writing to officials of the audited entity, unless inconsequential (par. 7.19).

A **questioned cost** arises from an audit finding, generally relating to noncompliance with a law, regulation, or agreement, whose costs are either not supported by adequate documentation or appear unreasonable. Cost principles to be followed by nonfederal entities in the administration of federal awards are prescribed in the OMB *Uniform Guidance*, which defines concepts such as direct and indirect costs, allowable and unallowable costs, and methods for calculating indirect cost rates. These cost principles are described in Chapter 12.

In auditing a major program, the *Uniform Guidance* requires that *known questioned costs* exceeding $25,000 shall be reported in the schedule of findings and questioned costs. A known questioned cost is one that the auditor has specifically identified in performing audit procedures. In evaluating the impact of a known questioned cost, the dollar impact also includes a best estimate of "likely questioned costs." Thus, the auditor must also report known questioned costs if the likely questioned costs exceed $25,000, even if the known dollar amount is zero. Nonmajor programs are not normally audited for compliance (except for audit follow-up of a program that was previously audited as a major program); however, if the auditor becomes aware of a known questioned cost in a nonmajor program, he or she must also report it in the schedule of findings and questioned costs.

Other Single Audit Requirements

The GAGAS (yellow book) requires that auditors make their audit personnel and audit documentation available to other auditors and to oversight officials from federal awarding agencies and cognizant agents, so that auditors may use others' work and avoid duplication of efforts. Federal agency access also includes the right to obtain copies of the working papers, which should be retained for a minimum of three years.

The *Uniform Guidance* provides that a **cognizant agency for audit responsibilities** will be designated for each nonfederal entity expending more than $50 million a year in federal awards. The cognizant agency will be the federal awarding agency that provides the predominant amount of direct funding unless the OMB specifically designates a different cognizant agency. Among the cognizant agency's responsibilities are providing technical audit advice and liaison to auditees and auditors, obtaining or conducting quality control reviews of selected audits made by nonfederal auditors, communicating to affected parties the deficiencies identified by quality control reviews (including, when necessary, referral of deficiencies to state licensing agencies and professional bodies for possible disciplinary action), and promptly communicating findings of irregularities and illegal acts to affected federal agencies and appropriate federal law enforcement agencies. Nonfederal entities expending less than $50 million in federal awards are assigned an **oversight agency.** The oversight agency is the

[21] Ibid.

agency that makes the predominant amount of direct funding to the nonfederal entity. An oversight agency has responsibilities similar to a designated cognizant agency, but they are less extensive.

SPECIAL TOPICS RELATED TO AUDITS OF GOVERNMENTS AND NOT-FOR-PROFITS

Single Audit Quality

Single Audit quality has been an area of concern for decades. It came to the forefront when a 1986 General Accounting Office (GAO) study revealed that 34 percent of the 120 governmental audits examined were substandard or problematic.[22] While subsequent professional guidance and educational requirements have helped to improve governmental audit quality, a 2007 project undertaken by the GAO, the OMB, the AICPA, the President's Council on Integrity and Efficiency (PCIE), and the National State Auditors Association indicated that some quality issues remain.

Results of the 2007 project's statistical analysis led researchers to conclude that 48.6 percent of the single audits were of acceptable quality.[23] Another 16.0 percent were of limited reliability (i.e., there were significant deficiencies), while 35.5 percent of the single audits were unacceptable (i.e., there were material reporting errors and/or deficiencies so severe that the opinion on at least one major program could not be relied upon). The most prevalent problems discovered related to not documenting an understanding of internal controls over compliance requirements (56.5 percent), not documenting the testing of internal controls on at least some compliance requirements (61.0 percent), and not documenting compliance testing of at least some compliance requirements (59.6 percent). As can be seen, the problem areas relate directly to and are unique to the single audit—major program compliance requirements.

As was the case in the mid-1980s, the AICPA, GAO, OMB, and other agencies are currently active in governmental audit activities. The AICPA has created a Governmental Audit Quality Center (*www.aicpa.org/gaqc*) to promote the importance of quality governmental audits and the value of such audits to purchasers of governmental audit services. The GAO and OMB provide frequent updates to GAGAS and federal fund audit requirements and guidelines. Furthermore, these organizations agree that auditor selection processes can serve a vital role in ensuring a quality governmental audit.[24]

When seeking an external auditor, governments and not-for-profits should prepare a formal request for proposal (RFP). Requests for proposals should include information about the governmental entity and cover the scope of services (financial audit, Single Audit, and any additional compliance auditing), the auditing standards to be followed (GAAS, GAGAS, or state-mandated standards), reports to be issued, assistance to be provided to the auditor, and other considerations. Engagement specifics, such as the timing of the audit, work schedules, estimated hours, prior year audit fees, and due date, are also important. Finally, the RFP should also specify the required

[22] U.S. General Accountability Office (U.S. GAO), *CPA Quality: Many Governmental Audits Do Not Comply with Professional Standards*, AFMD 86-33 (Washington, DC: Government Printing Office, 1986).

[23] The information in this paragraph is from the *Report on National Single Audit Sampling Project, June 2007* (Washington, DC: President's Council on Integrity and Efficiency, 2007).

[24] See Stephen J. Gauthier, *An Elected Official's Guide to Auditing* (Chicago: Government Finance Officers Association, 1992), for recommendations regarding the selection of auditing services for governmental entities.

qualifications of the auditing firm in terms of experience, staff size, licensing and training, and independence. Government officials should examine auditor proposals submitted in response to the RFP to evaluate potential auditors.

The Impact of SOX

The Sarbanes-Oxley (SOX) Act of 2002, Congress's response to corporate accounting scandals of the late 1990s and early 2000s, applies to publicly held companies, their public accounting firms, and other issuers.[25] However, some states, such as California, have passed SOX-type regulations for not-for-profit organizations (NFPs).

Indirectly, SOX has impacted governments and not-for-profits as the AICPA moves to align the GAAS standards with those issued by the Public Company Accounting Oversight Board (PCAOB). This alignment is reflected in the issuance of several new auditing standards since the enactment of SOX. SOX has also indirectly affected all entities by altering the funding status of the standards-setting bodies—FASB and GASB. Finally, members of not-for-profit boards of directors and elected officials frequently have business backgrounds. As a result, board members and officials are often interested in applying SOX-related practices used in business to the not-for-profits and governments they represent. Two areas where SOX can lead to improvements in government and not-for-profit governance are audit committees and internal controls.

The SOX legislation requires audit committees of public companies, subsets of the board of directors, to (1) appoint and oversee the auditor, (2) resolve disagreements between management and its auditor, (3) establish procedures to receive complaints from employees who "blow the whistle" on those responsible for fraud, (4) ensure auditor independence, and (5) review the audit report and other written communications. A state or local government or not-for-profit organization that establishes an audit committee, at a minimum, signals to the public that the auditors report to the board that hired them, not to management.[26]

Section 404 of SOX requires managers of publicly traded companies to accept responsibility for the effectiveness of the entity's internal control system. The act of "certifying" requires that managers present a written assertion not only that they have adopted some framework for internal controls, but also that they test these controls and can document the effectiveness of the internal control system. The OMB reexamined its internal control requirements for federal agencies in light of the Sarbanes-Oxley Act of 2002 and revised OMB *Circular A–123,* "Management's Responsibility for Internal Control." This circular "provides guidance to Federal managers on improving the accountability and effectiveness of Federal programs and operations by establishing, assessing, correcting, and reporting on internal control."[27]

Managers of government and not-for-profit entities could benefit from voluntarily adopting certain requirements of the Sarbanes-Oxley Act, such as creation of an audit committee, monitoring the independence of auditors, and certification of internal controls and financial statements by the chief executive or financial officer of the entity.

[25] For more detailed information, students are directed to the Act itself (P.L. 107–204) and the Public Company Accounting Oversight Board (PCAOB) Web site (*www.pcaobus.org*).

[26] The AICPA produced *Audit Committee Toolkits* for both government and not-for-profit organizations to provide guidance for establishing and working with audit committees.

[27] OMB *Circular A–123 revised,* "Management's Responsibility for Internal Control" (Washington, DC: OMB), December 21, 2004.

Auditing Guidance

As demonstrated throughout this chapter, audits of governments and not-for-profit organizations encompass unique issues for auditors. Fortunately, numerous resources are available to guide auditors in these specialized engagements. In addition to the often-mentioned version for state and local governments, the AICPA publishes industry-specific audit and accounting guides for not-for-profit organizations and health care entities. If a single audit or GAGAS audit is required, the audit guide entitled *Government Auditing Standards and Circular A-133 Audits* may be pertinent. The AICPA also issues annual audit risk alerts for each of the areas covered by an audit guide. State CPA societies and numerous professional organizations, such as the National Association of Nonprofit Accountants & Consultants, the National Association of College and University Business Officers, and the Healthcare Financial Management Association, also provide guidance for understanding and applying new accounting issuances, which can be helpful to the auditor.

Key Terms

Attestation engagements, *451*
Audit findings, *465*
Cognizant agency for audit responsibilities, *466*
Compliance audit, *462*
Engagement letter, *446*
Financial audits, *451*
Generally accepted auditing standards (GAAS), *442*
Generally accepted government auditing standards (GAGAS), *450*
Major programs, *462*
Material weakness, *465*
Materiality, *449*
Nonaudit work, *456*
Opinion units, *449*
Oversight agency, *466*
Performance audits, *451*
Program-specific audit, *458*
Questioned cost, *466*
Risk-based approach, *462*
Significant deficiency, *466*
Single audit, *457*

Selected References

American Institute of Certified Public Accountants. Audit and Accounting Guide. *State and Local Governments.* New York: AICPA, 2014.

———. Audit Guide. *Government Auditing Standards and Circular A–133 Audits.* New York: AICPA, 2014.

Comptroller General of the United States. *Government Auditing Standards.* Washington, DC: Superintendent of Documents, U.S. Government Printing Office, 2011.

Office of Management and Budget, *Uniform Administrative Requirements, Cost Principles, and Audit Requirements for Federal Awards,* 78 FR 78589, published in the Federal Register on December 26, 2013, available at *https://federalregister.gov/a/2013-30465.* (Upon implementation, this guidance will also be available on the OMB Web site.)

———. *Circular A–133, Compliance Supplement.* March 2014, available at *http://www.whitehouse.gov/omb/circulars/a133_compliance_supplement_2014*

President's Council on Integrity and Efficiency, Audit Committee. *Report on National Single Audit Sampling Project.* Washington, DC: Superintendent of Documents, U.S. Government Printing Office, June 2007.

Questions

11–1. What is the purpose of a financial audit? Who is responsible for setting standards for financial audits of government and not-for-profit organizations?

11–2. What are the three types of auditor services described in the Government Accountability Office's *Government Auditing Standards,* and how do they differ?

11–3. In the context of a government audit, what is an opinion unit, and of what significance is an opinion unit to the auditor?

11–4. Under the hierarchy of GAAP, what sources of accounting principles have the most authority for state and local governments, federal government entities, and nongovernmental entities? Where do accountants and auditors look when a particular item is not covered within the hierarchy?

11–5. As a newly hired staff auditor, you have been assigned to a governmental engagement that includes a single audit. Your supervisor asks you to familiarize yourself with OMB's *Uniform Administrative Requirements, Cost Principles, and Audit Requirements for Federal Awards,* the OMB *Compliance Supplement,* and the Government Accountability Office's *Government Auditing Standards*. Why are all three resources necessary?

11–6. What are some ways an audit report for a government differs from an audit report for a for-profit organization?

11–7. Define GAGAS, and describe how GAGAS differ from GAAS.

11–8. *Government Auditing Standards* specifically outline an auditor's responsibilities with respect to ethics and independence. What are the ethical principles and primary considerations with regard to independence, as identified in GAGAS? How do ethical principles relate to independence?

11–9. Explain how federal award programs are selected for audit under the risk-based approach.

11–10. What are the benefits of having an audit committee?

Cases

11–11 Audit Engagement. *Background.* Lake View Mental Health Affiliates, a nongovernmental not-for-profit organization, has contacted William Wise, CPA, about conducting an annual audit for its first year of operations. The governing board wishes to obtain an audit of the financial statements and, having received favorable information about Mr. Wise's ability to conduct such audits, has decided not to issue a request for proposals from other audit firms. Anne Bollin, president of the board, heard from a friend associated with a similar organization that $10,000 is an appropriate price for such an audit and has offered Mr. Wise the audit for that price. Although Mr. Wise agrees that $10,000 would be reasonable for a typical financial statement audit of an organization of Lake View's type and size, he refuses to contract for the audit at that price until he is able to estimate the extent of audit work that would be involved.

Facts. In discussions with Lake View's controller, Mr. Wise obtains the following information about the organization for the year just ended:

1. Lake View received a $200,000 grant from the City of Lake View, of which 50 percent was stated as being from federal sources. Of this amount, $150,000 was expended during the year, equally from federal and nonfederal sources.
2. Unrestricted gifts of $50,000 were received from private donors; $40,000 was spent during the year.

3. The organization received $300,000 from Medicare for mental health services rendered during the year.
4. Lake View received federal funding passed-through Highlands County of $350,000; $300,000 of the funds were spent for allowable costs.
5. Lake View carried out a program with the Federal Bureau of Prisons to provide alcohol and drug abuse counseling services for prisoners at a nearby federal prison. Services are provided on a "units of service" reimbursement basis. Each unit of service is reimbursed at the rate of $100 and the contract provides for maximum reimbursement of $400,000. Actual units of service for the year were 4,400. Direct costs incurred for these services amounted to $250,000 in total.

Required

a. Based on the foregoing facts, is Lake View Mental Health Affiliates required to have a single audit? Explain your answer.

b. Should Mr. Wise accept the audit engagement for a $10,000 fee? Why or why not?

c. Would Mr. Wise be considered independent according to *Government Auditing Standards* if he also prepares routine tax filings for the organization? How would this be determined?

(*Note:* The authors are indebted to James Brown, a partner with BKD, LLP in Springfield, Missouri, for providing the example on which Case 11–11 is based.)

11–12 Audit Considerations. A city has approached you concerning the audit of its 2017 financial statements. State law requires the city to have an audit and submit the audited financial report to the state. New elections at the beginning of the fiscal year resulted in a change in the administration of the city. Your firm and the audit firm that conducted the prior year's audit have been asked by the city to submit bids for the current year's audit. Since the new city administration is quite inexperienced, it has not provided you with a formal request for proposal (RFP). Therefore, you have the prior year's audit and financial reports, and little more information than the following for fiscal year 2017.

1. The new city controller is a certified public accountant who worked for a firm that specialized in government audits.
2. For the last three years the city has received a clean audit opinion. The prior auditor has declined the opportunity to perform the 2017 audit.
3. The city is receiving grants and other aid from state and federal sources totaling $3,977,000.
4. Total budgeted revenues for the year were $20,980,000 and expenditures were $25,749,000. Approximately 48 percent of revenues are from property taxes.
5. The city has six governmental funds, three enterprise funds, and an agency fund. You are also familiar with the city's downtown development district, which was not reported in the city's prior year financial statements.
6. It is five months until the end of fiscal year 2017.
7. You recently read in the newspaper that an employee at the city's wastewater facility has sued the city for wrongful termination. The employee was an accountant who claimed that wastewater billings were improperly being refunded to the new administrators and their families.

Required

Prior to determining whether you would be interested in submitting a bid for the audit, you decide to use the information you have to draw up a list of factors that would affect the cost of your bid. Provide your list and explain why each item would affect your fee bid.

11–13 Research Case—Single Audit. The chief administrator for a group of not-for-profit early education centers and outreach facilities has hired you to conduct an audit. A mission of the organization is to provide child care and early education to children in economically distressed areas of the county. The organization receives funds from several sources, including federal programs. The federal programs and the amount of funding expended from each program for the fiscal year are as follows:

Program	Funds Expended
Child Care and Development Block Grant	$280,000
National School Lunch Program	174,320
National School Breakfast Program	98,829
Special Milk Program for Children	8,112
Head Start	800,000
Maternal, Infant, and Early Childhood Home Visiting Program	195,000
Special Education—Grants for Infants and Families	25,000

Required

Use the Catalog of Federal Domestic Assistance (CFDA) Web site (*www.cfda.gov*) and the OMB *Compliance Supplement* (*www.whitehouse.gov/OMB/circulars*) to answer the following questions:

a. What federal departments are sponsoring the programs listed?

b. OMB allows "cluster programs" to be considered as a single program when conducting the risk-based approach to selecting programs for audit under the single audit. Of the programs listed, which (if any) are part of the same cluster?

c. Based on size alone, are there any Type A programs? Are there any programs that would be exempt from assessment under the risk-based approach?

d. Based on size alone, which programs would you select for audit and why?

e. If the not-for-profit has received an unmodified opinion in each of the last two years and the Head Start program was selected for audit in both years, would the programs you select for audit change? If not, why not? If so, what programs would you select and why?

11–14 Auditing a Federal Program. Custer County receives pass-through funds from the state's Department of Justice to assist in administering the federally funded Public Safety Partnership and Community Policing Grants program (also referred to as Community Oriented Policing Services [COPS] project grants). At the request of the state's Department of Justice, the county has engaged you to perform a program-specific audit of its expenditures related to the program.

Required

Utilize the Catalog of Federal Domestic Assistance (CFDA) Web site at *http://www.cfda.gov* and the *Compliance Supplement* link on the OMB Web site at *http://www.whitehouse.gov/OMB/circulars* to answer the following questions.

a. What is the CFDA number for this program?

b. Describe the program's objectives.

c. Review the matrix of compliance requirements within the *Compliance Supplement*. Which generic compliance requirements are applicable to this program?

d. As part of the overall funding, the county received a nonhiring Community Policing Development (CPD) grant and a hiring grant for COPS in schools (CIS). Determine whether the following costs are eligible for reimbursement under the grants:

(1) The county hosted a Fourth of July picnic, free to the public, at a cost of $75,000 to improve community relations.

(2) An entry-level law enforcement officer was hired for the COPS in schools program at an annual salary of $145,000.

(3) Civilian personnel were hired to develop a neighborhood watch program.

11–15 Auditor Selection and Independence. You are the finance director of White Rock City. Your current auditor informs you that he is retiring and selling his auditing practice. When you seek his advice regarding the hiring of the accounting firm that is currently helping to integrate a new accounting system for the city, he mentions that you would first want to check the new GAGAS threats to independence. He recently read an article about the seven threats, but because he was retiring, he did not pay much attention to their content. He also recommends preparing a request for proposal (RFP) for the audit services that would be published locally.

Required

a. Access the Government Accountability Office's *Government Auditing Standards* at *http://www.gao.gov/yellowbook*, and identify the seven threats to auditor independence. Do you think any of the threats apply to the accounting firm that is helping to integrate the new accounting system?

b. Prepare a list of items that you would like your accounting staff to include in an RFP.

11–16 GAAP Hierarchy. One of the responsibilities of an auditor is to determine the appropriate GAAP for the entity being audited. In December, 2013, GASB issued an exposure draft titled "The Hierarchy of Generally Accepted Accounting Principles for State and Local Governments." The deadline for comments for the exposure draft was December 31, 2014.

Required

a. Access the exposure draft through *www.gasb.org*. What was the purpose of the exposure draft and what types of organizations would be affected by it? What prompted GASB to address this issue?

b. What was the board's initial approach to revising the hierarchy of GAAP? What was the outcome of that deliberation? Explain the board's reasoning.

c. How is the proposed hierarchy different from the one presented in this text?

d. What is the current status of this project? What, if any, are the next steps?
e. Do you agree with the changes in the hierarchy? Why or why not?

11–17 Audit Committees. The city council members of Laurel City are considering establishing an audit committee as a subset of the council. Several members work for commercial businesses that have such committees. They have asked your advice as a partner in the public accounting firm that audits the city's annual financial statements. They are especially interested in whether the benefits of such a committee outweigh any costs to establishing one.

Required

a. What resources are available to the city to help it use this audit committee efficiently and effectively?
b. Provide a short report to the council that lists the benefits and costs of establishing an audit committee. Explain what qualifications would be expected of council members who sit on this committee and the tasks in which they would be engaged.

Exercises and Problems

11–18 Examine the CAFR. Using the CAFR you obtained for Exercise 1–16, answer the following questions:
a. Auditors. Was this CAFR audited by external certified public accountants (CPAs) or by state or local governmental auditors?
b. Audit Opinion. What type of opinion did this entity receive? If it was modified, what reason was given? What opinion units received an opinion? Was an opinion expressed on the supplementary information as well as the basic financial statements?
c. Auditing Standards. Did the auditor use generally accepted auditing standards (GAAS), generally accepted government auditing standards (GAS or GAGAS), or both?
d. Report Content. Does the introductory paragraph identify the financial statements being audited and, in particular, refer to the audit of the financial statements of each opinion unit? Does the report include an "Other Matters" section? What is discussed in this section? Is an "Other Information" section included? For what purpose? Does the auditor mention other responsibilities in addition to the auditor's responsibility under GAAS?
e. Single Audit. Can you tell whether this entity was required to have a single audit? If so, are the required single audit reports contained within the CAFR that you are examining? If the entity does receive federal financial assistance but you see no mention of the single audit in the auditor's report, where do you expect that single audit report to be?

11–19 Multiple Choice. Choose the best answer.
1. Under the hierarchy of GAAP for a state and local government, which of the following has the highest level of authority?
   a. AICPA Practice Bulletins if specifically made applicable to state and local governments by the AICPA (and cleared by the GASB).
   b. Technical releases of the Accounting and Auditing Policy Committee of the FASAB.
   c. Implementation guides ("Qs and As") published by the GASB staff.
   d. AICPA Industry Audit and Accounting Guides.

2. The scope of an auditing engagement is described in:
   a. GAAS.
   b. An engagement letter.
   c. The "Auditor's Responsibility" section of the audit report.
   d. GAGAS.
3. Ramon Fuentes is the new head of the State Department of Motor Vehicles. He has observed several situations that make him believe that there may be issues with the department's internal controls. He wants to engage a CPA to provide him with assurance that the department's internal controls is functioning as it should. This type of engagement is called:
   a. An attestation engagement.
   b. An operational audit.
   c. An internal control audit.
   d. A general audit.
4. The GAGAS conceptual framework for independence should be employed:
   a. Annually.
   b. At the end of the audit engagement, just prior to issuing the audit report.
   c. When taking on a nonaudit service engagement at an audited entity.
   d. All of the above.
5. An additional auditing standard imposed by GAGAS when compared to GAAS is:
   a. The auditor must maintain independence in mental attitude in all matters relating to the audit.
   b. The auditor must either express an opinion regarding the financial statements, taken as a whole, or state that an opinion cannot be expressed.
   c. The auditor must identify in the auditor's report those circumstances in which generally accepted accounting principles have not been consistently observed.
   d. Documentation should be provided concerning evidence of supervisory review of work performed.
6. Single audits performed pursuant to OMB's *Uniform Guidance*:
   a. Apply to all entities that receive $750,000 or more of federal funds in a fiscal year.
   b. Apply to not-for-profit organizations only.
   c. Require the auditor to use generally accepted government accounting standards when conducting the audit.
   d. Are triggered when federal funds are expended that are associated with a grant.
7. Under the GASB reporting model, materiality is determined:
   a. For opinion units.
   b. At the government-wide level.
   c. At the fund level.
   d. For governmental and business-type activities and the aggregate discretely presented component units only.
8. An auditor must audit as a major program:
   a. All Type A programs, unless the auditor has identified one as low risk.
   b. All Type A programs, including any the auditor considers low-risk programs.
   c. One-fourth of all Type B programs.
   d. At least 40 percent of all federal funds received.

9. Dan Cole is the head of the county's Division of Animal Control. The division receives funding from both the state and federal governments and is required to have its audit done using GAGAS. You and Dan were fraternity brothers at All State University, and your families often celebrate holidays and special occasions together. Dan has asked your audit firm to perform the division's financial audit this year. What should you do?
   a. Contact the state board of accountancy for authorization to accept the audit.
   b. Decline the audit because you want to avoid any perceived independence issues.
   c. Accept the audit but disclose your relationship in the engagement letter and audit report.
   d. Refer to the ethics guidance in GAGAS before making a decision to accept the engagement.
10. The auditor's responsibility for required supplementary information (RSI) is:
   a. The same as with the basic financial statements.
   b. To perform certain limited procedures to ensure that RSI is fairly presented in relation to the audited financial statements.
   c. The same as for all information in the financial section of a comprehensive annual financial report.
   d. To render an opinion as to the fairness of the RSI and whether it conforms to generally accepted accounting principles.

11–20 Continuing Professional Education. As part of your audit firm's quality control policies, it maintains a record of continuing profession education (CPE) taken by professional staff members. Following is information on some of the classes, sessions, workshops, and conferences that the auditors of your firm have attended in the past year.

______ 1. A session dealing with the source of current revenues and three-year projections of revenues for the state.
______ 2. A conference on estate planning.
______ 3. A workshop on partnerships between governments, businesses, and citizens.
______ 4. A session on updates to *Government Auditing Standards.*
______ 5. A session on conducting external quality control reviews.
______ 6. An online "Principles of Accounting" course.
______ 7. A workshop on "Federal Grant Administration."
______ 8. A session on GASB's pension standard.
______ 9. A conference on "Helping Individuals Meet Their Long-term Financial Goals" (a financial planning conference).
______10. A session on problems associated with implementing a balanced scorecard approach to performance measurement.

Required

It is your responsibility to determine whether the classes, sessions, workshops, and conferences attended by the auditors could be used to meet the GAGAS requirement that auditors earn 24 hours of CPE in government-related areas every two years. Access the GAO guide entitled *Government Auditing Standards: Guidance on GAGAS Requirements for Continuing Professional*

Education at the GAO Web site to perform research. In the space to the left of each item, indicate whether the item qualifies (Q) or does not qualify (DNQ).

11–21 Single Audit. Collier County had the following federal award activity during the most recent fiscal year:

Program #	Award Received	Award Expended	Major program in prior year (Y/N)	Audit findings in prior year (Y/N)
1	$8,000,000	$7,932,000	Y	N
2	450,000	434,000	N	N/A
3	3,500,000	1,069,000	N	N/A
4	2,000,000	963,000	N	N/A
5	6,000,000	4,712,000	Y	Y
6	500,000	389,000	N	N/A
7	5,000,000	661,000	N	N/A
8	250,000	74,000	N	N/A
9	1,000,000	746,000	Y	N
10	500,000	150,000	Y	Y

Required

a. Based on size, which programs would be considered Type A programs? Type B programs?

b. Based on the information provided above, list any low-risk Type A programs or high-risk Type B programs.

c. Collier County is not considered a low risk auditee. Based on the information provided, which programs would you select for audit? Why?

11–22 GAAS vs. GAGAS Standards. Gail McCook, the administrative assistant of a local CPA firm, merged the files listing GAAS standards and GAGAS standards. Because the firm performs both GAAS and GAGAS audits, it is important to identify which standards are applicable to which audits. The governmental audit partner, Gerald Henderson, has split up the list of standards among staff, and you have been assigned the standards below.

1. Pertinent information should be communicated to individuals contracting for or requesting the audit.
2. The auditor must maintain independence in mental attitude in all matters relating to the audit.
3. The auditor must adequately plan the work and must properly supervise any assistants.
4. When the audit findings involve deficiencies, the elements (criteria, condition, cause and effect) of the findings should be developed.
5. When the financial statement audit report contains an opinion or a disclaimer of opinion, a report on internal control over financial reporting and on compliance with laws, regulations, and provisions of contracts and grants must be provided as part of the report or as a separate report.
6. The auditor must identify in the auditor's report those circumstances in which such principles have not been consistently observed in the current period in relation to the preceding period.

7. The audit organization must establish a system of quality and have an external peer review at least once every 3 years.
8. Auditors apply certain limited procedures in connection with RSI to provide assurance that it is fairly presented *in relation to* the basic financial statements.
9. The auditor must exercise due professional care in the performance of the audit and the preparation of the report.
10. Known findings and recommendations from previous engagements that directly relate to the current audit should be considered in planning.

Required

For each item in the preceding list, indicate whether standards are GAAS or GAGAS standards.

11–23 Audit Report. Following is the audit report for the City of Prairie View.

Citizens of Prairie View:

Split Responsibility for Financial Statements

We have audited the accompanying financial statements of the City of Prairie View (the City) as of and for the year ended September 30, 2017. These financial statements are the responsibility of the City's management. Our responsibility is to express an opinion on these financial statements based on our audit.

We conducted our audit in accordance with generally accepted auditing standards and the standards applicable to financial audits contained in the Government Audit Standards, issued by the Comptroller General of the United States. Those standards require that we plan and perform the audit to obtain a reasonable assurance about whether the financial statements are free of material misstatement. An audit includes examining, on a test basis, evidence supporting the amounts and disclosures in the financial statements. An audit also includes assessing the accounting principles used and significant estimates made by management, as well as evaluating the overall financial statement presentation. We believe that our audit provides a reasonable basis for our opinion.

Opinion

In our opinion, the financial statements referred to above present fairly, in all material respects, the financial position of the City as of September 30, 2017, and the respective changes in financial position thereof for the year then ended in conformity with accounting principles generally accepted in the United States of America.

Other Matters

Our audit was conducted for the purpose of forming an opinion on the financial statements taken as a whole. The information presented in the Statistical Section is presented for the purpose of additional analysis and is not a required part of the basic financial statements. Such information has not been subjected to the auditing procedures applied in the audit of the basic financial statements and, accordingly, we express no opinion on it.

Raphael and VanEyck, LLP
March 12, 2018

Required

Based on your knowledge of audit reporting requirements for government audits, you have determined that the audit report issued by Raphael and VanEyck does not meet requirements. Provide a list of changes that would need to be made to the audit report to bring it into conformance with audit report requirements.

Chapter Twelve

Budgeting and Performance Measurement

Learning Objectives

After studying this chapter, you should be able to:

12-1 Explain the objectives of budgeting in the public sector.

12-2 Explain the differences among various budgeting approaches.

12-3 Describe the budgeting process for a state or local government, including the procedures involved in preparing specific types of budgets.

12-4 Describe methods of integrating planning, budgeting, performance measurement, and performance reporting.

12-5 Describe managerial tools used to improve performance.

12-6 Describe the budget and cost issues in grant accounting.

Budgeting is an important part of a manager's planning and control responsibilities in both public and private organizations. In governments, however, budgets take on added importance since they legally authorize managers to raise and expend resources to provide services to citizens. Legislation at the state and local government level also specifies what sanctions will be imposed if managers overspend appropriations. Chapter 3 described how fund accounting and the modified accrual basis of accounting are used to demonstrate legal compliance with the annual budget. Chapter 4 illustrated how the cost of governmental activities by function is measured using accrual accounting and reported in the government-wide statement of activities. This cost information is critical in developing budgets and assessing government financial performance, as seen in Chapter 10. As described in Chapter 17, the federal government has incorporated budgeting for results (or performance or outcomes) for federal agencies in required performance and accountability reports (PARs).

Not-for-profit organizations are somewhat different in that their budgets are not legal documents reflecting plans for spending resources from other governments or from tax and other revenues. However, a not-for-profit entity is accountable to its resource providers, such as donors and grantors, and the government that granted the organization its existence and tax-exempt status. The budgeting approaches described in this chapter are equally useful to not-for-profit managers, although the budgets of these organizations are most likely reviewed and approved by governing boards but not made available to the public. Budgeting and performance measures in the not-for-profit sector will be discussed in Chapter 14. In this chapter, the role of the budget as a communication and management tool in government and not-for-profit entities is explored.

OBJECTIVES OF BUDGETING IN THE PUBLIC SECTOR

Budgeting may be the most important and challenging responsibility of a government legislator or manager. Citizens expect government leaders to prioritize community program and service goals, authorize the expenditure of resources to meet those goals, comply with laws over spending appropriations, improve the quality of services in the near term, and demonstrate stewardship for public funds in the long term. The budget embodies management's plans to meet public expectations. Robert Bland describes the complex set of budgeting objectives in this way:

> The budget document, in its arduous journey through preparation to adoption, expresses the basic political values of a government. It reflects the compromises negotiated in the contentious process of budget adoption. It guides public administrators, defining government's economic and political role in a community and sanctioning, as well as limiting, administrative action. It not only represents plans for the future but also molds that future by the policies it contains . . . Thus, the budget is a tool for holding administrators accountable for performance expectations.[1]

A good budget should, at a minimum, have majority "buy-in" by all affected parties. Logistically, a budget needs to be enacted before the fiscal year begins and be integrated with the financial accounting system, so that actual results can be compared to budgeted plans at regular intervals. As illustrated in earlier chapters, the budget has always played a role in external financial reports through the required budget-to-actual comparison schedules or statements for those funds that have a legally approved budget. Also, integrating the budget into the accounting system allows management to oversee individual unit performance and react quickly to variances between actual results and budgeted plans.

The legalistic view is that a budget is a plan of financial operation embodying an estimate of proposed expenditures for a given period of time and the proposed means of financing them. In a much more general sense, budgets may be regarded as devices to aid management in operating an organization more effectively. Governments build budgets to facilitate compliance with laws and to communicate performance effectiveness. These two views of a budget are examined next.

Compliance with Laws

The GASB budgeting, budgetary control, and budgetary reporting principle provides that:

a. An annual budget(s) should be adopted by every governmental unit.

b. The accounting system should provide the basis for appropriate budgetary control.

c. Budgetary comparison should be presented for the General Fund and for each major special revenue fund that has a legally adopted annual budget. Governments are encouraged to present such budgetary comparison information in schedules as a part of required supplementary information (RSI). The budgetary

[1] Robert L. Bland, *A Budgeting Guide for Local Government* (Washington, DC: International City/County Management Association, 2013), p. 1–2.

comparison should present both (*a*) the original and (*b*) the final appropriated budgets for the reporting period as well as (*c*) actual inflows, outflows, and balances, stated on the government's budgetary basis.[2]

The budgeting principle is directly related to the accounting and reporting capabilities principle, which specifies that a governmental accounting system must make it possible for a government (1) to present fairly and with full disclosure the funds and activities of the governmental unit in conformity with generally accepted accounting principles (GAAP) and (2) to determine and demonstrate compliance with finance-related legal and contractual provisions.[3] Chapter 3 describes budgets as legal documents that bind the actions of administrators and illustrates how the integration of budgetary accounting into the formal accounting system makes it possible to prepare budgetary reports that demonstrate legal compliance. It is also concerned with budgetary comparisons required for the General Fund and major special revenue funds in conformity with the GASB reporting model. Recall that GASB allows governments to choose whether to present the budgetary comparison schedule after the notes to the financial statements as RSI or as a basic financial statement that compares budgeted to actual operating performance.

Communicate Performance Effectiveness

Budgeting is also an important tool for achieving efficient and effective management of resources. Because of public demand for improved transparency and accountability, performance measurement systems have been developed at all levels of government. Federal agencies submit strategic plans to Congress, develop annual performance plans, report annually on the results achieved in those performance plans, and integrate *accountability reports* with the Government Performance and Results Act (GPRA) performance reports.[4] Furthermore, as discussed later in this chapter, many state and local governments are identifying outcome measures of interest to citizens and publishing popular reports.

Several groups of professionals provide guidance for governments that communicate quality information to stakeholders about the budget and performance measures. The National Advisory Council on State and Local Budgeting, a cooperative of organizations, issued a document that describes nearly 60 *best* budget practices covering the planning, development, adoption, and execution phases of the budget process.[5] This document recognizes that budgeting is one of the most important activities undertaken by state and local governments in allocating scarce resources to programs and services.

The Government Finance Officers Association (GFOA) reviews budgets and presents distinguished awards to those governments that not only meet the goals described in traditional government principles, but go beyond that in their presentation of the budget as a policy document, financial plan, operations guide, and communications device. For over three decades, the GFOA's award program has recognized state and local governments that use the budgeting process to its fullest potential in demonstrating accountability for the use of public funds and improving the quality of government services provided. Illustration 12–1 lists the criteria the GFOA uses in its review of budget documents. Note that some of the criteria are mandatory (i.e., documents

[2] Governmental Accounting Standards Board, *Codification of Governmental Accounting and Financial Reporting Standards,* as of June 30, 2014 (Norwalk, CT: GASB, 2014), Sec. 1100.111, 2400.

[3] Ibid, Sec. 1100.

[4] See Chapter 17 for more discussion of the GPRA and performance reporting.

[5] See *www.gfoa.org,* "Best Practices and Advisories—Budgeting and Fiscal Policy."

ILLUSTRATION 12–1 Criteria for the GFOA's Distinguished Budget Presentation Award Program

Introduction and Overview

- A table of contents to make it easy to locate information in the document.*
- A coherent statement of organization-wide, strategic goals and strategies that address long-term issues.
- Short-term factors that influence the development of the budget.
- A budget message that articulates priorities and issues for the upcoming year.*
- An overview of significant budgetary items and trends within the budget document.*

Financial Structure, Policy, and Process

- Organization chart(s) for the entire entity.*
- A description of all funds that are subject to appropriation.
- Narrative, tables, schedules, or matrices to show the relationship between functional units, major funds, and nonmajor funds in the aggregate.
- An explanation of the basis of budgeting for all funds.
- A coherent statement of entity-wide long-term financial policies.*
- A description of the process for preparing, reviewing, adopting, and amending the budget.*

Financial Summaries

- A summary of budgeted major revenues, expenditures, other financing sources and uses.*
- Summaries of revenues, other financing sources, expenditures, and other financing uses for the prior year actual, the current year budget, and the proposed budget year.*
- Projected changes in fund balances or fund equity.*
- A description of major revenue sources, underlying assumptions, and significant trends.*
- An explanation of long-range financial plans and effects upon the budget and budget process.

Capital and Debt

- Budgeted capital expenditures.*
- Significant nonrecurring capital investments that will affect the entity's current and future operating budget and the services that the entity provides.
- Current debt obligations, debt levels and legal debt limits.*

Departmental Information

- Personnel or position counts for prior, current and budgeted years.*
- A description of activities, services or functions carried out by organizational units.*
- Clearly stated goals and objectives of organizational units.
- Objective measures of progress toward accomplishing the government's mission and specific goals and objectives.

Document-wide Criteria

- A description of the organization, its community, and population.
- A glossary for any terminology that is not easily understood.
- Charts, graphs, and narratives to convey financial information.
- A format that enhances understanding by the average reader.

* Indicates a mandatory criterion to receive the distinguished budget presentation award; that is, the budget "shall" include the item listed.

Source: Condensed from "Detailed Criteria Location Guide," available at *www.gfoa.org/downloads/BudgetDetailedCriteriaLocationGuideFY2011.pdf.*

"shall" include an item) in order for a government to receive the distinguished budget presentation award. Voluntary applications for this award increased from 113 in 1984, the year the program was initiated, to approximately 1,400 in 2014. While a majority of the applicants receive the award, unsuccessful applicants are provided confidential reviewer suggestions that permit them to subsequently qualify for the award.

BUDGETING APPROACHES

As the budget process has evolved from an accounting function with a control orientation to an executive tool to improve the management of operations and the assignment of priorities to public problems, so have the basic formats of budgets evolved. Governments use a variety of budgeting approaches in developing annual budgets. These budget approaches exhibit the perspective of the staff or area within the government with budget responsibilities. For example, the accounting department often focuses on line-item budgeting, the finance department can be associated with performance budgeting, an independent budget office may be concerned with program budgeting, and the chief executive office may focus on entrepreneurial budgeting.[6] These budget approaches are briefly discussed next.

Line-item Budgeting

A traditional approach to budgeting and the one that is most likely present in some portion of every government's budget today is line-item, or object-of-expenditure, budgeting. Line-item budgeting has remained a popular tool due to its simplicity and the accountability it allows.

A common approach to budgeting line-items is called **incremental budgeting.** In essence, an incremental budget is derived from the current year's budget by adding or subtracting amounts expected to be required by line items. Examples include salary and wage increases, increases in the cost of supplies and equipment, decreases that would result from shrinkage in the scale of operations forced by pressures such as spending limitations mandated by the electorate, and cuts in capital equipment purchases. Incremental budgeting focuses largely on controlling resource inputs and typically uses the *line-item* budget format in which the focus is on departmental expenditures for specified purposes or objects, such as personnel, supplies, equipment, and travel. The weakness of the incremental approach is that it focuses on government operations in terms of dollars spent in the prior year rather than what was accomplished by that spending.

In the 1970s, an approach to wed the legally required budget process to a rational process of allocating scarce resources among alternative uses was introduced: **zero-based budgeting,** or **ZBB.** As the name indicates, the basic concept of ZBB is that the very existence of each activity as well as the amounts of resources requested to be allocated to each activity must be justified each year, which is a move toward program budgeting. However, ZBB is described here as an example of line-item budgeting because it uses readily available objects of expenditures.

The ZBB approach has several advantages: It is easy to understand, uses readily available line-item data, and involves staff from the government that is going to incur the cost. Typically, staff prepare three types of budgets—one representing basic service needs, another reflecting the cost of delivering services at the current level, and a

[6] Bland, *A Budgeting Guide for Local Government,* Chapter 7.

third that captures the cost of extending services to meet new demand. It is hard to argue with the basic premise of annually re-evaluating the value that a program or department adds to total government operations. However, ZBB is time-intensive, and managers become skeptical of the approach when marginally successful programs continue to be funded to some degree.[7]

Performance Budgeting

The evolution of the concept of a budget from "an estimate of proposed expenditures and the proposed means of financing them" to an "operating plan" was a natural accompaniment to the development of the concept of professional management. In public administration, as in business administration, the concept of professionalism demanded that administrators or managers attempt to put the scarce resources of qualified personnel and money to the best possible uses. The legal requirement that administrators of governments submit appropriation requests to the legislative bodies in budget format provided a basis for adapting required budgetary estimates of proposed expenditures to broader management use. The legislative appropriation process has traditionally required administrators to justify budget requests. A logical justification of proposed expenditures is to relate the proposed expenditures of each governmental subdivision to the programs and activities to be accomplished by that subdivision during the budget period. The type of budgeting in which input of resources is related to output of services is sometimes known as **performance budgeting.** Performance budgeting is linked conceptually with *performance auditing* as defined in Chapter 11 of this text. Performance budgeting is a plan for relating resource inputs to the efficient production of outputs; performance auditing is the subsequent evaluation to determine that resources were in fact used efficiently and effectively in accordance with the plan.

Performance budgeting historically focused on the relation between inputs and outputs of each organizational unit rather than programs. The use of performance budgeting in governments received significant impetus from work the first Hoover Commission did for the federal government. Its report, presented to the Congress in 1949, led to the adoption in the federal government of budgets then known as *cost-based budgets* or *cost budgets.* The use of these designations suggests that a government desiring to use performance budgeting must have an accrual accounting system rather than a cash accounting system in order to routinely ascertain the costs of programs and activities. The recommendations of the second Hoover Commission led to the statutory requirement of both accrual accounting and cost-based budgeting for agencies of the executive branch of the federal government. Federal statutes also require the synchronization of budgetary and accounting classifications and the coordination of these with the organizational structure of the agencies. Entities that use performance budgeting consider it a financial management tool and not a subfield of accounting.[8]

Program Budgeting

Program budgeting is a term sometimes used synonymously with performance budgeting. However, the term is more generally used to refer to a budget format that discloses the full costs of programs or functions without regard to the number of organizational units that might be involved in performing the various aspects of the program or functions. Program budgets address the fundamental issues of whether

[7] Ibid., p. 20.

[8] Ibid., p. 21.

programs should exist at all and how to allocate scarce resources among competing programs. The integration of planning, programming, budgeting, and accounting has considerable appeal to persons concerned with public administration because an integrated system should, logically, provide legislators and administrators with much better information for the management of governmental resources than has been provided by separate systems. In the late 1960s, there was a concentrated effort to introduce a **planning-programming-budgeting system,** called **PPBS,** throughout the executive branch of the federal government, and to adapt the concept to state and local governments and other complex organizations. The advantage that program and PPBS budgeting offer compared to performance budgeting is the ability to address fundamental policy questions about whether the government or not-for-profit is better off operating certain programs.

As state and local governments have experimented with program budgeting, they have developed stand-alone budget offices to analyze the costs and benefits of programs that cut across department or division lines. These budget offices report directly to the highest level administrator, so budgeting is neither a subfield of accounting nor a responsibility of the finance department.[9]

Entrepreneurial Budgeting

Another evolution of budgeting that is also distanced from the purview of the accounting department is **entrepreneurial budgeting,** an approach where budgeting is the responsibility of the highest level person in the government, most often the chief executive officer. In this approach, strategic plans, incentives, and accountability are merged into the budget and communicated to citizens as a package that might be posted on the government's Web site.

Budgeting for outcomes is a different type of entrepreneurial budgeting that articulates government-wide goals, such as "improve community safety" or "improve environmental health," and all departments or units cast their budget requests in terms of advancing those goals.[10] An advantage of integrating strategic planning into a government's daily activities is that units (or departments or programs) remain focused on outcomes that improve the government's services to its citizens. A disadvantage is that market-based concepts, such as competition among units for scarce resources, are often seen as being at odds in a nonbusiness entity. Managers may find that the department and program personnel continue to operate in a traditional legalistic budget environment.

It is important to realize that a government does not choose a single budgeting approach to the exclusion of the others. An entity-wide budget may be constructed from program or department budgets using different approaches. Over time, changes in leadership, technological advances in data availability, and other circumstances will also result in variations on budget approaches for a government.

BUDGETING PROCESS IN A STATE OR LOCAL GOVERNMENT

Budgeting Governmental Appropriations

Appropriations budgets are an administration's requests for authorization to incur liabilities for goods, services, and facilities for specified purposes. The preparation of

[9] Ibid.

[10] Ibid., pp. 22–23.

appropriations budgets for any one year is closely tied to the administration's budget of revenues since the revenues budget is the plan for financing the proposed appropriations. During recessionary periods, governments at all levels face revenue shortages and consequently have to make difficult decisions regarding spending cuts. If the program or performance budget concept is followed, appropriations budgets are prepared for each existing and continuing work program or activity of each governmental subdivision; for each program authorized by action of past legislative bodies but not yet made operative; and for each new program the administration intends to submit to the legislative body for approval.

In budgeting, each ongoing program should be subjected to rigorous management scrutiny at budget preparation time to make sure there is a valid reason for continuing the program at all: This is the fundamental idea of zero-based budgeting. If the program should be continued, management must decide whether the prior allocation of resources to the program is optimal or whether changes should be made in the assignment of personnel, equipment, space, and money.

If the administration decides that a program should be continued, the preparation of the appropriations budget is delegated to those in charge of the program. In the case of a new program, the administration states the objectives of the program and sets general guidelines for the operation of the program and then delegates budget preparation to individuals who are expected to be in charge of the program when legislative authorization and appropriations are secured. State laws or local ordinances typically require that certain steps be followed in the budgeting process and may prescribe dates by which each step must be completed. These requirements are referred to as the **budget calendar.** A budget calendar (or cycle) for Chesapeake, Virginia is presented in Illustration 12–2. Notice that this budget plan includes two types of budgets—an operating budget, the primary budget discussed in the chapter, and a capital budget, which is also discussed intermittently throughout the chapter. The budget calendar could span a 10-month period. Many governments implement multiyear budgeting to enhance long-range planning, decrease staff time, and improve program evaluation. In these cases, the budget calendar should span the two-year period (or appropriate time frame) and refer to dates when mid-period forms and reports are due.

To ensure that administrative policies are actually used in budget preparation and that the budget calendar and other legal requirements are met, it is customary to designate someone in the central administrative office as budget officer. In addition to the responsibilities enumerated, the **budget officer** is responsible for providing technical assistance to the operating personnel who prepare the budgets.

Budgets prepared by departmental administrators should be reviewed by the central administration before submission to the legislative branch because the total of departmental requests frequently exceeds the total of estimated revenues, and it is necessary to trim the requests in some manner. Central review may also be necessary to make sure that enough is being spent on certain programs. Good financial management of the taxpayers' dollars is a process of trying to determine the optimum dollar input to achieve the desired service output, not a process of minimizing input. Even though the appropriations budget is a legally prescribed document, the administration should not lose sight of its managerial usefulness.

It should be emphasized that governmental budgets submitted to the legislative branch for action must be made available for a certain length of time for study by interested citizens, and one or more public hearings must be held before the legislative branch takes final action. Ordinarily, few citizens take the trouble to study the proposed budgets in detail; however, newspaper and television reporters often publicize

ILLUSTRATION 12–2 City of Chesapeake Budget Calendar for FY 2014–15

Date	Activity	Responsible Party
08/07/13	Review upcoming planning with department heads (Management Meeting)	Budget Director, City Manager
08/19/13 to 08/23/13	Initial budget targets and instructions distributed to departments for incorporation in the FY 2015 Operating Budget	City Manager, Departments, and Budget Office
09/09/13	Capital Budget framework to select departments	Budget Office
10/01/13	Five-Year Projections complete	Budget Office
10/01/13	Operating Budget Proposals due to Budget Office	All Departments
10/15/13	Capital Budget Data due to Budget Office	Select Departments
10/29/13	Strategic Planning Session: Five-Year Revenue and Expenditure Projections	City Council, City Manager, and Budget Office
12/06/13	Completion of analysis, review, and summarization of Operating and Capital Improvement Budget requests	Budget Office
12/09/13 to 01/31/14	Review of department funding proposals for Operating and Capital Improvement Budgets	City Manager, Deputy City Managers, Departments, and Budget Office
01/28/14	Strategic Planning Session	City Council, City Manager and Budget Office
02/10/14	Revenue and spending summaries to City Manager	Budget Office
02/24/14	Final date for revisions to Manager's proposed budget	Budget Office
03/07/14	Manager's budget message to Budget Office	City Manager
03/10/14	Operating and Capital Improvement Budgets to Printer	Budget Office
03/18/14 or 03/25/14	Operating and Capital Budgets presented to Council (April 1 is 90th Day Prior to July 1)	City Manager and Budget Director
03/25/14	Advertise Operating and Capital Budgets	City Clerk and City Attorney
04/08/14 to 05/13/14	Council Work Sessions	City Manager and City Council
04/22/14	Public Hearings on Operating and Capital	City Clerk and City Council
05/13/14	Improvement Budgets	
05/13/14	City Council scheduled to vote on the Operating and Capital Improvement Budgets	City Council
06/10/14	Amendments required by State Budget action are presented to City Council for action prior to July 1 implementation	City Manager and City Council

Source: City of Chesapeake, VA, available at *www.cityofchesapeake.net*.

proposed appropriations, especially those for programs, activities, and functions deemed particularly newsworthy. News reporters also publicize increases in taxes and fees proposed to finance budgeted appropriations or spending cuts to popular public programs. Representatives of organizations such as the state or local Chamber of Commerce and League of Women Voters analyze the budgets in detail and furnish analyses to their members, the public, and news media.

Generally, such broadly based organizations attempt to be evenhanded in their budget analyses. In many instances, however, members of special interest groups also sift through the proposed budget to determine the proposed allocation of resources to the programs, activities, and functions of interest to the groups they represent. Budget analyses by special interest groups are not intended to be evenhanded. If the proposed budget does not meet the interests of the groups as well as they think it should, the groups may be counted on to attempt to influence the members of the legislative branch to change the budget before it is enacted into law. Thus, it is evident that the governmental process involves political and social considerations and, at higher levels of government, aggregate economic considerations, all of which may be more important to many voters, administrators (bureaucrats), and legislators (politicians) than are financial considerations.

In public budgeting there is natural tension among these stakeholders that must be mediated by the government's chief executive officer. Illustration 12–3 shows sources of conflict that will arise during a budget process that serves to air community concerns and build consensus about which public services should be provided with available levels of public resources. For example, department heads and interest groups may advocate for more funding than they know the budget officials will approve. The public may want something different than officials believe is needed. Special interest groups may command a louder voice than the collective interests of the whole. Public administrators may have a concern for realism in the budget when politicians prefer a positive budget picture.[11] All these conflicts make the budget process a political one in which the budget emerges to communicate the plan of elected officials and management to meet the demands of its citizens subject to economic and other constraints.

Budgeting Governmental Revenues

In state and local governments, the availability of revenues is a necessary prerequisite to the incurring of expenditures. Some governments may operate at a deficit temporarily, but it is generally conceded that they may not do so for several consecutive periods. Thus, wise financial management calls for the preparation of revenues budgets, at least in rough form, prior to the preparation of detailed operating plans and finalizing appropriations budgets.

Revenues is a term that has a precise meaning in governmental accounting. The GASB states that the term *revenues* "means increases in (sources of) fund financial resources other than from interfund transfers and debt issue proceeds."[12] For purposes

ILLUSTRATION 12–3 Sources of Conflict in the Budget Process

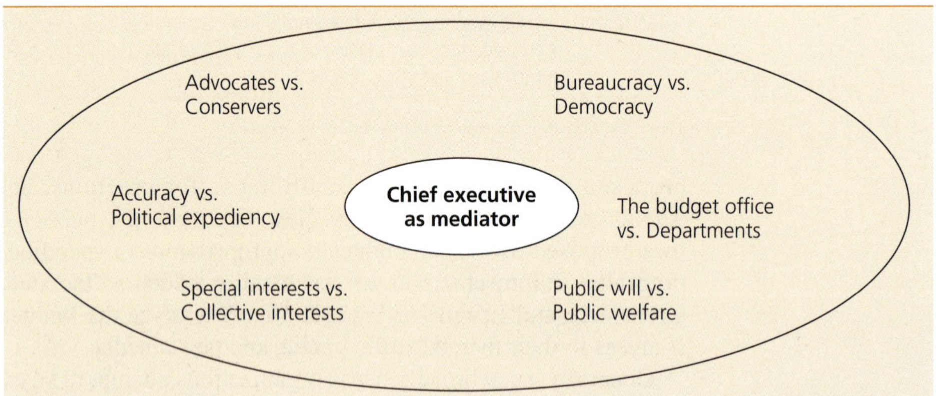

Source: Robert L. Bland *A Budgeting Guide for Local Government* (Washington, DC: International City/County Management Association, 2013), p. 187, Figure 8–3.

[11] Bland, *A Budgeting Guide for Local Government,* pp. 186–192.

[12] GASB, *Codification,* Sec. 1800, 130.

of budgeting inflows of financial resources of a fund, it does not seem particularly valuable to distinguish among revenues, as defined by the GASB, interfund transfers, and debt issue proceeds, other than to keep budgeting terminology consistent with accounting and financial reporting terminology.

Sources of revenue and other financial inflows available to a given local government are generally closely controlled by state law; state laws also establish procedures for the utilization of available sources and may impose ceilings on the amount of revenue a local government may collect from certain sources. Sources generally available for financing routine operations include property taxes, sales taxes, income taxes, license fees, fines, charges for services, grants or allocations from other governments, and revenue from the use of money or property. Chapter 3 of this text describes revenue sources and discusses revenue accounting in some detail. The present discussion is, therefore, limited to the broad aspects of governmental revenue budgeting.

Within the framework set by legal requirements and subject to the approval of the legislative body (which, in turn, reacts to the electorate), the determination of revenue policy is a prerogative of the administration. After policies have been established, the technical preparation of the revenues budget is ordinarily delegated to the budget officer. To facilitate budget preparation, experienced budget officers generally keep for each revenue source files containing (1) a copy of legislation authorizing the source and any subsequent legislation pertaining to the source; (2) historical experience relative to collections from the source, including collections as a percentage of billings, when applicable; (3) relevant administrative policies; and (4) specific factors that affect the yield from the source, including for each factor the historical relationship of the factor to revenue procedures to be used in projecting the trend of factors influencing yield and factors affecting collections. Finance officers of large governments use sophisticated statistical and econometric methods of revenue forecasting, particularly to evaluate alternative assumptions in the preparation of a legal revenues budget.

Budgeting Capital Expenditures

Accounting principles for business enterprises and for proprietary funds of governments require the cost of assets expected to benefit more than one period to be treated as a balance sheet item rather than as a charge against revenues of the period. No such distinction exists for governmental fund types. Expenditures for long-lived assets to be used in the general operations of a government are treated in the appropriations process in the same manner as are expenditures for salaries, wages, benefits, materials, supplies, and services to be consumed during the accounting period. Accounting control over long-lived assets used in governmental activities is established at the government-wide level.

Effective financial management requires the plans for any one year to be consistent with intermediate- and long-range plans. Governmental projects such as the construction or improvement of streets; construction of bridges and buildings; acquisition of land for recreational use, parking lots, and future building sites; and urban renewal may require a consistent application of effort over a span of years. Consequently, administrators need to present to the legislative branch and to the public a multiyear capital improvements program, as well as the budget for revenues, operating expenditures, and capital outlays requested for the forthcoming year.

Effective financial management also requires review and presentation of nonfinancial information such as physical measures of capital assets, their service condition, and their estimated replacement cost. Nonfinancial information of these types is useful for purposes of forecasting future asset repair and replacement schedules, repair and replacement costs, and financing requirements, and is required for certain eligible infrastructure assets.

Budgeting Cash Receipts

Revenues and expenditures budgets would best be prepared on the same basis of accounting as the accounts and financial reports: modified accrual, in the case of governmental funds—particularly the General Fund and special revenue funds. Although it is highly desirable for persons concerned with the financial management of governments (or any other organization) to foresee the effects of operating plans and capital improvement plans on receivables, payables, inventories, and facilities, it is absolutely necessary to foresee the effects on cash. An organization must have sufficient cash to pay employees, suppliers, and creditors the amounts due at the times due, or it risks labor troubles, an unsatisfactory credit rating, and consequent difficulties in maintaining its capacity to render services at levels acceptable to its residents. An organization that maintains cash balances in excess of needs fails to earn interest on temporary investments; therefore, it is raising more revenues than would otherwise be needed or failing to offer services.

In Chapter 4 it was noted that in a typical government, cash receipts from major sources of revenues of general and special revenue funds are concentrated in a few months of each fiscal year, whereas cash disbursements tend to be approximately level month by month. Under the heading "Tax Anticipation Notes" in Chapter 4, reference is made to cash forecasting done by the treasurer of the Town of Brighton in order to determine the amount of **tax anticipation notes** to be issued. The cash forecasting method illustrated in that chapter is quite crude but often reasonably effective if done by experienced persons. Sophisticated cash budgeting methods used in well-managed governments require additional data, such as historical records of monthly collections from each revenue source, including percentage of billings where applicable. In addition to the historical record of collections, the budget files should contain analyses of the factors affecting the collections from each source, so that adjustments to historical patterns may be made, if needed, for the budget year.

Property taxes are often the largest recurring cash receipt in a government; however, all other expected cash receipts must be included in the cash budget. More difficult to project are self-assessed taxes, such as income taxes; nonrecurring receipts, such as those from the sale of assets; and income earned on sweep accounts, arrangements by which a bank automatically "sweeps" cash that exceeds the target balance into short-term cash investments.

Managing cash flows involves accelerating the flow of cash receipts. This can be done by using techniques such as earlier billing, prompt payment discounts, and late payment penalties. Online payment systems, electronic fund transfers, and accepting credit cards for payment all help to reduce the time between when the payment is converted to cash and the government has the use of the funds.[13]

Budgeting Cash Disbursements

Except for provisions regarding expenditures of debt service funds, the expenditures of all other governmental funds are typically recognized and budgeted when they are

[13] William R. Voorhees and Jeongwoo Kim, "Cash Flow Forecasting: Principles," *Encyclopedia of Public Administration and Public Policy*, Taylor and Francis, 2008, p. 285.

expected to be incurred. Therefore, the conversion of the approved appropriations budget into a cash disbursements budget involves the knowledge of personnel policies, purchasing policies, and operating policies and plans, which should govern the timing of expenditures of appropriations and the consequent payment of liabilities. Information as to current and previous typical time intervals between the ordering of goods and contractual services, their receipt, and the related disbursements should be available from the appropriation expenditures ledgers and cash disbursement records. In the case of salaries and wages of governmental employees, the cash disbursements budget for each month is affected by the number of paydays that fall in the month rather than the number of working days in the month.

Monthly cash receipts budgets are prepared for all sources of revenues of each fund, and cash disbursements budgets are prepared for all organizational units. Management should then match the two in order to determine when and for how long cash balances will rise to unnecessarily high levels or fall to levels below those prudent management would require. Note that the preceding sentence concerns cash receipts and disbursements of all funds of a government, not of a single fund. There is no reason for bank accounts and fund cash accounts to agree, except in total. Effective cash planning and control suggests that *all* cash be put under control of the treasurer of the government.

Managing cash flows also involves minimizing or decelerating cash disbursements. Techniques that can be used include pooling cash balances into a central concentration account to permit better monitoring of payables and balances, using zero-balance accounts to reduce the amount of idle cash, and implementing expenditure controls to track and brake unnecessary early payments. Standard payment periods that are as long apart as possible can reduce processing costs and increase the predictability of payment amounts.[14]

As shown in Illustration 12–4, cash receipts for the Town of Brighton are highest in April, May, and November, presumably when taxes are collected. Disbursements are fairly constant across the year, except for January, which may be when capital assets are acquired. The pattern of short-term borrowing, repayment, and investment seems to indicate that the city's cash and investment policies include (1) a target monthly cash balance of at least $425,000, (2) new borrowing made in increments of $5,000, and (3) cash exceeding the target is used to repay short-term borrowing; any remaining excess is invested. A very small government that has few receipts and infrequent disbursements may be able to plan temporary investments and short-term borrowings on the basis of cash budgets for periods longer than one month, perhaps quarterly or semiannually. Conversely, a government with considerable cash activity involving large sums might need to budget cash receipts and cash disbursements on a daily basis to maintain adequate but not excessive cash balances.

Budgeting, by definition, involves planning on the basis of assumptions about economic conditions, salary levels, numbers of employees at each salary level, prices of supplies and capital acquisitions, and other factors that cannot be foreseen with great accuracy. Accordingly, it is necessary at intervals throughout the year to compare actual receipts with budgeted receipts, source by source, and actual disbursements with budgeted disbursements for each organizational unit, function, and object. This provides for control of the budget and, if necessary, revision of the budget in light of new knowledge about economic conditions, salary, price levels, and other factors affecting collections and disbursements.

[14] Ibid.

ILLUSTRATION 12–4

TOWN OF BRIGHTON
Budgeted Cash Receipts and Disbursements for FY 2017
(in thousands)

	January	February	March	April	May	June	July	August	September	October	November	December
Balance first of month	$ 610	$425	$425	$425	$ 425	$425	$425	$427	$427	$427	$ 427	$425
Expected receipts during month	165	250	295	570	1,096	134	280	370	285	270	892	116
Cash available	775	675	720	995	1,521	559	705	797	712	697	1,319	541
Expected disbursements during month	1,050	240	280	325	320	320	508	325	315	335	320	455
Provisional balance at end of month	(275)	435	440	670	1,201	239	197	472	397	362	999	86
Less: Temporary investments purchased	—	—	—	—	346	—	—	—	—	—	454	—
Less: Repayment of short-term borrowings	—	10	15	245	430	—	—	45	—	—	120	—
Add: Temporary investments sold	—	—	—	—	—	186	160	—	—	—	—	340
Add: Short-term borrowings	700	—	—	—	—	—	70	—	30	65	—	—
Balance at end of month	$ 425	$425	$425	$425	$ 425	$425	$427	$427	$427	$427	$ 425	$426

INTEGRATION OF PLANNING, BUDGETING, AND PERFORMANCE MEASUREMENT

As noted throughout this chapter, budgeting is a comprehensive endeavor that links financial accountability and managerial control over scarce resources used to meet community and entity goals. The concept of "managing for results" has taken hold in many governments as a commonsense way to focus the activities of employees toward the needs that the government is trying to address. These goals might include safe highways, healthy children, plentiful employment opportunities, and a culturally diverse citizenry. When planning, budgeting, and performance measurement are related, good performance is rewarded, and consequences exist for substandard performance, then public employees' behaviors will change. Highway patrol officers who are judged on accident rates for their highway beat, rather than on their output of tickets written or miles covered, have changed their behavior, writing tickets strategically to slow down drivers on the most hazardous stretches of roads, and reporting potholes that cause accidents to maintenance departments more often.[15]

Illustration 12–5 is a graphic representation of the interrelations among the processes of policy setting through a strategic plan, budgeting the resources needed to deliver services that accomplish the goals of the plan, monitoring operations and reporting on performance, and assessing performance as it relates to the strategic plan. Once a government identifies the public needs it is trying to address, then it should develop an overall strategic plan for addressing those needs; devise policies, programs, and services to meet those needs; implement budgeting, accounting, and management systems that support the strategic plan; and track cost and performance data that allow the government to gauge its progress in reaching its goals.[16]

Certain components of a results-oriented performance measurement system are critical for effective integration with budgeting, decision making, and communication to citizens. For example, clear identification of outputs (e.g., number of lane-miles of road repaired or the number of serious crimes reported) and outcomes (e.g., percentage of lane-miles of road maintained in excellent, good, or fair condition or the percentage of residents rating their neighborhood as safe or very safe) is essential. These performance indicators should be transparent; that is, they should be revealed in department budget requests, the executive budget itself, operating documents, and annual reports. Government managers should report performance measures over time (e.g., from budget development through the audit) and in a variety of activities (e.g., strategic planning, contract management, and personnel decisions). Leadership support and explicit, written management-for-results policies are also crucial for an integrated performance measurement system to be effective.[17]

In the past decade, the "Report Results" element of the Managing for Results cycle has dramatically expanded to include reporting performance measurements to

[15] James Fountain, Wilson Campbell, Terry Patton, Paul Epstein, and Mandi Cohn, *Special Report: Reporting Performance Information: Suggested Criteria for Effective Communication* (Norwalk, CT: GASB), August 2003, p. 13.

[16] Ibid.

[17] Julia Melkers and Katherine Willoughby, "Models of Performance-Measurement Use in Local Goverments: Understanding Budgeting, Communication, and Lasting Effects," *Public Administration Review*, vol. 65, no.2, March/April 2005.

ILLUSTRATION 12–5 Managing for Results Process

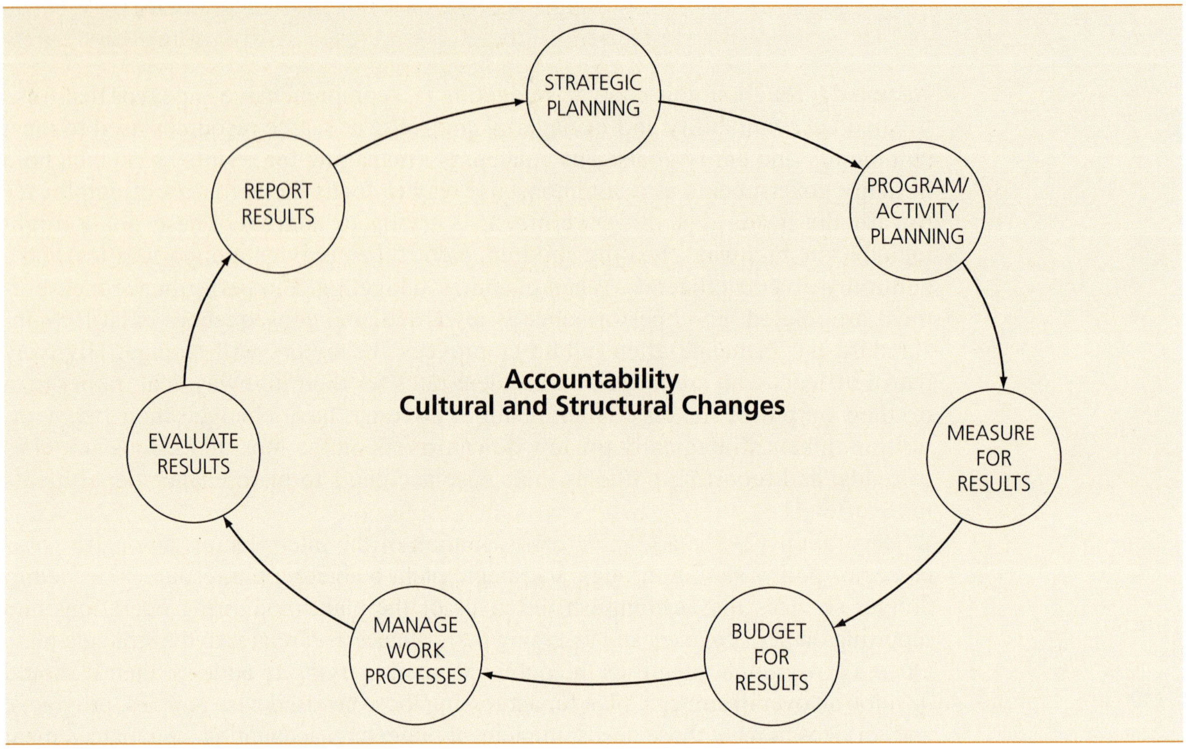

Source: Adapted from James Fountain, Wilson Campbell, Terry Patton, Paul Epstein, and Mandi Cohn, *Special Report: Reporting Performance Information: Suggested Criteria for Effective Communication* (Norwalk, CT: GASB), August 2003, p. 14.

citizens, a trend that has support from the GASB, the Government Finance Officers Association, and the Association of Government Accountants.[18] As mentioned in Chapter 9, many governments now publish popular reports, and the GASB published guidelines in 2010 for governments that elect to communicate *service efforts and accomplishments* performance information to citizens, elected officials, and other interested parties.

Service Efforts and Accomplishments (SEA)

In addition to traditional financial statement reporting and required budget-to-actual comparisons reported within the comprehensive annual financial report (CAFR), citizens, governmental officials, investors and creditors, and others having an interest in the government's performance are increasingly demanding *nonfinancial* measures of **service efforts and accomplishments (SEA)** for informed decision making. SEA information includes indicators of a government's actual performance in providing services to its citizens. In conjunction with information from other sources, SEA information aids users in assessing the economy, efficiency, and effectiveness of government.

[18] Judith Harris, Karen McKenzie, and Randall Rentfro, "Performance Reporting: Assessing Citizen Access to Performance Measures on State Government Web sites," *Journal of Public Budgeting, Accounting & Financial Management*, vol. 23, no. 1, Spring 2011.

SEA reporting is not required of any governments; however, as governments integrate strategic planning, budgeting, and performance measurement, information on service efforts and accomplishments is available and often provided to the public to demonstrate accountability and transparency regarding public funds. SEA reporting, also referred to as **citizen-centric reporting,** may take the form of a published report, an electronic report posted on a government's Web site, or a pamphlet designed to summarize an entity's service efforts and measurement results. The GASB, the Government Finance Officers Association (GFOA), and the Association of Government Accountants (AGA) have developed guidance to help state and local governments that choose to communicate SEA performance information to citizens, elected officials, and other interested parties do so effectively.[19]

GASB *Concepts Statement No. 2,* as amended by *Concepts Statement No. 5,* directly addresses SEA reporting. *Concepts Statement No. 2* clarifies the role of SEA reporting as complementary to CAFR reporting yet integral to broader general purpose external financial reporting. It also describes the elements of SEA reporting (discussed later), provides examples of quantitative and narrative information that should be included to help increase the usefulness of reported results for users, and identifies limitations of SEA performance information and methods of enhancing its usefulness. The GASB also published *Government Service Efforts and Accomplishment Performance Reports: A Guide to Understanding* in 2005 and issued *Suggested Guidelines for Voluntary Reporting, SEA Performance Information* in 2010. These documents provide suggested criteria for use in preparing reports on service efforts and accomplishment measures, describe essential components of an effective SEA report, and identify keys to effective communication.

The GASB identifies three broad categories of SEA measures: (1) measures of service efforts, (2) measures of service accomplishments, and (3) measures that relate efforts to accomplishments.[20] Measures of service efforts, or **input measures,** relate to the amount of financial and nonfinancial resources (such as money and materials) used in a program or process.[21] Measures of service accomplishments are of two types: outputs and outcomes. **Output measures** are quantity measures that reflect either the quantity of a service provided, such as the number of lane-miles of road repaired, or the quantity of service provided that meets a specified quality requirement, such as the number of lane-miles of road repaired to a specified minimum condition. **Outcome measures** gauge accomplishments, or the results of services provided, such as the percentage of lane-miles of road in excellent, good, or fair condition. Such measures are particularly useful when compared with established objectives or norms or with results from previous years. Finally, measures that relate efforts to accomplishments are referred to as **efficiency measures.** GASB *Concepts Statement 5* identifies two types of efficiency measures—those that relate service efforts to outputs of service and those that relate service efforts to outcomes or results of services. Efficiency measures that relate the quantity or cost of resources used to unit of output (e.g., cost per lane-mile of road repaired) provide information about an entity's relative efficiency that can be compared with previous

[19] See AGA citizen-centric reporting tools and resources available at *http://www.agacgfm.org.*

[20] Governmental Accounting Standards Board, *Concepts Statement No. 2,* "Service Efforts and Accomplishments Reporting" (Norwalk, CT: April 1994).

[21] The discussion of SEA measures in this paragraph is paraphrased from the discussion in *Concepts Statement No. 2,* pars. 50–53, as amended by *Concepts Statement No.* 5.

ILLUSTRATION 12–6 Performance Indicators for the City of Bellevue, Washington, Fire Department

Annual Snapshot of Fire Department Performance Measures

Performance Measure	2010 Actual	2011 Actual	2012 Actual	2012 Target	2012 Target Met or Exceeded (✓) Not Met (–)
Outcome: Safe Community					
Efficiency					
1. Complete 100% of fire and life safety inspections	100%	100%	99%	100%	–
2. Conduct 100% of required high-rise evacuation drills	100%	100%	100%	100%	✓
3. Violations cleared on re-inspection	87%	89%	85%	90%	–
Effectiveness					
4. % of incidents where total response time is less than 6 minutes	69%	67%	68%	90%	–
5. % of fires confined to room of origin**	88%	80%	83%	88%	–
6. Cardiac arrest survival rate (Utstein Criteria) 5 year-average	57%	51%	51%	45%	✓
7. % of residents who feel Bellevue is a safe community in which to live, learn, work, and play	96%	90%	97%	90%	✓
8. % of residents who agree that Bellevue plans for and is well prepared to respond to emergencies	95%	86%	91%	90%	✓
9. Total dollars loss from fire	$0.8M	$5.4M	$6.1M	$3M	–
10. Average City paramedic response time (urban)	6:57 mins	7:03 mins	7:08 mins	7:30 mins	✓
11. Maintain International Accreditation	Accredited	Accredited	Accredited	Accredited	✓
12. Maintain a Class 2 WA State Insurance Rating	Class II	Class II	Class II	Class II	✓
13. % of City employees trained in compliance with NIMS	95%	97%	95%	100%	–
Workload*					
14. Number of Fire/Suppression/EMS incidents	16,527	16,284	16,659	17,000	–
15. Individuals reached through community events and public outreach programs	5,887	4,500	13,150	3,500	✓
16. Individuals receiving CPR Training	393	449	445	600	–
17. Number of annual individual training hours	33,113	35,630	29,452	32,000	–

* Workload indicators gauge service demand but do not show goals are met.

** 2011 actuals were reported as 88% in last year's report and have been revised.

Source: City of Bellevue 2012 Annual Performance Report. See *www.bellevuewa.gov/citizen_outreach_performance.htm.*

results, internal goals, generally accepted norms or standards, or results achieved by similar jurisdictions. Measures that relate resource costs to outcomes are useful in evaluating how effectively service objectives are being met and at what cost (e.g., the cost per lane-mile of road maintained in excellent, good, or fair condition). They aid management, elected officials, and the public in assessing the value of the services provided by an entity.

Illustration 12–6 shows performance indicators for the fire department in Bellevue, Washington. The input measures (not shown) are the quantities and dollar amounts of resources used in providing fire services. The output and outcome indicators collectively indicate service accomplishments where outputs are workload (such as number of fire/suppression/EMS incidents) and outcomes indicate the effectiveness of activities in achieving desired objectives (such as the percentage of fires confined to room of origin). The city presents trend information and target values to assist users in the

ILLUSTRATION 12–7 Suggested Criteria and Purpose for Reporting Performance Information

Category I: The External Report on Performance Information

1. *Purpose and scope:* To inform users of the intent of the report and to identify the programs and services that are included.
2. *Statement of major goals and objectives:* To provide users with the goals and objectives and their source, so users can determine how they were established.
3. *Involvement in establishing goals and objectives:* To help users identify who established the goals and objectives and whether that includes those responsible for achieving results.
4. *Multiple levels of reporting:* To allow specific users to find the appropriate level of detail performance information for their needs.
5. *Analysis of results and challenges:* To present performance results with a discussion of challenges facing the organization.
6. *Focus on key measures:* To ensure that reports provide users with enough (and not too much) information to develop their own conclusions about the organization's performance.
7. *Reliable information:* To assist users in assessing the credibility of the reported performance information.

Category II: What Performance Information to Report

8. *Relevant measures of results:* To ensure performance measures reflect the degree to which those goals and objectives have been accomplished.
9. *Resources used and efficiency:* To facilitate an assessment of resources used and the efficiency, cost-effectiveness, and economy of programs and services.
10. *Citizen and customer perceptions:* To ensure that a more complete view of the results of programs and services results than is captured in other "objective" measures of outputs and outcomes.
11. *Comparisons for assessing performance:* To provide a clear frame of reference for assessing the performance of the organization, its programs, and its services.
12. *Factors affecting results:* To help users understand the factors that might have an effect on performance, including relevant conditions in the state, region, or community.
13. *Aggregation and disaggregation of information:* To provide performance information that is not misleading and is relevant to users with different interests and needs.
14. *Consistency:* To allow users to compare an organization's performance from period to period and to better understand changes in measures and reasons why measures changed.

Category III: Communication of Performance Information

15. *Easy to find, access, and understand:* To ensure that a broad group of potential users can access, understand, and use various forms of performance reports to reach conclusions.
16. *Regular and timely reporting:* To ensure that organizations report performance information on a regular and timely basis to be useful in decision making.

Source: Paul Epstein, James Fountain, Wilson Campbell, Terry Patton, and Kimberly Keaton, *Government Service Efforts and Accomplishment Performance Reports: A Guide to Understanding* (Norwalk, CT: GASB) July 2005, App. A, pp. 37–41.

analysis of effectiveness and efficiency measures. Presumably, some of these measures correspond to standard measures used nationally by fire-fighting agencies, further increasing the comparability value of this service efforts and accomplishments report.

The GASB has identified 16 suggested criteria for use in preparing reports on service efforts and accomplishment measures presented in three broad categories. Illustration 12–7 shows these measures and categories. It is important to note that these are criteria that suggest characteristics of performance reports and measures that are expected to lead to their usefulness by users. There is no suggestion as to what values of these measures would be considered good or bad. As SEA reporting continues to evolve additional guidelines and industry standards will become available.

MANAGERIAL TOOLS TO IMPROVE PERFORMANCE

During the last several decades, growth in service demands and cutbacks in unrestricted federal funding forced numerous state and local governments to examine tax structures and user fees. Fiscal reform and sustainability became popular platforms for politicians aspiring to key elective offices. The result was the adoption of management innovations in the private sector that might improve the efficiency of government operations and reduce the need for higher taxes. Several of those strategies are discussed in the sections that follow.

Total Quality Management

Total quality management (TQM) is attractive to many government officials because it links customer (taxpayer and other resource provider) satisfaction to improvements in the operating systems and processes used to provide goods and services. TQM seeks to continuously improve the government's ability to meet or exceed demands from customers who might be external, such as taxpayers and service recipients, or internal, such as the customers of an internal service fund. Central to TQM is using customer data to identify and correct problems.

The elements of TQM are consistent with those of the program budgeting approaches (particularly PPBS) previously discussed. Thus, governments that have implemented one of those budgeting approaches may find it less costly to implement a TQM structure. On the other hand, few governments possess adequate data on customer satisfaction. Moreover, the traditional emphases of government on line-item budgeting, rigid personnel classifications, restrictive procurement regulations, and so on, tend to reduce management autonomy and thus may be inconsistent with the need under TQM to empower employees to be "entrepreneurial" in improving processes and meeting customer demand. It should also be noted that the objective of TQM is not necessarily to reduce cost but to increase "value for the dollar." Insofar as a TQM program successfully adds value, it has the potential to improve the public perception of government in addition to improving service delivery.

Customer Relationship Management

Customer relationship management (CRM) systems, developed in the 1990s for businesses, have great potential for governments as they provide services to their customers—citizens. CRM systems create an integrated view of a customer to coordinate services from all channels of the organization with the intent to improve the long-term relationship the organization has with its customer. Examples some governments are using include obtaining licenses and making tax payments through a government Web site.

Activity-based Costing

Budgeting for performance requires sophisticated cost accounting systems to determine the full cost of programs or functions. Well-managed state and local governments are, therefore, actively developing improved cost accounting systems. One costing approach being implemented by some governments is activity-based costing (ABC). **Activity-based costing (ABC)** was developed for use by manufacturing companies when it became apparent that traditional cost accounting systems were producing distorted product costs. Thus, some products that were thought to be profitable were, on closer inspection, found to be unprofitable, and vice versa. Two Harvard

University professors, Robin Cooper and Robert S. Kaplan, made convincing arguments that typical cost accounting systems often understate profits on high-volume products and overstate profits on low-volume specialty items.[22] This problem is attributable, in part, to greater product diversity, shorter product life cycles, the shift in production technology from labor to automation, more diverse distribution channels, and greater quality demands, all of which are driven by the need to more effectively compete in the global marketplace. The net effect of these trends (which are also applicable to government, at least to some extent) is to create a larger infrastructure of "production support" activities and thus to shift costs from direct cost categories to indirect cost, or overhead, categories. Because a larger proportion of these costs is allocated to products, product cost distortions become a larger problem and may result in poor product decisions.

ABC essentially attempts to determine the cost of specific process-related activities, the "drivers" of those costs (e.g., labor-hours, machine-hours, or units of material), and the consumption of cost drivers in producing outputs of goods or services. Emphasis is placed on tracing the specific activities performed to specific outputs of goods or services rather than on allocating average costs to units of output as is done in conventional cost accounting systems. Determining the amount of each activity that is consumed in each product or service utilizes materials usage records, observation, and timekeeping systems but is often augmented with estimates obtained through employee interviews and other means.

An article by Bridget Anderson explains the objectives of ABC in a governmental environment as follows:

> The objectives of ABC are to preserve, at a minimum, the present quality and availability of core services but to acknowledge that some of the forces for greater expenditures have not been controlled. It seeks to reduce the costs of service outcomes by:
>
> - reducing the number of service units through program redesign,
> - finding lower cost alternatives,
> - making volume increases dependent on cost reductions, and
> - understanding and controlling the delivery/program design interaction.[23]

Administrative Costs

A very large part of governmental expenditures are incurred for administrative services of a general nature (such as the costs of the chief executive's office, costs of accounting and auditing, and costs of boards and commissions), which are somewhat remote from the results any given subdivision is expected to accomplish. Furthermore, in smaller units of government, many offices or departments perform such a variety of services that separating their costs is practically impossible under their present schemes of organization.

Given the importance and magnitude of key administrative offices, government officials should attempt to measure the efficiency and effectiveness of the activities of these offices just as they would other service activities. The primary difference is that many of these activities, such as those of the finance and legal

[22] Robin Cooper and Robert S. Kaplan, "Measure Costs Right: Make the Right Decisions," *Harvard Business Review,* September–October 1988, pp. 96–103.

[23] Bridget M. Anderson, "Using Activity-Based Costing for Efficiency and Quality," *Government Finance Review,* June 1993, pp. 7–9.

departments for example, mainly serve customers within the government rather than the general public. Activity-based costing would seem to be a useful tool for measuring the cost of such activities. Possible activities and cost drivers for selected offices follow.

Office	Activities	Cost Drivers
Tax collector	Preparing tax bills.	Number of bills prepared.
	Collecting tax bills.	Number of bills collected.
	Preparing receipts.	Number of receipts prepared.
	Mailing receipts.	Number of receipts mailed.
	Preparing deposits.	Number of deposits prepared.
Accounting	Recording revenues.	Number of revenue transactions.
	Recording expenditures.	Number of expenditure transactions.
	Processing payroll.	Number of employees.
	Recording purchase orders.	Number of orders.
Public recorder	Recording documents.	Number of documents or number of lines.

This table is intended to be illustrative of the types of activities and cost drivers that might apply to certain administrative offices. Although the list is incomplete, insofar as the activities and drivers are appropriate for a particular office, costs accumulated by activity could be useful both for internal performance review and pricing services to other offices. As an example of pricing services rendered, the costs of accounting services could be priced to other departments on the basis of the amount of accounting activities other departments consume. Assume that the Public Works department generates 30 percent of all purchase requisitions processed by the Accounting department. Arguably, Public Works should then be charged for 30 percent of the total cost of recording purchase orders in the accounting function. Similarly, the costs of recording expenditures could be charged to departments proportionate to the expenditures they make.

Activity-based costing is a managerial tool that can enhance decision making by creating a clearer picture of the costliest activities of a service. However, ABC only supplements traditional accounting systems; it does not replace them. Although an activity-based costing approach to costing central services seems technologically feasible, additional research is warranted to determine whether the benefits of a particular ABC approach would exceed the costs involved.

Balanced Scorecards

A **balanced scorecard** is an integrated set of performance targets, both financial and nonfinancial that are derived from an organization's strategies about how to achieve its goals. The concept was developed by Robert Kaplan and David Norton as a strategic management system for the business sector in 1992.[24] Performance measures are usually classified into four groups: *financial* (Has our financial performance improved?), *customer* (Do customers recognize that we are delivering more value?), *internal business processes* (Have business processes improved, so we can deliver more value?), and *learning and growth* of employees and the organization (Have we maintained our ability to adapt and improve?). Examples of measures in each of

[24] Robert Kaplan and David Norton, "The Balanced Scorecard—Measures that Drive Performance," *Harvard Business Review*, January/February 1992, pp. 71–79.

these groups include: return on investment (financial), number of customer complaints (customer), customer response time (internal business processes), and hours of training per employee (learning and growth). Governments and not-for-profit organizations must adapt financial indicators to meet their not-for-profit objectives, but indicators used by businesses in the other three groups likely match up well to public sector goals.

The City of Charlotte, North Carolina, was one of the first public sector entities to use the balanced scorecard concept as a management tool for planning. Charlotte was inducted into the Balanced Scorecard Hall of Fame in recognition of its ongoing use of the balanced scorecard. The City's focus areas have evolved over time. In its FY 2014–FY 2015 Strategic Operating Plan, Charlotte identifies the following five focus areas:[25]

1. *Community safety*—"Charlotte will be one of America's safest community."
2. *Housing and neighborhood development*—"Creating and sustaining communities of choice for living, working, and recreation."
3. *Transportation*—"Charlotte will be the premier city in the country for integrating land use and transportation choices."
4. *Economic development*—"Charlotte will be the most prosperous and livable city for all citizens through quality economic development."
5. *Environment:* "Charlotte will become a national leader in environmental sustainability, preserving our natural resources while balancing growth with sound fiscal policy."

The transportation focus includes goals, such as (*a*) enhance multimodal mobility, environmental quality, and long-term sustainability; (*b*) promote transportation choices; and (*c*) seek financial resources, external grants, and funding partnerships necessary to implement transportation programs and services. Some of the corresponding performance measures for these transportation goals are: (*a*) annual hours of congestion and commute time per traveler, (*b*) number of new bikeways and sidewalks, and (*c*) number of funding strategies and project lists for transportation improvements. The focus areas in Charlotte's balanced scorecard demonstrate that this is a management tool that works best when adapted by the government for its own mission, goals, and performance measures. Charlotte's focus areas have their roots in the management by objectives (MBO) performance measurement system in place since the early 1970s, but they have been modified over the years.

CONCLUSION

In spite of difficulties presented in this chapter, rational allocation of resources requires the best available information as to benefits expected to result from a proposed program to be matched with the best available information as to costs of the same program. Anticipated benefits from a program must be stated in monetary or quantitative terms or at least in explicit and operational terms to be of value in the management process. There is a crucial link among these benefits or performance measures, the government's budgetary process, and the cost of government services.

[25] The City of Charlotte's annual Strategic Operating Plan and Capital Investment Plan are available at *http://charmeck.org/city/charlotte/Budget/Pages/default.aspx.*

An entity that integrates its strategic planning, budgeting, and cost/benefit analysis with the management of the resources with which it is entrusted can more effectively document and report performance than if these financial management functions stand alone. The statement of anticipated benefits from a proposed program, activity, or grant should follow from a statement of objectives for it. The statement of objectives should be expanded into a plan of action to achieve the objectives, which in turn serves as a basis for planning costs to be incurred. Unless this course is followed, administrators and legislators will not be able to allocate resources of the governmental unit wisely, nor will administrators be able to manage resources committed to approved programs. Legislators and the public have a right to expect this integration of long-range analysis and fiscal period planning, so that they may evaluate the actions of the administrators in following the plan as well as the success of the programs in achieving the stated objectives. Managerial accounting takes on an even more important role in long-range fiscal planning as organizations evaluate the benefits of privatizing and outsourcing traditional functions.

Appendix

Budget and Cost Issues in Grant Accounting

Grant applications to federal and nonfederal granting organizations will include a statement of the program purpose, a needs assessment, the process proposed to conduct the program to meet those identified public needs, a program evaluation process, the credentials of the principal investigators, a timeline over which the goals of the program will be accomplished, and a budget detailing how the requested funds will be spent. The budget should be built with the cost principles of the granting agency in mind. A final report, and sometimes interim reports, will be required to match actual costs incurred against the approved budget. Very often requests to move funds from one line-item category to another must be approved in writing by the grantor.

FEDERAL GRANTS AND SPONSORED AGREEMENTS

State and local governments and not-for-profit entities, particularly colleges and universities, have found grants from and sponsored agreements with the federal government important, although diminishing, sources of financing. The United States Office of Management and Budget (OMB) issued a series of circulars to set forth *cost principles* to govern payments by the federal government under grant programs, contracts, and other agreements, to state and local governments, educational institutions, and other not-for-profit organizations. In late 2013, the OMB released an extensive document, *Uniform Administrative Requirements, Cost Principles, and Audit Requirements for Federal Awards,* which incorporates prior OMB circulars and provides streamlined guidelines for grant accounting and reporting.[26] Since the guidance replaces eight OMB circulars, it is often referred to as the *super circular or omni circular.*

[26] See United States Office of Management and Budget, *Uniform Administrative Requirements, Cost Principles, and Audit Requirements for Federal Awards,* 78 FR 78589, published in the Federal Register on December 26, 2013, available at *https://federalregister.gov/a/2013-30465*. Upon implementation, this guidance will also be available on the OMB Web site.

The cost principles provided by OMB guidance are based on fundamental premises that a nonfederal entity receiving a federal award maintains responsibility for the efficient and effective use of funds for their intended purposes. The principles are used in determining the allowable costs of work performed under federal awards. The super circular, and its predecessor circulars, provides that the total cost of a federal award is the sum of the allowable direct and allocable indirect costs less any applicable credits. Any costs incurred that are not allowable or allocable as part of the award will not be reimbursed by the granting organization.

Allowable Costs

To be an **allowable cost,** OMB guidance specifies that a cost must meet the following general criteria:

a. Be necessary and reasonable for the performance of the federal award and be allocable thereto under the OMB cost principles.
b. Conform to any limitations or exclusions set forth in the OMB cost principles or in the federal award as to types or amount of cost items.
c. Be consistent with policies and procedures that apply uniformly to both federally financed and other activities of the nonfederal entity.
d. Be accorded consistent treatment. A cost may not be assigned to a federal award as a direct cost if any other cost incurred for the same purpose in like circumstances has been allocated to the federal award as an indirect cost.
e. Be determined in accordance with generally accepted accounting principles (GAAP), except as otherwise provided for in the OMB guidance.
f. Not be included as a cost or used to meet cost sharing or matching requirements of any other federally financed program in either the current or a prior period.
g. Be adequately documented.[27]

A cost is defined as reasonable if, in its nature and amount, it "does not exceed that which would be incurred by a prudent person under the circumstances prevailing at the time the decision was made to incur the cost"; it is considered allocable to a particular federal award if the goods or services involved are chargeable or assignable to the federal award in accordance with relative benefits received.[28] Since the reasonableness and allocability of certain items of costs may be difficult to determine, nonfederal entities may seek the prior written approval of the federal awarding agency in advance of the incurrence of special or unusual costs.

Certain items of cost are generally allowable whether or not mentioned specifically in a grant, contract, or other agreement document. Certain other cost items are allowable only if specifically approved by the grantor agency, and certain other cost items are unallowable. *Subtitle VI* of the OMB guidance lists 38 selected cost categories ranging alphabetically from advertising to travel costs. Of the 38 cost categories, most are allowable whether direct or indirect to the extent of benefits received by federal awards. Depreciation and use allowances are included in the allowable cost items. As explained in Chapter 5, even though governmental funds do not record depreciation expense, it is reported for general capital assets at the government-wide level in the GASB reporting model. Moreover, public colleges and universities are also required to report depreciation expense as a business-type activity under GASB standards. Consequently, both governments and public

[27] Ibid, Sec. 200.403.
[28] Ibid., Sec. 200.404.

colleges and universities will find it relatively easy to charge depreciation to federal grants and contracts.

Several costs are allowable under highly restrictive conditions and generally require the explicit approval of the grantor agency. An example is advertising costs that are allowable only for such items as recruitment of personnel, procurement of goods and services, and disposal of scrap or surplus materials related to the performance of a federal award. Some cost items are *unallowable,* including items such as alcoholic beverages, bad debt expenses, contributions and donated services, fund-raising and investment management costs, entertainment, general expenses of the state or local government (e.g., salaries of the chief executive, legislatures, and judicial department officials), and lobbying.

Direct Costs

Direct costs are those that can be identified specifically with a particular cost objective. A **cost objective,** in federal terminology, is a program, function, activity, award, organizational subdivision, contract, or work unit established for the accumulation of costs. A final, or ultimate, cost objective is a particular award, internal project, or other direct activity (presumably one that provides resources for the activity under a grant, contract, or other agreement). A cost may be direct with respect to a given function or activity but indirect with respect to the grant or other final cost objective of interest to the grantor or contractor. Typical direct costs chargeable to grant programs include compensation of employees for the time and efforts devoted specifically to the execution of grant programs; cost of materials acquired, consumed, or expended specifically for the purpose of the grant; and other items of expense incurred specifically to carry out the grant agreement. If approved by the grantor agency, equipment purchased and other capital expenditures incurred for a certain grant or other final cost objective would be considered direct costs.

Indirect Costs

Indirect costs are those (1) incurred for a common or joint purpose benefiting more than one cost objective and (2) not readily assignable to the cost objectives specifically benefited without effort disproportionate to the results achieved.[29] The term *indirect costs* applies to costs originating in the grantee department as well as to those incurred by other departments in supplying goods, services, and facilities to the grantee department. For major not-for-profit organizations and institutions of higher learning, indirect costs must be classified within two broad categories termed *facilities* and *administration.* To ensure equitable distribution of indirect expenses to the cost objectives served, it may be necessary to establish a number of "pools" of indirect cost within the grantee department. Indirect cost pools should be distributed to benefited cost objectives on bases that equitably reflect relative benefits derived. In certain instances, grantees may negotiate annually with the grantor a predetermined fixed rate for computing indirect costs applicable to a grant or a lump-sum allowance for indirect costs, but generally grantees must prepare a cost allocation plan that conforms with instructions issued by the U.S. Department of Health and Human Services. Cost allocation plans of local governments will be retained for audit by a designated federal agency. (Audit of federal grants is discussed in some detail in Chapter 11 of this text.)

[29] Ibid., Sec. 200.56.

NONFEDERAL GRANTS

States make grants to local governments, and both states and local governments make grants to not-for-profit organizations. It is important for the recipient organization to recognize whether funds received are actually federal funds being passed through to them or nonfederal grants. Private foundations and community foundations often make grants to state and local governments and other not-for-profit organizations. Nonfederal grantors may not have specific cost requirements, as seen in the discussion of federal grants; however, they may explicitly deny or limit indirect cost recovery or grants for capital assets (e.g., computers or buildings). The more familiar the applicant is with the funding policies of the grantor, the more likely the organization will be successful in its bid for funds.

ACCOUNTING INFORMATION SYSTEMS

Whether funds come from federal or nonfederal sources, the recipient is expected to have an accounting information system with adequate internal controls that can deliver reliable information to compare the actual amount spent with budgeted amounts. Illustration A12–1 shows the relationship between programs and grantors and indicates some of the challenges for grantees in accounting for grants. A cost must be classified by these two dimensions, as well as by line-item (or object-of-expenditure), in order to prepare appropriate cost reports for submission to the funding organizations. For example, an organization may receive one grant to support a single program that has no other source of funds (e.g., Program A and Grant 1), or a program may be supported by multiple sources of funds (e.g., Program B and Grants 2 and 3), or a grant may support more than one program (e.g., Programs B and C and Grant 3). An accounting information system can be designed to allow reporting by grantor, by program (as is needed in a statement of functional expenses for an organization, described in Chapter 13), or by line-item. A well-structured chart of accounts is the key to reporting along multiple dimensions. Illustration A12–2 shows a chart of accounts for a not-for-profit organization that operates seven programs (e.g., Programs A through G) and receives funding from federal, state, local government, foundation, and church sources. Reports can then be generated based on the account numbering systems for revenues and expenses.

ILLUSTRATION A12–1 Relationship of Programs and Grantors in an Organization

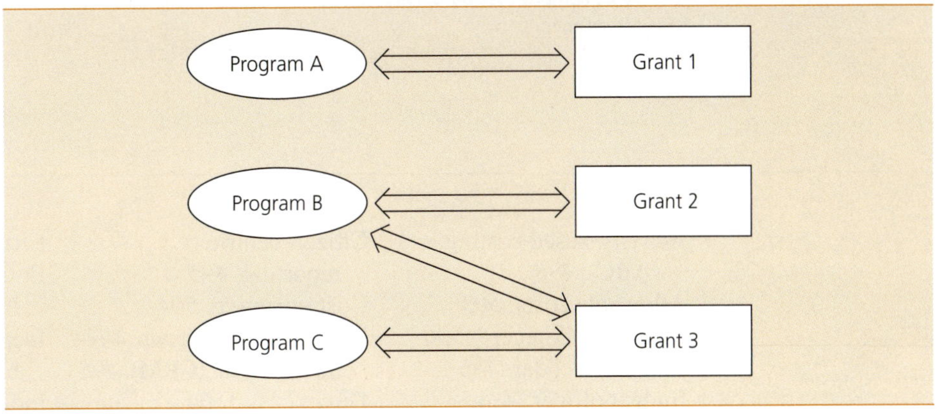

ILLUSTRATION A12–2 Chart of Accounts for a Not-for-Profit Organization
Account Number (X)–(XX)–(X)–(XX)

Type of Account X	Object XX	Program X	Funding Source XX
1 = Assets	10 = Cash		
	20 = Accounts receivable		
	30 = Inventory		
	40 = Prepaid expenses		
	50 = Investments		
	60 = Property, plant, and equipment		
	70 = Accumulated depreciation		
2 = Liabilities	10 = Accounts payable		
	20 = Accrued payroll		
	30 = Other accrued liabilities		
3 = Net assets	10 = Unrestricted net assets		
	20 = Unrestricted, designated net assets		
	30 = Temporarily restricted net assets		
	40 = Permanently restricted net assets		
4 = Revenues	10 = Contributions	A = Community Impact	01 = Federal grant
	20 = Grants	B = Youth Commission	02 = Community development block grant
	30 = Charges for services	C = Juvenile Court Advocacy	21 = State grant
	40 = Dues	D = Student Outreach	22 = County grant
	50 = Investment income	E = Safe Schools	23 = City grant
	60 = Special events	F = Parent Effectiveness Training	24 = City Housing Commission grant
	70 = Miscellaneous	G = Advocacy	30 = Ford Foundation grant
5 = Cost of programs	11 = Salaries and wages		31 = Kellogg Foundation grant
6 = Expenses (general and administrative; fund-raising)	12 = Fringe benefits and payroll taxes		32 = Smith Foundation grant
	20 = Travel		33 = Brown Foundation grant
	30 = Supplies, phone, postage, printing		43 = Universal Church
	40 = Occupancy costs		50 = United Way
	60 = Equipment maintenance		
	61 = Depreciation		
	70 = Legal and professional services		
	80 = Miscellaneous		

Key Terms

Activity-based costing (ABC), *498*
Allowable costs, *503*
Balanced scorecard, *500*
Budget calendar, *486*
Budget officer, *486*
Citizen-centric reporting, *495*
Cost objective, *504*
Customer relationship management (CRM), *498*
Direct costs, *504*
Efficiency measures, *495*
Entrepreneurial budgeting, *485*
Incremental budgeting, *483*
Indirect costs, *504*

Input measures, *495*
Outcome measures, *495*
Output measures, *495*
Performance budgeting, *484*
Planning-programming-budgeting system (PPBS), *485*
Program budgeting, *484*
Service efforts and accomplishments (SEA), *494*
Tax anticipation notes, *490*
Total quality management (TQM), *498*
Zero-based budgeting (ZBB), *483*

Selected References

Bland, Robert L. *A Budgeting Guide for Local Government,* 3rd ed. Washington, DC: International City/County Management Association, 2013.

Epstein, Paul, James Fountain, Wilson Campbell, Terry Patton, and Kimberly Keaton. *Government Service Efforts and Accomplishments Performance Reports: A Guide to Understanding.* Norwalk, CT: Government Accounting Standards Board, July 2005.

Fishbein, John. *Preparing High Quality Budget Documents.* Chicago, IL: GFOA, 2006.

Fountain, James, Wilson Campbell, Terry Patton, Paul Epstein, and Mandi Cohn. *Special Report: Reporting Performance Information: Suggested Criteria for Effective Communication.* Norwalk, CT: Government Accounting Standards Board, August 2003.

Government Finance Officers Association. *Best Practices in Public Budgeting.* Chicago, IL: GFOA, 2000 (on CD-ROM) at *www.gfoa.org.*

Lalli, William, ed., *Handbook of Budgeting,* 5th ed. New York: John Wiley & Sons, 2005, with 2006 Supplement.

Meyers, Roy T. *Handbook of Government Budgeting.* San Francisco, CA: Jossey-Bass, 1998.

National Advisory Council on State and Local Budgeting. *Recommended Budget Practices: A Framework for Improved State and Local Government Budgeting.* Chicago, IL: NACSLB, 1998.

Questions

12–1. Are governments and not-for-profit organizations required to prepare budgets?

12–2. What is the difference between two types of line-item budgeting approaches—incremental budgeting and zero-based budgeting?

12–3. Describe the advantages of performance budgeting and program budgeting over incremental budgeting in a governmental entity.

12–4. Robert Bland suggested that tensions may exist between stakeholders in a government's budget process. Identify the six sets of stakeholders or topics with potential conflict in Bland's model.

12–5. Identify some essential components of the annual budget process for a state or local government. How long might the process take?

12–6. Discussion at a local meeting of government financial officers centered on using a balanced scorecard to present information to the public on the government's Web site. Describe the components of a balanced scorecard and provide an example of how each component is applicable in a government setting.

12–7. Explain the GASB's role in developing standards for SEA reporting.

12–8. What are the three broad categories of service efforts and accomplishments (SEA) measures?

12–9. How might activity-based costing (ABC) be useful in a government setting?

12–10. A small city has been awarded a federal grant, and the finance director is curious as to what costs might be allowable under the grant. To what source could the finance officer go to determine what costs are allowable under federal grants?

Cases

12–11 Research Case—Distinguished Budget Presentation Award. You are a governmental accountant for a large municipality, and you have recently been assigned to the budget office and charged with building a better budget document—one that will be of the highest quality, so that citizens and others with an interest in the government's finances will be fully informed.

Required

a. Find out which other local governments in your state have received the GFOA's Distinguished Budget Presentation Award (*Hint:* the GFOA posts an annual report on award winners of the Distinguished Budget Presentation Program on its Web site at *www.gfoa.org* under the Award Programs link.)

b. Under the *Introduction and Overview* section of Illustration 12–1, note that the GFOA requires both a budget message that articulates priorities and issues for the upcoming year and an overview of significant budgetary items and trends within the budget document. To obtain ideas for budget improvement, examine budgets from two of the local governments in your state. (1) What are the key budgetary priorities and issues for each government? (2) Compare the budgetary trends described in the two budgets. How are the trends similar or different?

c. Under the *Document-wide Criteria* section of Illustration 12–1, guidelines recommend charts, graphs, and narratives to convey financial information. Using the two budgets from part *b,* identify what you believe to be the most unique or interesting graphical presentation found within either of the budgets and discuss how it helped convey financial information to you, the reader.

12–12 Research Case—Budgeting for Outcomes. The City of Fort Collins, Colorado, has adopted the budgeting for outcomes entrepreneurial budgeting method as a basis for its budgeting process.

Required

Locate the city's most recent budget materials and answer the following questions:

a. Why has the city adopted the budgeting for outcomes method?

b. Who identifies the outcomes?

c. What are the categories of budget outcomes specified for the current budget cycle?

d. How often does the city revise its budget outcomes?

e. Locate another municipality that uses budgeting for outcomes in its budgetary process. (*Hint:* perform a Google search using "budgeting for outcomes." Identify the entity's current outcomes. Are your interests more aligned with the budget outcomes for one of the two municipalities?

12–13 Allowable Costs under a Federal Grant. You work for an auditing firm that is performing a local government audit. The government has received federal grant funding, and the audit manager on the engagement has asked you to perform the necessary research and review the following costs charged to the federal grant to determine whether or not they are allowable: (1) travel to a conference overseas, the primary purpose of which is the dissemination of technical information; (2) the travel costs for a dependent child accompanying a parent employee to a conference; (3) charges for investment counsel incurred to enhance income from investments; (4) lobbying activities undertaken to obtain a grant; (5) entity membership in a professional organization; and (6) insurance.

Required

a. What document will you research to determine the allowability of the costs?

b. Write a short memo to document your opinion about whether each of these costs would be allowable indirect costs to be recovered in part by federal grants. If certain limitations or specifications must be met for allowability, note them in your memo.

Exercises and Problems

12–14 Examine the Budget. Obtain a copy of a recent operating budget document of a government.* Familiarize yourself with the organization of the operating budget document; read the letter of transmittal or any narrative that accompanies the budget.

Required

Answer the following questions, which aid in assessing the quality of the budget document you are reviewing.†

Introduction and Overview. Does the operating budget include a table of contents to help you locate information in the document? Does the budget document include a coherent statement of organization-wide goals and strategies that address long-term issues? Does the document address short-term factors that influence the development of the budget? Does it include a budget message that articulates priorities and issues for the upcoming year? Does the budget document provide an overview of significant budgetary items and trends within the budget document?

Financial Structure, Policy, and Process. Does the budget document include an organization chart? Does the budget document describe all funds that are subject to appropriation? Does the document include narrative, tables, schedules, or matrices to show the relationship between functional units, major funds, and nonmajor funds in the aggregate? Is the basis of budgeting explained for all funds—whether cash, modified accrual, or some other statutory basis? Is a coherent statement of entity-wide long-term financial policies included? Does the document address the process for preparing, reviewing, adopting, and amending the budget?

Financial Summaries. Does the document present a summary of major revenues and expenditures as well as other financing sources and uses? Does the document include summaries of revenues, other financing sources, and expenditures and other financing uses for prior-year actual, current-year

* Many operating budget documents are available on city, town, or county Web sites.

† These questions are paraphrased from the awards criteria established by the Government Finance Officers Association for its Distinguished Budget Presentation Awards Program.

budget and/or estimated current-year actual, and proposed budget year? Does the document include projected changes in fund balances for governmental funds included in the budget presentation, including all balances potentially available for appropriation? Are major revenue sources described? Does the budget document explain long-range financial plans and potential impacts upon the budget and budgeting process?

Capital and Debt. Does the budget document include budgeted capital expenditures (even if these are authorized in a separate capital budget)? Does the document describe whether, and to what extent, significant and nonroutine capital expenditures or other major capital spending will affect the entity's current and future operating budget? Are financial data on current debt obligations provided, describing the relationship between current debt levels and legal debt limits and explaining the effects of existing debt levels on current and future operations?

Departmental Information. Is a schedule(s) or summary table provided giving personnel or position counts for prior, current, and budget years? Does the operating budget document describe activities, services, or functions carried out by organizational units? Does it detail clearly stated goals and objectives of the organizational units? Are objective measures of progress toward accomplishing the government's mission, as well as goals and objectives, provided for specific units or programs?

Document-wide Criteria. Does the document include statistical and supplemental data that describe the organization and the community or population it serves and provide other pertinent background information related to services provided? Is there a glossary to define terms (including abbreviations and acronyms) that are not readily understood by a reasonably informed reader? Are charts and graphs used, where appropriate, to highlight financial and statistical information? Is narrative information provided when the messages conveyed by the charts and graphs are not self-evident? Finally, is the document produced and formatted in such a way as to enhance understanding by the average reader?

12–15 Multiple Choice. Choose the best answer.

1. Budgets of government entities:
   a. Are integrated with the financial accounting system.
   b. Enable governments to demonstrate compliance with laws and to communicate performance effectiveness.
   c. Are adopted by governments after required public hearings.
   d. All of the above.
2. Which of the following statements regarding budgets of not-for-profit organizations is true?
   a. Not-for-profit organization budgets are legal documents reflecting plans for spending resources.
   b. A not-for-profit entity may choose to prepare a budget to demonstrate accountability to its resource providers, such as donors and grantors.
   c. The budgeting approaches used for governments generally cannot be used by not-for-profit entities.
   d. All of the above statements are true.

3. Which of the following steps would *not* usually be part of the budgeting process?
   a. Heads of operating departments prepare budget requests.
   b. The chief executive (mayor or city manager, as appropriate) formally adopts the budget, thus giving it the force of law.
   c. One or more public budget hearings are held.
   d. Budget officer and other central administrators review and make adjustments to departmental requests.
4. The budgeting principle in generally accepted accounting principles (GAAP) for state and local governments states that:
   a. The accounting system should provide the basis for appropriate budgetary control.
   b. Budgetary comparison schedules should be presented as required supplementary information for the General Fund and each major special revenue fund that has a legally adopted budget.
   c. Annual budgets should be adopted by each government.
   d. All of the above.
5. The budgetary comparisons required of state and local governments under GASB standards:
   a. Can be presented as a schedule within required supplementary information (RSI) or as a statement in the basic financial statements.
   b. Must be a schedule included as part of RSI.
   c. Continues to be a statement included in the basic financial statements.
   d. Is no longer required.
6. An approach to budgeting that requires the very existence of each program and the amount of resources requested to be allocated to that program to be justified each year is called:
   a. Incremental budgeting.
   b. Zero-based budgeting.
   c. Performance budgeting.
   d. Planning-programming-budgeting.
7. Which of the following does *not* represent a performance measurement group under the balanced scorecard?
   a. Customer.
   b. Internal business processes.
   c. Economy and efficiency.
   d. Learning and growth.
8. Governments that choose to report service efforts and accomplishments (SEA):
   a. Must adhere to GASB SEA guidance.
   b. Must adhere to GASB SEA guidance only if the SEA report is part of the CAFR.
   c. Must adhere to guidance provided by the Association of Government Accountants (AGA) because GASB has not issued standards addressing SEA.
   d. May refer to guidance provided by the GASB, the AGA, or other professional organizations.

9. Efficiency measures, as the term is used in the service efforts and accomplishments (SEA) literature, can be described as:
   a. Measures that relate the quantity or cost of resources used to units of output.
   b. Measures that relate to the amount of financial and nonfinancial resources used in a program or process.
   c. Measures that relate costs to outcomes.
   d. Measures that reflect either the quantity or quality of a service provided.
10. Which of the following provides guidance to government managers and auditors in determining appropriate and allowable costs chargeable to federal grants?
    a. Financial Accounting Standards Board pronouncements.
    b. Government Finance Officers Association best practices documents.
    c. Principles published by the Association of Government Accountants.
    d. Guidelines issued by the Office of Management and Budget.

12–16 Police Department Budget. The police chief of the Town of Meridian submitted the following budget request for the police department for the forthcoming budget year 2017–18.

Item	Actual FY 2016	Budget FY 2017	Forecast FY 2017	Budget FY 2018
Personnel	$1,051,938	$1,098,245	$1,112,601	$1,203,157
Supplies	44,442	61,971	60,643	65,070
Maintenance	47,163	45,310	46,139	48,075
Miscellaneous	34,213	36,272	32,198	38,086
Capital outlay	65,788	69,433	67,371	117,905
Totals	$1,243,544	$1,311,231	$1,318,952	$1,472,293

Upon questioning by the newly appointed town manager, a recent masters graduate with a degree in public administration from a nearby university, the police chief explained that he had determined the amounts in the budget request by multiplying the prior year's budget amount by 1.05 (to allow for the expected inflation rate of 5 percent). In addition, the personnel category includes a request for a new uniformed officer at an estimated $50,000 for salary, payroll expenses, and fringe benefits. Capital outlay includes a request for a new patrol vehicle at an estimated cost of $45,000. The amount of $500 was added to the maintenance category for estimated maintenance on the new vehicle. The police chief is strongly resisting instructions from the town manager that he justify the need not only for the new uniformed position and additional vehicle but also for the existing level of resources in each category. The town manager has stated she will not request any increase in the police department's budget unless adequate justification is provided.

Required

a. Evaluate the strengths and weaknesses of the police chief's argument that his budget request is reasonable.

b. Are the town manager's instructions reasonable? Explain.
c. Would the town council likely support the town manager or the police chief in this dispute, assuming the police chief might take his case directly to the town council?
d. What other improvements could be made to the town's budgeting procedures?

12–17 Illustrations within a Budget Document. The City of Manhattan, Kansas, prepares an annual Budget Book, a comprehensive document that includes a citywide budget, as well as departmental budgets. The city has received the GFOA Distinguished Budget Award for more than 25 years. Following are graphical excerpts from the 2014 Budget Book that disclose typical tax-payer tax payments and primary revenue sources and functional expense categories.

Required

a. Examine the taxpayer calculation for the three-year period. What observations can you make from this illustration? What questions might you ask city budget officials at a public budget hearing?
b. Examine the pie charts and data provided for revenue sources and functional expenses. What are the primary revenue sources? What are the greatest expenditure categories? Taken together, do you have any questions regarding the city's finances?
c. As a citizen, did you find these illustrations user-friendly and relevant?

TAX COMPUTATION FOR TYPICAL HOMEOWNER

	2012	2013	2014
Increase in Valuation:	2.9%	3.1%	4.8%
Home Value:	238,308	245,695	257,488
Residential Appraisal Rate:			
(set by State law)	11.5%	11.5%	11.5%
Tax Value:	27,405	28,255	29,611

	2012 Budget		2013 Budget		2014 Budget	
	Mill Levy Rate 42.156	Taxes Paid	Mill Levy Rate 43.439	Taxes Paid	Mill Levy Rate 43.424	Taxes Paid
General Fund	2.445	$ 67	2.372	$ 67	3.669	$ 109
Library	4.238	$ 116	4.309	$ 122	4.215	$ 125
Library EBF	0.891	$ 24	0.932	$ 26	0.941	$ 28
Fire Equipment Reserve	0.111	$ 3	0.108	$ 3	0.451	$ 13
Bond & Interest	5.409	$ 148	5.412	$ 153	3.881	$ 115
Employee Benefit Fund	1.533	$ 42	1.487	$ 42	2.039	$ 60
KP&F	0.167	$ 5	0.162	$ 5	1.069	$ 32
RCPD	27.363	$ 750	28.657	$ 810	27.159	$ 804
Total City Tax Bill:	42.156	$1,155	43.439	$1,227	43.424	$1,286

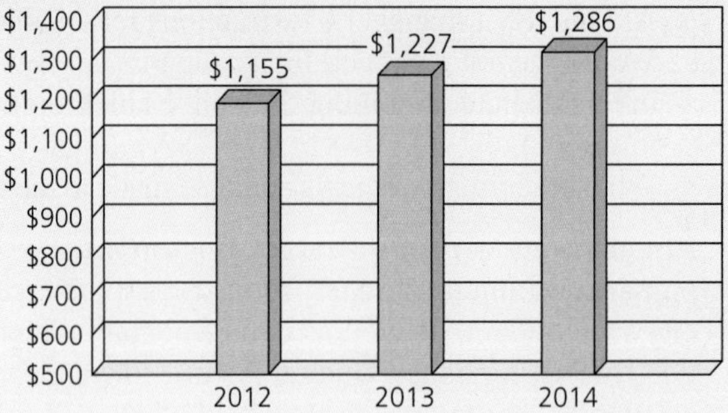

REVENUES AND EXPENSES BY CATEGORY
Primary Government Sources of Revenue

Revenues by Source	**2013 Budget**	**2014 Budget**
Beginning Fund Balance	$ 25,605,430	$ 27,920,683
State and Local Taxes	22,827,021	25,364,252
Property Taxes	20,108,343	21,332,588
Motor Vehicle Taxes	1,409,770	1,571,799
Special Assessments	5,946,969	5,983,234
Other Taxes & Fees	2,425,000	2,513,955
User Fees & Licenses	24,447,498	26,245,010
Investment Income	1,200,469	1,064,473
Transfers	10,331,789	10,953,835
Grants, Contributions, & Other Rev.	7,501,853	7,835,338
Total Revenues	$121,804,142	$130,785,167

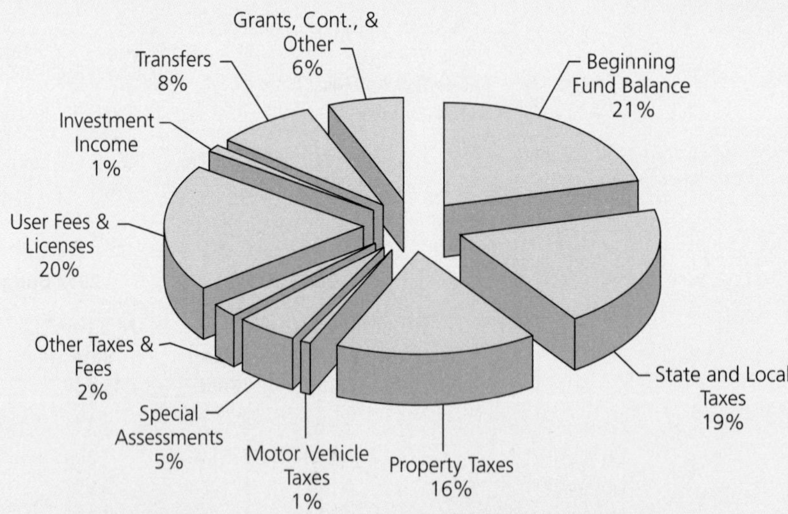

State & Local Sales Taxes: Includes city/county sales taxes, and franchise fees
Property Taxes: Includes ad valorem, delinquent taxes, and PILOT's
User Fees & Licenses: Includes licenses & permits, services & sales, program revenue, utility sales, and fines
Investment Income: Includes land rent, farm income, and misc. investment income
Transfers: Includes transfers for utility administrative services, sales tax, debt service, etc.
Grants, Cont., & Other Rev.: Includes contributions, grants, and misc. revenue

Primary Government Functional Expenses

Expenditures by Governmental Function	2013 Budget	2014 Budget
Utilities	$ 30,505,020	$ 32,747,404
Public Safety	21,311,601	22,253,273
Debt Service	24,495,886	27,651,662
Economic Development	7,734,100	9,037,730
Public Works	5,177,766	5,557,790
General Government	14,050,280	14,513,116
Culture and Recreation	10,855,801	11,429,854
Community Development	1,947,234	2,045,352
Transfers	5,726,454	5,548,986
Total Expenditures	$121,804,142	$130,785,167

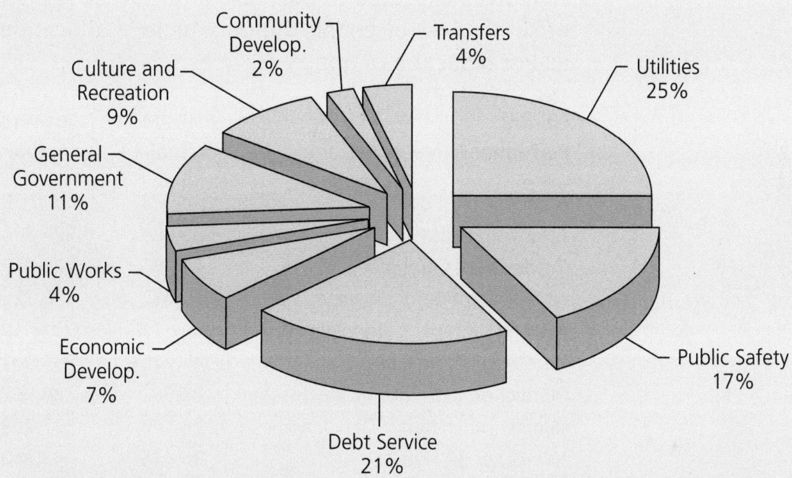

Utilities: Includes Water, Wastewater, and Stormwater operations
Public Safety: Includes Fire Operations, Administration, Technical Services, Building Maintenance, Fire Equipment Reserve, Fire Pension K. P. & F., and R.C.P.D
Debt Service: Includes all long-term debt payments
Economic Development: Includes General Improvement, Industrial Promotion, Economic Development Opportunity Fund, CIP Reserves, and Downtown Redevelopment T.I.F.
Public Works: Includes Admin., Streets, Engineering, Traffic, and Special Street & Highway
General Government: Includes General Government, Finance, Human Resources, Airport, Court, General Services, Outside Services, City University Fund, Employee Benefits, Special Alcohol Programs and Riley County Health Dept.
Culture & Recreation: Parks & Recreation, Zoo, Pools, Flint Hills Discovery Center, Library, and Library Employee Benefits
Community Development: Administration & Planning, Business Districts, and Tourism & Convention Fund
Transfers: Includes transfers from Sales Tax to General Fund & Special Revenue Funds

Source: City of Manhattan, Kansas, 2014 Budget Book, pp. 43 and 51.

12–18 SEA Reporting. The City of Ashcroft has produced a Service Efforts and Accomplishments report for the past four years in an attempt to answer the question, "How are we doing?" for its citizens. Reproduced here is an excerpt from the 2013–2017 SEA report that details library services. The report shows the efforts of library staff to offer more library programs to the increasing population and customer base in the city. Program participation has seen steady increases over the past four years, with some programs so high in demand waiting lists to participate are starting to occur.

Citizen Perceptions

The 2015 community survey reported that 86 percent of city residents rated library services as "good" or "excellent," only marginally down from 88 percent in 2013. For the variety of materials at the library, 79 percent of citizens rated the variety as "good" or "excellent," unchanged from 2013.

Library Budget

The owner of a house with a total assessed valuation of $200,000 paid property taxes of $67 in FY 2017 to support the library. Twenty-six percent (26%) of the library's FY 2017 budget depends upon support from Fairview County in return for services provided to rural Polk County residents. Fairview County's support is expected to decrease after FY 2017. Options being considered to offset the loss of county funding include allocation of General Fund monies and/or reduction in library services.

Library Performance Measures	2013–14 Actual	2014–15 Actual	2015–16 Actual	2016–17 Actual
Authorized FT Positions	8	8	8	8
Total Visitations	326,085	329,346	332,639	349,270
City Resident Cardholders	21,786	25,477	28,168	27,850
Non-Resident Cardholders	7,437	6,725	7,321	7,215
Average Visits per Cardholder	11	10	9	10
Number of Circulations	347,729	353,001	385,234	404,495
Number of Items for Circulation	82,952	86,567	91,251	94,900
Number of Reference Desk Inquiries	24,144	27,793	28,656	30,088
Number of PC Users	35,475	43,340	45,874	64,697
Number of PC Users per Available PC	1,313	1,495	1,582	2,021
Number of Special Programs	523	692	942	1,051
Number of Participants per Program	28	33	26	26
Cost per Registered Borrower	$38.50	$37.40	$35.20	$36.30
Cost per Circulation	$3.26	$3.40	$3.20	$3.14
Cost per Visitation	$3.48	$3.65	$3.71	$3.64

The material for this problem is adapted from the City of Ankeny, Iowa's 2006–2007 SEA report.

Required

a. Which of the performance measures best represents inputs, outputs, and outcomes?

b. How does the city demonstrate efficiency with respect to the General Fund budget it receives?

c. How would you address a citizen who feels he or she is not getting his or her money's worth?

12–19 Activity-based Costing in a Government. The midsize City of Orangeville funds an animal control program intended to minimize the danger stray dogs pose to people and property. The program is under scrutiny because of current budgetary constraints and constituency pressure.

An animal control warden responds to each complaint made by citizens about dogs running loose. Approximately one in six complaints results in the capture of a dog. When a dog is caught, the warden must drive it to a kennel 20 miles from the center of the city. Donna's Kennels, a privately owned animal boarding establishment, is under contract with the city to board, feed, and care for the impounded dogs. It is a no-kill shelter (i.e., it does not euthanize healthy animals), and dogs remain there until they are claimed by their owners or adopted.

Costs of Orangeville's animal control program are as follows. The city employs two animal control wardens, a clerk, and a program director. The task of the wardens is to respond to complaints, drive to the site, search for the dog, and deliver it (if it is found) to Donna's Kennels. The clerk is responsible for issuing licenses to dogs that are returned to their owners or are adopted, as well as tracking correspondence between Donna's Kennels and the city. The clerk also tracks program statistics and provides support to the program director.

The city owns and operates two vehicles specially designed for impounding and transporting stray dogs. For $10 per dog per day, Donna's Kennels provides shelter, food, and routine veterinary care. On average, 60 percent of impounded dogs are returned to their owners in seven days. The other 40 percent stay at Donna's Kennels for an average of 14 days before being adopted.

Critics of the animal control program argue that it costs too much to drive to the distant kennel to deliver an impounded dog. They have suggested that the city convert a vacant building within the city limits into an animal shelter to save on transportation costs. Prompted by the need to cut the city budget and address the public outcry, city officials are reviewing the budget proposal for the animal control program and are looking for ways to reduce the program's costs.

This problem is adapted from the International City/County Management Association *Service Report: Introduction to Activity-Based Costing,* February 1998, pp. 9–13.

Required

a. Identify (1) the activities related to the animal control program, (2) the resources required for each activity, and (3) the cost drivers for each activity.

b. Based upon the information provided and consideration of the activities and cost drivers identified in part *a*, identify any costs that could be reduced.

c. Would conversion of the vacant building be cost-effective?

12–20 SEA Reporting. The City of Greeley, Colorado's, fire department, prepares annual Performance Measures. Following are excerpts from the 2013 fire department performance report.

Required

a. Examine the following performance report. In what areas did the fire department perform well? If you are a citizen of Greeley, what are your concerns with the fire department's performance?

b. Compare and contrast the City of Greeley's fire department performance measures to the City of Bellevue's fire department performance measures found in Illustration 12–6.

Service Grouping

Program or Service: Greeley Fire Department (GFD) Emergency Response

Statement of Purpose:

Rapid response has been shown to save lives in medical emergencies and reduce property damage in fires. Reporting response times to medical incidents and comparing performance to national standards measures GFD performance. Tracking cardiac arrest save percentages provides an important community outcome. Another principle method to prevent community harm is through reduction of fire loss. Outcomes will be measured by tracking the total number of fires requiring fire department suppression sustained in the community and comparing that with the property value loss.

Program Activities:

GFD will equip response units with most advanced medical treatment technologies and maintain them in a state of readiness strategically placed throughout the community. Additionally, **GFD** will **support activities** designed to reduce fire incidence including fire education presentations and modern firefighting techniques calibrated to limit fire spread and damage.

Performance Measures				**Performance**				
Performance Measure	**Target**	**2007**	**2008**	**2009**	**2010**	**2011**	**2012**	**2013**
(1) Respond to emergency EMS service calls (paging tone to wheel stop at) within 5 minutes for 75% of calls:	75%	70.14%	71.23%	75.2%	73.4%	71.3%	72.8%	72.8%
• Overall average response time EMS incidents	5 mins	4 min 29 sec	4 min 27 sec	4 min 6 sec	4 min 12 sec	4 min 17 sec	4 min 14 sec	4 min 15 sec
• V-Tach, V-Fib cardiac arrest save rate[1]	15%	new	new	new	new	5%	18%	57%
(2) Respond to fire incidents (paging tone to wheel stop) within 5 minutes for first unit arrival within 5 minutes for 75% of calls:	75%	new	new	new	new	79%	67%	75%
• Overall average response time FIRE incidents	5 mins	8 min 31 sec	7 min 46 sec	5 min 48 sec	5 min 9 sec	5 min 43 sec	5 min 37 sec	5 min 39 sec
Total number of Fires	n/a	309	391	280	317	345	380	284
Total Community Fire Loss	n/a		1761216	2249840	1008290	1768640	1425690	1687980
Maintain community fire loss at or below the national average per capita	≤$30.70	$17.09	$14.45	$24.19	$10.84	$19.01	$15.33	17.40
Property Saved Value (Total property value − fire damage = values saved)[2]	n/a		3519595	2931090	6146463	2951210	2416711	3523020
(3) Total number of all fire and EMS responses	n/a	8,914	9,566	9,206	9,144	10,718	11,155	11,810

[1] This indicator tracks cardiac emergency calls where the patient is in ventricular tachycardia or ventricular fibrillation, two life threatening cardiac problems. Based on national averages a 15% survival rate is sought.

[2] This indicator provides perspective on the fire loss indicator given the total value of the incident property vs. the amount of damage equaling the amount saved.

Source: City of Greeley, Colorado Fire Department, available at http://greeleygov.com/Fire.

12–21 Allowable Costs under Federal Grants. The United States Office of Management and Budget (OMB) provides guidance on the allowability of costs under federal grant agreements in *Uniform Administrative Requirements, Cost Principles, and Audit Requirements for Federal Awards.* Following is a list of costs being considered for reimbursement under a federal grant:

_____1. Publication costs for electronic and print media, including distribution, promotion, and general handling.
_____2. Alcoholic beverages purchased to host a foreign dignitary.
_____3. Value Added Tax (VAT) charged for the purchase of goods or services that a nonfederal entity is legally required to pay to a foreign country.
_____4. Bad debts.
_____5. Recruiting costs.
_____6. Employee dependent care costs.
_____7. Costs of contributions and donations.
_____8. Necessary and reasonable expenses incurred for security to protect facilities, personnel, and work products.

Required

For each of the costs listed, indicate with an A (allowable) if the cost is always allowable under OMB guidance, an N (nonallowable) if the cost is not allowable under OMB guidance, and an M (may be allowable) if the cost is allowable under specific circumstances. For any costs marked with an M, explain the circumstance necessary for the cost to be allowable.

PART Three

ACCOUNTING AND FINANCIAL REPORTING FOR NOT-FOR-PROFIT ORGANIZATIONS AND THE FEDERAL GOVERNMENT

Chapter Thirteen

Accounting for Not-for-Profit Organizations

Learning Objectives

After studying this chapter, you should be able to:

13-1 Distinguish not-for-profit organizations (NFPs) from entities in the governmental and commercial sectors of the U.S. economy.

13-2 Identify the authoritative standards-setting body for establishing GAAP for nongovernmental NFPs.

13-3 Explain financial reporting and accounting for NFPs, including required financial statements; classification of net assets; accounting for revenue, gains, and support; accounting for expenses; accounting for assets; and accounting for NFP combinations and consolidations.

13-4 Prepare financial statements in accordance with the generally accepted accounting principles governing NFP organizations.

The not-for-profit sector serves a critically important role in the United States by providing a vast array of community services, including emergency and disaster assistance; health and human services; education and research; furthering the arts, sciences, and human development; and protecting the environment. From 2001 to 2011 the number of not-for-profit organizations (NFPs)[1] registering with the Internal Revenue Service (IRS) grew by more than 21 percent,[2] and in 2011, NFPs totaled 1.58 million (religious organizations and those with annual revenues of less than $5,000 are not required to register).[3] NFPs employed 13.7 million individuals in 2010,

[1] The Financial Accounting Standards Board (FASB) and the American Institute of CPAs (AICPA) prefer to call these organizations *not-for-profit organizations*, which is the term we use in this text. Within the industry and among the general public, however, the term *nonprofit organizations* is more commonly used, along with the abbreviations NPO, ONPO (other nonprofit organizations), and NGO (nongovernmental organizations, used in an international context). We use the abbreviation NFP interchangeably with the term *not-for-profit organization*.

[2] Sarah L. Pettijohn, *The Nonprofit Sector in Brief 2013* (Washington, DC: The Urban Institute Press, 2013), p. 1.

[3] National Center for Charitable Statistics. Available at http://nccsdataweb.urban.org/PubApps/profile1.php (accessed June 10, 2014).

representing approximately 10 percent of the workforce.[4] It is estimated that the NFP sector provided 5.5 percent of the gross domestic product, totaling $805 billion.[5] In 2011 charitable giving was estimated at $298.4 billion, a 4 percent increase over 2010 giving.[6]

DEFINING THE NOT-FOR-PROFIT SECTOR

Illustration 13–1 shows the various organization forms that comprise the for-profit and not-for-profit sectors in the United States. Chapter 1 identifies how NFP organizations differ from businesses. Consistent with the characteristics identified in Chapter 1, a widely accepted definition of an NFP is one whose goals involve something other than earning a profit for owners, usually the provision of services.[7] Lack of defined ownership and the related profit motive present control and reporting problems for not-for-profit managers. Rather than measuring success with profits, success is measured by how much the organization contributes to the public well-being with the resources available to it.[8] As shown in Illustration 13–1, the term *not-for-profit* encompasses the governmental entities described in Chapters 2 through 10 and the nongovernmental entities that are the focus in Chapters 13 through 16. Chapters 13 and 14 focus on nongovernmental NFPs in general, while the higher education and health care industries are the focus of Chapters 15 and 16. In Chapters 15 and 16, the focus is on comparing the accounting for nongovernmental NFPs with governmental and for-profit entities.

There are numerous ways that NFPs can be categorized. For example, the Internal Revenue Service classifies NFPs for tax-exempt purposes (discussed further in Chapter 14). Another organization that has developed classifications for NFPs is the National Center for Charitable Statistics (NCCS) of the Urban Institute. It developed a National Taxonomy of Exempt Entities (NTEE) that divides the largest set of tax-exempt entities, Internal Revenue Code Sec. 501(c)(3) and (c)(4) organizations, into 10 functional categories (arts, culture, and humanities; education; environment and animals; health; human services; international/foreign affairs; public/societal benefit; religion related; mutual/membership benefit; and unknown/unclassified) and 26 major group areas.[9]

However, to align most closely with accounting and auditing standards, the categories used in this textbook are voluntary health and welfare organizations, other nonprofit organizations, colleges and universities, and health care entities. **Voluntary health and welfare organizations (VHWO),** such as the American Diabetes Association, are organizations that receive contributions from the public at large.

[4] Independent Sector. Available at http://independentsector.org/economic_role#sthash.tVVGqAdX.dpbs (accessed June 10, 2014).

[5] Ibid.

[6] Ibid.

[7] David W. Young, *Management Control in Nonprofit Organizations,* 8th ed. (Cambridge, MA: The Crimson Press, 2008), p. 20.

[8] Ibid.

[9] This set of organizations, representing 75 percent of all tax-exempt organizations, is referred to as the *independent sector* because it includes private, self-governing organizations founded to serve a public purpose and foster volunteerism and philanthropy. Classifications available at *http://nccs.urban.org/classification/index.cfm.*

ILLUSTRATION 13–1 Organizational Forms

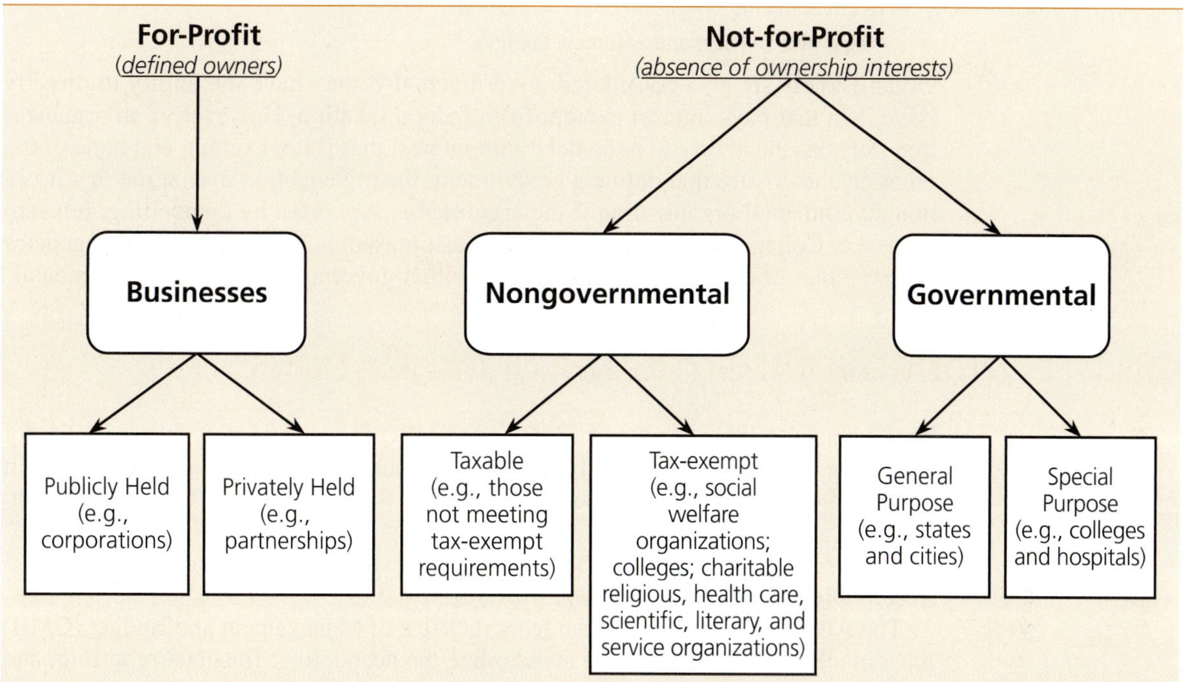

VHWOs use contributions for purposes related to solving health and welfare problems of society or for community services. In many cases VHWOs assist individuals by providing services for a nominal fee or for no fee at all. **Other nonprofit organizations (ONPOs)** encompass a wide variety of not-for-profit organizations serving a wide variety of purposes and include organizations such as cemetery organizations, civic organizations, fraternal organizations, labor unions, libraries, museums, cultural institutions, performing arts organizations, political parties, private schools, professional and trade associations, social and country clubs, research and scientific organizations, and religious organizations.

Determining Whether an NFP Organization Is Governmental

Although it may seem that the distinction between a government and a not-for-profit organization should be clear, that is not always the case. In practice, it may be difficult to determine whether some NFPs are governmental in nature, and thus which standards-setting body to look to for authoritative guidance. To provide additional guidance for auditors on this issue, the not-for-profit audit and accounting guide of the AICPA, with the tacit approval of both the FASB and the GASB, states:

> Governmental organizations that report in accordance with guidance promulgated by the GASB are public corporations and bodies corporate and politic, all of which are governmental organizations. Other organizations are governmental organizations if they have one or more of the following characteristics:
>
> *a.* Popular election of officers or appointment (or approval) of a controlling majority of the members of the organization's governing body by officials of one or more state or local governments,

b. the potential for unilateral dissolution by a government with the net assets reverting to a government,
c. the power to enact and enforce a tax levy.[10]

Organizations are also considered governmental if they have the ability to directly issue debt that pays interest exempt from federal taxation. However, if an organization only has the ability to issue debt with interest that is tax-exempt, and none of the other characteristics that define a government, the organization may argue that it is a nongovernmental organization if the argument is supported by compelling, relevant evidence. Colleges and universities, hospitals, museums, and social service agencies are examples of organizations that may be either governmental or nongovernmental.

GAAP FOR NONGOVERNMENTAL NFP ORGANIZATIONS

The Financial Accounting Standards Board (FASB) assumed primary responsibility for providing guidance on generally accepted accounting principles for not-for-profit entities in 1979.[11] The Governmental Accounting Standards Board (GASB) is responsible for governmental organizations including governmental not-for-profit organizations (see Illustration 1–1). These lines of responsibility are outlined in FASB *Accounting Standards Codification (ASC)* 105.

The AICPA, the FASB, and the federal Office of Management and Budget (OMB) have made a concerted effort to standardize the accounting, financial reporting, and auditing rules for the diverse set of entities in the not-for-profit sector and reduce the inconsistencies across segments of this sector. The FASB has codified accounting and reporting standards specific to NFPs under FASB *ASC* 958. However, unless specifically exempted, all FASB standards should be applied by NFPs. Additionally, the Single Audit Act and *OMB Circular A-133* apply to governmental and nongovernmental NFPs expending $750,000 or more in federal awards (see Chapter 11).

FINANCIAL REPORTING

As stated in Chapter 1, the FASB's objectives of financial reporting for not-for-profit organizations are to provide information useful in (1) making resource allocation decisions, (2) assessing services and ability to provide services, (3) assessing management stewardship and performance, and (4) assessing economic resources, obligations, net resources, and changes in them.[12] Common phrases heard today when speaking of financial reporting of any organization include accountability and transparency to stakeholders. Stakeholders of NFPs that use not-for-profit financial statements include donors, grantors, members, lenders, consumers, and others who provide resources to NFPs.

[10] American Institute of Certified Public Accountants, Audit and Accounting Guide, *Not-for-Profit Entities* (New York: AICPA, 2014), par. 1.04.

[11] Financial Accounting Standards Board, *Statement of Financial Accounting Standards No. 32,* "Specialized Accounting and Reporting Principles in AICPA Statements of Position and Guides on Accounting and Auditing Matters" (New York, 1979).

[12] Financial Accounting Standards Board, *Statement of Financial Accounting Concepts No. 4,* "Objectives of Financial Reporting by Nonbusiness Organizations" (Norwalk, CT, 1980), pp. 19–23.

Although some NFPs may use the cash basis of accounting for internal accounting, external financial statements must be prepared on the accrual basis to be in conformity with GAAP. FASB *ASC* 958-205-45-4 requires, as a minimum, that all NFPs present a statement of financial position, a statement of activities, and a statement of cash flows that present financial information for the entity as a whole. In addition, voluntary health and welfare organizations are required to present a statement of functional expenses. Comparative financial statements are encouraged but not required.[13] In addition to reporting financial information for the entity as a whole, FASB *ASC* 958-205-45-3 permits NFPs to present additional disaggregated information, such as fund information (see appendix to this chapter), that may be useful to internal management, donors, and others.

Financial statements for the American Diabetes Association, Inc., for the fiscal year ended December 31, 2013, are presented for illustrative purposes in Illustrations 13–2 through 13–5. Because the American Diabetes Association is a voluntary health and welfare organization, it is required to present a statement of functional expenses (see Illustration 13–5) in addition to a statement of financial position, a statement of activities, and a statement of cash flows.

Statement of Financial Position

This statement, also known as a balance sheet, shows total assets, total liabilities, and the difference, **net assets,** for the organization as a whole. As shown in Illustration 13–2, net assets for the American Diabetes Association are categorized into the three classes required by FASB *ASC* 958-205-45-2: unrestricted net assets, temporarily restricted net assets, and permanently restricted net assets. **Unrestricted net assets** can arise from the following sources: contributions for which either no donor restrictions exist or the restrictions have expired, revenues for services provided, and investment income. Unrestricted net assets can be separated into undesignated and board designated. **Board-designated net assets** are unrestricted net assets appropriated or set aside for specific purposes by the governing board rather than an external donor. Purposes for which the board may set aside net assets include future capital acquisitions or additions to an endowment (see quasi-endowment in the following paragraph). It is useful for the stakeholders if the specific board-designated purposes are identified on the face of the financial statement or in the notes.

Temporarily restricted net assets result from contributions on which the donor imposes restrictions as to purpose (how the asset may be used) or time (when the asset may be used). When the restrictions are met, these net assets are "released from restrictions" and reported as increases in unrestricted net assets (see Illustration 13–3). **Permanently restricted net assets** are assets for which the donor states that the assets be held in perpetuity but allows the organization to spend any income earned from investing those assets. These gifts are also called **endowments** and are nonexpendable. Endowments may take the form of *pure* or *permanent* endowments, *term* endowments, or *quasi*-endowments. Term endowments are classified as temporarily restricted net assets because as the term expires, the assets can be used at the discretion of the NFP. Quasi-endowments or "funds functioning as endowments" are those the board sets aside; however, since the board can reverse that decision, this form of endowment is classified as an unrestricted net asset. Permanently restricted net assets

[13] FASB *ASC* 958-205-45-7.

ILLUSTRATION 13–2

AMERICAN DIABETES ASSOCIATION
CONSOLIDATED BALANCE SHEET
December 31, 2013
(with comparative information as of December 31, 2012)
(in thousands of dollars)

	2013	2012
Assets		
Cash and cash equivalents	$ 17,549	7,529
Investments	38,975	33,422
Accounts receivable, net	9,540	11,244
Inventory and supplies, net	1,592	1,559
Prepaid expenses and other assets	5,551	3,987
Contributions receivable, net	67,787	76,446
Fixed assets, net	9,238	7,474
Interest in perpetual trusts	8,126	5,879
Total assets	$158,358	147,540
Liabilities and Net Assets		
Accounts payable and accrued liabilities	$ 14,266	15,492
Line of credit	10,000	2,280
Research grants payable	12,833	10,265
Deferred revenues	13,743	12,585
Total liabilities	50,842	40,622
Net assets:		
Unrestricted	7,387	17,734
Temporarily restricted	87,658	78,960
Permanently restricted	12,471	10,224
Total net assets	107,516	106,918
Total liabilities and net assets	$158,358	147,540

Notes (not provided here) are an integral part of the financial statements.

may also be in the form of artwork, land, or other assets that must be used for a certain purpose and may not be sold. Information on temporarily and permanently restricted net assets can be reported on the face of the statement of financial position or disclosed in the notes to the financial statements.

At a minimum, the FASB standards require that the statement of financial position provide the amounts for total assets, total liabilities, total net assets, and the totals for each of the net asset classifications. FASB *ASC* 958-205-45-2 also requires that assets and liabilities be reported in reasonably homogeneous groups and that information about liquidity be provided by either listing assets and liabilities by nearness to cash or by classifying them as current or noncurrent, or both, as presented on the American Diabetes Association statement of financial position (Illustration 13–2). Alternately, relevant information about liquidity can be disclosed in the notes to the financial statements.

In some instances there may be restrictions on an asset that limits its use to a long-term purpose. If an asset has such a limitation on its use, information on the restriction needs to be displayed on the statement of financial position or disclosed in the notes to the financial statements. When displaying the restriction on the statement of financial position, the asset would appear on a separate line under a heading such as "assets whose use is limited."

ILLUSTRATION 13–3

AMERICAN DIABETES ASSOCIATION
CONSOLIDATED STATEMENT OF ACTIVITIES
Year ended December 31, 2013
(with summarized information for the year ended December 31, 2012)
(in thousands of dollars)

	Unrestricted	Temporarily Restricted	Permanently Restricted	2013 Total	2012 Total
Revenue:					
Contributions and grants:					
Donations	$ 39,339	38,828	—	78,167	87,718
Special events	63,148	4,264	—	67,412	64,537
Less costs of direct benefits to donors	(9,127)	—	—	(9,127)	(8,384)
Bequests	16,938	8,746	1,851	27,535	25,663
Federated and nonfederated organizations	7,468	52	—	7,520	8,105
Total contributions and grants	117,766	51,890	1,851	171,507	177,639
Fees from exchange transactions:					
Subscriptions and other income from periodicals	20,583	—	—	20,583	21,865
Sales of materials	4,745	—	—	4,745	6,715
Program service fees	17,117	—	—	17,117	15,086
Investment income	3,266	604	396	4,266	3,431
Miscellaneous revenues	3,543	—	—	3,543	3,756
Total fees from exchange transactions	49,254	604	396	50,254	50,853
Net assets released from restrictions	43,796	(43,796)	—	—	—
Total revenues	210,816	8,698	2,247	221,761	228,492
Expenses:					
Program activities:					
Research	47,653	—	—	47,653	45,376
Information	57,939	—	—	57,939	55,284
Advocacy and public awareness	56,666	—	—	56,666	47,232
Total program activities	162,258	—	—	162,258	147,892
Supporting services:					
Management and general	9,540	—	—	9,540	11,061
Fundraising	49,365	—	—	49,365	47,244
Total supporting services	58,905	—	—	58,905	58,305
Total expenses	221,163	—	—	221,163	206,197
Change in net assets	(10,347)	8,698	2,247	598	22,295
Net assets, beginning of year	17,734	78,960	10,224	106,918	84,623
Net assets, end of year	$ 7,387	87,658	12,471	107,516	106,918

Notes (not provided here) are an integral part of the financial statements.

Statement of Activities

The statement of activities is an operating statement that presents, in aggregated fashion, all changes in unrestricted net assets, temporarily restricted net assets, permanently restricted net assets, and total net assets for the reporting period. These changes take the form of revenues, gains, expenses, and losses. A common format for presenting the changes in net assets is the four column display used by the American Diabetes Association (Illustration 13–3). In this format, a column is used to show changes occurring in each net asset class (unrestricted, temporarily restricted, and permanently restricted) during the reporting period. As seen in Illustration 13–3, for the American Diabetes Association, there is a line titled "Net Assets Released from Restrictions" indicating the reclassification of temporarily restricted support to unrestricted support in the year in which the donor stipulations were met. Reclassifications are made for (1) satisfaction of program or purpose restrictions, (2) satisfaction of equipment acquisition restrictions, sometimes measured by depreciation expense, and (3) satisfaction of time restrictions, either actual donor or implied restrictions.

FASB *ASC* 958-205-45-1 provides NFPs with considerable flexibility in presenting financial information as long as it is useful and understandable to the reader. If desired, NFPs can use additional classifications to report financial information, such as operating and nonoperating, expendable and nonexpendable, earned and unearned, and recurring and nonrecurring.

In general, revenues and expenses should be reported on the statement of activities at their gross amounts. Exceptions include activities peripheral to the entity's central operations and investment revenue, which may be reported net of related expenses, if properly disclosed. Although revenues are categorized into three net asset classes, notice in Illustration 13–3 that all expenses are reported as reductions of unrestricted net assets. In addition, expenses must be reported by their functional classification (e.g., program or supporting) either in the statement of activities or in the notes to the financial statements. Gains and losses on investments and other assets are reported as changes in unrestricted net assets unless their use is temporarily or permanently restricted.

Statement of Cash Flows

FASB *ASC* 230-10-15-2 and 3 require NFPs to prepare a statement of cash flows using the same guidance as business entities. As Illustration 13–4 shows, the American Diabetes Association reports its cash flows in three categories: operating, investing, and financing. Although the American Diabetes Association uses the indirect method for reporting its cash flows from operating activities, either the direct or indirect method may be used. If the direct method is used, a reconciliation showing the change in total net assets from the statement of activities to net cash used for operating activities must be presented at the bottom of the statement.

Donor-imposed restrictions are not separately reported in the cash flows statement; however, the statement does have some unique aspects. Unrestricted gifts are included with the operating activities. The receipt of temporarily and permanently restricted net assets given for long-term purposes, such as temporarily restricted gifts for use in acquiring buildings or equipment, are included in the financing activities section, as is any income earned from the gift. Sale of a donated financial asset that has no donor-imposed restrictions almost immediately after receiving the asset is reported as an operating cash flow rather than an investing cash flow. Acquisition of a building or equipment using temporarily restricted net assets would be reported as an investing activity. Noncash gifts or in-kind contributions (discussed later) are disclosed as noncash investing and financing activities in a separate section.

Statement of Functional Expenses

The FASB requires that VHWOs prepare a statement of functional expenses and encourages other NFPs to do so. The Financial Reporting Executive Committee (FinREC) of the AICPA has observed that there is inconsistency in applying this standard due to different interpretations of what constitutes a VHWO. As a result, the FinREC has encouraged organizations that receive support from the general public

ILLUSTRATION 13–4

AMERICAN DIABETES ASSOCIATION
CONSOLIDATED STATEMENT OF CASH FLOWS
Year ended December 31, 2013
(with comparative information for the year ended December 31, 2012)
(in thousands of dollars)

	2013	2012
Cash flows from operating activities:		
Change in net assets	$ 598	22,295
Adjustments to reconcile change in net assets to net cash provided by (used in) operating activities:		
Depreciation and amortization	3,099	3,108
Net unrealized and realized gain on investments	(1,344)	(1,173)
Loss on disposal of assets	86	15
Provisions for doubtful receivables and obsolete inventory	2,546	2,078
Contributions to third party perpetual trusts	(1,851)	(305)
Other contributions restricted for long-term investments	—	(5)
Adjustments for changes in operating assets and liabilities:		
Decrease (increase) in accounts receivable	1,118	(2,779)
Decrease (increase) in inventory and supplies	61	(582)
Increase in prepaid expenses and other assets	(1,564)	(107)
Decrease (increase) in contributions receivable	8,456	(29,409)
(Decrease) increase in accounts payable and accrued liabilities	(1,023)	218
Increase in research grants payable	2,568	1,289
Increase in deferred revenues	1,158	1,958
Net cash provided by (used in) operating activities	13,908	(3,399)
Cash flows from investing activities:		
Purchases of investments	(43,549)	(29,333)
Sales or maturities of investments	37,093	28,168
Purchase of fixed assets	(4,949)	(2,850)
Net cash used in investing activities	(11,405)	(4,015)
Cash flows from financing activities:		
Proceeds from contributions restricted for investment in endowment	—	5
Proceeds from borrowing on line of credit	7,720	2,280
Payments on line of credit	—	—
Payments on capital lease agreements	(203)	(369)
Net cash provided by financing activities	7,517	1,916
Net increase (decrease) in cash and cash equivalents	10,020	(5,498)
Cash and cash equivalents, beginning of year	7,529	13,027
Cash and cash equivalents, end of year	$17,549	7,529

Notes (not provided here) are an integral part of the financial statements.

(contributions of 20 percent or more of total revenue and support) to prepare a statement of functional expenses.[14] Illustration 13–5 for the American Diabetes Association shows the usual format with functional expenses reported in the columns and the natural classification of expenses shown as rows. *Functional expenses* are those that relate to either the program or mission of the organization (*program expenses*) or the

[14] AICPA, AAG-NFP Entities, par. 3.42 and 3.43.

ILLUSTRATION 13–5

AMERICAN DIABETES ASSOCIATION
CONSOLIDATED STATEMENT OF FUNCTIONAL EXPENSES
Year ended December 31, 2013
(with summarized information for the year ended December 31, 2012)
(in thousands of dollars)

	Program activities				Supporting services				
	Research	Information	Advocacy and Public awareness	Total	Management and general	Fundraising	Total	2013 Total	2012 Total
Grants	$35,516	115	12	35,643	—	—	—	35,643	34,753
Employee costs	2,883	21,379	24,037	48,299	5,146	19,707	24,853	73,152	66,538
Professional fees	1,454	6,339	5,147	12,940	1,332	4,787	6,119	19,059	20,603
Supplies	44	2,806	718	3,568	94	553	647	4,215	3,721
Telecommunications	96	712	812	1,620	170	658	828	2,448	2,469
Postage and shipping	389	5,386	3,512	9,287	107	6,287	6,394	15,681	14,685
Occupancy cost	361	4,466	2,658	7,485	570	2,147	2,717	10,202	10,103
Equipment rental and maintenance	49	410	412	871	76	339	415	1,286	1,373
Printing and publications	2,296	11,253	6,851	20,400	236	10,606	10,842	31,242	30,273
Travel	94	845	1,231	2,170	122	982	1,104	3,274	3,218
Conferences and meetings	4,015	1,545	2,142	7,702	84	403	487	8,189	7,409
Data processing	10	585	526	1,121	17	936	953	2,074	2,077
Depreciation and amortization	124	899	1,023	2,046	217	836	1,053	3,099	3,108
Miscellaneous	322	1,199	7,585	9,106	1,369	1,124	2,493	11,599	5,867
Total expenses	$47,653	57,939	56,666	162,258	9,540	49,365	58,905	221,163	206,197
Costs of direct benefits to donors								9,127	8,384
Total expenses and costs of direct benefits to donors								$230,290	214,581

Notes (not provided here) are an integral part of the financial statements.

management and general and fund-raising expenses required to support the programs (*support expenses*). The natural classification of expenses, or object of expense, includes salaries, supplies, occupancy costs, interest, and depreciation, among other categories the organization considers useful to the readers. Watchdog agencies, donors, and others often use the ratio of program expenses to total expenses as a measure of an NFP's performance. The AICPA Audit and Accounting Guide, *Not-for-Profit Entities,* indicates that expenses that relate to more than one function (such as occupancy costs and interest and other expenses) be allocated to the programs or functional expenses to which they pertain.[15] It is not difficult to assign direct expenses (such as travel) to various functions; however, in order to allocate indirect expenses (such as occupancy costs or interest expense), a reasonable allocation basis must be used. A reasonable basis might include square footage of space occupied by each program or personnel costs.

Notes to the Financial Statements

The notes to the financial statements are an integral part of the financial statements of NFPs. Disclosures include principles applicable to for-profit entities unless there is a specific exemption for not-for-profit organizations. Examples of required disclosures are those relating to financial instruments, commitments, contingencies, extraordinary items, prior-period adjustments, changes in accounting principles, employee benefits, and credit risks. In addition, the nature and amounts of unrestricted, temporarily restricted, and permanently restricted net assets must be disclosed if not displayed on the face of the financial statements. Notes are encouraged to report the detail of reclassifications, investments, and promises to give. Policy statements regarding whether restricted gifts received and expended in the same period are reported first as temporarily restricted must also be disclosed.

ACCOUNTING FOR NFP ORGANIZATIONS

Revenues and Gains

Not-for-profit organizations have traditionally distinguished revenues, gains, and support. **Revenues** in the traditional sense, represent increases in unrestricted net assets arising from **exchange transactions** in which the other party to the transaction is presumed to receive direct tangible benefit commensurate with the resources provided. Examples are membership dues, program service fees, sales of goods and services, and investment income. **Gains,** such as realized gains on investment transactions and gains on sale or disposal of equipment, are increases in net assets that relate to peripheral or incidental transactions of the entity and often are beyond the control of management. **Support** is a category of revenues arising from contributions of resources or **nonexchange transactions** and includes only amounts for which the donor derives no tangible benefits from the recipient agency. Membership dues may be part exchange revenue and part contribution revenue (support) if the value received by the member is less than the dues payment. A government grant is usually considered support unless it is essentially a purchase of services, in which case the recipient is considered a vendor and the grant is classified as exchange revenue. As shown in Illustration 13–3, NFPs often present one section in the statement of activities for revenues, gains, and other support, in which case these distinctions are less important. Revenues and gains

[15] AICPA, AAG-NFP Entities, par. 13.66.

generally should be recognized on the accrual basis and reported at gross amounts to be in conformity with GAAP, although some NFPs (e.g., colleges and universities) report some revenues net of certain deductions. Revenue that is restricted by an agreement, such as fees or dues dedicated for a specific purpose, is reported in unrestricted net assets because it does not arise from a restricted gift by a donor.

Contributions

Not-for-profit organizations, in particular voluntary health and welfare organizations, are heavily dependent on contribution revenue (i.e., support) for their operations. A **contribution** is a voluntary, unconditional and nonreciprocal transfer of cash or other asset to a NFP (or a settlement or cancellation of its liabilities) by an entity external to the NFP. In this section of the chapter, the discussion focuses on financial reporting guidance for donor and donee entities. If an entity is an agent, trustee, or intermediary, financial reporting guidance may differ. Additionally, this chapter does not focus on reporting for tax purposes.

Donors can give gifts without restrictions *(unrestricted)*. However, they can also require that their gift be used for a specific purpose *(purpose restriction),* or they can specify that their gift be used in a certain time period *(time restriction)*. As can be seen from the following examples, consideration must be given to the existence of restrictions on gifts and how the gift is classified for reporting purposes. In general, FASB requires that both unrestricted and restricted gifts be recognized as support and at fair value at the time the gift is given.[16] Depending on the type of restriction, the gift increases unrestricted, temporarily restricted, or permanently restricted net assets. If the provisions of a temporarily restricted contribution are met in the same period of the gift, the revenue *may* be reported in the unrestricted classification. For example, if, in the year the gift was given, the NFP incurred at least $1,000 in research expenses related to the $1,000 gift listed here, the NFP could classify the $1,000 as unrestricted. The discerning reader will recognize that documenting the donor's intentions in writing at the time of the contribution is critical for proper accounting and reporting.

Gifts Given	Type of Restriction	Net Asset Classification
$3,000 to be used as desired	None	Unrestricted
$1,000 to be used for research	Purpose	Temporary
$9,000 to be added to endowment	Purpose	Permanent
$5,000 to be used next year	Time	Temporary

Promises to give assets to an organization (commonly called *pledges*) can be conditional or unconditional. A **conditional promise to give** depends on the occurrence of a specified future and uncertain event to bind the promissor, such as obtaining matching gifts by the recipient. A conditional promise to give is *not* recognized as support until the conditions on which it depends have been substantially met. An **unconditional promise to give** depends only on the passage of time or demand by the promisee for performance. These promises are recorded as support in the year made. Unconditional promises to give that will not be received until future periods

[16] FASB *ASC* 958-310-35 provides an alternative for fair value measurement of receivables.

must be reported as temporarily restricted net assets unless explicit donor stipulations or the circumstances surrounding the promise make it clear that the donor intended the contribution to support activities of the current period. FASB *ASC* 958-605-30-6 indicates that if unconditional pledges will be received in less than a year, they can be recognized at net realizable value. To determine net realizable value, an NFP calculates the allowance for uncollectible pledges based on the NFP's history and expectations concerning the collectibility of the pledges. The NFP records the allowance in a manner similar to businesses, debiting an expense account such as Provision for Uncollectible Pledges and crediting Allowance for Uncollectible Pledges. Generally, long-term unconditional pledges (those that will not be collected within one year) are measured at fair value using guidance provided by FASB *ASC* 820. If the present value technique is used to value pledges, the difference between the pledged amount and the present value is recorded as a discount. For example, The Helping Hand entity received $90,000 in unconditional pledges that will be collected five years from the current date. Applying a 3 percent present value rate to the amount, the Helping Hand recorded the following journal entry:

	Debits	Credits
Contributions Receivable	90,000	
Contributions—Temporarily Restricted		77,634
Discount on Contributions Receivable		12,366

When the contributions are received, the discount is removed by recording a debit to the discount account and a credit to Contributions—Unrestricted. Pledges or intentions to give are not recorded until they have the characteristics of an unconditional promise to give, for example, a written document, partial payment, or a public announcement by the donor. An example of the required note disclosures for contributions receivable, documenting the net receivable value, is presented for the American Diabetes Association.

Selected American Diabetes Association Note Disclosures
Contributions Receivable

Unconditional promises to give are initially recorded at their fair value. These unconditional promises to give are nonrecurring fair value measurements classified as Level 3. Unconditional promises to give that are expected to be collected in future years are recorded at the present value of the amounts expected to be collected. The present value discount is calculated using a risk-adjusted rate at the time of the contribution ranging from 1.3 percent to 4.8 percent. The carrying value of contributions receivable approximates their fair value based on the relatively short-term maturity of these receivables.

Contributions receivable consist of the following amounts due as of December 31, 2013, and 2012 (in thousands):

	2013	2012
Within one year	$50,382	$55,803
In one to five years	6,419	13,052
In more than five years	1	104
Total contributions receivable	56,802	68,959
Less: allowance for doubtful accounts	(3,800)	(3,574)
Less: present value discount	(136)	(291)
Subtotal	52,866	65,094

Contributions can take the form of cash, securities, capital assets, materials, or services. Cash contributions require that a strong system of internal controls over the safeguarding of cash be in place; however, cash contributions pose no unusual accounting or reporting problems. Donated securities may be received for any purpose, although generally they are received as a part of the principal of an endowment. They are recorded at their fair value at the date of the gift. The fair value rule is also applied to capital assets received either as a part of an endowment or for use in the operations of the organization.

Donated Materials and Services

One of the basic characteristics that distinguishes not-for-profit organizations from commercial organizations is their reliance on noncash contributions or **gifts in kind.** Sheltered workshops for persons with disabilities often depend heavily on donations of clothing and furniture, thrift shops receive their inventory from donations, and health agencies may obtain contributions of drugs from pharmaceutical firms. Office space may be furnished rent free; and television, radio, and periodicals may publicize fund drives, special events, or the general work of NFPs at no charge. FASB *ASC* 958-605-30-11 requires that all unconditional gifts, including material amounts of donated materials, be reported at fair value. The gift would be regarded as both contribution revenue and an expense or a noncash asset. An objective, clearly measurable basis for fair value can be established by proceeds from resale by the organization, price lists, market quotations, or appraisals. FASB *ASC* 958-605-30-11 indicates consideration should be given to the quantity and quality of gifts when determining fair value. Donated materials used or consumed in providing services should be reported as part of the cost of the services.

The services of unpaid workers may well make the difference between an effective organization and one that fails to achieve its objectives. Voluntary health and welfare organizations typically rely on the efforts of volunteer workers to supplement the efforts of paid employees. FASB *ASC* 958-605-25-16 requires recognition of contributed services at their fair value if the services received (1) create or enhance nonfinancial assets or (2) require specialized skills, are provided by individuals possessing those skills, and typically would need to be purchased if not provided by donation (e.g., accountants). Although FASB does not provide an example of the first criterion, a logical example would be recognition of support for donated architectural, legal, or carpentry services related to construction of a building addition. In this example, a capital asset account rather than a program or support expense would be debited. In general, nonfinancial assets are assets other than cash and assets readily convertible into cash, such as consumable supplies and capital assets. The second criterion is quite restrictive and results in many donated services not being recognized. It should be noted that a donation of advertising time is considered to be a contributed asset rather than a contributed service. This is important since the criterion of "would need to be purchased" does not apply.[17] An example of the types of services and in-kind materials recognized by the American Diabetes Association is provided in its note disclosure.

[17] FASB *ASC* 958-605-55-23.

Selected American Diabetes Association Note Disclosures
Contributed Services and In-kind Contributions

The Association recognizes as contribution revenue and as professional fees expense the fair value of services donated by volunteers in conjunction with the peer review process by the Grant Review Panel of the American Diabetes Association Research Foundation, Inc. and medical services provided in conjunction with the Association's program activities, primarily camps held for children with diabetes. Contributed services for occupancy are recorded as occupancy expenses. The Association recognized approximately $2,493,000 and $2,395,000, in donated services provided in conjunction with the Association's activities during the years ended December 31, 2013, and 2012, respectively.

Many other volunteers made significant contributions of time to the Association's program and supporting functions. The values of those contributed services do not meet the criteria for recognition and, accordingly, are not recognized as revenues and expenses in the accompanying consolidated statement of activities.

In-kind contributions of supplies are recognized as contribution revenue and supplies expense and totaled approximately $2,121,000 and $1,668,000 for the years ended December 31, 2013, and 2012, respectively.

Donated Land, Building, and Equipment

At the time of donation, land, buildings, and equipment are recorded at their fair value. The donations are reported as contributions or support on the statement of activities and would be classified as unrestricted, temporarily restricted, or permanently restricted on the financial reports. If the donor does not indicate how the asset should be used, the gift is classified as unrestricted. If the donor does impose restrictions, such as how long the asset must be used as a building, or if the NFP has a policy implying a time restriction over the useful life of the asset, the contribution is classified as temporarily restricted. An NFP with a policy implying a time restriction should clearly state the policy in the notes to the financial statements.

For buildings and equipment classified as temporarily restricted, an amount equal to annual depreciation expense is typically reclassified from temporarily restricted to unrestricted net assets each year. The reclassification is intended to reflect that the cost of "using up" the asset's service potential satisfies the donor's imposed restriction.[18]

If an NFP receives the use of a building for a reduced rate, the difference between the rent paid and the fair market rental value should be reported as a contribution that is unrestricted. In certain cases an NFP could receive a donation of land, building or equipment that it intends to sell rather than use, in such cases the contribution should be reported as an increase in unrestricted net assets.

Special Events

Special events are fund-raising activities that provide a direct benefit to those attending. The contribution to attend the special event exceeds the cost (expense) of the direct benefit provided, resulting in contribution revenue for the entity sponsoring the event. Dinners, dances, golf outings, bazaars, card parties, fashion shows, concerts, and bake sales are typical "special events." The special events category of revenue is reserved for those events sponsored by the NFP or by an organization over which it has control. If a completely independent organization sponsors an event for the NFP's benefit, the amount given to the NFP should be reported as contribution revenue not special event revenue.

[18] FASB *ASC* 958-205-45-12.

FASB *ASC* 958-225-45-17 requires that revenues from special events be reported at gross with the direct expenses of providing the benefit reported separately. If the special event is peripheral to the NFP, the direct expenses can be netted against the revenues. If desired, NFPs can provide more detailed reporting of special events, either on the face of the statement of activities or in the notes to the financial statements. An example of a special event note follows.

Selected Bay Area Discovery Museum Note Disclosures
Special Events

Special event contributions, revenue, and direct donor-benefit costs during the year ended August 31, 2012, totaled as follows:

Event	Contributions and Revenue	Direct Costs	Net
Creativity Forum	$221,232	$ 66,696	$154,536
PlayDate	449,265	237,712	211,553
Goblin Jamboree	89,721	31,555	58,166
Totals	$760,218	$335,963	$424,255

PlayDate direct donor-benefit costs include the cost of in-kind contributions of goods and services sold at auction totaling $125,321.

Expenses of promoting and conducting special events, such as expenses of printing tickets and posters, mailings, fees and expenses of public relations and fund-raising consultants, and salaries of employees of the NFP attributable to planning, promoting, and conducting special events are reported as fund-raising expenses and are not charged against special events revenue.

Split-interest Gifts

Donors may arrange to divide the interest in a gift among several beneficiaries, including an NFP. In these cases, one party may receive the gift's investment income as an asset and the other party has the right to the gift's principal at some point in time (such as the donor's death). These complex legal agreements are discussed in greater detail in Chapter 15.

Contribution of Assets Involving an Intermediary

An NFP may receive contributions of assets from an agent, intermediary, or trustee. Additionally, an NFP may act as an agent, intermediary, or trustee providing contributions to others. While the terms *agent* and *trustee* were introduced in Chapter 8, the term *intermediary* is new. Similar to an agent and a trustee, an **intermediary** serves in a fiduciary capacity by helping with the transfer of assets between a donor and a beneficiary. The FASB provides guidance on when agents and intermediaries should recognize contribution revenue related to the assets they receive on behalf of other entities (i.e., the beneficiary organization). FASB *ASC* 958-605 states that generally the agent or intermediary will recognize an asset and a related liability when it receives a donation or contribution on behalf of the beneficiary organization. The agent or intermediary does not recognize any contribution revenue when it receives the asset because the asset does not belong to the agent or intermediary; rather, it belongs to the beneficiary organization. However, FASB does state there are instances when an agent or an intermediary could recognize the asset as contribution revenue rather than as a liability. If the agent or intermediary is interrelated to the beneficiary organization, or if it has variance power, contribution revenue is recognized. According to FASB *ASC* 958-20-20, entities are **financially interrelated** if (1) one of the entities has the ability to influence the operating and financial decisions of the other entity and (2) one of the entities has an ongoing economic interest in the net assets of the other. **Variance power** exists when the agent or intermediary has the ability to redirect the assets it receives to an entity other than the beneficiary organization. A short example related to how the agent or intermediary would recognize assets received may be helpful.

An intermediary received $5,000 in cash from a donor. The donor indicated that she wanted her donation to go to the local not-for-profit hospital.

Scenario 1—there is no financial relationship between the intermediary and the hospital. The intermediary would make the following journal entry.

	Debits	Credits
Cash	5,000	
Contributions Payable		5,000

Scenario 2—the intermediary and hospital are financially interrelated or the intermediary has variance power. The intermediary would make the following journal entry.

Cash	5,000	
Contributions-Unrestricted		5,000

Federated fund-raising organizations, such as the United Way, frequently report as in the first scenario. Foundations and fund-raising organizations of colleges, hospitals, and other entities frequently report as in the second scenario.

Accounting for Expenses

Generally accepted accounting principles require that all expenses of NFPs be measured on the accrual basis and be reported as decreases in unrestricted net assets on the statement of activities. Depreciation of capital assets with a limited life, including contributed capital assets, used in the operation of the organization is required by the FASB. Depreciation of art and historical collections is discussed later in this chapter.

Functional Expenses

NFPs have long been required to report expenses by functional classifications, such as major *program* and *support* classifications.[19] Program classifications result from the provision of goods or services that help achieve the major purposes or mission of the NFP. Support activities assist the NFP in carrying out its mission and include such functional classifications as fund-raising and management and general. The FASB allows the reporting of functional classifications on the face of the financial statements

[19] FASB *ASC* 958-720-45.

or in the notes to the statements. The American Diabetes Association has opted to provide functional classifications on the face of its financial statement as reflected in Illustration 13–3. The statement shows that the American Diabetes Association operates three programs: research, information, and advocacy and public awareness. Also listed are the two support functions, management and general, and fund-raising.

A fund-raising organization, such as the United Way, that is intended to allocate most of its inflows to participating agencies rather than to engage directly in offering program services to the public, will report program services that are quite different from those of other NFP organizations. For example, it may report under program services functions such as "campaign and public relations," and "investor relations." It would also report support functions such as "management and general," and "fund-raising."

Fund-raising—Allocation of Joint Costs

Not-for-profit organizations often conduct activities that combine a program or administrative activity with fund-raising. An example is a door-to-door campaign to improve neighborhood safety *and* solicit contributions. FASB *ASC* 958-720-45 provides guidance on allocating joint costs of such activities, making it more difficult to include fund-raising expenses as a part of program expenses. The FASB provides the following:

1. The total cost of activities that include a fund-raising appeal should be reported as fund-raising costs unless a *bona fide* program or management and general function has been conducted in conjunction with the appeal for funds.
2. The joint costs of a bona fide program or management and general function should be allocated between the bona fide program or management and general function and fund-raising using an equitable allocation method. An equitable allocation method is one that is rational and systematically applied to yield a reasonable allocation of the costs to fund-raising and a program and/or the management and general function.
3. Criteria of purpose, audience, and content must be met in order to conclude that a bona fide program or management and general function has been conducted in conjunction with the appeal for funds.

The criteria provided by FASB are quite detailed. A summary of those criteria is provided in the remainder of this paragraph. For those interested in additional information concerning the criteria, a flowchart is provided in FASB *ASC* 958-720. The *purpose* criterion may be met if the joint activity helps accomplish a program purpose or management function. Generally, the joint activity needs to ask the audience to take a specific action that will help accomplish the NFP's mission. The purpose criterion will not be met if the majority of the compensation or fees received by those conducting the joint activity are based on the contributions raised as part of the activity. The *audience* criterion is met if the audience was selected primarily for program or management reasons rather than its ability to make a contribution or donation. Finally, the *content* criterion is met if the content of the joint activity either motivates the audience to take action to further the NFP's mission, or the joint activity meets a management responsibility. If the NFP determines that joint costs can be allocated, the FASB requires that certain note disclosures be made.[20]

[20] State and local governments, including governmental colleges and universities, are subject to the same guidance when conducting joint activities. The guidance used by state and local governments is provided by the AICPA Statement of Position 98-2.

Fund-raising expenses include the costs of television and radio announcements that request contributions, including the costs of preparing the announcements and purchasing or arranging for the time; the costs of postage, addressing, and maintenance of mailing lists and other fund drive records; the costs of preparing or purchasing fund-raising materials; the costs of public meetings to "kick off" a fund drive; and an appropriate portion of the salaries of personnel who supervise fund-raising activities or keep records of activities.

Management and General Expenses

Management and general expenses include the cost of publicity and public relations activities designed to keep the organization's name before prospective contributors. Costs of informational materials that contain only general information regarding the NFP's program and the costs of informational materials distributed to potential contributors, but not as a part of a fund drive, are considered management and general expenses. The costs of budgeting, accounting, reporting, legal services, office management, purchasing, and similar activities are examples of expenses properly classifiable as management and general expenses.

Accounting for Assets

Generally, assets of NFPs are recorded in a manner similar to those of for-profit entities. The following topics identify some areas where accounting and reporting for NFP assets does differ.

Assets with Restrictions on Use

Assets that are not available for current operating purposes because *donors* have limited their use to a long-term purpose (e.g., capital asset acquisition) are considered *restricted*. The FASB *ASC* 958-210-45 indicates that such assets should be classified separately from current assets on the face of the statement of financial position. An example of how such assets could be recognized is provided in Illustration 13–6.

Investments

FASB *ASC* 958-320 provides guidance to NFPs on accounting for investments that is similar to the guidance provided to businesses. The guidance requires NFPs to value all purchases of investments in equity securities that have readily determinable fair values and all purchases of debt securities at acquisition price. Securities that are contributed are initially measured at *fair value*. Fair values are determined by quoted market prices, if available; selling price of similar securities; or valuation techniques, such as discounted cash flows. At subsequent measurement dates, such as fiscal year-end, NFPs report equity securities with readily determinable fair values and debt securities at fair value. Unlike businesses, but similar to governments, NFPs are not required to classify their investments into trading, available-for-sale, and held-to-maturity categories. Similar to businesses, the guidance provided by FASB *ASC* 958-320 does not apply to investments with no readily determinable fair value, securities reported under the equity method, or consolidations.

When reporting investments at fair value, the difference between the carrying value (book value) and the fair value of the investment can result in an unrealized gain or loss. Because NFPs do not report other comprehensive income, they report unrealized gains or losses on the current period's statement of activities. Similarly, realized gains and losses, along with income earned on the investments (i.e., interest and dividends) are reported on the current period's statement of activities.

Investment income, unrealized or realized gains, and unrealized or realized losses are reported as adjustments to unrestricted net assets unless their use is restricted by the donor or state law.[21] Based on the type of restriction, investment income is reported as an increase in either temporarily or permanently restricted net assets. Similarly, if a restriction exists, the type of restriction dictates whether the gains and losses on investments are reported as temporarily or permanently restricted. If a restriction exists and the restriction is satisfied in the same period the income or gain is earned, the income or gain may be reported as an increase in unrestricted net assets as long as the NFP has a similar policy for reporting contributions received, reports consistently from period to period, and discloses its accounting policy.

The rules concerning the reporting of gains and losses on investments also apply to endowment investments if the donor or law has not specified otherwise.[22] However, at the time this textbook was published, 49 states had adopted the Uniform Prudent Management of Investment Funds Act (UPMIFA), which provides rules on the use and reporting of endowment assets. As a result, there are few states without laws governing the accounting for endowment assets. Additional information about UPMIFA is provided in the Chapter 15 because colleges and universities traditionally hold large endowments. Additional information about UPMIFA can be obtained from the National Conference of Commissioners on Uniform State Laws at *www.nccusl.org.*

FASB *ASC* 958-320-50 requires extensive investment disclosures, such as (1) the makeup of the investment return, (2) a reconciliation of investment return to amounts reported in the statement of activities, (3) the aggregate carrying amount of investments by major type of investment (e.g., equity securities, U.S. Treasury securities, or corporate debt securities), (4) disclosures about all significant concentrations of credit risk arising from all financial instruments, (5) the nature of and carrying amount for each individual investment or group of investments that represents a significant concentration of market risk, and (6) information about realized and unrealized gains and losses and about historical costs of investments if it is useful.

NFPs must follow the guidance in FASB *ASC* 815 as it relates to derivative instruments and hedging activities.

Collection Items

Certain not-for-profit organizations, particularly museums and libraries, have significant collections. FASB *ASC* 958-360-20 defines **collections** as works of art, historical treasures, or similar assets that are

1. Held for public exhibition, education, or research in furtherance of public service rather than financial gain.
2. Protected, kept unencumbered, cared for, and preserved.
3. Subject to an organizational policy that requires the proceeds of items that are sold to be used to acquire other items for collection.

An NFP may adopt the policy of recognizing collections as assets or not recognizing them; however, selective capitalization is not allowed. The following note from the American Museum of Natural History shows that the Museum has elected not to capitalize its unusual collections. In accordance with FASB standards, the Museum defines its collections in terms of its policy for exhibiting, maintaining and investing in the collections.

[21] FASB *ASC* 958-225-45.

[22] FASB *ASC* 958-205.

Selected American Museum of Natural History Note Disclosures Collections

The Museum has extensive collections of specimens and artifacts that constitute a record of life on Earth. These valuable, and sometimes irreplaceable, collections have been acquired through field expeditions, contributions, and purchases since the Museum's inception and represent one of the largest natural history collections in the world. New collection areas include the Museum's frozen tissue collection of DNA and tissue samples and access to large scientific databases of genomic and astrophysical data. The collections provide a resource for scientists around the world and grows significantly each year.

In conformity with accounting policies generally followed by museums, the value of the Museum's collections are not reflected in the consolidated statement of net position. If the assets used to purchase the collection items are from restricted funds, proceeds from the sale of those items are recorded as increases in temporarily restricted net assets in that fund until an acquisition is made.

If an NFP capitalizes its collections, it should recognize the collections as assets in the period in which they are acquired, either at cost or fair market value, if contributed. Contributed collections should be recorded in the appropriate net asset category, depending on any restrictions placed on the contribution by the donor. If the organization chooses not to capitalize, it should provide note disclosure of its collections.

FASB *ASC* 958-360-35 states that capitalized art or historical treasures do not need to be depreciated so long as their economic benefit is used up so slowly that their estimated useful lives are extraordinarily long. This characteristic exists if (1) the assets individually have cultural, aesthetic, or historic value that is worth preserving perpetually and (2) the holder has the technological and financial ability to protect and preserve essentially undiminished the service potential of the asset and is doing that.[23]

CONSOLIDATIONS AND COMBINATIONS

Not-for-profit organizations can have financial relationships with for-profit entities, other NFP organizations, or governments. These relationships may result in the need for the consolidation of interests when reporting on the financial statements. As with businesses, NFPs can acquire or merge with other entities. Consolidations and combinations are briefly discussed in the following paragraphs. For those interested in additional information concerning consolidations and combinations, the FASB code sections are provided.

Consolidations

Consolidating entities for financial reporting purposes can vary by the type of entity being considered for consolidation.

Investments in For-profit Entities

According to FASB *ASC* 958-810, an NFP organization should consolidate a for-profit entity's financial information with its own if the NFP has a controlling financial interest through directly or indirectly owning a voting majority in the for-profit entity or if the NFP is a general partner that controls a limited partnership for-profit entity. However, if the NFP owns a noncontrolling interest, it should use the equity method to report investments in that entity.[24] Unlike for-profit entities, NFPs are not subject to variable interest entity standards.[25]

[23] FASB *ASC* 958-360-35-3.

[24] Ibid., 958-810.

[25] Ibid., 810-10.

Financially Interrelated NFPs

In the case of financially interrelated not-for-profit organizations, the NFP should consolidate another NFP in which it has a controlling financial interest and an economic interest. An economic interest exists (1) if one NFP holds or utilizes significant assets that must be used for the unrestricted or restricted purposes of another NFP, either directly or indirectly by producing income or generating services, or (2) if one NFP is responsible for the liabilities of another NFP.[26] If either control *or* an economic interest—but not both—exists, related party disclosures are required, as well as disclosures that identify the related organization and the nature of the relationship.

Component Units of Governmental Entities

Certain NFPs are created for the sole purpose of raising and holding economic resources for the direct benefit of a government. For example, public universities often create NFPs, collectively referred to as *institutionally related foundations,* for fund-raising, managing businesslike activities or endowment assets, conducting medical or other research, promoting athletics, or interacting with alumni of the university. Frequently, such NFPs must be reported as component units of the governmental entity. The criteria outlined in Chapter 9 for recognition of a component unit should be applied to determine whether an NFP is reported as part of a governmental entity.

Combinations

FASB *ASC* 958-805 provides that NFPs can recognize a combination of two or more NFP organizations as either a merger or an acquisition.

Mergers

A **merger** occurs when two or more NFPs combine to create a new NFP. At the date of the merger, the new NFP recognizes the assets and liabilities of the merging NFP organizations at the amounts reported on the GAAP prepared financial statements of the merging NFPs.[27]

Acquisitions

An **acquisition** occurs when an NFP obtains control of one or more NFP activities or businesses. The assets and liabilities of the acquired activities or businesses are initially recognized in the acquiring NFP financial statements using the acquisition method. This method is basically the same as that used by for-profit entities as outlined in FASB *ASC* 805.

ILLUSTRATIVE TRANSACTIONS—VOLUNTARY HEALTH AND WELFARE ORGANIZATIONS

Preceding sections of this chapter point out the fact that NFPs vary greatly regarding the kinds of program services provided and the sources of support and revenue utilized. Accordingly, the transactions and accounting entries presented in this section should be taken as illustrative of those considered appropriate for an organization that offers counseling, adoption, and foster home care; they are not necessarily typical of other NFPs. The transactions illustrated in this section are assumed to pertain to the

[26] Ibid., 958-810.

[27] Ibid., 958-805-25.

year 2017 of a hypothetical organization called the Community Family Service Agency, Inc. The trial balance of the Community Family Service Agency, Inc., as of December 31, 2016, is shown below.

The trial balance as of December 31, 2016, indicates that the capital assets (land, building, and equipment) are temporarily restricted, either explicitly by the donor or by an organization policy implying that donated capital assets will be restricted for the term of their useful life, or, in the case of land, for some specified period of time. An amount equal to depreciation expense is reclassified from temporarily restricted to unrestricted net assets each year. Donors of temporarily restricted gifts for programs, plant, or future periods have also restricted the specific asset or investments, in addition to net assets.

COMMUNITY FAMILY SERVICE AGENCY, INC.
Trial Balance
As of December 31, 2016

	Debits	*Credits*
Cash	$ 58,711	
Short-term Investments—Unrestricted	22,000	
Short-term Investments—Temporarily Restricted—Plant	20,000	
Accounts Receivable	2,485	
Allowance for Uncollectible Accounts Receivable		$ 135
Contributions Receivable—Unrestricted	5,424	
Allowance for Uncollectible Pledges—Unrestricted		259
Contributions Receivable—Temporarily Restricted	10,470	
Allowance for Uncollectible Pledges—Temporarily Restricted		288
Supplies	23,095	
Prepaid Expense	3,917	
Land—Temporarily Restricted	16,900	
Building—Temporarily Restricted	58,000	
Allowance for Depreciation—Building		4,640
Equipment—Temporarily Restricted	42,824	
Allowance for Depreciation—Equipment		9,136
Long-term Investments—Unrestricted	17,000	
Long-term Investments—Permanently Restricted	230,000	
Accounts Payable and Accrued Expenses		25,911
Mortgage Payable		55,000
Unrestricted Net Assets—Undesignated—Available for Operations		67,302
Unrestricted Net Assets—Designated for Special Outreach Project		30,000
Temporarily Restricted Net Assets—Programs		3,900
Temporarily Restricted Net Assets—Plant		79,130
Temporarily Restricted Net Assets—Time		5,125
Permanently Restricted Net Assets		230,000
Totals	$510,826	$510,826

Contributions received in 2016 but specified by donors for unrestricted use in 2017 were transferred from the temporarily restricted to the unrestricted net asset class, as shown by Entry 1.

		Debits	*Credits*
1.	Net Assets Released—Expiration of Time Restrictions—Temporarily Restricted	5,125	
	Net Assets Released—Expiration of Time Restrictions—Unrestricted		5,125

Pledges receivable resulting from the 2017 fund drive were recorded. Pledges of $69,500 were unrestricted; in addition, pledges of $16,500 were donor restricted for a special outreach project to be undertaken in 2017.

		Debits	Credits
2a.	Contributions Receivable—Unrestricted	69,500	
	Contributions—Unrestricted		69,500
2b.	Contributions Receivable—Temporarily Restricted	16,500	
	Contributions—Temporarily Restricted—Program		16,500

Collection on accounts receivable amounted to $2,200. Cash collected for unrestricted pledges totaled $68,500. Collections of cash for restricted pledges made this year totaled $16,500. Cash in the amount of $9,200 was collected for pledges given during a building fund drive in the preceding year.

3a.	Cash	70,700	
	Contributions Receivable—Unrestricted		68,500
	Accounts Receivable		2,200
3b.	Cash	16,500	
	Contributions Receivable—Temporarily Restricted		16,500
3c.	Cash	9,200	
	Contributions Receivable—Temporarily Restricted		9,200

The organization sponsored a bazaar to raise funds for the Special Outreach Project. Direct costs (expenses) of $3,000, not considered peripheral or incidental in nature, incurred for this event were paid in cash; the event yielded cash contributions of $10,000.

4a.	Cash	10,000	
	Contributions—Temporarily Restricted—Program		10,000
4b.	Direct Costs—Special Outreach Project—Program	3,000	
	Cash		3,000

For FY 2017, the Community Family Service Agency received $317,000 from the United Way. Of the amount received, $13,200 was recorded by the Community Family Service as a fund-raising expense paid to United Way, and the remainder was recorded as an unrestricted cash contribution.

5.	Cash	303,800	
	Fund-Raising Support Expenses	13,200	
	Contributions—Unrestricted		317,000

Salaries expense for the year totaled $265,000, employee benefits expense totaled $51,000, and payroll taxes expense was $20,300. As of year-end, $15,100 of these expenses were unpaid; the balance had been paid in cash.

		Debits	Credits
6.	Salaries Expense	265,000	
	Employee Benefits Expense	51,000	
	Payroll Taxes Expense	20,300	
	Cash		321,200
	Accounts Payable and Accrued Expenses		15,100

Expenses incurred for the Special Outreach Project were professional fees, $17,000; supplies, $4,500; and printing and publications, $1,600. All amounts were paid in cash.

7.	Professional Fees Expense	17,000	
	Supplies Expense	4,500	
	Printing and Publications Expense	1,600	
	Cash		23,100

Expenses for program services and supporting services were professional fees, $43,000; supplies, $7,800; telephone, $9,800; postage and shipping, $7,800; occupancy, $23,900; rental and maintenance of equipment, $8,700; printing and publications, $7,900; travel, $22,000; conferences, conventions, and meetings, $13,800; specific assistance to individuals, $35,500; membership dues, $700; costs of sales to the public, $900; and miscellaneous, $4,200. All expenses were credited to accounts payable and accrued expenses.

8.	Professional Fees Expense	43,000	
	Supplies Expense	7,800	
	Telephone Expense	9,800	
	Postage and Shipping Expense	7,800	
	Occupancy Expense	23,900	
	Rental and Maintenance of Equipment Expense	8,700	
	Printing and Publications Expense	7,900	
	Travel Expense	22,000	
	Conferences, Conventions, and Meetings	13,800	
	Specific Assistance to Individuals	35,500	
	Membership Dues	700	
	Cost of Sales to the Public	900	
	Miscellaneous Expense	4,200	
	Accounts Payable and Accrued Expenses		186,000

Unrestricted contributions and revenue were received in cash during 2017 from the following sources: legacies and bequests, $15,000; membership dues from individuals, $1,000; program service fees, $55,000; investment income, $2,900; and miscellaneous, $1,500. In addition, $250 of net incidental revenue was collected in cash from advertisers for the Special Outreach Project.

		Debits	Credits
9.	Cash	75,650	
	Contributions—Unrestricted		15,000
	Membership Dues		1,000
	Program Service Fees		55,000
	Investment Income—Unrestricted		2,900
	Miscellaneous Revenue		1,500
	Contributions—Temporarily Restricted—Program		250

Sales to the public amounted to $1,000 gross for the year. None of this amount was collected by year-end.

10.	Accounts Receivable	1,000	
	Sales to the Public		1,000

Accounts payable and accrued expenses paid in cash during 2017 totaled $182,864.

11.	Accounts Payable and Accrued Expenses	182,864	
	Cash		182,864

Contributions received in cash in 2017 amounted to $20,000, of which $10,000 was specified by donors for use in 2018, $6,000 was temporarily restricted for a program, and $4,000 was temporarily restricted for plant.

12.	Cash	20,000	
	Contributions—Temporarily Restricted—Time		10,000
	Contributions—Temporarily Restricted—Program		6,000
	Contributions—Temporarily Restricted—Plant		4,000

Interest of $4,540 and $6,500 on the principal of the mortgage were paid. Short-term investments that were restricted for plant were sold at par, $5,000; the proceeds were used to purchase equipment. The organization's policy is that there is an implied restriction on plant assets and that this restriction is satisfied as the assets are used (measured by depreciation expense).

13a.	Miscellaneous Expense	4,540	
	Mortgage Payable	6,500	
	Cash		11,040
13b.	Cash	5,000	
	Short-Term Investments—Temporarily Restricted—Plant		5,000
13c.	Equipment—Temporarily Restricted	5,000	
	Cash		5,000

Interest received in cash on short-term investments restricted for the plant amounted to $1,390. Interest received in cash on investments of endowment funds amounted to $12,780. This income was not restricted by the donor.

		Debits	Credits
14a.	Cash	1,390	
	Investment Income—Temporarily Restricted—Plant		1,390
14b.	Cash	12,780	
	Investment Income—Unrestricted		12,780

The Community Family Service Agency incurred $8,574 in expenses related to contracting for fund-raising services. These expenses were recorded as Professional Fees Expense.

15.	Professional Fees Expense	8,574	
	Cash		8,574

At the end of the year, a local family donated $100,000 in cash to be held in perpetuity with any investment income or gains and losses (realized or unrealized) to be used at the discretion of management.

16.	Cash	100,000	
	Contributions—Permanently Restricted		100,000

End-of-the-Year Adjusting Journal Entries

A physical count of supplies, valued at the lower of cost or market, indicated the proper balance sheet value should be $19,100, a decrease of $3,995 during the year. Prepaid expenses at year-end were $3,600; the decrease of $317 is chargeable to postage and shipping expense.

17a.	Supplies Expense	3,995	
	Supplies		3,995
17b.	Postage and Shipping Expense	317	
	Prepaid Expense		317

An analysis of the investment accounts indicated that the fair value of the long-term investments had decreased. The long-term investments for endowment had a fair value of $226,000 at the end of the year,[28] and the unrestricted long-term investments were valued at $14,000, a decrease of $4,000 and $3,000, respectively. Short-term investments and investments for land, building, and equipment did not change.

18.	Unrealized Loss on Investments—Permanently Restricted	4,000	
	Unrealized Loss on Investments—Unrestricted	3,000	
	Long-Term Investments—Permanently Restricted		4,000
	Long-Term Investments—Unrestricted		3,000

[28] The FASB requires that investment losses on endowments be reported as a decrease in either temporarily restricted or unrestricted net assets unless donor stipulations or law require that the loss be reported as a decrease in permanently restricted net assets. We assume that such a donor stipulation or law exists for this endowment.

The allowance for uncollectible accounts receivable appeared adequate and not excessive, but the allowance for uncollectible unrestricted pledges should be increased by $104. This adjustment relates to current period unrestricted contributions (see Entry 2a).

		Debits	Credits
19.	Provision for Uncollectible Pledges	104	
	Allowance for Uncollectible Pledges—Unrestricted		104

Depreciation on buildings and equipment belonging to the Community Family Service Agency is recorded in the amounts shown in Entry 20a. Since the depreciation reduced the carrying value of the capital assets, a reclassification is made for the net assets temporarily restricted for plant released from restriction.

20a.	Depreciation of Buildings and Equipment	4,185	
	Allowance for Depreciation—Building		1,145
	Allowance for Depreciation—Equipment		3,040
20b.	Net Assets Released—Satisfaction of Plant Restrictions—Temporarily Restricted	4,185	
	Net Assets Released—Satisfaction of Plant Restrictions—Unrestricted		4,185

End-of-the-Year Reclassification Journal Entries

Miscellaneous expenses for mortgage interest (in Entry 13a) and depreciation expense (in Entry 20a) were allocated to program services and supporting services. The allocation is assumed to be as shown in Entry 21.

21.	Counseling Program Expenses	2,480	
	Adoption Program Expenses	990	
	Foster Home Care Program Expenses	2,510	
	Special Outreach Project Program Expenses	2,050	
	Management and General Support Expenses	530	
	Fund-Raising Support Expenses	165	
	Miscellaneous Expense		4,540
	Depreciation of Buildings and Equipment		4,185

The natural classification of expenses in Entry 7 were allocated to the Special Outreach Project.

22.	Special Outreach Project Program Expenses	23,100	
	Professional Fees Expense		17,000
	Supplies Expense		4,500
	Printing and Publications Expense		1,600

Except for Cost of Sales to the Public (Entry 8), Provision for Uncollectible Pledges (Entry 19), and Professional Fees (see Entry 15), the remaining natural classification of expenses (in Entries 6, 8, and 17b) were allocated to the various program and support categories in the assumed amounts shown in Entry 23. Costs of Sales to the Public (Entry 8) will be netted with Sales to the Public. Provision for Uncollectible Pledges (Entry 19) was allocated to Management and General Expense.

		Debits	Credits
23.	Counseling Program Expenses	183,033	
	Adoption Program Expenses	68,570	
	Foster Home Care Program Expenses	170,021	
	Special Outreach Project Program Expenses	37,720	
	Management and General Support Expenses	52,659	
	Fund-raising Support Expenses	22,387	
	Salaries Expense		265,000
	Employee Benefits Expense		51,000
	Payroll Taxes Expense		20,300
	Professional Fees Expense		51,574
	Supplies Expense		11,795
	Telephone Expense		9,800
	Postage and Shipping Expense		8,117
	Occupancy Expense		23,900
	Rental and Maintenance of Equipment		8,700
	Printing and Publications Expense		7,900
	Travel Expense		22,000
	Conferences, Conventions, and Meetings		13,800
	Specific Assistance to Individuals		35,500
	Membership Dues		700
	Provision for Uncollectible Pledges		104
	Miscellaneous Expense		4,200

Unrestricted net assets that were designated by the board for the Special Outreach Project were deemed no longer necessary; the board authorized the return of the amount, $30,000, to Unrestricted Net Assets—Undesignated. Based on an analysis of transactions, management determined that $27,400 should be released from temporary restriction. This includes the temporarily restricted net assets on the 2016 trial balance ($3,900) and expenses of $23,500 that were incurred in the current reporting period.

24.	Unrestricted Net Assets—Designated for Special Outreach Project	30,000	
	Unrestricted Net Assets—Undesignated—Available for Operations		30,000
	Net Assets Released—Satisfaction of Program Restrictions—Temporarily Restricted	27,400	
	Net Assets Released—Satisfaction of Program Restrictions—Unrestricted		27,400

End-of-the-Year Closing Journal Entries

The following closing journal entries are made: (*a*) reclassifications for net assets released are closed into the appropriate categories of net assets, (*b*) unrestricted support and revenue are closed to unrestricted net assets, (*c*) program and support expenses are closed to unrestricted net assets, (*d*) temporarily restricted support for programs, plant, and time are closed to temporarily restricted net assets, (*e*) permanently restricted support is closed to permanently restricted net assets, if any, and (*f*) unrealized losses are closed to the appropriate net asset categories.

		Debits	Credits
25a.	Temporarily Restricted Net Assets—Time	5,125	
	Net Assets Released—Expiration of Time Restrictions—Unrestricted	5,125	
	Net Assets Released—Expiration of Time Restriction—Temporarily Restricted		5,125
	Unrestricted Net Assets—Undesignated—Available for Operations		5,125
	Temporarily Restricted Net Assets—Plant	4,185	
	Net Assets Released—Satisfaction of Plant Restrictions—Unrestricted	4,185	
	Net Assets Released—Satisfaction of Plant Restrictions—Temporarily Restricted		4,185
	Unrestricted Net Assets—Undesignated—Available for Operations		4,185
	Temporarily Restricted Net Assets—Program	27,400	
	Net Assets Released—Satisfaction of Program Restrictions—Unrestricted	27,400	
	Net Assets Released—Satisfaction of Program Restrictions—Temporarily Restricted		27,400
	Unrestricted Net Assets—Undesignated—Available for Operations		27,400
25b.	Contributions—Unrestricted	401,500	
	Sales to the Public	1,000	
	Membership Dues—Individuals	1,000	
	Program Service Fees	55,000	
	Investment Income—Unrestricted	15,680	
	Miscellaneous Revenue	1,500	
	Unrestricted Net Assets—Undesignated—Available for Operations		475,680
25c.	Unrestricted Net Assets—Undesignated—Available for Operations	580,315	
	Counseling Program Expenses		185,513
	Adoption Program Expenses		69,560
	Foster Home Care Program Expenses		172,531
	Special Outreach Project Program Expenses		62,870
	Cost of Sales to Public		900
	Management and General Support Expenses		53,189
	Fund-Raising Support Expenses		35,752
25d.	Contributions—Temporarily Restricted—Program	32,750	
	Contributions—Temporarily Restricted—Time	10,000	
	Contributions—Temporarily Restricted—Plant	4,000	
	Investment Income—Temporarily Restricted—Plant	1,390	
	Temporarily Restricted Net Assets—Program		29,750
	Temporarily Restricted Net Assets—Plant		5,390
	Temporarily Restricted Net Assets—Time		10,000
	Direct Costs—Special Outreach Project—Program		3,000
25e.	Contributions—Permanently Restricted	100,000	
	Permanently Restricted Net Assets		100,000

		Debits	Credits
25f.	Permanently Restricted Net Assets	4,000	
	Unrestricted Net Assets—Undesignated—Available for Operations	3,000	
	Unrealized Loss on Investments—Permanently Restricted		4,000
	Unrealized Loss on Investments—Unrestricted		3,000

Illustrations 13–6 through 13–8 present the statement of financial position, statement of activities, and statement of cash flows for the Community Family Service Agency, reflecting the effects of the illustrative transactions for the year. Since the agency is a voluntary health and welfare organization, it must also prepare a statement

ILLUSTRATION 13–6

COMMUNITY FAMILY SERVICE AGENCY, INC.
Statement of Financial Position
December 31, 2017, and 2016

	2017	2016
Assets:		
Cash	$ 28,953	$ 58,711
Short-term investments, at fair value	22,000	22,000
Accounts receivable (net)	1,150	2,350
Contributions receivable (net)	6,061	5,165
Supplies, at lower of cost or market	19,100	23,095
Prepaid expense	3,600	3,917
Assets restricted:		
For land, buildings, and equipment:		
Investments, at fair value	15,000	20,000
Contributions receivable (net)	982	10,182
For endowment:		
Cash	100,000	
Investments, at fair value	226,000	230,000
Land, buildings, and equipment, less allowance for accumulated depreciation of $17,961 and $13,776	104,763	103,948
Long-term investments	14,000	17,000
Total assets	$541,609	$496,368
Liabilities:		
Accounts payable and accrued expenses	$ 44,147	$ 25,911
8.25% mortgage payable, due 2029	48,500	55,000
Total liabilities	92,647	80,911
Net assets:		
Unrestricted	26,377	97,302
Temporarily restricted	96,585	88,155
Permanently restricted	326,000	230,000
Total net assets	448,962	415,457
Total liabilities and net assets	$541,609	$496,368

of functional expenses, which is presented in Illustration 13–9. As shown in Illustration 13–7, the statement of activities reports the increases and decreases that occurred during the year in each of the three categories of net assets—unrestricted, temporarily restricted, and permanently restricted. As the financial statements for the American Diabetes Association show (see Illustrations 13–2 through 13–5 earlier in this chapter), larger VHWOs will have more complex transactions than those illustrated for the hypothetical Community Family Service Agency.

ILLUSTRATION 13–7

COMMUNITY FAMILY SERVICE AGENCY, INC.
Statement of Activities
For the Year Ended December 31, 2017

	Unrestricted	Temporarily Restricted	Permanently Restricted	Total 2014
Revenues, gains and other support:				
Contributions	$401,500	$36,500	$100,000	$538,000
Special events		10,250		
Less: Direct costs		3,000		
Net special events		7,250		7,250
Program service fees	55,000			55,000
Membership dues	1,000			1,000
Sales to the public (net)	100			100
Investment income	15,680	1,390		17,070
Miscellaneous	1,500			1,500
Net assets released from restrictions:				
Satisfaction of program requirements	27,400	(27,400)		
Satisfaction of equipment acquisition restrictions	4,185	(4,185)		
Expiration of time restrictions	5,125	(5,125)		
Total revenues, gains, and other support	511,490	8,430	100,000	619,920
Expenses and losses:				
Program services:				
Counseling	185,513			185,513
Adoption	69,560			69,560
Foster home care	172,531			172,531
Special outreach project	62,870			62,870
Total program expenses	490,474			490,474
Support expenses:				
Management and general	53,189			53,189
Fund-raising	35,752			35,752
Total support expenses	88,941			88,941
Unrealized loss on investments	3,000		4,000	7,000
Total expenses and losses	582,415		4,000	586,415
Change in net assets	(70,925)	8,430	96,000	33,505
Net assets, December 31, 2016	97,302	88,155	230,000	415,457
Net assets, December 31, 2017	$ 26,377	$96,585	$326,000	$448,962

ILLUSTRATION 13–8

COMMUNITY FAMILY SERVICE AGENCY, INC.
Statement of Cash Flows
Year Ended December 31, 2017

Cash flows from operating activities:	
Cash received from contributors	$345,300
Cash collected on contributions receivable	68,500
Cash received from service recipients	57,200
Cash collected from members	1,000
Investment income	15,680
Miscellaneous receipts	1,750
Cash paid to employees and suppliers	(538,738)
Interest paid	(4,540)
Net cash used for operating activities	(53,848)
Cash flows from investing activities:	
Purchase of equipment	(5,000)
Proceeds from sale of investments	5,000
Net cash used by investing activities	0
Cash flows from financing activities:	
Proceeds from contributions restricted for:	
Investment in plant	13,200
Future operations	16,000
Endowments	100,000
Other financing activities:	
Interest and dividends restricted for plant acquisition	1,390
Repayment of long-term debt	(6,500)
Net cash provided by financing activities	124,090
Net increase (decrease) in cash	70,242
Cash, December 31, 2016	58,711
Cash, December 31, 2017 (Note A)	$128,953
Reconciliation of changes in net assets to net cash used for operating activities:	
Change in net assets	$ 33,505
Adjustments to reconcile changes in net assets to net cash provided by operating activities:	
Depreciation	4,185
Decrease in accounts receivable, net	1,200
Decrease in contributions receivable, net	8,304
Decrease in supplies	3,995
Decrease in prepaid expenses	317
Increase in accounts payable and accrued expenses	18,236
Gifts, grants, and bequests restricted for long-term investment	(129,200)
Interest restricted for long-term investment	(1,390)
Unrealized loss on investments	7,000
Cash used for operating activities	$ (53,848)

Note A: Includes regular operating cash and cash restricted for endowment.

ILLUSTRATION 13–9

COMMUNITY FAMILY SERVICE AGENCY, INC.
Statement of Functional Expenses
Year Ended December 31, 2017
(with comparative totals for 2016)

	Program Services					Supporting Services			Total Program and Supporting Services Expenses	
	Counseling	Adoption	Foster Home Care	Special Outreach Project	Total	Management and General	Fund-raising	Total	2017	2016
Salaries	$ 87,720	$36,559	$ 83,610	$13,738	$221,627	$35,153	$ 8,220	$43,373	$265,000	$232,170
Employee benefits	16,882	7,036	16,091	2,644	42,653	6,765	1,582	8,347	51,000	47,035
Payroll taxes	6,720	2,801	6,405	1,051	16,977	2,693	630	3,323	20,300	11,400
Total salaries and related expenses	111,322	46,396	106,106	17,433	281,257	44,611	10,432	55,043	336,300	290,605
Professional fees	25,107	3,929	11,643	18,143	58,822	1,178	8,574	9,752	68,574	54,600
Supplies	4,049	2,167	4,747	3,950	14,913	790	592	1,382	16,295	8,500
Telephone	3,897	1,430	3,350	190	8,867	600	333	933	9,800	9,610
Postage and shipping	2,840	1,073	2,402	908	7,223	684	210	894	8,117	6,750
Occupancy	8,772	1,415	8,078	2,586	20,851	2,468	581	3,049	23,900	24,600
Rental and maintenance of equipment	3,669	1,520	3,511	—	8,700	—	—	—	8,700	8,750
Printing and publications	2,761	1,420	1,352	1,462	6,995	940	1,565	2,505	9,500	7,200
Travel	7,700	1,500	7,500	5,000	21,700	300	—	300	22,000	24,000
Conferences, conventions, meetings	3,450	887	4,436	4,436	13,209	591	—	591	13,800	13,700
Specific assistance to individuals	9,000	6,500	16,100	3,900	36,500	—	—	—	36,500	28,500
Membership dues	234	187	93	93	607	93	—	93	700	677
Fee to United Way	—	—	—	—	—	—	13,200	13,200	13,200	—
Provision for uncollectible pledges	—	—	—	—	—	104	—	104	104	—
Miscellaneous	1,744	843	1,891	4,144	8,622	118	—	118	8,740	5,200
Total before depreciation	184,545	69,267	171,209	62,245	487,266	52,477	35,487	87,964	575,230	487,692
Depreciation of buildings and equipment	968	293	1,322	625	3,208	712	265	977	4,185	4,200
Total expenses	$185,513	$69,560	$172,531	$62,870	$490,474	$53,189	$35,752	$88,941	$579,415	$491,892

Appendix

Optional Fund Accounting

Fund accounting was defined and illustrated in Chapters 1 through 9 for governments as a method of segregating assets, liabilities, and fund balances into separate accounting entities associated with specific activities, donor-imposed restrictions, or obligations. Similarly, a fund accounting system makes it possible to determine compliance with laws, regulations, and agreements and to demonstrate that the NFP is meeting its stewardship responsibility to resource providers. Many NFPs still use this accounting method for internal management and grant reporting purposes. As mentioned previously, FASB permits not-for-profit organizations to also present disaggregated data classified by fund groups as long as the aggregated net asset statements are also presented. Fund categories described in the AICPA Audit and Accounting Guide, *Not-for-Profit Organizations,* follow:

- Unrestricted current or operating, or general funds.
- Restricted current or operating, or specific purpose, funds.
- Plant funds (or land, building, and equipment funds).
- Loan funds.
- Endowment funds.
- Annuity and life income (split-interest) funds.
- Agency funds (or custodian funds).[29]

All NFP funds are self-balancing sets of accounts that are both accounting entities and fiscal entities maintained on the full accrual basis—except the agency funds, which report only assets and liabilities. The residual difference between total assets and total liabilities in a fund is labeled *fund balance.* Net assets also represent residual interests, but net assets are not the same as fund balances, in part because all expenses reduce unrestricted net assets under FASB *ASC* 958-205 and in a fund accounting system, operating funds reflect both revenues and expenses.

Unrestricted current funds are used to account for all resources that may be used at the discretion of the governing board for carrying on the operations of the organization, including assets designated by the board for specific purposes. Restricted current funds account for resources that may be used for operations but have been *restricted* by the stipulations of donors or grantors. Current liabilities are recorded in the appropriate fund, depending on which funds will be used to pay them.

Plant funds are used to account for land, buildings, and equipment used by not-for-profit organizations in the conduct of their operations; liabilities relating to the acquisition or improvement of plant assets; and cash, investments, or receivables contributed specifically for acquiring, replacing, or improving the plant. Loan funds account for loans made to students, employees, and other constituents; consequently, they appear most often in accounting for colleges and universities.

The principal amounts of gifts and bequests that must, under the terms of agreements with donors, be maintained intact in perpetuity or until the occurrence of a specified event or for a specified time period are accounted for as endowment funds. Other gifts may take the form of split interests in which donors retain some of the gift (either the income or principal) for a period of time, sometimes until their death.

[29] AICPA, AAG-NFP Entities, pars. 16.01–16.25.

Annuity funds are used when the donor specifies an amount of income to be paid to the donor or to a designated third party for a specified period. A life income fund is used when the donor stipulates that all income will be paid to the donor or a designated third party, with the principal reverting to the NFP upon the donor's death or at some other specified time.

Agency or custodian funds are established to account for assets received by an organization to be held or disbursed only according to the instructions of the person or organization from whom they were received. Assets of a custodian fund belong to donors and are not assets of the organization; income generated from the assets is added to the appropriate liability account. For these reasons, neither the receipt of assets to be held in custody nor the receipt of income from those assets should be reported by the NFP organization as revenue or support. Assets of custodian funds and the offsetting liabilities should not be combined with assets and liabilities of other funds.

NFPs that use fund accounting recognize revenues and expenses for current operating funds. This practice makes it relatively easy for NFPs to prepare the aggregated entity-wide financial statements required by FASB. Unrestricted current fund balance is reported as unrestricted net assets, restricted current fund balances as temporarily restricted net assets, and *pure* endowment fund balance as permanently restricted net assets. The remaining fund balances can contain elements of each category, and the terms of their existence must be examined for donor restrictions. All interfund receivables and payables must be eliminated in preparing entity-wide statements. Fund accounting for not-for-profit entities is not illustrated in this chapter.

Key Terms

Acquisition, *544*
Board-designated net assets, *527*
Collections, *542*
Conditional promise to give, *534*
Contribution, *534*
Endowments, *527*
Exchange transactions, *533*
Federated fund-raising organization, *539*
Financially interrelated, *539*
Gains, *533*
Gifts in kind, *536*
Intermediary, *538*
Merger, *544*
Net assets, *527*
Nonexchange transactions, *533*
Other nonprofit organizations (ONPOs), *525*
Permanently restricted net assets, *527*
Promise to give, *534*
Revenue, *533*
Support, *533*
Temporarily restricted net assets, *527*
Unconditional promise to give, *534*
Unrestricted net assets, *527*
Variance power, *539*
Voluntary health and welfare organizations (VHWOs), *524*

Selected References

American Institute of Certified Public Accountants. Audit and Accounting Guide, *Not-for-Profit Entities.* New York: AICPA, 2014.

Berger, Steven. *Understanding Nonprofit Financial Statements,* 3rd ed. Washington, DC: BoardSource, 2008.

Financial Accounting Standards Board. *Accounting Standards Codification,* Section 958. Norwalk, CT: FASB (on-line).

McCarthy, John H., Nancy E. Shelmon, and John Mattie. *Financial Accounting Guide for Not-for-Profit Organizations,* 8th ed. New Jersey: John Wiley & Sons, 2012, and Cumulative Supplement, 2013.

Questions

13–1. This chapter divides not-for-profit entities into four categories that align with accounting and auditing standards. What are the four categories and what types of entities are included in each?

13–2. Discuss how characteristics of not-for-profit organizations and public sector organizations are similar and how they differ.

13–3. Discuss some of the differences in the preparation and presentation of the operating statements of nongovernmental not-for-profit entities and governmental not-for-profit entities reporting as business-type entities.

13–4. What are the three categories into which NFPs must classify their net assets? Describe which net assets are included in each category. Would *board-designated net assets* be reported as *temporarily restricted net assets*? Explain your answer.

13–5. What is the value of a statement of functional expenses? What is the FASB and the Financial Reporting Executive Committee's position on who should prepare a statement of functional expenses? Explain why you believe they have taken the positions they have.

13–6. What is the difference between an unconditional and a conditional pledge? How are the two pledges reported?

13–7. Distinguish between *program services* expenses and *supporting services* expenses. Why is it important that NFPs report expenses for program services separately from those for supporting services?

13–8. What criteria must be met before a not-for-profit organization can record donated services? If the criteria are met, how should donated services be recorded? Give examples to support your answer.

13–9. The new administrator for the art museum was concerned that the museum's collection of rare 17th-century American porcelain was not recognized on the financial statements. Explain to the administrator why the collection might not be recognized on the financial statements.

13–10. What are joint costs and how are joint costs recorded?

Cases

13–11 Temporarily Restricted Net Assets. For several years, Baytown Rehabilitative Camp for Disabled Children (hereafter referred to as the camp) has applied for an operating grant from the Baytown Area United Way. As the finance adviser for the local United Way allocation panel, it is your responsibility to evaluate the camp's budget request for the forthcoming year and its audited financial statements. The camp's most recent comparative statement of financial position and statement of activities are presented below.

BAYTOWN REHABILITATIVE CAMP FOR DISABLED CHILDREN
Statement of Financial Position
December 31, 2017, and 2016

	2017	2016
Assets		
Current assets		
Cash	$ 36,802	$ 12,248
Contributions receivable	28,728	16,372
Prepaid expenses	15,559	17,748
Total current assets	81,089	46,368

Investments—Temporarily restricted	90,434	122,368
Property, plant, and equipment		
Land	175,000	175,000
Buildings and building improvements (net of accumulated depreciation of $137,440 and $130,200)	449,768	457,008
Equipment (net of accumulated depreciation of $195,370 and $186,788)	185,342	171,924
Total property, plant, and equipment	810,110	803,932
Total assets	$981,633	$972,668
Liabilities and Net Assets		
Current liabilities		
Accounts payable	$ 23,852	$ 35,722
Accrued payroll and other accrued liabilities	5,289	5,064
Total current liabilities	29,141	40,786
Net assets		
Unrestricted	862,058	809,514
Temporarily restricted	90,434	122,368
Total net assets	952,492	931,882
Total liabilities and net assets	$981,633	$972,668

BAYTOWN REHABILITATIVE CAMP FOR DISABLED CHILDREN
Statement of Activities
For the Year Ended December 31, 2017

	Unrestricted	Temporarily Restricted	Total
Revenues and other support			
Contributions	$ 65,250	$ 20,000	$ 85,250
United Way allocation	25,000		25,000
Charges to clients	34,400		34,400
Donated goods and services	105,160		105,160
Interest	154	5,566	5,720
Miscellaneous	4,012		4,012
Net assets released from restriction satisfaction of purpose	57,500	(57,500)	-0-
Total revenues and other support	291,476	(31,934)	259,542
Expenses			
Program services	152,828		152,828
Management and general	77,604		77,604
Fund-raising	8,500		8,500
Total expenses	238,932		238,932
Increase (decrease) in net assets	52,544	(31,934)	20,610
Net assets, December 31, 2016	809,514	122,368	931,882
Net assets, December 31, 2017	$862,058	$ 90,434	$952,492

Additional Information: As reflected in the camp's 2017 statement of activities, the United Way agency allocated $25,000 to the camp for fiscal year 2017. However, the amount allocated was $5,000 less than the camp had requested in its fiscal year 2017 budget, reflecting the allocation panel's concern about the camp's financial reserves (representing about 12 days in 2016) and low ratio of program services expense to total expense (only 57 percent in 2016). As a condition for receiving the $25,000 fiscal year 2017 allocation, Baytown Rehabilitative Camp agreed to take actions to improve its financial reserves and its ratio of program services expense to total expense, including an increase in its fund-raising efforts and a reduction in its support payroll.

Another area of concern to the allocation panel has been the camp's long delay in using a restricted contribution of $100,000 received several years earlier. This gift was restricted by the donor for future expansion of a building used as a dining hall and for rehabilitative activities. This contribution has been invested in CDs and has grown to $122,368 as of December 31, 2016.

The camp is requesting a $35,000 United Way allocation for fiscal year 2018, based on a growing demand for its services and improvement made in its financial condition. As financial adviser for the local United Way allocation panel, however, you note that much of the improvement in unrestricted net assets resulted from $37,500 of temporarily restricted net assets that were released from restriction during fiscal year 2017, with no corresponding increase in the balance of the Buildings and Building Improvements account. (*Note:* $20,000 of the $57,500 released from restriction related to $20,000 of temporarily restricted contributions received during 2017.) You immediately contact the camp administrator for an explanation, whereupon she explains that the board of directors voted to use $37,500 of previously restricted investments for operating purposes after the administrator reported to the board that the original agreement with the donor could not be located and the donor was now deceased. She further indicated that the board may continue to use this pool of resources to further improve the camp's financial condition.

Required

a. As financial adviser, evaluate the camp's statement of financial position and statement of activities and prepare a report for the chair of the allocation committee indicating the extent to which the camp's financial situation has improved or worsened. In your analysis, you should look at the camp's unrestricted financial position, both including and excluding the use of the $37,500 of temporarily restricted net assets for operating purposes. As part of your analysis, you should consider liquidity (current and/or quick ratio), days of financial reserves, and effectiveness (program expenses/total expenses). Financial reserves ratio is calculated as working capital (current assets − current liabilities) divided by expenses. To calculate the number of days of financial reserves available to cover expenses, multiply the financial reserves ratio by 365 days.

b. What is your reaction to the board of directors' decision to use, for operating purposes, the $100,000 temporarily restricted net assets provided by a donor for building expansion?

c. What amount of United Way funds would you recommend be allocated to the camp for fiscal year 2018? Explain your recommendation.

13–12 Research Case—Not-for-Profit Reporting Model. In November of 2011, the FASB announced two new projects related to financial reporting of not-for-profit organizations. One of the projects was a research project that was subsequently dropped from the agenda; as a result, the standard-setting project was renamed "Financial Statements of Not-For-Profit Entities." As this textbook goes to press, the FASB has tentatively scheduled the release of an exposure draft in the second half of 2014. The board has reached tentative conclusions about several NFP issues, including reporting of net assets. The board proposes that net assets be reported in two net asset categories—net assets *with donor-imposed restrictions* and net assets *without donor-imposed restrictions*—instead of the currently required three net asset categories of unrestricted net assets, temporarily restricted net assets, and permanently restricted net assets.

Required

a. Research the current status of the FASB project. (*Hint:* the FASB Web site is *www.fasb.org*. However, you may wish to also search for other current articles about the project.) Write a summary of the current reporting requirement for net assets and compare that with the proposed reporting requirement for net assets.

b. Why is the FASB proposing this change in net asset reporting? In other words, how will the proposed changes improve financial reporting for NFP organizations?

c. In addition to the net asset classification component of the project, there was one other overall objective. Identify the objective and discuss what, if any, proposals are being considered as part of this objective.

d. After having performed this research, what is your opinion? Do you believe the proposed changes will in fact improve financial reporting? Explain the rationale for the position you take.

13–13 Research Case—Governmental or Not-for-Profit Entity? In partnership with Jefferson County, Mound City recently established a Native American Heritage Center and Museum, organized as a tax-exempt not-for-profit organization. Although the facility does not charge admission, signs at the information desk in the entry lobby encourage gifts of $3.00 for adults and $1.00 for children, 12 and under. Many visitors make the recommended contribution, some contribute larger amounts, and some do not contribute at all. Such contributions comprise 40 percent of the museum's total annual revenues, with net proceeds from fund-raising events and governmental grants comprising the remaining 60 percent. The center operates from a city-owned building for which it pays a nominal $1 per year in rent. Except for a full-time executive director and a part-time assistant, the center is staffed by unpaid volunteers. The center is governed by a six-member board of directors, each appointed for a three-year term. Two of the directors are appointed by the Mound City Council, one by the Jefferson County

Commission, two by the Mound City/Jefferson County Business Council, and one director is a Native American appointed by the local Tribe to represent Tribal interests. Should the center cease to operate, its charter provides that net assets be allocated as follows: all artifacts will revert to the local Tribe; of the remaining net assets, 25 percent will go to the city, 15 percent will go to the county, and the remaining amount will be donated to the State Historical Society.

At the end of its first year of operation, the board of directors decided to engage a local CPA to conduct an audit of the center's financial statements. The board expects to receive an unqualified (clean) audit opinion stating that its financial statements are presented fairly in conformity with generally accepted accounting principles.

Required

Assume you are the CPA who has been engaged to conduct this audit. To which standards-setting body (or bodies) would you look for accounting and financial reporting standards to assist you in determining whether the center's financial statements are in conformity with generally accepted accounting principles? Explain how you arrived at this conclusion.

Exercises and Problems

13–14 Multiple Choice. Choose the best answer.

1. Which of the following organizations would be considered a nongovernmental not-for-profit organization?
   a. An organization that provides shelter for men who have been victims of domestic violence and has been designated as a not-for-profit organization by the IRS. The board of trustees is composed of county commissioners, but in the case of the dissolution of the organization, any remaining funds would be donated to the United Way. Funding for the organization comes entirely from contributions.
   b. An organization that provides services to persons who wish to learn English as their second language. The organization is incorporated and is funded by fees charged to the learners. All profits are reinvested in the organization to provide further services. The organization has applied for not-for-profit status with the IRS.
   c. An organization classified by the IRS as a not-for-profit organization that employs individuals with disabilities in a workshop where the workers make custom stationery out of recycled goods. The organization receives cash and in-kind contributions as well as the proceeds from the sale of the stationery. The organization's board is composed of local businessmen and women.
   d. An organization that provides fund-raising services for other not-for-profit organizations. The organization is funded by fees for its services and was incorporated by the former chairperson of the local United Way organization. The organization distributes 40 percent of its profits to local charities.
2. According to GAAP, all not-for-profit organizations are required to prepare
   a. A statement of activities, a statement of functional expense, and a statement of cash flows using accrual accounting.
   b. A statement of activities, a balance sheet, and a statement of cash flows using accrual accounting.

c. A statement of financial position, a statement of activities, a statement of cash flows and a statement of functional expenses using accrual accounting.
d. A statement of cash flows, a statement of activities, and a statement of financial position using either cash basis or accrual basis accounting.

3. Jane's Planes is an organization that provides air transportation for critically ill children. A friend of Jane's Planes, Richard Bucks donated a plane to be used over its remaining life solely for transportation of critically ill children. In addition, he donated a substantial amount of investments that were to be used strictly to generate income to help fund the organization's expenses. These donations would be included in the organization's net assets as:

	Plane	***Investments***
a.	Permanently restricted	Permanently restricted
b.	Temporarily restricted	Permanently restricted
c.	Permanently restricted	Temporarily restricted
d.	Temporarily restricted	Temporarily restricted

4. In a local NFP elementary school's statement of cash flows, a contribution restricted for use on a new building project would be reported as:
   a. A financing activity.
   b. A capital and related financing activity.
   c. An investing activity.
   d. An operating activity.
5. A wealthy donor promised $1 million to the local art museum to expand the size of its building, contingent on the museum obtaining a grant from the State Endowment for the Arts of at least $500,000. Upon completing a signed agreement with the donor, the museum should:
   a. Record a debit to Contributions Receivable—Temporarily Restricted in the amount of $1,000,000.
   b. Record a debit to Contributions Receivable—Temporarily Restricted in the amount of $500,000.
   c. Not make a journal entry until the conditions of the agreement have been met.
   d. Either *a* or *c* are permissible, depending on the museum's established policy.
6. Orlando Perez, president of a local information systems company, volunteered his time to help develop software for Best Friends, a local no-kill pet shelter. The software will allow the organization to track intake, placement, and statistics of animals in its three locations. Without Mr. Perez's assistance, Best Friends would have needed to hire someone to develop this software. Best Friends should record the value of Mr. Perez's time as:
   a. Program revenue and supporting services expense.
   b. Contribution revenue and supporting services expense.
   c. Program revenue and program expense.
   d. Contribution revenue and a program expense.

7. The Maryville Cultural Center recently conducted a successful talent show in which local talent performed for a nominal prize. The talent show is an ongoing major event and is central to the center's mission. The event raised $4,800 in gross revenue. Expenses related to the event included $1,000 to rent an auditorium, $1,200 to advertise the event, $500 for trophies and other awards for the winner and the runners up, and $100 for printing and mailing tickets. The center believes there was no monetary value received by donors (attendees). To report this event in its statement of activities, the center will report:
   a. Special event revenue of $4,800 and special event expense of $1,500.
   b. Special event revenue of $4,800 and fund-raising expense of $1,300.
   c. Special event revenue of $2,300 and fund-raising expense of $1,300.
   d. Both *a* and *b* are correct.
8. Many not-for-profit organizations attempt to classify fund-raising expenses as program services expenses by making the activities look educational in nature or advocating for the mission of the organization. For such expenses to be reported as program services expenses, they must meet which of the following three criteria:
   a. Purpose, mission-related, and benefit to the public.
   b. Purpose, audience, and content.
   c. Purpose, expand donor base, and content.
   d. Reasonable, improve financial condition, and benefit to the public.
9. Save Our Beaches, a NFP organization, prepared and distributed a tri-fold flyer to individuals and families at White Sands Beach, a popular beach for both residents and tourists. The flyer provided information about beach pollution and invited the public to participate in the organization's semi-annual beach cleanup. In addition, one segment of the flyer solicited contributions to the organization to help fund its activities. The cost of the flyer and its distribution would be considered:
   a. A fund-raising cost.
   b. A program cost.
   c. Both a fund-raising and program cost.
   d. A management and general expense.
10. A particular organization functions as an intermediary between donors and other beneficiary organizations. The intermediary organization must report contribution revenue from donors if:
    a. The organization has variance power.
    b. The organization elects to consistently report such donor gifts as contribution revenue.
    c. The beneficiary organization requests a delay in receiving the contribution from the intermediary organization.
    d. All of the above are correct.

13–15 Classification of Revenues and Contributions. For each of the independent transactions listed in the left-hand column below, indicate which of the revenue or contribution classifications apply by choosing one or more of the letters from the listed items in the right-hand column. Choose all that apply.

	Transaction	Revenue and Contribution Classifications
________	1. A museum gift shop sold prints of famous paintings.	*a.* Revenue
________	2. At the end of the year a donor agreed to contribute $400,000 to a local artists' fund if the museum raised a matching amount in the first quarter of the upcoming year.	*b.* Contributions—Unrestricted
________	3. A registered nurse volunteered 10 hours a week to a local agency for disabled persons.	*c.* Contributions—Temporarily Restricted
________	4. A donor contributed $1 million to a not-for-profit hospital for a new clinic.	*d.* Contributions—Permanently Restricted
________	5. An NFP art association hosted its annual art exhibition for the association's major contributors.	*e.* None of the above
________	6. A donor contributed securities valued at $10 million to be permanently invested. Earnings thereon are stipulated by the donor to be used for eye research.	
________	7. A local computer store donated computers for children's use at an NFP hands-on children's museum.	
________	8. A local PTA received cash contributions of $2,000 to be used for its operating activities.	

13–16 Donated Services. Indicate whether each of the following donated services situations would require a journal entry for contribution revenue and a related expense or asset by circling Y for yes or N for no.

Y N 1. Volunteers worked as sales assistants in a not-for-profit hospital snack shop.

Y N 2. An architect provided *pro bono* design services for the planned remodeling of a local museum.

Y N 3. A member of a church volunteered to repaint the church's activities room to make it more attractive. Church leaders had not planned to repaint the room.

Y N 4. Several local persons used their cars to deliver meals to senior citizens for Meals on Wheels.

Y N 5. A psychiatrist volunteered several hours each week at a not-for-profit counseling center to assist persons with alcohol and drug addiction.

Y N 6. A local CPA firm performed the regular annual financial statement audit for the university's chapter of Beta Alpha Psi.

Y N 7. A local pastor donated several hours weekly to the local food bank run by an NFP.

Y N 8. A registered dietitian donates several hours each summer providing dietary instruction to children with diabetes who are attending a camp sponsored by the local chapter of the American Diabetes Association.

13–17 Joint Activities with a Fund-Raising Appeal. Consider the following scenarios relating to activities that include a fund-raising appeal:

1. The Green Group's mission is to protect the environment by increasing the portion of waste recycled by the public. The group conducts a door-to-door canvass of communities that recycle a low portion of their waste. The canvassers share their knowledge about the environmental problems caused by not recycling with households, asking them to change their recycling habits. The canvassers also ask for charitable contributions to continue this work, although these canvassers have not participated in fund-raising activities before.
2. The mission of Kid's Camp is to provide summer camps for economically disadvantaged youths. It conducts a door-to-door solicitation campaign for its camp programs by sending volunteers to homes in upper-class neighborhoods. The volunteers explain the camp's programs and distribute leaflets explaining the organization's mission. Solicitors say, "Although your own children most likely are not eligible to attend this camp, we ask for your financial support, so that children less fortunate can have this summer camp experience."
3. The Save the Ridley Turtles Society is a NFP organization whose mission it is to save the Ridley turtles from extinction and educate the public about the turtles. The society invites the citizens of the coastal areas where the turtles nest to a lecture on the nesting habits of the turtle. It also explains how people can play a role in improving the successful hatching of the turtle eggs in their area. At the conclusion of the lecture, the members of the society request donations to help prevent the extinction of the Ridley turtle.
4. The Citizens for Firefighters is a NFP organization that supports the mission of the city's firefighters. The organization sponsored a telephone campaign in which it called homes in the fire district and provided a list of five simple activities the homeowner could take to help reduce the probability of fires. The caller recommended that these simple steps be taken by the homeowner. Additionally, the caller asked for a donation and said that with the donation the homeowner would receive a pamphlet outlining the five activities along with other suggestions. The Citizens for Firefighters hired a firm to conduct its campaign. The firm conducting the campaign charged a 60 percent fee on the gross contributions received.

Required

Determine for each scenario whether its purpose, audience, and content meet the criteria described in this chapter and FASB *ASC* 958-720-45, so that the joint costs can be allocated between programs and support expenses. Explain your reasons.

13–18 Identify Departures from GAAP. The statement of activities for the ECE Children's Learning Center for fiscal year 2017, prepared by a newly hired budget employee with no NFP experience, is presented on the following page.

ECE CHILDREN'S' LEARNING CENTER
Statement of Activities
For the Period Ended June 30, 2017

	Unrestricted	Temporarily Restricted	Permanently Restricted	Total
Revenues:				
Admission fees	$ 732,000	$ —	$ —	$ 732,000
Special events revenue	125,000	—	—	125,000
Program fees	554,450	—	150,000	704,450
Contributions	792,320	539,770	300,000	1,632,090
Grants	50,000	—	—	50,000
Investment income	955	112	213,096	214,163
Total revenues	2,254,725	539,882	663,096	3,457,703
Expenses:				
Center for creativity	947,173	582,834	—	1,530,007
Outdoor experiences	522,297	—	311,854	834,151
Management & fund-raising	603,337	—	—	603,337
Depreciation	10,735	—	—	10,735
Total expenses	2,083,542	582,834	311,854	2,978,230
Decrease in net assets	171,183	(42,952)	351,242	479,473
Beginning net assets	798,011	33,245	2,500,767	3,332,023
Ending net assets	$ 969,194	$ (9,707)	$2,852,009	$3,811,496

Required

a. Because you are taking a not-for-profit course, a friend who sits on the board of the ECE has asked you to review its statement of activities. Your friend has a concern about the statement since it doesn't look quite the same as it did last year. Given that the ECE opted to hire someone without NFP experience, your friend has concerns that the statement may not be properly presented. Make a list of modifications or corrections that you believe should be made to the statement to ensure it is presented in conformance with GAAP.

b. Your friend indicates that the center is facing an upcoming audit. What concern would you have for the ECE regarding its audit, based on the financial statement it has prepared?

13–19 Statement of Activities. The Atkins Museum recently hired a new controller. His experience with managerial accounting and strong communication skills were extremely attractive. The new controller sent each member of the Board of Trustees' Finance Committee a set of the financial statements one week before the monthly meeting for their review. The set included the following statement of activities.

THE ATKINS MUSEUM
Statement of Activities
For the Year Ended June 30, 2017
(in hundreds of dollars)

	Public Exhibits	Abstract Exhibit	Mgt. & General	Total
Revenues:				
Contributions	$ 61,400	$50,000	$ 0	$111,400
Charges for services	478,800	0	0	478,800
Interest income	0	0	2,500	2,500
Total revenues	540,200	50,000	2,500	592,700
Expenses:				
Salaries and wages	381,900	24,700	44,200	450,800
Occupancy costs	38,100	12,000	14,900	65,000
Supplies	7,100	2,300	8,300	17,700
Equipment	5,000	0	6,500	11,500
Travel and development	2,800	0	6,900	9,700
Depreciation	12,000	1,500	6,300	19,800
Interest	0	0	3,700	3,700
Total variable expenses	446,900	40,500	90,800	578,200
Allocated management and general expenses	85,300	5,500	(90,800)	0
Total costs	532,200	46,000	0	578,200
Excess of revenues over expenses	$ 8,000	$ 4,000	$ 2,500	$ 14,500

Other information: The management and general expenses are first allocated to the programs to which they directly relate; for example, the executive director's salary is allocated to the Public Exhibit Program according to the percentage of time spent working on the program. Remaining unallocated management and general expenses are allocated to the programs as indirect costs based on the relative amount of salaries and wages to total salaries and wages for the programs.

Required

As a member of The Atkins Museum's Board of Directors Finance Committee, review this statement and answer the following questions:

a. Is the statement in proper form according to FASB standards?

b. What questions do you have for the controller?

c. The Atkins Museum would like to open an Impressionists exhibit. If its operating expenses are expected to be similar to that of the Abstract Exhibit, how much should the organization solicit in contributions or grants to cover the full cost of the program?

d. If you were a potential contributor to the Atkins Museum, do you think you have enough information from this statement on which to base your decision to donate?

13–20 Recording Revenue and Related Expense Transactions. The Shannon Community Kitchen provides hot meals to homeless and low-income individuals and families; it is the organization's only program. It is the policy of the community kitchen to use temporarily restricted resources for which the purpose has been met before unrestricted resources. The Kitchen had the following revenue and expense transactions during the 2017 fiscal year.

1. Unrestricted cash donations of $25,000 were received. A local philanthropist also contributed $3,000, which was to be used for the purchase of Thanksgiving dinner foodstuffs.
2. A local grocery store provided fresh produce with a fair value of $100. The produce was immediately used.
3. Volunteers from the local university contributed 100 hours to preparation and serving of meals. The estimated fair value of their labor was $750.
4. The Kitchen received a $5,000 federal grant for the purchase of institutional kitchen appliances.
5. At Thanksgiving time, the Kitchen spent $4,100 on foodstuffs for preparation of the Thanksgiving dinner.

Required

Make all necessary journal entries to record these transactions.

13–21 Recording and Reporting Transactions. INVOLVE was incorporated as a not-for-profit voluntary health and welfare organization on January 1, 2017. During the fiscal year ended December 31, 2017, the following transactions occurred.

1. A business donated rent-free office space to the organization that would normally rent for $35,000 a year.
2. A fund drive raised $185,000 in cash and $100,000 in pledges that will be paid within one year. A state government grant of $150,000 was received for program operating costs related to public health education.
3. Salaries and fringe benefits paid during the year amounted to $208,560. At year-end, an additional $16,000 of salaries and fringe benefits were accrued.
4. A donor pledged $100,000 for construction of a new building, payable over five fiscal years, commencing in 2019. The discounted value of the pledge is expected to be $94,260.
5. Office equipment was purchased for $12,000. The useful life of the equipment is estimated to be five years. Office furniture with a fair value of $9,600 was donated by a local office supply company. The furniture has an estimated useful life of 10 years. Furniture and equipment are considered unrestricted net assets by INVOLVE.
6. Telephone expense for the year was $5,200, printing and postage expense was $12,000 for the year, utilities for the year were $8,300, and supplies expense was $4,300 for the year. At year-end, an immaterial amount of supplies remained on hand and the balance in accounts payable was $3,600.
7. Volunteers contributed $15,000 of time to help with answering the phones, mailing materials, and various other clerical activities.
8. It is estimated that 90 percent of the pledges made for the 2018 year will be collected. Depreciation expense is recorded for the full year on the assets recorded in item 5.

9. Salaries and wages were allocated to program services and support services in the following percentages: public health education, 35 percent; community service, 30 percent; management and general, 20 percent; and fund-raising, 15 percent. All other expenses were allocated in the following percentages: public health education, 35 percent; community service, 20 percent; management and general, 25 percent; and fund-raising, 20 percent.
10. Net assets were released to reflect satisfaction of state grant requirements that the grant resources be used for public health education program purposes.
11. All nominal accounts were closed to the appropriate net asset accounts.

Required

a. Make all necessary journal entries to record these transactions. Expense transactions should be initially recorded by object classification; in entry 10 expenses will be allocated to functions.
b. Prepare a statement of activities for the year ended December 31, 2017.
c. Prepare a statement of financial position for the year ended December 31, 2017.
d. Prepare a statement of cash flows for the year ended December 31, 2017.
e. Prepare a statement of functional expenses for the year ended December 31, 2017.

13–22 Recording and Reporting Transactions. The Art League is a not-for-profit organization dedicated to promoting the arts within the community. There are two programs conducted by the Art League: (1) exhibition and sales of members' art (referred to as Exhibition) and (2) Community Art Education. Activities of the Art League are conducted by a part-time administrator, a part-time secretary-bookkeeper, and several part-time volunteers. The volunteers greet visitors, monitor the security of the exhibit hall, and handle the sales of art to the public. Art on exhibit is considered the property of the member artists, not the Art League.

The post-closing trial balance for the Art League as of June 30, 2016, is shown here.

ART LEAGUE
Post-closing Trial Balance
June 30, 2016

	Debits	Credits
Cash	$ 3,015	
Short-term Investments	12,111	
Grants Receivable	4,600	
Prepaid Expense	1,060	
Equipment	9,345	
Allowance for Depreciation—Equipment		$ 2,426
Long-term Investments—Permanently Restricted	5,767	
Accounts Payable and Accrued Expenses		2,649
Deferred Revenue		2,800
Unrestricted Net Assets		9,011
Temporarily Restricted Net Assets		13,245
Permanently Restricted Net Assets		5,767
Totals	$35,898	$35,898

Following is information summarizing the transactions of the Art League for the year ended June 30, 2017.

1. During the year, unrestricted cash was received from the following sources: grants, $11,600, of which $4,600 had been reported as receivable on June 30, 2016; annual contributions from fund drives and other unrestricted gifts, $13,861; membership dues, $16,285; tuition and fees for educational workshops, $6,974; and sales of members' art, $12,010, of which 20 percent represents commissions earned by the Art League.
2. Interest earnings were as follows: interest on unrestricted investments totaled $686; interest on temporarily restricted investments totaled $925; interest on permanently restricted investments totaled $344 (these investment earnings are temporarily restricted for program use).
3. Grants receivable as of year-end totaled $5,020, of which $3,120 was earned in the current year (thus unrestricted) and $1,900 was reported as deferred revenue.
4. The Art League receives free rent from the city at an estimated value of $18,000 a year.
5. Expenses incurred during the year were as follows: salaries and fringe benefits, $46,900; utilities $3,080; postage and supplies, $1,310; and miscellaneous, $640. As of year-end, the balances of the following accounts were: Prepaid Expenses, $840; Accounts Payable and Accrued Expenses, $2,746.
6. During the year, $2,900 of short-term investments were sold, with the proceeds used to purchase two computers and printer at a cost of $2,835. The resources used were temporarily restricted for the purchase of equipment. It is the policy of the Art League to record the equipment as temporarily restricted net assets.
7. In accordance with the terms of the Art League endowment, income earned by the endowment for the provision of free art instruction for handicapped children was provided at a cost of $825. This amount was allocated to community art education.
8. Depreciation on equipment in the amount of $1,642 was recorded.
9. Expenses for the year were allocated 30 percent to Exhibition Program, 30 percent to Community Art Education, 25 percent to Management and General Expenses, and 15 percent to Fund-Raising. (Round to the nearest dollar.)
10. Proceeds of art sales, net of commissions charged by the Art League, totaled $9,608. This amount was paid to member artists during the year.
11. All nominal accounts were closed a year-end.

Required

a. On the advice of its independent auditor, the Art League does not record support and expenses related to the value of services donated by the volunteers. Discuss the criteria for recognition of donated services, and comment on the auditor's likely rationale for not recognizing them in this case.

b. Make all necessary journal entries to record these transactions. Expense transactions should be initially recorded by object classification unless otherwise instructed; in entry 9, expenses will be allocated to functions.

c. Prepare a statement of activities for the year ended June 30, 2017.

d. Prepare a statement of financial position for the year ended June 30, 2017.

13–23 Identify Statement of Financial Position Departures from GAAP. The Center to Advance Student Learning has presented its statement of financial position for the 2017 fiscal year.

CENTER TO ADVANCE STUDENT LEARNING
Statement of Financial Position
As of December 31, 2017

Assets	
Cash and cash equivalents	$ 286,802
Short and long-term investments	1,371,143
Contributions receivable	286,372
Supplies and other prepaid expenses	43,258
Land	210,000
Buildings (net of accumulated depreciation of $63,420)	561,627
Equipment (net of accumulated depreciation of $92,642)	144,230
Total assets	$2,903,432
Liabilities and Net Assets	
Accounts payable	$ 45,722
Mortgage payable	495,000
Accrued liabilities	24,963
Unrestricted	503,980
Temporarily restricted	
Donor restricted for operations	196,892
Debt-covenant restricted	61,875
Permanently restricted	
Donor restricted	1,225,000
Board-designated	350,000
Total liabilities and net assets	$2,903,432

Required

Upon reviewing the statement, you realize that it is not presented in compliance with the FASB standards. To help the Center to Advance Student Learning correct the statement, please make a list of the corrections or modifications that should be made to the statement, so it can be presented in the proper format.

13–24 Prepare Financial Statements. The Kare Counseling Center was incorporated as a not-for-profit voluntary health and welfare organization 10 years ago. Its adjusted trial balance as of June 30, 2017, follows.

	Debits	Credits
Cash	$126,500	
Pledges Receivable—Unrestricted	41,000	
Estimated Uncollectible Pledges		$ 4,100
Inventory	2,800	
Investments	178,000	
Furniture and Equipment	210,000	
Accumulated Depreciation—Furniture and Equipment		120,000
Accounts Payable		20,520
Unrestricted Net Assets		196,500
Temporarily Restricted Net Assets		50,500
Permanently Restricted Net Assets		140,000
Contributions—Unrestricted		348,820

Continued

	Debits	Credits
Contributions—Temporarily Restricted		38,100
Investment Income—Unrestricted		9,200
Net Assets Released from Restrictions—Temporarily Restricted	22,000	
Net Assets Released from Restrictions—Unrestricted		22,000
Salaries and Fringe Benefit Expense	288,410	
Occupancy and Utility Expense	38,400	
Supplies Expense	6,940	
Printing and Publishing Expense	4,190	
Telephone and Postage Expense	3,500	
Unrealized Gain on Investments		2,000
Depreciation Expense	30,000	
Totals	$951,740	$951,740

1. Salaries and fringe benefits were allocated to program services and supporting services in the following percentages: counseling services, 40 percent; professional training, 20 percent; community service, 10 percent; management and general, 20 percent; and fund-raising, 10 percent. Occupancy and utility, supplies, printing and publishing, and telephone and postage expense were allocated to the programs in the same manner as salaries and fringe benefits. Depreciation expense was divided equally among all five functional expense categories.
2. The organization had $165,314 of cash on hand at the beginning of the year. During the year, the center received cash from contributors: $310,800 that was unrestricted and $38,100 that was restricted for the purchase of equipment for the center. It had $9,200 of income earned and received on long-term investments. The center spent cash of $288,410 on salaries and fringe benefits, $22,000 on the purchase of equipment for the center, and $86,504 for operating expenses. Other pertinent information follows: net pledges receivable increased $6,000, inventory increased $1,000, accounts payable decreased $102,594, and there were no salaries payable at the beginning of the year.

Required

a. Prepare a statement of financial position as of June 30, 2017, following the format in Illustration 13–6.

b. Prepare a statement of functional expenses for the year ended June 30, 2017, following the format in Illustration 13–9.

c. Prepare a statement of activities for the year ended June 30, 2017, following the format in Illustration 13–7.

d. Prepare a statement of cash flows for the year ended June 30, 2017, following the format in Illustration 13–8.

Chapter Fourteen

Not-for-Profit Organizations—Regulatory, Taxation, and Performance Issues

Learning Objectives

After studying this chapter, you should be able to:

14-1 Identify oversight bodies and the source of their authority over not-for-profit organizations (NFPs).

14-2 Describe how and why states regulate NFPs and describe the following:
- Not-for-profit incorporation laws.
- Registration, licenses, and tax exemption.

14-3 Identify how the federal government regulates NFPs and describe the following:
- Tax-exempt status—public charities and private foundations.
- Unrelated business income tax.
- Restricting political activity.
- Excessive benefits received by officers.
- Reorganization and dissolution.

14-4 Describe governance issues of NFP boards, including incorporating documents and board membership.

14-5 Identify how benchmarks and performance measures can be used to evaluate NFPs.

As discussed at the beginning of Chapter 13, the not-for-profit sector is a very large and diverse sector of the U.S. economy. The compassion and generosity of individuals supplies the not-for-profit sector with tremendous amounts of resources. The amount of resources, combined with the opportunity for unscrupulous fund-raisers and illegal scams, means that not-for-profit organizations (NFPs) need to be held accountable for how contributions are used. In addressing the issue of the accountability of NFPs, it is important to understand the legal and governance structure of NFPs. Therefore, this chapter examines regulation, taxation, and performance issues related to ensuring that NFPs are accountable to their various stakeholders.

In general, NFPs are accountable to the state government that grants them their legal existence; the federal government, which grants them tax-exempt status; their own governing board; individual donors and grantors; consumers of their services; and the public at large. It is important to note that churches, while certainly part of the nongovernmental, not-for-profit sector, do not require the state and federal governments to grant them legal and tax-exempt status because of the historic constitutional separation of church and state in the United States. However, many activities in which churches engage are subject to state and federal regulations. Accountants and auditors play a critical role in assuring stakeholders that all NFPs have complied with applicable laws and regulations and, in the process, have efficiently and effectively used the assets with which they were entrusted.

The process that has evolved for individuals who wish to operate an NFP is to first request recognition from a state as a legal entity and then to apply to the Internal Revenue Service for exemption from federal taxes. With these two steps, the organization accepts oversight, and responsibility for transparency and performance accountability. Watchdog organizations, which are often NFPs themselves, have sprung up to help ensure that data are available for stakeholders to evaluate the effectiveness and efficiency of NFPs in meeting their public purpose.

STATE REGULATION

This section provides general information about state regulation of not-for-profit organizations. Anyone with an interest in a specific state's requirements related to NFPs is encouraged to contact that state government. A useful Web site for locating the appropriate state agency is maintained by the National Association of State Charity Officials and the National Association of Attorneys' General (*www.multistatefiling.org*).

A state has the power to give legal life to an NFP, either in the form of a not-for-profit corporation or limited liability company or in the state's recognition of a charitable trust. Once an organization is recognized by the state as an NFP, the state has a responsibility to represent public beneficiaries of charities and contributors. The state's responsibilities include detecting cases when managers or directors have diverted resources, mismanaged, or defrauded the charity and the public. To assist with oversight, some states require NFPs to register with a specified department of the state (e.g., Attorney General, Secretary of State, Consumer Affairs, Regulatory Affairs, or Commerce) or apply for a license in order to solicit funds, hold property, do business in the state, or lobby. For the most part, state and local governments require fees to accompany registration and licenses in order to defray the cost of regulation and monitoring. Failure to file required reports may result in automatic dissolution of the NFP.

Legislation regulating NFPs varies greatly across states. However, there are some common methods used by states and sometimes adopted by local governments to ensure that the public good is protected as NFPs solicit charitable contributions and conduct business. In an effort to increase uniformity across governments, states' attorneys general and others involved in the regulation of the not-for-profit sector have collaborated in establishing policies and best practices in the areas of incorporation, investments, solicitation, and volunteers. A model not-for-profit corporation act developed by the American Bar Association and a model charitable solicitation act prepared by the National Association of Attorneys General provide a basic framework of best practices that have been used by many states and by many NFP organizations. The Uniform Prudent Management of Investment Funds Act (UPMIFA) of 2006 relates to the investing of funds and the spending of endowment income by NFP organizations that manage charitable funds. In the remainder of this section, general information concerning state regulation of NFPs is provided.

Not-for-Profit Incorporation Laws

A group of individuals who share a philanthropic or other vision may operate as an unincorporated association if the association is small or if the organizers expect the endeavor to have a limited life; however, organizers are treated as partners and share liability for any debts incurred by the association. If the organization plans to grow into a long-lived operation, organizers may choose to file articles of incorporation with a state under the not-for-profit corporation statutes or charitable trust laws to create a legal entity and limit the liability of the incorporators and directors.

Incorporation laws differ across the 50 states, but states generally have built into the not-for-profit corporation laws the requirement that organizers (1) choose a name that is not misleading or in use by another corporation, (2) designate a resident agent and address, (3) state a clear purpose for the entity, (4) appoint a board of directors, (5) write by-laws that delineate board responsibilities and operating structure, (6) call at least one board meeting a year, and (7) require management to report on financial condition and operations at least once a year. Not-for-profit incorporation statutes also state the extent to which directors are individually liable for the misapplication of assets through neglect or failure to exercise reasonable care and prudence in administration of the affairs of the corporation. Upon conferring the NFP legal status separate from the incorporators, the state bears oversight responsibility for the NFP.

Licenses to Solicit Contributions or for Other Purposes

Some states protect citizens from competitive fund-raising requests by requiring the NFP to obtain a license to solicit charitable contributions. **Charitable solicitation** is the direct or indirect request for money, credit, property, financial assistance, or other things of value on the representation that these assets will be used for a charitable purpose.

States granting licenses usually impose annual compliance reporting on NFPs. A few states require audited annual financial reports to be filed when the level of public support exceeds a certain threshold, such as $250,000. Some states require a license when an NFP compensates someone for fund-raising, such as a professional fund-raiser or solicitor, and a fee may be required of the organization for the right of each fund-raiser to solicit. Many states also require specific disclosures be put on all written materials mailed to potential donors to indicate that financial information about the organization may be on file with the state. In addition to the state, local governments may regulate charitable solicitation, although sometimes more for its fee revenue potential than for regulatory purposes.

States or local governments may require an NFP organization to get a license or permit for gaming events, such as bingo and raffles, with maximum prize limits set. Often licenses or permits are granted for one-day beer, wine, and liquor sales for events.

For those NFPs considering raising funds over the Internet, state registration requirements are frequently guided by the Charleston Principles (*www.nasconet.org*). State officials are encouraged to use these principles, which were developed by the National Association of Charity Officials.

Taxes

NFPs are often exempted from the taxes levied by state and local governments, such as sales, real or personal property, transfer, employment, or excise taxes. This privilege varies across the country and, in the case of property taxes, is being both challenged by interest groups suspicious of some NFPs' charitable mission and defended by not-for-profit coalitions. To be relieved from the tax, the NFP may have to file for specific tax exemption and document that the property is *in use* for charitable purposes. Fund-raising events often give rise to sales tax reporting, both collection of tax from customers and exemption from sales tax paid on the purchase of goods. Often overlooked by the NFP are the excise taxes on telephone and utility bills for which they may not be liable and could recover by filing for a refund.

Lobbying and Political Activity

Some NFPs are organized specifically as political parties, campaign committees, or political action committees. These NFPs are discussed later in the chapter in a discussion of Section 527 political organizations. However, the majority of NFPs do not exist for political or lobbying purposes. To avoid sanctions, these NFPs need to be aware of what constitutes allowable and unallowable lobbying and political activity.

States have their own regulations over lobbying and political activity for NFPs that differ somewhat from each other and from that of the federal government. States regulate lobbying for all organizations through lobbying acts. These laws require organizations to register with the state and then account for lobbying activities. The NFP must determine whether it, or someone it hires to influence others, is a lobbyist or lobbyist agent and, consequently, subject to these regulations. **Influencing** means to promote, support, affect, modify, oppose, or delay by any means.

The impact of excessive political activity on NFPs can be significant due to the harsh sanctions for violating these laws, as well as negative publicity that may harm future fund-raising efforts. The ultimate penalty is revocation of exemption from taxes, but more often fines are imposed for engaging in prohibited behavior. Illustration 14–1

ILLUSTRATION 14–1 **Regulations over Not-for-Profit Organizations (varies by state)**

State and/or Local Government Regulations
Application to operate under an assumed name.
Application to incorporate as a not-for-profit corporation or a limited liability company.
Annual compliance reporting.
Special licenses with particular state departments to operate a health care facility (public health), housing corporation (housing authority), residential care facility (social service), school (education), or to handle food.
Application for exemption from income, franchise, sales, use, real, and personal property taxes.
Employer registration, including payroll tax returns, withholding of state taxes, and unemployment.
License to solicit charitable contributions.
Registration of political lobbyists, lobbying agents, or lobbying activities.
License for one-day beer, wine, and liquor sales.
License to conduct charitable games (e.g., bingo, raffles, millionaire parties).
Policies on conflict of interest and self-dealing with directors.
License to collect sales and use taxes as a vendor.
Freedom of Information Act (FOIA) (if a substantial amount of funds are public).
Open Meetings Act (if governmental in nature).
Notice of plans to merge with another agency.
Notice of plans to dissolve, including tax clearance.

presents a list of typical regulations for nongovernmental not-for-profit organizations at the state and local levels.

FEDERAL REGULATION

Because charities serve the common good, the federal government has encouraged not-for-profit associations and charitable contributions since the first revenue act in 1894. The public expects the federal government to monitor organizations receiving tax benefits to ensure that these privileges are not abused. NFPs must follow general laws that govern businesses (such as fair labor standards, older workers' benefits protection, equal employment opportunities acts, disabilities acts, civil rights laws, drug-free workplace laws, immigration laws, antidiscrimination and harassment laws, and veterans and whistleblowers' protection) unless they are specifically exempted. This section describes federal law and regulations that are unique to NFPs.

Illustration 14–2 is a chart depicting how a public charity interacts with the Internal Revenue Service (IRS) during its existence.

ILLUSTRATION 14–2 Operating a Public Charity

Starting Out

- Organizing documents (such as articles of incorporation, and charter)
- By-laws
- Employer identification number (EIN)
- Charitable solicitation registration
- See Pub. 557, *Tax Exempt Status for Your Organization,* for information on starting a tax-exempt organization

Applying to IRS

- Application for 503(c)(3) tax-exempt status using Form 1023, and Pub. 4220, *Applying for 501(c)(3) Tax-exempt Status*
- Application for 501(a) tax-exempt status using Form 1024

Required Annual Filings

- Annual exempt organizations information return (Forms 990, 990-EZ, 990-N)
- Unrelated business income tax (UBIT) (Form 990-T, and Pub. 598, *Tax on Unrelated Business Income for Exempt Organizations*)

Ongoing Compliance

- Jeopardizing exemption (private benefit, political activity); failure to file, inurement, intermediate sanctions for excessive officer benefits, lobbying/political activity
- Employment taxes
- Substantiation and disclosure (e.g., noncash contributions) (see Pub. 1771, *Charitable Contributions—Substantiation and Disclosure Requirements* and Pub. 561, *Determining the Value of Donated Property*)
- Public disclosure requirements
- Retirement plan compliance
- Compliance Guide for 501(c)(3) Public Charities (Pub. 4221-PC)

Significant Events

- Notifying the IRS of significant changes (e.g., mergers, terminations)
- Private letter rulings and determination letters
- Audits of exempt organizations

Source: Internal Revenue Service "Life Cycle of a Public Charity" with examples and links to appropriate forms, available at *www.irs.gov/Charities-&-Non-Profits/Charitable-Organizations/Life-Cycle-of-a-Public-Charity.*

Tax-exempt Status

Even though a state may have conferred not-for-profit corporation status on an organization that NFP must still apply to the IRS for exemption from federal income tax.[1] Religious organizations, including churches, synagogues, temples, mosques, and integrated auxiliaries of religious organizations, and any organization that has gross receipts in each taxable year of normally not more than $5,000 do not have to file Form 1023 to be considered tax-exempt under Sec. 501(c)(3).

The stated purpose of the NFP and the services it will perform determine the Internal Revenue Code (IRC) section under which the NFP requests exemption. Illustration 14–3 shows some of the many classifications of statutory exemptions under which tax-exempt organizations fall. The most common classification under IRC Section 501 is Sec. 501(c)(3), which is an organization operated for philanthropic, educational, or similar purposes. The **organizational test** for tax-exempt status is that the articles of incorporation must limit the organization's purposes to those described in the classifications in IRC Sec. 501, cannot benefit private interests, and may not attempt to influence

ILLUSTRATION 14–3 Tax-exempt Status According to the Internal Revenue Code (selected)

Section of Internal Revenue Code	Description of Organization and Its Activities
501(c)(1)	Corporations organized under acts of Congress, such as the Federal Deposit Insurance Corporation
501(c)(2)	Title-holding corporation for exempt organizations
501(c)(3)	Charitable, religious, scientific, literary, educational, testing for public safety
501(c)(4)	Civic leagues, social welfare organizations, local employee associations
501(c)(5)	Labor, agricultural and horticultural organizations
501(c)(6)	Business leagues, chambers of commerce, real estate boards
501(c)(7)	Social and recreational clubs
501(c)(8)	Fraternal beneficiary society and associations
501(c)(9)	Voluntary employees' beneficiary associations to provide insurance or other benefits to members
501(c)(10)	Domestic fraternal societies and associations
501(c)(11)	Teacher retirement fund associations
501(c)(13)	Cemetery companies; burial activities
501(c)(14)	State-chartered credit unions, mutual reserve fund
501(c)(18)	Employee funded pension trust
501(c)(19)	Veterans' organizations or armed forces members' posts
501(d)	Religious and apostolic associations; religious communities
501(e)	Cooperative hospital service organizations
501(f)	Cooperative service organization of operating educational organizations
501(k)	Child care organizations
521(a)	Farmers; cooperative associations
527	Political parties, campaign committees, political action committees
529	Qualified state tuition programs

[1] IRS Instructions for Form 1023.

legislation as a substantial part of its activities. Some not-for-profit organizations, such as hospitals, have been criticized for not providing an adequate amount of free services as a benefit to society, as stated in their application for tax-exempt status.

An individual can receive a charitable contribution tax deduction by making a donation to a Sec. 501(c)(3) organization (and certain other exempt organizations), but only if the gift is used for charitable purposes. Gifts are nonexchange transactions (discussed in Chapters 4 and 13) for which the donor receives no benefit in exchange for the contribution. For a single charitable contribution of $75 or more, the NFP must provide the contributor with written disclosure of the contribution amount. NFPs are subject to penalties for failure to provide such disclosures. Another advantage of tax exemption under Sec. 501(c)(3) is the opportunity to apply for grants from foundations and government agencies, which often limit funding to public charities.

Many categories of tax-exempt organizations, such as business leagues, social clubs, and cooperatives, cannot offer donors the advantage of a charitable deduction from income taxes because they operate primarily for the benefit of members, not the public at large. An organization that is not a Sec. 501(c)(3) organization must disclose to donors that contributions are *not* tax deductible.

Independent charitable organizations may voluntarily join together as a **federated fund-raising organization** to raise and distribute money among themselves. An example of such a federation is the United Way.

Public Charities versus Private Foundations

As indicated in IRS publication 557, every organization that qualifies as an IRC Section 501(c)(3) organization is considered a private foundation unless it meets the requirements of Section 509(a) to be excluded from consideration as a private foundation. Two ways to be excluded as a private foundation are through the nature of an organization's mission (e.g., religious organizations, educational organizations, or hospitals) or by meeting the public support requirements to be considered a public charity. A **private foundation** is one that receives its support from a small number of individuals or corporations and investment income rather than from the public at large. It exists to make grants to public charities. Private foundations file an annual Form 990-PF and are subject to several excise taxes: (1) for failure to take certain actions (such as distribute a minimum amount to public charities), (2) for prohibited behavior (such as self-dealing transactions with disqualified persons and excess business holdings), and (3) on net investment income.[2]

Public charities are funded, operated, and monitored by the public at large rather than by a limited number of donors. Public charities receive preferential treatment over private foundations because of their broad base of support. They are not subject to the excise taxes mentioned for private foundations, and donors do not face the same limitations when giving to a public charity.

New tax-exempt organizations are presumed to be private foundations unless they request that they be considered a public charity. If the organization applies for public charity status and it can reasonably expect to meet the public support test during its first five years of operation, the IRS will classify it as a public charity.[3] However, in the sixth year the data must indicate that the public support test has been met for the organization to avoid being classified as a private foundation.

[2] IRS publication 557, 2013.

[3] Ibid.

The public support test is generally met if an NFP normally receives at least one-third of its total support from governments, contributions made directly or indirectly by the general public, or some combination of these sources. There is a limitation on the amount any one individual can make and have it count toward the one-third calculation. If an individual makes a contribution of 2 percent or more of the total support, only an amount up to 2 percent of the total support can be counted toward public support (numerator), while the full amount is counted toward total support (denominator) when making the one-third calculation.[4] The one-third support test for the current tax year is calculated based on the aggregate of the four preceding tax years.

Sec. 527 Political Organizations

Political action committees (PACs), political parties, and campaign committees for candidates for government office are considered **political organizations** and are subject to special reporting and disclosures requirements. Like all tax-exempt organizations, a political organization must meet an organizational test; that is, it must document the purpose and intent of the founding members. A political organization does not need to be incorporated, but it does need to have a separate bank account into which funds are deposited and disbursed. Federal Election Commission filing papers or resolutions arising from meetings of the founding members will also serve as documentation of the organization's purpose. As part of campaign finance reform laws, political organizations must meet two requirements. The first is to provide an initial notice to the IRS that an organization is to be treated as an IRC Sec. 527 organization, unless an exception applies. Second, the organization must periodically report on Form 8872 the names and addresses of persons contributing at least $200 annually and persons receiving expenditures of at least $500 annually.

Political Activity

Early legislative attempts at restricting political activity of public charities were intended to deny a charitable contribution income tax deduction for a selfish contribution made merely to advance the personal interests of the donor through his/her contribution to a charity conducting political activities. If any of the activities of the NFP consist of participating in any political campaign on behalf of (or in opposition to) any candidate for public office, the organization will not qualify for tax-exempt status and may have its tax-exempt status revoked. This includes contributions to political campaign funds, public statements of position on behalf of the organization in favor of (or in opposition to) any candidate for public office, and the publication or distribution of political statements. However, the facts and circumstances on the amount of money, time, and energy spent on each case determine whether the organization can be tax-exempt. For example, certain voter education activities or public forums conducted in a nonpartisan manner may not be considered prohibited political activity. The key is whether the activities encourage people to vote for or against a particular candidate, even if that is not the intent of the NFP.

While the political activities just described are absolutely barred for charitable entities, a different set of rules applies to lobbying or legislative activities, and these rules are different at the federal and state levels. The general rule is that no substantial part of a charity's activities may involve conducting propaganda or otherwise attempting to influence legislation. **Propaganda** is information skewed toward a

[4] Ibid.

particular belief with a tendency to have little or no factual basis. **Legislation** is generally action by Congress, a state legislative body, or a local council to establish laws, statutes, or ordinances.

If an organization passes the "no *substantial* amount of propaganda or influencing legislation" hurdle and is granted tax-exempt status, it still faces limitations on the amount of political activity it can conduct. The severest penalty is loss of tax-exempt status. Less extreme is a tax on excessive political expenditures.[5] An exempt organization other than a religious organization is allowed to make limited expenditures to influence legislation if properly elected on Form 5768.[6] A permissible amount of direct **lobbying** (i.e., testifying at legislative hearings, corresponding or conferring with legislators or their staffs, or publishing documents advocating specific legislative action) is allowed. The allowable amount is referred to as the lobbying nontaxable amount and it is the lesser of a specified percentage of an organization's exempt purpose expenditures or $1 million annually. Additionally, NFPs are allowed to conduct a limited amount of **grass-roots lobbying** (i.e., an appeal to the general public to contact legislators or to take other action regarding a legislative matter). The limit on grass-roots lobbying is 25 percent of the lobbying nontaxable amount in any given tax year. It should be noted that lobbying does not include distributing nonpartisan studies, providing technical advice to a governmental body, opposing legislation that negatively affects the organization, exchanging information among organization members, and communicating on routine matters with governmental officials. Schedule C on the revised Form 990 provides a significant amount of information on legislative and political activities. Federal penalties for excess political activity are in addition to those that might be assessed by a state for lobbying.

Annual Compliance Reporting

Form 990 is the primary tool the federal government uses to collect information about the NFP and its activities. The IRS expands the form as Congress requires more information to be furnished by tax-exempt organizations. The form must be made available to the public for three years.[7] Failure to file this form brings significant penalties, unless an extension is granted. Annual reporting requirements do not apply to federal agencies and religious organizations and their affiliates.

The IRS overhauled the Form 990 effective for returns filed for the 2008 tax year, the first substantive change in annual reporting for tax-exempt organizations since 1979. The changes are designed to enhance transparency about the organization, allow the IRS to efficiently assess noncompliance, and minimize the burden of filing on tax-exempt organizations. The form is comprised of a 12-page core return and 16 schedules that may apply to only some organizations (increased from a 9-page core return and 2 schedules). Some information is new, some information has been deleted, and much of it has been reorganized. Illustration 14–4 delineates the information that is required on the annual reporting Form 990.

[5] IRC Sec. 4955.

[6] IRC Sec. 4911.

[7] Public disclosure regulations issued in 1999 require that tax-exempt organizations provide a copy of their three most recently filed Form 990s and exempt application immediately upon personal request or within 30 days for a written request. Penalties can be avoided if the organization makes these forms widely available on the Internet [Treas. Reg. Sec. 301.6104(d)]. Similar regulations were passed for private foundations and their Form 990-PFs in 2000.

ILLUSTRATION 14–4 Parts of the IRS Form 990

	Core Form
Part I	Summary
Part II	Signature block
Part III	Statement of program service accomplishments
Part IV	Checklist of required schedules
Part V	Statements regarding other IRS filings and tax compliance
Part VI	Governance, management, and disclosure
Part VII	Compensation of officers, directors, trustees, key employees, highest compensated employees, and independent contractors
Part VIII	Statement of revenue
Part IX	Statement of functional expenses
Part X	Balance sheet
Part XI	Reconciliation of net assets
Part XII	Financial statements and reporting
	Schedules
A	Public charity status and public support
B	Schedules of contributors
C	Political campaign and lobby activities
D	Supplemental financial statements
E	Schools
F	Statement of activities outside the United States
G	Supplemental information regarding fund-raising or gaming activities
H	Hospitals
I	Grants and other assistance to organizations, governments, and individuals in the U.S.
J	Compensation information
K	Supplemental information on tax-exempt bonds
L	Transactions with interested persons
M	Noncash contributions
N	Liquidation, termination, dissolution, or significant disposition of assets
O	Supplemental information to Form 990 or 990-EZ
R	Related organizations and unrelated partnerships

With few exceptions (e.g., religious organizations and governmental NFPs), tax-exempt organizations will file one of three forms of the Form 990. The form filed will depend on the size of the organization. Small tax-exempt entities with gross receipts normally $50,000 or less per year will file a Form 990-N "e-postcard." Form 990-EZ will be filed by tax-exempt entities with annual gross receipts of between $50,000 and $200,000, and with less than $500,000 in total assets. Larger NFP organizations will file the Form 990. Private foundations, discussed in the next section, will prepare an annual Form 990-PF.

Unrelated Business Income Tax

Owners of small businesses have long complained that NFPs compete with them in businesslike activities with the unfair advantage of lower costs due to exemption from income taxes. For example, college bookstores sell clothing, credit unions operate travel agencies, YMCAs run health clubs, and universities operate veterinary clinics.[8] In 1950 Congress passed the first unrelated business income tax (UBIT), which assesses tax at corporate rates on income that NFPs derive from activities not substantially related to their charitable or tax-exempt mission.[9] UBIT requirements apply to all not-for-profit organizations and public colleges and universities except federal corporations and certain charitable trusts.

The IRS is primarily interested in how the unrelated business income was earned, not in how it is used, even if it is used to further the organization's tax-exempt purpose. **Unrelated business income (UBI)** is calculated as the gross income from an unrelated trade or business engaged in on a *regular* basis less directly connected expenses, certain net operating losses, and qualified charitable contributions. The first $1,000 of unrelated business income is excluded from taxation. Unrelated trade or business activities are those that are *substantially* unrelated to carrying out the organization's exempt purpose. Stated differently, unless activities make an important contribution to the accomplishment of the organization's exempt purpose, they will be considered unrelated. The activities that must be carefully examined include sponsorships, advertising, affinity credit card arrangements, sale of mailing lists, travel tour services, and fund-raising events. The UBIT is reported on a Form 990-T, which must be publicly available.

To determine whether the business activity is substantially related to the organization's exempt purpose, the relationship between the business activity and the exempt purpose is examined. Unrelated business income does not include dividends, interest, royalties, fees for use of intangible property, gains on the sale of property (unless that property was used in an unrelated trade or business), or income from activities in which substantially all of the work is done by volunteers, income from the sale of donated merchandise, income from legally conducted games of chance, rents from real property, or when the trade is conducted primarily for the convenience of its members, such as a laundry in a college dorm. However, rents from debt-financed property, rents based on a percentage of net income rather than gross income, and rents on personal property are considered to be unrelated business income. Excluded from UBI is income from advertising done in the form of corporate sponsorships for particular events if (1) the corporate sponsor does not get any substantial benefit in return for its payment other than the promotion of its name, (2) the display does not advertise the company's products or services, and (3) the amount of payment is not contingent on the level of attendance at the event. Corporate sponsorships that appear in regularly published periodicals are still UBI. Special rules apply to bingo and distribution of low-cost items, such as pens or stickers.

Feeder Organizations

NFPs may control a **feeder organization** that is organized to carry on a trade or business for the benefit of the exempt organization and remit its profits to the NFP. The income passed from the feeder to the not-for-profit organization in the form of interest, rents, royalties, and annuities is subject to unrelated business income tax. *Control* is defined as more than 50 percent of the voting stock of a feeder organization. Some activities not subject to the feeder organization rules are those that (1) generate rental income that would be excluded from rent for UBIT, (2) use volunteers for substantially all the work, and (3) sell merchandise that was substantially all contributed.

[8] See *www.irs.gov/charities,* then search for "UBIT" for general rules and current developments.

[9] IRC Secs. 511–513. Unrelated business income is also subject to the alternative minimum tax.

Unrelated Debt-financed Income

If an NFP has income from an asset that is mortgaged or **debt-financed income** (e.g., rental of real estate on which the NFP holds a mortgage) that income is UBI. The unrelated business income is the total income times the proportion to which the property is financed by debt. However, there are many exceptions to this general rule, such as property that is substantially used to achieve the organization's exempt purpose.

Excessive Benefits Received by Officers

This section addresses sanctions that can be imposed for excessive economic benefits received by officers of NFPs. While an NFP's tax-exempt status can be revoked for provision of excess benefits to officers, it is more likely the IRS will apply an intermediate sanction. **Intermediate sanctions** are penalties assessed when a transaction confers a substantial benefit on a disqualified person. A **disqualified person** is one who has substantial influence over the organization's affairs. Examples of **excess benefit transactions** include unreasonable compensation, sales of assets at bargain prices, and lease arrangements.[10] The law applies to public charities but may be extended to other classifications of exempt organizations. The first-tier penalty is a tax of 25 percent of the excess benefit on the disqualified person in addition to repayment of the excess benefit. If the organization's managers are aware the transaction is improper, the NFP is assessed a tax of 10 percent of the excess benefit. A second-tier penalty of 200 percent of the excess benefit is assessed on the disqualified person if the transaction is not corrected within the taxable period. Careful structuring of management compensation contracts along with documentation of comparable salaries of similar positions is critical in avoiding intermediate sanctions.

Reorganization and Dissolution

If an NFP finds that the societal needs initially described in the tax-exemption application are no longer met, it may redefine its mission, merge, or choose to dissolve the organization. The accounting issues involved in a dissolution include ensuring that (1) all creditors are paid, (2) all federal, state, and local taxes are paid, and (3) all assets are appropriately transferred (e.g., to another tax-exempt organization). If the incorporating documents are silent about the distribution of assets, state law or IRS regulations dictate. The IRS has said that if an NFP liquidates, dissolves, or terminates, its assets have to be distributed for another exempt purpose or be given to the federal or a state or local government.[11] Involuntary dissolution may occur due to failure to file an annual report or as a result of a state attorney general's determination of fraud or unlawful conduct.

GOVERNANCE

Managers of tax-exempt, not-for-profit organizations are directly accountable to the board of the organization, which in turn is ultimately responsible to the public and governmental oversight bodies. This relationship is not different from that among corporate managers, boards of directors, and stockholders. What is different, however, is the importance of incorporating documents that define the philanthropic or not-for-profit mission of the organization and the (sometimes underestimated) responsibilities of board members who may be invited to serve on the board, without compensation, more for their fund-raising ability than their financial management expertise.

[10] IRC Sec. 4958.

[11] Rev. Proc. 82-2, 1982-1 CB 367.

Incorporating Documents

The incorporating documents include the articles of incorporation, which has an external focus and describe the purpose of the organization without being too restrictive, and the by-laws, which has an internal focus and describe the functional rules of the organization. In the articles of incorporation, the organization declares its charitable intentions. An important factor in a charity, as opposed to other not-for-profits, is that the prospective beneficiary is undetermined and unknown; therefore, it can be said that the public at large, and not a specific interest group, benefits from the charity. Other important documents to the accountant include minutes of board meetings (i.e., the legal history of the organization) and written policies. They establish the charitable or exempt purpose for which the organization was organized and for which it should be held accountable. Expectations of resource providers, such as donors and grantors, as well as federal and state governments requiring reporting on the financial management of assets devoted to the exempt purpose, are revealed in these documents. State laws may govern the type of information that must be included in some of these documents; for example, the articles of incorporation is required to list name, purpose, organizational activities, registered office, and the incorporators.

Not-for-profit corporations can take the form of (1) a membership in which there is voting or nonvoting stock (for example, property owners association) or (2) a directorship in which the board is self-perpetuating (i.e., it elects itself). In the case of a directorship, there is little threat of removal by the membership at large. The significance of the form of the NFP corporation for accountants is that the stakeholders or users of financial information and their needs may differ depending on the organizational form.

Board Membership

Board members are responsible for all authorized activities generating financial support on the organization's behalf.[12] They set policy and provide fiscal guidance and ongoing governance. Characteristics of a quality board include diversity, leadership, sensitivity, direction, and, probably the most important, the ability of each member to contribute and attract funds. Treasurers of boards have specific duties articulated in the incorporating documents that require them to have custody of corporate funds and securities, keep full and accurate records of all receipts and disbursements, and deposit money and valuables in designated depositories until funds are authorized to be disbursed. Internal board members, managers, and employees of the organization may have competing objectives from those of external board members who are outside the daily operations of the organization and who have no financial stake in the organization. Board members may carry errors and omissions insurance and require that indemnification clauses be included in the articles of incorporation to protect them from lawsuits.

To satisfy its fiduciary responsibilities, the board should require managers to regularly summarize the activities of administering the entity. It should regularly review the organization's policies, programs, and operations. Incentive performance contracts can be made with managers to encourage certain goals and outcomes. By-laws or policies may call for continuous quality improvement, so boards can assess performance against benchmarks and predetermined performance goals.

Not-for-profit boards are increasingly adopting best practices. In particular, many boards have established audit committees. The advantage of a committee that is separate from the board and finance committee is that it helps the board fulfill its oversight

[12] Boardsource, *Twelve Principles of Governance That Power Exceptional Boards* (Washington, DC: Boardsource, 2005).

responsibilities by working directly with the public accounting firm throughout the year. The audit committee will hire the auditors, sign the engagement letter, approve any permitted nonaudit services, assess the independence and qualifications of the auditor (including whether a rotation of the audit partner and auditing firm is warranted), review the audit scope and approach, and resolve any disagreements between management and the auditors. Members of this committee should be financially literate and at least one member should be designated as a financial expert. Further, the audit committee members should be fully knowledgeable about the internal control system of the organization and have a healthy level of skepticism that allows them to ask probing questions of both management and the auditors.

BENCHMARKING AND PERFORMANCE MEASURES

Oversight bodies, such as boards of directors, not-for-profit watchdog agencies, and an increasing number of states, are tracking performance measures of exempt organizations. Financial and operational results are compared to specified performance targets as well as benchmarked to comparable organizations in the industry. Not-for-profit agencies collecting information about entities in the not-for-profit sector include Guidestar Inc., the BBB Wise Giving Alliance, the American Institute of Philanthropy, the Tax-Exempt/Government Entities (TE/GE) Division of the IRS, Independent Sector, and the Urban Institute, among other regional associations supporting NFPs.[13] These organizations are likely to provide standards for charitable solicitation useful for donors, but information necessary to benchmark one NFP to its peer organizations or other organizations is just at the early stages of development in the not-for-profit sector.

With a sector of the economy as diverse as the not-for-profit sector, a classification scheme is extremely helpful in identifying organizations that are similar enough to allow for comparisons. The National Center for Charitable Statistics (NCCS) at the Urban Institute was instrumental in developing a National Taxonomy of Exempt Entities (NTEE). This classification system is sorted into 26 different categories related to the purpose, type, or major function of an organization. Illustration 14–5 presents these categories, which are further broken down into more detail (not shown). The NCCS developed a parallel classification taxonomy, called the Nonprofit Program Classification (NPC) System that focuses on programs. The NPC has 671 different programs that tie into the NTEE by using one of the 26 letter codes as the first placeholder in the code. These codes may eventually be used on the Form 990, so that data can be more easily captured and summarized for use in establishing benchmarks for similar organizations.

Financial Performance Measures

Generally, NFPs need to demonstrate accountability to their stakeholders for effective and efficient operations, compliance with laws and regulations, financial management (short- and long-term), fiduciary responsibility of managers and board members, sustainability of the organization over time, and community impact or "making a

[13] The respective Web sites of these organizations are *www.guidestar.org, www.give.org, www.charitywatch.org, www.irs.gov, www.independentsector.org,* and *www.nccs.urban.org.* Guidestar Inc. makes available the Form 990s of many NFP organizations. One regional organization that provides much information for users and preparers of NPO financial information is the Maryland Association of Nonprofit Organizations at *www.marylandnonprofits.org.*

ILLUSTRATION 14–5 National Taxonomy of Exempt Entities (NTEE) Core Codes

A	Arts, culture and humanities
B	Education
C	Environment
D	Animal-related
E	Health care
F	Mental health and crisis intervention
G	Voluntary health associations and medical disciplines
H	Medical research
I	Crime and legal-related
J	Employment
K	Food, agriculture and nutrition
L	Housing and shelter
M	Public safety, disaster preparedness and relief
N	Recreation and sports
O	Youth development
P	Human services
Q	International, foreign affairs and national security
R	Civil rights, social action and advocacy
S	Community improvement and capacity building
T	Philanthropy, voluntarism (grantmaking foundations)
U	Science and technology
V	Social science
W	Public and societal benefit
X	Religion-related
Y	Mutual and membership benefit
Z	Unknown (not classified elsewhere)

Source: National Center for Charitable Statistics, *www.nccs.urban.org,* revised May 2005.

difference." Illustration 14–6 shows some financial ratios that can be computed from financial statement information and used as performance indicators that can be tracked over time and shared with stakeholders.

Several limitations of financial ratio analysis should be considered. For instance, donors may incorrectly assume that federal and state laws govern the percentage of annual revenue that a charity must spend on its programs or that there are limits on the percentage of revenue that is spent on fund-raising. Another limitation is the lack of benchmarks for comparable not-for-profit organizations that provide generally accepted targets for fund-raising efficiency, debt coverage, and capital structure, among other financial ratios. The percentage of total expenses spent on the program, rather than supporting the program, is such a well-publicized measure of effectiveness that organizations are quite careful to allocate as much to the program category as possible. At issue has been the joint costs of advocacy or educational materials that have a fund-raising appeal. As explained in Chapter 13 the amount of such costs that can be classified as program expenses is limited. Another way to increase the proportion of program expenses to total expenses is to recognize the fair value of gifts in kind (i.e., contributions of tangible items) and contributed services used in the operations of the program as expenses. Generally accepted accounting principles do require that this type of gift be recognized as both income and expense if fair value can be objectively

ILLUSTRATION 14–6 Performance Indicators

Type of Ratio	Indicator	Ratio
Liquidity	Can the organization pay its current debts?	Current assets (cash, A/R, inventory) / Current liabilities
		Quick assets (cash and A/R) / Current liabilities
Going concern	Are revenues sufficient to cover expenses?	Revenues / Expenses
	How many months of operating expenses can be covered by unrestricted net assets?	Unrestricted net assets / Operating expenses
Capital structure	Does the organization rely more on debt or equity to finance its operations?	Debt / Total assets; Debt / Net assets
Program effectiveness	Is an appropriate amount spent on accomplishing the NFP's goals?	Program expenses / Total expenses
Efficiency	Is the cost per achieved output decreasing over time?	Program expenses / Number of clients served
Leverage and debt coverage	Is the debt service expense adequately covered by income?	Revenue, support, and gains plus interest and depreciation expenses / Annual debt service expense
Fund-raising ratio	What percent of contributions remains after adjusting for the cost of raising the contributions?	Total contributions − fund-raising costs / Total contributions
Fund-raising efficiency	Are the costs of raising contributions an appropriately small percentage of the contributions received?	Fund-raising expenses / Public support
Investment performance	Is the rate of total return on investments reasonable?	Interest and dividend income ± realized and unrealized gains/losses / Average fair value of investments [(balance at the beginning of the year + end of the year)/2]

determined, the amounts are material, expenses related to services require specialized skills, are provided by an individual with specialized skills and would have been incurred even without the donation.[14] At issue is whether fair market value is objective, particularly for corporate contributions of obsolete inventory. If the contribution is overstated, the public interest is not served.

Form 990 provides a substantial amount of information that can be used in evaluating tax-exempt entities; however, this information is not audited. There is a required schedule in Form 990 that reconciles the audited financial statements and the Form 990. These two statements may differ if they use different bases of accounting (i.e., cash vs. accrual) or if there are unrealized gains and losses and gifts-in-kind (which are reported according to generally accepted accounting principles on the audited financial statements, but not on the Form 990).

[14] FASB *ASC* 958-605-25-16.

ILLUSTRATION 14–7 Ten Largest Charitable NFPs and Selected Performance Measures (2013)

Rank		Private Donations (in billions)	Total Revenue (in billions)	Fund-raising Ratio* (percentage)	Program Effectiveness† (percentage)
1	United Way	$3.93	$4.26	91	86
2	Salvation Army	1.86	4.08	89	82
3	Task Force for Global Health	1.66	1.66	100	100
4	Feeding America	1.51	1.55	98	98
5	Catholic Charities USA	1.45	4.39	95	86
6	Goodwill Industries International	0.95	4.90	97	88
7	Food for the Poor	0.89	0.90	97	96
8	American Cancer Society	0.89	0.93	76	72
9	YMCA	0.83	6.24	85	85
10	World Vision	0.83	1.01	87	85

*Fund-raising ratio is calculated as (total contributions − fund-raising costs)/total contributions.

†For the calculation of program effectiveness, see Illustration 14–6.

Sources: William Barrett, contributor to *Forbes,* "The 5 Largest US Charities," November 13, 2013, *http://www.forbes.com/top-charities/* (accessed June 21, 2014).

In addition to financial information, Form 990 asks for a description of significant program service accomplishments in the charity's own words. Illustration 14–7 provides two performance measures for some of the nation's largest public charities based on private contributions.

As the federal government requires outcome and performance measures of its agencies, we should expect those agencies to require the same information from the organizations that receive public funds. Many NFPs are voluntarily reporting some type of service efforts and accomplishments in their annual reports. As this practice becomes more widespread, NFPs are expected to report similar statistics for charitable gifts to stay competitive.

Nonfinancial Performance Measures

Donors, creditors, grantors, and others who review financial performance measures in making decisions about providing resources to a not-for-profit organization also want to know whether the organization is effective in meeting its mission and goals. Nonfinancial performance measures are critical in addressing questions of effectiveness and efficiency. Several NFPs have collaborated to set up a common framework for measuring performance, with core indicators to guide NFPs in the development of their own performance measurement systems.

The Panel on the Nonprofit Sector, set up by the Independent Sector, has recommended that NFPs establish procedures for measuring and evaluating their program accomplishments based on their goals and objectives. In response, the Urban Institute and The Center for What Works have collaborated in the Outcome Indicators Project to develop a common outcome indicators framework. The group has developed a sample outcome monitoring chart and indicators for 14 different program areas, which are available at *www.urban.org/nonprofits/index.cfm.* Program areas include adult education and family literacy, affordable housing, emergency shelter, performing arts, and youth mentoring, among others. Although an NFP program will never be able to show that its actions were entirely responsible for outcomes, the attempt to measure and draw correlations is a valiant effort at accountability for the scarce dollars entrusted to NFPs to make a difference.

SUMMARY

This chapter provides a general description of tax laws and other state and federal regulations, so that accountants and decision makers using financial information are familiar with the environment within which tax-exempt organizations operate. It should be clear that a thorough understanding of current case law about exempt organizations is also important. More specific details are available in Internal Revenue Service literature available on its Web site (*www.irs.gov*) and books on taxation of tax-exempt organizations. NFPs can expect increased scrutiny and accountability for performance outcomes as a more well-informed public demands it and as technology enables government agencies, such as the IRS, to audit and monitor tax-exempt organizations.

Key Terms

Charitable solicitation, *577*
Debt-financed income, *586*
Disqualified person, *586*
Excess benefit transaction, *586*
Federated fund-raising organization, *581*
Feeder organization, *585*
Grass-roots lobbying, *583*
Influencing, *578*
Intermediate sanctions, *586*
Legislation, *583*
Lobbying, *583*
Organizational test, *580*
Political organization, *582*
Private foundation, *581*
Propaganda, *582*
Public charity, *581*
Unrelated business income, (UBI), *585*

Selected References

John H. McCarthy, Nancy E. Shelmon, and John Mattie. *Financial and Accounting Guide for Not-for-Profit Organizations*, 8th ed. New York: John Wiley & Sons, 2012.

Internal Revenue Service, Department of Treasury. *Application for Recognition of Exemption under Sec. 501(c)(3) of the Internal Revenue Code.* Instructions and Form 1023.

______. Pub. 557. *Tax-Exempt Status for Your Organization.*

______. Pub. 598. *Tax on Unrelated Business Income of Exempt Organizations.*

______. Pub. 1771. *Charitable Contributions Substantiation & Disclosure Requirements.*

______. Pub. 4221-PC. *Compliance Guide for 501(c)(3) Public Charities.*

Ober Kaler. Attorneys at Law *The Nonprofit Legal Landscape.* Washington, DC: Boardsource, 2005.

Roeger, Katie L., Amy Blackwood, and Sarah Pettijohn. *The Nonprofit Almanac.* Washington, DC: The Urban Institute Press, 2012.

Web sites for Not-for-Profit Support Organizations

American Institute of Philanthropy, *www.charitywatch.org*
BBB Wise Giving Alliance, *www.give.org*
Boardsource, Inc., *www.boardsource.org*
Guidestar, Inc., *www.guidestar.org*
Independent Sector, *www.independentsector.org*
National Center for Charitable Statistics, at the Urban Institute, *www.nccs.urban.org*

Periodicals

Chronicle of Philanthropy, http://philanthropy.com.

Nonprofit Management and Leadership, Wiley Periodicals, Inc.

Nonprofit and Voluntary Sector Quarterly, Association for Research on Nonprofit Organizations and Voluntary Action (ARNOVA), *www.arnova.org.*

Exempt Organization Tax Review. Tax Analysts.

The Nonprofit Times, http://www.nptimes.com.

Questions

14–1. Identify which level(s) of government regulate(s) NFP organizations and identify the source of authority.

14–2. Explain a major difference between a 501(c)(3) tax-exempt organization and a 501(c)(7) tax-exempt organization.

14–3. What is the purpose of the Form 990? Because there are different types of Form 990, explain how an NFP would know which type it must file.

14–4. What are the distinguishing characteristics between a public charity and a private foundation? What is a public support test and how does it relate to public charities and private foundations?

14–5. Discuss what, if any, political activity can be undertaken by a charitable NFP organization.

14–6. How can a not-for-profit museum ensure that its gift shop activities will not result in an unrelated business income tax liability?

14–7. What is an IRC Sec. 527 organization? Are these organizations tax-exempt? What filing requirements have been imposed on 527 organizations by campaign finance laws?

14–8. What are excessive benefits and what are the consequences of paying/receiving excessive benefits?

14–9. The financial manager of a not-for-profit child care center wants to improve the monthly report to the board and has decided to include performance measures. What are the benefits of providing performance measures? How will board members be able to determine if the centers' performance is "good" or "poor"?

14–10. What are articles of incorporation and how do they differ from by-laws of a NFP organization?

Cases

14–11 Research Case—Analysis of a Not-for-Profit Organization. Go to the Web site for the American Institute of Certified Public Accountants (AICPA) (*www.aicpa.org*). Information relevant to the following questions can be located under the tab that provides information about the organization.

Required

a. Under what IRC code section does the AICPA receive its tax-exempt status? What is the AICPA's primary source of revenue and does it appear to support the IRC tax-exempt classification of the AICPA?

b. The AICPA lists preferred stock in the net asset section of its statement of financial position. Would you normally expect to see issued stock on the statement of a NFP organization? Explain why the AICPA has preferred stock listed in its net asset section.

c. Is the AICPA subject to unrelated business income tax (UBIT)? Support your answer.

d. What is the AICPA's program effectiveness ratio (see Illustration 14–6 for calculation)? How does the AICPA's ratio compare to the ratios of the charitable organizations listed on Illustration 14–7? Would you expect the ratios to be similar? Why or why not?

e. What evidence is provided that indicates that the AICPA practices good governance?

14–12 Research Case—Unrelated Business Income Tax. Phyllis Gene is a certified human resource manager who serves on the board of a local professional association of human resource managers. The association puts on an annual conference for its members at which there are educational workshops and keynote speakers. For the first time, the board is considering setting up an exhibit space for vendors. The board believes that the sale of exhibit space to vendors could result in substantial revenues, which could be used to support the association's mission. A concern of Ms. Gene's is whether the revenues generated would be subject to unrelated business income tax. As a result, Gene has asked your assistance, as an accounting student, in helping determine any tax implications related to the proposal.

Required

a. Create a list of questions to pose to the executive director of the association about the proposed advertising, so that the board has all the relevant facts on hand.

b. What resources are available to investigate whether income from advertising is subject to unrelated business income tax?

c. Prepare a memo to Ms. Gene that outlines the key issues and suggest an approach to minimize any tax effects.

14–13 Research Case—Performance Measures. Go to the Internet Web sites of any five of the charitable organizations listed in Illustration 14–7 and search for financial information and performance measures they may disclose on their Web sites.

Required

a. For the most recent year provided on the organization's Web site, calculate the program effectiveness ratio for each organization (as a percentage of total expenses) as well as the fund-raising ratio (contributions − fund-raising costs/contributions). How do the ratios you calculated compare to the values provided in Illustration 14–7?

b. Select other financial performance measures from Illustration 14–6 and calculate those measures.

c. How many years of financial information is provided by each organization? Why is it valuable to have multiple years of financial data available?

d. Prepare a table showing the five charities and the performance measures calculated for each. Which charity would you consider the most efficient and effective? Why?

14–14 Research Case—Evaluating Charity Organizations. In 2013, the *Tampa Bay Times* published a series of four articles uncovering some of the worst charities in America. Read the articles *(www.tampabay.com/topics/specials/worst-charities.page)* and answer the following questions.

Required

a. What performance measurements did the *Tampa Bay Times* use to determine which charities were the worst? Do you believe these measurements were the right ones to use? If so, explain why you agree; if not, suggest other measures and explain why you think they are more relevant.

b. There are several other Web sites that provide information about the performance of charities. For each of the following, identify what performance measures are used.

(1) Charity Navigator *(www.charitynavigator.org)*

(2) CharityWatch *(www.charitywatch.org)*

(3) Guidestar *(www.guidestar.org)*

(4) Better Business Bureau Wise Giving Alliance *(www.bbb.org/us/charity/)*

c. Review the *Times*'s list of the 50 worst charities and pick two. Also pick two charities not on the list to which you have contributed or to which you would consider contributing. Rank the four charities you have selected from best to worst, using information obtained from at least two of the Web sites listed in part *b*. Explain what measures you used to rank the charities. How does your evaluation of the two worst charities compare to the *Times*'s evaluation?

14–15 Research Case—Performance Evaluation of a Not-for-Profit. You are considering making a contribution to the Conservation Fund. However, as an accountant you decide to conduct "due diligence" related to the efficiency and effectiveness of the Conservation Fund before making your contribution. You are aware of two Web sites that can assist you in your research; the first is operated by the American Institute of Philanthropy *(www.charitywatch.org)*, and the other is operated by the Better Business Bureau *(www.give.org)*.

Required

a. What grade (or rating) did the Conservation Fund receive from the American Institute of Philanthropy (AIP)? What criteria are used by AIP in assigning grades? Interpret the grade received by the Conservation Fund.

b. Does the Conservation Fund meet the Better Business Bureau's (BBB) standards for charity accountability? Why or why not?

c. Using the BBB Web site, provide statistics on the Conservation Fund's program effectiveness and fund-raising efficiency.

d. Based on your answers to parts *a–c*, does it appear the Conservation Fund is efficient and effective?

Exercises and Problems

14–16 Multiple Choice. Choose the best answer.

1. Jan and Dean decided to form a charitable organization, I Love Rock N Rollers, to provide funding to assist former rock and roll group members who have become homeless. They are planning to hold a "mini-Woodstock" event to raise money, with music by groups from the '60s and '70s. The event will offer food and beverages and the sale of memorabilia related to the event. Before they go any further, Jan and Dean need to:

   a. Prepare articles of incorporation and by-laws, obtain an EIN from the IRS if the organization will have employees, apply for permission to solicit charitable contributions, and apply for 501(c)(3) status from the IRS.

b. Prepare articles of incorporation and by-laws and file them with the state, obtain an EIN from the IRS if the organization will have employees, apply for permission to solicit charitable contributions, and apply for 501 (a) status from the IRS.
c. Prepare articles of incorporation and by-laws and file them with the state, obtain an EIN from the IRS, apply for permission to solicit charitable contributions, and apply for 501 (c) (3) status from the IRS.
d. Prepare articles of incorporation and by-laws, obtain an EIN from the IRS, apply for permission to solicit charitable contributions, and apply for 501 (a) status from the IRS.

2. When organizers and directors apply for not-for-profit status from a state, they are subject to which of the following?
   a. Oversight, transparency, and accountability for performance.
   b. Supervision, transparency, and profitability.
   c. Oversight, reliability, and transparency of performance.
   d. Responsibility for performance, accountability, and liability.
3. Approval from the IRS of 501(c)(3) status exempts an organization from which of the following?
   a. All taxes.
   b. Federal income taxes.
   c. Federal and state income taxes.
   d. Income taxes and sales taxes.
4. Under the IRC, public charities are allowed to conduct direct lobbying activity. What, if any, limit is placed on such lobbying?
   a. There is no limit provided no propaganda is distributed by the charity.
   b. There is no limit provided no individual or group contributes more than $500 to lobbying activity in any one year.
   c. There is no limit provided the lobbying activity directly affects the NFP's charitable purpose.
   d. There is a limit of up to $1,000,000 a year based on the size of the NFP's exempt program costs.
5. A not-for-profit organization that is exempt from federal income taxes under IRC Sec. 501(c)(3), exists to make grants to public charities, and receives its support from a small number of individuals or corporations and investment income rather than from the public at large is called a:
   a. Private foundation.
   b. Public charity.
   c. Nongovernmental organization.
   d. Public foundation.
6. An organization was formed solely to support the creation of a high-speed rail system between two major metropolitan areas. The organization will be offering voter education seminars to be sure that the public is educated about the benefits of the rail system before the proposal is presented to the legislature. Under what circumstances would the organization be able to maintain charitable tax-exempt status?
   a. Information in its brochures is strictly based on confirmable facts.
   b. The brochures provide information only about the benefits of the system but do not directly attempt to persuade voters to vote for the system.

c. The organization properly elects to make expenditures to influence legislation on Form 5768.
d. The organization would not be eligible for charitable tax-exempt status.

7. Artists Unlimited was formed to support the local art community. Which of the following activities would be considered unrelated business income?
a. Income from the sale of tee shirts that feature art reproductions by local artists, produced and sold by volunteers.
b. Interest and dividend income from investments that were donated by a major retail company.
c. Sponsorship of an event by an art supply company, whose name was prominently displayed at the event.
d. Monthly rental fees for office space used by two small legal firms. The rental fees are used to make mortgage and interest payments on Artists Unlimited's building.

8. You are considering contributing to a local charity whose primary function is to provide after-school care for underprivileged children. However, you saw in the paper that the president of the organization just bought a house that is located in a very expensive gated community, and you are concerned that more money is going to the president's salary than to the actual after-school care. Before you donate, you want to feel comfortable that this is not the case. Which of the following is a financial measurement that might help you in determining the amount of resources going to after-school care?
a. Fund-raising efficiency.
b. Program effectiveness.
c. Fund-raising ratio.
d. Efficiency.

9. The tool the IRS most likely will use when key officers in a tax-exempt entity receive excess economic benefits from transactions with the not-for-profit organization is:
a. Fines and forfeits.
b. Revocation of the organization's tax-exempt status.
c. Intermediate sanctions.
d. Public display of offenders on the IRS's Web site.

10. When a tax-exempt organization dissolves, the managers must ensure that:
a. All assets are appropriately transferred to another tax-exempt organization.
b. All creditors get paid.
c. All federal, state, and local taxes are paid.
d. All of the above.

14–17 Public Charity. The Let's Read organization is a public charity under IRC Sec. 501(c)(3). It had total support of the following:

United Way support	$ 10,000
Grant from the state	25,000
Grant from the city	10,000
Contributions from individuals	261,000
Investment income	1,000
Revenue from the sale of books	12,000
	$319,000

Of the $261,000 received from contributors, $240,000 came from four contributors, each of whom gave $60,000; the other $21,000 came from small individual contributions.

Required

a. Calculate the total amount of support that qualifies as "public support" in meeting the public support test to escape private foundation status.
b. Is the organization considered a public charity? Why?
c. If the organization had received $200,000 from one individual, and the remaining $61,000 from many small individual contributions, would the NFP still be classified the same as in your response to part *b*?

14–18 Identifying Tax-exempt Status. Use Illustration 14–3 as a guide in completing this exercise.

______ 1. Fredericksburg Chamber of Commerce
______ 2. American Diabetes Association
______ 3. American Legion
______ 4. American Museum of Natural History
______ 5. American Institute of Certified Public Accountants
______ 6. Wee Care Daycare
______ 7. Allentown Racquetball Association
______ 8. Citizen's to Elect Harvey

Required

In the space to the left of each number indicate under which Internal Revenue Code section each of the above NFP entities is most likely to be exempt from federal income tax.

14–19 Unrelated Business Income Tax. The Silverton Symphony Orchestra Hall is a well-established not-for-profit organization exempt under IRC Sec. 501(c)(3) that owns a facility that is home to the local symphony orchestra. Its mission is to increase access to the arts for the community of Silverton. The facility is used throughout the year for many activities.

	Subject to UBIT	Not Subject to UBIT
1. Sale of Silverton Symphony Orchestra Concert CDs in the facility's gift shop.		
2. Rental of the facility to the high school drama club.		
3. Rental of two apartments in the facility to the symphony.		
4. Sale of the season ticket membership list to a local music store.		
5. Rental of the facility to the state CPA association for continuing professional education events.		
6. Internet sales of gift shop items with the Silverton Symphony Orchestra logo.		
7. Lease of the facility's parking lot to the local university on football game days.		

Required

In the boxes provided, check whether the regularly conducted activity of Silverton Symphony Hall is/is not subject to unrelated business income tax. (*Hint:* IRS Publication 598 may be helpful in answering this question. It is available at *www.irs.gov* under "Charities and Non-Profits" and "UBIT.")

14–20 Intermediate Sanctions. Listed are four independent situations involving transactions between individuals and an NFP organization.

1. Jane is president of an IRC Sec. 501(c)(3) public charity and personally owns a building that she has decided to sell to the not-for-profit organization. The appraisal value is $200,000, and the agreed-upon selling price is $250,000.
2. A large public charity is very happy with its president's performance and offers him a new compensation agreement for the coming year. He will receive a base salary plus a percentage of the increase in the gross revenues of the organization with no limitation as to the maximum amount.
3. Ann is a member and the director of a symphony association. She receives 20 free admission tickets as a member of the organization.
4. The local chapter of the United Way recently hired Joe Curtis as its new president at a salary of $200,000. The outgoing president was paid $150,000. Mr. Curtis had other offers that ranged from $95,000 to $190,000. The minutes of the meeting reflected that he was exceptionally talented and would not have accepted the position for a lower salary.

Required

For each of the independent transactions, determine whether the NFP is at risk for receiving intermediate sanctions from the Internal Revenue Service for conferring excess economic benefits on disqualified persons. If so, indicate how the organization can minimize those sanctions.

14–21 Performance Measures. Information from the 2012 Form 990 and the 2013 annual report for Feeding America, follows. Although the Form 990 indicates it is for 2012, it is actually for the period July 1, 2012, to June 30, 2013, the same time period as the 2013 annual report. Use the following information to complete the exercise.

Required

a. Compute the following performance measures using the Form 990 data presented in this exercise and comment on what information they convey to a potential donor without comparing them to prior years or other comparable agencies.
   1. Current ratio—liquidity.
   2. Revenues/expenses—going concern.
   3. Program expenses/total expenses—program effectiveness.
   4. Public support/fund-raising expenses—fund-raising efficiency.

b. Using the annual financial statements provided in this exercise, calculate the same ratios listed in requirement *a.* Comment on any differences.

c. Discuss the advantages of analyzing financial performance using audited annual financial statement information versus IRS Form 990 information.

Form 990 (2012) Page 9

Part VIII Statement of Revenue

Check if Schedule O contains a response to any question in this Part VIII . . . . . ☐

Section	Line	Description	Sub-line	Amount	(A) Total revenue	(B) Related or exempt function revenue	(C) Unrelated business revenue	(D) Revenue excluded from tax under sections 512, 513, or 514
Contributions, Gifts, Grants and Other Similar Amounts	1a	Federated campaigns	1a					
	b	Membership dues	1b					
	c	Fundraising events	1c					
	d	Related organizations	1d					
	e	Government grants (contributions)	1e					
	f	All other contributions, gifts, grants, and similar amounts not included above	1f	1,855,398,787.				
	g	Noncash contributions included in lines 1a-1f: $ 1,783,122,499.						
	h	**Total.** Add lines 1a-1f ▶			1,855,398,787.			
Program Service Revenue			Business Code					
	2a	FOOD PROCUREMENT REVENUE	900099		14,910,058.	14,910,058.		
	b	MEMBER FEES	900099		2,969,803.	2,969,803.		
	c	CONFERENCE REVENUE	900099		996,480.	996,480.		
	d	TRAINING	900099		68,288.	68,288.		
	e	INTEREST INCOME	900099		19,956.	19,956.		
	f	All other program service revenue						
	g	**Total.** Add lines 2a-2f ▶			18,964,585.			
Other Revenue	3	Investment income (including dividends, interest, and other similar amounts) ▶			376,537.			376,537.
	4	Income from investment of tax-exempt bond proceeds ▶			0			
	5	Royalties ▶			16,417,505.			16,417,505.
			(i) Real	(ii) Personal				
	6a	Gross rents	49,114.					
	b	Less: rental expenses	61,373.					
	c	Rental income or (loss)	-12,259.					
	d	Net rental income or (loss) ▶			-12,259.			-12,259.
			(i) Securities	(ii) Other				
	7a	Gross amount from sales of assets other than inventory	10,819,000.	187,427.				
	b	Less: cost or other basis and sales expenses	10,862,628.	192,427.				
	c	Gain or (loss)	-43,628.	-5,000.				
	d	Net gain or (loss) ▶			-48,628.			-48,628.
	8a	Gross income from fundraising events (not including $ ____ of contributions reported on line 1c). See Part IV, line 18	a					
	b	Less: direct expenses	b					
	c	Net income or (loss) from fundraising events ▶			0			
	9a	Gross income from gaming activities. See Part IV, line 19	a					
	b	Less: direct expenses	b					
	c	Net income or (loss) from gaming activities ▶			0			
	10a	Gross sales of inventory, less returns and allowances	a	51,043,799.				
	b	Less: cost of goods sold	b	51,001,425.				
	c	Net income or (loss) from sales of inventory ▶			42,374.	42,374.		
		Miscellaneous Revenue	Business Code					
	11a	OTHER FEES	900099		1,754,835.	1,754,835.		
	b	PUBLICATIONS AND MATERIALS FEE	900099		464,891.	464,891.		
	c							
	d	All other revenue						
	e	**Total.** Add lines 11a-11d ▶			2,219,726.			
	12	**Total revenue.** See instructions ▶			1,893,358,627.	21,226,685.		16,733,155.

Form **990** (2012)

Part IX Statement of Functional Expenses

Section 501(c)(3) and 501(c)(4) organizations must complete all columns. All other organizations must complete column (A).

Check if Schedule O contains a response to any question in this Part IX . . . . [X]

Do not include amounts reported on lines 6b, 7b, 8b, 9b, and 10b of Part VIII.	(A) Total expenses	(B) Program service expenses	(C) Management and general expenses	(D) Fundraising expenses
1 Grants and other assistance to governments and organizations in the United States. See Part IV, line 21	1,812,857,224.	1,812,857,224.		
2 Grants and other assistance to individuals in the United States. See Part IV, line 22	12,500.	12,500.		
3 Grants and other assistance to governments, organizations, and individuals outside the United States. See Part IV, lines 15 and 16	0			
4 Benefits paid to or for members	0			
5 Compensation of current officers, directors, trustees, and key employees	2,837,929.	1,091,164.	1,461,519.	285,246.
6 Compensation not included above, to disqualified persons (as defined under section 4958(f)(1)) and persons described in section 4958(c)(3)(B)	0			
7 Other salaries and wages	17,232,872.	10,809,414.	2,699,932.	3,723,526.
8 Pension plan accruals and contributions (include section 401(k) and 403(b) employer contributions)	802,073.	483,867.	143,021.	175,185.
9 Other employee benefits	1,889,271.	1,297,898.	91,420.	499,953.
10 Payroll taxes	1,453,039.	856,437.	322,228.	274,374.
11 Fees for services (non-employees):				
a Management	0			
b Legal	28,937.		28,937.	
c Accounting	194,828.		177,402.	17,426.
d Lobbying	183,544.	183,544.		
e Professional fundraising services. See Part IV, line 17	3,352,444.			3,352,444.
f Investment management fees	45,358.		45,358.	
g Other. (If line 11g amount exceeds 10% of line 25, column (A) amount, list line 11g expenses on Schedule O.)	6,317,055.	3,592,758.	760,042.	1,964,255.
12 Advertising and promotion	2,239,042.	1,123,828.		1,115,214.
13 Office expenses	936,184.	760,809.	80,678.	94,697.
14 Information technology	2,366,587.	1,785,854.	183,626.	397,107.
15 Royalties	0			
16 Occupancy	1,638,819.	1,097,146.	120,425.	421,248.
17 Travel	1,346,568.	1,066,021.	92,643.	187,904.
18 Payments of travel or entertainment expenses for any federal, state, or local public officials	0			
19 Conferences, conventions, and meetings	1,232,538.	1,114,260.	92,674.	25,604.
20 Interest	30,472.	30,472.		
21 Payments to affiliates	0			
22 Depreciation, depletion, and amortization	378,142.	232,417.	66,650.	79,075.
23 Insurance	96,240.	55,747.	19,057.	21,436.
24 Other expenses. Itemize expenses not covered above (List miscellaneous expenses in line 24e. If line 24e amount exceeds 10% of line 25, column (A) amount, list line 24e expenses on Schedule O.)				
a PRODUCE	17,865,868.	17,865,868.		
b POSTAGE & PRINTING	9,435,655.			9,435,655.
c DISASTER PURCHASES & TRANSPO	1,585,081.	1,585,081.		
d MISCELLANEOUS	640,450.	162,581.	436,426.	41,443.
e All other expenses				
25 **Total functional expenses.** Add lines 1 through 24e	1,886,998,720.	1,858,064,890.	6,822,038.	22,111,792.
26 **Joint costs.** Complete this line only if the organization reported in column (B) joint costs from a combined educational campaign and fundraising solicitation. Check here ▶ [ ] if following SOP 98-2 (ASC 958-720)	0			

Form 990 (2012) Page 11

Part X Balance Sheet

Check if Schedule O contains a response to any question in this Part X . . . . ☐

			(A) Beginning of year		(B) End of year
Assets	1	Cash - non-interest-bearing	16,418,663.	1	24,906,039.
	2	Savings and temporary cash investments	0	2	0
	3	Pledges and grants receivable, net	23,661,170.	3	21,689,039.
	4	Accounts receivable, net	4,608,740.	4	4,543,820.
	5	Loans and other receivables from current and former officers, directors, trustees, key employees, and highest compensated employees. Complete Part II of Schedule L	0	5	0
	6	Loans and other receivables from other disqualified persons (as defined under section 4958(f)(1)), persons described in section 4958(c)(3)(B), and contributing employers and sponsoring organizations of section 501(c)(9) voluntary employees' beneficiary organizations (see instructions). Complete Part II of Schedule L	0	6	0
	7	Notes and loans receivable, net	0	7	0
	8	Inventories for sale or use	245,971.	8	0
	9	Prepaid expenses and deferred charges	911,286.	9	974,092.
	10a	Land, buildings, and equipment: cost or other basis. Complete Part VI of Schedule D — 10a — 4,042,955.			
	b	Less: accumulated depreciation — 10b — 2,457,402.	1,931,961.	10c	1,585,553.
	11	Investments - publicly traded securities	14,269,430.	11	17,527,004.
	12	Investments - other securities. See Part IV, line 11	29,581.	12	33,527.
	13	Investments - program-related. See Part IV, line 11	476,363.	13	682,128.
	14	Intangible assets	0	14	0
	15	Other assets. See Part IV, line 11	23,210.	15	23,218.
	16	**Total assets.** Add lines 1 through 15 (must equal line 34)	62,576,375.	16	71,964,420.
Liabilities	17	Accounts payable and accrued expenses	8,902,357.	17	12,915,046.
	18	Grants payable	6,075,567.	18	5,043,646.
	19	Deferred revenue	350,152.	19	618,895.
	20	Tax-exempt bond liabilities	0	20	0
	21	Escrow or custodial account liability. Complete Part IV of Schedule D	476,198.	21	465,607.
	22	Loans and other payables to current and former officers, directors, trustees, key employees, highest compensated employees, and disqualified persons. Complete Part II of Schedule L	0	22	0
	23	Secured mortgages and notes payable to unrelated third parties	0	23	0
	24	Unsecured notes and loans payable to unrelated third parties	1,625,000.	24	1,125,000.
	25	Other liabilities (including federal income tax, payables to related third parties, and other liabilities not included on lines 17-24). Complete Part X of Schedule D	2,380,450.	25	2,590,936.
	26	**Total liabilities.** Add lines 17 through 25	19,809,724.	26	22,759,130.
Net Assets or Fund Balances		**Organizations that follow SFAS 117 (ASC 958), check here ▶ [X] and complete lines 27 through 29, and lines 33 and 34.**			
	27	Unrestricted net assets	15,467,988.	27	17,037,259.
	28	Temporarily restricted net assets	25,731,620.	28	30,592,480.
	29	Permanently restricted net assets	1,567,043.	29	1,575,551.
		Organizations that do not follow SFAS 117 (ASC 958), check here ▶ [ ] and complete lines 30 through 34.			
	30	Capital stock or trust principal, or current funds		30	
	31	Paid-in or capital surplus, or land, building, or equipment fund		31	
	32	Retained earnings, endowment, accumulated income, or other funds		32	
	33	Total net assets or fund balances	42,766,651.	33	49,205,290.
	34	Total liabilities and net assets/fund balances	62,576,375.	34	71,964,420.

Form **990** (2012)

FEEDING AMERICA
Statements of Financial Position
June 30, 2013 and 2012
(In thousands)

	2013	2012
Assets		
Current assets:		
Cash	$ 24,906	16,419
Short-term investments	2,370	2,353
Contributions receivable, net	16,487	16,263
Accounts receivable, net	4,544	4,218
Notes receivable, net	426	390
Other assets	974	1,157
Total current assets	49,707	40,800
Long-term investments	15,191	11,946
Contributions receivable, net	5,202	7,399
Notes receivable, net	256	476
Other assets	23	23
Furniture and equipment, net of accumulated depreciation of $2,457 and $2,268 in 2013 and 2012, respectively	1,586	1,932
Total assets	$ 71,965	62,576
Liabilities and Net Assets		
Current liabilities:		
Accounts payable and accrued expenses	$ 17,570	12,576
Deferred revenue	619	350
Other obligations	74	75
Current portion of loan payable	562	500
Current portion of leases payable	220	146
Total current liabilities	19,045	13,647
Loan payable	563	1,125
Leases payable	2,334	2,234
Other obligations	817	2,803
Total liabilities	22,759	19,809
Net assets:		
Unrestricted	17,036	15,468
Temporarily restricted	30,594	25,732
Permanently restricted	1,576	1,567
Total net assets	49,206	42,767
Total liabilities and net assets	$ 71,965	62,576

FEEDING AMERICA
Statements of Activities
Years ended June 30, 2013 and 2012 (In thousands)

	2013				2012			
	Unrestricted	Temporarily restricted	Permanently restricted	Total	Unrestricted	Temporarily restricted	Permanently restricted	Total
Operating activities:								
Public support and revenue:								
Public support:								
Individual contributions	$ 28,813	1,378	—	30,191	28,540	586	—	29,126
Corporate contributions	23,663	15,048	—	38,711	18,840	9,681	—	28,521
Foundations	2,247	507	—	2,754	1,371	582	—	1,953
Corporate promotions	14,652	1,765	—	16,417	14,704	4,007	—	18,711
Total fundraising	69,375	18,698	—	88,073	63,455	14,856	—	78,311
Donated goods and services	1,784,017	—	—	1,784,017	1,451,995	—	—	1,451,995
Total public support	1,853,392	18,698	—	1,872,090	1,515,450	14,856	—	1,530,306
Revenue:								
Member fees	2,970	—	—	2,970	2,427	—	—	2,427
Conference fees	996	—	—	996	1,245	—	—	1,245
Other revenue	2,317	—	—	2,317	618	—	—	618
Food procurement revenue	65,980	—	—	65,980	62,603	—	—	62,603
Investment income	83	—	—	83	121	—	—	121
Investment return designated for operations	—	—	—	—	401	—	—	401
Net assets released from restriction	13,689	(13,689)	—	—	20,449	(20,449)	—	—
Total public support and revenue	1,939,427	5,009	—	1,944,436	1,603,314	5,593	—	1,597,721
Expenses:								
Program services:								
Member services	34,151	—	—	34,151	38,591	—	—	38,591
Food procurement	1,864,444	—	—	1,864,444	1,522,192	—	—	1,522,192
Public awareness and education	3,769	—	—	3,769	4,269	—	—	4,269
Public programs and policy	3,639	—	—	3,639	3,638	—	—	3,638
Research and analysis	4,099	—	—	4,099	1,841	—	—	1,841
Total program services	1,910,102	—	—	1,910,102	1,570,531	—	—	1,570,531
Supporting services:								
Management and general	7,148	—	—	7,148	7,434	—	—	7,434
Fund development	22,143	—	—	22,143	24,730	—	—	24,730
Total supporting services	29,291	—	—	29,291	32,164	—	—	32,164
Total expenses	1,939,393	—	—	1,939,393	1,602,695	—	—	1,602,695
Increase (decrease) in net assets as a result of operations	34	5,009	—	5,043	619	(5,593)	—	(4,974)
Nonoperating activities:								
Wills and bequests	746	—	—	746	451	—	—	451
Individual contributions	—	—	4	4	—	—	30	30
Investment return	801	170	—	971	(321)	(58)	—	(379)
Other	(8)	(317)	5	(320)	(19)	(412)	—	(431)
Investment return designated for operations	—	—	—	—	(401)	—	—	(401)
Loss on disposition of furniture and equipment	(5)	—	—	(5)	(33)	—	—	(33)
Changes in net assets	1,568	4,862	9	6,439	296	(6,063)	30	(5,737)
Net assets at beginning of year	15,468	25,732	1,567	42,767	15,172	31,795	1,537	48,504
Net assets at end of year	$ 17,036	30,594	1,576	49,206	15,468	25,732	1,567	42,767

Chapter **Fifteen**

Accounting for Colleges and Universities

Learning Objectives

After studying this chapter, you should be able to:

15-1 Distinguish between generally accepted accounting principles for public and private colleges and universities.

15-2 Describe financial reporting for public and private colleges and universities.

15-3 Discuss accounting and reporting issues for all colleges and universities, such as accounting for assets, liabilities, and net assets/net position; accounting for revenues and expenses; and accounting for cash flows.

15-4 Journalize transactions and prepare financial statements for private colleges and universities.

15-5 Discuss issues related to colleges and universities, such as planned giving, auditing, and federal financial assistance.

Institutions of higher learning have long been dichotomized into public colleges and universities, which are governmental in nature, and private colleges and universities, which are nongovernmental not-for-profit organizations. Because traditionally, the terms *public* and *private,* rather than *governmental* and *not-for-profit* are used to distinguish these two type of institutions, the text uses the terms *public* and *private*.

Public institutions generally receive significantly more of their total revenues from state appropriations and research grants, than private institutions, which depend to a larger extent on student tuition and fees, private gifts, and research grants. Also governmental in nature, community colleges are supported in large part by local property tax assessments. More recently, for-profit corporations have joined the higher education market. The National Center for Education Statistics lists 4,706 degree-granting postsecondary institutions in 2011–2012.[1] These institutions enroll approximately 20.6 million students and expended over $488 billion in 2011–2012.[2]

[1] National Center for Education Statistics (NCES), Digest of Education Statistics, 2013, Table 317.10 available at *http://nces.ed.gov/programs/digest/2013menu_tables.asp.*

[2] Ibid., Tables 303.25, 334.10, and 334.70.

The focus of this chapter is on accounting and reporting that is unique to colleges and universities. Comparisons are also made between the accounting and reporting for private and public colleges and universities.

ACCOUNTING AND FINANCIAL REPORTING STANDARDS

For most of the 20th century, the majority of institutions in the higher education industry followed a single set of accounting and financial reporting standards. This guidance was described in the AICPA Audit Guide *Audits of Colleges and Universities* and included standards set by the American Institute of Certified Public Accountants (AICPA) in cooperation with committees of the National Association of College and University Business Officers (NACUBO) and task forces of groups related to the U.S. Department of Education.

In 1984, the GASB was given jurisdiction over accounting and financial reporting standards for public colleges and universities. Jurisdiction for private and for-profit colleges and universities was retained by the FASB. From 1984 until 1993 reporting for public and private colleges and universities was not significantly different. In 1993 the FASB changed the reporting model for private and for-profit colleges and universities, standardizing the way all nongovernmental not-for-profit entities report to the public, making them report more like businesses and less like governments. An important presumption was that decision makers would find this format more useful, even though comparability between public and private colleges and universities would be made more difficult.[3]

One of the most significant changes in the reporting model was the elimination of fund reporting. While external financial reports of private colleges and universities no longer provide fund information, many colleges and universities may continue to use fund accounting for internal purposes. For these institutions, a worksheet can be used to convert fund accounting information to institution-wide information necessary for the basic financial statements. Fund information may also be included as supplementary information in the financial report. The most commonly used funds are unrestricted current funds, restricted current funds, plant funds, loan funds, endowment funds, annuity and life-income funds, and agency funds. Additional information concerning funds can be found in the AICPA Audit and Accounting Guide, *Not-for-Profit Entities.*

Generally accepted accounting principles (GAAP) for private and for-profit colleges and universities are found in the FASB *Codification.* Information provided in the AICPA Audit and Accounting Guide, *Not-for-Profit Entities,* and information provided by NACUBO serve as guidance for private and for-profit colleges and universities but are not considered GAAP unless incorporated into the codification.

After much due process, the GASB changed the public colleges and universities reporting model in 1999. Under the model adopted in 1999, public colleges and universities use the same reporting model as special purpose governments and possibly enterprise funds or component units of another governmental entity (see Chapters 3–9).[4] As a result of GASB's actions, comparability between public and private entities is again possible.

[3] John H. Engstrom and Connie Esmond-Kiger, "Different Formats, Same User Needs: Do the FASB and GASB College and University Reporting Models Meet User Needs?" *Accounting Horizons* 11 (September 1997), pp. 16–34.

[4] See Appendices A and B in *GASBS 35* for details on the due process and other background information, pars. 13–20.

GAAP for public colleges and universities are found in the GASB standards. The GASB[5] incorporated the AICPA Audit and Accounting Guides into the GAAP hierarchy as category (b) accounting principles. Guidance from NACUBO would be considered as category (d) accounting principles under the hierarchy.

Because many of the accounting and financial reporting requirements for private colleges and universities were addressed in Chapter 13, and those for public colleges and universities were addressed in Chapter 7, this chapter focuses on accounting and reporting issues typically found in the higher education industry. Particular attention is given to identifying differences in accounting and reporting for private versus public colleges and universities.

Private Colleges and Universities

The FASB requires private colleges and universities to report on the changes in unrestricted, temporarily restricted, and permanently restricted net assets of the entity as a whole, the same as the nongovernmental not-for-profit organizations described in Chapter 13. The reader is directed to that chapter for more information on the definitions of net asset classifications and the considerable discretion that is allowed by FASB in presenting financial information, including optional display of supplementary fund accounting information, if desired. Later in this chapter, Illustrations 15–4, 15–5, and 15–6 present the statement of financial position, statement of activities, and statement of cash flows, respectively, for Valley College, a hypothetical private not-for-profit college. These statement formats are generally the same as those illustrated in Chapter 13.

Public Colleges and Universities

When issuing their financial reports, public colleges and universities are permitted to use the guidance for special purpose governments engaged only in business-type activities, engaged only in governmental activities, or engaged in both.[6] Most public colleges and universities follow the model for public institutions engaged only in business-type activities. For that reason, the discussion of public colleges and universities in this chapter is based on the business-type activity reporting model. The basic financial statements for Midwest University, a hypothetical public university reporting as a business-type activity are presented in Illustrations 15–1, 15–2, and 15–3. These statements include the statement of net position (Illustration 15–1), the statement of revenues, expenses, and changes in net position (Illustration 15–2), and the statement of cash flows (Illustration 15–3). Since the reporting model is that used by business-type activities, the statements are similar in format to Illustrations 7–6, 7–7, and 7–8 for proprietary funds. If a college or university has a component unit, such as a university hospital, it is presented discretely from the primary institution.

Some public higher education institutions, such as community colleges, have "taxing authority," the power to assess special taxes on local residents. These institutions may elect to report as "engaged in governmental-type activities only" or "engaged in both governmental and business-type activities." The basic financial statements are the same as those discussed for state and local governments in Chapters 1 through 9 and shown in Illustrations A2–1 through A2–11 using revenue and expenditure/expense classifications appropriate to colleges and universities. These institutions would use fund accounting, based on the authoritative guidance provided by GASB.

[5] GASB, *Codification,* Sec. 1000.101

[6] GASB, *Codification,* Sec. Co5.

ILLUSTRATION 15–1

MIDWEST UNIVERSITY
Statement of Net Position
June 30, 2017
(in thousands)

	Primary Institution	Component Unit Hospital
Assets		
Current assets:		
Cash and cash equivalents	$ 1,568	$ 98
Short-term investments	428	225
Accounts receivable, net	110	953
Inventories	95	127
Deposits with bond trustee	373	—
Prepaid expenses	29	47
Total current assets	2,603	1,450
Noncurrent assets:		
Endowment investments	10,450	—
Loans receivable, net	613	—
Long-term investments	7,063	646
Capital assets, net of depreciation	63,440	3,260
Total noncurrent assets	81,566	3,906
Total assets	84,169	5,356
Liabilities		
Current liabilities:		
Accounts payable and accrued liabilities	274	291
Unearned revenue	35	—
Deposits held in custody for others	350	—
Annuities and income payable	1,855	—
Long-term liabilities—current portion	1,050	99
Total current liabilities	3,564	390
Noncurrent liabilities:		
Notes payable	600	
Bonds payable	24,000	220
Total noncurrent liabilities	24,600	220
Total liabilities	28,164	610
Net Position		
Net investment in capital assets	37,790	2,941
Restricted for:		
Nonexpendable:		
Scholarships and fellowships	10,496	—
Expendable:		
Research	1,459	228
Instructional department uses	3,417	—
Loans	756	—
Capital projects	2,185	91
Debt service	430	15
Unrestricted	(528)	1,471
Total net position	$56,005	$4,746

Source: Adapted from GASB, *Codification*, Sec. Co5.902.

ILLUSTRATION 15–2

MIDWEST UNIVERSITY
Statement of Revenues, Expenses, and Changes in Net Position
For the Year Ended June 30, 2017
(in thousands)

	Primary Institution	Component Unit Hospital
Operating Revenues		
Tuition and fees (net)	$ 2,690	
Patient services (net)		$4,629
Federal grants and contracts	35	747
Auxiliary activities	2,300	—
Other operating revenues	—	43
Total operating revenues	5,025	5,419
Operating Expenses		
Salaries and wages	5,346	2,699
Benefits	998	775
Scholarships and fellowships	135	—
Utilities	1,211	912
Supplies and other services	215	734
Depreciation	3,000	297
Other operating expenses	302	—
Total operating expenses	11,207	5,417
Operating income (loss)	(6,182)	2
Nonoperating Revenues (Expenses)		
Federal appropriations	438	—
State appropriations	4,170	—
Gifts	1,621	32
Investment income	975	49
Change in fair value of investments	189	—
Interest expense	(1,850)	(3)
Net nonoperating revenues	5,543	78
Income before changes in capital assets and endowments	(639)	80
Capital grants and gifts	220	71
Additions to permanent endowments	2,186	—
Increase in net position	1,767	151
Net Position		
Net position—beginning of year	54,238	4,595
Net position—end of year	$56,005	$4,746

(*Note:* Operating expenses are displayed here using object classification; however, expenses could be shown using functional classification as in Illustration 15–5.)

Source: Adapted from GASB, *Codification,* Sec. Co5.902.

ILLUSTRATION 15–3

MIDWEST UNIVERSITY
Statement of Cash Flows
For the Year Ended June 30, 2017
(in thousands)

	Primary Institution	Component Unit Hospital
Cash Flows from Operating Activities		
Cash received from students for tuition and fees	$ 2,775	—
Research grants and contracts	35	—
Cash received from auxiliary activities	2,300	—
Cash received from patients and third-party payors	—	$1,858
Cash received from Medicaid and Medicare	—	3,164
Payments to suppliers and others	(1,322)	(1,308)
Payments to students—scholarships	(135)	—
Payments to employees	(6,344)	(3,299)
Payments to annuitants	(250)	—
Other payments	(447)	(100)
Net cash provided (used) by operating activities	(3,388)	315
Cash Flows from Noncapital Financing Activities		
Federal appropriations	438	—
State appropriations	4,170	—
Gifts and grants received for endowment purposes	4,192	—
Net cash flows provided by noncapital financing activities	8,800	—
Cash Flows from Capital and Related Financing Activities		
Capital grants and gifts received	220	71
Proceeds from capital debt	500	—
Purchase of capital assets	(1,490)	(195)
Principal paid on capital debt	(550)	(13)
Interest paid on capital debt	(1,850)	(3)
Net cash used by capital and related financing activities	(3,170)	(140)
Cash Flows from Investing Activities		
Proceeds from sales and maturities of investments	2,664	284
Investment income	975	7
Loans	(163)	—
Purchase of investments	(4,825)	(454)
Net cash provided (used) by investing activities	(1,349)	(163)
Net Increase in Cash and Cash Equivalents	893	12
Cash and cash equivalents—beginning of year	675	86
Cash and cash equivalents—end of year	$ 1,568	$ 98
Reconciliation of Net Operating Revenues (Expenses) to Net Cash Provided (Used) by Operating Activities		
Operating income (loss)	$(6,182)	$ 2
Adjustments to reconcile net income (loss) to net cash provided (used) by operating activities:		
Depreciation expense	3,000	297

continued

ILLUSTRATION 15–3 (*Continued*)

	Primary Institution	Component Unit Hospital
Change in assets and liabilities:		
Receivables, net	70	33
Inventories	(15)	(16)
Short-term investments	(128)	—
Deposit with bond trustee	(23)	—
Prepaid expenses	(9)	8
Accounts payable	119	(8)
Unearned revenue	15	—
Deposits held in custody for others	15	—
Annuities payable	(250)	(1)
Net cash provided (used) by operating activities	$(3,388)	$ 315

Source: Adapted from GASB, *Codification,* Sec. Co5.902.

REPORTING AND ACCOUNTING ISSUES

Due to the unique nature of the industry, both private and public colleges and universities often need to look for guidance on issues not specifically addressed by the FASB and GASB standards. Two sources of such guidance are the NACUBO's *Financial Accounting and Reporting Manual for Higher Education (FARM),* and NACUBO's Accounting Principles Council, which studies issues and publishes guidance in the form of implementation guides. Any instances where information is presented in accordance with NACUBO guidance rather than FASB or GASB standards are identified. As indicated earlier, only reporting and accounting issues typical of colleges and universities are presented in the chapter, with differences between public and private institutions identified.

It might be helpful during the following discussion of selected elements of the financial statements to refer periodically to the illustrative financial statements for Midwest University (Illustrations 15–1 through 15–3), a hypothetical public university, and to those of Valley College (Illustrations 15–4 through 15–6, shown later), a hypothetical private college.

Statement of Net Position or Financial Position

Illustration 15–1 presents a statement of net position for a public university, and Illustration 15–4 presents a statement of financial position (or balance sheet) for a private college. Some of the accounting issues related to assets, liabilities, and net assets/position of colleges and universities are discussed next.

Loan Assets

Assets that are loanable to students, faculty, and staff of an educational institution are provided by gifts, grants, and income from endowments. In some cases, loans may also be made to the institution for the purpose of extending loans to eligible individuals. When a loan is made to an individual the college or university would recognize a loan receivable. At the time the loan is collected, the receivable would be removed (credited) and any interest collected on the loan would be recognized as revenue. With the exception of recording any restrictions on loan assets, the recording is the same under the FASB and GASB standards.

Assets that are loanable are classified according to any restrictions. For example, if a donor makes a cash contribution that is to be used for student loans, the cash would be classified as temporarily restricted net assets by private colleges and universities and as restricted net position by public colleges and universities. However, if the board designates cash for loans to students, the cash would be considered unrestricted, designated net assets or net position by private and public colleges and universities, respectively. Finally, if a loan of cash is made to the college or university for the purpose of extending loans to students, it would be recorded as a liability.

Interest earned on loans and interest earned or gains on temporary investments of loan assets are expected to offset wholly or partially the cost of administration of loan activities and the loss from uncollectible loans. Interest on loans should be credited on the accrual basis to appropriate revenue accounts. To the extent that the costs of administering loan activities, losses on investments of loan assets, provision for losses on loans (either estimated or actual), and related expenses and losses exceed interest earnings and gains there will be a reduction in loan net asset balances.

Capital Assets

The recording and reporting of capital assets by colleges and universities is similar under FASB and GASB standards. For example, at initial recognition both use historical cost, which includes all costs necessary to bring the capital asset to a condition and place for its intended use, and both use depreciation to reflect the change in the productivity of the asset subsequent to initial measurement. Although both have similar asset categories, the GASB recognizes two capital asset classifications that are not recognized by FASB: intangible assets and infrastructure assets. The following two paragraphs discuss some differences in capital asset reporting under FASB and GASB standards.

FASB standards require that intangible assets be reported as a separate classification, generally below property, plant, and equipment (capital assets). Since the FASB does not have an infrastructure classification, assets similar to infrastructure, such as sidewalks and streets, could be reported as land improvements. Note disclosures for capital assets include the amount of depreciation expense for the year, end-of-year balances of major classes of depreciable assets, accumulated depreciation, and depreciation method.

GASB standards include intangible assets as a classification within capital assets. Since intangible assets are recorded as a classification with capital assets, all of the recording and reporting requirements for capital assets apply to intangible assets. Because the GASB allows colleges and universities to report infrastructure as a separate classification, colleges and universities may also use the modified approach for reporting infrastructure at reporting dates subsequent to initial acquisition. Under the modified approach, the college or university would implement an asset management system that would document that eligible infrastructure assets are being preserved at a level established by the asset management system. The expenditures incurred to ensure that the assets are maintained at the established level would be expensed in the period incurred. These maintenance costs are reported instead of depreciation expense. Chapter 5 provides additional information on the modified approach. Note disclosures for capital assets should provide detail by asset class in a schedule that includes beginning of the year balances, additions, sales or other dispositions, and end-of-year balances for each asset classification. The notes should also provide information on current period depreciation expense with a disclosure on the amount of depreciation charged to each function of the college or university.

Collections

Many colleges and universities have historical archives, libraries, and museums containing valuable works of art, historical treasures, and similar assets. Both FASB and

GASB provide for note disclosure of such assets rather than reporting them on the balance sheet; both FASB and GASB permit nonrecognition only if the donated items are added to **collections** that meet the conditions outlined in Chapter 13.

Liabilities

One somewhat unfamiliar short-term liability that may appear on college and university statements is Deposits Held in Custody for Others. This account is used to record events such as students making cash deposits for housing, equipment, or services. If the college or university is obligated to return some or all of the deposit at a future date, it should be accounted for as a liability. As an example, assume that a university received from students $50,000 in refundable deposits for dormitory rooms. The college would record the following entry.

	Debits	Credits
Cash	50,000	
Deposits Held in Custody for Others		50,000

When the deposits are returned, the liability would be debited and cash would be credited. If a student owes a university for outstanding charges (e.g., dormitory rent or damages), an adjustment to the deposit returned would result. When an outstanding charge exists, the university would credit cash and the outstanding receivable for the amount owed. Reporting of deposits is the same under FASB and GASB standards.

Net Assets or Net Position

FASB and GASB standards have colleges and universities separate the total assets minus total liabilities residual into three categories; however, the categories are different.

FASB standards indicate the residual, to be titled net assets, should be separated into unrestricted, temporarily restricted, and permanently restricted. Unrestricted net assets are those on which there are no external contributor restrictions related to purpose or time. Private colleges and universities classify net assets as temporarily restricted if an external contributor imposes a restriction as to purpose or time. Net assets are classified as permanently restricted when a donor requires that the assets be held in perpetuity, or when assets must be held for a certain purpose and cannot be sold (e.g., artwork or collections).

GASB standards indicate the residual, to be titled net position, should be separated into unrestricted, restricted, and net investment in capital assets. Unrestricted net position is the amount of the net position remaining after adjustments have been made for restricted net position and net investment in capital assets. Restricted net position will include resources that are restricted by external contributors, creditors, law or regulation of governments (other than the college or university itself), or constitutional provisions. You will notice that the definition of restricted net position used by public colleges and universities is broader in scope than the definition of temporarily or permanently restricted net assets used by private colleges and universities. Net investment in capital assets is determined by the value of capital assets adjusted for accumulated depreciation and any debt that is attributable to capital assets. If there are deferred inflows or deferred outflows of resources related to capital assets, the capital asset value would be further adjusted.

Under both FASB and GASB standards accounts and reports must be in sufficient detail to demonstrate that the restrictions and any board policies are being met. Of particular importance to colleges and universities are the resources received through fund-raising efforts. Due to the importance of long-term commitments to colleges and universities that arise through fund-raising, the topic of planned giving is discussed in a separate section later in the chapter.

Operating Statements

As will be noticed, there are differences and similarities in the operating statements for public and private colleges and universities.

FASB standards require private colleges and universities to prepare a statement of activities (Illustration 15–2). Private colleges and universities have discretion in deciding the reporting format for the statement of activities, in that the entity can use a single-step format where all revenues and gains are reported, followed by all expenses and losses, or a multistep format where the entity would separate the revenues and expenses into operating and nonoperating. The FASB requires that private colleges and universities disclose the amount of net assets released from restrictions due to the meeting of purpose or time restrictions, and changes in the net asset categories on the financial statement (Illustration 15–5).

GASB standards require that colleges and universities following a business-type model separately report operating activity from nonoperating activity on the financial statement (Illustration 15–2). The title of the operating statement for public entities following a business-type model is statement of revenues, expenses, and changes in net position.

Revenues

All colleges and universities should recognize revenues on the accrual basis. Revenue accounts typically used by colleges and universities are those recommended by NACUBO. Examples include:

Tuition and Fees
Appropriations (typically state)
Grants and Contracts (which can be divided into federal, state, local, and private)
Contributions
Investment Income
Auxiliary Services

All of the account titles listed are control accounts and should be supported by appropriately named subsidiary accounts. For example, Tuition and Fees may be supported by subsidiary accounts for the regular session, summer school, extension, continuing education, and any other accounts providing useful information for a given educational institution.

Under both FASB[7] and GASB standards gross tuition and fees should be recorded as revenue even though some of the revenue will be offset by tuition waivers, scholarships, and fellowships. To recognize offsets to tuition and fees, discount and allowance accounts are used. For example, if a university billed $25,000 in tuition and fees, expecting to provide $5,000 in scholarships to students, the transaction would be recorded as follows:

	Debits	Credits
Tuition and Fees Receivable	20,000	
Tuition and Fees Discount and Allowances	5,000	
Tuition and Fees—Unrestricted		25,000

Using contra accounts allows for the reporting of net tuition and fees on the financial statements.

[7] FASB *ASC* 958-605-45.

Two additional accounting issues related to tuition and fees are tuition waivers received as part of compensation and tuition refunds. Tuition waivers received as part of compensation should be recorded as an expense rather than a contra-revenue account. For example, if a student receives a tuition waiver as part of his or her compensation for serving as a teaching assistant, the waiver would be recorded as an instructional expense. Refunds of tuition or fees are charged directly against the Tuition and Fees—Unrestricted account.

It should be noted that because college and university fiscal years and academic years rarely coincide, it is common for tuition and fees collected near the end of a fiscal year to relate in large portion to services to be rendered by the institution during the ensuing fiscal year. Both FASB and GASB standards indicate that using accrual principles revenue should be recognized in the period in which it is available and earned. If *earned* is defined as providing the service to the student, it is possible that tuition and fee revenue collected in one fiscal year could be recorded as unearned revenue until the service is provided in the subsequent fiscal year. NACUBO indicates that determining when an institution earns tuition revenue is a matter of professional judgment.[8] Therefore, recognition of such tuition revenues may vary by institution.

Both private and public colleges and universities show tuition and fee revenues net of any estimated uncollectible amounts. Public colleges and universities can use a contra-revenue account, such as Provision for Bad Debts (see Chapter 7), to account for estimated uncollectible tuition and fees. Whereas, NACUBO indicates that private colleges and universities should show tuition and fees net of any estimated uncollectible amounts, directly adjusting the revenue account for the estimate.[9] For example, at the end of the year, a private university estimated that it needed to increase its Allowance for Doubtful Accounts by $1,000. Using NACUBO guidance, it would make the following adjusting journal entry:

	Debits	Credits
Tuition and Fees—Unrestricted	1,000	
Allowance for Doubtful Accounts		1,000

Contributions

GASB (discussed in Chapter 4), and FASB (discussed in Chapter 13) provide guidance to public and private colleges and universities, respectively, when they are the recipients of contributions and grants in nonexchange transactions. Private colleges and universities may depend more on contributions from alumni and other supporters to keep tuition costs reasonable than do public institutions that receive relatively more state funding. However, this distinction is becoming less evident as public universities recognize the benefits of increasing endowments to decrease reliance on volatile state funding and constrained tuition support. Because contributions are so important to colleges and universities, the information provided in earlier chapters concerning recording and reporting of contributions is briefly restated in this section.

The standard setters define nonexchange transactions, such as contributions, as those in which the donor does not expect anything of value in return. Contributions by donors are considered nonexchange transactions as long as the donor does not receive any direct benefits from the donation.

[8] NACUBO, *FARM*, Sec. 360.4.

[9] Ibid., Sec. 360.5.

GASB standards require that public colleges and universities recognize contributions as nonexchange revenue when all eligibility requirements and time restrictions have been met. GASB *Codification* N50 identifies eligibility requirements as relating to (1) characteristics of the recipients for which the contribution is intended, (2) incurrence of reimbursable costs for which the contribution is intended, and/or (3) ability to meet a stated contingency related to the contribution. Contributions with a purpose restriction but no eligibility requirement are recognized as revenue and reported as restricted net position. Public colleges and universities can also receive promises to give. Nonexchange revenue from promises to give is recognized in the same manner as contributions. Generally, the time requirement relating to promises to give will not be met until cash or other assets are received. Estimates for any uncollectible promises to give must be made. A contra-revenue account such as Provision for Uncollectible Pledges would be used.

FASB Standards require that private colleges and universities recognize contributions as income in the period in which the contributions are made and report increases as either unrestricted, temporarily restricted, or permanently restricted net assets, depending on the stipulation of the donor. This also applies to promises to give, even though they may not be legally enforceable. Estimates for uncollectible Pledges Receivable must also be made. If the pledges are expected to be collected within a year the estimate for the uncollectible amount is recorded by debiting an expense account such as Provision for Uncollectible Pledges and crediting a contra asset account such as Allowance for Uncollectible Pledges. It should be recalled (Chapter 13), that under FASB standards, estimating an uncollectible amount applies only to current or short-term pledges. The FASB standards generally require that long-term Pledges Receivable be shown at fair value on the financial statements.

If a contribution to a private or public college or university is contingent upon a future event, such as obtaining matching funds, the university waits until the condition has been met before recording the contribution revenue. *Intentions to give,* such as naming a university in a will, are not recognized as revenue or considered a promise by universities because the potential donor can change the will at any time.

Grants and Awards

Colleges and universities often receive significant dollar amounts of grants and other assistance from governments, foundations, and corporations. Whether the assistance is recorded as a nonexchange or exchange transaction depends upon whether the resource provider directly benefits by receiving something of value through the transaction. The facts and circumstances of each award should be examined. For example, a federal research grant given to a university in which the value received by the agency is incidental to the public benefit from using the assets transferred is considered a contribution and would be recorded using the rules for contributions. On the other hand, if a federal agency enters into a contract in which the university tests a product and any patent or other results of the activity are retained by the federal agency, that transaction is considered an exchange transaction, not a contribution; consequently, this transaction results in an increase in unrestricted net assets/position because an exchange transaction cannot result in restricted net assets/position.[10] Colleges and universities should not report grants as exchange transactions or operating revenue without careful consideration of the terms of the grant.

[10] FASB, *ASC* 958-605-45; GASB, *Codification,* Sec. 1800.157.

Expenses

Expenses are recognized on the accrual basis by private and public colleges and universities. The classification of expenses can be on a natural basis (as seen in Illustration 15–2) or on a functional basis (as demonstrated later in Illustration 15–5). Most private and public colleges and universities use the NACUBO functional classifications for reporting expenses. Functional classifications provided by NACUBO for educational and general expenses include the following:

Instruction
Research
Public Service
Academic Support
Student Services
Institutional Support
Scholarships and Fellowships
Operations and Maintenance
Auxiliary Enterprises

An astute reader will notice that the NACUBO functional expense accounts do not clearly define program and support functions. To be in compliance with FASB standards, private colleges and universities need to disclose program and support expenses in the notes to the financial statements if not included on the face of the statement.[11]

Within each of the functional expense account categories just listed, accounts are kept by organizational unit, project, or other classification that provides useful information for internal or external users of the financial statements. A third level of analysis of expenses is provided by an object classification—personnel compensation and supplies expense are suggested as object classifications in the NACUBO chart of accounts. Further detail under each of these object classifications is usually kept to facilitate planning and control. For example, personnel compensation may be subdivided into salaries, other personnel services, and personnel benefits, with each of these further subdivided as desired by the administrators of a given college or university.

Statement of Cash Flows

FASB standards allow private colleges and universities the option of preparing the statement of cash flows using either the direct or the indirect method, as described in Chapter 13. Illustration 15–6 shows a statement of cash flows for the sample private university.

GASB standards applicable to colleges and universities require a statement of cash flows to be prepared using the direct method. In addition, institutions using GASB reporting standards must categorize cash flow information into operating, investing, noncapital financing, and capital and related financing activities. Illustration 15–3 shows a statement of cash flows for a public university. Note that state appropriations are reported as nonoperating revenues in Illustration 15–2 and as cash flow from noncapital financing activities in Illustration 15–3. For additonal information on the types of activities reported under each cash flow category, the reader is referred to Chapter 7.

[11] NACUBO, *FARM,* Sec. 506.5.

Segment Reporting

GASB requires that public institutions that use business-type reporting present segment information in the notes to the financial statements.[12] A segment is an identifiable activity for which one or more revenue bonds or other revenue-backed debt instruments are outstanding, for example, revenue bonds for residence halls or bookstores. Required disclosures include a condensed statement of net position; a statement of revenues, expenses, and changes in net position; and a statement of cash flows. FASB *ASC* 280-10-15 exempts private colleges and universities from segment reporting.

ILLUSTRATIVE TRANSACTIONS FOR PRIVATE COLLEGES AND UNIVERSITIES

This section presents journal entries for selected illustrative transactions for Valley College, a hypothetical private college. This information is then summarized in the financial statements presented in Illustrations 15–4 through 15–6. The account balances as of July 1, 2016, the beginning of Valley College's fiscal year, are provided in the following trial balance.

VALLEY COLLEGE
Postclosing Trial Balance
As of June 30, 2016

	Debits	*Credits*
Cash and Cash Equivalents	$ 675,000	
Tuition and Fees Receivable	298,000	
Allowance for Doubtful Accounts		$ 18,000
Pledges Receivable	800,000	
Allowance for Doubtful Pledges		50,000
Discount on Pledges Receivable		100,000
Loans Receivable	460,000	
Allowance for Doubtful Loans		10,000
Inventories	80,000	
Deposits with Trustees	350,000	
Prepaid Expenses	20,000	
Long-term Investments	16,163,000	
Property, Plant, and Equipment	85,745,000	
Accumulated Depreciation		21,795,000
Accounts Payable		140,000
Accrued Liabilities		15,000
Deposits Held in Custody for Others		335,000
Unearned Revenue		350,000
Notes Payable		700,000
Bonds Payable		25,000,000
Net Assets—Unrestricted		37,158,000
Net Assets—Temporarily Restricted		2,200,000
Net Assets—Permanently Restricted		16,720,000
Total	$104,591,000	$104,591,000

[12] GASB, *Codification,* Sec. 2500.

During the fiscal year ended June 30, 2017, the following receivables were recorded:

Receivables:	
Tuition and fees	5,990,000
Federal grants and contracts	1,075,000
Pledges	
Unrestricted	4,850,000
Temporarily restricted	1,000,000

Student scholarships in the amount of $450,000 were awarded, reducing the amount of the Tuition and Fees Receivable to $5,540,000 and creating the contra-revenue account Tuition and Fees Discount and Allowances. The temporarily restricted pledges receivable will be collected over five succeeding fiscal years. FASB standards require pledges that will not be collected in less than a year's time to be reported at fair value. Valley College has opted to use the present value technique[13] to determine the fair value of the pledges receivable for years 2 through 5. Based on the discount rate selected, the present value calculation results in a discount of $74,000 on the pledges receivable.[14] Entry 1 records the recognition of the receivables and related revenue for fiscal year 2017.

		Debits	Credits
1.	Tuition and Fees Receivable	5,540,000	
	Grants Receivable	1,075,000	
	Pledges Receivable	5,850,000	
	Tuition and Fees Discount and Allowances	450,000	
	Tuition and Fees—Unrestricted		5,990,000
	Federal Grants and Contracts—Unrestricted		1,075,000
	Contributions—Unrestricted		4,850,000
	Contributions—Temporarily Restricted		926,000
	Discount on Pledges Receivable		74,000

In addition to the recording of receivables, Valley College recorded the following cash collections:

Cash items collected:	
Investment income	
Unrestricted	700,000
Temporarily restricted	280,000
Student deposits	20,000
Auxiliary enterprises	2,300,000

[13] FASB *ASC* 820-10.

[14] If Valley College had made a fair value election in conformity with FASB *ASC* 825-10, the discount would not be amortized over the period; rather, a current discount rate would be used to determine fair value at each measurement date.

Entry 2 records the collection of cash.

		Debits	Credits
2.	Cash	3,300,000	
	Investment Income—Unrestricted		700,000
	Investment Income—Temporarily Restricted		280,000
	Deposits Held in Custody for Others		20,000
	Auxiliary Enterprises—Unrestricted		2,300,000

In the preceding year, unearned revenue was recorded for cash collected from students for classes offered in the current year. In the current year, the unearned revenue amount ($350,000) is reclassified as Tuition and Fees.

3.	Unearned Revenue	350,000	
	Tuition and Fees—Unrestricted		350,000

Entry 4 records the collections of cash for tuition and fees receivable amounting to $5,650,000, grants receivable of $1,075,000, and $4,945,000 in pledges receivable. For those pledges collected from prior periods, $14,000 of the Discount on Pledges Receivable was amortized and recorded as unrestricted contributions.

4a.	Cash	11,670,000	
	Tuition and Fees—Receivable		5,650,000
	Grants Receivable		1,075,000
	Pledges Receivable		4,945,000
4b.	Discount on Pledges Receivable	14,000	
	Contributions—Unrestricted		14,000

Entry 5 records operating expenses incurred in accomplishing the goals of the college. In addition, operating expenses for auxiliary enterprises are recorded.

5.	Instruction Expense	4,321,000	
	Public Service Expense	1,123,460	
	Academic Support Expense	129,630	
	Student Services Expense	2,592,600	
	Institutional Support Expense	2,872,170	
	Auxiliary Enterprises Expense	2,116,000	
	Accounts Payable		3,936,500
	Accrued Liabilities		9,218,360

Accounts payable and accrued liabilities were paid in the amounts of $4,003,500 and $9,133,900, respectively. Refunds of students' deposits amounted to $10,000.

		Debits	Credits
6.	Accounts Payable	4,003,500	
	Accrued Liabilities	9,133,900	
	Deposits Held in Custody for Others	10,000	
	Cash		13,147,400

Inventories and prepaid expenses increased during the year in the amounts shown in Entry 7. These increases reduced expenses in instruction and institutional support, as shown.

7.	Inventories	15,000	
	Prepaid Expenses	9,000	
	Instruction Expense		13,200
	Institutional Support Expense		10,800

Contributions restricted for the purpose of research were received.

8.	Cash	1,109,000	
	Contributions—Temporarily Restricted		1,109,000

Expenses for the restricted research purposes described in Entry 8 were incurred during the period in the amount of $1,025,000.

9a.	Research Expense	1,025,000	
	Accrued Liabilities		10,000
	Cash		1,015,000
9b.	Net Assets Released from Restrictions—Temporarily Restricted	1,025,000	
	Net Assets Released from Restrictions—Unrestricted		1,025,000

Entry 10 records the receipt of state grants that are temporarily restricted for student loans.

10.	Cash	208,000	
	State Grants and Contracts—Temporarily Restricted		208,000

Loans were made to students during the year in the amount of $260,000, and other student loans were repaid in the amount of $95,000 with an additional amount of $7,000 received as interest revenue on these loans. There are no imposed stipulations on the interest earned. Entries 11a and 11b record the loan transactions.

		Debits	Credits
11a.	Loans Receivable	260,000	
	Cash		260,000
11b.	Cash	102,000	
	Loans Receivable		95,000
	Interest Income—Unrestricted		7,000

During the year, cash of $500,000 for construction of a new laboratory building was received from a private foundation and 8 percent term bonds maturing in five years were issued in the amount of $2,000,000.

12.	Cash	2,500,000	
	Bonds Payable		2,000,000
	Contributions—Temporarily Restricted		500,000

During the year, the new laboratory building was completed at a cost of $2,000,000. Equipment costs amounted to $350,000. Renovations to the old laboratory building totaled $250,000; however, none of the renovations met the criteria for capitalization.

13a.	Buildings	2,000,000	
	Equipment	350,000	
	Research Expense	250,000	
	Cash		2,600,000
13b.	Net Assets Released from Restrictions—Temporarily Restricted	500,000	
	Net Assets Released from Restrictions—Unrestricted		500,000

Valley College received endowment gifts during the year in the amount of $2,423,000. Entry 14 records the effect of the endowment gifts.

14.	Cash	2,423,000	
	Contributions—Permanently Restricted		2,423,000

Long-term investments were made using $2,400,000 from the endowment.

15.	Long-term Investments	2,400,000	
	Cash		2,400,000

Entry 16 records the interest and principal payments on outstanding bonds and notes. The interest is allocated to the instruction function.

		Debits	Credits
16.	Instruction Expense	1,850,000	
	Bonds Payable	500,000	
	Notes Payable	50,000	
	Cash		2,400,000

Near the end of the current fiscal year, the college collected tuition and fees in the amount of $350,000 for classes that will be held in the following fiscal year. The college recognizes an unearned revenue liability since the fees are related to educational programs conducted in the following fiscal year.

17.	Cash	350,000	
	Unearned Revenue		350,000

Adjusting Entries

Entry 18 records the accrual of instructional and public service expenses at June 30, 2017, in the amounts shown.

18.	Instruction Expense	51,000	
	Public Service Expense	21,000	
	Accounts Payable		65,000
	Accrued Liabilities		7,000

At the end of the year, a pre-audit review of the loans receivable and pledges receivable indicates that the balances in the allowance accounts are sufficient. However, the Allowance for Doubtful Accounts related to tuition and fees is increased for expected write-offs in the amount of $2,000.

19.	Tuition and Fees—Unrestricted	2,000	
	Allowance for Doubtful Accounts		2,000

As of June 30, 2017, the fair value of long-term investments increased by $7,800 from the value reported in the college's financial records. The gain is permanently restricted.

20.	Long-term Investments	7,800	
	Unrealized Gain on Investments		7,800

Capital assets are depreciated as shown in Entry 21. For simplicity, the total expense is charged to instruction.

		Debits	Credits
21.	Instruction Expense	300,000	
	Accumulated Depreciation		300,000

Closing Entries

All revenue and expense accounts were closed to the appropriate net asset accounts.

22a.	Tuition and Fees—Unrestricted	6,338,000	
	Federal Grants and Contracts—Unrestricted	1,075,000	
	Contributions—Unrestricted	4,864,000	
	Interest Income—Unrestricted	7,000	
	Investment Income—Unrestricted	700,000	
	Auxiliary Enterprises—Unrestricted	2,300,000	
	Net Assets—Unrestricted	1,793,860	
	Instruction Expense		6,508,800
	Public Service Expense		1,144,460
	Academic Support Expense		129,630
	Student Services Expense		2,592,600
	Institutional Support Expense		2,861,370
	Auxiliary Enterprises Expense		2,116,000
	Research Expenses		1,275,000
	Tuition and Fees Discount and Allowances		450,000
22b.	Contributions—Temporarily Restricted	2,535,000	
	State Grants—Temporarily Restricted	208,000	
	Investment Income—Temporarily Restricted	280,000	
	Net Assets—Temporarily Restricted		3,023,000
22c.	Contributions—Permanently Restricted	2,423,000	
	Unrealized Gain on Investments	7,800	
	Net Assets—Permanently Restricted		2,430,800

Net assets released from restrictions are closed in the following entry:

23.	Net Assets—Temporarily Restricted	1,525,000	
	Net Assets Released from Restrictions—Unrestricted	1,525,000	
	Net Assets—Unrestricted		1,525,000
	Net Assets Released from Restrictions—Temporarily Restricted		1,525,000

The financial statements for Valley College are presented in Illustrations 15–4, 15–5, and 15–6 for the fiscal year ended June 30, 2017. Valley college discloses restrictions on assets in the notes, rather than recognizing them on the face of the statement.

ILLUSTRATION 15–4

VALLEY COLLEGE
Statement of Financial Position
June 30, 2017

Assets	
Cash and cash equivalents	$ 514,600
Tuition and fees receivable, less allowance for doubtful accounts of $20,000	168,000
Pledges receivable, less allowance for doubtful pledges of $50,000 and a discount of $160,000	1,495,000
Loans receivable, less allowance for doubtful loans of $10,000	615,000
Inventories, at average cost	95,000
Prepaid expenses	29,000
Deposits with trustees	350,000
Long-term investments, at fair value, cost of $18,563,000	18,570,800
Property, plant, and equipment, net of accumulated depreciation of $22,095,000	66,000,000
Total assets	$87,837,400
Liabilities and Net Assets	
Liabilities:	
Accounts payable	$ 138,000
Accrued liabilities	116,460
Deposits held in custody for others	345,000
Unearned revenue	350,000
Notes payable	650,000
Bonds payable	26,500,000
Total liabilities	28,099,460
Net Assets:	
Unrestricted	36,889,140
Temporarily restricted	3,698,000
Permanently restricted	19,150,800
Total net assets	59,737,940
Total liabilities and net assets	$87,837,400

PLANNED GIVING

Endowments

Endowments are donor-restricted resources that are nonexpendable as of the date of reporting and are or can be invested for the purpose of producing income. Generally, endowments are in one of two forms—permanent (identified as permanently restricted net assets by private institutions and restricted—nonexpendable net position by public institutions) or term (identified as restricted by both public and private institutions). **Permanent endowments** are gifts, for which donors or other external agencies have stated that as a condition of the gift the principal must be maintained intact in perpetuity. The principal is invested in order to earn income. The use of the income may be restricted by the donor; if so, the income is considered an addition to restricted net assets for private institutions or restricted net position for public institutions. If the use of the income is unrestricted, the income is considered an increase to unrestricted net assets/net position. Under **term endowments,** the principal is to be maintained intact until the happening of a particular event or the passage of a stated period of time. Once the event has occurred or the time has passed, all or a portion of the principal can be expended.

ILLUSTRATION 15–5

VALLEY COLLEGE
Statement of Activities
Year Ended June 30, 2017

	Unrestricted	Temporarily Restricted	Permanently Restricted	Total
Revenues and gains:				
Student tuition and fees (net)	$ 5,888,000			$ 5,888,000
Government grants and contracts	1,075,000	$ 208,000		1,283,000
Investment and interest income	707,000	280,000		987,000
Contributions	4,864,000	2,535,000	$ 2,423,000	9,822,000
Auxiliary enterprise sales and services	2,300,000			2,300,000
Gain on investments			7,800	7,800
Net assets released from restrictions	1,525,000	(1,525,000)		0
Total revenues and gains	16,359,000	1,498,000	2,430,800	20,287,800
Expenses and losses:				
Educational and general expenses:				
Instruction	6,508,800			6,508,800
Public service	1,144,460			1,144,460
Academic support	129,630			129,630
Research	1,275,000			1,275,000
Student services	2,592,600			2,592,600
Institutional support	2,861,370			2,861,370
Total educational and general expenses	14,511,860			14,511,860
Auxiliary enterprises	2,116,000			2,116,000
Total expenses and losses	16,627,860			16,627,860
Total change in net assets	(268,860)	1,498,000	2,430,800	3,659,940
Net assets, beginning of the year	37,158,000	2,200,000	16,720,000	56,078,000
Net assets, end of the year	$36,889,140	$3,698,000	$19,150,800	$59,737,940

When investing endowment assets, the objective of many educational institutions has focused on the return of the investment portfolio. In determining the return on the portfolio, changes in the market value of the portfolio are considered. This concept is known as **total return.** Total return is calculated as the sum of net realized and unrealized appreciation or shrinkage in portfolio value plus dividend and interest yield. Total return has another aspect; this is the determination of **spending rate,** the proportion of total return that may prudently be used by an institution for current purposes. The adoption of total return as a policy requires the approval of legal counsel and formal approval of the governing board. The total return concept appears to be used by an increasing number of colleges and universities.

Split-interest Agreements

Split-interest agreements occur when a donor enters into an arrangement with the college or university (institution) requiring the institution to share the benefits received from the donor's gift with another beneficiary. Split-interest agreements can be revocable or irrevocable. A *revocable* agreement allows donors to take back their gifts in certain situations. Alumni and others often use split-interest agreements as a form of planned giving to the institution. There are four widely used types of split-interest agreements: charitable lead trusts, charitable remainder trusts, charitable gift annuities, and pooled (life) income funds.

ILLUSTRATION 15–6

VALLEY COLLEGE
Statement of Cash Flows
Year Ended June 30, 2017

Cash Flows from Operating Activities	
Increase in net assets	$ 3,659,940
Adjustments to reconcile increase in net assets to net cash provided by operating activities:	
Depreciation	300,000
Increase in pledges receivable (net)	(845,000)
Decrease in tuition and fees receivable (net)	112,000
Increase in accounts payable and accrued expenses	99,460
Increase in deposits	10,000
Increase in prepaid expenses	(9,000)
Increase in inventories	(15,000)
Gains restricted for long-term purpose	(7,800)
Contributions restricted for long-term investment	(2,423,000)
Net cash provided for operating activities	881,600
Cash Flows from Investing Activities	
Purchases of investments	(2,400,000)
Purchases of property, plant, and equipment	(2,350,000)
Loans to students and faculty	(260,000)
Collections of loans to students and faculty	95,000
Net cash used for investing activities	(4,915,000)
Cash Flows from Financing Activities	
Proceeds from contributions restricted for long-term investment	2,423,000
Issuance of long-term debt	2,000,000
Repayment of long-term debt	(550,000)
Net cash provided by financing activities	3,873,000
Net decrease in cash and cash equivalents	(160,400)
Cash and cash equivalents, beginning of year	675,000
Cash and cash equivalents, end of year	$ 514,600

As indicated, the institution shares either the income from the investment of the donor's gift or the investment itself with another beneficiary, which may include the donor. The donor gift can be placed in a trust with the trust assets held by a third party. If the institution has an interest in an irrevocable split-interest agreement, the assets should be recorded at fair value. When the agreement includes promises to give noncash assets (e.g., land or real property), a present value or other fair value technique as described in FASB *ASC* 820-10 can be used. Any liabilities accepted, such as to pay the donor-stipulated amounts of an annuity agreement, should also be recorded at the time of the agreement. Any difference between assets and liabilities is either a restricted or unrestricted net asset, depending on the agreement with the donor. The remainder of this section briefly discusses two of the four types of irrevocable split-interest agreements.

Annuity Agreements

Annuity agreements are used to account for assets given to an institution under conditions that bind the institution to pay a fixed amount periodically to the donors or other designated individuals for a period of time specified in the agreements or for the lifetime of the donor or other designated individual. Under a **pooled (life) income fund,**

the donor's assets become part of a managed pool of investments. The income fund is divided into units and each donor is assigned a pro rata share of the income fund's units, based on the fair value of the donor's contributions to the total fair value of the fund.[15] The donor is paid the total income earned on the fund units the donor holds. Upon the donor's death, the value of the assigned units reverts to the institution.[16]

The acceptance of annuity funds by a not-for-profit organization is subject to regulation by the Internal Revenue Service (IRS) and, in many jurisdictions, by agencies of the appropriate state government. The Internal Revenue Code and regulations state the conditions under which (for IRS purposes) an annuity trust may be established and administered. State agencies may specify the types of investments in which annuity assets may be invested.

It is possible to have an annuity agreement in which liabilities exceed initial assets. Entering into an annuity agreement that has initial deficit net assets would not appear to be in the institution's best interests. Agreements with potential donors of annuities should be carefully drawn by attorneys experienced with such agreements in consultation with accountants and investment managers in order to protect the interests of the receiving institution as well as the donor. The definition of *income* is one of the matters needing most careful attention. From the accounting point of view, *income* should be defined in accrual terms. It is also in the interest of the institution that an equitable allocation of indirect administrative expenses be permitted as well as a deduction for direct expenses of administering each annuity.

Annuity payments are debited to a liability account that is created when the agreement is initiated. Periodically, an adjustment is made between the liability and restricted net assets/position to record the actuarial gain or loss due to recomputation of the liability based on revised life expectancy and anticipated return on investments. On termination of an annuity agreement, the principal of the annuity is transferred to the net asset category specified in the agreement; if the agreement is silent on the point, the principal of the terminated annuity fund should be transferred to unrestricted net assets/position and identified, so readers of the financial statements will not infer that a new gift has been received.

Pooled (Life) Income Funds

Life income fund agreements differ from annuity agreements. The primary difference is that the life income fund agreement provides that the income earned by the donated assets will be paid to the donors over a specified period rather than in a fixed amount. Because the amount to be paid can vary from period to period as the income produced by the life income fund assets varies, it is not practical or necessary to compute the present value of the stream of unknown future payments. Accordingly, the liabilities of life income fund agreements consist of payments currently due and any indebtedness against the life income fund assets. With this exception, accounting for life income fund agreements is similar to annuity agreements.

If the college or university is party to a revocable split-interest agreement, the assets are recorded at fair value when received. However, a refundable advance (liability) rather than contribution revenue is recognized as the credit entry for the transaction. Contribution revenue is recognized when the agreement becomes irrevocable or when the assets are distributed to the institution for its unconditional use.[17]

[15] American Institute of Certified Public Accountants, Audit and Accounting Guide, *Not-for-Profit Entities* (New York: AICPA, 2014), par. 6.79.

[16] Ibid.

[17] Ibid., par. 6.07.

While the discussion in this section has related to GASB and FASB requirements, endowment and split-interest agreements may be subject to other standards and laws as well. For example, states have adopted the Uniform Prudent Management of Institutional Funds Act, which deals with the management of endowment funds.

Uniform Prudent Management of Institutional Funds Act

The Uniform Prudent Management of Investment Funds Act (UPMIFA) of 2006 relates to not-for-profit organizations that manage funds for charitable purposes. Charitable purposes is defined somewhat broadly and incudes activities such as the relief of poverty, advancement of education or religion, promotion of health, promotion of a governmental purpose, or other activities that are beneficial to the community.[18] This act revises its predecessor, the Uniform Management of Institutional Funds Act (UMIFA). Both acts are designed to provide guidance in the absence of explicit donor stipulations. Forty-nine states have enacted UPMIFA. UPMIFA supports two general principles: (1) assets should be invested prudently in diversified investments that allow for growth as well as income, and (2) appreciation of investments may be prudently spent for the purpose of the endowment fund.[19] Three areas of the act that are of primary importance to NFP organizations relate to investments, expenditures, and release or modification of restrictions on net assets. These three areas are briefly discussed. More information about the act is available at *www.upmifa.org*.

Investments

UPMIFA requires investment "in good faith and with the care an ordinarily prudent person in a like position would exercise under similar circumstances."[20] It requires prudence in incurring investment costs. Investment decisions are to be made in relation to the overall resources of the NFP and its charitable purposes, with consideration given to the entire investment portfolio. An investment strategy should be developed "having risk and return objectives reasonably suited to the fund and to the institution."[21]

Expenditures

UPMIFA does not specify limitations on expenditures, instead providing criteria for the NFP to consider regarding its spending policies. The seven criteria that should be considered as part of a spending policy are:

1. Duration and preservation of the endowment fund.
2. The purposes of the institution and the endowment fund.
3. The general economic conditions.
4. The effect of inflation or deflation.
5. The expected total return from income and the appreciation of investments.
6. Other resources of the NFP.
7. The investment policy of the institution.[22]

UPMIFA does allow states, within limits, to enact specific rules regarding excessive expenditure.

[18] UPMIFA, Sec. 2(1).

[19] AICPA, AAG-NFP Entities, par. 15.51.

[20] UPMIFA, Sec. 3(b).

[21] Ibid., Sec. 3(e)(2).

[22] Ibid., Sec. 4(a).

Release or Modification of Restrictions on Net Assets

A donor has the right to release restrictions on funds he or she has provided. However, if the donor is no longer available to release or modify restrictions, the NFP can ask for court approval of a modification of the restriction under UPMIFA. UPMIFA authorizes a modification that a court determines is in accordance with the donor's probable wishes regarding his or her donation.

UPMIFA also has a provision that allows a charity to modify a restriction on a small (less than $25,000) and old (more than 20 years old) fund without going to court.[23] If a restriction has become impracticable or wasteful, the charity can notify the state charitable regulator; wait 60 days; and then unless the regulator objects, modify the restriction in a manner consistent with the purposes expressed in the documents that were part of the original donation/gift.[24]

OTHER ACCOUNTING ISSUES

Performance Measures

Public colleges and universities are encouraged to present nonfinancial and nonquantitative information, such as service efforts and accomplishments, that document how well the organization accomplished its mission.[25] However, many accrediting agencies, and an increasing number of states, are requiring assessment of student outcomes, sometimes as a determining factor in funding levels. Some states are requiring standardized norm-based objective exams, although more often the institution is allowed to develop its own measure of outcomes based on mission-based objectives. This approach recognizes that the mission of higher education institutions differs in the weight each one places on instruction, research, and service. Outputs, for example, might be graduation statistics, such as time to degree, number of graduates, and job placements.[26] Outcomes differ from outputs in that they measure the benefits derived by constituents, such as performance on nationally ranked exams or student/employer satisfaction with education quality. Many colleges and universities have projects on developing improvement processes and benchmarking for improvement. The best measures are those that capture the "value added" to the student through the educational process. Although doing so is difficult, colleges and universities are increasingly attempting to capture data from alumni and employers concerning the effectiveness of the educational process. There is more discussion about performance evaluation in Chapters 12 and 14.

Recently the federal government has shown an interest in developing a college-ratings system that would measure colleges' and universities' performance based on metrics such a affordability and graduation rates.[27] It is proposed that federal financial

[23] Ibid., Sec. 6(d).

[24] Ibid.

[25] Governmental Accounting Standards Board, *Concepts Statement No. 2,* "Service Efforts and Accomplishments" (Norwalk, CT: GASB, 1994).

[26] Teresa Gordon and Mary Fischer, "Communicating Performance: The Extent and Effectiveness of Performance Reporting by U.S. Colleges and Universities," *Public Budgeting, Accounting & Financial Management* 20, no. 2 (2008), pp. 217–255.

[27] Porter, Caroline, "Obama Focuses on Education in 2015 Budget; Discretionary Spending Would be Cut by 3.7%," *The Wall Street Journal* (Online), March 4, 2014.

aid would be tied to a college or university's rating as early as 2018.[28] A national ratings system would provide data for benchmarking; however, it is important to remember that national data cannot take into account differences in missions or other factors that could impact the "value added" for the student.

Auditing Colleges and Universities

Most colleges and universities, whether private or public, publish audited financial statements. More and more often, financial statements appear on their Web sites. At a minimum, audits of colleges and universities are performed in conformity with the generally accepted auditing standards (GAAS) promulgated by the AICPA, as discussed in Chapter 11. Additionally, many colleges and universities, as a condition of accepting federal financial awards, are audited under the auditing standards established by the U.S. Government Accountability Office in its publication *Government Auditing Standards* (GAS), also known as the "yellow book," as discussed in Chapter 11. Specifically, if a college or university expends $750,000 or more in federal awards in a given fiscal year, it must have a "single audit" in accordance with the provisions of Office of Management and Budget (OMB) *Uniform Administrative Requirements, Cost Principles, and Audit Requirements for Federal Awards.* Since the audit requirements for the single audit are described in considerable detail in Chapter 11, they need not be reiterated here.

Due to the large number of dollars involved and decentralized controls, an item of special concern in auditing colleges and universities is ensuring that only costs allowable under OMB *Uniform Guidance*[29] are charged, either as direct costs or indirect costs, to federal grants or contracts. The federal government devotes considerable resources to auditing educational institutions that receive federal assistance, in particular their compliance with cost principles, as well as unrelated business income. The administrative requirements for grants and other agreements with the federal government are addressed in the *Uniform Guidance*. Compliance with the requirements is also subject to audit. The tax issues involving unrelated business income are discussed in Chapter 14. As with state and local governments, single audits of colleges and universities place heavy emphasis on evaluating the system of internal controls and compliance with applicable laws and regulations in addition to the traditional audit of the financial statements.

Federal Financial Assistance

The federal government supports institutions of higher learning in the form of research grants and student loan funds. As mentioned in the previous section on auditing issues, acceptance of federal funds requires reporting to the grantor and conformance with various cost accounting rules as well as administrative requirements.

Sponsored Research Funds

Research funds received from the federal government are most likely to be in the form of contracts and grants in which the government is expecting periodic activity reports and a report at the end of the grant period as to how the funds were used. In some instances, the organization may contract with the federal government for a specific product for the funds paid. The terms of the grant or contract are critical factors in

[28] State Higher Education Executive Officers Association, "Postsecondary Institutional Ratings System (PIRS) Update," February, 2014, available at *http://www.sheeo.org/resources/publications/sheeo-postsecondary-institutional-ratings-system-pirs-update-february-2014.*

[29] Office of Management and Budget, *Uniform Administrative Requirements, Cost Principles, and Audit Requirements for Federal Awards,* 78 FR 78589, § 200.38.

determining whether it is an exchange or a nonexchange transaction. Some colleges and universities may have a policy to classify all federal grants as exchange transactions, but the facts and circumstances of each grant should be examined.

Student Grants and Loans

Student assistance takes various forms: loans or grants, subsidized or unsubsidized, held by the institution or given directly to the student. A Pell Grant is one in which the federal government provides pass-through funds to the institution, which then disperses the funds to the recipient based on federal payment schedules.[30]

Related Entities

Public and private colleges and universities can be complex in their organizational structure, including majority-owned subsidiaries for intellectual property and businesslike enterprises; clinical and research facilities; financing corporations; and controlled affiliates for fund-raising, alumni relations, and management of assets. At issue is whether there is sufficient control of one organization over another to combine their financial information under one reporting entity. Information related to reporting related entities is provided in Chapter 13 for private colleges and universities and in Chapter 9 for public colleges and universities.

[30] Catalog of Federal Domestic Assistance (CFDA) #84.063. See: *http://www.cfda.gov.*

Key Terms

Annuity agreements, *627*
Collections, *613*
Endowments, *625*
Permanent endowments, *625*
Pooled (life) income fund, *627*
Spending rate, *626*
Split-interest agreements, *626*
Term endowments, *625*
Total return, *626*

Selected References

American Institute of Certified Public Accountants. Audit and Accounting Guide. *Not-for-Profit Entities.* New York: AICPA, 2014.

Financial Accounting Standards Board. *Accounting Standards Codification,* Sections 958 and 820. Norwalk, CT: FASB (on-line).

Governmental Accounting Standards Board. *Codification of Governmental Accounting and Financial Reporting Standards as of June 30, 2014.* Norwalk, CT, 2014.

National Association of College and University Business Officers. *Financial Accounting and Reporting Manual for Higher Education* (*e-FARM*). Washington, DC. (on-line).

Questions

15–1. Identify the financial statements that must be prepared by a private college or university and those that must be prepared by a public college or university.

15–2. For each of the following situations explain how a private and a public university would record the transaction (assume the grants are nonexchange): notification of a grant to be received in the next fiscal year; receipt of a grant with a purpose restriction; notification of a grant payable for only allowable costs related to the grant.

15–3. Private colleges and universities report temporarily and permanently restricted net assets. What, if any, comparable reporting is provided by public universities?

15–4. How do private colleges and universities account for bad debts related to tuition and fees? Compare the accounting to that of public and for-profit (corporate) colleges and universities.

15–5. When would receipt of a grant be recorded as revenue rather than a contribution? Give an example of a transaction in which a grant would be recorded as revenue.

15–6. A private college has received pledges that are due within one year and pledges that are long-term (that is, due in more than one year). How will the college report the pledges in its financial statements?

15–7. The NACUBO expense accounts typically used by colleges and universities do not identify the program and support functions. Discuss whether colleges and universities are required to identify program and support expenses and how this is accomplished if the entity uses the NACUBO accounts.

15–8. What is a split interest agreement, and why do you believe a donor or a university would enter into such an agreement?

15–9. What is UPMIFA, and why is it important to colleges and universities? Does UPMIFA apply only to colleges and universities?

15–10. Discuss whether colleges and universities are subject to audits under Government Auditing Standards (GAS).

Cases

15–11 Review of Annual Financial Report. Obtain the most recent copy of the annual report for your college or university (school). Using the annual report, answer the following.

Required

a. Does your school follow GASB or FASB standards? Use the financial statements to explain how you can tell which GAAP is being applied.

b. Do the financial statements appear to follow the reporting standards of the appropriate standards-setting body? Identify examples to support your answer. Identify any instances where you believe the reporting standards are not being met. (*Hint:* It may be helpful to refer to the financial statement illustrations presented in this chapter.)

c. What percentage of total revenue comes from student tuition and fees? What percentage of total tuition and fees are student discounts and/or scholarship allowances?

d. What percentage of total revenue comes from grants and contracts?

e. Under FASB standards, not-for-profit entities must clearly identify the expenses that are program related from those expenses that are management and general and fund-raising. What percentage of total expenses is your college or university spending on its programs? Discuss what if any benefit you believe this information has when the entity is funded primarily by user charges (tuition and other fees) versus contributions? (*Hint:* You may need to search the footnotes.)

f. Has an audit been included with the financial report? Discuss the content of the audit report.

15–12 Comparison of Public and Private Universities. Following are the operating statements for a public and private college. The operating statements have been adapted from the annual reports of a public and a private university. As would be expected, the reports are somewhat different. Catherine College is over 150 years old and has a student enrollment of 5,000. Midland State College is relatively new at 50 years of age and has a student enrollment of 6,704.

CATHERINE COLLEGE
Statements of Activities
Years Ended June 30, 2017 and 2016

	2017				2016			
	Unrestricted	Temporarily Restricted	Permanently Restricted	Total	Unrestricted	Temporarily Restricted	Permanently Restricted	Total
Revenue								
Tuition and Fees	$102,917,430	$ —	$ —	$102,917,430	$100,467,638	$ —	$ —	$100,467,638
Less:								
Allowances and Scholarships	34,145,296	—	—	34,145,296	31,188,166	—	—	31,188,166
Tuition Waivers	1,883,642	—	—	1,883,642	1,827,471	—	—	1,827,471
Net Student Tuition and Fees	66,888,492	—	—	66,888,492	67,452,001	—	—	67,452,001
Government Grants	105,266	2,136,597	—	2,241,863	98,313	2,021,517	—	2,119,830
Contributions	2,270,381	3,434,187	3,316,016	9,020,584	1,786,013	8,638,031	1,177,496	11,601,540
Investment Income, Net	899,119	2,393,324	330,702	3,623,145	802,668	2,367,500	(184,757)	2,985,411
Sale of Educational Activities	320,949	201,480	—	522,429	465,399	354,475	—	819,874
Change in Value of Split-Interest Agreements	—	313,770	251,451	565,221	—	(528,895)	105,820	(423,075)
Other Sources	1,298,818	(437,800)	(644,915)	216,103	1,333,078	(483,888)	(502,284)	346,906
Auxiliary Enterprises	8,536,763	—	—	8,536,763	8,010,408	—	—	8,010,408
Net Assets Released from Restrictions	7,873,344	(7,873,344)	—	—	6,897,955	(6,897,955)	—	—
Total Revenues	88,193,132	168,214	3,253,254	91,614,600	86,845,835	5,470,785	596,275	92,912,895
Expenses								
Instruction	33,037,790	—	—	33,037,790	34,102,230	—	—	34,102,230
Academic Support	14,328,597	—	—	14,328,597	15,588,271	—	—	15,588,271
Research	178,717	—	—	178,717	189,643	—	—	189,643
Public Service	1,429,026	—	—	1,429,026	1,653,880	—	—	1,653,880
Student Services	13,775,201	—	—	13,775,201	13,092,600	—	—	13,092,600
Institutional Support	14,114,290	—	—	14,114,290	12,966,389	—	—	12,966,389
Auxiliary Enterprises	11,329,426	—	—	11,329,426	9,533,062	—	—	9,533,062
Total Expenses	88,193,047	—	—	88,193,047	87,126,075	—	—	87,126,075
Change in Assets	85	168,214	3,253,254	3,421,553	(280,240)	5,470,785	596,275	5,786,820
Net Assets-Beginning of Year	53,219,881	30,271,067	61,190,187	144,681,135	53,500,121	24,800,282	60,593,912	138,894,315
Net Assets - End of Year	$ 53,219,966	$30,439,281	$64,443,441	$148,102,688	$ 53,219,881	$30,271,067	$61,190,187	$144,681,135

MIDLAND STATE COLLEGE
Statements of Revenues, Expenses, and Changes in Net Position
For the Years Ended June 30, 2017 and 2016
(in Thousands)

	2017	**2016**
Operating Revenues		
Tuition and fees, net	$ 14,939	$ 14,390
Auxiliary sales, net	1,456	1,403
Restricted student payments, net	6,215	5,639
Other income	110	47
Total operating revenues	22,720	21,479
Operating Expenses		
Salaries and benefits	30,555	28,864
Purchased services	6,547	6,230
Supplies	1,767	2,332
Repairs and maintenance	826	724
Depreciation	3,740	3,780
Financial aid, net	653	321
Other expense	2,167	2,205
Total operating expenses	46,255	44,456
Operating loss	(23,535)	(22,977)
Nonoperating Revenues (Expenses)		
State appropriations	14,514	14,120
Federal grants	5,173	5,044
State grants	2,303	1,933
Private grants	1,324	896
Interest income	125	124
Interest expense	(890)	(968)
Total nonoperating revenues (expenses)	22,549	21,149
Loss Before Other Revenues, Expenses, Gains, or Losses	(986)	(1,828)
State capital appropriations	675	1,498
Capital grants	—	73
Gain on disposal of capital assets	74	2
Change in net position	(237)	(255)
Total Net Position, Beginning of Year	66,993	67,248
Total Net Position, End of Year	$ 66,756	$ 66,993

Required

a. Identify the reporting standards under which each statement was prepared and identify some of the format differences that are the result of the different reporting standards.

b. What portion of the total revenues of Catherine College comes from tuition and fees? From state appropriations? From grants and contributions? How do those amounts compare to those for Midland State College? Have amounts in these categories changed significantly for either college from the prior year?

c. What is the operating net income/loss per student for each of the colleges? Do the colleges appear to be generating much income per student? Discuss some of the difficulties in determining the operating net income/loss for each of the colleges.

d. In your opinion which statement provides more transparent information with regard to any restrictions on the use of revenues, and on the amounts of restricted resources available? Provide support for your opinion.

15–13 Research Case—Rating Colleges and Universities. A federal government initiative to rate public colleges and universities has been undertaken by the U.S. Department of Education. Performance measures for K–12 education have been part of the federal funding initiative for many years with such programs as No Child Left Behind. However, ratings for colleges and universities by the government or not-for-profit organizations have not been developed. To learn more about the federal initiative two Web sites will be helpful—the U.S. Department of Education (*www.ed.gov/college-affordability/college-ratings-and-paying-performance*) and the State Higher Education Executive Officers Association (SHEEO) (*www.sheeo.org*). Use these Web sites and other resources to complete this case.

Required

a. What is the purpose of and who will primarily be affected by the U.S. Department of Education's proposal to rate colleges and universities?
b. What is PIRS?
c. What are the three key metrics that will be used in the rating system?
d. When is the rating system projected to be implemented?
e. What are some strengths and weaknesses of such a system?

15–14 Research Case—UPMIFA. Carol Hernandez has recently been appointed director of the foundation for a private university located in the state of Minnesota. She is intent on learning as much as she can about the foundation's responsibilities concerning the management and investment of the endowment and other contributions received by the foundation. In particular, she has questions concerning UPMIFA and its impact on the operation of the foundation.

The foundation is a not-for-profit organization of the university and operates solely for the benefit of the university. It receives substantial support in the form of annual contributions and endowments from alumni. There are two items related to its endowment funds about which Ms. Hernandez has concerns. The first is the spending rate established by the foundation. Currently, the spending rate is set at 4 percent, and it appears that this rate has been in effect for a *very* long time. To Ms. Hernandez, this rate seems somewhat high given that the total return to the foundation's portfolio has averaged 4.5 percent over the last three years. The second concern is an endowment that is 50 years old. The endowment document indicates that the income generated by the endowment is to be used to fund research and scholarship related to fossil discoveries along Lake Superior. The problem is two-fold: (1) the donor has passed away, and (2) the paleontology department was one of the departments eliminated in the budget cut 10 years ago. As a result, the endowment fund has been collecting income on investments but has been unable to spend any of the income to carry out the purpose of the endowment.

Ms. Hernandez has asked you to provide her answers for several questions she has related to this information.

Required

a. Are organizations in Minnesota subject to UPMIFA? (*Hint:* The UPMIFA Web site is *www.upmifa.org*.)
b. Is the foundation subject to UPMIFA? Explain why or why not.

c. Is the spending rate (4 percent for the foundation) set by UPMIFA? If it is, is there flexibility in determining the rate? If not, what does UPMIFA say about spending or expenditure of funds? How might Ms. Hernandez use UPMIFA guidance in addressing her concern?

d. In accordance with UPMIFA, what recourse is available with regard to the 50-year-old endowment?

Exercises and Problems

15–15 Multiple Choice. Choose the best answer.

1. Colleges and universities look to which standard-setting body for GAAP?
   a. The GASB.
   b. The FASB.
   c. The NACUBO.
   d. It depends on whether the entity is public, private, or for-profit.
2. Which of the following statements is prepared by both a private and public college or university?
   a. Statement of net assets.
   b. Statement of cash flows.
   c. Statement of activities.
   d. Statement of net position.
3. Which of the following is a true statement about tuition revenue in a college or university?
   a. Scholarships should always be reported as expenses.
   b. Tuition receivables estimated to be uncollectible should be reported as an operating expense.
   c. Refunds should be reported as deductions from gross revenue.
   d. All of these statements are true.
4. A university expended $2,475,000 on a new parking facility. The transaction was reported as an investing activity on its direct method statement of cash flows. What type of university prepared the statement of cash flows?
   a. A public university.
   b. A for-profit university.
   c. A private university.
   d. Either b or c.
5. Last year Zelnick College showed a positive revenue over expenses number for the first time in several years. The college is funded with contributions, grants, two government appropriations (state and local), and tuition and fees. Zelnick College is most likely what type of college?
   a. A private for-profit college.
   b. A private not-for-profit college.
   c. A public university engaged primarily in governmental activities
   d. A public university engaged primarily in business-type activities.
6. Gresham College is a local private college. When reviewing the college's financial reports, you would expect to see which of the following categories on its statement of assets and liabilities?
   a. Unrestricted net assets, temporarily restricted net assets, and permanently restricted net assets.
   b. Unrestricted net position, temporarily restricted net position, and permanently restricted net position.

   c. Unrestricted net position, restricted net position, and net investment in capital assets.
   d. Unrestricted net assets, restricted net assets, and net investment in capital assets.

7. How would a university account for funds received from an external donor that are to be retained and invested, with the related earnings restricted to the purchase of library books?
   a. Temporarily restricted net assets in a private university.
   b. Permanently restricted net position in a private university.
   c. Unrestricted net assets/position in either a private or public university.
   d. Nonspendable, endowment in a public university.
8. Which of the following statements is *incorrect* concerning the financial reports of colleges and universities?
   a. The NACUBO account titles are frequently used for reporting revenues and expenses by both private and public entities.
   b. State appropriations are reported as nonoperating revenues by public entities.
   c. Intangible assets are reported as a classification within capital assets by private entities.
   d. Conditional contributions are not recognized by public or private entities.
9. Many endowment management policies establish a spending rate for the college or university's endowment funds. A spending rate is best defined as:
   a. The portion of the total return that can currently be used to carry out the endowment purpose.
   b. The average rate of return earned on the endowment investments for the current fiscal year.
   c. The moving average rate of return earned on endowment investments over a set period of time, such as a five-year moving average.
   d. The percentage of the endowment corpus that can be used to carry out the endowment purpose.
10. Which of the following is a performance measure of an outcome?
   a. Farley College students complete an undergraduate degree in an average of 4.3 years.
   b. A state survey of employers showed that 70 percent of employers ranked Beasley State University's graduates as "very well prepared" to enter the workforce.
   c. Within six months of graduation, 75 percent of undergraduate students at Gravette College have a job in their field.
   d. Faculty members at Ballard University published an average of two peer-reviewed papers each year.

15–16 Identifying the Appropriate GAAP. Section A lists a number of reporting requirements for colleges and universities. Section B lists the standard-setting body(ies) imposing the reporting requirements.

Section A

_____ 1. Patents are classified as capital assets.
_____ 2. Sidewalks are classified as land improvements.
_____ 3. Revenues and expenses must be categorized as operating and nonoperating.
_____ 4. Tuition and fees must be shown net of any estimated uncollectible amounts.

_____ 5. Expenses must be reported by program and support (management and general, and fund-raising) function classifications.
_____ 6. Statement of cash flows must be prepared using the direct method.
_____ 7. The purchase of a building is reported as an investing activity on the statement of cash flows.
_____ 8. The receipt of student deposits for housing is reported as a liability, Deposits Held in Custody for Others.
_____ 9. The cash from a debt issuance is reported in the capital and related financing activities section on the statement of cash flows.
_____10. The collection of historical first editions can be reported as a note rather than on the face of the financial statement provided certain conditions are met.

Section B

a. FASB standards
b. GASB standards
c. FASB and GASB standards

Required

Using the choices provided in Section B, identify whether the reporting requirement listed in Section A is a FASB standard, a GASB standard, or both a FASB and a GASB standard.

15–17 Private College Transactions. Steiner College's statement of financial position for the year ended June 30, 2016, is presented here. Steiner is a private college.

STEINER COLLEGE
Statement of Financial Position
June 30, 2016
(amounts in thousands)

Assets		
Cash and cash equivalents		$ 734
Short-term investments		7,666
Tuition and fees receivable (net of doubtful accounts of $12)		230
Pledges receivable (net of doubtful accounts of $280)		5,872
Prepaid assets		1,364
Property, plant, and equipment (net of accumulated depreciation of $104,240)		281,404
Investments (at fair value, cost of $162,000)		158,400
Total assets		$ 455,670
Liabilities and Net Assets		
Liabilities:		
Accounts payable and accrued liabilities		$ 21,130
Deposits held in custody for others		700
Unearned revenue		900
Bonds payable		99,000
Total liabilities		121,730
Net Assets:		
Unrestricted	$104,000	
Temporarily restricted	33,040	
Permanently restricted	196,900	
Total net assets		333,940
Total liabilities and net assets		$ 455,670

The following transaction information (amounts in thousands) pertains to the year ended June 30, 2017.

1. During the year charges for tuition and fees were $244,500; scholarships were $16,300; and tuition waivers for scholastic achievement were $5,100. After payment was received, tuition refunds of $11,200 were given. Tuition waivers of $17,300 for students serving as teaching assistants for instruction were accrued.
2. The college received unrestricted cash contributions of $2,080, pledges to be collected in 2018 of $550, and cash contributions to the endowments of $335. It also collected $820 of Pledges Receivable that were unrestricted.
3. Collections on Tuition and Fees Receivable totaled $222,600
4. Net deposits returned to students totaled $10.
5. Expenses were incurred for:

Instruction	$86,100
Academic support	23,300
Student services	37,700
Institutional support	28,500

   Related to the expenses incurred: prepaid assets of $534 were used, $4,776 of the expenses were accrued, and the remaining expenses were paid. Expenses incurred resulted in the release of $7,320 in temporarily restricted net assets.
6. The ending balance in Accounts Payable and Accrued Liabilities was $1,935.
7. Investment earnings received for the period were $3,960, of which $2,070 was temporarily restricted.
8. Adjusting entries for the period were made to increase Allowance for Doubtful Accounts by $20, to record depreciation expense of $26,400 (charged 70 percent to instruction and 30 percent to academic support), to adjust tuition revenue for an increase in unearned revenue of $10, and to recognize an increase in fair value of investments of $4,700 ($790 was related to temporarily restricted net assets, $1,610 was related to permanently restricted net assets, the remainder was related to unrestricted net assets).
9. Nominal accounts were closed.

Required

a. Prepare journal entries in good form to record the foregoing transactions for the year ended June 30, 2017.
b. Prepare a statement of activities for the year ended June 30, 2017.
c. Prepare a statement of financial position for the year ended June 30, 2017.

15–18 Private College Transactions. Elizabeth College, a small private college, had the following transactions in fiscal year 2017.

1. Gross tuition and fees revenue totaled $5,600,000. Tuition waivers and scholarships of $346,000 were granted. Of the tuition waivers granted $276,400 was for teaching assistantships, which is an instruction expense.
2. Students received tuition refunds of $101,670.
3. During the year the college received $1,891,000 cash in unrestricted private gifts, $575,200 cash in temporarily restricted grants, and $1,000,000 in securities for an endowment.
4. A pledge campaign generated $1,090,000 in pledges. Of the amount pledged, $573,200 was for the capital construction campaign, $300,000 was for endowments, and the remainder of the pledges had no purpose restrictions. The pledges will all be collected in 2018.

5. Auxiliary enterprises provided goods and services that generated $94,370 in cash.
6. Collections of tuition receivable totaled $5,080,000.
7. Unrestricted cash of $1,000,000 was invested.
8. The college purchased computer equipment at a cost of $10,580.
9. During the year the following expenses were paid:

Instruction	$3,566,040
Academic support	1,987,000
Student services	87,980
Institutional support	501,130
Auxiliary enterprises	92,410

10. Instruction provided $450,000 in services related to the temporarily restricted grant recorded in transaction 2.
11. At year-end, the allowance for uncollectible tuition and fees was increased by $7,200. The fair value of investments had increased $11,540; of this amount, $3,040 was allocated to permanently restricted net assets, the remainder was allocated to unrestricted net assets. Depreciation on plant and equipment was allocated $34,750 to instruction, $41,000 to auxiliary enterprises, and $12,450 to academic support.
12. All nominal accounts were closed.

Required

a. Prepare journal entries in good form to record the foregoing transactions for the fiscal year ended June 30, 2017.

b. Prepare a statement of activities for the year ended June 30, 2017. Assume beginning net asset amounts of $7,518,000 unrestricted, $200,000 temporarily restricted, and $5,000,000 permanently restricted.

15–19 Public University Transactions. The Statement of Net Position of South State University, a governmentally owned university, as of the end of its fiscal year June 30, 2016, follows.

SOUTH STATE UNIVERSITY
Statement of Net Position
June 30, 2016

Assets		
Cash		$ 340,000
Accounts receivable (net of doubtful accounts of $15,000)		370,000
Investments		250,000
Capital assets	$1,750,000	
Accumulated depreciation	275,000	1,475,000
Total assets		2,435,000
Liabilities		
Accounts payable		105,000
Accrued liabilities		40,000
Unearned revenue		25,000
Bonds payable		600,000
Total liabilities		770,000
Net Position		
Net investment in capital assets		875,000
Restricted		215,000
Unrestricted		575,000
Total net position		$1,665,000

The following information pertains to the year ended June 30, 2017:

1. South billed tuition and fees totaling $1,500,000 and provided $250,000 in scholarship waivers.
2. Unearned revenue at June 30, 2016, was earned during the year ended June 30, 2017.
3. Notification was received from the federal government that up to $50,000 in funds could be received in the current year for costs incurred in developing student performance measures.
4. During the year, the University received an unrestricted appropriation of $3,000,000 from the state.
5. Equipment for the student computer labs was purchased for cash in the amount of $525,000.
6. During the year, $800,000 in cash contributions was received from alumni. Of the amount contributed, $200,000 is to be used for construction of a new library.
7. Interest expense on the bonds payable in the amount of $48,000 was paid.
8. Student tuition refunds of $113,000 were made. Cash collections of tuition and fees totaled $1,458,700, $138,000 of which applied to the semester beginning in August 2017. Investment income of $13,000 was earned and collected during the year.
9. General expenses of $4,684,000 related to the administration and operation of academic programs, and research expenses of $37,000 related to the development of student performance measures were recorded in the voucher system. At June 30, 2017, the accounts payable balance was $75,000.
10. Accrued liabilities at June 30, 2016, were paid.
11. At year-end, adjusting entries were made. Depreciation on capital assets totaled $90,000. The Allowance for Doubtful Accounts was adjusted to $17,000. Accrued interest on investments was $1,250. The fair value of investments at year-end was $262,000. Of the income earned on investments, $5,230 was restricted.
12. Nominal accounts were closed and net position amounts were reclassified as necessary.

Required

a. Prepare journal entries in good form to record the foregoing transactions for the year ended June 30, 2017.

b. Prepare a statement of net position for the year ended June 30, 2017.

15–20 Various Unrelated Transactions. Following are several transactions involving a university.

1. In fiscal year 2017, the university was notified by the federal government that in 2018 it would receive a $500,000 grant for wetlands research.
2. The university received a $500,000 endowment.
3. For the fiscal year, the university recorded $2,500,000 in tuition and fees revenue. Cash refunds of $325,000 were given.
4. The university provided $12,600 in tuition waivers for students with outstanding academic performance.
5. During the year, the university constructed a new street, to allow for the expansion of its student housing efforts. The cost of the street was $1,980,000.

6. The biology department spent $25,000 on wetland research.
7. At year-end, $1,670 of estimated uncollectible tuition and fees was recorded.

Required

a. Prepare journal entries to record the foregoing transactions, assuming the university is a private institution.
b. Prepare journal entries to record the foregoing transactions, assuming the university is a public institution.

15–21 Financial Statements—Private University. The following is the preclosing trial balance for Allen University as of June 30, 2017. Additional information related to net assets and the statement of cash flows is also provided.

ALLEN UNIVERSITY
Preclosing Trial Balance
June 30, 2017

	Debits	***Credits***
Cash and Cash Equivalents	$ 516,600	
Investments	3,200,000	
Tuition and Fees Receivable	372,400	
Allowance for Doubtful Accounts		$ 75,600
Pledges Receivable	223,000	
Allowance for Doubtful Pledges		79,000
Property, Plant, and Equipment	2,196,160	
Accumulated Depreciation		658,720
Accounts Payable		103,000
Accrued Liabilities		37,500
Deposits Held in Custody for Others		17,570
Unearned Revenue		62,150
Bonds Payable		792,000
Net Assets—Unrestricted		3,353,110
Net Assets—Temporarily Restricted		340,600
Net Assets—Permanently Restricted		980,000
Net Assets Released from Restrictions—Temporarily Restricted	426,850	
Net Assets Released from Restrictions—Unrestricted		426,850
Tuition and Fees		1,290,750
Tuition and Fees Discount and Allowances	327,000	
Contributions—Unrestricted		310,200
Contributions—Temporarily Restricted		177,000
Contributions—Permanently Restricted		150,000
Grants and Contracts—Temporarily Restricted		324,000
Investment Income—Unrestricted		50,500
Investment Income—Temporarily Restricted		29,500
Other Revenue		13,250
Auxiliary Enterprise Sales and Services		153,560
Gain on Sale of Investments		70,000
Unrealized Gain on Investments		179,200
Instruction Expense	1,044,630	
Research Expense	571,800	
Academic Support Expense	240,560	
Student Services Expense	193,000	
Institutional Support Expense	203,360	
Auxiliary Enterprise Expenses	158,700	
Total	$9,674,060	$9,674,060

Additional Information

Net assets released from temporary restrictions totaled $426,850. The gain resulting from sale of investments was unrestricted. Twenty percent of the unrealized gain is related to permanently restricted net assets and 10 percent is related to temporarily restricted net assets, with the remainder related to unrestricted net assets.

Additional information is as follows:

The balance in cash and cash equivalents as of July 1, 2016, was $615,540.
Tuition and Fees Receivable increased by $10,230.
Pledges Receivable decreased by $1,560.
Allowance for Doubtful Accounts was increased by $770 (the bad debt was netted against Tuition and Fees).
Accounts Payable decreased by $2,900.
Accrued Liabilities decreased by $1,120.
Unearned Revenue increased by $6,200.
Depreciation Expense was $30,070.
Cash of $100,000 was used to retire bonds.
Investments were sold for $1,500,000 (at a gain of $70,000) and others were purchased for $1,250,000.
Unrestricted net assets were used to purchase equipment at a cost of $33,000.

Required

a. Prepare a statement of activities for the year ended June 30, 2017.
b. Prepare a statement of financial position for June 30, 2017.
c. Prepare a statement of cash flows for the year ended June 30, 2017.

15–22 Financial Statements—Public College. The following balances come from the trial balance of Wilson State College as of the end of the 2017 fiscal year.

WILSON STATE COLLEGE
Preclosing Trial Balance
June 30, 2017
(000s omitted)

	Debits	***Credits***
Cash and Cash Equivalents	$ 3,278	
Investments	29,387	
Accounts Receivable	1,957	
Allowance for Uncollectible Receivables		$ 137
Due from State	79,626	
Inventories	869	
Cash and Cash Equivalents—Restricted	6,716	
Investments—Restricted	71,883	
Depreciable Capital Assets	184,620	
Accumulated Depreciation		28,850
Nondepreciable Assets	89,481	
Accounts Payable		2,306
Accrued Liabilities		2,039
Unearned Revenue		13,789
Compensated Absences—Current Portion		1,538
Bonds Payable		92,116

continued

	Debits	Credits
Compensated Absences		37,662
Net Position—Net Investment in Capital Assets		158,715
Net Position—Restricted for Debt Service—Expendable		1,157
Net Position—Restricted for Capital Projects—Expendable		49,272
Net Position—Restricted for Endowment—Nonexpendable		39,959
Net Position—Unrestricted		36,559
Tuition and Fees		30,095
Tuition and Fees Discount and Allowances	7,565	
Grants and Contracts Revenue		18,196
Auxiliary Enterprise Sales		14,595
Investment Income		1,745
State Appropriations		44,894
Capital Appropriations		12,785
Institutional Support Expenses	26,268	
Academic Support Expenses	58,940	
Scholarships and Fellowships Expense	7,664	
Depreciation Expense	5,580	
Interest Expense	378	
Auxiliary Enterprise Expenses	12,197	
Totals	$586,409	$586,409
Information on Cash and Cash Equivalents Activity		
Beginning Cash Balance	$ 8,067	
Received Tuition and Fees (net)	23,609	
Received Grants and Contracts	12,940	
Received from Auxiliary Enterprises	13,765	
Payments to Employees	58,220	
Payments to Vendors	21,711	
Payments to Students for Scholarships and Fellowships	7,664	
Received State Appropriations	39,894	
Received Capital Appropriations	20,540	
Purchase of Capital Assets	20,634	
Interest Paid on Debt	2,095	
Interest Income	1,503	

Required

a. Prepare a statement of revenues, expenses, and changes in net position for the year ended June 30, 2017, in good form. See Illustrations 15–2 and 7–6; however, display expenses using functional classifications as shown in Illustration 15–6.

b. Prepare a statement of net position as of June 30, 2017, in good form. For the period, net position restricted for capital projects increased by $3,000, and net position restricted for debt service increased by $150; all bonded debt relates to capital assets. See Illustration 15–1.

c. Prepare a statement of cash flows for the year ended June 30, 2017. Information on changes in assets and liabilities is as follows: Accounts Receivable (net) increased by $2,551; Due from State decreased by $14,842; Inventories increased by $23; Accounts Payable and Accrued Liabilities increased by $1,962; and Unearned Revenue decreased by $1,763. See Illustration 15–3.

Chapter Sixteen

Accounting for Health Care Organizations

Learning Objectives

After studying this chapter, you should be able to:

16-1 Identify the different organizational forms and the related authoritative accounting literature for health care organizations.

16-2 Explain unique accounting and reporting issues in health care organizations.

16-3 Journalize transactions and prepare the basic financial statements for not-for-profit and governmental health care organizations.

16-4 Describe other accounting issues in the health care industry, including legislation, auditing, taxation and regulation, prepaid health care services, and continuing care retirement communities.

16-5 Explain financial and operational analysis of health care organizations.

The health care industry in the United States changed dramatically in the last century and continues to see dramatic change. Today, health care organizations are complex entities that cross the private, public, and not-for-profit sectors; spiraling costs outpace inflation; capital construction requires extensive financing; and professional managers face increasing public scrutiny and government oversight. Technological advances brought dramatic changes in the delivery and quality of health care services but also contributed greatly to rising costs. Health care spending in 2012 was $2.8 trillion, representing 17.2 percent of gross domestic product. It is projected to grow to 19.9 percent of the gross domestic product by 2022.[1]

Political, social, and economic factors explain the tremendous change in the health care industry. The initiation of entitlement programs, such as Medicare and Medicaid in the 1960s, reflected public policy efforts to make health care a basic right to be regulated at the federal level. In the 1980s, employers and insurance companies initiated managed care systems in an attempt to bring down the cost of providing health care coverage. In the 1990s, comprehensive health care reform became a political issue at the federal level. As a result of concerns about increasing health care costs and health care coverage, the Patient Protection and Affordability Act was passed in 2010.

Today, over half of the nonfederal *hospital* health care is provided by not-for-profit organizations, with the remaining care being provided by approximately an equal

[1] Centers for Medicare and Medicaid Services, National Health Expenditure Data, *www.cms.gov/Research-Statistics-Data-and-Systems/Statistics-Trends-and-Reports/NationalHealthExpendData/index.html*.

ILLUSTRATION 16–1 **Classification of Health Care Organizations**

By Legal Structure and Sponsors

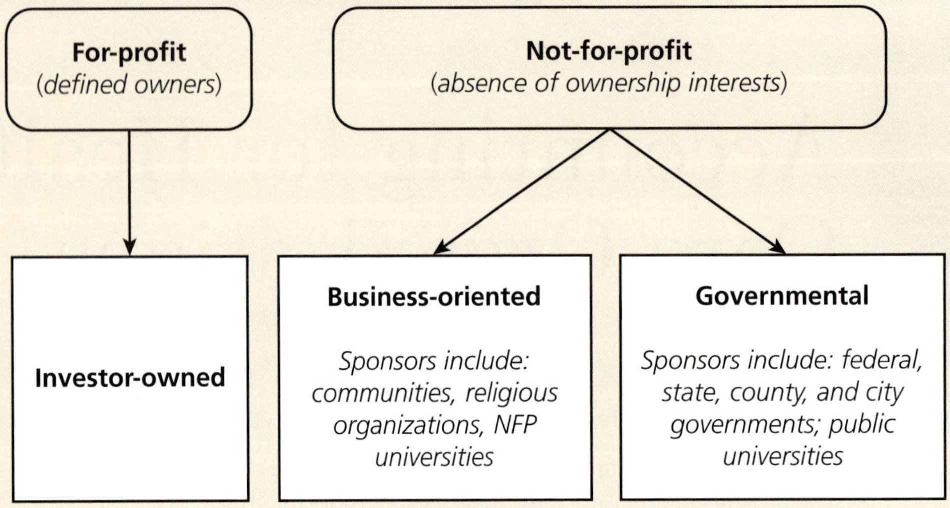

By Type of Health Care Organization

Clinics, medical group practices, individual practice associations, individual practitioners, and other ambulatory care organizations.

Continuing care retirement communities (CCRCs).

Health maintenance organizations (HMOs) and similar prepaid health care plans.

Home health agencies.

Hospitals.

Nursing homes that provide skilled, intermediate, and a less-intensive level of health care.

Drug and alcohol rehabilitation centers and other rehabilitation facilities.

Integrated systems that include one or more of the above entity types.

Source: Constructed from information in FASB *ASC* 954-10.

number of governmental and for-profit hospitals.[2] Illustration 16–1 shows classifications of health care organizations by legal structure as well as by the nature of services they provide.

This chapter focuses on the financial reporting and accounting issues of not-for-profit (NFP) and governmental entities that charge patients or third parties for the services provided. Since many of the accounting and financial reporting requirements for NFPs were addressed in Chapter 13, and those for governmental business-type entities were

[2] American Hospital Association, "Fast Facts on US Hospitals," *http://www.aha.org/research/rc/stat-studies/fast-facts.shtml* (accessed June 30, 2014).

addressed in Chapter 7, this chapter focuses on accounting and reporting issues typically found in the health care industry. Particular attention is given to identifying differences in accounting and reporting for NFP versus governmental health care entities.

GAAP FOR HEALTH CARE PROVIDERS

Generally accepted accounting principles (GAAP) for hospitals and other health care organizations have evolved through and are influenced by the efforts of the American Hospital Association (AHA), the Healthcare Financial Management Association (HFMA), and the American Institute of Certified Public Accountants (AICPA). Currently, GAAP for health care entities is determined by the Financial Accounting Standards Board (FASB) and the Governmental Accounting Standards Board (GASB).

FASB is the sole authoritative source of GAAP for nongovernmental NFP and for-profit health care entities. The AICPA Audit and Accounting Guide *Health Care Entities* provides nonauthoritative guidance for nongovernmental and for-profit health care entities. The focus of this chapter is on authoritative guidance unless otherwise indicated.

Governmental hospitals and health care providers are considered special purpose governments, that is, legally separate entities that may be either component units of another government or stand-alone governmental entities. GASB is the authoritative source of GAAP for entities engaged in either governmental or business-type activities or both. According to the GASB the AICPA Audit and Accounting Guide is considered category (b) authority for governmental entities, which means that GASB statements take precedence.[3]

Given that different authoritative guidance exists, accounting and reporting rules may differ, depending on whether the health care provider is legally structured as an investor-owned, not-for-profit, or governmental organization. Some of the differences relate to accounting and reporting for contributions and financial reporting display, cash flows, and investments, as seen in Illustration 16–2. This chapter illustrates financial accounting and reporting for not-for-profit health care organizations, the largest segment of the in-patient health care industry, and points out differences unique to governmental health care providers. The reader is directed to Chapter 13 for a more thorough discussion of not-for-profit organizations, and to Chapter 7 for a discussion of business-type enterprises of government.

REPORTING AND ACCOUNTING ISSUES

The financial statements for health care organizations serve a broad set of users. However, the statements can vary based on the standards under which they are prepared.

FASB standards require that not-for-profit health care organizations prepare: (1) a balance sheet or statement of financial position; (2) a statement of operations; (3) a statement of cash flows; and (4) a statement of changes in net assets. Although the FASB allows the statement of changes in equity to be combined with the statement of operations, health care organizations often prefer to issue separate statements because they view operating activity as separate from investment and donor activities. The FASB allows considerable flexibility in displaying financial information.

[3] Governmental Accounting Standards Board, *Codification of Governmental Accounting and Financial Reporting Standards, as of June 30, 2014* (Norwalk, CT, 2014), Sec. 1000.101.

ILLUSTRATION 16–2 GAAP for Health Care Entities in Different Sectors

	Health Care Providers		
Accounting and Reporting Issue	**Investor-Owned**	**Not-for-Profit**	**Governmental**
Reporting entity	FASB *ASC* 954-810-15	FASB *ASC* 954-810-15	GASB *Codification*, Sec. 2100
Contributions and financial statement display	FASB *ASC* 954-225, 958-205, 958-225 and 958-605 (includes donated services)	FASB *ASC* 954-225, 958-205, 958-225 and 958-605 (includes donated services)	GASB *Codification*, Secs. N50 and 2200 (donated services not addressed)
Cash flows	FASB *ASC* 230	Same as investor owned plus FASB *ASC* 958-230	GASB *Codification*, Sec. 2450
Deposits with financial institutions	FASB *ASC* 305-45	Same as investor owned plus FASB *ASC* 954-305-45	GASB *Codification*, Sec. C20
Investments	FASB *ASC* 320 and 825	Same as investor owned plus FASB *ASC* 958-320 and 958-325	GASB *Codification*, Sec. I50
Operating leases	FASB *ASC* 840-20	Same as investor owned plus FASB *ASC* 958-840	GASB *Codification*, Sec. L20
Prepaid health care arrangements and self-insurance programs	FASB *ASC* 954-405-50 and AAG-HCE Chs. 8 and 14 (includes reoccupancy)	Same as investor owned (includes reoccupancy)	GASB *Codification*, Secs. C50 and Po20
Compensated absences	FASB *ASC* 710-25	Same as investor owned	GASB *Codification*, Sec. C60
Debt refundings	FASB *ASC* 470-50	Same as investor owned	GASB *Codification*, Sec. D20
Pensions	FASB *ASC* 715, 960 and 962	Same as investor owned	GASB *Codification*, Sec. P20
Risk and uncertainties	AICPA *SOP* 94-6	Same as investor owned	GASB *Codification*, Sec. C50
Postemployment benefits	FASB *ASC* 712 and 965	Same as investor owned	GASB *Codification*, Sec. C50
Fair value measurements	FASB *ASC* 820	Same as investor owned	None
Net patient revenue	FASB *ASC* 954-310	Same as investor owned	GASB *Codification*, Sec. P80

Abbreviated citations: FASB *ASC* is the FASB *Accounting Standards Codification*™; GASB *Codification* is the GASB *Codification of Governmental Accounting and Financial Reporting* Standards; AAG-HCE is the AICPA Audit and Accounting Guide, *Health Care Entities*; AICPA *SOP* is the AICPA *Statement of Position*.

Sources: Adapted from the AICPA *Audit and Risk Alert, Health Care Industry Developments—2001.02* (New York: AICPA, 2002), par. 121 (out of print). Updated and expanded for subsequent changes in standards.

Examples of statements for a not-for-profit hospital are presented in Illustrations 16–3, 16–4, and 16–5.

GASB standards require that the financial statements of a governmental health care provider include: (1) a statement of net position; (2) a statement of revenues, expenses, and changes in net position; and (3) a statement of cash flows. With the exception of the statement of cash flows, the financial statements required for governmental health care organizations that follow proprietary fund accounting—the most common case—are similar to the balance sheet and operating statements illustrated for not-for-profit health care organizations. Thus, these statements are not illustrated in this chapter. Readers should refer to Chapter 7 for illustrations of the formats of proprietary fund statements. Differences in the statements of cash flow are discussed later in the chapter.

A health care organization may choose to use fund accounting for internal purposes, in part, to account for revenues and expenses associated with grants (or because it is a governmental entity). For organizations using fund accounting, the fund structure should include general unrestricted funds and donor-restricted funds (e.g., specific purpose, plant replacement and expansion, and endowment).

ILLUSTRATION 16–3

SIERRA REGIONAL HOSPITAL
Balance Sheet
As of September 30, 2017

Assets		**Liabilities and Net Assets**	
Current assets:		Current liabilities:	
Cash	$ 172,100	Accounts payable	$ 259,000
Accounts and notes receivable, net of allowance for uncollectibles of $135,000	353,000	Accrued expenses payable	173,500
Pledges receivable, net of allowance for uncollectibles of $114,300	548,700		
Accrued interest receivable	44,000		
Inventory	160,000		
Prepaid expenses	8,000		
Short-term investments	1,778,000		
Total current assets	3,063,800	Total current liabilities	432,500
Assets limited as to use:		Long-term debt:	
Internally designated for capital acquisition—cash	6,500	Mortgages payable	6,000,000
		Total liabilities	6,432,500
Internally designated for capital acquisition—investments	778,000		
Total assets limited as to use	784,500	Net assets:	
Long-term investments	146,000	Unrestricted—undesignated	8,536,600
Property, plant, and equipment:		Unrestricted—designated	784,500
		Temporarily restricted—plant	2,392,700
Land	1,080,000	Temporarily restricted—programs	25,000
Buildings, net of accumulated depreciation of $1,365,000	9,685,000	Permanently restricted	178,000
		Total net assets	11,916,800
Equipment, net of accumulated depreciation of $1,702,000	3,590,000		
Total property, plant, and equipment	14,355,000		
Total assets	$18,349,300	Total liabilities and net assets	$18,349,300

Balance Sheet or Statement of Net Position

The balance sheet presented in Illustration 16–3 is for Sierra Regional Hospital, a hypothetical not-for-profit health care entity. Although the name of the statement may differ, the format of the statement is similar for NFP, governmental, and for-profit health care organizations. One significant difference is that the residual resulting when liabilities are deducted from assets is named and classified differently under the different legal structures. The net assets section of a not-for-profit organization balance sheet is classified into unrestricted, temporarily restricted, and permanently restricted categories, as described in Chapter 13. Governmental organizations prepare a statement of net position and classify net position into net investment in capital assets; restricted; and unrestricted, as illustrated in Chapters 1 through 9. The equity section on the balance sheet of an investor-owned health care provider shows stockholders' equity separated into capital stock and retained earnings.

Assets Limited as to Use

FASB standards have NFP health care entities identify **assets limited as to use.** These are unrestricted assets whose use is limited by the governing board or contracts or agreements with outside parties *other than* donors or grantors.[4] Examples include proceeds of debt issues deposited with a trustee and limited as to use by the debt agreement; self-insurance funding arrangements, such as medical malpractice funding arrangements; statutory reserve requirements (i.e., those required under state law for health maintenance organizations); and a limitation placed on the assets by the board of directors or trustees (e.g., for capital acquisition). Information about significant contractual limits should be disclosed in the notes to the financial statements. Internally designated funds should be reported separately from externally designated funds on the face or in the notes to the financial statements.[5] Assets that are held in trust by other parties are not reported on the balance sheet of the health care entity; however, their existence should be disclosed in the notes. Assets limited as to use differ from *assets with restrictions* on use, which are assets with long-term purpose donor-imposed restrictions (see Chapter 13).

GASB standards do not provide for reporting of assets limited as to use; therefore, governmental health care entities generally do not identify assets limited as to use. However, governmental entities do report restricted assets, which are assets restricted by external parties, including restrictions by donors or contracts and other agreements.

Investments

Generally, health care organizations report their investments at fair value, although exact treatment of specific assets depends on the legal structure of the organization, as seen in Illustration 16–2.

FASB standards (FASB *ASC* 954-320) followed by NFP organizations require that all investments in equity securities with readily determinable values and all debt securities be reported at fair value with the realized and unrealized gains and losses reported as changes in net assets. FASB *ASC* 820 provides guidance on measuring fair value. As with other NFP organizations, health care entities are not required to identify investments as trading, available-for-sale, or held-to-maturity. However, many health care entities do separate investments into these three categories, enabling them to exclude unrealized gains and losses from their operating performance indicator, which is discussed later in the chapter.

GASB standards followed by governmental entities require that changes in the fair value of certain investments be reported in the statement of revenues, expenses, and changes in net position. Changes in fair value are recognized as part of investment income or revenue. The changes in fair value should not be displayed separately from realized gains and losses on the financial statement.[6]

Investor-owned entities follow FASB *ASC* 320, which is the most complicated set of rules in that investments are required to be separated into trading, available-for-sale, and held-to-maturity categories with different accounting treatment for each category.

[4] FASB *ASC* 954-210-45-2.

[5] FASB *ASC* 954-210-45-4.

[6] GASB, *Codification,* Sec. I50, par. 112.

Receivables

Amounts due from patients and third-party payors (e.g., insurance companies) result in several asset and contra-asset accounts on the balance sheet: Accounts Receivable, Allowance for Uncollectible Accounts, Interim Payments, and Settlement accounts. **Settlement accounts** are the receivables (or payables) arising from differences between original payment estimates by third-party payors, cash received and paid, and final determinations. The rate-setting process in the health care industry is complex. In the revenue section, some of the financial accounting aspects related to the rates received by health care entities are discussed. However, discussion related to the negotiation process used to establish rates is not discussed because it does not directly relate to recognition and reporting of receivables and revenues.

Commitments and Contingencies

Contingencies that are common for health care providers arise from malpractice claims, risk contracting, third-party payor payment programs, obligations to provide uncompensated care, and contractual agreements with physicians. Other commitments and contingencies found in most business enterprises also apply to health care organizations, such as those that arise from construction contracts, pension plans, operating leases, purchase commitments, and loan guarantees. The cost of these claims against the health care organization should be accrued if they can be reasonably estimated, and it is probable they will have to be paid.[7] Accruals should be made for unasserted claims at the best estimates based on industry experience.

Operating Statement

Not-for-profit health care entities call their operating statement the statement of operations; whereas, governmental health care entities call it the statement of revenues, expenses, and changes in net position. As you will see in this section, except for the differences noted, the reporting requirements for the operating statement are similar under FASB and the GASB standards.

FASB standards, as shown in Illustration 16–4, allow not-for-profits, such as Sierra Regional Hospital, considerable flexibility in displaying the results of operations. Flexibility is allowed in classifying results of operations as operating and nonoperating, earned and unearned, or recurring and nonrecurring. FASB concepts statements provide guidance on distinguishing operating items (i.e., those arising from ongoing major activities, such as service revenue) from nonoperating items (i.e., those arising from transactions peripheral or incidental to the delivery of health care, such as investment income and unrestricted contributions).[8]

Not-for-profit health care organizations should include a **performance indicator** to report the results of operations. The intent of the performance indicator is to provide an operating measure that is equivalent to income from continuing operations of for-profit health care organizations. The principal components of a performance indicator are unrestricted revenues, gains, and other support; expenses; and other income. Examples of performance indicators include excess of revenues over expenses, revenues and gains over expenses and losses, earned income, and performance earnings. In accordance with FASB *ASC* 954-225, investment income, realized gains and losses, and unrealized gains and losses on trading securities should be reported in the

[7] FASB, *ASC* 450-20; and GASB, *Codification,* Sec. C50.

[8] Financial Accounting Standards Board, *Concepts Statement No. 6,* "Elements of Financial Statements" (Norwalk, CT: FASB, 1985).

ILLUSTRATION 16–4 Illustration of a Two-Part Statement of Operations

SIERRA REGIONAL HOSPITAL
Statement of Operations
Year Ended September 30, 2017

Unrestricted revenues, gains, and other support:		
Net patient service revenue		$ 8,981,000
Other revenue		48,800
Contributions		297,900
Investment income		36,100
Total revenues and gains		9,363,800
Expenses and losses:		
Nursing services	$4,577,500	
Other professional services	1,286,420	
General services	2,016,660	
Fiscal and administrative services	1,307,120	
Total expenses		9,187,700
Loss on disposal of equipment		1,500
Total expenses and losses		9,189,200
Excess of revenue and gains over expenses and losses		174,600
Net assets released from restrictions:		
Satisfaction of equipment acquisition restrictions		100,000
Increase in unrestricted net assets		$ 274,600

Statement of Changes in Net Assets
Year Ended September 30, 2017

Unrestricted net assets (see Part 1 above):	
Excess of revenue and gains over expenses and losses	$ 174,600
Net assets released from restrictions	100,000
Increase in unrestricted net assets	274,600
Temporarily restricted net assets:	
Contributions	25,000
Investment income	77,000
Increase in provision for uncollectible pledges	(66,300)
Loss on sale of investments	(26,000)
Net assets released from restrictions	(100,000)
Decrease in temporarily restricted net assets	(90,300)
Permanently restricted net assets:	
Contributions	24,000
Increase in permanently restricted net assets	24,000
Increase in net assets	208,300
Net assets at beginning of year	11,708,500
Net assets at end of year	$11,916,800

performance indicator; however, the following items should be reported separately from the performance indicator:

- Transactions with owners acting in that capacity.
- Equity transfers involving other related entities.
- Receipt of temporarily and permanently restricted contributions.

- Contributions of (and assets released from donor restrictions related to) long-lived assets.
- Unrealized gains and losses on investments other than trading securities.
- Investment returns restricted by donors or by law.
- Other items that are required by GAAP to be reported separately, such as extraordinary items, the effect of discontinued operations, or the cumulative effect of accounting changes.

Notice that the format of the statement of operations in Illustration 16–4 is different from the format of the statement of activities prepared by other types of NFP organizations. The net assets released from restrictions is not reported in the revenue section; rather it is reported below excess of revenue and gains over expenses and losses. Since the release of net assets from restrictions is not included in the calculation of the performance indicator, it is shown below the activity representing income from continuing operations. Changes in temporarily and permanently restricted net assets are not reflected on the statement of operations; they are only shown on the statement of changes in net assets.

GASB standards allow for less flexibility in the display of operations, requiring that governmental health care entities display operating activity separately from nonoperating activity. Although not specifically identified as a performance indicator, governmental health care entities are required to report operating income.

Revenues

Health care organizations receive the majority of their revenue in the form of fees for services. The principal sources of service revenue are (1) patient service revenue; (2) premium revenue derived from **capitation fees,** which are fixed fees per person paid periodically, regardless of services provided, by a health maintenance organization; and (3) resident service revenue, such as maintenance or rental fees in an extended care facility. Payors of service revenues include the patient and third-party payors such as: the government, in the form of Medicare or Medicaid payments; Blue Cross/Blue Shield or other private insurance companies; or contracts with other private health care companies.

Under the FASB and GASB standards, service revenue is recorded at the gross amount when services are rendered. **Contractual adjustments (or allowances)** are recorded as contra-revenue accounts for the difference between the gross patient service revenue and the negotiated payment by third-party payors (discussed in the next section) in arriving at net patient service revenue. For example, if a hospital determined it had contractual adjustments of $50,000 on $125,000 of patient service revenue it had already billed to a third-party payor, it would record the adjustment to receivables as follows.

	Debits	Credits
Contractual Adjustments	50,000	
Accounts Receivable		50,000

When reported in the financial statements the contractual adjustment will be subtracted from the $125,000 of patient service revenue, resulting in net patient service revenue of $75,000.

Prepaid health care plans that earn revenues from *agreements to provide* services record revenue at the point that agreements are made, not when services are rendered. The variety of payment plans with third-party payors makes accounting for patient service revenue a complicated accounting task. For example, payments can be made on a per case, per service performed, per diem, or per person (capitated) basis. In addition, interim payments are often received with final settlement at a later point in time.

Third-Party Payors

Contracts with Medicare, Medicaid, Blue Cross and other insurance companies, and state and local welfare agencies customarily provide for payment by **third-party payors** according to allowable costs or a predetermined (prospective) contractual rate rather than paying the service rates billed by the health care provider. For example, under Medicare's **Prospective Payment System (PPS),** payments are based on allowable service costs for medical procedures within the same diagnosis-related group rather than on the length of the patient's hospital stay or the actual cost of services rendered.

The **diagnosis related group (DRG)** is a case-mix classification scheme that is used to determine the payment provided to the hospital for inpatient services, regardless of how much the hospital spends to treat a patient. For example, the DRG relative weighting factor for chest pain may be 0.6 relative to the norm of 1.0, while the DRG for a kidney transplant may provide a relative weight of 3.15. These relative numbers are multiplied by the federal standard rate as determined by the Centers for Medicare & Medicaid Services (CMS). Many other third-party payors regularly negotiate contractual services and contract payment rates with health care providers. Health care providers, therefore, have an incentive to determine actual costs of services rendered: to keep their costs commensurate with payments for services. It is now common for most hospitals to have sophisticated systems to capture costs by procedure. Some payment methods, such as capitation fees in prepaid health care plans, shift a considerable amount of risk to the provider. That is, the fixed amount of revenue received per patient may not cover the costs of providing the service.

Charity Service

Governmental and NFP health care entities are expected to provide some level of **charity care,** services to persons with a demonstrated inability to pay. Because charity service is never expected to result in an inflow of resources, it is neither recognized as revenue nor receivables nor bad debt expense.[9] Therefore, if the health care organization's policy is not to pursue collection of amounts determined by its policy to qualify as charity care, those amounts are never reported as revenue. Although the GASB standards do not specifically address disclosure requirements related to charity care FASB *ASC* 954-605-50 requires that health care entities disclose their policies for providing charity care and the level of charity care provided. According to FASB *ASC* 954-605-50, the level of charity care is to be measured based on the costs of providing the care. If gifts or grants are received to pay for charity care the gifts or grants are to be separately disclosed.

In practice, it is often difficult to distinguish bad debt from charity service. However, it is important to disclose management's charity care policies and the level of charity care provided for several reasons. Some third-party payors reimburse for a portion of bad debts but not charity service. The Hill-Burton Act of 1946 requires that hospitals receiving federal assistance for construction projects perform some charity care. NFP

[9] FASB *ASC* 954-605-25.

health care entities are under additional scrutiny since the IRS and local tax authorities question the tax-exempt status of some NFP health care providers that do not appear to deliver an adequate amount of charity service to justify their tax exemption, although regulations do not specify levels of adequacy.

Other Revenue and Support

For all health care entities, other revenue includes auxiliary sales (e.g., sales to nonpatients of medical supplies and cafeteria meals), fees (e.g., for educational programs or transcripts), rental of facilities other than to residents, and investment income and gains. Also considered other revenue would be nonexchange or support revenues that come from unrestricted contributions and grants, and endowment income restricted by donors to finance charity care. It is important to realize that research grants or contracts may be considered exchange transactions or nonexchange transactions (i.e., contributions) depending on whether the resource provider directly benefits by receiving something of value through the transaction.

GASB standards make the classification of grants or contracts of particular concern to governmental health care organizations since they are required to separate operating from nonoperating revenues. A type of other revenue and support that is unique to governmental health care entities is tax or intergovernmental revenue. In some instances, health care entities may be supported in part by such revenues, which would be classified as nonoperating.

Donated Materials and Services

Because health care entities can receive donated materials and services, accounting for such donations is briefly discussed. A more complete discussion is provided in Chapter 13.

FASB standards (*ASC* 958-605-25-16) require that material amounts of donated materials be reported at fair value as both contribution revenue and an expense or a noncash asset. Donated materials used or consumed in providing services should be reported as part of the cost of the services. The FASB requires recognition of contributed services at their fair value if the services received (1) create or enhance nonfinancial assets or (2) require specialized skills, are provided by individuals possessing those skills, and typically would need to be purchased if not provided by donation (e.g., accountants).

GASB standards require recognition of donations of materials at fair value. However, the standards do not provide for recognition of donated services.

Expenses

All health care providers use the accrual basis of accounting, and the accrual of expenses is generally the same as for any business organization. Expenses can be reported using either a natural presentation (e.g., salaries, supplies, and occupancy costs) or a functional presentation (e.g., inpatient services, ancillary outpatient services, and fiscal and administrative services). Functional expenses should be based on full cost allocations.

As a result of recent changes to the FASB *ASC*, both the FASB and the GASB standards require estimates for uncollectible patient accounts receivable to be recorded using contra-revenue accounts rather than expense accounts. NFP and government hospitals recognize a debit to an account such as Provision for Bad Debts and a credit to Allowance for Uncollectible Receivables. FASB *ASC* 954-605-45 recommends that the Provision for Bad Debts be separately disclosed on the face of the operating statement.

FASB standards have not changed the manner in which estimates for uncollectible accounts other than patient accounts receivable are recorded and reported.

For estimated uncollectible amounts other than patient accounts receivable, a debit is made to Bad Debt Expense and a credit is made to Allowance for Uncollectible Receivables.

Under FASB standards, health care organizations must disclose functional classifications in the notes to the financial statements if they report expenses using a natural classification. The categories of functional expenses displayed or disclosed in the notes can be as simple as distinguishing between health care services and support services, such as general/administrative expenses. In accordance with FASB standards, NFP organizations must at a minimum recognize program and support expenses separately. In Illustration 16–4, Sierra Regional Hospital displays functional expenses. As required by the FASB, all expenses are reported as decreases in unrestricted net assets.

Statement of Changes in Net Assets

NFP health care entities are required to prepare a statement of changes in net position. The statement can be a separate statement or it can be combined with the statement of operations. Sierra Regional Hospital has prepared a separate statement, which is shown in the bottom half of Illustration 16–4. The statement shows increases and decreases in the three classes of net assets for a not-for-profit organization: unrestricted, temporarily restricted, and permanently restricted. Net assets released from restrictions increase unrestricted net assets and decrease temporarily restricted net assets. Net gains on permanently restricted endowments are shown as increases to the permanently restricted net assets in Illustration 16–4; however, the accounting treatment of net gains will depend on donor stipulations, state law, and organizational policy. While this statement may be combined with the statement of operations, NFP health care entities generally view operating activity as separate from the changes that result from restricted revenues or investments; thus, separate statements are commonly used by NFP health care entities. Governmental health care entities do not have a statement comparable to the statement of changes in net assets.

Statement of Cash Flows

FASB standards require a statement of cash flows similar to the one presented in Illustration 16–5. Sierra Regional Hospital has prepared its statement in accordance with FASB *ASC* 230, adjusted for NFP entities. The direct method is presented with a reconciliation of changes in net assets to net changes provided by operating activities. Under FASB standards, Sierra has the option of presenting the statement using the direct or the indirect method. The statement is divided into three sections: operating, investing, and financing. With few adjustments, preparation of the statement of activities under FASB standards is the same for NFP and investor-owned entities. One adjustment to the statement of cash flows for NFP entities relates to the reporting of interest. Interest paid and received by an NFP entity is generally reported in the operating activities section, unless the interest income is to be added to temporarily or permanently restricted net assets. Such restricted income is reported as a financing activity. NFPs also receive more gifts and contributions than investor-owned entities; unrestricted contributions are reported as operating activity.

GASB standards require that the statement of cash flows be prepared using the direct method.[10] An additional difference between the statements for an NFP and a governmental health care entity is that the governmental statement is divided into four sections:

[10] Governmental Accounting Standards Board, *Codification of Governmental Accounting and Financial Reporting Standards as of June 30, 2014* (Norwalk, CT, 2014), Sec. 2200.195.

ILLUSTRATION 16–5 Illustration of Statement of Cash Flows—Not-for-Profit Organizations

SIERRA REGIONAL HOSPITAL
Statement of Cash Flows
Year Ended September 30, 2017

Cash Flows from Operating Activities	
Cash received from patients and third-party payors	$8,842,000
Other receipts from operations	48,800
Interest received on assets limited as to use	36,100
Receipts from unrestricted gifts	297,900
Cash paid to employees and suppliers	(8,014,200)
Interest paid	(160,000)
Net cash provided by operating activities	1,050,600
Cash Flows from Investing Activities	
Purchase of property and equipment	(400,000)
Purchase of long-term investments	(737,000)
Proceeds from sale of securities	59,000
Proceeds from sale of equipment	500
Net cash used by investing activities	(1,077,500)
Cash Flows from Financing Activities	
Proceeds from contributions restricted for:	
Investment in plant	292,000
Future operations	5,000
	297,000
Other financing activities:	
Interest and dividends restricted to endowment	69,000
Repayment of long-term debt	(400,000)
	(331,000)
Net cash used by financing activities	(34,000)
Net increase (decrease) in cash	(60,900)
Cash and cash equivalents, September 30, 2016	239,500
Cash and cash equivalents, September 30, 2017	$ 178,600

Reconciliation of Changes in Net Assets to Net Cash Provided by Operating Activities

Changes in net assets	$ 208,300
Adjustments to reconcile change in net assets to net cash provided by operating activities:	
Depreciation	783,000
Loss on disposal of equipment	1,500
Increase in patient accounts receivable, net	(139,000)
Increase in supplies	(80,000)
Increase in accounts payable and accrued expenses	306,500
Decrease in prepaid expenses	4,000
Gifts, grants, and bequests restricted for long-term investment	(49,000)
Interest restricted for long-term investment	(77,000)
Loss on sale of investments	26,000
Increase in provision for uncollectible pledges	66,300
Net cash provided by operating activities	$1,050,600

ILLUSTRATION 16–6 Illustration of Statement of Cash Flows—GASB Standards

BLOOMFIELD HOSPITAL
Statement of Cash Flows
Year Ended September 30, 2017

Cash Flows from Operating Activities	
Cash received from patients and third-party payors	$8,842,000
Cash paid to employees and suppliers	(8,014,200)
Other receipts from operations	48,800
Net cash provided by operating activities	876,600
Cash Flows from Noncapital Financing Activities	
Unrestricted gifts and income from endowments	306,000
Gifts restricted for future operations	5,000
Net cash provided by noncapital financing activities	311,000
Cash Flows from Capital and Related Financing Activities	
Purchase of property and equipment	(400,000)
Principal paid on mortgage	(400,000)
Interest paid	(160,000)
Collection of pledges receivable	292,000
Proceeds from sale of equipment	500
Net cash used for capital and related financing activities	(667,500)
Cash Flows from Investing Activities	
Proceeds from sale of securities	59,000
Interest received on assets limited as to use	28,000
Interest received on donor-restricted assets	69,000
Cash invested in assets limited as to use	(378,000)
Cash invested in donor-restricted assets	(359,000)
Net cash used by investing activities	(581,000)
Net increase (decrease) in cash	(60,900)
Cash and cash equivalents, September 30, 2016	239,500
Cash and cash equivalents, September 30, 2017	$ 178,600

Reconciliation of Operating Income to Net Cash Provided by Operating Activities

Operating income (loss)	$ (157,900)
Adjustments:	
Depreciation	783,000
Increase in patient accounts receivable, net	(139,000)
Increase in inventory	(80,000)
Increase in accounts payable	149,000
Increase in accrued expenses	157,500
Decrease in prepaid expenses	4,000
Interest paid in cash (Note 1)	160,000
Net cash provided by operating activities and gains and losses	$ 876,600

Note 1: Interest was classified as an operating expense on the income statement but as cash flows from capital and related financing activities on the cash flows statement prepared in conformity with GASB standards.

operating, noncapital financing, capital and related financing, and investing. Because of these differences in structure, Illustration 16–6 provides an example of a statement of cash flows for a governmental health care entity. Due to the different number of sections, there are also differences in the activities reported in each section. The GASB requires that interest received be reported as an investing activity. However, interest paid would be reported as either a noncapital financing or a capital and related financing activity, depending on the nature of the borrowing on which the interest is being paid. Acquisitions of land, buildings, and equipment are reported as capital and related financing activities under GASB standards. Unrestricted contributions are shown as noncapital financing activities. In the reconciliation schedule that must be prepared under the direct method, the statement shows the reconciliation of *operating income (loss)* to cash flows from operating activities, this is different than the FASB statement, which reconciles changes in net assets to cash flows from operating activities.

ILLUSTRATIVE CASE FOR A NOT-FOR-PROFIT HEALTH CARE ORGANIZATION

The illustrative transactions provided in this section are for a hypothetical not-for-profit hospital, Sierra Regional Hospital. Hospitals continue to be the dominant form of health care organization and usually exhibit a greater range of operating activities and transactions than other forms of health care organizations. Typical hospital transactions are illustrated for Sierra Regional Hospital following the post-closing trial balance as of September 30, 2016, the end of its fiscal year.

SIERRA REGIONAL HOSPITAL
(A Not-for-Profit Organization)
Post-closing Trial Balance
As of September 30, 2016

	Debits	*Credits*
Cash	$ 233,000	
Short-term Investments	1,480,000	
Accrued Interest Receivable	36,000	
Accounts and Notes Receivable	300,000	
Allowance for Uncollectible Receivables		$ 86,000
Pledges Receivable	960,000	
Allowance for Uncollectible Pledges		73,000
Inventory	80,000	
Prepaid Expenses	12,000	
Assets Limited as to Use—Cash	6,500	
Assets Limited as to Use—Investments	400,000	
Long-term Investments	146,000	
Land	1,080,000	
Buildings	11,050,000	
Equipment	4,920,000	
Accumulated Depreciation—Buildings		1,050,000
Accumulated Depreciation—Equipment		1,260,000
Accounts Payable		110,000
Accrued Expenses Payable		16,000
Mortgages Payable		6,400,000
Net Assets—Unrestricted, Undesignated		8,640,000
Net Assets—Unrestricted, Designated		406,500
Net Assets—Temporarily Restricted—Plant		2,508,000
Net Assets—Permanently Restricted		154,000
	$20,703,500	$20,703,500

During fiscal year 2017, the gross revenues for patient services from all responsibility centers totaled $9,261,000. It is the practice of Sierra Regional Hospital to debit receivable accounts for the gross charges for all services rendered to patients except for charity care patients. The following entry should be made:

		Debits	Credits
1.	Accounts and Notes Receivable	9,261,000	
	Patient Service Revenue		9,261,000

The preceding entry recorded the revenues the hospital would have earned if all services rendered to each patient (other than charity care patients) were to be collected from the patients or third-party payors as billed. Customers of profit-seeking businesses do not all pay their bills in full, and neither do hospital patients or patients' insurance companies. The variety of third-party payment policies makes estimation of net patient service revenue difficult, but such estimation is necessary for sound financial management and proper financial reporting. For the FY 2017, it is assumed the estimated provision for bad debts is $180,000 and contractual adjustments from third-party payors is $100,000. The entry to record this information is:

2.	Provision for Bad Debts	180,000	
	Contractual Adjustments	100,000	
	Allowance for Uncollectible Receivables		180,000
	Accounts and Notes Receivable		100,000

Provision for Bad Debts and Contractual Adjustments are contra-accounts deducted from Patient Service Revenue with only the net amount reported as revenues of the period.

Examples of *other revenues* for hospitals include tuition from nursing students, interns, or residents; cafeteria and gift shop revenues; parking fees; fees for copies of medical records; and other activities related to the ongoing major or central operations of the hospital. Assuming a total of $48,800 in other revenue was received in cash during FY 2017, Entry 3 is appropriate:

3.	Cash	48,800	
	Other Revenue		48,800

Apart from items previously described, hospitals may receive unrestricted donations of money or services. Ordinarily, such donations should be classified as nonoperating gains rather than revenues. Hospitals often receive donated medicines and other materials. If such medicines and materials would otherwise have to be purchased, it is appropriate to record these donations at fair value as other revenue. Hospitals also routinely receive benefits from the services of volunteer workers; however, the value of such services is recorded as a revenue or gain (and as an expense) only if the restrictive conditions required by FASB standards for recognition are met (see Chapter 13).

Assume that total contributions were received in cash in the amount of $297,900 and unrestricted endowment income was $8,100.

		Debits	Credits
4.	Cash	306,000	
	Contributions—Unrestricted		297,900
	Investment Income—Unrestricted		8,100

One piece of capital equipment, which had a historical cost of $28,000 and a book value of $2,000 as of September 30, 2016, was sold early in the 2017 fiscal year for $500 cash. The entry to record the disposal of the asset at a loss is:

5.	Cash	500	
	Loss on Disposal of Equipment	1,500	
	Accumulated Depreciation—Equipment	26,000	
	Equipment		28,000

New capital equipment costing $400,000 was purchased during FY 2017 by Sierra Regional Hospital, $100,000 with temporarily restricted net assets and $300,000 with unrestricted net assets. The entries should be:

6a.	Equipment	400,000	
	Cash		400,000
6b.	Net Assets Released from Restrictions—Temporarily Restricted—Plant	100,000	
	Net Assets Released from Restrictions—Unrestricted		100,000

During the year, the following items were recorded as accounts payable: the $16,000 accrued expenses payable as of September 30, 2016; nursing services expenses, $4,026,000; other professional services expenses, $947,200; general services expenses, $1,650,000; fiscal and administrative services expenses, $1,124,000; and supplies added to inventory, $400,000. The following entry summarizes that activity:

7.	Accrued Expenses Payable	16,000	
	Nursing Services Expenses	4,026,000	
	Other Professional Services Expenses	947,200	
	General Services Expenses	1,650,000	
	Fiscal and Administrative Services Expenses	1,124,000	
	Inventory	400,000	
	Accounts Payable		8,163,200

Collections on accounts and notes receivable during the year amounted to $8,842,000; accounts and notes receivable totaling $131,000 were written off:

		Debits	Credits
8.	Cash	8,842,000	
	Allowance for Uncollectible Receivables	131,000	
	Accounts and Notes Receivable		8,973,000

The following cash disbursements were made during FY 2017: accounts payable, $8,014,200; a principal payment in the amount of $400,000 was made to reduce the mortgage liability; and interest amounting to $160,000 on mortgages was paid:

9.	Accounts Payable	8,014,200	
	Mortgages Payable	400,000	
	Interest Expense	160,000	
	Cash		8,574,200

Supplies issued during the year cost $320,000 ($20,000 of the total was for use by fiscal and administrative services; $120,000 for use by general services; and the remainder for use by other professional services):

10.	Other Professional Services Expenses	180,000	
	General Services Expenses	120,000	
	Fiscal and Administrative Services Expenses	20,000	
	Inventory		320,000

Accrued expenses as of September 30, 2017, included $160,000 interest on mortgages; fiscal and administrative services expenses, $8,700; and other professional services expenses, $4,800. Prepaid expenses, consisting of general services expense items, declined $4,000 during the year:

11.	Interest Expense	160,000	
	Fiscal and Administrative Services Expenses	8,700	
	Other Professional Services Expenses	4,800	
	General Services Expenses	4,000	
	Accrued Expenses Payable		173,500
	Prepaid Expenses		4,000

Depreciation of plant and equipment for FY 2017 was in the amounts shown in the following journal entry:

		Debits	Credits
12.	Depreciation Expense	783,000	
	Accumulated Depreciation—Buildings		315,000
	Accumulated Depreciation—Equipment		468,000

The hospital received cash of $28,000 for interest on investments held in the Assets Limited as to Use—Investments account. Entry 13 records the receipt of cash and the corresponding credit.

13.	Cash	28,000	
	Investment Income—Unrestricted		28,000

The $28,000 received in cash for interest (see Entry 13) was reinvested in investments to be held for eventual use for expansion of facilities; the hospital governing board decided to purchase an additional $350,000 of investments for the same purpose. Entries 14a and 14b reflect the purchase of the investments and the increase in unrestricted designated net assets.

14a.	Assets Limited as to Use—Investments	378,000	
	Cash		378,000
14b.	Net Assets—Unrestricted, Undesignated	378,000	
	Net Assets—Unrestricted, Designated		378,000

Cash in the amount of $361,000 was received. The cash was from the collection of $292,000 in pledges, $36,000 in interest that was accrued as of the end of FY2016, and $33,000 in interest earned on investments restricted for plant expansion.

15.	Cash	361,000	
	Pledges Receivable		292,000
	Accrued Interest Receivable		36,000
	Investment Income—Temporarily Restricted—Plant		33,000

Short-term investments restricted for use in plant expansion were sold. The investments had a carrying value of $85,000 and were sold for $59,000. The loss on the sale reduces the amount of net assets restricted for use in plant expansion. At year-end, the loss will be closed to Net Assets—Temporarily Restricted—Plant.

Proceeds from the sale of the investments plus $300,000 in cash were used to purchase marketable securities (short-term investments).

		Debits	Credits
16a.	Cash	59,000	
	Loss on Sale of Investments—Temporarily Restricted—Plant	26,000	
	Short-term Investments		85,000
16b.	Short-term Investments	359,000	
	Cash		359,000

A review of pledges receivable indicated pledges restricted for plant acquisition in the amount of $25,000 should be written off, and the allowance for uncollectible pledges should be increased by $66,300.

17a.	Allowance for Uncollectible Pledges	25,000	
	Pledges Receivable		25,000
17b.	Provision for Uncollectible Pledges	66,300	
	Allowance for Uncollectible Pledges		66,300

The fair values of short-term investments and assets limited as to use have not changed during the year. At the end of FY 2017, the amount of interest accrued on marketable securities is $44,000. This amount is temporarily restricted for plant acquisition.

18.	Accrued Interest Receivable	44,000	
	Investment Income—Temporarily Restricted—Plant		44,000

Sierra Regional Hospital did not have any net assets temporarily restricted for programs as of September 30, 2016. In September 2017, however, a civic organization donated $5,000 to the hospital to be used to augment the physician residency program. The organization pledged an additional sum of $20,000 to be paid in the coming year for the same purpose.

19.	Cash	5,000	
	Pledges Receivable	20,000	
	Contributions—Temporarily Restricted—Programs		25,000

The governing board and administration of Sierra Regional Hospital expect the civic organization to honor its pledge; therefore, no Allowance for Uncollectible Pledges is created. Because the gift was received shortly before the end of FY 2017, no expenses for the program were incurred during the year.

The hospital has a small endowment fund, the principal of which must be retained in perpetuity. During FY 2017, the hospital received an additional $24,000 in marketable securities for its endowment fund.

20.	Short-term Investments	24,000	
	Contributions—Permanently Restricted		24,000

Natural expenses of depreciation and interest were allocated to the functional expenses based on an allocation basis established by the hospital.

		Debits	Credits
21.	Nursing Services Expenses	551,500	
	Other Professional Services Expenses	154,420	
	General Services Expenses	242,660	
	Fiscal and Administrative Services Expenses	154,420	
	Depreciation Expense		783,000
	Interest Expense		320,000

The pre-closing trial balance for Sierra Regional Hospital as of September 30, 2017, is shown here. Financial statements reflecting the preceding transactions for Sierra Regional Hospital were shown earlier in this chapter as Illustrations 16–3, 16–4, and 16–5.

SIERRA REGIONAL HOSPITAL
Pre-closing Trial Balance
As of September 30, 2017

	Debits	Credits
Cash	$ 172,100	
Short-term Investments	1,778,000	
Accrued Interest Receivable	44,000	
Accounts and Notes Receivable	488,000	
Allowance for Uncollectible Receivables		$ 135,000
Pledges Receivable	663,000	
Allowance for Uncollectible Pledges		114,300
Inventory	160,000	
Prepaid Expenses	8,000	
Assets Limited as to Use—Cash	6,500	
Assets Limited as to Use—Investments	778,000	
Long-term Investments	146,000	
Land	1,080,000	
Buildings	11,050,000	
Equipment	5,292,000	
Accumulated Depreciation—Buildings		1,365,000
Accumulated Depreciation—Equipment		1,702,000
Accounts Payable		259,000
Accrued Expenses Payable		173,500
Mortgages Payable		6,000,000
Net Assets—Unrestricted, Undesignated		8,262,000
Net Assets—Unrestricted, Designated		784,500
Net Assets—Temporarily Restricted—Plant		2,508,000
Net Assets—Permanently Restricted		154,000
Patient Service Revenue		9,261,000
Provision for Bad Debts	180,000	
Contractual Adjustments	100,000	

	Debits	Credits
Other Revenue		48,800
Contributions—Unrestricted		297,900
Contributions—Temporarily Restricted—Programs		25,000
Contributions—Permanently Restricted		24,000
Investment Income—Unrestricted		36,100
Investment Income—Temporarily Restricted—Plant		77,000
Net Assets Released from Restrictions—Unrestricted		100,000
Net Assets Released from Restrictions—Temporarily Restricted	100,000	
Nursing Services Expenses	4,577,500	
Other Professional Services Expenses	1,286,420	
General Services Expenses	2,016,660	
Fiscal and Administrative Services Expenses	1,307,120	
Loss on Disposal of Equipment	1,500	
Provision for Uncollectible Pledges	66,300	
Loss on Sale of Investments—Temporarily Restricted—Plant	26,000	
	$31,327,100	$31,327,100

End-of-Year Closing Journal Entries

Unrestricted revenues and expenses that pertain to FY 2017 are closed to the Net Assets—Unrestricted, Undesignated account as follows:

		Debits	Credits
22.	Patient Service Revenue	9,261,000	
	Other Revenue	48,800	
	Contributions—Unrestricted	297,900	
	Investment Income—Unrestricted	36,100	
	Provision for Bad Debts		180,000
	Contractual Adjustments		100,000
	Nursing Services Expenses		4,577,500
	Other Professional Services Expenses		1,286,420
	General Services Expenses		2,016,660
	Fiscal and Administrative Services Expenses		1,307,120
	Loss on Disposal of Equipment		1,500
	Net Assets—Unrestricted, Undesignated		174,600

Restricted revenues that pertain to FY 2017 are closed to the restricted net asset accounts as shown:

23.	Contributions—Temporarily Restricted—Programs	25,000	
	Contributions—Permanently Restricted	24,000	
	Investment Income—Temporarily Restricted—Plant	77,000	
	Net Assets—Temporarily Restricted—Plant	15,300	
	Provision for Uncollectible Pledges		66,300
	Loss on Sale of Investments—Temporarily Restricted—Plant		26,000
	Net Assets—Temporarily Restricted—Programs		25,000
	Net Assets—Permanently Restricted		24,000

Net assets released from restrictions are closed out in the following entry:

		Debits	Credits
24.	Net Assets Released from Restrictions—Unrestricted	100,000	
	Net Assets—Temporarily Restricted—Plant	100,000	
	Net Assets Released from Restrictions—Temporarily Restricted—Plant		100,000
	Net Assets—Unrestricted, Undesignated		100,000

OTHER HEALTH CARE ISSUES

Related Entities

Health care organizations have long been associated with separate fund-raising foundations, medical research foundations, auxiliaries, and guilds. More recently, organizations have begun networking with other organizations in an effort to integrate health care services, control costs, increase efficiency, and ultimately improve the quality of health care. Reaction to the Patient Protection and Affordability Act (also known as the Affordable Care Act) has resulted in increasing numbers of acquisitions, mergers, and consolidations among health care entities. Financial reporting guidance comes from the FASB in existing statements on consolidations and affiliated organizations and from the GASB in statements on the reporting entity and affiliated organizations. If one entity controls another, the financial statements of the two organizations should be consolidated in order to be most useful to the decision maker. Additional information on consolidating or combining related entities is provided in Chapter 13.

Auditing

Auditing issues of particular significance to the health care industry relate to contingencies, third-party payors, related entities, and restructuring. Renewed efforts on the part of the federal government to curb health care fraud and illegal acts also affect auditors and their clients. Congress has instituted several laws to aid in detection and punishment of fraud and illegal acts. Some of the laws include the Health Insurance Portability and Accountability Act (HIPAA) of 1996, False Claims Act, Stark Laws, and the Patient Protection and Affordability Act. Investigations center on improper billing and coding, improper care, and kickbacks. Auditors must also understand OMB *Uniform Guidance* and its application to hospitals and health care organizations that receive federal financial assistance, as described in Chapter 11 of this text.

Taxation and Regulatory Issues

Since a large number of health care providers are legally structured as tax-exempt organizations under IRC Sec. 501(c)(3), the regulations and activities of the Internal Revenue Service should be of concern to the accountant working with health care organizations. For example, the penalties for private inurement or excess economic benefits to individuals, introduced in the Taxpayer Bill of Rights 2 of 1996, apply to health care administrators and persons with substantial influence over the organization. The IRS closely reviews physician recruiting incentives, joint operating agreements for exemption applications, unrelated business income (such as hospital pharmacy sales to the general public), private-activity bonds, and independent contractor (versus employee) status. Congressional and public scrutiny over the accountability for assets of not-for-profit organizations and the amount of charity care provided by tax-exempt hospitals is high. Sanctions are economically significant and may involve loss of tax-exempt status or eligibility for tax-exempt financing. Health care providers may also be regulated by states that have laws governing the granting of licenses and the scope of services to be rendered.

In addition, the Patient Protection and Affordability Act has imposed additional Form 990 reporting requirements on 501(c)(3) hospitals. Under the act, NFP hospitals need to provide information related to policies on financial assistance and emergency medical care. Every three years hospitals are required to conduct and report on a community health needs assessment (CHNA). Failure to meet the CHNA requirement results in increased reporting requirements and imposition of an excise tax.[11]

Patient Protection and Affordability Act

The Patient Protection and Affordability Act (also known as the Affordable Care Act) was signed into law (P.L. 111-148) on March 23, 2010. The law states it is primarily intended to provide health insurance reform that will result in improved quality of health care. Provisions of the law increase insurance companies' accountability, attempt to lower health care costs, and provide more health care choices for individuals. Comprehensive in scope, the law contains more than 45 individual provisions that were enacted over the time period 2010 through 2014.[12] Because the law primarily focuses on the health insurance industry and individuals, it is unclear exactly how, the law will affect the financial accounting and reporting discussed in this chapter There is agreement that the act has a far-reaching effect, but given the newness of some of the most significant requirements the ultimate impact of the act on delivery, cost and compensation of services remains uncertain.[13]

A review of some of the provisions of the law indicates possible areas where the degree of accounting by health care entities could be affected. Examples of a few provisions that could impact accounting include (1) physician pay tied to quality of care,[14] (2) medical services bundled for Medicare payment,[15] and (3) records moved to electronic form to reduce paperwork and standardize billing.[16] If physician pay is increasingly tied to quality of care, it is possible that accounting measures and accounting information systems will need to be developed that can capture the necessary information for tying pay and quality. Bundling is being considered for use with federal programs such as Medicare. It would require that all services related to a medical procedure be bound together and submitted for one flat rate payment. This would

[11] Internal Revenue Service, "New Requirements for 501(c)(3) Hospitals Under the Affordable Care Act," March, 2014, *http://www.irs.gov/Charities-&-Non-Profits/Charitable-Organizations/New-Requirements-for-501(c)(3)-Hospitals-Under-the-Affordable-Care-Act* (accessed July 1, 2014).

[12] Public Law 111-148 is accessible through the Department of Health and Human Services Web site *www.healthcare.gov*.

[13] American Institute of Certified Public Accountants, Audit and Accounting Guide, *Health Care Entities*, AICPA, (NYC, 2013), par. 1.13.

[14] Public Law 111-148, Title III, Subtitle A.

[15] Ibid., Title II, Subtitle I and Title III, Subtitle A.

[16] Ibid., Title 1, Subtitle B.

replace the current system, where each service related to a medical procedure (e.g., angioplasty) is submitted for separate payment. Charts of accounts and accounting information systems may need to be developed/modified to clearly identify all services related to a medical procedure. Finally, moving records to electronic form has serious implications for accounting information systems, the most important of which is probably security and integrity of the system.

Prepaid Health Care Plans

Prepaid health care plans, such as **health maintenance organizations (HMOs)** and **preferred provider organizations (PPOs),** function as brokers between the consumer or patient demanding the services and the providers of health care, such as health care professionals or hospitals. Contractual arrangements among these parties, including employers, are complex and varied. The revenue received from prepaid plans is referred to as **premium revenue.** According to FASB *ASC* 954-605, premium revenue is recorded as earned revenue when an agreement is entered into to provide care. Costs of providing care under a prepaid plan are recorded as accrued. Depending on contract terms, health care entities may be required to continue accruing costs for care beyond those costs covered by premium revenue or premium period.[17]

Continuing Care Retirement Communities

There are more than 1,800 **continuing care retirement communities (CCRCs)** in the United States that are operated primarily by not-for-profit organizations.[18] CCRCs provide residential care in a facility, along with some level of long-term medical care that is less intensive than hospital care. There are many ways to structure contracts between the patient/resident and the CCRC; however, most plans require advance payment of an entrance fee and periodic fees to cover operating costs in exchange for current use of the facilities and the promise to provide some level of health and residential services in the future. Under FASB *ASC* 954-430, the amount of an advance fee that is nonrefundable under the terms of the CCRC contract is to be recorded and reported as deferred revenue. In accordance with contract terms, the deferred revenue is then amortized to income over future periods. Estimated amounts expected to be refunded under terms of the contract are reported as a refund liability.

Financial and Operational Analysis

The goal of financial and operational analysis depends, of course, on the needs of the decision maker. For example, managers are directly accountable for performance, financial analysts determine the creditworthiness of organizations issuing debt, and third parties determine appropriate payment based on costs. Consumers may want nonfinancial performance and quality measures, such as the success rate for various procedures or the value received for money spent.

Health care entities are evaluated using a variety of ratios and benchmarks, some of which are unique to hospitals and others that are similar to those applied to other business organizations. The Healthcare Financial Management Association (HFMA)

[17] FASB *ASC* 954-405.

[18] AICPA, AAG-Health Care Entities, Sec. 14.02.

reports annual benchmark data compiled from bond-rating agencies and other national organizations for 11 financial indicators that are key measures used to determine the financial health of hospitals. Formulas for calculating the financial indicators are provided to members and subscribers at *www.hfma.org*. When combined with patient volume (e.g., average length of stay and occupancy rate) and patient and payout mix (e.g., Medicare, Medicaid, third-party payors, self-pay, charity care, etc.), ratios such as these can provide important information about liquidity, solvency, and financial performance. The 11 financial indicators are:[19]

1. Operating margin (%)
2. Excess margin (%)
3. Debt services coverage
4. Current ratio
5. Cash on hand (days)
6. Cushion ratio
7. Accounts receivable (days)
8. Average payment period (days)
9. Average age of plant (years)
10. Debt-to-capitalization (%)
11. Capital expense (%)

Other organizations, such as the Health Care Accounting and Finance Benchmarking Association, an organization of over 140,000 accounting and finance professionals in the health care industry, provide benchmarking databases to members and participants.

Several organizations maintain quality-of-care benchmarking databases that report both medical process and outcome data for numerous hospitals and other health care organizations. These include databases such as the national Consumer Assessment of Healthcare Providers and Systems (CAHPS) benchmarking database, which is publicly accessible at the *hospitalcompare* Web site (*www.hospitalcompare.hhs.gov*). This site was created by the Centers for Medicare and Medicaid Services (CMS), the U.S. Department of Health and Human Services, and the Hospital Quality Alliance (HQA), an alliance of numerous national health care and other organizations.

CONCLUSION

A single chapter on accounting for health care organizations can touch on only the most fundamental features. Variations in the reporting and accounting procedures for individual health care entities exist due to the variety in the type and size of health care providers, the range of services offered, the dependence of these entities on third-party payors, and the financial sophistication of the governing board, administrator, and finance director. For further information, the references cited in the Selected References section are recommended.

[19] Adapted from Steven Berger, "Making the Most of Key Hospital Financial Metrics," *Strategic Financial Planning Newsletter*, Fall 2006. Source: Healthcare Financial Management Association, *www.hfma.org/publications/know_newsletter/030707.htm*.

Key Terms

Assets limited as to use, *652*
Capitation fees, *655*
Charity care, *656*
Continuing care retirement communities (CCRCs), *671*
Contractual adjustments (or allowances), *655*
Diagnosis-related groups (DRGs), *656*
Health maintenance organization (HMO), *671*
Performance indicator, *653*
Preferred provider organization (PPO), *671*
Premium revenue, *671*
Prospective Payment System (PPS), *656*
Settlement accounts, *653*
Third-party payor, *656*

Selected References

American Institute of Certified Public Accountants. Audit and Accounting Guide. *Health Care Entities.* New York, 2013.

Financial Accounting Standards Board. *Accounting Standards Codification,* Sections 954 and 958. Norwalk, CT: FASB (on-line).

Governmental Accounting Standards Board. *Codification.* "Section Ho5." Norwalk, CT, 2014.

Periodicals

Healthcare Financial Management. The journal of the Healthcare Financial Management Association, Oak Brook, IL.

Hospital Progress. The journal of the Catholic Hospital Association, St. Louis, MO.

Hospitals and Health Networks. The journal of the American Hospital Association, Chicago, IL.

Questions

16–1. Since the FASB sets the standards for both not-for-profit health care entities and investor-owned entities, the financial reporting requirements are the same for these two entities. Do you agree with this statement? Why or why not?

16–2. What are the required financial statements for (*a*) a not-for-profit health care entity and (*b*) a governmental health care entity reporting only business-type activities?

16–3. How do the accounting treatments for charity services, patient discounts, contractual adjustments, and provision for bad debts differ in terms of their effects on patient service revenues and related receivables? What, if any, differences exist in the accounting or reporting treatment under the FASB and GASB standards?

16–4. What is an example of a performance indicator and to what would it compare in investor-owned financial reporting?

16–5. Discuss some of the presentation differences between the operating statements of not-for-profit and business-type governmental health care entities.

16–6. Tupper Memorial Hospital received from a donor a $50,000 contribution and a $50,000 pledge payable in one year. The donor required that the funds be used for heart research. Explain differences in accounting for the donor's contribution and pledge if Tupper is (*a*) a government hospital and (*b*) a not-for-profit hospital.

16–7. What are *assets limited as to use* and how do they differ from restricted assets?

16–8. What is premium revenue, and when is it recognized? Discuss the recognition of revenue relative to the revenue recognition and matching concepts in accounting.

16–9. What is the Patient Protection Affordability Act, and what impact has it had on NFP hospitals' financial reporting and tax filing?

16–10. A board member of an NFP hospital has asked you what resources are available to help him in assessing the financial and operational performance of the hospital. Where would you direct him to obtain benchmarking data to help him with his assessment?

Cases

16–11 Charity Care. The local newspaper of a large urban area printed a story titled "Charity Care by Hospitals Stirs Debate." The story quotes one legislator who wants "to ensure that the state's not-for-profit hospitals are fulfilling their obligation; that is to provide charity care at least equal to the tax exemption they receive as a not-for-profit entity." The following table is provided:

Comparison of Selected Factors in Three Not-for-profit Hospitals (dollars in millions)

	Hope Hospital	St. Pat's Hospital	Capitol Hospital
Estimated taxes the hospitals would pay if they were not tax-exempt	$ 6.8	$2.2	$4.5
Contract adjustments with third-party payors (including Medicaid and Medicare)	$10.8	$3.1	$3.5
Charity care	$ 3.7	$2.0	$1.3
Nonreimbursed research and graduate medical education	$ 2.0	$0.7	n.a.

n.a. = Not available.

Required

a. What are the obligations of IRC Sec. 501(c)(3) organizations to provide charity care?

b. Do you agree that the hospitals are not fulfilling their obligations? Why or why not?

c. What additional information would you like to have? Do you expect to find this information in the audited annual financial statements?

16–12 Research Case—Determining Community Benefit. The Internal Revenue Service (IRS) initiated a study of not-for-profit hospitals in 2006. One purpose of the study was to help the IRS better understand the community benefit provided by not-for-profit hospitals. Community benefit is a critical factor in the determination of whether a hospital is granted 501(c)(3) status, which may result in significant savings in income and other taxes. The final report on the project was issued in February 2009 and combined with the Affordable Care Act, resulted in new reporting requirements for not-for-profit hospitals. The reporting is required under IRC Section 501(r) and is accomplished by completing Schedule H of Form 990.

Required

a. Using the IRS Web site (*www.irs.gov*), examine the executive summary and final report of the IRS Exempt Organizations Hospital Study. How many hospitals participated in the study? What types of information related to community benefit did the IRS request from the hospitals surveyed?

What two primary demographics were used to summarize the data, and what categories were used in each demographic? Why do you believe these demographics were selected?

b. Select a not-for-profit hospital located in your region or state and locate its most recent Form 990 using Guidestar (*www.guidestar.org*). Using the information found on Schedule H, answer the following questions. (Note: You can register, at no cost, to access Form 990s available through Guidestar.)

1. What were the hospital's total revenues? Total expenses?
2. What was the total cost of community benefit reported by the hospital? How much of that amount was for uncompensated care (referred to as Total Financial Assistance and Means-Tested Government Programs)? Identify the other types of community benefit provided by the hospital and the associated costs.
3. Compute the percentage of community benefit to total revenue and total expenses. How does your hospital compare to hospitals of similar size in the IRS study?

c. How do you think the new IRS requirements will affect future accounting and financial reporting for not-for-profit hospitals? Give examples to support your discussion.

16–13 Patient Protection and Affordability Act. In 2010, Congress passed and the President signed into law the Patient Protection and Affordability Act. The act provides for sweeping changes to health care and has been extremely controversial. To learn more about this act, go to *www.healthcare.gov* to answer the following questions.

Required

a. What is (are) the purpose(s) of the act?

b. How long has it taken to implement the act? For individuals covered by the act, what are some of the major coverage provisions?

c. In addition to cost, one of the most controversial provisions of the act relates to the purchase of health insurance. What is the Insurance Marketplace, does it allow for the purchase of government health insurance, and can you purchase insurance at any time? Why do you believe purchasing insurance is controversial?

16–14 Internet Case—Evaluating the Quality of Health Care. The U.S. Department of Health and Human Services maintains the Web site *www.hospitalcompare.hhs.gov,* which provides an array of measures that report on individual hospitals and other types of health care providers. Access the Web site for help in completing this case.

Required

a. What is the purpose of the Hospital Compare site?

b. The site allows you to find a hospital and assess how it compares to state and/or federal statistics. There are several categories of measures including: general information; survey of patients' experiences; timely and effective care; readmissions, complications, and deaths; use of medical imaging; Medicare payment; and number of Medicare patients. Enter information to locate a hospital of interest to you. Once the hospital is located complete the following.

1. Compare and evaluate the survey of patients' experiences relative to state and federal statistics.
2. Compare and evaluate timely and effective care for emergency department care relative to state (if available) and federal statistics.
3. Compare and evaluate under readmission, complications, and deaths the 30-day outcome information relative to state (if available) and federal statistics.
4. Overall how would you rate the hospital you selected? Explain your rating.

c. Explain how such factors as patient mix, occupancy rate, average length of stay, payor mix (i.e., Medicare, Medicaid, third-party insurers, self-pay, and charity care), and the hospital's financial condition may affect the quality of care.

Exercises and Problems

16–15 Multiple Choice. Choose the best answer.

1. The AICPA Audit and Accounting Guide *Health Care Entities* is considered category b authoritative guidance that can be used by which of the following?
   a. A business-type government hospital.
   b. A not-for-profit hospital.
   c. A for-profit hospital.
   d. All of the above.
2. A not-for-profit hospital would present all of the following financial statements, *except* a:
   a. Balance sheet or statement of financial position.
   b. Statement of functional expenses.
   c. Statement of operations.
   d. Statement of cash flows.
3. Which of the following is a true statement regarding a *performance indicator*?
   a. All health care organizations are required to report a performance indicator.
   b. Only governmental health care organizations are required to report a performance indicator.
   c. The purpose of reporting a performance indicator is to make it easier to compare the results of operations of not-for-profit health care organizations to those of for-profit health care organizations.
   d. The purpose of reporting a performance indicator is to assist in evaluating the efficiency and effectiveness of a health care organization's operating activities.
4. Fees received by a hospital for a "healthy heart" workshop offered to patients should be reported as:
   a. Patient service revenue.
   b. Administrative service revenue.
   c. Other revenue.
   d. Nonoperating gains.
5. Which of the following is an example of an asset limited as to use?
   a. Real estate donated to build a clinic for the homeless.
   b. Contributed cash that the board is considering setting aside for self-insurance.

c. Investments bequeathed to the health care organization where the income is to be used to fund operating costs for a cancer clinic.
d. Funds from a sale of bonds that are required by covenant to be used to build a new hospital.

6. Why are health care organizations motivated to track the actual costs of services?
   a. Both GASB and FASB require it.
   b. They must report their actual expenses, so that third-party payors will reimburse them.
   c. Third-party payors contract with the organization to reimburse a set amount, and the organization risks a loss if costs are greater than the amount reimbursed.
   d. Any amount not reimbursed by a third-party payor or paid by the patient must be included in the amount reported as charity care.
7. The controller for Bloomingfield Regional Hospital estimated that the uncollectible patient accounts have increase by $152,000. The controller's journal entry included a debit to Bad Debt Expense and a credit to Allowance for Uncollectible Receivables. Based on this, Bloomingfield Regional Hospital is
   a. An investor-owned health care organization.
   b. A nongovernmental not-for-profit health care organization.
   c. A governmental not-for-profit health care organization.
   d. Properly recording the estimate for uncollectible accounts under the FASB and GASB standards.
8. Wellness Psychiatric Clinic received a large contribution from the family of a former patient. The contribution came with a request that the funds be used or invested to support any activities that the clinic felt would be best. On this not-for-profit clinic's statement of cash flows, this contribution would be reported in which section?
   a. Noncapital financing activities.
   b. Operating activities.
   c. Financing activities.
   d. Investing activities.
9. The Patient Protection and Affordability Act, passed in 2010,
   a. Is unlikely to impact accounting and financial reporting for health care organizations.
   b. May or may not impact Form 990 filings for 501(c)(3) health care organizations.
   c. Requires health care organizations to implement new cost accounting systems where each service related to a medical procedure is tracked and submitted for payment separately.
   d. Could impact the security and integrity of a health organization's accounting information system.
10. Which of the following would be most useful for evaluating the financial profitability of a not-for-profit health care organization?
    a. Current ratio.
    b. Debt-to-capitalization.
    c. Excess margin.
    d. Debt services coverage.

16–16 Revenue Classifications. Caring Community Hospital, a not-for-profit hospital, recorded the following transactions.

1. Received $20 as co-pay from a patient for an out-patient visit. Billed $500 to insurance.
2. Gift shop sales amounted to $1,500.
3. Citizen's Health Insurance paid $350 as final payment on the $500 billed for the patient in transaction 1.
4. The hospital provided medical care valued at $20,000 for homeless citizens.
5. A grateful patient contributed $1,000 for unrestricted use by the hospital.
6. The hospital received $500 for CPR training it provided to the city fire department.
7. The local retirees association contributed $2,000 of labor at the hospital information desk.
8. The hospital received a $10,000 federal grant to provide immunizations to children.
9. Patient accounts of $500 were written off as uncollectible.
10. Pharmaceutical firms donated recently approved drugs valued at $8,000. The hospital uses a similar type drug in its operations.

a. Patient service revenue
b. Contractual adjustments
c. Other revenue (exchange)
d. Other revenue (nonexchange)
e. No revenue

Required

For each transaction, indicate which revenue classification would be affected by selecting the letter or letters of that (those) classification(s) from the list in the right-hand column.

16–17 Various Unrelated Transactions. Following are several unrelated transactions involving a hospital.

1. The hospital has a contractual agreement with a lender requiring that $500,000 in cash be set aside to meet its future debt payment.
2. The hospital accrued $1,500,000 in patient service revenues. Charity services of $415,000 were also provided. Contractual adjustments total $535,000.
3. An increase of $45,000 was recorded for bad debts.
4. General services of $100,000 were donated by technicians. Normally, the hospital would have purchased these specialized services.
5. An endowment contribution of $1,500,000 was received.
6. Investments held by the hospital increased in fair value by $32,000.
7. The hospital purchased $837,000 in equipment with resources that had been contributed in prior years for such a purchase.

Required

a. Prepare journal entries to record the foregoing transactions, assuming the hospital is a not-for-profit facility.
b. Prepare journal entries to record the foregoing transactions, assuming the hospital is a business-type government facility.

16–18 Performance Indicator. The Kyle Sports Medicine facility is a not-for-profit health care facility that is trying to determine what transaction information should be included in its calculation of the performance indicator it uses to report its results of operations. Indicate whether each of the following transactions being considered should be included in the operating performance indicator by circling Y for yes or N for no.

Y	N	1.	An unrealized gain was recorded on the facility's trading securities.
Y	N	2.	Temporarily restricted contributions were received.
Y	N	3.	A loss on the sale of equipment was recorded.
Y	N	4.	Contractual adjustments to patient service revenue were recorded.
Y	N	5.	Fund-raising expenses were recorded.
Y	N	6.	The Geriatric Sports Division was classified as a discontinued operation, resulting in a net loss on operations.
Y	N	7.	The facility transferred cash to its parent organization.
Y	N	8.	A research grant to study football injuries was received from a local sports club (research is not part of Kyle's normal activities).
Y	N	9.	A gain on the sale of unrestricted investments was recorded.
Y	N	10.	Taxes were paid on unrelated business income.

16–19 Revenue and Related Transactions. During its current fiscal year, Evanston General Hospital, a not-for-profit health care organization, had the following revenue-related transactions (amounts summarized for the year).

1. Services provided to inpatients and outpatients amounted to $9,600,000, of which $450,000 was for charity care, $928,000 was paid by uninsured patients, and $8,222,000 was billed to Medicare, Medicaid, and insurance companies.
2. Donated pharmaceuticals and medical supplies valued at $265,000 were received and utilized as general expenses.
3. Medicare, Medicaid, and third-party payors (insurance companies) approved and paid $5,365,000 of the $8,222,000 billed by the hospital during the year (see transaction 1).
4. An unconditional contribution of $5,000,000 was received in cash from a donor to construct a new facility for care of Alzheimers patients. The full amount is expendable for that purpose. No activity occurred on this project during the current year.
5. A total of $965,000 was received from the following activities/sources: cafeteria and gift shop sales, $710,000; medical seminars, 125,000; unrestricted transfers from the Evanston General Hospital Foundation, $75,000; and fees for medical transcripts, $55,000.
6. Uncollectible accounts totaling $3,250 were written off. The allowance for uncollectible receivables was increased by $1,170.

Required

a. Record the preceding transactions in general journal form.
b. Prepare the *unrestricted revenues, gains, and other support* section of Evanston General Hospital's statement of operations for the current year, following the format in Illustration 16–4.
c. On which statement would restricted contributions be reported? Explain.

16–20 Governmental Hospital. During 2017, the following selected events and transactions were recorded by Milos County Hospital.

1. Gross charges for hospital services, all charged to accounts and notes receivable, were as follows:

Patient service revenues	$1,664,900

2. The hospital cafeteria and gift shop had cash sales of $295,300.
3. Additional information determined subsequently to recording patient service revenues and relating to the current-year is as follows:

Contractual adjustments	$632,000
Provision for bad debts	30,200
Charity care	261,400

4. A federal cost reimbursement research grant of $350,000 was awarded. As of the end of the year, $200,000 in expenses related to the grant had been made. (*Hint:* See Chapter 4 for eligibility requirements.)
5. Vouchers totaling $1,326,540 were issued for the following items:

Fiscal and administrative services expenses	$194,440
General services expenses	253,100
Nursing services expenses	585,000
Other professional services expenses	185,600
Inventory	101,200
Expenses accrued at December 31, 2017	7,200

6. Collections of accounts receivable totaled $1,159,000. Accounts written off as uncollectible amounted to $11,900.
7. Cash payments on vouchers payable (paid to employers and suppliers) during the year were $1,031,200.
8. Supplies of $99,770 were issued to nursing services.
9. On December 31, 2017, accrued interest income on investments was $800.
10. Depreciation of buildings and equipment was as follows:

Buildings	$51,000
Equipment	73,000

11. On December 31, 2017, closing entries were made in the general journal.

Required

a. Show in general journal form the entries that should be made for each of the transactions and the closing entries in accordance with the standards for a governmental health care entity that follows proprietary fund accounting, as discussed in this chapter and Chapter 7.

b. Using the available information, calculate the net patient service revenue that would be reported on the statement of revenues, expenses, and changes in net position.

16–21 Financial Statements—Not-for-Profit Hospital. The following is the pre-closing trial balance for Christina Rehabilitation Hospital as of September 30, 2017.

CHRISTINA REHABILITATION HOSPITAL
Pre-closing Trial Balance
September 30, 2017
(000s omitted)

	Debits	Credits
Cash and Cash Equivalents	$ 45,525	
Accounts Receivable	61,850	
Allowance for Uncollectible Receivables		$ 16,550
Inventory	8,410	
Prepaid Expenses	6,610	
Assets Limited as to Use—Investments	49,440	
Investments	198,000	
Pledges Receivable	3,820	
Discount on Pledges Receivable		910
Land	7,580	
Buildings	324,440	
Accumulated Depreciation—Buildings		142,960
Equipment	259,160	
Accumulated Depreciation—Equipment		118,040
Accounts Payable		20,730
Accrued Payables		26,790
Interest Payable		1,070
Bonds Payable		173,000
Other Long-term Liabilities		126,700
Net Assets—Unrestricted		221,105
Net Assets—Temporarily Restricted		78,600
Net Assets—Permanently Restricted		27,110
Patient Service Revenue		1,063,360
Contractual Adjustments	550,980	
Other Operating Revenue		11,330
Contributions—Temporarily Restricted		6,540
Contributions—Permanently Restricted		130
Investment Income—Unrestricted		7,300
Investment Income—Temporarily Restricted		470
Unrealized Gain on Investments—Temporarily Restricted		590
Salary Expense	338,520	
Supplies Expense	140,610	
Provision for Uncollectible Accounts	17,030	
Depreciation Expense	25,230	
Interest Expense	5,130	
Unrealized Loss on Investments—Unrestricted	950	
Total	$2,043,285	$2,043,285

Required

a. Prepare a statement of operations and a statement of changes in net assets for the year ended September 30, 2017. Not included on the trial balance is the fact that $1,010 has been released from temporary purpose restrictions.

b. Prepare a balance sheet as of September 30, 2017. The pledges and investments are both long-term. Not included on the trial balance is the fact that $15,000 of bonds will be due in 2018 and must be reclassified on the balance sheet.

16–22 Not-for-Profit Hospital. The Edwards Lake Community Hospital balance sheet as of December 31, 2016, follows.

EDWARDS LAKE COMMUNITY HOSPITAL
Balance Sheet
As of December 31, 2016

Assets		
Current assets:		
Cash and cash equivalents		$ 259,300
Accounts and notes receivable (net of uncollectible accounts of $15,800)		26,500
Inventory		71,000
Total current assets		356,800
Assets limited as to use:		
Cash	$ 17,140	
Investments	229,220	
Total assets limited as to use		246,360
Property, plant, and equipment:		
Land	210,100	
Buildings (net of accumulated depreciation of $1,623,000)	2,893,000	
Equipment (net of accumulated depreciation of $1,024,500)	1,858,800	
Total property, plant, and equipment		4,961,900
Total assets		$5,565,060
Liabilities and Net Assets		
Current liabilities:		
Accounts payable		$ 19,200
Accrued payroll		45,000
Current portion of mortgage payable		500,000
Total current liabilities		564,200
Long-term debt—mortgage payable		2,500,000
Total liabilities		3,064,200
Net assets:		
Unrestricted		
Undesignated	2,082,760	
Designated for plant	246,360	
Temporarily restricted	171,740	2,500,860
Total liabilities and net assets		$5,565,060

Required

a. Record in general journal form the effect of the following transactions during the fiscal year ended December 31, 2017, assuming that Edwards Lake Community Hospital is a not-for-profit hospital.

(1) Information related to accrual of revenues and gains is as follows:

Patient services revenue, gross	$3,500,900
Charity care	211,260
Contractual adjustments to patient service revenues	1,520,000
Other operating revenues	998,750

(2) Cash received includes:

Interest on investments in Assets Limited as to Use	7,350
Collections of receivables	2,960,600

(3) Expenses of $891,000 were recorded in accounts payable and $1,454,390 in accrued payroll. Since some of the nursing expenses met a temporary net asset restriction, $94,000 was released from temporary restrictions.

Administration expenses	446,480
General services expenses	524,360
Nursing services expenses	1,031,800
Other professional services expenses	342,750

(4) Cash paid includes:

Interest expense (allocated half to nursing services and half to general services)	280,000
Payment on mortgage principal	500,000
Accounts payable for purchases	836,800
Accrued payroll	1,279,500

(5) Interest of $1,180 accrued on investments in Assets Limited as to Use.

(6) Depreciation charges for the year amounted to $117,000 for the buildings and $128,500 for equipment. Depreciation was allocated 45 percent to nursing services, 15 percent to other professional services and 20 percent to each administrative and general services.

(7) Other information:

(*a*) Provision for uncollectible receivables was determined to be adequate.

(*b*) Supplies inventory balances:

	12/31/2016	12/31/2017
Administration	$ 8,000	$ 7,300
General services	8,700	9,000
Nursing services	17,000	16,800
Other professional services	37,300	40,000
Totals	$71,000	$73,100

(*c*) Portion of mortgage payable due within one year, $500,000.

(8) A $663 unrealized loss on investments occurred.

(9) Nominal accounts were closed. Necessary adjustments were made to increase the Net Assets—Unrestricted, Designated for Plant.

b. Prepare a balance sheet as of December 31, 2017.

c. Prepare a statement of operations for the year ended December 31, 2017.

d. Prepare a statement of cash flows for the year ended December 31, 2017.

16–23 Not-for-profit Statements of Operations and Changes in Net Assets. You have recently started work as the controller for a small community hospital. The financial statements for the just completed fiscal year have been provided for your review.

DANKER COMMUNITY HOSPITAL
Statement of Operations
For the year ended June 30, 2017

Unrestricted revenue, gains, and other support:		
Patient service revenue (net of charity care)		$1,974,240
Other operating revenue		293,890
Investment income		103,910
Unrealized gain on investments		770
Net assets released from restrictions		42,040
Total revenue and gains		2,414,850
Expenses:		
Salary and employee benefit expense	$742,170	
Supplies expense	245,740	
Utilities expense	41,700	
Contractual adjustments	889,690	
Provision for uncollectible accounts	31,170	
Depreciation expense	140,420	
Interest expense	29,840	
Total expenses		2,120,730
Increase in unrestricted net assets		$ 294,120

DANKER COMMUNITY HOSPITAL
Statement of Changes in Net Assets
For year ended June 30, 2017

Unrestricted net assets:	
Increase in unrestricted net assets	$ 294,120
Restricted net assets:	
Contributions	30,460
Investment income	7,220
Unrealized loss on investments	(590)
Net assets released from restrictions	(42,040)
Decrease in restricted net assets	(4, 950)
Increase in net assets	289,170
Net assets at beginning of the year	1,642,450
Net assets at end of the year	$1,931,620

Required

After reviewing the statement you realize that it is not in the proper FASB format. To help your staff correct the statements, make a list of all of the modifications or corrections that should be made to the statement, so that it can be presented in the proper format.

Chapter Seventeen

Accounting and Reporting for the Federal Government

Learning Objectives

After studying this chapter, you should be able to:

17-1 Describe the financial management structure and the process for establishing generally accepted accounting principles for the federal government.

17-2 Explain the concepts underlying federal accounting and financial reporting.

17-3 Describe federal government-wide and agency performance and financial reporting requirements.

17-4 Understand and record budgetary and proprietary journal entries and prepare financial statements for federal agencies.

17-5 Compare accounting for state and local governments with federal agencies.

The federal government of the United States of America is the largest reporting entity in the world and is growing. Total outlays of all federal agencies grew from $107 billion in 1962 to $3.5 trillion in 2013 and are projected to be $4.7 trillion in 2019.[1] In FY 2013 $546 billion of the federal outlays (or 15.6%) went to state and local governments in the form of grants.[2] Other grants are made to not-for-profit organizations to operate a wide variety of programs to meet public needs.

Federal elected officials and managers are accountable for public funds raised to meet the cost of government services today, as they have been from as far back as 1789 when a federal accounting structure was first put into place.

Major institutional change since the 1980s has provided the impetus for many significant changes in federal accounting. Among these changes are the Federal Managers Fiscal and Integrity Act (FMFIA) of 1982, the Chief Financial Officers Act (CFO) of 1990, the creation of the Federal Accounting Standards Advisory Board (FASAB) in 1990, the Government Performance and Results Act of 1993 (GPRA), the Government Management Reform Act of 1994 (GMRA), the Federal Financial Management

[1] A table of federal government outlays by agency for 1962–2019 (est.) is available at *www.whitehouse.gov/omb/budget/historical,* Table 4.1.

[2] A table of summary comparisons of total outlays for grants to state and local governments is available at *www.whitehouse.gov/omb/budget/historical*, Table 12.1.

Improvement Act of 1996, the Reports Consolidation Act of 2000, and the Accountability of Tax Dollars Act (ATDA) of 2002.

Systems put in place to demonstrate accountability for federal funds are similar to those used by state and local governments, as described in Chapters 1 through 10. Budgetary accounting is integrated with financial reporting to demonstrate compliance with annual budgets, and accrual-based entity-wide statements are also produced to give citizens information about the financial condition and sustainability of the government. In this chapter, accountability issues focusing on the federal government as a whole are discussed, followed by the unique aspects of accounting for federal agencies.

FEDERAL GOVERNMENT FINANCIAL MANAGEMENT STRUCTURE

The U.S. government is a complex set of branches, offices, and departments, as can be seen in Illustration 17–1, as well as independent establishments and government corporations, such as the U.S. Postal Service, the Securities and Exchange Commission, and the Central Intelligence Agency (not shown).[3] The United States Code (31 U.S.C. §3512) requires the head of each executive agency to establish, evaluate, and maintain adequate systems of accounting and internal control. To help ensure that federal agencies establish and maintain effective financial management systems, Congress enacted the **Federal Financial Management Improvement Act of 1996 (FFMIA).** The act states:

> To rebuild the accountability and credibility of the Federal Government, and restore public confidence in the Federal Government, agencies must incorporate accounting standards and reporting objectives established for the Federal Government into their financial management systems so that all the assets and liabilities, revenues, and expenditures or expenses, and the full costs of programs and activities of the Federal Government can be consistently and accurately recorded, monitored, and uniformly reported throughout the Federal Government.[4]

The FFMIA further requires that each agency "shall implement and maintain financial management systems that comply substantially with federal financial management systems requirements, applicable federal accounting standards, and the U.S. Government Standard General Ledger at the transaction level."[5]

Twenty-four major agencies of the federal government must submit performance and accountability reports (PAR). Two components of a PAR are the annual performance report (APR) required by the Government Performance and Results Act (GPRA) (P.L. 103-62), and the audited annual financial statements (AFR) required by the CFO Act of 1990 (P.L. 101-576). If so desired, agencies can separately submit the reports rather than consolidate the reports into a PAR. Those agencies not covered by the CFO Act, are required under the Accountability of Tax Dollars Act of 2002 (P.L. 107-289)

[3] There are also federally chartered corporations, such as the Federal Home Loan Mortgage Corporation (Freddie Mac), and the Federal National Mortgage Association (Fannie Mae), that are shareholder owned. Financial information about these entities is not included in the financial statements of the U.S. government because they do not meet the criteria for a federal entity, as described in *Statement of Federal Financial Accounting Concepts (SFFAC) No. 1,* "Entity and Display."

[4] Public Law 104-208, 104th Congress, Federal Financial Management Improvement Act of 1996, Sec. 802(a)(5).

[5] Ibid., Sec. 803(a).

ILLUSTRATION 17–1 The U.S. Government

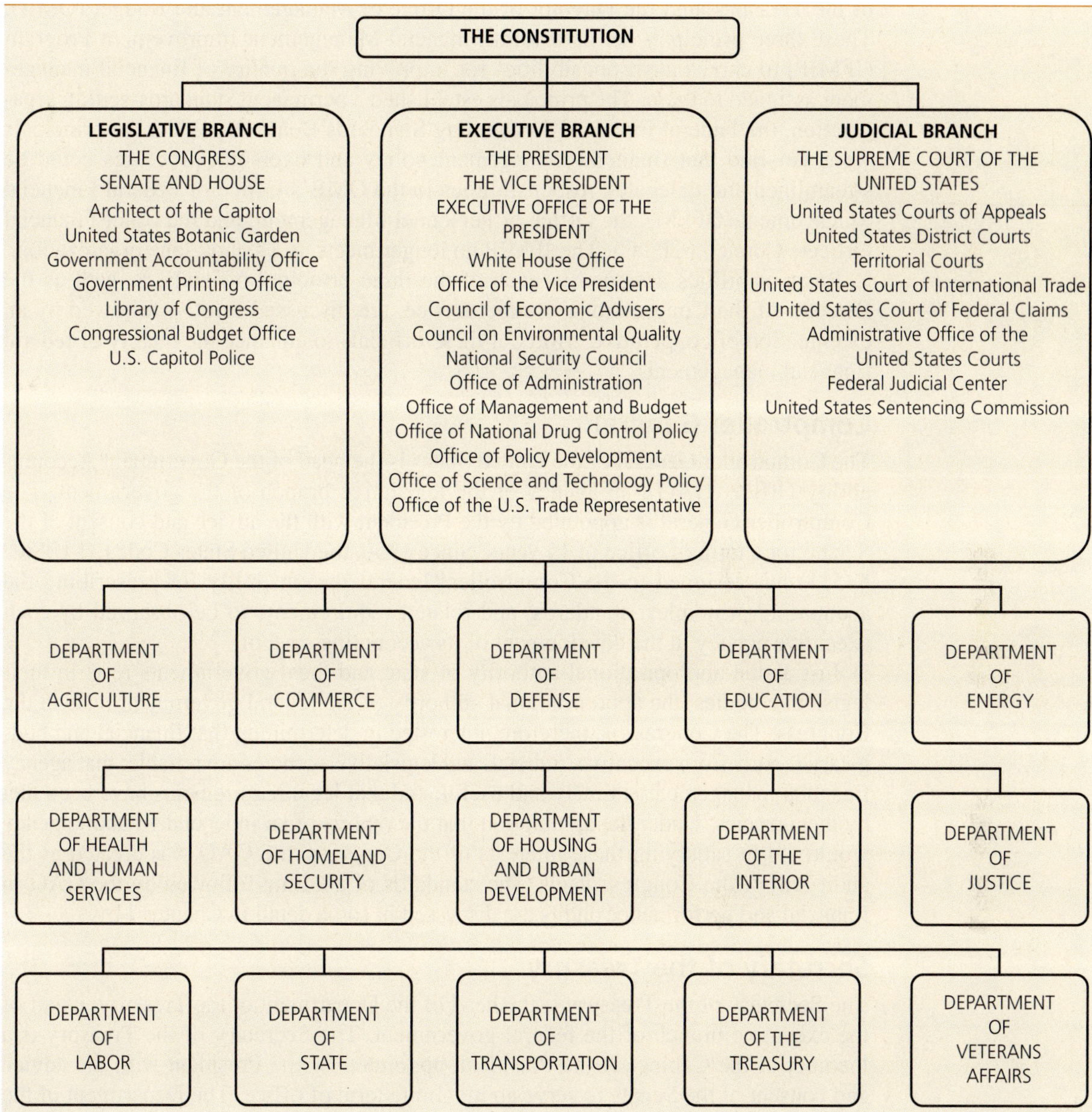

Source: 2013 *Financial Report of the United States Government,* Management's Discussion and Analysis, p. 2.
Note that only significant reporting entities are included on the chart.

to submit audited financial reports to the Office of Management and Budget (OMB) and Congress.[6]

Federal statutes (Budget and Accounting Procedures Act of 1950 and the Chief Financial Officers (CFO) Act of 1990) assign responsibility for establishing and maintaining a sound financial management structure for the federal government as a whole

[6] Office of Management and Budget *Circular A–136, Financial Reporting Requirements,* revised September 21, 2013.

to three principal officials: the Comptroller General of the United States, the Secretary of the Treasury, and the Director of the Office of Management and Budget (OMB). These three principals set up a Joint Financial Management Improvement Program (JFMIP) to carry out responsibilities for improving the quality of financial management assigned to them. The principals established a permanent standards-setting organization, the Federal Financial Accounting Standards Board. By 2004, the principals were satisfied that financial management policy and oversight processes could be streamlined and delegated responsibilities to the OMB's Office of Federal Financial Management (OFFM), the Office of Personnel Management, and the Chief Financial Officers Council (CFOC). The JFMIP no longer meets as a stand-alone organization.

Responsibilities assigned to each of the three principal officials, as well as the Director of the Congressional Budget Office, are discussed briefly, followed by an examination of cooperative efforts of these officials to enhance the quality of federal financial management.

Comptroller General

The Comptroller General of the United States is the head of the Government Accountability Office (GAO), an agency of the legislative branch of the government. The Comptroller General is appointed by the President with the advice and consent of the Senate for a term of office of 15 years. Since 1950, the United States Code (31 U.S.C. §3511) has assigned to the Comptroller General responsibility for prescribing the accounting principles, standards, and related requirements to be observed by each executive agency in the development of its accounting system.

Just as the appropriational authority of state and local governments rests in their legislative bodies, the appropriational authority of the federal government rests in the Congress. The Congress is, therefore, interested in determining that financial and budgetary reports from executive, judicial, and legislative agencies are reliable; that agency financial management is timely and useful; and that legal requirements have been met by the agencies. Under the assumption that the reports of an independent audit agency would aid in satisfying these interests of the Congress, the GAO was created as the audit arm of the Congress itself. The standards of auditing followed by the GAO in financial and performance audits are discussed in some detail in Chapter 11.

Secretary of the Treasury

The Secretary of the Treasury is the head of the Department of the Treasury, a part of the executive branch of the federal government. The Secretary of the Treasury is a member of the Cabinet of the President, appointed by the President with the advice and consent of the Senate to serve an indefinite term of office. The Department of the Treasury was created in 1789 to receive, keep, and disburse monies of the United States, and to account for them. The Internal Revenue Service, active in the enforcement of the collections of revenues due the federal government, is part of the Department of the Treasury, as are the U. S. Mint, the Bureau of Engraving and Printing, the Bureau of Fiscal Service, the Office of Treasurer of the United States, and the Financial Management Service. The Secretary of the Treasury is responsible for the preparation of reports that will inform the President, the Congress, and the public on the financial condition and operations of the government (31 U.S.C. §3513).

An additional responsibility of the Secretary of the Treasury is the maintenance of a system of central accounts of the public debt and cash to provide a basis for consolidation of the accounts of the various executive agencies. The Department of the Treasury's Financial Management Service (FMS) maintains the U.S. Government Standard

Deposit Funds

Combined receipt and expenditure accounts established to account for receipts held in suspense temporarily and later refunded or paid to some other fund or receipts held by the government as a banker or agent for others and paid out at the discretion of the owner are classified within the federal government as deposit fund accounts. They are similar in nature to the agency funds established for state and local governments.

REQUIRED FINANCIAL REPORTING—U.S. GOVERNMENT-WIDE

In FY 1997, the Department of the Treasury began issuing an annual *Financial Report of the United States Government* that follows FASAB standards and is audited by the Government Accountability Office. Prototype "Consolidated Financial Statements" had been issued since the early 1980s; however, the Government Performance and Results Act of 1993 expanded the requirements of the Chief Financial Officers Act of 1990 and required that 24 federal agencies be audited and comprehensive government-wide financial statements be prepared. For every year since audits of the Consolidated Financial Statements have been conducted, a disclaimer of opinion by the Comptroller General of the United States has been issued. The most recent disclaimer reads as follows:

> Because of the significance of the related matters described in the Basis for Disclaimer of Opinion paragraphs above, we were not able to obtain sufficient appropriate audit evidence to provide a basis for an audit opinion on the accrual-based consolidated financial statements. Accordingly, we do not express an opinion on the accrual-based consolidated financial statements as of and for the fiscal years ended September 30, 2013, and 2012.[11]

The Comptroller General attributes the inability to issue an opinion on the government's consolidated financial statements to three major issues, which have been ongoing:

> (1) serious financial management problems at the Department of Defense (DOD) that have prevented DOD's financial statements from being auditable, (2) the federal government's inability to adequately account for and reconcile intragovernmental activity and balances between federal entitites, and (3) the federal government's ineffective process for preparing the consolidated financial statements.[12]

Given the difficulties that agencies have experienced in complying with federal GAAP, it may be surprising that 20 of 24 agencies *did* receive unqualified (unmodified) opinions.

Since the CFO Act, federal accounting and reporting has greatly improved, attributed in part to congressional mandate and the increasingly high professional skills and dedication of governmental accountants, auditors, and agency managers. However, it is apparent financial management issues remain, some of which have proven difficult to resolve. Given the complexity of the government and the fact that the Comptroller General has not been able to render an opinion on the federal

[11] FY 2013 Financial Report of the United States Government, p. 225, available at *www.fms.treas.gov/fr/index.html*. Prior to the disclaimer, the report identifies specific issues that led to the disclaimer (see the full report for detail).

[12] Ibid., p. 27.

ILLUSTRATION 17–2

UNITED STATES GOVERNMENT
Balance Sheets
As of September 30, 2013, and September 30, 2012
(In billions of dollars)

	2013	2012 (Restated)
Assets:		
Cash and other monetary assets	206.3	206.2
Accounts and taxes receivable, net	103.2	111.2
Loans receivable, net	1,022.3	859.6
TARP direct loans and equity investments, net	17.9	40.2
Inventories and related property, net	311.1	299.0
Property, plant, and equipment, net	896.7	855.0
Debt and equity securities	107.8	110.2
Investments in GSEs	140.2	109.3
Other assets	162.8	157.6
Total assets	2,968.3	2,748.3
Stewardship land and heritage assets*		
Liabilities:		
Accounts payable	66.2	65.2
Federal debt securities held by the public and accrued interest	12,028.4	11,332.3
Federal employee and veteran benefits payable	6,538.3	6,274.0
Environmental and disposal liabilities	349.1	339.0
Benefits due and payable	174.3	166.2
Insurance and guarantee program liabilities	130.0	156.4
Loan guarantee liabilities	59.2	74.6
Liabilities to GSEs	—	9.0
Other liabilities	532.1	432.6
Total liabilities	19,877.6	18,849.3
Contingencies and Commitments		
Net position:		
Funds from Dedicated Collections	3,143.7	3,147.8
Funds other than those from Dedicated Collections	(20,053.0)	(19,248.8)
Total net position	(16,909.3)	(16,101.0)
Total liabilities and net position	2,968.3	2,748.3

The accompanying notes are an integral part of these financial statements.
*Described in notes, no amount reported here.

government's financial statements, it may be helpful to look at the "big picture" provided by the government-wide statements before studying GAAP and reporting for federal agencies. The comparative balance sheets for the U.S. government for FY 2012 and FY 2013, as shown in Illustration 17–2, report a $16.9 billion deficit in net position on September 30, 2013. The cost of government operations in FY 2013 exceeded revenues for the year by $800.1 billion, as seen in the Statement of Operations in Illustration 17–3, which led to the increase in the net position deficit from the prior year. The GAO does provide a resource for understanding the U.S. government's annual financial report, which is referenced at the end of this chapter.

ILLUSTRATION 17–3

UNITED STATES GOVERNMENT
Statements of Operations and Changes in Net Position
For the Year Ended September 30, 2013
(In billions of dollars)

	Funds Other Than Those from Dedicated Collections (Combined)	Funds from Dedicated Collections (Combined)	Eliminations	Consolidated
Revenue:				
Individual income tax and tax withholdings	1,294.0	902.4	—	2,196.4
Corporation income taxes	270.4	—	—	270.4
Excise taxes	32.8	52.8	—	85.6
Unemployment taxes	—	54.0	—	54.0
Customs duties	30.6	—	—	30.6
Estate and gift taxes	18.8	—	—	18.8
Other taxes and receipts	139.7	36.4	(0.6)	175.5
Miscellaneous earned revenues	7.0	4.2	—	11.2
Intragovernmental interest	—	119.6	(119.6)	—
Total revenue	1,793.3	1,169.4	(120.2)	2,842.5
Net Cost of Government Operations:				
Net cost	2,175.2	1,482.0	(0.6)	3,656.6
Intragovernmental interest	119.6	—	(119.6)	—
Total net cost	2,294.8	1,482.0	(120.2)	3,656.6
Intragovernmental transfers	(307.6)	307.6	—	—
Unmatched transactions and balances	9.0	—	—	9.0
Net operating (cost)/revenue	(800.1)	(5.0)	—	(805.1)
Net position, beginning of period	(19,248.8)	3,147.8	—	(16,101.0)
Prior period adjustments—changes in accounting principles	(4.1)	0.9	—	(3.2)
Net operating (cost)/revenue	(800.1)	(5.0)	—	(805.1)
Net position, end of period	(20,053.0)	3,143.7	—	(16,909.3)

The accompanying notes are an integral part of these financial statements.

REQUIRED FINANCIAL REPORTING—GOVERNMENT AGENCIES

The Chief Financial Officers (CFO) Council and OMB provide guidance for federal agencies in meeting the financial and performance management requirements of various federal statutes. The form and content of these reports have changed over the years. The most recent guidance for agencies is provided in OMB *Circular A-136*, "Financial Reporting Requirements." The 2013 revision of *Circular A-136* indicates which agencies are required to prepare an annual performance report (APR) and an annual financial report (AFR). The reports can be presented using a consolidated performance and accountability report (PAR), or they can be separately issued. In addition to the APR and AFR reports, agencies are required to issue a separate Summary of Performance and Financial Information. Federal agencies prepare the PAR annually but are also required to submit unaudited interim reports to OMB on a quarterly basis. Interim reports are to be submitted within 21 calendar days of the end of each quarter.

The consolidated PAR is composed of several parts. In addition to an agency head message, the PAR includes the four main sections: an APR, an AFR, management's discussion and analysis, and other accompanying information. Within the sections, the reader can find several reports, including an audit report, reports on management's assessment of internal control and other accountability issues, and the Inspector General's assessment of management and performance challenges. The next five sections of the text briefly discuss the agency head message and the four main sections of the PAR.

Agency Head Message

The top administrator for the agency is required to include a transmittal letter explaining the agency's mission, goals, and accomplishments. An assessment on the reliability and completeness of the information in the report, along with identification of material internal control weaknesses and actions the agency is taking to resolve them, is also required in the transmittal letter. If the agency is issuing a separate APR and AFR, rather than a PAR, that must also be explained in the transmittal letter.

Management's Discussion and Analysis (MD&A)

SFFAS No. 15 requires that an MD&A be included in a federal agency's PAR. The conceptual basis for the role and importance of the MD&A was described earlier in the chapter with the discussion of *SFFAC No. 3*. *SFFAS No. 15* lists requirements for the MD&A, which include providing a clear description of the entity's mission and organizational structure; performance goals, objectives, and results; financial statements; and systems, controls, and legal compliance.

Annual Performance Reports (APR)

The APR provides information on the agency's actual performance and progress in achieving the goals in its strategic plan and performance budget. There is no prescribed format for this report; however, OMB *Circular A–11,* "Preparation, Submission, and Execution of the Budget," provides guidance on what should be included in the report. The performance budget included in the APR is the basis for preparing the President's annual budget, which is submitted to Congress for approval.

Annual Financial Statements (AFR)

OMB *Circular A–136* specifies essentially the same financial statements recommended by *SFFAC No. 2*. It also provides detailed descriptions and instructions for completing each part of each statement and providing the accompanying notes to the financial statements. These statements include the following:

1. Balance sheet
2. Statement of net cost
3. Statement of changes in net position
4. Statement of budgetary resources
5. Statement of custodial activity
6. Statement of social insurance (for specified programs)
7. Statement of net changes in social insurance amounts (for specified programs)

Each of these statements is discussed briefly in the following paragraphs. The FY 2013 principal financial statements of the U.S. Department of the Interior are presented in Illustrations 17–4 through 17–9. The statements consolidate the various units of the Department of the Interior, such as the Bureau of Indian Affairs, the National Park Service, the U.S. Fish and Wildlife Service, the Bureau of Land Management, the Bureau of Land Reclamation, and the U.S. Geological Survey, among others. The department received an unqualified audit opinion from the public accounting firm KMPG for FY 2013.[13]

Balance Sheet

The U.S. Department of the Interior's Balance Sheet for FY 2013 is presented in Illustration 17–4. Agencies have considerable latitude regarding the level of aggregation to be used in preparing the financial statements. Agencies can use either a single-column (consolidated) format or a multicolumn format displaying financial information for component units or lines of business. If consolidated reporting is used, a separate column showing the intraentity transactions (for example, eliminations of intercomponent unit receivables and payables) is required in the *consolidating* statements, which underlie the consolidated statements. As shown, when consolidated financial information is provided, comparative totals for the prior year must be presented for the balance sheet, the statement of budgetary resources, and the statement of custodial activity.

Assets A streamlined format is required in which *entity assets* are combined with *nonentity assets*; however, *intragovernmental assets* are reported separately from *governmental assets*. **Entity assets** are those the reporting entity has authority to use in its operations, whereas **nonentity assets** are held by the entity but are not available for the entity to spend. An example of a nonentity asset is federal income taxes collected and held by the Internal Revenue Service for the U.S. government. Nonentity assets should be disclosed in the notes. **Intragovernmental assets (liabilities)** are claims by (against) a reporting entity that arise from transactions among federal entities. **Governmental assets (liabilities)** arise from transactions of the federal government or an entity of the federal government with nonfederal entities.

SFFAS No. 1 provides specific standards relating to Cash, Fund Balance with Treasury, Accounts Receivable, Interest Receivable, and various other asset categories. In most federal agencies *Fund Balance with Treasury* is used rather than *Cash* to indicate that the agency has a claim against the U.S. Treasury on which it may draw to pay liabilities. Only a few large federal departments and agencies, such as the Department of Defense, are authorized to write and issue checks directly against their balances with the Treasury. Most departments and agencies must request that the Treasury issue checks to pay their liabilities. If a federal agency does have the right to maintain one or more bank accounts, bank balances would be reported as *Cash*.

Consistent with the manner in which business entities report inventories, *SFFAS No. 3* distinguishes inventory from consumable supplies. Inventory is defined as "tangible personal property that is (1) held for sale, (2) in the process of production for sale, or (3) to be consumed in the production of goods for sale or in the provision of services for a fee" (p. 4). Inventory may be valued at either historical cost or latest acquisition cost. Supplies to be consumed in normal operations are reported as *operating materials and supplies*.

[13] Complete versions of these statements are available at *www.doi.gov/pfm*.

ILLUSTRATION 17–4

U.S. DEPARTMENT OF INTERIOR
Balance Sheet
As of September 30, 2013 and 2012
(dollars in thousands)

	FY 2013	FY 2012 Restated
ASSETS		
Intragovernmental Assets:		
Fund Balance with Treasury	$48,595,659	$44,596,626
Investments, Net	7,552,860	6,849,501
Accounts, and Interest Receivable	1,811,045	1,949,324
Loans and Interest Receivable, Net	3,352,753	3,164,122
Other	2,688	701
Total Intragovernmental Assets	$61,315,005	$56,560,274
Cash	437	447
Investments, Net	16	18
Accounts and Interest Receivable, Net	2,482,214	3,185,912
Loans and Interest Receivable, Net	61,622	63,116
Inventory and Related Property, Net	130,066	140,304
General Property, Plant and Equipment, Net	21,963,995	21,041,652
Other	247,322	206,468
Total Assets	$86,200,677	$81,198,191
Stewardship Assets*		
LIABILITIES		
Intragovernmental Liabilities:		
Accounts Payable	$ 632,208	$ 666,872
Debt	97,329	94,368
Other		
Resources Payable to Treasury	1,887,892	1,850,922
Advances and Deferred Revenue	303,101	343,269
Custodial Liability	873,276	1,144,050
Other Liabilities	910,633	889,325
Total Intragovernmental Liabilities	$ 4,704,439	$ 4,988,806
Accounts Payable	971,896	815,838
Loan Guarantee Liability	29,445	29,425
Federal Employee and Veteran Benefits	1,509,331	1,498,248
Environmental and Disposal Liabilities	192,142	176,510
Other		
Contingent Liabilities	1,035,563	4,387,944
Trust Land Consolidation Program	1,896,910	—
Asbestos Cleanup liability	537,601	—
Advances and Deferred Revenue	745,443	836,149
Payments Due to States	1,013,107	1,240,226
Grants Payable	415,795	496,655
Other Liabilities	1,147,112	1,006,954
Total Liabilities	$14,198,784	$15,476,755
Commitments and Contingencies*		
Net Position		
Unexpended Appropriations-Funds from Dedicated Collections	489,938	573,615
Unexpended Appropriations-Other Funds	4,612,820	4,760,058
Cumulative Results of Operations-Funds from Dedicated Collections	61,849,547	59,167,026
Cumulative Results of Operations-Other Funds	5,049,588	1,220,737
Total Net Position	$72,001,893	$65,721,436
Total Liabilities And Net Position	$86,200,677	$81,198,191

The accompanying notes (not shown here) are an integral part of these financial statements.

*Described in notes, no amounts reported here.

The federal government's property, plant, and equipment (PP&E) include assets that are unique to the federal government. **General PP&E** is used to provide general government goods and services, as well as military weapon systems and space exploration equipment.

Stewardship assets are of two types: heritage assets and stewardship land. **Heritage assets** are unique in that they have historical or natural significance; cultural, artistic, or educational significance; or are architecturally significant. The Washington Monument would be an example of a heritage asset. Generally, heritage assets are expected to be maintained indefinitely. **Stewardship land** is not used by the federal government for operating purposes. Examples of stewardship land include national parks and land used for wildlife.

The FASAB has concluded that many of the unique federal assets should be included in categories of assets that are well defined in the professional accounting literature and familiar to report users. For example, *SFFAS No. 23* categorizes national defense property, plant and equipment as general PP&E that are capitalized and depreciated (except for land). *SFFAS No. 29* requires that heritage assets and stewardship land be accounted for as basic financial information with a note on the balance sheet that discloses information about them, but without any asset dollar amount shown. The notes will disclose information such as a description of major categories of heritage, multi-use heritage, and stewardship land; physical units added and withdrawn during the year; methods of acquisition and withdrawal; and condition information.

Liabilities *SFFAS No. 1* and *SFFAS No. 2* provide specific accounting standards for Accounts Payable, Interest Payable, and Other Current Liabilities. Liabilities covered by budgetary resources (funded) and liabilities not covered by budgetary resources (unfunded) are combined on the face of the balance sheet. *Liabilities covered by budgetary resources* are those for which monies have been made available either through congressional appropriations or current earnings of the entity. *Liabilities not covered by budgetary resources* result from the receipt of goods or services in the current or prior periods but for which monies have not yet been made available through congressional appropriations or current earnings of the entity. Examples of the latter are liabilities for accrued leave, capital leases, and pensions. These should be disclosed in the notes.

SFFAS No. 5 establishes standards for liabilities not covered in *SFFAS No. 1* and *No. 2*. The statement defines a *liability* as "a probable future outflow or other sacrifice of resources as a result of past transactions or events" (par. 19). Recognition criteria is provided for liabilities arising from exchange and nonexchange transactions, government-related or acknowledged events, contingencies, capital leases, federal debt, pension and other postemployment benefits, and insurance and guarantee programs. *SFFAS No. 5* also requires disclosure in the notes to the financial statements of the condition and estimated cost to remedy deferred maintenance on PP&E. In addition, it provides standards for measurement and recognition of expenses and liabilities related to environmental cleanup and closure costs from removing general PP&E from service.

Net Position The fund balances of the entity's funds are reported in the balance sheet as **net position.** There are two components of net position. The first is **unexpended appropriations,** which is the amount of the entity's appropriations represented by undelivered orders and unobligated balances. The second component is the **cumulative results of operations,** representing the net difference between expenses/losses and financing sources, including appropriations, revenues, and gains, since the inception of the activity. Cumulative results of operations would also include any other items that would affect the net position, including, for example, the fair market value of donated assets and assets (net of liabilities) transferred to or from other federal entities without reimbursement.

ILLUSTRATION 17–5

U.S. DEPARTMENT OF INTERIOR
Statement of Net Cost
For the years ended September 30, 2013 and 2012
(dollars in thousands)

	FY 2013	FY 2012
Provide Natural and Cultural Resource Protection		
Gross Costs	$ 8,143,558	$ 8,525,594
Less: Earned Revenue	933,285	914,622
Net Cost	7,210,273	7,610,972
Manage Energy, Water & Natural Resources		
Gross Costs	3,723,092	5,613,721
Less: Earned Revenue	1,870,900	1,846,803
Net Cost	1,852,192	3,766,918
Advance Government to Government Relationships		
Gross Costs	3,793,235	4,806,140
Less: Earned Revenue	295,788	341,386
Net Cost	3,497,447	4,464,754
Provide a Scientific Foundation for Decision Making		
Gross Costs	1,532,820	1,582,292
Less: Earned Revenue	372,442	387,155
Net Cost	1,160,378	1,195,137
Building a 21st Century Department of the Interior		
Gross Costs	354,438	421,437
Less: Earned Revenue	8,390	2,892
Net Cost	346,048	418,545
Reimbursable Activity and other		
Gross Costs	3,749,915	3,649,155
Less: Earned Revenue	1,593,528	1,872,634
Net Cost	2,156,387	1,776,521
TOTAL		
Gross Costs	21,297,058	24,598,339
Less: Earned Revenue	5,074,333	5,365,492
Net Cost of Operations	$16,222,725	$19,232,847

The accompanying notes (not shown here) are an integral part of these financial statements.

Statement of Net Cost

Illustration 17–5 presents the Department of the Interior's statement of net cost. This statement shows the components of net cost for the major programs (e.g., Resource Protection) of the reporting entity and the reporting entity as a whole. Major programs relate to the major goals and outputs described in the entity's strategic plans required by the Government Performance and Results Act. If the reporting entity has a complex organizational structure, it may need to provide supporting schedules in the notes to the financial statements.

Statement of Changes in Net Position

The Department of the Interior's consolidated statement of changes in net position is shown in Illustration 17–6. The purpose of this statement is to communicate all

ILLUSTRATION 17–6

U.S. DEPARTMENT OF INTERIOR
Statement of Changes in Net Position
For the years ended September 30, 2013 and 2012
(dollars in thousands)

	FY 2013 Consolidated	**FY 2012** (Restated) Consolidated
Unexpended Appropriations		
Beginning Balance	$ 5,333,673	$ 6,041,022
Budgetary Financing Sources		
Appropriations Received, General Funds	12,688,480	12,036,767
Appropriations Transferred In/(Out)	14,363	18,571
Appropriations—Used	(12,305,595)	(12,644,015)
Other Adjustments	(628,163)	(118,672)
Net Change	(230,915)	(707,349)
Ending Balance–Unexpended Appropriations	$ 5,102,758	$ 5,333,673
Cumulative Results of Operations		
Beginning Balance	$60,387,763	$57,391,119
Adjustments		
Change in Accounting Principle	(537,601)	—
Beginning Balance, as adjusted	59,850,162	57,391,119
Budgetary Financing Sources		
Appropriations—Used	12,305,595	12,644,015
Royalties Retained	4,132,882	6,046,924
Non-Exchange Revenue	1,298,565	1,057,700
Transfers In/(Out) without Reimbursement	2,468,564	371,509
Donations and Forfeitures of Cash and Cash Equivalents	43,097	46,963
Other Adjustments	—	—
Other Financing Sources		
Donations and Forfeitures of Property	274,730	131,913
Transfers In/(Out) without Reimbursement	560,087	8,172
Imputed Financing from Costs Absorbed by Others	2,416,725	2,102,193
Other Non-Budgetary Financing Sources/(Uses)	(228,547)	(179,898)
Total Financing Sources	23,271,698	22,229,491
Net Cost of Operations	(16,222,725)	(19,232,847)
Net change	7,048,973	2,996,644
Ending Balance-Cumulative Results of Operations	$66,899,135	$60,387,763
Total Net Position	$72,001,893	$65,721,436

The accompanying notes (not shown here) are an integral part of these financial statements. Columns that break the consolidated totals into dedicated and all other amounts for each year are omitted for the sake of brevity.

changes in the reporting entity's net position through the use of the two sections called unexpended appropriations and cumulative results of operation. Net cost of operations is shown at the bottom of the statement in the cumulative results of operations section (see Illustration 17–5). It includes gross costs less any exchange (earned) revenues. Further changes in net position can arise from additions or deductions resulting from prior-period adjustments (due to material errors or accounting changes), changes in cumulative results of operations, and unexpended appropriations.

Statement of Budgetary Resources

The statement of budgetary resources for the Department of the Interior (see Illustration 17–7) presents the availability of budgetary resources and the status of those resources at year-end. This statement is derived from the entity's budgetary general ledger and is designed to show consistency between budgetary information presented in the financial statement and the budget of the U.S. government. OMB *Circular A–11,* "Preparation, Submission, and Execution of the Budget," provides the definitions and guidance for budgetary accounting and reporting. As shown in Illustration 17–7, total budgetary resources is equal to the total status of budgetary resources. **Budgetary resources** include new budgetary authority for the period plus unobligated budgetary authority carried over from the prior period, any transfers in or out of budgetary resources, recoveries of obligations from the prior period, and any budgetary adjustments. The *Status of Budgetary Resources* section is intended to show the status of budgetary resources at the end of the period. It consists of obligations incurred (that is, budget authority expended and amounts reserved for undelivered orders) plus any current budgetary authority that is still available to finance operations of the current period or those of prior periods. The lower portion of the statement of budgetary resources reconciles obligations incurred during the period to total budgetary outlays for the period, after adjusting for offsetting collections and budgetary adjustments, and the change in obligations during the year is carried forward.

Statement of Custodial Activity

Entities that "collect nonexchange revenue for the General Fund of the Treasury, a trust fund, or other recipient entities" prepare a statement of custodial activity (see Illustration 17–8). As shown in Illustration 17–8, the Department of the Interior's statement of custodial activity essentially reports on the agency's fiduciary activities related to how much has been collected and accrued and how the monies were distributed.

Statement of Social Insurance

A limited number of federal agencies are required to prepare a statement of social insurance. Accounting for federal social insurance programs—Social Security, Medicare and Supplementary Medical Insurance (Part B), Railroad Retirement benefits, Black Lung benefits, and Unemployment Insurance is very complex. In general, *SFFAS No. 17* (as amended by *SFFAS No. 37*) requires a liability to be recognized when payments are due and payable to beneficiaries or service providers. Supplementary stewardship information is required to help in assessing long-term sustainability of programs and the government's ability to raise resources from future program participants to pay benefits to current participants. The FASAB acknowledges that although *SFFAS No. 17* was a major step forward in federal financial reporting, there is much more work to do in properly accounting for social insurance. Social insurance is a unique blend of nonexchange transactions, such as annual governmental assistance programs, and exchange transactions, such as long-term pension programs.

SFFAS No. 25 directs four of the five social insurance programs listed in the prior paragraph to present a Statement of Social Insurance (SOSI). Although the fifth program, Unemployment Insurance, does not present an SOSI, it does provide required supplementary information (RSI). The SOSI presents (1) the actuarial present value

ILLUSTRATION 17–7

U.S. DEPARTMENT OF INTERIOR
Statement of Budgetary Resources
For the years ended September 30, 2013 and 2012
(dollars in thousands)

	Total Budgetary Accounts	
	FY 2013	**FY 2012**
Budgetary Resources:		
Unobligated balance brought forward, October 1	$ 6,493,319	$ 7,520,693
Recoveries of prior year unpaid obligations	607,245	545,389
Other Changes in unobligated balance	(24,046)	(7,961)
Unobligated balance from prior year budget authority, net	7,076,518	8,058,121
Appropriations (discretionary and mandatory)	19,096,882	16,906,091
Borrowing authority (discretionary and mandatory)	—	—
Spending authority from offsetting collections (discretionary and mandatory)	5,207,970	5,593,397
Total Budgetary Resources	$31,381,370	$30,577,609
Status of Budgetary Resources:		
Obligations incurred:	$22,190,928	$24,064,290
Unobligated balance, end of year:		
Apportioned	9,032,371	6,352,370
Exempt from apportionment	59	59
Unapportioned	158,012	140,890
Total unobligated balance, end of year	9,190,442	6,493,319
Total Status of Budgetary Resources	$31,381,370	$30,557,609
Change in Obligated Balance:		
Unpaid obligations:		
Unpaid obligations, brought forward, October 1	$10,575,801	$10,975,256
Obligations incurred	22,190,928	24,064,290
Outlays (gross) (-)	(22,127,621)	(23,918,356)
Recoveries of prior year unpaid obligations (-)	(607,245)	(545,389)
Unpaid obligations, end of year	10,031,863	10,575,801
Uncollected payments:		
Uncollected payments, Federal sources, brought forward, October 1	(2,737,350)	(2,654,681)
Adjustment to uncollected payments, Federal sources, start of year	—	—
Change in uncollected payments, Federal sources	25,740	(82,669)
Uncollected payments, Federal sources, end of year	(2,711,610)	(2,737,350)
Obligated balance, start of Year	$ 7,838,451	$ 8,320,575
Obligated Balance, end of year	$ 7,320,253	$ 7,838,451
Budget Authority and Outlays, Net:		
Budget authority, gross (discretionary and mandatory)	$24,304,854	$22,499,493
Actual offsetting collections (discretionary and mandatory)	(5,249,521)	(5,546,688)
Change in uncollected customer payments from Federal sources	25,740	(82,669)
Budget authority, net (discretionary and mandatory)	$19,081,073	$16,870,136
Outlays, gross (discretionary and mandatory)	22,127,621	23,918,356
Actual offsetting collections (discretionary and mandatory)	(5,249,521)	(5,546,688)
Outlays, net (discretionary and mandatory)	16,878,100	18,371,668
Distributed offsetting receipts (-)	(5,410,103)	(5,553,460)
Agency Outlays Net (Discretionary and Mandatory)	$11,467,997	$12,818,208

The accompanying notes (not shown here) are an integral part of these financial statements. Columns that identify nonbudgetary credit program financing are omitted for the sake of brevity.

ILLUSTRATION 17–8

U.S. DEPARTMENT OF INTERIOR
Statement of Custodial Activity
For the years ended September 30, 2013 and 2012
(dollars in thousands)

	FY 2013	FY 2012
Revenues on Behalf of the Federal Government		
Mineral Lease Revenue		
Rents and Royalties	$10,091,011	$ 9,901,697
Onshore Lease Sales	236,185	2,107,090
Offshore Lease Sales	2,304,960	1,095,070
Total Revenue	$12,632,156	$13,103,857
Disposition of Revenue		
Distribution to Department of the Interior		
Departmental Offices	2,074,225	2,088,585
National Park Service Conservation Funds	1,045,580	1,047,141
Bureau of Reclamation	1,593,537	1,654,847
Bureau of Ocean Energy Management	162,802	160,952
Bureau of Safety and Environmental Enforcement	52,602	52,474
Bureau of Land Management	20,389	31,313
Fish and Wildlife Service	2,655	2,302
Distribution to Other Federal Agencies		
Department of the Treasury	8,293,960	6,049,167
Department of Agriculture	110,457	134,303
Department of Energy	50,000	50,000
Distribution to Indian Tribes and Agencies	9	11
Distribution to States and Others	46,648	36,658
Change in Untransferred Revenue	(820,708)	1,796,104
Total Disposition of Revenue	$12,632,156	$13,103,857
Net Custodial Activity	$ —	$ —

The accompanying notes (not shown here) are an integral part of these financial statements.

for the projection period of all future contributions and tax income received from or on behalf of current and future participants; (2) the actuarial present value for the projection period of estimated future scheduled expenditures paid to or on behalf of current and future participants; and (3) the actuarial present value for the projection period of the estimated future excess of contributions and tax income (excluding interest) over future scheduled expenditures. Information for the current year and separate estimates for each of the preceding four years should be provided. Since the Department of Interior does not prepare a statement of social insurance, Illustration 17–9 provides the statement of social insurance from the financial report of the Social Security Administration. As shown, Social Security (Old Age, Survivors and Disability Insurance) is running a projected deficit, which has been increasing over the past five years.

Statement of Net Changes in Social Insurance Amounts

SFFAS No. 37 requires the preparation of a statement of net changes in social insurance at the government-wide level and at the agency level for those agencies affected by social insurance programs. The purpose of the statement is to reconcile beginning

ILLUSTRATION 17–9

STATEMENT OF SOCIAL INSURANCE
Old-Age, Survivors, and Disability Insurance
as of January 1, 2013
(in billions)

		Estimates from Prior Years			
	2013	**2012**	**2011**	**2010**	**2009**
Present value for the 75-year projection period from or on behalf of:					
Participants who, in the starting year of the projection period, have attained eligibility age (age 62 and over):					
Noninterest income	$ 908	$ 847	$ 726	$ 672	$ 575
Cost for scheduled future benefits	11,021	9,834	8,618	8,096	7,465
Future noninterest income less future cost	−10,112	−8,988	−7,892	−7,424	−6,890
Participants who have not yet attained retirement eligibility age (ages 15-61):					
Noninterest income	24,591	22,703	20,734	19,914	18,559
Cost for scheduled future benefits	40,591	37,753	34,042	32,225	30,207
Future noninterest income less future cost	−16,000	−15,050	−13,309	−12,311	−11,647
Present value of future noninterest income less future cost for current participants (closed group measure)	−26,113	−24,038	−21,201	−19,735	−18,537
Combined OASI and DI Trust Fund asset reserves at start of period	2,732	2,678	2,609	2,540	2,419
Closed group-Present value of future noninterest income less future cost for current participants *plus* combined OASI and DI Trust Fund asset reserves at start of period	−$23,381	−$21,360	−$18,592	−$17,195	−$16,118
Present value for the 75-year projection period from or on behalf of:					
Future participants (those under age 15 and to be born and to immigrate during period):					
Noninterest income	23,419	21,649	20,144	19,532	18,082
Cost for scheduled future benefits	9,600	8,890	8,100	7,744	7,223
Future noninterest income less future cost	13,819	12,759	12,044	11,789	10,860
Present value of future noninterest income less future cost for current and future participants (open group measure)	−12,294	−11,278	−9,157	−7,947	−7,677
Combined OASI and DI Trust Fund asset reserves at start of period	2,732	2,678	2,609	2,540	2,419
Open group-Present value of future noninterest income less future cost for current and future participants *plus* combined OASI and DI Trust Fund asset reserves at start of period	−$ 9,562	−$ 8,601	−$ 6,548	−$ 5,406	−$ 5,258

Totals do not necessarily equal the sum of rounded components. The accompanying notes are an integral part of these financial statements.

and ending balances of social insurance. It should present information about significant changes occurring during the period (e.g., changes in valuation; interest on the obligation due to present valuation; the changes in demographic, economic, and health care assumptions; and changes in law, regulation, and policy).

Required Supplemental Information

Many FASAB statements address required disclosures to be included in the notes to the financial statements. Disclosures for stewardship PP&E, deferred maintenance on PP&E, and stewardship investments are examples. **Stewardship investments** are beneficial investments of the government in items such as nonfederal physical property (property financed by the federal government but owned by state or local governments), human capital, and research and development. There are other required disclosures about environmental cleanup costs, detail of budgetary resources and obligations, and incidental amounts of custodial collections and distributions that may not warrant separate reporting in a statement of custodial activity.

Other Accompanying Information

The last section in the PAR provides information on a set of topics not covered in the previous sections. A summary table of the financial statement audit indicates the type of audit opinion the agency received and includes a list of any material weaknesses and whether or not they were resolved. Another table summarizes management's assurances on internal controls over operations and financial reporting as required under the Federal Managers Fiscal and Integrity Act of 1982 and discussed in OMB *Circular A–123,* Appendix D. The Inspector General's statements indicating the agency's most serious management and performance challenges are also found in this section.

DUAL-TRACK ACCOUNTING SYSTEM

Financial reports of federal agencies must be based on historical costs to indicate whether an entity has complied with laws and regulations (e.g., 31 U.S.C. §1341). Congressional policy as expressed in 31 U.S.C. §3512 and the Federal Financial Management Improvement Act of 1996 calls for using cost information in budgeting and in managing operations. This law also provides for using cost-based budgets, at such time as may be determined by the President, in developing requests for appropriations. All departments and agencies, therefore, should have budget and accounting systems that have the capability to produce cost-based budgets. In this context, cost is the value of goods and services used or consumed by a government agency within a given period, regardless of when they were ordered, received, or paid. In any given year, the obligations incurred may be less than, equal to, or greater than the costs recognized for that period due to changes in inventories, obligations, and so on. At the completion of a program, however, obligations and costs are identical.

The accounting system of a federal agency must provide information needed for financial management as well as information needed to demonstrate that agency managers have complied with budgetary and other legal requirements. Accordingly, federal agency accounting is based on a *dual-track system,* one track being a self-balancing set of *proprietary* (accrual based) accounts intended to provide information for agency management and the other track being the self-balancing

ILLUSTRATION 17–10 **Summary of Key Differences between Budgetary and Proprietary Accounting in Recognition of Events That Constitute Transactions**

Budgetary Accounting	Proprietary Accounting
Entries are made for commitment of funds in advance of preparing orders to procure goods and services.	Entries are not made for commitments.
Entries are made for obligation of funds at the time goods and services are ordered.	Entries are not made for obligations.
Entries are made to expend appropriations when goods and services chargeable to the appropriation are received, regardless of when they are used and regardless of when they are paid.	Goods and services that will last more than a year and otherwise meet the criteria to qualify as assets are capitalized and expensed when consumed, regardless of what appropriation funded them and when they are paid.
Entries are only made against an appropriation for transactions funded by the appropriation.	Goods and services consumed in the current period for which payment is to be made from one or more subsequent appropriations is recognized as an expense in the current period.
Entries are not made against an appropriation for transactions not funded by the appropriation.	Goods and services consumed in the current period but paid for in prior periods are expensed in the current period.

Source: U.S. General Accounting Office, *GAO Accounting Guide: Basic Topics Relating to Appropriations and Reimbursables* (Washington, DC: GAO, 1990), p. 3–2.

set of *budgetary accounts* needed (1) to ensure that available budgetary resources and authority are not over expended or over obligated and (2) to facilitate standardized budgetary reporting requirements. Illustration 17–10 summarizes key differences between budgetary and proprietary track accounting in terms of the timing of the recognition of events and transactions. The use of the dual-track system is illustrated in the next section.

The basic budgetary authority for a federal agency can come from many different sources. Only one of those sources is illustrated here—basic operating appropriations.[14] The flow of budgetary authority generally follows several steps from congressional appropriation to expenditure by the agencies. The sequence of the budgetary steps is shown in Illustration 17–11 and described as follows:

1. The Congressional **appropriation** is enacted into law and provides budget authority to fund an agency's operations for the year.
2. An **apportionment,** usually quarterly, is approved by the Office of Management and Budget and may be used by the agency to procure goods and services for the quarter.
3. The head of the agency or his or her designee authorizes an **allotment** of the apportionment for procurement of goods and services.

[14] The illustrative journal entries shown in this section are modeled on the account titles prescribed by the U.S. Government Standard General Ledger except that we have added fiscal year designations after certain accounts for instructional purposes. The financial statements that follow are based on those specified by OMB *Circular A–136.*

ILLUSTRATION 17–11 Relationship among Budgetary Accounts

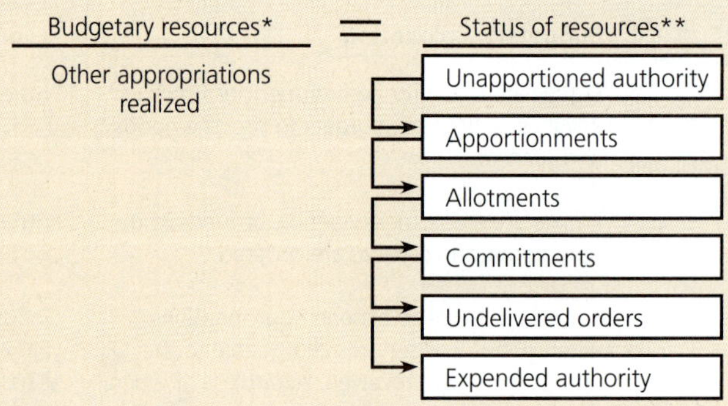

* Normal debit balance.** Normal credit balance.

4. Authorized agency employees reserve allotted budget authority in the estimated amount of an order as a **commitment** prior to the actual ordering of goods and services.
5. **Obligation** of the allotment occurs when a formal order for acquisition of goods and services is placed, charging the allotment with the latest estimate of the cost of goods or services ordered.
6. An **expended appropriation** occurs when goods or services have been received.

It should be noted that the term *expended appropriation* means that the budget authority has been used and is no longer available to provide for goods and services. It does not necessarily mean that cash has been disbursed; it may be that only a liability has been incurred. A *commitment* (item 4) does not legally encumber an appropriation, but its use is recommended for effective planning and fund control. Some agencies, however, use commitments only for certain spending categories. An *obligation* (item 5) does encumber an appropriation. The account title used to record an obligation is *Undelivered Orders*. As with state and local governments, agencies may opt not to use obligations if the costs are recurring.

As shown in Illustration 17–11, the full amount of an agency's appropriation for the year is reported as a budgetary resource that, at a given point during the period, is distributed among the budgetary accounts (shown under "Status of Resources" in Illustration 17–11). As discussed earlier and in the following illustrative transactions, budgetary authority normally flows down the accounts, culminating ultimately in expended authority.

Illustrative Transactions and Entries

The account titles and transactions used by the federal government are quite different from those presented in Chapters 1 through 9 for state and local governments. To assist with understanding the accounts used in the following illustrative transactions and entries, Illustration 17–12 is provided. In this illustration, a comparison is provided between state and local government fund journal entries and those that are used by the federal government. As can be seen, the federal government flow of resources from Congress, through OMB, to agency heads and authorized agency employees has no equivalent in state and local governments. As you see the flow of budgetary

ILLUSTRATION 17–12 Comparison of Accounting for State and Local Governmental Funds and Federal Agencies (journal entries)

Item	State and Local Government Funds Compliance Track Only[1]	Federal Agency	
		Budgetary Track	**Proprietary Track**
1. Passage of appropriations (and for state and local governments, revenue) bills	Estimated Revenues Appropriations Budgetary Fund Balance	Other Appropriations Realized Unapportioned Authority	Fund Balance with Treasury Unexpended Appropriations
2. Revenues accrued (at expected collectible amount)	Taxes Receivable Estimated Uncollectible Taxes Revenues	No equivalent for taxes; user charges, if any, recognized as billed	Taxes Receivable Allowance for Uncollectible Taxes Earned Income from the Public
3. Apportionment by OMB	No equivalent	Unapportioned Authority Apportionments	No entry
4. Allotment by agency head	No equivalent[2]	Apportionments Allotments	No entry
5. Budget authority reserved prior to ordering goods or services	No equivalent	Allotments Commitments	No entry
6. Goods or services ordered	Encumbrances Encumbrances Outstanding	Commitments Undelivered Orders[3]	No entry
7. Goods or services received	Encumbrances Outstanding Encumbrances Expenditures Accounts Payable	Undelivered Orders Expended Authority	Expense or asset account Accounts Payable Unexpended Appropriations Appropriations Used
8. Liability paid (expenditure recorded in 7)	Accounts Payable Cash	No entry	Accounts Payable Fund Balance with Treasury[4]
9. Supplies used	No entry	No entry	Operating/Program Expenses Inventory for Agency Operations
10. Physical inventory (consumption method assumed for state and local governments)	Inventory Expenditures Fund Balance—Unassigned Fund Balance—Nonspendable—Inventory of Supplies	No entry	Entry for (7) assumes perpetual inventory; would need entry for (10) if physical inventory and book inventory differed
11. Depreciation computed	No entry (computation used for cost reimbursements and management information)	No entry (Not an expenditure of appropriations; will never require a check to be drawn on U.S. Treasury)	Depreciation and Amortization Accumulated Depreciation (on general property, plant, and equipment but not certain military assets and stewardship assets)
12. Closing entries	Appropriations Estimated Revenues Budgetary Fund Balance Encumbrances Outstanding[5] Encumbrances Revenues Expenditures Fund Balance—Unassigned	Expended Authority Other Appropriations Realized; (Also must close any budgetary accounts associated with expired budget authority)	Cumulative Results of Operations Operating/Program Expenses Appropriations Used Cumulative Results of Operations

[1] Funds that use modified accrual basis of accounting.

[2] As discussed in Chapter 3, some local governments utilize allotment accounting. In such cases, the credit in Entry 1 will be to Unallotted Appropriations, and in Entry 4 it will be necessary to record the debit to that account and the credit to Allotments.

[3] As illustrated by Entry 4, and by Entry 5, some agencies opt to use the interim account Commitments to improve planning for procurement of goods and services. If commitments are not recorded in advance of placing orders, the debit for the budgetary track will be to Allotments.

[4] As indicated in this chapter, the account credited here might be Disbursements in Transit rather than Fund Balance with Treasury.

[5] Required only if the encumbrances must be re-appropriated in the next year; optional otherwise.

ILLUSTRATION 17–13

FEDERAL AGENCY
Post-closing Trial Balance
As of September 30, 2016

	Debits	Credits
Proprietary Accounts:		
Fund Balance with Treasury—2016	$ 675,000	
Operating Materials and Supplies	610,000	
Equipment	3,000,000	
Accumulated Depreciation on Equipment		$ 600,000
Accounts Payable		275,000
Unexpended Appropriations—2016		400,000
Cumulative Results of Operations		3,010,000
	$4,285,000	$4,285,000
Budgetary Accounts:		
Other Appropriations Realized—2016	$ 400,000	
Undelivered Orders—2016		$ 400,000
	$ 400,000	$ 400,000

resources identified in Illustration 17–11 results in several of the transactions (1, 3, 4 and 5) shown in Illustration 17–12. This budgetary flow of resources is unique to the federal government budgetary track. Studying Illustration 17–12 will be helpful in understanding the following journal entries.

Consider the agency whose September 30, 2016, post-closing trial balance is shown in Illustration 17–13. If this agency receives from Congress a one-year appropriation for fiscal year 2017 (FY 2017) in the amount of $2,500,000, the Treasury's Bureau of Government Financial Operations would prepare a formal notice to the agency after the appropriation act has been signed by the President. The following entries would be made in the agency accounts:

		Debits	Credits
1a.	*Budgetary:*		
	Other Appropriations Realized—2017	2,500,000	
	Unapportioned Authority—2017		2,500,000
1b.	*Proprietary:*		
	Fund Balance with Treasury—2017	2,500,000	
	Unexpended Appropriations—2017		2,500,000

The *Other Appropriations Realized* account is used in the U.S. Standard General Ledger to distinguish basic operating appropriations from appropriation authority that earmarks appropriations for specific purposes.

When the Office of Management and Budget approves the quarterly apportionment, the agency would be notified. Assuming that the OMB approved apportionments of $2,500,000 during FY 2017, the agency would record the apportionments as follows:[15]

		Debits	Credits
2.	*Budgetary:*		
	Unapportioned Authority—2017	2,500,000	
	Apportionments—2017		2,500,000

If, during FY 2017, the agency head allotted to subunits within the agency the entire apportionment, the event would be recorded in the agency accounts in the following manner:

3.	*Budgetary:*		
	Apportionments—2017	2,500,000	
	Allotments—2017		2,500,000

All three entries—for the annual appropriation, for the apportionment by the OMB, and for the agency allotments—would be made as of October 1, the first day of fiscal year 2017. Although journal entries are made the first day of the fiscal year, in some years the appropriation bill might not have actually been enacted by that date. The substance of the three entries is that agency managers had obligational spending authority for the year totaling $2,500,000 to finance agency operations. As discussed in Chapters 3 and 4 for state and local government accounting, federal agencies are legally constrained to manage the activities of the agency so obligational authority is not exceeded. It should also be noted that if the OMB should withhold any portion of the annual appropriations, that amount would not be available to the agency. Furthermore, for single-year appropriations, any apportionments and allotments not expended or obligated ordinarily must be returned to the U.S. Treasury at the end of the fiscal year.

Commitments were recorded during FY 2017 in the amount of $1,150,000. Operations of the agency for FY 2017 are summarized in the following journal entries:

4.	*Budgetary:*		
	Allotments—2017	1,150,000	
	Commitments—2017		1,150,000

Purchase orders and contracts for goods and services were issued in the amount of $1,144,000 during the year.

5.	*Budgetary:*		
	Commitments—2017	1,144,000	
	Undelivered Orders—2017		1,144,000

[15] OMB ordinarily does not have authority to withhold apportionments. If OMB does withhold a portion of an apportionment, special accounts would be used.

Checks to vendors as of October 1 were requested from the Treasury. The Accounts Payable balance was for materials received in fiscal year 2016 in the amount of $90,000 and equipment received in the amount of $185,000. This event does not reduce the agency's Fund Balance with Treasury until the checks are actually issued by the Treasury. Instead, most agencies would credit the account *Disbursements in Transit* until notified by the Treasury that the requested checks have been issued. Disbursements in Transit is a current liability account since liabilities to vendors and creditors cannot be considered settled until the checks have actually been issued. If this agency had been one of the few with authority to issue checks directly, then Fund Balance with Treasury would have been credited immediately. Since this agency is not assumed to have check-writing authority, the following entry would be made:

		Debits	Credits
6.	*Proprietary:*		
	Accounts Payable	275,000	
	Disbursements in Transit—2016		275,000

The agency received notification from the Treasury that the checks requested in Transaction 6 had been issued. This notification would be recorded as follows:

		Debits	Credits
7.	*Proprietary:*		
	Disbursements in Transit—2016	275,000	
	Fund Balance with Treasury—2016		275,000

Goods and equipment ordered in FY 2016 (prior fiscal year) are reported in Illustration 17–13 in the net position account, Unexpended Appropriations—2016, a proprietary account, as amounting to $400,000. A budgetary account Undelivered Orders—2016 also exists in the same amount, as does its offsetting account Other Appropriations Realized—2016. (All other budgetary accounts for 2016 were closed at the end of that fiscal year because all unobligated appropriation authority expired at year-end.) Assuming that all the goods and equipment ordered in 2016 were received during the first quarter of FY 2017, one entry is necessary in the budgetary accounts to show that fiscal 2016 obligations are now liquidated and that the prior-year appropriation is expended in the same amount. Entries in proprietary accounts are required to record the debit to Unexpended Appropriations—2016 and the offsetting credit to the Appropriations Used account, as well as debits to asset accounts and a credit to Accounts Payable. These entries follow:

		Debits	Credits
8a.	*Budgetary:*		
	Undelivered Orders—2016	400,000	
	Expended Authority—2016		400,000
8b.	*Proprietary:*		
	Operating Materials and Supplies	150,000	
	Equipment	250,000	
	Accounts Payable		400,000
	Unexpended Appropriations—2016	400,000	
	Appropriations Used		400,000

Operating materials and supplies were received from suppliers during FY 2017 at an actual cost of $1,010,000, for which Undelivered Orders—2017 had been recorded in the estimated amount of $1,005,000. Budgetary track and proprietary track entries for these transactions are shown in Entries 9a and 9b. Because the actual cost of materials and supplies exceeded the estimated amount recorded previously as Undelivered Orders—2017, the $5,000 excess must be debited to Allotments—2017 to record the additional expenditure of obligational authority.

		Debits	Credits
9a.	*Budgetary:*		
	Undelivered Orders—2017	1,005,000	
	Allotments—2017	5,000	
	Expended Authority—2017		1,010,000
9b.	*Proprietary:*		
	Operating Materials and Supplies	1,010,000	
	Accounts Payable		1,010,000
	Unexpended Appropriations—2017	1,010,000	
	Appropriations Used		1,010,000

Payrolls for FY 2017 amounted to $1,188,000. Utilities in the amount of $120,000 were also approved for payment during the year. (The agency does not record commitments or obligations for payrolls and other recurring operating expenses.) Checks totaling $1,308,000 were requested from the Treasury for these expenses. The debit in the first proprietary track entry is to the control account Operating/Program Expenses. Each agency would have a subsidiary expense ledger or more detailed expense accounts in its general ledger tailored to its specific needs. The required entries are:

10a.	*Budgetary:*		
	Allotments—2017	1,308,000	
	Expended Authority—2017		1,308,000
10b.	*Proprietary:*		
	Operating/Program Expenses	1,308,000	
	Disbursements in Transit—2017		1,308,000
	Unexpended Appropriations—2017	1,308,000	
	Appropriations Used		1,308,000

Materials and supplies used in the operating activities during FY 2017 amounted to $1,620,000. The entries would be:

11.	*Proprietary:*		
	Operating/Program Expenses	1,620,000	
	Operating Materials and Supplies		1,620,000

Accounts Payable in the amount of $1,410,000 (see Entries 8b and 9b) were approved for payment and checks were requested from the Treasury. Of this amount, $400,000 will be charged against the FY 2016 Fund Balance with

Treasury and $1,010,000 against the FY 2017 Fund Balance with Treasury. The required entry is:

		Debits	Credits
12.	*Proprietary:*		
	Accounts Payable	1,410,000	
	Disbursements in Transit—2016		400,000
	Disbursements in Transit—2017		1,010,000

The Treasury notified the agency that checks in the amount of $2,718,000 (including $400,000 for Accounts Payable arising from fiscal year 2016—see Entry 12) had been issued during FY 2017. Of the $2,318,000 charged against the FY 2017 Fund Balance with Treasury, $1,010,000 was for operating materials and supplies (see Entry 9b), $1,188,000 was for payrolls, and $120,000 was for utilities expense.

13.	*Proprietary:*		
	Disbursements in Transit—2016	400,000	
	Disbursements in Transit—2017	2,318,000	
	Fund Balance with Treasury—2016		400,000
	Fund Balance with Treasury—2017		2,318,000

Adjusting Entries

To prepare accrual-based financial statements, the following items were taken into account: (1) payroll accrued for the last week of the fiscal year amounts to $27,000 and (2) invoices or receiving reports for goods received but for which payment has not yet been approved total $105,000, of which $36,000 has been used in operations and $69,000 remains in ending inventory. Because the obligations for the items in (1) and (2) have become certain in amount and relevant expense accounts or inventory accounts can be charged, the amounts should be shown in the financial statements as current liabilities. This is reflected in the following journal entries. It is assumed that the goods received had been previously obligated in the amount of $105,000, but no commitment or obligation had been recorded for the accrued payroll. The required entries are:

14a.	*Budgetary:*		
	Allotments—2017	27,000	
	Undelivered Orders—2017	105,000	
	Expended Authority—2017		132,000
14b.	*Proprietary:*		
	Operating/Program Expenses	63,000	
	Operating Materials and Supplies	69,000	
	Accounts Payable		105,000
	Accrued Funded Payroll and Benefits		27,000
	Unexpended Appropriations—2017	132,000	
	Appropriations Used		132,000

Depreciation of equipment was computed as $300,000 for FY 2017. Inasmuch as depreciation is not an expense chargeable against the appropriation, the accrual of depreciation expense does not affect any of the appropriation, allotment, or obligation accounts. However, it is recorded as in business accounting to measure the cost of activities on an accrual basis. The credit to Accumulated Depreciation reduces the book value of the equipment.

		Debits	Credits
15.	*Proprietary:*		
	Depreciation and Amortization	300,000	
	Accumulated Depreciation on Equipment		300,000

Although not illustrated here, federal agencies also accrue some expenses such as accrued annual leave that will be funded by future-period appropriations. These unfunded accrued expenses require entries in the proprietary track but require no entries in the budgetary track. The effect of these unfunded expenses is to reduce the balance of Cumulative Results of Operations since the expenses are not offset by a financing source.

Illustrative Financial Statements

After entries just illustrated have been made, the federal agency balance sheet at the end of FY 2017 and the other required statements can be prepared. As discussed earlier in this chapter, OMB *Circular A–136* prescribes the form and content of financial statements required to be prepared by most executive agencies and departments. The content of each agency's *annual financial statement* and examples of the basic financial statements were provided as Illustrations 17–4 through 17–9 earlier in this chapter.

In this section, basic financial statements are shown (see Illustrations 17–15 through 17–17) for the simple federal agency whose transactions were just discussed. These statements include a balance sheet, a statement of changes in net position, and a statement of budgetary resources. Since the example federal agency used in this chapter had no material custodial activities, no statement of custodial activities is needed. The agency also does not administer a social insurance program, so there is no need for a statement of social insurance. The statement of net cost is omitted, and no supplemental financial and management information is provided. In the case of an actual federal entity, such as the Department of Defense, for example, there would be numerous funds, programs, and organizational units and thus the need for consolidating and consolidated financial statements, as well as required supplemental information.

Prior to preparing the illustrative financial statements, as of and for the fiscal year ended September 30, 2017, lapsed budgetary authority should be closed and a pre-closing general ledger trial balance should be prepared such as that presented in Illustration 17–14. Note that it is standard practice to prepare the U.S. Standard General Ledger *pre-closing* trial balance after the expended and withdrawn budgetary authority accounts have been closed but before the other temporary proprietary accounts are closed. Closing of expended and withdrawn budgetary authority is discussed here.

Total credits to the Expended Authority—2017 account (Entries 9a, 10a, and 14a) amounted to $2,450,000. Thus, the total *unexpended* budgetary authority at the end of FY 2017 is $50,000 ($2,500,000−$2,450,000). Of the $50,000 unexpended amount, $34,000 is reserved in the Undelivered Orders—2017 for goods or services still on order at year-end (Entries 4, 9a, and 14a). However, the $6,000 balance in Commitments—2017 and $10,000 in Allotments—2017 have not been reserved and must be returned to Treasury. The following journal entries are needed to record the lapse of obligational authority for the $16,000 not obligated or reserved by fiscal year-end. As the first entry in Entry 16a shows, unused commitments and allotments (as well as apportionments if there had been a year-end balance) are closed to Other Appropriations Realized—2017, as is the amount of appropriations that was expended. In addition, the $400,000 balance

ILLUSTRATION 17–14

FEDERAL AGENCY
Pre-closing Trial Balance
As of September 30, 2017

	Debits	Credits
Proprietary accounts:		
Fund Balance with Treasury—2017	$ 166,000	
Operating Materials and Supplies	219,000	
Equipment	3,250,000	
Accumulated Depreciation on Equipment		$ 900,000
Disbursements in Transit—2017		0
Accounts Payable		105,000
Accrued Funded Payroll and Benefits		27,000
Unexpended Appropriations—2017		34,000
Cumulative Results of Operations		3,010,000
Appropriations Used—2016		400,000
Appropriations Used—2017		2,450,000
Operating/Program Expenses	2,991,000	
Depreciation and Amortization	300,000	
	$6,926,000	$6,926,000
Budgetary accounts:		
Appropriations Realized but Withdrawn—2017	$ 16,000	
Other Appropriations Realized—2017	34,000	
Unapportioned Authority—2017		$ 0
Apportionments—2017		0
Allotments—2017		0
Commitments—2017		0
Undelivered Orders—2017		34,000
Restorations, Write-offs, and Withdrawals—2017		16,000
	$ 50,000	$ 50,000

in Expended Authority—2016 is closed to Other Appropriations Realized—2016, which also has a $400,000 balance prior to closing. To establish a record of withdrawn appropriations, the second budgetary entry that follows should also be made. In addition, temporary proprietary accounts would be closed as shown in Entry 16b.

		Debits	Credits
16a.	*Budgetary:*		
	Commitments—2017	6,000	
	Allotments—2017	10,000	
	Expended Authority—2016	400,000	
	Expended Authority—2017	2,450,000	
	Other Appropriations Realized—2016		400,000
	Other Appropriations Realized—2017		2,466,000
	Appropriations Realized but Withdrawn—2017	16,000	
	Restorations, Write-offs, and Withdrawals—2017		16,000
16b.	*Proprietary:*		
	Unexpended Appropriations—2017	16,000	
	Fund Balance with Treasury—2017		16,000

Accounting procedures also exist to reverse the second entry under Entry 16a to the extent that the actual cost of goods or services received early in FY 2018 exceeds the $34,000 estimated in Undelivered Orders. Essentially, a portion of the budgetary authority that was withdrawn in Entry 16a would be *restored* in this case.

Temporary proprietary accounts should be closed to update the net position accounts, so the end-of-period balance sheet can be prepared. The necessary closing entry would be:

		Debits	Credits
17.	*Proprietary:*		
	Appropriations Used	2,850,000	
	Cumulative Results of Operations	441,000	
	Operating/Program Expenses		2,991,000
	Depreciation and Amortization		300,000

The balance sheet for the example federal agency whose pre-closing trial balance is shown in Illustration 17–14 is presented in Illustration 17–15. More complex agencies usually prepare a consolidated balance sheet like the one shown in Illustration 17–4. The example federal agency is assumed to have only entity assets (those that can be used for the agency's operations) and, except for Fund Balance with Treasury, the remaining assets are governmental. All liabilities (Accounts Payable and Accrued Funded Payroll and Benefits) are assumed to be

ILLUSTRATION 17–15

FEDERAL AGENCY
Balance Sheet
As of September 30, 2017

Assets	
Intragovernmental:	
Fund balance with Treasury	$ 166,000
Governmental:	
Operating materials and supplies	219,000
Equipment (net of accumulated depreciation of $900,000)	2,350,000
Total assets	$2,735,000
Liabilities	
Governmental liabilities:	
Accounts payable	$ 105,000
Accrued funded payroll and benefits	27,000
Total liabilities	132,000
Net Position	
Unexpended appropriations	34,000
Cumulative results of operations	2,569,000
Total net position	2,603,000
Total liabilities and net position	$2,735,000

ILLUSTRATION 17–16

FEDERAL AGENCY
Statement of Changes in Net Position
For the Year Ended September 30, 2017

	Cumulative Results of Operations	Unexpended Appropriations
Beginning balances	$3,010,000	$ 400,000
Prior period adjustments	0	0
Beginning balances, as adjusted	3,010,000	400,000
Budgetary financing sources:		
Appropriations received		2,484,000
Appropriations used	2,850,000	(2,850,000)
Other financing sources		
Total financing sources	5,860,000	34,000
Net cost of operations (+−) Note A	3,291,000	
Ending balances	$2,569,000	$ 34,000

Note A: These amounts are taken from the bottom line of the statement of net costs, which is not included here for sake of brevity.

governmental. Furthermore, all liabilities are covered by budgetary resources. As discussed earlier in this chapter, the *net position* consists of only two items, Unexpended Appropriations ($34,000 reserved for goods and services on order at year-end) and Cumulative Results of Operations.

A statement of net cost for the U.S. Department of the Interior was presented in Illustration 17–5. Because the federal agency used in our example is assumed to have a simple organizational structure and no earned revenues, its statement of net cost would be very simple; net cost would be the same as gross cost. Moreover, since the agency's net suborganization or program costs are reported on the first line of the statement of changes in net position presented in Illustration 17–16, a statement of net cost is not presented in this chapter. While the statement of changes in net position is quite simple, it is informative nonetheless.

The final statement presented for the simple federal agency in our example is a statement of budgetary resources (see Illustration 17–17). The astute reader will note that the equation applicable to the top portion of this statement is budgetary resources = status of budgetary resources. Budgetary resources in this case are $2,884,000, consisting of current-year appropriations of $2,500,000 less expired appropriations of $16,000 plus $400,000 carried forward from prior-year appropriations to cover undelivered orders at the end of the prior year. Since there are no unobligated appropriations that can be carried forward at year-end, the status of budgetary resources in this case is simply the amount of budgetary resources expended ($2,450,000) plus $34,000 obligated for goods on order at the end of FY 2017 that had not yet been expended. Outlays are reported in the bottom section of the statement of budgetary resources and are the same as the total amount expended during the year, or $2,850,000 ($2,450,000 chargeable to the current-year appropriation and $400,000 chargeable to the prior-year appropriation). Subtracting the excess of outlays ($2,850,000) over obligations incurred ($2,484,000) from the beginning obligated balance of $400,000 equals the ending obligated balance of $34,000.

ILLUSTRATION 17–17

FEDERAL AGENCY
Statement of Budgetary Resources
For the Year Ended September 30, 2017 (Note A)

Budgetary resources:	
Budgetary authority (Note B)	$2,484,000
Status of budgetary resources:	
Obligations incurred (Note C)	$2,484,000
Total status of budgetary resources	$2,484,000
Change in obligated balance:	
Unpaid obligations, beginning of year	$ 400,000
Obligations incurred	2,484,000
Outlays (disbursements) (Note D)	(2,850,000)
Unpaid obligations, end of year	$ 34,000

(The net outlays section of the statement is omitted since there are no adjustments to outlays.)

Note A: Comparative totals should also be presented for the prior year. Those totals are omitted in this example.

Note B: Total available budgetary authority for the current year was the $2,500,000 appropriation less $16,000 that expired.

Note C: Obligations incurred equals the expended authority of $2,450,000 plus $34,000 obligated for undelivered orders.

Note D: Outlays for the year include all authority expended during the year, $400,000 from 2016 and $2,450,000 from 2017.

SUMMARY OF ACCOUNTING AND REPORTING FOR FEDERAL GOVERNMENT AGENCIES

Federal agency accounting takes into consideration certain accruals (supplies used and depreciation) generally ignored in state and local government fund accounting, although the Governmental Accounting Standards Board (GASB) reporting model requires the use of accrual accounting by state and local governments at the government-wide level.

The head of each agency in the executive branch of the federal government has the statutory responsibility for the establishment and maintenance of systems of accounting and internal control in conformity with principles, standards, and requirements established by the Comptroller General, the Secretary of the Treasury, and the Director of the OMB. Federal agency accounting is directed at providing information for intelligent financial management of agency activities and programs to the end that they may be operated with efficiency and economy, as well as providing evidence of adherence to legal requirements. As emphasized by the headings of Illustration 17–12 and by the discussions in earlier chapters, accounting for governmental funds presently focuses on legal compliance. The focus of federal agency accounting, in contrast, is broadened to include information needed for the management of agency resources (the *proprietary* track) as well as for compliance with fund control requirements (the *budgetary* track). However, as discussed in Chapters 1 through 9 of this text, the authors have introduced dual-track accounting for state and local government accounting to meet the accrual accounting needs at the government-wide level while continuing to focus on legal compliance within the governmental funds. International public sector accounting standards consider funds an element of internal control and not a focal point of external reporting.

Key Terms

Allotment, *709*
Apportionment, *709*
Appropriation, *709*
Budget accounts, *692*
Budgetary resources, *704*
Commitment, *710*
Cumulative results of operations, *701*
Entity assets, *699*
Expended appropriation, *710*
Federal Financial Management Improvement Act of 1996 (FFMIA), *686*
General PP&E, *701*
Governmental assets (liabilities), *699*
Heritage assets, *701*
Intragovernmental assets (liabilities), *699*
Net position, *701*
Nonentity assets, *699*
Obligation, *710*
Stewardship assets, *701*
Stewardship investments, *708*
Stewardship land, *701*
Unexpended appropriations, *701*

Selected References

Financial Management Services, a Bureau of the U.S. Department of the Treasury. *U.S. Government Standard General Ledger,* available at *www.fms.treas.gov/ussgl/index.html.*

Government Accountability Office. *Understanding the Primary Components of the Annual Financial Report of the United States Government,* GAO-09-946SP, September 2009.

Office of Management and Budget. *Circular A–136,* "Financial Reporting Requirements," 2013.

———. *Circular A–134,* "Financial Accounting Principles and Standards," 1993.

Tierney, Cornelius E., Roldan Fernandez, Edward F. Kearney, and Jeffrey W. Green. *Federal Accounting Handbook: Policies, Standards, Procedures, Practices*, 2nd edition. New York: Wiley, 2007.

Questions

17–1. Explain the role of the Government Accountability Office (GAO), the Department of the Treasury, and the Office of Management and Budget (OMB) in the financial accounting and reporting of the federal government.

17–2. Compare the GAAP hierarchy for the federal government to that for state and local governments (see Chapter 11).

17–3. According to the FASAB conceptual framework, there are four objectives for federal financial reporting. Discuss the four objectives and explain why the focus of the FASAB objectives differs from that of the FASB or the GASB.

17–4. Explain the differences among these accounts: (1) *Estimated Revenues* used by state and local governments, (2) *Other Appropriations Realized* used by federal agencies in their budgetary track, and (3) *Fund Balance with Treasury* used by federal agencies in their proprietary track.

17–5. "Net position for a federal agency is similar to net position of a state or local government." Do you agree or disagree? Explain.

17–6. Defining the reporting entity at the federal level is complicated by different perspectives from which the federal government can be viewed. What are the three perspectives? How are they defined? How do they interrelate?

17–7. The federal government uses two groups of funds. Identify the two fund groups, and the funds associated with each group. Compare the funds to those used by state and local governments.

17–8. What are stewardship assets? How does the accounting for a stewardship asset differ from that for general property, plant, and equipment?

17–9. What are the two tracks in the dual-track accounting system? Explain the purpose of each track. Relate each track to state and local governmental "dual-track" accounting.

17–10. What are the components of the PAR and where would a federal agency go to find out the requirements for preparing a PAR?

Cases

17–11 Agency PAR and Audit. In 2013, 22 of 24 CFO Act agencies received unqualified (unmodified) audit opinions. The Comptroller General disclaimed an opinion on one agency, and one agency received a qualified opinion. The one agency receiving a qualified opinion was HUD (Housing and Urban Development). Go to the HUD Web site *(www.hud.gov)* and find its PAR, which can be used to answer the following.

Required

a. Briefly identify the HUD financial situation by answering the following questions.

(1) What portion of HUD's assets is composed of cash (i.e., fund balance with treasury)?

(2) What was the increase or decrease in HUD's net position for the period examined?

b. Who conducted the HUD audit? What audit standards did the auditor apply? In your opinion, what, if any, independence issues would need to be addressed?

c. Why did HUD receive a qualified opinion in FY 2013? Since FY 2013, has HUD received an unqualified (unmodified) opinion or are there ongoing problems?

17–12 Research Case—FASAB. The source of authoritative guidance for federal financial accounting and reporting is the Federal Accounting Standards Advisory Board. To better understand the FASAB, access its Web site at *www.fasab.gov* to answer the following.

Required

a. What is the mission of the FASAB?

b. What is the composition of the FASAB, and how are the board members selected/appointed?

c. How is the FASAB funded?

d. Discuss whether you believe the FASAB is an independent standard-setting body. Do you believe it is more or less independent than FASB or GASB? Explain your answer.

e. Identify and briefly describe at least three active projects on which the FASAB is currently working.

f. The FASB and GASB standards are proprietary in that a user must pay to access the standards. Are the FASAB standards proprietary?

17–13 Audit of U.S. Government-wide Annual Report. Obtain the most recent audited annual financial report of the U.S. government. It is available from the Government Accountability Office (GAO).

Required

a. Did the GAO give the federal government an unqualified (unmodified), qualified, adverse, or disclaimer of opinion?
b. What were the material weaknesses cited by the Comptroller General?
c. What CFO Act federal agencies received an unqualified (unmodified) opinion for this fiscal year? (*Hint:* Read the Management's Discussion and Analysis.)
d. Did the statements of social insurance receive a clean opinion? If not, why not?

17–14 Analysis of the U.S. Government Budget Deficit and Net Cost of Operations. Access the most recent Financial Report of the U.S. Government at the U.S. Treasury Department Web site, *www.fms.treas.gov/fr*, and answer the following questions.

Required

a. What are amounts of the total budget deficit and net operating cost for each of the three most recent fiscal years?
b. How do these two measures of federal government fiscal health differ? (*Hint:* Refer to the *Citizen's Guide* that accompanies the report.)
c. What are the main factors that explain the three-year trend in each of these measures?
d. For the most recent fiscal year, identify the five largest components of the net cost of operations of the U.S. government?

Exercises and Problems

17–15 Multiple Choice. Choose the best answer.

1. Which of the following represents one of the roles of the Government Accountability Office in federal financial accounting and reporting?
   a. Providing an independent assessment of the financial reports of the federal government.
   b. Providing the chart of accounts for the standard general ledger used by federal agencies.
   c. Providing forward-looking financial information, such as estimated future revenues.
   d. Providing information to federal agencies on financial reporting requirements.
2. Which of the following is an important aid in assisting federal agencies in preparing their performance and accountability reports?
   a. *Statement of Federal Financial Accounting Concepts No. 1.*
   b. *Statement of Federal Financial Accounting Concepts No. 6.*
   c. OMB *Circular A-134.*
   d. OMB *Circular A-136.*
3. Which of the following is the highest level of GAAP for the federal government?
   a. The FASAB's technical bulletins.
   b. The FASAB's concepts statements.
   c. The FASAB's interpretations.
   d. The FASB standards if adopted by FASAB.
4. Objectives that are identified by *Statement of Federal Financial Accounting Concepts (SFFAC) No. 1* for federal financial reporting include all of the following except:
   a. Budgetary integrity.
   b. Adequacy of controls.

c. Stewardship.
d. Relevance and reliability of information.

5. Which of the following is a required basic financial statement for federal agencies?
   a. Balance sheet.
   b. Statement of cash flows.
   c. Statement of operations.
   d. Statement of budgetary revenues and expenditures.
6. Assuming that an agency's unused appropriations expire at year-end but appropriations continue in effect for obligated amounts (purchase orders, etc.), which of the following budgetary accounts would likely be found in the agency's post-closing trial balance at year-end?
   a. Commitments and Other Appropriations Realized.
   b. Undelivered Orders and Other Appropriations Realized.
   c. Expended Authority and Undelivered Orders.
   d. Commitments and Undelivered Orders.
7. Which of the following is a correct mathematical relationship among proprietary account balances?
   a. Net Position equals Total Assets minus Total Liabilities.
   b. Fund Balance with Treasury equals Unexpended Appropriations.
   c. Cumulative Results of Operations equals Revenues and Financing Sources minus Operating/Program Expenses.
   d. Disbursements in Transit equals Fund Balance with Treasury minus Accounts Payable and Other Current Liabilities.
8. Which of the following is *not* a component of a consolidated performance and accountability report (PAR)?
   a. MD&A.
   b. The basic financial statements.
   c. Statistical information section.
   d. A transmittal letter from the agency head.
9. Fund Balance with the Treasury would be considered equivalent to which of the following accounts?
   a. Cash.
   b. Other Appropriations Realized.
   c. Allotments.
   d. Both *a* and *b*.
10. Which of the following is *not* a true statement about the difference between accounting and reporting for federal government agencies versus state and local governments?
   a. State and local governments record material amounts of inventory at the fund and government-wide level, as does the federal government at the budgetary and proprietary levels.
   b. State and local governments use accrual accounting in the government-wide statements as well as proprietary and fiduciary funds; federal agencies use only the cash basis of accounting.
   c. The budget is recorded in the general ledger of a state or local government and a federal agency.
   d. State and local governments do not account for apportionments and most do not account for allotments.

17–16 Identifying Account Types and Normal Balances. Following is a list of a number of accounts used by federal agencies.

	Column A P or B	*Column B* Dr or Cr
1. Unexpended Appropriations	____	____
2. Office Materials and Supplies	____	____
3. Undelivered Orders	____	____
4. Commitments	____	____
5. Accumulated Depreciation	____	____
6. Fund Balance with Treasury	____	____
7. Other Appropriations Realized	____	____
8. Disbursements in Transit	____	____
9. Accounts Payable	____	____
10. Cumulative Results of Operations	____	____

Required

For each of the accounts listed indicate in Column A whether the account is a proprietary account (P) or a budgetary account (B). In Column B indicate whether the account has a normal debit (Dr) or credit (Cr) balance.

17–17 Fund Balance with U.S. Treasury. One amount is missing in the following trial balance of proprietary accounts, and another is missing from the trial balance of budgetary accounts of the Save Our Resources Commission of the federal government. This trial balance was prepared before budgetary accounts were adjusted, such as returning unused appropriations. The debits are not distinguished from the credits.

SAVE OUR RESOURCES COMMISSION
Pre-closing Trial Balance
September 30, 2017

Proprietary accounts:	
Accounts Payable	$ 134,000
Accumulated Depreciation—Plant and Equipment	5,350,000
Appropriations Used	4,500,000
Fund Balance with Treasury—2017	?
Operating Materials and Supplies	63,000
Cumulative Results of Operations—10/1/16	1,009,000
Operating/Program Expenses	2,150,000
Depreciation and Amortization	750,000
Plant and Equipment	8,111,000
Unexpended Appropriations—2017	410,000
Budgetary accounts:	
Other Appropriations Realized—2017	?
Expended Authority—2017	4,500,000
Undelivered Orders—2017	310,000
Allotments—2017	100,000

Required

a. Compute each missing amount in the pre-closing trial balance.

b. Compute the net additions (or reductions) to assets other than Fund Balance with Treasury during fiscal year 2017. Clearly label your computations and show all work in good form.

c. In general journal form, prepare entries to close the budgetary accounts as needed and to close the operating statement proprietary accounts.

17–18 Federal Commission Financial Statements. Use the data from Problem 17–17 for this assignment. In completing the assignment assume that all assets are *entity assets,* Fund Balance with Treasury is an *intragovernmental asset,* and all other assets are *governmental.* Also, assume that Other Appropriations Realized—2016 were zero.

Required

In good form, prepare the following statements for the Save Our Resources Commission for 2017:

a. A statement of budgetary resources using Illustration 17–17 as an example.

b. A statement of changes in net position using Illustration 17–16 as an example.

c. A balance sheet using Illustration 17–15 as an example.

17–19 Statement of Net Cost. The Rural Assistance Agency operates three major programs as responsibility centers—the Food Bank, Housing Services, and Credit Counseling. Clients pay a fee for services on a sliding scale based on income. The following information is drawn from the accounting records of the agency for the year ended September 30, 2017. Earned revenue from the three programs was as follows: Food Bank, $2,611,900; Housing Services, $1,237,400; and Credit Counseling, $87,000. Costs for the same period were: Food Bank, $9,632,800; Housing Services, $7,438,500; and Credit Counseling, $2,391,000.

Required

Prepare a statement of net cost for the Rural Assistance Agency for the year ended September 30, 2017.

17–20 Statement of Budgetary Resources. The trial balance of the Federal Antiquities Administration, as of August 31, 2017, follows:

	Debits	Credits
Budgetary Accounts		
Other Appropriations Realized—2017	$4,894,855	
Other Appropriations Realized—2016	1,210,210	
Allotments—2017		$ 600,000
Commitments—2017		150,000
Undelivered Orders—2017		664,131
Expended Authority—2017		3,480,724
Expended Authority—2016		1,210,210
Total Budgetary Accounts	$6,105,065	$6,105,065

Required

Prepare a statement of budgetary resources for the 11 months ended August 31, 2017, assuming that goods on order at the end of the prior year amounted to $1,210,210.

17–21 Transaction Analysis and Statements. Congress authorized the Flood Control Commission to start operations on October 1, 2017.

Required

a. Record the following transactions in general journal form as they should appear in the accounts of the Flood Control Commission. Record all expenses in the Operating/Program Expenses account.

(1) The Flood Control Commission received official notice that the one-year appropriation passed by Congress and signed by the President amounted to $7,000,000 for operating expenses.

(2) The Office of Management and Budget notified the Commission of the following schedule of apportionments: first quarter, $2,000,000; second quarter, $2,000,000; third quarter, $1,500,000; and fourth quarter, $1,500,000.

(3) The Flood Control Commissioner allotted $1,000,000 for the first month's operations.

(4) Obligations were recorded for salaries and fringe benefits, $400,000; furniture and equipment, $270,000; materials and supplies, $250,000; and rent and utilities, $50,000. The Commission does not record commitments prior to recording obligations.

(5) Payroll for the first two weeks in the amount of $170,000 was paid.

(6) Invoices approved for payment totaled $395,000; of the total, $180,000 was for furniture and equipment, $175,000 for materials and supplies, and $40,000 for rent.

(7) A liability was recorded for the payroll for the second two weeks, $160,000, and for the employer's share of FICA taxes for the four weeks, $23,000. (*Note:* Credit to Accrued Funded Payroll and Benefits.)

(8) Accounts payable totaling $189,000 were paid, and this included liabilities for materials and supplies, $149,000, and rent, $40,000. Accrued Funded Payroll and Benefits in the amount of $183,000 were paid.

(9) Accruals recorded at month-end were salaries, $30,000, and utilities, $10,000. Materials and supplies costing $60,000 were used during the month. Depreciation of $2,500 was recorded on furniture and equipment for the month. (*Note:* In practice, this would likely be done in worksheet form for monthly reporting purposes.)

(10) Necessary closing entries were prepared as of October 31, 2017. (*Note:* Again, for monthly statements, this would be a worksheet entry only.)

b. Prepare the Balance Sheet of the Flood Control Commission as of October 31, 2017, assuming that all of the Commission's assets are entity assets, Fund Balance with Treasury is intragovernmental, and all other assets are governmental.

c. Prepare the Statement of Changes in Net Position of the Flood Control Commission for the month ended October 31, 2017.

d. Prepare the Statement of Budgetary Resources of the Flood Control Commission for the month ended October 31, 2017.

17–22 Financial Statement Analysis of the Federal Government. The complexity and uniqueness of the federal government makes it difficult to conduct a meaningful analysis of its financial condition. However, conducting a financial statement analysis does provide a better understanding of the federal government. To assist in the financial statement analysis, use Illustrations 17–2 and 17–3 along with the following excerpts from the 2013 *Financial Report of the United States Government.* (*Hint:* When using revenues or net costs, use the consolidated amounts, which are adjusted for intra-entity activity.)

UNITED STATES GOVERNMENT
Statements of Changes in Cash Balance from Unified Budget and Other Activities
For the Years Ended September 30
(In billions of dollars)

	2013		2012	
Unified budget deficit		(680.3)		(1,089.4)
Adjustments for Noncash Outlays Included in the budget:				
Interest accrued by Treasury on debt held by the public	242.7		240.1	
TARP yearend re-estimates	(0.9)		32.3	
TARP Subsidy (income)	(11.9)		(10.8)	
Other Federal entity subsidy (income)	(63.4)		(29.4)	
Subtotal		166.5		232.2
Items Affecting the Cash Balance Not Included in the budget:				
Net Transactions from financing activity:				
Borrowings from the public	8,145.4		7,766.9	
Repayment of debt held by the public	(7,444.0)		(6,614.0)	
Agency securities	0.7		(0.4)	
Subtotal		702.1		1,152.5
Transactions from monetary and other activity:				
Interest paid by Treasury on debt held by the public	(248.7)		(234.3)	
Net TARP direct loans and equity investments activity	31.7		52.3	
Net GSEs-mortgage-backed securities activity	—		70.6	
Net loan receivable activity	(125.6)		(153.7)	
Allocations of special drawing rights	(0.2)		(0.7)	
Uninvested principal from the Thrift Savings Plan (TSP)				
G Fund	119.9		—	
Other	34.7		(0.3)	
Subtotal		(188.2)		(266.1)
Cash and other monetary assets:				
Increase in Cash and other monetary assets		0.1		29.2
Balance, beginning of period		206.2		177.0
Balance, end of period		206.3		206.2

The accompanying notes are an integral part of these financial statements.

Property, Plant, and Equipment
As of September 30, 2013
(In billions of dollars)

	Cost		Accumulated Depreciation/ Amortization		Net	
	Defense	All Others	Defense	All Others	Defense	All Others
Buildings, structures, and facilities	269.8	249.7	127.9	130.0	141.9	119.7
Furniture, fixtures, and equipment	983.6	165.1	547.5	102.5	436.1	62.6
Construction in progress	46.6	41.6	N/A	N/A	46.6	41.6
Land	10.8	12.5	N/A	N/A	10.8	12.5
Internal use software	11.0	25.0	8.0	14.2	3.0	10.8
Assets under capital lease	0.6	3.3	0.4	1.7	0.2	1.6
Leasehold improvements	0.4	8.6	0.2	4.5	0.2	4.1
Other property, plant, and equipment	1.0	7.6	—	3.6	1.0	4.0
Subtotal	1,323.8	513.4	684.0	256.5	639.8	256.9
Total property, plant, and equipment, net		1,837.2		940.5		896.7

Required

a. To provide an indication of the government's financial capability answer the following:

(1) What percentage of total revenues comes from individual income taxes and withholdings?

(2) What is the debt service as calculated by the ratio of principal and interest payments on debt held by the public to total revenue?

b. To provide an indication of the government's financial performance, answer the following:

(1) What is interperiod equity, as calculated by the ratio of revenue to net costs?

c. To provide an indication of the government's financial position answer the following:

(1) What is the ratio of non-dedicated collections funds to total revenue?

(2) What is the quick ratio (use known current liabilities in the calculation)?

(3) What is the capital asset condition as calculated by the ratio of accumulated depreciation to the cost of depreciable capital assets?

d. Based on the ratios you have calculated, how would you assess the financial condition of the federal government for FY 2013? (*Hint:* Chapter 10 may help provide a context/benchmark for the value of some of the ratios you have calculated.)

Glossary

Some of these definitions were adapted from publications of the Government Finance Officers Association. Others were taken from specialized publications cited in the text; the remainder were supplied by the authors. The letters *q.v.* signify "which see"; that is, the preceding word is defined elsewhere in the glossary.

A

Abatement A complete or partial cancellation of a levy imposed by a government. Abatements usually apply to tax levies, special assessments, and service charges.

Accountability Being obliged to explain one's actions, to justify what one does; the requirement for government to answer to its citizenry—to justify the raising of public resources and expenditure of those resources. Also, in the GASB's view, the obligation to report whether the government operated within appropriate legal constraints; whether resources were used efficiently, economically, and effectively; whether current-year revenues were sufficient to pay for the services provided in the current year; and whether the burden for services previously provided will be shifted to future taxpayers.

Accounting Period A period at the end of which and for which financial statements are prepared. *See also* Fiscal Period.

Accounting System The total structure of records and procedures that discover, record, classify, and report information on the financial position and operations of a government or any of its funds, and organizational components.

Accounts Receivable Amounts owing on open account from private persons, firms, or corporations for goods and services furnished by a government. Taxes Receivable and Special Assessments Receivable are recorded separately. Amounts due from other funds or from other governments should be reported separately.

Accrual Basis The basis of accounting under which revenues are recorded when earned and expenditures (or expenses) are recorded as soon as they result in liabilities for benefits received, notwithstanding that the receipt of cash or the payment of cash may take place, in whole or in part, in another accounting period. *See also* Accrue and Levy.

Accrue To record revenues when earned and to record expenditures (or expenses) as soon as they result in liabilities for benefits received, notwithstanding that the receipt of cash or payment of cash may take place, in whole or in part, in another accounting period. *See also* Accrual Basis, Accrued Expenses, and Accrued Revenue.

Accrued Expenses Expenses incurred during the current accounting period but not payable until a subsequent accounting period. *See also* Accrual Basis and Accrue.

Accrued Interest on Investments Purchased Interest accrued on investments between the last interest payment date and the date of purchase.

Accrued Interest Payable A liability account that represents the amount of interest expense accrued at the balance sheet date but not due until a later date.

Accrued Revenue Revenue earned during the current accounting period but not to be collected until a subsequent accounting period. *See also* Accrual Basis and Accrue.

Accrued Taxes Payable A liability for taxes that have accrued since the last payment date.

Accrued Wages Payable A liability for wages earned by employees between the last payment date and the balance sheet date.

Acquisition A transaction or other event in which a not-for-profit acquirer obtains control of one or more nonprofit activities or businesses and initially recognizes their assets and liabilities in the acquirer's financial statements.

Acquisition Adjustment Difference between amount paid by a utility for plant assets acquired from another utility and the original cost (*q.v.*) of those assets less depreciation to date of acquisition.

Activity A specific and distinguishable line of work performed by one or more organizational components of a government for the purpose of accomplishing a function for which the government is responsible. For example, food inspection is an activity performed in the discharge of the health function. *See also* Function, Subfunction, and Subactivity.

Activity-Based Costing (ABC) A cost accounting system that identifies specific factors (cost drivers) that drive the costs of service or production activities and tracks the consumption of cost drivers in producing outputs of goods or services. *See also* Cost Determination.

Activity Classification A grouping of expenditures on the basis of specific lines of work performed by organization units. For example, sewage treatment and disposal, solid waste collection, solid waste disposal, and street cleaning are activities performed in carrying out the function of sanitation, and the segregation of the expenditures made for each of these activities constitutes an activity classification.

Actuarial Basis A basis used in computing the amount of contributions to be made periodically to a fund so that the total contributions plus the compounded earnings thereon will equal the required payments to be made out of the fund. The factors taken into account in arriving at the amount of these contributions include the length of time over which each contribution is to be held and the rate of return compounded on such contribution over its life.

Ad Valorem Property Taxes In proportion to value. A basis for levy of taxes on property.

Advance Refunding The issuance of debt instruments to refund existing debt before the existing debt matures or is callable.

Agency Funds Funds consisting of resources received and held by the government as an agent for others; for example, taxes collected and held by a municipality for a school district. *Note:* Sometimes resources held by a government for other organizations are handled through an agency fund known as a *pass-through agency fund.*

Agent Multiple Employer Pension Plan A pension plan under which plan assets of numerous employers are pooled for investment purposes but accounts are maintained for the individual employer participants.

Allocate To divide a lump-sum appropriation into parts that are designated for expenditure by specific organization units and/or for specific purposes, activities, or objects.

Allotment A part of an appropriation (or, in federal usage, parts of an apportionment) that may be encumbered (obligated) or expended during an allotment period.

Allotments Available for Commitment/Obligation The portion of a federal agency's allotments not yet obligated by issuance of purchase orders, contracts, or other evidence of commitment.

Allowable Costs Costs that meet specific criteria determined by the resource provider, generally used in the context of federal financial assistance.

Allowance for Amortization The account in which the amounts recorded as amortization (*q.v.*) of the intangible asset are accumulated.

Allowance for Depreciation The account in which the amounts recorded as depreciation (*q.v.*) of the related asset are accumulated.

Allowance for Funds Used during Construction For construction work in progress, the net cost for the period of construction of borrowed funds used for construction purposes and a reasonable rate on other funds so used.

Amortization (1) Gradual reduction, redemption, or liquidation of the balance of an account according to a specified schedule of times and amounts. (2) Provision for the extinguishment of a debt by means of a debt service fund (*q.v.*).

Annuity A series of equal money payments made at equal intervals during a designated period of time. In governmental accounting, the most frequent annuities are accumulations of debt service funds for term bonds and payments to retired employees or their beneficiaries under public employee retirement systems.

Annuity Agreements Assets given to an organization subject to an agreement that binds the organization to pay stipulated amounts periodically to the donor(s).

Annuity Serial Bonds Bonds for which the amount of annual principal repayments is scheduled to increase each year by approximately the same amount that interest payments decrease.

Apportionment A distribution made of a federal appropriation by the Office of Management and Budget into amounts available for specified time periods.

Appropriation Act, Bill, Ordinance, Resolution, or Order A legal action giving the administration of a government authorization to incur on behalf of the government liabilities for the acquisition of goods, services, or facilities to be used for purposes specified in the act, ordinance, or so on, in amounts not to exceed those specified for each purpose. The authorization usually expires at the end of a specified term, most often one year.

Appropriations Authorizations granted by a legislative body to incur liabilities for purposes specified in the Appropriation Act (*q.v.*). *Note:* An appropriation is usually limited in amount and as to the time when it may be expended. *See*, however, Indeterminate Appropriation.

Appropriations Budget Appropriations requested by departments or by the central administration of a government for a budget period. When the appropriations budget has been adopted in accord with procedures specified by relevant law, the budget becomes legally binding on the administration of the government for which the budget has been adopted.

Appropriations Used An account used in federal government accounting to indicate resources provided by current- or prior-period appropriations that were consumed during the current fiscal period.

Arbitrage Earning a higher interest rate from investing borrowed funds than is applicable to the entity's tax-exempt debt. Federal tax regulations require governments to rebate the investment earnings in excess of that permitted. *See also* Arbitrage Rebate.

Assess To value property officially for the purpose of taxation. *Note:* The term is also sometimes used to denote the levy of taxes, but such usage is not correct because it fails to distinguish between the valuation process and the tax levy process.

Assessed Valuation A valuation set on real estate or other property by a government as a basis for levying taxes.

Assessment (1) The process of making the official valuation of property for purposes of taxation. (2) The valuation placed on property as a result of this process.

Asset Impairment A significant, unexpected decline in the service utility of a capital asset (*q.v.*).

Assets Probable future economic benefits obtained or controlled by a particular entity as a result of past transactions or events.

Assets Limited as to Use Assets whose use is limited by contracts or agreements with outside parties (such as proceeds of debt issues, funds deposited with a trustee, self-insurance funding arrangements, and statutory reserve requirements) other than donors or grantors. The term also includes limitations placed on assets by the board of directors or trustees.

Assigned Fund Balance Fund balance amounts that are constrained by the government's intent to be used for specific purposes but are neither restricted nor committed. Intent should be expressed by (1) the governing body itself or (2) a body (e.g., a budget or finance committee) or official to which the governing body has delegated the authority to assign amounts to be used for specific purposes.

Attestation Engagements Services related to internal control, compliance, MD&A presentation, allowability and reasonableness of proposed contract amounts, final contract costs, and reliability of performance measures.

Audit The examination of documents, records, reports, systems of internal control, accounting and financial procedures, and other evidence for one or more of the following purposes:

1. To determine whether the financial statements or other financial reports and related items are fairly presented in accordance with generally accepted accounting principles or other established or stated criteria.
2. To determine whether the entity has complied with laws and regulations and other specific financial compliance requirements that may have a material effect on the financial statements or that may affect other financial reports or the economy, efficiency, or effectiveness of program activities.
3. To determine whether the entity is acquiring, protecting, and using its resources economically and efficiently.
4. To determine whether the desired program results or benefits established by the legislature or other authorizing body are being achieved.

Audit Committee A committee of the governing board whose function it is to help select the auditor, monitor the audit process, review results of the audit, assist the governing board in understanding the results of the audit, and participate with both management and the independent auditor in resolving internal control or other deficiencies identified during the audit.

Audit Findings Items identified by the auditors in the course of the audit, such as internal control weaknesses, instances of noncompliance, questioned costs, fraud, and material misrepresentations (by the auditee).

Auditor's Opinion or Report A statement signed by an auditor stating that he or she has examined the financial statements in accordance with generally accepted auditing standards (with exceptions, if any) and expressing his or her opinion on the financial condition and results of operations of the reporting entity, as appropriate.

Authority A government or public agency created to perform a single function or a restricted group of related activities. Usually such governments are financed from service charges, fees, and tolls, but in some instances they also have taxing powers. An authority may be completely independent of other governments, or in some cases it may be partially dependent on other governments for its creation, its financing, or the exercise of certain powers.

Auxiliary Enterprises Activities of a college or university that furnish a service to students, faculty, or staff on a user-charge basis. The charge is directly related but not necessarily equal to the cost of the service. Examples include college unions, residence halls, stores, faculty clubs, and intercollegiate athletics.

Available Collectible within the current period or soon enough thereafter to be used to pay liabilities of the current period.

B

Balance Sheet A statement that reports the balances of assets, liabilities, reserves, and equities of a fund, government, or not-for-profit entity at a specified date, properly classified to exhibit financial position of the fund or unit at that date.

Balanced Scorecard An integrated set of performance targets, both financial and nonfinancial, that are derived from an organization's strategies about how to achieve its goals.

Basic Financial Statements Term used in GASB standards to describe required government-wide and fund financial statements.

Basis of Accounting The standard(s) used to determine the point in time when assets, liabilities, revenues, and expenses (expenditures) should be measured and recorded as such in the accounts of an entity. *See* Accrual Basis, Cash Basis, and Modified Accrual Basis.

Bearer Bond A bond that requires the holder to present matured interest coupons or matured bonds to the issuer or a designated paying agent for payment. Payments are made to the bearer since the issuer maintains no record of current bond ownership.

Benchmarking The method of identifying a number that represents a target to which actual results are compared, or a basis for comparison; for example, industry averages.

Betterment An addition made to or change made in a capital asset that is expected to prolong its life or to increase its efficiency over and above that arising from maintenance (*q.v.*) and the cost of which is, therefore, added to the book value of the asset. *Note:* The term is sometimes applied to sidewalks, sewers, and highways, but these should preferably be designated as improvements or infrastructure assets (*q.v.*).

Blended Presentation The method of reporting the financial data of a component unit in a manner similar to that in which the financial data of the primary government are presented. Under this method the component unit data are usually combined with the appropriate fund types of the primary government and reported in the same columns as the data for the primary government except General Funds. *See* Discrete Presentation.

Block Grants Federal monies given to state or local governments with the discretion to administer for many projects and to many recipients and for which no matching requirement exists.

Board-Designated Funds Funds created to account for assets set aside by the governing board of an organization for specified purposes.

Board-Designated Net Assets Unrestricted net assets that the not-for-profit organization's board decides to set aside or "designate" for specific purposes.

Bond A written promise to pay a specified sum of money, called the *face value* or *principal amount,* at a specified date or dates in the future, called the *maturity date(s),* together with periodic interest at a specified rate. *Note:* The difference between a note and a bond is that the latter runs for a longer period of time and requires greater legal formality.

Bond Anticipation Notes (BANs) Short-term interest-bearing notes issued by a government in anticipation of bonds to be issued at a later date. The notes are retired from proceeds of the bond issue to which they are related. *See also* Interim Borrowing.

Bond Discount The excess of the face value of a bond over the price for which it is acquired or sold. *Note:* The price does not include accrued interest at the date of acquisition or sale.

Bond Indenture The contract between an entity issuing bonds and the trustees or other body representing prospective and actual holders of the bonds.

Bond Ordinance or Resolution An ordinance (*q.v.*) or resolution (*q.v.*) authorizing a bond issue.

Bond Premium The excess of the price at which a bond is acquired or sold over its face value. *Note:* The price does not include accrued interest at the date of acquisition or sale.

Bonded Debt That portion of indebtedness represented by outstanding bonds. *See* Gross Bonded Debt and Net Bonded Debt.

Bonds Authorized and Unissued Bonds that have been legally authorized but not issued and that can be issued and sold without further authorization. *Note:* This term must not be confused with the terms *margin of borrowing power* or *legal debt margin,* either one of which represents the difference between the legal debt limit of a government and the debt outstanding against it.

Book Value Value (*q.v.*) as shown by the books of account. *Note:* In the case of assets subject to reduction by valuation allowances, *book value* refers to cost or stated value less the appropriate allowance. Sometimes a distinction is made between *gross* book value and *net* book value, the former designating value before deduction of related allowances and the latter after their deduction. In the absence of any modifier, however, the term *book value* is understood to be synonymous with net book value.

Budget A plan of financial operation embodying an estimate of proposed expenditures for a given period and the proposed means of financing them. Used without any modifier, the term usually indicates a financial plan for a single fiscal year.

Budget Accounts Accounts used in federal agencies that are broad in scope, for which appropriations are made, and that are not the same as the standard general ledger accounts used for accounting purposes.

Budget Calendar A schedule of certain steps to be followed in the budgeting process and the dates by which each step must be completed.

Budget Document The instrument used by the budget-making authority to present a comprehensive financial program to the appropriating body. The budget document usually consists of three parts: (1) a message from the budget-making authority with a summary of the proposed expenditures and the means of financing them; (2) schedules supporting the summary; and (3) drafts of the appropriation, revenue, and borrowing measures necessary to put the budget into effect.

Budget Officer A person, usually in the central administrative office, designated to ensure that administrative policies are actually used in budget preparation and that the budget calendar and other legal requirements are met.

Budgetary Accounts Those accounts that reflect budgetary operations and condition, such as estimated revenues, appropriations, and encumbrances, as distinguished from proprietary accounts. *See also* Proprietary Accounts.

Budgetary Control The control or management of a government or enterprise in accordance with an approved budget for the purpose of keeping expenditures within the limitations of available appropriations and available revenues.

Budgetary Resources A term that includes new budgetary authority for the period plus unobligated budgetary authority carried over from the prior period and offsetting collections, if any, plus or minus any budgetary adjustments in a federal agency.

Budgetary Solvency A government's ability to generate enough revenue over its normal budgetary period to meet its expenditures and not incur deficits.

Buildings A capital asset account that reflects the acquisition value of permanent structures used to house persons and property owned by a government. If buildings are purchased or constructed, this account includes the purchase or contract price of all permanent buildings and fixtures attached to and forming a permanent part of such buildings. If buildings are acquired by gift, the account reflects their appraised value at time of acquisition.

Business-Type Activities Commercial-type activities of a government, such as public utilities (e.g., electric, water, gas, and sewer utilities), transportation systems, toll roads, toll bridges, hospitals, parking garages and lots, liquor stores, golf courses, and swimming pools.

C

Callable Bond A type of bond that permits the issuer to pay the obligation before the stated maturity date by giving notice of redemption in a manner specified in the bond contract. Also called optional bond.

Capital Assets Assets of a long-term character that are intended to continue to be held or used, such as land, buildings, machinery, furniture, and other equipment. *Note:* The term does not indicate the immobility of an asset, which is the distinctive character of "fixture" (*q.v.*). Also called *fixed assets.*

Capital Budget A plan of proposed capital outlays and the means of financing them for the current fiscal period. It is usually a part of the current budget. If a capital program is in operation, it will be the first year thereof. A capital program is sometimes referred to as a capital budget. *See also* Capital Program.

Capital Expenditures *See* Capital Outlays.

Capital Lease A lease that substantively transfers the benefits and risks of ownership of property to the lessee. Any lease that meets certain criteria specified in applicable accounting and reporting standards is a capital lease. *See also* Operating Lease.

Capital Outlays Expenditures that result in the acquisition of or addition to capital assets.

Capital Program A plan for capital expenditures to be incurred each year over a fixed period of years to meet capital needs arising from a long-term work program or otherwise. It sets forth each project or other contemplated expenditure in which the government is to have a part and specifies the full resources estimated to be available to finance the projected expenditures.

Capital Projects Funds (CPFs) Funds used to account for and report financial resources that are restricted, committed, or assigned to expenditure for capital outlays, including the acquisition or construction of capital facilities and other capital assets. Capital projects funds exclude those types of capital-related outflows financed by proprietary funds or for assets that will be held in trust for individuals, private organizations, or other governments.

Capitation Fees Fixed dollar amount of fees per person paid periodically by a third-party payor to a health care organization, regardless of services provided.

Cash Currency, coin, checks, money orders, and bankers' drafts on hand or on deposit with an official or agent designated as custodian of cash and bank deposits. *Note:* All cash must be recorded as a part of the fund to which it belongs. Any restrictions or limitations as to its availability must be indicated in the records and statements. It is not necessary, however, to have a separate bank account for each fund unless required by law.

Cash Basis The basis of accounting under which revenues are recorded when received in cash and expenditures (or expenses) are recorded when cash is disbursed.

Cash Discount An allowance received or given if payment is completed within a stated period of time.

Cash Equivalents Short-term, highly liquid investments that are both readily convertible into known amounts of cash and so near their maturity that they present insignificant risk of changes in value due to changes in interest rates.

Cash Solvency A government's ability to generate enough cash over a 30- or 60-day period to pay its bills.

Certificate of Participation (COP) A long-term debt instrument authorized for construction of municipal facilities, typically issued by a quasi-independent authority but secured by a long-term lease with a general-purpose local government.

Character A basis for distinguishing expenditures according to the periods they are presumed to benefit. *See also* Character Classification.

Character Classification A grouping of expenditures on the basis of the fiscal periods they are presumed to benefit. The three groupings are (1) current expenditures, presumed to benefit the current fiscal period, (2) debt service, presumed to benefit prior fiscal periods primarily but also present and future periods, and (3) capital outlays, presumed to benefit the current and future fiscal periods. *See also* Activity, Activity Classification, Expense, Function, Functional Classification, Object, and Object Classification.

Charitable Solicitation The direct or indirect request for money, credit, property, financial assistance, or other things of value on the representation that these assets will be used for a charitable purpose.

Charity Care Service provided by a health care organization to persons with a demonstrated inability to pay.

Check A bill of exchange drawn on a bank and payable on demand; a written order on a bank to pay on demand a specified sum of money to a named person, to his or her order, or to the bearer, from money on deposit to the credit of the maker. *Note:* A check differs from a warrant in that the latter is not necessarily payable on demand and may not be negotiable. It differs from a voucher in that the latter is not an order to pay.

Citizen-centric Reporting Abbreviated government reports that are often visually appealing and understandable to the general public, sometimes synonymous with service efforts and accomplishments reporting.

Claims and Judgments Potential liabilities, including lawsuits or demands for payment of damages related to the occurrence of an event, such as the destruction or damage of property and related injuries.

Clearing Account An account used to accumulate total charges or credits for the purpose of distributing them later among the accounts to which they are allocable or for the purpose of transferring the net differences to the proper account. Also called *suspense account.*

Cognizant Agency for Audit Responsibilities The federal awarding agency that provides the predominant amount of direct funding to a nonfederal entity expending more than $50 million in federal awards, as determined by the OMB.

Collateralized Secured with the pledge of assets to minimize the risk of loss. Deposits, investments, or loans are often required to be collateralized.

Collections Works of art, historical treasures, or similar assets that are (1) held for public exhibition, education, or research in furtherance of public service rather than financial gain; (2) protected, kept unencumbered, cared for, and preserved; and (3) subject to an organizational policy that requires the proceeds of items that are sold to be used to acquire other items for collection.

Combining Financial Statement A financial statement that displays nonmajor governmental or enterprise funds in columns with totals that agree with those reported in the basic financial statements.

Commitment In federal government usage, a reservation of an agency's allotment in the estimated amount of orders for goods or services, prior to actually placing the orders. *See also* Obligation.

Committed Fund Balance Fund balance amounts that can only be used for specific purposes pursuant to constraints imposed by formal action of the government's highest level of decision-making authority should be reported as committed fund balance. Those committed amounts cannot be used for any other purpose unless the government removes or changes the specified use by taking the same type of action (e.g., legislation, resolution, ordinance) it employed to previously commit those amounts.

Common Rule An OMB related term that describes administrative requirements that must be met by a state or local government receiving federal financial assistance.

Compensated Absences Leaves of absence for which employees earn the right to be paid, such as vacation or sick leave.

Compliance Audit An audit designed to provide reasonable assurance that a government has complied with applicable laws and regulations. Required for every audit performed in conformity with generally accepted governmental auditing standards.

Component Units Separate governments, agencies, or not-for-profit corporations that, pursuant to the criteria in the GASB *Codification,* Section 2100, are combined with other component units to constitute the reporting entity (*q.v.*).

Comprehensive Annual Financial Report (CAFR) A government's annual report that contains three sections—introductory, financial, and statistical. A CAFR provides financial information beyond the general purpose external financial statements and conforms to guidance in the GASB *Codification.*

Conditional Promise to Give A promise to make a contribution to an organization that depends on the occurrence of a specified future and uncertain event to bind the promisor, such as obtaining matching gifts by the recipient.

Construction Work in Progress The cost of construction work that has been started but not yet completed.

Consumption Method A method of recording supplies as inventory when purchased and as expenditures when used or consumed. The alternative method is called the *purchases method.*

Contingency Fund Assets or other resources set aside to provide for unforeseen expenditures, anticipated expenditures, or an uncertain amount(s).

Contingent Liabilities Items that may become liabilities as a result of conditions undetermined at a given date, such as guarantees, pending lawsuits, judgments under appeal, unsettled disputed claims, unfilled purchase orders, and uncompleted contracts.

Continuing Appropriation An appropriation that, once established, is automatically renewed without further legislative action, period after period, until altered or revoked. *Note:* The term should not be confused with *indeterminate appropriation* (*q.v.*).

Continuing Care Retirement Community (CCRC) A facility that provides residential care along with some level of long-term nursing or medical care, generally to elderly or retired persons.

Contractual Adjustments (or Allowances) The difference between the gross patient service revenue and the negotiated payment by third-party payors in arriving at net patient service revenue.

Contribution An amount given to an individual or to an organization for which the donor receives no direct private benefits. Contributions may be in the form of pledges, cash, securities, materials, services, or capital assets.

Control Account An account in the general ledger in which is recorded the aggregate of debit and credit postings to a number of identical or related accounts called *subsidiary accounts.* For example, the Taxes Receivable account is a control account supported by the aggregate of individual balances in individual property taxpayers' accounts.

Cost The amount of money or money's worth exchanged for property or services. *Note:* Costs may be incurred even before money is paid, that is, as soon as a liability is incurred. Ultimately, however, money or money's worth must be given in exchange. Again, the cost of some property or service may, in turn, become a part of the cost of another property or service. For example, the cost of part or all of the materials purchased at a certain time will be reflected in the cost of articles made from such materials or in the cost of services provided using such materials.

Cost Accounting The branch of accounting that provides for the assembling and recording of all elements of cost incurred to accomplish a purpose, to carry on an activity or operation, or to complete a unit of work or a specific job.

Cost Determination The use of statistical procedures to determine or estimate the cost of goods or services as opposed to accumulating such costs in a formal cost accounting system.

Cost Objective In federal terminology, an organization unit, function, activity, project, cost center, or pool established for the accumulation of costs.

Cost-sharing Multiple-Employer Pension Plan A pension plan under which the pension obligations of many employers are pooled. The plan assets can be used to pay the benefits to employees of any employer that provides pensions through the pension plan.

Cost Unit A term used in cost accounting to designate the unit of product or service whose cost is computed. These units are selected for the purpose of comparing the actual cost with a standard cost or with actual costs of units produced under different circumstances or at different places and times. *See also* Unit Cost.

Coupon Rate The interest rate specified on interest coupons attached to a bond. The term is synonymous with nominal interest rate (*q.v.*) for coupon bonds.

Covered Payroll The amount of payroll on which contributions to a pension plan are based.

Credit Risk The risk that a debt issuer will not pay interest and principal when due. *See also* Default.

Cumulative Results of Operations A term generally used in federal agencies to refer to the net difference between expenses/losses and financing sources, including appropriations, revenues, and gains, since the inception of the activity.

Current A term applied to budgeting and accounting that designates the operations of the present fiscal period as opposed to past or future periods.

Current Assets Those assets that are available or can be made readily available to meet the cost of operations or to pay current liabilities. Some examples are cash, temporary investments, and taxes receivable.

Current Financial Resources Cash or items expected to be converted into cash during the current period or soon enough thereafter to pay current period liabilities.

Current Fund In governmental accounting, sometimes used as a synonym for General Fund.

Current Funds Funds whose resources are expended for operating purposes during the current fiscal period. Colleges and universities and voluntary health and welfare organizations may use fund types called Current Funds—Unrestricted and Current Funds—Restricted for Internal Purposes.

Current Liabilities Liabilities payable within a relatively short period of time, usually no longer than a year. *See also* Floating Debt.

Current Resources Resources (*q.v.*) to which recourse can be had to meet current obligations and expenditures. Examples are estimated revenues of a particular period not yet realized, transfers from other funds authorized but not received, and, in the case of certain funds, bonds authorized and unissued.

Current Special Assessments (1) Special assessments levied and becoming due during the current fiscal period from the date special assessment rolls are approved by the proper authority to the date on which a penalty for nonpayment is attached. (2) Special assessments levied in a prior fiscal period but becoming due in the current fiscal period from the time they become due to the date on which a penalty for nonpayment is attached.

Current Taxes (1) Taxes levied and becoming due during the current fiscal period from the time the amount of tax levy is first established to the date on which a penalty for nonpayment is attached. (2) Taxes levied in the preceding fiscal period but becoming due in the current fiscal period from the time they become due until a penalty for nonpayment is attached.

Customer Relationship Management (CRM) Systems that create an integrated view of a customer to coordinate services from all channels of the organization with the intent to improve long-term relationships.

Cycle Billing A practice to bill part of the customers each working day during a month instead of billing all customers as of a certain day of the month. It is followed by utilities, retail stores, and other organizations with a large number of credit customers.

D

Data Processing (1) The preparation and handling of information and data from source media through prescribed procedures to obtain specific end results such as classification, problem solution, summarization, and reports. (2) Preparation and handling of financial information wholly or partially by use of computers.

Debt A liability resulting from the borrowing of money or from the purchase of goods and services. Debts of governments include bonds, time warrants, notes, and floating debt. *See also* Bond, Notes Payable, Time Warrant, Floating Debt, Long-term Debt, and General Long-term Liabilities.

Debt-Financed Income Income from property that is subject to debt, such as rental income from a building that has been financed with a mortgage.

Debt Limit The maximum amount of gross or net debt that is legally permitted.

Debt Margin The difference between the amount of the debt limit (*q.v.*) and the net amount of outstanding indebtedness subject to the limitation.

Debt Service Funds (DSFs) Funds used to account for and report financial resources that are restricted, committed, or assigned to expenditure for principal and interest. Debt service funds should be used to report resources if legally mandated. Financial resources that are being accumulated for principal and interest maturing in future years also should be reported in debt service funds.

Default Failure of a debtor to pay interest or repay the principal of debt when legally due.

Defeasance A transaction in which the liability for a debt is substantively settled and is removed from the accounts even though the debt has not actually been paid. *See also* Legal Defeasance and In-Substance Defeasance.

Deferred Inflow of Resources An acquisition of net assets by the government that is applicable to a future reporting period.

Deferred Outflow of Resources A consumption of net assets by the government that is applicable to a future reporting period.

Deferred Serial Bonds Serial bonds (*q.v.*) in which the first installment does not fall due for two or more years from the date of issue.

Deficiency A general term indicating the amount by which anything falls short of some requirement or expectation. The term should not be used without qualification.

Deficit (1) The excess of liabilities and reserved equity of a fund over its assets. (2) The excess of expenditures over revenues during an accounting period or, in the case of enterprise and internal service funds, of expense over revenue during an accounting period.

Defined Benefit Plan A pension plan that provides a specified amount of benefits based on a formula that may include factors such as age, salary, and years of employment.

Defined Contribution Plan A pension plan that specifies the amount or rate of contribution, often a percentage of covered salary, that the employer and employees must contribute to the members' accounts.

Delinquent Special Assessments Special assessments remaining unpaid on and after the date on which a penalty for nonpayment is attached.

Delinquent Taxes Taxes remaining unpaid on and after the date on which a penalty for nonpayment is attached. Even though the penalty may be subsequently waived and a portion of the taxes may be abated or canceled, the unpaid balances continue to be delinquent taxes until abated, canceled, paid, or converted into tax liens. *Note:* The term is sometimes limited to taxes levied for the fiscal period or periods preceding the current one, but such usage is not entirely correct. *See also* Current Taxes and Prior-Years' Tax Levies.

Deposit Warrant A financial document prepared by a designated accounting or finance officer authorizing the treasurer of a government to accept for deposit sums of money collected by various departments and agencies of the government.

Deposits Money deposited with a financial institution that must be released upon the "demand" of the depositor; for example, demand deposits (checking) and time deposits (savings accounts). These funds are generally insured by the Federal Deposit Insurance Corporation (up to a limit) and are distinguished from investments.

Depreciation (1) Expiration of the service life of capital assets other than wasting assets attributable to wear and tear, deterioration, action of the physical elements, inadequacy, and obsolescence. (2) The portion of the cost of a capital asset other than a wasting asset that is charged as an expense during a particular period.

Derivative A financial instrument or other contract that has one or more reference rates and one or more notional amounts (e.g., face amount), requires little or no initial investment, and requires or permits net settlement.

Derived Tax Revenues A classification of nonexchange transactions, such as income or sales taxes.

Designated A term that describes assets or equity set aside by action of the governing board; as distinguished from assets or equity set aside in conformity with requirements of donors, grantors, or creditors.

Diagnosis-Related Groups (DRGs) A case-mix classification scheme instituted by Congress in 1983 in relation to the Medicare program that is used to determine the reimbursement received by a hospital for inpatient services. Payment is made based on the patient's diagnosis regardless of how much the hospital spends to treat a patient.

Direct Costs Costs incurred because of some definite action by or for an organization unit, function, activity, project, cost center, or pool; costs identified specifically with a cost objective (*q.v.*).

Direct Debt The debt that a government has incurred in its own name or assumed through the annexation of territory or consolidation with another government. *See also* Overlapping Debt.

Direct Expenses Those expenses that can be charged directly as a part of the cost of a product or service or of a department or operating unit as distinguished from overhead and other indirect costs that must be prorated among several products or services, departments, or operating units.

Disbursements Payments in cash.

Discount on Taxes A cash discount offered to taxpayers to encourage early payment of taxes.

Discrete Presentation The method of reporting financial data of component units in a column(s) separate from the financial data of the primary government.

Disqualified Person A person who has substantial influence over the affairs of a not-for-profit organization, such as an officer or manager.

Donated Assets Noncash contributions (*q.v.*) that may be in the form of securities, land, buildings, equipment, or materials.

Donated Materials *See* Donated Assets.

Donated Services The services of volunteer workers who are unpaid or are paid less than the market value of their services.

Donor-imposed Restrictions Donor stipulations that specify use for a contributed asset that is more specific than broad limits resulting from the nature of the not-for-profit entity, the environment in which it operates, or the purposes specified in its articles of incorporation or bylaws. A donor-imposed restriction may be temporary or permanent.

Double Entry A system of bookkeeping that requires that for every entry made to the debit side of an account or accounts an entry for a corresponding amount or amounts to the credit side of another account or accounts be made. *Note:* Double-entry bookkeeping involves maintaining a balance between assets on the one hand and liabilities and equities on the other.

Due Diligence Formal disclosure and discovery of all relevant information about a transaction or organization, particularly about risks.

E

Earnings *See* Income and Revenue.

Economic Condition A composite of a government's financial health and its ability and willingness to meet its financial obligations and its commitments to provide services.

Economic Interest An interest in another organization because it holds or utilizes significant resources that must be used for the purposes of the reporting organization or the reporting organization is responsible for the liabilities of the other entity.

Economic Resources Measurement Focus Attention on measuring the total economic resources that flow in and out of the government rather than on measuring *current financial resources* only.

Economic Size The minimum possible size to be able to provide services without long-term damage to the organization's financial base.

Effective Interest Rate The rate of earning on a bond investment based on the actual price paid for the bond, the maturity date, and the length of time between interest dates, in contrast with the nominal interest rate (*q.v.*).

Effectiveness Measures Measures that relate cost to outcomes.

Efficiency Measures Measures that relate quantity or cost of resources used to unit of output.

Eligibility Requirements Specified characteristics that program recipients must possess or reimbursement provisions and contingencies tied to required actions by the recipient.

Enabling Legislation Legislation that authorizes a government to assess, levy, charge, or otherwise mandate payment of resources (from external resource providers) and includes a legally enforceable requirement that those resources be used only for the specific purposes stipulated in the legislation.

Encumbrances Accounts used to record the estimated amount of purchase orders, contracts, or salary commitments chargeable to an appropriation. The account is credited when goods or services are received and the actual expenditure of the appropriation is known.

Encumbrances Outstanding A budgetary account that allows a double bookkeeping entry for originating encumbrances when purchase orders are placed and for reversing encumbrances when goods or services are received or purchase orders are canceled.

Endowment A gift whose principal must be maintained inviolate but whose income may be expended.

Engagement Letter Written agreement between an auditor and the audited entity that describes the scope of work to be completed, among other things.

Enterprise Debt Debt that is to be retired primarily through the earnings of governmentally owned and operated enterprises. *See also* Revenue Bonds.

Enterprise Fund (EF) A fund established to finance and account for the acquisition, operation, and maintenance of governmental facilities and services that are entirely or predominantly self-supporting by user charges; or for when the governing body of the government has decided periodic determination of revenues earned, expenses incurred, and/or net income is appropriate. Governmentally owned utilities and hospitals are ordinarily accounted for by enterprise funds.

Entitlement The amount of payment to which a state or local government is entitled as determined by the federal government pursuant to an allocation formula contained in applicable statutes.

Entity Assets Those assets of a federal agency that the reporting entity has authority to use in its operations as opposed to holding but not available to spend.

Entitywide Perspective A view of the net position of the organization as a whole, rather than as a collection of separate funds.

Entrepreneurial Budgeting A budgeting approach that positions budgeting at the highest level and merges strategic plans, incentives, and accountability into the budget to communicate to citizens as a package.

Entry (1) The record of a financial transaction in its appropriate book of account. (2) The act of recording a transaction in the books of account.

Equipment Tangible property of a more or less permanent nature (other than land, buildings, or improvements) that is useful in carrying on operations. Examples are machinery, tools, trucks, cars, furniture, and furnishings.

Estimated Expenditures The estimated amounts of expenditures included in budgeted appropriations. *See also* Appropriations.

Estimated Other Financing Sources Amounts of financial resources estimated to be received or accrued during a period by a governmental or similar type fund from interfund transfers or from the proceeds of noncurrent debt issuance.

Estimated Other Financing Uses Amounts of financial resources estimated to be disbursed or accrued during a period by a governmental or similar type fund for transfer to other funds.

Estimated Revenues For revenue accounts kept on an accrual basis (*q.v.*), this term designates the amount of revenue estimated to accrue during a given period regardless of whether or not it is all to be collected during the period. For revenue accounts kept on a cash basis (*q.v.*), the term designates the amount of revenue estimated to be collected during a given period. Under the modified accrual basis (*q.v.*), estimated revenues are those that are measurable and available. *See also* Revenue, Cash Basis, Accrual Basis, and Modified Accrual Basis.

Estimated Uncollectible Accounts Receivable (or Current Taxes, Delinquent Taxes or Interest Receivable) That portion of receivables that it is estimated will never be collected. The account is deducted from the Accounts Receivable account on the balance sheet in order to arrive at the net amount of accounts receivable.

Excess Benefit Transaction A transaction that results in unfair benefits to a person who has substantial influence over a not-for-profit organization, for example, unreasonable compensation, sales of assets at bargain prices, and lease arrangements.

Exchange Transaction A transaction in which each party receives direct tangible benefits commensurate with the resources provided, for example, sales between a buyer and a seller.

Exchange-like Transaction A transaction in which the values exchanged, though related, may not be quite equal or in which the direct benefits may not be exclusively for the parties to the transaction, unlike a "pure" exchange transaction.

Exemption A statutory reduction in the assessed valuation of taxable property accorded to certain taxpayers, such as senior citizens and war veterans.

Expendable Assets and resources may be converted into cash and used in their entirety for purposes of the fund.

Expended Appropriation A charge against an appropriation for the actual cost of items received; the appropriation is no longer available to acquire additional goods and services.

Expenditures Expenditures are recorded when liabilities are incurred pursuant to authority given in an appropriation (*q.v.*). If the accounts are kept on the accrual basis (*q.v.*) or the modified accrual basis (*q.v.*), this term designates the cost of goods delivered or services rendered, whether paid or unpaid, including expenses, provision for debt retirement not reported as a liability of the fund from which retired, and capital outlays. When the accounts are kept on the cash basis (*q.v.*), the term designates only actual cash disbursements for these purposes. *Note:* Encumbrances are not expenditures.

Expenditure Responsibility The responsibility of one public charity over another to which it has given a grant to ensure that the grant was used exclusively for the purpose for which it was made.

Expenses Charges incurred, whether paid or unpaid, for operation, maintenance, interest, and other charges presumed to benefit the current fiscal period.

External Investment Pool Centrally managed investment portfolios (pools) that manage the investments of participants (e.g., other governments and not-for-profit organizations) outside the reporting entity of the government that administers the pool.

External Support Test One of two parts of the broad public support test to determine if an organization is a public charity rather than a private foundation. It is met if at least one-third of the organization's total revenue comes from the government or general public in the form of contributions, grants, membership dues, charges for services, or sales of merchandise.

Extraordinary Items Unusual and infrequent material gains or losses.

F

Face Value As applied to securities, the amount of liability stated in the security document.

Facilities and Administrative Costs (F&A) Costs that are not readily assignable to one program or cost objective in a college or university but are incurred for a joint purpose. These costs are called *indirect costs* in some OMB circulars. *See also* Indirect Costs.

Federal Financial Management Improvement Act of 1996 (FFMIA) Act of Congress in 1996 that requires each federal agency to maintain a financial management system that applies federal accounting standards and provides the information necessary to report whether the agency is in compliance with those standards.

Federal Funds In federal government accounting, accounts used to record resources derived from the general taxation and revenue powers of the government or from business operations of the government.

Federated Fund-Raising Organization An organization composed of independent charitable organizations that have voluntarily joined together to raise and distribute money among themselves.

Feeder Organization An entity controlled by a not-for-profit organization and formed to carry on a trade or business for the benefit of an exempt organization and remit its profits to the exempt organization.

Fidelity Bond A written promise to indemnify against losses from theft, defalcation, and misappropriation of public funds by government officers and employees. *See also* Surety Bond.

Fiduciary Activities Activities in which the government acts in a fiduciary capacity either as an agent or trustee for parties outside the government, for example in the collection of taxes or amounts bequeathed from private citizens, as well as assets held for employee pension plans.

Fiduciary Funds Any fund held by a government in a fiduciary capacity for an external party, ordinarily as agent or trustee. Also called *trust and agency funds.*

Financial Audit One of the two major types of audits defined by the U.S. Government Accountability Office (*see* Performance Audit for the other major type). A financial audit provides an auditor's opinion that financial statements present fairly an entity's financial position and results of operations in conformity with generally accepted accounting principles or that other financial reports comply with specified finance-related criteria.

Financial Condition The probability that a government will meet its financial obligations as they become due and its service obligations to constituencies, both currently and in the future. *See* Financial Position.

Financial Position The adequacy of cash and short-term claims to cash to meet current obligations and those expected in the near future. *See* Financial Condition.

Financial Reporting Entity *See* Reporting Entity.

Financial Transparency Relevant financial information that is fully and freely available to users.

Financially Accountable When a primary government either appoints a voting majority of an organization's governing board and can impose its will on the organization, or the organization can provide specific benefits to (or impose specific burdens on) the primary government. *See* Accountability.

Financially Interrelated A recipient entity and a specified beneficiary are financially interrelated entities if (1) one of the entities has the ability to influence the operating and financial decisions of the other entity and (2) one of the entities has an ongoing economic interest in the net assets of the other.

Fiscal Accountability Current-period financial position and budgetary compliance reported in fund-type financial statements of governments. *See also* Financial Accountability.

Fiscal Agent A bank or other corporate fiduciary that performs the function of paying, on behalf of the government or other debtor, interest on debt or principal of debt when due.

Fiscal Capacity A government's ongoing ability and willingness to raise revenues, incur debt, and meet its financial obligations as they become due.

Fiscal Period Any period at the end of which a government determines its financial position and the results of its operations.

Fiscal Year A 12-month period of time to which the annual budget applies and at the end of which a government determines its financial position and the results of its operations. For example, FY14 refers to the year that ends in 2014 (e.g., 7-1-13 to 6-30-14).

Fiscally dependent Conditions whereby an organization provides specific financial benefits to, or imposes specific financial burdens on, the primary government.

Fixed Assets *See* Capital Assets.

Fixed Charges Expenses (*q.v.*) the amount of which is set by agreement. Examples are interest, insurance, and contributions to pension funds.

Fixtures Attachments to buildings that are not intended to be removed and that cannot be removed without damage to the latter. *Note:* Those fixtures with a useful life presumed to be as long as that of the building itself are considered a part of the building; all others are classed as equipment.

Floating Debt Liabilities other than bonded debt and time warrants that are payable on demand or at an early date. Examples are accounts payable, notes, and bank loans. *See also* Current Liabilities.

Forfeiture The automatic loss of cash or other property as a punishment for not complying with legal provisions and as compensation for the resulting damages or losses. *Note:* The term should not be confused with *confiscation.* The latter term designates the actual taking over of the forfeited property by the government. Even after property has been forfeited, it cannot be said to be confiscated until the government claims it.

Franchise A special privilege granted by a government permitting the continuing use of public property, such as city streets, and usually involving the elements of monopoly and regulation.

Full Cost The total cost of providing a service or producing a good; the sum of both direct costs (*q.v.*) and indirect costs (*q.v.*).

Full Faith and Credit A pledge of the general taxing power for the payment of debt obligations. *Note:* Bonds carrying such pledges are usually referred to as *general obligation bonds.*

Function A group of related activities aimed at accomplishing a major service or regulatory responsibility for which a government is responsible. For example, public health is a function. *See also* Subfunction, Activity, Character, and Object.

Functional Classification A grouping of expenditures on the basis of the principal purposes for which they are made. Examples are public safety, public health, and public welfare. *See also* Activity, Character, and Object Classification.

Fund A fiscal and accounting entity with a self-balancing set of accounts recording cash and other financial resources together with all related liabilities and residual equities or balances, and changes therein, which are segregated for the purpose of carrying on specific activities or attaining certain objectives in accordance with special regulations, restrictions, or limitations.

Fund Accounting An accounting system organized on the basis of funds, each of which is considered a separate accounting entity. Accounting for the operations of each fund is accomplished with a separate set of self-balancing accounts that comprise its assets, liabilities, fund equity, revenues, and expenditures, or expenses, as appropriate. Resources are allocated to and recorded in individual funds based upon purposes for which they are to be spent and the means by which spending activities are controlled. Fund accounting is used by states and local governments and internally by not-for-profit organizations that need to account for resources the use of which is restricted by donors or grantors.

Fund Balance The difference between governmental fund assets and liabilities, the fund equity (*q.v.*). Fund balance for governmental funds should be reported in classifications that comprise a hierarchy based primarily on the extent to which the government is bound to honor constraints on the specific purposes for which amounts in those funds can be spent. *See* Assigned Fund Balance, Committed Fund Balance, Nonspendable Fund Balance, Restricted Fund Balance, and Unassigned Fund Balance.

Fund Balance Sheet A balance sheet for a single fund. *See* Fund and Balance Sheet.

Fund Balance with Treasury An asset account of a federal agency representing cash balances held by the U.S. Treasury upon which the agency can draw. The Treasury will disburse cash on behalf of and at the request of the agency to pay for authorized goods and services.

Fund Financial Statements A category of the basic financial statements that assist in assessing fiscal accountability.

Fund Type A classification of funds that are similar in purpose and character.

Funded Deficit A deficit eliminated through the sale of bonds issued for that purpose. *See also* Funding Bonds.

Funding The conversion of floating debt or time warrants into bonded debt (*q.v.*).

Funding Bonds *See* Refunding Bonds.

Funds Functioning as Endowments Funds established by the governing board of an institution, usually a college or university, to account for assets to be retained and invested. Also called *quasi-endowment funds.*

G

GAAP Hierarchy The list in Section 1000 of the GASB *Codification* that shows the relative weight to be placed on authoritative and other material for nongovernmental entities, state and local governments, and federal governmental entities.

Gains Increases in net position from peripheral or incidental transactions of an entity.

General Capital Assets (GCA) Those capital assets of a government that are not recognized by a proprietary or fiduciary fund.

General Fund A fund used to account for all transactions of a government that are not accounted for in another fund. *Note:* The General Fund is used to account for the ordinary operations of a government that are financed from taxes and other general revenues.

General Long-Term Liabilities Long-term debt legally payable from general revenues and backed by the full faith and credit of a governmental entity. *See* Long-Term Debt.

General Obligation (GO) Bonds Bonds for whose payment the full faith and credit of the issuing body is pledged. More commonly, but not necessarily, general obligation bonds are considered to be those payable from taxes and other general revenues. In some states, these bonds are called *tax-supported bonds. See also* Full Faith and Credit.

General Property, Plant, and Equipment Property, plant, and equipment used to provide general government goods and services in a federal agency.

General Purpose Governments Governments that provide many categories of services to their residents, such as states, counties, municipalities, and townships. Typical services include public safety, road maintenance, and health and welfare.

General Revenues Revenues that are not directly linked to any specific function or do not produce a net revenue.

Generally Accepted Accounting Principles (GAAP) The body of accounting and financial reporting standards, conventions, and practices that have authoritative support from standards-setting bodies such as the Governmental Accounting Standards Board and the Financial Accounting Standards Board, or for which a degree of consensus exists among accounting professionals at a given point in time. Generally accepted accounting principles are continually evolving as changes occur in the reporting environment.

Generally Accepted Auditing Standards (GAAS) Standards prescribed by the American Institute of Certified Public Accountants to provide guidance for planning, conducting, and reporting on audits by certified public accountants.

Generally Accepted Government Auditing Standards (GAGAS) *See* Government Auditing Standards.

Gifts in kind Contributions of tangible items to a tax-exempt organization.

Government Auditing Standards (GAS) Auditing standards set forth by the Comptroller General of the United States to provide guidance for federal auditors, state and local governmental auditors, and public accountants who audit federal organizations, programs, activities, and functions. Also referred to as *generally accepted government auditing standards (GAGAS).*

Government-Mandated Nonexchange Transactions A category of nonexchange transactions, such as certain education, social welfare, and transportation services, mandated and funded by a higher level of government.

Governmental Accounting The composite activity of analyzing, recording, summarizing, reporting, and interpreting the financial transactions of governments and agencies. The term generally is used to refer to accounting for state and local governments rather than the U.S. federal government.

Governmental Activities Core governmental services, such as protection of life and property (e.g., police and fire protection), public works (e.g., streets and highways, bridges, and public buildings), parks and recreation facilities and programs, and cultural and social services. Also includes general administrative support, such as data processing, finance, and personnel.

Governmental Assets (Liabilities) Assets (or liabilities) that arise from transactions of the federal government or an entity of the federal government with nonfederal entities.

Governmental Funds A generic classification used by the GASB to refer to all funds other than proprietary and fiduciary funds. The General Fund, special revenue funds, capital projects funds, debt service funds, and permanent funds are the types of funds referred to as *governmental funds.*

Government-wide Financial Statements Two statements prescribed by GASB standards designed to provide a highly aggregated overview of a government's net position and results of financial activities.

Grant A contribution by one entity to another, usually made to aid in the support of a specified function (for example, education), but sometimes for general purposes or for the acquisition or construction of capital assets.

Grants in Aid *See* Grant.

Grass-Roots Lobbying An appeal to the general public to contact legislators or to take other action regarding a legislative matter.

Gross Bonded Debt The total amount of direct debt of a government represented by outstanding bonds before deduction of any assets available and earmarked for their retirement. *See also* Direct Debt.

H

Health Maintenance Organization (HMO) A prepaid health care plan that functions as a broker of health care between the consumer/patient requiring services and health care providers. HMOs differ depending, in part, on whether or not the health care provider is an employee of the HMO. Similar to *preferred provider organizations (PPOs).*

Heritage Assets Federal capital assets (*q.v.*), such as the Washington Monument, that possess educational, cultural, or natural characteristics.

Historical Cost The amount paid or liability incurred by an accounting entity to acquire an asset and make it ready to render the services for which it was acquired.

Human Service Organization *See* Voluntary Health and Welfare Organization.

I

Imposed Nonexchange Revenue A category of nonexchange revenue, such as property taxes and most fines and forfeitures.

Improvements Buildings, other structures, and other attachments or annexations to land that are intended to remain so attached or annexed, such as sidewalks, trees, drives, tunnels, drains, and sewers. *Note:* Sidewalks, curbing, sewers, and highways are sometimes referred to as *betterments,* but the term *improvements other than buildings* is preferred. *Infrastructure assets* is also a term used.

Improvements Other than Buildings A capital asset account that reflects the acquisition value of permanent improvements, other than buildings, that add value to land. Examples of such improvements are fences and retaining walls. If the improvements are purchased or constructed, this account contains the purchase or contract price. If improvements are obtained by gift, it reflects fair value at time of acquisition.

Income A term used in accounting for governmental enterprises to represent the excess of revenues earned over the expenses incurred in carrying on the enterprise's operations. It should not be used without an appropriate modifier, such as operating, nonoperating, or net. *See also* Operating Income, Nonoperating Income, and Net Income. *Note:* The term *income* should not be used in lieu of *revenue* (*q.v.*) in nonenterprise funds.

Incremental Budgeting A budgeting approach that is simply derived from the current-year's budget by multiplying by a factor (i.e., an incremental increase equal to inflation) or by adding amounts expected to be required by salary and other cost increases and deducting expenses not needed when the scope of operations is reduced.

Indeterminate Appropriation An appropriation that is not limited to any definite period of time and/or to any definite amount. *Note:* A distinction must be made between an indeterminate appropriation and a continuing appropriation. A continuing appropriation is indefinite only as to time, an indeterminate appropriation is indefinite as to both time and amount. Even indeterminate appropriations that are indefinite only as to time are to be distinguished from continuing appropriations in that such indeterminate appropriations may eventually lapse.

Indirect Costs Costs incurred that cannot be identified specifically with a cost objective (*q.v.*) but benefit multiple cost objectives (e.g., a hospital cafeteria, central data processing department, and general management costs).

Indirect Expenses Those expenses that are not directly linked to an identifiable function or program.

Industrial Aid Bonds Bonds issued by governments, the proceeds of which are used to construct plant facilities for private industrial concerns. Lease payments made by the industrial concern to the government are used to service the bonds. Such bonds may be in the form of general obligation bonds (*q.v.*) or revenue bonds (*q.v.*). Also called *industrial development bonds (IDBs).*

Influencing Promoting, supporting, affecting, modifying, opposing, or delaying by any means. Often used in the context of "influencing" legislation or political candidates.

Infrastructure Assets Roads, bridges, curbs and gutters, streets, sidewalks, drainage systems, and lighting systems installed for the common good. *See also* Improvements.

Input Measures Measures of service efforts, or financial and nonfinancial resources used in a program or process.

In-Substance Defeasance A transaction in which low-risk U.S. government securities are placed into an irrevocable for the benefit of debtholders, and the liability for the debt is removed from the accounts of the entity even though the debt has not been repaid. *See* Defeasance and Legal Defeasance.

Intangible Assets Capital assets that lack physical substance, have a useful life of more than one reporting period, and are nonfinancial in nature.

Inter-Activity Transactions Interfund loans or transfers that occur between a governmental fund (or internal service fund) and an enterprise fund.

Interest and Penalties Receivable on Taxes The uncollected portion of interest and penalties due on taxes.

Interest Receivable on Investments The amount of interest receivable on investments, exclusive of interest purchased. Interest purchased should be shown in a separate account.

Interest Receivable—Special Assessments The amount of interest receivable on unpaid installments of special assessments.

Interfund Accounts Accounts in which transactions between funds are reflected. *See* Interfund Transfers.

Interfund Loans Loans made by one fund to another.

Interfund Transfers Amounts transferred from one fund to another.

Intergovernmental Revenue Revenue from other governments. Grants, shared revenue, and entitlements are types of intergovernmental revenue.

Interim Borrowing (1) Short-term loans to be repaid from general revenues during the course of a fiscal year. (2) Short-term loans in anticipation of tax collections or bonds issuance. *See* Bond Anticipation Notes, Tax Anticipation Notes, and Revenue Anticipation Notes.

Interim Statement A financial statement prepared before the end of the current fiscal year and covering only financial transactions during the current year to date.

Intermediary A recipient entity that acts as a facilitator for the transfer of assets between a potential donor and a potential beneficiary (donee) but is neither an agent or trustee nor a donee and donor.

Intermediate Sanctions Penalties imposed by the IRS in the form of excise taxes on private inurement to disqualified persons resulting from excess economic benefit transactions. For example, excessive salaries paid to a manager of a not-for-profit organization or rents higher than fair market value paid to a board member who owns the building the organization occupies.

Internal Balances An account reported on the government-wide statement of net position with a debit or credit balance, which represents activity between the governmental funds and enterprise funds (business-type activities). Amounts receivable by governmental activities from business-type activities are reported as an asset by governmental activities and as a contra-asset by business-type activities.

Internal Control A plan of organization under which employees' duties are so arranged and records and procedures so designed as to make it possible to exercise effective accounting control over assets, liabilities, revenues, and expenditures. Under such a system, the work of employees is subdivided, so that no single employee performs a complete cycle of operations. For example, an employee handling cash would not post the accounts receivable records. Moreover, under such a system, the procedures to be followed are definitely laid down and require proper authorizations by designated officials for all actions to be taken.

Internal Service Funds (ISFs) Funds established to finance and account for services and commodities furnished by a designated department or agency to other departments and agencies within a single government or to other governments. Amounts expended by the fund are restored thereto either from operating earnings or by transfers from other funds, so that the original fund capital is kept intact. Formerly called a *working capital fund* or *intragovernmental service fund.*

Internal Support Test One of two tests of broad public support to determine if an organization is a public charity rather than a private foundation. The test is met if the not-for-profit organization does not receive more than one-third of its total support from investment income and unrelated business income.

Interperiod Equity A term coined by the Governmental Accounting Standards Board indicating the extent to which current-period revenues are adequate to pay for current-period services.

Intra-Activity Transactions Transactions that occur between two governmental funds (or between a governmental fund and an internal service fund) or between two enterprise funds.

Intra-Entity Transactions Exchange or nonexchange transactions between the primary government and its blended or discretely presented component units.

Intragovernmental Assets (Liabilities) Claims by or against a reporting entity that arise from transactions between that entity and other reporting entities.

Inventory A detailed list showing quantities, descriptions, and values of property and frequently units of measure and unit prices.

Investment Trust Funds Funds used to account for the assets, liabilities, net position, and changes in net position corresponding to the equity of the external participants.

Investments Securities and real estate held for the production of income in the form of interest, dividends, rentals, or lease payments. The term does not include capital assets used in governmental operations.

Irregular Serial Bonds Bonds payable in which the total principal is repayable, but the repayment plan does not fit the definitions of regular serial bonds, deferred serial bonds, or term bonds.

J

Job Order Cost Cost accounting system most appropriate for recording costs chargeable to specific jobs, grants, programs, projects, activities, or departments.

Joint Venture A legal entity that results from a contractual arrangement that is owned, operated, or governed by two or more participants as a separate and specific activity subject to joint control.

Jointly Governed Organizations A regional government or other multigovernmental arrangement that is governed by representatives.

Judgment An amount to be paid or collected by a government as the result of a court decision, including a condemnation award in payment for private property taken for public use.

Judgment Bonds Bonds issued to pay judgments (*q.v.*). *See also* Funding.

Judgments Payable Amounts due to be paid by a government as the result of court decisions, including condemnation awards in payment for private property taken for public use.

L

Land A capital asset account that reflects the carrying value of land owned by a government. If land is purchased, this account shows the purchase price and costs such as legal fees and filling and excavation costs that are incurred to put the land in condition for its intended use. If land is acquired by gift, the account reflects its appraised value at time of acquisition.

Lapse (Verb) As applied to appropriations, to terminate an appropriation. *Note:* Except for indeterminate appropriations (*q.v.*) and continuing appropriations (*q.v.*), an appropriation is made for a certain period of time. At the end of this period, any unexpended and unencumbered balance thereof lapses unless otherwise provided by law.

Leasehold The right to the use of real estate by virtue of a lease, usually for a specified term of years, for which a consideration is paid.

Legal Defeasance A transaction in which debt is legally satisfied based on certain provisions in the debt instrument (e.g., third-party guarantor assumes the debt) even though the debt has not been repaid. *See also* Defeasance and In-Substance Defeasance.

Legal Enforceability Conditions whereby a government can be compelled by an external party—such as citizens, public interest groups, or the judiciary—to use resources created by enabling legislation only for the purposes specified by the legislation.

Legislation Action by Congress, a state legislative body, or a local council to establish laws, statutes, and ordinances.

Levy (Verb) To impose taxes, special assessments, or service charges for the support of governmental activities. (Noun) The total amount of taxes, special assessments, or service charges imposed by a government.

Liabilities Probable future sacrifices of economic benefits arising from present obligations of a particular entity to transfer assets or provide services to other entities in the future as a result of past transactions or events. *Note:* The term does not include encumbrances (*q.v.*).

Life Income Fund Funds, ordinarily of colleges and universities and not-for-profit organizations, established to account for assets given to the organization subject to an agreement to pay to the donor or designee the income earned by the assets over a specified period of time. Also called *pooled (life) income funds*.

Limited Obligation Debt Debt secured by a pledge of the collections of a certain specified tax (rather than by all general revenues).

Limited Purpose Governments *See* Special Purpose Governments.

Line Item Budget A detailed expense or expenditure budget, generally classified by object within each organizational unit and often classified within each object as to authorized number of employees at each salary level within each job classification, and so on.

Loans Receivable Amounts that have been loaned to persons or organizations, including notes taken as security for such loans.

Lobbying Communicating directly with a public official in either the executive or legislative branch of the state government for the purpose of influencing legislation.

Local Education Agency (LEA) A broad term that is used to include school districts, public schools, intermediate education agencies, and school systems.

Long-Run Solvency A government's ability in the long run to pay all of the costs of doing business.

Long-Term Budget A budget prepared for a period longer than a fiscal year, or, in the case of some state governments, a budget prepared for a period longer than a biennium. If the long-term budget is restricted to capital expenditures, it is called a *capital program* (*q.v.*) or a *capital improvement program.*

Long-Term Debt Debt with a maturity of more than one year after the date of issuance.

Losses Decreases in net assets from peripheral or incidental transactions of an entity.

Lump-Sum Appropriation An appropriation made for a stated purpose or for a named department without specifying further the amounts that may be spent for specific activities or for particular objects of expenditure. An example of such an appropriation would be one for the police department that does not specify the amount to be spent for uniform patrol, traffic control, and so on, or for salaries and wages, materials and supplies, travel, and so on.

M

Machinery and Equipment *See* Equipment.

Maintenance The upkeep of physical properties in condition for use or occupancy. Examples are the inspection of equipment to detect defects and the making of repairs.

Major Funds Funds are classified as major if they are significantly large with respect to the whole government. A fund is "major" if

1. total assets, liabilities, revenues, or expenditures/expenses of the individual governmental or enterprise fund are at least 10 percent of the corresponding total of assets, liabilities, revenues, or expenditures/expenses for all funds of that category or type (total governmental or total enterprise funds), and
2. total assets, liabilities, revenues, or expenditures/expenses of the individual governmental fund or enterprise fund are at least 5 percent of the corresponding total for all governmental and enterprise funds combined.

Major Programs All federal programs identified by the auditor through a risk-based process that will be audited as part of a single audit.

Management's Discussion and Analysis (MD&A) Narrative information, in addition to the basic financial statements, in which management provides a brief, objective, and easily readable analysis of the government's financial performance for the year and its financial position at year-end. An MD&A is required for state and local governments and federal agencies.

Market Risk The risk of loss arising from increases in market rates of interest or other factors that reduce market value of securities.

Material Weakness A deficiency in internal control such that there is a reasonable possibility that a material misstatement of the entity's financial statements will not be prevented, or detected and corrected, on a timely basis.

Materiality An auditor's judgment as to the level at which the quantitative or qualitative effects of missstatements will have a significant impact on users' evaluations.

Matured Bonds Payable Bonds that have reached their maturity date but remain unpaid.

Matured Interest Payable Interest on bonds that has matured but remains unpaid.

Measurable Capable of being expressed in monetary terms.

Measurement Focus The nature of the resources, claims against resources, and flows of resources that are measured and reported by a fund or other entity. For example, governmental funds currently measure and report available financial resources, whereas proprietary and fiduciary funds measure and report economic resources.

Merger A transaction or other event in which the governing boards of two or more not-for-profit entities cede control of those entities to create a new not-for-profit entity.

Modified Accrual Basis Under the modified accrual basis of accounting, required for use by governmental funds (*q.v.*), revenues are recognized in the period in which they become available and measurable, and expenditures are recognized at the time a liability is incurred pursuant to appropriation authority.

Modified Approach An approach that allows the government to elect *not* to depreciate certain eligible infrastructure assets provided certain requirements are met.

Modified Cash Basis Sometimes same as Modified Accrual Basis, sometimes a plan under which revenues are recognized on the cash basis but expenditures are recognized on the accrual basis.

Mortgage Bonds Bonds secured by a mortgage against specific properties of a government, usually its public utilities or other enterprises. If primarily payable from enterprise revenues, they are also classed as revenue bonds. *See also* Revenue Bonds.

Multiple-employer Pension Plan Pension plans under which benefits are provided to the employees of more than one employer.

Municipal In its broadest sense, an adjective that denotes the state and all subordinate units of government. As defined for census statistics, the term denotes a city, town, or village as opposed to other units of local government.

Municipal Bond A bond (*q.v.*) issued by a state or local government.

Municipal Corporation A body politic and corporate established pursuant to state authorization for the purpose of providing governmental services and regulations for its inhabitants. A municipal corporation has defined boundaries and population and is usually organized with the consent of its residents. It usually has a seal and may sue and be sued. Cities and towns are examples of municipal corporations. *See also* Quasi-Municipal Corporation.

N

Net Assets A term used in accounting for not-for-profit organizations indicating the difference between total assets and total liabilities.

Net Bonded Debt Gross bonded debt (*q.v.*) less cash or other assets available and earmarked for its retirement.

Net Income A term used in accounting for governmental enterprises to designate the excess of total revenues (*q.v.*) over total expenses (*q.v.*) for an accounting period. *See also* Income, Operating Revenues, Operating Expenses, Nonoperating Income, and Nonoperating Expenses.

Net Investment in Capital Assets The component of net position that consists of capital assets, including restricted capital assets, net of accumulated depreciation reduced by the outstanding balances of bonds, mortgages, notes, or other borrowings and deferred inflows of resources that are attributable to the acquisition, construction, or improvement of those assets.

Net Pension Liability The difference between the total pension liability and plan fiduciary net position.

Net Position The residual of all other elements presented in a statement of financial position. It is measured as the difference between (1) assets and deferred outflows of resources and (2) liabilities and deferred inflows of resources.

Net Revenue Available for Debt Service Gross operating revenues of an enterprise less operating and maintenance expenses but exclusive of depreciation and bond interest. *Net revenue* as thus defined is used to compute "coverage" of revenue bond issues. *Note:* Under the laws of some states and the provisions of some revenue bond indentures, net revenues used for computation of coverage are required to be on a cash basis rather than an accrual basis.

Nominal Interest Rate The contractual interest rate shown on the face and in the body of a bond and representing the amount of interest to be paid, in contrast to the effective interest rate (*q.v.*). *See also* Coupon Rate.

Nonaudit Work Work that is solely for the benefit of the entity requesting the work and does not provide for a basis for conclusions, recommendations, or opinions.

Nonentity Assets Those assets of a federal agency that the reporting entity is holding but are not available for the entity to spend.

Nonexchange Revenue *See* Derived Tax Revenues, Imposed Nonexchange Revenues, Voluntary Nonexchange Transactions, and Government-Mandated Nonexchange Transactions.

Nonexchange Transactions Transactions in which the donor derives no direct tangible benefits from the recipient agency, for example, a contribution to or support for a government or not-for-profit organization.

Nonexpendable The principal and sometimes the earnings of a gift that may not be expended. *See also* Endowment.

Nonexpenditure Disbursements Disbursements not chargeable as expenditures; for example, a disbursement made for the purpose of paying a liability previously recorded on the books.

Nonoperating Expenses Expenses (*q.v.*) incurred for nonoperating properties or in the performance of activities not directly related to supplying the basic service by a governmental enterprise. An example of a nonoperating expense is interest paid on outstanding revenue bonds. *See also* Nonoperating Properties.

Nonoperating Income Income of governmental enterprises that is not derived from the basic operations of such enterprises. An example is interest on investments or on bank time deposits.

Nonoperating Properties Properties owned by a governmental enterprise but not used in the provision of basic services for which the enterprise exists.

Nonoperating Revenue Revenue arising from transactions peripheral or incidental to the delivery of basic operations, including investment income, gains and losses, and unrestricted contributions.

Nonrevenue Receipts Collections other than revenue (*q.v.*), such as receipts from loans whose liability is recorded in the fund in which the proceeds are placed and receipts on account of recoverable expenditures.

Nonspendable Fund Balance The fund balance classification that includes amounts that cannot be spent because they are either (1) not in spendable form or (2) legally or contractually required to be maintained intact. The "not in spendable form" criterion includes items that are not expected to be converted to cash (e.g., inventories and prepaid amounts). It also includes the long-term amount of loans and notes receivable, as well as property acquired for resale.

Not-for-Profit (Nonprofit) Organizations An entity that is distinguished from a business enterprise by these characteristics: (1) contributions by providers who do not expect commensurate returns, (2) operating purposes other than to earn a profit, and (3) absence of ownership interests. The AICPA prefers the term *not-for-profit* over *nonprofit.* The term *nongovernmental organization* (*NGO*) is used in an international context.

Notes Payable In general, an unconditional written promise signed by the maker to pay a certain sum in money on demand or at a fixed or determinable time either to the bearer or to the order of a person designated therein.

Notes Receivable A note payable held by an entity.

O

Object A basis for distinguishing expenditures by the article purchased or the service obtained (as distinguished from the results obtained from expenditures). Examples are personal services, contractual services, materials, and supplies.

Object Classification A grouping of expenditures on the basis of goods or services purchased, for example, personal services, materials, supplies, and equipment. *See also* Functional Classification, Activity Classification, and Character Classification.

Objects of Expenditure *See* Object.

Obligated Group A group of independent organizations that have joined together for a specific purpose, for example, to obtain financing in which case all parties are obligated in some way to repay the debt.

Obligation Generally, an amount that a government may be required legally to meet out of its resources. Included are actual liabilities, as well as unliquidated encumbrances. In federal usage, obligation has essentially the same meaning as encumbrance in state and local governmental accounting.

Obsolescence The decrease in the value of capital assets resulting from economic, social, technological, or legal changes.

Operating Budget A budget that applies to all outlays other than capital outlays. *See* Budget.

Operating Cycle The cycle of an organization that includes forecasting cash flows; collecting revenues; investing excess cash; tracking the performance and security of investments; making disbursements for various purposes; and monitoring, evaluating, and auditing cash flows.

Operating Expenses (1) As used in the accounts of governmental enterprises, those costs that are necessary to the maintenance of the enterprise, the rendering of services, the sale of merchandise, the production and disposition of commodities produced, and the collection of enterprise revenues. (2) Sometimes used to describe expenses for general governmental purposes.

Operating Fund The fund used to account for all assets and related liabilities used in the routine activities of a hospital. Also sometimes used by governments as a synonym for General Fund.

Operating Income Income of a governmental enterprise derived from the sale of its goods and/or services. For example, income from the sale of water by a municipal water utility is operating income. *See also* Operating Revenues.

Operating Lease A rental-type lease in which the risks and benefits of ownership are substantively retained by the lessor, and thus do not meet the criteria defined in applicable accounting and reporting standards for a capital lease (*q.v.*).

Operating Revenues Revenues derived from the primary operations of governmental enterprises of a business character.

Operating Statement A statement summarizing the financial operations of a government for an accounting period as contrasted with a balance sheet (*q.v.*) that shows financial position at a given moment in time.

Operational Accountability Information useful in assessing operating results and short- and long-term financial position and the cost of providing services from an economic perspective reported in entitywide financial statements.

Opinion Units In the GASB reporting model, these are (1) governmental activities, (2) business-type activities, (3) aggregate discretely presented component units, (4) each major governmental and enterprise fund, and (5) the aggregate remaining fund information.

Order A formal legislative enactment by the governing body of certain local governmental entities that has the full force and effect of law. For example, county governing bodies in some states pass orders rather than laws or ordinances.

Ordinance A formal legislative enactment by the council or governing body of a municipality. If it is not in conflict with any higher form of law, such as a state statute or constitutional provision, it has the full force and effect of law within the boundaries of the municipality to which it applies. *Note:* The difference between an ordinance and a resolution (*q.v.*) is that the latter requires less legal formality and has a lower legal status.

Organization Unit Units or departments within an entity, such as police department or city attorney department.

Organizational Test A not-for-profit organization meets the organizational test if its articles of incorporation limit the organization's purposes to those described in IRC Sec. 501 and does not empower it to engage in activities that are not in furtherance of those purposes.

Original Cost The total of assets given and/or liabilities assumed to acquire an asset. In utility accounting, the original cost is the cost to the first owner who dedicated the plant to service of the public.

Other Appropriations Realized A budgetary account used in federal government accounting to record an agency's basic operating appropriations for a fiscal period.

Other Comprehensive Basis of Accounting (OCBOA) A term used to encompass bases of accounting that are not GAAP (*q.v.*). Bases included are cash, modified cash, regulatory basis, income tax basis, and substantial support criteria basis.

Other Financing Sources An operating statement classification in which financial inflows other than revenues are reported, for example, proceeds of long-term debt and transfers in.

Other Financing Uses An operating statement classification in which financial outflows other than expenditures are reported, for example, transfers out.

Other Nonprofit Organizations (ONPOs) A wide variety of not-for-profit organizations, such as cemetery organizations, civic organizations, fraternal organizations, labor unions, libraries, museums, cultural institutions, performing arts organizations, political parties, private schools, professional and trade associations, social and country clubs, research and scientific organizations, and religious organizations.

Other Postemployment Benefits (OPEB) Benefits, other than pensions, provided to employees subsequent to employment. Included would be items such as health care and life insurance.

Other Stand-Alone Government A legally separate governmental organization that does not have a separately elected governing body and is not a component unit.

Outcome Measures Accomplishments, or the results of services provided.

Outlays Sometimes synonymous with disbursements. *See also* Capital Outlays.

Output Measures Quantity measures reflecting either the total quantity of service provided or the quantity of service provided that meets a specified quality requirement.

Overhead Those elements of cost necessary in the production of an article or the performance of a service that are of such a nature that the amount applicable to the product or service cannot be determined accurately or readily. Usually they relate to those objects of expenditure that do not become an integral part of the finished product or service, such as rent, heat, light, supplies, management, or supervision.

Overlapping Debt The proportionate share of the debts of local governments located wholly or in part within the limits of the government reporting entity that must be borne by property within each government. *Note:* Except for special assessment debt, the amount of debt of each unit applicable to the reporting unit is arrived at by (1) determining what percentage of the total assessed value of the overlapping jurisdiction lies within the limits of the reporting unit and (2) applying this percentage to the total debt of the overlapping jurisdiction. Special assessment debt is allocated on the basis of the ratio of assessments receivable in each jurisdiction that will be used wholly or in part to pay off the debt to total assessments receivable that will be used wholly or in part for this purpose.

Oversight Agency The federal agency that makes the predominant amount of direct funding to the nonfederal entity receiving less than $50 million in federal awards. An oversight agency's responsibilities are similar to those of a cognizant agency but are less extensive.

P

Pay-as-You-Go Basis A term used to describe the financial policy of a government that finances all of its capital outlays from current revenues rather than by borrowing. A government that pays for some improvements from current revenues and others by borrowing is said to be on a *partial* or *modified pay-as-you-go basis.*

Penalty A legally mandated addition to a tax on the day it became delinquent (generally, the day after the day the tax is due).

Pension Trust Funds (PTFs) *See* Public Employee Retirement Systems.

Performance and Accountability Report (PAR) A report required to be prepared by major federal departments and agencies under the Office of Management and Budget's (OMB) *Circular A-136.* It includes an annual performance report (APR), annual financial statements, and a variety of management reports on internal control and other accountability issues.

Performance Audit One of the two major types of audits defined by the U.S. Government Accountability Office (*see* Financial Audit for the other type). A performance audit provides an auditor's independent determination (but not an opinion) of the extent to which government officials are efficiently, economically, and effectively carrying out their responsibilities.

Performance Budgeting Budget format that relates the input of resources and the output of services for each organizational unit individually. Sometimes used synonymously with program budget (*q.v.*).

Performance Indicator A measure of how well a health care organization has performed. Examples include "excess of revenues over expenses," "revenues and gains over expenses and losses," "earned income," and "performance earnings."

Permanent Endowments Gifts for which donors or other external agencies have stated that as a condition of the gift the principal must be maintained intact in perpetuity.

Permanent Funds Funds used to account for and report resources that are restricted to the extent that only earnings, and not principal, may be used for purposes that support the reporting government's programs—that is, for the benefit of the government or its citizenry. Permanent funds do not include private-purpose trust funds, which should be used to report situations in which the government is required to use the principal or earnings for the benefit of individuals, private organizations, or other governments.

Permanently Restricted Net Assets A term used in accounting for not-for-profit organizations indicating the amount of net assets whose use is permanently restricted by an external donor. *See* Endowment and Net Assets.

Perpetual Inventory A system whereby the inventory of units of property at any date may be obtained directly from the records without resorting to an actual physical count. A record is provided for each item or group of items to be inventoried and is so divided as to provide a running record of goods ordered, received, and withdrawn, and the balance on hand, in units and frequently also in value.

Petty Cash A sum of money set aside for the purpose of making change or paying small obligations for which the issuance of a formal voucher and check would be too expensive and time-consuming. Sometimes called a *petty cash fund,* with the term *fund* here being used in the commercial sense of earmarked liquid assets.

Planning-Programming-Budgeting System (PPBS) A budgeting approach that integrates planning, programming, and budgeting into one system; most popular in the federal government during the 1960s.

Plant Acquisition Adjustment *See* Acquisition Adjustment.

Political Activity Activity designed to influence legislation or that relates to a candidate's campaign for political office.

Political Organization Entities described in IRC Sec. 527, such as political action committees, political parties, and campaign committees for candidates for government office.

Pollution Remediation Obligations Obligations that arise from responsibilities related to the cleanup of hazardous waste resulting from existing pollution.

Pooled (Life) Income Fund *See* Life Income Fund.

Pooled Investments Investments that may be pooled or merged to simplify portfolio management, obtain a greater degree of investment diversification for individual endowments or trusts, and reduce brokerage, taxes, and bookkeeping expenses.

Popular Reports Highly condensed financial information, including budgets, summaries, and narrative descriptions.

Postaudit An audit made after the transactions to be audited have taken place and have been recorded or approved for recording by designated officials if such approval is required. *See also* Preaudit.

Posting The act of transferring to an account in a ledger the data, either detailed or summarized, contained in a book or documentary of original entry.

Preaudit An examination for the purpose of determining the propriety of proposed financial transactions and financial transactions that have already taken place but have not yet been recorded, or, if such approval is required, before the approval of the financial transactions by designated officials for recording.

Preferred Provider Organization (PPO) *See* Health Maintenance Organization.

Premium Revenue Revenue received from prepaid health care plans.

Prepaid Expenses Expenses entered in the accounts for benefits not yet received. Prepaid expenses differ from deferred charges in that they are spread over a shorter period of time than deferred charges and are regularly recurring costs of operations. Examples of prepaid expenses are prepaid rent, prepaid interest, and premiums on unexpired insurance.

Prepayment of Taxes The deposit of money with a government on condition that the amount deposited is to be applied against the tax liability of a designated taxpayer after the taxes have been levied and such liability has been established. *See also* Taxes Collected in Advance.

Primary Government A state government or general purpose local government. Also, a special purpose government that has a separately elected governing body is legally separate and is fiscally independent of other state or local governments.

Prior-Years' Tax Levies Taxes levied for fiscal periods preceding the current one.

Private Foundation An organization exempt from federal income taxes under IRC Sec. 501(a) that (1) receives its support from a small number of individuals or corporations and investment income rather than from the public at large and (2) exists to make grants to public charities.

Private-Purpose Trust Funds Funds that account for contributions received under a trust agreement in which the investment income of an endowment is intended to benefit an external individual, organization, or government.

Private Trust Fund A trust fund (*q.v.*) that will ordinarily revert to private individuals or will be used for private purposes, for example, a fund that consists of guarantee deposits.

Pro Forma For form's sake; an indication of form; an example. The term is used in conjunction with a noun to denote merely a sample form, document, statement, certificate, or presentation, the contents of which may be either wholly or partially hypothetical, actual facts, estimates, or proposals.

Program Budgeting A budget wherein inputs of resources and outputs of services are identified by programs without regard to the number of organizational units involved in performing various aspects of the program. *See also* Performance Budgeting.

Program Revenues Revenues linked to a specific function or program and reported separately from general revenues on the government-wide statement of activities.

Program-Specific Audit An audit of one specific federal program as opposed to a single audit of the whole entity.

Programs Activities, operations, or organizational units grouped together because they share purposes or objectives.

Project A plan of work, job, assignment, or task. Also refers to a job or task.

Promise to Give A pledge or promise to make a contribution that may be unconditional or conditional.

Propaganda Information that is skewed toward a particular belief with a tendency to have little or no factual basis.

Property Assessment A process by which each parcel of taxable real and personal property owned by each taxpayer is assigned a valuation.

Property Taxes Taxes levied by a legislative body against agricultural, commercial, residential, or personal property pursuant to law and in proportion to the assessed valuation of said property, or other appropriate basis. *See* Ad Valorem Property Taxes.

Proprietary Accounts Those accounts that show actual financial position and operations, such as actual assets, liabilities, reserves, fund balances, revenues, and expenditures, as distinguished from budgetary accounts (*q.v.*).

Proprietary Funds Sometimes referred to as *income-determination, business-like,* or *commercial-type* funds of a state or local government. Examples are enterprise funds and internal service funds.

Prospective Payment System (PPS) Medicare's system in which payments are based on allowed service costs for medical procedures within the same diagnosis-related group rather than on the length of the patient's hospital stay or actual cost of services rendered.

Public Authority *See* Authority.

Public Charity An organization exempt from taxes under IRC Sec. 501(a) that receives its support from the public at large rather than from a limited number of donors. Most often public charities are exempt from federal income taxes under IRC Sec. 501(c)(3).

Public Corporation *See* Municipal Corporation and Quasi-Municipal Corporation.

Public Employee Retirement Systems (PERS) The organizations that collect retirement and other employee benefit contributions from government employers and employees, manage assets, and make payments to qualified retirants, beneficiaries, and disabled employees.

Public-Purpose Trust Contributions received under a trust agreement in which the investment income or an endowment must be used to benefit a public program or function or the citizenry.

Public Trust Fund A trust fund (*q.v.*) whose principal, earnings, or both must be used for a public purpose, for example, a pension or retirement fund.

Purchase Order A document that authorizes the delivery of specified merchandise or the rendering of certain services and the making of a charge for them.

Purchases Method A method of recording supplies as Expenditures when purchased. If inventory levels have risen at the end of the month, the asset Supplies Inventory is debited and Fund Balance—Reserve for Inventory is credited. An alternative method is called the *consumption method.*

Purpose Restrictions Specifications by resource providers of the purposes for which resources are required to be used.

Q

Quasi-Endowments *See* Funds Functioning as Endowments.

Quasi-External Transaction *See* Internal Exchange Transactions.

Quasi-Municipal Corporation An agency established by the state primarily for the purpose of helping to carry out its functions, for example, a county or school district. *Note:* Some counties and other agencies ordinarily classified as quasi-municipal corporations have been granted the powers of municipal corporations by the state in which they are located. *See also* Municipal Corporation.

Questioned Cost A cost identified by an auditor in an audit finding that generally relates to noncompliance with a law, regulation, or agreement, when the costs are either not supported by adequate documentation or appear unreasonable. OMB cost circulars identify, for different kinds of organizations, which costs are allowable and unallowable.

R

Rate Base The value of utility property used in computing an authorized rate of return as authorized by law or a regulatory commission.

Realize To convert goods or services into cash or receivables. Also to exchange for property that is a current asset or can be converted immediately into a current asset. Sometimes applied to conversion of noncash assets into cash.

Rebates Abatements (*q.v.*) or refunds (*q.v.*).

Receipts This term, unless otherwise qualified, means cash received.

Recoverable Expenditure An expenditure made for or on behalf of another government, fund, or department or for a private individual, firm, or corporation that will subsequently be recovered in cash or its equivalent.

Refunding Bonds Bonds issued to retire bonds already outstanding. The refunding bonds may be sold for cash and outstanding bonds redeemed in cash, or the refunding bonds may be exchanged with holders of outstanding bonds.

Registered Bond A bond the owner of which is registered with the issuing government and that cannot be sold or exchanged without a change of registration.

Registered Warrant A warrant that is registered by the paying officer for future payment on account of present lack of funds and that is to be paid in the order of its registration. In some cases, such warrants are registered when issued; in others, they are registered when first presented to the paying officer by the holders. *See also* Warrant.

Regular Serial Bonds Bonds payable in which the total principal is repayable in a specified number of equal annual installments.

Regulatory Accounting Principles (RAP) The accounting principles prescribed by federal or state regulatory commissions for investor-owned and some governmentally owned utilities. Also called *statutory accounting principles (SAP).* RAP or some SAP may differ from GAAP.

Reimbursement Cash or other assets received as a repayment of the cost of work or services performed or of other expenditures made for or on behalf of another government or department or for an individual, firm, or corporation.

Replacement Cost The cost as of a certain date of a property that can render similar service (but need not be of the same structural form) as the property to be replaced. *See also* Reproduction Cost.

Reporting Entity The primary government and all related component units, if any, combined in accordance with GASB *Codification* Section 2100 constitute the governmental reporting entity.

Reproduction Cost The cost as of a certain date of reproducing an exactly similar new property in the same place.

Repurchase Agreement An agreement wherein a government transfers cash to a financial institution in exchange for securities and the financial institution agrees to repurchase the same securities at an agreed-upon price.

Required Supplementary Information (RSI) Information that is required by generally accepted accounting principles to be included with the audited annual financial statements, usually directly following the notes to the general purpose external financial statements.

Requisition A written demand or request, usually from one department to the purchasing officer or to another department, for specified articles or services.

Reserve An account that records a portion of the fund equity that must be segregated for some future use and that is, therefore, not available for further appropriation or expenditure.

Resolution A special or temporary order of a legislative body; an order of a legislative body requiring less legal formality than an ordinance or statute. *See also* Ordinance.

Resources Legally budgeted revenues of a state or local government that have not been recognized as revenues under the modified accrual basis of accounting as of the date of an interim balance sheet.

Restricted Assets Assets (usually of an enterprise fund) that may not be used for normal operating purposes because of the requirements of regulatory authorities, provisions in bond indentures, or other legal agreements, but that need not be accounted for in a separate fund.

Restricted Fund A fund established to account for assets the use of which is limited by the requirements of donors or grantors. Hospitals may use three types of restricted funds for internal purposes: specific purpose funds, endowment funds, and plant replacement and expansion funds. The governing body or administration cannot restrict the use of assets; they may only designate the use of assets. *See* Board-Designated Funds.

Restricted Fund Balance Fund balance amounts that are restricted to specific purposes. Fund balance should be reported as restricted when constraints placed on the use of resources are either externally imposed by creditors (such as through debt covenants), grantors, contributors, or laws or regulations of other governments or imposed by law through constitutional provisions or enabling legislation.

Restricted Net Assets A term used in accounting for not-for-profit organizations indicating the portion of the residual of assets and liabilities (i.e., net assets) that has been restricted in purpose or time by parties external to the organization.

Restricted Net Position The component of net position that consists of restricted assets, other than capital assets included in the net investment in capital assets component of net position, reduced by liabilities and deferred inflows of resources related to those assets.

Retirement Fund A fund out of which retirement annuities and/or other benefits are paid to authorized and designated public employees. The accounting for a retirement fund is the same as that for a pension trust fund (*q.v.*).

Revenue The inflow of economic resources resulting from the delivery of services or activities that constitute the organization's major or central operations rather than from interfund transfers (*q.v.*) and debt issue proceeds.

Revenue Anticipation Notes (RANS) Notes issued in anticipation of the collection of revenues, usually from specified sources, and to be repaid upon the collection of the revenues.

Revenue Bonds Bonds whose principal and interest are payable exclusively from earnings of a public enterprise. In addition to a pledge of revenues, such bonds sometimes contain a mortgage on the enterprise's property and are then known as *mortgage revenue bonds.*

Revenues Budget A legally adopted budget authorizing the collection of revenues from specified sources and estimating the amounts to be collected during the period from each source.

Revenues Collected in Advance A liability account that represents revenues collected before they are earned.

Revolving Fund *See* Internal Service Funds.

Risk-Based Approach This approach, used by auditors to determine which programs will be audited as part of the single audit, is a five-step process designed to select federal programs that are relatively large as well as likely to have problems. The auditors can use their professional judgment to classify programs that have been audited recently without audit findings, have had no significant changes in personnel or systems, or have a high level of oversight by awarding agencies as "low risk."

Risk Contract An insurance policy used to protect a prepaid health care plan from losses arising from excess of actual cost of providing health care over the fixed (capitation) fee.

S

Schedules (1) The explanatory or supplementary statements that accompany the balance sheet or other principal statements periodically prepared from the accounts. (2) The accountant's or auditor's principal work papers covering their examination of the books and accounts. (3) A written enumeration or detailed list in orderly form.

Securities Bonds, notes, mortgages, or other forms of negotiable or nonnegotiable instruments. *See also* Investments.

Self-Supporting or Self-Liquidating Debt Debt obligations whose principal and interest are payable solely from the earnings of the enterprise for the construction or improvement of which they were originally issued. *See also* Revenue Bonds.

Serial Annuity Bonds Serial bonds in which the annual installments of bond principal are so arranged that the combined payments for principal and interest are approximately the same each year.

Serial Bonds Bonds the principal of which is repaid in periodic installments over the life of the issue. *See* Serial Annuity Bonds and Deferred Serial Bonds.

Service Capacity A government's ongoing ability and willingness to supply the capital and human resources needed to meet its commitments to provide services.

Service Concession Arrangements (SCA) An arrangement between a transferor (a government) and an operator (governmental or nongovernmental entity) in which (1) the transferor conveys to an operator the right and related obligation to provide services through the use of infrastructure or another public asset (a "facility") in exchange for significant consideration and (2) the operator collects and is compensated by fees from third parties.

Service Cost The portion of the actuarial present value of projected pension benefit payments that is attributed to the current year.

Service Efforts and Accomplishments (SEA) A conceptualization of the resources consumed (inputs), tasks performed (outputs), goals attained (outcomes), and the relationship among these items in providing services in selected areas (e.g., police protection, solid waste garbage collection, and elementary and secondary education).

Service-level Solvency A government's ability to provide services at the level and quality that are required for the health, safety, and welfare of the community and that its citizens desire.

Settlement Accounts Receivables (or payables) arising from differences between original payment estimates by third-party payors, cash received and paid, and final determinations in health care organizations.

Shared Revenue Revenue levied by one governmental unit but shared, usually on a predetermined basis, with another unit of government or class of governments.

Short-Term Debt Debt with a maturity of one year or less after the date of issuance. Short-term debt usually includes floating debt, bond anticipation notes, tax anticipation notes, and interim warrants.

Significant Deficiency A deficiency in internal control that is less severe than a material weakness (*q.v.*), yet important enough to merit attention by those charged with governance.

Single Audit An audit prescribed by federal law for state and local governments and not-for-profit organizations that expend federal financial assistance above a specified amount. Such an audit is to be conducted in conformity with the Office of Management and Budget guidelines. Such an audit is conducted on an organizationwide basis rather than on the former grant-by-grant basis. The Single Audit Act of 1984, as amended in 1996, and the circular cited impose uniform and rigorous requirements for conducting and reporting on single audits.

Single-Employer Pension Plan Pension plan under which benefits are provided only to employees of the employer.

Sinking Fund *See* Debt Service Fund.

Sinking Fund Bonds Bonds issued under an agreement that requires the government to set aside periodically out of its revenues a sum that, with compound earnings thereon, will be sufficient to redeem the bonds at their stated date of maturity. Sinking fund bonds are usually also term bonds (*q.v.*).

Special Assessment A compulsory levy made against certain properties to defray part or all of the cost of a specific improvement or service that is presumed to be a general benefit to the public and of special benefit to such properties.

Special Assessment Bonds Bonds payable from the proceeds of special assessments (*q.v.*). If the bonds are payable only from the collections of special assessments, they are known as *special-special assessment bonds.* If, in addition to the assessments, the full faith and credit of the government is pledged, they are known as *general obligation special assessment bonds.*

Special Assessment Liens Receivable Claims that a government has on properties until special assessments (*q.v.*) levied against them have been paid. The term normally applies to those delinquent special assessments for the collection of which legal action has been taken through the filing of claims.

Special Assessment Roll The official list showing the amount of special assessments (*q.v.*) levied against each property presumed to be benefited by an improvement or service.

Special District An independent unit of local government organized to perform a single governmental function or a restricted number of related functions. Special districts usually have the power to incur debt and levy taxes; however, certain types of special districts are entirely dependent on enterprise earnings and cannot impose taxes. Examples of special districts are water districts, drainage districts, flood control districts, hospital districts, fire protection districts, transit authorities, port authorities, and electric power authorities.

Special District Bonds Bonds issued by a special district. *See* Special District.

Special Fund Any fund that must be devoted to some special use in accordance with specific regulations and restrictions. Generally, the term applies to all funds other than the General Fund (*q.v.*).

Special Items Operating statement items that are either unusual or infrequent and are within management control.

Special-Purpose Framework A term used to refer to financial reporting prepared on an other comprehensive basis of accounting rather than GAAP.

Special Purpose Governments Governments that provide only a single function or a limited number of functions, such as independent school districts and special districts. Formerly called *limited purpose governments.*

Special Revenue Funds (SRFs) Funds used to account for and report the proceeds of specific revenue sources that are restricted or committed to expenditure for specified purposes other than debt service or capital projects. After the fund is established, it usually continues year after year until discontinued or revised by proper legislative authority. An example is a motor fuel tax fund used to finance highway and road construction.

Special-Special Assessment Bonds *See* Special Assessment Bonds.

Spending Rate The proportion of total return that may prudently be used by an institution for current purposes.

Split-Interest Agreements Forms of planned giving by donors who divide the rights to investment income on assets and assets themselves with intended beneficiary organizations in a predetermined manner.

Statute A written law enacted by a duly organized and constituted legislative body. *See also* Ordinance, Resolution, and Order.

Statutory Accounting Principles (SAP) *See* Regulatory Accounting Principles.

Stewardship Assets Heritage assets and stewardship land reported by the federal government.

Stewardship Investments Beneficial investments of the federal government in items such as nonfederal physical property (property financed by the federal government but owned by state or local governments), human capital, and research and development.

Stewardship Land Federal land other than that included in general property, plant, and equipment (e.g., national parks).

Stores Materials and supplies on hand in storerooms subject to requisition and use.

Straight Serial Bonds Serial bonds (*q.v.*) in which the annual installments of a bond principal are approximately equal.

Subactivity A specific line of work performed in carrying out a governmental activity. For example, replacing defective street lamps would be a subactivity under the activity of street light maintenance.

Subfunction A grouping of related activities within a particular governmental function. For example, police is a subfunction of the public safety function.

Subsidiary Account One of a group of related accounts that support in detail the debit and credit summaries recorded in a control account, for example, the individual property taxpayers' accounts for taxes receivable in the general ledger. *See also* Control Account and Subsidiary Ledger.

Subsidiary Ledger A group of subsidiary accounts (*q.v.*) the sum of the balances of which is equal to the balance of the related control account. *See also* Control Account and Subsidiary Account.

Support The increase in net assets arising from contributions of resources or nonexchange transactions and includes only amounts for which the donor receives no direct tangible benefits from the recipient agency.

Surety Bond A written promise to pay damages or to indemnify against losses caused by the party or parties named in the document through nonperformance or through defalcation. An example is a surety bond given by a contractor or by an official handling cash or securities.

Surplus Receipts A term sometimes applied to receipts that increase the balance of a fund but are not a part of its normal revenue, for example, collection of accounts previously written off. Sometimes used as an account title.

Suspense Fund or Account A fund or account established to account separately for certain receipts pending the distribution or disposal thereof. *See also* Agency Funds.

Syndicate, Underwriting A group formed for the marketing of a given security issue too large for one member to handle expeditiously after which the group is dissolved.

T

Tax Anticipation Note (TAN) Note (sometimes called *warrant*) issued in anticipation of collection of taxes usually retirable only from tax collections and frequently only from the proceeds of the tax levy whose collection they anticipate.

Tax Certificate A certificate issued by a government as evidence of the conditional transfer of title to tax-delinquent property from the original owner to the holder of the certificate. If the owner does not pay the amount of the tax arrearage and other charges required by law during the special period of redemption, the holder can foreclose to obtain title. Also called *tax sale certificate* and *tax lien certificate* in some jurisdictions. *See also* Tax Deed.

Tax Deed A written instrument by which title to property sold for taxes is transferred unconditionally to the purchaser. A tax deed is issued on foreclosure of the tax lien (*q.v.*) obtained by the purchaser at the tax sale. The tax lien cannot be foreclosed until the expiration of the period during which the owner may redeem his or her property through paying the delinquent taxes and other charges. *See also* Tax Certificate.

Tax Expenditure A revenue loss attributable to provisions of federal tax laws that allow a special exclusion, exemption, or deduction from gross income or that provide a special credit, a preferential rate of tax, or a deferral of tax liability.

Tax Increment Debt Debt secured by an incremental tax earmarked for servicing the debt, such as a half-cent sales tax, or payable from taxes derived from incremental growth in the tax base that was financed by the tax increment debt.

Tax Levy *See* Levy.

Tax Levy Ordinance An ordinance (*q.v.*) by means of which taxes are levied.

Tax Liens Claims that governments have on properties until taxes levied against them have been paid. *Note:* The term is sometimes limited to those delinquent taxes for the collection of which legal action has been taken through the filing of liens.

Tax Liens Receivable Legal claims against property that have been exercised because of nonpayment of delinquent taxes, interest, and penalties. The account includes delinquent taxes, interest, penalties receivable up to the date the lien becomes effective, and the cost of holding the sale.

Tax Rate Limit The maximum rate at which a government may levy a tax. The limit may apply to taxes raised for a particular purpose or to taxes imposed for all purposes and to a single government, a class of governments, or all governments operating in a particular area. Overall tax rate limits usually restrict levies for all purposes and of all governments, state and local, having jurisdiction in a given area.

Tax Roll The official list showing the amount of taxes levied against each taxpayer or property. Frequently, the tax roll and the assessment roll are combined but even in these cases the two can be distinguished.

Tax Supplement A tax levied by a local government that has the same base as a similar tax levied by a higher level of government, such as a state. The local tax supplement is frequently administered by the higher level of government along with its own tax. A locally imposed, state-administered sales tax is an example of a tax supplement.

Tax Title Notes Obligations secured by pledges of the government's interest in certain tax liens or tax titles.

Taxable Property All property except that, which is exempt from taxation; examples of exempt property are property owned by governments and property used by some religious and charitable organizations.

Taxes Compulsory charges levied by a government for the purpose of financing services performed for the common benefit. *Note:* The term does not include either specific charges made against particular persons or property for current or permanent benefits such as special assessments or charges for services rendered only to those paying such charges as, for example, sewer service charges.

Taxes Collected in Advance A liability for taxes collected before the tax levy has been made or before the amount of taxpayer liability has been established.

Taxes Levied for Other Governments Taxes levied by the reporting government for other governments, which, when collected, are to be paid over to these governments.

Taxes Paid in Advance Same as Taxes Collected in Advance. Also called *prepaid taxes.*

Taxes Receivable—Current The uncollected portion of taxes that a government has levied but that are not yet delinquent.

Taxes Receivable—Delinquent Taxes remaining unpaid on and after the date on which a penalty for nonpayment is attached. Even though the penalty may be subsequently waived and a portion of the taxes may be abated or canceled, the unpaid balances continue to be delinquent taxes until paid, abated, canceled, or converted into tax liens.

Temporarily Restricted Net Assets A term used in accounting for not-for-profit organizations indicating the amount of net assets temporarily restricted by an external donor for use in a future period or for a particular purpose. *See* Net Assets.

Term Bonds Bonds the entire principal of which matures on one date.

Term Bonds Payable A liability account that records the face value of general obligation term bonds issued and outstanding.

Term Endowments Assets for which donors or other external agencies have stipulated, as a condition of the gift, that the principal is to be maintained intact for a stated period of time (or term).

Termination Benefits Benefits provided to employees as a result of the voluntary or involuntary termination of employment.

Third-Party Payor Term used in health care organizations to refer to the entity other than the patient/client that pays for services such as an insurance company or federal insurance program.

Time Requirements Restrictions that relate to the period when resources are required to be used or when use may begin.

Time Warrant A negotiable obligation of a government having a term shorter than bonds and frequently tendered to individuals and firms in exchange for contractual services, capital acquisitions, or equipment purchases.

Total Pension Liability The portion of the present value of projected benefit payments to be provided through a pension plan that is attributed to past periods of employee service.

Total Quality Management (TQM) A management approach in which an organization seeks to continuously improve its ability to meet or exceed customer demands, where *customer,* in government or not-for-profit organization usage, may be broadly defined to include such parties as taxpayers, service recipients, students, and members.

Total Return A comprehensive measure of rate of investment return in which the sum of net realized and unrealized appreciation or shrinkage in portfolio value is added to dividend and interest yield.

Transfers *See* Interfund Transfers.

Trial Balance A list of the balances of the accounts in a ledger kept by double entry (*q.v.*), with the debit and credit balances shown in separate columns. If the totals of the debit and credit columns are equal or their net balance agrees with a control account, the ledger from which the figures are taken is said to be "in balance."

Trust and Agency Funds *See* Agency Funds, Trust Funds, and Fiduciary Funds.

Trust Funds In federal government accounting, accounts that are used to record resources held and managed by the government in the capacity of custodian or trustee.

Trust Funds Funds consisting of resources received and held by the government as trustee, to be expended or invested in accordance with the conditions of the trust. *See also* Endowment, Pension Trust Funds, Private-Purpose Trust Funds, and Public-Purpose Trust.

U

Unallotted Balance of Appropriation An appropriation balance available for allotment (*q.v.*).

Unamortized Discounts on Bonds Sold That portion of the excess of the face value of bonds over the amount received from their sale that remains to be written off periodically over the life of the bonds.

Unamortized Premiums on Bonds Sold An account that represents that portion of the excess of bond proceeds over par value and that remains to be amortized over the remaining life of such bonds.

Unapportioned Authority The amount of a federal appropriation made by the Congress and approved by the President but not yet apportioned by the Office of Management and Budget. *See* Other Appropriations Realized and Apportionment.

Unassigned Fund Balance The residual classification for the general fund that represents fund balance that has not been assigned to other funds and that has not been restricted, committed, or assigned to specific purposes within the general fund. The general fund should be the only fund that reports a positive unassigned fund balance amount.

Unbilled Accounts Receivable An account that designates the estimated amount of accounts receivable for services or commodities sold but not billed. For example, if a utility bills its customers bimonthly but prepares monthly financial statements, the amount of services rendered or commodities sold during the first month of the bimonthly period would be reflected in the balance sheet under this account title.

Unconditional Promise to Give A promise to make contributions to an organization that depends only on the passage of time or demand by the promisee for performance.

Underwriting Syndicate *See* Syndicate, Underwriting.

Undistributed Change in Fair Value of Investments An account used by a cash and investment pool to accumulate realized and unrealized gains and losses on sales of investments pending distribution to pool participants. *See* Undistributed Earnings.

Undistributed Earnings An account used by a cash and investment pool to accumulate investment earnings pending distribution to pool participants.

Unencumbered Allotment That portion of an allotment not yet expended or encumbered.

Unencumbered Appropriation That portion of an appropriation not yet expended or encumbered.

Unexpended Allotment That portion of an allotment not yet expended.

Unexpended Appropriation The equity of a federal agency provided by an appropriation that has not yet been expended.

Unit Cost A term used in cost accounting to denote the cost of producing a unit of product or rendering a unit of service, for example, the cost of treating and purifying a thousand gallons of sewage.

Unrealized Revenue *See* Accrued Revenue.

Unrelated Business Income Gross income from trade or business regularly carried on by a tax-exempt organization less directly connected expenses, certain net operating losses, and qualified charitable contributions that is not related to its exempt purpose. If more than $1,000, the income is subject to federal income tax at corporate tax rates.

Unrestricted Assets Assets that may be utilized at the discretion of the governing board of a not-for-profit entity.

Unrestricted Funds Funds established to account for assets or resources that may be utilized at the discretion of the governing board.

Unrestricted Net Assets The portion of the excess of total assets over total liabilities that may be utilized at the discretion of the governing board of a not-for-profit entity. *See* Net Assets, Temporarily Restricted Net Assets, and Permanently Restricted Net Assets.

Unrestricted Net Position The component of net position that represents the net amount of the assets, deferred outflows of resources, liabilities, and deferred inflows of resources that are not included in the determination of the net investment in capital assets or restricted components of net position.

User Charge A charge levied against users of a service or purchasers of a product.

Utility Plant Acquisition Adjustment An account that captures the premium paid on a utility plant purchased by a government. Similar to goodwill except that the premium is the difference between the purchase price and the depreciated original cost of the utility rather than the difference between the purchase price and fair value.

V

Value As used in governmental accounting, this term designates (1) the act of describing anything in terms of money or (2) the measure of a thing in terms of money. The term should not be used without further qualification. *See also* Book Value, Face Value, and Fair Value.

Variance Power The unilateral power of an organization to redirect donated assets to a beneficiary different from the third party initially indicated by the donor.

Voluntary Health and Welfare Organization Not-for-profit organizations that receive contributions from the public at large and provide health and welfare services for a nominal or no fee. Also known as *human service organizations.*

Voluntary Nonexchange Transactions A category of nonexchange transaction that includes certain grants and entitlements and most donations.

Voucher A written document that evidences the propriety of transactions and usually indicates the accounts in which they are to be recorded.

Voucher System A system that calls for the preparation of vouchers (*q.v.*) for transactions involving payments and for the recording of such vouchers in a special book of original entry (*q.v.*), known as a *voucher register,* in the order in which payment is approved.

Vouchers Payable Liabilities for goods and services evidenced by vouchers that have been preaudited and approved for payment but not paid.

W

Warrant An order drawn by the legislative body or an officer of a government on its treasurer, directing the latter to pay a specified amount to the person named or to the bearer. It may be payable on demand, in which case it usually circulates the same as a bank check, or it may be payable only out of certain revenues when and if received, in which case it does not circulate as freely. *See also* Registered Warrant and Deposit Warrant.

Warrants Payable The amount of warrants outstanding and unpaid.

Work Order A written order authorizing and directing the performance of a certain task and issued to the person who is to direct the work. Among the items of information shown on the order are the nature and location of the job, specifications of the work to be performed, and a job number that is referred to in reporting the amount of labor, materials, and equipment used.

Working Capital Fund *See* Internal Service Funds.

Y

Yield Rate *See* Effective Interest Rate.

Z

Zero-Based Budgeting (ZBB) A budget based on the concept that the very existence of each activity, as well as the amounts of resources requested to be allocated to each activity, must be justified each year.

Governmental and Not-for-Profit Organizations

AAA	**American Accounting Association** An organization of accounting educators and practitioners involved in education whose objectives are to contribute to the development of accounting theory, to encourage and sponsor accounting research, and to improve the quality of accounting education.
ABFM	**Association for Budgeting and Financial Management** A section of the American Society for Public Administration that advances the science, processes, and art of public administration as it relates to budgeting and financial management.
ACE	**American Council on Education** An organization founded in 1918 to influence public policy on higher education issues through advocacy, research, and program initiatives.
AFGI	**Association of Financial Guaranty Insurors** The trade association of the insurers and reinsurers of municipal bonds and asset-backed securities.
AGA	**Association of Government Accountants** An association formed in 1950 to serve the professional development of governmental finance professionals by providing education, research, and professional certifications, such as the certified government financial manager (CGFM).
AHA	**American Hospital Association** An association organized in the early 1900s by hospital administrators to promote economy and efficiency in hospital management. Its current mission is to take a leadership role in public policy, representation and advocacy, and health services.
AICPA	**American Institute of Certified Public Accountants** The professional organization to which certified public accountants (CPAs) belong. In addition to providing educational and lobbying services on behalf of its members, the AICPA is responsible for promulgating auditing standards applicable to private companies, governments, and not-for-profit organizations.
APPA	**American Public Power Association** The national trade association representing state and local government-owned electric utilities.
ARNOVA	**Association for Research on Nonprofit Organizations** An international group committed to strengthening the research about nonprofit organizations, voluntary action, philanthropy and civil society.
ASBOI	**Association of School Business Officials International** A professional association of school business management professionals that provides programs and services to promote the

highest standards of school business management practices, professional growth, and the effective use of educational resources.

BBBWGA **BBB Wise Giving Alliance** A 2001 merger of the National Charities Information Bureau and the Philanthropic Advisory Service of the Council of Better Business Bureaus Foundation.

CBO **Congressional Budget Office** An office of the legislative branch of the federal government established in 1974 that gathers information for the House and Senate budget committees with respect to the budget submitted to the executive branch, appropriations bills, other bills providing budget authority, tax expenditures, and other analysis.

CSG **Council of State Governments** An association of state financial officers that forecasts policy trends for states, commonwealths, and territories and champions state sovereignty.

FAF **Financial Accounting Foundation** The organization that finances and appoints members of the Financial Accounting Standards Board and Governmental Accounting Standards Board.

FASAB **Federal Accounting Standards Advisory Board** The nine-member standards-setting body that recommends federal governmental accounting and financial reporting standards to the U.S. Comptroller General, Secretary of the Treasury, and Director of the Office of Management and Budget.

FASAC **Financial Accounting Standards Advisory Council** The council that advises the Financial Accounting Standards Board on policy matters, agenda items, project priorities, technical issues, and task forces.

FASB **Financial Accounting Standards Board** The designated organization in the private sector for establishing standards of financial accounting and reporting since 1973.

GAO **Government Accountability Office** An agency of the legislative branch of the federal government responsible for prescribing accounting principles for federal agencies; the auditing arm of Congress.

GASAC **Governmental Accounting Standards Advisory Council** The council that advises the Governmental Accounting Standards Board on policy matters, agenda items, project priorities, technical issues, and task forces. Its members are broadly representative of preparers, attestors, and users of financial information.

GASB **Governmental Accounting Standards Board** The independent agency established under the Financial Accounting Foundation in 1984 as the official body designated by the AICPA to set accounting and financial reporting standards for state and local governments.

GFOA **Government Finance Officers Association** An association of government finance managers founded in 1906 as the Municipal Finance Officers Association to promote the professional management of governments. The GFOA administers the Certificate of Achievement program to reward excellence in financial reporting, budgeting, and other areas.

GRA — **Governmental Research Association** A national organization, founded in 1914, of individuals professionally engaged in governmental research.

HFMA — **Healthcare Financial Management Association** A not-for-profit organization of financial management professionals employed by hospitals and other health care providers established in 1946 to provide professional development opportunities, influence health care policy, and communicate information and technical data.

ICMA — **International City/County Management Association** An organization founded in 1914 that is the professional and educational organization for appointed administrators serving cities, towns, counties, and regional entities around the world.

IPSASB — **International Public Sector Accounting Standards Board** An independent standards-setting body, designated by the International Federation of Accountants (IFAC) to develop high quality accounting standards for use by public sector entities around the world.

MSRB — **Municipal Securities Rulemaking Board** A body created under the Securities Acts Amendments of 1975 to protect investors, state and local governments and other municipal entities, and the public interest by promoting a fair and efficient municipal securities market.

NABL — **National Association of Bond Lawyers** An organization of bond lawyers that educates its members and others in the laws relating to state and municipal bonds.

NACo — **National Association of Counties** An organization created in 1935 by county officials to provide legislative, research, technical, and public affairs assistance to members and ensure that the concerns of over 3,000 counties in the United States are heard at the federal level of government.

NACUBO — **National Association of College & University Business Officers** A not-for-profit professional organization founded in 1962 representing chief administrative and financial officers at colleges and universities whose mission is to promote sound management and financial practices at institutions of higher education.

NAFOA — **Native American Finance Officers Association** An association of tribal officers, controllers, treasurers, accountants, auditors, financial advisors, tribal leaders, and others that provides educational forums and resources about finance and accounting best practices.

NASACT — **National Association of State Auditors, Comptrollers, and Treasurers** An organization formed in 1915 for state officials who deal with the financial management of state government.

NASBO — **National Association of State Budget Officers** The professional organization for state budget and finance officers through which the states and U.S. territories have collectively advanced state budget practices since 1945.

NASRA — **National Association of State Retirement Administrators** An organization comprised of directors of the nation's public retirement systems for the 50 states, the District of Columbia, and U.S. territories.

NCSL — **National Conference of State Legislatures** A bipartisan association that serves the legislators and staffs of the nation's states, commonwealths, and territories by providing research, technical assistance, and opportunities for policy makers to exchange ideas on state issues.

NFMA — **National Federation of Municipal Analysts** An association chartered in 1983 to promote professionalism in municipal credit analysis and to further the skill level of its members through educational programs and industry communication.

NGA — **National Governors' Association** A bipartisan organization of the nation's governors founded in 1908 to promote visionary state leadership, share best practices, and speak with a unified voice on national policy.

NLC — **National League of Cities** An organization founded in 1924 as the American Municipal Association to represent municipal governments and strengthen and support cities.

OMB — **Office of Management and Budget** An office of the executive branch of the federal government that has responsibility for establishing policies and procedures for approving and publishing financial accounting principles and standards to be followed by executive branch agencies. It also has the authority to control the size and nature of appropriations requested of each Congress.

PCIE — **President's Council on Integrity and Efficiency** A federal agency established by executive order that is comprised of all presidentially appointed Inspectors General, as well as other federal agency members. Its charge is to conduct interagency and interentity audits and inspect and investigate projects in order to effectively and efficiently deal with government-wide issues of fraud, waste, and abuse.

SIFMA — **Securities Industry and Financial Markets Association** A merger of The Bond Market Association and The Securities Industry Association representing member firms in all financial markets with the broad mission to strengthen markets and support investors.

USCM — **U.S. Conference of Mayors** A nonpartisan organization established in 1932 representing U.S. cities with populations of 30,000 or more. The conference aids the development of effective national urban policy, strengthens federal–city relationships, ensures that federal policy meets urban needs, and provides mayors with leadership and management tools of value in their cities.

Index